ENCYCLOPEDIA OF FAMILIAR QUOTATIONS

ENCYCLOPEDIA OF

Familiar Quotations

CONTAINING FIVE THOUSAND SELECTIONS FROM SIX HUNDRED AUTHORS, WITH A COMPLETE GENERAL INDEX AND AN INDEX OF AUTHORS

COMPILED BY

ELFORD EVELEIGH TREFFRY

W. & R. CHAMBERS, LIMITED
EDINBURGH: 43-45 Annandale Street
1907

This edition published 1984 by
New Orchard Editions Ltd.
Robert Rogers House,
New Orchard,
Poole, Dorset
England BH15 1LU

ISBN 185079 010 8 (Paperback edition)

NEW ORCHARD EDITIONS
POOLE DORSET

Printed and bound in Great Britain by
Hazell Watson & Viney Limited,
Member of the BPCC Group,
Aylesbury, Bucks.

PREFACE

IN presenting to the public a new collection of familiar quotations, a brief explanation of the aim and the nature of the work seems to be demanded.

At the outset, the difficulty is encountered of determining the scope of the work, and the classes of readers to which it is to appeal. The primary object of a collection of "familiar quotations" is to furnish information as to the author of a fugitive line or passage, such as sometimes haunts the brain, and also the exact locality in that author's works where such line or passage may be found.

But from this restricted field others open, until it is rendered more and more difficult to determine where the lines governing admission or rejection shall be drawn. One seeks a well-turned phrase that may embody a wish or a compliment for a friend; the orator or statesman desires some epigrammatic passage with which he can adroitly illustrate a point or make a well-rounded peroration. Instinctively all such turn to the book of "familiar quotations," in the hope of finding therein the sentiments they desire to express. And so the circles widen until little can be considered but the feasibility of compiling a good "working" collection of condensed crystallized philosophy and apt descriptions, necessarily bounded in its scope by the ordinary limitations of handiness of reference.

Any attempt to limit the terms of admission by a test of "familiarity" must necessarily fail; as what is familiar to one may be unknown to another seeker of the kinds mentioned above. With the enormous increase of genuine literature, not to mention books of merit but of unstable reputation, familiarity with the bulk of the world's literary treasures is to-day beyond the capability of all but a few. The mind that is stored with the lofty imagery of Milton, or the graphic but too often prosy descriptions of Homer and other classical writers, has little in common with that of the reader of humor-

ous works, such as those of Hood and Barham, Mark Twain and Kipling. To cater exclusively to one class is to exclude the other from participation in whatever advantages a collection of quotations may possess; and practically neither class would be satisfied with the result, yet with the best endeavours, the question will repeatedly be asked of any collection,—and doubtless at times with impatience,—"Why is this passage given room while that is omitted?" No answer can be given that will prove satisfactory to every querist. The omission of one passage may be justified by its very familiarity, it being assumed that nearly every one would recognize its language and its source, and the space thus afforded may give room to some phrase newly coming into favour. The insertion of another may be due to its familiarity in certain circles of readers.

To constitute familiarity a quotation must present, in pleasing and compact form, some noteworthy truth or idea,—be the latter philosophical or humorous. It must be incisive, to create an impression on the mind; it must be brief, to retain a hold, however slight, upon the memory. A line or a few words will linger for years in some unused chamber of the brain, until occasion furnishes the connection between the present and the past. Then like a flash comes recollection,—sometimes clear, but more often confused and indistinct,—of having that idea presented to the mind before. According to the strength of the mental faculties and the amount of their training, more or less assistance must be called for to reproduce the complete image, and the mere suggestion of a word may suffice to establish the train of thought. But to frame a complete list of quotations which should supply the mental yearnings of every one would be an impossible task. Many men have many minds—to quote a hoary thought—and no collection—however comprehensive—of crystallized ideas could ever begin to supply the demands of human mental activities.

Too many books of this nature follow one another blindly, even in many cases justifying the suspicion that little originality was used in their compilation. In the present work, however, the selection of quotations has been made directly from the sources, with the purpose of bringing together as

varied a collection as possible,—a collection which should appeal to a large number of readers through both its literary value and its practical usefulness. This has made it possible to avoid following the exact lines of the older collections, and to present to the public a work fresh and original. The advantage of the present volume as a book of reference is that it contains many phrases and verses, the source of which is not generally known or easily found; thus making it exceptionally interesting and suggestive to the general reader on account of the number and variety of the quotations, many of which are from literary fields not generally gleaned from in similar works.

In the present collection, but little attempt has been made to tap the great fountain of foreign or classical literature, or to trace to their original sources the sentences which contain the crystallized wisdom of ages. In the world of thought there is comparatively little new. Old ideas are reclothed in newer language; but many of the gems of English literature have their basic germ in the thought of thousands of years ago. The logic of a Bacon, the imagery of a Milton, or the keen exposition of human nature of a Shakespeare can often be traced back to the philosophers, poets, orators, and historians of Greece and Rome. Still further back, the thread may be followed through Egyptian lore till we find familiar ideas impressed on Assyrian and Babylonian tablets and cylinders. Beyond this point who can say that human wisdom shall be ultimately traced? And yet it can hardly be said that scientific exploration will not at some time reveal evidence of more remote civilizations with rich literature. For this reason little or no attempt has been made in these pages to detect the earliest known exponent of an idea. Space, to say nothing of other limitations upon such a scheme, would naturally forbid more than has been attempted,—the citation of some author of ability or repute who has at some time given form and utterance to a happy description, a quaint conceit, or an immortal truth.

The field of this book is therefore narrowed practically to English and American literature. Within this field every effort has been made to include a wide range of authors, subjects and literary styles. There has been no intent to limit

the quotations to authors of classical rank; for humble ideas will often survive where polished form will perish. Considerable use has, however, been made of such translations from the classics and the writings of foreign authors as have reproduced in poetic form in our own tongue the glories of the Greek and Latin writers.

The storehouse of language and thought which lies within the covers of the Bible has purposely been drawn upon very scantily, and then more by way of annotation than of direct quotation. More than sufficient material has been found in more modern fields to fill the space originally allotted to this volume, and to enter the sacred field without reaping an ample harvest would prove but an aggravation to the seeker after Biblical lore.

For the quotations that are given, a glance at the index of authors will suffice to show that there is an unusually large number of authors cited,—more than in any other such collection of similar size and scope; and that they represent all classes from the great poets to obscure writers who are remembered only by some one poem, or perhaps by a single verse or phrase which through some value of its own has impressed itself upon the minds of men. Among these many authors, even at the risk of sacrificing some old favourites, the most modern writers have been well represented; for many of their apt phrases and forcible words have already made their impression upon the public mind, and if not actually "familiar" are rapidly becoming so, and are likely to remain so. Among those cited may be mentioned Austin Dobson and Kipling, President Roosevelt and not a few American writers whose works are too little known in Britain. The introduction of such names is a distinguishing characteristic of this volume, and will contribute to its usefulness.

In citing the different quotations, each one has been taken from the most trustworthy available editions of the works of the authors cited, and variorum readings have been supplied in many cases. When possible, such different readings have been given in the text enclosed in brackets; but when the variation is considerable and the insertion of both renderings in the text awkward or impossible, one of the readings has been given in the form of a footnote. Painstaking effort

has been made to secure accuracy in specific reference, but on account of variances between editions, it is possible that the passages quoted may be found in certain editions a few lines distant from the citations given in this volume; though in some instances varying citations are given.

In reference to the general plan of the book, it is to be noted that the quotations are arranged under "key-words" —that is under some word occurring in the text of the passage selected, which seems most readily to suggest the idea of the whole, and most likely to occur to any one seeking the particular passage in question. This arrangement has been deemed superior to the arrangement by authors, because likely to give the most satisfactory aid to the reader who is seeking the accurate reference for a phrase he but imperfectly remembers, or the one who is looking for a passage illustrating and enforcing a certain idea. In either case such key-word is the one thing most likely to be remembered or sought for, and the desired passage can always most readily be found by this means. Both of these uses of the book may be illustrated by a single case. Let us suppose that one vaguely remembers a passage in which occurs the reference, "Life's final star is brotherhood," or that he wishes to have at hand a number of passages in which *brotherhood* is the leading idea. In either case he has but to open the book at the word *brotherhood*. Under this word he will find the passage, in which the given expression occurs, cited from Markham, and he will also find such other passages as the book contains, in which *brotherhood* is the leading word.

Naturally there might be a difference of opinion as to what the key-word should be, especially in certain passages where two words seem to be equally significant and suggestive, or, on the other hand, the reader's remembrance of the quotation he is seeking may be vague, and some less important word may have for some reason or other impressed itself upon his memory. In all cases of either kind the general index is well calculated effectually to aid him in his search. The general index is very full and gives a reference for every important word in every quotation, with enough of the phrase given to distinguish it. Key-words are indicated by italics; and when the quotations under any key-

word cover more than one page the inclusive page references are given. This word is not again indexed for any quotation arranged under such key-word; but is indexed for every other passage in which it has any importance. Take, for example, the word *love;* the quotations grouped under this as a key-word cover several pages, and the page references are accordingly given in the index. Tennyson's

> "Love took up the glass of Time, and turned it in his glowing hands"

is included in these pages; hence *love* is not again indexed for this specific passage, but it is separately indexed in the phrase "a sigh for those who *love* me"—which is elsewhere found under a different key-word.

The footnotes—aside from the variorum readings already mentioned—consist, for the most part, of parallel passages from other authors than those cited, which express ideas more or less similar to those illustrated in the text; thus bringing together a number of quotations related in thought, if not similar in language and expression, which might otherwise be separated; and serving to illustrate how a thought may be consciously or unconsciously passed on from one writer to another, or may occur to more than one almost simultaneously. Less frequently passages from the same author are given, especially when the thought suggested is frequently repeated in his works.

With this explanation of the aim and plan of the book, and with the hope that it will be a real help to those who use it, it is submitted to their kindly judgment.

ENCYCLOPEDIA OF FAMILIAR QUOTATIONS

Abbey.— To the hush of our dread high-altars
Where the Abbey makes us *We.*
KIPLING, *The Native-Born*, st. 12

A B C. F. R. S. and LL. D.
Can only spring from A B C. ELIZA COOK, *A B C*

Sorting and puzzling with a deal of glee
Those seeds of science called his A B C.
COWPER, *Conversation*, lines 13, 14

Abed. He who once has won a name may lie abed till eight. G. W. THORNBURY, *The Jester's Sermon*

Abra.— Abra was ready ere I called her name;
And, though I called another, Abra came. PRIOR,
Solomon on the Vanity of the World, II, lines 362, 363

Abridgment.—An abridgment of all that was pleasant in man.
GOLDSMITH, *Retaliation*, st. 8

Absalom.— That 't is a common grief
Bringeth but slight relief;
Ours is the bitterest loss,
Ours is the heaviest cross;[1]
And for ever the cry will be
"Would God I had died for thee,
O Absalom, my son!"
LONGFELLOW, *The Chamber Over the Gate*, st. 7

Absence.— Absence makes the heart grow fonder;
Isle of Beauty, fare thee well!
T. H. BAYLY, *Isle of Beauty*

There is not one among them but I dote on his very absence, and I pray God grant them a fair departure.
SHAKESPEARE, *Merchant of Venice*, i, 2

---

[1] That loss is common would not make
My own less bitter, rather more.—TENNYSON, *In Memoriam*, vi, st. 1

Oh! never say that I was false of heart,
Though absence seemed my flame to qualify.
SHAKESPEARE, *Sonnet* cix

Accompt.— He can write and read and cast accompt.
SHAKESPEARE, *King Henry VI, Part II*, iv, 2

Aches. I'll rack thee with old cramps,
Fill all thy bones with aches.
SHAKESPEARE, *The Tempest*, i, 2

Achieving.— Let us, then, be up and doing,
With a heart for any fate;[1]
Still achieving, still pursuing,
Learn to labour and to wait.
LONGFELLOW, *Psalm of Life*, st. 9

Acorns.— Large streams from little fountains flow,
Tall oaks from little acorns grow.
D. EVERETT, *Lines Written for a School Declamation*

Action.— Action is eloquence, and the eyes of the ignorant
More learned than the ears.
SHAKESPEARE, *Coriolanus*, iii, 2

Suit the action to the word, the word to the action.
SHAKESPEARE, *Hamlet*, iii, 2

Acts.— Our acts our angels are, or good or ill,
Our fatal shadows that walk by us still.
BEAUMONT AND FLETCHER,
An Honest Man's Fortune, Epilogue

Adam.— When Eve upon the first of men
The apple pressed with specious cant,
Oh, what a thousand pities then
That Adam was not Adamant!
HOOD, *Epigram xx: A Reflection*

In Adam's fall
We sinned all. *New England Primer*

Adam was a gardener.
SHAKESPEARE, *King Henry VI, Part II*, iv, 2

Adieu.— Adieu, adieu! my native shore
Fades o'er the waters blue;
The night-winds sigh, the breakers roar,
And shrieks the wild sea-mew.
BYRON, *Childe Harold's Pilgrimage*, Canto i, st. 13 (1)

---

[1] Here's a heart for every fate. BYRON, *To Thomas Moore*, st. 2

He turned his charger as he spake,
  Upon the river shore,
He gave his bridle-reins a shake,
  Said "Adieu for evermore,
                    My love!
And adieu for evermore."

SCOTT, *Rokeby*, Canto iii, st. 28

Admiration.— A Society of Mutual Admiration.

HOLMES, *Autocrat of the Breakfast-Table*, i

Adorned. Loveliness
Needs not the foreign aid of ornament,
But is, when unadorned, adorned the most.

THOMSON, *The Seasons*, Autumn, lines 204–206

Adversity. O summer friendship,[1]
Whose flattering leaves, that shadowed us in
Our prosperity, with the least gust drop off
In the autumn of adversity.

PHILIP MASSINGER, *The Maid of Honour*

Sweet are the uses of adversity,
Which, like the toad, ugly and venomous,
Wears yet a precious jewel in his head;
And this our life, exempt from public haunt,
Finds tongues in trees, books in the running brooks,
Sermons in stones, and good in everything.[2]

SHAKESPEARE, *As You Like It*, ii, 1

Let me embrace thee, sour adversity,
For wise men say it is the wisest course.

SHAKESPEARE, *King Henry VI, Part III*, iii, 1

Advice.— Good but rarely came from good advice.

BYRON, *Don Juan*, Canto xiv, st. 66

Affection.— Skins may differ, but affection
Dwells in white and black the same.

COWPER, *The Negro's Complaint*, st. 2

Surely a woman's affection
Is not a thing to be asked for, and had for only the asking.
When one is truly in love, one not only says it, but shows it.

LONGFELLOW, *Courtship of Miles Standish*, iii, lines 125–127

---

[1] Like summer friends,
Flies of estate and sunneshine.—G. HERBERT, *The Answer*.

[2] God is seen God
In the star, in the stone, in the flesh, in the soul, and the clod.
ROBERT BROWNING, *Saul*, xvii

Affection is a coal that must be cooled;
Else, suffered, it will set the heart on fire.
SHAKESPEARE, *Venus and Adonis*, lines 387, 388

Affliction. Henceforth I'll bear
Affliction till it do cry out itself
"Enough, enough!" and die.
SHAKESPEARE, *King Lear*, iv, 6

Affront.— A moral, sensible, and well-bred man
Will not affront me, and no other can.
COWPER, *Conversation*, lines 193, 194

Afloat.— I'm afloat — I'm afloat — on the fierce rolling tide;
The ocean's my home! and my bark is my bride.
ELIZA COOK, *Rover's Song*, st. 1

Afternoon. Sleeping within my [mine] orchard,
My custom always of [in] the afternoon.
SHAKESPEARE, *Hamlet*, i, 5

Age.— A lady of "a certain age," which means
Certainly aged. BYRON, *Don Juan*, Canto vi, st. 69

I am not of this people, nor this age.
BYRON, *Prophecy of Dante*, Canto i, line 143

When he's forsaken,
Withered and shaken,
What can an old man do but die?
Love will not clip him,
Maids will not lip him,
Maud and Marian pass him by;
Youth it is sunny,
Age has no honey,—
What can an old man do but die? HOOD, *Ballad*

He was not of an age, but for all time!
BEN JONSON, *To the Memory of Shakespeare*, line 43

Old age is still old age.
It is the waning, not the crescent moon;
The dusk of evening, not the blaze of noon:
It is not strength, but weakness; not desire,
But its surcease; not the fierce heat of fire,
The burning and consuming element,
But that of ashes and of embers spent,
In which some living sparks we still discern,
Enough to warm, but not enough to burn.
LONGFELLOW, *Morituri Salutamus*, st. 26

Old age ne'er cools the Douglas blood.
SCOTT, *Marmion*, vi, 15

Age cannot wither her, nor custom stale
Her infinite variety: other women cloy
The appetites they feed: but she makes hungry
Where most she satisfies.

SHAKESPEARE, *Antony and Cleopatra*, ii, 2

Your lordship, though not clean past your youth, hath yet some smack of age in you, some relish of the saltness of time.

SHAKESPEARE, *King Henry IV, Part II*, i, 2

When the age is in, the wit is out.

SHAKESPEARE, *Much Ado about Nothing*, iii, 5

Crabbed age and youth cannot live together:
Youth is full of pleasance, age is full of care;
Youth like summer morn, age like winter weather;
Youth like summer brave, age like winter bare.

SHAKESPEARE, *Passionate Pilgrim*, st. 12

Thoughts of my age,
  Dread ye not the cold sod;
Hopes of my age,
  Be ye fixed on your God.

ST. GEORGE TUCKER, *Days of My Youth*, st. 3

Agony.— Charm ache with air, and agony with words.

SHAKESPEARE, *Much Ado about Nothing*, v, 1

Air.— *Hamlet*. The air bites shrewdly; it is very cold.
Horatio. It is a nipping and an eager air.

SHAKESPEARE, *Hamlet*, i, 4

The air, a chartered libertine.

SHAKESPEARE, *King Henry V*, i, 1

Alarum.— Hear the loud alarum bells —
Brazen bells!
What a tale of terror, now, their turbulency tells.

POE, *The Bells*, st. 3

Albatross.— "Why look'st thou so?"—"With my cross-bow I shot the albatross."

COLERIDGE, *Ancient Mariner*, lines 81, 82

Alcalde.— He whose father is alcalde, of his trial hath no fear.

BRET HARTE, *Concepcion de Arguello*, iii, st. 15

Alcoholic.— The alcoholic virtues don't wash; but until the water takes their colours out, the tints are very much like those of the true celestial stuff.

HOLMES, *Autocrat of the Breakfast-Table*, viii

Ale.— Then to the spicy nut-brown ale.[1]
MILTON, *L'Allegro*, line 100

I would give all my fame for a pot of ale and safety.
SHAKESPEARE, *King Henry V*, iii, 2

A quart of ale is a dish for a king.
SHAKESPEARE, *Winter's Tale*, iv, 3 [2]

I cannot eat but little meat,—
My stomach is not good;
But, sure, I think that I can drink
With him that wears a hood. . . .
Back and side, go bare, go bare;
Both foot and hand go cold;
But, belly, God send thee good ale enough,
Whether it be new or old.
JOHN STILL, *Good Ale*, st. 1

Alexandrine.— A needless Alexandrine ends the song
That, like a wounded snake, drags its slow length along.
POPE, *Essay on Criticism*, lines 356, 357

Algebra. He, by geometric scale,
Could take the size of pots of ale;
Resolve, by sines and tangents straight,
If bread or butter wanted weight;
And wisely tell what hour o' th' day
The clock does strike, by algebra.
BUTLER, *Hudibras*, I, i, lines 121–126

Allegory.— As headstrong as an allegory on the banks of the Nile.
SHERIDAN, *The Rivals*, v, 3

Alley.— Of all the girls that are so smart
There's none like pretty Sally;
She is the darling of my heart,
And she lives in our alley.
H. CAREY, *Sally in Our Alley*, st. 1

Alliances.— Peace, commerce, and honest friendship, with all nations,— entangling alliances with none.
THOMAS JEFFERSON, *Inaugural Address, March* 4, 1801

Alliteration.— Apt alliteration's artful aid.
C. CHURCHILL, *The Prophecy of Famine*

Almighty.— The Almighty has his own purposes.
ABRAHAM LINCOLN, *Inaugural Address, March* 4, 1865

---

[1] Foamed forth in floods the nut-brown ale.
SCOTT, *Lay of the Last Minstrel*, Canto VI, viii

Alms.— That is no true alms which the hand can hold;
He gives only the worthless gold
Who gives from a sense of duty.
LOWELL, *Vision of Sir Launfal*, i, st. 6

Alone.— Alone, alone, all, all alone,
Alone on a wide, wide sea!
COLERIDGE, *Ancient Mariner*, lines 232, 233, 598

Alone I did it. SHAKESPEARE, *Coriolanus*, v, 6 [5]

Altar-stairs.— Upon the great world's altar-stairs
That slope through darkness up to God.
TENNYSON, *In Memoriam*, lv, st. 4

Ambassador.— An ambassador is an honest man sent to lie abroad for the good of his country.
SIR HENRY WOTTON, adapted and translated by Izaak Walton in his *Life of Wotton*

Ambition.— Till pride and worse ambition threw me down.
MILTON, *Paradise Lost*, IV, line 40

What will not ambition and revenge
Descend to? who aspires must down as low
As high he soared. *Ibid.*, IX, lines 168–170

Lowliness is young ambition's ladder,
Whereto the climber-upward turns his face;
But when he once attains the upmost round,
He then unto the ladder turns his back,
Looks in the clouds, scorning the base degrees
By which he did ascend.
SHAKESPEARE, *Julius Cæsar*, ii, 1

Ambition should be made of sterner stuff. *Ibid.*, iii, 2

Cromwell, I charge thee, fling away ambition:
By that sin fell the angels; how can man, then,
The image of his Maker, hope to win by it?
SHAKESPEARE, *King Henry VIII*, iii, 2

Vaulting ambition, which o'erleaps itself.
SHAKESPEARE, *Macbeth*, i, 7

Ambitious.— As Cæsar loved me, I weep for him; as he was fortunate, I rejoice at it; as he was valiant, I honour him: but, as he was ambitious, I slew him. There is tears for his love; joy for his fortune; honour for his valour; and death for his ambition.
SHAKESPEARE, *Julius Cæsar*, iii, 2

No man's pie is freed
From his ambitious finger.
SHAKESPEARE, *King Henry VIII*, i, 1

Amen. "Amen"
Stuck in my throat. SHAKESPEARE, *Macbeth*, ii, 2

America.— This day is a glorious day for America.
SAMUEL ADAMS, quoted in Tudor's *Life of James Otis*

America! half-brother of the world!
With something good and bad of every land.
P. J. BAILEY, *Festus*, Scene—The Surface

My Lords, you cannot conquer America.
WILLIAM PITT, EARL OF CHATHAM,
Speech on the American War, Nov. 18, 1777

American.— I am an American,— and wherever I look up and see the stars and stripes overhead, that is home to me! HOLMES, *Professor at the Breakfast-Table*, iv

The apron-strings of an American mother are made of india-rubber. Her boy belongs where he is wanted; and . . . his home [is] wherever the stars and stripes [blow] over his head. *Ibid.*, xii

To think of trying to waterproof the American mind against the questions that Heaven rains down upon it shows a misapprehension of our new conditions; . . . for what the Declaration means is the right to question everything, even the truth of its own fundamental proposition. *Ibid.*

The kindly-earnest, brave, foreseeing man [Lincoln],
Sagacious, patient, dreading praise, not blame,
New birth of our new soil, the first American.
LOWELL, *Commemoration Ode*, st. 6

If I were an American, as I am an Englishman, while a foreign troop was landed in my country, I never would lay down my arms—never—never—never!
WILLIAM PITT, EARL OF CHATHAM,
Speech on the American War, Nov. 18, 1777

Amorous.— Whosoever esteemeth too much of amorous affection, quitteth both riches and wisdom.
BACON, *Essay X: Of Love*

Anchor.— Our anchor soon must change his bed of fiery rich array
For a hammock at the roaring bows, or an oozy couch of clay.
SIR S. FERGUSON, *The Forging of the Anchor*, st. 4

Cast all your cares on God; that anchor holds.
TENNYSON, *Enoch Arden*, line 222

Angel.— Thou hast called me thy angel in moments of bliss,
And thy angel I'll be, 'mid the horrors of this,—
Through the furnace, unshrinking, thy steps to pursue,
And shield thee, and save thee,—or perish there too!
THOMAS MOORE, *Come, Rest in This Bosom*, st. 3

Methinks an angel spake.—SHAKESPEARE, *King John*, v, 2

Till my bad angel fire my good one out.
SHAKESPEARE, *Sonnet cxliv; Passionate Pilgrim*, st. 2

Angels.—The angels all were singing out of tune,
And hoarse with having little else to do,
Excepting to wind up the sun and moon,
Or curb a runaway young star or two.
BYRON, *Vision of Judgment*, st. 2

I know that the angels are whispering with thee.
S. LOVER, *The Angel's Whisper*

Like angels' visits, short and bright.[1]
JOHN NORRIS, *The Parting*

Angels and ministers of grace defend us!
SHAKESPEARE, *Hamlet*, i, 4

Anger.— Like women's anger, impotent and loud.
DRYDEN, *Epistle to Sir Godfrey Kneller*, line 84

Anger's my meat; I sup upon myself,
And so shall starve with feeding.
SHAKESPEARE, *Coriolanus*, iv, 2

Anger is like
A full-hot horse, who being allowed his way,
Self-mettle tires him.
SHAKESPEARE, *King Henry VIII*, i, 1

Anger hath a privilege.—SHAKESPEARE, *King Lear*, ii, 2

Angle. Angle on; and beg to have
A quiet passage to a welcome grave.
IZAAK WALTON, *The Angler's Wish*, st. 4

---

[1] Like angel-visits, few and far between.
THOMAS CAMPBELL, *Pleasures of Hope*, ii, st. 28

Visits
Like those of angels, short and far between.
R. BLAIR, *The Grave*, ii

Angling.— Angling is somewhat like poetry, men are to be born so. Izaak Walton, *The Complete Angler*, i

We may say of angling as Dr. Boteler said of strawberries: "Doubtless God could have made a better berry, but doubtless God never did." And so, if I might be judge, God never did make a more calm, quiet, innocent recreation than angling. *Ibid.*

All that are lovers of virtue . . . be quiet and go a-angling. *Ibid.*, xxi

Anguish.— Beloved one, if anguish would fall where fall it may,
If sorrow could be won by gifts to barter prey for prey,
There is an arm would wither, so thine revived might be;
A lip which would be still and mute, to make thy music free;
An eye which would forget to wake, to bid thy morning shine;
A heart whose very strings would break, to steal one pang from thine. Praed, *To* ———, st. 2

Anointed.— The Lord's anointed.
Shakespeare, *King Richard III*, iv, 4

Answer.— You shall never take her without her answer, unless you take her without her tongue.
Shakespeare, *As You Like It*, iv, 1

Answers.— I am not bound to please thee with my answers.
Shakespeare, *Merchant of Venice*, iv, 1

Anthem.— Where, through the long-drawn aisle and fretted vault,
The pealing anthem swells the note of praise.
Gray, *Elegy Written in a Country Churchyard*, st. 11

The hundredth Psalm, the grand old Puritan anthem.
Longfellow, *Courtship of Miles Standish*, iii, line 40

Anti.— Lean, hungry, savage, anti-everythings.
Holmes, *A Modest Request*, The Speech, line 40

Antiquity.— Antiquity appears to have begun
Long after thy primeval race was run.
Horace Smith, *Address to a Mummy*, st. 6

Apes.— I must dance barefoot on her wedding-day,
And, for your love to her, lead apes in hell.[1]
Shakespeare, *Taming of the Shrew*, ii

---

[1] I will . . . lead his apes into hell.
Shakespeare, *Much Ado about Nothing*, ii, 1

Apology.— Apology is only egotism wrong side out.
HOLMES, *Professor at the Breakfast-Table*, vi

Apostles.— Parson Wilbur sez he never heerd in his life
Thet th' Apostles rigged out in their swaller-tail coats,
An' marched round in front of a drum an' a fife,
To git some on 'em office, an' some on 'em votes;
But John P.
Robinson he
Sez they did n't know everythin' down in Judee.
LOWELL, *Biglow Papers*, I, iii, st. 8

Apothecary.— An apothecary on a white horse
Rode by, on his vocation;
And the Devil thought of his old friend,
Death, in the Revelation.
SOUTHEY, *The Devil's Walk*, st. 7

Apparel.— Costly thy habit as thy purse can buy,
But not expressed in fancy; rich, not gaudy;
For the apparel oft proclaims the man.
SHAKESPEARE, *Hamlet*, i, 3

Appetite.— Appetite comes with eating. RABELAIS, I, v

She would hang on him,
As if increase of appetite had grown
By what it fed on. SHAKESPEARE, *Hamlet*, i, 2

Applaud.— I would applaud thee to the very echo,
That should applaud again.
SHAKESPEARE, *Macbeth*, v, 3

Applause.— The applause of listening senates[1] to command.
GRAY, *Elegy Written in a Country Churchyard*, st. 17

Apple.— An evil soul producing holy witness
Is like a villain with a smiling cheek,
A goodly apple rotten at the heart.
SHAKESPEARE, *Merchant of Venice*, i, 3

Apples.— Lord love us, how we apples swim.
DAVID MALLETT,[2] *Tyburn*

There's small choice in rotten apples.
SHAKESPEARE, *Taming of the Shrew*, i, 1

Approbation.— Approbation from Sir Hubert Stanley is praise indeed.
THOMAS MORTON, *A Cure for the Heart-ache*, v, 2

---

[1] While listening senates hang upon thy tongue.
THOMSON, *The Seasons, Autumn*, line 15

[2] Also attributed to Swift.

'T is approbation strikes the string of joy.
YOUNG, *Night Thoughts*, VIII, line 85

Arab.— Because thou com'st, a weary guest,
Unto my tent, I bid thee rest.
This cruse of oil, this skin of wine,
These tamarinds and dates are thine.

. . . . .

Even so
An Arab chieftain treats a foe,
Holds him as one without a fault
Who breaks his bread and tastes his salt;
And, in fair battle, strikes him dead
With the same pleasure that he gives him bread.
T. B. ALDRICH, *An Arab Welcome*

Archer.— Insatiate archer! could not one suffice?
Thy shaft flew thrice, and thrice my peace was slain;
And thrice, ere thrice yon moon had filled her horn.
YOUNG, *Night Thoughts*, I, lines 212–214

Are.— We know what we are, but know not what we may be.
SHAKESPEARE, *Hamlet*, iv, 5

Argue.— In arguing, too, the parson owned his skill,
For e'en though vanquished, he could argue still.
GOLDSMITH, *The Deserted Village*, st. 14

Ark.— Presume to lay their hand upon the ark
Of her magnificent and awful cause.
COWPER, *The Task: The Time-Piece*, lines 231, 232

Arm.— Arm! arm! it is — it is — the cannon's opening roar!
BYRON, *Childe Harold's Pilgrimage*, Canto iii, st. 22

Arm-chair.— I love it, I love it; and who shall dare
To chide me for loving that old arm-chair?

. . . . .

Would ye learn the spell? — a mother sat there;
And a sacred thing is that old arm-chair.
ELIZA COOK, *The Old Arm-chair*, st. 1

Armed.— Thrice is he armed that hath his quarrel just,[1]
And he but naked, though locked up in steel,
Whose conscience with injustice is corrupted.
SHAKESPEARE, *King Henry VI, Part II*, iii, 2

Arms.— My soul's in arms, and eager for the fray.
COLLEY CIBBER, *Richard III, Adapted*, v, 5

---

[1] My strength is as the strength of ten,
Because my heart is pure.
TENNYSON, *Sir Galahad*

Arms and the man I sing, who, forced by Fate,
And haughty Juno's unrelenting hate.[1]
DRYDEN, *Virgil's Æneid*, Book I, lines 1, 2

The arms are fair,
When the intent of bearing them is just.
SHAKESPEARE, *King Henry IV, Part I*, v, 2

Art.— All things are artificial, for nature is the art of God.[2]
SIR THOMAS BROWNE, *Religio Medici*, sect. xvi

When the flush of a new-born sun fell first on Eden's green and gold,
Our father Adam sat under the Tree and scratched with a stick in the mould;
And the first rude sketch that the world had seen was joy to his mighty heart,
Till the Devil whispered behind the leaves: "It's pretty, but is it art?"
KIPLING, *The Conundrum of the Workshop*

Artificer.— Another lean unwashed artificer.
SHAKESPEARE, *King John*, iv, 2

Artillery.— Then shook the hills with thunder riven;
Then rushed the steed, to battle driven;
And louder than the bolts of Heaven
Far flashed the red artillery.
THOMAS CAMPBELL, *Hohenlinden*, st. 4

Arts.— Arts that thrive at Number Five
Don't take at Number One. HOOD, *Number One*, st. 3

Ashes.— Take them, O Father, in immortal trust!
Ashes to ashes, dust to kindred dust,
Till the last angel rolls the stone away,
And a new morning brings eternal day!
HOLMES, *Dedication of the Pittsfield Cemetery*, st. 9

Ass.— Oh, that he were here to write me down an ass! But, masters, remember that I am an ass; though it be not written down, yet forget not that I am an ass . . . Oh, that I had been writ down an ass. . . . Do not forget to specify, when time and place shall serve, that I am an ass.
SHAKESPEARE, *Much Ado about Nothing*, iv, 2; v, 1

---

[1] And angry Juno's unrelenting hate.
DRYDEN, *Palamon and Arcite*, line 698

[2] The course of nature is the art of God.
YOUNG, *Night Thoughts*, IX, line 1269

Asses.— Its proper power to hurt, each creature feels;
Bulls aim their horns, and asses lift their heels.
POPE *Imitations of Horace.*
Satire I, Book ii, lines 85, 86

Theseus. I wonder if the lion be to speak.
Demetrius. No wonder, my lord: one lion may, when many asses do.
SHAKESPEARE, *Midsummer-Night's Dream*, v, 1

Assurance. I 'll make assurance doubly sure,
And take a bond of fate.—SHAKESPEARE, *Macbeth*, iv, 1

Assyrian.— The Assyrian came down like the wolf on the fold,
And his cohorts were gleaming in purple and gold.
BYRON, *Destruction of Sennacherib*, st. 1

Astronomer.— An undevout astronomer is mad.
YOUNG, *Night Thoughts*, IX, line 773

Atheism.— A little philosophy inclineth man's mind to atheism; but depth in philosophy bringeth men's minds about to religion. . . . Atheism is rather in the lip than in the heart of man. BACON, *Essay XVI: Of Atheism*

Atheist.— By night an atheist half believes a god.
YOUNG, *Night Thoughts*, V, line 176

Atlantis.— The lost Atlantis of our youth!
LONGFELLOW, *Ultima Thule*, Dedication, st. 2

Attempt.— Attempt the end, and never stand to doubt;
Nothing 's so hard, but search will find it out.
HERRICK, *Seek and Find*

Attractive.— Here 's metal more attractive.
SHAKESPEARE, *Hamlet*, iii, 2

Auld Lang Syne.—Should auld acquaintance be forgot,
And never brought to min'?
. . . . .
We'll tak' a cup o' kindness yet,
For auld lang syne. BURNS, *Auld Lang Syne*

Austrian.— An Austrian army, awfully arrayed,
Boldly by battery besieged Belgrade.
ANONYMOUS, *Siege of Belgrade*

Authors.— Authors, like coins, grow dear as they grow old;
It is the rust we value, not the gold.
POPE, *Imitations of Horace*, Epistle I, Book ii, lines 35, 36

Avarice.— So, for a good old gentlemanly vice,
I think I must take up with avarice.
BYRON, *Don Juan*, Canto i, st. 216

Avenged.— 'T is an old tale and often told;
But did my fate and wish agree,
Ne'er had been read in story old
Of maiden true betrayed for gold
That loved or was avenged like me!
SCOTT, *Marmion*, ii, st. 27

O God! if my deep prayers cannot appease thee,
But thou wilt be avenged on my misdeeds,
Yet execute thy wrath in [on] me alone;
Oh, spare my guiltless wife and my poor children!
SHAKESPEARE, *King Richard III*, i, 4

Avenging.— So wills the fierce avenging Sprite,
Till blood for blood atones!
Ay, though he's buried in a cave,
And trodden down with stones,
And years have rotted off his flesh,—
The world shall see his bones!
HOOD, *The Dream of Eugene Aram*

Awake.— Awake, arise, or be for ever fallen!
MILTON, *Paradise Lost*, I, line 33

Aweary. Cassius is aweary of the world;
Hated by one he loves; braved by his brother;
Checked like a bondman; all his faults observed,
Set in a note-book, learned, and conned by rote,
To cast into my teeth.
SHAKESPEARE, *Julius Cæsar*, iv, 3

Axe.— When I see a merchant over-polite to his customers, begging them to taste a little brandy, and throwing half his goods on the counter, thinks I, that man has an axe to grind. C. MINOR, *Who'll Turn Grindstones?*

Axis.— The axis of the earth sticks out visibly through the centre of each and every town or city.
HOLMES, *Autocrat of the Breakfast-Table*, vi

Baby.— Who can tell what a baby thinks?
Who can follow the gossamer links
By which the mannikin feels his way
Out from the shore of the great unknown,
Blind, and wailing, and alone,
Into the light of day? J. G. HOLLAND, *Bitter Sweet:* First Movement — The Question Stated

"Where did you come from, baby dear?"
"Out of the everywhere into the here."
G. MACDONALD, *The Baby*, st. 1

Oh, hush thee, my baby, thy sire was a knight,
Thy mother a lady both lovely and bright.
SCOTT, *Lullaby of an Infant Chief*, st. 1

Bacchus.— Bacchus, ever fair and young,
Drinking joys did first ordain;
Bacchus' blessings are a treasure,
Drinking is the soldier's pleasure:
Rich the treasure,
Sweet the pleasure,
Sweet is pleasure after pain.
DRYDEN, *Alexander's Feast*, lines 54–60

Bachelor.— When I said I would die a bachelor, I did not think I should live till I were married.
SHAKESPEARE, *Much Ado about Nothing*, ii, 3

Bachelor's Hall.— Bachelor's Hall, what a quare-lookin' place it is!
Kape me from such all the days of my life!
Sure but I think what a burnin' disgrace it is,
Niver at all to be gettin' a wife.

Pots, dishes, pans, an' such grasy commodities,
Ashes and praty-skins, kiver the floor;
His cupboard's a storehouse of comical oddities,
Things that had niver been neighbours before.
JOHN FINLEY, *Bachelor's Hall*, st. 1, 2

Bad.— 'Tis no shame to be bad, because 'tis so common.
CYRIL TOURNEUR, *The Revenger's Tragedy*, ii, 1

Bairns.— Oh, bairnies, cuddle doon!
ALEXANDER ANDERSON, *Cuddle Doon*

They say barnes are blessings.
SHAKESPEARE, *All's Well That Ends Well*, i, 3

Bait.— Bait the hook well; this fish will bite.
SHAKESPEARE, *Much Ado about Nothing*, ii, 3

Balance.— I called the New World into existence to redress the balance of the Old. CANNING, *The King's Message*

Ballads.— I knew a very wise man that believed that if a man were permitted to make all the ballads he need not care who should make the laws of a nation.
ANDREW FLETCHER OF SALTOUN, *Letter to the Marquis of Montrose*

Balm.—"Is there — is there balm in Gilead? — tell me — tell me, I implore!"
Quoth the raven, "Nevermore!"
POE, *The Raven*, st. 15

Banishment.— The bitter bread of banishment.
SHAKESPEARE, *King Richard II*, iii, 1

Bank.— I know a bank where the wild thyme blows,
Where oxlips and the nodding violet grows.
SHAKESPEARE, *Midsummer-Night's Dream*, ii, 1

Banner.— For ever float that standard sheet!
Where breathes the foe but falls before us,
With Freedom's soil beneath our feet,
And Freedom's banner streaming o'er us?
DRAKE, *The American Flag*, st. 5

Oh, say, can you see, by the dawn's early light,
What so proudly we hailed at the twilight's last gleaming?
Whose broad stripes and bright stars, through the perilous fight,
O'er the ramparts we watched, were so gallantly streaming;
And the rocket's red glare, the bombs bursting in air,
Gave proof through the night that our flag was still there;
Oh, say, does that star-spangled banner yet wave
O'er the land of the free and the home of the brave?
F. S. KEY, *The Star-Spangled Banner*, st. 1

Our glorious Semper Eadem, the banner of our pride.
MACAULAY, *The Armada*, line 30

Banners.— Hang out our banners on the outward walls;
The cry is still "They come!" our castle's strength
Will laugh a siege to scorn.—SHAKESPEARE, *Macbeth*, v, 5

Banquet-hall.— I feel like one
Who treads alone
Some banquet-hall deserted,
Whose lights are fled,
Whose garlands dead,
And all but he departed.
T. MOORE, *Oft in the Stilly Night*, st. 2

Bar.— Sunset and evening star,
And one clear call for me!
And may there be no moaning of the bar,
When I put out to sea.[1]

---

[1] Raise ye no cry, and let no moan
Be made when I depart.—FELICIA HEMANS, *The Cid's Deathbed*, st. 9

But such a tide as moving seems asleep,
  Too full for sound and foam,[1]
When that which drew from out the boundless deep[2]
  Turns again home.

Twilight and evening bell,
  And after that the dark!
And may there be no sadness of farewell,
  When I embark. TENNYSON, *Crossing the Bar*

Barbarism.— There is a moral of all human tales;
  'T is but the same rehearsal of the past,
  First freedom, and then glory — when that fails,
  Wealth, vice, corruption,— barbarism at last.
BYRON, *Childe Harold's Pilgrimage*, Canto iv, st. 108

Barbered.— Being barbered ten times o'er.
SHAKESPEARE, *Antony and Cleopatra*, ii, 2

Bard.— A bard here dwelt, more fat than bard beseems.
JAMES THOMSON, *The Castle of Indolence*, Canto i, st. 68

Bargain.— So clap hands and a bargain.
SHAKESPEARE, *King Henry V*, v, 2

Bark. That fatal and perfidious bark,
  Built in the eclipse, and rigged with curses dark.
MILTON, *Lycidas*, lines 100, 101

Barleycorn.— John Barleycorn was a hero bold,
    Of noble enterprise,
  For if you do but taste his blood,
    'T will make your courage rise.
BURNS, *John Barleycorn*, st. 13

---

[1] How still the plains of the water be!
The tide is in his ecstasy.
The tide is at his highest height:
And it is night.—LANIER, *The Marshes of Glynn*, st. 10

[2] Out of the deep, my child, out of the deep,
Where all that was to be, in all that was,
Whirled for a million æons through the vast
Waste dawn of multitudinous-eddying light —

. . . . . .

And last in kindly curves, with gentlest fall,
By quiet fields, a slowly-dying power,
To that last deep where we and thou are still.
TENNYSON, *De Profundis*, i

Out of the deep, Spirit, out of the deep,
With this ninth moon, that sends the hidden sun
Down yon dark sea, thou comest, darling boy.
TENNYSON, *De Profundis*, ii, st. 1

Where is he who knows?
From the great deep to the great deep he goes.
TENNYSON, *Coming of Arthur*, lines 409, 410

Inspiring, bold John Barleycorn!
What dangers thou canst mak' us scorn!
Wi' tippenny we fear nae evil;
Wi' usquebae we'll face the devil!
BURNS, *Tam O' Shanter*, st. 11

Bastion.— A looming bastion fringed with fire.
TENNYSON, *In Memoriam*, xv, st. 5

Battle.— Battle's magnificently-stern array! BYRON,
Childe Harold's Pilgrimage, Canto iii, st. 28

While the battle rages loud and long
And the stormy winds do blow.
CAMPBELL, *Ye Mariners of England*

Wut 's words to them whose faith an' truth
On War's red techstone rang true metal,
Who ventered life an' love an' youth
For the gret prize o' death in battle?
LOWELL, *Biglow Papers*, II, x, st. 17

And hark! like the roar of the billows on the shore,
The cry of battle rises along their charging line!
For God! for the cause! for the Church! for the Laws!
For Charles, King of England, and Rupert of the Rhine!
MACAULAY, *The Battle of Naseby*, st. 5

On the perilous edge
Of battle.—MILTON, *Paradise Lost*, I, lines 276, 277

Battles.— Soothed with the sound the king grew vain;
Fought all his battles o'er again;
And thrice he routed all his foes; and thrice he slew the slain.
DRYDEN, *Alexander's Feast*, lines 66–68

Be.— To be, or not to be: that is the question:
Whether 'tis nobler in the mind to suffer
The slings and arrows of outrageous fortune,
Or to take arms against a sea of troubles,
And by opposing end them?—SHAKESPEARE, *Hamlet*, iii, 1

Beak.—"Take thy beak from out my heart, and take thy form from off my door!"
Quoth the raven, "Nevermore!"
POE, *The Raven*, st. 17

Bear.— To bear, to nurse, to rear,
To watch, and then to lose:
To see my bright ones disappear,
Drawn up like morning dews.
JEAN INGELOW, *Songs of Seven: Seven Times Six*, st. 1

She will sing the savageness out of a bear.
SHAKESPEARE, *Othello*, iv, 1

Beast. The beast
With many heads. SHAKESPEARE, *Coriolanus*, iv, 1

A beast, that wants discourse of reason,
Would have mourned longer.—SHAKESPEARE, *Hamlet*, i, 2

Move upward, working out the beast,
And let the ape and tiger die.
TENNYSON, *In Memoriam*, cxviii, st. 7

Beaten.— Some have been beaten till they know
What wood a cudgel's of by th' blow;
Some kicked, until they can feel whether
A shoe be Spanish or neat's leather.
BUTLER, *Hudibras*, II, i, lines 221–224

Beautiful.— With other articles of ladies fair,
To keep them beautiful, or leave them neat.
BYRON, *Don Juan*, Canto i, st. 143

Make no deep scrutiny
Into her mutiny
Rash and undutiful;
Past all dishonour,
Death has left on her
Only the beautiful. HOOD, *The Bridge of Sighs*, st. 5

Beautiful as sweet!
And young as beautiful! and soft as young!
And gay as soft! and innocent as gay!
YOUNG, *Night Thoughts*, III, lines 81–83

Beauty.— My love in her attire doth show her wit,
It doth so well become her:
For every season she hath dressings fit,
For winter, spring, and summer.
No beauty she doth miss
When all her robes are on:
But Beauty's self she is
When all her robes are gone.
ANONYMOUS, *Madrigal: My Love in Her Attire*

Old as I am, for ladies' love unfit,
The power of beauty I remember yet,
Which once inflamed my soul, and still inspires my wit.[1]
DRYDEN, *Cymon and Iphigenia*, lines 1–3

A thing of beauty is a joy for ever.
KEATS, *Endymion*, i, line 1

---

[1] Oh, the days are gone when beauty bright
My heart's chain wove,
When my dream of life from morn to night
Was love, still love!
T. MOORE, *Love's Young Dream*

Beauty provoketh thieves sooner than gold.
SHAKESPEARE, *As You Like It*, i, 3

The goodness that is cheap in beauty makes beauty brief in goodness.
SHAKESPEARE, *Measure for Measure*, iii, 1

Beauty too rich for use, for earth too dear!
SHAKESPEARE, *Romeo and Juliet*, i, 5

'Tis beauty truly blent, whose red and white
Nature's own sweet and cunning hand laid on:
Lady, you are the cruellest she alive,
If you will lead these graces to the grave
And leave the world no copy.
SHAKESPEARE, *Twelfth Night*, i, 5

Bed.— Oh, bed! oh, bed! delicious bed!
That heaven upon earth to the weary head.
HOOD, *Miss Kilmansegg*, Her Dream

Weary with toil, I haste me to my bed,
The dear repose for limbs with travel tired;
But then begins a journey in my head,
To work my mind, when body's work's expired.
SHAKESPEARE, *Sonnet* xxvii

Of all the foes that man should dread
The first and worse one is a bed

. . . . . .

For I've been born and I've been wed —
All of man's peril comes of bed.
C. H. WEBB, *Dum Vivimus Vigilamus*, st. 1, 2

Bedclothes.— He took lodgings for rain or shine
Under green bedclothes in '69.
HOLMES, *Parson Turell's Legacy*, st. 1

Bedfellows.— Misery acquaints a man with strange bedfellows.[1]
SHAKESPEARE, *The Tempest*, ii, 2

Bee.— Where the bee sucks, there suck I:
In a cowslip's bell I lie.

. . . . . .

Merrily, merrily shall I live now,
Under the blossom that hangs on the bough.
SHAKESPEARE, *The Tempest*, v, 1 (Ariel's Song)

---

[1] In they go,
Beggar and banker, porter and gentleman,
The cinder wench and the white-handed lady,
Into one pit: oh, rare, rare bedfellows!
There they all lie in uncomplaining sleep.
WILSON

Do not all go to one place?
Ecclesiastes, vi, 6

Beef.— When mighty roast beef was the Englishman's food,
It ennobled our hearts, and enriched our blood;
Our soldiers were brave, and our courtiers were good.
Oh, the roast beef of old England,
And oh, the old English roast beef!
FIELDING, *The Roast Beef of Old England*, st. 1

What say you to a piece of beef and mustard?
SHAKESPEARE, *Taming of the Shrew*, iv, 3

Beer.— Doth it not show vilely in me to desire small beer?
SHAKESPEARE, *King Henry IV, Part II*, ii, 2

Taps, that in our day were famous,
Have given place to lager bier.
STEDMAN, *The Ballad of Lager Bier*, st. 1

Beetle.— If I do, fillip me with a three-man beetle.
SHAKESPEARE, *King Henry IV, Part II*, i, 2

Beggar. Whiles I am a beggar, I will rail
And say there is no sin but to be rich;
And, being rich, my virtue then shall be
To say there is no vice but beggary.
SHAKESPEARE, *King John*, ii, 1 [2]

Beggars.— Beggars mounted run their horse to death.
SHAKESPEARE, *King Henry VI, Part III*, i, 4

Bell.— The sound of the church-going bell.
COWPER, *Alexander Selkirk*, st. 4

His death, which happened in his berth,
At forty-odd befell:
They went and told the sexton, and
The sexton tolled the bell.
HOOD, *Faithless Sally Brown*, st. 17

If the midnight bell
Did, with his iron tongue and brazen mouth,
Sound on into the drowsy ear of night.
SHAKESPEARE, *King John*, iii, 3

Bell, book and candle.[1] *Ibid.*

---

[1]The Cardinal rose with a dignified look,
He called for his candle, his bell, and his book.
R. H. BARHAM, *Ingoldsby Legends*, The Jackdaw of Rheims

Go fetch me a book!— go fetch me a bell
As big as a dustman's!— and a candle as well!
I'll send him — *where* good manners won't let me tell!
R. H. BARHAM, *Ingoldsby Legends*, The Ingoldsby Penance

It is done!
Clang of bell and roar of gun
Send the tidings[1] up and down.
How the belfries rock and reel!
How the great guns, peal on peal,
Fling the joy from town to town!
WHITTIER, *Laus Deo*, st. 1

Bells.— Oh, the merry Christ-Church bells!
ANONYMOUS, *The Merry Bells of Oxford*

Those evening bells! those evening bells!
How many a tale their music tells,
Of youth and home and that sweet time
When last I heard their soothing chime.
T. MOORE, *Those Evening Bells*, st. 1

Hear the sledges with the bells —
Silver bells!
What a world of merriment their melody foretells!
How they tinkle, tinkle, tinkle,
In the icy air of night!
While the stars that oversprinkle
All the heavens seem to twinkle
With a crystalline delight.[2]— POE, *The Bells*, st. 1

If ever you have looked on better days,
If ever been where bells have knolled to church,
If ever sat at any good man's feast,
If ever from your eyelids wiped a tear
And know what 't is to pity and be pitied,
Let gentleness my strong enforcement be.
SHAKESPEARE, *As You Like It*, ii, 7

The time draws near the birth of Christ:
The moon is hid, the night is still;
A single church below the hill
Is pealing, folded in the mist.

A single peal of bells below,
That wakens at this hour of rest
A single murmur in the breast,
That these are not the bells I know.
TENNYSON, *In Memoriam*, civ

Ring out, wild bells, to the wild sky. *Ibid.*, cvi, st. 1

---

[1] Of the passage of the Thirteenth Amendment to the Constitution of the United States abolishing slavery.

[2] Jingle, jingle, clear the way,
'T is the merry, merry sleigh!
As it swiftly scuds along,
Hear the burst of happy song,
See the gleam of glances bright,
Flashing o'er the pathway white!
Jingle, jingle, past it flies,
Sending shafts from hooded eyes.
G. W. PETTEE, *Sleigh Song*.

Belly.— He had a broad face, and a little round belly,
That shook, when he laughed, like a bowl full of jelly.
C. C. MOORE, *A Visit from St. Nicholas*

Benefits.— Freeze, freeze, thou bitter sky,
Thou dost not bite so nigh
As benefits forgot:
Though thou the waters warp,
Thy sting is not so sharp
As friend remembered not.
SHAKESPEARE, *As You Like It*, ii, 7

Benison.— God's benison go with you; and with those
That would make good of bad, and friends of foes!
SHAKESPEARE, *Macbeth*, ii, 4

Best.— Grow old along with me!
The best is yet to be.
R. BROWNING, *Rabbi Ben Ezra*, st. 1

No doubt everything is for the best.
BYRON, *Don Juan*, Canto vi, st. 1

Who does the best his circumstance allows,
Does well, acts nobly; angels could no more.
YOUNG, *Night Thoughts*, II, lines 91, 92

Betimes.— Not to be a-bed after midnight is to be up betimes.
SHAKESPEARE, *Twelfth Night*, ii, 3

Beware.— I know a maiden fair to see,
Take care!
She can both false and friendly be,
Beware! Beware!
Trust her not,
She is fooling thee!
LONGFELLOW, *Translation from the German: Beware!* st. 1

Bible.— Slowly the Bible of the race is writ,
And not on paper leaves nor leaves of stone;
Each age, each kindred, adds a verse to it,
Texts of despair or hope, of joy or moan.[1]
LOWELL, *Bibliolatres*, st. 6

Bier.— They bore him barefaced on the bier.
SHAKESPEARE, *Hamlet*, iv, 5

Bile.— There are but two bad things in this world — sin and bile.
HANNAH MORE

---

[1] Out from the heart of Nature rolled
The burdens of the Bible old;
The litanies of nations came,
Like the volcano's tongue of flame,
Up from the burning core below,—
The canticles of love and woe.
EMERSON, *The Problem*, st. 2

Bilious.— No solemn sanctimonious face I pull,
Nor think I'm pious when I'm only bilious.
HOOD, *Ode to Rae Wilson, Esquire*, st. 4

Billiards.— Let's to billiards.
SHAKESPEARE, *Antony and Cleopatra*, ii, 5

Bird.— The bird that hath been limèd in a bush,
With trembling wings misdoubteth every bush.
SHAKESPEARE, *King Henry VI, Part III*, v, 6

The ruddy square of comfortable light,
Far-blazing from the rear of Philip's house,
Allured him, as the beacon-blaze allures
The bird of passage, till he madly strikes
Against it and beats out his weary life.
TENNYSON, *Enoch Arden*, lines 722–726

Birdie.— What does little birdie say
In her nest at peep of day?
TENNYSON, *Sea Dreams*, lines 281, 282

Birnam.— Till Birnam wood remove to Dunsinane.
SHAKESPEARE, *Macbeth*, v, 3

Birth.— The owl shrieked at thy birth,— an evil sign;
The night-crow cried, aboding luckless time;
Dogs howled, and hideous tempests [tempest] shook down trees;
The raven rooked her on the chimney's top,
And chattering pies in dismal discords sung.
SHAKESPEARE, *King Henry VI, Part III*, v, 6

Our birth is but a sleep and a forgetting:
The soul that rises with us, our life's star,
Hath had elsewhere its setting,
And cometh from afar:
Not in entire forgetfulness,
And not in utter nakedness,
But trailing clouds of glory do we come
From God, who is our home.
WORDSWORTH, *Ode on Intimations of Immortality*, st. 5

Birthdays.— What different dooms our birthdays bring!
HOOD, *Miss Kilmansegg*, Her Birth

Birthright. Thy blood and virtue
Contend for empire in thee, and thy goodness
Share with thy birthright!
SHAKESPEARE, *All's Well That Ends Well*, i, 1

Biscay.— Loud roared the dreadful thunder,
The rain a deluge showers,
The clouds were rent asunder
By lightning's vivid powers;
The night both drear and dark,
Our poor devoted bark,
Till next day, there she lay,
In the Bay of Biscay, O!
ANDREW CHERRY, *The Bay of Biscay*, st. 1

Bite.— And having looked to government for bread, in the very first scarcity they will turn and bite the hand that fed them. BURKE, *Thoughts and Details on Scarcity.*

Bivouac.— On fame's eternal camping-ground
Their silent tents are spread,
And glory guards, with solemn round,
The bivouac of the dead.
THEODORE O'HARA, *The Bivouac of the Dead*, st. 1

Blackguards.— "*Arcades ambo,*" *id est* — blackguards both.
BYRON, *Don Juan*, Canto iv, st. 93

Black-jack.— Our vicar still preaches that Peter and Poule
Laid a swingeing long curse on the bonny brown bowl,
That there's wrath and despair in the jolly black-jack,
And the seven deadly sins in a flagon of sack;
Yet whoop, Barnaby! off with thy liquor,
Drink upsees out, and a fig for the vicar.
SCOTT, *Lady of the Lake*, Canto vi, st. 5

Blade.— The trenchant blade, Toledo trusty,
For want of fighting had grown rusty,
And ate into itself, for lack
Of some body to hew and hack.[1]
BUTLER, *Hudibras*, I, i, lines 359-362

Blaize.— Good people all, with one accord,
Lament for Madam Blaize;
Who never wanted a good word —
From those who spoke her praise.
GOLDSMITH, *Elegy on Mrs. Mary Blaize*, st. 1

Blameless.— Wearing the white flower of a blameless life.
TENNYSON, *Idylls of the King: Dedication*, line 24

Blank.— That man may last, but never lives,
Who much receives but nothing gives;
Whom none can love, whom none can thank,
Creation's blot, creation's blank.
T. GIBBONS, *When Jesus Dwelt*

---

[1] A sword laid by,
Which eats into itself, and rusts ingloriously.
BYRON, *Childe Harold's Pilgrimage*, Canto iii, st. 44

Blessed.— A spring of love gushed from my heart,
And I blessed them unaware.
COLERIDGE, *Ancient Mariner*, lines 284, 285

Blessings.— How blessings brighten as they take their flight.
YOUNG, *Night Thoughts*, II, line 606

Blind.— A blind man is a poor man, and blind a poor man is;
For the former seeth no man, and the latter no man sees.
LONGFELLOW, *Poverty and Blindness*, from the German of F. von Logau

Bliss.— That dearest bliss, the power of blessing thee!
THOMSON, *The Seasons*, Spring, lines 1170–1176

Scenes where love and bliss immortal reign.
Ibid., Spring, lines 1170–1176

Blocks.— You blocks, you stones, you worse than senseless things!
SHAKESPEARE, *Julius Cæsar*, i, 1

Blood. When I touched the lifeless clay,
The blood gushed out amain.
HOOD, *The Dream of Eugene Aram*, st. 18

That is best blood that hath most iron in 't,
To edge resolve with, pouring without stint
For what makes manhood dear.
LOWELL, *Commemoration Ode*, st. 10

Pleased to the last, he crops the flow'ry food,
And licks the hand just raised to shed his blood.
POPE, *Essay on Man*, Epistle i, lines 83, 84

There is no sure foundation set on blood,
No certain life achieved by others' death.
SHAKESPEARE, *King John*, iv, 2

Fie, foh, and fum,
I smell the blood of a British man.
SHAKESPEARE, *King Lear*, iii, 4

Lay the summer's dust with showers of blood.
SHAKESPEARE, *King Richard II*, iii, 3

Blood will have blood. SHAKESPEARE, *Macbeth*, iii, 4

He forfeits his own blood that spills another.
SHAKESPEARE, *Timon of Athens*, iii, 5

Where blood with gold is bought and sold.
SHELLEY, *Prometheus Unbound*, i

Blood-avenging.— And now, from forth the frowning sky,
From the Heaven's topmost height,
I heard a voice — the awful voice
Of the blood-avenging sprite[1]—
"Thou guilty man! take up thy dead
And hide it from my sight!"
HOOD, *The Dream of Eugene Aram*, st. 20

Bludgeonings.— In the fell clutch of circumstance
I have not winced nor cried aloud.
Under the bludgeonings of chance
My head is bloody, but unbowed.
W. E. HENLEY, *Out of the Night That Covers Me*, st. 2

Blue.— Under the laurel, the Blue,
Under the willow, the Gray.
F. M. FINCH, *The Blue and the Gray*, st. 2

Blunder.— Sire, it is worse than a crime, it is a blunder.
JOSEPH FOUCHÉ, cited by Barbère de Vieuzac

In men this blunder still you find,
All think their little set—mankind.
HANNAH MORE, *Florio*, I

Blunt.— Though he be blunt, I know him passing wise.
SHAKESPEARE, *Taming of the Shrew*, iii, 2

Blushes.— The man that blushes is not quite a brute.
YOUNG, *Night Thoughts*, VII, line 496

Boat.— My boat is on the shore,
And my bark is on the sea.—BYRON, *Lines to Moore*, st. 1

Bodies.— Our bodies are [our] gardens, to the which our wills are gardeners. SHAKESPEARE, *Othello*, i, 3

Body.— A dem'd, damp, moist, unpleasant body.
DICKENS, *Nicholas Nickleby*, xxxiv

The human body is a furnace which keeps in blast threescore years and ten, more or less. . . . When the fire slackens, life declines; when it goes out, we are dead.
HOLMES, *Autocrat of the Breakfast Table*, vii

Bold.— Write on your door the saying wise and old,
"Be bold! be bold!" and everywhere — "Be bold;
Be not too bold!" Yet better the excess
Than the defect; better the more than less;
Better like Hector in the field to die,[2]
Than like a perfumed Paris turn and fly.
LONGFELLOW, *Morituri Salutamus*, st. 11

---

[1] Blood, though it sleep a time, yet never dies:
The gods on murderers fix revengeful eyes. CHAPMAN, *Widow's Tears*

[2] Better to sink beneath the shock,
Than moulder piecemeal on the rock! BYRON, *The Giaour*, lines 969, 970

A bold bad man.[1]—SPENSER, *Faerie Queene*, I, i, st. 37

Bolt.— Don't you remember sweet Alice, Ben Bolt?
T. D. ENGLISH, *Ben Bolt*, st. 1

Bond.— Let him look to his bond. . . . I have sworn an oath that I will have my bond. . . . Is it so nominated in the bond? . . . I cannot find it; 't is not in the bond.
SHAKESPEARE, *Merchant of Venice*, iii, 1, 3; iv, 1

Bondman.— Who is here so base that would be a bondman?
SHAKESPEARE, *Julius Cæsar*, iii, 2

Bonds.— His words are bonds, his oaths are oracles,
His love sincere, his thoughts immaculate,
His tears pure messengers sent from his heart,
His heart as far from fraud as heaven from earth.
SHAKESPEARE, *Two Gentlemen of Verona*, ii, 7

Bondsmen.— Hereditary bondsmen! know ye not
Who would be free themselves must strike the blow?
BYRON, *Childe Harold's Pilgrimage*, Canto ii, st. 76

Bones.— The knight's bones are dust,
And his good sword rust;
His soul is with the saints, I trust.
S. T. COLERIDGE, *The Knight's Tomb*

Good frend for Jesus sake forbeare
To digg the dust encloased heare,
Bleste be y[e] man y[t] spares thes stones,
And curst be he y[t] moves my bones.[2]
SHAKESPEARE, *Inscription over His Tomb*

An old man, broken with the storms of state,
Is come to lay his weary bones among ye;
Give him a little earth for charity!
SHAKESPEARE, *King Henry VIII*, iv, 2

Thy bones are marrowless, thy blood is cold;
Thou hast no speculation in those eyes
Which thou dost glare with.—SHAKESPEARE, *Macbeth*, iii, 4

---

[1] This bold bad man. SHAKESPEARE, *King Henry VIII*, ii, 2

[2] What needs my Shakespeare for his honoured bones
The labour of an age in piled stones?
Or that his hallowed reliques should be hid
Under a star-ypointing pyramid? MILTON, *On Shakespeare*, 1630

Ill fare the hands that heaved the stones
Where Milton's ashes lay,
That trembled not to grasp the bones
And steal his dust away!
COWPER, *On the Liberties Taken with the Remains of Milton*, st. 5

Bonnet.— Tying her bonnet under her chin,
She tied her raven ringlets in;
But not alone in the silken snare
Did she catch her lovely floating hair,
For, tying her bonnet under her chin,
She tied a young man's heart within.

NORA PERRY, *The Love Knot*, st. 1

Book.— 'Tis pleasant, sure, to see one's name in print;
A book's a book, although there's nothing in't.

BYRON, *English Bards and Scotch Reviewers*, lines 51, 52

The Holy Book by which we live and die.

R. H. MESSINGER, *A Winter Wish*, st. 3

A good book is the precious life-blood of a master spirit, embalmed and treasured up on purpose to a life beyond life. MILTON, *Areopagitica*

As good almost kill a man as kill a good book; who kills a man kills a reasonable creature, God's image; but he who destroys a good book kills reason itself.— *Ibid.*

He hath never fed of the dainties that are bred in a book; he hath not eat paper, as it were; he hath not drunk ink: his intellect is not replenished.

SHAKESPEARE, *Love's Labour's Lost*, iv, 2

Was ever book containing such vile matter
So fairly bound? Oh, that deceit should dwell
In such a gorgeous palace!

SHAKESPEARE, *Romeo and Juliet*, iii, 2

Painter. When comes your book forth?
Poet. Upon the heels of my presentment, sir.

SHAKESPEARE, *Timon of Athens*, i, 1

Bookful.— The bookful blockhead, ignorantly read,
With loads of learned lumber in his head.

POPE, *Essay on Criticism*, lines 612, 613

Book-learned.— But of all plagues, the greatest is untold;
The book-learned wife in Greek and Latin bold,
The critic-dame, who at her table sits,
Homer and Virgil quotes, and weighs their wits.

DRYDEN, *Juvenal, Satire VI*, lines 560–563

Books.— Some books are to be tasted, others to be swallowed, and some few to be chewed and digested.

BACON, *Essay L: Of Studies*

Some books are lies frae end to end.

BURNS, *Death and Doctor Hornbook*

I trust in God — and good books.
CAMPBELL, cited by John Hogben, in
Biographical Sketch, 1886

Books cannot always please, however good;
Minds are not ever craving for their food.
G. CRABBE, *The Borough*, Letter xxiv, lines 402, 403

Learning hath gained most by those books by which the printers have lost. J. FULLER, *Of Books*

Reading new books is like eating new bread,
One can bear it at first, but by gradual steps he
Is brought to death's door of a mental dyspepsy.
LOWELL, *Fable for Critics*, lines 104–106

Knowing I loved my books, he furnish'd me
From mine own library with volumes that
I prize above my dukedom.
SHAKESPEARE, *The Tempest*, i, 2

Bore.— No iron gate, no spiked and panelled door,
Can keep out death, the postman, or the bore.
HOLMES, *A Modest Request*, The Scene, lines 17, 18

Bores.— Got the ill name of augurs, because they were bores.
LOWELL, *Fable for Critics*, line 55

Borrower.— Neither a borrower nor a lender be;
For loan oft loses both itself and friend,
And borrowing dulls the edge of husbandry.[1]
SHAKESPEARE, *Hamlet*, i, 3

Bosom.— Come, rest in this bosom, my own stricken deer,
Though the herd have fled from thee, thy home is still here;
Here still is the smile, that no cloud can o'ercast,
And a heart and a hand all thy own to the last.
T. MOORE, *Come, Rest in This Bosom*, st. 1

Boston. Stern-eyed Puritans, who first began
To spread their roots in Georgius Primus' reign,
Nor dropped till now, obedient to some plan,
Their century fruit,— the perfect Boston man.
BRET HARTE, *Cadet Grey*, Canto i, st. 2

Boston has opened, and kept open, more turnpikes that lead straight to free thought and free speech and free deeds than any other city of live men or dead men.
HOLMES, *Professor at the Breakfast Table*, i

---

[1] Who goeth a borrowing,
Goeth a sorrowing.
TUSSER, *Five Hundred Points of Good Husbandry:* June's Abstract

Solid men of Boston,[1] banish long potations;
Solid men of Boston, make no long orations![2]
CHARLES MORRIS, *Lyra Urbanica*

So, long as Boston shall Boston be,
And her bay-tides rise and fall,
Shall Freedom stand in the Old South Church,
And plead for the rights of all!
WHITTIER, *In the Old South*, st. 13

Bottle.— Pardon me, the bottle stands with you.
COWPER, *Hope*, line 380

Leave the bottle on the chimley-piece, and don't ask me to take none, but let me put my lips to it when I am so dispoged. DICKENS, *Martin Chuzzlewit*, xix

Bouillabaisse.— This bouillabaisse a noble dish is —
A sort of soup or broth, or brew,
Or hotchpotch of all sorts of fishes,
That Greenwich never could outdo:
Green herbs, red peppers, mussels, saffron,
Soles, onions, garlic, roach, and dace:
All these you eat at Terré's tavern,
In that one dish of bouillabaisse.
THACKERAY, *The Ballad of Bouillabaisse*, st. 2

Bounty. For his bounty,
There was no winter in 't; an autumn 't was
That grew the more by reaping.
SHAKESPEARE, *Antony and Cleopatra*, v, 2

Bowed.— My God has bowed me down to what I am;
My grief and solitude have broken me.
TENNYSON, *Enoch Arden*, lines 852, 853

Bowl.— Troll the bowl, the jolly nut-brown bowl,
And here, kind mate, to thee!
Let 's sing a dirge for Saint Hugh's soul,
And down it merrily.
DEKKER, *The Second Three Men's Song*, in
The Shoemaker's Holiday, v, 4

---

[1] A solid man of Boston,
A comfortable man, with dividends,
And the first salmon, and the first green peas.
LONGFELLOW, *New England Tragedies:* John Endicott, iv, 1

[2] Also quoted in this form:
Solid men of Boston, make no long orations;
Solid men of Boston, banish strong potations!

Box.— The whole machinery of the State, all the apparatus of the system, and its varied workings, end in simply bringing twelve good men into a box.
BROUGHAM, *Present State of the Law*

Boxes.— A beggarly account of empty boxes.
SHAKESPEARE, *Romeo and Juliet*, v, 1

Boy.— Ah! happy years! once more who would not be a boy?[1]
BYRON, *Childe Harold's Pilgrimage*, Canto ii, st. 23

A boy's will is the wind's will,
And the thoughts of youth are long, long thoughts.
LONGFELLOW, *My Lost Youth*

Oh, 'tis a parlous [perilous] boy;
Bold, quick, ingenious, forward, capable.
SHAKESPEARE, *King Richard III*, iii, 1

Bowls. Fill our bowls once more;[2]
Let's mock the midnight bell.
SHAKESPEARE, *Antony and Cleopatra*, iii, 13 [11]

Brain.— With curious art the brain, too finely wrought,
Preys on herself, and is destroyed by thought.
C. CHURCHILL, *Epistle to Hogarth*

This is the very coinage of your brain.
SHAKESPEARE, *Hamlet*, iii, 4

The brain may devise laws for the blood, but a hot temper leaps o'er a cold decree.
SHAKESPEARE, *Merchant of Venice*, i, 2

Brains.— Our brains are seventy-year clocks. The Angel of Life winds them up once for all, then closes the case, and gives the key into the hand of the Angel of the Resurrection. HOLMES, *Autocrat of the Breakfast Table*, viii

Cudgel thy brains no more about it, for your dull ass will not mend his pace with beating.
SHAKESPEARE, *Hamlet*, v, 1

O God, that men should put an enemy in their mouths to steal away their brains!—SHAKESPEARE, *Othello*, ii, 3

---

[1] Perhaps 'twas boyish love, yet still,
O listless woman, weary lover!
To feel once more that fresh, wild thrill
I'd give — but who can live youth over?
STEDMAN, *The Doorstep*, st. 12

[2] "Fill our bowls; once more,"— according to differing versions.

Brandy.— Claret is the liquor for boys: port for men: but he who aspires to be a hero must drink brandy. . . . Brandy will do soonest for a man what drinking *can* do for him.

SAMUEL JOHNSON, *Life*, by Boswell, April 7, 1779

Brass.— Men's evil manners live in brass; their virtues
We write in water.

SHAKESPEARE, *King Henry VIII*, iv, 2

Brave.— How sleep the brave who sink to rest
By all their country's wishes blest!

. . . . . .

By fairy hands their knell is rung,
By forms unseen their dirge is sung:
There Honour comes, a pilgrim grey,
To bless the turf that wraps their clay,
And Freedom shall awhile repair
To dwell a weeping hermit there!

WILLIAM COLLINS, *Ode Written in* 1746

None but the brave deserves the fair.

DRYDEN, *Alexander's Feast*, line 15

Then to side with Truth is noble when we share her wretched crust,
Ere her cause bring fame and profit, and 't is prosperous to be just;
Then it is the brave man chooses, while the coward stands aside,
Doubting, in his abject spirit, till his Lord is crucified,
And the multitude make virtue of the faith they had denied.

LOWELL, *The Present Crisis*, st. 11

The bravest of the brave.[1]

NAPOLEON BONAPARTE, *Life*, by Sloane, IV, 2

The heart's-blood of the brave.

L. H. SIGOURNEY, *Return of Napoleon from St. Helena*, st. 9

Bravest.— The bravest are the tenderest,—
The loving are the daring.

BAYARD TAYLOR, *The Song of the Camp*, st. 11

Bread.— Besides, they always smell of bread and butter.

BYRON, *Beppo*, st. 39

Not a deed would he do, nor a word would he utter,
Till he weighed its relation to plain bread and butter.

LOWELL, *Fable for Critics*, lines 186, 187

---

[1] A characterization of Marshal Ney.

This day, be bread and peace my lot:
  All else beneath the sun,
Thou know'st if best bestowed or not;
  And let Thy will be done.
POPE, *The Universal Prayer*, st. 12

Bread is the staff of life.[1] SWIFT, *Tale of a Tub*

Chalk and alum and plaster are sold to the poor for bread,
And the spirit of murder works in the very means of life.
TENNYSON, *Maud*, I, st. 10

Break.— Break, break, break,
  On thy cold grey stones, O Sea!
And I would that my tongue could utter
  The thoughts that arise in me.
TENNYSON, *Break, Break*, st. 1

Break not, O woman's heart, but still endure.
TENNYSON, *Idylls of the King, Dedication*, line 43

Breakers.— The breakers licked them off; and some were crushed,
Some swallowed in the yeast, some flung up dead,
The dear breath beaten out of them.
JEAN INGELOW, *Brothers, and a Sermon*

Breakfast. Then to breakfast with
What appetite you have.
SHAKESPEARE, *King Henry VIII*, iii, 2

Breast.— On some fond breast the parting soul relies,
  Some pious drops the closing eye requires;
E'en from the tomb the voice of Nature cries,
  E'en in our ashes live their wonted fires.
GRAY, *Elegy Written in a Country Churchyard*, st. 24

So perish all whose breast ne'er learned to glow
For others' good, or melt at others' woe.
POPE, *Elegy to an Unfortunate Lady*, lines 45, 46

Now is done thy long day's work;
Fold thy palms across thy breast,[2]
Fold thine arms, turn to thy rest.
TENNYSON, *A Dirge*, st. 1

Breath.— With bated breath and whispering humbleness.
SHAKESPEARE, *Merchant of Venice*, i, 3

---

[1] Bread which strengtheneth man's heart. Ps. civ, 15

[2] Two hands upon the breast,
  And labor's done. D. M. CRAIK, *Now and Afterwards*

Breathing.— We watched her breathing through the night,
Her breathing soft and low,
As in her breast the wave of life
Kept heaving to and fro.—HOOD, *The Death-Bed*, st. 1

Breech.—But Hudibras gave him a twitch
As quick as lightning in the breech,
Just in the place where honour's lodged,
As wise philosophers have judged,
Because a kick in that part more
Hurts honour than deep wounds before.
BUTLER, *Hudibras*, II, iii, lines 1065–1070

Brevity.— Brevity is the soul of wit.
SHAKESPEARE, *Hamlet*, ii, 2

Bribe. Examine well
His milk-white hand; the palm is hardly clean—
But here and there an ugly smutch appears.
Foh! 't was a bribe that left it: he has touched
Corruption! Whoso seeks an audit here
Propitious, pays his tribute, game or fish,
Wild-fowl or venison; and his errand speeds.
COWPER, *The Task: The Winter Evening*, lines 606–612

This prints my letters,[1] that expects a bribe,
And others roar aloud, "Subscribe, subscribe."
POPE, *Epistle to Dr. Arbuthnot*, lines 113, 114

Bribes. What! shall one of us,
That struck the foremost man of all this world
But for supporting robbers,— shall we now
Contaminate our fingers with base bribes,
And sell the mighty space of our large honours
For so much trash as may be grasped thus?
I had rather be a dog, and bay the moon,
Than such a Roman.—SHAKESPEARE, *Julius Cæsar*, iv, 3

Bricks.— Sir, he made a chimney in my father's house, and the bricks are alive at this day to testify it.
SHAKESPEARE, *King Henry VI, Part II*, iv, 2

Bride.— The bride hath paced into the hall,
Red as a rose is she;
Nodding their heads before her goes
The merry minstrelsy.
COLERIDGE, *Ancient Mariner*, lines 33–36

Bride-bed.— I thought thy bride-bed to have decked, sweet maid,
And not [to] have strewed thy grave.
SHAKESPEARE, *Hamlet*, v, 1

---

[1] Some of Pope's letters to Cromwell had been surreptitiously printed.

Bridge.— In yon strait path a thousand
May well be stopped by three.
Now who will stand on either hand,
And keep the bridge with me?
MACAULAY, *Horatius*, st. 29

Brief.— Brief let me be. SHAKESPEARE, *Hamlet*, i, 5

Briers.— Oh, how full of briers is this working-day world!
SHAKESPEARE, *As You Like It*, i, 3

Britain.— When Britain first, at Heaven's command,
Arose from out the azure main,
This was the charter of the land,
And guardian angels sung this strain:
"Rule, Britannia, rule the waves,
Britons never will be slaves."—THOMSON, *Alfred*, ii, 5

British.—Wherever there is water to float a ship, there is to be found a British standard.
NAPOLEON BONAPARTE, *Life*, by Sloane, IV, 214

Britons. Britons rarely swerve
From law, however stern, which tends their strength to nerve.
BYRON, *Childe Harold's Pilgrimage*, Canto ii, st. 19

Broken-hearted.— Had we never loved sae kindly,
Had we never loved sae blindly,
Never met—or never parted,
We had ne'er been broken-hearted.
BURNS, *Ae Fond Kiss*, st. 2

Brook.— A noise like of a hidden brook
In the leafy month of June,
That to the sleeping woods all night
Singeth a quiet tune.
S. T. COLERIDGE, *Ancient Mariner*, lines 369–372

Brother.— Tam lo'ed him like a vera brither;
They had been fou for weeks thegither.
BURNS, *Tam O' Shanter*, st. 5

My father's brother, but no more like my father
Than I to Hercules. SHAKESPEARE, *Hamlet*, i, 2

There spake my brother; there my father's grave
Did utter forth a voice.
SHAKESPEARE, *Measure for Measure*, iii, 1

"Where wert thou, brother, those four days?"
There lives no record of reply.
TENNYSON, *In Memoriam*, xxxi, st. 2

Brotherhood.— There is no flesh in man's obdurate heart,
It does not feel for man; the natural bond
Of brotherhood is severed as the flax
That falls asunder at the touch of fire.
COWPER, *The Task: The Time-Piece*, lines 8–11

The crest and crowning of all good,
Life's final star, is Brotherhood.
EDWIN MARKHAM, *Brotherhood*, st. 1

Brothers.— Then let us pray that come it may,
As come it will for a' that,
That sense and worth, o'er a' the earth,
May bear the gree [*palm*] and a' that.
For a' that and a' that,
It 's coming yet, for a' that.
That man to man, the warld o'er,
Shall brothers be for a' that.[1]
BURNS, *Is There for Honest Poverty*, st. 5

More than my brothers are to me.
TENNYSON, *In Memoriam*, lxxix, st. 1

Brow. This man's brow, like to a title-leaf,
Foretells the nature of a tragic volume.
SHAKESPEARE, *King Henry IV, Part II*, i, 1

Brown. Old Brown,
Osawatomie Brown,
Said, "Boys, the Lord will aid us!" and he shoved his ramrod down.
STEDMAN, *How Old Brown Took Harper's Ferry*, st. 2

Brute.— A bitter sorrow 'tis to lose a brute
Friend, dog or horse, for grief must then be mute,—
So many smile to see the rivers shed
Of tears for one poor, speechless creature dead.
T. W. PARSONS, *Obituary*, lines 11–14

Bubble.— Only propose to blow a bubble,
And Lord! what hundreds will subscribe for soap!
HOOD, *A Black Job*, st. 2

Who sees with equal eye, as God of all,
A hero perish, or a sparrow fall,
Atoms or systems into ruin hurled,
And now a bubble burst, and now a world.
POPE, *Essay on Man*, Epistle i, lines 87–90

---

[1] Hope on, hope ever, yet the time shall come,
When man to man shall be a friend and brother.
GERALD MASSEY, *Hope On, Hope Ever*

Bubbles.— The Eternal Sáki from that bowl has poured
Millions of bubbles like us, and will pour.
OMAR KHAYYÁM, *Rubáiyát* (trans. Fitzgerald), st. 46

The earth hath bubbles, as the water hath.
SHAKESPEARE, *Macbeth*, i, 3

Bucket.— The old oaken bucket, the iron-bound bucket,
The moss-covered bucket, which hung in the well.
S. WOODWORTH, *The Bucket*

Buckets. The toil
Of dropping buckets into empty wells,
And growing old in drawing nothing up.
COWPER, *The Task: The Garden*, lines 188–190

Now up, now down, as buckets in a well.
DRYDEN, *Palamon and Arcite*, line 692

Budge.— I will not budge for no man's pleasure, I.
SHAKESPEARE, *Romeo and Juliet*, iii, 1

Bugle-horn.— Where, where was Roderick then![1]
One blast upon his bugle-horn
Were worth a thousand men.[2]
SCOTT, *Lady of the Lake*, Canto vi, st. 18

Bugles.— Our bugles sang truce, for the night-cloud had lowered,
And the sentinel stars set their watch in the sky;
And thousands had sunk on the ground overpowered,
The weary to sleep, and the wounded to die.
CAMPBELL, *The Soldier's Dream*, st. 1

Build.— Build sure in the beginnin'.
An' then don't never tech the underpinnin'.
LOWELL, *Biglow Papers*, II, ii, lines 309, 310

Builded.— The hand that rounded Peter's dome
And groined the aisles of Christian Rome
Wrought in a sad sincerity;
Himself from God he could not free;
He builded better than he knew;
The conscious stone to beauty grew.
EMERSON, *The Problem*, st. 2

---

[1] Oh! where was Rupert in that hour
Of danger, toil, and strife?
It would have been to all brave men
Worth a hundred years of life.
SIR FRANCIS HASTINGS DOYLE, *The Old Cavalier*, st. 8

[2] Oh, for a blast of that dread horn,
On Fontarabian echoes borne,
That to King Charles did come!
SCOTT, *Marmion*, Canto vi, st. 33

Building.— We've gut to fix this thing for good an' all;
It's no use buildin' wut's a-goin' to fall.
I'm older 'n you, an' I've seen things an' men,
An' my experunce,— tell ye wut it's ben:
Folks thet wurked thorough was the ones thet thriv,
But bad work follers ye ez long's ye live;
You can't git red on't; jest ez sure ez sin,
It's ollers askin' to be done agin.

LOWELL, *Biglow Papers*, II, ii, lines 269–276

Built.— Heroic built, though of terrestrial mould.

MILTON, *Paradise Lost*, IX, line 485

Bulldog.— Stick to your aim; the mongrel's hold will slip,
But only crowbars loose the bulldog's grip.

HOLMES, *A Rhymed Lesson*, st. 33

Hold on with a bulldog grip, and chew and choke as much as possible.

ABRAHAM LINCOLN, *Telegram to Gen. U. S. Grant, August* 17, 1864

Bunker's Hill.— "Drink, John," she said, "'twill do you good,— poor child, you'll never bear
This working in the dismal trench, out in the midnight air;
And if — God bless me! — you were hurt, 'twould keep away the chill;"
So John did drink,— and well he wrought that night at Bunker's Hill!

HOLMES, *On Lending a Punch-Bowl*, st. 10

Burden.— The daily burden for the back.

TENNYSON, *In Memoriam*, xxv, st. 1

Burgundy.— The mellow-tasted Burgundy.

THOMSON, *The Seasons*, Autumn, line 705

Burial.— Rider and horse,— friend, foe,— in one red burial blent.

BYRON, *Childe Harold's Pilgrimage*, Canto iii, st. 28

Burthen. A burthen
Too heavy for a man that hopes for heaven.

SHAKESPEARE, *King Henry VIII*, iii, 2

Bush.— Good wine needs no bush.

SHAKESPEARE, *As You Like It*, v, 4

Business.— To business that we love we rise betime,
And go to't with delight.

SHAKESPEARE, *Antony and Cleopatra*, iv, 4

Come home to men's business and bosoms.

BACON, *Dedication of Essays*

But.— *Messenger.* But yet, madam,—
Cleopatra. I do not like "But yet," it does allay
The good precedence; fie upon "But yet"!
"But yet" is as a gaoler to bring forth
Some monstrous malefactor.
SHAKESPEARE, *Antony and Cleopatra*, ii, 5

Butcher.— Who finds the heifer dead and bleeding fresh,
And sees, fast by, a butcher with an axe,
But will suspect 'twas he that made the slaughter?[1]
SHAKESPEARE, *King Henry VI, Part II*, iii, 2

Butterfly.— Who breaks a butterfly upon a wheel?
POPE, *Epistle to Dr. Arbuthnot*, line 308

Buxom.— Buxom, blithe, and debonair.
MILTON, *L'Allegro*, line 24

Buy.— I will buy with you, sell with you, talk with you, walk with you, and so following; but I will not eat with you, drink with you, nor pray with you.
SHAKESPEARE, *Merchant of Venice*, i, 3

Cabined. Now I am cabined, cribbed, confined,[2] bound in
To saucy doubts and fears. SHAKESPEARE, *Macbeth*, iii, 4

Cæsar.— Not that I loved Cæsar less, but that I loved Rome more. SHAKESPEARE, *Julius Cæsar*, iii, 2

Cake.—Would'st thou both eat thy cake, and have it?
G. HERBERT, *The Size*, st. 3

My cake is dough.[3]
SHAKESPEARE, *Taming of the Shrew*, v, 1

He that will have a cake out of the wheat must [needs] tarry the grinding.
SHAKESPEARE, *Troilus and Cressida*, i, 1

Calamity.— Calamity is man's true touchstone.[4]
BEAUMONT AND FLETCHER, *Four Plays in One: The Triumph of Honour*, sc. 1

---

[1] Who finds the partridge in the puttock's nest,
But may imagine how the bird was dead,
Although the kite soar with unbloodied beak?
SHAKESPEARE, *King Henry VI, Part II*, iii, 2

[2] Cabined, cribbed, confined.
BYRON, *Childe Harold's Pilgrimage*, Canto iv, 127

[3] Our cake 's dough on both sides.—SHAKESPEARE, *Taming of the Shrew*, i, 1

[4] Times of general calamity and confusion have ever been productive of the greatest minds. The purest ore is produced from the hottest furnace, and the brightest thunderbolt from the darkest storm.
C. C. COLTON, *Lacon*.

Calf.— To worship the golden calf of Baal; . . . to barter away that precious jewel, self-esteem, and cringe to any mortal creature — for eighteen shillings a week! . . . Had it been for the sake of a ribbon, star, or garter; sleeves of lawn, a great man's smile, a seat in Parliament, a tap upon the shoulder from a courtly sword; a place, a party, or a thriving lie, or eighteen thousand pounds, or even eighteen hundred: — but to worship the golden calf for eighteen shillings a week! oh, pitiful, pitiful! DICKENS, *Martin Chuzzlewit*, x

Calumny.—Be thou as chaste as ice, as pure as snow, thou shalt not escape calumny.[1]—SHAKESPEARE, *Hamlet*, iii, 1

Camel.— It is as hard to come as for a camel
To thread the postern of a small needle's eye.[2]
SHAKESPEARE, *King Richard II*, v, 5

Camp.— After eighteen hundred years' profession of the creed of peace, Christendom is an armed camp.
LECKY, *The Map of Life*, vii

Cancer.— There's nothin' for a cancer but the knife,
Onless you set by 't more than by your life.
LOWELL, *Biglow Papers*, II, ii, lines 291, 292

Candidate.— Ez to my princerples I glory
In hevin' nothin' o' the sort;
I ain't a Wig, I ain't a Tory,
I'm jest a candidate, in short.
LOWELL, *Biglow Papers*, I, vii, st. 10

Candle.— How far that little candle throws his beams!
So shines a good deed in a naughty world.
SHAKESPEARE, *Merchant of Venice*, v

Cannon.— Cannon to right of them,
Cannon to left of them,
Cannon in front of them
Volleyed and thundered.
TENNYSON, *Charge of the Light Brigade*, st. 3

Cannon-shot.— Cannon-shot, musket-shot, volley on volley, and yell upon yell.—TENNYSON, *Defence of Lucknow*, st. 3

---

[1] No might nor greatness in mortality
Can censure 'scape; back-wounding calumny
The whitest virtue strikes. What king so strong
Can tie the gall up in the slanderous tongue?
SHAKESPEARE, *Measure for Measure*, iii, 2

[2] Matt. xix, 24; Mark x, 25; Luke xviii, 25.

Canopy.— *Third Servant.* Where dwellest thou?
Coriolanus. Under the canopy.

. . . . . .

Third Servant. Where's that?
Coriolanus. I' the city of kites and crows.
SHAKESPEARE, *Coriolanus*, iv, 5

Caps. They threw their caps[1]
As they would hang them on the horns o' the moon,
Shouting their emulation.—SHAKESPEARE, *Coriolanus*, i, 1

Captain.— That in the captain's but a choleric word,
Which in the soldier is flat blasphemy.
SHAKESPEARE, *Measure for Measure*, ii, 2

Great in council and great in war,
Foremost captain of his time,
Rich in saving common sense,
And, as the greatest only are,
In his simplicity sublime.—TENNYSON, *Ode on the Death of the Duke of Wellington*, st. 4

O Captain! my Captain! our fearful trip is done,
The ship has weathered every rack, the prize we sought is won,
The port is near, the bells I hear, the people all exulting,
While follow eyes the steady keel, the vessel grim and daring;
But O heart! heart! heart!
O the bleeding drops of red,
Where on the deck my Captain lies,
Fallen cold and dead.
WALT WHITMAN, *O Captain! My Captain!* st. 1

Card.— How absolute the knave is! we must speak by the card, or equivocation will undo us.
SHAKESPEARE, *Hamlet*, v, 1

Care.— I know not where His islands lift
Their fronded palms in air;
I only know I cannot drift
Beyond His love and care.[2]
WHITTIER, *The Eternal Goodness*, st. 20

---

[1] You are they
That made the air unwholesome, when you cast
Your stinking, greasy caps in hooting at Coriolanus' exile.
SHAKESPEARE, *Coriolanus*, iv, 6

The rabblement hooted [shouted] and clapped their chapped [chopped] hands and threw up their sweaty night-caps.
SHAKESPEARE, *Julius Cæsar*, i, 2

[2] I cannot go
Where Universal Love not smiles around.
THOMSON, *A Hymn*, lines 111, 112

Cares. Gi'e me a canny hour at e'en,
My arms about my dearie, oh!
An' warly cares, an' warly men,
May a' gae tapsalteerie, oh!
BURNS, *Green Grow the Rashes*, st. 3

And the night shall be filled with music,
And the cares that infest the day
Shall fold their tents, like the Arabs,
And as silently steal away.
LONGFELLOW, *The Day Is Done*, st. 11

His cares are now all ended.
SHAKESPEARE, *King Henry IV, Part II*, v, 2

Case.— A rotten case abides no handling.
SHAKESPEARE, *King Henry IV, Part II*, iv, 1

Cash.— Some for the glories of this world; and some
Sigh for the Prophet's paradise to come;
Ah, take the cash, and let the credit go,
Nor heed the rumble of a distant drum!
OMAR KHAYYÁM, *Rubáiyát* (trans. Fitzgerald), st. 13

Cast.— Slave! I have set my life upon a cast,
And I will stand the hazard of the die.
SHAKESPEARE, *King Richard III*, v, 4

Castle.— A man's house is his castle.[1]
SIR EDWARD COKE, *Third Institute*

Cat.— Should ever anything be missed—milk, coals, umbrellas, brandy—
The cat's pitched into with a boot or anything that's handy.
C. S. CALVERLEY, *Sad Memories*, st. 5

What female heart can gold despise?
What cat's averse to fish?
THOMAS GRAY, *On a Favourite Cat*, st. 4

Now puss, while folks are in their beds, treads leads,
And sleepers, waking, grumble —"Drat that cat!"
Who in the gutter caterwauls, squalls, mauls
Some feline foe, and screams in shrill ill will.
HOOD, *A Nocturnal Sketch*, lines 22–25

---

[1] The poorest man may in his cottage bid defiance to all the force of the crown. It may be frail; its roof may shake; the wind may blow through it; the storms may enter; the rain may enter,— but the King of England cannot enter! All his forces dare not cross the threshold of the ruined tenement.
WILLIAM PITT, EARL OF CHATHAM, *Speech Against the Excise on Cider*

What d'ye think of that, my cat?
What d'ye think of that, my dog?
HOOD, *The Bachelor's Dream*

Let Hercules himself do what he may,
The cat will mew and dog will have his day.
SHAKESPEARE, *Hamlet*, v, 1

As vigilant as a cat to steal cream.
SHAKESPEARE, *King Henry IV, Part I*, iv, 2

Letting "I dare not" wait upon "I would,"
Like the poor cat i' the adage.
SHAKESPEARE, *Macbeth*, i, 7

Thrice the brinded cat hath mewed. *Ibid.*, iv, 1

A harmless necessary cat.
SHAKESPEARE, *Merchant of Venice*, iv, 1

What though care killed a cat, thou hast mettle enough in thee to kill care.
SHAKESPEARE, *Much Ado about Nothing*, v, 1

Catastrophe.— I'll tickle your catastrophe.
SHAKESPEARE, *King Henry IV, Part II*, ii, 1

Catechism.— Love! Honour! And Obey! Overhaul your catechism till you find that passage, and when found turn the leaf down. DICKENS, *Dombey and Son*, iv

Cathay.— Better fifty years of Europe than a cycle of Cathay.
TENNYSON, *Locksley Hall*, line 184

Cats.— When cats run home and light is come.
TENNYSON, *The Owl*, st. 1

Cauldron.— Round about the cauldron go.
SHAKESPEARE, *Macbeth*, i, 1

Cause.— His cause being just and his quarrel honourable.
SHAKESPEARE, *King Henry V*, iv, 1

Caviare.— The play, I remember, pleased not the million; 'twas caviare to the general.
SHAKESPEARE, *Hamlet*, ii, 2

Cavil.— I'll cavil on the ninth part of a hair.
SHAKESPEARE, *King Henry IV, Part I*, iii, 1

Cecilia.— At last divine Cecilia came,
Inventress of the vocal frame.
DRYDEN, *Alexander's Feast*, lines 161, 162

Celerity.— Celerity is never more admired
Than by the negligent.
SHAKESPEARE, *Antony and Cleopatra*, iii, 7

Censure.— Careless of censure, nor too fond of fame;
Still pleased to praise, yet not afraid to blame,
Averse alike to flatter, or offend;
Not free from faults, nor yet too vain to mend.
POPE, *Essay on Criticism*, lines 741–744

Censure is the tax a man pays to the public for being eminent. SWIFT, *Thoughts on Various Subjects*

Chair.— To see the vacant chair, and think,
"How good! how kind! and he is gone!"
TENNYSON, *In Memoriam*, xx, st. 5

Chaise.— A chaise breaks down, but doesn't wear out.[1]
HOLMES, *The Deacon's Masterpiece*, st. 3

Champagne. Quick
As is the wit it gives, the gay champagne.
THOMSON, *The Seasons*, Autumn, lines 705, 706

Champion.— His square-turned joints and strength of limb
Showed him no carpet knight so trim,
But in close fight a champion grim,
In camps a leader sage. SCOTT, *Marmion*, i, 5

Chance.— Have a care o' th' main chance.
BUTLER, *Hudibras*, II, ii, line 502

Chance is like an amberill,— it don't take twice to lose it.
LOWELL, *Biglow Papers*, II, i, st. 1

Change.— The time is ripe, and rotten-ripe, for change;
Then let it come.
LOWELL, *A Glance Behind the Curtain*, lines 230, 231

Change is the watchword of Progression. When
We tire of well-worn ways, we seek for new.
This restless craving in the souls of men
Spurs them to climb, and seek the mountain view.
ELLA WHEELER WILCOX, *The Year Outgrows the Spring*, st. 5

Chaos.— A shout that tore Hell's concave, and beyond
Frighted the reign of Chaos and old Night.[2]
MILTON, *Paradise Lost*, I, lines 542, 543

---

[1] Have you heard of the wonderful one-hoss shay
That was built in such a logical way
It ran a hundred years to a day?
HOLMES, *The Deacon's Masterpiece*, st. 1

[2] I sung of Chaos and eternal Night. MILTON, *Paradise Lost*, III, line 18
Daughter of Chaos and eternal Night. POPE, *The Dunciad*, I, line 12

Charge.— With dying hand, above his head,
He shook the fragment of his blade
And shouted "Victory!
Charge, Chester, charge! On, Stanley, on!"
Were the last words of Marmion.—SCOTT, *Marmion*, vi, 32

Charmer.— How happy could I be with either,
Were t'other dear charmer away!
JOHN GAY, *The Beggar's Opera*, ii, 2 [10]

Charms.— Believe me, if all those endearing young charms,
Which I gaze on so fondly to-day,
Were to change by to-morrow, and fleet in my arms,
Like fairy-gifts fading away.—T. MOORE, *Believe Me*, st. 1

Honoured well are charms to sell
If priests the selling do.—N. P. WILLIS, *Unseen Spirits*, st. 3

Charter. A glorious charter, deny it who can,
Is breathed in the words "I'm an Englishman!"
ELIZA COOK, *The Englishman*, st. 4

Chaste.— As chaste as unsunned snow.
SHAKESPEARE, *Cymbeline*, ii, 5

Chastity.— So dear to Heaven is saintly chastity,
That, when a soul is found sincerely so,
A thousand liveried angels lackey her,
Driving far off each thing of sin and guilt.
MILTON, *Comus*, lines 453-456

Chat.— This bald unjointed chat.
SHAKESPEARE, *King Henry IV, Part I*, i, 3

We sit to chat as well as eat.
SHAKESPEARE, *Taming of the Shrew*, v, 2

Chaucer.— Dan Chaucer, well of English undefyled,
On Fame's eternall beadroll worthie to be fyled.
SPENSER, *Faerie Queene*, IV, ii, st. 32

Cheap.— As cheap as stinking mackerel.
SHAKESPEARE, *King Henry IV, Part I*, ii, 4

Cheat.— Doubtless the pleasure is as great
Of being cheated as to cheat.
BUTLER, *Hudibras*, II, iii, lines 1, 2

Cheek.— See, how she leans her cheek upon her hand!
Oh, that I were a glove upon that hand,
That I might touch that cheek!
SHAKESPEARE, *Romeo and Juliet*, ii, 2

Cheer.— Cheer, boys! cheer! no more of idle sorrow,
Courage, true hearts, shall bear us on our way!
Hope points before, and shows the bright to-morrow,
Let us forget the darkness of to-day!
Cheer, boys! cheer! for England, mother England!
Cheer, boys! cheer! the willing strong right hand,
Cheer, boys! cheer! there's work for honest labour—
Cheer, boys! cheer! — in the new and happy land.
CHARLES MACKAY, *Cheer, Boys! Cheer!*

You shall have better cheer
Ere you depart; and thanks to stay and eat it.
SHAKESPEARE, *Cymbeline*, iii, 6

Cheerful.— A man he seems of cheerful yesterdays
And confident to-morrows.
WORDSWORTH, *The Excursion: VII, The Churchyard Among the Mountains*, lines 562–563

Cheese.— With the exception of the heel of a Dutch cheese — which is not adapted to the wants of a young family — there is really not a scrap of anything in the larder.
DICKENS, *David Copperfield*, I, xi

I dare not fight; but I will wink and hold out mine iron: it is a simple one; but . . . it will toast cheese.
SHAKESPEARE, *King Henry V*, ii, 1

Cherish.— Something the heart must have to cherish,
Must love and joy and sorrow learn,
Something with passion clasp, or perish,
And in itself to ashes burn.
LONGFELLOW, *Forsaken*, st. 1

Love thyself last; cherish those hearts that hate thee.
SHAKESPEARE, *King Henry VIII*, iii, 2

Cherries.— No man can gather cherries in Kent at the season of Christmas!
LONGFELLOW, *Courtship of Miles Standish*, ix, line 48

Cherub.— There's a sweet little cherub that sits up aloft,
To keep watch for the life of poor Jack.
C. DIBDIN, *Poor Jack*, st. 2

Chess-board.— We called the chess-board white,— we call it black. ROBERT BROWNING, *Bishop Blougram's Apology*, line 214

Chickens.— To swallow gudgeons ere th're catched,
And count their chickens ere th're hatched.[1]
BUTLER, *Hudibras*, II, iii, lines 923, 924

---

[1] This moral, I think, may be safely attached,—
"Reckon not on your chickens before they are hatched."
J. TAYLOR, *The Milkmaid*

What! all my pretty chickens and their dam
At one fell swoop? SHAKESPEARE, *Macbeth*, iv, 3

Chief.— Hail to the chief who in triumph advances!
Honoured and blessed be the ever-green Pine!
Long may the tree, in his banner that glances,
Flourish, the shelter and grace of our line.
SCOTT, *Lady of the Lake*, Canto ii, st. 19

Child. I never seed nothing that could or can
Jest git all the good from the heart of a man
Like the hands of a little child.
JOHN HAY, *Golyer*, st. 4

A child don't not feel like a child till you miss him.
HOOD, *The Lost Heir*

Never shalt thou the heavens see,
Save as a little child thou be.[1]
LANIER, *The Symphony*, lines 333, 334

Behold the child, by Nature's kindly law,
Pleased with a rattle, tickled with a straw:
Some livelier plaything gives his youth delight,
A little louder, but as empty quite:
Scarfs, garters, gold, amuse his riper stage,
And beads and prayer-books are the toys of age:
Pleased with this bauble still, as that before;
Till tired he sleeps, and life's poor play is o'er.
POPE, *Essay on Man*, Epistle ii, lines 275–282

How sharper than a serpent's tooth it is
To have a thankless child!
SHAKESPEARE, *King Lear*, i, 4

The child is father of the man.[2]
WORDSWORTH, *My Heart Leaps Up When I Behold*

Childhood.— How dear to this heart are the scenes of my childhood,
When fond recollection presents them to view!
The orchard, the meadow, the deep-tangled wildwood,
And every loved spot which my infancy knew!
S. WOODWORTH, *The Bucket*, st. 1

Childishness.— Second childishness and mere oblivion,
Sans teeth, sans eyes, sans taste, sans everything.
SHAKESPEARE, *As You Like It*, ii, 7

---

[1] Matt. xviii, 3.

[2] The childhood shows the man
As morning shows the day. MILTON, *Paradise Lost*, v, lines 220, 221

Children.— Children sweeten labours, but they make misfortune more bitter; they increase the cares of life, but they mitigate the remembrance of death.
BACON, *Essay VII: Of Parents and Children*

Between the dark and the daylight,
When the night is beginning to lower,
Comes a pause in the day's occupations,
That is known as the Children's Hour.
LONGFELLOW, *The Children's Hour*, st. 1

Our children's children
Shall see this, and bless heaven.
SHAKESPEARE, *King Henry VIII*, v, 5 [4]

Chimney.— He is a little chimney, and heated hot in a moment.[1]
LONGFELLOW, *Courtship of Miles Standish*, vi, line 87

Chinee. For ways that are dark
And for tricks that are vain,
The heathen Chinee is peculiar.—BRET HARTE,
Plain Language from Truthful James, st. 1

Chinese.— We are ruined by Chinese cheap labor.
Ibid., st. 7

Chivalry.— I thought that ten thousand swords would have leaped from their scabbards to avenge even a look that threatened her [Marie Antoinette] with insult. But the age of chivalry is gone. That of sophisters, economists, and calculators has succeeded.
EDMUND BURKE, *Reflections on the Revolution in France*

Choir. The choir invisible
Of those immortal dead who live again
In minds made better by their presence.
GEORGE ELIOT, *O, May I Join the Choir Invisible*, st. 1

She thought no v'ice hed sech a swing
Ez his'n in the choir;
My! when he made Ole Hunderd ring,
She knowed the Lord was nigher.
LOWELL, *The Courtin'*, st. 11

Choler.— Must I give way and room to your rash choler?
Shall I be frightened when a madman stares?
SHAKESPEARE, *Julius Cæsar*, iv, 3

What! drunk with choler?
SHAKESPEARE, *King Henry IV, Part I*, i, 3

---

[1] Were not I a little pot, and soon hot.
SHAKESPEARE, *Taming of the Shrew*, iv, 1

Chord. I struck one chord of music,
Like the sound of a great Amen.
. . . . .
I have sought, but I seek it vainly,
That one lost chord divine,
Which came from the soul of the organ,
And entered into mine.

It may be that Death's bright angel
Will speak in that chord again;
It may be that only in heaven
I shall hear that grand Amen.
A. A. PROCTER, *A Lost Chord*, st. 2, 6, 7

Chowder-kettle.— You should have been with us that day round the chowder-kettle.
WALT WHITMAN, *Song of Myself*, 10

Christ.— Ring in the Christ that is to be.
TENNYSON, *In Memoriam*, cvi, st. 8

Christian.— A Christian is the highest style of man.[1]
YOUNG, *Night Thoughts*, IV, line 789

Christians.— Christians have burned each other, quite persuaded
That all the apostles would have done as they did.
BYRON, *Don Juan*, Canto i, st. 83

O father Abram, what these Christians are,
Whose own hard dealings teaches them suspect
The thoughts of others!
SHAKESPEARE, *Merchant of Venice*, i, 3

Christmas. My song I troll out, for Christmas stout,
The hearty, the true, and the bold;
A bumper I drain, and with might and main
Give three cheers for this Christmas old!
DICKENS, *Pickwick Papers*, xxviii, A Christmas Carol

'Twas the night before Christmas, when all through the house
Not a creature was stirring, not even a mouse;
The stockings were hung by the chimney with care,
In hopes that Saint Nicholas soon would be there.
C. C. MOORE, *A Visit from St. Nicholas*

God rest ye merry, gentlemen; let nothing you dismay,
For Jesus Christ, our Saviour, was born on Christmas Day.
DINAH M. MULOCK, *A Christmas Carol*, st. 1

---

[1] A Christian is God Almighty's gentleman.—J. C. HARE, *Guesses at Truth*
His tribe were God Almighty's gentlemen.
DRYDEN, *Absalom and Achitophel*, i, line 645

The time draws near the birth of Christ:
  The moon is hid, the night is still;
  The Christmas bells from hill to hill
Answer each other in the mist.

Four voices of four hamlets round,
  From far and near, on mead and moor,
  Swell out and fail, as if a door
Were shut between me and the sound:

Each voice four changes on the wind,
  That now dilate and now decrease,
  Peace and good will, good will and peace,
Peace and good will, to all mankind.[1]

TENNYSON, *In Memoriam*, xxviii, st. 1–3

Again at Christmas did we weave
  The holly round the Christmas hearth.

TENNYSON, *In Memoriam*, lxxviii, st. 1

At Christmas play and make good cheere,
  For Christmas comes but once a yeere.

TUSSER, *Five Hundred Points of Good Husbandry:* The Farmer's Daily Diet, st. 6

Church. That spiritual pinder,
  Who looks on erring souls as straying pigs,
  That must be lashed by law, wherever found,
  And driven to church as to the parish pound.

HOOD, *Ode to Rae Wilson, Esquire*, st. 11

A man may cry Church! Church! at ev'ry word,
With no more piety than other people —
A daw's not reckoned a religious bird
Because it keeps a-cawing from a steeple.
The Temple is a good, a holy place,
But quacking only gives it an ill savour;
While saintly mountebanks the porch disgrace,
And bring religion's self into disfavour!

Ibid., st. 17

---

[1] Tall spire, from which the sound of cheerful bells
Just undulates upon the listening ear.

COWPER, *The Task: The Sofa*, lines 174, 175

How soft the music of those village bells,
Falling at intervals upon the ear
In cadence sweet! now dying all away,
Now pealing loud again, and louder still,
Clear and sonorous, as the gale comes on!

COWPER, *The Task: Winter Walk at Noon*, lines 6–10

Dear bells! how sweet the sounds of village bells
  When on the undulating air they swim!
Now loud as welcomes! faint, now, as farewells!
And trembling all about the breezy dells
  As fluttered by the wings of Cherubim.

HOOD, *Ode to Rae Wilson, Esquire*, st. 16

Who builds a church to God, and not to Fame,
Will never mark the marble with his name.
POPE, *Moral Essays*, Epistle iii, lines 285, 286

An I have not forgotten what the inside of a church is made of, I am a peppercorn, a brewer's horse.
SHAKESPEARE, *King Henry IV, Part I*, iii, 3

Till holy Church incorporate two in one.
SHAKESPEARE, *Romeo and Juliet*, ii, 6

Cider.— The piercing cider for the thirsty tongue.
THOMSON, *The Seasons*, Autumn, line 643

Cigar.— A woman is only a woman, but a good cigar is a smoke.[1] KIPLING, *The Betrothed*, st. 25

Cigar-box.— Open the old cigar-box, get me a Cuba stout,
For things are running crossways, and Maggie and I are out. KIPLING, *The Betrothed*, st. 1

Circle. As when
A stone is flung into some sleeping tarn
The circle widens till it lip the marge.[2]
TENNYSON, *Pelleas and Etarre*, lines 88–90

---

[1] They tell me Nancy Low
Has married Mr. R——;
The jilt! but I can live,
So I have my cigar.
HOOD, *The Cigar*, st. 14

[2] If that thou
Throw on water now a stoon,
Wel wost thou, hit wol make anoon
A litel roundel as a cercle,
Paraventure brood as a covercle;
And right anoon thou shalt see weel,
That wheel wol cause another wheel,
And that the thridde, and so forth, brother,
Every cercle causing other,
Wyder than himselve was;
And thus fro roundel to compas,
Ech aboute other goinge,
Caused of otheres steringe,
And multiplying ever-mo,
Til that hit be so fer y-go
That hit at bothe brinkes be.
CHAUCER, *The House of Fame*, II, lines 280–295

As the small pebble stirs the peaceful lake;
The centre moved, a circle straight succeeds,
Another still, and still another spreads.
POPE, *Essay on Man*, Epistle iv, lines 364–366

Glory is like a circle in the water,
Which never ceaseth to enlarge itself
Till by broad spreading it disperse to nought.
SHAKESPEARE, *King Henry VI, Part I*, i, 2

Circumlocution.— The Circumlocution Office was . . . the most important Department under government. No public business of any kind could possibly be done at any time without the acquiescence of the Circumlocution Office. Its finger was in the largest public pie, and in the smallest public tart. It was equally impossible to do the plainest right and to undo the plainest wrong without the express authority of the Circumlocution Office. . . . Whatever was required to be done, the Circumlocution Office was beforehand with all the public departments in the art of perceiving — How not to do it.
DICKENS, *Little Dorrit*, x

Citizen.— The first requisite of a good citizen in this republic of ours is that he shall be able and willing to pull his weight; that he shall not be a mere passenger, but shall do his share in the work that each generation of us finds ready to hand.[1]
THEODORE ROOSEVELT, *Speech before the New York Chamber of Commerce*, November 11, 1902

Civet.— I cannot talk with civet in the room,
A fine puss gentleman that 's all perfume.
COWPER, *Conversation*, lines 283, 284

Civic.— Ring out false pride in place and blood,
The civic slander and the spite.
TENNYSON, *In Memoriam*, cvi, st. 6

Civil. The intestine shock
And furious close of civil butchery.
SHAKESPEARE, *King Henry IV, Part I*, i, 1

Where civil blood makes civil hands unclean.
SHAKESPEARE, *Romeo and Juliet*, Prologue

Civilizes.— The sex whose presence civilizes ours.
COWPER, *Conversation*, line 254

Clanging.— Trailing like a wounded duck, working out her soul;
Clanging like a smithy-shop after every roll;
Just a funnel and a mast lurching through the spray —
So we threshed the "Bolivar" out across the Bay!
KIPLING, *Ballad of the Bolivar*, st. 4

Clapper-clawing.— Have always been at daggers-drawing,
And one another clapper-clawing.
BUTLER, *Hudibras*, II, ii, lines 79, 80

---

[1] The true Christian is the true citizen, lofty of purpose, resolute in endeavour, ready for a hero's deeds, . . . and in this world doing all that in him lies, so that when death comes he may feel that mankind is in some degree better because he has lived.
THEODORE ROOSEVELT, *Sp. bef. Y. M. C. A.*, Dec. 30, 1900

Claret.— The claret smooth, red as the lips we press
In sparkling fancy, while we drain the bowl.
THOMSON, *The Seasons*, Autumn, lines 703, 704

Classes.— I have seen some nations like o'erloaded asses
Kick off their burthens — meaning the high classes.
BYRON, *Don Juan*, Canto xi, st. 84

Classic.— Still I seem to tread on classic ground.
ADDISON, *Letter from Italy*, line 12

Clay.— "She is dead!" they said to him. "Come away;
Kiss her! and leave her! — thy love is clay!"
SIR EDWIN ARNOLD, *She and He*, st. 1

Some must follow, and some command,
Though all are made of clay.
LONGFELLOW, *Kéramos*, st. 1

Clean.— Let your hands and your conscience
Be honest and clean;
Scorn to touch or to think of
The thing that is mean;
But hold on to the pure
And the right with firm grip,
And though hard be the task,
"Keep a stiff upper lip!"
PHŒBE CARY, *Keep a Stiff Upper Lip*, st. 3

Cleanliness.— Cleanliness is indeed next to godliness.
WESLEY, *Sermon on Dress*

Clergy.— The clergy have played the part of the fly-wheel in our modern civilization.
HOLMES, *Professor at the Breakfast-Table*, i

Climb.— Fain would I climb but that I fear to fall.[1]
RALEIGH, *Line Written on Window of Queen Elizabeth's Pavilion*

To climb steep hills
Requires slow pace at first.
SHAKESPEARE, *King Henry VIII*, i, 1

Clock.— From that chamber, clothed in white,
The bride came forth on her wedding night;
There, in that silent room below,
The dead lay in his shroud of snow;
And in the hush that followed the prayer,
Was heard the old clock on the stair,—
"For ever — never!
Never — for ever!"
LONGFELLOW, *The Old Clock on the Stairs*, st. 7

[1] If thy mind fail thee, do not climb at all.
QUEEN ELIZABETH, *Line Written Beneath Raleigh's Inscription*

Orlando. There's no clock in the forest.
Rosalind. Then there is no true lover in the forest; else sighing every minute and groaning every hour would detect the lazy foot of Time as well as a clock.
SHAKESPEARE, *As You Like It*, iii, 2

Cloister.— For aye to be in shady cloister mewed,
To live a barren sister all your life,
Chanting faint hymns to the cold fruitless moon [1]
SHAKESPEARE, *Midsummer-Night's Dream*, i, 1

Cloud. There does a sable cloud
Turn forth her silver lining on the night.
MILTON, *Comus*, lines 223, 224

Hamlet. Do you see yonder cloud that's almost in shape of a camel? [2]
Polonius. By the mass, and 't is like a camel, indeed.
Hamlet. Methinks it is like a weasel.
Polonius. It is backed like a weasel.
Hamlet. Or like a whale.
Polonius. Very like a whale.
SHAKESPEARE, *Hamlet*, iii, 2

Can such things be,
And overcome us like a summer's cloud,
Without our special wonder?
SHAKESPEARE, *Macbeth*, iii, 4

Clouds.— I saw two clouds at morning,
Tinged with the rising sun;
And in the dawn they floated on,
And mingled into one.
J. G. C. BRAINARD, *Epithalamium*, st. 1

Coaches.— What are we . . . but coaches? . . . Our passions are the horses, and rampant animals, too. . . . We start from The Mother's Arms, and we run to The Dust Shovel. DICKENS, *Martin Chuzzlewit*, viii

Coarse. Thou shalt lower to his level day by day,
What is fine within thee growing coarse to sympathize with clay. TENNYSON, *Locksley Hall*, lines 45, 46

---

[1] I was not good enough for man,
And so am given to God. KINGSLEY, *The Ugly Princess*, st. 4

[2] Sometime we see a cloud that's dragonish;
A vapour sometime like a bear or lion,
A towered citadel, a pendent rock,
A forked mountain, or blue promontory
With trees upon't, that nod unto the world,
And mock our eyes with air: . . .
That which is now a horse, even with a thought
The rack dislimns, and makes it indistinct,
As water is in water. SHAKESPEARE, *Antony and Cleopatra*, iv, 14 [12]

Coat.— There's a hole made in your best coat.
SHAKESPEARE, *Merry Wives of Windsor*, iii, 5

Cobwebs.— And with as delicate a hand,
Could twist as tough a rope of sand;
And weave fine cobwebs, fit for skull
That's empty when the moon is full;
Such as take lodgings in a head
That's to be let unfurnished.
BUTLER, *Hudibras*, I, i, lines 157–162

Cock.— *Bernardo*. It was about to speak when the cock crew.
Horatio. And then it started like a guilty thing
Upon a fearful summons.[1] — SHAKESPEARE, *Hamlet*, i, 1

The early village cock
Hath twice done salutation to the morn.
SHAKESPEARE, *King Richard III*, v, 3

Cockle.— How should I your true love know
From another one?
By his cockle hat and staff,
And his sandal shoon. SHAKESPEARE, *Hamlet*, iv, 5

Coffee.— Coffee, which makes the politician wise,
And see through all things with his half-shut eyes.
POPE, *Rape of the Lock*, iii, lines 117, 118

Cold.— For this relief much thanks: 't is bitter cold,
And I am sick at heart. SHAKESPEARE, *Hamlet*, i, 1

I had a true-love, none so dear,
And a friend both leal and tried:
I had a cask of good old beer,
And a gallant horse to ride.

. . . . .

My lady fell to shame and hell,
And with her took my friend;
My cask ran sour, my horse went lame,
So alone in the cold I end.
LORD DE TABLEY, *Fortune's Wheel*, st. 1, 3

Coliseum.— While stands the Coliseum, Rome shall stand;
When falls the Coliseum, Rome shall fall;
And when Rome falls — the world.
BYRON, *Childe Harold's Pilgrimage*, Canto iv, st. 145

---

[1] The cock he crew; the fiends they flew
From the voice of the morning away.
SOUTHEY, *The Old Woman of Berkeley*, st. 27

Collar.— His lockèd, lettered, braw brass collar
Showed him the gentleman and scholar.
BURNS, *The Twa Dogs*, st. 3

Cologne.— The river Rhine, it is well known,
Doth wash your city of Cologne;
But tell me, Nymphs! what power divine
Shall henceforth wash the river Rhine?
S. T. COLERIDGE, *Cologne*, lines 7–10

Colonel.— I personally wish ——— to be appointed colonel . . .; and this regardless of whether he can tell the exact shade of Julius Cæsar's hair.—ABRAHAM LINCOLN, *Note to Secretary Stanton, November* 11, 1863

Colossus.— Why, man, he doth bestride the world
Like a Colossus, and we petty men
Walk under his huge legs and peep about
To find ourselves dishonourable graves.
SHAKESPEARE, *Julius Cæsar*, i, 2

Colour.— Deem our nation brutes no longer,
Till some reason ye shall find
Worthier of regard, and stronger
Than the colour of our kind.
Slaves of gold, whose sordid dealings
Tarnish all your boasted powers,
Prove that you have human feelings
Ere you proudly question ours.
COWPER, *The Negro's Complaint*, st. 7

Colours.— Stood for his country's glory fast,
And nailed her colours to the mast.[1]
SCOTT, *Marmion*, Introd. to Canto i

Colt.— Your colt's tooth is not cast yet.
SHAKESPEARE, *King Henry VIII*, i, 3

Columbia.— Columbia, Columbia, to glory arise,
The queen of the world, and the child of the skies!
TIMOTHY DWIGHT, *Columbia*, st. 1

Hail, Columbia! happy land!
Hail, ye heroes, heaven-born band!
Who fought and bled in Freedom's cause!
JOSEPH HOPKINSON, *Hail, Columbia!* st. 1

---

[1] Through childhood, through manhood,
Through life to the end,
Struggle bravely and stand
By your colours, my friend.
Only yield when you must;
Never "give up the ship,"
But fight on to the last
"With a stiff upper lip!" PHŒBE CARY, *Keep a Stiff Upper Lip*, st. 4

Column.— Where London's column, pointing at the skies,
Like a tall bully, lifts the head, and lies.
POPE, *Moral Essays*, Epistle iii, lines 339, 340

Comb.— To comb your noddle with a three-legged stool.
SHAKESPEARE, *Taming of the Shrew*, i, 1

Come.— Come in the evening, or come in the morning,
Come when you're looked for, or come without warning,
Kisses and welcome you'll find here before you,
And the oftener you come here the more I'll adore you!
T. O. DAVIS, *The Welcome*, st. 1

That it should come to this!
SHAKESPEARE, *Hamlet*, i, 2

Comfort. That comfort comes too late;
'T is like a pardon after execution.[1]
SHAKESPEARE, *King Henry VIII*, iv, 2

Commandments.— Old as the Ten Commandments.
KIPLING, *Cleared*, st. 12

Could I come near your beauty with my nails,
I'd set my ten commandments in your face.
SHAKESPEARE, *King Henry VI, Part II*, i, 3

Commerce.— Saw the heavens fill with commerce, argosies of magic sails,
Pilots of the purple twilight, dropping down with costly bales.
TENNYSON, *Locksley Hall*, lines 121, 122

Common.— I am not in the roll of common men.
SHAKESPEARE, *King Henry IV, Part I*, iii, 1

'T is the common lot;
In this shape, or in that, has Fate entailed,
The mother's throes on all of woman born,
Not more the children than sure heirs of pain.
YOUNG, *Night Thoughts*, I, lines 238–241

Commonwealth.— An independent, peaceful, law-abiding, well-governed, and prosperous commonwealth; . . . a state without king or nobles; . . . a church without a bishop; . . . a people governed by grave magistrates which it had selected, and equal laws which it had framed.
RUFUS CHOATE, *Address before the New England Association, December*, 1843

---

[1] "After dying all reprieve's too late."
DRYDEN, *Song, "Fair, Sweet, and Young,"* line 18

Company.— Villainous company hath been the spoil of me.
SHAKESPEARE, *King Henry IV, Part I*, iii, 3

Comparisons.— She and comparisons are odious.[1]
DONNE, *Elegy VIII: The Comparison*

Compass. That trembling vassal of the Pole,
The feeling compass, navigation's soul.
BYRON, *The Island*, Canto i, st. 5

Watched the compass chase its tail like a cat at play —
That was on the "Bolivar," south across the Bay.
KIPLING, *Ballad of the Bolivar*, st. 8

Complexion.— Mislike me not for my complexion,
The shadowed livery of the burnished sun,
To whom I am a neighbour and near bred.
SHAKESPEARE, *Merchant of Venice*, ii, 1

Compromise.— They enslave their children's children who make compromise with sin.
LOWELL, *The Present Crisis*, st. 9

Conclusion.— O most lame and impotent conclusion!
SHAKESPEARE, *Othello*, ii, 1

But this denoted a foregone conclusion. *Ibid.*, iii, 3

Confess. Confess yourself to heaven;
Repent what 's past; avoid what is to come;
And do not spread the compost on the weeds,
To make them ranker. SHAKESPEARE, *Hamlet*, iii, 4

I confess nothing, nor I deny nothing.
SHAKESPEARE, *Much Ado about Nothing*, iv, 1

Confidence.— Confidence is a plant of slow growth in an aged bosom.—WILLIAM PITT, EARL OF CHATHAM,
Speech, January 14, 1766

Conflict.— It is an irrepressible conflict between opposing and enduring forces.—W. H. SEWARD, *Speech, October* 25, 1858

Congenial.— Congenial spirits part to meet again.
THOMAS CAMPBELL, *Pleasures of Hope*, ii, st. 29

Congress.— So, wen one 's chose to Congriss, ez soon ez he 's in it,
A collar grows right round his neck in a minnit,
An' sartin it is thet a man cannot be strict
In bein' himself, wen he gits to the Deestrict,
Fer a coat thet sets wal here in ole Massachusetts,
Wen it gits on to Washin'ton, somehow askew sets.
LOWELL, *Biglow Papers*, I, iv, lines 39–44

---

[1] Comparisons are odorous.—SHAKESPEARE, *Much Ado about Nothing*, iii, 5

Conquer.— Though mine arm should conquer twenty worlds,
There's a lean fellow beats all conquerors.
THOMAS DEKKER, *Old Fortunatus*, i, 1

Conquered.— I sing the hymn of the conquered, who fell in the Battle of Life,—
The hymn of the wounded, the beaten, who died overwhelmed in the strife;
. . . . .
The hymn of the low and the humble, the weary, the broken in heart,
Who strove and who failed, acting bravely a silent and desperate part.
W. W. STORY, *Io Victis*, st. 1

Conscience. That fierce thing
They call a conscience![1]
HOOD, *Lamia*, Scene vii

I keep a conscience clear,
I've a hundred pounds a year,
And I manage to exist and to be glad, John Brown.
CHARLES MACKAY, *John Brown*, st. 4

What conscience dictates to be done,
Or warns me not to do,
This, teach me more than hell to shun,
That, more than heaven pursue.
POPE, *The Universal Prayer*, st. 4

Conscience is but [For conscience is] a word that cowards use,
Devised at first to keep the strong in awe.
SHAKESPEARE, *King Richard III*, v, 3

Conscience has no more to do with gallantry than it has with politics.
R. B. SHERIDAN, *The Duenna*, ii, 4

---

[1] With his departing breath,
A form shall hail him at the gates of death,
The spectre Conscience,— shrieking through the gloom,
Man, we shall meet again beyond the tomb.
JAMES MONTGOMERY, *The West Indies*, iii, st. 10

Thus conscience does make cowards of us all;
And thus the native hue of resolution
Is sicklied o'er with the pale cast of thought,
And enterprises of great pith and moment
With this regard their currents turn awry
And lose the name of action.
SHAKESPEARE, *Hamlet*, iii, 1

O coward conscience, how dost thou afflict me!
. . . . .
My conscience hath a thousand several tongues,
And every tongue brings in a several tale,
And every tale condemns me for a villain.
SHAKESPEARE, *King Richard III*, v, 3

Trust that man in nothing who has not a conscience in everything.

STERNE, *Tristram Shandy*, II, xvii; *Sermon* xxvii

Consent.— And whispering "I will ne'er consent," consented.

BYRON, *Don Juan*, Canto i, st. 117

Considering.— "I am pretty well, considering." Mrs. Pipchin always used that form of words. It meant, considering her virtues, sacrifices, and so forth.

DICKENS, *Dombey and Son*, xi

Consistency.— He's ben on all sides thet give places or pelf;
But consistency still wuz a part of his plan,—
He's ben true to *one* party,— an' thet is himself.

LOWELL, *Biglow Papers*, I, iii, st. 3

Constable. Thou hast
Out-run the constable at last.

BUTLER, *Hudibras*, I, iii, lines 1367, 1368

Constant. I am constant as the northern star,
Of whose true-fixed and resting quality
There is no fellow in the firmament.

SHAKESPEARE, *Julius Cæsar*, iii, 1

Content.— Happy the man that, when his day is done,
Lies down to sleep with nothing of regret —
The battle he has fought may not be won —
The fame he sought be just as fleeting yet;
Folding at last his hands upon his breast,
Happy is he, if hoary and forespent,
He sinks into the last, eternal rest,
Breathing these only words: "I am content."

EUGENE FIELD, *Contentment*, st. 1

Contentment.— The noblest mind the best contentment has.

SPENSER, *Faerie Queene*, Canto i, st. 35

Conversation.— When you stick on conversation's burrs,
Don't strew your pathway with those dreadful *urs*.

HOLMES, *A Rhymed Lesson*, st. 45

Conversations. Conversations, dull and dry,
Embellished with — He said, and So said I.

COWPER, *Conversation*, lines 211, 212

Cook.— 'T is an ill cook that cannot lick his own fingers.

SHAKESPEARE, *Romeo and Juliet*, iv, 2

Cookery.— But his neat cookery! he cut our roots
In characters,
And sauced our broths, as Juno had been sick
And he her dieter. SHAKESPEARE, *Cymbeline*, iv, 2

Cooks.— We may live without poetry, music, and art;
We may live without conscience, and live without heart;
We may live without friends; we may live without books;
But civilized man cannot live without cooks.
He may live without books,— what is knowledge but grieving?
He may live without hope,— what is hope but deceiving?
He may live without love,— what is passion but pining?
But where is the man that can live without dining?

OWEN MEREDITH, *Lucile*, II, xix

Cooks must live by making tarts,
And wits by making verses.

PRAED, *Twenty-Eight and Twenty-Nine*, st. 2

Copies.— We took him setting of boys' copies.

SHAKESPEARE, *King Henry VI, Part II*, iv, 2

Copper.— All in a hot and copper sky,
The bloody sun, at noon,
Right up above the mast did stand,
No bigger than the moon.

COLERIDGE, *Ancient Mariner*, lines 111–114

Corinth.— The khan and the pachas are all at their post;
The vizier himself at the head of the host.
When the culverin's signal is fired, then on;
Leave not in Corinth a living one —
A priest at her altars, a chief in her halls,
A hearth in her mansions, a stone on her walls.
God and the Prophet! — Alla Hu!
Up to the skies with that wild halloo!

BYRON, *Siege of Corinth*, st. 22

Cormorant.— Thence up he flew, and on the Tree of Life,
The middle tree and highest there that grew,
Sat like a cormorant.[1]

MILTON, *Paradise Lost*, IV, lines 194–196

Cornishmen.— By Tre, Pol, and Pen[2] ye may know Cornishmen.

R. S. HAWKER, *Gate Song of Stowe*, st. 4

---

[1] Myself sate like a cormorant once
Upon the Tree of Knowledge. SOUTHEY, *The Devil's Walk*, st. 14

[2] What! will they scorn Tre, Pol, and Pen,
And shall Trelawney die? R. S. HAWKER, *Song of the Western Men*

A good sword and a trusty hand,
A merry heart and true,
King James's men shall understand
What Cornish lads can do.
And have they fixed the where and when,
And shall Trelawney die?
Then twenty thousand Cornishmen
Will know the reason why!

R. S. HAWKER, *Song of the Western Men*, st. 1

Corporations.— Corporations cannot commit treason, nor be outlawed, nor excommunicated, for they have no souls.
SIR EDWARD COKE, 10 *King's Bench Reports*, 32

Corruption. Most base is he who, 'neath the shade
Of Freedom's ensign plies Corruption's trade.[1]
T. MOORE, *Corruption*

Corruption wins not more than honesty.
SHAKESPEARE, *King Henry VIII*, iii, 2

Corsair.— He left a corsair's name to other times,
Linked with one virtue, and a thousand crimes.
BYRON, *The Corsair*, Canto iii, st. 24

Coughs.— Coughs are ungrateful things. You find one out in the cold, take it up and nurse it and make everything of it, dress it up warm, give it all sorts of balsams and other food it likes, and carry it round in your bosom as if it were a miniature lapdog. And by-and-by its little bark grows sharp and savage, and — confound the thing! — you find it is a wolf's whelp that you have got there, and he is gnawing in the breast where he has been nestling so long.
HOLMES, *Professor at the Breakfast-Table*, vi

Counsel. I pray thee, cease thy counsel,
Which falls into mine ears as profitless
As water in a sieve.
SHAKESPEARE, *Much Ado about Nothing*, v, 1

Country.— To be suspected, thwarted, and withstood,
E'en when he labours for his country's good.
COWPER, *Table Talk*, lines 141, 142

God made the country, and man made the town.[2]
COWPER, *The Task: The Sofa*, line 749

'Twas for the good of my country that I should be abroad.[3]
GEORGE FARQUHAR, *The Beaux Stratagem*, iii, 2

---

[1] That party-coloured mass which nought can warm
But rank Corruption's heat — whose quickened swarm
Spread their light wings in Bribery's golden sky,
Buzz for a period, lay their eggs, and die;
That greedy vampire which from Freedom's tomb
Comes forth with all the mimicry of bloom
Upon its lifeless cheek and sucks and drains
A people's blood to feed its putrid veins! T. MOORE, *Corruption*

[2] God the first garden made, and the first city Cain.
COWLEY, *Essay V: The Garden*

[3] True patriots all; for, be it understood,
We left our country for our country's good.
G. BARRINGTON, *Prologue to a Play Performed by Convicts in New South Wales*

My country! 't is of thee,
Sweet land of liberty,
  Of thee I sing;[1]
Land where my fathers died,
Land of the Pilgrims' pride,
From every mountain-side
  Let freedom ring. S. F. SMITH, *America*, st. 1

Courage. 'Tis true that we are in great danger;
The greater therefore should our courage be.[2]
SHAKESPEARE, *King Henry V*, iv, 1

Court.— A friend i' the court is better than a penny in purse.
SHAKESPEARE, *King Henry IV, Part II*, v, 1

Courtesies.— Since when I have been debtor to you for courtesies, which I will be ever to pay and yet pay still. SHAKESPEARE, *Cymbeline*, i, 4 [5]

Courtesy.— I am the very pink of courtesy.
SHAKESPEARE, *Romeo and Juliet*, ii, 4

---

[1] Our country! in her intercourse with foreign nations, may she always be in the right; but our country, right or wrong.
S. DECATUR, Toast at Norfolk, April, 1816

There is a land of every land the pride,
Beloved by Heaven o'er all the world beside;
Where brighter suns dispense serener light,
And milder moons emparadise the night;
A land of beauty, virtue, valour, truth,
Time-tutored age, and love-exalted youth.
JAMES MONTGOMERY, *The West Indies*, iii, st. 1

Breathes there the man, with soul so dead,
Who never to himself hath said,
  This is my own, my native land!
Whose heart hath ne'er within him burned,
As home his footsteps he hath turned,
  From wandering on a foreign strand!
If such there breathe, go, mark him well;
For him no minstrel raptures swell;
High though his titles, proud his name,
Boundless his wealth as wish can claim;
Despite those titles, power, and pelf,
The wretch, concentred all in self,
Living, shall forfeit fair renown,
And, doubly dying, shall go down
To the vile dust, from whence he sprung,
Unwept, unhonored, and unsung.*
SCOTT, *Lay of the Last Minstrel*, Canto vi, st. 6

Who is here so vile that will not love his country?
SHAKESPEARE, *Julius Cæsar*, iii, 2

[2] Courage, then! what cannot be avoided
'Twere childish weakness to lament or fear.
SHAKESPEARE, *King Henry VI, Part III*, v, 4

Courage mounteth with occasion. SHAKESPEARE, *King John*, ii, 1

---

*Unwept, unnoted, and for ever dead. POPE, *Odyssey*, V, line 402

Courtier.— Sir, I have lived a courtier all my days,
And studied men, their manners, and their ways;
And have observed this useful maxim still,
To let my betters always have their will.
Nay, if my lord affirmed that black was white,
My word was this, Your honour's in the right.
POPE, *January and May*, lines 156–161

Coward.— When all the blandishments of life are gone,
The coward sneaks to death, the brave live on.
DR. GEORGE SEWELL, *The Suicide*,
from Martial, XI, Epistle 56

The man that lays his hand upon a woman,
Save in the way of kindness, is a wretch
Whom 'twere gross flattery to name a coward.
JOHN TOBIN, *The Honeymoon*, ii, 1

Cowards.— Cowards die many times before their deaths;
The valiant never taste of death but once.
SHAKESPEARE, *Julius Cæsar*, ii, 2

A plague of all cowards!
SHAKESPEARE, *King Henry IV, Part I*, ii, 4

Craft.— Built for freight, and yet for speed,
A beautiful and gallant craft.
LONGFELLOW, *Building of the Ship*, st. 4

Crazed.— Crazed with care, or crossed in hopeless love.
GRAY, *Elegy Written in a Country Churchyard*, st. 28

Creed.— Sapping a solemn creed with solemn sneer.
BYRON, *Childe Harold's Pilgrimage*, Canto iii, st. 107

Cricket.— The cricket on the hearth.[1]
MILTON, *Il Penseroso*, line 82

Crime. Many a crime deemed innocent on earth
Is registered in heaven. COWPER, *The Task: Winter Walk at Noon*, lines 439, 440

A mighty yearning, like the first
Fierce impulse unto crime!
HOOD, *The Dream of Eugene Aram*, st. 26

Crispian.— This day is called the feast of Crispian:
He that outlives this day, and comes safe home,
Will stand a-tiptoe when this day is named,
And rouse him at the name of Crispian.
SHAKESPEARE, *King Henry V*, iv, 3

[1] Crickets sing at the oven's mouth.— SHAKESPEARE, *Pericles*, iii, Prologue

Critic.— Fear not to lie, 'twill seem a lucky hit;
Shrink not from blasphemy, 'twill pass for wit;
Care not for feeling — pass your proper jest,
And stand a critic, hated yet caressed.[1] BYRON,
English Bards and Scotch Reviewers, lines 71–74

Critical.— I am nothing, if not critical.
SHAKESPEARE, *Othello*, ii, 1

Cross.— Not she with trait'rous kiss her Saviour stung,
Not she denied him with unholy tongue,
She, while apostles shrank, could danger brave,
Last at his cross, and earliest at his grave.
E. S. BARRETT, *Woman*, i

The cross that our own hands fashion is the heaviest cross of all. K. E. CONWAY,
The Heaviest Cross of All, st. 1

No cross,— no crown.
HON. MRS. CHARLES HOBART,
The Changed Cross, st. 14

Those holy fields
Over whose acres walked those blessed feet
Which fourteen hundred years ago were nailed
For our advantage on the bitter cross.
SHAKESPEARE, *King Henry IV, Part I*, i, 1

Crow.— You and I must pull a crow.[2]
BUTLER, *Hudibras*, II, ii, line 500

Crowd.— We met,— 'twas in a crowd.[3]
T. H. BAYLY, *We Met*

---

[1] As soon
Seek roses in December, ice in June;
Hope constancy in wind, or corn in chaff;
Believe a woman, or an epitaph,
Or any other thing that's false, before
You trust in critics who themselves are sore.
BYRON, *English Bards and Scotch Reviewers*, lines 75–80

Nature fits all her children with something to do,
He who would write and can't write, can surely review,
Can set up a small booth as critic and sell us his
Petty conceit and his pettier jealousies.
LOWELL, *Fable for Critics*, lines 1785–1788

Did some more sober critic come abroad;
If wrong, I smiled; if right, I kissed the rod.
Pains, reading, study, are their just pretence,
And all they want is spirit, taste, and sense.
Commas and points they set exactly right,
And 'twere a sin to rob them of their mite.
POPE, *Epistle to Dr. Arbuthnot*, lines 157–162

[2] We'll pluck a crow together.—SHAKESPEARE, *Comedy of Errors*, iii, 1

[3] We met,—'t was in a mob.—*Parody by Hood.*

Far from the madding crowd's ignoble strife,[1]
  Their sober wishes never learned to stray;[2]
Along the cool, sequestered vale of life
  They kept the noiseless tenor of their way.
GRAY, *Elegy Written in a Country Churchyard*, st. 20

Crown.— Upon the summit of my crown
  I have a trifling patch;
A little white amidst the brown,
  An opening in the thatch.
H. S. LEIGH, *The Sword of Damocles*, st. 5

Young Jamie lo'ed me weel, and sought me for his bride;
But saving a croun he had naething else beside:
To make the croun a pund, young Jamie gaed to sea;
And the croun and the pund were baith for me.
LADY ANNE LINDSAY, *Auld Robin Gray*, st. 2

Uneasy lies the head that wears a crown.
SHAKESPEARE, *King Henry IV, Part II*, iii, 1

Cruel.— I must be cruel, only to be kind.
SHAKESPEARE, *Hamlet*, iii, 4

Crutch.— The broken soldier, kindly bade to stay,
Sat by his fire, and talked the night away;
Wept o'er his wounds, or, tales of sorrow done,
Shouldered his crutch, and showed how fields were won.
GOLDSMITH, *The Deserted Village*, st. 10

Cry.— Oh! would I were dead now,
Or up in my bed now,
To cover my head now,
  And have a good cry!
HOOD, *A Table of Errata*, st. 15

I could find in my heart to disgrace my man's apparel and to cry like a woman; but I must comfort the weaker vessel, as doublet and hose ought to show itself courageous to petticoat.—SHAKESPEARE, *As You Like It*, ii, 4

Cup.— Then fill a fair and honest cup, and bear it straight
  to me;
The goblet hallows all it holds, whate'er the liquid be;
And may the cherubs on its face protect me from the sin,
That dooms one to those dreadful words,— "My dear,
  where *have* you been?"
HOLMES, *On Lending a Punch-Bowl*, st. 13

---

[1] Far from gay cities and the ways of men.
POPE, *The Odyssey*, XIV, line 410

[2] Their wants but few, their wishes all confined.
GOLDSMITH, *The Traveller*, st. 17

The cup of water in His name.
LONGFELLOW, *Inscription on the Shanklin Fountain*

Fill the cup and fill the can,
Have a rouse before the morn;
Every moment dies a man,
Every moment one is born.
TENNYSON, *The Vision of Sin*, lines 95-98

Cupid.— Love looks not with the eyes, but with the mind;
And therefore is winged Cupid painted blind.
SHAKESPEARE, *Midsummer-Night's Dream*, i, 1

Curfew.— The curfew tolls the knell of parting day;
The lowing herd winds slowly o'er the lea;
The ploughman homeward plods his weary way,
And leaves the world to darkness and to me.
GRAY, *Elegy Written in a Country Churchyard*, st. 1

Current. We must take the current when it serves,
Or lose our ventures.—SHAKESPEARE, *Julius Cæsar*, iv, 3

Curs.— You common cry of curs! whose breath I hate
As reek o' the rotten fens, whose loves I prize
As the dead carcasses of unburied men
That do corrupt my air, I banish you!
SHAKESPEARE, *Coriolanus*, iii, 3

Curse.— Why, be this juice the growth of God, who dare
Blaspheme the twisted tendril as a snare?
A blessing, we should use it, should we not?
And if a curse — why, then, who set it there?
OMAR KHAYYÁM, *Rubáiyát* (trans. Fitzgerald), st. 61

Thou shalt seek Death to release thee in vain;
Thou shalt live in thy pain, while Kehama shall reign,
With a fire in thy heart, and a fire in thy brain;
And Sleep shall obey me, and visit thee never,
And the curse shall be on thee for ever and ever.
SOUTHEY, *Curse of Kehama*, II

Cursed.— "A jolly place," said he, "in times of old!
But something ails it now: the spot is cursed."[1]
WORDSWORTH, *Hart-Leap Well*, ii, st. 7

Curtain.— Draw this curtain, and let's see your picture.[2]
SHAKESPEARE, *Troilus and Cressida*, iii, 2

---

[1] O'er all there hung a shadow and a fear;
A sense of mystery the spirit daunted,
And said, as plain as whisper in the ear,
The place is haunted. HOOD, *The Haunted House*, i, st. 8

[2] We will draw the curtain and show you the picture.
SHAKESPEARE, *Twelfth Night*, i, 5

The play is done; the curtain drops,
  Slow falling to the prompter's bell:
A moment yet the actor stops,
  And looks around, to say farewell.

THACKERAY, *The End of the Play*, st. 1

Custom. Though I am native here
And to the manner born, it is a custom
More honoured in the breach than in the observance.

SHAKESPEARE, *Hamlet*, i, 4

A thing of custom.[1] SHAKESPEARE, *Macbeth*, iii, 4

Customs. New customs,
Though they be never so ridiculous,
Nay, let 'em be unmanly, yet are followed.

SHAKESPEARE, *King Henry VIII*, i, 3

Cut.— This was the most unkindest cut of all.

SHAKESPEARE, *Julius Cæsar*, iii, 2

Cynic.— The cynic is one who never sees a good quality in a man, and never fails to see a bad one. He is the human owl, vigilant in darkness and blind to light, mousing for vermin, and never seeing noble game. H. W. BEECHER, *Lectures to Young Men*, The Portrait Gallery, The Cynic

Cynosure.— The cynosure of neighbouring eyes.

MILTON, *L'Allegro*, line 80

Dagger.— Is this a dagger which I see before me,
The handle toward my hand? Come, let me clutch thee.
I have thee not, and yet I see thee still.
Art thou not, fatal vision, sensible
To feeling as to sight? or art thou but
A dagger of the mind, a false creation,
Proceeding from the heat-oppressed brain?

SHAKESPEARE, *Macbeth*, ii, 1

This is the air-drawn dagger. *Ibid.*, iii, 4

Daggers. Infirm of purpose!
Give me the daggers. SHAKESPEARE, *Macbeth*, ii, 2

Dalliance.— Look thou be true: do not give dalliance
Too much the rein; the strongest oaths are straw
To the fire i' the blood: be more abstemious,
Or else, good-night your vow!

SHAKESPEARE, *The Tempest*, iv, 1

---

[1] *Hamlet.* Has this fellow no feeling of his business, that he sings at grave-making?
Horatio. Custom hath made it in him a property of easiness.
Hamlet. 'Tis e'en so: the hand of little employment hath the daintier sense. SHAKESPEARE, *Hamlet*, v, 1

Dame. When my old wife lived, upon
This day she was both pantler, butler, cook,
Both dame and servant; welcomed all, served all;
Would sing her song and dance her turn; now here,
At upper end o' the table, now i' the middle;
On his shoulder, and his; her face o' fire
With labour and the thing she took to quench it,
She would to each one sip.
SHAKESPEARE, *Winter's Tale*, iv, 4 [3]

Damn.— Damn with faint praise, assent with civil leer,
And, without sneering, teach the rest to sneer;
Willing to wound, and yet afraid to strike,
Just hint a fault, and hesitate dislike.
POPE, *Epistle to Dr. Arbuthnot*, lines 201–204

Damnation.— Let not this weak, unknowing hand
Presume thy bolts to throw,
And deal damnation round the land,
On each I judge thy foe.
POPE, *The Universal Prayer*, st. 7

The deep damnation of his taking-off.
SHAKESPEARE, *Macbeth*, i, 7

Damnations.— There's a great text in Galatians,
Once you trip on it, entails
Twenty-nine distinct damnations,
One sure, if another fails.
R. BROWNING, *Soliloquy of the Spanish Cloister*, st. 7

Dance.— On with the dance! let joy be unconfined;
No sleep till morn when youth and pleasure meet,
To chase the glowing hours with flying feet.
BYRON, *Childe Harold's Pilgrimage*, Canto iii, st. 22

To dance attendance on their lordships' pleasure.
SHAKESPEARE, *King Henry VIII*, v, 2

Dancing.— A very merry, dancing, drinking,
Laughing, quaffing, and unthinking time.
DRYDEN, *The Secular Masque*, lines 44, 45

Many a youth, and many a maid,
Dancing in the chequered shade;
And young and old come forth to play
On a sunshine holy-day.—MILTON, *L'Allegro*, lines 95–98

You and I are past our dancing days.
SHAKESPEARE, *Romeo and Juliet*, i, 5

Dangerous. Though I am not splenitive and rash,
Yet have I something in me [in me something] dangerous,
Which let thy wiseness [wisdom] fear.
SHAKESPEARE, *Hamlet*, v, 1

Daniel.—*Shylock.* A Daniel come to judgment! yea, a Daniel!
O wise young judge, how I do honour thee!

. . . . . .

Gratiano. A second Daniel, a Daniel, Jew!
Now, infidel, I have you on the hip.

. . . . . .

A Daniel, still say I, a second Daniel!
I thank thee, Jew, for teaching me that word.
SHAKESPEARE, *Merchant of Venice*, iv, 1

Danube. Never
Can I forget that night in June,
Adown the Danube river.
H. AÏDÉ, *The Danube River*, st. 1

Dare.—I dare do all that may become a man;[1]
Who dares do more is none.—SHAKESPEARE, *Macbeth*, i, 7

Daring. The fierce native daring which instils
The stirring memory of a thousand years.
BYRON, *Childe Harold's Pilgrimage*, Canto iii, st. 26

Dark.— It was so dark, Hal, that thou could'st not see thy hand. SHAKESPEARE, *King Henry IV, Part I*, ii, 4

Darkness.— Strange, is it not? that of the myriads who
Before us passed the door of Darkness through,
Not one returns to tell us of the Road,
Which to discover we must travel too.
OMAR KHAYYÁM, *Rubáiyát* (trans. Fitzgerald), st. 64

Yet from those flames
No light, but rather darkness visible.
MILTON, *Paradise Lost*, I, lines 62, 63

Ring out the darkness of the land.
TENNYSON, *In Memoriam*, cvi, st. 8

Darling.— 'T is no spell of enchantment, no magical art,
But the way he says "Darling" that goes to my heart!
PHŒBE CARY, *The Old Man's Darling*, st. 2

Darlings.— The wealthy curled darlings of our nation.
SHAKESPEARE, *Othello*, i, 2

Dash.— Six precious souls, and all agog
To dash through thick and thin.
COWPER, *John Gilpin*, st. 10

---

[1] What man dare, I dare:
Approach thou like the rugged Russian bear,
The armed rhinoceros, or the Hyrcan tiger;
Take any shape but that, and my firm nerves
Shall never tremble SHAKESPEARE, *Macbeth*, iii, 4

Dashest.— And send'st him, shivering in thy playful spray
And howling, to his gods, where haply lies
His petty hope in some near port or bay,
And dashest him again to earth: — there let him lay.
BYRON, *Childe Harold's Pilgrimage*, Canto iv, st. 180

Daughter.— There came to port last Sunday night
The queerest little craft,
Without an inch of rigging on;
I looked and looked — and laughed!
It seemed so curious that she
Should cross the Unknown water,
And moor herself within my room —
My daughter! O, my daughter![1]
GEORGE W. CABLE, *The New Arrival*, st. 1

With a little hoard of maxims preaching down a daughter's heart. TENNYSON, *Locksley Hall*, line 94

Stern Daughter of the Voice of God.
WORDSWORTH, *Ode to Duty*, st. 1

Day.— Sweet day, so cool, so calm, so bright,
The bridal of the earth and sky.
GEORGE HERBERT, *Virtue*, st. 1

The gilded car of day. MILTON, *Comus*, line 95

Would I had met my dearest foe in heaven
Or ever I had seen that day!—SHAKESPEARE, *Hamlet*, i, 2

The livelong day. SHAKESPEARE, *Julius Cæsar*, i, 1

"I've lost a day!"[2] — the prince who nobly cried,
Had been an emperor without his crown.
YOUNG, *Night Thoughts*, II, lines 99, 100

Daylight.— Noiselessly as the daylight
Comes when the night is done,
And the crimson streak on ocean's cheek
Grows into the great sun.
C. F. ALEXANDER, *Burial of Moses*, st. 2

---

[1] My daughter! O, my daughter!
CAMPBELL, *Lord Ullin's Daughter*, st. 13; SHAKESPEARE, *Othello*, i, 3

[2] Lost! lost! lost!
A gem of countless price,
Cut from the living rock,
And graved in Paradise;
Set round with three times eight
Large diamonds, clear and bright,
And each with sixty smaller ones,
All changeful as the light. L. H. SIGOURNEY, *Advertisement of a Lost Day*, st. 1

Days.— Of all the days that 's in the week
I dearly love but one day —
And that 's the day that comes betwixt
A Saturday and Monday;
For then I 'm dressed all in my best
To walk abroad with Sally;
She is the darling of my heart,
And she lives in our alley.
HENRY CAREY, *Sally in Our Alley*, st. 4

The best of all ways
To lengthen our days,
Is to steal a few hours from the night, my dear!
T. MOORE, *The Young May Moon*, st. 1

Come hither lads and hearken, for a tale there is to tell,
Of the wonderful days a-coming, when all shall be better than well. W. MORRIS, *The Day Is Coming*, st. 1

We have seen better days. SHAKESPEARE,
As You Like It, ii, 7; *Timon of Athens*, iv, 2

Jesus, [Oh,] the days that we have seen![1]
SHAKESPEARE, *King Henry IV*, *Part II*, iii, 2

Deacon.— The Deacon swore, as deacons do,
With an "I dew vum," or an "I tell yeou."
HOLMES, *The Deacon's Masterpiece*, st. 4

Dead.— Faithful friends! It lies, I know,
Pale and white and cold as snow;
And ye say, "Abdallah's dead!"
Weeping at the feet and head,
I can see your falling tears,
I can hear your sighs and prayers;
Yet I smile and whisper this,—
"*I* am not the thing you kiss;
Cease your tears, and let it lie;
It *was* mine, it is not *I*."
SIR EDWIN ARNOLD, *After Death in Arabia*, st. 2

All that tread
The globe are but a handful to the tribes
That slumber in its bosom. Take the wings
Of morning, pierce the Barcan wilderness,
Or lose thyself in the continuous woods
Where rolls the Oregon, and hears no sound

---

[1] Eyah! those days, those days!—KIPLING, *The Courting of Dinah Shadd*

That time,— O times! SHAKESPEARE, *Antony and Cleopatra*, ii, 5

We'll talk of sunshine and of song,
And summer days, when we were young,
Sweet childish days, that were as long
As twenty days are now. WORDSWORTH, *To a Butterfly*, st. 2

Save his own dashings,— yet the dead are there!
And millions in those solitudes, since first
The flight of years began, have laid them down
In their last sleep,— the dead reign there alone!
BRYANT, *Thanatopsis*, lines 48–57

The light has come upon the dark benighted way. Dead, your Majesty! Dead, my Lords and gentlemen! Dead, Right Reverends and Wrong Reverends of every order! Dead, men and women, born with heavenly compassion in your hearts! And dying thus around us every day! DICKENS, *Bleak House*, xlvii

When once the Fates have cut the mortal thread,
The man as much to all intents is dead,
Who dies to-day, and will as long be so,
As he who died a thousand years ago. DRYDEN,
Translation of Lucretius, III, lines 318–321

Twelve hundred million men are spread
About this earth, and I and You
Wonder, when You and I are dead,
What will those luckless millions do?
KIPLING, *The Last Department*

Dead he lay among his books!
The peace of God was in his looks.
LONGFELLOW, *Bayard Taylor*, st. 1

Some
Have long been dead who think themselves alive,
Because not buried.
LONGFELLOW, *Michael Angelo*, III, i

Nothing in Nature's aspect intimated
That a great man was dead.
LONGFELLOW, *Warden of the Cinque Ports*, st. 12

"Odious! in woollen! 't would a saint provoke!"
(Were the last words that poor Narcissa spoke),
"No, let a charming chintz, and Brussels lace
Wrap my cold limbs, and shade my lifeless face:
One would not, sure, be frightful when one's dead —
And — Betty — give this cheek a little red."
POPE, *Moral Essays*, Epistle i, lines 246–251

Dead, for a ducat, dead! SHAKESPEARE, *Hamlet*, iii, 4

He is dead and gone, lady,
He is dead and gone;
At his head a grass-green turf,
At his heels a stone. *Ibid.*, iv, 5

Come not, when I am dead,
  To drop thy foolish tears upon my grave,
To trample round my fallen head,
  And vex the unhappy dust thou wouldst not save.
TENNYSON, *Fragment*, st. 1

Home they brought her warrior dead;
  She nor swooned nor uttered cry:
All her maidens, watching, said,
  "She must weep or she will die."
TENNYSON, *The Princess*, v

Nothing is dead, but that which wished to die;
Nothing is dead, but wretchedness and pain;
Nothing is dead, but what encumbered, galled,
Blocked up the pass, and barred from real life.
YOUNG, *Night Thoughts*, VI, lines 41–44

Dead Sea. The apples on the Dead Sea's shore,
All ashes to the taste.
BYRON, *Childe Harold's Pilgrimage*, Canto iii, 34

Death.— Weep awhile, if ye are fain,—
Sunshine still must follow rain;
Only not at death,— for death,
Now I know, is that first breath
Which our souls draw when we enter
Life, which is of all life centre.[1]
SIR EDWIN ARNOLD, *After Death in Arabia*, st. 6

I would tell *you*, darling, if I were dead,
And 'twere your hot tears upon *my* brow shed.

. . . . .

You should not ask, vainly, with streaming eyes,
Which in Death's touch was the chiefest surprise.

. . . . .

What a strange delicious amazement is Death,
To be without body and breathe without breath.
SIR EDWIN ARNOLD, *She and He*, st. 27, 29, 35

There was another heavy sound,
  A hush and then a groan;
And darkness swept across the sky —
  The work of death was done!
W. E. AYTOUN, *The Execution of Montrose*, st. 18

---

[1] There is no death! What seems so is transition;
  This life of mortal breath
Is but a suburb of the life elysian,
  Whose portal we call death.
LONGFELLOW, *Resignation*, st. 5

Revenge triumphs over death; love slights it; honour aspireth to it; grief flieth to it; fear preoccupateth it.
BACON, *Essay II: On Death*

Men fear death as children fear to go into the dark.
Ibid.

Like the hand which ends a dream,
Death, with the might of his sunbeam,
Touches the flesh, and the soul awakes.
R. BROWNING, *The Flight of the Duchess*, xv

What is death but parting breath?
BURNS, *Macpherson's Farewell*, st. 2

For the angel of death spread his wings on the blast,
And breathed in the face of the foe as he passed;
And the eyes of the sleepers waxed deadly and chill,
And their hearts but once heaved, and for ever grew still.
BYRON, *Destruction of Sennacherib*, st. 3

Ere Sin could blight or Sorrow fade,
Death came with friendly care;
The opening bud to Heaven conveyed,
And bade it blossom there.
S. T. COLERIDGE, *Epitaph on an Infant*

The child who enters life comes not with knowledge or intent,
So those who enter death must go as little children sent.
Nothing is known. But I believe that God is overhead;
And as life is to the living, so death is to the dead.
MARY MAPES DODGE, *The Two Mysteries*, st. 5

The world 's an inn, and death the journey's end.[1]
DRYDEN, *Palamon and Arcite*, line 2164

He trumped Death's ace for me that day,
And I 'm not goin'. back on him!
JOHN HAY, *Banty Tim*, st. 7

Death rides on every passing breeze,
He lurks in every flower.—R. HEBER, *At a Funeral*, st. 3

Death saw two players playing at cards,
But the game wasn't worth a dump,
For he quickly laid them flat with a spade,
To wait for the final trump![2] HOOD, *Death's Ramble*

---

[1] And, as the cock crew, those who stood before
The Tavern shouted —"Open then the door!
You know how little while we have to stay,
And, once departed, may return no more."
OMAR KHAYYÁM, *Rubáiyát* (trans. Fitzgerald), st. 3

[2] There card-players wait till the last trump be played.
LOWELL, *Fable for Critics*, line 1659

Death—*Continued*

But why do I talk of death?
  That phantom of grisly bone,
I hardly fear his terrible shape,
  It seems so like my own —
  It seems so like my own,
  Because of the fasts I keep;
O God! that bread should be so dear,
  And flesh and blood so cheap!

HOOD, *The Song of the Shirt*, st. 5

Ah, well, friend Death, good friend thou art:
  I shall be free when thou art through.
Take all there is — take hand and heart:
  There must be somewhere work to do.

HELEN FISKE JACKSON, *Habeas Corpus*, ad finem

Death stands above me, whispering low
  I know not what into my ear:
Of his strange language all I know
  Is, there is not a word of fear.[1]

W. S. LANDOR, *Last Fruit off an Old Tree*, xcv

Death, thou 'rt a cordial old and rare:
Look how compounded, with what care!
Time got his wrinkles reaping thee
Sweet herbs from all antiquity.

. . . . .

Then, Time, let not a drop be spilt:
Hand me the cup whene'er thou wilt;
'T is thy rich stirrup-cup to me;
I 'll drink it down right smilingly.

LANIER, *The Stirrup-Cup*, st. 1–3

---

[1] Fear death?— to feel the fog in my throat,
  The mist in my face,
When the snows begin, and the blasts denote
  I am nearing the place

. . . . .

Where he stands, the Arch Fear, in a visible form,
  Yet the strong man must go:
For the journey is done and the summit attained,
  And the barriers fall,
Though a battle's to fight ere the guerdon be gained,
  The reward of it all.
I would hate that death bandaged my eyes, and forbore,
  And bade me creep past.
No! let me taste the whole of it, fare like my peers
  The heroes of old,
Bear the brunt, in a minute pay glad life's arrears
  Of pain, darkness, and cold.
For sudden the worst turns the best to the brave,
  The black minute's at end,
And the elements' rage, the fiend-voices that rave,
  Shall dwindle, shall blend,
Shall change, shall become first a peace out of pain,
  Then a light.

R. BROWNING, *Prospice*, lines 1–26

Death takes us by surprise,
And stays our hurrying feet;
The great design unfinished lies,
Our lives are incomplete.
LONGFELLOW, *Charles Sumner*, st. 5

Our years are fleet,
And, to the weary, death is sweet.
LONGFELLOW, *Kéramos*, st. 15

There is a Reaper, whose name is Death.
LONGFELLOW, *The Reaper and the Flowers*, st. 1

Death the Ploughman wanders in all lands,
And to the last of earth his furrow stands.
EDWIN MARKHAM, *The Last Furrow*, st. 1

Death hath a thousand doors to let out life,
I shall find one. MASSINGER, *A Very Woman*, v, 4

Death 's but one more to-morrow. S. W. MITCHELL,
Of One Who Seemed to Have Failed, line 1

It is curious how forgetful we are of death, how little we think that we are dying daily, and that what we call life is really death, and death the beginning of a higher life. MAX MÜLLER, *Letter to Miss Mary Müller*, April 18, 1883, *Life*, by His Wife, II, xxvi

Tell me, my soul, can this be death?
POPE, *Dying Christian to His Soul*, st. 2

Now, men of death, work forth your will,
For I can suffer and be still;
And come he slow, or come he fast,
It is but death who comes at last.
SCOTT, *Marmion*, ii, st. 30

Is it sin
To rush into the secret house of death,
Ere death dare come to us?
SHAKESPEARE, *Antony and Cleopatra*, iv. 15 [13]

The stroke of death is as a lover's pinch,
Which hurts, and is desired. *Ibid.*

Who would [Who 'd] fardels bear,
To grunt and sweat under a weary life,
But that the dread of something after death,
The undiscovered country from whose bourne
No traveller returns, puzzles the will
And makes us rather bear those ills we have
Than fly to others that we know not of?[1]
SHAKESPEARE, *Hamlet*, iii, 1

---

[1] A secret prepossession
To plunge with all your fears — but where?
BYRON, *Don Juan*, Canto xiv, st. 6

Death—*Continued*

This fell sergeant, Death,
Is strict in his arrest. SHAKESPEARE, *Hamlet*, v, 2

It seems to me most strange that men should fear;
Seeing that death, a necessary end,
Will come when it will come.
SHAKESPEARE, *Julius Cæsar*, ii, 2

Where hateful death put on his ugliest mask.
SHAKESPEARE, *King Henry IV*, *Part II*, i, 1

Warwick. So bad a death argues a monstrous life.
King. Forbear to judge, for we are sinners all.[1]
Close up his eyes and draw the curtains close;
And let us all to meditation.
SHAKESPEARE, *King Henry VI*, *Part II*, iii, 3

Nothing can we call our own but death
And that small model of the barren earth
Which serves as paste and cover to our bones.
SHAKESPEARE, *King Richard II*, iii, 2

The sense of death is most in apprehension;
And the poor beetle, that we tread upon,
In corporal sufferance finds a pang as great
As when a giant dies.
SHAKESPEARE, *Measure for Measure*, iii, 1

Thy best of rest is sleep,
And that thou oft provok'st; yet grossly fear'st
Thy death, which is no more. *Ibid.*

Holy men at their death have good inspirations.
SHAKESPEARE, *Merchant of Venice*, i, 2

I would fain die a dry death.
SHAKESPEARE, *The Tempest*, i, 1

Out of the jaws of death.[2]
SHAKESPEARE, *Twelfth Night*, iii, 4

---

[1] Fools and blind!
This Czar, this emperor, this disthroned corpse,
Lying so straightly in an icy calm
Grander than sovereignty, was but as ye—
No better and no worse: Heaven mend us all!
DINAH M. MULOCK CRAIK, *The Dead Czar*, st. 6

[2] Stormed at with shot and shell,
While horse and hero fell,
They that had fought so well
Came through the jaws of death,
Back from the mouth of hell,
All that was left of them,
Left of six hundred.—TENNYSON, *Charge of the Light Brigade*, st. 5

I could lie down like a tired child,
And weep away the life of care
Which I have borne, and yet must bear
Till death like sleep might steal on me. SHELLEY,
Stanzas Written in Dejection near Naples, st. 4

How wonderful is Death,
Death and his brother Sleep![1]
SHELLEY, *Queen Mab*, i, st. 1

You, proud monarchs, must obey
And mingle with forgotten ashes, when
Death calls ye to the crowd of common men.
J. SHIRLEY, *The Last Conqueror*, st. 1

Virtue alone has majesty in death.
YOUNG, *Night Thoughts*, II, line 656

Death is the crown of life:
Was death denied, poor man would live in vain;
Was death denied, to live would not be life;
Was death denied, even fools would wish to die.
Ibid., III, lines 527–530

Man makes a death which Nature never made.
Ibid., IV, line 15

While man is growing, life is in decrease,
And cradles rock us nearer to the tomb.
Our birth is nothing but our death begun,
As tapers waste that instant they take fire.
Ibid., V, lines 717–720

Death loves a shining mark, a signal blow;
A blow, which, while it executes, alarms;
And startles thousands with a single fall.
Ibid., V, lines 1011–1013

Death-bed.— A death-bed 's a detector of the heart.
Here tired Dissimulation drops her mask,
Through life's grimace, that mistress of the scene.
YOUNG, *Night Thoughts*, II, lines 645–647

Death-fires.— About, about, in reel and rout
The death-fires danced at night;
The water, like a witch's oils,
Burnt green and blue and white.
COLERIDGE, *Ancient Mariner*, lines 127–130

---

[1] Care-charmer Sleep, son of the sable Night,
Brother to Death. S. DANIEL, *Sonnet* liv

Death it seemed, and not his cousin Sleep.
HOOD, *Hero and Leander*, st. 61

Sleep, Death's twin-brother. TENNYSON, *In Memoriam*, lxviii, st. 1

Debating.— The ancient Goths . . . had . . . a wise custom of debating everything of importance . . . twice, — once drunk and once sober,— drunk,— that their councils might not want vigour; and sober,— that they might not want discretion.

STERNE, *Tristram Shandy*, VI, xvii

Debt.— What! from his helpless creature be repaid
Pure gold for what he lent him dross-allayed —
Sue for a debt he never did contract,
And cannot answer — Oh, the sorry trade!

OMAR KHAYYÁM, *Rubáiyát* (trans. Fitzgerald), st. 79

Poor is the man in debt.

YOUNG, *Night Thoughts*, VI, line 532

Debts.— He that dies pays all debts.[1]

SHAKESPEARE, *The Tempest*, iii, 2

Decay.— A general flavour of mild decay.

HOLMES, *The Deacon's Masterpiece*, st. 9

Deceit. That is good deceit
Which mates him first that first intends deceit.[2]

SHAKESPEARE, *King Henry VI, Part II*, iii, 1

Deceits.— The tongues of men are full of deceits.

SHAKESPEARE, *King Henry V*, v, 2

Deceive.— Kiss me, though you make believe;
Kiss me, though I almost know
You are kissing to deceive:
Let the tide one moment flow
Backward ere it rise and break,
Only for poor pity's sake.

ALICE CARY, *Make Believe*, st. 1

Oh, what a tangled web we weave[3]
When first we practise to deceive![4]

SCOTT, *Marmion*, vi, 17

---

[1] The end of life cancels all bonds.

SHAKESPEARE, *King Henry IV, Part I*, iii, 2

Since . . it is impossible I should live, all debts are cleared between you and I. SHAKESPEARE, *Merchant of Venice*, iii, 2

[2] Do unto the other feller the way he'd like to do unto you — an' do it fust. E. N. WESTCOTT, *David Harum*, Preface

[3] When one fib becomes due, as it were, you must forge another to take up the old acceptance; and so the stock of your lies in circulation inevitably multiplies, and the danger of detection increases every day.

THACKERAY, *Vanity Fair*, lxvi

[4] I will not practise to deceive. SHAKESPEARE, *King John*, i

Deceived.— To be deceived in your true heart's desire
Was bitterer than a thousand years of fire!
JOHN HAY, *A Woman's Love*, st. 11

Deceiver.— Where shall the traitor rest,
He, the deceiver,
Who could win maiden's breast,
Ruin and leave her?
In the lost battle,
Borne down by the flying,
Where mingles war's rattle
With groans of the dying.—SCOTT, *Marmion*, iii, st. 11

Deceivers.— Sigh no more, ladies, sigh no more,
Men were deceivers ever,[1]
One foot in sea and one on shore,
To one thing constant never.
SHAKESPEARE, *Much Ado about Nothing*, ii, 3

Decency.— Immodest words admit of no defence;
For want of decency is want of sense.
EARL OF ROSCOMMON, *Essay on Translated Verse*

Decide.— Once to every man and nation comes the moment to decide,
In the strife of Truth with Falsehood, for the good or evil side. LOWELL, *The Present Crisis*, st. 5

Deed.—*Macbeth.* I have done the deed![2] Didst thou not hear a noise?
Lady Macbeth. I heard the owl scream and the crickets cry. SHAKESPEARE, *Macbeth*, ii, 2

One good deed dying tongueless
Slaughters a thousand waiting upon that.
SHAKESPEARE, *Winter's Tale*, i, 2

Deeds.— Foul deeds will rise. SHAKESPEARE, *Hamlet*, i, 2

How oft the sight of means to do ill deeds
Make deeds ill done [ill deeds done]!
SHAKESPEARE, *King John*, iv, 2

My deeds upon my head! I crave the law,
The penalty and forfeit of my bond.
SHAKESPEARE, *Merchant of Venice*, iv, 1

---

[1] Trust not a man: we are by nature false,
Dissembling, subtle, cruel and inconstant. T. OTWAY, *The Orphan*, ii, 1

[2] A deed of dreadful note. SHAKESPEARE, *Macbeth*, iii, 2
A deed without a name. *Ibid.*, iv, 1

Speaking in deeds, and deedless in his tongue;
Not soon provoked, nor, being provoked, soon calmed;
His heart and hand both open and both free;
For what he has he gives, what thinks he shows;
Yet gives he not till judgment guide his bounty.
SHAKESPEARE, *Troilus and Cressida*, iv, 5

Deep.— The very deep did rot.
COLERIDGE, *Ancient Mariner*, line 123

Though deep yet clear, though gentle yet not dull;
Strong without rage, without o'erflowing full.
SIR J. DENHAM, *Cooper's Hill*

Rocked in the cradle of the deep
I lay me down in peace to sleep;
Secure I rest upon the wave,
For thou, O Lord! hast power to save.
I know thou wilt not slight my call,
For thou dost mark the sparrow's fall;
And calm and peaceful shall I sleep,
Rocked in the cradle of the deep.
E. H. WILLARD, *Rocked in the Cradle of the Deep*, st. 1

Deer.— Why, let the stricken deer go weep,
The hart ungalled play;
For some must watch, while some must sleep,
So [Thus] runs the world away.
SHAKESPEARE, *Hamlet*, iii, 2

Defence.— What boots it at one gate to make defence,
And at another to let in the foe?
MILTON, *Samson Agonistes*, lines 560, 561

In cases of defence 't is best to weigh
The enemy more mighty than he seems.
SHAKESPEARE, *King Henry V*, ii, 4

Defer.— Defer not till to-morrow to be wise,
To-morrow's sun to thee may never rise.[1]
WILLIAM CONGREVE, *Letter to Lord Cobham*, 1729, lines 61, 62

Defiance.— A cry of defiance and not of fear,
A voice in the darkness, a knock at the door,
And a word that shall echo for evermore.
LONGFELLOW, *Paul Revere's Ride*, st. 14

Degenerate.— Not two strong men th' enormous weight could raise,
Such men as live in these degenerate days.
POPE, *Iliad*, V, lines 371, 372

---

[1] Be wise to-day; 't is madness to defer.
Next day the fatal precedent will plead;
Thus on, till wisdom is pushed out of life.
YOUNG, *Night Thoughts*, I, lines 390–392

Deliberates.— When love once pleads admission to our hearts
(In spite of all the virtue we can boast),
The woman that deliberates is lost.—ADDISON, *Cato*, iv, 1

Deliberation. With grave
Aspect he rose, and in his rising seemed
A pillar of state. Deep on his front engraven
Deliberation sat, and public care;
And princely counsel in his face yet shone,
Majestic, though in ruin.
MILTON, *Paradise Lost*, II, lines 300–305

Demeanour.— You will find it serviceable, in the formation of a demeanour, if you sometimes say to yourself in company — on entering a room, for instance — Papa, potatoes, poultry, prunes, and prism.
DICKENS, *Little Dorrit*, II, v

Den. And darest thou then
To beard the lion in his den,
The Douglas in his hall? SCOTT, *Marmion*, vi, 14

Depolarize.— Depolarize every fixed religious idea in the mind by changing the word which stands for it.
HOLMES, *Professor at the Breakfast-Table*, i

Depths.— He sinks into thy depths with bubbling groan,
Without a grave, unknelled, uncoffined, and unknown.
BYRON, *Childe Harold's Pilgrimage*, Canto iv, st. 179

Descent.— And made a preachment of your high descent.
SHAKESPEARE, *King Henry VI, Part III*, i, 4

Desert.— Oh! that the desert were my dwelling-place,
With one fair spirit for my minister,[1]
That I might all forget the human race,
And, hating no one, love but only her!
BYRON, *Childe Harold's Pilgrimage*, Canto iv, st. 177

In dark Cimmerian desert. MILTON, *L'Allegro*, line 10

Fly to the desert, fly with me,
Our Arab tents are rude for thee;
But oh! the choice what heart can doubt,
Of tents with love or thrones without?
T. MOORE, *Lalla Rookh: The Light of the Harem*

I never will desert Mr. Micawber.
DICKENS, *David Copperfield*, I, xii

---

[1] A book of verses underneath the bough,
A jug of wine, a loaf of bread — and Thou
Beside me singing in the wilderness —
Oh, wilderness were paradise enow!
OMAR KHAYYÁM, *Rubáiyát* (trans. Fitzgerald), st. 12

Deserted.— Deserted, at his utmost need,
By those his former bounty fed;
On the bare earth exposed he lies,
With not a friend to close his eyes.
DRYDEN, *Alexander's Feast*, lines 80–83

Desire.— From the desert I come to thee
On a stallion shod with fire;
And the winds are left behind
In the speed of my desire.
BAYARD TAYLOR, *Bedouin Song*, st. 1

Desires.— Your heart's desires be with you!
SHAKESPEARE, *As You Like It*, i, 2

Despairing. The daring
Last look of despairing
Fixed on futurity. HOOD, *The Bridge of Sighs*, st. 16

Desperate.— Beware of desperate steps. The darkest day,
Live till to-morrow, will have passed away.
COWPER, *The Needless Alarm: Moral*

Diseases desperate grown
By desperate appliance are relieved,[1]
Or not at all. SHAKESPEARE, *Hamlet*, iv, 3

Despised.— Ay, do despise me, I'm the prouder for it; I like to be despised.—ISAAC BICKERSTAFFE, *The Hypocrite*, v, 1

Destiny. What if thou withdraw
In silence from the living, and no friend
Take note of thy departure? All that breathe
Will share thy destiny.
BRYANT, *Thanatopsis*, lines 58–61

Destiny never swerves,
Nor yields to men the helm;
He shoots his thought, by hidden nerves,
Throughout the solid realm.
EMERSON, *The World-Soul*, st. 10

Think you I bear the shears of destiny?
Have I commandment on the pulse of life?
SHAKESPEARE, *King John*, iv, 2

Hanging and wiving goes by destiny.[2]
SHAKESPEARE, *Merchant of Venice*, ii, 9

---

[1] 'Tis not amiss, ere ye're given o'er,
To try one desperate medicine more:
For where your case can be no worse,
The desp'rat'st is the wisest course.
BUTLER, *Hudibras*, Epistle to Sidrophel, lines 5–8

[2] Love is not in our choice, but in our fate.
DRYDEN, *Palamon and Arcite*, line 328
Your marriage comes by destiny.
SHAKESPEARE, *All's Well That Ends Well*, i, 3

Destroyer.— For in the night, unseen, a single warrior,
In sombre harness mailed,
Dreaded of man, and surnamed the Destroyer,
The rampart wall had scaled.
. . . . .
He did not pause to parley or dissemble,
But smote the Warden hoar;
Ah! what a blow! that made all England tremble,
And groan from shore to shore.
LONGFELLOW, *Warden of the Cinque Ports*, st. 9, 11

Devil.— Bid the devil take the hindmost.[1]
BUTLER, *Hudibras*, I, Canto ii, line 633

Here Francis C—— lies. Be civil;
The rest God knows — perhaps the Devil.
POPE, *Epitaph*

The devil was sick, the devil a monk would be;
The devil was well, the devil a monk was he.
RABELAIS, IV, xxiv

How then was the Devil dressed?
Oh! he was in his Sunday's best;
His coat was red, and his breeches were blue,
And there was a hole where his tail came through.
SOUTHEY, *The Devil's Walk*, st. 3

And in he came with eyes of flame,
The Devil, to fetch the dead;
And all the church with his presence glowed
Like a fiery furnace red.
SOUTHEY, *The Old Woman of Berkeley*, st. 40

He must needs go, that the devil drives.
SHAKESPEARE, *All's Well That Ends Well*, i, 3

He must have a long spoon that must eat with the devil.
SHAKESPEARE, *Comedy of Errors*, iv, 3

Give the devil his due.[2]
SHAKESPEARE, *King Henry V*, iii, 7

Lest the devil cross my prayer.[3]
SHAKESPEARE, *Merchant of Venice*, iii, 1

---

[1] This expression has become proverbial, and is used by Prior, Pope, Burns and others.

[2] And so give his due to the devil.
ALEXANDER BROME, *The Holy Pedlar*, st. 5

He will give the devil his due.
SHAKESPEARE, *King Henry IV, Part I*, i, 2

[3] Wherever God erects a house of prayer,
The Devil always builds a chapel there;
And 't will be found upon examination,
The latter has the largest congregation.
DANIEL DEFOE, *The True-born Englishman*, I, lines 1-4

No man means evil but the devil, and we shall know him by his horns.
SHAKESPEARE, *Merry Wives of Windsor*, v, 2

One of those gentle ones that will use the devil himself with courtesy. SHAKESPEARE, *Twelfth Night*, iv, 2

Devion. With devotion's visage
And pious action we do sugar o'er
The devil himself. SHAKESPEARE, *Hamlet*, iii, 1

Dewlapped.— Who would believe that there were mountaineers
Dewlapped like bulls,[1] whose throats had hanging at them
Wallets of flesh? or that there were such men
Whose heads stood in their breasts.[2]
SHAKESPEARE, *The Tempest*, iii, 3

Dial.— True as the dial to the sun,[3]
Although it be not shined upon.
BUTLER, *Hudibras*, III, ii, lines 175, 176

Diamond. Spots quadrangular of diamond form,
Ensanguined hearts, clubs typical of strife,
And spades, the emblem of untimely graves.
COWPER, *The Task: The Winter Evening*, lines 217–219

Diamonds.— Diamonds cut diamonds; they who will prove
To thrive in cunning, must cure love with love.
JOHN FORD, *The Lover's Melancholy*, i, 3 [1]

Die.— It is as natural to die as to be born.
BACON, *Essay II: On Death*

A voice within us speaks the startling word,
"Man, thou shalt never die!" R. H. DANA,
The Husband and Wife's Grave, lines 56, 57

The pure, the bright, the beautiful,
That stirred our hearts in youth,
The impulse to a wordless prayer,
The dreams of love and truth;
The longings after something lost,
The spirit's yearning cry,
The strivings after better hopes —
These things can never die.
SARAH DOUDNEY, *Things That Never Die*, st. 1

---

[1] Dewlapped like Thessalian bulls.
SHAKESPEARE, *Midsummer-Night's Dream*, iv, 1

[2] Men whose heads
Do grow beneath their shoulders. SHAKESPEARE, *Othello*, i, 3

[3] True as the needle to the pole
Or as the dial to the sun. BARTON BOOTH, *Song*

And could we choose the time, and choose aright,
'Tis best to die, our honour at the height,
When we have done our ancestors no shame,
But served our friends, and well secured our fame;
Then should we wish our happy life to close,
And leave no more for fortune to dispose:
So should we make our death a glad relief
From future shame, from sickness, and from grief.
DRYDEN, *Palamon and Arcite*, lines 2364–2371

To die is landing on some silent shore,
Where billows never break, nor tempests roar;
E'er well we feel the friendly stroke 'tis o'er.
S. GARTH, *The Dispensary*, Canto iii, lines 225–227

To every man upon this earth
  Death cometh soon or late.
And how can man die better
  Than facing fearful odds,
For the ashes of his fathers,
  And the temples of his gods,

And for the tender mother
  Who dandled him to rest,
And for the wife who nurses
  His baby at her breast?
MACAULAY, *Horatius*, st. 27, 28

Whether I ought to die or not
  My doctors cannot quite determine;
It's only clear that I shall rot,
  And be, like Priam, food for vermin.
My debts are paid; — but Nature's debt
  Almost escaped my recollection!
Tom! we shall meet again; and yet
  I cannot leave you my direction!
PRAED, *Quince*, st. 13

All that lives [live] must die,
Passing through nature to eternity.
SHAKESPEARE, *Hamlet*, i, 2

A man can die but once: we owe God a death.
SHAKESPEARE, *King Henry IV, Part II*, iii, 2

What is pomp, rule, reign, but earth and dust?
And, live we how we can, yet die we must.
SHAKESPEARE, *King Henry VI, Part III*, v, 2

As good to die and go, as die and stay.
SHAKESPEARE, *King John*, iv, 3

Die—*Continued*

The times have been,
That, when the brains were out, the man would die,
And there an end; but now they rise again,
With twenty mortal murders on their crowns,
And push us from our stools.
SHAKESPEARE, *Macbeth*, iii, 4

Blow, wind! come, wrack!
At least we'll die with harness on our back.[1]—*Ibid.*, v, 5

If I must die,
I will encounter darkness as a bride,
And hug it in mine arms.
SHAKESPEARE, *Measure for Measure*, iii, 1

Ay, but to die, and go we know not where;
To lie in cold obstruction and to rot;
This sensible warm motion to become
A kneaded clod; and the delighted spirit
To bathe in fiery floods, or to reside
In thrilling region of thick-ribbed ice;
To be imprisoned in the viewless winds,
And blown with restless violence round about
The pendent world.[2] *Ibid.*, iii, 1

Not though the soldier knew
Some one had blundered:
Theirs not to make reply,
Theirs not to reason why,
Theirs but to do and die,[3]
Into the valley of Death
Rode the six hundred.
TENNYSON, *Charge of the Light Brigade*, st. 2

---

[1] Fallen from his fellow's side,
The steed beneath is lying;
In harness here he died,
His only fault was dying.
Epitaph on a Coach Horse, near the Foot of Helvellyn

The Englishman is proud when it can be said, "He died in harness."
MAX MÜLLER, *Letter to Crown Prince Friedrich Wilhelm*, —— —, 1888, *Life*, by his Wife, II, xxix

[2] Who would lose,
Though full of pain, this intellectual being,
Those thoughts that wander through eternity,
To perish rather, swallowed up and lost
In the wide womb of uncreated Night,
Devoid of sense and motion? MILTON, *Paradise Lost*, II, lines 146–151

[3] They went where duty seemed to call,
They scarcely asked the reason why;
They only knew they could but die,
And death was not the worst of all! WHITTIER, *Lexington*, st. 5

'T was there of just and good he reasoned strong,
Cleared some great truth, or raised some serious song:
There patient showed us the wise course to steer,
A candid censor and a friend severe;
There taught us how to live, and (Oh, too high
The price for knowledge!) taught us how to die.

T. TICKELL, *To the Earl of Warwick, on the Death of Addison*, lines 77–82

The good die first,
And they whose hearts are dry as summer dust
Burn to the socket. WORDSWORTH, *The Excursion, The Wanderer*, lines 504–506

Died.— Most persons have died before they expire,— died to all earthly longings, so that the last breath is only, as it were, the locking of the door of the already deserted mansion. HOLMES, *Professor at the Breakfast Table*, xi

"I give and I devise (old Euclio said,
And sighed) my lands and tenements to Ned."—
"Your money, sir?"—"My money, sir, what, all?
Why,— if I must — (then wept) I give it Paul."—
"The manor, sir?"—"The manor! hold," he cried,
"Not that,— I cannot part with that,"— and died.

POPE, *Moral Essays*, Epistle i, lines 256–261

Dies.— Stand, stand to your glasses, steady!
'T is all we have left to prize:
One cup to the dead already —
Hurrah for the next that dies!

BARTHOLOMEW DOWLING, *Revel of the Dying*, st. 8

He that dies this year is quit for the next.

SHAKESPEARE, *King Henry IV, Part II*, iii, 2

He dies, and makes no sign.

SHAKESPEARE, *King Henry VI, Part II*, iii, 3

Digestion.— Now, good digestion wait on appetite,
And health on both! SHAKESPEARE. *Macbeth*, iii, 4

Diminished.— Ye little stars! hide your diminished rays.

POPE, *Moral Essays*, Epistle iii, line 282

Dimple.— Cheek or chin, or knuckle or knee,
Where shall the baby's dimple be?
Where shall the angel's finger rest
When he comes down to the baby's nest?
Where shall the angel's touch remain
When he awakens my babe again? J. G. HOLLAND, *Where Shall the Baby's Dimple Be*, st. 2

Dine.— The hungry judges soon the sentence sign,
And wretches hang that jurymen may dine.[1]
POPE, *Rape of the Lock*, iii, lines 21, 22

Dinner.— A dinner lubricates business.
LORD STOWELL, quoted in Boswell, *Life of Johnson*, April 15, 1781

Dinner-bell.— That all-softening, o'erpowering knell,
The tocsin of the soul — the dinner-bell.
BYRON, *Don Juan*, Canto v, st. 49

Direct.— Think it more honour to direct in chief than to be busy in all. BACON, *Essay XI: Of Great Place*

Directors.— However, as is usual in our city,
They had a sort of Managing Committee,
A board of grave, responsible Directors —
A Secretary, good at pen and ink —
A Treasurer, of course, to keep the chink,
And quite an army of Collectors!
. . . .
With many of those persevering ones,
Who mite by mite would beg a cheese!
HOOD, *A Black Job*, st. 8

Dirt. Dirt?— Jacob, what is dirt?
If matter,— why, the delicate dish that tempts
An o'ergorged epicure, to the last morsel
That stuffs him to the throat-gates, is no more.
SOUTHEY, *The Pig*, lines 57–60

Dirty. The last charge,— he lived
A dirty life. Here I could shelter him
With noble and right-reverend precedents,
And show by sanction of authority
That 'tis a very honourable thing
To thrive by dirty ways.[2] *Ibid.*, lines 49–54

Disappointed.— What ardently I wished, I long believed,
And, disappointed still, was still deceived.
By expectation every day beguiled,
Dupe of to-morrow even from a child. COWPER, *On the Receipt of My Mother's Picture*, lines 38–41

---

[1] A good, contented, well-breakfasted juryman is a capital thing to get hold of. Discontented or hungry jurymen . . . always find for the plaintiff. . . . If it's near dinner-time, the foreman takes out his watch when the jury has retired, and says, "Dear me, gentlemen, ten minutes to five, I declare! I dine at five." . . . "So do I," says everybody else, except two men who ought to have dined at three, and seem more than half-disposed to stand out in consequence. The foreman smiles and puts up his watch: "Well, gentlemen, what do we say,— plaintiff or defendant? . . . I *rather* think the plaintiff's the man. DICKENS, *Pickwick Papers*, xxxiv

[2] The public path of life
Is dirty. YOUNG, *Night Thoughts*, VIII, lines 373, 374

Disasters.— Well had the boding tremblers learned to trace
The day's disasters in his morning face;
Full well they laughed with counterfeited glee
At all his jokes, for many a joke had he.
GOLDSMITH, *The Deserted Village*, st. 14

Discontent.— Here comes a man of comfort, whose advice
Hath often stilled my brawling discontent.
SHAKESPEARE, *Measure for Measure*, iv, 1

Discontent,— the nobleman's consumption.
CYRIL TOURNEUR, *The Revenger's Tragedy*, i, 1

Discord.— From hence, let fierce contending nations know
What dire effects from civil discord flow.
ADDISON, *Cato*, v, 4

Discourse.— Bid me discourse, I will enchant thine ear.
SHAKESPEARE, *Venus and Adonis*, line 145

Discretion.— Let your own discretion be your tutor.
SHAKESPEARE, *Hamlet*, iii, 2

Disease.— Ring out old shapes of foul disease.
TENNYSON, *In Memoriam*, cvi, st. 7

Disobedience.— Of man's first disobedience, and the fruit
Of that forbidden tree, whose mortal taste
Brought death into the world, and all our woe.
MILTON, *Paradise Lost*, I, lines 1–3

Disobey.— God bade me act for him: I dared not disobey!
R. BROWNING, *Ivan Ivanovitch*, line 300

Dissemble.— Perhaps it was right to dissemble your love,
But why did you kick me downstairs?
J. P. KEMBLE, *The Panel*

Distance.— 'Tis distance lends enchantment to the view.
CAMPBELL, *Pleasures of Hope*, i, st. 1

Distinguish.— He could distinguish, and divide
A hair 'twixt south and southwest side.
BUTLER, *Hudibras*, I, i, lines 67, 68

Ditch.— I will die in the last ditch.
WILLIAM, PRINCE OF ORANGE, cited by Hume, *History of England*

Diver. Are there not, dear Michal,
Two points in the adventure of the diver,
One — when, a beggar, he prepares to plunge,
One — when, a prince, he rises with his pearl?
R. BROWNING, *Paracelsus*, I

Divine.— It is a good divine that follows his own instructions.
SHAKESPEARE, *Merchant of Venice*, i, 2

Divinely.— A daughter of the gods, divinely tall,[1]
And most divinely fair.[2]
TENNYSON, *Dream of Fair Women*, lines 87, 88

Divinity.— There's a divinity that shapes our ends,
Rough-hew them how we will.
SHAKESPEARE, *Hamlet*, v, 2

Dixie.— Southrons, hear your country call you!
Up, lest worse than death befall you!
To arms! To arms! To arms, in Dixie!

. . . . .

Advance the flag of Dixie!
Hurrah! Hurrah!
For Dixie's land we take our stand,
And live or die for Dixie! A. PIKE, *Dixie*, st. 1

Do.— So much to do, so little done!
But when it's o'er,— the victory won,—
Oh! then, my soul, this strife and sorrow
Will end in that great, glad To-morrow.
J. R. GILMORE, *Three Days*, st. 3

And all may do what has by man been done.
YOUNG, *Night Thoughts*, VI, line 606

Doctor.— Joy and Temperance and Repose
Slam the door on the doctor's nose. LONGFELLOW,
The Best Medicines, from the German of F. von Logau

Doctors.— So lived our sires, ere doctors learned to kill,
And multiplied with theirs the weekly bill.
DRYDEN, *Epistle to John Dryden*, lines 71, 72

Talk of your science! after all is said
There's nothing like a bare and shiny head;
Age lends the graces that are sure to please;
Folks want their doctors mouldy, like their cheese.
HOLMES, *Rip Van Winkle, M.D.*, II, st. 4

Who shall decide, when doctors disagree,
And soundest casuists doubt, like you and me?
POPE, *Moral Essays*, Epistle iii, lines 1, 2

---

[1] Her stature tall — I hate a dumpy woman. BYRON, *Don Juan*, st. 61

[2] Divinely fair. MILTON, *Paradise Lost*, IX, line 489

Doctrine.— What makes all doctrine plain and clear?
About two hundred pounds a year.
And that which was proved true before
Proved false again?— Two hundred more.
BUTLER, *Hudibras*, III, i, lines 1277–1280

Dog.— My dog howls at the gate.
BYRON, *Childe Harold's Pilgrimage*, Canto i, st. 13 (2)

The dog, to gain some private ends,
Went mad and bit the man.

. . . . .

The man recovered of the bite,
The dog it was that died!
GOLDSMITH, *Elegy on the Death of a Mad Dog*, st. 8

I am his Highness' dog at Kew;
Pray tell me, sir, whose dog are you?
POPE, *Epigram Engraved on the Collar of a Dog Given to His Royal Highness*

Celia. Why, Rosalind! . . . not a word?
Rosalind. Not one to throw at a dog.
SHAKESPEARE, *As You Like It*, i, 3

Mine enemy's dog,
Though he had bit me, should have stood that night
Against my fire. SHAKESPEARE, *King Lear*, iv, 7

Hath a dog money? Is it possible
A cur can lend three thousand ducats?
SHAKESPEARE, *Merchant of Venice*, i, 3

Thou call'dst me dog before thou hadst a cause;
But, since I am a dog, beware my fangs. *Ibid.*, iii, 3

An he had been a dog that should have howled thus, they would have hanged him.
SHAKESPEARE, *Much Ado about Nothing*, ii, 3

Dogrose.— A dogrose blushin' to a brook
Ain't modester nor sweeter.
LOWELL, *The Courtin'*, st. 7

Dogs.— The little dogs and all,
Tray, Blanch, and Sweet-heart, see, they bark at me!
SHAKESPEARE, *King Lear*, iii, 6

Let dogs delight to bark and bite,
For God hath made them so;
Let bears and lions growl and fight,
For 't is their nature to. ISAAC WATTS, *Song*, xvi

Doing.— What is worth doing is worth doing well; and with a little more trouble at first, much trouble afterwards may be avoided.— MAX MÜLLER, *Letter to John Bellows*, July 18, 1866, *Life*, by His Wife, I, xv

Doll.— I once had a sweet little doll, dears,
The prettiest doll in the world;
. . . . .
Yet for old sakes' sake she is still, dears,
The prettiest doll in the world.
KINGSLEY, *Songs from the Water Babies*, IV, st. 1, 2

Dollar.— The Almighty Dollar.
WASHINGTON IRVING, *The Creole Village*

A short-weight dollar is not an honest dollar to pay full-weight-dollar debts with.
THEODORE ROOSEVELT, cited by Jacob Riis in *Theodore Roosevelt the Citizen*, xii

Done.— What men have done can still be done,
And shall be done to-day!
G. BARLOW, *The Song of Abou Klea*, st. 2

That 's what I always say; if you wish a thing to be well done,
You must do it yourself, you must not leave it to others!
LONGFELLOW, *Courtship of Miles Standish*, ii, lines 28, 29

If it were done when 'tis done, then 'twere well
It were done quickly. SHAKESPEARE, *Macbeth*, i, 7

What's done cannot be undone. *Ibid.*, v, 1

Door.— Open the door with shame, if ye have sinned;
If ye be sorry, open it with sighs.
Albeit the place be bare for poverty,
And comfortless for lack of plenishing,
Be not abashed for that, but open it,
And take Him in that comes to sup with thee;
"Behold!" He saith, "I stand at the door and knock!"
JEAN INGELOW, *Brothers, and a Sermon*

The door is open, sir; there lies your way;
You may be jogging whiles your boots are green.
SHAKESPEARE, *Taming of the Shrew*, iii, 2

Dormouse.— But a child — that bids the world good-night,
In downright earnest and cuts it quite —
A cherub no art can copy,—
'Tis a perfect picture to see him lie
As if he had supped on dormouse pie
(An ancient classical dish by the by),
With a sauce of syrup of poppy.
HOOD, *Miss Kilmansegg*, Her Dream

Doubt.— Doubt thou the stars are fire;
Doubt that the sun doth move;
Doubt truth to be a liar;
But never doubt I love.— SHAKESPEARE, *Hamlet*, ii, 2

To be once in doubt
Is once to be resolved. SHAKESPEARE, *Othello*, iii, 3

Perplexed in faith, but pure in deeds,
At last he beat his music out.
There lives more faith in honest doubt,
Believe me, than in half the creeds.
TENNYSON, *In Memoriam*, xcvi, st. 3

Doubts. Our doubts are traitors,
And make us lose the good we oft might win
By fearing to attempt.
SHAKESPEARE, *Measure for Measure*, i, 4 [5]

Douglas.— Like Douglas conquer, or like Douglas die.
JOHN HOME, *Douglas*, v, 1

Could ye come back to me, Douglas, Douglas,
In the old likeness that I knew,
I would be so faithful, so loving, Douglas,
Douglas, Douglas, tender and true.
D. M. MULOCK CRAIK, *Too Late*, st. 1

The hand of Douglas is his own
And never shall in friendly grasp
The hand of such as Marmion clasp.
SCOTT, *Marmion*, vi, 13

Dove. The tender fierceness of the dove,
Pecking the hand that hovers o'er her mate.
BYRON, *Childe Harold's Pilgrimage*, Canto i, st. 57

Oh, had I the wings of a dove!
COWPER, *Alexander Selkirk*, st. 3

Coo, dove, to thy married mate —
She has two warm eggs in her nest:
Tell her the hours are few to wait
Ere life shall dawn on their rest;
And thy young shall peck at the shells, elate
With a dream of her brooding breast.
JEAN INGELOW, *Brothers, and a Sermon*

Down.— He that is down need fear no fall,[1]
He that is low, no pride.
BUNYAN, *Pilgrim's Progress*, II, Stage v

---

[1] I am not now in Fortune's power,
He that is down can fall no lower.— BUTLER, *Hudibras*, I, iii, lines 857, 858

Dragon.— Come not between the dragon and his wrath.
Shakespeare, *King Lear*, i, 1

Dream.— I had a dream, which was not all a dream.
Byron, *Darkness*, line 1

A change came o'er the spirit of my dream.
Byron, *The Dream*

The people's prayer, the glad diviner's theme,
The young men's vision, and the old men's dream![1]
Dryden, *Absalom and Achitophel*, I, lines 238, 239

To die, to sleep;
To sleep; perchance to dream:[2] ay, there's the rub;
For in that sleep of death what dreams may come
When we have shuffled off this mortal coil, must give us pause.
Shakespeare, *Hamlet*, iii, 1

With that, methought, a legion of foul fiends
Environed me [about], and howled in mine ears
Such hideous cries, that with the very noise
I trembling waked, and for a season after
Could not believe but that I was in hell,
Such terrible impression made the [my] dream.
Shakespeare, *King Richard III*, i, 4

There is some ill a-brewing towards my rest,
For I did dream of money-bags to-night.
Shakespeare, *Merchant of Venice*, ii, 5

Or I am mad, or else this is a dream:
Let fancy still my sense in Lethe steep;
If it be thus to dream, still let me sleep.
Shakespeare, *Twelfth Night*, iv, 1

Dreaming. Sorrow returned with the dawning of morn,
And the voice in my dreaming ear melted away.[3]
Campbell, *The Soldier's Dream*, st. 6

Dreams.— My dreams were always beautiful, my thoughts were high and fine;
No life was ever lived on earth to match those dreams of mine.
Henry van Dyke, *Another Chance*, st. 3

---

[1] Your old men shall dream dreams, your young men shall see visions.
Joel, ii, 28

[2] How happy they who wake no more!
Yet that were vain, if dreams infest the grave.
Young, *Night Thoughts*, I, lines 7, 8

[3] But oh, as to embrace me she inclined,
I waked, she fled, and day brought back my night.
Milton, *On His Deceased Wife*

As vessels starting from ports thousands of miles apart pass close to each other in the naked breadth of the ocean nay, sometimes even touch, in the dark, with a crack of timbers, a gurgling of water, a cry of startled sleepers,—a cry mysteriously echoed in warning dreams, as the wife of some Gloucester fisherman, some coasting skipper, wakes with a shriek, calls the name of her husband, and sinks back to uneasy slumbers upon her lonely pillow,—a widow. HOLMES, *Professor at the Breakfast-Table*, iii

Unknown facts of guilty acts
Are seen in dreams from God!
HOOD, *The Dream of Eugene Aram*, st. 11

Dhrames always go by conthrairies, my dear.
SAMUEL LOVER, *Rory O'More*, st. 2

You laugh when boys or women tell their dreams.
SHAKESPEARE, *Antony and Cleopatra*, v

Oh! I have passed a miserable night,
So full of ugly sights, of ghastly dreams,[1]
That, as I am a Christian faithful man,
I would not spend another such a night,
Though 'twere to buy a world of happy days,—
So full of dismal terror was the time!
SHAKESPEARE, *King Richard III*, i, 4

Let not our babbling dreams affright our souls.
Ibid., v, 3

Dreams,
Which are the children of an idle brain,
Begot of nothing but vain fantasy.
SHAKESPEARE, *Romeo and Juliet*, i, 4

Dressed.— Still to be neat, still to be dressed,
As you were going to a feast.
BEN JONSON, *The Silent Woman*, i, 1

Drink.— Drink to me only with thine eyes,
And I will pledge with mine;
Or leave a kiss but in the cup,
And I'll not look for wine.

. . . . .

I sent thee late a rosie wreath,
Not so much honouring thee,
As giving it a hope that there
It could not withered be.
But thou thereon didst only breathe,
And sent'st it back to me:

---

[1] "So full of fearful dreams, of ugly sights," according to other versions.

Drink—*Continued*

Since when it grows, and smells, I swear,
  Not of itself, but thee.[1]
BEN JONSON, *The Forest: To Celia*

Drink of this cup; you'll find there's a spell in
  Its every drop 'gainst the ills of mortality;
Talk of the cordial that sparkled for Helen!
  Her cup was a fiction, but this is reality.
T. MOORE, *Drink of This Cup*, st. 1

While you live,
Drink! — for, once dead, you never shall return.
OMAR KHAYYÁM, *Rubáiyát* (trans. Fitzgerald), st. 35

Drink! for you know not whence you came, nor why:
Drink! for you know not why you go, nor where.
Ibid., st. 74

The more you drink, the more you crave. POPE,
Imitations of Horace, II, Epistle ii, line 212

I never drink but at my hours. RABELAIS, I, v

We'll teach you to drink deep ere you depart.
SHAKESPEARE, *Hamlet*, i, 2

I can drink with any tinker in his own language.
SHAKESPEARE, *King Henry IV, Part I*, ii, 4

And let me the cannikin clink, clink;
And let me the cannikin clink:
  A soldier's a man;
  A life's but a span;
Why, then, let a soldier drink.
SHAKESPEARE, *Othello*, ii, 3

'Tis evermore the prologue to his sleep:
He'll watch the horologe a double set,
If drink rock not his cradle. *Ibid.*

Great men should drink with harness on their throats.
SHAKESPEARE, *Timon of Athens*, i, 2

---

[1] The utmost share
  Of my desire shall be
Only to kiss that air
  That lately kissed thee.
HERRICK, *To Electra, I Dare not Ask a Kiss*, st. 2

I took the wreath, whose inmost twine
Breathed of him and blushed with wine.— T. MOORE, *Odes of Anacreon*, i

If thou art inclined to gratify thy lover, send him back the remains of the garland, no longer breathing of roses only, but also of thee!
PHILOSTRATUS, *Erotica*, cited by Moore, note to *Odes of Anacreon*, i

He has a sin that often
Drowns him, and takes his valour prisoner:
If there were no foes, that were enough
To overcome him: in that beastly fury
He has been known to commit outrages,
And cherish factions: 'tis inferred to us,
His days are foul and his drink dangerous.—*Ibid.*, iii, 5

We keep the day. With festal cheer,
With books and music, surely we
Will drink to him whate'er he be,
And sing the songs he loved to hear.
TENNYSON, *In Memoriam*, cvii, st. 6

Drink, pretty creature, drink!
WORDSWORTH, *The Pet Lamb*, st. 1

Drinking.— The thirsty earth soaks up the rain,[1]
And drinks, and gapes for drink again.
The plants suck in the earth, and are
With constant drinking fresh and fair;
The sea itself (which one would think
Should have but little need of drink)
Drinks twice ten thousand rivers up,
So filled that they o'erflow the cup
. . . . .
Nothing in nature's sober found,
But an eternal health goes round.
Fill up the bowl then, fill it high,
Fill all the glasses there; for why
Should every creature drink but I;
Why, man of morals, tell me why?
COWLEY, *Anacreontiques: Drinking*

Drinking all night and dozing all the day.
DRYDEN, *Essay upon Satire*, line 189

There is no drinking after death.[2]
JOHN FLETCHER, *Drink To-Day*, st. 1

---

[1] Observe when mother earth is dry,
She drinks the droppings of the sky;
And then the dewy cordial gives
To every thirsty plant that lives.
The vapours, which at evening weep,
Are beverage to the swelling deep;
And when the rosy sun appears,
He drinks the ocean's misty tears.
The moon too quaffs her paly stream
Of lustre, from the solar beam.
Then, hence with all your sober thinking!
Since Nature's holy law is drinking;
I'll make the laws of nature mine,
And pledge the universe in wine. T. MOORE, *Odes of Anacreon*, xxi

[2] I know in the tombs
There's no carousing. HERRICK, *Anacreontic, Born Was I to Be Old*

The habit of drinking is often a vice, no doubt,— sometimes a misfortune,— as when an almost irresistible hereditary propensity exists to indulge in it,— but oftenest of all a punishment.
HOLMES, *Autocrat of the Breakfast-Table*, viii

They call drinking deep, dyeing scarlet.[1]
SHAKESPEARE, *King Henry IV, Part I*, ii, 4

The dry divan
Close in firm circle; and set, ardent, in
For serious drinking.
THOMSON, *The Seasons:* Autumn, lines 531–533

Dross.— What men call treasure, and the gods call dross.
LOWELL, *Commemoration Ode*, st. 4

Drown.— Lord, Lord! [O Lord!] methought, what pain it was to drown!
What dreadful noise of water[s] in mine ears!
What ugly sights of [sights of ugly] death within mine eyes!
Methought I saw a thousand fearful wrecks;
Ten [A] thousand men that fishes gnawed upon;
Wedges of gold, great anchors, heaps of pearl,
Inestimable stones, unvalued jewels,
All scattered in the bottom of the sea.
SHAKESPEARE, *King Richard III*, i, 4

Drudgery.— A servant with this clause
Makes drudgery divine:
Who sweeps a room, as for thy laws,
Makes that and the action fine.
G. HERBERT, *The Elixir*, st. 5

Drum.— Not a drum was heard, not a funeral note,
As his corpse to the rampart we hurried.
CHARLES WOLFE, *Burial of Sir John Moore*, st. 1

Drunk.— Then hasten to be drunk, the business of the day.[2]
DRYDEN, *Cymon and Iphigenia*, line 408

All loud alike,
All learned, and all drunk! COWPER, *The Task: The Winter Evening*, lines 477, 478

Drunkenness.— Whenever the wandering Demon of Drunkenness finds a ship adrift,— no steady wind in its sails, no thoughtful pilot directing its course,— he steps on board, takes the helm, and steers straight for the maelstrom. HOLMES, *Autocrat of the Breakfast-Table*, viii

---

[1] *Cf.* the modern phrase, "Paint the town red."

[2] Let other hours be set apart for business.
To-day it is our pleasure to be drunk. FIELDING, *Tom Thumb*, i, 2

Ducats.— You'll ask me, why I rather choose to have
A weight of carrion flesh than to receive
Three thousand ducats: I'll not answer that:
But say it is my humour.

. . . . . .

If every ducat in six thousand ducats
Were in six parts, and every part a ducat,
I would not draw them; I would have my bond.
SHAKESPEARE, *Merchant of Venice*, iv, 1

Dupes.— The history of human-kind to trace
Since Eve — the first of dupes — our doom unriddled,
A certain portion of the human race
Has certainly a taste for being diddled.[1]
HOOD, *A Black Job*, st. 1

Durance.— In durance vile here must I wake and weep.
BURNS, *Epistle from Esopus to Maria*, st. 3

Dust.— Ah, make the most of what we yet may spend,
Before we too into the dust descend;
Dust into dust, and under dust to lie,
Sans wine, sans song, sans singer, and — sans end!
OMAR KHAYYÁM, *Rubáiyát* (trans. Fitzgerald), st. 24

Fear no more the heat o' the sun,
Nor the furious winter's rages;
Thou thy worldly task hast done,
Home art gone, and ta'en thy wages:
Golden lads and girls all must,
As chimney-sweepers, come to dust.

. . . . . .

The sceptre, learning, physic, must
All follow this, and come to dust.[2]
SHAKESPEARE, *Cymbeline*, iv, 2

And give to dust that is a little gilt
More laud than gilt [gold] o'er-dusted.
SHAKESPEARE, *Troilus and Cressida*, iii, 3

---

[1] Those good and easy innocents in fact,
Who, willingly receiving chaff for corn,

. . . .

Still find a secret pleasure in the act
Of being plucked and shorn.
HOOD, *A Black Job*, st. 16

[2] Death is master of lord and clown;
Shovel the clay in, tread it down.
ALFRED AUSTIN, *Songs from "Prince Lucifer,"* st. 3

Sceptre and crown
Must tumble down,
And in the dust be equal made
With the poor crooked scythe and spade.
J. SHIRLEY, *Dirge: Death the Leveller*, st. 1

Thou wilt not leave us in the dust:
  Thou madest man, he knows not why;
  He thinks he was not made to die;
And thou hast made him: thou art just.
TENNYSON, *In Memoriam*, Introduction, st. 3

Why all this toil for triumphs of an hour?
What though we wade in wealth, or soar in fame?
Earth's highest station ends in, "Here he lies;"
And "Dust to dust" concludes her noblest song.
YOUNG, *Night Thoughts*, IV, lines 98–101

Duty.— So nigh is grandeur to our dust,
  So near is God to man,
When Duty whispers low, "Thou must,"
  The youth replies, "I can."—EMERSON, *Voluntary III*

He seen his duty, a dead-sure thing,—
  And went for it thar and then;
And Christ ain't a-going to be too hard
  On a man that died for men.
JOHN HAY, *Jim Bludso of the Prairie Belle*, st. 7

I slept and dreamed that life was Beauty:
I woke and found that life was Duty.
E. S. HOOPER, *Duty*

England expects every man to do his duty.
HORATIO, VISCOUNT NELSON, quoted by Southey, *Life of Nelson*, ix

I will turn
To the straight path of Duty.
. . . . .
  Labour shall be my lot:
My kindred shall be joyful in my praise;
And Fame shall twine for me in after-days
  A wreath I covet not:

  And, if I cannot make,
Dearest, thy hope my hope, thy trust my trust,
Yet will I study to be good and just
  And blameless, for thy sake.
PRAED, *A Retrospect*, st. 10–12

My duty then shall pay me for my pains.
SHAKESPEARE, *All's Well That Ends Well*, ii, 1

I do perceive here a divided duty.
SHAKESPEARE, *Othello*, i, 3

And keep the soldier firm, the statesman pure;
Till in all lands and through all human story
The path of duty be the way to glory.—TENNYSON, *Ode on the Death of the Duke of Wellington*, st. 8

I have fought for Queen and Faith like a valiant man
and true;
I have only done my duty as a man is bound to do.
TENNYSON, *The Revenge*, st. 13

Dying.— Our very hopes belied our fears,
Our fears our hopes belied —
We thought her dying when she slept,
And sleeping when she died.

For when the morn came dim and sad,
And chill with early showers,
Her quiet eyelids closed — she had
Another morn than ours.[1]
HOOD, *The Death-Bed*, st. 3, 4

Oh, the pain, the bliss of dying!
POPE, *Dying Christian to His Soul*, st. 1

I am dying, Egypt, dying.
SHAKESPEARE, *Antony and Cleopatra*, iv, 15 [13]

Oh! but they say the tongues of dying men
Enforce attention like deep harmony:
Where words are scarce, they are seldom spent in vain,
For they breathe truth that breathe their words in pain.
He that no more must say is listened more
Than they whom youth and ease have taught to glose;
More are men's ends marked than their lives before.
SHAKESPEARE, *King Richard II*, ii, 1

---

[1] Her suffering ended with the day,
Yet lived she at its close,
And breathed the long, long night away
In statue-like repose.

But when the sun in all his state
Illumed the eastern skies,
She passed through glory's morning gate,
And walked in Paradise. JAMES ALDRICH, *A Death-Bed*

She thought our good-night kiss was given,
And like a lily her life did close;
Angels uncurtained that repose,
And the next waking dawned in heaven.
GERALD MASSEY, *Ballad of Babe Christabel*

She's from a world of woe relieved,
And blooms, a rose, in heaven. BURNS, *On the Poet's Daughter*, st. 2

So softly death succeeded life in her:
She did but dream of heaven, and she was there.
DRYDEN, *Eleonora*, lines 315, 316

Gently!
She is sleeping,
She has breathed her last!
Gently!
While you're weeping
She to heaven has past! C. G. EASTMAN, *Dirge*, st. 3

Eagle.— Like an eagle in a dove-cote.
SHAKESPEARE, *Coriolanus*, v, 6 [5]

Men that in a narrower day —
Unprophetic rulers they —
Drove from out the mother's nest
That young eagle of the West
To forage for herself alone. TENNYSON,
Opening of the Indian and Colonial Exhibition, st. 3

The eagle's fate and mine are one,
Which, on the shaft that made him die,
Espied a feather of his own,
Wherewith he wont to soar so high.[1]
EDMUND WALLER, *To a Lady, Singing a Song of His Own Composing*

Eagles.— Wrens make prey where eagles dare not perch.
SHAKESPEARE, *King Richard III*, i, 3

Ear.— Her small and shell-like ear.
HOOD, *Bianca's Dream*, st. 31

Where more is meant than meets the ear.
MILTON, *Il Penseroso*, line 120

Ear-kissing.— Ear-kissing arguments.
SHAKESPEARE, *King Lear*, ii, 1

Ears.— Pitchers have ears.
SHAKESPEARE, *Taming of the Shrew*, iv, 4

Earth.— This is the last of earth.
J. Q. ADAMS, Last Words, *Life*, by Josiah Quincy, xiv

The earth goes on the earth glittering in gold,
The earth goes to the earth sooner than it wold;
The earth builds on the earth castles and towers,
The earth says to the earth — All this is ours.
ANONYMOUS, *Inscription on Melrose Abbey*

He saw with his own eyes the moon was round,
Was also certain that the earth was square,
Because he had journeyed fifty miles, and found
No sign that it was circular anywhere.
BYRON, *Don Juan*, Canto v, st. 150

---

[1] 'T was thine own genius gave the final blow,
And helped to plant the wound that laid thee low:
So the struck eagle, stretched upon the plain,
No more through rolling clouds to soar again,
Viewed his own feather on the fatal dart,
And winged the shaft that quivered in his heart.
BYRON, *English Bards and Scotch Reviewers*, lines 824–829

The duped people, hourly doomed to pay
The sums that bribe their liberties away,—
Like a young eagle who has lent his plume
To fledge the shaft by which he meets his doom,—
See their own feathers plucked, to wing the dart
Which rank corruption destines for their heart! — T. MOORE, *Corruption*

Above the smoke and stir of this dim spot,
Which men call Earth. MILTON, *Comus*, lines 5, 6

Said one among them — "Surely not in vain
My substance of the common earth was ta'en
  And to this figure moulded, to be broke,
Or trampled back to shapeless earth again."

Then said a second — "Ne'er a peevish boy
Would break the bowl from which he drank in joy;
  And He that with his hand the vessel made
Will surely not in after-wrath destroy."[1]
OMAR KHAYYÁM, *Rubáiyát* (trans. Fitzgerald), st. 84, 85

Ease.— Born to write, converse, and live with ease.
POPE, *Epistle to Dr. Arbuthnot*, line 196

East.— If you've 'eard the East a-callin', you won't never 'eed naught else. KIPLING, *Mandalay*

High on a throne of royal state, which far
Outshone the wealth of Ormus and of Ind,
Or where the gorgeous East, with richest hand,
Showers on her kings barbaric pearl and gold,[2]
Satan exalted sat, by merit raised
To that bad eminence.
MILTON, *Paradise Lost*, II, lines 1–6

Eaten.— He hath eaten me out of house and home.
SHAKESPEARE, *King Henry IV, Part II*, ii, 1

Eaves.— The martin-haunted eaves.
TENNYSON, *Aylmer's Field*, line 163

Echo.— Hark! to the hurried question of despair:
"Where is my child?" an echo answers — "Where?"
BYRON, *Bride of Abydos*, Canto ii, st. 27

Education.— 'T is education forms the common mind,
Just as the twig is bent, the tree 's inclined.
POPE, *Moral Essays*, Epistle i, lines 149, 150

---

[1]If we are only as the potter's clay
Made to be fashioned as the artist wills,
And broken into shards if we offend
The eye of Him who made us, it is well.

. . . . . .

Or is it only clay,
Bleeding and aching in the potter's hand,
Yet all his own to treat it as he will,
And when he will to cast it at his feet,
Shattered, dishonoured, lost for evermore?
HOLMES, *Rights*, lines 26–29, 52–56

[2]The exhaustless East
Poured in her lap all gems in sparkling showers.
BYRON, *Childe Harold's Pilgrimage*, Canto iv, st. 2

Though her[1] mien carries much more invitation than command, to behold her is an immediate check on loose behaviour; to love her was a liberal education.
STEELE, *The Tatler*, No. 49

Egg.— We shall sooner have the fowl by hatching the egg than by smashing it.
ABRAHAM LINCOLN, *Last Public Address*, April 11, 1865

One likes the pheasant's wing, and one the leg;
The vulgar boil, the learned roast an egg. POPE, *Imitations of Horace*, II, Epistle ii, lines 84, 85

Eggs. They say we are
Almost as like as eggs.—SHAKESPEARE, *Winter's Tale*, i, 2

Egotist. You, foul-tongued
Fanatic or ambitious egotist,
Who thinks God stoops from His high majesty
To lay his finger on your puny head,
And crown it — that you henceforth may parade
Your maggotship throughout the wondering world —
"I am the Lord's anointed!"
D. M. MULOCK CRAIK, *The Dead Czar*, st. 5

Elder.— How much more elder art thou than thy looks!
SHAKESPEARE, *Merchant of Venice*, iv, 1

Elms.— Beneath those rugged elms, that yew-tree's shade,
Where heaves the turf in many a mouldering heap,
Each in his narrow cell for ever laid,
The rude forefathers of the hamlet sleep.
GRAY, *Elegy Written in a Country Churchyard*, st. 5

Eloquent.— That old man eloquent.[2]
MILTON, *Sonnet: To the Lady Margaret Ley*

Embers.— Thou hast but taken thy lamp and gone to bed;
I stay a little longer, as one stays
To cover up the embers that still burn.
LONGFELLOW, *Three Friends of Mine*, iv

Embrace.— Better thou and I were lying, hidden from the heart's disgrace,
Rolled in one another's arms, and silent in a last embrace.[3]
TENNYSON, *Locksley Hall*, lines 57, 58

---

[1] Lady Elizabeth Hastings.

[2] The Earl of Marlborough, Lord-President of the Council to King James I.

[3] Would that we two were lying
Beneath the churchyard sod,
With our limbs at rest in the green earth's breast,
And our souls at home with God.
C. KINGSLEY, *The Saint's Tragedy*, ii, 9

Emetics.— I [cannot] believe that a man could contract so strong an appetite for emetics during temporary illness as to persist in feeding upon them during the remainder of his healthful life.— ABRAHAM LINCOLN, *Letter to Erastus Corning*, June 12, 1863

Emigrated.— Oh, write of me, not "Died in bitter pains,"
But "Emigrated to another star!"
HELEN FISKE JACKSON, *Emigravit*, lines 12, 13

Empire.— Westward the course of empire takes its way;[1]
The first four acts already past,
A fifth shall close the drama with the day;
Time's noblest offspring is the last.
GEORGE BERKELEY, *The Prospect of Planting Arts and Learning in America*, st. 6

Stop!—for thy tread is on an empire's dust!
An earthquake's spoil is sepulchred below!
BYRON, *Childe Harold's Pilgrimage*, Canto iii, st. 17

Some heart once pregnant with celestial fire;
Hands that the rod of empire might have swayed,
Or waked to ecstasy the living lyre.
GRAY, *Elegy Written in a Country Churchyard*, st. 13

End.— The end must justify the means.
MATTHEW PRIOR, *Hans Carvel*, line 67

The true beginning of our end.
SHAKESPEARE, *Midsummer-Night's Dream*, v, 1

The end crowns all,
And that old common arbitrator, Time,
Will one day end it.
SHAKESPEARE, *Troilus and Cressida*, iv, 5

Ended.— All was ended now, the hope, and the fear, and the sorrow,
All the aching of heart, the restless, unsatisfied longing,[2]
All the dull, deep pain, and constant anguish of patience!
And, as she pressed once more the lifeless head to her bosom,
Meekly she bowed her own, and murmured, "Father, I thank thee!"
LONGFELLOW, *Evangeline*, II, v, lines 125–129

Ending.— Great is the art of beginning, but greater the art is of ending;
Many a poem is marred by a superfluous verse.
LONGFELLOW, *Elegiac Verse*, st. 14

---

[1] The star of empire glitters in the west.
CHARLES MACKAY, *Cheer, Boys! Cheer!* st. 2

[2] A vague unrest
And a nameless longing filled her breast.— WHITTIER, *Maud Muller*, st. 5

Endure.— O ye gods, ye gods! must I endure all this?
SHAKESPEARE, *Julius Cæsar*, iv, 3

Enemies.— Lands intersected by a narrow frith
Abhor each other. Mountains interposed
Make enemies of nations, who had else
Like kindred drops been mingled into one.[1]
COWPER, *The Task: The Time-Piece*, lines 16–19

Enemy.— A weak invention of the enemy.
COLLEY CIBBER, *Richard III*, v, 6

We have met the enemy and they are ours.
OLIVER H. PERRY, *Report of the Battle of Lake Erie*

Engineer.— For 't is the sport to have the engine[e]r
Hoist with his own petar: and 't [it] shall go hard
But I will delve one yard below their mines,
And blow them at the moon.
SHAKESPEARE, *Hamlet*, iii, 4

England.— Ye Mariners of England,
That guard our native seas!
Whose flag has braved, a thousand years,
The battle and the breeze.
CAMPBELL, *Ye Mariners of England*, st. 1

The meteor flag of England. *Ibid.*, st. 4

The foeman will find neither coward nor slave
'Neath the Red Cross of England — the flag of the Brave.
ELIZA COOK, *The Red Cross of England*, st. 1

England, with all thy faults, I love thee still —
My country![2] and, while yet a nook is left
Where English minds and manners may be found,
Shall be constrained to love thee.
COWPER, *The Task: The Time-Piece*, lines 206–209

---

[1] Once we thought it right to foster
Local jealousies and pride;
Right to hate another nation
Parted from us by a tide;
Right to go to war for glory,
Or extension of domain;
Right, through fear of foreign rivals,
To refuse the needful grain;
Right to bar it out till Famine
Drew the bolt with fingers wan.
Old opinions! rags and tatters!
Get you gone! get you gone!
CHARLES MACKAY, *Old Opinions*, st. 4

[2] "England! with all thy faults I love thee still" . . .
I like the freedom of the press and quill; * . . .
I like the taxes, when they're not too many;
I like a sea-coal fire, when not too dear;
I like a beefsteak, too, as well as any;
Have no objection to a pot of beer,
I like the weather, when it is not rainy,
That is, I like two months of every year.— BYRON, *Beppo*, st. 47, 48

---

* Because bold Britons have a tongue and free quill,
At which all modern nations vainly aim.
BYRON, *Don Juan*, Canto xiii, st. 20

[England] is the cradle and the refuge of free principles, though often persecuted; the school of religious liberty, the more precious for the struggles through which it has passed; the tombs of those who have reflected honour on all who speak the English tongue; it is the birthplace of our fathers, the home of the Pilgrims.

EDWARD EVERETT, *Oration Delivered at Plymouth, Mass., Dec.* 22, 1824

What should they know of England who only England know?
KIPLING, *The English Flag*, st. 1

What is the flag of England? Winds of the world, declare!
Ibid., st. 2

She's [England's] all thet's honest, honnable, an' fair,
An' when the vartoos died they made her heir.
LOWELL, *Biglow Papers*, II, ii, lines 136, 137

She [England] an' Columby's gut to be fas' friends:
For the world prospers by their privit ends:
'T would put the clock back all o' fifty years
Ef they should fall together by the ears.
. . . . .
We're boun' to be good friends, an' so we'd oughto,
In spite of all the fools both sides the water.
Ibid., lines 209–230

Attend, all ye who list to hear our noble England's praise:
I tell [sing] of the thrice famous deeds she wrought in ancient days,
When that great fleet invincible against her bore in vain
The richest spoils of Mexico, the stoutest hearts of Spain.
MACAULAY, *The Armada*, lines 1–4

The freshening breeze of eve unfurled that banner's massy fold;
The parting gleam of sunshine kissed that haughty scroll of gold;
Night sank upon the dusky beach, and on the purple sea,
Such night in England ne'er had been, nor e'er again shall be.
Ibid., lines 31–34

Now all the youth of England are on fire,
And silken dalliance in the wardrobe lies.
SHAKESPEARE, *King Henry V*, ii, Prologue

That island of England breeds very valiant creatures.
Ibid., iii, 7

England—*Continued*

This England never did, nor never shall,
Lie at the proud foot of a conqueror,
But when it first did help to wound itself.[1]
Now these her princes are come home again,
Come the three corners of the world in arms,
And we shall shock them. Nought shall make us rue,
If England to itself do rest but true.
SHAKESPEARE, *King John*, v, 7

This royal throne of kings, this sceptred isle,
This earth of majesty, this seat of Mars,
This other Eden, demi-paradise,
This fortress built by Nature for herself
Against infection and the hand of war,
This happy breed of men, this little world,
This precious stone set in the silver sea,
Which serves it in the office of a wall
Or as a moat defensive to a house,
Against the envy of less happie[r] lands,
This blessed plot, this earth, this realm, this England.
SHAKESPEARE, *King Richard II*, ii, 1

England, where indeed, they are most potent in potting. SHAKESPEARE, *Othello*, ii, 3

Shot through the staff or the halyard, but ever we raised thee anew,
And ever upon the topmost roof our banner of England blew. TENNYSON, *Defence of Lucknow*, st. 1

A power, to which, for purposes of foreign conquest and subjugation, Rome in the height of her glory is not to be compared,— a power which has dotted over the surface of the whole globe with her possessions and military posts, whose morning drum-beat, following the sun, and keeping company with the hours, circles the earth with one continuous and unbroken strain of the martial airs of England.[2]— DANIEL WEBSTER, *Speech in the Senate*, May 7, 1834

---

[1] No foreign foe could quell
Thy soul, till from itself it fell. BYRON, *The Giaour*, lines 138, 139

[2] From India's morning-bugle
To the last sunset-gun.— G. BARLOW, *England, Ho! for England*, st. 1

The Briton may traverse the pole or the zone,
And boldly claim his right;
For he calls such a vast domain his own,
That the sun never sets on his might.
ELIZA COOK, *The Englishman*, st. 4

Take 'old o' the wings o' the mornin',
An' flop 'round the earth till you're dead;
But you won't get away from the tune that they play
To the bloomin' old Rag over'ead.— KIPLING, *The Widow at Windsor*

English.— 'Tis the hard grey weather
Breeds hard English men.
C. KINGSLEY, *Ode to the Northeast Wind*, lines 51, 52

Never was isle so little, never was sea so lone,
But over the scud and the palm-trees an English flag has flown. KIPLING, *The English Flag*, st. 7

Never the lotos closes, never the wild-fowl wake,
But a soul goes out on the East Wind that died for England's sake —
Man or woman or suckling, mother or bride or maid —
Because on the bones of the English the English flag is stayed.[1] *Ibid.*, st. 12

An old abusing of God's patience and the king's English. SHAKESPEARE, *Merry Wives of Windsor*, i, 4

Handful of men as we were, we were English in heart and in limb,
Strong with the strength of the race to command, to obey, to endure,
Each of us fought as if hope for the garrison hung but on him. TENNYSON, *Defence of Lucknow*, st. 4

Englishman.— There's a land that bears a world-known name,
Though it is but a little spot;
. . . . .
'Tis the star of earth, deny it who can;
The island home of an Englishman.
ELIZA COOK, *The Englishman*, st. 1

Where'er I wander, boast of this I can,
Though banished, yet a trueborn Englishman.
SHAKESPEARE, *King Richard II*, i, 3

Ennoble.— What can ennoble sots, or slaves, or cowards?
Alas! not all the blood of all the Howards!
POPE, *Essay on Man*, Epistle iv, lines 215, 216

---

[1] We have fed our sea for a thousand years,
And she calls us, still unfed,
Though there's never a wave of all her waves
But marks our English dead:*
We have strawed our best to the weed's unrest,
To the shark and the sheering gull.
If blood be the price of admiralty,
Lord God, we ha' paid in full!
KIPLING, *A Song of the English*, II, st. 1

* Wave may not foam, nor wild wind sweep,
Where rest not England's dead.
FELICIA HEMANS, *England's Dead*, st. 2

Ensign.— Ay, tear her tattered ensign down!
Long has it waved on high,
And many an eye has danced to see
That banner in the sky.—HOLMES, *Old Ironsides*, st. 1

Envy. Can envy dwell
In heavenly breasts?
MILTON, *Paradise Lost*, IX, lines 729, 730

There is not a passion so strongly rooted in the human heart as envy. SHERIDAN, *The Critic*, i, 1

Base envy withers at another's joy,
And hates that excellence it cannot reach.
THOMSON, *The Seasons*, Spring, lines 284, 285

Epitaph.— Let there be no inscription upon my tomb; let no man write my epitaph. . . . Let my character and my motives repose in obscurity and peace till other times and other men can do them justice. Then shall my character be vindicated; then may my epitaph be written.—ROBERT EMMET, *Speech from the dock on his conviction for high treason*, Sept. 19, 1803

Thy ignominy sleep with thee in the grave,
But not remembered in thy epitaph.
SHAKESPEARE, *King Henry IV, Part I*, v 4

Epithet.— A kind of maddened John the Baptist,
To whom the harshest word comes aptest,
Who, struck by stone or brick ill-starred,
Hurls back an epithet as hard,
Which, deadlier than stone or brick,
Has a propensity to stick.
LOWELL, *Letter from Boston*, lines 135–140

Epitome.— In the first rank of these did Zimri stand;
A man so various that he seemed to be
Not one, but all mankind's epitome;
Stiff in opinions, always in the wrong;
Was everything by starts, and nothing long;
But, in the course of one revolving moon,
Was chymist, fiddler, statesman, and buffoon.
DRYDEN, *Absalom and Achitophel*, I, lines 544–550

Equalized.— One place there is — beneath the burial sod —
Where all mankind are equalized by death;
Another place there is — the Fane of God —
Where all are equal who draw living breath;
Juggle who will elsewhere with his own soul,
Playing the Judas with a temporal dole —

He who can come beneath that awful cope,
In the dread presence of a Maker just,
Who metes to ev'ry pinch of human dust
One even measure of immortal hope —
He who can stand within that holy door,
With soul unbowed by that pure spirit-level,
And frame unequal laws for rich and poor,—
Might sit for Hell and represent the Devil.
HOOD, *Ode to Rae Wilson, Esquire*, st. 14

Era.— At the birth of each new Era, with a recognizing start,
Nation wildly looks at nation, standing with mute lips apart,
And glad Truth's yet mightier man-child leaps beneath the Future's heart.—LOWELL, *The Present Crisis*, st. 2

Erin.— Erin mavournin, Erin go bragh![1]
CAMPBELL, *The Exile of Erin*, st. 5

Euchred.— Just a pack o' rotten plates puttied up with tar,
In we came, an' time enough, 'cross Bilbao Bar.
Cverloaded, undermanned, meant to founder, we
Euchred God Almighty's storm, bluffed the Eternal Sea.
KIPLING, *Ballad of the Bolivar*, st. 11

Evanescence.— Statue of flesh — immortal of the dead!
Imperishable type of evanescence!
Posthumous man, who quitt'st thy narrow bed,
And standest undecayed within our presence,
Thou wilt hear nothing till the Judgment morning,
When the Great Trump shall thrill thee with its warning.
HORACE SMITH, *Address to a Mummy*, st. 12

Eve.— One of Eve's family. HOOD, *The Bridge of Sighs*

But if the first Eve
Hard doom did receive,
When only one apple had she,
What a punishment new
Shall be found out for you,
Who, tasting, have robbed the whole tree?
POPE, *To Lady Mary Wortley Montagu*, st. 5

Even.— Even is come; and from the dark Park, hark,
The signal of the setting sun — one gun!
And six is sounding from the chime, prime time
To go and see the Drury-Lane Dane slain,—
Or hear Othello's jealous doubt spout out,
Or Macbeth raving at that shade-made blade,
Denying to his frantic clutch much touch.
HOOD, *A Nocturnal Sketch*, lines 1–7

[1] Ireland my darling! Ireland for ever!

Evening.— Now stir the fire, and close the shutters fast,
Let fall the curtains, wheel the sofa round,
And while the bubbling and loud hissing urn
Throws up a steamy column, and the cups,
That cheer but not inebriate, wait on each,
So let us welcome peaceful evening in.
COWPER, *The Task: The Winter Evening*, lines 36–41

Now came still evening on, and twilight grey
Had in her sober livery all things clad.
MILTON, *Paradise Lost*, IV, lines 598, 599

And still on that evening, when pleasure fills up
To the highest top sparkle each heart and each cup,
Where'er my path lies, be it gloomy or bright,
My soul, happy friends, shall be with you that night;
Shall join in your revels, your sports, and your wiles,
And return to me, beaming all o'er with your smiles —
Too blest, if it tells me that, 'mid the gay cheer
Some kind voice had murmured, "I wish he were here!"
T. MOORE, *Farewell!— But Whenever You Welcome the Hour*, st. 2

Ever.— It may be for years, and it may be for ever!
L. M. CRAWFORD, *Kathleen Mavourneen*

For ever and a day.—SHAKESPEARE, *As You Like It*, iv, 1

Men may come and men may go,
But I go on for ever. TENNYSON, *The Brook*

Evil.— The wounds I might have healed!
The human sorrow and smart!
And yet it never was in my soul
To play so ill a part:
But evil is wrought by want of thought,
As well as want of heart!
HOOD, *The Lady's Dream*, st. 16

And out of good still to find means of evil.
MILTON, *Paradise Lost*, I, line 165

Though fallen on evil days,
On evil days though fallen, and evil tongues.
Ibid., VII, lines 25, 26

The evil that men do lives after them;
The good is oft interred with their bones.
SHAKESPEARE, *Julius Cæsar*, iii, 2

Evils.— Of two evils the less is alway to be chosen.
THOMAS À KEMPIS, *Imitation of Christ*, III, xii, 2

Executors.— Let's choose executors and talk of wills.
SHAKESPEARE, *King Richard II*, iii, 2

Expectation.— 'Tis expectation makes a blessing dear;
Heaven were not Heaven, if we knew what it were.
SIR JOHN SUCKLING, *Against Fruition*, st. 4

Expediency.— No man is justified in doing evil on the ground of expediency.
THEODORE ROOSEVELT, *The Strenuous Life: Latitude and Longitude Among Reformers*

Experience.— Experience is bitter, but its teachings we retain;
It has taught me this,— who once has loved, loves never on earth again!

. . . . .

Experience is bitter indeed,— I have learned at a heavy cost
The secret of love's persistency: I, too, have loved and lost.
G. ARNOLD, *Introspection*, vi

Experience keeps a dear school, but fools will learn in no other, and scarse in that.
BENJAMIN FRANKLIN, *Poor Richard's Almanac*

Unless experience be a jewel that I have purchased at an infinite rate.
SHAKESPEARE, *Merry Wives of Windsor*, ii, 2

Explanation.— I wish he would explain his explanation.
BYRON, *Don Juan*, Dedication, st. 2

Extenuate.— Speak of me as I am; nothing extenuate,
Nor set down aught in malice.
SHAKESPEARE, *Othello*, v, 2

Extremes.— Extremes in nature equal good produce,
Extremes in man concur to gen'ral use.
POPE, *Moral Essays*, Epistle iii, lines 161–162

Eye.— The love-light in her eye.
HARTLEY COLERIDGE, *She Is Not Fair to Outward View*

He holds him with his glittering eye.
S. T. COLERIDGE, *Ancient Mariner*, line 13

The bright black eye, the melting blue,—
I cannot choose between the two.
HOLMES, *The Dilemma*, st. 1

I trowe that countenance cannot lie,
Whose thoughts are legible in the eie.
MATTHEW ROYDON, *Elegy on a Friend's Passion for His Astrophill* (Sir Philip Sidney)

Faster than his tongue
Did make offence his eye did heal it up.

SHAKESPEARE, *As You Like It*, iii, 5

Where is any author in the world
Teaches such beauty [learning] as a woman's eye?

SHAKESPEARE, *Love's Labour's Lost*, iv, 3

Stabbed with a white wench's black eye; shot through the ear with a love-song; the very pin of his heart cleft with the blind bow-boy's butt-shaft.

SHAKESPEARE, *Romeo and Juliet*, ii, 4

Eyes.— Her eyes are sapphires set in snow.

T. LODGE, *Rosaline*, st. 1

From women's eyes[1] this doctrine I derive:
They sparkle still the right Promethean fire;
They are the books,[2] the arts, the academes,
That show, contain, and nourish all the world.

SHAKESPEARE, *Love's Labour's Lost*, iv, 3

Eyes, look your last!
Arms, take your last embrace! and, lips, O you
The doors of breath, seal with a righteous kiss
A dateless bargain to engrossing death.

SHAKESPEARE, *Romeo and Juliet*, v, 3

Those perplexed and patient eyes were dim.

TOM TAYLOR, *Abraham Lincoln*, st. 15

Face.— Human face divine.

MILTON, *Paradise Lost*, III, line 44

The tartness of his face sours ripe grapes.

SHAKESPEARE, *Coriolanus*, v, 4

I have heard of your paintings too, well enough; God has [hath] given you one face, and you make yourselves another. SHAKESPEARE, *Hamlet*, iii, 1

Are you like the painting of a sorrow,
A face without a heart? *Ibid.*, iv, 7

Wet my cheeks with artificial tears,
And frame my face to all occasions.

SHAKESPEARE, *King Henry VI, Part III*, iii, 2

---

[1] The light that lies
In woman's eyes. MOORE, *The Time I've Lost in Wooing*

[2] My only books
Were woman's looks,
And folly's all they've taught me. *Ibid.*

I think there's never a man in Christendom
That can less[er] hide his love or hate than he;
For by his face straight shall you know his heart.
SHAKESPEARE, *King Richard III*, iii, 4

What's the matter,
That you have such a February face,
So full of frost, of storm and cloudiness?
SHAKESPEARE, *Much Ado about Nothing*, v, 4

Her angels face,
As the great eye of heaven, shyned bright,
And made a sunshine in the shady place.
SPENSER, *Faerie Queene*, I, iii, st. 4

There's a new foot on the floor, my friend,
And a new face at the door, my friend,
A new face at the door.[1]
TENNYSON, *Death of the Old Year*

Faces.— Sea of upturned faces.[2]
SCOTT, *Rob Roy*, xx, DANIEL WEBSTER, *Speech in Boston*, Sept. 30, 1842

Menas. All men's faces are true, whatso[m]e'er their hands are.
Enobarbus. But there is never a fair woman has a true face. SHAKESPEARE, *Antony and Cleopatra*, ii, 6

Though men can cover crimes with bold, stern looks,
Poor women's faces are their own faults' books.
SHAKESPEARE, *Rape of Lucrece*, lines 1252, 1253

Facts. Facts are chiels that winna ding [*cannot be overthrown*]
An' downa [*will not*] be disputed.—BURNS, *A Dream*, st. 4

Fail.— In the lexicon of youth, which fate reserves
For a bright manhood, there is no such word
As — fail. E. G. BULWER-LYTTON, *Richelieu*, ii, 2

Macbeth. If we should fail?
Lady Macbeth. We fail!
But screw your courage to the sticking place,
And we'll not fail. SHAKESPEARE, *Macbeth*, i, 7

Failings. E'en his failings leaned to virtue's side.
GOLDSMITH, *The Deserted Village*, line 164

[1] I heard a sick man's dying sigh,
And an infant's idle laughter.
The Old Year went mourning by—
The New came dancing after!
PRAED, *Twenty-Eight and Twenty-Nine*, st. 1

[2] An avalanche of men,
. . . . . .
A sea, a sea of men! EBENEZER ELLIOTT, *The Corn-Law Hymn*, st. 2

Faint.— Faint heart ne'er won fair lady.
Proverbial, and quoted in various forms by many authors.[1]

Who is so faint, that dare not be so bold
To touch the fire, the weather being cold?
SHAKESPEARE, *Venus and Adonis*, lines 401, 402

Fair.— Is she not passing fair?
SHAKESPEARE, *Two Gentlemen of Verona*, iv, 4

Shall I, wasting in despair,
Die, because a woman's fair?
G. WITHER, *The Author's Resolution*, st. 1

Fairer.— Fairer than Rachel by the palmy well,
Fairer than Ruth among the fields of corn.
TENNYSON, *Aylmer's Field*, lines 679, 680

Faith.— Learn to win a lady's faith
Nobly, as the thing is high,
Bravely, as for life and death,
With a loyal gravity.
E. B. BROWNING, *The Lady's Yes*, st. 5

His faith, perhaps, in some nice tenets might
Be wrong; his life, I'm sure, was in the right.[2]
COWLEY, *On the Death of Crashaw*, lines 55, 56

I consider faith and prayers
Amongst the privatest of men's affairs.
HOOD, *Ode to Rae Wilson, Esquire*, st. 6

They only the victory win
Who have fought the good fight, and have vanquished the demon that tempts us within;
Who have held to their faith unseduced by the prize that the world holds on high;
Who have dared for a high cause to suffer, resist, fight, —if need be, to die.
W. W. STORY, *Io Victis*, st. 2

A bending staff I would not break,
A feeble faith I would not shake,
Nor even rashly pluck away
The error which some truth may stay,
Whose loss might leave the soul without
A shield against the shafts of doubt.
WHITTIER, *Questions of Life*, lines 1–6

---

[1]Faint heart ne'er wan [*won*]
A lady fair.
BURNS, *Epistle to Dr. Blacklock*, st. 8

[2]For modes of faith let graceless zealots fight;
His can't be wrong whose life is in the right.
POPE, *Essay on Man*, Epistle iii, lines 305, 306

One in whom persuasion and belief
Had ripened into faith, and faith become
A passionate intuition. WORDSWORTH,
The Excursion: Despondency Corrected, lines 1302–1304

Faithful.— But the noblest thing which perished there
Was that young faithful heart!
FELICIA HEMANS, *Casabianca*, st. 10

Among the faithless, faithful only he.
MILTON, *Paradise Lost*, V, line 897

Falcon.— A falcon, towering in her pride of place,
Was by a mousing owl hawked at and killed.
SHAKESPEARE, *Macbeth*, ii, 4

Fall.— Oh, what a fall was there, my countrymen!
Then I, and you, and all of us fell down,
Whilst bloody treason flourished over us.
SHAKESPEARE, *Julius Cæsar*, iii, 2

Fallen.— Fallen, fallen, fallen, fallen,
Fallen from his high estate.
DRYDEN, *Alexander's Feast*, lines 77, 78

So fallen! so lost! the light withdrawn
Which once he wore!
The glory from his grey hairs gone
For evermore!

. . . . .

Then, pay the reverence of old days
To his dead fame;
Walk backward, with averted gaze,
And hide the shame! WHITTIER, *Ichabod*, st. 1, 9

Falling.— Press not a falling man too far!
SHAKESPEARE, *King Henry VIII*, iii, 2

'T is a cruelty
To load a falling man. *Ibid.*, v, 3 [2]

Falling-off.— O Hamlet, what a falling-off was there!
SHAKESPEARE, *Hamlet*, i, 5

Falls.— Some falls are means the happier to arise.
SHAKESPEARE, *Cymbeline*, iv, 2

When he falls, he falls like Lucifer,[1]
Never to hope again.
SHAKESPEARE, *King Henry VIII*, iii, 2

False.—One false step is ne'er retrieved.
GRAY, *On a Favourite Cat*, st. 7

All was false and hollow; though his tongue
Dropped manna, and could make the worse appear
The better reason.
MILTON, *Paradise Lost*, II, lines 112–114

False face must hide what the false heart doth know.
SHAKESPEARE, *Macbeth*, i, 7

Framed to make women false.—SHAKESPEARE, *Othello*, i, 3

Thou art false as hell. *Ibid.*, iv, 2

Ring out the false, ring in the true.
TENNYSON, *In Memoriam*, cvi, st. 2

Falsehood. Falsehood
Is worse in kings than beggars.
SHAKESPEARE, *Cymbeline*, iii, 6

Oh, what a goodly outside falsehood hath!
SHAKESPEARE, *Merchant of Venice*, i, 3

Had I a heart for falsehood framed,
I ne'er could injure you. SHERIDAN, *The Duenna*, i, 5

Falsehoods.— There are some falsehoods . . . on which men mount, as on bright wings, towards heaven. There are some truths, cold, bitter, taunting truths, wherein your worldly scholars are very apt and punctual, which bind men down to earth with leaden chains.
DICKENS, *Martin Chuzzlewit*, xiii

Fame. Fate that then denied him,
And envy that decried him,
And malice that belied him,
Have cenotaphed his fame
J. H. BONER, *Poe's Cottage at Fordham*, st. 7

---

[1] Thrown by angry Jove
Sheer o'er the crystal battlements: from morn
To noon he fell, from noon to dewy eve,
A summer's day; and with the setting sun
Dropped from the zenith like a falling star.
MILTON, *Paradise Lost*, I, lines 741–745

I have touched the highest point of all my greatness;
And, from that full meridian of my glory,
I haste now to my setting: I shall fall
Like a bright exhalation in the evening,
And no man see me more. SHAKESPEARE, *King Henry VIII*, iii, 2

Men the most infamous are fond of fame,
And those who fear not guilt yet start at shame.
CHURCHILL, *The Author*, lines 233, 234

The aspiring youth that fired the Ephesian dome,
Outlives in fame the pious fool that raised it.
COLLEY CIBBER, *Richard III, Adapted*, iii, 2

Fame is the spur that the clear spirit doth raise
(That last infirmity of noble mind)
To scorn delights, and live laborious days;
But the fair guerdon when we hope to find,
And think to burst out into sudden blaze,
Comes the blind Fury with the abhorred shears,
And slits the thin-spun life.—MILTON, *Lycidas*, lines 70–76

Air and fame, as poets sing,
Are both the same, the self-same thing;
Yet bards are not chameleons quite,
And heavenly food is very light;
Who ever dined or supped on fame,
And went to bed upon a name? J. MONTGOMERY,
The Pleasures of Imprisonment, Epistle i, st. 4

Life is a lightning-flash of breath,
Fame but a thunder-clap at death.
J. MONTGOMERY, *Winter-Lightning*, st. 2

Do good by stealth, and blush to find it fame.
POPE, *Epilogue to the Satires*, I, line 136

If parts allure thee, think how Bacon shined,
The wisest, brightest, meanest of mankind:
Or ravished with the whistling of a name,
See Cromwell, damned to everlasting fame![1]
POPE, *Essay on Man*, Epistle iv, lines 281–284

What is fame? the meanest have their day,
The greatest can but blaze, and pass away.[2] POPE,
Imitations of Horace, I, Epistle vi, lines 46, 47

---

[1] All crowd, who foremost shall be damned to fame.
POPE, *The Dunciad*, iii, line 158

What rage for fame attends both great and small!
Better be damned than mentioned not at all.
J. WOLCOT ("PETER PINDAR"), *Ode ix*

[2] What is the end of fame? 'T is but to fill
A certain portion of uncertain paper;
Some liken it to climbing up a hill,
Whose summit, like all hills, is lost in vapour;
For this men write, speak, preach, and heroes kill;
And bards burn what they call their "midnight taper,"
To have, when the original is dust,
A name, a wretched picture, and worse bust.
BYRON, *Don Juan*, Canto i, st. 218

Unblemished let me live, or die unknown;
Oh, grant an honest fame, or grant me none.
POPE, *Temple of Fame*, lines 523, 524

Man dreams of Fame while woman wakes to love.
TENNYSON, *Merlin and Vivien*, line 458

Fame is the shade of immortality,
And in itself a shadow.
YOUNG, *Night Thoughts*, VII, lines 365, 366

Familiar.— Be thou familiar, but by no means vulgar.
SHAKESPEARE, *Hamlet*, i, 3

Family.— I go for the man with the gallery of family portraits against the one with the twenty-five-cent daguerreotype, unless I find out that the last is the better of the two.— HOLMES, *Autocrat of the Breakfast-Table*, i

Famous.— I awoke one morning and found myself famous.
BYRON, *Life*, by T. Moore, xiv

If thou wilt be constant then,
And faithful of thy word,
I'll make thee glorious by my pen,
And famous by my sword.
I'll serve thee in such noble ways
Was never heard before;
I'll crown and deck thee with all bays,
And love thee evermore.
JAMES GRAHAM, MARQUIS OF MONTROSE,
My Dear and Only Love, st. 5

Fancy. Gloomy as usual, . . .
Brooding on fancy's eggs.
GEORGE MACDONALD, *Within and Without*, i, 1

Chewing the food [cud] of sweet and bitter fancy.
SHAKESPEARE, *As You Like It*, iv, 3

Tell me where is fancy bred,
Or in the heart or in the head?
How begot, how nourished?
Reply, Reply.
It is engendered in the eyes,
With gazing fed; and fancy dies
In the cradle where it lies.
Let us all ring fancy's knell:
I'll begin it,— Ding, dong, bell.
SHAKESPEARE, *Merchant of Venice*, iii, 2

Farewell.— But still her lips refused to send — "Farewell!"
For in that word — that fatal word — howe'er
We promise — hope — believe — there breathes despair.
BYRON, *The Corsair*, Canto i, st. 15

Farewell! if ever fondest prayer
  For other's weal availed on high,
Mine will not all be lost in air,
  But waft thy name beyond the sky.

BYRON, *Farewell*, st. 1

I only know we loved in vain —
I only feel — Farewell! — Farewell! *Ibid.*, st. 2

Fare thee well; and if for ever,
  Still for ever, fare thee well;
Even though unforgiving, never
  'Gainst thee shall my heart rebel.

BYRON, *Fare Thee Well*, st. 1

Farewell! — but whenever you welcome the hour,
That awakens the night-song of mirth in your bower,
Then think of the friend who once welcomed it too,
And forgot his own griefs to be happy with you.

T. MOORE, *Farewell!— But Whenever*, etc., st. 1

Farewell, my best beloved; beloved, fare thee well!
I may not mourn where thou dost weep, nor be where thou dost dwell;
But when the friend I trusted all coldly turns away,
When the warmest feelings wither, and the dearest hopes decay,
To thee — to thee — thou knowest, whate'er my lot may be,
For comfort and for happiness, my spirit turns to thee.

PRAED, *To* ———, st. 6

  Whether we shall meet again I know not.
Therefore our everlasting farewell take:
For ever, and for ever, farewell, Cassius!
If we do meet again, why, we shall smile;
If not, why then, this parting was well made.

SHAKESPEARE, *Julius Cæsar*, v, 1

  Oh, now, for ever
Farewell the tranquil mind! farewell content!
Farewell the plumed troop, and the big wars,
That make ambition virtue! oh, farewell!
Farewell the neighing steed, and the shrill trump,
The spirit-stirring drum, the ear-piercing fife,
The royal banner, and all quality,
Pride, pomp, and circumstance of glorious war!
And O you mortal engines, whose rude throats
The immortal Jove's dread clamours counterfeit,
Farewell! Othello's occupation 's gone.

SHAKESPEARE, *Othello*, iii, 3

Farewell! thou art too dear for my possessing.

SHAKESPEARE, *Sonnet* lxxxvii

Fashion.— The fashion wears out more apparel than the man.
SHAKESPEARE, *Much Ado about Nothing*, iii, 3

Fashions.— In words, as fashions, the same rule will hold;
Alike fantastic if too new or old:
Be not the first by whom the new are tried,
Nor yet the last to lay the old aside.
POPE, *Essay on Criticism*, lines 333-336

Old fashions please me best.
SHAKESPEARE, *Taming of the Shrew*, iii, 1

Fast.— Fast bind, fast find;
A proverb never stale in thrifty mind.
SHAKESPEARE, *Merchant of Venice*, ii, 5

Fat.— Who drives fat oxen should himself be fat.
SAMUEL JOHNSON, *Life*, by Boswell, 1784

Let me have men about me that are fat:
Sleek-headed men and such as sleep o' nights:
Yond Cassius has a lean and hungry look;
He thinks too much: such men are dangerous.
. . . . .
Would he were fatter! But I fear him not:
Yet, if my name were liable to fear,
I do not know the man I should avoid
So soon as that spare Cassius. He reads much;
He is a great observer, and he looks
Quite through the deeds of men.
SHAKESPEARE, *Julius Cæsar*, i, 2

As fat as butter.
SHAKESPEARE, *King Henry IV, Part I*, ii, 4

If to be fat be to be hated, then Pharaoh's lean kine are to be loved. *Ibid.*

Fate.— He either fears his fate too much,
Or his deserts are small,
That dares not put it to the touch,
To win or lose it all. JAMES GRAHAM,
MARQUIS OF MONTROSE, *My Dear and Only Love*, st. 2

It matters not how strait the gate,
How charged with punishments the scroll,
I am the master of my fate;
I am the captain of my soul.[1]
W. E. HENLEY, *Out of the Night That Covers Me*, st. 4

[1] Arise, O soul, and gird thee up anew,
Though the black camel Death kneel at thy gate;
No beggar thou that thou for alms shouldst sue;
Be the proud captain still of thine own fate!
J. B. KENYON, *A Challenge*

Cf. FORTUNE.

O God! that one might read the book of fate![1]
SHAKESPEARE, *King Henry IV, Part II*, iii, 1

Before I trust my fate to thee,
Or place my hand in thine,
Before I let thy future give
Colour and form to mine,
Before I peril all for thee, question thy soul to-night for me.
A. A. PROCTER, *A Woman's Question*, st. 1

There is no armour against fate;
Death lays his icy hand on kings.
J. SHIRLEY, *Dirge: Death the Leveller*, st. 1

This net [of fate] was twisted by the sisters three;
Which, when once cast o'er hardened wretch, too late
Repentance comes: replevy cannot be
From the strong iron grasp of vengeful destiny.
THOMSON, *Castle of Indolence*, ii, 32

The farthest from the fear
Are often nearest to the stroke of fate.
YOUNG, *Night Thoughts*, V, lines 790, 791

Fates.— Men at some time are masters of their fates:
The fault, dear Brutus, is not in our stars,
But in ourselves, that we are underlings.[2]
SHAKESPEARE, *Julius Cæsar*, i, 2

Father.— Father of all, in ev'ry age,
In ev'ry clime adored,
By saint, by savage, and by sage,
Jehovah, Jove, or Lord!
POPE, *The Universal Prayer*, st. 1

God help thee, poor monkey! But how wilt thou do for a father? SHAKESPEARE, *Macbeth*, iv, 2

It is a wise father that knows his own child.
SHAKESPEARE, *Merchant of Venice*, ii, 2

---

[1] Heav'n from all creatures hides the book of Fate,
All but the page prescribed, their present state.
POPE, *Essay on Man*, Epistle i, lines 77, 78

[2] Man is his own star, and the soul that can
Render an honest and a perfect man
Commands all light, all influence, all fate.
Nothing to him falls early, or too late.
J. FLETCHER, *Upon an Honest Man's Fortune*

It is the stars,
The stars above us, govern our conditions.—SHAKESPEARE, *King Lear*, iv, 3

'Tis in ourselves that we are thus or thus.—SHAKESPEARE, *Othello*, i, 3

Fathers.— Thy free, proud fathers slumber at thy side;
Live as they lived, or perish as they died!
HOLMES, *A Rhymed Lesson*, st. 71

Fault. Oftentimes excusing of a fault
Doth make the fault the worse by the excuse,
As patches set upon a little breach
Discredit more in hiding of the fault
Than did the fault before it was so patched.
SHAKESPEARE, *King John*, iv, 2

Every man has his fault, and honesty is his.
SHAKESPEARE, *Timon of Athens*, iii, 1

Faultless.— Whoever thinks a faultless piece to see,
Thinks what ne'er was, nor is, nor e'er shall be.[1]
POPE, *Essay on Criticism*, lines 253, 254

Faultily faultless, icily regular, splendidly null,
Dead perfection, no more. TENNYSON, *Maud*, ii

Yet graceful ease, and sweetness void of pride,
Might hide her faults, if belles had faults to hide:
If to her share some female errors fall,
Look on her face, and you'll forget 'em all.
POPE, *Rape of the Lock*, ii, lines 15-18

A friendly eye could never see such faults.
SHAKESPEARE, *Julius Cæsar*, iv, 3

Oh, what a world of vile ill-favoured faults
Looks handsome in three hundred pounds a year.
SHAKESPEARE, *Merry Wives of Windsor*, iii, 4

Fear.— Early and provident fear is the mother of safety.
BURKE, *On the Unitarian Petition*, May 11, 1792

Like one, that on a lonesome road
Doth walk in fear and dread,
And having once turned round walks on,
And turns no more his head;
Because he knows, a frightful fiend
Doth close behind him tread.
COLERIDGE, *Ancient Mariner*, lines 446-451

In the night, imagining some fear,
How easy is a bush supposed a bear!
SHAKESPEARE, *Midsummer-Night's Dream*, v, 1

Feared. Wheresoever he appeared,
Full twenty times was Peter feared
For once that Peter was respected.
WORDSWORTH, *Peter Bell*, i, st. 3

---

[1] 'T is true, perfection none must hope to find
In all this world, much less in womankind.
POPE, *January and May*, lines 190, 191

Feast.— Meanwhile, welcome joy and feast,
Midnight shout and revelry,
Tipsy dance and jollity.—MILTON, *Comus*, lines 102-104

The feast is sold . . .
'Tis given with welcome: to feed were best at home;
From thence the sauce to meat is ceremony;
Meeting were bare without it.
SHAKESPEARE, *Macbeth*, iii, 4

Feast, and your halls are crowded;
Fast, and the world goes by;
Succeed and give, and it helps you live,
But no man can help you die.
ELLA WHEELER WILCOX, *Solitude*, st. 3

Feeble.— 'Tis not enough to help the feeble up,
But to support him after.
SHAKESPEARE, *Timon of Athens*, i, 1

Feeling.— The warm, champagny, old-particular, brandy-punchy feeling. HOLMES, *Nux Postcœnatica*, st. 17

Feelings.— Every person's feelings have a front-door and a side-door by which they may be entered. The front-door is on the street . . . The side-door opens at once into the secret chambers. There is almost always at least one key to this side-door. This is carried for years hidden in a mother's bosom. Fathers, brothers, sisters, and friends, often, but by no means so universally, have duplicates of it. The wedding-ring conveys a right to one; alas, if none is given with it!
HOLMES, *Autocrat of the Breakfast-Table*, vi

Some feelings are to mortals given,
With less of earth in them than heaven.
SCOTT, *Lady of the Lake*, Canto ii, st. 22

Feet.— Muse of the many-twinkling feet!—BYRON, *Waltz*, line 1

Her feet beneath her petticoat,
Like little mice, stole in and out,
As if they feared the light:[1]
But oh! she dances such a way!
No sun upon an Easter day
Is half so fine a sight.[2]
SIR JOHN SUCKLING, *Ballad upon a Wedding*, st. 8

---

[1] Her feet fell patter, cheep, like little mice.
ROBERT BUCHANAN, *The Widow Mysie*, st. 7

Her pretty feet
Like snails did creep
A little out, and then,
As if they started at bo-peep,
Did soon draw in again. HERRICK, *Upon Her Feet*

[2] And then she danced — oh, heaven! her dancing!
PRAED, *Belle of the Ball-Room*, st. 2

Fell.— He fought, he conquered, and he fell.[1]
SOUTHEY, *Inscription xxii: Epitaph*

Fellows.— If he be not fellow with the best king, thou shalt find the best king of good fellows.[2]
SHAKESPEARE, *King Henry V*, v, 2

Felony.— There shall be in England seven halfpenny loaves sold for a penny; the three-hooped pot shall have ten hoops; and I will make it felony to drink small beer: all the realm shall be in common.
SHAKESPEARE, *King Henry VI, Part II*, iv, 2

Ferryman.— That grim [sour] ferryman which poets write of.
SHAKESPEARE, *King Richard III*, i, 4

Feud.— Ring out the feud of rich and poor.
TENNYSON, *In Memoriam*, cvi, st. 3

Feuds.— In their faces stern defiance,
In their hearts the feuds of ages,
The hereditary hatred,
The ancestral thirst of vengeance.— LONGFELLOW,
Song of Hiawatha: The Peace-Pipe, lines 75–78

Field.— Their dearest action in the tented field.
SHAKESPEARE, *Othello*, i, 3

Fight. When the fight begins within himself,
A man's worth something.— R. BROWNING, *Bishop Blougram's Apology*, lines 699, 700

For those that fly may fight again,
Which he can never do that 's slain.[3]
BUTLER, *Hudibras*, III, iii, lines 243, 244

---

[1]General Sir John Moore, killed in the battle of Coruña, Jan. 16, 1809.

[2]The king o' guid fellows and wale of auld men.
BURNS, *Auld Rob Morris*, st. 1

[3]That same man, that runnith awaie,
Maie again fight an other daie. ERASMUS, *Apothegms*, (trans. Udall)

For he who fights and runs away
May live to fight another day;
But he who is in battle slain
Can never rise and fight again.—GOLDSMITH, *Art of Poetry on a New Plan*

He that fights and runs away
May turn and fight another day;
But he that is in battle slain
Will never rise to fight again. RAY, *History of the Rebellion*

We shall live to fight again and to strike another blow.
TENNYSON, *The Revenge*, st. 12

Sometimes we fight and we conquer,
And sometimes we fight and we run.
THACKERAY, *The Chronicle of the Drum*, i, st. 6

If you do fight, fight it out;[1] and don't give in while you can stand and see.

T. HUGHES, *Tom Brown's School Days*, II, vii

'Twun't du to think thet killin' ain't perlite,—
You've gut to be in airnest, ef you fight.

LOWELL, *Biglow Papers*, II, ii, lines 281, 282

Fifty-four-forty or fight!

Political (Democratic) slogan in the United States Presidential Campaign of 1844[2]

Fighting.— He rushed into the field, and, foremost fighting, fell.—BYRON, *Childe Harold's Pilgrimage*, Canto iii, st. 23

His bellyful [belly full] of fighting.

SHAKESPEARE, *Cymbeline*, ii, 1

Fig-tree.— Train up a fig-tree in the way it should go, and when you are old sit under the shade on it.

DICKENS, *Dombey and Son*, xix

Fine.— Fine by degrees, and beautifully less.

PRIOR, *Henry and Emma*, line 430

Fire.— Those that with haste will make a mighty fire
Begin it with weak straws.

SHAKESPEARE, *Julius Cæsar*, i, 3

A little fire is quickly trodden out,
Which, being suffered, rivers cannot quench.

SHAKESPEARE, *King Henry VI, Part III*, iv, 8

Ye blew the fire that burns ye.

SHAKESPEARE, *King Henry VIII*, v, 3 [2]

One fire burns out another's burning,
One pain is lessened by another's anguish.

SHAKESPEARE, *Romeo and Juliet*, i, 2

Fire that's closest kept burns most of all.

SHAKESPEARE, *Two Gentlemen of Verona*, i, 2

Thus have I shunned the fire, for fear of burning,
And drenched me in the sea, where I am drowned.

Ibid., i, 3

---

[1] Stand back to back, in God's name, and fight it to the last.

MACAULAY, *The Battle of Naseby*, st. 7

I have fought a good fight. 2 *Tim.* iv, 7

[2] Referring to the dispute with Great Britain over the Oregon boundary.

Any captain not under fire is not at his post, and a signal to recall him would be a disgrace.[1]

VILLENEUVE, cited by W. M. Sloane in *Napoleon Bonaparte*, II, xxxii

Fires. Where two raging fires meet together,
They do consume the thing that feeds their fury:
Though little fire grows great with little wind,
Yet extreme gusts will blow out fire and all.

SHAKESPEARE, *Taming of the Shrew*, ii

Poor men, when yule is cold,
Must be content to sit by little fires.

TENNYSON, *The Holy Grail*, lines 612, 613

Firmament.— The spacious firmament on high,
With all the blue ethereal sky,
And spangled heavens, a shining frame,
Their great Original proclaim.

ADDISON, *Ode*

First.— To the memory of the man, first in war, first in peace, and first in the hearts of his countrymen.

HENRY LEE, *Eulogy on Washington*

Fish.—Neither fish, nor flesh, nor good red herring.

DRYDEN, *Epilogue to the Duke of Guise*

Fishers.— Three fishers went sailing away to the west,—
Away to the west as the sun went down;
Each thought on the woman who loved him the best,
And the children stood watching them out of the town;
For men must work, and women must weep,
And there's little to earn, and many to keep,
Though the harbor bar be moaning.

. . . . .

Three corpses lay out on the shining sands
In the morning gleam as the tide went down,
And the women are weeping and wringing their hands
For those who will never come back to the town;
For men must work, and women must weep,
And the sooner it's over, the sooner to sleep,
And good-bye to the bar and its moaning.

KINGSLEY, *The Three Fishers*, st. 1, 3

Fishes.— O blest south wind that toots his horn
Through every hole and crack!
I'm off at eight to-morrow morn,
To bring *such* fishes back.

KINGSLEY, *The Southwest Wind*, st. 3

---

[1] The signal made by the French admiral at the opening of the battle of Trafalgar.

Fishes that tipple in the deep.
LOVELACE, *To Althea from Prison*, st. 2

Third Fisherman. I marvel how the fishes live in the sea.

First Fisherman. Why, as men do a-land; the great ones eat up the little ones: I can compare our rich misers to nothing so fitly as to a whale; a' plays and tumbles, driving the poor fry before him, and at last devours them all at a mouthful: such whales have I heard on o' the land, who never leave gaping till they 've swallowed the whole parish, church, steeple, bells, and all.

. . . . .

Third Fisherman. But if the good King Simonides were of my mind, . . . we would purge the land of these drones, that rob the bee of her honey.
SHAKESPEARE, *Pericles*, ii, 1

Fish-hook.— It 's a good sight easier to git a fish-hook in 'n 'tis to git it out. E. N. WESTCOTT, *David Harum*, i

Fit.— The fit is momentary; upon a thought
He will again be well. SHAKESPEARE, *Macbeth*, iii, 4

Fits.— 'Twas sad by fits, by starts 'twas wild.
WILLIAM COLLINS, *The Passions*

Flag.— Many a one on our decks knew then for the first time how tame a sight his country's flag is at home compared to what it is in a foreign land. To see it is to have a vision of home itself and all its idols, and feel a thrill that would stir a very river of sluggish blood.
S. L. CLEMENS ("MARK TWAIN"), *The Innocents Abroad*, vii

There 's a flag that waves o'er every sea,
No matter when or where;
And to treat that flag as aught but the free
Is more than the strongest dare.
For the lion-spirits that tread the deck
Have carried the palm of the brave;
And that flag may sink with a shot-torn wreck,
But never float over a slave.
ELIZA COOK, *The Englishman*, st. 2

Nail to the mast her holy flag,
Set every threadbare sail,
And give her to the god of storms,
The lightning and the gale!
HOLMES, *Old Ironsides*, st. 3

One life, one flag, one fleet, one throne!
TENNYSON, *Opening of the Indian and Colonial Exhibition*, st. 4

Flags.— Forty flags with their silver stars,
Forty flags with their crimson bars.
WHITTIER, *Barbara Frietchie*, st. 7

Flatteries. He does me double wrong
That wounds me with the flatteries of his tongue.
SHAKESPEARE, *King Richard II*, iii, 2

Flattery.— Flattery is the bellows blows up sin.
SHAKESPEARE, *Pericles*, i, 2

Flattery's the food for fools.
SWIFT, *Cadenus and Vanessa*

Flea.— That's a valiant flea that dare eat his breakfast on the lip of a lion. SHAKESPEARE, *King Henry V*, iii, 7

So, naturalists observe, a flea
Has smaller fleas that on him prey;
And these have smaller still to bite 'em;
And so proceed *ad infinitum*.—SWIFT, *Poetry, a Rhapsody*

Fleas.— A reasonable amount o' fleas is good fer a dog — keeps him from broodin' over bein' a dog.
E. N. WESTCOTT, *David Harum*, xxxii

Flesh. Flesh of my flesh,
Bone of my bone thou art,[1] and from thy state
Mine never shall be parted, bliss or woe.
MILTON, *Paradise Lost*, IX, lines 914–916[2]

Oh, that this too too solid flesh would melt,
Thaw and resolve itself into a dew!
Or that the Everlasting had not fixed
His canon 'gainst self-slaughter!
SHAKESPEARE, *Hamlet*, i, 2

A pound of that same merchant's flesh is thine:
The court awards it, and the law doth give it.

. . . . .

Take then thy bond, take thou thy pound of flesh;
But, in the cutting of it, if thou dost shed
One drop of Christian blood, thy lands and goods
Are, by the laws of Venice, confiscate
Unto the state of Venice.
SHAKESPEARE, *Merchant of Venice*, iv, 1

O flesh, flesh, how art thou fishified!
SHAKESPEARE, *Romeo and Juliet*, ii, 4

---

[1] Thou art a collop of my flesh.
SHAKESPEARE, *King Henry VI, Part I*, v, 4

[2] See also *Paradise Lost*, IV, line 483; VIII, line 495; IX, lines 958, 959

Flibbertigibbet.— This is the foul fiend Flibbertigibbet; he begins at curfew, and walks till the first cock; he gives the web and the pin, squints the eye, and makes the hare-lip; mildews the white wheat, and hurts the poor creature of earth. SHAKESPEARE, *King Lear*, iii, 4

Flint. The fire i' the flint
Shows not till it be struck.
SHAKESPEARE, *Timon of Athens*, i, 1

Flog.— O ye! who teach the ingenious youth of nations,
Holland, France, England, Germany, or Spain,
I pray ye flog them upon all occasions,
It mends their morals, never mind the pain.
BYRON, *Don Juan*, Canto ii, st. 1

Flogging.— There is now less flogging in our great schools than formerly, but then less is learned there; so that what the boys get at one end they lose at the other.
SAMUEL JOHNSON, *Life*, by Boswell, 1775

Flood.— You may as well go stand upon the beach
And bid the main flood bate his usual height.
SHAKESPEARE, *Merchant of Venice*, iv, 1

Flower.— 'Tis but a little faded flower,
But oh, how fondly dear!
ELLEN C. HOWARTH, *'Tis but a Little Faded Flower*, st. 1

One thing is certain, and the rest is Lies;
The flower that once has blown for ever dies.
OMAR KHAYYÁM, *Rubáiyát* (trans. Fitzgerald), st. 63

Flower in the crannied wall,
I pluck you out of the crannies,
I hold you here, root and all, in my hand,
Little flower — but if I could understand
What you are, root and all, and all in all,
I should know what God and man is.
TENNYSON, *Flower in the Crannied Wall*

Flowers.— He who hunts for flowers will find flowers; and he who loves weeds may find weeds.— H. W. BEECHER, *Lectures to Young Men*, Portrait Gallery, The Cynic

Flunked.— A keerless man in his talk was Jim,
And an awkward hand in a row;
But he never flunked, and he never lied,—
I reckon he never knowed how.
JOHN HAY, *Jim Bludso of the Prairie Belle*, st. 2

Fly.— His back against a rock he bore,
And firmly placed his foot before:—
"Come one, come all! this rock shall fly
From its firm base as soon as I."
SCOTT, *Lady of the Lake*, Canto v, st. 10

Foam.— The cruel crawling foam.
KINGSLEY, *The Sands of Dee*, st. 4

Foe.— Whispering with white lips — "The foe! They come! they come!"[1]
BYRON, *Childe Harold's Pilgrimage*, Canto iii, st. 25

Heat not a furnace for your foe so hot
That it do singe yourself.
SHAKESPEARE, *King Henry VIII*, i, 1

Folly.— When lovely woman stoops to folly,
And finds too late that men betray,—
What charm can soothe her melancholy,
What art can wash her guilt away?
The only art her guilt to cover,
To hide her shame from every eye,
To give repentance to her lover
And wring his bosom, is — to die.
GOLDSMITH, *The Vicar of Wakefield*, II, 5

Shoot folly as it flies.
POPE, *Essay on Man*, Epistle i, line 13

Where lives a man that has not tried,
How mirth can into folly glide,
And folly into sin!
SCOTT, *Bridal of Triermain*, Canto i, st. 21

Folly in fools bears not so strong a note
As foolery in the wise,[2] when wit doth dote.
SHAKESPEARE, *Love's Labour's Lost*, v, 2

Fool.— A fool must now and then be right by chance.
COWPER, *Conversation*, line 96

A fool there was and he made his prayer
(Even as you and I)
To a rag and a bone and a hank of hair
(We called her the woman who did not care),
But the fool he called her his lady fair
(Even as you and I!).
KIPLING, *The Vampire*, st. 1

---

[1]And the neigh of the steed and the multitude's hum,
And the clash and the shout, "They come! they come!"
BYRON, *The Siege of Corinth*, st. 22

[2]So doth a little folly him that is in reputation for wisdom and honor.
Ecclesiastes, x, 1

No creature smarts so little as a fool.
POPE, *Epistle to Dr. Arbuthnot*, line 84

A fool, a fool! I met a fool i' the forest,
A motley fool.
. . . . .
"Good morrow, fool," quoth I. "No, sir," quoth he,
"Call me not fool till heaven hath sent me fortune."
. . . . .
O noble fool!
A worthy fool! Motley 's the only wear.
SHAKESPEARE, *As You Like It*, ii, 7

Jaques. I was seeking for a fool when I found you.
Orlando. He is drowned in the brook: look but in, and you shall see him. *Ibid.*, iii, 2

The fool doth think he is wise, but the wise man knows himself to be a fool. *Ibid.*, v, 1

They fool me to the top of my bent.
SHAKESPEARE, *Hamlet*, iii, 2

How ill white hairs become a fool and jester!
SHAKESPEARE, *King Henry IV*, *Part II*, v, 5

A fool's bolt is soon shot.
SHAKESPEARE, *King Henry V*, iii, 7

Lear. Dost thou call me fool, boy?
Fool. All thy other titles thou hast given away; that thou wast born with.
SHAKESPEARE, *King Lear*, i, 4

Better a witty fool than a foolish wit.
SHAKESPEARE, *Twelfth Night*, i, 5

There 's no fool like the old one.
TENNYSON, *The Grandmother*, st. 11

Be wise with speed,
A fool at forty is a fool indeed.
YOUNG, *Love of Fame*, Satire ii, lines 281, 282

Foolery.— Thou little thinkest what a little foolery governs the world. JOHN SELDEN, *Table Talk: Pope*

Fools.— Fools for arguments use wagers.
BUTLER, *Hudibras*, II, i, line 298

We think our fathers fools, so wise we grow,
Our wiser sons, no doubt, will think us so.
POPE, *Essay on Criticism*, lines 438, 439

Fools rush in where angels fear to tread.—*Ibid.*, line 625

What fools these mortals be!
SHAKESPEARE, *Midsummer-Night's Dream*, iii, 2

She was a wight, if ever such wight were,— . . .
To suckle fools and chronicle small beer.
SHAKESPEARE, *Othello*, ii, 1

Men may live fools, but fools they cannot die.
YOUNG, *Night Thoughts*, IV, line 843

Foot.— Now as they bore him off the field,
Said he, "Let others shoot,
For here I leave my second leg,
And the Forty-Second Foot!"
HOOD, *Faithless Nelly Gray*

His very foot has music in 't
As he comes up the stair.
W. J. MICKLE, *The Sailor's Wife*, st. 5

My foot is on my native heath, and my name is MacGregor. SCOTT, *Rob Roy*, xxxiv

Footprints.— Lives of great men all remind us
We can make our lives sublime,
And, departing, leave behind us
Footprints on the sands of time;[1]

Footprints, that perhaps another,
Sailing o'er life's solemn main,
A forlorn and shipwrecked brother,
Seeing, shall take heart again.[2]
LONGFELLOW, *Psalm of Life*, st. 7, 8

Forbear.— The kindest and the happiest pair
Will find occasion to forbear;
And something every day they live
To pity, and perhaps forgive.
COWPER, *Mutual Forbearance*, lines 37–40

Forbearance.— There is, however, a limit at which forbearance ceases to be a virtue. BURKE

---

[1] So from the bosom of darkness our days come roaring and gleaming,
Chafe and break into foam, sink into darkness again.
But on the shores of Time each leaves some trace of its passage,
Though the succeeding wave washes it out from the sand.
LONGFELLOW, *A Fragment*, August 4, 1856

[2] So when a great man dies,
For years beyond our ken,
The light he leaves behind him lies
Upon the paths of men. LONGFELLOW, *Charles Sumner*, st. 9

Force. Who overcomes
By force hath overcome but half his foe.
MILTON, *Paradise Lost*, I, lines 648, 649

Do we must what force will have us do.
SHAKESPEARE, *King Richard II*, iii, 3

Foreign.— By foreign hands thy dying eyes were closed,
By foreign hands thy decent limbs composed,
By foreign hands thy humble grave adorned,
By strangers honoured, and by strangers mourned.
POPE, *Elegy to an Unfortunate Lady*, lines 51-54

Forest.— This is the forest primeval.
LONGFELLOW, *Evangeline*, Introduction, line 1

Forever.— Forever! 'Tis a single word!
And yet our fathers deemed it two:
Nor am I confident they erred;
Are you? C. S. CALVERLY, *Forever*, st. 9

Forget.— The tumult and the shouting dies,—
The Captains and the Kings depart,—
Still stands Thine ancient sacrifice,
An humble and a contrite heart.
Lord God of Hosts, be with us yet,
Lest we forget — lest we forget!

Far-called, our navies melt away,—
On dune and headland sinks the fire,
Lo, all our pomp of yesterday
Is one with Nineveh and Tyre!
Judge of the Nations, spare us yet,
Lest we forget — lest we forget!
KIPLING, *Recessional*, st. 2, 3

Of all affliction taught a lover yet,
'Tis sure the hardest science to forget!
POPE, *Eloïsa to Abélard*, lines 189, 190

Urge me no more, I shall forget myself;
Have mind upon your health, tempt me no further.
SHAKESPEARE, *Julius Cæsar*, iv, 3

Pray you now, forget and forgive.
SHAKESPEARE, *King Lear*, iv, 7

Forgetfulness.— For who, to dumb forgetfulness a prey,
This pleasing, anxious being e'er resigned,
Left the warm precincts of the cheerful day,
Nor cast one longing, lingering look behind?
GRAY, *Elegy Written in a Country Churchyard*, st. 23

Forgetting.— How happy is the blameless vestal's lot!
The world forgetting, by the world forgot.
POPE, *Eloïsa to Abélard*, lines 207, 208

Forgive.— To err is human, to forgive, divine.[1]
POPE, *Essay on Criticism*, line 525

Forgiven. I think, in the lives of most women and men,
There's a moment when all would go smooth and even,
If only the dead could find out when
To come back, and be forgiven.
E. R. BULWER-LYTTON ("OWEN MEREDITH"),
Aux Italiens, st. 27

Forgiveness.— Forgiveness to the injured does belong;
But they ne'er pardon who have done the wrong.[2]
DRYDEN, *Conquest of Granada*, Part II, i, 2

Stretch out your hand to me, Douglas, Douglas,
Drop forgiveness from heaven like dew;
As I lay my heart on your dead heart, Douglas,
Douglas, Douglas, tender and true.
D. M. MULOCK CRAIK, *Too Late*, st. 5

Forgiving.— Our sex are still forgiving at their heart;
And did not wicked custom so contrive,
We'd be the best good-natured things alive.
POPE, *Epilogue to Rowe's Jane Shore*, lines 12–14

Forgotten. When I am forgotten, as I shall be,
And sleep in dull, cold marble, where no mention
Of me more must be heard of, say, I taught thee;
Say, Wolsey, that once trod the ways of glory,
And sounded all the depths and shoals of honour,
Found thee a way, out of his wreck, to rise in;
A sure and safe one, though thy master missed it.
SHAKESPEARE, *King Henry VIII*, iii, 2

Form. Who would keep an ancient form
Through which the spirit breathes no more?
TENNYSON, *In Memoriam*, cv, st. 5

Fortress.— A mighty fortress is our God.
MARTIN LUTHER, *Hymn* (trans. F. H. Hedge), st. 1

---

[1] Father, forgive them; for they know not what they do. *Luke* xxiii, 34

Yet, Lorde, I thee desire,
For that they doe to me,
Let them not taste the hire
Of their iniquitie. ANNE ASKEW, *The Fight of Faith*, st. 14

[2] The offender never pardons. GEORGE HERBERT, *Jacula Prudentum*

Fortune.— Too poor for a bribe, and too proud to importune;
He had not the method of making a fortune.[1]
THOMAS GRAY, *Of Himself*

Fortune, men say, doth give too much to many,
But yet she never gave enough to any.
SIR J. HARRISON, *Epigram*

Nor was it hard to move the lady's mind;
When Fortune favours, still the Fair are kind.
POPE, *January and May*, lines 303, 304

Fortune brings in some boats that are not steered.
SHAKESPEARE, *Cymbeline*, iv, 3

Turn, Fortune, turn thy wheel, and lower the proud;
Turn thy wild wheel through sunshine, storm, and cloud;
. . . . . .
Smile and we smile, the lords of many lands;
Frown and we smile, the lords of our own hands;
For man is man and master of his fate.[2]
TENNYSON, *The Marriage of Geraint*, lines 347-355

Fortunes. We are ready to try our fortunes
To the last man.
SHAKESPEARE, *King Henry IV, Part II*, iv, 2

All the unsettled humours of the land,
. . . . . .
Have sold their fortunes at their native homes,
Bearing their birthrights proudly on their backs,
To make a hazard of new fortunes here.
SHAKESPEARE, *King John*, ii, 1

All my fortunes are at sea.
SHAKESPEARE, *Merchant of Venice*, i, 1

Fossils. The way they heaved those fossils in their anger was a sin,
Till the skull of an old mammoth caved the head of Thompson in.
BRET HARTE, *The Society upon the Stanislaus*, st. 8

Foul. As foul
As Vulcan's stithy. SHAKESPEARE, *Hamlet*, iii, 2

---

[1] Though equal to all things, for all things unfit,
Too nice for a statesman, too proud for a wit:
For a patriot too cool; for a drudge disobedient;
And too fond of the right to pursue the expedient.
GOLDSMITH, *Retaliation*, st. 3

[2] *Cf.* FATE.

Fowls.— When fowls have no feathers, and fish have no fin.
SHAKESPEARE, *Comedy of Errors*, iii, 1

Fox. When the fox hath once got in his nose,
He 'll soon find means to make the body follow.
SHAKESPEARE, *King Henry VI, Part III*, iv, 7

Frailty.— Ye high, exalted, virtuous dames,
Tied up in godly laces,
Before ye gi'e poor Frailty names,
Suppose a change o' cases;
A dear-loved lad, convenience snug,
A treacherous inclination —
But, let me whisper i' your lug,
Ye 're aiblins nae temptation.
BURNS, *Address to the Unco Guid*, st. 6

Frailty, thy name is woman!
SHAKESPEARE, *Hamlet*, i, 2

France.— They order . . . this matter better in France.
STERNE, *A Sentimental Journey*, Introduction

Free.— Free soil, free speech, free labour, and free men.[1]
Slogan of the Free Soil Party, adopted August, 1848

Freedom. Freedom's battle once begun,
Bequeathed by bleeding sire to son,
Though baffled oft, is ever won.
BYRON, *The Giaour*, lines 123–125

Oh, bloodiest picture in the book of Time,
Sarmatia fell, unwept, without a crime;
Found not a generous friend, a pitying foe,
Strength in her arms, nor mercy in her woe!
Dropped from her nerveless grasp the shattered spear,
Closed her bright eye, and curbed her high career —
Hope, for a season, bade the world farewell[2]
And Freedom shrieked — as Kosciusko fell.
CAMPBELL, *Pleasures of Hope*, i, st. 36

What is freedom, but the unfettered use
Of all the powers which God for use had given?
S. T. COLERIDGE, *The Destiny of Nations*, st. 3

The sun that rose on freedom rose in blood. *Ibid.*

---

[1] Free speech, free press, free soil, free men, Frémont, and victory.
Slogan of the Republican Party in the Campaign of 1856

[2] Hope withering fled — and Mercy sighed farewell!*
BYRON, *The Corsair*, Canto i, st. 9

**Cf.* HOPE.

Up with our standard, wide and high, when glory leads the fight,
And let the nations fear our cry of "Freedom and the right."
ELIZA COOK, *Freedom and the Right*, lines 15, 16

Freedom has a thousand charms to show,
That slaves, howe'er contented, never know.
COWPER, *Table Talk*, lines 260, 261

They that fight for freedom undertake
The noblest cause mankind can have at stake.
Ibid., lines 284, 285

What avail the plough or sail,
Or land or life, if freedom fail? EMERSON, *Boston*

Freedom ain't a gift
Thet tarries long in han's o' cowards!
LOWELL, *Biglow Papers*, II, x, st. 21

When a deed is done for Freedom, through the broad earth's aching breast
Runs a thrill of joy prophetic, trembling on from east to west,
And the slave, where'er he cowers, feels the soul within him climb
To the awful verge of manhood, as the energy sublime
Of a century bursts full-blossomed on the thorny stem of Time. LOWELL, *The Present Crisis*, st. 1

Once we thought that holy Freedom
Was a cursed and tainted thing;
Foe of Peace, and Law, and Virtue;
Foe of Magistrate and King;
That all vile degraded passion
Ever followed in her path;
Lust and Plunder, War and Rapine,
Tears and Anarchy and Wrath;
That the angel was a cruel,
Haughty, blood-stained Amazon.
Old opinions! rags and tatters!
Get you gone! get you gone!
CHARLES MACKAY, *Old Opinions*, st. 3

Thus Freedom now so seldom wakes.
The only throb she gives,
Is when some heart indignant breaks,
To show that still she lives.— T. MOORE, *The Harp That Once Through Tara's Halls*, st. 2

Of old sat Freedom on the heights.
TENNYSON, *Of Old Sat Freedom*, st. 1

A land of settled government,
A land of just and old renown,
Where Freedom slowly broadens down
From precedent to precedent.
TENNYSON, *You Ask Me Why*, st. 3

Wherever outraged Nature
Asks word or action brave,
Wherever struggles labour,
Wherever groans a slave,—

Wherever rise the peoples,
Wherever sinks a throne,
The throbbing heart of Freedom finds
An answer in his own.
WHITTIER, *The Hero*, st. 24, 25

Freeman.— He is the freeman whom the truth makes free,
And all are slaves beside.— COWPER, *The Task: The Winter Morning Walk*, lines 733, 734

When your youngest, the mealy-mouthed rector,
Lets your soul rot asleep to the grave,
You will find in your God the protector
Of the freeman you fancied your slave.
KINGSLEY, *The Bad Squire*,[1] st. 19

A weapon that comes down as still
As snow-flakes fall upon the sod;
But executes a freeman's will,
As lightning does the will of God.[2]
JOHN PIERPONT, *A Word from a Petitioner*, st. 14

Showed their fierce zeal a worthier cause,
And brought the freeman's arm to aid the freeman's laws.
SCOTT, *Marmion*, Introd. to Canto i

Frenchman.— The Frenchman's darling [mignonette].
COWPER, *The Task: The Winter Evening*, line 765

Fret.— Fret till your proud heart breaks.
SHAKESPEARE, *Julius Cæsar*, iv, 3

---

[1] Also known as "A Rough Rhyme on a Rough Matter."

[2] Not lightly fall
Beyond recall
The written scrolls a breath can float;
The crowning fact,
The kingliest act
Of Freedom is the freeman's vote!—WHITTIER, *The Eve of Election*, st. 8

Friar.— It was a friar of orders grey[1]
Walked forth to tell his beads;
And he met with a lady fair
Clad in a pilgrim's weeds.
THOMAS PERCY, *The Friar of Orders Grey* (Adapted from old ballads), st. 1

Friend.— To mark a friend's remains these stones arise —
I never knew but one, and here he lies.
BYRON, *Inscription on the Monument of a Newfoundland Dog*, lines 25, 26

Give me the avowed, the erect, the manly foe,
Bold I can meet — perhaps may turn his blow;
But of all plagues, good Heaven, thy wrath can send,
Save, save, oh! save me from the candid friend!
G. CANNING, *New Morality*

A cheer, then, for the noble breast that fears not danger's post;
And, like the lifeboat, proves a friend when friends are wanted most.
ELIZA COOK, *The Lifeboat Is a Gallant Bark*, st. 2

A friend should bear his friend's infirmities,
But Brutus makes mine greater than they are.
SHAKESPEARE, *Julius Cæsar*, iv, 3

The dearest friend to me, the kindest man,
The best-conditioned and unwearied spirit
In doing courtesies, and one in whom
The ancient Roman honour more appears
Than any that draws breath in Italy.
SHAKESPEARE, *Merchant of Venice*, iii, 2

He makes no friend who never made a foe.
TENNYSON, *Lancelot and Elaine*, line 1082

Friends.— None wrote his epitaph, nor saw the beauty
Of the pure love that reached into the grave,
Nor how in unobtrusive ways of duty
He kept, despite the dark; but men less brave
Have left great names, while not a willow bends
Above his dust,— poor Jo, he had no friends!
ALICE CARY, *Uncle Jo*, st. 10

He[2] cast off his friends, as a huntsman his pack,
For he knew when he pleased he could whistle them back.
GOLDSMITH, *Retaliation*, st. 8

---

[1] It was the friar of orders grey,
As he forth walked on his way.
SHAKESPEARE, *Taming of the Shrew*, iv, 1

[2] David Garrick.

Yes, we must ever be friends; and of all who offer you friendship
Let me be ever the first, the truest, the nearest and dearest!

LONGFELLOW, *Courtship of Miles Standish*, vi, lines 72, 73

We have been friends together —
Shall a light word part us now?—LADY CAROLINE NORTON, *We Have Been Friends Together*

Where are my friends? — I am alone,
No playmate shares my beaker —
Some lie beneath the churchyard stone,
And some before the Speaker;
And some compose a tragedy,
And some compose a rondo;
And some draw sword for liberty,
And some draw pleas for John Doe.

PRAED, *School and School-Fellows*, st. 5

Old friends are best. King James used to call for his old shoes; they were easiest for his feet.

JOHN SELDEN, *Table Talk: Friends*

Those [The] friends thou hast, and their adoption tried,
Grapple them to thy soul with hoops of steel;
But do not dull thy palm with entertainment
Of each new-hatched, unfledged comrade.

SHAKESPEARE, *Hamlet*, i, 3

You knot of mouth-friends!

SHAKESPEARE, *Timon of Athens*, iii, 6

Friendship.— Friendship's the wine of life; but friendship new
(Not such was his) is neither strong nor pure.

YOUNG, *Night Thoughts*, II, lines 588, 589

Friendships.— So vanish friendships only made in wine.

TENNYSON, *Geraint and Enid*, line 479

Front.— To front a lie in arms and not to yield.

LOWELL, *Commemoration Ode*, st. 5

Frown.— Fear no more the frown o' the great;
Thou art past the tyrant's stroke.

SHAKESPEARE, *Cymbeline*, iv, 2

Fruit.— The ripest fruit first falls.

SHAKESPEARE, *King Richard II*, ii, 1

The weakest kind of fruit
Drops earliest to the ground.

SHAKESPEARE, *Merchant of Venice*, iv, 1

The tree that bears no fruit deserves no name.
YOUNG, *Night Thoughts*, V, line 774

Fuel.— Adding fuel to the flame.
MILTON, *Samson Agonistes*, line 1351

Fun.— There's fun in everything we meet,—
The greatest, worst, and best;
Existence is a merry treat,
And every speech a jest.
J. R. DRAKE, *The Man Who Frets at Strife*, st. 2

Funeral. The funeral baked meats
Did coldly furnish forth the marriage tables.
SHAKESPEARE, *Hamlet*, i, 2

Future.— Trust no Future, howe'er pleasant!
Let the dead Past bury its dead!
LONGFELLOW, *Psalm of Life*, st. 6

O masters, lords and rulers in all lands,
How will the Future reckon with this man?
How answer his brute question in that hour
When whirlwinds of rebellion shake the world?
How will it be with kingdoms and with kings
With those who shaped him to the thing he is —
When this dumb Terror shall reply to God,
After the silence of the centuries?
EDWIN MARKHAM, *The Man with the Hoe*, st. 6

I know not what the future hath
Of marvel or surprise,
Assured alone that life and death
His mercy underlies.
WHITTIER, *The Eternal Goodness*, st. 16

Fuzzy-Wuzzy.— So 'ere's *to* you, Fuzzy-Wuzzy, at your 'ome in the Soudan;
You're a pore benighted 'eathen, but a first-class fightin' man;
An ere's *to* you, Fuzzy-Wuzzy, with your 'ayrick 'ead of 'air —
You big black boundin' beggar — for you broke a British square!
KIPLING, *Fuzzy-Wuzzy*

Gaberdine.— You call me misbeliever, cut-throat dog,
And spit upon my Jewish gaberdine,
And all for use of that which is mine own.
SHAKESPEARE, *Merchant of Venice*, i, 3

Gale. The gale was high,
The sea was all a boiling seething froth,
And God Almighty's guns were going off,
And the land trembled.
JEAN INGELOW, *Brothers, and a Sermon*

Gall.— Let there be gall enough in thy ink, though thou write with a goose-pen. SHAKESPEARE, *Twelfth Night*, iii, 2

Game.— There's blood on your new foreign shrubs, squire,
There's blood on your pointer's feet;
There's blood on the game you sell, squire,
And there's blood on the game you eat.
KINGSLEY, *The Bad Squire*,[1] st. 8

The game is up. SHAKESPEARE, *Cymbeline*, iii, 3

Gangrened. Gangrened members must be lopped away,
Before the nobler parts are tainted to decay.
DRYDEN, *Ovid's Metamorphoses*, I, lines 248, 249

Garden.— Come into the garden, Maud,
For the black bat, night, has flown,
Come into the garden, Maud,
I am here at the gate alone.
TENNYSON, *Maud*, xxii, st. 1

Gardener.— Trust me, Clara Vere de Vere,
From yon blue heavens above us bent
The gardener Adam and his wife
Smile at the claims of long descent.
Howe'er it be, it seems to me,
'T is only noble to be good.[2]
Kind hearts are more than coronets,
And simple faith than Norman blood.
TENNYSON, *Lady Clara Vere de Vere*, st. 7

Garret.— Born in the garret, in the kitchen bred.
BYRON, *Sketch from Private Life*, st. 1

Gate.— Claps the gate behind thee.
COWPER, *On a Mischievous Bull*, st. 6

Gay.— Lady, when first your mirth
Flung magic o'er my way,
Mine was the gayest soul on earth
When all the earth was gay;
My songs were full of joy,—
You might have let them flow;
My heart was every woman's toy,—
You might have left it so! PRAED, *The Parting*, st. 5

Gazelle.— I never nursed a dear gazelle
To glad me with its soft black eye,
But when it came to know me well
And love me it was sure to die!
T. MOORE, *Lalla Rookh: The Fire-Worshippers*

---

[1] Also known as "A Rough Rhyme on a Rough Matter."

[2] We'll shine in more substantial honours,
And to be noble we'll be good. ANONYMOUS, *Winifreda*, st. 2

Gem.— Full many a gem of purest ray serene
The dark, unfathomed caves of ocean bear;
Full many a flower is born to blush unseen,
And waste its sweetness on the desert air.
GRAY, *Elegy Written in a Country Churchyard*, st. 15

If thou hast crushed a flower,
The root may not be blighted;
If thou hast quenched a lamp,
Once more it may be lighted:
. . . . .
But if upon the troubled sea
Thou hast thrown a gem unheeded,
Hope not that wind or wave will bring
The treasure back when needed.
FELICIA HEMANS, *If Thou Hast Crushed a Flower*, st. 1, 2

Gems.— Rich and rare were the gems she wore,
And a bright gold ring on her wand she bore;
But oh! her beauty was far beyond
Her sparkling gems, or snow-white wand.
T. MOORE, *Rich and Rare, etc.*, st. 1

Generalities.— The glittering and sounding generalities of natural right which make up the Declaration of Independence.—RUFUS CHOATE, *Letter to Maine Whig Committee*, Aug. 9, 1856

Genteelly.— Heaven grant him now some noble nook,
For, rest his soul! he 'd rather be
Genteelly damned beside a Duke,
Than saved in vulgar company.
T. MOORE, *Epitaph on a Tuft-Hunter*, st. 5

Gentleman.— I 'll sing you a good old song,
Made by a good old pate,
Of a fine old English gentleman
Who had an old estate,
And who kept up his old mansion
At a bountiful old rate;
With a good old porter to relieve
The old poor at his gate,
Like a fine old English gentleman
All of the olden time.
ANONYMOUS, *The Fine Old English Gentleman*, st. 1

When Adam dolve, and Eve span,
Who was then the gentleman?
Of uncertain origin; alleged to be cited by JOHN BALL during Wat Tyler's Rebellion

That gentilman Jhesus.
JULIANA BERNERS, *Heraldic Blazonry*

Loke who that is most vertuous alway,
Privee and apert, and most entendeth ay
To do the gentil dedes that he can,[1]
And tak him for the grettest gentilman.
CHAUCER, *The Wife of Bath's Tale*, lines 257–260

First Clown. There is no ancient gentlemen but gardeners, ditchers, and grave-makers: they hold up Adam's profession.
Second Clown. Was he a gentleman?
First Clown. He was the first that ever bore arms.
SHAKESPEARE, *Hamlet*, v, 1

A kinder gentleman treads not the earth.
SHAKESPEARE, *Merchant of Venice*, ii, 8

And thus he bore without abuse
The grand old name of gentleman,
Defamed by every charlatan,
And soiled with all ignoble use.
TENNYSON, *In Memoriam*, cxi, st. 6

O selfless man and stainless gentleman,
Who would'st against thine own eye-witness fain
Have all men true and leal, all women pure.
TENNYSON, *Merlin and Vivien*, lines 790–792

Come wealth or want, come good or ill,
Let young and old accept their part,
And bow before the Awful Will,
And bear it with an honest heart,
Who misses or who wins the prize.
Go, lose or conquer as you can;
But if you fail, or if you rise,
Be each, pray God, a gentleman.
THACKERAY, *The End of the Play*, st. 9

Gentlemen.— The would-be wits and can't-be gentlemen.
BYRON, *Beppo*, st. 76

Like two single gentlemen rolled into one.
G. COLMAN THE YOUNGER, *Lodgings for Single Gentlemen*

---

[1] He is gentil that doth gentil dedis.
CHAUCER, *The Wife of Bath's Tale*, line 314

The gentle minde by gentle deeds is knowne,
For a man by nothing is so well betrayd
As by his manners. SPENSER, *Faerie Queene*, VI, Canto iii, st. 1

German.— A graceless, worthless wight thou must be;
No German maid desires thee,
No German song inspires thee,
No German Rhine-wine fires thee.
Forth in the van,
Man by man,
Swing the battle-sword who can.
KARL T. KÖRNER, *Men and Boys* (trans. C. T. Brooks), st. 1

Getting-up.— Let Taylor preach upon a morning breezy,
How well to rise while nights and larks are flying —
For my part getting up seems not so easy
By half as *lying*.

. . . . .

Talk not to me of bees and such like hums,[1]
The smell of sweet herbs at the morning prime —
Only lie long enough, and bed becomes
A bed of *time*.

. . . . .

An early riser Mr. Gray has drawn,
Who used to haste the dewy grass among,
"To meet the sun upon the upland lawn"—
Well — he died young.
HOOD, *Morning Meditations*, st. 1, 3, 8

Ghosts.— Mysterious one, and proud!
In the land where shadows reign,
Hast thou met the flocking ghosts of those
Who at thy nod were slain?
Oh, when the cry of that spectral host
Like a rushing blast shall be,
What will thine answer be to them?
And what thy God's to thee?— L. H. SIGOURNEY,
The Return of Napoleon from St. Helena, st. 14

Giant. Oh! it is excellent
To have a giant's strength; but it is tyrannous
To use it like a giant.
SHAKESPEARE, *Measure for Measure*, ii, 2

Giddy.— He that is giddy thinks the world turns round.
SHAKESPEARE, *Taming of the Shrew*, v, 2

Gift-horse. Loth
To look a gift-horse in the mouth.[2]
BUTLER, *Hudibras*, I, i, lines 489, 490

---

[1] A colloquial abbreviation of "humbugs."

[2] He always looked a gift-horse in the mouth. RABELAIS, I, xi

Gild.— To gild refined gold, to paint the lily,
To throw a perfume on the violet,
To smooth the ice, or add another hue
Unto the rainbow, or with taper-light
To seek the beauteous eye of heaven to garnish,
Is wasteful and ridiculous excess.[1]
SHAKESPEARE, *King John*, iv, 2

Girdle.— I'll put a girdle round about the earth
In forty minutes.[2]
SHAKESPEARE, *Midsummer-Night's Dream*, ii, 1

Glad.— Be glad, and your friends are many;
Be sad, and you lose them all;
There are none to decline your nectared wine,
But alone you must drink life's gall.
ELLA WHEELER WILCOX, *Solitude*, st. 2

Gladiator.— I see before me the gladiator lie:
He leans upon his hand — his manly brow
Consents to death, but conquers agony.
BYRON, *Childe Harold's Pilgrimage*, Canto iv, st. 140

Glass.— And when like her, oh Sáki, you shall pass
Among the guests star-scattered on the grass,
And in your joyous [blissful] errand reach the spot
Where I made one — turn down an empty glass.
OMAR KHAYYÁM, *Rubáiyát* (trans. Fitzgerald), st. 101

The generous glass . . . inspired to wake
The life-refining soul of decent wit.
THOMSON, *The Seasons*, Autumn, lines 88, 89

Glisten.— God made sech nights, all white and still
Fur 'z you can look or listen,
Moonshine an' snow on field an' hill,
All silence an' all glisten.—LOWELL, *The Courtin'*, st. 1

Glory.— The combat deepens. On, ye brave,
Who rush to glory, or the grave![3]
CAMPBELL, *Hohenlinden*, st. 7

---

[1] True coral needs no painter's brush,
Nor need be daubed with red.
G. W. THORNBURY, *The Jester's Sermon*, st. 14

[2] Away! away! through the sightless air
Stretch forth your iron thread!
For I would not dim my sandals fair
With the dust ye tamely tread!
Ay, rear it up on its million piers,
Let it circle the world around,
And the journey ye make in a hundred years
I'll clear at a single bound!
G. W. CUTTER, *Song of the Lightning*, st. 1

[3] Who track the steps of glory to the grave.
BYRON, *Death of Sheridan*, line 74

Mine eyes have seen the glory of the coming of the Lord:
He is trampling out the vintage where the grapes of wrath are stored;
He hath loosed the fateful lightning of his terrible swift sword:
His truth is marching on.—JULIA WARD HOWE,
Battle-Hymn of the Republic, st. 1

Go where glory waits thee. T. MOORE, *Irish Melodies*

I have ventured,
Like little wanton boys that swim on bladders,
This many summers in a sea of glory,
But far beyond my depth: my high-blown pride
At length broke under me, and now has left me,
Weary and old with service, to the mercy
Of a rude stream, that must for ever hide me.
SHAKESPEARE, *King Henry VIII*, iii, 2

Slowly and sadly we laid him down,
From the field of his fame fresh and gory;
We carved not a line, and we raised not a stone —
But we left him alone with his glory.
CHARLES WOLFE, *Burial of Sir John Moore*, st. 8

Gloves.— Wear seemly gloves; not black, nor yet too light,
And least of all the pair that once was white;

. . . . .

Shave like the goat, if so your fancy bids,
But be a parent,— don't neglect your kids.
HOLMES, *A Rhymed Lesson*, st. 49

Glow-worm.— The glow-worm shows the matin to be near,
And 'gins to pale his ineffectual fire.
SHAKESPEARE, *Hamlet*, i, 5

Goblet.— Alas for the loved one! too spotless and fair
The joys of his banquet to chasten and share;
Her eye lost its light that his goblet might shine,
And the rose of her cheek was dissolved in his wine.
HOLMES, *Song for a Temperance Dinner*, st. 3

Goblins.— The Gobble-uns 'll git you ef you don't watch out!
JAMES WHITCOMB RILEY, *Little Orphant Annie*

God.— It were better to have no opinion of God at all than such an opinion as is unworthy of Him.
BACON, *Essay XVII: Of Superstition*

Earth's crammed with heaven,
And every common bush afire with God.
E. B. BROWNING, *Aurora Leigh*, VII, lines 850, 851

God—*Continued*

I smiled to think God's greatness flowed around our incompleteness,—
'Round our restlessness, His rest.— ELIZABETH B. BROWNING, *Rhyme of the Duchess May, ad finem*

God's in his heaven —
All's right with the world![1]
R. BROWNING, *Pippa Passes*, i

The Muezza's call doth shake the minaret,
"There is no god but God! — to prayer — lo! God is great!"
BYRON, *Childe Harold's Pilgrimage*, Canto ii, st. 59

We hailed it in God's name.
COLERIDGE, *Ancient Mariner*, line 66

So lonely 'twas, that God himself
Scarce seemed there to be. *Ibid.*, lines 599, 600

Earth, with her thousand voices, praises God.
S. T. COLERIDGE, *Hymn Before Sunrise*, line 85

God moves in a mysterious way
His wonders to perform;
He plants his footsteps in the sea,
And rides upon the storm.[2]
COWPER, *Light Shining out of Darkness*, st. 1

---

[1]God reigneth. All is well! HOLMES, *Hymn*, 3

When the wind blows, the blossoms fall,
But a good God reigns over all!
CHARLES MACKAY, *The Child and the Mourners*

Before me, even as behind,
God is, and all is well! WHITTIER, *My Birthday*, st. 2

[2]God hath his mysteries of grace,
Ways that we cannot tell;
He hides them deep, like the secret sleep
Of him he loved so well. C. F. ALEXANDER, *Burial of Moses*, st. 10

God is a spirit,* veiled from human sight,
In secret darkness of eternal light;
Through all the glory of his works we trace
The hidings of his council and his face;
Nature, and time, and change, and fate fulfil,
Unknown, unknowing, his mysterious will;
Mercies and judgments mark him, every hour,
Supreme in grace, and infinite in power.
JAMES MONTGOMERY, *The West Indies*, iii, st. 15

---

*God is a spirit. *John* iv, 24

God is his own interpreter[1]
  And he will make it plain. *Ibid.*, st. 6

Oh! for a closer walk with God!
COWPER, *Walking with God*, st. 1

With ravished ears
The monarch hears,
    Assumes the god,
    Affects to nod,
And seems to shake the spheres.
DRYDEN, *Alexander's Feast*, lines 37–41

To thee I turn, to thee I make my prayer,
    God of the open air.
. . . . .

For men have dulled their eyes with sin,
And dimmed the light of heaven with doubt,
And built their temple walls to shut thee in,
And framed their iron creeds to shut thee out.
HENRY VAN DYKE, *God of the Open Air*, st. 1, 3

"Come to thy God in time!"
Rang out Tintagel chime.
"Youth, manhood, old age, past,
Come to thy God at last!"
R. S. HAWKER, *Silent Tower of Bottreaux*, st. 3

    One unquestioned text we read,
  All doubt beyond, all fear above,
Nor crackling pile nor cursing creed
  Can burn or blot it: God is Love![2]
HOLMES, *What We All Think*, st. 10

Man proposes, but God disposes.
THOMAS À KEMPIS, *Imitation of Christ*, I, xix, 2

---

[1] Do not tell me the Almighty Master
  Would work a miracle to save the one,
And yield the other up to dire disaster,*
  By merely human justice thus outdone!

Vainly we weep and wrestle with our sorrow—
  We cannot see his roads, they lie so broad:
But his eternal day knows no to-morrow,
  And life and death are all the same with God.
CELIA THAXTER, *Wherefore*, st. 10, 11

[2] God! Thou art love! I build my faith on that.
R. BROWNING, *Paracelsus*, v

* Alluding to the narrow escape of one ship from wreck on an iceberg, and the destruction of another without warning.

God—*Continued*

As the marsh-hen secretly builds on the watery sod,
Behold I will build me a nest on the greatness of God:

. . . . .

By so many roots as the marsh-grass sends in the sod
I will heartily lay me a-hold on the greatness of God.
LANIER, *The Marshes of Glynn*, st. 8

Ye whose hearts are fresh and simple,
Who have faith in God and Nature,
Who believe, that in all ages
Every human heart is human,
That in even savage bosoms
There are longings, yearnings, strivings
For the good they comprehend not,
That the feeble hands and helpless
Groping blindly in the darkness,
Touch God's right hand in that darkness
And are lifted up and strengthened;
Listen to this simple story,
To this song of Hiawatha!—LONGFELLOW, *Song of Hiawatha*, Introduction, lines 88–100

Ef you take a sword an' dror it,
An' go stick a feller thru,
Guv'ment ain't to answer for it,
God'll send the bill to you.
LOWELL, *Biglow Papers*, I, i, 6

I ha'n't no patience with sech swellin' fellers ez
Think God can't forge 'thout them to blow the bellerses.
Ibid., II, ii, lines 169, 170

O God! thy arm was here;
And not to us, but to thy arm alone,
Ascribe we all.

. . . . .

And be it death proclaimed through our host
To boast of this or take that praise from God
Which is his only.

. . . . .

Let there be sung "Non nobis" and "Te Deum."
SHAKESPEARE, *King Henry V*, iv, 8

You are one of those that will not serve God, if the devil bid you. SHAKESPEARE, *Othello, i*, 1

God b' wi' you, with all my heart.
SHAKESPEARE, *Troilus and Cressida*, iii, 3

By the splendour of God![1]
Cited in STERNE, *Tristram Shandy*, III, xii

[1] The favourite oath of William the Conqueror.

A God all mercy is a God unjust.
YOUNG, *Night Thoughts*, IV, line 234

Goddess.— Vows for thee broke deserve not punishment.
A woman I forswore; but I will prove,
Thou being a goddess, I forswore not thee:
My vow was earthly, thou a heavenly love.
SHAKESPEARE, *Love's Labour's Lost*, iv, 3

Godlike.— The seeds of Godlike power are in us still.
MATTHEW ARNOLD, *Written in Emerson's Essays*, st. 4

Gods. What can be avoided
Whose end is purposed by the mighty gods?
SHAKESPEARE, *Julius Cæsar*, ii, 2

God's-Acre.— I like that ancient Saxon phrase, which calls
The burial-ground God's-Acre! It is just;
It consecrates each grave within its walls,
And breathes a benison o'er the sleeping dust.
LONGFELLOW, *God's-Acre*, st. 1

Going. Men must endure
Their going hence, even as their coming hither:
Ripeness is all. SHAKESPEARE, *King Lear*, v, 2

Stand not upon the order of your going,
But go at once. SHAKESPEARE, *Macbeth*, iii, 4

Gold.— Gold! Gold! Gold! Gold!
Bright and yellow, hard and cold,
Molten, graven, hammered, and rolled:
Heavy to get, and light to hold;
Hoarded, bartered, bought, and sold,
Stolen, borrowed, squandered, doled:
Spurned by the young, but hugged by the old
To the very verge of the churchyard mould;
Price of many a crime untold;
Gold! Gold! Gold! Gold:
Good or bad a thousandfold!
How widely its agencies vary —
To save — to ruin — to curse — to bless —
As even its minted coins express,
Now stamped with the image of Good Queen Bess,
And now of a Bloody Mary![1]
HOOD, *Miss Kilmansegg*, Her Moral

[1] Gold hath the hue of hell flames.— BAILEY, *Festus*, Scene — Anywhere.

That gold, for which unpitied Indians fell,
That gold, at once the snare and scourge of hell,
Thenceforth by righteous Heaven was doomed to shed
Unmingled curses on the spoiler's head;
For gold the Spaniard cast his soul away,—
His gold and he were every nation's prey.
JAMES MONTGOMERY, *The West Indies*, i, st. 12

He buys, he sells, he steals, he kills for gold. *Ibid.*, iii, st. 9

Gold provokes the world to arms.
T. MOORE, *Odes of Anacreon*, xxix

Judges and senates have been bought for gold,[1]
Esteem and love were never to be sold.
POPE, *Essay on Man*, Epistle iv, lines 187, 188

Gold must be tried by fire,
As a heart must be tried by pain!
A. A. PROCTER, *Cleansing Fires*, st. 1

All gold and silver rather turn to dirt!
And [As] 't is no better reckoned, but of those
Who worship dirty gods.—SHAKESPEARE, *Cymbeline*, iii, 6

All, as they say, that glitters, is not gold.[2]
DRYDEN, *The Hind and the Panther*, line 787

There is thy gold, worse poison to men's souls,
Doing more murders in this loathsome world,
Than these poor compounds that thou mayst not sell.
SHAKESPEARE, *Romeo and Juliet*, v, 1

Though authority be a stubborn bear, yet he is oft led by the nose with gold: show the inside of your purse to the outside of his hand, and no more ado.
SHAKESPEARE, *Winter's Tale*, iv, 4 [3]

Ring out the narrowing lust of gold.
TENNYSON, *In Memoriam*, cvi, st. 7

Gone.— Not dead but gone before.[3] ROGERS, *Human Life*

---

[1] Saint-seducing gold. SHAKESPEARE, *Romeo and Juliet*, i, 1

[2] Al thing, which that shyneth as the gold
Nis nat gold, as that I have herd it told.
CHAUCER, *The Chanouns Yemannes Tale*, lines 409, 410

Nor all that glisters gold. GRAY, *On a Favourite Cat*, st. 7

All is not gold that glisters. HERBERT, *Jacula Prudentum*

All is not golde that outward sheweth bright.
LYDGATE, *On Human Affairs*

All is not gold that glisteneth. MIDDLETON, *A Fair Quarrel*, v, 1

All that glisters is not gold. SHAKESPEARE, *Merchant of Venice*, ii, 7

Yet gold al is not that doth golden seeme.
SPENSER, *Faerie Queene*, II, 8, st. 14

[3] Gone before
To that unknown and silent shore. LAMB, *Hester*

Good.— It's wiser being good than bad;[1]
It's safer being meek than fierce:
It's fitter being sane than mad.
My own hope is, a sun will pierce
The thickest cloud earth ever stretched;
That, after Last, returns the First,
Though a wide compass 'round be fetched;
That what began best, can't end worst,
Nor what God blessed once, prove accursed.
R. BROWNING, *Apparent Failure*, st. 7

Too high for common selfishness, he could
At times resign his own for others' good,
But not in pity, not because he ought,
But in some strange perversity of thought,
That swayed him onward with a secret pride
To do what few or none would do beside.
BYRON, *Lara*, Canto i, st. 18

The strong gods pine for my abode,
And pine in vain the sacred Seven;
But thou, meek lover of the good!
Find me, and turn thy back on heaven.
EMERSON, *Brahma*, st. 4

Learn the luxury of doing good.
GOLDSMITH, *The Traveller*, st. 2

There's a good time coming, boys,
A good time coming:
We may not live to see the day,
But earth shall glisten in the ray
Of the good time coming.
Cannon-balls may aid the truth,
But thought's a weapon stronger;
We'll win our battle by its aid;
Wait a little longer.
CHARLES MACKAY, *The Good Time Coming*, st. 1

When the good man yields his breath
(For the good man never dies),
Bright beyond the gulf of death,
Lo! the land of promise lies.—JAMES MONTGOMERY,
The Wanderer of Switzerland, v, st. 1

Can one desire too much of a good thing?
SHAKESPEARE, *As You Like It*, iv, 1

It is not nor it cannot come to good.
SHAKESPEARE, *Hamlet*, i, 2

---

[1] Better, though difficult, the right way to go,
Than wrong,— though easy, where the end is woe.
BUNYAN, *Pilgrim's Progress*, I, stage iii

It was alway[s] yet the trick of our English nation, if they have a good thing, to make it too common.
SHAKESPEARE, *King Henry IV, Part II*, i, 2

What care I who calls me well or ill,
So you o'er-green my bad, my good allow?
SHAKESPEARE, *Sonnet* cxii

Oh, yet we trust that somehow good
Will be the final goal of ill,
To pangs of nature, sins of will,
Defects of doubt, and taints of blood;

That nothing walks with aimless feet;
That not one life shall be destroyed,
Or cast as rubbish to the void,
When God hath made the pile complete;

That not a worm is cloven in vain;
That not a moth with vain desire
Is shrivelled in a fruitless fire,
Or but subserves another's gain.
TENNYSON, *In Memoriam*, liv, st. 1-3

Ring in the common love of good. *Ibid.*, cvi, st. 6

From seeming evil still educing good.
JAMES THOMSON, *Hymn on the Seasons*, line 114

Prayers of love like rain-drops fall,
Tears of pity are cooling dew,
And dear to the heart of our Lord are all
Who suffer like Him in the good they do!
WHITTIER, *The Robin*, st. 7

Goodness.— There is some soul of goodness in things evil,
Would men observingly distil it out.
SHAKESPEARE, *King Henry V*, iv, 1

A most incomparable man, breathed, as it were,
To an untirable and continuate goodness.
SHAKESPEARE, *Timon of Athens*, i, 1

The wrong that pains my soul below
I dare not throne above:
I know not of His hate,— I know
His goodness and His love.
WHITTIER, *The Eternal Goodness*, st. 13

Good-night.— My native land — good-night!
BYRON, *Childe Harold's Pilgrimage*. Canto i, st. 13 (1)

Gordian.— Turn him to any cause of policy,
The Gordian knot of it he will unloose,
Familiar as his garter.—SHAKESPEARE, *King Henry V*, i, 1

Gorgons.— Gorgons, and Hydras, and Chimæras dire.
MILTON, *Paradise Lost*, II, line 628

Gospel.— The gospel's sound, diffused from pole to pole,
Where winds can carry, and where waves can roll.
DRYDEN, *The Hind and the Panther*, lines 1124, 1125

Gossips.— By this the lazy gossips of the port,
Abhorrent of a calculation crossed,
Began to chafe as at a personal wrong.
TENNYSON, *Enoch Arden*, lines 469–471

Govern.— The right divine of kings to govern wrong.
POPE, *The Dunciad*, IV, line 188

Government.— Th' older a guv'ment is, the better 't suits;
New ones hunt folks's corns out like new boots.
LOWELL, *Biglow Papers*, II, ii, lines 311 312

For forms of government let fools contest;
Whate'er is best administered is best;
POPE, *Essay on Man*, Epistle iii, lines 303, 304

Governments.— To secure these rights, governments are instituted among men, deriving their just powers from the consent of the governed.
THOMAS JEFFERSON, *Declaration of Independencc*

Gown.— I never saw a better-fashioned gown,
More quaint, more pleasing, nor more commendable.
SHAKESPEARE, *Taming of the Shrew*, iv, 3

I passed beside the reverend walls
In which of old I wore the gown.
TENNYSON, *In Memoriam*, lxxxvii, st. 1

Grace.— Grace was in all her steps, heaven in her eye,
In every gesture dignity and love.
MILTON, *Paradise Lost*, VIII, lines 488, 489

Break, break, break,
At the foot of thy crags, O Sea!
But the tender grace of a day that is dead
Will never come back to me.
TENNYSON, *Break, Break*, st. 4

Gracious. He is gracious, if he be observed:
He hath a tear for pity, and a hand
Open as day for melting charity:
Yet notwithstanding, being incensed, he's flint,
As humourous as winter, and as sudden
As flaws congealed in the spring of day.
SHAKESPEARE, *King Henry IV*, *Part II*, iv, 4

Graduates.— With prudes for proctors, dowagers for deans,
And sweet girl-graduates in their golden hair.
TENNYSON, *The Princess*, Prologue, lines 141, 142

Granary.— The exhaustless granary of a world.
THOMSON, *The Seasons*, Spring, line 77

Grandam. Go to it grandam, child;
Give grandam kingdom, and it grandam will
Give it a plum, a cherry, and a fig:
There's a good grandam.
SHAKESPEARE, *King John*, ii, 1

Grant.— "I was with Grant" —the stranger said;
Said the farmer, "Say no more,
But rest thee here at my cottage porch,
For thy feet are weary and sore."
. . . . .
Said the aged man,
"[I] should have remarked before,
That I was with Grant,— in Illinois,—
Some three years before the war."
BRET HARTE, *The Aged Stranger*, st. 1, 7

Grape.— The Grape that can with logic absolute
The two-and-seventy jarring sects confute;[1]
The sovereign Alchemist that in a trice
Life's leaden metal into gold transmute.
OMAR KHAYYÁM, *Rubáiyát* (trans. Fitzgerald), st. 59

Grass.— He gave it for his opinion, that whoever could make two ears of corn, or two blades of grass, to grow upon a spot of ground where only one grew before, would deserve better of mankind, and do more essential service to his country, than the whole race of politicians put together. SWIFT, *Voyage to Brobdingnag*, vii

Grave. The grave, dread thing!
Men shiver when thou 'rt named; Nature, appalled,
Shakes off her wonted firmness.
R. BLAIR, *The Grave*, lines 9–11

Happy who in his verse can gently steer,
From grave to light; from pleasant to severe.[2]
DRYDEN, *Art of Poetry*, lines 75, 76

---

[1] These principles your jarring sects unite,
When differing doctors and disciples fight.
DRYDEN, *The Hind and the Panther*, lines 686, 687

[2] Formed by thy converse, happily to steer
From grave to gay, from lively to severe.
POPE, *Essay on Man*, Epistle iv, lines 379, 380

The boast of heraldry, the pomp of power,
  And all that beauty, all that wealth e'er gave,
Await alike the inevitable hour;
  The paths of glory lead but to the grave.
GRAY, *Elegy Written in a Country Churchyard*, st. 10

Thou art gone to the grave; but we will not deplore thee,
Though sorrows and darkness encompass the tomb.
R. HEBER, *At a Funeral*, ii

Sat by some nameless grave, and thought that perhaps in its bosom
He was already at rest, and she longed to slumber beside him.
LONGFELLOW, *Evangeline*, II, i, lines 32, 33

Where are the others? Voices from the deep
Caverns of darkness answer me: "They sleep!"
I name no names; instinctively I feel
Each at some well-remembered grave will kneel,
And from the inscription wipe the weeds and moss,
For every heart best knoweth its own loss.
LONGFELLOW, *Morituri Salutamus*, st. 13

Art is long, and Time is fleeting,
  And our hearts, though stout and brave,
Still, like muffled drums, are beating
  Funeral marches to the grave.
LONGFELLOW, *Psalm of Life*, st. 4

Lend, lend your wings! I mount! I fly!
O Grave! where is thy victory?
  O Death! where is thy sting?
POPE, *Dying Christian to His Soul*, st. 3

Quiet consummation have;
And renowned be thy grave!
SHAKESPEARE, *Cymbeline*, iv, 2

Taking the measure of an unmade grave.
SHAKESPEARE, *Romeo and Juliet*, iii, 3

The earth can yield me but a common grave.
SHAKESPEARE, *Sonnet* lxxxi

Under the wide and starry sky,
Dig the grave and let me lie.
Glad did I live and gladly die,
  And I laid me down with a will.

This be the verse you grave for me:
Here he lies where he longed to be;
Home is the sailor, home from sea,
  And the hunter home from the hill.
R. L. STEVENSON, *Requiem*

Who knows the inscrutable design?
  Blessed be He who took and gave!
Why should your mother, Charles, not mine,
  Be weeping at her darling's grave?

THACKERAY, *The End of the Play*, st. 6

With one foot in the grave.

WORDSWORTH, *Michael*, line 90

Grave-maker.— What is he that builds stronger than either the mason, the shipwright, or the carpenter? . . . When you are asked this question next, say "a grave-maker": the houses that he makes last till domes-day.

SHAKESPEARE, *Hamlet*, v, 1

Graves.— Let 's talk of graves, of worms, and epitaphs;
Make dust our paper, and with rainy eyes
Write sorrow on the bosom of the earth.

SHAKESPEARE, *King Richard II*, iii, 2

Grease.— Melted him in his own grease.

SHAKESPEARE, *Merry Wives of Windsor*, ii, 1

Great.— Great on the bench, great in the saddle.

BUTLER, *Hudibras*, I, i, line 23

The great man never falls.

W. W. LORD, *On the Defeat of a Great Man*, st. 1

Rightly to be great
Is not to stir without great argument,
But greatly to find quarrel in a straw
When honour 's at the stake.

SHAKESPEARE, *Hamlet*, iv, 4

Some are born great, some achieve greatness, and some have greatness thrust upon 'em [them].

SHAKESPEARE, *Twelfth Night*, ii, 5

Greater.— Four things greater than all things are,
Women and horses and power and war.

KIPLING, *Ballad of the King's Jest*, st. 4

Greatness.— Farewell, a long farewell to all my greatness!
This is the state of man: to-day he puts forth
The tender leaves of hope; to-morrow blossoms,
And bears his blushing honours thick upon him;
The third day comes a frost, a killing frost,
And, when he thinks, good easy man, full surely
His greatness is a-ripening, nips his root,
And then he falls, as I do.

SHAKESPEARE, *King Henry VIII*, iii, 2

Greed.— Down all the stretch of hell to its last gulf
There is no shape more terrible than this —
More tongued with censure of the world's blind greed —
More filled with signs and portents for the soul —
More fraught with menace to the universe.
EDWIN MARKHAM, *The Man With the Hoe*, st. 2

Greek.— Beside, 't is known he could speak Greek
As naturally as pigs squeak;
That Latin was no more difficile
Than to a blackbird 't is to whistle.
BUTLER, *Hudibras*, I, i, lines 51–54

It was Greek to me. SHAKESPEARE, *Julius Cæsar*, i, 2

Greeks.— When Greeks joined Greeks, then was the tug of war. NATHANIEL LEE, *Alexander the Great*, iv, 2

Green.— Green grow the rashes, oh!
Green grow the rashes, oh!
The sweetest hours that e'er I spent,
Were spent amang the lasses, oh!
BURNS, *Green Grow the Rashes*

On the dry smooth-shaven green.
MILTON, *Il Penseroso*, line 66

Greenwood.— Under the greenwood tree
Who loves to lie with me.
SHAKESPEARE, *As You Like It*, ii, 5

Grief.— Inward grief was writhing o'er its task,
As heart-sick jesters weep behind the mask.
HOOD, *Hero and Leander*, st. 29

Grief fills the room up of my absent child,
Lies in his bed, walks up and down with me;
Puts on his pretty looks, repeats his words,
Remembers me of all his gracious parts,
Stuffs out his vacant garments with his form:
Then, have I reason to be fond of grief.
SHAKESPEARE, *King John*, iii, 4

Grief makes one hour ten.
SHAKESPEARE, *King Richard II*, i, 3

Give sorrow words; the grief that does not speak
Whispers the o'er-fraught heart, and bids it break.
SHAKESPEARE, *Macbeth*, iv, 3

Every one can master a grief but he that has it.
SHAKESPEARE, *Much Ado about Nothing*, iii, 2

Patch grief with proverbs. *Ibid.*, v, 1

When griping grief the heart doth wound,
And doleful dumps the mind oppress.
SHAKESPEARE, *Romeo and Juliet*, iv, 5

What 's gone and what 's past help
Should be past grief.—SHAKESPEARE, *Winter's Tale*, iii, 2

Great griefe will not be tould,
And can more easily be thought than said.
SPENSER, *Faerie Queene*, I, Canto vii, st. 41

Ring out the grief that saps the mind.
TENNYSON, *In Memoriam*, cvi, st. 3

Griefs.— Some griefs are med'cinable.
SHAKESPEARE, *Cymbeline*, iii, 2

Grieving.— Grieving, if aught inanimate e'er grieves,
Over the unreturning brave.
BYRON, *Childe Harold's Pilgrimage*, Canto iii, st. 27

Grind.— My life is one dem'd horrid grind.
DICKENS, *Nicholas Nickleby*, lxiv

Ground.— A time there was, ere England's griefs began,
When every rood of ground maintained its man.
GOLDSMITH, *The Deserted Village*, st. 4

When she took the ground,
She went to pieces like a lock of hay
Tossed from a pitchfork.
JEAN INGELOW, *Brothers, and a Sermon*

Growed.— I 'spect I growed. Don't think nobody never made me. H. B. STOWE, *Uncle Tom's Cabin*, xx

Grudge.— If I can catch him once upon the hip,
I will feed fat the ancient grudge I bear him.
SHAKESPEARE, *Merchant of Venice*, i, 3

Grundy.— What will Mrs. Grundy say?
T. MORTON, *Speed the Plough*, i, 1

Guard.— The Guard dies, but never surrenders!
Attributed to GEN. CAMBRONNE, at Waterloo[1]

Guards.— Up, Guards, make ready![2]
DUKE OF WELLINGTON, at Waterloo;
cited by W. M. SLOANE, *Napoleon Bonaparte*, IV, 202

---

[1]The tradition is denied by W. M. SLOANE, *Napoleon Bonaparte*, IV, 202.

[2]Commonly quoted as "Up, Guards, and at 'em!" Its authenticity has been frequently denied.

Guest.— Welcome the coming, speed the going guest.[1]
POPE, *Imitations of Horace*, II, Satire ii, line 160

Guests.— The guests are met, the feast is set.
COLERIDGE, *Ancient Mariner*, line 7

Guide.— Thou wert my guide, philosopher, and friend![2]
POPE, *Essay on Man*, Epistle iv, line 390

Guilt.— And peace went with them, one and all,
And each calm pillow spread;
But Guilt was my grim Chamberlain
That lighted me to bed;
And drew my midnight curtains round,
With fingers bloody red!
HOOD, *The Dream of Eugene Aram*, st. 24

Guinea.— I've a guinea I can spend,
I've a wife, and I've a friend,
And a troop of little children at my knee, John Brown.
CHARLES MACKAY, *John Brown*, st. 1

Gun.— For this is England's greatest son,
He that gained a hundred fights,
Nor ever lost an English gun.
TENNYSON, *Ode on the Death of the Duke of Wellington*, st. 6

H.— 'Twas whispered in heaven,[3]
'Twas muttered in hell.
C. M. FANSHAWE, *Enigma: The Letter H*

Habit.— How use doth breed a habit in a man!
SHAKESPEARE, *Two Gentlemen of Verona*, v, 4

Habits.— Small habits, well pursued betimes,
May reach the dignity of crimes.
HANNAH MORE, *Florio*, I

Ill habits gather by unseen degrees,
As brooks make rivers, rivers run to seas.
DRYDEN, *Ovid's Metamorphoses*, XV

---

[1] Welcome the coming, speed the parting guest.
POPE, *Odyssey*, xv, line 84

Time is like a fashionable host
That slightly shakes his parting guest by the hand,
And with his arms outstretched, as he would fly,
Grasps in the comer. SHAKESPEARE, *Troilus and Cressida*, iii, 3

[2] Is this my guide, philosopher, and friend?
POPE, *Imitations of Horace*, I, Epistle i, line 177

[3] Another version reads: "'Twas in heaven pronounced, and 't was," etc.

Hack.— Here lies poor Ned Purdon, from misery freed,
Who long was a bookseller's hack;
He led such a damnable life in this world,—
I don't think he 'll wish to come back.[1]
GOLDSMITH, *Epitaph on Edward Purdon*

Haggard. If I do prove her haggard,
Though that her jesses were my dear heart-strings,
I 'd whistle her off and let her down the wind,
To prey at fortune. SHAKESPEARE, *Othello*, iii, 3

Hair.— My hair is grey, but not with years.
BYRON, *Prisoner of Chillon*, st. 1

With hairy springes we the birds betray,
Slight lines of hair surprise the finny prey,
Fair tresses man's imperial race ensnare,
And beauty draws us with a single hair.[2]
POPE, *Rape of the Lock*, ii, lines 25–28

There 's many a man hath more hair than wit.[3]
SHAKESPEARE, *Comedy of Errors*, ii, 2

Halcyon.— Saint Martin's summer, halcyon days.
SHAKESPEARE, *King Henry VI, Part I*, i, 2

Half.— My dear, my better half.[4]
SIR PHILIP SIDNEY, *Arcadia*, III

Hampden.— Some village Hampden, that, with dauntless breast,
The little tyrant of his fields withstood;
Some mute, inglorious Milton here may rest;
Some Cromwell, guiltless of his country's blood.
GRAY, *Elegy Written in a Country Churchyard*, st. 16

---

[1] Well, then, poor G—— lies under ground!
So there's an end of honest Jack.
So little justice here he found,
'T is ten to one he'll ne'er come back. POPE, *Epitaph*

[2] And though it be a two-foot trout,
'T is with a single hair pulled out.—BUTLER, *Hudibras*, II, iii, lines 13, 14

Can draw you to her with a single hair.
DRYDEN, *Persius*, Satire v, line 247

Here in her hairs
The painter plays the spider and hath woven
A golden mesh to entrap the hearts of men
Faster than gnats in cobwebs. SHAKESPEARE, *Merchant of Venice*, iii, 2

[3] She hath more hair than wit, and more faults than hairs.
SHAKESPEARE, *Two Gentlemen of Verona*, iii, 1

[4] He is the half part of a blessed man,
Left to be finished by such as she;
And she a fair divided excellence,
Whose fulness of perfection lies in him.
SHAKESPEARE, *King John*, ii, 1 [2]

Hand. My red right hand[1] grows raging hot,
Like Cranmer's at the stake.
HOOD, *The Dream of Eugene Aram*

If the veriest cur would lick my hand,
I could love it like a child! HOOD, *The Last Man*

I 'll follow thee and make a heaven of hell,
To die upon the hand I love so well.
SHAKESPEARE, *Midsummer-Night's Dream*, ii, 1

Ferdinand. Here's my hand.
Miranda. And mine, with my heart in't.
SHAKESPEARE, *The Tempest*, iii, 1

I think we do know the sweet Roman hand.[2]
SHAKESPEARE, *Twelfth Night*, iii, 4

And the stately ships go on
To their haven under the hill;
But oh, for the touch of a vanished hand,
And the sound of a voice that is still.
TENNYSON, *Break, Break*, st. 3

Hands.— Cross her hands humbly,
As if praying dumbly,
Over her breast! HOOD, *The Bridge of Sighs*, st. 17

Will these hands ne'er be clean?

. . . . .

All the perfumes of Arabia will not sweeten this little hand.[3] SHAKESPEARE, *Macbeth*, v, 1

Hanged.— I 'll see thee hanged first.
SHAKESPEARE, *King Henry IV, Part I*, ii, 1

He that drinks all night, and is hanged betimes in the morning, may sleep the sounder all the next day.
SHAKESPEARE, *Measure for Measure*, iv, 3

Born to be hanged. SHAKESPEARE, *The Tempest*, i, 1

Hanging.— They 're hangin' Danny Deever in the mornin'.
KIPLING, *Danny Deever*

---

[1] His red right hand. MILTON, *Paradise Lost*, II, line 174

[2] I know the hand: in faith, 't is a fair hand;
And whiter than the paper it writ on
Is the fair hand that writ. SHAKESPEARE, *Merchant of Venice*, ii, 4

[3] What if this cursed hand
Were thicker than itself with brother's blood,
Is there not rain enough in the sweet heavens
To wash it white as snow? SHAKESPEARE, *Hamlet*, iii, 3

Will all great Neptune's ocean wash this blood
Clean from my hand? No, this my hand will rather
The multitudinous seas incarnadine,
Making the green one red. SHAKESPEARE, *Macbeth*, ii, 2

Hanover.— The illustrious House of Hanover,
And Protestant succession,
To these I do allegiance swear,—
While they can keep possession.
ANONYMOUS, *The Vicar of Bray*, st. 6

Happened.— I put myself in the way of things happening, and they happened.
THEODORE ROOSEVELT, quoted by JACOB RIIS in *Theodore Roosevelt, The Citizen*, ii

Happier.— And feel that I am happier than I know.
MILTON, *Paradise Lost*, VIII, line 282

Happiness.— How bitter a thing it is to look into happiness through another man's eyes!
SHAKESPEARE, *As You Like It*, v, 2

One feast, one house, one mutual happiness.
SHAKESPEARE, *Two Gentlemen of Verona*, v, 4

Happy. Happy thou art not;
For what thou hast not, still thou striv'st to get,
And what thou hast, forget'st.
SHAKESPEARE, *Measure for Measure*, iii, 1

Hark.— Hark! they whisper; Angels say,
Sister Spirit, come away.
POPE, *Dying Christian to His Soul*, st. 2

Harmony.— The hidden soul of harmony.
MILTON, *L'Allegro*, line 144

Harp.— The harp that once through Tara's halls
The soul of music shed,
Now hangs as mute on Tara's walls,
As if that soul were fled. T. MOORE, *The Harp That Once Through Tara's Halls*, st. 1

I hold it truth, with him who sings
To one clear harp in divers tones,
That men may rise on stepping-stones
Of their dead selves to higher things.[1]
TENNYSON, *In Memoriam*, i, st. 1

A harp of thousand strings.
ISAAC WATTS, *Hymns and Spiritual Songs*, ii, 19

---

[1] Saint Augustine! well hast thou said,
That of our vices we can frame
A ladder, if we will but tread
Beneath our feet each deed of shame!

. . . .

Nor deem the irrevocable Past,
As wholly wasted, wholly vain,
If, rising on its wrecks, at last
To something nobler we attain.
LONGFELLOW, *The Ladder of Saint Augustine*, st. 1, 12

Harping.— Still harping on my daughter.
SHAKESPEARE, *Hamlet*, ii, 2

Haste. Make haste; the better foot before.
. . . . .
Be Mercury, set feathers to thy heels,
And fly like thought. SHAKESPEARE, *King John*, iv, 2

Hat.— A hat not much the worse for wear.
COWPER, *John Gilpin*, st. 46

Virtue may flourish in an old cravat,
But man and nature scorn the shocking hat.[1]
HOLMES, *A Rhymed Lesson*, st. 50

Hate.— The lust of booty, and the thirst of hate.
BYRON, *Lara*, Canto ii, st. 11

Folks never understand the folks they hate.
LOWELL, *Biglow Papers*, II, ii, line 176

Hater.— A good hater.
SAMUEL JOHNSON, *Johnsoniana*, Piozzi, 39

Head.— All you've got to do is to lay your head well to the wind, and we'll fight through it!
DICKENS, *Dombey and Son*, ix

But first I would remark, that it is not a proper plan
For any scientific gent to whale his fellow-man,
And, if a member don't agree with his peculiar whim,
To lay for that same member for to "put a head" on him.
BRET HARTE, *The Society upon the Stanislaus*, st. 2

Head of the army! NAPOLEON BONAPARTE, last words, *Life*, by Sloane, IV, 219

Off with his head![2]
SHAKESPEARE, *King Richard III*, iii, 4

I never knew so young a body with so old a head.
SHAKESPEARE, *Merchant of Venice*, iv, 1

O good grey head which all men knew.[3]
TENNYSON, *Ode on the Death of the Duke of Wellington*, st. 4

---

[1] Shabby gentility has nothing so characteristic as its hat. There is always an unnatural calmness about its nap, and an unwholesome gloss, suggestive of a wet brush. The last effort of decayed fortune is expended in smoothing its dilapidated castor. The hat is the *ultimum moriens* of "respectability."
HOLMES, *Autocrat of the Breakfast-Table*, viii

[2] Off with his head — so much for Buckingham.
COLLEY CIBBER, *Richard III, Adapted*, iv, 4

[3] O honest face, which all men knew!
R. H. STODDARD, *Abraham Lincoln*, st. 35

Heads.— Their heads sometimes so little, that there is no room for wit; sometimes so long, that there is no wit for so much room. T. FULLER, *Of Natural Fools*

At whose sight all the stars
Hide their diminished heads.
MILTON, *Paradise Lost*, IV, lines 34, 35

Health.— From labour health, from health contentment springs.[1] JAMES BEATTIE, *The Minstrel*

And he that will this health deny,
Down among the dead men let him lie.
DYER, *Down Among the Dead Men*

Love and health to all; . . .
I drink to the general joy of the whole table.
SHAKESPEARE, *Macbeth*, iii, 4

The wealth
Of simple beauty and rustic health.
WHITTIER, *Maud Muller*, st. 2

Hear.— He cannot choose but hear.
COLERIDGE, *Ancient Mariner*, line 18

Heart.— Not all the lip can speak is worth
The silence of the heart.
J. Q. ADAMS, *The Lip and the Heart*, st. 4

The agonies we suffer, when the heart is left alone,
For every sin of humanity should fully and well atone!
GEORGE ARNOLD, *Introspection*, v

Who made the heart, 't is He alone
Decidedly can try us,
He knows each chord — its various tone,
Each spring — its various bias:
Then at the balance let 's be mute,
We never can adjust it;
What 's done we partly may compute,
But know not what 's resisted.
BURNS, *Address to the Unco Guid*, st. 8

The heart will break, yet brokenly live on.
BYRON, *Childe Harold's Pilgrimage*, Canto iii, st. 32

---

[1]Better to hunt in fields for health unbought,
Than fee the doctor for a nauseous draught.
The wise for cure on exercise depend;
God never made his work for man to mend.
DRYDEN, *Epistle to John Dryden*, lines 92–95

There's a heart that leaps with burning glow,
The wronged and the weak to defend;
And strikes as soon for a trampled foe,
As it does for a soul-bound friend.
It nurtures a deep and honest love;
It glows with faith and pride;
And yearns with the fondness of a dove,
To the light of its own fireside.

ELIZA COOK, *The Englishman*, st. 3

I learned how much the heart can bear,
When I saw her die in that old arm-chair.

ELIZA COOK, *The Old Arm-chair*, st. 4

A heart to resolve, a head to contrive, and a hand to execute.[1]

GIBBON, *Decline and Fall of the Roman Empire*, xlviii

My heart's wound up just like a watch,
As far as springs will take,—
It wants but one more evil turn,
And then the cords will break! HOOD, *Epigram vii*

A woman's heart, and its whole wealth of love,
Are all embarked upon that little boat.

HOOD, *Hero and Leander*, st. 24

The full heart's a Psalter,
Rich in deep hymns of gratitude and love!

HOOD, *Ode to Rae Wilson, Esquire*, st. 40

The beating of my own heart
Was all the sound I heard.

LORD HOUGHTON, *The Brook-Side*

There are moments in life, when the heart is so full of emotion,
That if by chance it be shaken, or into its depths like a pebble
Drops some careless word, it overflows, and its secret,
Spilt on the ground like water, can never be gathered together.

LONGFELLOW, *Courtship of Miles Standish*, vi, lines 12–15

Snows may o'er his head be flung,
But his heart — his heart is young.

T. MOORE, *Odes of Anacreon*, xxxix

---

[1]A hand to do, a head to plan,
A heart to feel and dare.— EBENEZER ELLIOTT, *A Poet's Epitaph*

Heart to conceive, the understanding to direct, or the hand to execute.
JUNIUS, *Letter* xxxvii

For the heart must speak when the lips are dumb.
KATE P. OSGOOD, *Driving Home the Cows*, st. 12

Taught by time, my heart has learned to glow
For others' good, and melt at others' woe.
POPE, *The Odyssey*, XVIII, lines 269, 270

More, much more, the heart may feel
Than the pen may write or the lip reveal.
PRAED, *To* ———, st. 5

My heart is in the coffin there with Cæsar.
SHAKESPEARE, *Julius Cæsar*, iii, 2

My heart
Is true as steel.
SHAKESPEARE, *Midsummer-Night's Dream*, ii, 1

One heart, one bed, two bosoms, and one troth.[1]
Ibid., ii, 2

He hath a heart as sound as a bell, and his tongue is the clapper; for what his heart thinks, his tongue speaks.
SHAKESPEARE, *Much Ado about Nothing*, iii, 2

I will live in thy heart, die in thy lap, and be buried in thy eyes. *Ibid.*, v, 2

Jog on, jog on, the foot-path way,
And merrily hent the stile-a:
A merry heart goes all the day,
Your sad tires in a mile-a.
SHAKESPEARE, *Winter's Tale*, iv, 3 [2]

A heart has throbbed beneath that leathern breast,
And tears adown that dusky cheek have rolled.
HORACE SMITH, *Address to a Mummy*, st. 11

Bearing a lifelong hunger in his heart.
TENNYSON, *Enoch Arden*, line 79

The larger heart, the kindlier hand.
TENNYSON, *In Memoriam*, cvi, st. 8

You thought to break a country heart
For pastime, ere you went to town.
TENNYSON, *Lady Clara Vere de Vere*, st. 1

---

[1] I have one heart, one bosom, and one truth.
SHAKESPEARE, *Twelfth Night*, iii, 1

It is not art, but heart, which wins the wide world over.
ELLA WHEELER WILCOX, *Art and Heart*, st. 8

Hearth.— Little inmate, full of mirth,
Chirping on my kitchen hearth.
COWPER, *The Cricket*, st. 1

For them no more the blazing hearth shall burn,
Or busy housewife ply her evening care;
No children run to lisp their sire's return,
Or climb his knees the envied kiss to share.
GRAY, *Elegy Written in a Country Churchyard*, st. 7

Keep a clean hearth and a clear fire for me.[1]
TENNYSON, *Enoch Arden*, line 192

Hearts.— Hearts, like apples, are hard and sour,
Till crushed by pain's resistless power;
And yield their juices rich and bland
To none but sorrow's heavy hand.
J. G. HOLLAND, *Bitter Sweet:* First Movement—First Episode

There are inscriptions on our hearts, which, like that on Dighton Rock, are never to be seen except at dead-low-tide. HOLMES, *Autocrat of the Breakfast-Table*, x

Can your lady patch hearts that are breaking
With handfuls of coals and rice,
Or by dealing out flannel and sheeting
A little below cost price?
KINGSLEY, *The Bad Squire*,[2] st. 15

When hearts have once mingled
Love first leaves the well-built nest.
SHELLEY, *When the Lamp Is Shattered*, st. 3

The kind hearts, the true hearts, that loved the place of old. R. L. STEVENSON, *Wandering Willie*, st. 2

Our hoard is little, but our hearts are great.[3]
TENNYSON, *The Marriage of Geraint*, line 374

---

[1]A clear fire, a clean hearth, and the rigour of the game.
CHARLES LAMB, *Mrs. Battle's Opinions on Whist*

[2]Also known as "A Rough Rhyme on a Rough Matter."

[3]Large of heart, though of very small estate.
CHARLES MACKAY, *John Brown*, st. 1

Heaven.— What kind of dwelling-place was heaven above?
And was it full of flowers? and were there schools
And dominies there? and was it far away?
Then, with a look that made your eyes grow dim,
Clasping his wee white hands 'round Donald's neck,
"Do doggies gang to heaven?"[1] he would ask.
ROBERT BUCHANAN, *Willie Baird*, lines 192–197

To appreciate heaven well,
'Tis good for a man to have some fifteen minutes of hell.
W. CARLETON, *Gone With a Handsomer Man*, st. 20

Whispers breathing less of earth than heaven.[2]
FELICIA HEMANS, *To the Memory of a Sister-in-Law*, st. 5

One of those faces that small children loathe without knowing why, and which give them that inward disgust for heaven so many of the little wretches betray, when they hear that these are "good men," and that heaven is full of such.
HOLMES, *Professor at the Breakfast Table*, viii

It [*my soul*] will not own a notion so unholy,
As thinking that the rich by easy trips
May go to heaven, whereas the poor and lowly
Must work their passage, as they do in ships.
HOOD, *Ode to Rae Wilson, Esquire*, st. 13

Earth gets its price for what Earth gives us;
The beggar is taxed for a corner to die in,
The priest hath his fee who comes and shrives us,
We bargain for the graves we lie in;

---

[1] But the poor dog, in life the firmest friend,
The first to welcome, foremost to defend,
Whose honest heart is still his master's own,
Who labours, fights, lives, breathes for him alone,
Unhonoured falls, unnoticed all his worth,
Denied in heaven the soul he had on earth:
While man, vain insect! hopes to be forgiven,
And claims himself a sole exclusive heaven.
BYRON, *Inscription on the Monument of a Newfoundland Dog*, lines 7–14

Lo, the poor Indian! whose untutored mind
Sees God in clouds, or hears him in the wind: . . .
To be contents his natural desire,
He asks no angel's wing, no seraph's fire;
But thinks, admitted to that equal sky,
His faithful dog shall bear him company.
POPE, *Essay on Man*, Epistle i, lines 99—112

[2] A form so fair, that, like the air,
'Tis less of earth than heaven.
EDWARD COATE PINKNEY, *A Health*, st. 1

At the devil's booth are all things sold,
Each ounce of dross costs its ounce of gold;
For a cap and bells our lives we pay,
Bubbles we buy with a whole soul's tasking:
'T is heaven alone that is given away,
'T is only God may be had for the asking;
No price is set on the lavish summer;
June may be had by the poorest comer.
LOWELL, *Vision of Sir Launfal*, Prelude to Part I, st. 4

Heaven's last, best gift.
MILTON, *Paradise Lost*, V, lines 18, 19

Heaven is not always angry when he strikes,
But most chastises those whom most he likes.
JOHN POMFRET, *To a Friend under Affliction*, lines 89, 90

Heaviness.— Let us not burthen our remembrance with
A heaviness that 's gone.
SHAKESPEARE, *The Tempest*, V, 1

Heedless.— Alas! I have walked through life
Too heedless where I trod;
Nay, helping to trample my fellow worm,
And fill the burial sod —
Forgetting that even the sparrow falls
Not unmarked of God!
HOOD, *The Lady's Dream*, st. 13

Heights.— The heights by great men reached and kept
Were not attained by sudden flight,
But they, while their companions slept,
Were toiling upward in the night.
LONGFELLOW, *Ladder of Saint Augustine*, st. 10

Helen.— Like another Helen, fired another Troy.
DRYDEN, *Alexander's Feast*, line 150

Hell.— Deep in yon cave Honorius long did dwell,
In hope to merit heaven by making earth a hell.
BYRON, *Childe Harold's Pilgrimage*, Canto i, st. 20

Me miserable! which way shall I fly
Infinite wrath and infinite despair?

Hell—*Continued*

Which way I fly is hell; myself am hell;[1]
And in the lowest deep a lower deep[2]
Still threatening to devour me opens wide,
To which the hell I suffer seems a heaven.
MILTON, *Paradise Lost*, IV, lines 73–78

All hell broke loose.[3]
MILTON, *Paradise Lost*, IV, line 918

All hell shall stir for this.
SHAKESPEARE, *King Henry V*, v, 1

Some there are who tell
Of one who threatens he will toss to hell
The luckless pots he marred in making[4] — Pish!
He's a good fellow, and 't will all be well.
OMAR KHAYYÁM, *Rubáiyát* (trans. Fitzgerald), st. 88

To rest, the cushion and soft Dean invite,
Who never mentions hell to ears polite.
POPE, *Moral Essays*, Epistle iv, lines 149, 150

Go thou, and fill another room in hell.
SHAKESPEARE, *King Richard II*, v, 5

The cunning livery of hell.
SHAKESPEARE, *Measure for Measure*, iii, 1

That deep torture may be called a hell
When more is felt than one hath power to tell.
SHAKESPEARE, *Rape of Lucrece*, lines 1287, 1288

---

[1] Horror and doubt distract
His troubled thoughts, and from the bottom stir
The hell within him; for within him hell
He brings, and round about him, nor from hell
One step, no more than from himself, can fly
By change of place. MILTON, *Paradise Lost*, IV, lines 18–23

I myself am Heaven and Hell.
OMAR KHAYYÁM, *Rubáiyát* (trans. Fitzgerald), st. 66

[2] The Devil's Cellar,— underneath the bottomless pit.
Proverbial Expression

Still there lies
An outer distance when the first is hailed,
And still for ever yawns before our eyes
An utmost — that is veiled.
JEAN INGELOW, *Honours*, II, st. 40

See ever so far, there is limitless space outside of that,
Count ever so much, there is limitless time around that.
WALT WHITMAN, *Song of Myself*, 45

[3] Hell is empty,
And all the devils are here. SHAKESPEARE, *The Tempest*, i, 2

[4] What! did the hand then of the Potter shake?
OMAR KHAYYÁM, *Rubáiyát* (trans. Fitzgerald), st. 89

Hell-broth.— Eye of newt and toe of frog,
Wool of bat and tongue of dog,
Adder's fork and blind-worm's sting,
Lizard's leg and owlet's wing,
For a charm of powerful trouble,
Like a hell-broth boil and bubble.
SHAKESPEARE, *Macbeth*, iv, 1

Helmet.— Now by the lips of those ye love, fair gentlemen of France,
Charge for the golden lilies,— upon them with the lance,
A thousand spurs are striking deep, a thousand spears in rest,
A thousand knights are pressing close behind the snow-white crest:
And in they burst, and on they rushed, while, like a guiding star,
Amidst the thickest carnage blazed the helmet of Navarre.
MACAULAY, *Ivry*, st. 4

Help.— God helps them that help themselves.
BENJAMIN FRANKLIN, *Poor Richard's Almanac*

What I can help thee to thou shalt not miss.
SHAKESPEARE, *All's Well That Ends Well*, i, 3

Herb.— She was the sweet-marjoram of the salad, or, rather, the herb of grace.
SHAKESPEARE, *All's Well That Ends Well*, iv, 5

Hereafter.— How is it, I wonder, hereafter? Faith teaches us little, here,
Of the ones we have loved and lost on earth,— do you think they will still be dear?
Shall we live the lives we might have led? will those who are severed now
Remember the pledge of a lower sphere, and renew the broken vow?
GEORGE ARNOLD, *Introspection*, v

Hero.— Be not like dumb, driven cattle!
Be a hero in the strife!—LONGFELLOW, *Psalm of Life*, st. 5

Nature, they say, doth dote,
And cannot make a man
Save on some worn-out plan,
Repeating us by rote:
For him [*Lincoln*] her Old-World moulds aside she threw,
And, choosing sweet clay from the breast
Of the unexhausted West,
With stuff untainted shaped a hero new,
Wise, steadfast in the strength of God, and true.
LOWELL, *Commemoration Ode*, st. 6

There is no trade or employment but the young man following it may become a hero.
WALT WHITMAN, *Song of Myself*, 48

Heroes. It's Tommy this, an' Tommy that, an' "Tommy, 'ow's yer soul?"
But it's "Thin red line of 'eroes" when the drums begin to roll.
KIPLING, *Tommy*

Herod.— It out-herods Herod.—SHAKESPEARE, *Hamlet*, iii, 2

Herse.— Underneath this sable herse
Lies the subject of all verse,
Sidney's sister, Pembroke's mother;
Death! ere thou hast slain another,
Learned and fair, and good as she,
W. BROWNE,[1] *Epitaph on the Countess of Pembroke*

Hills. The hills,
Rock-ribbed, and ancient as the sun.
BRYANT, *Thanatopsis*, lines 37, 38

Over the hills and far away.
GAY, *The Beggar's Opera*, i, 1

Himself.— Richard's himself again!
COLLEY CIBBER, *Richard III, Adapted*, v, 5

Hindrance.— Something between a hindrance and a help.
WORDSWORTH, *Michael*, line 189

Hisses.— And then he heard the hisses change to cheers.
TOM TAYLOR, *Abraham Lincoln*, st. 13

History.— History . . . is, indeed, little more than the register of the crimes, follies, and misfortunes of mankind.
GIBBON, *Decline and Fall of the Roman Empire*, iii

Hit.— A hit, a very palpable hit.—SHAKESPEARE, *Hamlet*, v, 2

Hobby-horse.— A man's hobby-horse is as tender a part as he has about him. STERNE, *Tristram Shandy*, II, xii

Hoe.— Bowed by the weight of centuries he leans
Upon his hoe and gazes on the ground,
The emptiness of ages in his face,
And on his back the burden of the world.
EDWIN MARKHAM, *The Man With the Hoe*, st. 1

[1] This poem has been sometimes ascribed to others. Whalley assigns it to Ben Jonson, but a concourse of opinion seems to attribute its authorship to Browne.

Hog.— The fattest hog in Epicurus' sty.
WILLIAM MASON, *Heroic Epistle*

Holiday.— There were his young barbarians all at play,
There was their Dacian mother — he, their sire,
Butchered to make a Roman holiday.
BYRON, *Childe Harold's Pilgrimage*, Canto iv, st. 141

Hollands.— He poured the fiery Hollands in,— the man that never feared,—
He took a long and solemn draught, and wiped his yellow beard;
And one by one the musketeers — the men that fought and prayed —
All drank as 'twere their mother's milk, and not a man afraid.

That night, affrighted from his nest, the screaming eagle flew,
He heard the Pequot's ringing whoop, the soldier's wild halloo;
And there the sachem learned the rule he taught to kith and kin,
"Run from the white man when you find he smells of Hollands gin!"
HOLMES, *On Lending a Punch-Bowl*, st. 7, 8

Holly.— To-night ungathered let us leave
This laurel, let this holly stand:[1]
We live within the stranger's land,
And strangely falls our Christmas-eve.
TENNYSON, *In Memoriam*, cv, st. 1

Holy.— Where'er we tread 't is haunted, holy ground.
BYRON, *Childe Harold's Pilgrimage*, Canto ii, st. 88

Holy Supper.— The Holy Supper is kept, indeed,
In whatso we share with another's need;
Not what we give, but what we share,
For the gift without the giver is bare;
Who gives himself with his alms feeds three,
Himself, his hungering neighbour, and Me.[2]
LOWELL, *Vision of Sir Launfal*, ii, st. 8

---

[1] An earlier reading is:
This holly by the cottage eave
To-night, ungathered shall it stand.

[2] He serveth his Maker who aideth the poor. ELIZA COOK, *Winter*, st. 8

Home.—Such is the patriot's boast, where'er we roam,
His first, best country ever is at home.[1]
GOLDSMITH, *The Traveller*, st. 7

Mid pleasures and palaces though we may roam,
Be it ever so humble, there's no place like home;
A charm from the sky seems to hallow us there,
Which, seek through the world, is ne'er met with elsewhere.
Home, home, sweet, sweet home!
There's no place like home! there's no place like home![2]
JOHN HOWARD PAYNE, *Home, Sweet Home*, st. 1

Home was home then, my dear, full of kindly faces.
R. L. STEVENSON, *Wandering Willie*, st. 2

Homeless. Homeless near a thousand homes I stood,[3]
And near a thousand tables pined and wanted food.
WORDSWORTH, *Guilt and Sorrow*, st. 41

Homely.— Home-keeping youth have ever homely wits.
SHAKESPEARE, *Two Gentlemen of Verona*, i, 1

---

[1] Where shall that land, that spot of earth be found?
Art thou a man? — a patriot? — look around;
Oh, thou shalt find, howe'er thy footsteps roam,
That land *thy* country, and that spot *thy* home.
JAMES MONTGOMERY, *The West Indies*, iii, st. 1

[2] Cling to thy home! if there the meanest shed
Yield thee a hearth and shelter for thy head,
And some poor plot, with vegetables stored,
Be all that Heaven allots thee for thy board,—
Unsavoury bread, and herbs that scattered grow
Wild on the river brink or mountain brow,
Yet e'en this cheerless mansion shall provide
More heart's repose than all the world beside.
ROBERT BLAND, *Home*, From the Greek of Leonidas

If solid happiness we prize,
Within our breast this jewel lies;
And they are fools who roam:
The world has nothing to bestow;
From our own selves our joys must flow,
And that dear hut — our home. N. COTTON, *The Fireside*, st. 3

[3] Alas! for the rarity
Of Christian charity
Under the sun!
Oh! it was pitiful!
Near a whole city full,
Home she had none! HOOD, *The Bridge of Sighs*, st. 9

The poor white man sat down beneath our tree,
Weary and faint, and far from home was he:
For him no mother fills with milk the bowl,
No wife prepares the bread to cheer his soul.
JAMES MONTGOMERY, *The West Indies*, iii, st. 4

Home,— what home? had he a home?
TENNYSON, *Enoch Arden*, line 664

Homer.— Seven cities warred for Homer being dead;
Who living had no roofe to shrowd his head.[1]
T. Heywood, *The Hierarchie of the Blessed Angells*

Honest.— An honest man, close-buttoned to the chin,
Broadcloth without, and a warm heart within.
Cowper, *Epistle to Joseph Hill*, lines 62, 63

A wit's a feather, and a chief a rod;
An honest man's the noblest work of God.[2]
Pope, *Essay on Man*, Epistle iv, lines 247, 248

To be honest, as this world goes, is to be one man picked out of ten thousand.—Shakespeare, *Hamlet*, ii, 2

I am myself indifferent honest.[3]
Shakespeare, *Hamlet*, iii, 1

A free and open nature,
That thinks men honest that but seem to be so.
Shakespeare, *Othello*, i, 3

To be direct and honest is not safe. *Ibid.*, iii, 3

Honesty.— Honesty is the best policy.
Byrom, *The Nimmers*, line 18; Franklin, *Poor Richard's Almanac*

No legacy is so rich as honesty.
Shakespeare, *All's Well That Ends Well*, iii, 5

Rich honesty dwells like a miser, sir, in a poor house; as your pearl in your foul oyster.
Shakespeare, *As You Like It*, v, 4

Honesty's a fool
And loses that it works for.[4] Shakespeare, *Othello*, iii,

---

[1] Seven wealthy towns contend for Homer dead,
Through which the living Homer begged his bread. Anonymous

[2] Princes and lords are but the breath of kings,
"An honest man's the noblest work of God."
Burns, *The Cotter's Saturday Night*, st. 19

[3] I am as honest as any man living that is an old man and no honester than I. Shakespeare, *Much Ado about Nothing*, iii, 4

[4] But conscience was tough: it was not enough;*
And their honesty never swerved;
And they bade him go, with Mister Joe,
To the Devil, as he deserved.

. . . . . .

But they wavered not long, for conscience was strong,
And they thought they might get more;
And they refused the gold, but not
So rudely as before.

. . . . . .

And they could not stand the sound in his hand,
For he made the guineas chink.
Southey, *The Surgeon's Warning*, st. 25, 30, 34

*A proffered bribe of one guinea, increased in the following stanzas to two and three guineas.

Honey. When was ever honey made
With one bee in a hive? HOOD, *The Last Man*

Where'er ye shed the honey, the buzzing flies will crowd;
Where'er ye fling the carrion, the raven's croak is loud;[1]
Where'er down Tiber garbage floats, the speedy pike ye see;
And wheresoe'er such lord is found, such client still will be. MACAULAY, *Virginia*, st. 2

Honour.— And had he not high honour?
The hillside for a pall;
To lie in state while angels wait
With stars for tapers tall;
And the dark rock-pines, like tossing plumes,
Over his bier to wave,
And God's own hand, in that lonely land,
To lay him in his grave!
CECIL FRANCES ALEXANDER, *Burial of Moses*, st. 8

The fear o' hell 's a hangman's whip
To haud the wretch in order;
But where ye feel your honour grip,
Let that aye be your border.
BURNS, *Epistle to a Young Friend*, st. 8

If he that in the field is slain,
Be in the bed of honour lain,
He that is beaten may be said
To lie in honour's truckle-bed.
BUTLER, *Hudibras*, I, iii, lines 1047–1050

Seek no friend save Honour,
Dread no foe but Debt.
D. M. MULOCK CRAIK, *An Honest Valentine*, st. 5

I could not love thee, dear, so much,
Loved I not honour more. RICHARD LOVELACE,
To Lucasta, On Going to the Warres, st. 3

Honour and shame from no condition rise;
Act well your part, there all the honour lies.
POPE, *Essay on Man*, Epistle iv, lines 193, 194

Honour pricks me on. Yea, but how if honour prick me off when I come on? — how then? Can honour set to a leg? — no: or an arm? — no: or take away the grief of a wound? — no. Honour hath no skill in surgery, then? — no. What is honour? — a word. What

[1] Wheresoever the carcass is, there will the eagles be gathered together.
Matt. xxiv, 28

is in that word honour? — what is that honour? — air. A trim reckoning! Who hath it? — he that died o' Wednesday. Doth he feel it? — no. Doth he hear it? — no. 'T is insensible, then. Yea, to the dead. But will it not live with the living? — no. Why? — detraction will not suffer it. Therefore I 'll none of it. Honour is a mere scutcheon: and so ends my catechism.

SHAKESPEARE, *King Henry IV, Part I*, v, 1

If we are marked to die, we are enough
To do our country loss; and if to live,
The fewer men, the greater share of honour.

. . . . .

But if it be a sin to covet honour
I am the most offending soul alive.

SHAKESPEARE, *King Henry V*, iv, 3

The jingling of the guinea helps the hurt that honour feels. TENNYSON, *Locksley Hall*, line 105

We crave
The austere virtues strong to save,
The honour proof to place or gold,
The manhood never bought nor sold!

WHITTIER, *Centennial Hymn*, st. 5

Honours.— He gave his honours to the world again,
His blessed part to heaven, and slept in peace.

SHAKESPEARE, *King Henry VIII*, iv, 2

Hope.— All hope abandon, ye who enter here.

DANTE, *Inferno*, Canto iii, line 9

While there is life, there 's hope.[1]

GAY, *The Sick Man and the Angel*, line 49

A hope beyond the shadow of a dream.

KEATS, *Endymion*, i, line 857

None without hope e'er loved the brightest fair,
But love can hope[2] where reason would despair.

LORD LYTTELTON, *Epigram*

---

[1] The wretch condemned with life to part,
Still, still on hope relies;
And every pang that rends the heart,
Bids expectation rise.

Hope, like the glimmering taper's light,
Adorns and cheers the way;
And still, as darker grows the night,
Emits a brighter ray.

GOLDSMITH, *The Captivity*, ii

[2] Hope! thou nurse of young desire.

I. BICKERSTAFFE, *Love in a Village*, st. 1

Twining subtle fears with hope.
A. MARVELL, *Horatian Ode upon Cromwell's Return from Ireland*, st. 13

Hope on, hope ever! though to-day be dark,
The sweet sunburst may smile on thee to-morrow.
GERALD MASSEY, *Hope On, Hope Ever*

So farewell hope,[1] and, with hope, farewell fear,
Farewell remorse! All good to me is lost;
Evil, be thou my good.
MILTON, *Paradise Lost*, IV, lines 108–110

Hope springs eternal in the human breast:
Man never is, but always to be blessed:
The soul, uneasy and confined from home,
Rests and expatiates in a life to come.
POPE, *Essay on Man*, Epistle i, lines 95–98

True hope is swift, and flies with swallow's wings;
Kings it makes gods, and meaner creatures kings.
SHAKESPEARE, *King Richard III*, v, 2

Hope is a lover's staff.
SHAKESPEARE, *Two Gentlemen of Verona*, iii, 1

Ah, well! for us all some sweet hope lies
Deeply buried from human eyes;

And, in the hereafter, angels may
Roll the stone from its grave away!
WHITTIER, *Maud Muller*, st. 54, 55

Hornet.— 'Tis dangerous to disturb a hornet's nest.
DRYDEN, *The Cock and the Fox*, line 566

Horror.— On horror's head horrors accumulate.
SHAKESPEARE, *Othello*, iii, 3

Horse. At my door the Pale Horse stands
To carry me to unknown lands.
JOHN HAY, *The Stirrup Cup*, st. 1

I would not have the horse I drive
So fast that folks must stop and stare;
An easy gait — two, forty-five —
Suits me; I do not care;
Perhaps, for just a single spurt,
Some seconds less would do no hurt.
HOLMES, *Contentment*, st. 7

[1] *Cf.* FREEDOM.

The ways of a man with a maid be strange, yet simple and tame
To the ways of a man with a horse, when selling or racing the same.[1] KIPLING, *Certain Maxims of Hafiz*, st. 13

They sell the pasture now to buy the horse.
SHAKESPEARE, *King Henry V*, ii, Prologue

Give me another horse! bind up my wounds!
SHAKESPEARE, *King Richard III*, v, 3

A horse! a horse! my kingdom for a horse! *Ibid.*, v, 4

He doth nothing but talk of his horse.
SHAKESPEARE, *Merchant of Venice*, i, 2

Pity for a horse o'er-driven,
And love in which my hound has part.
TENNYSON, *In Memoriam*, lxiii, st. 1

Horsemanship.— As if an angel dropped down from the clouds,
To turn and wind a fiery Pegasus
And witch the world with noble horsemanship.
SHAKESPEARE, *King Henry IV*, *Part I*, iv, 1

Horses.— Orses and dorgs is some men's fancy. They're wittles and drink to me — lodging, wife, and children — reading, writing, and 'rithmetic — snuff, tobacker, and sleep. DICKENS, *David Copperfield*, I, xix

Hospitable.— On hospitable thoughts intent.
MILTON, *Paradise Lost*, V, line 332

Hot. Now,
While it is hot, I'll put it to the issue
SHAKESPEARE, *King Henry VIII*, v, 1

Hour.— Some wee short hour ayont the twal.
BURNS, *Death and Doctor Hornbook*, st. 31

House.— The house with the narrow gate.
SHAKESPEARE, *All's Well That Ends Well*, iv, 5

Like a fair house built on another man's ground.
SHAKESPEARE, *Merry Wives of Windsor*, ii, 2

---

[1] When one that hath a horse on sale
Shall bring his merit to the proof,
Without a lie for every nail
That holds the iron on the hoof.—HOLMES, *Latter-Day Warnings*, st. 5

A feller may be straighter 'n a string in ev'ythin' else, an' never tell the truth — that is, the hull truth —about a hoss.
E. N. WESTCOTT, *David Harum*, xviii

Housewife.— I'll play the housewife for this once.
SHAKESPEARE, *Romeo and Juliet*, iv, 2

Hub.— Boston State-House is the hub of the solar system. You could n't pry that out of a Boston man if you had the tire of all creation straightened out for a crowbar.
HOLMES, *Autocrat of the Breakfast-Table*, vi

Hum.— The busy hum of men.—MILTON, *L'Allegro*, line 118

Human.— Then gently scan your brother man,
Still gentler sister woman;
Though they may gang a kennin wrang,
To step aside is human.
BURNS, *Address to the Unco Guid*, st. 7

Human nature in its shirt-sleeves.
HOLMES, *Professor at the Breakfast Table*, i

Humanity.— The traitor to humanity is the traitor most accursed.—LOWELL, *On the Capture of Fugitive Slaves near Washington*, st. 5

Through this dread shape the suffering ages look;
Time's tragedy is in that aching stoop;
Through this dread shape humanity betrayed,
Plundered, profaned, and disinherited,
Cries protest to the Judges of the World,
A protest that is also prophecy.
EDWIN MARKHAM, *The Man With the Hoe*, st. 4

The still, sad music of humanity.
WORDSWORTH, *Tintern Abbey*, line 93

Humidity.— O blessed breathing sun, draw from the earth
Rotten humidity!—SHAKESPEARE, *Timon of Athens*, iv, 2

Humility.—That very thing so many Christians want —
Humility. HOOD, *Ode to Rae Wilson, Esquire*, st. 21

Hundred.— While one with moderate haste might tell a hundred. SHAKESPEARE, *Hamlet*, i, 2

Hurrahs.— One stormy gust of long-suspended Ahs!
One whirlwind chaos of insane hurrahs!
HOLMES, *A Modest Request: The Speech*, lines 49, 50

Hurricane.— One night came on a hurricane,
The sea was mountains rolling.
WILLIAM PITT (of Malta), *The Sailor's Consolation*, st. 1

Hurt.— *Romeo.* Courage, man! the hurt cannot be much.
Mercutio. No, 't is not so deep as a well, nor so wide as a church door; but 't is enough, 't will serve.
SHAKESPEARE, *Romeo and Juliet*, iii, 1

I 'll not hurt thee,[1] . . . go, poor devil, get thee gone, why should I hurt thee? This world surely is wide enough to hold both thee and me.
STERNE, *Tristram Shandy*, II, xii

Husband.— And truant husband should return, and say,
"My dear, I was the first who came away."
BYRON, *Don Juan*, Canto i, st. 141

She who ne'er answers till a husband cools,
Or, if she rules him, never shows she rules.
POPE, *Moral Essays*, Epistle ii, line 261

Get thee a good husband, and use him as he uses thee.
SHAKESPEARE, *All's Well That Ends Well*, i, 1

Here 's my husband,
And so much duty as my mother showed
To you, preferring you before her father,
So much I challenge that I may profess
Due to the Moor my lord. SHAKESPEARE, *Othello*, i, 3

Thy husband is thy lord, thy life, thy keeper,
Thy head, thy sovereign; one that cares for thee,
And for thy maintenance commits his body
To painful labour both by sea and land,
To watch the night in storms, the day in cold,
While thou liest warm at home, secure and safe;
And craves no other tribute at thy hands
But love, fair looks, and true obedience;
Too little payment for so great a debt.[2]
SHAKESPEARE, *Taming of the Shrew*, v, 2

As the husband is, the wife is; thou are mated with a clown,
And the grossness of his nature will have weight to drag thee down. TENNYSON, *Locksley Hall*, lines 47, 48

---

[1] A fly which "Uncle Toby" had caught after it had tormented him cruelly all dinner-time.

[2] *Galatea.* What is a man?
Pygmalion. A being strongly framed
To wait on woman, and protect her from
All ills that strength and courage can avert;
To work and toil for her, that she may rest;
To weep and mourn for her, that she may laugh;
To fight and die for her, that she may live!
Galatea. I'm glad I am a woman.
W. S. GILBERT, *Pygmalion and Galatea*, i, 1

Husbands.— Fools are as like husbands as pilchards are to herrings. SHAKESPEARE, *Twelfth Night*, iii, 1

Hypocrisy.— Oh for a forty-parson power to chaunt
Thy praise, hypocrisy!
BYRON, *Don Juan*, Canto x, st. x, 34

Ice.— Ice, mast-high, came floating by.
S. T. COLERIDGE, *Ancient Mariner*, line 53

The ice was here, the ice was there,
The ice was all around:[1]
It cracked and growled, and roared and howled,
Like noises in a swound! *Ibid.*, lines 59–62

Icicles.— When icicles hang by the wall,
And Dick the shepherd blows his nail,
And Tom bears logs into the hall,
And milk comes frozen home in pail.
SHAKESPEARE, *Love's Labour's Lost*, v, 2

Ideal.— The human ideal will be the desire to transform life into something better and grander than itself.
CHARLES WAGNER, *The Simple Life*, ii

Ideality.— Infinite Ideality!
Immeasurable Reality!
Infinite Personality!—TENNYSON, *The Human Cry*, st. 1

Ides.— Beware the ides of March.[2]
SHAKESPEARE, *Julius Cæsar*, i, 2

Idle.— Satan finds some mischief still
For idle hands to do. WATTS, *Divine Songs*, Song 20

Idler.— An idler is a watch that wants both hands;
As useless if it goes as if it stands.
COWPER, *Retirement*, lines 681, 682

Ignorance. Where ignorance is bliss,
'T is folly to be wise.[3] THOMAS GRAY, *Ode on a Distant Prospect of Eton College*, st. 10

---

[1] 'T was ice around, behind, before —
My God! there is no sea.
G. H. BOKER, *Ballad of Sir John Franklin*, st. 15

[2] *Cæsar.* The ides of March are come.
Soothsayer. Ay, Cæsar, but not gone.—SHAKESPEARE, *Julius Cæsar*, iii, 1

Remember March, the ides of March remember! *Ibid.*, iv, 3

[3] From ignorance our comfort flows;
The only wretched are the wise. PRIOR, *to Montague*

Ill.— The good are better made by ill,
As odours crushed are sweeter still.
S. ROGERS, *Jacqueline*, st. 3

Ill wind never said well.
SHAKESPEARE, *King Henry V*, iii, 7

Ills.— Kings may be blest, but Tam was glorious,
O'er a' the ills o' life victorious!
BURNS, *Tam O' Shanter*, st. 6

Imagination.— We must temper the imagination . . . with judgment.—KEATS, *Letter to G. and G. Keats*, April 28, 1819

Who can hold a fire in his hand
By thinking on the frosty Caucasus?
Or cloy the hungry edge of appetite
By bare imagination of a feast?
Or wallow naked in December snow
By thinking on fantastic summer's heat?
SHAKESPEARE, *King Richard II*, i, 3

Immortal.— The soul, secured in her existence, smiles
At the drawn dagger, and defies its point.
The stars shall fade away, the sun himself
Grow dim with age, and nature sink in years.
But thou shalt flourish in immortal youth,
Unhurt amidst the wars of elements,
The wrecks of matter, and the crush of worlds.
ADDISON, *Cato*, v, 1

How can he be dead
Who lives immortal in the hearts of men?
LONGFELLOW, *Michael Angelo*, II, iv

The man immortal, rationally brave,
Dares rush on death — because he cannot die.
YOUNG, *Night Thoughts*, VII, lines 197, 198

Immortality.— The old, old fashion! The fashion that came in with our first garments, and will last unchanged until our race has run its course, and the wide firmament is rolled up like a scroll. The old, old fashion — Death! Oh, thank God, all who see it, for that older fashion yet, of Immortality! DICKENS, *Dombey and Son*, xvi

Impeachment.— I own the soft impeachment.
R. B. SHERIDAN, *The Rivals*, v, 3

Improve.— Men might be better if we better deemed
Of them.[1] The worst way to improve the world
Is to condemn it.
P. J. BAILEY, *Festus*, Scene—A Mountain—Sunrise

---

[1] The surest plan to make a man
Is, think him so.—LOWELL, *Biglow Papers*, II, ii, *Jonathan to John*, st. 9

Income.— Annual income twenty pounds, annual expenditure nineteen nineteen six, result happiness. Annual income twenty pounds, annual expenditure twenty pounds ought and six, result misery.
DICKENS, *David Copperfield*, I, xii

Indebted.— And stand indebted, over and above,
In love and service to you evermore.
SHAKESPEARE, *Merchant of Venice*, iv, 1

Independence.— Independence now and independence for ever!—DANIEL WEBSTER, *Eulogy on Adams and Jefferson*, Boston, August 2, 1826

Index learning. Index-learning turns no student pale,
Yet holds the eel of science by the tail.
POPE, *The Dunciad*, I, lines 279, 280

Infant.— An infant crying in the night;
An infant crying for the light;
And with no language but a cry.
TENNYSON, *In Memoriam*, liv, st. 5

Infinity.— How can finite grasp infinity?
DRYDEN, *The Hind and the Panther*, line 105

Ingratitude.— Ingratitude, more strong than traitors' arms,
Quite vanquished him: then burst his mighty heart.
SHAKESPEARE, *Julius Cæsar*, iii, 2

Ingratitude, thou marble-hearted fiend,
More hideous when thou show'st thee in a child
Than the sea-monster! SHAKESPEARE, *King Lear*, i, 4

Inhumanity.— Man's inhumanity to man
Makes countless thousands mourn!
BURNS, *Man was Made to Mourn*, st. 7

Injury. His injury
The gaoler to his pity. SHAKESPEARE, *Coriolanus*, v, 1

Ink.— But words are things, and a small drop of ink,
Falling like dew upon a thought, produces
That which makes thousands, perhaps millions, think.
BYRON, *Don Juan*, Canto iii, st. 88

Inn.— There is nothing which has yet been contrived by man, by which so much happiness is produced as by a good tavern or inn.[1]
SAMUEL JOHNSON, *Life*, by BOSWELL, March 21, 1776

---

[1] Whoe'er has travelled life's dull round,
Where'er his stages may have been,
May sigh to think he still has found
The warmest welcome at an inn.
W. SHENSTONE, *Written on a Window of an Inn*

Shall I not take mine ease in mine inn but I shall have my pocket picked?
SHAKESPEARE, *King Henry IV, Part I*, iii, 3

Innocents.— Some innocents 'scape not the thunderbolt.[1]
SHAKESPEARE, *Antony and Cleopatra*, ii, 5

Insipid.— Insipid as the queen upon a card.
TENNYSON, *Aylmer's Field*, line 28

Instruction.— Pleasure with instruction should be joined;
So take the corn, and leave the chaff behind.
DRYDEN, *The Cock and the Fox*, lines 820, 821

Instrument.— He made an instrument to know
If the moon shine at full or no.
BUTLER, *Hudibras*, II, iii, lines 261, 262

Intentions.— Hell is paved with good intentions.[2]
SAMUEL JOHNSON, *Life*, by Boswell, April 14, 1775

Interest.— His simple rule of interest being all comprised in the one golden sentence, "two pence for every half-penny" . . . a familiar precept . . . strongly recommended to the notice of . . . money-brokers and bill discounters. DICKENS, *Nicholas Nickleby*, i

I don't believe in princerple,
But oh, I du in interest.
LOWELL, *Biglow Papers*, I, vi, st. 9

He hates our sacred nation, and he rails,
Even there where merchants most do congregate,
On me, my bargains and my well-won thrift,
Which he calls interest. Cursed be my tribe,
If I forgive him!
SHAKESPEARE, *Merchant of Venice*, i, 3

Intoxication.— Man, being reasonable, must get drunk;
The best of life is but intoxication:
Glory, the grape, love, gold, in these are sunk
The hopes of all men, and of every nation.
BYRON, *Don Juan*, Canto ii, st. 179

Ire.— Arise! ye Goths, and glut your ire.
BYRON, *Childe Harold's Pilgrimage*, Canto iv, st. 141

---

[1] Those eighteen, upon whom the tower in Siloam fell, and slew them, think ye that they were sinners above all men that dwelt in Jerusalem?
Luke xiii, 4

[2] Hell is full of good meanings and wishings.— HERBERT, *Jacula Prudentum*

Ireland.— Heartsome Ireland, winsome Ireland,

. . . . .

Tender, comely, valiant Ireland,
Songful, soulful, sorrowful Ireland.
LANIER, *Ireland*, st. 1–3

Irishman.— A wild, tremendous Irishman,
A tearing, swearing, thumping, bumping, ranting, roaring Irishman.

. . . . .

The whiskey-devouring Irishman,
The great he-rogue with his wonderful brogue — the fighting, rioting Irishman.

. . . . .

The rattling, battling Irishman,
The stamping, ramping, swaggering, staggering, leathering swash of an Irishman.
WILLIAM MAGINN, *The Irishman and the Lady*, st. 1, 3

Iron. This iron age. SHAKESPEARE, *King John*, iv, 1

Iscariot. The Bridegroom stood at the open door,
And beckoned, smiling sweet;
'Twas the soul of Judas Iscariot
Stole in, and fell at his feet.

"The Holy Supper is spread within,
And the many candles shine,
And I have waited long for thee
Before I poured the wine!"

The supper wine is poured at last,
The lights burn bright and fair,
Iscariot washes the Bridegroom's feet,
And dries them with his hair.
ROBERT BUCHANAN, *The Ballad of Judas Iscariot*, st. 47–49

Island.— O, it's a snug little island!
A right little, tight little island!
Search the globe round, none can be found
So happy as this little island.
T. DIBDIN, *The Tight Little Island*

Isle.— Our little mother isle, God bless her!
HOLMES, *A Good Time Coming*, st. 6

Ivy.— Oh, a dainty plant is the ivy green,
That creepeth o'er ruins old!

. . . . .

Creeping where no life is seen,
A rare old plant is the ivy green.

. . . . .

For the stateliest building man can raise
Is the ivy's food at last.

DICKENS, *Pickwick Papers*, vi, *The Ivy Green*

Jade.— We that have free souls, it touches us not: let the galled jade wince, our withers are unwrung.

SHAKESPEARE, *Hamlet*, iii, 2

Jaundiced.— All seems infected that th' infected spy,
As all looks yellow to the jaundiced eye.

POPE, *Essay on Criticism*, lines 558, 559

Jaw.— Who loosened and let down this brutal jaw?
Whose was the hand that slanted back this brow?
Whose breath blew out the light within this brain?

EDWIN MARKHAM, *The Man With the Hoe*, st. 1

Jays.— We'll teach him to know turtles from jays.

SHAKESPEARE, *Merry Wives of Windsor*, iii, 3

Jealousy.— Green-eyed jealousy.[1]

SHAKESPEARE, *Merchant of Venice*, iii, 2

Jest.— Of all the griefs that harass the distressed,
Sure the most bitter is a scornful jest.[2]

SAMUEL JOHNSON, *London*, (adapted from the Third Satire of Juvenal)

---

[1] Beware, my lord, of jealousy!
It is the green-eyed monster which doth mock [make]
The meat it feeds on. SHAKESPEARE, *Othello*, iii, 3

Jealous souls will not be answered so;
They are not ever jealous for the cause,
But jealous for they are [they're] jealous: 'tis a monster
Begot upon itself, born on itself. *Ibid.*, 4

I'll see before I doubt; when I doubt, prove;
And, on the proof,* there is no more but this,—
Away at once with love or jealousy! *Ibid.*, 3

[2] Nothing in poverty so ill is borne,
As its exposing men to grinning scorn.
JOHN OLDHAM, *Adaptation from the Third Satire of Juvenal*

---

* Trifles light as air
Are to the jealous confirmation strong
As proofs of holy writ. SHAKESPEARE, *Othello*, iii, 3

Haste thee, Nymph, and bring with thee
Jest and youthful jollity,
Quips and cranks and wanton wiles,
Nods and becks and wreathed smiles.

MILTON, *L'Allegro*, lines 25–28

It would be argument for a week, laughter for a month, and a good jest for ever.

SHAKESPEARE, *King Henry IV*, *Part I*, ii, 2

Maria. Not a word with him but a jest.[1]
Boyet. And every jest but a word.

SHAKESPEARE, *Love's Labour's Lost*, ii

A jest's prosperity lies in the ear
Of him that hears it, never in the tongue
Of him that makes it.

Ibid., v, 2

Great men may jest with saints; 'tis wit in them,
But in the less foul profanation.

SHAKESPEARE, *Measure for Measure*, ii, 2

Jesus.— If Jesus Christ is a man,—
And only a man,— I say
That of all mankind I cleave to him,
And to him will I cleave alway.

If Jesus Christ is a God,—
And the only God,— I swear
I will follow Him through heaven and hell,
The earth, the sea, and the air!

R. W. GILDER, *The Song of a Heathen*

---

[1] A trusty villain, sir, that very oft,
When I am dull with care and melancholy,
Lightens my humour with his merry jests.

SHAKESPEARE, *Comedy of Errors*, i, 2

A merrier man,
Within the limit of becoming mirth,*
I never spent an hour's talk withal:
His eye begets occasion for his wit;
For every object that the one doth catch,
The other turns to a mirth-moving jest,
Which his fair tongue (conceit's expositor)
Delivers in such apt and gracious words
That aged ears play truant at his tales
And younger hearings are quite ravished;
So sweet and voluble is his discourse.

SHAKESPEARE, *Love's Labour's Lost*, ii

From the crown of his head to the sole of his foot, he is all mirth.

SHAKESPEARE, *Much Ado about Nothing*, iii, 2

---

*I do enjoy this bounteous beauteous earth;
And dote upon a jest
Within the limits of becoming mirth.

HOOD, *Ode to Rae Wilson, Esquire*, st. 4

Jew.— I am a Jew else, an Ebrew Jew.
SHAKESPEARE, *King Henry IV, Part I*, ii, 4

I'll seal to such a bond
And say there is much kindness in the Jew.
SHAKESPEARE, *Merchant of Venice*, i, 3

Hath not a Jew eyes? hath not a Jew hands, organs, dimensions, senses, affections, passions? fed with the same food, hurt with the same weapons, subject to the same diseases, healed by the same means, warmed and cooled by the same winter and summer, as a Christian is? If you prick us, do we not bleed? if you tickle us, do we not laugh? if you poison us, do we not die? and if you wrong us, shall we not revenge? If we are like you in the rest, we will resemble you in that. If a Jew wrong a Christian, what is his humility? Revenge. If a Christian wrong a Jew, what should his sufferance be by Christian example? Why, revenge. The villainy you teach me, I will execute, and it shall go hard but I will better the instruction. *Ibid.*, iii, 1

Jewel. Man, she is mine own,
And I as rich in having such a jewel,
As twenty seas, if all their sand were pearl,
The water nectar, and the rocks pure gold.
SHAKESPEARE, *Two Gentlemen of Verona*, ii, 4

Jewels.— Win her with gifts, if she respect not words:
Dumb jewels often, in their silent kind,
More quick than words, do move a woman's mind.
Two Gentlemen of Verona, iii, 1

Jews.— On her white breast a sparkling cross she wore,
Which Jews might kiss, and infidels adore.
POPE, *Rape of the Lock*, ii, lines 7, 8

Johnny.— A kind of a little Johnny, you know.
HOLMES, *Professor at the Breakfast-Table*, vii

Joke.— Rare compound of oddity, frolic, and fun!
Who relished a joke, and rejoiced in a pun;
Whose temper was generous, open, sincere;
A stranger to flattery, a stranger to fear.
GOLDSMITH, *Sequel to Retaliation*

Jolly.— Any man may be in good spirits and good temper when he's well dressed. There ain't much credit in that. If I was very ragged and very jolly, then I should begin to feel I had gained a point.
DICKENS, *Martin Chuzzlewit*, I, v

There might be some credit in being jolly with a wife, 'specially if the children had the measles and that, and was very fractious indeed.

DICKENS, *Martin Chuzzlewit*, I, v

There'd be some credit in being jolly, with an inflammation of the lungs. *Ibid.*

Journeys.— Journeys end in lovers meeting.

SHAKESPEARE, *Twelfth Night*, ii, 3

Joy.— He chortled in his joy.—C. L. DODGSON ("LEWIS CARROLL"), *Through the Looking-Glass*, i

Things won are done; joy's soul lies in the doing.

SHAKESPEARE, *Troilus and Cressida*, i, 2

Joy is an exchange;
Joy flies monopolists; it calls for two.

YOUNG, *Night Thoughts*, II, lines 509, 510

Joys.— Joys too exquisite to last.

JAMES MONTGOMERY, *The Little Cloud*, st. 10

Judas.— If that ain't Judas on the largest scale!

HOLMES, *A Modest Request: The Scene*, line 50

Judge.— Judge not; the workings of his brain
And of his heart thou canst not see;
What looks to thy dim eyes a stain,
In God's pure light may only be
A scar, brought from some well-won field,
Where thou wouldst only faint and yield.

ADELAIDE A. PROCTER, *Judge Not*, st. 1

Gently to hear, kindly to judge.

SHAKESPEARE, *King Henry V*, Prologue

Judged.— Thank God! man is not to be judged by man:
Or, man by man, the world would damn itself.

P. J. BAILEY, *Festus*, Scene—A Gathering of Kings and Peoples

Judges.— Judges ought to remember that their office is . . . to interpret law, and not to make law.

BACON, *Essay LVI: Of Judicature*

Judging.— Judging each step, as though the way were plain

TOM TAYLOR, *Abraham Lincoln*, st. 3

Judgment.— His years but young, but his experience old;
His head unmellowed, but his judgment ripe.

SHAKESPEARE, *Two Gentlemen of Verona*, ii, 4

Judgments.— Fondly do we hope — fervently do we pray — that this mighty scourge of war may speedily pass away. Yet, if God wills that it continue until all the wealth piled by the bondsman's two hundred and fifty years of unrequited toil shall be sunk, and until every drop of blood drawn with the lash shall be paid by another drawn with the sword, as was said three thousand years ago, so still it must be said, "The judgments of the Lord are true and righteous altogether."

LINCOLN, *Second Inaugural Address*, March 4, 1865

Judicious.— Make the judicious grieve.

SHAKESPEARE, *Hamlet*, iii, 2

June. What is so rare as a day in June?
Then, if ever, come perfect days.

LOWELL, *Vision of Sir Launfal*, Prelude to Part I, st. 5

Jury.— A jury too frequently has at least one member more ready to hang the panel than to hang the traitor.

LINCOLN, *Letter to Erastus Corning*, June 12, 1863

Just.— Only the actions of the just
Smell sweet, and blossom in their dust.[1]

J. SHIRLEY, *Dirge: Death the Leveller*, st. 3

Justice.— Justice conquers evermore,
. . . . .
And he who battles on her side,
God, though he were ten times slain,
Crowns him victor glorified,
Victor over death and pain. EMERSON, *Voluntary IV*

Yet I shall temper so
Justice with mercy.—MILTON, *Paradise Lost*, X, lines 77,78

And then the justice,
In fair round belly with good capon lined,
With eyes severe and beard of formal cut,
Full of wise saws and modern instances.

SHAKESPEARE, *As You Like It*, ii, 7

Liberty plucks justice by the nose.

SHAKESPEARE, *Measure for Measure*, i, 3 [4]

Shylock. Is that the law?
Portia. Thyself shalt see the act:
For, as thou urgest justice, be assured
Thou shalt have justice, more than thou desirest.
. . . . .
He hath refused it in the open court:
He shall have merely justice and his bond.

SHAKESPEARE, *Merchant of Venice*, iv, 1

[1] The memory of the just is blessed.—*Proverbs* x, 7

Justify.— Justify the ways of God to men.[1]
MILTON, *Paradise Lost*, I, line 26

Kangaroos.— Von only happy moment I have had
Since here I come to be a farmer's cad,
And then I cotched a vild beast in a snaoze,
And picked her pouch of three young kangarooi.
HOOD, *The Forlorn Shepherd's*[2] *Complaint*, st. 6

Katydid.— Thou testy little dogmatist,
Thou pretty katydid![3]
HOLMES, *To an Insect*, st. 1

Keel.— Without a breeze, without a tide,
She steadies with upright keel!
S. T. COLERIDGE, *Ancient Mariner*, lines 169, 170

See! she stirs!
She starts,— she moves,— she seems to feel
The thrill of life along her keel.
LONGFELLOW, *Building of the Ship*, st. 21

I hear the noise about thy keel;
I hear the bell struck in the night;
I see the cabin-window bright;
I see the sailor at the wheel.
TENNYSON, *In Memoriam*, x, st. 1

Kentucky.— We'll sing one song for the old Kentucky home.
S. C. FOSTER, *My Old Kentucky Home*

---

[1] Just are the ways of God,
And justifiable to men,
Unless there be who think not God at all:
If any be, they walk obscure;
For of such doctrine never was there school,
But the heart of the fool,
And no man therein doctor but himself.
MILTON, *Samson Agonistes*, lines 293–299

Vindicate the ways of God to man.
POPE, *Essay on Man*, Epistle i, line 16

[2] "The Forlorn Shepherd,"— a London pickpocket transported to Australia, and put to sheep-herding.

[3] Oh, tell me where did Katy live,
And what did Katy do?
And was she very fair and young,
And yet so wicked, too?
Did Katy love a naughty man,
Or kiss more cheeks than one?
I warrant Katy did no more
Than many a Kate has done.* HOLMES, *To an Insect*, st. 3

---

*Tell me, what did Caty do?
Did she mean to trouble you?
Why was Caty not forbid
To trouble little Caty-did? PHILIP FRENEAU, *To a Caty-Did*, st. 5

Kick.— A kick, that scarce would move a horse,
May kill a sound divine.
COWPER, *The Yearly Distress*, st. 16

Kickshaws.— Any pretty little tiny kickshaws.
SHAKESPEARE, *King Henry IV, Part II*, v, 1

Kidney.— A man of my kidney.
SHAKESPEARE, *Merry Wives of Windsor*, iii, 5

Kill.— Let 's kill him boldly, but not wrathfully;
Let 's carve him as a dish fit for the gods,
Not hew him as a carcass fit for hounds.
SHAKESPEARE, *Julius Cæsar*, ii, 1

Kind.— A fellow-feeling makes one wondrous kind.
DAVID GARRICK, *Prologue on Quitting the Stage, June*, 1776

Be to her virtues very kind;
Be to her faults a little blind.[1]
MATTHEW PRIOR, *English Padlock*, lines 78, 79

If she be not so to me
What care I how kind she be?
GEORGE WITHER, *The Author's Resolution*, st. 2

Kindness.— A way to kill a wife with kindness.
SHAKESPEARE, *Taming of the Shrew*, iv, 1

Kindness in women, not their beauteous looks,
Shall win my love. *Ibid.*, iv, 2

That best portion of a good man's life,
His little, nameless, unremembered acts
Of kindness and of love.
WORDSWORTH, *Tintern Abbey*, lines 34–36

Kindred.— All that inhabit this great earth,
Whatever be their rank or worth
Are kindred and allied by birth,
And made of the same clay.
LONGFELLOW, *Kéramos*, st. 21

King.— Wha last beside his chair shall fa',
He is the king amang us three!
BURNS, *Oh, Willie Brewed a Peck o' Maut*, st. 4

God save our gracious king,
Long live our noble king,
God save our king. H. CAREY, *God Save the King*

[1] Be a little, nay, intensely blind. HOLMES, *A Rhymed Lesson*, st. 54

The king himself has followed her —
When she has walked before.
GOLDSMITH, *Elegy on Mrs. Mary Blaize*, st. 5

Here lies our sovereign lord the king,
Whose word no man relies on;
He never says a foolish thing,
Nor ever does a wise one.
EARL OF ROCHESTER, *Written on the Bedchamber Door of Charles II*

A king of shreds and patches.
SHAKESPEARE, *Hamlet*, iii, 4

There's such divinity doth hedge a king,
That treason can but peep to what it would.—*Ibid.*, iv, 5

Was never subject longed to be a king
As I do long and wish to be a subject.
SHAKESPEARE, *King Henry VI, Part II*, iv, 9

Ay, every inch a king. SHAKESPEARE, *King Lear*, iv, 6

The king's name is a tower of strength.
SHAKESPEARE, *King Richard III*, v, 3

The king of France, with forty thousand men,
Went up a hill, and so came down agen.
RICHARD TARLTON, *The Pigges Corantoe*

He is king who has the power.
POPE ZACHARIAS (A. D. 752), cited by W. M. SLOANE, *Napoleon Bonaparte*, II, 208

Kings.— Kings then at last have but the lot of all:
By their own conduct they must stand or fall.
COWPER, *Table Talk*, lines 106, 107

Kings must have slaves;
Kings climb to eminence
Over men's graves.—AUSTIN DOBSON, *Before Sedan*, st. 2

Others thought kings a useless heavy load,
Who cost too much, and did too little good.
DRYDEN, *Absalom and Achitophel*, I, lines 505, 506

Kings cannot reign unless their subjects give.
DRYDEN, *Epistle to Sir Godfrey Kneller*, line 142

Kiss. Maids must kiss no men
Till they do for good and all.
NICHOLAS BRETON, *Phillida and Corydon*, st. 3

Ae fond kiss, and then we sever.[1]
BURNS, *Ae Fond Kiss*, st. 1

Gin a body meet a body
  Coming through the rye,
Gin a body kiss a body —
  Need a body cry?
BURNS, *Coming Through the Rye*, st. 2

Love's first snowdrop, virgin kiss![2]
BURNS, *To a Kiss*, st. 1

The kiss, dear maid! thy lip has left,
  Shall never part from mine,
Till happier hours restore the gift
  Untainted back to thine.[3] BYRON, *On Parting*, st. 1

Since there's no helpe,— come, let us kisse and parte.
MICHAEL DRAYTON, *Come, Let Us Kisse and Parte*, st. 1

The sound of a kiss is not so loud as that of a cannon, but its echo lasts a deal longer.
HOLMES, *Professor at the Breakfast-Table*, xi

Alas, for the love that's linked with gold!
Better — better a thousand times told —
  Most honest, happy, and laudable,
The downright loving of pretty Cis,
Who wipes her lips, though there's nothing amiss,
And takes a kiss, and gives a kiss,
  In which her heart is audible!
HOOD, *Miss Kilmansegg*, Her Courtship

There grows a flower on every bough,
Its petals kiss — I'll show you how:
    Sing heigh-ho, and heigh-ho!
  Young maids must marry.
KINGSLEY, *Sing Heigh-Ho*, st. 2

Alas, how easily things go wrong!
A sigh too much, or a kiss too long,
And there follows a mist and a weeping rain,
And life is never the same again.
GEORGE MACDONALD, *Sir Aglovaile*

---

[1] One kind kiss before we part. ROBERT DODSLEY, *The Parting Kiss*

[2] How delicious is the winning
Of a kiss at love's beginning,
When two mutual hearts are sighing
For the knot there's no untying!
T. CAMPBELL, *Song: How Delicious is the Winning*, st. 1

[3] The kiss that she left on my lip,
  Like a dewdrop shall lingering lie.
T. MOORE, Paraphrase of Epigram from the Anthologia, in note *Odes of Anacreon*, xliii

Sweetheart,
I were unmannerly to take you out
And not to kiss you.

SHAKESPEARE, *King Henry VIII*, i, 4

Seal the bargain with a holy kiss.

SHAKESPEARE, *Two Gentlemen of Verona*, ii, 2

The sunlight clasps the earth,
And the moonbeams kiss the sea —
What are all these kissings worth,[1]
If thou kiss not me? SHELLEY, *Love's Philosophy*, st. 2

O Love, O fire! once he drew
With one long kiss my whole soul through
My lips, as sunlight drinketh dew.[2]

TENNYSON, *Fatima*, st. 3

Kissed.— Jenny[3] kissed me when we met,
Jumping from the chair she sat in.
Time, you thief! who love to get
Sweets into your list, put that in.
Say I'm weary, say I'm sad;
Say that health and wealth have missed me;
Say I'm growing old, but add —
Jenny kissed me!

LEIGH HUNT, *Jenny Kissed Me*

Kisses. A something on her cheek that smacked
(Tho' quite in silence) of ambrosial sweetness.
That made her think all other kisses lacked
Till then, but what she knew not, of completeness:
Being used but sisterly salutes to feel,
Insipid things — like sandwiches of veal.

HOOD, *Bianca's Dream*, st. 33

Then her lip, so rich in blisses,
Sweet petitioner for kisses.

T. MOORE, *Odes of Anacreon*, xvi

---

[1]Another reading is: What is all this sweet work worth?

[2]Their lips drew near, and clung into a kiss;

A long, long kiss, a kiss of youth and love,
And beauty, all concentrating, like rays
Into one focus kindled from above;
Such kisses as belong to early days,
Where heart, and soul, and sense, in concert move,
And the blood's lava, and the pulse ablaze,
Each kiss a heart-quake,— for a kiss's strength,
I think it must be reckoned by its length.

BYRON, *Don Juan*, Canto ii, st. 185, 186

As if he plucked up kisses by the roots.— SHAKESPEARE, *Othello*, iii, 3

[3]Jane Carlyle.

Dear as remembered kisses after death,
And sweet as those by hopeless fancy feigned
On lips that are for others.

TENNYSON, *The Princess*, iv, lines 36–38

Come, Chloe, and give me sweet kisses,
For sweeter sure never girl gave;
But why, in the midst of my blisses,
Do you ask me how many I 'd have?
. . . . .
Go number the stars in the heaven,
Count how many sands on the shore,
When so many kisses you 've given,
I still shall be craving for more.

SIR CHARLES H. WILLIAMS, *Come, Chloe*
(cited by MOORE, *The Numbering of the Clergy*)

The wretch who can number his kisses,
With few will be ever content. *Ibid.*

Kissing. A hand that kings
Have lipped, and trembled kissing.

SHAKESPEARE, *Antony and Cleopatra*, ii, 5

His kissing is as full of sanctity as the touch of holy bread. SHAKESPEARE, *As You Like It*, iii, 4

Kitten.— I had rather be a kitten and cry mew
Than one of these same metre ballad-mongers.

SHAKESPEARE, *King Henry IV, Part I*, iii, 1

Knave.— An honest man may take a knave's advice,
But idiots only may be cozened twice:
Once warned is well bewared.

DRYDEN, *The Cock and the Fox*, lines 797–799

Now will I show myself to have more of the serpent than the dove; that is, more knave than fool.

C. MARLOWE, *The Jew of Malta*, ii, 3

A knave 's a knave, to me, in ev'ry state.

POPE, *Epistle to Dr. Arbuthnot*, line 361

Knaves.— Three misbegotten knaves in Kendal green.

SHAKESPEARE, *King Henry IV, Part I*, ii, 4

Whip me such honest knaves.—SHAKESPEARE, *Othello*, i, 1

Knell. The bell invites me.
Hear it not, Duncan; for it is a knell
That summons thee to heaven or to hell.

SHAKESPEARE, *Macbeth*, ii, 1

The mournful surges
That ring the dead seaman's knell.

SHELLEY, *When the Lamp Is Shattered*, st. 2

Knew.— The village all declared how much he knew;
'Twas certain he could write and cipher too.
GOLDSMITH, *The Deserted Village*, st. 14

Knife.— The hardest knife ill-used doth lose his edge.
SHAKESPEARE, *Sonnet xcv*

Knocker.— Shut, shut the door, good John, fatigu'd I said,
Tie up the knocker, say I'm sick, I'm dead.
POPE, *Epistle to Dr. Arbuthnot*, lines 1, 2

Knocks.— What's he that knocks as he would beat down the gate? SHAKESPEARE, *Taming of the Shrew*, v, 1

Knot.— A knot that gold and silver can buy
Gold and silver may yet untie,
Unless it is tightly fastened.
E. C. STEDMAN, *The Diamond Wedding*, st. 13

Knots.— His owne two hands the holy knotts did knitt,
That none but death for ever can divide.
SPENSER, *Faerie Queene*, I, Canto xii, st. 37

Know.— Know, not for knowing's sake,
But to become a star to men for ever;
Know, for the gain it gets, the praise it brings,
The wonder it inspires, the love it breeds:
Look one step onward, and secure that step!
R. BROWNING, *Paracelsus*, i

Well didst thou speak, Athena's wisest son!
"All that we know is, nothing can be known."
Why should we shrink from what we cannot shun?
BYRON, *Childe Harold's Pilgrimage*, Canto ii, st. 7

I know what I know.
SHAKESPEARE, *Comedy of Errors*, iii, 1; *Measure for Measure*, iii, 2

Knowing.— 'Tain't a knowin' kind o' cattle
Thet is ketched with mouldy corn.
LOWELL, *The Biglow Papers*, I, i, st. 1

Knowledge.— Knowledge itself is a power.
BACON, *Meditationes Sacræ: Heresies*

Knowledge by suffering entereth,
And life is perfected by death.
E. B. BROWNING, *A Vision of Poets*, Conclusion, st. 62

Knowledge is of two kinds. We know a subject ourselves, or we know where we can find information upon it. SAMUEL JOHNSON, *Life*, by Boswell, April 11, 1775

Knows. He that tossed you down into the field,
He knows about it all — HE knows — HE knows!
OMAR KHAYYÁM, *Rubáiyát* (trans. Fitzgerald), st. 70

Labour.— The many still must labour for the one.
BYRON, *The Corsair*, Canto i, st. 8

Toiling in the naked fields,
Where no bush a shelter yields,
Needy Labour dithering stands,
Beats and blows his numbing hands,
And upon the crumping snows
Stamps in vain to warm his toes.
JOHN CLARE, *The Labourer*, st. 1

They who tread the path of labour follow where My feet have trod;
They who work without complaining do the holy will of God.
. . . . .
Nevermore thou needest seek Me; I am with thee everywhere;
Raise the stone, and thou shalt find Me; cleave the wood, and I am there.—HENRY VAN DYKE, *Toiling of Felix*, Legend, st. 83, 88

Work — work — work!
My labour never flags;
And what are its wages? A bed of straw,
A crust of bread — and rags.
HOOD, *The Song of the Shirt*

Slave of the wheel of labour, what to him
Are Plato and the swing of Pleiades?
What the long reaches of the peaks of song,
The rift of dawn, the reddening of the rose?
EDWIN MARKHAM, *The Man With the Hoe*, st. 3

Ask not if neighbour
Grind great or small:
Spare not *your* labour,
Grind *your* wheat all.
D. M. MULOCK CRAIK, *The Mill*, st. 1

---

[1] The singers have sung and the builders have builded,
The painters have fashioned their tales of delight;
For what and for whom hath the world's book been gilded,
When all is for these but the blackness of night?
WILLIAM MORRIS, *The Message of the March Wind*, st. 11

Two hands upon the breast,
And labour 's done;
Two pale feet crossed in rest —
The race is won;
Two eyes with coin-weights shut,
And all tears cease;
Two lips where grief is mute,
Anger at peace.
D. M. MULOCK CRAIK, *Now and Afterwards*, st. 1

Labour is worship.—F. S. OSGOOD, *To Labour Is to Pray*

I have had my labour for my travail [travel].
SHAKESPEARE, *Troilus and Cressida*, i, 1

He who does not love his labour and does not put interest or dignity into it is a bad workman.
CHARLES WAGNER, *The Simple Life*, viii

Labourer.— I am long past wailing and whining —
I have wept too much in my life:
I 've had twenty years of pining
As an English labourer's wife.

A labourer in Christian England,
Where they cant of a Saviour's name,
And yet waste men's lives like the vermin's
For a few more brace of game.
KINGSLEY, *The Bad Squire*,[1] st. 6, 7

Labouring.— Labourin' man an' labourin' woman
Hev one glory an' one shame.
Ev'ythin' thet 's done inhuman
Injers all on 'em the same.
LOWELL, *The Biglow Papers*, I, i, st. 10

Laced.— They braced my aunt against a board,
To make her straight and tall;
They laced her up, they starved her down,
To make her light and small;
They pinched her feet, they singed her hair,
They screwed it up with pins; —
Oh never mortal suffered more
In penance for her sins. HOLMES, *My Aunt*, st. 4

Ladder.— Heaven is not reached at a single bound;
But we build the ladder by which we rise
From the lowly earth to the vaulted skies,
And we mount to its summit round by round.
J. G. HOLLAND, *Gradatim*

[1] Also known as "A Rough Rhyme on a Rough Matter."

Lady. When a lady 's in the case,
You know, all other things give place.
GAY, *The Hare and Many Friends*, lines 41, 42

I 'll make my heaven in a lady's lap.
SHAKESPEARE, *King Henry VI, Part III*, iii, 2

Lamb.— O Cassius! you are yoked with a lamb
That carries anger as the flint bears fire,
Who, much enforced, shows a hasty spark,
And straight is cold again.
SHAKESPEARE, *Julius Cæsar*, iv, 3

God tempers the wind to the shorn lamb.[1]
STERNE, *A Sentimental Journey*, Maria

Lamp.—When the lamp is shattered
The light in the dust lies dead —
When the cloud is scattered
The rainbow's glory is shed.
When the lute is broken,
Sweet tones are remembered not;
When the lips have spoken,
Loved accents are soon forgot.
SHELLEY, *When the Lamp Is Shattered*, st. 1

Land.— "I hear thee speak of the better land,
Thou call'st its children a happy band;
Mother! oh, where is that radiant shore?
Shall we not seek it, and weep no more?"
. . . . .
"Eye hath not seen it, my gentle boy!
Ear hath not heard its deep songs of joy;
Dreams cannot picture a world so fair —
Sorrow and death may not enter there:
Time doth not breathe on its fadeless bloom,
For beyond the clouds, and beyond the tomb,
It is there, it is there, my child!"
FELICIA HEMANS, *The Better Land*, st. 1, 4

Landlord.— The landlord's laugh was ready chorus.
BURNS, *Tam O'Shanter*, st. 5

Landscape.— Now fades the glimmering landscape on the sight,
And all the air a solemn stillness holds.
GRAY, *Elegy Written in a Country Churchyard*, st. 2

---

[1] To a close-shorn sheep, God gives wind by measure.
GEORGE HERBERT, *Jacula Prudentum*

Language.— I love the language, that soft bastard Latin,
Which melts like kisses from a female mouth,
And sounds as if it should be writ on satin,
With syllables which breathe of the sweet South,
And gentle liquids gliding all so pat in,
That not a single accent seems uncouth,
Like our harsh Northern whistling, grunting guttural,
Which we're obliged to hiss, and spit, and sputter all.
BYRON, *Beppo*, st. 44

Language is a solemn thing,— I said.— It grows out of life,— out of its agonies and ecstasies, its wants and its weariness.—HOLMES, *Professor at the Breakfast-Table*, ii

Where nature's end of language is declined,
And men talk only to conceal the mind.
YOUNG, *Love of Fame*, Satire ii, line 207

Lards. Falstaff sweats to death,
And lards the lean earth as he walks along.
SHAKESPEARE, *King Henry IV, Part I*, ii, 2

Lark.— Merrily rose the lark, and shook
The dewdrop from its wing.
HOOD, *The Dream of Eugene Aram*

Rise with the lark, and with the lark to bed.[1]
JAMES HURDIS, *The Village Curate*

Hark, hark! the lark at heaven's gate sings.[2]
SHAKESPEARE, *Cymbeline*, ii, 3

Lass.— A penniless lass wi' a lang pedigree.
LADY NAIRNE, *The Laird o' Cockpen*, st. 2

Let the toast pass,
Drink to the lass,
I'll warrant she'll prove an excuse for the glass.
SHERIDAN, *School for Scandal*, iii, 3

---

[1]At what precise minute that little airy musician doffs his night gear, and prepares to tune up his unseasonable matins, we are not naturalists enough to determine. But for a mere human gentleman — that has no orchestra business to call him from his warm bed to such preposterous exercises — we take ten, or half after ten, . . . to be the very earliest hour at which he can begin to think of abandoning his pillow. . . . To do it in earnest requires another half-hour's good consideration.
CHARLES LAMB, *Popular Fallacies*, XIV

[2]Lost to sight th' ecstatic lark above
Sings, like a soul beatified, of love.
HOOD, *Ode to Rae Wilson, Esquire*, st. 16

The lark so shrill and clear,
Now at heaven's gate she claps her wings.— JOHN LYLY, *Campaspe*, v, 1

Like to the lark, at break of day arising
From sullen earth, sings hymns at heaven's gate.
SHAKESPEARE, *Sonnet*, xxix

Lasses.— Auld nature swears the lovely dears
Her noblest work she classes, oh!
Her 'prentice han' she tried on man,
An' then she made the lasses, oh!
BURNS, *Green Grow the Rashes*, st. 5

Lassie.— What can a young lassie do wi' an auld man?
BURNS, *What Can a Young Lassie Do?* st. 1

Last.— My dreams have boded all too right —
We part — for ever part — to-night!
I knew, I knew it could not last —
'Twas bright, 'twas heavenly, but 'tis past!
T. MOORE, *Lalla Rookh: The Fire Worshippers*

Although the [our] last, not least.
SHAKESPEARE, *King Lear*, i, 1

Late.— While we send for the napkin the soup gets cold,
While the bonnet is trimming the face grows old,
When we've matched our buttons the pattern is sold,
And everything comes too late — too late!
FITZ HUGH LUDLOW, *Too Late*, st. 2

It is so very very late,
That we may call it early by and by.[1]
SHAKESPEARE, *Romeo and Juliet*, iii, 4

Late, late, so late! and dark the night and chill!
Late, late, so late! but we can enter still.
Too late, too late! ye cannot enter now.[2]
TENNYSON, *Guinevere*, lines 166–168

Better late than never.
THOMAS TUSSER, *Five Hundred Points of Good Husbandry: An Habitation Enforced*

Latin.—Small Latin and less Greek.
BEN JONSON, *To the Memory of Shakespeare*, line 31

Oh, I smell false Latin!
SHAKESPEARE, *Love's Labour's Lost*, v, 1

Laugh.— The loud laugh that spoke the vacant mind.
GOLDSMITH, *The Deserted Village*, line 121

---

[1] I am glad I was up so late; for that's the reason I was up so early.
SHAKESPEARE, *Cymbeline*, ii, 3

[2] Changeless sentence of mortal fate,
Freezing the marrow with — Too late!
E. C. STEDMAN, *Alice of Monmouth*, xii, st. 3

I believe she could spread a horse-laugh through the pews of a tabernacle.

GOLDSMITH, *The Good-Natured Man*, i

They laugh that win. SHAKESPEARE, *Othello*, iv, 1

Laugh, and the world laughs with you;
 Weep, and you weep alone;
For the sad old earth must borrow its mirth,
 But has trouble enough of its own.

ELLA WHEELER WILCOX, *Solitude*, st. 1

Laughter. Methinks the older that one grows
Inclines us more to laugh than scold, though laughter
Leaves us so doubly serious shortly after.

BYRON, *Beppo*, st. 79

Launched.— How hard it is for some people to get out of a room after their visit is really over. . . . One would think they had been built in your parlour or study, and were waiting to be launched.

HOLMES, *Autocrat of the Breakfast-Table*, i

Laurel.— No more shall the war-cry sever,
 Or the winding rivers be red;
They banish our anger for ever
 When they laurel the graves of our dead.

F. M. FINCH, *The Blue and the Gray*, st. 7

Law.—Of law there can be no less acknowledged, than that her seat is the bosom of God, her voice the harmony of the world; all things in heaven and earth do her homage, the very least as feeling her care, and the greatest as not exempted from her power.

R. HOOKER, *Ecclesiastical Polity*, I

There's never a law of God or man runs north of 'Fifty-three. KIPLING, *The Rhyme of the Three Sealers*

The law is a sort of hocus-pocus science, that smiles in yeer face while it picks your pocket; and the glorious uncertainty of it is of mair use to the professors than the justice of it. C. MACKLIN, *Love à la Mode*, ii, 1

Why, law an' order, honour, civil right,
Ef they ain't wuth it, wut is wuth a fight?

LOWELL, *Biglow Papers*, II, ii, lines 297, 298

 The plough, the axe, the mill,
All kin's o' labour an' kin's o' skill,
Would be a rabbit in a wile-cat's claw,
Ef 't warn't for thet slow critter, 'stablished law.

Ibid., lines 299–302

Men of most renowned virtue have sometimes by transgressing most truly kept the law.[1]

MILTON, *Tetrachordon*

First Clown. He that is not guilty of his own death shortens not his own life.
Second Clown. But is this law?
First Clown. Ay, marry, is 't; crowner's quest law.

SHAKESPEARE, *Hamlet*, v, 1

Old father antic the law.

SHAKESPEARE, *King Henry IV, Part I*, i, 2

I have been a truant in the law,
And never yet could frame my will to it;
And therefore frame the law unto my will.

SHAKESPEARE, *King Henry VI, Part I*, ii, 4

Between two hawks, which flies the higher pitch;
Between two dogs, which hath the deeper mouth;
Between two blades, which bears the better temper;
Between two horses, which doth bear him best;
Between two girls, which hath the merriest eye;
I have perhaps some shallow spirit of judgment:
But in these nice sharp quillets of the law,
Good faith, I am no wiser than a daw. *Ibid.*

In law, what plea so tainted and corrupt,
But, being seasoned with a gracious voice,
Obscures the show of evil?

SHAKESPEARE, *Merchant of Venice*, iii, 2

If you deny me, fie upon your law!
There is no force in the decrees of Venice.
I stand for judgment: answer; shall I have it?

Ibid., iv, 1

The intent and purpose of the law
Hath full relation to the penalty,
Which here appeareth due upon the bond. *Ibid.*

---

[1] Man is more than Constitutions; better rot beneath the sod,
Than be true to Church and State while we are doubly false to God!

LOWELL, *On the Capture of Fugitive Slaves near Washington*, st. 5

There is a higher law than the Constitution.

W. H. SEWARD, *Speech*, March 11, 1850

And I beseech you,
Wrest once the law to your authority:
To do a great right, do a little wrong,
And curb this cruel devil of his will.

SHAKESPEARE, *Merchant of Venice*, iv, 1

Here's a fish hangs in the net, like a poor man's right in the law; 't will hardly come out.
SHAKESPEARE, *Pericles*, ii, 1

Do as adversaries do in law,
Strive mightily, but eat and drink as friends.
SHAKESPEARE, *Taming of the Shrew*, i, 2

Still you keep o' the windy side of the law.
SHAKESPEARE, *Twelfth Night*, iii, 4

Let the law go whistle.
SHAKESPEARE, *Winter's Tale*, iv, 4 [3]

The lawless science of our law,
The codeless myriad of precedent,
The wilderness of single instances,
Through which a few, by wit or fortune led,
May beat a pathway out to wealth and fame.
TENNYSON, *Aylmer's Field*, lines 435–438

And joy was duty and love was law.
WHITTIER, *Maud Muller*, st. 49

Laws.— Laws grind the poor, and rich men rule the law.
GOLDSMITH, *The Traveller*, st. 29

Lawyer.— Why may not that be the skull of a lawyer? Where be his quiddities [quiddits] now, his quillets, his cases, his tenures, and his tricks? why does he suffer this rude knave now to knock him about the sconce with a dirty shovel, and will not tell him of his action of battery?
SHAKESPEARE, *Hamlet*, v, 1

Lawyers.— When lawyers take what they would give,
And doctors give what they would take.
HOLMES, *Latter-Day Warnings*, st. 4

Lay.— I'll lay my head to any good man's hat.
SHAKESPEARE, *Love's Labour's Lost*, i, 1

Lay on, Macduff,
And damned be him [he] that first cries "Hold, enough!"[1]
SHAKESPEARE, *Macbeth*, v, 8 [7]

Lead.—Lead, kindly Light, amid the encircling gloom,
Lead thou me on!
J. H. NEWMAN, *The Pillar of the Cloud*, st. 1

[1] Foul fall him that blenches first. SCOTT, *Marmion*, vi, 12

Leaking.— Racketing her rivets loose, smoke-stack white as snow,
All the coals adrift a deck, half the rails below,
Leaking like a lobster-pot, steering like a dray —
Out we took the "Bolivar," out across the bay.
KIPLING, *Ballad of the Bolivar*, st. 2

Leal.— I'm wearing awa', Jean,
Like snaw when it 's thaw, Jean,
I'm wearing awa'
To the land o' the leal.
There 's nae sorrow there, Jean,
There 's neither cauld nor care, Jean,
The day is aye fair,
In the land o' the leal.
LADY NAIRNE, *The Land o' the Leal*, st. 1

Learn. She is not yet so old
But she may learn.
SHAKESPEARE, *Merchant of Venice*, iii, 2

Learning.— Whence is thy learning? hath thy toil
O'er books consumed the midnight oil?
GAY, *The Shepherd and the Philosopher*, lines 15, 16

A little learning is a dangerous thing;
Drink deep, or taste not the Pierian spring.
There shallow draughts intoxicate the brain,
And drinking largely sobers us again.
POPE, *Essay on Criticism*, lines 215–218

A progeny of learning. SHERIDAN, *The Rivals*, i, 2

Leave.— And wilt thou leave me thus?
That hath loved thee so long?
In wealth and woe among:
And is thy heart so strong
As for to leave me thus?
Say nay! say nay!
SIR T. WYATT, *An Earnest Suit to His Unkind Mistress Not to Forsake Him*, st. 2

Leaves.— Nothing but leaves; the spirit grieves
Over a wasted life;
Sin committed while conscience slept,
Promises made, but never kept,
Hatred, battle, and strife;
Nothing but leaves!
L. E. AKERMAN, *Nothing but Leaves*, st. 1

Like the leaves of the forest when summer is green,
That host with their banners at sunset were seen:
Like the leaves of the forest when autumn hath blown,
That host on the morrow lay withered and strown.
BYRON, *Destruction of Sennacherib*, st. 2

The book of Nature
Getteth short of leaves. HOOD, *The Season*, st. 2

Thick as autumnal leaves that strow the brooks
In Vallombrosa.—MILTON, *Paradise Lost*, I, lines 302, 303

Leek.— I 'll knock his leek about his pate
Upon Saint Davy's day.
SHAKESPEARE, *King Henry V*, iv, 1

I will make him eat some part of my leek, or I will peat his pate four days. Pite, I pray you; it is goot for your green wound and your ploody coxcomb.—*Ibid.*, v, 1

Leg. His leg, then broke,
Had got a deputy of oak;
For when a shin in fight is cropped,
The knee with one of timber 's propped,
Esteemed more honourable than the other,
And takes place, though the younger brother.
BUTLER, *Hudibras*, I, ii, lines 141–146

Legislators.— When legislators keep the law,
When banks dispense with bolts and locks,
HOLMES, *Latter-Day Warnings*, st. 1

Letter.— Any man that can write may answer a letter.
SHAKESPEARE, *Romeo and Juliet*, ii, 4

Letters.— Heav'n first taught letters for some wretch's aid,
Some banished lover, or some captive maid;
They . . .
Speed the soft intercourse from soul to soul,
And waft a sigh from Indus to the Pole.[1]
POPE, *Eloïsa to Abélard*, lines 51–58

Letter-writing.—She 'll vish there wos more, an' that 's the great art o' letter-writin'.
DICKENS, *Pickwick Papers*, xxxiii

---

[1] Whilst all the stars that round her burn,
And all the planets in their turn,
Confirm the tidings as they roll,
And spread the truth from pole to pole.*
ADDISON, *Hymn: The Spacious Firmament on High*, st. 2

* Like a sea of glory
It spreads from pole to pole. R. HEBER, *Missionary Hymn*, st. 4

Level.— We met upon the level an' we parted on the square.
KIPLING, *The Mother-Lodge*, st. 2

Levite. You, Levite small,
Who shut your saintly ears, and prate of hell
And heretics, because outside church-doors,
Your church-doors, congregations poor and small
Praise heaven in their own way.
D. M. MULOCK CRAIK, *The Dead Czar*, st. 5

Liar.— Thou liar of the first magnitude!
CONGREVE, *Love for Love*, ii, 5 [1]

Liberty.— O Liberty! the prisoner's pleasing dream,
The poet's muse, his passion, and his theme.
COWPER, *Table Talk*, lines 288, 289

Is life so dear, or peace so sweet, as to be purchased at the price of chains and slavery? Forbid it, Almighty God! — I know not what course others may take; but as for me, give me liberty, or give me death.
PATRICK HENRY, *Speech in the Virginia Assembly*, March 23, 1775

The God who gave us life, gave us liberty at the same time.—JEFFERSON, *Summary View of the Rights of British America*

Make way for liberty! he cried,
Make way for liberty, and died.
. . . . .
Thus Switzerland again was free;
Thus death made way for liberty.
JAMES MONTGOMERY, *The Patriot's Password*, st. 1, 9

O'er the wild mountains and luxuriant plains,
Nature in all the pomp of beauty reigns,
In all the pride of freedom.— Nature free
Proclaims that Man was born for liberty.
JAMES MONTGOMERY, *The West Indies*, i, st. 14

Give me again my hollow tree,
A crust of bread, and liberty!
POPE, *Imitations of Horace*, II, Satire vi, lines 220, 221

O Liberty! Liberty! how many crimes are committed in thy name![1] M. J. P. ROLAND

I must have liberty
Withal, as large a charter as the wind,
To blow on whom I please; for so fools have.
SHAKESPEARE, *As You Like It*, ii, 7

---

[1] License they mean when they cry liberty. MILTON, *On Detraction*

Liberty and Union, now and for ever, one and inseparable. —DANIEL WEBSTER, *Second Speech on Foote's Resolution*, January, 1830

Library. My library
Was dukedom large enough.
SHAKESPEARE, *The Tempest*, i, 2

Lie.— If the devil, to serve his turn,
Can tell truth; why the saints should scorn,
When it serves theirs, to swear and lie,
I think there's little reason why.
BUTLER, *Hudibras*, II, ii, lines 123–126

After all, what is a lie? 'T is but
The truth in masquerade; and I defy
Historians, heroes, lawyers, priests, to put
A fact without some leaven of a lie.
BYRON, *Don Juan*, Canto xi, st. 37

Dare to be true. Nothing can need a lie:
A fault, which needs it most, grows two thereby.[1]
GEORGE HERBERT, *The Church Porch*, st. 13

Sin has many tools, but a lie is the handle which fits them all.[2] HOLMES, *Autocrat of the Breakfast-Table*, vi

He will lie, sir, with such volubility, that you would think truth were a fool.
SHAKESPEARE, *All's Well That Ends Well*, iv, 3

Jaques. Can you nominate in order now the degrees of the lie?

. . . . . .

Touchstone. I will name you the degrees. The first, the Retort Courteous; the second, the Quip Modest; the third, the Reply Churlish; the fourth, the Reproof Valiant; the fifth, the Countercheck Quarrelsome; the sixth, the Lie with Circumstance; the seventh, the Lie Direct. All these you may avoid but the Lie Direct, and you may avoid that, too, with an If.[3]
SHAKESPEARE, *As You Like It*, v, 4

If I tell thee a lie, spit in my face, call me horse.
SHAKESPEARE, *King Henry IV, Part I*, ii, 4

---

[1] He that does one fault at first,
And lies to hide it, makes it two. ISAAC WATTS, *Song xv*

[2] Who dares think one thing, and another tell,
My heart detests him as the gates of hell.—POPE, *Iliad*, IX, lines 412–413

[3] Your If is the only peace-maker; much virtue in If.
SHAKESPEARE, *As You Like It*, v, 4

You lie in your throat.
SHAKESPEARE, *King Henry IV, Part II*, i, 2

Like one
Who having into truth, by telling of it,
Made such a sinner of his memory,
To credit his own lie, he did believe
He was indeed the duke.—SHAKESPEARE, *The Tempest*, i, 2

You lie — under a mistake —
For this is the most civil sort of lie
That can be given to a man's face.[1]
SHELLEY, *Scenes from the Magico Prodigioso*, Scene I

And the parson made it his text that week, and he said likewise
That a lie which is half a truth is ever the blackest of lies,
That a lie which is all a lie may be met and fought with outright,
But a lie which is part a truth is a harder matter to fight.
TENNYSON, *The Grandmother*, st. 8

Life.— Life's but a series of trifles at best.[2]
ANONYMOUS, cited in *Memoir of Laurence Sterne*

Is life worth living? Yes, so long
As there is wrong to right,
Wail of the weak against the strong,
Or tyranny to fight;
Long as there lingers gloom to chase,
Or streaming tear to dry,
One kindred woe, one sorrowing face
That smiles as we draw nigh.
. . . . .
So long as faith with freedom reigns
And loyal hope survives,
And gracious charity remains
To leaven lowly lives;

[1] Should captains the remark, or critics, make,
They also lie too — under a mistake.— BYRON, *Don Juan*, Canto i, st. 208

[2] Life is the rose's hope while yet unblown;
The reading of an ever-changing tale;
The light uplifting of a maiden's veil;
A pigeon tumbling in clear summer air;
A laughing schoolboy, without grief or care,
Riding the springy branches of an elm.
KEATS, *Sleep and Poetry*, lines 90–95

Life is a jest,* and all things show it:
I thought so once, but now I know it. GAY, *My Own Epitaph*

* Man's life is but a jest,
A dream, a shadow, bubble, air, a vapour at the best.
G. W. THORNBURY, *The Jester's Sermon*

Life—*Continued*

While there is one untrodden tract
For intellect or will,
And men are free to think and act,
Life is worth living still.
ALFRED AUSTIN, *Is Life Worth Living*, st. 4

Life's more than breath and the quick round of blood,—
It is a great spirit and a busy heart.
P. J. BAILEY, *Festus*, Scene — A Country Town — Market-place — Noon

Life! I know not what thou art,
But know that thou and I must part;
And when, or how, or where we met
I own to me's a secret yet.
. . . .
Life! we've been long together
Through pleasant and through cloudy weather,
'T is hard to part when friends are dear —
Perhaps 't will cost a sigh, a tear;
Then steal away, give little warning,
Choose thine own time;
Say not Good Night,— but in some brighter clime
Bid me Good Morning.
A. L. BARBAULD, *Life! I Know Not*, etc., st. 1, 3

Life treads on life, and heart on heart;
We press too close in church and mart
To keep a dream or grave apart.
E. B. BROWNING, *A Vision of Poets*, Conclusion, st. 1

Life's enchanted cup but sparkles near the brim.
BYRON, *Childe Harold*, Canto iii, st. 8

If when for life's prizes
You're running, you trip,
Get up, start again —
"Keep a stiff upper lip!"
PHŒBE CARY, *Keep a Stiff Upper Lip*, st. 2

Side by side, for the way was one,
The toilsome journey of life was done,
And all who in Christ the Saviour died
Came out alike on the other side;
No forms, or crosses, or books had they,
No gowns of silk, or suits of grey,
No creeds to guide them, or MSS.,
For all had put on Christ's righteousness.
MRS. CLEVELAND, *No Sect in Heaven*, st. 23

To know, to esteem, to love,— and then to part,—
Makes up life's tale to many a feeling heart.
S. T. COLERIDGE, *The Two Sisters*, lines 1, 2

Life, that dares send
A challenge to his end,
And when it comes, say, "Welcome, friend."
R. CRASHAW, *Wishes to His Supposed Mistress*, st. 29

Life, what is it but a dream?[1]
C. L. DODGSON ("LEWIS CARROLL"), *Through the Looking-Glass*, Ad Finem

Every life has pages vacant still,
Whereon a man may write the thing he will.
HENRY VAN DYKE, *A Legend of Service*, st. 2

Life protracted is protracted woe.—SAMUEL JOHNSON, *The Vanity of Human Wishes*, line 258

I have fought my fight, I have lived my life,
I have drunk my share of wine;
From Trier to Coln there was never a knight
Led a merrier life than mine.[2]
KINGSLEY, *The Knight's Leap*, st. 3

Our cradle is the starting-place,
Life is the running of the race,
We reach the goal
When, in the mansions of the blest,
Death leaves to its eternal rest
The weary soul.—LONGFELLOW, *Translation: Coplas de Manrique*, st. 10

---

[1] Time fleets, youth fades, life is an empty dream.
ROBERT BROWNING, *Paracelsus*, ii

[2] Be fair, or foul, or rain, or shine,
The joys I have possessed, in spite of fate, are mine.
Not heaven itself upon the past has power;
But what has been, has been, and I have had my hour.
DRYDEN, *Paraphrase of Horace*, III, Ode 29, lines 69–72

I warmed both hands before the fire of life;
It sinks, and I am ready to depart.
WALTER SAVAGE LANDOR, *On Himself*

I have worked — I have felt — I have lived — I have loved.*
D. M. MULOCK CRAIK, *The Good of It* — Moral

*I've lived and loved.— COLERIDGE, trans. of Schiller's *Wallenstein*, I, ii, 6

And I have lived and loved, and closed the door.
R. L. STEVENSON, *I Have Trod the Upward and the Downward Slope*

Life—*Continued*

A few more goings in and out these doors,
A few more chimings of these convent bells,
A few more prayers, a few more sighs and tears,
And the long agony of this life will end.[1]
LONGFELLOW, *Michael Angelo*, II, ii

Tell me not in mournful numbers,
Life is but an empty dream!
For the soul is dead that slumbers,
And things are not what they seem.

Life is real! Life is earnest!
And the grave is not its goal;
Dust thou art, to dust returnest,
Was not spoken of the soul.
LONGFELLOW, *Psalm of Life*, st. 1, 2

This speck of life in time's great wilderness,
This narrow isthmus 'twixt two boundless seas,[2]
The past, the future, two eternities!— T. MOORE,
Lalla Rookh: The Veiled Prophet of Khorassan

I've wandered east, I've wandered west,
Through mony a weary way;
But never, never can forget
The luve o' life's young day!
WILLIAM MOTHERWELL, *Jeanie Morrison*, st. 1

In life, as in a football game, the principle to follow is: Hit the line hard; don't foul and don't shirk, but hit the line hard. THEODORE ROOSEVELT, cited by JACOB RIIS in *Theodore Roosevelt the Citizen*, i

The life that is worth living is worth working for.
THEODORE ROOSEVELT, *Speech at La Crosse, Wisconsin*, 1903

Uncertain life, and sure death.
SHAKESPEARE, *All's Well That Ends Well*, ii, 3

The web of our life is of a mingled yarn, good and ill together. *Ibid.*, iv, 3

---

[1]A few more years shall roll,
A few more seasons come,
And we shall be with those that rest
Asleep within the tomb.
H. BONAR, *A Hymn for the Closing Year*, st. 1

[2]These sands betwixt two tides.
E. B. BROWNING, *Aurora Leigh*, VII, line 1064

Life is a narrow vale between the cold and barren peaks of two eternities.
ROBERT G. INGERSOLL, *Oration at the Funeral of His Brother, E. C. Ingersoll*

I do not set my life at a pin's fee;
And for my soul, what can it do to that,
Being a thing immortal as itself?
SHAKESPEARE, *Hamlet*, i, 4

Nothing in his life
Became him like the leaving it.
SHAKESPEARE, *Macbeth*, i, 4

After life's fitful fever he sleeps well;
Treason has done his worst: nor steel, nor poison,
Malice domestic, foreign levy, nothing,
Can touch him further. *Ibid.*, iii, 2

I have lived long enough: my way of life
Is fallen into the sear, the yellow leaf;[1]
And that which should accompany old age,
As honour, love, obedience, troops of friends,
I must not look to have; but, in their stead,
Curses, not loud but deep, mouth-honour, breath,
Which the poor heart would fain deny, and [but] dare not.
Ibid., v, 3

I am married to a wife
Which is as dear to me as life itself;
But life itself, my wife, and all the world,
Are not with me esteemed above thy life.
SHAKESPEARE, *Merchant of Venice*, iv, 1

You take my house when you do take the prop
That doth sustain my house. You take my life
When you do take the means whereby I live. *Ibid.*

Where is the life that late I led?
SHAKESPEARE, *Taming of the Shrew*, iv, 1

Gonzalo. Here is everything advantageous to life.
Antonio. True; save means to live.
SHAKESPEARE, *The Tempest*, ii, 1

It seems that life is all a void,
On selfish thoughts alone employed;
That length of days is not a good,
Unless their use be understood.
JANE TAYLOR, *The Toad's Journal*

---

[1] Now my sere fancy "falls into the yellow leaf."
BYRON, *Don Juan*, Canto iv, st. 3

My days are in the yellow leaf;
The flowers and fruits of love are gone;
The worm, the canker, and the grief,
Are mine alone! — BYRON, *On Completing His Thirty-Sixth Year*, st. 2

Two children in two neighbour villages
Playing mad pranks along the heathy leas;
Two strangers meeting at a festival;
Two lovers whispering by an orchard wall;
Two lives bound fast in one with golden ease;[1]
Two graves grass-green beside a grey church-tower,
Washed with still rains and daisy-blossomed;
Two children in one hamlet born and bred:
So runs the round of life from hour to hour.
TENNYSON, *Circumstance*

Through all this changing world of changeless law,
And every phase of ever-heightening life.
TENNYSON, *De Profundis*, i

Shadow and shine is life, little Annie, flower and thorn.
TENNYSON, *The Grandmother*, st. 15

The tree of deepest root is found
Least willing still to quit the ground;
'Twas therefore said, by ancient sages,
That love of life increased with years
So much, that in our later stages,
When pains grow sharp, and sickness rages,
The greatest love of life appears.
HESTER L. THRALE (PIOZZI), *The Three Warnings*

He sins against this life who slights the next.
YOUNG, *Night Thoughts*, III, line 400

That life is long which answers life's great end.
Ibid., V, line 773

Light. Not by eastern windows only,
When daylight comes, comes in the light.
In front the sun climbs slow, how slowly,
But westward, look, the land is bright!
A. H. CLOUGH, *Say Not the Struggle Nought Availeth*, st. 4

---

[1] Two souls with but a single thought,
Two hearts that beat as one.— MARIA LOVELL, *Ingomar the Barbarian*

So we grew together,
Like to a double cherry, seeming parted,
But yet an union in partition;
Two lovely berries moulded on one stem;
So, with two seeming bodies, but one heart.
SHAKESPEARE, *Midsummer-Night's Dream*, iii, 2

We still have slept together,
Rose at an instant, learned, played, eat together,
And wheresoe'er we went, like Juno's swans,
Still we went coupled and inseparable.
SHAKESPEARE, *As You Like It*, i, 3

There's a fount about to stream,
There's a light about to beam,
There's a flower about to blow,
There's a warmth about to glow,
There's a midnight darkness changing
Into grey,
Men of thought and men of action,
Clear the way!—CHARLES MACKAY, *Clear the Way*, st. 1

Storied windows richly dight,
Casting a dim religious light.
MILTON, *Il Penseroso*, lines 159, 160

But, soft! what light through yonder window breaks?
It is the east,[1] and Juliet is the sun.
SHAKESPEARE, *Romeo and Juliet*, ii, 2

The light that never was, on sea or land.
WORDSWORTH, *Elegiac Stanzas on a Picture of Peele Castle*, st. 4

Likeness.— As sometimes in a dead man's face,
To those that watch it more and more,
A likeness, hardly seen before,
Comes out — to some one in his race.
TENNYSON, *In Memoriam*, lxxiv, st. 1

Lilies.— In the beauty of the lilies Christ was born across the sea,
With a glory in his bosom that transfigures you and me:
As he died to make men holy, let us die to make men free,
While God is marching on.
JULIA WARD HOWE, *Battle-Hymn of the Republic*, st. 5

Lily.— A most unspotted lily.
SHAKESPEARE, *King Henry VIII*, v, 5 [4]

Lincoln.— You lay a wreath on murdered Lincoln's bier,
You, who with mocking pencil wont to trace,
Broad for the self-complacent British sneer,
His length of shambling limb, his furrowed face.
TOM TAYLOR, *Abraham Lincoln*, st. 1

Linden.— On Linden, when the sun was low,
All bloodless lay the untrodden snow;
And dark as winter was the flow
Of Iser, rolling rapidly.—CAMPBELL, *Hohenlinden*, st. 1

Line.— "I see you a shaving of a baker, . . . last week," said the coal-heaver.—"It's necessary to draw the line somewheres," replied [the barber] . . . "We can't go beyond bakers." DICKENS, *Nicholas Nickleby*, lii

[1] The East is unveiled, the East hath confessed
A flush. LANIER, *Sunrise*, lines 120, 126

Linen.— It is not linen you 're wearing out,
But human creatures' lives!
HOOD, *The Song of the Shirt*, st. 4

They 'll find linen enough on every hedge.
SHAKESPEARE, *King Henry IV, Part I*, iv, 2

Linnets.— I do but sing because I must,
And pipe but as the linnets sing.
TENNYSON, *In Memoriam*, xxi, st. 6

Lion.— Old England! thy name shall yet warrant thy fame,
If the brow of the foeman should scowl;
Let the Lion be stirred by too daring a word,
And beware of his echoing growl.
ELIZA COOK, *The Red Cross of England*, st. 1

The lion's paw is all the law.
LOWELL, *Biglow Papers*, II, ii, *Jonathan to John*, st. 1

The man that once did sell the lion's skin
While the beast lived, was killed with hunting him.
SHAKESPEARE, *King Henry V*, iv, 3

When the lion fawns upon the lamb,
The lamb will never cease to follow him.
SHAKESPEARE, *King Henry VI, Part III*, iv, 8

Oh, well did he become that lion's robe,
That did disrobe the lion of that robe.
SHAKESPEARE, *King John*, ii, 1

Thou wear a lion's hide! doff it for shame,
And hang a calf's skin on those recreant limbs.
Ibid., iii, 1

There is a lion in the way.[1]
TENNYSON, *The Holy Grail*, line 643

Lip.— Our vicar he calls it damnation to sip
The ripe ruddy dew of a woman's dear lip,[2]
Says, that Beelzebub lurks in her kerchief so sly,
And Apollyon shoots darts from her merry black eye;
Yet whoop, Jack! kiss Gillian the quicker,
Till she bloom like a rose, and a fig for the vicar!
SCOTT, *Lady of the Lake*, Canto vi, st. 2

---

[1] He espied two lions in the way. . . . The lions were chained, but he saw not the chains. BUNYAN, *Pilgrim's Progress*, I, iii

[2] You have witchcraft in your lips.— SHAKESPEARE, *King Henry V*, v, 2

Oh, how ripe in show
Thy lips, those kissing cherries, tempting grow!
SHAKESPEARE, *Midsummer-Night's Dream*, iii, 2

Her lips were red; and one was thin,
Compared to that was next her chin;
(Some bee had stung it newly).
SIR JOHN SUCKLING, *Ballad Upon a Wedding*, st. 11

Many an evening by the waters did we watch the stately ships,
And our spirits rushed together at the touching of the lips.
TENNYSON, *Locksley Hall*, lines 37, 38

Lips.— Oh, that those lips had language! Life has passed
With me but roughly since I heard thee last.
COWPER, *On the Receipt of My Mother's Picture*, lines 1, 2

My lips are no common, though several they be.
SHAKESPEARE, *Love's Labour's Lost*, ii

Live.— We live in deeds, not years;[1] in thoughts, not breaths;
In feelings, not in figures on a dial.
We should count time by heart-throbs.
P. J. BAILEY, *Festus*, Scene — A Country Town — Market-place — Noon

So live, that when thy summons comes to join
The innumerable caravan that moves
To that mysterious realm where each shall take
His chamber in the silent halls of death,
Thou go not, like the quarry-slave at night,
Scourged to his dungeon, but, sustained and soothed
By an unfaltering trust, approach thy grave
Like one who wraps the drapery of his couch
About him, and lies down to pleasant dreams.[2]
BRYANT, *Thanatopsis*, lines 73–81

On parent knees, a naked new-born child,
[Naked on parent knees, a new-born child]
Weeping thou sat'st while all around thee smiled;
So live, that, sinking in thy last long sleep,
Calm thou [Thou then] mayst smile, while all around thee weep.—CALIDASA, *The Babe* (trans. SIR WILLIAM JONES)

Live while you live, the epicure would say,
And seize the pleasures of the present day;
Live while you live, the sacred preacher cries,
And give to God each moment as it flies.
Lord, in my views, let both united be;
I live in pleasure when I live to thee.
DODDRIDGE, *Epigram on his Family Arms* (*Dum vivimus vivamus*)

---

[1] He most lives
Who thinks most — feels the noblest — acts the best.
P. J. BAILEY, *Festus*, Scene — A Country Town — Market-place — Noon

Trust not in words, but deeds.—YOUNG, *Night Thoughts*, VII, line 1005

[2] Live well, and fear no sudden fate;
When God calls virtue to the grave,
Alike 't is justice, soon or late,
Mercy alike to kill or save.
Virtue unmoved can hear the call,
And face the flash that melts the ball.
POPE, *Epitaphs on John Hughes and Sarah Drew*, st. 2

So mayst thou live, till, like ripe fruit, thou drop
Into thy mother's lap, or be with ease
Gathered, not harshly plucked, for death mature.
MILTON, *Paradise Lost*, XI, lines 535-537

I would not live alway: I ask not to stay
Where storm after storm rises dark o'er the way.
W. A. MUHLENBERG, *I Would Not Live Alway*, st. 2

He knows to live, who keeps the middle state,
And neither leans on this side, nor on that.—POPE,
Imitations of Horace, II, Satire ii, lines 61, 62

"Let me not live," quoth he,
"After my flame lacks oil, to be the snuff
Of younger spirits."[1]
SHAKESPEARE, *All's Well That Ends Well*, i, 2

Lived.— She lived.[2]— What further can be said
Of all the generations dead?
She died.— What else can be foretold
Of all the living, young or old?
JAMES MONTGOMERY, *Epitaph*

Livery.— He was a man
Who stole the livery of the court of heaven
To serve the devil in.
POLLOK, *The Course of Time*, VIII, lines 616-618

Lives.—Our lives are rivers, gliding free
To that unfathomed, boundless sea,
The silent grave!
Thither all earthly pomp and boast
Roll, to be swallowed up and lost
In one dark wave.
LONGFELLOW, *Translation: Coplas de Manrique*, st. 5

---

[1] Learn to live well, or fairly make your will;
You've played, and loved, and eat, and drank your fill:
Walk sober off; before a sprightlier age
Comes titt'ring on, and shoves you from the stage.
POPE, *Imitations of Horace*, II, Epistle ii, lines 322-325

[2] Once in the flight of ages past,
There lived a man: — and who was he?
—Mortal! howe'er thy lot be cast,
That Man resembled thee.

. . . . .

The annals of the human race,
Their ruins, since the world began,
Of him afford no other trace
Than this,— There lived a man.
JAMES MONTGOMERY, *The Common Lot*, st. 1, 10

Living.— How good is man's life, the mere living! how fit to employ
All the heart and the soul and the senses for ever in joy!
R. BROWNING, *Saul*, ix

Thank Heaven! the crisis —
The danger is past,
And the lingering illness
Is over at last —
And the fever called "Living"
Is conquered at last.
POE, *For Annie*, st. 1

Not what we would, but what we must,
Makes up the sum of living.
R. H. STODDARD, *The Country Life*, st. 1

No means of stopping for breath, to have one hour's quiet for reposeful thought, nor to exchange a peaceful word. No, this is not living!
CHARLES WAGNER, *The Simple Life*, i

Plain living and high thinking.
WORDSWORTH, *Sonnet: London*, 1802

Loafe.— I loafe and invite my soul.
WALT WHITMAN, *Song of Myself*, 1

Lochaber.— Farewell to Lochaber! and farewell, my Jean,
Where heartsome with thee I hae mony day been;
For Lochaber no more, Lochaber no more,
We 'll maybe return to Lochaber no more!
ALLAN RAMSAY, *Lochaber No More*, st. 1

Lochinvar.—Oh, young Lochinvar is come out of the west!
SCOTT, *Marmion*, v, 12

Locks.— Thou canst not say I did it: never shake
Thy gory locks at me. SHAKESPEARE, *Macbeth*, iii, 4

Lodge.— Oh for a lodge in some vast wilderness,
Some boundless contiguity of shade,
Where rumor of oppression and deceit,
Of unsuccessful or successful war,
Might never reach me more.
COWPER, *The Task: The Time-Piece*, lines 1–5

Lodgings.— Brave lodgings for one, brave lodgings for one,
A few feet of cold earth, when life is done;
A stone at the head, a stone at the feet,
A rich, juicy meal for the worms to eat;
Rank grass over head, and damp clay around,
Brave lodgings for one, these, in holy ground.
DICKENS, *Pickwick Papers*, xxix

Logic.— Logic is logic. That 's all I say.
HOLMES, *The Deacon's Masterpiece*, st. 12

Logs.— Bring in great logs and let them lie,
To make a solid core of heat.
TENNYSON, *In Memoriam*, cvii, st. 5

Lone.— A poor lone woman.[1]
SHAKESPEARE, *King Henry IV, Part II*, ii, 1

Loneliness.— But it was something still to know
Thy dawn and dusk were mine,
And that we felt the same breeze blow,
And saw the same star shine:
And still the shadowy hope was rife
That once in this waste weary life
My path might cross with thine,
And one brief gleam of beauty bless
My spirit's utter loneliness. PRAED, *A Farewell*, st. 4

Long-ago.— The lusty days of long-ago,
When you were Bill and I was Joe.
HOLMES, *Bill and Joe*, st. 1

Longings. I have
Immortal longings in me.[2]
SHAKESPEARE, *Antony and Cleopatra*, v, 2

Look. Look before you ere you leap;
For, as you sow, y' re like to reap.[3]
BUTLER, *Hudibras*, II, ii, lines 503, 504

Looked.— Sighed and looked unutterable things.
THOMSON, *The Seasons: Summer*, line 1188

Lopping.— Lopping away of the limb by the pitiful-pitiless knife,—
Torture and trouble in vain,— for it never could save us a life. TENNYSON, *Defence of Lucknow*, st. 6

Lord.— They never sought in vain that sought the Lord aright! BURNS, *The Cotter's Saturday Night*, st. 6

---

[1] I am a lone lorn creetur and everythink goes contrairy with me.
DICKENS, *David Copperfield*, I, iii

[2] I had immortal feelings. R. BROWNING, *Paracelsus*, iii

I feel the infinite in me.— NAPOLEON BONAPARTE, *Life*, by Sloane, IV, 231

[3] Looke ere thou leape, see ere thou go.
THOMAS TUSSER, *Five Hundred Points of Good Husbandry: Of Wiving and Thriving*

But let a lord once own the happy lines,
How the wit brightens! how the style refines!
Before his sacred name flies every fault,
And each exalted stanza teems with thought!

POPE, *Essay on Criticism*, lines 420–423

Lords. These old pheasant-lords,
These partridge-breeders of a thousand years.

TENNYSON, *Aylmer's Field*, lines 381, 382

Lose.— Oh, misery! must I lose that too?

THOMAS MOORE, *Lalla Rookh: The Fire-Worshippers*

Loss.— Wise men ne'er sit and wail their loss,
But cheerly seek how to redress their harms.
What though the mast be now blown overboard,
The cable broke, the holding-anchor lost,
And half our sailors swallowed in the flood!
Yet lives our pilot still.

SHAKESPEARE, *King Henry VI, Part III*, v, 4

Lost.— For 't is a truth well known to most,
That whatsoever thing is lost,
We seek it, ere it comes to light,
In every cranny but the right.

COWPER, *The Retired Cat*

What though the field be lost?
All is not lost;[1] the unconquerable will,
And study of revenge, immortal hate,
And courage never to submit or yield.

MILTON, *Paradise Lost*, I, lines 105–108

The quiet sense of something lost.

TENNYSON, *In Memoriam*, lxxviii, st. 2

Lothario.— Is this that haughty gallant, gay Lothario?

N. ROWE, *The Fair Penitent*, v, 1

Love.— Love will find out the way.

ANONYMOUS, *The Great Adventurer*, st. 1, quoted
in Richard Brome's *Sparagus Garden*

But had I wist, before I kissed,
  That love had been sae ill to win,
I'd locked my heart in a case o' gowd,
  And pinned it wi' a siller pin.

ANONYMOUS, *Waly, Waly*, st. 5

Be ye certain all seems love,
Viewed from Allah's throne above;

---

[1] All is lost save honour.
FRANCIS I, *Letter after his defeat at Pavia*, February 24, 1525

Love—*Continued*

Be ye stout of heart, and come
Bravely onward to your home!
La Allah illa Allah! yea!
Thou love divine! Thou love alway!
SIR EDWIN ARNOLD, *After Death in Arabia*, st. 7

I loved thee once, I 'll love no more,
Thine be the grief as is the blame;
Thou art not what thou wast before,
What reason I should be the same?
He that can love unloved again,
Hath better store of love than brain:
God sends me love my debts to pay,
While unthrifts fool their love away.
SIR R. AYTON, *Woman's Inconstancy*, st. 1

Nuptial love maketh mankind; friendly love perfecteth it; but wanton love corrupteth and embaseth[1] it.
BACON, *Essay X: Of Love*

Love is the art of hearts and heart of arts.
P. J. BAILEY, *Festus*, Scene — Home

Wilt thou cure thine heart
Of love, and all its smart,—
Then die, dear, die!
T. L. BEDDOES, *If Thou Wilt Ease Thine Heart*

Many a soul, o'er life's drear desert faring,
Love's pure congenial spring unfound, unquaffed,
Suffers — recoils — then, thirsty and despairing
Of what it would, descends and sips the nearest draught!
M. G. BROOKS, *Disappointment*

If you loved only what were worth your love,
Love were clear gain.
R. BROWNING, *James Lee's Wife*, vii, st. 2

No torment is so bad as love. BURTON, *Anatomy of Melancholy*, The Author's Abstract, line 61

Love is a boy, by poets styled,
Then spare the rod, and spoil the child.
BUTLER, *Hudibras*, II, i, lines 843, 844

Man's love is of man's life a thing apart,
'T is woman's whole existence.[2]
BYRON, *Don Juan*, Canto i, st. 194

---

[1] Love did embase him
Into a kitchen drudge. THIRTEENTH CENTURY BALLAD

[2] In her first passion woman loves her lover,
In all the others all she loves is love.
BYRON, *Don Juan*, Canto iii, st. 3

Most men know love but as a part of life. TIMROD, *Sonnet*, line 1

The cold in clime are cold in blood,
  Their love can scarce deserve the name,
But mine was like the lava flood
  That boils in Ætna's breast of flame.
I cannot prate in puling strain
Of ladye-love, and beauty's chain:
If changing cheek, and scorching vein,
Lips taught to writhe, but not complain,
If bursting heart, and madd'ning brain,
And daring deed, and vengeful steel,
And all that I have felt, and feel,
Betoken love — that love was mine,
And shown by many a bitter sign.
'Tis true I could not whine nor sigh,
I knew but to obtain or die.
I die — but first I have possessed,
And, come what may, I have been blest.[1]
BYRON, *The Giaour*, lines 1099–1115

Yes, love indeed is light from heaven,
  A spark of that immortal fire
With angels shared, by Allah given,
  To lift from earth our low desire.
Devotion wafts the mind above,
But heaven itself descends in love;
A feeling from the Godhead caught,
To wean from self each sordid thought;
A ray of him who formed the whole;
A glory circling round the soul! *Ibid.*, lines 1131–1140

Time shall make the bushes green;
  Time dissolve the winter snow;
Winds be soft, and skies serene;
  Linnets sing their wonted strain:
    But again
Blighted love shall never blow.— LUIS DE CAMOENS,
Blighted Love (trans. Lord Strangford), st. 3

Love's a fire that needs renewal
Of fresh beauty for its fuel;
Love's wing moults when caged and captured,[2]
Only free, he soars enraptured.
CAMPBELL, *Song: How Delicious is the Winning*, st. 1

---

[1] *Cf.* LIFE.

[2] How the light, light love, he has wings to fly
  At suspicion of a bond. R. BROWNING, *James Lee's Wife*, iv, st. 8

Curse on all laws but those which love has made.
Love, free as air, at sight of human ties,
Spreads his light wings, and in a moment flies.
POPE, *Eloïsa to Abélard*, lines 74–76

Love—*Continued*

Then fly betimes, for only they
Conquer love that run away.
THOMAS CAREW, *Conquest by Flight*, st. 2

All thoughts, all passions, all delights,
Whatever stirs this mortal frame,
All are but ministers of love,
And feed his sacred flame.
S. T. COLERIDGE, *Love*, st. 1

Two people who cannot afford to play cards for money sometimes sit down to a quiet game for love.
DICKENS, *Nicholas Nickleby*, i

Love 's the subject of the comic muse.
DRYDEN, *Cymon and Iphigenia*, line 24

Love, studious how to please, improves our parts
With polished manners, and adorns with arts.
Ibid., lines 31, 32

Since love is held the master-passion,
Its loss must be the pain supreme.
P. L. DUNBAR, *Lyrics of Lowly Life*, Ione, i

O, dinna ask me gin I lo'e ye:
Troth, I daurna tell!
Dinna ask me gin I lo'e ye,—
Ask it o' yoursel'.
JOHN DUNLOP, *Dinna Ask Me*, st. 1

Love is joy and grief,
And trembling doubt, and certain-sure belief,
And fear, and hope, and longing unexpressed,
In pain most human, and in rapture brief
Almost divine.
HENRY VAN DYKE, *Music: The Symphony*, st. 2

If with love thy heart has burned;
If thy love is unreturned;
Hide thy grief within thy breast,
Though it tear thee unexpressed.
EMERSON, *To Rhea*, st. 2

The bashful virgin's sidelong looks of love
GOLDSMITH, *The Deserted Village*, st. 1

My dear and only love.—JAMES GRAHAM, MARQUIS OF MONTROSE, *My Dear and Only Love*, st. 1

Pray love me little, so you love me long.
HERRICK, *Love Me Little, Love Me Long*

We die with love, and never dream we're dead.
HOLMES, *Prologue, ad finem*

Love prays devoutly when it prays for love.
HOOD, *Hero and Leander*, st. 20

You say — Sir Andrew and his love of law,
And I — the Saviour with his law of love.
HOOD, *Ode to Rae Wilson, Esquire*, st. 11

Love thwarted in bad temper oft has vent.
KEATS, *The Cap and Bells*, st. 20

Love never dies, but lives, immortal Lord.
KEATS, *Isabella, or the Pot of Basil*, st. 50

Love in a hut, with water, and a crust,
Is — Love, forgive us! — cinders, ashes, dust;
Love in a palace is perhaps at last
More grievous torment than a hermit's fast.
KEATS, *Lamia*, ii, st. 1

What do the doves say? Curuck-coo,
You love me and I love you.[1]
KINGSLEY, *Juventus Mundi*, lines 75, 76

The light of love shines over all;
Of love, that says not mine and thine,
But ours, for ours is thine and mine.
LONGFELLOW, *Hanging of the Crane*, ii, st. 2

Tell me, my heart, if this be love.
LORD LYTTLETON, *Tell Me, My Heart*, st. 1

I love the song of birds,
And the children's early words,
And a loving woman's voice, low and sweet, John Brown.
CHARLES MACKAY, *John Brown*, st. 2

Come live with me and be my love,
And we will all the pleasures prove
That hills and valleys, dales and fields,
Woods or steepy mountain yields.
MARLOWE, *The Passionate Shepherd to His Love*, st. 1

---

[1] The lark is so brimful of gladness and love,
The green fields below him, the blue sky above,
That he sings, and he sings; and for ever sings he —
I love my love, and my love loves me.
S. T. COLERIDGE, *Answer to a Child's Question*, lines 9–12

I love my love, because I know
My love loves me. MACKAY, *I Love My Love*

I love my love, and my love loves me.— GERALD MASSEY, *I Love My Love*

My true-love hath my heart, and I have his.—SIR PHILIP SIDNEY, *The Countess of Pembroke's Arcadia, Heart-Exchange*

Love—*Continued*

Too often Love's insidious dart
Thrills the fond soul with wild desire,
But kills the heart.
JAMES MONTGOMERY, *The Grave*, st. 21

Oh! what was love made for, if 'tis not the same
Through joy and through torment, through glory and shame?
I know not, I ask not, if guilt 's in that heart,
I but know that I love thee, whatever thou art.
T. MOORE, *Come, Rest in This Bosom*, st. 2

Oh! the days are gone, when Beauty bright
My heart's chain wove;
When my dream of life, from morn till night,
Was love, still love.
New hope may bloom,
And days may come,
Of milder, calmer beam,
But there 's nothing half so sweet in life
As love's young dream:
No, there 's nothing half so sweet in life
As love's young dream.
T. MOORE, *Love's Young Dream*, st. 1

We loved with a love that was more than love.
POE, *Annabel Lee*, st. 2

But our love it was stronger by far than the love
Of those who were older than we —
Of many far wiser than we —
And neither the angels in heaven above,
Nor the demons down under the sea,
Can ever dissever my soul from the soul
Of the beautiful Annabel Lee. *Ibid.*, st. 5

Thou would'st be loved? — then let thy heart
From its present pathway part not!
Being everything which now thou art,
Be nothing which thou art not.
So with the world thy gentle ways,
Thy grace, thy more than beauty,
Shall be an endless theme of praise,
And love — a simple duty.
POE, To F —— S. O —— D

Is it, in heav'n, a crime to love too well?
To bear too tender or too firm a heart,
To act a lover's or a Roman's part?
POPE, *Elegy to an Unfortunate Lady*, lines 6–8

Fame, wealth, and honour! what are you to love?
POPE, *Eloïsa to Abélard*, line 80

Who love too much, hate in the like extreme,
And both the golden mean alike condemn.
POPE, *Odyssey*, XV, lines 79, 80

I think that you will love me still,
  Though far our fates may be;
And that your heart will fondly thrill
  When strangers ask of me;
My praise will be your proudest theme
  When these dark days are past:
If this be all an idle dream,
    It is my last! PRAED, *The Last*, st. 4

If all the world and love were young,
And truth on every shepherd's tongue,
These pleasures might my passion move
To live with thee, and be thy love.
RALEIGH, *Reply to Marlowe's Passionate Shepherd*, st. 1

Love rules the court, the camp, the grove,
And men below, and saints above;[1]
For love is heaven, and heaven is love.
SCOTT, *Lay of the Last Minstrel*, Canto iii, st. 2

True love's the gift which God has given
To man alone beneath the heaven:
  It is not fantasy's hot fire,
    Whose wishes, soon as granted, fly;
  It liveth not in fierce desire,
    With dead desire it doth not die;
It is the secret sympathy,
The silver link, the silken tie,
Which heart to heart, and mind to mind,
In body and in soul can bind. *Ibid.*, Canto v, st. 13

Love will still be lord of all. *Ibid.*, Canto vi, st. 11

A laggard in love and a dastard in war.
SCOTT, *Marmion*, v, 12

Countess. Love you my son?
Helena. Do you not love him, madam?[2]
SHAKESPEARE, *All's Well That Ends Well*, i, 3

There's beggary in the love that can be reckoned.
SHAKESPEARE, *Antony and Cleopatra*, i, 1

---

[1] It is the imponderables that move the world,— heat, electricity, love.
HOLMES, *Autocrat of the Breakfast-Table*, vi

[2] *Mrs. Bagot.* Are you so fond of him?
Trilby. *Fond* of him? Are n't *you?*
Mrs. Bagot. I'm his mother, my good girl! — DU MAURIER, *Trilby*, iv

Love—*Continued*

Down on your knees,
And thank heaven, fasting, for a good man's love.
SHAKESPEARE, *As You Like It*, iii, 5

Men have died from time to time, and worms have eaten them, but not for love. *Ibid.*, iv, 1

This is the very ecstasy of love.
SHAKESPEARE, *Hamlet*, ii, 1

Ophelia. 'T is brief, my lord.
Hamlet. As woman's love. *Ibid.*, iii, 2

Where love is great, the littlest doubts are fear;
Where little fears grow great, great love grows there.
Ibid.

Though last, not least in love.
SHAKESPEARE, *Julius Cæsar*, iii, 1

When love begins to sicken and decay,
It useth an enforced ceremony. *Ibid.*, iv, 2

I know no ways to mince it in love, but directly to say "I love you." SHAKESPEARE, *King Henry V*, v, 2

My love 's
More richer than my tongue.
SHAKESPEARE, *King Lear*, i, 1

This love is as mad as Ajax.
SHAKESPEARE, *Love's Labour's Lost*, iv, 3

Love, whose month is ever May. *Ibid.*

What! do I love her,
That I desire to hear her speak again,
And feast upon her eyes?
SHAKESPEARE, *Measure for Measure*, ii, 2

There 's something tells me (but it is not love)
I would not lose you.
SHAKESPEARE, *Merchant of Venice*, iii, 2

If there be no great love in the beginning, yet heaven may decrease it upon better acquaintance, when we are married, and have more occasion to know one another: I hope upon familiarity will grow more contempt.
SHAKESPEARE, *The Merry Wives of Windsor*, i, 1

For aught that I could ever read,
Could ever hear by tale or history,
The course of true love never did run smooth.
SHAKESPEARE, *Midsummer-Night's Dream*, i, 1

Speak low, if you speak love.
SHAKESPEARE, *Much Ado about Nothing*, ii, 1

If he be not in love with some woman, there is no believing old signs:[1] a' brushes his hat o' mornings; what should that bode? *Ibid.*, iii, 2

"Suffer love!"—a good epithet! *Ibid.*, v, 2

Excellent wretch! Perdition catch my soul,
But I do love thee! and when I love thee not,
Chaos is come again. SHAKESPEARE, *Othello*, iii, 3

With love's light wings did I o'erperch these walls;
For stony limits cannot hold love out:
And what love can do, that dares love attempt.
SHAKESPEARE, *Romeo and Juliet*, ii, 2

This bud of love, by summer's ripening breath,
May prove a beauteous flower when next we meet.—*Ibid.*

My bounty is as boundless as the sea,
My love as deep; the more I give to thee,
The more I have, for both are infinite. *Ibid.*

Love goes toward love, as schoolboys from their books,
But love from love, toward school with heavy looks.—*Ibid.*

So true a fool is love, that in your will,
Though you do any thing, he thinks no ill.
SHAKESPEARE, *Sonnet* lvii

What is love? 't is not hereafter;
Present mirth hath present laughter;
What 's to come is still unsure:
In delay there lies no plenty;
Then come kiss me, sweet-and-twenty,
Youth 's a stuff will not endure.
SHAKESPEARE, *Twelfth Night*, ii, 3

---

[1] There is none of my uncle's marks upon you: he taught me how to know a man in love. . . . A lean cheek, . . . a blue eye and sunken . . . an unquestionable spirit, . . . a beard neglected, . . . then your hose should be ungartered, your bonnet unbanded, your sleeve unbuttoned, your shoe untied, and everything about you demonstrating a careless desolation. SHAKESPEARE, *As You Like It*, iii, 2

I do love: and it hath taught me to rhyme and to be melancholy. *Ibid.*

Valentine. Why, how know you that I am in love?
Speed. Marry, by these special marks: first, you have learned like Sir Proteus, to wreathe your arms, like a malcontent; to relish a love-song, like a robin-redbreast; to walk alone, like one that had the pestilence; to sigh, like a schoolboy that had lost his A B C; to weep, like a young wench that had buried her grandam; to fast, like one that takes diet; to watch, like one that fears robbing; to speak puling, like a beggar at Hallowmas. You were wont, when you laughed, to crow like a cock; when you walked, to walk like one of the lions; when you fasted, it was presently after dinner; when you looked sadly, it was for want of money: and now you are metamorphosed with a mistress, that, when I look on you, I can hardly think you my master. SHAKESPEARE, *Two Gentlemen of Verona*, ii, 1

Love—*Continued*

Love sought is good, but given unsought is better.
Ibid., iii, 1

Oh, how this spring of love resembleth
The uncertain glory of an April day,
Which now shows all the beauty of the sun,
And by and by a cloud takes all away!
SHAKESPEARE, *Two Gentlemen of Verona*, i, 3

Speed. If you love her, you cannot see her.
Valentine. Why?
Speed. Because Love is blind. *Ibid.*, ii, 1

Though the chameleon Love can feed on the air, I am one that am nourished by my victuals and would fain have meat. *Ibid.*

Love, thou know'st, is full of jealousy. *Ibid.*, ii, 4

Love is a spirit all compact of fire,
Not gross to sink, but light, and will aspire.
SHAKESPEARE, *Venus and Adonis*, lines 149, 150

Prosperity's the very bond of love,
Whose fresh complexion and whose heart together
Affliction alters.
SHAKESPEARE, *The Winter's Tale*, iv, 4 [3]

Love was love, and better than money;
The slyer the theft, the sweeter the honey;
And kissing was clover, all the world over,
Wherever Cupid might wander.
E. C. STEDMAN, *The Diamond Wedding*, st. 2

If of herself she will not love,
Nothing can make her:
The Devil take her! SIR JOHN SUCKLING, *Song: Why So Pale and Wan*, st. 3

Wheresoe'er I am, below, or else above you,
Wheresoe'er you are, my heart shall truly love you.
J. SYLVESTER, *Wheresoe'er I Am*

Open the door of thy heart,
And open thy chamber door,
And my kisses shall teach thy lips
The love that shall fade no more
Till the sun grows cold,
And the stars are old,
And the leaves of the Judgment Book unfold.
BAYARD TAYLOR, *Bedouin Song*, st. 3

They sang of love, and not of fame;
  Forgot was Britain's glory:
Each heart recalled a different name,
  But all sang ' Annie Laurie."
BAYARD TAYLOR, *The Song of the Camp*, st. 5

I cannot understand: I love.
TENNYSON, *In Memoriam*, xcvii, st. 9

Love, art thou sweet? then bitter death must be:
Love, thou art bitter; sweet is death to me.
O Love, if death be sweeter, let me die.
TENNYSON, *Lancelot and Elaine*, lines 1003–1005

In the spring a fuller crimson comes upon the robin's breast;
In the spring the wanton lapwing gets himself another crest;

In the spring a livelier iris changes on the burnished dove;
In the spring a young man's fancy lightly turns to thought of love.
TENNYSON, *Locksley Hall*, lines 17–20

Love took up the glass of Time, and turned it in his glowing hands;
Every moment, lightly shaken, ran itself in golden sands.

Love took up the harp of Life, and smote on all the chords with might;
Smote the chord of Self, that, trembling, passed in music out of sight. *Ibid.*, lines 31–34

In love, if love be love, if love be ours,
Faith and unfaith can ne'er be equal powers:
Unfaith in aught is want of faith in all.
TENNYSON, *Merlin and Vivien*, lines 385–387

Luvv? What's luvv? thou can luvv thy lass an' 'er munny too,[1]
Maäkin' 'em goä togither, as they've good right to do.
Could'n I luvv thy muther by cause o' 'er munny laaïd by?
Naäy — fur I luvved 'er a vast sight moor fur it: reason why. TENNYSON, *Northern Farmer, New Style*, st. 9

We talked of love as coolly as we talked of nebulæ,
And thought no more of being one than we did of being three. W. B. TERRETT, *Platonic*

---

[1]And play for love and money too.—BUTLER, *Hudibras*, III, i, line 1008

Thou who hast faith in the Christ above,
Shall the Koran teach thee the law of love?
O Christian! — open thy heart and door,
Cry east and west to the wandering poor:
"Whoever thou art whose need is great,
In the name of Christ, the Compassionate
And Merciful One, for thee I wait!"
ELIZABETH H. WHITTIER, *Charity*, st. 2

A love that makes heaven or hell for a man.
ELLA WHEELER WILCOX, *The Duet*, st. 5

Love, to endure life's sorrow and earth's woe,
Needs friendship's solid mason-work below.
ELLA WHEELER WILCOX, *Upon the Sand*, st. 2

Loved.— I only know we loved in vain —
I only feel — Farewell! — Farewell!
BYRON, *Farewell*, st. 2

Who ever loved that loved not at first sight?[1]
MARLOWE, *Hero and Leander*, I, line 176; SHAKESPEARE, *As You Like It*, iii, 5

One that loved not wisely but too well.
SHAKESPEARE, *Othello*, v, 2

'T is better to have loved and lost
Than never to have loved at all.
TENNYSON, *In Memoriam*, xxvii, st. 4; lxxxv, st. 1

Lover.— When Psyche's friend becomes her lover,
How sweetly these conditions blend!
But oh, what anguish to discover
Her lover has become—her friend!—MARY AINGE DE VERE ("MADELINE BRIDGES"), *Friend and Lover*

As true a lover
As ever sighed upon a midnight pillow.
SHAKESPEARE, *As You Like It*, ii, 4

The lover,
Sighing like a furnace, with a woeful ballad
Made to his mistress' eyebrow. *Ibid.*, 7

Lovers.— Sing the lovers' litany: —
"Love like ours can never die!"
KIPLING, *The Lovers' Litany*

---

[1]None ever loved but at first sight they loved.
CHAPMAN, *The Blind Beggar of Alexandria*

No sooner met but they looked, no sooner looked but they loved, no sooner loved but they sighed, no sooner sighed but they asked one another the reason, no sooner knew the reason but they sought the remedy; and in these degrees have they made a pair of stairs to marriage.
SHAKESPEARE, *As You Like It*, v, 2

Love is blind, and lovers cannot see
The pretty follies that themselves commit.
SHAKESPEARE, *Merchant of Venice*, ii, 6

Lovers and madmen have such seething brains,
Such shaping fantasies, that apprehend
More than cool reason ever comprehends.
SHAKESPEARE, *Midsummer-Night's Dream*, v, 1

Loves.— God be thanked, the meanest of his creatures
Boasts two soul-sides, one to face the world with,
One to show a woman when he loves her!
R. BROWNING, *One Word More*, xvii

If a man really loves a woman, of course he wouldn't marry her for the world, if he were not quite sure that he was the best person she could by any possibility marry.
HOLMES, *Autocrat of the Breakfast-Table*, x

Oh, what damned minutes tells he o'er
Who dotes, yet doubts, suspects, yet strongly loves!
SHAKESPEARE, *Othello*, iii, 3

I think there is not half a kiss to choose
Who loves another best.
SHAKESPEARE, *Winter's Tale*, iv, 4 [3]

Lovest.— No more of that, Hal, an thou lovest me!
SHAKESPEARE, *King Henry IV, Part I*, ii, 4

Loving.— Women are apt to love the man who they think has the largest capacity of loving.
HOLMES, *Professor at the Breakfast-Table*, vii

Loving is a painful thrill,
And not to love more painful still;
But oh, it is the worst of pain,
To love and not be loved again!
T. MOORE, *Odes of Anacreon*, xxix

So loving to my mother
That he might not beteem the winds of heaven
Visit her face too roughly. SHAKESPEARE, *Hamlet*, i, 2

When you shall see her, tell her that I died
Blessing her, praying for her, loving her;
Save for the bar between us, loving her
As when she laid her head beside my own.
TENNYSON, *Enoch Arden*, lines 874–877

Loyalty. I will follow thee,
To the last gasp, with truth and loyalty.
SHAKESPEARE, *As You Like It*, ii, 3

Luck. There 's nae luck about the house,
There 's nae luck at a'.
There 's little pleasure in the house
When our gudeman 's awa'.
W. J. MICKLE, *The Sailor's Wife*

No ill luck stirring but what lights on my shoulders.
SHAKESPEARE, *Merchant of Venice*, iii, 1

As good luck would have it.
SHAKESPEARE, *Merry Wives of Windsor*, iii, 5

Wheresoe'er thou move, good luck
Shall fling her old shoe after. TENNYSON, *Will Waterproof's Lyrical Monologue*, lines 215, 216

Lucky. 'T is lucky for the boats! Our eyes
Were drawn to him as either fain would say,
What! do they send the psalm up in the spire
And pray because 't is lucky for the boats?
JEAN INGELOW, *Brothers, and a Sermon*

Lying.— The Lord forgi'e me for lying!
BURNS, *Last May a Braw Wooer*, st. 2

'T is as easy as lying. SHAKESPEARE, *Hamlet*, iii, 2

Lord, Lord, how this world is given to lying![1]
SHAKESPEARE, *King Henry IV, Part I*, v, 4

Lyre.— Proud, mad, but not defiant,
He touched at heaven and hell.
Fate found a rare soul pliant
And rung her changes well.
Alternately his lyre,
Stranded with strings of fire,
Led earth's most happy choir,
Or flashed with Israfel.
J. H. BONER, *Poe's Cottage at Fordham*, st. 5

Mad.— Mad from life's history,
Glad to death's mystery,
Swift to be hurled —
Anywhere, anywhere,
Out of the world! HOOD, *The Bridge of Sighs*

I am *not* mad, but soon shall be.
MATTHEW GREGORY LEWIS, *The Maniac*, st. 7

[1] How subject we old men are to this vice of lying.
SHAKESPEARE, *King Henry IV, Part II*, iii, 2

The one thet fust gits mad 's 'most ollers wrong.
LOWELL, *Biglow Papers*, II, ii, line 151

I am but mad north-northwest: when the wind is southerly I know a hawk from a handsaw.
SHAKESPEARE, *Hamlet*, ii, 2

Hamlet. How came he mad?

. . . . .

First Clown. Faith, e'en with losing his wits.
Ibid., v, 1

Madmen.— For virtue's self may too much zeal be had;
The worst of madmen is a saint run mad.—POPE,
Imitations of Horace, I, Epistle vi, lines 26, 27

Madness.— His madness was not of the head, but heart.
BYRON, *Lara*, Canto i, st. 18

Great wits are sure to madness near allied,
And thin partitions do their bounds divide.[1]
DRYDEN, *Absalom and Achitophel*, I, lines 163, 164

Though this be madness, yet there 's method in 't.
SHAKESPEARE, *Hamlet*, ii, 2

Magazine.— A would-be satirist, a hired buffoon,
A monthly scribbler of some low lampoon,
Condemned to drudge the meanest of the mean,
And furnish falsehoods for a magazine.—BYRON,
English Bards and Scotch Reviewers, lines 975-978

Magistrate. After much debate,
The man prevailed above the magistrate.
DRYDEN, *Cymon and Iphigenia*, lines 462, 463

Magnet.— Long lay the ocean paths from man concealed;
Light came from heaven,— the magnet was revealed,
A surer star to guide the seaman's eye
Than the pale glory of the northern sky;
Alike ordain'd to shine by night and day,
Through calm and tempest, with unsetting ray;
Where'er the mountains rise, the billows roll,
Still with strong impulse turning to the pole
True as the sun is to the morning true,
Though light as film, and trembling as the dew.
JAMES MONTGOMERY, *The West Indies*, i, st. 2

---

[1] What thin partitions sense from thought divide!
POPE, *Essay on Man*, Epistle i, line 226

Maid.—"Where are you going, my pretty maid?"
"I am going a-milking, sir," she said.
"May I go with you, my pretty maid?"
"You're kindly welcome, sir," she said.
"What is your father, my pretty maid?"
"My father's a farmer, sir," she said.
"What is your fortune, my pretty maid?"
"My face is my fortune, sir," she said.
"Then I won't marry you, my pretty maid?"
"Nobody asked you, sir," she said.
ANONYMOUS, *Where Are You Going, My Pretty Maid?*

Neither maid, widow, nor wife.
SHAKESPEARE, *Measure for Measure*, v

Here's to the maid with a bosom of snow;[1]
Now to her that's as brown as a berry;
Here's to the wife with a face full of woe;
And now to the damsel that's merry!
SHERIDAN, *The School for Scandal*, iii, 3

Maiden.— Maiden! with the meek, brown eyes,
In whose orbs a shadow lies
Like the dusk in evening skies!

. . . . .

Standing, with reluctant feet,
Where the brook and river meet,
Womanhood and childhood fleet!
LONGFELLOW, *Maidenhood*, st. 1, 3

This maiden she lived with no other thought
Than to love and be loved by me.
POE, *Annabel Lee*, st. 1

"Tell this soul with sorrow laden if, within the distant Aidenn,
It shall clasp a sainted maiden whom the angels name Lenore —
Clasp a rare and radiant maiden whom the angels name Lenore."
Quoth the raven "Nevermore!"
POE, *The Raven*, st. 1

Nor would I break for your sweet sake
A heart that dotes on truer charms.
A simple maiden in her flower
Is worth a hundred coats-of-arms.
TENNYSON, *Lady Clara Vere de Vere*, st. 2

---

[1] Here's to the girl with a voice sweet and low,
The eye all of fire and the bosom of snow.
J. K. PAULDING, *The Old Man's Carousal*, st. 2

Main.— Strong and free, strong and free;
The floodgates are open, away to the sea.
Free and strong, free and strong,
Cleansing my streams as I hurry along
To the golden sands, and the leaping bar,
And the taintless tide that awaits me afar,
As I lose myself in the infinite main,
Like a soul that has sinned and is pardoned again.
Undefiled, for the undefiled;
Play by me, bathe in me, mother and child.
KINGSLEY, *Songs from the Water Babies*, I, st. 3

Majority.— One man with God is a majority.
WENDELL PHILLIPS, *Speech at Brooklyn*, November 1, 1859

Maker.— Who adores the Maker needs must love his work.
MICHELANGELO BUONARROTI (trans. by J. E. Taylor), *If It Be True That Any Beauteous Thing*

Makes.— This movement makes or mars me.[1]
NAPOLEON BONAPARTE, *Life*, by Sloane, IV, 121

Malady. Where the greater malady is fixed,
The lesser is scarce felt.
SHAKESPEARE, *King Lear*, iii, 4

Malice. It must appear
That malice bears down truth.
SHAKESPEARE, *Merchant of Venice*, iv, 1

Malthus.— I want to read, but really can't get on —
Let the four twins, Mark, Matthew, Luke, and John,
Go — to their nursery — go — I never can
Enjoy my Malthus among such a clan.
HOOD, *Ode to Mr. Malthus*

Mammon.— Behold yon servitor of God and Mammon,
Who, binding up his Bible with his ledger,
Blends Gospel texts with trading gammon,
A black-leg saint, a spiritual hedger,
Who backs his rigid Sabbath, so to speak,
Against the wicked remnant of the week,
A saving bet against his sinful bias —
"Rogue that I am," he whispers to himself,
"I lie — I cheat — do any thing for pelf,
But who on earth can say I am not pious?"
HOOD, *Ode to Rae Wilson, Esquire*, st. 18

---

[1] This is the night
That either makes me or fordoes me quite.— SHAKESPEARE, *Othello*, v, 1

Who see pale Mammon pine amidst his store,
Sees but a backward steward for the poor;
This year a reservoir to keep and spare;
The next, a fountain spouting through his heir,
In lavish streams to quench a country's thirst,
And men and dogs shall drink him till they burst.

POPE, *Moral Essays*, Epistle iii, lines 171–176

Man.— Man is of kin to the beasts by his body; and, if he be not of kin to God by his spirit, he is a base and ignoble creature.[1] BACON, *Essay XVI: Of Atheism*

Let each man think himself an act of God,
His mind a thought, his life a breath of God;
And let each try, by great thoughts and good deeds,
To show the most of Heaven he hath in him.[2]

P. J. BAILEY, *Proem*, lines 163–167

Never an age, when God has need of him,
Shall want its Man, predestined by that need,
To pour his life in fiery word or deed,—
The strong Archangel of the Elohim!

G. S. BURLEIGH, *A Prayer for Life*

A man's a man for a' that![3]

BURNS, *Is There for Honest Poverty*

---

[1] Yon brawny fool,
Who swaggers, swears, and a' that,
And thinks because his strong right arm
Might fell an ox and a' that,
That he's as noble, man for man,
As Duke or Lord and a' that,
Is but an animal at best,
And *not* a man for a' that.

CHARLES MACKAY, *A Man's a Man for A' That*, st. 3

[2] For a' that and a' that,
'Tis soul and heart and a' that
That makes the king a gentleman,
And not his crown and a' that.
And whether he be rich or poor,
The best is he for a' that
Who stands erect in self-respect,
And acts the man for a' that.

CHARLES MACKAY, *A Man's a Man for A That*, st. 6

[3] "A man's a man," says Robert Burns,
"For a' that, and a' that;"
But though the song be clear and strong,
It lacks a note for a' that.
The lout who'd shirk his daily work,
Yet claim his wage and a' that,
Or beg when he might earn his bread,
Is *not* a man for a' that.

CHARLES MACKAY, *A Man's a Man for A' That*, st. 1

The rank is but the guinea's stamp,
  The man's the gowd for a' that.[1] *Ibid.*, st. 1

A man may drink and no be drunk;
  A man may fight and no be slain;
A man may kiss a bonny lass,
  And aye be welcome back again.
BURNS, *There Was a Lass*, st. 3

Every man is as God hath made him, and sometimes a great deal worse.—CERVANTES, *Don Quixote* (Tudor translation, ed. Henley), II, iv

Man wants but little here below,
  Nor wants that little long.[2]
GOLDSMITH, *The Hermit*, st. 8

He's true to God who's true to man.
LOWELL, *On the Capture of Fugitive Slaves near Washington*, st. 7

He was six foot o' man, A 1,
  Clear grit an' human natur';
None couldn't quicker pitch a ton
  Nor dror a furrer straighter.
LOWELL, *The Courtin'*, st. 8

Man is a moral, accountable being.
LOWELL, *Fable for Critics*, line 237

Man is an animal unfledged,
A monkey with his tail abridged;
. . . . .
His body flexible and limber,
And headed with a knob of timber;
A being frantic and unquiet,
And very fond of beef and riot.
. . . . .
His own best friend, and, you must know,
His own worst enemy by being so!
JAMES MONTGOMERY, *Definition of Man*

---

[1] It comes to this, dear Robert Burns,
  The truth is old and a' that,
"The rank *is* but the guinea's stamp,
  The man's the gowd for a' that."
And though you'd put the self-same mark
  On copper, brass, and a' that,
The lie is gross, the cheat is plain,
  And will not pass for a' that.
CHARLES MACKAY, *A Man's a Man for A' That*, st. 5

[2] Man wants but little drink below,
  But wants that little strong.— HOLMES, *A Song of Other Days*, st. 2

Man wants but little; nor that little, long.
YOUNG, *Night Thoughts*, IV, line 119

Man—*Continued*

Know then thyself, presume not God to scan;
The proper study of mankind[1] is man.[2]
POPE, *Essay on Man*, Epistle ii, lines 1, 2

Like leaves on trees the race of man is found,
Now green in youth, now withering on the ground:
Another race the following spring supplies;
They fall successive, and successive rise.
POPE, *Iliad*, VI, lines 181–184

A man is master of his liberty.
SHAKESPEARE, *Comedy of Errors*, ii, 1

He was a man,[3] take him for all in all,
I shall not look upon his like again.
SHAKESPEARE, *Hamlet*, i, 2

An old man is twice a child. *Ibid.*, ii, 2

I could have better spared a better man.
SHAKESPEARE, *King Henry IV*, *Part I*, v, 4

---

[1] Virtue only makes our bliss below;
And all our knowledge is, ourselves to know.
POPE, *Essay on Man*, Epistle iv, lines 397, 398

[2] According to the first edition: "The only science of mankind is man."

[3] He's a rare man,
Our parson; half a head above us all.
JEAN INGELOW, *Brothers, and a Sermon*

God's plan
And measure of a stalwart man,
Limbèd like the old heroic breeds,
Who stands self-poised on manhood's solid earth,
Not forced to frame excuses for his birth,
Fed from within with all the strength he needs.
LOWELL, *Commemoration Ode*, st. 5

See, what a grace was seated on this brow;
Hyperion's curls; the front of Jove himself;
An eye like Mars, to threaten and command;
A station like the herald Mercury
New-lighted on a heaven-kissing hill;
A combination and a form indeed,
Where every god did seem to set his seal,
To give the world assurance of a man. SHAKESPEARE, *Hamlet*, iii, 4

Thou art the ruins of the noblest man
That ever lived in the tide of times.— SHAKESPEARE, *Julius Cæsar*, iii, 1

His life was gentle, and the elements
So mixed in him that Nature might stand up
And say to all the world, "This was a man!" *Ibid.*, v, 5

He is a proper man's picture.— SHAKESPEARE, *Merchant of Venice*, i, 2

If thou kill'st me, boy, thou shalt kill a man.
SHAKESPEARE, *Much Ado about Nothing*, v, 1

Let the end try the man.
SHAKESPEARE, *King Henry IV, Part II*, ii, 2

I am a very foolish fond old man.
SHAKESPEARE, *King Lear*, iv, 7

I cannot draw a cart, nor eat dried oats:
If it be man's work, I'll [I will] do it. *Ibid.*, v, 3

Lady Macbeth. Are you a man?
Macbeth. Ay, and a bold one, that dare look on that
Which might appal the devil.
SHAKESPEARE, *Macbeth*, iii, 4

Man, proud man,
Dressed in a little brief authority,
Most ignorant of what he's most assured,
His glassy essence, like an angry ape,
Plays such fantastic tricks before high heaven
As make the angels weep.
SHAKESPEARE, *Measure for Measure*, ii, 2

God made him, and therefore let him pass for a man.
SHAKESPEARE, *Merchant of Venice*, i, 2

What a pretty thing man is when he goes in his doublet and hose and leaves off his wit!
SHAKESPEARE, *Much Ado about Nothing*, v, 1

There is no man suddenly either excellently good or extremely evil. SIR PHILIP SIDNEY, *Arcadia*, I

How poor, how rich, how abject, how august,
How complicate, how wonderful is man.
YOUNG, *Night Thoughts*, I, lines 68, 69

At thirty, man suspects himself a fool;
Knows it at forty, and reforms his plan;
At fifty, chides his infamous delay,
Pushes his prudent purpose to resolve;
In all the magnanimity of thought
Resolves, and re-resolves; then dies the same.
Ibid., lines 417–422

Manacle. For my sake wear this;
It is a manacle of love.—SHAKESPEARE, *Cymbeline*, i, 1 [2]

Mandalay.— By the old Moulmein Pagoda, lookin' eastward to the sea,
There's a Burma girl a-settin', and I know she thinks o' me;

For the wind is in the palm-trees, and the temple-bells
they say:
"Come you back, you British soldier; come you back to
Mandalay!"

. . . . .

On the road to Mandalay,
Where the flyin' fishes play,
An' the dawn comes up like thunder outer China 'crost
the Bay! KIPLING, *Mandalay*

Manhood.— There was a manhood in his look,
That murder could not kill!
HOOD, *The Dream of Eugene Aram*, st. 16

Mankind.— The common curse of mankind, folly and ignorance. SHAKESPEARE, *Troilus and Cressida*, ii, 3

Manners.— Of manners gentle, of affections mild;
In wit, a man; simplicity, a child.
POPE, *Epitaph on Gay*, lines 1, 2

Ring in the nobler modes of life,
With sweeter manners, purer laws.[1]
TENNYSON, *In Memoriam*, cvi, st. 4

Many.— The mutable, rank-scented many.
SHAKESPEARE, *Coriolanus*, iii, 1

Maps.— So geographers, in Afric maps,
With savage pictures fill their gaps,
And o'er unhabitable downs
Place elephants for want of towns.
SWIFT, *On Poetry, a Rhapsody*, lines 177–180

Marble.— Water is soft, and marble hard; and yet
We see soft water through hard marble eat.[2]
DRYDEN, *Ovid's Art of Love*, I, lines 542, 543

Marbles.— The mossy marbles rest
On the lips that he has pressed
In their bloom,
And the names he loved to hear
Have been carved for many a year
On the tomb. HOLMES, *The Last Leaf*, st. 4

---

[1] In the light of fuller day,
Of purer science, holier laws.
KINGSLEY, *On the Death of a Certain Journal*, st. 5

[2] Much rain wears the marble.
SHAKESPEARE, *King Henry VI, Part III*, iii, 2

Stones with drops of rain are washed away.
DRYDEN, *Lucretius, IV*, line 298

Mare.— When the grey mare 's the better horse.[1]
BUTLER, *Hudibras*, II, ii, line 698

The grey mare
Is ill to live with, when her whinny shrills
From tile to scullery.
TENNYSON, *The Princess*, v, lines 441–443

Mariner.— I fear thee, ancient Mariner!
I fear thy skinny hand!
And thou art long, and lank, and brown,
As is the ribbed sea-sand.
S. T. COLERIDGE, *Ancient Mariner*, lines 224–227

Marriage.— Is not marriage an open question, when it is alleged, from the beginning of the world, that such as are in the institution wish to get out, and such as are out wish to get in?[2]
R. W. EMERSON, *Representative Men: Montaigne*

Pleasant the snaffle of courtship, improving the manners and carriage;
But the colt who is wise will abstain from the terrible thorn-bit of marriage.
KIPLING, *Certain Maxims of Hafiz*, st. 11

Such a mad marriage never was before.
SHAKESPEARE, *Taming of the Shrew*, iii, 2

Every kiss
Has a price for its bliss,
In the modern code of marriage;
And the compact sweet
Is not complete,
Till the high contracting parties meet
Before the altar of Mammon.
E. C. STEDMAN, *The Diamond Wedding*, st. 4

Marriages.— Marriages are made in Heaven.
TENNYSON, *Aylmer's Field*, line 188

Married. She
Was married, charming, chaste, and twenty-three.
BYRON, *Don Juan*, Canto i, st. 59

---

[1] The grey mare is, I'm sure, the better horse.
ANONYMOUS, *The Eggs and the Horses*, st. 16

[2] Wedlock, indeed, hath oft compared been
To public feasts, where meet a public rout,
Where they that are without would fain go in,
And they that are within would fain go out.
SIR J. DAVIES, *Contention Betwixt a Wife, etc.*

A young man married is a man that's marred.
SHAKESPEARE, *All's Well That Ends Well*, ii, 3

Benedick, the married man.
SHAKESPEARE, *Much Ado about Nothing*, i, 1; v, 1, 4

If he be married,
My grave is like to be my wedding-bed.
SHAKESPEARE, *Romeo and Juliet*, i, 5

She's not well married that lives married long;
But she's best married that dies married young.
SHAKESPEARE, *Romeo and Juliet*, iv, 5

I knew a wench married in an afternoon as she went to the garden for parsley to stuff a rabbit.
SHAKESPEARE, *Taming of the Shrew*, iv, 4

Marry.— I'm o'er young to marry yet;
I'm o'er young —'t wad be a sin
To tak' me frae my mammy yet.
BURNS, *I'm O'er Young to Marry Yet*

Choose not alone a proper mate,
But proper time to marry.
COWPER, *Pairing-Time Anticipated: Moral*

We'll drink our can, we'll eat our cake,
There's beer in the barrel, there's bread in the bake,
The world may sleep, the world may wake,
But I shall milk and marry.
S. DOBELL, *The Milkmaid's Song*

They that marry ancient people, merely in expectation to bury them, hang themselves, in hope that one will come and cut the halter.
THOMAS FULLER, *The Holy and Profane State: Of Marriage*

Then be not coy, but use your time,
And while ye may, go marry;
For having lost but once your prime,
You may forever tarry.—HERRICK, *To the Virgins*, st. 4

A person of genius should marry a person of character.
HOLMES, *Professor at the Breakfast-Table*, xii

There sits a bird on every tree,
And courts his love, as I do thee;
Sing heigh-ho, and heigh-ho!
Young maids must marry.
KINGSLEY, *Sing Heigh-Ho*, st. 1

The men that women marry,
And why they marry them, will always be
A marvel and a mystery to the world.
LONGFELLOW, *Michael Angelo*, I, vi

If thou wilt needs marry, marry a fool; for wise men know well enough what monsters you make of them.
SHAKESPEARE, *Hamlet*, iii, 1

That 's as much as to say, they are fools that marry.
SHAKESPEARE, *Julius Cæsar*, iii, 3

This I set down as a positive truth. A woman with fair opportunities, and without an absolute hump, may marry whom she likes.[1] THACKERAY, *Vanity Fair*, iv

Martyr. Ever the blind world
Knows not its angels of deliverance
Till they stand glorified 'twixt earth and heaven.
It stones the martyr; then, with praying hands,
Sees the God mount his chariot of fire,
And calls sweet names, and worships what it spurned.
GERALD MASSEY, *Hood*, lines 1–6

Maryland.— The despot's heel is on thy shore,
Maryland!
His torch is at thy temple door,
Maryland!
J. R. RANDALL, *My Maryland*, st. 1

Master.— I am meat for your master.
SHAKESPEARE, *King Henry IV., Part II*, ii, 4

Such mistris, such Nan,
Such maister, such man.
THOMAS TUSSER, *Five Hundred Points of Good Husbandry: April's Abstract*, st. 22

Masters.— We cannot all be masters.
SHAKESPEARE, *Othello*, i, 1

Matrimony.— I asked of Echo, t' other day
(Whose words are few and often funny),
What to a novice she could say
Of courtship, love, and matrimony.
Quoth Echo, plainly,—"Matter-o'-money!"
J. G. SAXE, *Echo*, st. 1

[1] I should like to see any kind of a man, distinguishable from a gorilla, that some good and even pretty woman could not shape a husband out of.
HOLMES, *Professor at the Breakfast Table*, vii

There swims no goose so grey, but soon or late,
She finds some honest gander for her mate.
POPE, *The Wife of Bath*, lines 98, 99

Matter.— When Bishop Berkeley said "there was no matter,"
And proved it —'t was no matter what he said.
BYRON, *Don Juan*, Canto xi, st. 1

Though the forms decay,
Eternal matter never wears away.
DRYDEN, *Palamon and Arcite*, lines 2306, 2307

May.— As it fell upon a day,
In the merry month of May,
R. BARNFIELD, *An Ode*, lines 1–2

You must wake and call me early, call me early, mother dear;
To-morrow 'ill be the happiest time of all the glad New Year;
Of all the glad New Year, mother, the maddest, merriest day;
For I'm to be Queen o' the May, mother,
I'm to be Queen o' the May.
TENNYSON, *The May Queen*, st. 1

Mayor. Our mayor's a noddy;
And as for our corporation — shocking.
R. BROWNING, *The Pied Piper of Hamelin*, st. 3

Meadows.— Meadows trim, with daisies pied.
MILTON, *L'Allegro*, line 75

Meals.— Man is a carnivorous production,
And must have meals, at least one meal a day;
He cannot live like woodcocks, upon suction,
But, like the shark and tiger, must have prey.
BYRON, *Don Juan*, Canto ii, st. 67

Meaning.— A very mean meaning.
SHAKESPEARE, *Taming of the Shrew*, v, 2

Meanness.— Like a peach thet's got the yellers,
With the meanness bustin' out.
LOWELL, *The Biglow Papers*, I, i, st. 14

Meant.— The mind that never meant amiss.
SIR THOMAS WYATT, *A Supplication*, st. 4

Measures.— Measures, not men,[1] have always been my mark.
GOLDSMITH, *The Good-Natured Man*, ii

---

[1] The cant of "not men, but measures."
BURKE, *Thoughts on the Present Discontents*

Meat.— Some ha'e meat and canna eat,
And some wad eat that want it;
But we ha'e meat and we can eat,
And sae the Lord be thankit.—BURNS, *The Selkirk Grace*

There is cold meat i' the cave; we 'll browse on that.
SHAKESPEARE, *Cymbeline*, iii, 6

Meditation.— In maiden meditation, fancy free.
SHAKESPEARE, *Midsummer-Night's Dream*, ii, 1

Meet.— In our course through life we shall meet the people who are coming to meet us from many strange places and by many strange roads; and what it is set to us to do to them, and what it is set to them to do to us, will all be done. DICKENS, *Little Dorrit*, I, ii

First Witch. When shall we three meet again,
In thunder, lightning, or in rain?
Second Witch. When the hurlyburly 's done;
When the battle 's lost and won.
SHAKESPEARE, *Macbeth*, i, 1

Meeting.— Here 's our next joyous meeting — and oh when we meet,
May our wine be as bright, and our union as sweet.
T. MOORE, *Hip, Hip, Hurra!* st. 5

Melancholy.— The melancholy days are come, the saddest of the year,
Of wailing winds, and naked woods, and meadows brown and sere. BRYANT, *The Death of the Flowers*, st. 1

There is a kindly mood of melancholy
That wings the soul and points her to the skies.[1]
J. DYER, *The Ruins of Rome*

Here rests his head upon the lap of earth,
A youth to fortune and to fame unknown;
Fair science frowned not on his humble birth,
And melancholy marked him for her own.
GRAY, *Elegy Written in a Country Churchyard*, st. 31

There 's not a string attuned to mirth,
But has its chord in melancholy.[2]
HOOD, *Ode to Melancholy*

---

[1] Nothing's so dainty sweet as lovely melancholy.
JOHN FLETCHER, *Melancholy*

[2] I can suck melancholy out of a song, as a weasel sucks eggs.
SHAKESPEARE, *As You Like It*, ii, 5

Hence, loathed Melancholy![1] MILTON, *L'Allegro*, line 1

I am as melancholy as a gib cat or a lugged bear.
SHAKESPEARE, *King Henry IV, Part I*, i, 2

We are high-proof melancholy.
SHAKESPEARE, *Much Ado about Nothing*, v, 1

Memories.— Long, long be my heart with such memories filled!
Like the vase, in which roses have once been distilled —
You may break, you may shatter the vase, if you will,
But the scent of the roses will hang round it still.
T. MOORE, *Farewell! — But Whenever You Welcome the Hour*, st. 3

Memory.— For my name and memory, I leave it to men's charitable speeches, to foreign nations, and to the next ages. BACON, *His Last Will*

How cruelly sweet are the echoes that start,
When memory plays an old tune on the heart!
ELIZA COOK, *Old Dobbin*, st. 16

Oft in the stilly night,
Ere Slumber's chain has bound me,
Fond Memory brings the light
Of other days around me;
The smiles, the tears,
Of boyhood's years,
The words of love then spoken;
The eyes that shone,
Now dimmed and gone,
The cheerful hearts now broken!
T. MOORE, *Oft in the Stilly Night*, st. 1

There's hope a great man's memory may outlive his life half a year. SHAKESPEARE, *Hamlet*, iii, 2

Begot in the ventricle of memory, nourished in the womb of pia mater, and delivered upon the mellowing of occasion. SHAKESPEARE, *Love's Labour's Lost*, iv, 2

Memory, the warder of the brain.
SHAKESPEARE, *Macbeth*, i, 7

Hope links her to the future,— but the link
That binds her to the past is memory.
AMELIA B. WELBY, *The Old Maid*

---

[1] Moping melancholy. MILTON, *Paradise Lost*, XI, line 485

Sable-coloured melancholy. SHAKESPEARE, *Love's Labour's Lost*, i, 1

Men.— God give us men! A time like this demands
Strong minds, great hearts, true faith, and ready hands;
Men whom the lust of office does not kill;
Men whom the spoils of office cannot buy;
Men who possess opinions and a will;
Men who have honour,— men who will not lie;
Men who can stand before a demagogue,
And damn his treacherous flatteries without winking!

J. G. HOLLAND, *Wanted*

God be thanked — whate'er comes after, I have lived and toiled with men! KIPLING, *The Galley Slave*

Our country claims our fealty; we grant it so, but then
Before Man made us citizens, great Nature made us men.

LOWELL, *On the Capture of Fugitive Slaves near Washington*, st. 6

I grew up in the field, and a man like me troubles himself little about a million men.

NAPOLEON BONAPARTE, *Life*, by Sloane, IV, 46

If we must fall, let us fall like men.

WILLIAM PITT, EARL OF CHATHAM, *Last Speech in Parliament*, April 7, 1778

The fate of all extremes is such,
Men may be read, as well as books, too much.

POPE, *Moral Essays*, Epistle i, lines 9, 10

I loathe all men; such unromantic creatures!
The coarsest tastes, and, ah! the coarsest features!
Betty! — the salts! — I'm sick with mere vexation,
To hear them called the Lords of the Creation:
They swear fierce oaths, they seldom say their prayers;
And then, they shed no tears,— unfeeling bears.

PRAED, *Prologue for The Honeymoon*, st. 2

There live not three good men unhanged in England; and one of them is fat and grows old.

SHAKESPEARE, *King Henry IV, Part I*, ii, 4

Men of few words are the best men.

SHAKESPEARE, *King Henry V*, iii, 2

Oh, what men dare do! what men may do! what men daily do, not knowing what they do!

SHAKESPEARE, *Much Ado about Nothing*, iv, 1

The world knows nothing of its greatest men.

SIR H. TAYLOR, *Philip van Artevelde*, I, i, 5

For men at most differ as heaven and earth,
But women, worst and best, as heaven and hell.

TENNYSON, *Merlin and Vivien*, lines 812, 813

Mended.— And I oft have heard defended
Little said is soonest mended.[1]
G. WITHER, *The Shepherd's Hunting*

Mercy.— Teach me to feel another's woe,
To hide the fault I see;
That mercy I to others show,
That mercy show to me.[2]
POPE, *The Universal Prayer*, st. 10

There is no more mercy in him than there is milk in a male tiger. SHAKESPEARE, *Coriolanus*, v, 4

Whereto serves mercy
But to confront the visage of offence?
And what 's in prayer but this twofold force,
To be forestalled ere we come to fall,
Or pardoned being down?—SHAKESPEARE, *Hamlet*, iii, 3

The gates of mercy shall be all shut up.
SHAKESPEARE, *King Henry V*, iii, 3

No ceremony that to great ones 'longs,
Not the king's crown, nor the deputed sword,
The marshal's truncheon, nor the judge's robe,
Become them with one half so good a grace
As mercy does.[3]
SHAKESPEARE, *Measure for Measure*, ii, 2

Merit.— Charms strike the sight, but merit wins the soul.
POPE, *Rape of the Lock*, v, line 34

---

[1] You know the proverb, the less as is said, the sooner the chiney's mended.
HOOD, *The China-Mender*

[2] Teach me to love and to forgive,
Exact my own defects to scan. GRAY, *Hymn to Adversity*, st. 6

How shalt thou hope for mercy, rendering none?
SHAKESPEARE, *Merchant of Venice*, iv, 1

[3] The quality of mercy is not strained,
It droppeth as the gentle rain from heaven
Upon the place beneath: it is twice blest;
It blesseth him that gives and him that takes:
'T is mightiest in the mightiest: it becomes
The throned monarch better than his crown;
His sceptre shows the force of temporal power,
The attribute to awe and majesty,
Wherein doth sit the dread and fear of kings;
But mercy is above this sceptred sway;
It is enthroned in the hearts of kings,
It is an attribute to God himself;
And earthly power doth then show likest God's
When mercy seasons justice.

. . . . .

In the course of justice, none of us
Should see salvation: we do pray for mercy;
And that same prayer doth teach us all to render
The deeds of mercy. SHAKESPEARE, *Merchant of Venice*, iv, 1

Merits.— Would you ask for his merits? alas! he had none;
What was good was spontaneous, his faults were his own.
GOLDSMITH, *Retaliation*, st. 4

Merriest.— Men are merriest when they are from home.[1]
SHAKESPEARE, *King Henry V*, i, 2

Merry.— I had rather have a fool to make me merry than experience to make me sad.
SHAKESPEARE, *As You Like It*, iv, 1

'T is merry in hall when beards wag all.
SHAKESPEARE, *King Henry IV, Part II*, v, 3;
THOMAS TUSSER, *Five Hundred Points of Good Husbandry: August Abstract*

As merry as the day is long.[2]
SHAKESPEARE, *Much Ado about Nothing*, ii, 1

Though he be merry, yet withal he 's honest.
SHAKESPEARE, *Taming of the Shrew*, iii, 2

Metaphysic.— He knew what 's what,[3] and that 's as high
As metaphysic wit can fly.
BUTLER, *Hudibras*, I, i, lines 149, 150

Method.— There is a method in man's wickedness,
It grows up by degrees.
BEAUMONT AND FLETCHER, *A King and No King*, v, 4

Mice.— The best-laid schemes o' mice and men
Gang aft a-gley [*wrong*].
BURNS, *To a Mouse*, st. 7

Mice and rats, and such small deer,
Have been Tom's food for seven long year.
SHAKESPEARE, *King Lear*, iii, 4

Midnight.— Once upon a midnight dreary, while I pondered, weak and weary,
Over many a quaint and curious volume of forgotten lore —
While I nodded, nearly napping, suddenly there came a tapping
As of some one gently rapping, rapping at my chamber door.
"'T is some visitor," I muttered, "tapping at my chamber door —
Only this and nothing more."
POE, *The Raven*, st. 1

---

[1] He hangs up his fiddle behind the door.— ANONYMOUS, *Anecdotal Saying*

[2] So I were out of prison, and kept sheep,
I should be merry as the day is long.— SHAKESPEARE, *King John*, iv, 1

[3] He sees with larger, other eyes,
Athwart all mysteries —
He knows what's Swat.— G. T. LANIGAN, *A Threnody*, st. 3 [On the Death of the Ahkoond of Swat]

We have heard the chimes at midnight.
SHAKESPEARE, *King Henry IV, Part II*, iii, 2

The iron tongue of midnight hath told twelve.
SHAKESPEARE, *Midsummer-Night's Dream*, v, 1

Mildest.— He was the mildest-mannered man
That ever scuttled ship or cut a throat.
BYRON, *Don Juan*, Canto iii, st. 41

Miles.— We must measure twenty miles to-day.
SHAKESPEARE, *Merchant of Venice*, iii, 4

Milk.— The milk of human kindness.
SHAKESPEARE, *Macbeth*, i, 5

Miller.— There was a jolly miller once,
Lived on the river Dee;
He worked and sung from morn till night,
No lark more blithe than he.
ISAAC BICKERSTAFFE, *Love in a Village*, i, 2

Mills.— Though the mills of God grind slowly, yet they grind exceeding small;
Though with patience he stands waiting, with exactness grinds he all.—LONGFELLOW, *Retribution*, from the German of F. von Logau

Mind. A heart
Susceptible of pity, or a mind
Cultured and capable of sober thought.
COWPER, *The Task: The Garden*, lines 322–324

My mind to me a kingdom is.[1]
EDWARD DYER, *My Mind to Me a Kingdom Is*, st. 1

High walls and huge the body may confine,
And iron gates obstruct the prisoner's gaze,
And massive bolts may baffle his design,
And vigilant keepers watch his devious ways;
But scorns the immortal mind such base control:
No chains can bind it and no cell enclose.
Swifter than light it flies from pole to pole,
And in a flash from earth to heaven it goes.
W. L. GARRISON, *Sonnet, Written in Prison*

---

[1] My mind to me a kingdom is,
Such perfect joy therein I find,
As far exceeds all earthly bliss
That God and Nature hath assigned.
BYRD, *Psalmes, Sonnets, etc.*, 1588

A mind content both crown and kingdom is.
ROBERT GREENE, *Farewell to Follie*, st. 2

At last he shut the ponderous tome,
With a fast and fervent grasp
He strained the dusky covers close,
And fixed the brazen hasp:
"Oh, God! could I so close my mind,
And clasp it with a clasp!"
HOOD, *The Dream of Eugene Aram*, st. 6

The mind is its own place, and in itself
Can make a heaven of hell, a hell of heaven.[1]
MILTON, *Paradise Lost*, I, lines 254, 255

Oh, what a noble mind is here o'erthrown!
The courtier's, soldier's, scholar's eye, tongue, sword;
The expectancy and rose of the fair state,
The glass of fashion and the mould of form,[2]
The observed of all observers, quite, quite down!
SHAKESPEARE, *Hamlet*, iii, 1

The mind shall banquet, though the body pine.
SHAKESPEARE, *Love's Labour's Lost*, i, 1

Canst thou not minister to a mind diseased,
Pluck from the memory a rooted sorrow,
Raze out the written troubles of the brain,
And with some sweet oblivious antidote
Cleanse the stuffed bosom of that perilous stuff
Which weighs upon the heart?
SHAKESPEARE, *Macbeth*, v, 3

Were I so tall to reach the pole,
Or grasp the ocean with my span,
I must be measured by my soul:
The mind 's the standard of the man.
WATTS, *Horæ Lyricæ*, ii, False Greatness

Mine.— An ill-favoured thing, sir, but mine own.
SHAKESPEARE, *As You Like It*, v, 4

What 's mine is yours, and what is yours is mine.
SHAKESPEARE, *Measure for Measure*, v

'T is mine, and I will have it.[3]
SHAKESPEARE, *Merchant of Venice*, iv, 1

Minister.— The minister kissed the fiddler's wife,
An' could na preach for thinkin' o't.
BURNS, *My Love She's But a Lassie Yet*, st. 2

---

[1] *Cf.* HELL.

[2] He was the mark and glass, copy and book,
That fashioned others. SHAKESPEARE, *King Henry IV, Part II*, ii, 3

[3] I will be master of what is mine own.
SHAKESPEARE, *Taming of the Shrew*, iii, 2

Minster.— In the great minster transept,
Where lights like glories fall,
And the sweet choir sings and the organ rings
Along the emblazoned wall.[1]
C. F. ALEXANDER, *Burial of Moses*, st. 6

The minster bell tolls out
Above the city's rout
And noise and humming;
They 've hushed the minster bell:
The organ 'gins to swell:
She 's coming, coming!
THACKERAY, *At the Church Gate*, st. 2

Mirth.— The mirth and fun grew fast and furious.
BURNS, *Tam O' Shanter*, st. 12

Oh, mirth and innocence! Oh, milk and water!
Ye happy mixtures of more happy days!
BYRON, *Beppo*, st. 80

Come, thou Goddess fair and free,
In heaven ycleped Euphrosyne,
And by men, heart-easing Mirth.
MILTON, *L'Allegro*, lines 11–13

Mirth cannot move a soul in agony.
SHAKESPEARE, *Love's Labour's Lost*, v, 2

You have displaced the mirth, broke the good meeting
With most admired disorder.
SHAKESPEARE, *Macbeth*, iii, 4

Let me play the fool:
With mirth and laughter let old wrinkles come,
And let my liver rather heat with wine
Than my heart cool with mortifying groans.
Why should a man, whose blood is warm within,
Sit like his grandsire cut in alabaster?
Sleep when he wakes, and creep into the jaundice
By being peevish?—SHAKESPEARE, *Merchant of Venice*, i, 1

Misery.— A great silent-moving misery puts a new stamp on us in an hour or a moment,— as sharp an impression as if it had taken half a lifetime to engrave it.
HOLMES, *Autocrat of the Breakfast-Table*, ii

Sharp misery had worn him to the bones.
SHAKESPEARE, *Romeo and Juliet*, v, 1

---

[1] Beneath some ample hallowed dome
The warrior's bones are laid,
And blazoned on the stately tomb
His martial deeds displayed.
JAMES MONTGOMERY, *Introduction to Verses on R. Reynolds*

Misfortune.— As if Misfortune made the throne her seat,
And none could be unhappy but the great.
N. ROWE, *The Fair Penitent*, Prologue

Misfortune, like a creditor severe,
But rises in demand for her delay;
She makes a scourge of past prosperity,
To sting thee more, and double thy distress.
YOUNG, *Night Thoughts*, I, lines 318–321

Misfortunes.— I am convinced that we have a degree of delight, and that no small one, in the real misfortunes and pains of others.
BURKE, *Ideas of the Sublime and Beautiful*, xiv

I never knew any man in my life who could not bear another's misfortunes perfectly like a Christian.[1]
POPE, *Thoughts on Various Subjects*

Misquote.— With just enough of learning to misquote.
BYRON, *English Bards and Scotch Reviewers*, line 66

Mistakes.— In short, year after year the same
Absurd mistakes went on;
And when I died, the neighbors came
And buried brother John!
H. S. LEIGH, *The Twins*, st. 4

Mistletoe.— The mistletoe hung in the castle hall,
The holly branch shone on the old oak wall;
And the baron's retainers were blithe and gay,
And keeping their Christmas holiday.
T. H. BAYLY, *The Mistletoe Bough*, st. 1

Mite.— Too small for any marketable shift,
What purpose can there be for coins like these?
Hush, hush, good Sir! — Thus charitable thrift
May give a mite to him who wants a cheese!
HOOD, *Epigram on the New Half-Farthings*

Mites.— Two mites, two drops (yet all her house and land),
Fall from a steady heart, though trembling hand:
The other's wanton wealth foams high and brave,
The other cast away, she only gave.
CRASHAW, *Divine Epigrams: The Widow's Mites*

Modest.— On their own merits, modest men are dumb.
GEO. COLMAN, JR., *The Heir-at-Law*, Epilogue

---

[1] The tame spectator of another's woe.
HOOLE, *Demophoon* (trans. from Metastasio), i, 3 [1]

Modesty.— Not stepping o'er the bounds of modesty.
SHAKESPEARE, *Romeo and Juliet*, iv, 2

Monarch.— I am monarch of all I survey,
My right there is none to dispute.
COWPER, *Alexander Selkirk*, st. 1

A merry monarch, scandalous and poor.
EARL OF ROCHESTER, *On the King*

Monarchy.— The trappings of a monarchy would set up an ordinary commonwealth.
SAMUEL JOHNSON, *Life of Milton*

Money.— Money is like muck, not good except it be spread.
BACON, *Essay XV: Of Seditions and Troubles*

For what is worth in any thing
But so much money as 'twill bring?
BUTLER, *Hudibras*, II, i, lines 465, 466

Fine young girls sittin', like shopkeepers behind their goods, waitin' and waitin' and waitin', 'n' no customers, — and the men lingerin' round and lookin' at the goods, like folks that want to be customers, but haven't got the money! — HOLMES, *Professor at the Breakfast-Table*, vii

To bring such visionary scenes to pass,
One thing was requisite, and that was — money!

. . . . .

Money — the root of evil — dross and stuff!
But oh! how happy ought the rich to feel,
Whose means enabled them to give enough
To blanch an African from head to heel!
How blessed — yea, thrice blessed — to subscribe
Enough to scour a tribe!
While he whose fortune was at best a brittle one,
Although he gave but pence, how sweet to know
He helped to bleach a Hottentot's great toe,
Or little one! HOOD, *A Black Job*, st. 8, 9

Get money; still get money, boy;
No matter by what means.[1]
BEN JONSON, *Every Man in His Humour*, ii, 3

---

[1] London's voice: "Get money, money still!
And then let Virtue follow, if she will."
POPE, *Imitations of Horace*, I, Epistle i, lines 79, 80

Get place and wealth, if possible, with grace;
If not, by any means get wealth and place.
Ibid., lines 103, 104

I can raise no money by vile means:
By heaven, I had rather coin my heart,
And drop my blood for drachmas, than to wring
From the hard hands of peasants their vile trash
By any indirection.—SHAKESPEARE, *Julius Cæsar*, iv, 3

There shall be no money; all shall eat and drink on my score.—SHAKESPEARE, *King Henry VI, Part II*, iv, 2

If money go before, all ways do lie open.
SHAKESPEARE, *Merry Wives of Windsor*, ii, 2

I knawed a Quaäker feller as often 'as towd ma this:
"Doänt thou marry for munny, but goä wheer munny is!" TENNYSON, *Northern Farmer, New Style*, st. 5

The love of money is the root of all evil.
1 *Timothy* vi, 10

Money-making.— I was not made merely for money-making.
GERALD MASSEY, *A Song in the City*

Monk.— The solitary monk who shook the world.
R. MONTGOMERY, *Luther*, Man's Need and God's Supply, st. 4

Monkey. The strain of man's bred out
Into baboon and monkey.
SHAKESPEARE, *Timon of Athens*, i, 1

Monks.— The monks of Melrose made gude kail
On Fridays when they fasted,
Nor wanted they gude beef and ale,
As long's their neighbours' lasted.[1]
Cited by F. T. PALGRAVE, Introduction to SCOTT, *Lay of the Last Minstrel*

Monument. When old Time shall lead him to his end,
Goodness and he fill up one monument![2]
SHAKESPEARE, *King Henry VIII*, ii, 1

Moon.— I saw the new moon, late yestreen,
Wi' the auld moon in her arm;
And if we gang to sea, master,
I fear we'll come to harm.[3]
ANONYMOUS, *Sir Patrick Spens*, st. 13

---

[1] Have drunk the monks of St. Bothan's ale,
And driven the beeves of Lauderdale.— SCOTT, *Marmion*, Canto i, st. 19

[2] Go, build his monument: — and let it be
Firm as the land, but open as the sea.
Low in his grave the strong foundations lie,
Yet be the dome expansive as the sky,
On crystal pillars resting from above,
Its sole supporters — works of faith and love.
JAMES MONTGOMERY, *A Good Man's Monument*, st. 7

[3] There are many versions of this ballad.

The wandering moon,[1]
Riding near her highest noon,
Like one that has been led astray
Through the heaven's wide pathless way,
And oft, as if her head she bowed,
Stooping through a fleecy cloud.
MILTON, *Il Penseroso*, lines 67–72

What may this mean,
That thou, dead corse, again in complete steel
Revisit'st thus the glimpses of the moon,
Making night hideous; and we fools of nature
So horridly to shake our disposition
With thoughts beyond the reaches of our souls?
SHAKESPEARE, *Hamlet*, i, 4

The moon, like to a silver bow
New-bent in heaven.
SHAKESPEARE, *Midsummer-Night's Dream*, i, 1

Romeo. Lady, by yonder blessed moon I swear
That tips with silver all these fruit-tree tops,—
Juliet. Oh, swear not by the moon, the inconstant moon,
That monthly changes in her circled orb,
Lest that thy love prove likewise variable.
SHAKESPEARE, *Romeo and Juliet*, ii, 2

That orbed maiden with white fire laden,
Whom mortals call the moon. SHELLEY, *The Cloud*

Moonlight.— As moonlight unto sunlight, and as water unto wine. TENNYSON, *Locksley Hall*, line 52

---

[1] The moon is at her full, and, riding high,
Floods the calm fields with light. BRYANT, *The Tides*, st. 1

Now glowed the firmament
With living sapphires: Hesperus, that led
The starry host, rode brightest, till the Moon,
Rising in cloudy majesty, at length,
Apparent queen, unveiled her peerless light,
And o'er the dark her silver mantle threw.
MILTON, *Paradise Lost*, IV, lines 604–609

How beautiful is night!
A dewy freshness fills the silent air,
No mist obscures, nor cloud, nor speck, nor stain,
Breaks the serene of heaven:
In full-orbed glory yonder moon divine
Rolls through the dark blue depths.*
Beneath her steady ray
The desert-circle spreads,
Like the round ocean, girdled with the sky.
How beautiful is night! SOUTHEY, *Thalaba the Destroyer*, I, st. 1

---

* Heaven's ebon vault,
Studded with stars unutterably bright,
Through which the moon's unclouded grandeur rolls.
SHELLEY, *Queen Mab*, iv

Moor.— Could you on this fair mountain leave to feed,
And batten on this moor?—SHAKESPEARE, *Hamlet*, iii, 4

Moral.— The moral market had the usual chills
Of virtue suffering from protested bills.
HOLMES, *The Banker's Dinner*, st. 8

The temple of my youth
Was strong in moral purpose; once I felt
The glory of philosophy, and knelt
In the pure shrine of truth.
PRAED, *A Retrospect*, st. 4

Morals. Where faith, law, morals, all began,
All end, in love of God, and love of Man.
POPE, *Essay on Man*, Epistle iv, lines 339, 340

Morn.— The sun had long since, in the lap
Of Thetis, taken out his nap,
And, like a lobster boiled, the morn
From black to red began to turn.
BUTLER, *Hudibras*, II, ii, lines 29–32

The breezy call of incense-breathing morn.
GRAY, *Elegy Written in a Country Churchyard*, st. 6

Look, the morn, in russet mantle clad,
Walks o'er the dew of yon high eastward [eastern] hill.
SHAKESPEARE, *Hamlet*, i, 1

Morning.— The night is past, and shines the sun
As if that morn were a jocund one.
Lightly and brightly breaks away
The morning from her mantle of grey,
And the noon will look on a sultry day.
BYRON, *Siege of Corinth*, st. 22

But, soft! methinks I scent the morning air.
SHAKESPEARE, *Hamlet*, i, 5

Mortal.— Oh, why should the spirit of mortal be proud?
Like a swift-fleeting meteor, a fast-flying cloud,
A flash of the lightning, a break of the wave,
He passeth from life to his rest in the grave.
WILLIAM KNOX, *Oh, Why Should the Spirit, etc.*, st. 1

All men think all men mortal but themselves.
YOUNG, *Night Thoughts*, I, line 424

Mortality.— To smell to a turf of fresh earth is wholesome for the body; no less are thoughts of mortality cordial to the soul.
THOMAS FULLER, *The Holy and the Profane State: The Court Lady*

We cannot hold mortality's strong hand.
SHAKESPEARE, *King John*, iv, 2

From this instant,
There's nothing serious in mortality: . . .
The wine of life is drawn, and the mere lees[1]
Is left this vault to brag of.
SHAKESPEARE, *Macbeth*, ii, 3

Motes.— The gay motes that people the sunbeams.
MILTON, *Il Penseroso*, line 8

Mother.— Thou wilt scarce be a man before thy mother.[2]
BEAUMONT AND FLETCHER, *Love's Cure*, ii, 2

The mother, wi' her needle an' her shears,
Gars [*makes*] auld claes look amaist as weel's the new.
BURNS, *The Cotter's Saturday Night*, st. 5

A mother is a mother still,
The holiest thing alive.
S. T. COLERIDGE, *The Three Graves*, III, st. 10

Where yet was ever found a mother
Who'd give her booby for another?
GAY, *The Mother, the Nurse, and the Fairy*, lines 33, 34

Taint not thy mind, nor let thy soul contrive
Against thy mother aught: leave her to heaven,
And to those thorns that in her bosom lodge
To prick and sting her. SHAKESPEARE, *Hamlet*, i, 5

Mother [in Law].— When Susan came to live with me,
Her mother came to live with her!
HOOD, *The Bachelor's Dream*, st. 3

Mothers.— Dishonour not your mothers.
SHAKESPEARE, *King Henry V*, iii, 1

Moths.— Maidens, like moths, are ever caught by glare,
And Mammon wins his way where seraphs might despair.
BYRON, *Childe Harold's Pilgrimage*, Canto i, st. 9

Mount.— Mount, mount, my soul! thy seat is up on high;
Whilst my gross flesh sinks downward, here to die.
SHAKESPEARE, *King Richard II*, v, 5

Mountain.— The labouring mountain must bring forth a mouse. DRYDEN, *Art of Poetry*, line 701

---

[1] The wine of life is on the lees.— SCOTT, *Marmion*, Introduction to Canto i

[2] Strive still to be a man before your mother.
COWPER, *Motto of No. III, Connoisseur*

Mounting.— And there was mounting in hot haste: the steed,
The mustering squadron, and the clattering car,
Went pouring forward with impetuous speed,
And swiftly forming in the ranks of war.
BYRON, *Childe Harold's Pilgrimage*, Canto iii, st. 25

Mourn.— They truly mourn, that mourn without a witness.
R. BARON, *Mirza*

Man was made to mourn.
BURNS, *Man Was Made to Mourn*, st. 3

To mourn a mischief that is past and gone
Is the next way to draw new [more] mischief on.
SHAKESPEARE, *Othello*, i, 3

Mourning.— Let us bury the Great Duke
To the noise of the mourning of a mighty nation;
Mourning when their leaders fall,
Warriors carry the warrior's pall,
And sorrow darkens hamlet and hall.
TENNYSON, *Ode on the Death of the Duke of Wellington*, st. 1

Mouse.— The mouse that always trusts to one poor hole,
Can never be a mouse of any soul.[1]
POPE, *The Wife of Bath, Her Prologue*, lines 298, 299

I never killed a mouse, nor hurt a fly:
I trod upon a worm against my will,
But I wept for it. SHAKESPEARE, *Pericles*, iv, 1

Mouth.— Peace! I will stop your mouth [*kissing her*].
SHAKESPEARE, *Much Ado about Nothing*, v, 4

God sendeth and giveth both mouth and the meat.
THOMAS TUSSER, *Five Hundred Points of Good Husbandry*

Muddle.—'T is a' a muddle. DICKENS, *Hard Times*, II, xi

Multitude.— A swinish multitude.
BURKE, *Reflections on the Revolution in France*

The multitude is always in the wrong.
EARL OF ROSCOMMON, *Essay on Translated Verse*, line 184

The many-headed multitude.
SHAKESPEARE, *Coriolanus*, ii, 3

Was ever feather so lightly blown to and fro as this multitude?—SHAKESPEARE, *King Henry VI, Part II*, iv, 8

[1] I holde a mouses herte nat worth a leek,
That hath but oon hole for to sterte to.—CHAUCER, *Canterbury Tales: The Wife of Bath's Prologue*, lines 572, 573

Murder. Methought, last night, I wrought
A murder, in a dream.
HOOD, *The Dream of Eugene Aram*, st. 13

Ninepunce a day fer killin' folks comes kind o' low fer murder. LOWELL, *The Biglow Papers*, I, ii, line 10

One murder made a villain,
Millions a hero. Princes were privileged
To kill, and numbers sanctified the crime.[1]
PORTEOUS, *Death*, lines 154–156

Murder most foul, as in the best it is;
But this most foul, strange, and unnatural.
SHAKESPEARE, *Hamlet*, i, 5

Oh, my offence is rank, it smells to heaven;
It hath the primal eldest curse upon 't,
A brother's murder! *Ibid.*, iii, 3

Murder cannot be hid long.[2]
SHAKESPEARE, *Merchant of Venice*, ii, 2

Murders. Murders disguised by philosophic name.[3]
SCOTT, *Harold the Dauntless*, Introduction, st. 3

Muse.— Oh for a Muse of fire, that would ascend
The brightest heaven of invention!
SHAKESPEARE, *King Henry V*, Prologue

Music.— When Music, heavenly maid, was young.
WILLIAM COLLINS, *The Passions*, st. 1

Music has charms to soothe a savage breast,
To soften rocks, or bend a knotted oak.
CONGREVE, *Mourning Bride*, i, 1

The music of the spheres.[4]
DRYDEN, *Elegy on Mrs. Killigrew*, line 49; POPE, *Essay on Man*, Epistle i, line 202

---

[1] One to destroy is murder, by the law,
And gibbets keep the lifted hand in awe;
To murder thousands takes a specious name,—
War's glorious art,— and gives immortal fame.
YOUNG, *Love of Fame*, Satire vii, lines 55–58

[2] Mordre wol out, that see we day by day.
CHAUCER, *The Nonnes Preestes Tale*, line 232

Murder, though it have no tongue, will speak
With most miraculous organ. SHAKESPEARE, *Hamlet*, ii, 2

[3] Vivisection *et id genus omne*.

[4] There's music in the sighing of a reed;
There's music in the gushing of a rill;
There's music in all things, if men had ears:
Their earth is but an echo of the spheres.
BYRON, *Don Juan*, Canto xv, st. 5

Music is Love in search of a word.
LANIER, *The Symphony*, line 368

Music, moody food
Of us that trade in love.
SHAKESPEARE, *Antony and Cleopatra*, ii, 5

Let music sound while he doth make his choice;
Then, if he lose, he makes a swan-like end,
Fading in music.[1]
SHAKESPEARE, *Merchant of Venice*, iii, 2

I am never merry when I hear sweet music.[2] *Ibid.*, v

The general so likes your music, that he desires you, for love's sake, to make no more noise with it.
SHAKESPEARE, *Othello*, iii, 1

If music be the food of love, play on:
Give me excess of it, that, surfeiting,
The appetite may sicken, and so die.
That strain again! it had a dying fall:
Oh, it came o'er my ear like the sweet sound [south[3]]
That breathes upon a bank of violets,
Stealing and giving odour.
SHAKESPEARE, *Twelfth Night*, i, 1

Till at the last she set herself to man,
Like perfect music unto noble words.
TENNYSON, *The Princess*, vii, lines 269, 270

Must.— What must be shall be.
SHAKESPEARE, *Romeo and Juliet*, iv, 1

Nails.—"When you see Ned Cuttle bite his nails, . . . then you may know that Ned Cuttle's aground."
DICKENS, *Dombey and Son*, xv

---

[1] So, on Mæander's banks, when death is nigh,
The mournful swan sings her own elegy.
DRYDEN, *Dido to Æneas*, lines 1, 2

'Tis strange that death should sing.
I am the cygnet to this pale faint swan,
Who chants a doleful hymn to his own death,
And from the organ-pipe of frailty sings
His soul and body to their lasting rest.—SHAKESPEARE, *King John*, v, 7

I will play the swan,
And die in music. SHAKESPEARE, *Othello*, v, 2

The wild swan's death-hymn. TENNYSON, *The Dying Swan*, st. 3

[2] The man that hath no music in himself,
Nor is not moved with concord of sweet sounds,
Is fit for treasons, stratagems, and spoils;
The motions of his spirit are dull as night
And his affections dark as Erebus:
Let no such man be trusted. SHAKESPEARE, *Merchant of Venice*, v

[3] A change suggested by Pope.

Naked.— The naked every day he clad —
When he put on his clothes.
GOLDSMITH, *Elegy on the Death of a Mad Dog*, st. 3

Name.— A little breath, love, wine, ambition, fame,
Fighting, devotion, dust — perhaps a name.
BYRON, *Don Juan*, Canto ii, st. 4

Oh! Amos Cottle! — Phœbus! what a name
To fill the speaking-trump of future fame.
BYRON, *English Bards and Scotch Reviewers*, lines 398, 399[1]

Who hath not owned, with rapture-smitten frame,
The power of grace, the magic of a name.
CAMPBELL, *Pleasures of Hope*, ii, lines 5, 6

And lastly, when summoned to drink to my flame,
Let her guess why I never once mention her name,
Though herself and the woman I love are the same.[2]
COWPER, *Symptoms of Love*, st. 6

He left the name at which the world grew pale,
To point a moral, or adorn a tale.—SAMUEL JOHNSON, *The Vanity of Human Wishes*, lines 221, 222

Here lies one whose name was writ in water.[3]
KEATS, *Epitaph, by Himself*

Oh! breathe not his name, let it sleep in the shade,
Where cold and unhonoured his relics are laid.
. . . . .
And the tear that we shed, though in secret it rolls,
Shall long keep his memory green in our souls.
T. MOORE, *Oh! Breathe Not His Name*, st. 1, 2

---

[1] Some versions vary in the number of lines.

[2] And oft in crowds I might rejoice
To hear thy uttered name,
Though haply from an unknown voice
The welcome echo came:
How coldly would I shape reply,
With lingering lip, and listless eye,
That none might doubt or blame,
Or guess that idle theme could be
A mine of afterthought to me! PRAED, *A Farewell*, st. 5

They shall never know from me,
On any one condition,
Whose health made bright my Burgundy,
Whose beauty was my vision! PRAED, *To* ———, I, st. 5

Whatsoe'er the hour or place,
No bribe or prayer shall win me
To say whose voice, or form, or face,
That spell awoke within me! *Ibid.*, III, st. 9

[3] Below lies one whose name was traced in sand.
DAVID GRAY, *My Epitaph*

Good name in man and woman, dear my lord,
Is the immediate jewel of their souls:
Who steals my purse steals trash; 'tis something, nothing;
'Twas mine, 'tis his, and has been slave to thousands:
But he that filches from me my good name
Robs me of that which not enriches him
And makes me poor indeed.— SHAKESPEARE, *Othello*, iii, 3

What 's in a name? that which we call a rose
By any other name would smell as sweet;
So Romeo would, were he not Romeo called,
Retain that dear perfection which he owes
Without that title.

SHAKESPEARE, *Romeo and Juliet*, ii, 2

Sweetheart, I love you so well that your good name is mine.[1] TENNYSON, *The Grandmother*, st. 13

Another name was on the door.

TENNYSON, *In Memoriam*, lxxxvii, st. 5

Names.— Call all things by their names. Hell, call thou hell;
Archangel, call archangel; and God, God.

P. J. BAILEY, *Festus*, Scene — Home

At thirty we are all trying to cut our names in big letters upon the walls of this tenement of life; twenty years later we have carved it, or shut up our jack-knives.

HOLMES, *Autocrat of the Breakfast-Table*, iv

Then shall our names,
Familiar in his mouth as household words, . . .
Be in their flowing cups freshly remembered.

SHAKESPEARE, *King Henry V*, iv, 3

And if his name be George, I 'll call him Peter;
For new-made honour doth forget men's names.

SHAKESPEARE, *King John*, i

Now sign your names, which shall be read,
Mute symbols of a joyful morn,
By village eyes as yet unborn.
The names are signed, and overhead

Begins the clash and clang that tells
The joy to every wandering breeze;
The blind wall rocks, and on the trees
The dead leaf trembles to the bells.

TENNYSON, *In Memoriam*, Conclusion, st. 15, 16

---

[1] My name, once mine, now thine, is closelier mine,
For fame, could fame be mine, that fame were thine,
And shame, could shame be thine, that shame were mine,
So trust me not at all or all in all.

TENNYSON, *Merlin and Vivien*, lines 444-447

Narrow.— To live in narrow ways with little men.
BYRON, *Prophecy of Dante*, Canto i, line 161

Narrower.— Some minds improve by travel, others, rather,
Resemble copper wire, or brass,
Which gets the narrower by going farther!
HOOD, *Ode to Rae Wilson, Esquire*, st. 23

Nation.— The Power that has made and preserved us a nation!
F. S. KEY, *The Star-Spangled Banner*, st. 4

A nation spoke to a nation,
A Queen sent word to a throne:
Daughter am I in my mother's house,
But mistress in my own.
The gates are mine to open
As the gates are mine to close,
And I abide in my mother's house,
Said our Lady of the Snows.
KIPLING, *Our Lady of the Snows*, st. 6

It is for us, the living, rather, to be dedicated here to the unfinished work, which they have thus far so nobly advanced. It is rather for us to be here dedicated to the great task remaining before us that from these honoured dead, we take increased devotion to that cause for which they gave the last full measure of devotion; that we here highly resolve that these dead shall not have died in vain; that this nation under God, shall have a new birth of freedom; and that government of the people, by the people, for the people, shall not perish from the earth.[1]
LINCOLN, *Address at Gettysburg*, Nov. 19, 1863

God had sifted three kingdoms to find the wheat for this planting,
Then had sifted the wheat, as the living seed of a nation.
LONGFELLOW, *Courtship of Miles Standish*, iv, lines 105, 106

The fate of a nation was riding that night.
LONGFELLOW, *Paul Revere's Ride*, st. 8

[1]Let us, the Living, rather dedicate
Ourselves to the unfinished work, which they
Thus far advanced so nobly on its way,
And save the imperilled State!
Let us, upon this field where they, the brave,
Their last full measure of devotion gave,
Highly resolve they have not died in vain!—
That, under God, the Nation's later birth
Of Freedom, and the people's gain
Of their own sovereignty, shall never wane
And perish from the circle of the earth!
BAYARD TAYLOR, *Gettysburg Ode*, st. 1

Earth's biggest country 's gut her soul
An' risen up earth's greatest nation.
LOWELL, *Biglow Papers*, II, vii, st. 21

A nation saved, a race delivered! *Ibid.*, x, st. 21

The pith and marrow of a nation
Drawing force from all her men,
Highest, humblest, weakest, all,
For her time of need, and then
Pulsing it again through them.
LOWELL, *Commemoration Ode*, st. 11

Methinks I see in my mind a noble and puissant nation rousing herself like a strong man after sleep, and shaking her invincible locks: methinks I see her as an eagle mewing her mighty youth, and kindling her undazzled eyes at the full midday beam. MILTON, *Areopagitica*

Nativity. *Glendower*. At my nativity
The front of heaven was full of fiery shapes,
Of burning cressets; and at my birth
The frame and huge foundation of the earth
Shaked like a coward.

Hotspur. Why, so it would have done at the same season, if your mother's cat had but kittened, though yourself had never been born.

. . . . .

Diseased nature oftentimes breaks forth
In strange eruptions.
SHAKESPEARE, *King Henry IV, Part I*, iii, 1

Nature.— I love not man the less, but Nature more.
BYRON, *Childe Harold's Pilgrimage*, Canto iv, st. 178

Nature, a jealous mistress, laid him low,
He wooed and won her; and, by love made bold,
She showed him more than mortal man should know,
Then slew him lest her secret should be told.
SYDNEY DOBELL, *Epigram on the Death of Edward Forbes*

Art may err, but Nature cannot miss.[1]
DRYDEN, *The Cock and the Fox*, line 452

He who Nature scorns and mocks,
By Nature is mocked and scorned.
JOHN HAY, *The Monks of Basle*, iv, st. 2

Nature and time were twins.—JAMES MONTGOMERY, *The Pelican Island*, Canto iv, st. 1

---

[1] Nature is always wise in every part.
LORD THURLOW, *To a Bird*

Slave to no sect, who takes no private road,
But looks through Nature up to Nature's God.
POPE, *Essay on Man*, Epistle iv, lines 331, 332

Nature teaches beasts to know their friends.
SHAKESPEARE, *Coriolanus*, ii, 1

As is the osprey to the fish, who takes it
By sovereignty of nature. *Ibid.*, iv, 7

How hard it is to hide the sparks of nature!
SHAKESPEARE, *Cymbeline*, iii, 3

O'erstep not the modesty of nature.
SHAKESPEARE, *Hamlet*, iii, 2

To hold, as 't were, the mirror up to nature.[1] *Ibid.*

He's walked the way of nature;
And to our purposes he lives no more.
SHAKESPEARE, *King Henry IV*, *Part II*, v, 2

One touch of nature makes the whole world kin.
SHAKESPEARE, *Troilus and Cressida*, iii, 3

I have no debt but the debt of Nature; and I want but patience of her, and I will pay her every farthing I owe her. STERNE, *Tristram Shandy*, VII, vii

Nautilus.— Learn of the little nautilus to sail,
Spread the thin oar, and catch the driving gale.
POPE, *Essay on Man*, Epistle iii, lines 177, 178

Navy.— A load would sink a navy.
SHAKESPEARE, *King Henry VIII*, iii, 2

Nearer.— Nearer, my God, to Thee,
Nearer to Thee!
E'en though it be a cross
That raiseth me;
Still all my song shall be,
Nearer, my God, to Thee,
Nearer to Thee.[2]—SARAH F. ADAMS, *Nearer, My God, to Thee*, st. 1

---

[1] Lo, where the stage, the poor, degraded stage,
Holds its warped mirror to a gaping age. C. SPRAGUE, *Curiosity*

[2] Nearer my Father's house,
Where the many mansions be;
Nearer the great white throne,
Nearer the crystal sea;

Nearer the bound of life,
Where we lay our burdens down;
Nearer leaving the cross,
Nearer gaining the crown! PHŒBE CARY, *Nearer Home*, st. 2, 3

Here in the body pent,
Absent from Him I roam;
Yet nightly pitch my moving tent
A day's march nearer home.
JAMES MONTGOMERY, *At Home in Heaven*, i, st. 2

Necessary.— A necessary act incurs no blame.
COWPER, *The Task: Winter Walk at Noon*, line 573

Necessities. Are these things then necessities?
Then let us meet them like necessities.
SHAKESPEARE, *King Henry IV, Part II*, iii, 1

Necessity.— Necessity invented stools,
Convenience next suggested elbow chairs.
COWPER, *The Task: The Sofa*, lines 87, 88

If necessity be the mother of invention.[1]
GEORGE FARQUHAR, *The Twin Rivals*, i, 1

Necessity,
The tyrant's plea.[2]
MILTON, *Paradise Lost*, IV, lines 393, 394

To make a virtue of necessity.[3]
SHAKESPEARE, *Two Gentlemen of Verona*, iv, 1;
DRYDEN, *Palamon and Arcite*, line 2361

Necessity, thou mother of the world.
SHELLEY, *Queen Mab*, vi, st. 10

Needle.— Spontaneously to God should tend the soul,
Like the magnetic needle to the Pole;
But what were that intrinsic virtue worth,
Suppose some fellow, with more zeal than knowledge,
Fresh from Saint Andrew's College,
Should nail the conscious needle to the north?[4]
HOOD, *Ode to Rae Wilson, Esquire*, st. 12

Needs.— The more goods a man has, the more he thinks he needs. CHARLES WAGNER, *The Simple Life*, i

---

[1] Necessity,— thou best of peacemakers as well as surest prompter of invention. SCOTT, *Peveril of the Peak*, xxvi

[2] Necessity is the argument of tyrants, it is the creed of slaves.
WILLIAM PITT, EARL OF CHATHAM, *Speech on the Indian Bill*, November, 1773

[3] To maken vertu of necessitee. CHAUCER, *The Knight's Tale*, line 2184

Orpheus, who found no remedy,
Made virtue of necessity.
WILLIAM KING, *Orpheus and Eurydice*, lines 193, 194

He did make of necessity virtue. RABELAIS, I, xi

There is no virtue like necessity.— SHAKESPEARE, *King Richard II*, i, 3

[4] If I put a weathercock on my house, Sir, I want it to tell which way the wind blows up aloft. . . . I don't want a weathercock with a winch in an old gentleman's study that he can take hold of and turn, so that the vane shall point west when the great wind overhead is blowing east with all its might. HOLMES, *Professor at the Breakfast-Table*, ii

Neglect.— A wise and salutary neglect.
BURKE, *Speech on Conciliation with America*, March 22, 1775

Nell.— And then, while round them shadows gathered faster,
And as the firelight fell,
He read aloud the book wherein the Master
Had writ of "Little Nell."
BRET HARTE, *Dickens in Camp*, st. 4

Nepenthe.— Quaff, oh, quaff this kind nepenthe and forget this lost Lenore! POE, *The Raven*, st. 14

Nerve.— It is better to lose a pint of blood from your veins than to have a nerve tapped.
HOLMES, *Autocrat of the Breakfast-Table*, i

Nest.— There are no birds in last year's nest.
LONGFELLOW, *It Is Not Always May*, st. 3

Nets.— Though 'tis pleasant weaving nets,
'Tis wiser to make cages.[1]
T. MOORE, *Nets and Cages*, st. 5

Nettle.— Tender-handed stroke a nettle,
And it stings you for your pains;
Grasp it like a man of mettle,
And it soft as silk remains.

'Tis the same with common natures:
Use 'em kindly, they rebel;
But be rough as nutmeg-graters,
And the rogues obey you well. AARON HILL,
Verses Written on a Window in Scotland

Out of this nettle, danger,[2] we pluck this flower, safety.
SHAKESPEARE, *King Henry IV, Part I*, ii, 3

Never. From its station in the hall
An ancient timepiece says to all,—
"For ever — never!
Never — for ever!"[3]
LONGFELLOW, *The Old Clock on the Stairs*, st. 1

---

[1] The reason why so few marriages are happy is because young ladies spend their time in making nets, not in making cages.
SWIFT, *Thoughts on Various Subjects*

In vain in the sight of the bird is the net of the fowler displayed.
KIPLING, *Certain Maxims of Hafiz*, st. 18

[2] Making the nettle danger soft for us as silk.
LOWELL, *Commemoration Ode*, st. 8

[3] "Tick-tock, tick-tock!"— for so the clock
Tells of a life to be;
"Tick-tock, tick-tock!"—'tis so the clock
Tells of eternity. EUGENE FIELD, *New Year's Eve*, st. 2

New.— New times demand new measures and new men.[1]
LOWELL, *A Glance Behind the Curtain*, line 193

New England.— A sup of New England's air is better than a whole draught of Old England's ale.
FRANCIS HIGGINSON, *New England's Plantation*, Of the Air of New England

News.— Evil news rides post, while good news baits.
MILTON, *Samson Agonistes*, line 1538

Though it be honest, it is never good
To bring bad news.
SHAKESPEARE, *Antony and Cleopatra*, ii, 5

The first bringer of unwelcome news
Hath but a losing office.
SHAKESPEARE, *King Henry IV, Part II*, i, 1

No news so bad abroad as this at home.
SHAKESPEARE, *King Richard III*, i, 1

Newton.— Nature and Nature's laws lay hid in night:
God said, Let Newton be! and all was light.
POPE, *Epitaph Intended for Sir Isaac Newton*

Nice.— Some people are more nice than wise.
COWPER, *Mutual Forbearance*, line 20

A nice man is a man of nasty ideas.
SWIFT, *Thoughts on Various Subjects*

Nick.— Nick Machiavel had ne'er a trick,
Though he gave 's [gave his] name to our Old Nick.
BUTLER, *Hudibras*, III, i, lines 1313, 1314

Nigger.— Whar you finds de nigger — dar 's de banjo an' de 'possum! IRWIN RUSSELL, *De Fust Banjo*, st. 11

Night.— The night has a thousand eyes,
And the day but one;
Yet the light of the bright world dies
With the dying sun.

The mind has a thousand eyes,
And the heart but one;
Yet the light of a whole life dies
When love is done.
F. W. BOURDILLON, *The Night Has a Thousand Eyes*

---

[1] New occasions teach new duties; Time makes ancient good uncouth;
They must upward still, and onward, who would keep abreast of Truth;
Lo, before us gleam her camp-fires! we ourselves must Pilgrims be,
Launch our Mayflower, and steer boldly through the desperate winter sea,
Nor attempt the Future's portal with the Past's blood-rusted key.
LOWELL, *The Present Crisis*, st. 18

Roused from their slumbers,
In grim array the grisly spectres rise,
Grin horrible, and, obstinately sullen,
Pass and repass, hushed as the foot of night.
Again the screech-owl shrieks. I'll hear no more,
It makes my blood run chill. BLAIR, *The Grave*

All night I lay in agony,
From weary chime to chime.
HOOD, *The Dream of Eugene Aram*, st. 26

The day is done, and the darkness
Falls from the wings of Night,[1]
As a feather is wafted downward
From an eagle in his flight.
LONGFELLOW, *The Day Is Done*, st. 1

Silence, ye wolves! while Ralph to Cynthia howls,
And makes night hideous — Answer him, ye owls!
POPE, *The Dunciad*, III, lines 165, 166

Come, night; end, day!
SHAKESPEARE, *All's Well That Ends Well*, iii, 2

One that converses more with the buttock of the night than with the forehead of the morning.
SHAKESPEARE, *Coriolanus*, ii, 1

In the dead vast and middle of the night.
SHAKESPEARE, *Hamlet*, i, 2

'Tis now the very witching time of night,
When churchyards yawn and hell itself breathes out
Contagion to this world.[2] *Ibid.*, iii, 2

'Tis a naughty night to swim in.
SHAKESPEARE, *King Lear*, iii, 4

Good things of day begin to droop and drowse,
Whiles night's black agents to their preys do rouse.
SHAKESPEARE, *Macbeth*, iii, 2

Macbeth. What is the night?
Lady Macbeth. Almost at odds with morning, which is which. *Ibid.*, iii, 4

The night is long that never finds the day. *Ibid.*, iv, 3

Nightcap.— A nightcap decked his brows instead of bay,
A cap by night — a stocking all the day!
GOLDSMITH, *Description of an Author's Bed-chamber*, lines 19, 20

---

[1] Smoothing the raven down
Of darkness. MILTON, *Comus*, lines 251, 252

[2] Now it is the time of night
That the graves all gaping wide,
Every one lets forth his sprite,
In the church-way paths to glide.
SHAKESPEARE, *Midsummer-Night's Dream*, v, 1 [2]

Nightingale.— Wilt thou be gone? it is not yet near day:[1]
It was the nightingale, and not the lark,
That pierced the fearful hollow of thine ear.
SHAKESPEARE, *Romeo and Juliet*, iii, 5

Nightly.— When by my bed I saw my mother kneel,
And with her blessing took her nightly kiss.[2]
W. ALLSTON, *Boyhood*

Niobe.— The Niobe of nations.[3]
BYRON, *Childe Harold's Pilgrimage*, Canto iv, 79

No.— I can march up to a fortress and summon the place to surrender,
But march up to a woman with such a proposal, I dare not.
I'm not afraid of bullets, nor shot from the mouth of a cannon,
But of a thundering "No!" point-blank from the mouth of a woman,
That I confess I'm afraid of, nor am I ashamed to confess it!
LONGFELLOW, *Courtship of Miles Standish*, ii, lines 84–88

To say why gals acts so or so,
Or don't 'ould be presumin';
Mebby to mean *yes* an' say *no*
Comes nateral to women.
LOWELL, *The Courtin'*, st. 18

At his birth an evil spirit
Charms and spells around him flung,
And, with well-concocted malice.
Laid a curse upon his tongue;
. . . .
He could plead, expound, and argue;
Fire with wit, with wisdom glow;
But one word for ever failed him,
Source of all his pain and woe,
Luckless wight! he could not say it —
Could not — dared not answer No!
CHARLES MACKAY, *My Neighbour*, st. 6, 7

---

[1] She says, "The cock crows,— hark!"
He says, "No! still 'tis dark."
She says, "The dawn grows bright,"
He says, "O no, my Light!"
. . . . .
She says, "Then quick depart:
Alas! you now must start;
But give the cock a blow
Who did begin our woe!"—ANONYMOUS, *The Parting Lovers*, from the Chinese (trans. by W. R. Alger)

[2] Thy nightly visits to my chamber made,
That thou mightst know me safe and warmly laid.
COWPER, *On the Receipt of my Mother's Picture*, lines 58, 59

[3] The Niobe of isles. J. B. O'REILLY, *My Native Land*

Nobility.— Let wealth and commerce, laws and learning die,
But leave us still our old nobility.— LORD JOHN MANNERS, *England's Trust*, III, lines 227, 228

Noble.— Noble thought produces
Noble ends and uses,
Noble hopes are part of Hope wherever she may be,
Noble thought enhances
Life and all its chances,
And noble self is noble song,— all this I learn from thee!
ROBERT BUCHANAN, *To David in Heaven*, st. 17

Noisy.— Vociferated logic kills me quite,
A noisy man is always in the right.
I twirl my thumbs, fall back into my chair,
Fix on the wainscot a distressful stare,
And, when I hope his blunders are all out,
Reply discreetly — "To be sure — no doubt!"
COWPER, *Conversation*, lines 113–118

Noon.— With twelve great shocks of sound, the shameless noon
Was clashed and hammered from a hundred towers.
TENNYSON, *Godiva*, lines 74, 75

North.— The pale, unripened beauties of the North.
ADDISON, *Cato*, i, 4

From the caves of the North
Mid the Night's dominions,
I come tempesting forth
On mine ice-ribbed pinions,
And the snows are my robe, and the frost is my crown, and the clouds are my minions.

. . . . .

But none ever dare to lay bare the cold lair of my dark generation.[1]
H. BERNARD CARPENTER, *Liber Amoris*, Wind-Song, st. 1, 4

Ask where's the North? — at York, 'tis on the Tweed;
In Scotland, at the Orcades; and there,
At Greenland, Zembla, or the Lord knows where.
No creature owns it in the first degree,
But thinks his neighbour further gone than he.
POPE, *Essay on Man*, Epistle ii, lines 222–226

---

[1] "I barred my gates with iron, I shuttered my doors with flame,
Because to force my ramparts your nutshell navies came;
I took the sun from their presence, I cut them down with my blast,
And they died, but the flag of England blew free ere the spirit passed."
KIPLING, *The English Flag*, st. 4

Nor'wester.— A strong nor'wester 's blowing, Bill;
Hark! don't ye hear it roar now?
Lord help 'em, how I pities them
Unhappy folks on shore now!—WILLIAM PITT (of Malta), *The Sailor's Consolation*, st. 1

Nose.— Knows he that never took a pinch,
Nosey, the pleasure thence which flows?
Knows he the titillating joys
Which my nose knows?
O nose, I am as proud of thee
As any mountain of its snows;
I gaze on thee, and feel that pride
A Roman knows!—A. A. FORRESTER, *To My Nose*

O jest unseen, inscrutable, invisible,
As a nose on a man's face, or a weathercock on a steeple!
SHAKESPEARE, *Two Gentlemen of Verona*, ii, 1

Noses.—'Tis said that people ought to guard their noses
Who thrust them into matters none of theirs.
HOOD, *Ode to Rae Wilson, Esquire*, st. 6

Note.— "In the Proverbs of Solomon you will find the following words, 'May we never want a friend in need, nor a bottle to give him!' When found, make a note of."
DICKENS, *Dombey and Son*, xv

Nothing.—'Twas doing nothing was his curse,
Is there a vice can plague us worse?
HANNAH MORE, *Florio*, I

Nothing will come of nothing. . . .
Nothing can be made out of nothing.
SHAKESPEARE, *King Lear*, i, 1, 4

Novel.— Some play the devil, and then write a novel.
BYRON, *Don Juan*, Canto ii, st. 201

November.— No sun — no moon!
No morn — no noon —
No dawn — no dust — no proper time of day —
. . . . .
No warmth — no cheerfulness — no healthful ease —
No comfortable feel in any member —
No shade — no shine — no butterflies — no bees —
No fruits — no flowers — no leaves — no birds —
November! HOOD, *No!*

Numbers.— They say there is divinity in odd numbers.[1]
SHAKESPEARE, *Merry Wives of Windsor*, v, 1

Nunnery.— Get thee to a nunnery.
SHAKESPEARE, *Hamlet*, iii, 1

Nursed.— Once when I had a fever — I won't forget it soon —
I was hot as a basted turkey and crazy as a loon;
Never an hour went by me when she was out of sight —
She nursed me true and tender, and stuck to me day and
night. W. CARLETON, *Betsey and I Are Out*, st. 17

Nut.— Sweetest nut hath sourest rind,
Such a nut is Rosalind.
SHAKESPEARE, *As You Like It*, iii, 2

Oak. Here's to the oak, the brave old oak,
Who stands in his pride alone;
And still flourish he, a hale green tree,
When a hundred years are gone!
H. F. CHORLEY, *The Brave Old Oak*

The hollow oak our palace is,
Our heritage the sea.—A. CUNNINGHAM, *A Wet Sheet and a Flowing Sea*, st. 3

Come cheer up, my lads! 't is to glory we steer,
The prize more than all to an Englishman dear;
To honour we call you as freemen, not slaves,
For who are so free as the sons of the waves?
Hearts of oak are our ships,
Hearts of oak are our men,
We always are ready,
Steady, boys, steady!
We'll fight and we'll conquer again and again.[2]
GARRICK, *Hearts of Oak*, st. 1

Oar.— The light drip of the suspended oar.
BYRON, *Childe Harold*, Canto iii, st. 86

Oars.— Faintly as tolls the evening chime,
Our voices keep tune and our oars keep time.[3]
T. MOORE, *Canadian Boat Song*, st. 1

---

[1] "Now Rory, leave off, sir; you'll hug me no more,
That's eight times to-day you have kissed me before."
"Then here goes another," says he, "to make sure,
For there's luck in odd numbers," says Rory O'More.
S. LOVER, *Rory O'More; or Good Omens*, st. 3

[2] There are many versions of this song.

[3] And all the way, to guide their chime,
With falling oars they kept the time.
ANDREW MARVELL, *Song of the Emigrants in Bermuda*

The measured pulse of racing oars.
TENNYSON, *In Memoriam*, lxxxvii, st. 3

Oath.— A good mouth-filling oath.
SHAKESPEARE, *King Henry IV, Part I*, iii, 1

It is great sin to swear unto a sin,
But greater sin to keep a sinful oath.
Who can be bound by any solemn vow . . .
And have no other reason for this wrong
But that he was bound by a solemn oath?
SHAKESPEARE, *King Henry VI, Part II*, v, 1

A terrible oath, with a swaggering accent sharply twanged off, gives manhood more approbation than ever proof itself would have earned him.
SHAKESPEARE, *Twelfth Night*, iii, 4

The accusing spirit, which flew up to Heaven's chancery with the oath,[1] blushed as he gave it in; and the recording angel, as he wrote it down, dropped a tear upon the word and blotted it out for ever.
STERNE, *Tristram Shandy*, VI, viii

Oaths.—As false as dicers' oaths. SHAKESPEARE, *Hamlet*, iii, 4

Obey.— No man doth safely rule, but he that hath learned gladly to obey.
THOMAS À KEMPIS, *Imitation of Christ*, I, xx, 2

Now these are the laws of the jungle, and many and mighty are they;
But the head and the hoof of the law and the haunch and the hump is — Obey!
KIPLING, *The Law of the Jungle*, st. 18

Observation.— The bearings of this observation lays in the application on it. DICKENS, *Dombey and Son*, xxiii

Obstinacy.— Obstinacy's ne'er so stiff,
As when 'tis in a wrong belief.
BUTLER, *Hudibras*, III, ii, lines 483, 484

Occasion.— How to occasion's height he rose.
TOM TAYLOR, *Abraham Lincoln*, st. 6

---

[1]The context is given here to illustrate the nature of the offence and the kindly spirit of the offender.

"In a fortnight . . . he might march," added my uncle Toby——"He will never march . . . in this world," said the Corporal; . . . "the poor soul will die."——"He shall not die, by God!" cried my uncle Toby.

Sad as angels for the good man's sin,
Weep to record, and blush to give it in!
CAMPBELL, *Pleasures of Hope*, ii, st. 26

Occasions.— There is occasions and causes why and wherefore in all things. SHAKESPEARE, *King Henry V*, v, 1

Ocean.[1]— Old ocean's grey and melancholy waste.
BRYANT, *Thanatopsis*, line 43

Roll on, thou deep and dark-blue[2] ocean — roll!
Ten thousand fleets sweep over thee in vain;
Man marks the earth with ruin — his control
Stops with the shore.
BYRON, *Childe Harold's Pilgrimage*, Canto iv st. 179

And I have loved thee, Ocean! and my joy
Of youthful sports was on thy breast to be
Borne, like thy bubbles, onward: from a boy
I wantoned with thy breakers . . .
For I was as it were a child of thee,
And trusted to thy billows far and near,
And laid my hand upon thy mane[3]— as I do here.
BYRON, *Ibid.*, st. 184

The spirits of your fathers
Shall start from every wave —
For the deck it was their field of fame,
And ocean was their grave.
CAMPBELL, *Ye Mariners of England*, st. 2

Strongly it bears us along in swelling and limitless billows,
Nothing before and nothing behind but the sky and the ocean.—S. T. COLERIDGE, *The Homeric Hexameter* (trans. from SCHILLER)

We own the ocean, tu, John:
You mus' n' take it hard,
Ef we can't think with you, John,
It 's jest your own back yard.
LOWELL, *Biglow Papers*, II, ii, *Jonathan to John*, st. 6

A life on the ocean wave,
A home on the rolling deep,
Where the scattered waters rave,
And the winds their revels keep!
EPES SARGENT, *A Life on the Ocean Wave*, st. 1

October.— Nor wanting is the brown October, drawn,
Mature and perfect, from his dark retreat
Of thirty years; and now his honest front
Flames in the light refulgent, not afraid
Even with the vineyard's best produce to vie,
To cheat the thirsty moments.
THOMSON, *The Seasons: Autumn*, lines 519–524

---

[1] Cf. SEA.

[2] Darkly, deeply, beautifully blue.—SOUTHEY, *Madoc in Wales*, quoted by BYRON in *Don Juan*, Canto iv, st. 110

[3] He laid his hand upon "the ocean's mane,"
And played familiar with his hoary locks.
POLLOK, *The Course of Time*, iv, line 389

Offence.— In the corrupted currents of this world
Offence's gilded hand may shove by justice,
And oft 't is seen the wicked prize itself
Buys out the law: but 't is not so above;
There is no shuffling, there the action lies
In his true nature; and we ourselves compelled,
Even to the teeth and forehead of our faults,
To give in evidence. SHAKESPEARE, *Hamlet*, iii, 3

In such a time as this it is not meet
That every nice offence should bear his comment.
SHAKESPEARE, *Julius Cæsar*, iv, 3

Offences.— All offences, my lord, come from the heart.
SHAKESPEARE, *King Henry V*, iv, 8

Offender.— She hugged the offender, and forgave the offence,[1]
Sex to the last.
DRYDEN, *Cymon and Iphigenia*, lines 367, 368

Office.— If a due participation of office is a matter of right, how are vacancies to be obtained? Those by death are few; by resignation, none. THOMAS JEFFERSON,
Letter to Elias Shipman, July 12, 1801

A dog 's obeyed in office.
SHAKESPEARE, *King Lear*, iv, 6

Officer. Cassio, I love thee;
But never more be officer of mine.
SHAKESPEARE, *Othello*, ii, 3

Official.— As it was in the beginning
Is to-day official sinning,
And shall be for evermore.
KIPLING, *Departmental Ditties, General Summary*, st. 5

Officials.— Public officials are the trustees of the people, and hold their places and exercise their powers for the benefit of the people.[2]— GROVER CLEVELAND, *Speech before the City Convention, Buffalo*, Oct. 25, 1881

Oily.— A little, round, fat, oily man of God.
THOMSON, *Castle of Indolence*, i, 6

---

[1] And love th' offender, yet detest th' offence.
POPE, *Eloïsa to Abélard*, line 192

[2] Public officers are the servants and agents of the people to execute laws which the people have made, and within the limits of a constitution which they have established.— GROVER CLEVELAND, *Letter Accepting Nomination for Governor*, Oct. 7, 1882

Old.— The old tree is leafless in the forest,
The old year is ending in the frost,
The old wound, if stricken, is the sorest,
The old hope is hardest to be lost.
E. B. BROWNING, *The Cry of the Children*, st. 2

I love everything that's old: old times, old manners, old books, old wine.
GOLDSMITH, *She Stoops to Conquer*, i, 1

When all the world is old, lad,
And all the trees are brown;
And all the sport is stale, lad,
And all the wheels run down;
Creep home, and take your place there,
The spent and maimed among:
God grant you find one face there,
You loved when all was young!
KINGSLEY, *Songs from The Water Babies*, II, st. 2

If to be old and merry be a sin, then many an old host that I know is damned.
SHAKESPEARE, *King Henry IV, Part I*, ii, 4

Once.— Better once than never.
SHAKESPEARE, *Taming of the Shrew*, v, 1

One.— It's very hard! — and so it is,
To live in such a row,—
And witness this that every Miss
But me, has got a beau.—
For Love goes calling up and down,
But here he seems to shun;
I'm sure he has been asked enough
To call at Number One. HOOD, *Number One*, st. 1

The ring is on,
The "Wilt thou" answered, and again
The "Wilt thou" asked, till out of twain
Her sweet "I will" has made ye one.
TENNYSON, *In Memoriam*, Conclusion, st. 14

Opinion.— He that complies against his will
Is of his own opinion still.
BUTLER, *Hudibras*, III, iii, lines 547, 548

Opinions. I have bought
Golden opinions from all sorts of people.
SHAKESPEARE, *Macbeth*, i, 7

Oppressed.— Holdin' up a beacon peerless
To the oppressed of all the world!
LOWELL, *The Biglow Papers*, I, i, st. 16

Oracle.— There are a sort of men whose visages
Do cream and mantle like a standing pond,
And do a wilful stillness entertain,
With purpose to be dressed in an opinion
Of wisdom, gravity, profound conceit;
As who would say "I am Sir Oracle,
And when I ope my lips let no dog bark!"
SHAKESPEARE, *Merchant of Venice*, i, 1

Orator.— I am no orator, as Brutus is;
But, as you know me all, a plain blunt man,
That love my friend.
SHAKESPEARE, *Julius Cæsar*, iii, 2

Order.— Order is Heaven's first law.
POPE, *Essay on Man*, Epistle iv, line 49

Organ. Let the pealing organ blow,
To the full-voiced quire below.
MILTON, *Il Penseroso*, lines 161, 162

Seated one day at the organ,
I was weary and ill at ease,
And my fingers wandered idly
Over the noisy keys.
A. A. PROCTER, *A Lost Chord*, st. 1

Organs.— And heard once more in college fanes
The storm their high-built organs make,
And thunder-music, rolling, shake
The prophets blazoned on the panes.
TENNYSON, *In Memoriam*, lxxxvii, st. 2

Original.— The honourable gentleman has said much that is original, and much that is good, but the good is not original, and I am sorry to add, the original is not good. But one other comment is necessary,— the gentleman has drawn upon his memory for his eloquence, and upon his imagination for his facts.[1]
R. B. SHERIDAN, *Speech in Reply to Mr. Dundas*

Orion.— Great Orion sloping slowly to the west.
TENNYSON, *Locksley Hall*, line 8

Orthodoxy.— Orthodoxy, my lord, is my *doxy*, and heterodoxy is another man's *doxy*.
THOMAS WARBURTON, cited in Priestley's *Memoirs*

[1]Another reading is: Is indebted to his memory for his jests, and to his imagination for his facts.

Out.— Launcelot and I are out.[1]
SHAKESPEARE, *Merchant of Venice*, iii, 5

Outcast.— But suffer me to pace
Round the forbidden place,
Lingering a minute,
Like outcast spirits who wait,
And see through heaven's gate
Angels within it.
THACKERAY, *At the Church Gate*, st. 5

Outswear.— But we 'll outface them, and outswear them too.
SHAKESPEARE, *Merchant of Venice*, iv, 2

Overrunning. We may outrun
By violent swiftness that which we run at,
And lose by overrunning.
SHAKESPEARE, *King Henry VIII*, i, 1

Owe.— *Prince.* Sirrah, do I owe you a thousand pound?
Falstaff. A thousand pound, Hal! a million: thy love is worth a million: thou owest me thy love.
SHAKESPEARE, *King Henry IV, Part I*, iii, 3

Owes.— And looks the whole world in the face,
For he owes not any man.
LONGFELLOW, *The Village Blacksmith*, st. 2

Owl.— Alone and warming his five wits,
The white owl in the belfry sits.[2]
TENNYSON, *The Owl*, st. 1

Own.— Stand for your own.
SHAKESPEARE, *King Henry V*, i, 2

Ox.— Like an ox jumped half over a fence and liable to be torn by dogs front and rear without a fair chance to gore one way or kick the other. LINCOLN,
Telegram to Gen. Joseph Hooker, June 5, 1863

Oyster.— It is unseasonable and unwholesome in all months that have not an R in their name to eat an oyster.
BUTLER, *Dyet's Dinner*

"There take" (says Justice) "take ye each a shell,
We thrive at Westminster on fools like you:"
'Twas a fat oyster — Live in peace — Adieu!
POPE, *Verbatim from Boileau*, lines 10–12

---

[1] Draw up the papers, lawyer, and make 'em good and stout;
For things at home are crossways, and Betsey and I are out.
W. CARLETON, *Betsey and I are Out*, st. 1

[2] From yonder ivy-mantled tower,
The moping owl does to the moon complain
Of such as, wandering near her secret bower,
Molest her ancient, solitary reign.
GRAY, *Elegy Written in a Country Churchyard*, st. 3

Why, then the world 's mine oyster,
Which I with sword will open.
SHAKESPEARE, *Merry Wives of Windsor*, ii, 2

An oyster may be crossed in love.
R. B. SHERIDAN, *The Critic*, iii, 1

Pagan. Great God! I 'd rather be
A Pagan suckled in a creed outworn;
So might I, standing on this pleasant lea,
Have glimpses that would make me less forlorn;
Have sight of Proteus rising from the sea,
Or hear old Triton blow his wreathed horn.
WORDSWORTH, *The World Is Too Much With Us*, lines 9–14

Page.— You shall see a beautiful quarto page, where a neat rivulet of text shall meander through a meadow of margin. R. B. SHERIDAN, *School for Scandal*, i, 1

Paid.— He is well paid that is well satisfied.
SHAKESPEARE, *Merchant of Venice*, iv, 1

Pain.— See the wretch who long has tossed
On the thorny bed of pain,
At length repair his vigour lost,
And breathe and walk again;
The meanest floweret of the vale,
The simplest note that swells the gale,
The common sun, the air, the skies,
To him are opening Paradise. GRAY, *Ode on the Pleasure of Arising from Vicissitude*, st. 7

To kiss thine eyelids, when they droop with heaviness and pain,
To pour sad tears upon thy hand, the heart's most precious rain,
To mark the changing colour as it flits across thy cheek,
To feel thy very wishes ere the feverish lip can speak,
To listen for the weakest word, watch for the lightest token,
Oh, bliss, that such a dream should be! oh, pain, that it is broken! PRAED, *To ———*, st. 5

The depth of the abyss may be
The measure of the height of pain.
And love and glory that may raise
This soul to God in after-days.
A. A. PROCTER, *Judge Not*, st. 4

Painter.— A flattering painter, who made it his care
To draw men as they ought to be, not as they are.[1]
GOLDSMITH, *Retaliation*, st. 6

Pair. Hand in hand they passed, the loveliest pair
That ever since in love's embraces met.
MILTON, *Paradise Lost*, IV, lines 321, 322

Pale.— Why so pale and wan, fond lover?
Pr'ythee, why so pale?
Will, when looking well can't move her,
Looking ill prevail? SIR JOHN SUCKLING,
Song: Why So Pale and Wan, st. 1

Pallas.— 'Tis Pallas, Pallas gives this deadly blow.
DRYDEN, *Virgil's Æneid*, XII, line 1373

Pall Mall.—"Why Pall Mall Gazette?" asked Wagg. "Because the editor was born in Dublin, the sub-editor at Cork, because the proprietor lives in Paternoster Row, and the paper is published in Catherine Street, Strand."
THACKERAY, *Pendennis*, xxxiv

Palm. You yourself
Are much condemned to have an itching palm;
To sell and mart your offices for gold
To undeservers. SHAKESPEARE, *Julius Cæsar*, iv, 3

Pan.— I'll cross him, and wrack him, until I heartbreak him,
And then his auld brass will buy me a new pan.
BURNS, *What Can a Young Lassie Do?* st. 4

Pansies.— There is pansies, that's for thoughts.
SHAKESPEARE, *Hamlet*, iv, 5

Pantaloon. The lean and slippered Pantaloon,
With spectacle on nose and pouch on side,
His youthful hose, well saved, a world too wide
For his shrunk shank; and his big manly voice,
Turning again toward childish treble, pipes
And whistles in his sound.
SHAKESPEARE, *As You Like It*, ii, 7

Pants.— The things named "pants" in certain documents,
A word not made for gentlemen, but "gents."
HOLMES, *A Rhymed Lesson*, st. 47

---

[1] Here lies the man
Who drew them as they are.
EBENEZER ELLIOTT, *A Poet's Epitaph* (Burns)

Paradise.— Must I thus leave thee, Paradise?
MILTON, *Paradise Lost*, XI, line 269

A fool's paradise.[1]
SHAKESPEARE, *Romeo and Juliet*, ii, 4

Parallel.— None but himself can be his parallel.
THEOBALD, *The Double Falsehood*

Parchment.— Is not this a lamentable thing, that of the skin of an innocent lamb should be made parchment? that parchment, being scribbled o'er, should undo a man?
SHAKESPEARE, *King Henry VI, Part II*, iv, 2

Pardoned.— May one be pardoned and retain the offence?
SHAKESPEARE, *Hamlet*, iii, 3

Parlour.— Imagination fondly stoops to trace
The parlour splendours of that festive place;
The whitewashed wall, the nicely sanded floor,
The varnished clock that clicked behind the door;
The chest contrived a double debt to pay,
A bed by night, a chest of drawers by day.
GOLDSMITH, *The Deserted Village*, st. 15

Parrot.— That ever this fellow should have fewer words than a parrot, and yet the son of a woman!
SHAKESPEARE, *King Henry IV, Part I*, ii, 4

Parson.— For me, I neither know nor care
Whether a parson ought to wear
A black dress or a white dress;[2]
Filled with a trouble of my own,—
A wife who preaches in her gown,
And lectures in her night-dress!
HOOD, *The Surplice Question*, st. 2

A parson, much bemus'd in beer.
POPE, *Epistle to Dr. Arbuthnot*, line 15

Part.— Some weep because they part,
And languish broken-hearted,
And others — O my heart! —
Because they never parted.
T. B. ALDRICH, *Quatrain* 19: *The Difference*

---

[1] In this fool's paradise he drank delight.
G. CRABBE, *The Borough*, Letter xii, line 166

The Paradise of Fools, to few unknown.
MILTON, *Paradise Lost*, III, line 496

[2] Referring to the dispute in the Church of England concerning the use in the pulpit of the white surplice or the black gown.

Come, let us kiss and part,—
Nay I have done, you get no more of me;
And I am glad, yea, glad with all my heart
That thus so cleanly I myself can free.
Shake hands for ever, cancel all our vows,
And when we meet at any time again,
Be it not seen, on either of our brows,
That we one jot of former love retain.[1]
M. DRAYTON, *Sonnet: Come, Let Us Kiss and Part*

Parted.— We parted in silence, we parted by night,
On the banks of that lonely river;
Where the fragrant limes their boughs unite,
We met — and we parted for ever![2]
JULIA CRAWFORD, *We Parted In Silence*, st. 1

We parted — months and years rolled by;
We met again four summers after;
Our parting was all sob and sigh —
Our meeting was all mirth and laughter;
For in my heart's most secret cell
There had been many other lodgers;
And she was not the ball-room's belle,
But only—Mrs. Something Rogers!
PRAED, *Belle of the Ball-Room*, st. 13

Parting.— Good night, good night! parting is such sweet sorrow,
That I shall say good night till it be morrow.
SHAKESPEARE, *Romeo and Juliet*, ii, 2

The honey-fee of parting.
SHAKESPEARE, *Venus and Adonis*, line 538

Partings. Sudden partings, such as press
The life from out young hearts.
BYRON, *Childe Harold's Pilgrimage*, Canto iii, st. 24

Partington.— In the midst of this sublime and terrible storm, Dame Partington . . . was seen at the door of her house, with mop and pattens, trundling her mop, squeezing out the sea-water, and vigorously pushing away the Atlantic Ocean. The Atlantic was roused.

---

[1] I hold it fit that we shake hands and part.
SHAKESPEARE, *Hamlet*, i, 5

[2] When we two parted
In silence and tears,
Half broken-hearted
To sever for years,
Pale grew thy cheek and cold,
Colder thy kiss;
Truly that hour foretold
Sorrow to this.
BYRON, *When We Two Parted*, st. 1

Mrs. Partington's spirit was up; but I need not tell you that the contest was unequal. The Atlantic Ocean beat Mrs. Partington. She was excellent at a slop, or a puddle, but she should not have meddled with a tempest.
SYDNEY SMITH, *Speech on the Reform Bill, delivered at Taunton, Eng.*, Oct. 12, 1831

Parts.— All are but parts of one stupendous whole.
POPE, *Essay on Man*, Epistle i, line 267

Party.— Party faithlessness is party dishonour. . . . Party honesty is party duty, and party courage is party expediency.—GROVER CLEVELAND, *Speech before the Business Men's Democratic Association, New York*, Jan. 8, 1892

Hans Breitmann gife a barty—
Where ish dat barty now?[1]
Where ish de lofely golden cloud
Dat float on de moundain's prow?
Where ish de himmelstrahlende Stern—
De shtar of de sphirit's light?
All goned afay mit de Lager Beer—
Afay in de Ewigkeit!
C. G. LELAND, *Hans Breitmann's Party*, st. 6

Party is the madness of many for the gain of a few.
POPE, *Thoughts on Various Subjects*

Passion.— We are ne'er like angels till our passion dies.
T. DEKKER, *The Honest Whore*, II, i, 2

Your ruling passion strong in death.[2]
POPE, *Moral Essays*, Epistle i, line 263

'Twixt two extremes of passion, joy and grief.
SHAKESPEARE, *King Lear*, v, 3

He will hold thee, when his passion shall have spent its novel force,
Something better than his dog, a little dearer than his horse.
TENNYSON, *Locksley Hall*, lines 49, 50

Passions.— Its passions will rock thee
As the storms rock the ravens on high.
SHELLEY, *When the Lamp Is Shattered*, st. 4

---

[1] "Hans Breitmann gif a barty,— vhere is dot barty now?"
On every shelf where wit is stored to smooth the careworn brow.
HOLMES, *Post-Prandial*, st. 7

[2] The ruling passion, be it what it will,
The ruling passion conquers reason still.
POPE. *Moral Essays*, Epistle iii, lines 153, 154

Ye, whose clay-cold heads and lukewarm hearts can argue down or mask your passions, tell me, what trespass is it that man should have them? or how his spirit stands answerable to the Father of Spirits but for his conduct under them!

STERNE, *A Sentimental Journey*, The Conquest

Path.— I will walk the long path with you.

HOLMES, *Autocrat of the Breakfast-Table*, xi

Patience. I do oppose
My patience to his fury.

SHAKESPEARE, *Merchant of Venice*, iv, 1

She never told her love,
But let concealment, like a worm i' the bud,
Feed on her damask cheek:[1] she pined in thought,
And with a green and yellow melancholy
She sat like patience on a monument,
Smiling at grief. SHAKESPEARE, *Twelfth Night*, ii, 4

Patient.— Beware the fury of a patient man.

DRYDEN, *Absalom and Achitophel*, I, line 1005

Patriotism.— Patriotism is the last refuge of a scoundrel.[2]

SAMUEL JOHNSON, *Life*, by Boswell, 1775

Paunches.— Fat paunches have lean pates, and dainty bits
Make rich the ribs, but bankrupt quite the wits.

SHAKESPEARE, *Love's Labour's Lost*, i, 1

Pauper.— There's a grim one-horse hearse in a jolly round trot,—
To the churchyard a pauper is going, I wot;
The road it is rough, and the hearse has no springs;
And hark to the dirge which the mad driver sings:
Rattle his bones over the stones!
He's only a pauper whom nobody owns!

T. NOEL, *The Pauper's Drive*, st. 1

Peace.— Hark! how the holy calm that breathes around
Bids every fierce tumultuous passion cease;
In still small accents whispering from the ground
The grateful earnest of eternal peace.[3]

GRAY, *Elegy Written in a Country Churchyard*, st. 4

---

[1] Sorrow concealed, like an oven stopped,
Doth burn the heart to cinders.— SHAKESPEARE, *Titus Andronicus*, ii, 4 [5]

[2] Often the resort of desperate men, the profession of a patriot.
JAMES PRIOR, *Life of Burke*, xi

[3] This stanza was removed by the author from the original poem.

The preservation of the general government in its whole constitutional vigour, as the sheet anchor of our peace at home and safety abroad.

THOMAS JEFFERSON, *Inaugural Address*, March 4, 1801

Peace wun't keep house with Fear:
Ef you want peace, the thing you 've gut to du
Is jes' to show you 're up to fightin', tu.

LOWELL, *Biglow Papers*, II, ii, lines 232–234

Better thet all our ships an' all their crews
Should sink to rot in ocean's dreamless ooze,
Each torn flag wavin' chellenge ez it went,
An' each dumb gun a brave man's moniment,
Than seek sech peace ez only cowards crave:
Give me the peace of dead men or of brave!

Ibid., lines 241–246

Come, Peace! not like a mourner bowed
For honour lost an' dear ones wasted,
But proud, to meet a people proud,
With eyes thet tell o' triumph tasted!—*Ibid.*, x, st. 20

The inglorious arts of peace.

A. MARVELL, *Horatian Ode upon Cromwell's Return From Ireland*, st. 3

Where peace
And rest can never dwell.

MILTON, *Paradise Lost*, I, lines 65, 66

Peace hath her victories
No less renowned than war.

MILTON, *Sonnet to the Lord General Cromwell*

Oh, come ye in peace here, or come ye in war?

SCOTT, *Marmion*, v, 12

The time of universal peace is near.

SHAKESPEARE, *Antony and Cleopatra*, iv, 6

This peace is nothing, but to rust iron, increase tailors, and breed ballad-makers.

SHAKESPEARE, *Coriolanus*, iv, 5

God send us peace!

SHAKESPEARE, *King Henry IV*, *Part II*, iii, 2

Still in thy right hand carry gentle peace,
To silence envious tongues.

SHAKESPEARE, *King Henry VIII*, iii, 2

I know myself now; and I feel within me
A peace above all earthly dignities,
A still and quiet conscience. *Ibid.*

In this weak piping time of peace.
SHAKESPEARE, *King Richard III*, i, 1

Ring in the thousand years of peace.
TENNYSON, *In Memoriam*, cvi, st. 7

"Hate hath no harm for love," so ran the song;
"And peace unweaponed conquers every wrong!"
WHITTIER, *Disarmament*, lines 31, 32

The bridal time of Law and Love,
The gladness of the world's release,
When, war-sick, at the feet of Peace
The hawk shall nestle with the dove!
WHITTIER, *Lexington*, st. 9

Peaceful.— What peaceful hours I once enjoyed!
How sweet their memory still!
But they have left an aching void,
The world can never fill.
COWPER, *Walking with God*, st. 3

When once their slumbering passions burn,
The peaceful are the strong!
HOLMES, *A Voice of the Loyal North*, st. 5

Pearl.— From the rough shell they picked the luscious food,
And left a prince's ransom in the pearl.
JAMES MONTGOMERY, *The Pelican Island*,
Canto v, st. 8

Peasant.— The might that slumbers in a peasant's arm.
CAMPBELL, *Pleasures of Hope*, I, st. 44

Peasantry.— Ill fares the land, to hastening ills a prey,
Where wealth accumulates, and men decay:
Princes and lords may flourish, or may fade;
A breath can make them, as a breath has made:
But a bold peasantry, their country's pride,
When once destroyed, can never be supplied.
GOLDSMITH, *The Deserted Village*, st. 3

Pedigree.— Whose pedigree, traced to earth's earliest years,
Is longer than anything else but their ears.
LOWELL, *Fable for Critics*, lines 121, 122

Pelf.— Excess of ill-got, ill-kept pelf
Does only death and danger breed;
Whilst one rich worldling starves himself
With what would thousand others feed.
CHARLES COTTON, *Contentation*, st. 9

Pen.— Beneath the rule of men entirely great
The pen is mightier than the sword.

. . . . . .

Take away the sword —
States can be saved without it.
E. G. Bulwer-Lytton, *Richelieu*, ii, 2

The feather, whence the pen
Was shaped that traced the lives of these good men,
Dropped from an angel's wing.[1]
Wordsworth, *Ecclesiastical Sonnets*, iii, 5

Penitence.— By penitence the Eternal's wrath 's appeased.
Shakespeare, *Two Gentlemen of Verona*, v, 4

Penny.— An I had but one penny in the world, thou shouldst have it to buy gingerbread.
Shakespeare, *Love's Labour's Lost*, v, 1

Pension.— Give 'im a letter —
Can't do no better,
Late Troop-Sergeant Major, an'— runs with a letter!
Think what 'e 's been,
Think what 'e 's seen,
Think of his pension, an'—
Gawd save the Queen! Kipling, *Shillin' a Day*, st. 2

'Tis no matter if I do halt; I have the wars for my colour, and my pension shall seem the more reasonable. A good wit will make use of anything: I will turn diseases to commodity.
Shakespeare, *King Henry IV, Part II*, i, 2

Penury.— Chill penury repressed their noble rage,
And froze the genial current of the soul.
Gray, *Elegy Written in a Country Churchyard*, st. 14

People. The People's voice is odd,
It is, and it is not, the voice of God.— Pope, *Imitations of Horace*, II, Epistle i, lines 89, 90

Slowly comes a hungry people,[2] as a lion, creeping nigher,
Glares at one that nods and winks behind a slowly-dying fire. Tennyson, *Locksley Hall*, lines 135, 136

---

[1] The pen wherewith thou dost so heavenly sing
Made of a quill from an angel's wing. H. Constable, *Sonnet*

[2] Wake not thou the giant
Who drinks hot blood for wine.
Ebenezer Elliott, *The Corn-Law Hymn*, st. 2

An Œdipus-people is coming fast,
With swelled feet limping on.

. . . . .

The people will come to their own at last,—
God is not mocked forever.
John Hay, *The Sphinx of the Tuileries*, st. 5

Perfect.— A perfect form in perfect rest. TENNYSON,
The Day-Dream, The Sleeping Beauty, st. 3

Perfection.— The very pink of perfection.
GOLDSMITH, *She Stoops to Conquer*, i, 1

Whenever you hear a man dissuading you from attempting to do well, on the ground that perfection is "Utopian," beware of that man.
RUSKIN, *Architecture and Painting*, ii

Perfume.— A strange invisible perfume.
SHAKESPEARE, *Antony and Cleopatra*, ii, 2

Peril.— Alack, there lies more peril in thine eye
Than twenty of their swords: look thou but sweet,
And I am proof against their enmity.
SHAKESPEARE, *Romeo and Juliet*, ii, 2

Perils.— Ay me! what perils do environ
The man that meddles with cold iron.
BUTLER, *Hudibras*, I, iii, lines 1, 2

Perjuries. At lovers' perjuries,[1]
They say, Jove laughs.
SHAKESPEARE, *Romeo and Juliet*, ii, 2

Perjury.— The witnesses may commit perjury, but the smoke cannot. LINCOLN, *Letter to J. R. Underwood*, Oct. 26, 1864

Perseverance.— Perseverance gains its meed,
And patience wins the race.
BERNARD BARTON, *Bruce and the Spider*, st. 5

Perverse.— Still so perverse and opposite,
As if they worshipped God for spite.
BUTLER, *Hudibras*, I, i, lines 217, 218

Peter.— By robbing Peter he paid Paul. RABELAIS, I, xi

Phantom.— She was a phantom of delight
When first she gleamed upon my sight;
A lovely apparition, sent
To be a moment's ornament.
WORDSWORTH, *She Was a Phantom of Delight*, st. 1

Phantoms.— I clasped the phantoms, and I found them air.
YOUNG, *Night Thoughts*, I, line 202

---

[1] Fool, not to know that love endures no tie,
And Jove but laughs at lovers' perjury.
DRYDEN, *Palamon and Arcite*, lines 758, 759

Philosophy.— In the calm lights of mild philosophy.
ADDISON, *Cato*, i, 1

Philosophy is a good horse in the stable, but an arrant jade on a journey.
GOLDSMITH, *The Good-Natured Man*, i

There are more things in heaven and earth, Horatio,
Than are dreamt of in your philosophy.
SHAKESPEARE, *Hamlet*, i, 5

Adversity's sweet milk, philosophy.
SHAKESPEARE, *Romeo and Juliet*, iii, 3

Phrases.— A man in all the world's new fashion planted,
That hath a mint of phrases in his brain.
SHAKESPEARE, *Love's Labour's Lost*, i, 1

Phyllis. Herbs and other country messes,
Which the neat-handed Phyllis dresses.
MILTON, *L'Allegro*, lines 85–86

Physic.— Throw physic to the dogs; I'll none of it.
SHAKESPEARE, *Macbeth*, v, 3

Physician. Trust not the physician;
His antidotes are poison.
SHAKESPEARE, *Timon of Athens*, iv, 3

Pickaxe.— A pickaxe, and a spade, a spade,
For and a shrouding sheet:
Oh, a pit of clay for to be made
For such a guest is meet!
SHAKESPEARE, *Hamlet*, v, 1

Pickers.— These pickers and stealers.
SHAKESPEARE, *Hamlet*, iii, 2

Pickwickian.— A Pickwickian construction.
DICKENS, *Pickwick Papers*, i

Picture.— Look here, upon this picture, and on this,
The counterfeit presentment[1] of two brothers.
SHAKESPEARE, *Hamlet*, iii, 4

Pieces.— It went to pieces all at once,[2]—
All at once, and nothing first,—
Just as bubbles do when they burst.
HOLMES, *The Deacon's Masterpiece*, st. 11

---

[1] Fair Portia's counterfeit. SHAKESPEARE, *Merchant of Venice*, iii, 2
[2] *Cf.* GROUND.

Pig.— Some men there are love not a gaping pig;
Some, that are mad if they behold a cat.
SHAKESPEARE, *Merchant of Venice*, iv, 1

Jacob! I do not like to see thy nose
Turned up in scornful curve at yonder pig.[1]
It would be well, my friend, if we, like him,
Were perfect in our kind!— SOUTHEY, *The Pig*, lines 1–4

Pillow.— Fair thoughts be your fair pillow!
SHAKESPEARE, *Troilus and Cressida*, iii, 1

Pilot.— O pilot! 'tis a fearful night,
There's danger on the deep.— T. H. BAYLY, *The Pilot*

Here's to the pilot that weathered the storm.[2]
CANNING, *The Pilot That Weathered the Storm*, st. 1

Pinch.— Pinch him, and burn him, and turn him about,[3]
Till candles and starlight and moonshine be out.
SHAKESPEARE, *Merry Wives of Windsor*, v, 5

Pine.— And on that grave where English oak and holly
And laurel wreaths entwine,
Deem it not all a too presumptuous folly,
This spray of Western pine!
BRET HARTE, *Dickens in Camp*, st. 10

Pins.— Pricking her fingers with those cursed pins,
Which surely were invented for our sins,—

Making a woman like a porcupine,
Not rashly to be touched.
BYRON, *Don Juan*, Canto vi, st. 61, 62

---

[1] I cannot bear to hear thee slandered, Goose!
L. H. SIGOURNEY, *To a Goose*, line 1

[2] A daring pilot in extremity;
Pleased with the danger, when the waves went high
He sought the storms; but for a calm unfit,
Would steer too nigh the sands to boast his wit.
DRYDEN, *Absalom and Achitophel*, I, lines 159–162

With Palinure's unaltered mood,
Firm at his dangerous post he stood;
Each call for needful rest repelled,
With dying hand the rudder held. SCOTT, *Marmion*, Introd. to Canto i

[3] Dare you haunt our hallowed green?
None but fairies here are seen.
Down and sleep,
Wake and weep;
Pinch him black, and pinch him blue,
That seeks to steal a lover true!
When you come to hear us sing,
Or to tread our fairy ring,
Pinch him black, and pinch him blue!
Oh, thus our nails shall handle you! ANONYMOUS, *The Fairies' Dance*

Pious.— O ye wha are sae guid yoursel',
Sae pious and sae holy,
Ye 've nought to do but mark and tell
Your neebours' faults and folly!
BURNS, *Address to the Unco Guid*, st. 1

Young Obadias,
David, Josias,—
All were pious. *New England Primer*

Pipe.— Do you think I am easier to be played on than a pipe? Call me what instrument you will, though you can fret me, [yet] you cannot play upon me.
SHAKESPEARE, *Hamlet*, iii, 2

Pity.— Careless their merits, or their faults to scan,
His pity gave ere charity began.
GOLDSMITH, *The Deserted Village*, st. 10

No flocks that range the valley free
To slaughter I condemn:
Taught by that Power that pities me,
I learn to pity them.
GOLDSMITH, *The Hermit*, st. 6

Such pity as my rapier's point affords.
SHAKESPEARE, *King Henry VI, Part III*, i, 3

But yet the pity of it, Iago! O Iago, the pity of it!
SHAKESPEARE, *Othello*, iv, 1

Pity 's akin to love.[1]
THOMAS SOUTHERNE, *Oroonoka*, ii, 1

Now pity is the touch of God
In human hearts,
And from that way He ever trod
He ne'er departs.
WALTER C. SMITH, *The Self-Exiled*, st. 25

Place.— All rising to great place is by a winding stair.[2]
BACON, *Essay XI: Of Great Place*

To place and power all public spirit tends
In place and power all public spirit ends.
T. MOORE, *Corruption*

---

[1] Of all the paths lead to a woman's love
Pity 's the straightest.
BEAUMONT AND FLETCHER, *The Knight of Malta*, i, 1

Pity melts the mind to love. DRYDEN, *Alexander's Feast*, line 96

Pity swells the tide of love. YOUNG, *Night Thoughts*, III, line 106

[2] The ascent to high office is steep, the summit slippery, the descent precipitous. BACON, *Essay XI: Of Great Place*

Plague.— A plague o' both your houses!
SHAKESPEARE, *Romeo and Juliet*, iii, 1

Plain.— One of those still plain men that do the world's rough work.— LOWELL, *On a Bust of General Grant*, st. 6

Plain-song. That is the very plain-song of it.
SHAKESPEARE, *King Henry V*, iii, 2

Planet.— They 'll search a planet's house, to know
Who broke and robbed a house below;
Examine Venus and the moon,
Who stole a thimble or a spoon;
. . . . .
They 'll question Mars, and, by his look,
Detect who 't was that nimmed a cloak.[1]
BUTLER, *Hudibras*, I, i, lines 589–598

Plant.— Fixed like a plant on his peculiar spot,
To draw nutrition, propagate, and rot;
Or, meteor-like, flame lawless through the void,
Destroying others, by himself destroyed.
POPE, *Essay on Man*, Epistle ii, lines 63–66

Play.— In play, there are two pleasures for your choosing —
The one is winning, and the other losing.
BYRON, *Don Juan*, Canto xiv, st. 12

Though this may be play to you,
'T is death to us.
L'ESTRANGE, *The Boys and the Frogs*

And laughed, and blushed, and oft did say,
Her pretty oath by Yea, and Nay,
She could not, would not, durst not play!
SCOTT, *Marmion*, v, st. 11

The play 's the thing
Wherein I 'll catch the conscience of the king.
SHAKESPEARE, *Hamlet*, ii, 2

Play out the play.
SHAKESPEARE, *King Henry IV*, *Part I*, ii, 4

---

[1] They 'll find, i' th' physiognomies
O' th' planets, all men's destinies;
. . . . .
They 'll feel the pulses of the stars,
To find out agues, coughs, catarrhs;
And tell what crisis does divine
The rot in sheep, or mange in swine;
In men, what gives or cures the itch,
What made them cuckolds, poor, or rich;
What gains, or loses, hangs, or saves,
What makes men great, what fools, or knaves;
But not what wise, for only 'f those
The stars, they say, cannot dispose.
BUTLER, *Hudibras*, I, i, lines 601–618

Player.— Is it not monstrous that this player here,
But in a fiction, in a dream of passion,
Could force his soul so to his own conceit
That from her working all his visage wanned,
Tears in his eyes, distraction in 's aspect,
A broken voice, and his whole function suiting
With forms to his conceit? and all for nothing!
For Hecuba!
What 's Hecuba to him, or he to Hecuba,
That he should weep for her?[1]

SHAKESPEARE, *Hamlet*, ii, 2

Playmates.— I have had playmates, I have had companions
In my days of childhood, in my joyful school days;
All, all are gone, the old familiar faces.

LAMB, *The Old Familiar Faces*, st. 1

Please.— We that live to please must please to live.

SAMUEL JOHNSON, *Prologue on the Opening of Drury Lane Theatre*

Pleasure.— It spoils the pleasure of the time.

SHAKESPEARE, *Macbeth*, iii, 4

Pleasure will be paid, one time or another.

SHAKESPEARE, *Twelfth Night*, ii, 4

Pledge.— For the support of this declaration, with a firm reliance on the protection of Divine Providence, we mutually pledge to each other our lives, our fortunes, and our sacred honour.

THOMAS JEFFERSON, *Declaration of Independence*

Plenty.— I was na fou, but just had plenty.

BURNS, *Death and Doctor Hornbook*, st. 3

Ploughman.— While the ploughman near at hand
Whistles o'er the furrowed land,
And the milkmaid singeth blithe,
And the mower whets his scythe,
And every shepherd tells his tale
Under the hawthorn in the dale.

MILTON, *L'Allegro*, lines 63–68

Pluck.— Be firm! one constant element in luck
Is genuine, solid, old Teutonic pluck.

HOLMES, *A Rhymed Lesson*, st. 32

His was the surly English pluck, and there is no tougher or truer, and never was, and never will be.

WALT WHITMAN, *Song of Myself*, 35

---

[1] I can counterfeit the deep tragedian;
Speak, and look back, and pry on every side,
Tremble and start at wagging of a straw,
Intending deep suspicion. SHAKESPEARE, *King Richard III*, iii, 5

Plume.— Right graciously he smiled on us, as rolled from wing to wing,
Down all our line a deafening shout, "God save our Lord the king!"
And if my standard-bearer fall, as fall full well he may,
For never saw I promise yet of such a bloody fray,
Press where ye see my white plume shine, amidst the ranks of war,
And be your oriflamme to-day the helmet of Navarre.
MACAULAY, *Ivry*, st. 3

Plutarch.— Here was a type of the true elder race,
And one of Plutarch's men talked with us face to face.
LOWELL, *Commemoration Ode*, st. 6

Plymouth.— In the Old Colony days, in Plymouth the land of the Pilgrims.
LONGFELLOW, *Courtship of Miles Standish*, I, line 1

Poem.— Now it is not one thing nor another alone
Makes a poem, but rather the general tone,
The something pervading, uniting the whole,
The before unconceived, unconceivable soul,
So that just in removing this trifle or that, you
Take away, as it were, a chief limb of the statue;
Roots, wood, bark, and leaves singly perfect may be,
But, clapped hodge-podge together, they don't make a tree.
LOWELL, *Fable for Critics*, lines 540–547

Poet.— A wandering poet, who thought it his duty
To feed upon nothing but bowls and beauty;
Who worshipped a rhyme, and detested a quarrel,
And cared not a single straw for a laurel,
Holding that Grief was Sobriety's daughter,
And loathing critics and cold water.
PRAED, *The Modern Nectar*, lines 13–18

Never durst poet touch a pen to write
Until his ink were tempered with Love's sighs.
SHAKESPEARE, *Love's Labour's Lost*, iv, 3

The poet's eye, in a fine frenzy rolling,
Doth glance from heaven to earth, from earth to heaven;
And, as imagination bodies forth
The forms of things unknown, the poet's pen
Turns them to shapes and gives to airy nothing
A local habitation and a name.
SHAKESPEARE, *Midsummer-Night's Dream*, v, 1

Poetic.— Mingling poetic honey with trade wax.
HOOD, *Sonnet: Literary Reminiscences*

Poetry.— Poetry is itself a thing of God.
P. J. BAILEY, *Festus*, Proem, line 5

Don't ever think the poetry is dead in an old man because his forehead is wrinkled, or that his manhood has left him when his hand trembles! If they ever were there, they are there still!
HOLMES, *Autocrat of the Breakfast-Table*, v

It is not poetry, but prose run mad.[1]
POPE, *Epistle to Dr. Arbuthnot*, line 188

The truest poetry is the most feigning.
SHAKESPEARE, *As You Like It*, iii, 3

I had rather hear a brazen canstick turned,
Or a dry wheel grate on the [an] axle-tree;
And that would set my teeth nothing on edge,
Nothing so much as mincing poetry:
'Tis like the forced gait of a shuffling nag.
SHAKESPEARE, *King Henry IV, Part I*, iii, 1

Poets.— Three poets in three distant ages born,
Greece, Italy, and England did adorn.
The first, in loftiness of thought surpassed;
The next, in majesty; in both the last.
The force of Nature could no further go;
To make a third, she joined the other two.
DRYDEN, *Lines Under Milton's Picture*

What are our poets, take them as they fall,
Good, bad, rich, poor, much read, not read at all?
They and their works in the same class you'll find;
They are the mere *waste-paper* of mankind.
FRANKLIN, *Paper*, st. 10

Plain hoss-sense in poetry-writin'
Would jes knock sentiment a-kitin'!
Mostly poets is all star-gazin'
And moanin' and groanin' and paraphrasin'!
J. W. RILEY, *A Wholly Unscholastic Opinion*

Point.— Not to put too fine a point upon it.
DICKENS, *Bleak House*, xxxii

Poison.— What's one man's poison, signor,
Is another's meat or drink.
BEAUMONT AND FLETCHER, *Love's Cure*, iii, 2

---

[1] Poetic souls delight in prose insane.
BYRON, *English Bards and Scotch Reviewers*, line 38 [243]

Politicians.— It is the weaker sort of politicians that are the greatest dissemblers.
BACON, *Essay VI: Of Simulation and Dissimulation*

Politics.— I should be glad to drink your honour's health in
A pot of beer, if you will give me sixpence;
But for my part, I never love to meddle
With politics, sir.—CANNING, *The Friend of Humanity and the Knife-Grinder*, st. 8

Practical politics must not be construed to mean dirty politics. . . . The most practical of all politicians is the politician who is clean and decent and upright.
THEODORE ROOSEVELT, cited by Jacob Riis in *Theodore Roosevelt the Citizen*, xvii

Pomp.— Vain pomp and glory of this world, I hate ye!
SHAKESPEARE, *King Henry VIII*, iii, 2

Poor.— Let not ambition mock their useful toil,
Their homely joys, and destiny obscure;
Nor grandeur hear with a disdainful smile
The short and simple annals of the poor.
GRAY, *Elegy Written in a Country Churchyard*, st. 9

He who ordained the Sabbath loves the poor.
HOLMES, *A Rhymed Lesson*, st. 22

My friends were poor, but honest; so's my love.
SHAKESPEARE, *All's Well That Ends Well*, i, 3

A poor, infirm, weak, and despised old man.
SHAKESPEARE, *King Lear*, iii, 2

As poor as Job.
SHAKESPEARE, *Merry Wives of Windsor*, v, 5

Taäke my word for it, Sammy, the poor in a loomp is bad.
TENNYSON, *Northern Farmer, New Style*, st. 12

Poor-house.— Over the hill to the poor-house I'm trudgin' my weary way.
W. CARLETON, *Over the Hill to the Poor-house*, st. 1

Pope.— Nor do I know what is become
Of him, more than the Pope of Rome.
BUTLER, *Hudibras*, I, iii, lines 263, 264

Pork.— In converting Jews to Christians, you raise the price of pork. SHAKESPEARE, *Merchant of Venice*, iii, 5

Porridge.— The halesome parritch, chief o' Scotia's food.
BURNS, *The Cotter's Saturday Night*, st. 11

Posterity. As though there were a tie
And obligation to posterity,
We get them, bear them, breed and nurse.
What has posterity done for us,
That we, lest they their rights should lose,
Should trust our necks to gripe of noose?
J. TRUMBULL, *McFingal*, ii

Positivist.— There was an ape in the days that were earlier;
Centuries passed, and his hair grew curlier;
Centuries more gave a thumb to his wrist,
Then he was a Man and a Positivist.
MORTIMER COLLINS, *Darwin*

Possibilities.—Seven hundred pounds and possibilities is good gifts.—SHAKESPEARE, *Merry Wives of Windsor*, i, 1

Potatoes.— Let the sky rain potatoes; let it thunder to the tune of Green Sleeves. *Merry Wives of Windsor*, v, 3

Potomac.— All quiet along the Potomac to-night;
No sound save the rush of the river;
While soft falls the dew on the face of the dead —
The picket 's off duty forever!—ETHEL LYNN BEERS,
All Quiet Along the Potomac, st. 6

Potter.— Who is the Potter, pray, and who the Pot?[1]
OMAR KHAYYÁM, *Rubáiyát* (trans. Fitzgerald), st. 87

Poverty.— Content with poverty, my soul I arm;
And virtue, though in rags, will keep me warm.
DRYDEN, *Paraphrase of Horace*, III, Ode 29, lines 86, 87

Apothecary. My poverty, but not my will, consents.
Romeo. I pay thy poverty, and not thy will.
SHAKESPEARE, *Romeo and Juliet*, v, 1

Pow.— John Anderson my jo, John,
When we were first acquent
Your locks were like the raven,
Your bonnie brow was brent;
But now your brow is beld, John,
Your locks are like the snow;
But blessing on your frosty pow,
John Anderson my jo.
ROBERT BURNS, *John Anderson*, st. 1

Powder.— Put your trust in God, my boys, and keep your powder dry COL. BLACKER, *Oliver's Advice*

---

[1] Another reading is: Who makes — who sells — who buys — who *is* the Pot?

Food for powder; they'll fill a pit as well as better.
SHAKESPEARE, *King Henry IV, Part I*, iv, 2

Something upon the soldier's cheek
Washed off the stains of powder.
BAYARD TAYLOR, *Song of the Camp*, st. 7

Power-house.— The power-house of the Line!
KIPLING, *The Native-Born*, st. 12

Practised. He practised what he preached.
J. ARMSTRONG, *Art of Preserving Health*

Praise.— He praised me at a time when praise was of value to me. SAMUEL JOHNSON, *Life*, by Boswell, 1745

Of whom to be dispraised were no small praise.
MILTON, *Paradise Regained*, III, line 56

With much to praise, little to be forgiven.
TOM TAYLOR, *Abraham Lincoln*, st. 19

Praise is the salt that seasons right to man,
And whets his appetite for moral good.
YOUNG, *Night Thoughts*, VII, lines 420, 421

Pray.— Two went to pray? Oh rather say,
One went to brag, th' other to pray:

One stands up close and treads on high,
Where th' other dares not lend his eye.

One nearer to God's altar trod,
The other to the altar's God.
RICHARD CRASHAW, *Divine Epigrams: Two Went up into the Temple*

Weep for the frail that err, the weak that fall,
Have thine own faith,— but hope and pray for all!
HOLMES, *A Rhymed Lesson*, st. 30

Church is "a little heaven below,
I have been there and still would go,"—
Yet I am none of those who think it odd
A man can pray unbidden from the cassock,
And, passing by the customary hassock,
Kneel down remote upon the simple sod,
And sue *in forma pauperis* to God.
HOOD, *Ode to Rae Wilson, Esquire*, st. 20

King Ferdinand. You shall fast a week with bran and water.
Costard. I had rather pray a month with mutton and porridge. SHAKESPEARE, *Love's Labour's Lost*, i, 1

Prayed.— Yet Enoch as a brave God-fearing man
Bowed himself down, and in that mystery
Where God-in-man is one with man-in-God,
Prayed for a blessing on his wife and babes.
TENNYSON, *Enoch Arden*, lines 185–188

There he would have knelt, but that his knees
Were feeble, so that falling prone he dug
His fingers into the wet earth, and prayed.[1]
Ibid., lines 774–776

Prayer.— I stretch my hands out in the empty air;
I strain my eyes into the heavy night;
Blackness of darkness! —— Father, hear my prayer ——
Grant me to see the light!
GEORGE ARNOLD, *In the Dark*

Ah! He who prayed the prayer of all mankind
Summed in those few brief words the mightiest plea
For erring souls before the courts of heaven,—
Save us from being tempted,— lest we fall!
HOLMES, *Rights*, lines 22–25

Prayer is the soul's sincere desire,
Uttered or unexpressed,
The motion of a hidden fire
That trembles in the breast.[2]
JAMES MONTGOMERY, *What is Prayer*, st. 1

Oh, what form of prayer
Can serve my turn? SHAKESPEARE, *Hamlet*, iii, 3

Prayers.— Thou child of many prayers!
LONGFELLOW, *Maidenhood*, st. 9

Few and short were the prayers we said,
And we spoke not a word of sorrow,
But we steadfastly gazed on the face of the dead,
And we bitterly thought of the morrow.
CHARLES WOLFE, *Burial of Sir John Moore*, st. 4

Prayeth.— He prayeth well, who loveth well
Both man and bird and beast.

---

[1] And here all hope soured on me
Of my feller-critter's aid,—
I jest flopped down on my marrow-bones,
Crotch-deep in the snow, and prayed.— JOHN HAY, *Little Breeches*, st. 5

[2] It is not the words of the prayer, but the yearning back of the praying.
ELLA WHEELER WILCOX, *Art and Heart*, st. 5

My words fly up, my thoughts remain below:
Words without thoughts never to heaven go.
SHAKESPEARE, *Hamlet*, iii, 3

He prayeth best, who loveth best
All things both great and small;
For the dear God who loveth us,
He made and loveth all.[1]
COLERIDGE, *Ancient Mariner*, lines 612–617

Praying.— Mr. Chadbands he wos a-prayin' wunst at Mr. Snagsby's and I heard him, but he sounded as if he wos a-speaking to hisself, and not to me. He prayed a lot, but I couldn't make out nothink on it. Different times, there was other gentlemen come down Tom-all-Alone's a-prayin', but they all mostly sed as the t'other wuns prayed wrong, and all mostly sounded to be a-talkin' to theirselves, or a-passin' blame on the t'others, and not a-talkin' to us. DICKENS, *Bleak House*, xlvii

Preached.— I preached as never sure to preach again,
And as a dying man to dying men.
RICHARD BAXTER, *Love Breathing Thanks and Praise*

Preacher.— Look! you can see from this window my brazen howitzer planted
High on the roof of the church, a preacher who speaks to the purpose,
Steady, straightforward, and strong, with irresistible logic,
Orthodox, flashing conviction right into the hearts of the heathen.

. . . . .

Truly the only tongue that is understood by the savage
Must be the tongue of fire that speaks from the mouth of the cannon. LONGFELLOW, *Courtship of Miles Standish*, i, lines 46–49; iv, lines 126, 127

This is what makes him,[2] the crowd-drawing preacher,
There's a background of God to each hard-working feature,
Every word that he speaks has been fierily furnaced
In the blast of a life that has struggled in earnest:

. . . . .

But his periods fall on you, stroke after stroke,
Like the blows of a lumberer felling an oak,
You forget the man wholly, you're thankful to meet
With a preacher who smacks of the field and the street.
LOWELL, *Fable for Critics*, lines 801–812

---

[1] He serves thee best who loveth most
His brothers and thy own. WHITTIER, *Our Master*, st. 35

[2] Theodore Parker.

Preachers.— When preachers tell us all they think,
And party leaders all they mean.
HOLMES, *Latter-Day Warnings*, st. 3

Precedent.— It must not be; there is no power in Venice
Can alter a decree established:
'Twill be recorded for a precedent,
And many an error by the same example
Will rush into the state: it cannot be.
SHAKESPEARE, *Merchant of Venice*, iv, 1

Preferment. 'Tis the curse of service,
Preferment goes by letter and affection,
And not by [the] old gradation, where each second
Stood heir to the first. SHAKESPEARE, *Othello*, i, 1

Prescient.— One sails toward me o'er the bay,
And what he comes to do and say

I can foretell. A prescient lore
Springs from some life outlived of yore.
P. H. HAYNE, *Pre-Existence*

Presentiment.— A man . . . has seldom an offer of kindness to make to a woman but she has a presentiment of it some moments before.
STERNE, *A Sentimental Journey*, The Remise, Calais

President.— The President of the United States is only the engine-driver of our broad-gauge mail train; and every honest, independent thinker has a seat in the first-class cars behind him.
HOLMES, *Professor at the Breakfast-Table*, v

Press.— What need of help? He knew how types were set,
He had a dauntless spirit, and a press.
LOWELL, *To W. L. Garrison*, st. 2

Presume.— Do not presume too much upon my love;
I may do that I shall be sorry for.
SHAKESPEARE, *Julius Cæsar*, iv, 3

Price.— All those[1] men have their price.[2]
SIR ROBERT WALPOLE, cited in his *Life*, by Coxe

Pride.— Pride is one of the seven deadly sins; but it cannot be the pride of a mother in her children, for that is a compound of two cardinal virtues — faith and hope.
DICKENS, *Nicholas Nickleby*, xliii

---

[1] Walpole here spoke specifically of certain pretended patriots, not of mankind in general.

[2] I know my price, I am worth no worse a place.
SHAKESPEARE, *Othello*, i, 1

Pride in their port,[1] defiance in their eye.
GOLDSMITH, *The Traveller*, st. 25

A pride there is of rank — a pride of birth,
A pride of learning, and a pride of purse,
A London pride — in short, there be on earth
A host of prides, some better and some worse;
But of all prides, since Lucifer's attaint,
The proudest swells a self-elected saint.
HOOD, *Ode to Rae Wilson, Esquire*, st. 32

In pride, in reas'ning pride, our error lies;
All quit their sphere, and rush into the skies.
Pride still is aiming at the blessed abodes,
Men would be Angels, Angels would be Gods.
POPE, *Essay on Man*, Epistle i, lines 123–126

He owned with a grin
That his favorite sin
Is pride that apes humility.
SOUTHEY, *The Devil's Walk*, st. 8

Once, when I was up so high in pride
That I was half way down the slope to hell,
By overthrowing me you threw me higher.
TENNYSON, *Geraint and Enid*, lines 789–791

Pride, like an eagle, builds among the stars;
But Pleasure, lark-like, nests upon the ground.
YOUNG, *Night Thoughts*, V, lines 19, 20

Priest.— A decent priest, where monkeys were the gods.
POPE, *The Dunciad*, III, line 208

Primrose.— A primrose by a river's brim
A yellow primrose was to him,
And it was nothing more.[2]
WORDSWORTH, *Peter Bell*, i, st. 12

Primroses. Pale primroses,
That die unmarried, ere they can behold
Bright Phœbus in his strength — a malady
Most incident to maids.
SHAKESPEARE, *Winter's Tale*, iv, 4 [3]

---

[1] His was the lofty port — the distant mien,
That seems to shun the sight — and awes if seen.
BYRON, *The Corsair*, Canto i, st. 16

There was pride in the head she carried so high,
Pride in her lip, and pride in her eye,
And a world of pride in the very sigh
That her stately bosom was fretting!
J. G. SAXE, *The Proud Miss MacBride*

[2] Now a flower is just a flower:
Man, bird, beast are but beast, bird, man.
ROBERT BROWNING, *Asolando*, Prologue, st. 2

Prince.— When a prince to the fate of the peasant has yielded,
The tapestry waves dark round the dim-lighted hall;
With scutcheons of silver the coffin is shielded,
And pages stand mute by the canopied pall.
SCOTT, *Helvellyn*, st. 4

That prince, and that alone, is truly great,
Who draws the sword reluctant, gladly sheaths;
On empire builds what empire far outweighs,
And makes his throne a scaffold to the skies.
YOUNG, *Night Thoughts*, VI, lines 362–365

Princes.— Princes are like to heavenly bodies, which cause good or evil times, and which have much veneration, but no rest. BACON, *Essay XIX: Of Empire*

Print.— Some said, "John, print it;" others said, "Not so,"
Some said, "It might do good;" others said, "No."
BUNYAN, *Apology for His Book*, st. 4

A chiel's amang you, taking notes,
And, faith, he'll prent it.
BURNS, *On Captain Grose's Peregrinations*, st. 1

Printers.— I'll wish he had to write his song beneath a midnight taper;
On pittance that would scarcely pay for goose-quill, ink, and paper;
And then, to crown his misery, and break his heart in splinters;
I'll wish he had to see his proofs, his publishers, and printers. ELIZA COOK, *Lines on a Nightingale*, st. 14

Printing.— Thou hast most traitorously corrupted the youth of the realm in erecting a grammar school: and whereas, before, our forefathers had no other books but the score and the tally, thou hast caused printing to be used, and, contrary to the king, his crown and dignity, thou hast built a paper-mill. It will be proved to thy face that thou hast men about thee that usually talk of a noun and a verb, and such abominable words as no Christian ear can endure to hear.
SHAKESPEARE, *King Henry VI, Part II*, iv, 7

Prior.— Nobles and heralds, by your leave,
Here lies what once was Matthew Prior,
The son of Adam and of Eve;
Can Bourbon or Nassau go higher?
MATTHEW PRIOR, *Epitaph on Himself*

Prison.— Stone walls doe not a prison make,
Nor iron bars a cage.[1]
RICHARD LOVELACE, *To Althea from Prison*, st. 4

Prize.— Let a man contend to the uttermost
For his life's set prize, be it what it will!
ROBERT BROWNING, *The Statue and the Bust*, st. 81

Men prize the thing ungained more than it is.
SHAKESPEARE, *Troilus and Cressida*, i, 2

The prize be sometimes with the fool,
The race not always to the swift.
THACKERAY, *The End of the Play*, st. 5

Procrastination.— Procrastination is the thief of time.
YOUNG, *Night Thoughts*, I, line 393

Profession.— I hold every man a debtor to his profession; from the which, as men of course do seek to receive countenance and profit, so ought they of duty to endeavour themselves, by way of amends, to be a help and ornament thereunto. BACON, *Law Tracts: Preface*

Progress. Progress is
The law of life, man is not Man as yet.
. . . . .
When all mankind alike is perfected,
Equal in full-blown powers — then, not till then,
I say, begins man's general infancy.
ROBERT BROWNING, *Paracelsus*, v

Promise.— Bate me some and I will pay you some, and, as most debtors do, promise you infinitely.
SHAKESPEARE, *King Henry IV, Part II*, v, Epilogue

Be these juggling fiends no more believed,
That palter with us in a double sense;
That keep the word of promise to our ear,
And break it to our hope.
SHAKESPEARE, *Macbeth*, v, 8 [7]

All promise is poor dilatory man.
YOUNG, *Night Thoughts*, I, line 412

---

[1] That which the world miscalls a jail
A private closet is to me;
Whilst a good conscience is my bail,
And innocence my liberty:
Locks, bars, and solitude together met,
Make me no prisoner, but an anchoret.
SIR ROGER L'ESTRANGE, *In Prison*, st. 2

Promises.— Bad promises are better broken than kept.[1]
LINCOLN, *Last Public Address*, April 11, 1865

Pronouns.— Who would succeed in the world should be wise in the use of his pronouns.
Utter the *You* twenty times where you once utter the *I*.
JOHN HAY, *Distichs*, xiii

Property.— Proputty, proputty sticks, an' proputty, proputty graws. TENNYSON, *Northern Farmer, New Style*, st. 4

He hath no need of property
Who knows not how to spend it.
THACKERAY, *The King of Brentford's Testament*, st. 38

Prophesy.— Don't never prophesy — onless ye know.
LOWELL, *Biglow Papers*, II, ii, line 38

Prophet.— The mariner curseth the warning bird
Who bringeth him news of the storm unheard!
Ah! thus does the prophet of good or ill
Meet hate from the creatures he serveth still.
B. W. PROCTER, *The Stormy Petrel*, st. 3

Propose.— Why don't the men propose, mamma,
Why don't the men propose?
T. H. BAYLY, *Why Don't the Men Propose?*

Prose.— Things unattempted yet in prose or rhyme.
MILTON, *Paradise Lost*, I, line 16

Prosper.— God prosper your affairs!
SHAKESPEARE, *King Henry IV, Part II*, iii, 2

Prosperous.— So long as I was prosperous, I'd dinners by the dozen,
Was well-bred, witty, virtuous, and everybody's cousin;
If luck should turn, as well she may, her fancy is so flexile,
Will virtue, cousinship, and all return with her from exile?
LOWELL, *Translation of Mapes's Imitation of Petronius*

Protests.— The lady protests [doth protest] too much, methinks. SHAKESPEARE, *Hamlet*, iii, 2

Proud.— The proud are always most provoked by pride.
COWPER, *Conversation*, line 160

---

[1] This is, however, proverbial.

Proud of her wit, and proud of her walk,
Proud of her teeth, and proud of her talk,
Proud of "knowing cheese from chalk,"
On a very slight inspection.

J. G. SAXE, *The Proud Miss MacBride*

He that is proud eats up himself: pride is his own glass, his own trumpet, his own chronicle.

SHAKESPEARE, *Troilus and Cressida*, ii, 3

Prove.— Free to prove[1] all things, and hold fast the best.

COWPER, *Table Talk*, line 273

I put this question hopelessly,
To every one I knew —
What would you do, if you were me,
To prove that you were you?

H. S. LEIGH, *The Twins*, st. 3

I 'll prove it on his body.

SHAKESPEARE, *Much Ado about Nothing*, v, 1

Proverb.— My definition of a proverb is, the wit of one man and the wisdom of many.

LORD JOHN RUSSELL, *To Sir J. Mackintosh*

Providence. Don't give up afore the ship goes down:
It 's a stiff gale, but Providence wun't drown;
An' God wun't leave us yit to sink or swim,
Ef we don't fail to du wut 's right by Him.

LOWELL, *Biglow Papers*, II, ii, lines 315–318

There 's a special providence in the fall of a sparrow.[2]

SHAKESPEARE, *Hamlet*, v, 2

Prudes.— By fools insulted, and by prudes accused.

Epitaph of Laurence Sterne

Publican.— How like a fawning publican he looks!

SHAKESPEARE, *Merchant of Venice*, i, 3

Publishers.— When publishers no longer steal,
And pay for what they stole before

HOLMES, *Latter-Day Warnings*, st. 8

---

[1] Prove all things; hold fast that which is good. *1 Thess.* v, 21

[2] Are not two sparrows sold for a farthing? and one of them shall not fall on the ground without your Father. *Matt.* x, 29

Are not five sparrows sold for two farthings, and not one of them is forgotten before God? *Luke* xii, 6

Punch.—"Jack," said my lady, "is it grog you 'll try,
Or punch, or toddy, if perhaps you 're dry?"
"Ah," said the sailor, "though I can 't refuse,
You know, my lady, 'tain't for me to choose;
I 'll take the grog to finish off my lunch,
And drink the toddy while you mix the punch."
HOLMES, *A Modest Request, The Scene*, lines 55–60

Puns.— People that make puns are like wanton boys that put coppers on the railroad tracks. They amuse themselves and other children, but their little trick may upset a freight-train of conversation for the sake of a battered witticism. HOLMES, *Autocrat of the Breakfast-Table*, i

Purgatory.— As the Celt said of purgatory,
One might go farther and fare worse.
WHITTIER, *The Wreck of Rivermouth*, st. 19

Puritans.— The Puritans hated bear-baiting, not because it gave pain to the bear, but because it gave pleasure to the spectators. MACAULAY, *History of England*, I, ii

Purity.— We maids would far, far whiter be
If that our eyes might sometimes see
Men maids in purity.
LANIER, *The Symphony*, lines 300–302

By the pattern of mine own thoughts I cut out
The purity of his.—SHAKESPEARE, *Winter's Tale*, iv, 4 [3]

Purpose.— Ah, many a one has started forth with hope and purpose high;
Has fought throughout a weary life, and passed all pleasure by;
Has burst all flowery chains by which men aye have been enthralled;
Has been stone-deaf to voices sweet, that softly, sadly called;
Has scorned the flashing goblet with the bubbles on its brim;
Has turned his back on jewelled hands that madly beckoned him;
Has, in a word, condemned himself to follow out his plan
By stern and lonely labor,— and has died, a conquered man! GEORGE ARNOLD, *Wool-Gathering*, iii

I want that glib and oily art,
To speak and purpose not.
SHAKESPEARE, *King Lear*, i, 1

Yet I doubt not through the ages one increasing purpose runs,[1]
And the thoughts of men are widened with the process of the suns.— TENNYSON, *Locksley Hall*, lines 137, 138

Purse.— Consumption of the purse.
SHAKESPEARE, *King Henry IV, Part II*, i, 2

Put money in thy purse. SHAKESPEARE, *Othello*, i, 3

Pygmies.— Pygmies are pygmies still, though perched on Alps;
And pyramids are pyramids in vales.
Each man makes his own statue, builds himself:
Virtue alone outbuilds the Pyramids;
Her monuments shall last when Egypt's fall.
YOUNG, *Night Thoughts*, VI, lines 309–313

Pyramids.— Forty centuries look down upon you from the summit of the Pyramids.
NAPOLEON BONAPARTE, *Life*, by Sloane, II, 41

Quality.— Give us a taste of your quality.
SHAKESPEARE, *Hamlet*, ii, 2

Quarrel.— Rather than fail, they will defy
That which they love most tenderly,
Quarrel with minced-pies, and disparage
Their best and dearest friend — plum-porridge;
Fat pig and goose itself oppose,
And blaspheme custard through the nose.[2]
BUTLER, *Hudibras*, I, i, lines 225–230

Beware
Of entrance to a quarrel; but, being in,
Bear't that the opposed may beware of thee.
SHAKESPEARE, *Hamlet*, i, 3

---

[1] These struggling tides of life that seem
In wayward, aimless course to tend,
Are eddies of the mighty stream
That rolls to its appointed end. BRYANT, *The Crowded Street*, st. 11

One God, one law, one element:
And one far-off divine event
To which the whole creation moves.
TENNYSON, *In Memoriam*, Conclusion, st. 36

[2] Why, thou wilt quarrel with a man that hath a hair more, or a hair less, in his beard, than thou hast: thou wilt quarrel with a man for cracking nuts, having no other reason but because thou hast hazel eyes: what eye but such an eye would spy out such a quarrel? Thy head is as full of quarrels as an egg is full of meat, and yet thy head hath been beaten as addle as an egg for quarrelling: thou hast quarrelled with a man for coughing in the street, because he hath wakened thy dog that hath lain asleep in the sun: didst thou not fall out with a tailor for wearing his new doublet before Easter? with another, for tying his new shoes with old riband? and yet thou wilt tutor me from quarrelling. SHAKESPEARE, *Romeo and Juliet*, iii, 1

The quarrel is a very pretty quarrel as it stands; we should only spoil it by trying to explain it.
SHERIDAN, *The Rivals*, iv, 3

Quarrelled.— We quarrelled like brutes, and who wonders?
What self-respect could we keep,
Worse housed than your hacks and your pointers,
Worse fed than your hogs and your sheep?
KINGSLEY, *The Bad Squire* [*A Rough Rhyme on a Rough Matter*], st. 13

Quarrelling.— Besides that he 's a fool, he 's a great quarreller; and, but that he hath the gift of a coward to allay the gust he hath in quarrelling, 'tis thought among the prudent he would quickly have the gift of a grave.
SHAKESPEARE, *Twelfth Night*, i, 3

Quarrels. Those who in quarrels interpose
Must often wipe a bloody nose.
GAY, *Fables: The Mastiffs*

Queen.— Her court was pure; her life serene;
God gave her peace; her land reposed;
A thousand claims to reverence closed
In her as Mother, Wife, and Queen.
TENNYSON, *To the Queen*

Queer.— I know it is a sin
For me to sit and grin
At him here;
But the old three-cornered hat,
And the breeches, and all that,
Are so queer! HOLMES, *The Last Leaf*, st. 7

Questions.— Ask me no questions, and I 'll tell you no fibs.
GOLDSMITH, *She Stoops to Conquer*, iii

Quiet.— Quiet to quick bosoms is a hell.
BYRON, *Childe Harold's Pilgrimage*, Canto iii, st. 42

For she was jest the quiet kind
Whose naturs never vary,
Like streams that keep a summer mind
Snowhid in Jenooary. LOWELL, *The Courtin'*, st. 22

Quietus.— Who would bear the whips and scorns of time,
The oppressor's wrong, the proud man's contumely,
The pangs of despised [disprized] love, the law's delay,
The insolence of office, and the spurns
That patient merit of the unworthy takes,
When he himself might his quietus make
With a bare bodkin? SHAKESPEARE, *Hamlet*, iii, 1

Quips.— Thy quips and thy quiddities.
SHAKESPEARE, *King Henry IV, Part I*, i, 2

Race.— Not to the swift, the race:
Not to the strong, the fight:
Not to the righteous, perfect grace:
Not to the wise, the light.

But often faltering feet
Come surest to the goal;
And they who walk in darkness meet
The sunrise of the soul.
HENRY VAN DYKE, *Reliance*, st. 1, 2

Radish.— If I fought not with fifty of them, I am a bunch of radish. SHAKESPEARE, *King Henry IV, Part I*, ii, 4

Rage.— The wine of passion — rage.
BYRON, *The Island*, Canto i, st. 3

Heaven has no rage like love to hatred turned,
Nor hell a fury like a woman scorned.
CONGREVE, *Mourning Bride*, iii, 2

In rage deaf as the sea, hasty as fire.
SHAKESPEARE, *King Richard II*, i, 1

Raggedy-man.— Ain't he a' awful good raggedy-man?
J. W. RILEY, *The Raggedy-man*

Ragings.— Think when your castigated pulse
Gi'es now and then a wallop,
What ragings must his veins convulse,
That still eternal gallop.
BURNS, *Address to the Unco Guid*, st. 4

Railing.— Railing and praising were his usual themes;
And both, to show his judgment, in extremes:
So over violent, or over civil,
That every man with him was God or Devil.
DRYDEN, *Absalom and Achitophel*, I, lines 555–558

Rail-splitter.— To make me own this hind of princes peer,
This rail-splitter a true-born king of men.
TOM TAYLOR, *Abraham Lincoln*, st. 5

Rain.— 'T will surely rain; I see with sorrow
Our jaunt must be put off to-morrow.
EDWARD JENNER, *Signs of Rain*

I list to this refrain
Which is played upon the shingles
By the patter of the rain.
COATES KINNEY, *Rain On the Roof*

The rain it raineth every day.
SHAKESPEARE, *King Lear*, iii, 2; *Twelfth Night*, v

Rake.— Men, some to bus'ness, some to pleasure take;
But every woman is at heart a rake:
Men, some to quiet, some to public strife;
But ev'ry lady would be queen for life.
POPE, *Moral Essays*, Epistle ii, lines 215–218

Rascals.— All the cankers wasting town and state,
The mob of rascals, little thieves and great,
Dealers in watered milk and watered stocks,
Who lead us lambs to pasture on the rocks,
Shepherds — Jack Sheppards — of their city flocks —
The rings of rogues that rob the luckless town,
Those evil angels creeping up and down
The Jacob's ladder of the Treasury stairs,
Not stage, but real, Turpins and Macaires.
HOLMES, *Address for the Opening of the Fifth Avenue Theatre, New York*, st. 11

Rat.— Quoth Hudibras, "I smell a rat;
Ralpho, thou dost prevaricate."
BUTLER, *Hudibras*, I, i, lines 821, 822

What if my house be troubled with a rat
And I be pleased to give ten thousand ducats
To have it baned.
SHAKESPEARE, *Merchant of Venice*, iv, 1

Rats. The very rats
Instinctively had quit it.
SHAKESPEARE, *The Tempest*, i, 2

Raven.— Open here I flung the shutter, when, with many a flirt and flutter,
In there stepped a stately raven of the saintly days of yore.
Not the least obeisance made he; not a minute stopped or stayed he,
But, with mien of lord or lady, perched above my chamber door —
Perched upon a bust of Pallas just above my chamber door —
Perched, and sat, and nothing more.
POE, *The Raven*, st. 7

The raven doth not hatch a lark.
SHAKESPEARE, *Titus Andronicus*, ii, 3

Did ever raven sing so like a lark? *Ibid.*, iii, 1

The raven croaked as she sat at her meal,
And the old woman knew what he said;
And she grew pale at the raven's tale,
And sickened and went to her bed.
SOUTHEY, *The Old Woman of Berkeley*, st. 1

Ravens. He that doth the ravens feed,
Yea, providently caters for the sparrow,
Be comfort to my age.
SHAKESPEARE, *As You Like It*, ii, 3

Razors.— A fellow in a market-town,
Most musical, cried razors up and down,
And offered twelve for eighteen pence;
. . . . .
"Friend," quoth the razor-man, "I'm not a knave;
As for the razors you have bought,
Upon my soul, I never thought
That they would shave."
"Not think they'd shave!" quoth Hodge, with wondering eyes,
And voice not much unlike an Indian yell;
"What were they made for, then, you dog?" he cries.
"Made," quoth the fellow with a smile,—"to sell."
JOHN WOLCOT ("PETER PINDAR") *The Razor-Seller*, st. 1, 8

Read. A worthy gentleman,
Exceedingly well read.
SHAKESPEARE, *King Henry IV, Part I*, iii, 1

Reading.— Reading maketh a full man; conference a ready man; and writing an exact man.
BACON, *Essay L: Of Studies*

Reaper.— The hand of the reaper
Takes the ears that are hoary,
But the voice of the weeper
Wails manhood in glory.
The autumn winds rushing
Waft the leaves that are serest,
But our flower was in flushing
When blighting was nearest.
SCOTT, *Lady of the Lake*, Canto III, xvi, st. 2

Reason.— I do not love thee, Doctor Fell,
The reason why I cannot tell;[1]
But this alone I know full well,
I do not love thee, Doctor Fell.
TOM BROWN (following classical and other authors)

Reason is the light of the law;[2] nay, the common law itself is nothing but reason. . . . The law which is perfection of reason.
SIR EDWARD COKE, *Institutes*, I, 976

What can we reason, but from what we know?
POPE, *Essay on Man*, Epistle i, line 18

There St. John mingles with my friendly bowl
The feast of reason and the flow of soul.
POPE, *Imitations of Horace*, II, Satire i, lines 127, 128

Now see that noble and most sovereign reason,
Like sweet bells jangled, out of tune and harsh.
SHAKESPEARE, *Hamlet*, iii, 1

If with the sap of reason you would quench,
Or but allay, the fire of passion.
SHAKESPEARE, *King Henry VIII*, i, 1

Reason the root, fair faith is but the flower;
The fading flower shall die; but reason lives
Immortal.— YOUNG, *Night Thoughts*, IV, lines 752–754

Reasons.— If reasons were as plentiful [plenty] as blackberries, I would give no man a reason upon compulsion.
SHAKESPEARE, *King Henry IV*, *Part I*, ii, 4

Gratiano speaks an infinite deal of nothing . . . His reasons are as two grains of wheat hid in two bushels of chaff: you shall seek all day ere you find them; and when you have them, they are not worth the search.
SHAKESPEARE, *Merchant of Venice*, i, 1

---

[1] I love thee and hate thee, but if I can tell
The cause of my love and my hate, may I die.
I can feel it, alas! I can feel it too well,
That I love thee and hate thee, but cannot tell why.
T. MOORE, in note to *Fragment of Odes of Anacreon*

So can I give no reason, nor I will not,
More than a lodged hate and a certain loathing.
SHAKESPEARE, *Merchant of Venice*, iv, 1

I have no other but a woman's reason:
I think him so because I think him so.
SHAKESPEARE, *Two Gentlemen of Verona*, i, 2

[2] Reason is the soul of the law; the reason of the law being changed, the law is also changed. 7 *Coke's King's Bench Report*, 7

Let us consider the reason of the case, for nothing is law that is not reason.
SIR J. POWELL, *Coggs vs. Bernard*, 2 Ld Raym., 912

Rebellion.— Rebellion to tyrants is obedience to God.
Inscription on a cannon near the burial-place of John Bradshaw, cited by STILES, *History of the Three Judges of King Charles I*

Rebels.— Kings will be tyrants from policy when subjects are rebels from principle.
BURKE, *On the French Revolution*

Rebuff. Welcome each rebuff
That turns earth's smoothness rough,
Each sting that bids nor sit nor stand but go!
Be our joys three parts pain!
Strive, and hold cheap the strain;
Learn, nor account the pang; dare, never grudge the throe!
R. BROWNING, *Rabbi Ben Ezra*, st. 6

Reckless.— Thus from your presence forth I go,
A lost and lonely man;
Reckless alike of weal or woe,
Heaven's benison or ban:
He who has known the tempest's worst,[1]
May bare him to the blast;
Blame not these tears; they are the first —
Are they the last?
PRAED, *The Last*, st. 6

I am one, my liege,
Whom the vile blows and buffets of the world
Have so incensed that I am reckless what
I do to spite the world.— SHAKESPEARE, *Macbeth*, iii, 1

Redeemer.— For sure he must be sainted man,
Whose blessed feet have trod the ground
Where the Redeemer's tomb is found.
SCOTT, *Marmion*, v, 21

Redress.— Ring in redress to all mankind.
TENNYSON, *In Memoriam*, cvi, st. 3

Refusal.— Who listens once will listen twice:
Her heart, be sure, is not of ice,
And one refusal no rebuff.
BYRON, *Mazeppa*, st. 6

---

[1] Through many a clime 't is mine to go,
With many a retrospection cursed;
And all my solace is to know,
Whate'er betides, I've known the worst.

What is that worst? Nay, do not ask —
In pity from the search forbear:
Smile on — nor venture to unmask
Man's heart, and view the hell that's there.
BYRON, *Childe Harold's Pilgrimage*, Canto I, st. 84 (8, 9)

Refuse.— For ane I'll get better, it's waur I'll get ten —
I was daft to refuse the Laird o' Cockpen.
LADY NAIRNE, *The Laird o' Cockpen*, st. 8

Reign.— Here we may reign secure; and, in my choice,
To reign is worth ambition though in Hell:
Better to reign in Hell than serve in Heaven.
MILTON, *Paradise Lost*, I, lines 261–263

How monarchs die is easily explained,
And thus it might upon the tomb be chiselled;
"As long as George the Fourth could reign he reigned,
And then he mizzled."
HOOD, *Epigram on a Royal Demise*

Rejoice.— Rejoice, and men will seek you;
Grieve, and they turn and go;
They want full measure of all your pleasure,
But they do not need your woe.
ELLA WHEELER WILCOX, *Solitude*, st. 2

Religion.— For his religion, it was fit
To match his learning and his wit;
'Twas Presbyterian, true blue;
For he was of that stubborn crew
Of errant saints, whom all men grant
To be the true Church Militant;
Such as do build their faith upon
The holy text of pike and gun;
Decide all controversies by
Infallible artillery;
And prove their doctrine orthodox
By apostolic blows and knocks;
Call fire, and sword, and desolation,
A godly, thorough Reformation,
Which always must be carried on
And still be doing, never done;
As if religion were intended
For nothing else but to be mended.
BUTLER, *Hudibras*, I, i, lines 189–206

My little woman, said Mr. Snagsby, likes to have her religion rather sharp. DICKENS, *Bleak House*, xix

And this was all the religion he had,—
To treat his engine well;
Never be passed on the river;
To mind the pilot's bell;
And if ever the Prairie Belle took fire,—
A thousand times he swore,
He'd hold her nozzle agin the bank
Till the last soul got ashore.
JOHN HAY, *Jim Bludso of the Prairie Belle*, st. 3

I don't go so much on religion,
  I never ain't had no show;
But I've got a middlin' tight grip, sir,
  On the handful o' things I know.
I don't pan out on the prophets,
  And free-will, and that sort of thing,—
But I b'lieve in God and the angels,
  Ever sence one night last spring.

JOHN HAY, *Little Breeches*, st. 1

With sweet kind natures, as in honeyed cells,
Religion lives, and feels herself at home;
But only on a formal visit dwells
Where wasps instead of bees have formed the comb.

HOOD, *Ode to Rae Wilson, Esquire*, st. 32

Now conscience chills her, and now passion burns;
And atheism and religion take their turns;
A very heathen in the carnal part,
Yet still a sad, good Christian at her heart.

POPE, *Moral Essays*, Epistle ii, lines 65–68

In religion,
What damned error, but some sober brow
Will bless it and approve it with a text,
Hiding the grossness with fair ornament.

SHAKESPEARE, *Merchant of Venice*, iii, 2

Religions.— Even gods must yield — religions take their turn:
  'Twas Jove's —'tis Mahomet's — and other creeds
  Will rise with other years, till man shall learn
  Vainly his incense soars, his victim bleeds;
  Poor child of doubt and death, whose hope is built on reeds.

BYRON, *Childe Harold's Pilgrimage*, Canto ii, st. 3

Remedies.— Our remedies oft in ourselves do lie,
Which we ascribe to heaven.

SHAKESPEARE, *All's Well That Ends Well*, i, 1

Remedy.— The remedy is worse than the disease.

DRYDEN, *Juvenal*, Satire xvi, line 31

Remember.— I sit beside my lonely fire,
  And pray for wisdom yet:
For calmness to remember,
  Or courage to forget.

HAMILTON AÏDÉ, *Remember or Forget*, st. 4

I remember, I remember,
The house where I was born,
The little window where the sun
Came peeping in at morn;

He never came a wink too soon
Nor brought too long a day,
But now I often wish the night
Had borne my breath away!

. . . .

I remember, I remember,
The fir-trees dark and high;
I used to think their slender tops
Were close against the sky:
It was a childish ignorance,
But now 't is little joy
To know I 'm farther off from heaven
Than when I was a boy.[1]

HOOD, *I Remember, I Remember*, st. 1, 4

Other arms may press thee,
Dearer friends caress thee,
All the joys that bless thee,
Sweeter far may be;
But when friends are nearest,
And when joys are dearest,
Oh! then remember me!

T. MOORE, *Go Where Glory Waits Thee*, st. 1

Remember thee!
Ay, thou poor ghost, while memory holds a seat
In this distracted globe. Remember thee!
Yea, from the table [tables] of my memory
I 'll wipe away all trivial fond records,
All saws of books, all forms, all pressures past,
That youth and observation copied there;
And thy commandment all alone shall live
Within the book and volume of my brain,
Unmixed with baser matter.

SHAKESPEARE, *Hamlet*, i, 5

---

[1] There was a time when I was very small,
When my whole frame was but an ell in height.

. . . .

Then seemed to me this world far less in size,
Likewise it seemed to me less wicked far.

. . . .

They perished, the blithe days of boyhood perished,
And all the gladness, all the peace I knew!
Now have I but their memory, fondly cherished;
God! may I never lose that too!

LONGFELLOW, *Childhood*, from the Danish of J. I. Baggesen, st. 1, 3, 9

I remember — I remember
How my childhood fleeted by,—
The mirth of its December,
And the warmth of its July;
On my brow, love — on my brow, love,
There are no signs of care;
But my pleasures are not now, love,
What childhood's pleasures were.

PRAED, *I Remember, I Remember*, st. 1

Remote.— Remote, unfriended, melancholy, slow.
GOLDSMITH, *The Traveller*, st. 1

Removes.— Three removes are as bad as a fire.
FRANKLIN, *Poor Richard's Almanac*

Remuneration.— Remuneration! Oh! that's the Latin word for three farthings: . . . Remuneration! why, it is a fairer name than French crown.
SHAKESPEARE, *Love's Labour's Lost*, iii

Repentance.— He who seeks repentance for the past
Should woo the angel Virtue in the future!
E. G. BULWER-LYTTON, *The Lady of Lyons*, v, 2

Is there no place
Left for repentance, none for pardon left?
None left but by submission.
MILTON, *Paradise Lost*, IV, lines 79–81

Who by repentance is not satisfied
Is nor of heaven nor earth.
SHAKESPEARE, *Two Gentlemen of Verona*, v, 4

Reproof.— Fear not the anger of the wise to raise;
Those best can bear reproof, who merit praise.
POPE, *Essay on Criticism*, lines 582, 583

That man is not alive
Might so have tempted him as you have done,
Without the taste of danger and reproof.
SHAKESPEARE, *King Henry IV*, *Part I*, iii, 1

Reptile.— Every foul bird comes abroad and every dirty reptile rises up. LINCOLN, *Letter to C. D. Drake*, Oct. 5, 1863

Reputation.— At ev'ry word a reputation dies.
POPE, *Rape of the Lock*, iii, line 16

My reputation is at stake;[1]
My fame is shrewdly gored.
SHAKESPEARE, *Troilus and Cressida*, iii, 3

Requiem.— A requiem for the chief,
Whose fiat millions slew,
The soaring eagle of the Alps,
The crushed at Waterloo:
The banished who returned,
The dead who rose again,
And rode in his shroud the billows proud
To the sunny banks of Seine.
L. H. SIGOURNEY, *The Return of Napoleon from St. Helena*, st. 8

---

[1] Oh, I have lost my reputation! I have lost the immortal part of myself, and what remains is bestial. SHAKESPEARE, *Othello*, ii, 3

Resign.— With a sigh I resign
What I once thought was mine,
And forgive her deceit with a tear.
BYRON, *The Tear*, st. 9

Resolute.— The star of the unconquered will,
He rises in my breast,
Serene, and resolute, and still,
And calm, and self-possessed.
LONGFELLOW, *Light of the Stars*, st. 7

Rest.— Peace waits us on the shores of Acheron:
There no forced banquet claims the sated guest,
But silence spreads the couch of ever-welcome rest.[1]
BYRON, *Childe Harold's Pilgrimage*, Canto ii, st. 7

Absence of occupation is not rest;[2]
A mind quite vacant is a mind distressed.
COWPER, *Retirement*

Let us cross over the river and rest under the shade of the trees.—STONEWALL JACKSON, *Last Words*, quoted in J. E. COOKE, *Life of Stonewall Jackson*, xxxviii

For some we loved, the loveliest and the best
That from his Vintage rolling Time has pressed,
Have drunk their cup a round or two before,
And one by one crept silently to rest.
OMAR KHAYYÁM, *Rubáiyát* (trans. Fitzgerald), st. 22

So may he rest; his faults lie gently on him!
SHAKESPEARE, *King Henry VIII*, iv, 2

Silvia. And so, good rest.
Proteus. As wretches have o'ernight
That wait for execution in the morn.
SHAKESPEARE, *Two Gentlemen of Verona*, iv, 2

I am sick of Time,
And I desire to rest.
TENNYSON, *Come Not When I Am Dead*, st. 2

---

[1] There is a calm for those who weep,
A rest for weary pilgrims found,
They softly lie and sweetly sleep
Low in the ground. JAMES MONTGOMERY, *The Grave*, st. 1

[2] Rest is not quitting
The busy career;
Rest is the fitting
Of self to its sphere. J. S. DWIGHT, *True Rest*, st. 4

For ever and for ever, all in a blessed home —
And there to wait a little while till you and Effie come —
To lie within the light of God, as I lie upon your breast —
And the wicked cease from troubling, and the weary are
at rest.[1]

TENNYSON, *The May Queen*, Conclusion, st. 15

Resting-place.— Yet not to thine eternal resting-place
Shalt thou retire alone,— nor couldst thou wish
Couch more magnificent. Thou shalt lie down
With patriarchs of the infant world,— with kings,[2]
The powerful of the earth,— the wise, the good,
Fair forms, and hoary seers of ages past,
All in one mighty sepulchre.

BRYANT, *Thanatopsis*, lines 31–37

Rests.— So peaceful rests, without a stone, a name,
What once had beauty, titles, wealth, and fame.
How loved, how honoured once, avails thee not,
To whom related, or by whom begot;
A heap of dust alone remains of thee,
'Tis all thou art, and all the proud shall be!

POPE, *Elegy to an Unfortunate Lady*, lines 69–74

Retreat.— Let us make an honourable retreat; though not with bag and baggage.

SHAKESPEARE, *As You Like It*, iii. 2

Return.— You know how little while we have to stay,
And, once departed, may return no more.[3]

OMAR KHAYYÁM, *Rubáiyát* (trans. Fitzgerald), st. 3

Revelry.— There was a sound of revelry by night,
And Belgium's capital had gathered then
Her beauty and her chivalry, and bright
The lamps shone o'er fair women and brave men;
A thousand hearts beat happily; and when
Music arose with its voluptuous swell,
Soft eyes looked love to eyes that spake again,
And all went merry as a marriage-bell;
But hush! hark! a deep sound strikes like a rising knell!

BYRON, *Childe Harold's Pilgrimage*, Canto iii, st. 21

Revenge.— A man that studieth revenge keeps his own wounds green, which otherwise would heal and do well.

BACON, *Essay IV: Of Revenge*

Sweet is revenge — especially to women.

BYRON, *Don Juan*, Canto i, st. 124

---

[1] There the wicked cease from troubling, and the weary be at rest.
Job iii. 17

[2] Kings have no such couch as thine,
As the green that folds thy grave.
TENNYSON, *A Dirge*, st. 6

[3] And once departed come no more.
LONGFELLOW, *A Fragment*, st. 1

The fairest action of our human life
Is scorning to revenge an injury:
For who forgives without a further strife
His adversary's heart to him doth tie:
And 'tis a firmer conquest truly said
To win the heart than overthrow the head.
LADY ELIZABETH CAREW, *Revenge of Injuries*,
(from *The Tragedy of Marian*)

Revenge, at first though sweet,
Bitter ere long back on itself recoils.
MILTON, *Paradise Lost*, IX, lines 171, 172

Cæsar's spirit, ranging for revenge,
With Ate by his side come hot from hell,
Shall in these confines with a monarch's voice
Cry "Havoc!" and let slip the dogs of war.
SHAKESPEARE, *Julius Cæsar*, iii, 1

If it will feed nothing else, it will feed my revenge.
SHAKESPEARE, *Merchant of Venice*, iii, 1

Patience is the honest man's revenge.
CYRIL TOURNEUR, *The Atheist's Tragedy*, v, 2

Reverence.— But yesterday the word of Cæsar might
Have stood against the world; now lies he there,
And none so poor to do him reverence.
SHAKESPEARE, *Julius Cæsar*, iii, 2

Rhetoric.— For rhetoric, he could not ope
His mouth, but out there flew a trope.
BUTLER, *Hudibras*, I, i, lines 81, 82

Rhyme.— For rhyme the rudder is of verses,
With which, like ships, they steer their courses.
BUTLER, *Hudibras*, I, i, lines 463, 464

Those that write in rhyme still make
The one verse for the other's sake;
For one for sense, and one for rhyme,
I think 's sufficient at one time. *Ibid.*, II, i, lines 27–30

I'll rhyme you so eight years together.
SHAKESPEARE, *As You Like It*, iii, 2

Neither rhyme nor reason.[1] *Ibid.*

---

[1] 'T is hard to fit the reason to the rhyme.— DRYDEN, *Art of Poetry*, line 328

Valentine. How now, sir! what are you reasoning with yourself?
Speed. Nay, I was rhyming: 'tis you that have the reason.
SHAKESPEARE, *Two Gentlemen of Verona*, ii, 1

I was promised on a time,
To have reason for my rhyme;
From that time unto this season,
I received nor rhyme nor reason.
SPENSER, *Lines on His Promised Pension*

As much love in rhyme
As would be crammed up in a sheet of paper,
Writ o' both sides the leaf, margent and all,
That he was fain to seal on Cupid's name.
SHAKESPEARE, *Love's Labour's Lost*, v, 2

Rhymes.— Ring out, ring out my mournful rhymes,
But ring the fuller minstrel in.
TENNYSON, *In Memoriam*, cvi, st. 5

Rhyming.— I was not born under a rhyming planet.
SHAKESPEARE, *Much Ado about Nothing*, v, 2

Rialto.— What news on the Rialto?
SHAKESPEARE, *Merchant of Venice*, i, 3; iii, 1

Riband.— Just for a handful of silver he left us,
Just for a riband to stick in his coat.
R. BROWNING, *The Lost Leader*, lines 1, 2

Rich.— A man he was to all the country dear,
And passing rich with forty pounds a year.
GOLDSMITH, *The Deserted Village*, st. 10

If thou art rich, thou 'rt poor;
For, like an ass whose back with ingots bows,
Thou bear'st thy heavy riches but a journey,
And death unloads thee.
SHAKESPEARE, *Measure for Measure*, iii, 1

When thou art old and rich,
Thou hast neither heat, affection, limb, nor beauty,
To make thy riches pleasant. *Ibid.*

Rage canine of dying rich;
Guilt's blunder! and the loudest laugh of hell.
YOUNG, *Night Thoughts*, IV, lines 108, 109

Riches.— Riches make them wings, and they
Do as an eagle fly away.[1] HOLMES, *After the Fire*

Let none admire
That riches grow in Hell; that soil may best
Deserve the precious bane.
MILTON, *Paradise Lost*, I, lines 690–692

What riches give us, let us then inquire?
Meat, fire, and clothes. What more? Meat, clothes, and fire.
Is this too little?
POPE, *Moral Essays*, Epistle iii, lines 79–81

---

[1] *Prov.* xxiii, 5.

Richmonds.— I think there be six Richmonds in the field;
Five have I slain to-day instead of him.
SHAKESPEARE, *King Richard III*, v, 4

Ride.— An two men ride of a horse, one must ride behind.
SHAKESPEARE, *Much Ado about Nothing*, iii, 4

Rift.— It is the little rift within the lute,
That by and by will make the music mute,
And ever widening slowly silence all.

The little rift within the lover's lute,
Or little pitted speck in garnered fruit,
That rotting inward slowly moulders all.
TENNYSON, *Merlin and Vivien*, lines 388–393

Right.— One who never turned his back, but marched breast forward,
Never doubted clouds would break,
Never dreamed, though right were worsted, wrong would triumph,
Held we fall to rise, are baffled to fight better,
Sleep to wake.
R. BROWNING, *Asolando*, Epilogue, st. 3

Blest, too, is he who can divine
Where real right doth lie,
And dares to take the side that seems
Wrong to man's blindfold eye.

For right is right, since God is God;
And right the day must win;
To doubt would be disloyalty,
To falter would be sin.
F. W. FABER, *The Right Must Win*

Let us have faith that right makes might, and in that faith let us to the end dare to do our duty as we understand it. LINCOLN, *Address at Cooper Institute, New York*, Feb. 27, 1860

With malice toward none; with charity for all; with firmness in the right, as God gives us to see the right, let us strive on to finish the work we are in; to bind up the nation's wounds; to care for him who shall have borne the battle, and for his widow, and his orphan — to do all which may achieve and cherish a just and lasting peace among ourselves, and with all nations.
LINCOLN, *Second Inaugural Address*, March 4, 1865

All nature is but art, unknown to thee;
All chance, direction, which thou canst not see;

All discord, harmony not understood;
All partial evil, universal good:
And, spite of pride, in erring Reason's spite,
One truth is clear, Whatever is, is right.
POPE, *Essay on Man*, Epistle i, lines 289–294;
Epistle iv, lines 145, 394

God and our right![1] SHAKESPEARE, *King John*, ii, 1

Follow you the star that lights a desert pathway, yours or mine.
Forward, till you see the Highest Human Nature is divine.

Follow Light, and do the Right — for man can half-control his doom —
Till you find the deathless Angel seated in the vacant tomb. TENNYSON, *Locksley Hall Sixty Years After*, lines 275–278

Rights.— They made and recorded a sort of institute and digest of anarchy, called the Rights of Man.
BURKE, *Speech on the Army Estimates*, February, 1790

They have rights who dare maintain them.
LOWELL, *The Present Crisis*, st. 17

Every man must be guaranteed his liberty and his right to do as he likes with his property or his labour, so long as he does not infringe the rights of others.
THEODORE ROOSEVELT, *Message to Congress*, January, 1904

Ring.— Your wedding-ring wears thin, dear wife; ah, summers not a few,
Since I put it on your finger first, have passed o'er me and you;
And, love, what changes we have seen,— what cares and pleasures, too,—
Since you became my own dear wife, when this old ring was new!
W. C. BENNETT, *The Worn Wedding Ring*, st. 1

I 'll tell you a story that 's not in Tom Moore:—
Young Love likes to knock at a pretty girl's door:
So he called upon Lucy —'t was just ten o'clock —
Like a spruce single man, with a smart double knock.

. . . . .

The meeting was bliss; but the parting was woe;
For the moment will come when such comers must go:
So she kissed him, and whispered—poor innocent thing—
"The next time you come, love, pray come with a ring."
HOOD, *Please to Ring the Belle*

[1]God defend the right! SHAKESPEARE, *King Richard II*, i, 3
Heaven still guards the right. *Ibid.*, iii, 2

Ring out the old, ring in the new.
TENNYSON, *In Memoriam*, cvi, st. 2

Ring out a slowly dying cause,
And ancient forms of party strife. *Ibid.*, st. 4

Ringlet.— [He] preferred in his heart the least ringlet that curled
Down her exquisite neck to the throne of the world.
T. MOORE, *Lalla Rookh: The Light of the Harem*

Rival.— Light me another Cuba; I hold to my first-sworn vows,
If Maggie will have no rival, I'll have no Maggie for spouse.[1] KIPLING, *The Betrothed*, st. 26

Rivals.— Of all the torments, all the cares,
With which our lives are cursed;
Of all the plagues a lover bears,
Sure rivals are the worst!
W. WALSH, *Rivalry in Love*

River.— Over the river they beckon to me,
Loved ones who've crossed to the farther side.
The gleam of their snowy robes I see,
But their voices are lost in the dashing tide.
N. A. W. PRIEST, *Over the River*

Rivulets.— Even as rivulets twain, from distant and separate sources,
Seeing each other afar, as they leap from the rocks, and pursuing
Each one its devious path, but drawing nearer and nearer,
Rush together at last, at their trysting-place in the forest;
So these lives that had run thus far in separate channels,
Coming in sight of each other, then swerving and flowing asunder,
Parted by barriers strong, but drawing nearer and nearer,
Rushed together at last, and one was lost in the other.
LONGFELLOW, *Courtship of Miles Standish*, viii, lines 94–101

Roar.— I will roar you as gently as any sucking dove; I will roar you an 'twere any nightingale.
SHAKESPEARE, *Midsummer-Night's Dream*, i, 2

---

[1] The ardent flame of love
My bosom cannot char,
I smoke, but do not burn,
So I have my cigar. HOOD, *The Cigar*, st. 13

Robbed.— He that is robbed, not wanting what is stolen,
Let him not know 't, and he 's not robbed at all.
SHAKESPEARE, *Othello*, iii, 3

Robe. My robe,
And my integrity to heaven, is all
I dare now call my own.
SHAKESPEARE, *King Henry VIII*, iii, 2

Robin Adair.— Come to my heart again,
Robin Adair;
Never to part again,
Robin Adair;
And if thou still art true,
I will be constant too,
And will wed none but you,
Robin Adair!
LADY CAROLINE KEPPEL, reputed author of *Robin Adair*

Rock.— Backward, turn backward, O Time, in your flight,
Make me a child again just for to-night!
Mother, come back from the echoless shore,
Take me again to your heart as of yore;
Kiss from my forehead the furrows of care,
Smooth the few silver threads out of my hair;
Over my slumbers your loving watch keep,—
Rock me to sleep, mother, rock me to sleep!
E. A. ALLEN, *Rock Me to Sleep*, st. 1

"Rock of ages, cleft for me,"
'Twas a woman sung them now,
Pleadingly and prayerfully;
Every word her heart did know.
Rose the song as storm-tossed bird
Beats with weary wing the air,
Every note with sorrow stirred,
Every syllable a prayer,—
"Rock of ages, cleft for me,
Let me hide myself in thee."
E. H. RICE, "*Rock of Ages*"

He smote the rock of the national resources, and abundant streams of revenue gushed forth. He touched the dead corpse of public credit, and it sprung upon its feet.
DANIEL WEBSTER, *Speech on Alexander Hamilton*

Rocket.— And the final event to himself [*Mr. Burke*] has been that as he rose like a rocket, he fell like the stick.
THOMAS PAINE, *Letter to the Addressers*

Rocks.— Now I hold it is not decent for a scientific gent
To say another is an ass,— at least, to all intent;
Nor should the individual who happens to be meant
Reply by heaving rocks at him, to any great extent.
BRET HARTE, *The Society upon the Stanislaus*, st. 6

Rod.— Severe by rule, and not by nature mild,
He never spoils the child and spares the rod,
But spoils the rod and never spares the child,
And so with holy rule deems he is reconciled.
HOOD, *The Irish Schoolmaster*, st. 12

And wilt thou . . . kiss the rod?[1]
SHAKESPEARE, *King Richard II*, v, 1

Rogue.— Damnable both-sides rogue.
SHAKESPEARE, *All's Well That Ends Well*, iv, 3

A pestilence on him for a mad rogue!
SHAKESPEARE, *Hamlet*, v, 1

Roller.— The league-long roller thundering on the reef.
TENNYSON, *Enoch Arden*, line 580

Roman.— Let's do it after the high Roman fashion.
SHAKESPEARE, *Antony and Cleopatra*, iv, 15 [13]

Who is here so rude that would not be a Roman?[2]
SHAKESPEARE, *Julius Cæsar*, iii, 2

This was the noblest Roman of them all.
SHAKESPEARE, *Julius Cæsar*, v, 5

Romans.— For Romans in Rome's quarrels
Spared neither land nor gold,
Nor son nor wife, nor limb nor life,
In the brave days of old.

Then none was for a party;
Then all were for the state;
Then the great man helped the poor,
And the poor man loved the great:
Then lands were fairly portioned;
Then spoils were fairly sold:
The Romans were like brothers
In the brave days of old.
MACAULAY, *Horatius*, st. 31, 32

Friends, Romans, countrymen, lend me your ears;
I come to bury Cæsar, not to praise him.
SHAKESPEARE, *Julius Cæsar*, iii, 2

---

[1] Whate'er thy lot,— whoe'er thou be,—
Confess thy folly,— kiss the rod,
And in thy chastening sorrows see
The hand of God. JAMES MONTGOMERY, *The Grave*, st. 24

How wayward is this foolish love,
That, like a testy babe, will scratch the nurse,
And presently, all humbled, kiss the rod!
SHAKESPEARE, *Two Gentlemen of Verona*, i, 2

[2] *Cf.* speech of Lord Palmerston in the Don Pacifico case, cited by JUSTIN McCARTHY, *History of Our Own Times*, xix.

Rome.— Rome shall perish — write that word
In the blood that she has spilt;
Perish, hopeless and abhorred,
Deep in ruin as in guilt. COWPER, *Boadicea*, st. 4

Rome, Rome! thou art no more
As thou hast been!
On thy seven hills of yore
Thou sat'st a queen.
FELICIA HEMANS, *Roman Girl's Song*, st. 1

The holy Church,
The great metropolis and see of Rome.
SHAKESPEARE, *King John*, v, 2

Romeo.— O Romeo, Romeo! wherefore art thou Romeo?
SHAKESPEARE, *Romeo and Juliet*, ii, 2

Rose.— The rose that all are praising
Is not the rose for me.
T. H. BAYLY, *The Rose That All Are Praising*

'Tis the last rose of summer
Left blooming alone;[1]
All her lovely companions
Are faded and gone.
T. MOORE, *The Last Rose of Summer*, st. 1

"Would," thought he, as the picture grows,
"I on its stalk had left the rose!
Oh, why should man's success remove
The very charms that wake his love?"[2]
SCOTT, *Marmion*, iii, st. 17

[1] One rose of the wilderness left on its stalk,
To mark where a garden had been. CAMPBELL, *Lines Written on Visiting a Scene in Argyleshire*, st. 2

The one red leaf, the last of its clan.
S. T. COLERIDGE, *Christabel*, I, line 49

One sad, ungathered rose
On my ancestral tree. HOLMES, *My Aunt*, st. 6

Earthlier happy is the rose distilled,
Than that which withering on the virgin thorn
Grows, lives, and dies in single blessedness.
SHAKESPEARE, *Midsummer-Night's Dream*, i, 1

[2] The butterfly from flower to flower
The urchin chased; and, when at last
He caught it in my lady's bower,
He cried, "Ha, Ha!" and held it fast.

Awhile he laughed, but soon he wept,
When looking at the prize he'd caught
And found he had to ruin swept
The very glory he had sought. JOSEPH SKIPSEY, *The Butterfly*

He that sweetest rose will find
Must find love's prick and Rosalind.
SHAKESPEARE, *As You Like It*, iii, 2

The rose upon my balcony the morning air perfuming,
Was leafless all the winter time and pining for the spring;
You ask me why her breath is sweet, and why her cheek
is blooming:
It is because the sun is out and birds begin to sing.
THACKERAY, *The Rose upon My Balcony*, st. 1

Go, lovely rose!
Tell her, that wastes her time and me,
That now she knows,
When I resemble her to thee,
How sweet and fair she seems to be.
WALLER, *Go, Lovely Rose*, st. 1

Rosebud.— A rosebud set with little wilful thorns,
And sweet as English air could make her, she.
TENNYSON, *The Princess*, Prologue, lines 153, 154

Rosebuds.— Gather ye rosebuds while ye may,[1]
Old Time is still a-flying;
And this same flower that smiles to-day,
To-morrow will be dying.
HERRICK, *To the Virgins, to Make Much of Time*

Rosemary.— There's rosemary, that's for remembrance.[2]
SHAKESPEARE, *Hamlet*, iv, 5

Roses.— There is a garden in her face,
Where roses and white lilies blow.
RICHARD ALLISON, *An Houre's Recreation in Musicke*

She wore a wreath of roses
The night that first we met.
T. H. BAYLY, *She Wore a Wreath of Roses*, st. 1

Poor Peggie hawks nosegays from street to street,
Till — think of that, who find life so sweet! —
She hates the smell of roses!
HOOD, *Miss Kilmansegg*, Her Birth

Fresh-blown roses washed in dew.[3]
MILTON, *L'Allegro*, line 22

---

[1] Let us crown ourselves with rosebuds before they be withered.
SOLOMON, *Wisdom*, ii, 8

[2] For you there's rosemary and rue; these keep
Seeming and savour all the winter long:
Grace and remembrance be to you both,
And welcome to our shearing. SHAKESPEARE, *Winter's Tale*, iv, 4 [3]

[3] As clear
As morning roses newly washed with dew.
SHAKESPEARE, *Taming of the Shrew*, ii

Rotten.— Something is rotten in the state of Denmark.
SHAKESPEARE, *Hamlet*, i, 4

Rove.— We hold our greyhound in our hand,
Our falcon in our glove;
But where shall we find leash or band
For dame that loves to rove?
Let the wild falcon soar her swing,
She 'll stoop when she has tired her wing.
SCOTT, *Marmion*, i, st. 17

Row.— A darned long row to hoe.
LOWELL, *Biglow Papers*, I, i, st. 13

Row, brothers, row, the stream runs fast,
The rapids are near and the daylight 's past.[1]
T. MOORE, *Canadian Boat Song*, st. 1

Rue.— There 's rue for you; and here 's some for me: we may call it herb-grace [herb of grace] o' Sundays.
SHAKESPEARE, *Hamlet*, iv, 5

Ruin.— With ruin upon ruin, rout on rout,
Confusion worse confounded.
MILTON, *Paradise Lost*, II, lines 995, 996

Rum.— There 's naught, no doubt, so much the spirit calms
As rum and true religion.
BYRON, *Don Juan*, Canto ii, st. 34

Rum I take to be the name which unwashed moralists apply alike to the product distilled from molasses and the noblest juices of the vineyard. "Burgundy[2] in all its sunset glow" is rum. Champagne, soul of "the foaming grape of Eastern France," is rum. Hock, which our friend, the Poet, speaks of as—
"The Rhine's breastmilk, gushing cold and bright,
Pale as the moon, and maddening as her light"[3]
—is rum.
HOLMES, *Autocrat of the Breakfast-Table*, viii

Running. In running, every pace
Is but between two legs a race,
In which both do their uttermost
To get before, and win the post;

---

[1] O comrades, hold! the longest reach is past;
The stream runs swift, and we are flying fast.
LAMPMAN, *Between the Rapids*, st. 2

[2] Burgundy in all its sunset glow. BYRON, *Don Juan*, Canto ii, st. 180

[3] HOLMES, *The Banker's Dinner*, st. 5.

Yet when they 're at their races' ends,
They 're still as kind and constant friends,
And, to relieve their weariness,
By turns give one another ease.

BUTLER, *Hudibras*, III, i, lines 895–902

With that, he gave his able horse the head,
And, bending forward, struck his armed heels
Against the panting sides of his poor jade
Up to the rowel-head, and, starting so,
He seemed in running to devour the way,
Staying no longer question.

SHAKESPEARE, *King Henry IV, Part II*, i, 1

Runs.— He that runs may read.[1]

COWPER, *Tirocinium*, line 80

Rust.— I were better to be eaten to death with [a] rust than to be scoured to nothing with perpetual motion.

SHAKESPEARE, *King Henry IV, Part II*, i, 2

Rusty.— Something to keep our souls from getting rusty.

HOLMES, *How Not to Settle It*, st. 6

Sabbath.— Raise not your scythe, suppressors of our vice!
Reforming saints, too delicately nice!
By whose decrees, our sinful souls to save,
No Sunday tankards foam, no barbers shave,
And beer undrawn and beards unmown display
Your holy reverence for the Sabbath day.[2]

BYRON, *English Bards and Scotch Reviewers*, lines 632–637

Did wisely from expensive sins refrain,
And never broke the Sabbath, but for gain:
Nor was he ever known an oath to vent,
Or curse, unless against the government.

DRYDEN, *Absalom and Achitophel*, I, lines 587–590

---

[1] Make it plain upon tables, that he may run that readeth it.

Habakkuk, ii, 2

[2] What! shut the Gardens! * lock the latticed gate!
Refuse the shilling and the Fellow's ticket!
And hang a wooden notice up to state,
"On Sundays no admittance at this wicket!"
The birds, the beasts, and all the reptile race
Denied to friends and visitors till Monday!
Now, really, this appears the common case
Of putting too much Sabbath into Sunday —
But what is your opinion, Mrs. Grundy?

HOOD, *An Open Question*, st. 1

* The Zoölogical Gardens, London.

Sack.— O monstrous! but one halfpenny-worth of bread to this intolerable deal of sack.
SHAKESPEARE, *King Henry IV, Part I*, ii, 4

If I do grow great, I 'll grow less; for I 'll purge, and leave sack, and live cleanly, as a nobleman should do.
Ibid., v, 4

Sad.— In sooth, I know not why I am so sad.
SHAKESPEARE, *Merchant of Venice*, i, 1

To make a sweet lady sad is a sour offence.
SHAKESPEARE, *Troilus and Cressida*, iii, 1

'T is impious, in a good man, to be sad.
YOUNG, *Night Thoughts*, IV, line 676

Sadder.— A sadder and a wiser man,
He rose the morrow morn.
COLERIDGE, *Ancient Mariner*, lines 624, 625

Saddest.— Of all sad words of tongue or pen,
The saddest are these: "It might have been."
WHITTIER, *Maud Muller*, st. 53[1]

Safety-valve.— So she came tearin' along that night —
The oldest craft on the line —
With a nigger squat on her safety-valve,
And her furnace crammed, rosin and pine.
JOHN HAY, *Jim Bludso, of the Prairie Belle*, st. 4

Sage.— He thought as a sage, though he felt as a man.
JAMES BEATTIE, *The Hermit*, st. 1

Sailor.— Lives like a drunken sailor on a mast,
Ready, with every nod, to tumble down
Into the fatal bowels of the deep.
SHAKESPEARE, *King Richard III*, iii, 4

Cease, rude Boreas, blustering railer!
List, ye landsmen, all to me;
Messmates, hear a brother sailor
Sing the dangers of the sea.
G. A. STEVENS, *The Storm*, st. 1

---

[1] Few poems have been parodied as much as this. The following humourous imitations are selected as examples of this form of poetical wit·

If, of all words of tongue and pen,
The saddest are, "It might have been,"
More sad are these we daily see:
"It is, but had n't ought to be."
BRET HARTE, *Mrs. Judge Jenkins*, st. 23, 24

These words are the saddest of tongue or of pen:
"Mr. Billings of Louisville touched me for ten."
EUGENE FIELD, *Mr. Billings of Louisville*, st 4

O mother, praying God will save
  Thy sailor,— while thy head is bowed,
  His heavy-shotted hammock-shroud
Drops in his vast and wandering grave.
TENNYSON, *In Memoriam*, vi, st. 4

The greatest sailor since our world began.
TENNYSON, *Ode on the Death of the Duke of Wellington*, st. 6

The sailor's wife the sailor's star shall be.
F. E. WEATHERLY, *Nancy Lee*

Sailors.— Believe not what the landsmen say
  Who tempt with doubts thy constant mind:
They 'll tell thee, sailors, when away,
  In every port a mistress find.
J. GAY, *Black-Eyed Susan*, st. 5

I recollect how sailors' rights was won,
Yard locked in yard, hot gun-lip kissin' gun.
LOWELL, *Biglow Papers*, II, ii, lines 235, 236

We know what risks all landsmen run,
  From noblemen to tailors;
Then, Bill, let us thank Providence,
  That you and I are sailors.
WILLIAM PITT (of Malta), *The Sailor's Consolation*

Saint. I 'm not a saint,
Not one of those self-constituted saints,
Quacks — not physicians — in the cure of souls
Censors who sniff out moral taints,
And call the devil over his own coals —
Those pseudo Privy Councillors of God,
Who write down judgments with a pen hard-nibbed;
  Ushers of Beelzebub's Black Rod,
Commending sinners, not to ice thick-ribbed,
But endless flames, to scorch them up like flax,—
Yet sure of heaven themselves, as if they 'd cribbed
Th' impression of Saint Peter's keys in wax!
HOOD, *Ode to Rae Wilson, Esquire*, st. 2

Able to corrupt a saint.
SHAKESPEARE, *King Henry IV, Part I*, i, 2

O cunning enemy, that, to catch a saint,
With saints dost bait thy hook! Most dangerous
Is that temptation that doth goad us on
To sin in loving virtue.
SHAKESPEARE, *Measure for Measure*, ii, 2

Kneel undisturbed, fair saint!
Pour out your praise or plaint
  Meekly and duly;
I will not enter there,
To sully your pure prayer
  With thoughts unruly.

THACKERAY, *At the Church Gate*, st. 4

Saint Keyne.— A well there is in the West country,
  And a clearer one never was seen;
There is not a wife in the West country
  But has heard of the Well of Saint Keyne.

. . . . .

'If the husband of this gifted well
  Shall drink before his wife,
A happy man henceforth is he,
  For he shall be master for life.

"But if the wife should drink of it first,
  Heaven help the husband then!"
The stranger stooped to the well of Saint Keyne,
  And drank of the water again.

SOUTHEY, *The Well of Saint Keyne*, st. 1, 10, 11

Saint Patrick.— Oh, St. Patrick was a gentleman,
  Who came of decent people;
He built a church in Dublin town,
  And on it put a steeple.
His father was a Gallagher;
  His mother was a Brady;
His aunt was an O'Shaughnessy,
  His uncle an O'Grady.

H. BENNETT, *St. Patrick Was a Gentleman*, st. 1

On the eighth day of March it was, some people say,
That St. Pathrick at midnight he first saw the day;
While others declare 't was the ninth he was born,
And 't was all a mistake between midnight and morn;
For mistakes will occur in a hurry and shock,
And some blamed the babby—and some blamed the clock —
Till with all their cross-questions sure no one could know
If the child was too fast, or the clock was too slow.

S. LOVER, *The Birth of St. Patrick*, st. 1

Saints. Saints will aid if men will call:
For the blue sky bends over all!

S. T. COLERIDGE, *Christabel*, I, lines 330, 331

We are n't no thin red 'eroes, nor we are n't no blackguards too,
But single men in barricks, most remarkable like you;
An' if sometimes our conduck is n't all your fancy paints:
Why, single men in barricks don't grow into plaster saints.
KIPLING, *Tommy*

Salad.— Our Garrick's a salad; for in him we see
Oil, vinegar, sugar, and saltness agree.
GOLDSMITH, *Retaliation*, st. 1

My salad days,
When I was green in judgment.
SHAKESPEARE, *Antony and Cleopatra*, i, 5

To make this condiment your poet begs
The pounded yellow of two hard-boiled eggs;
Two boiled potatoes, passed through kitchen sieve,
Smoothness and softness to the salad give;
Let onion atoms lurk within the bowl,
And, half suspected, animate the whole;
Of mordant mustard add a single spoon,
Distrust the condiment that bites too soon;
But deem it not, thou man of herbs, a fault
To add a double quantity of salt.
Four times the spoon with oil from Lucca crown,
And twice with vinegar, procured from town;
And lastly, o'er the flavoured compound toss
A magic *soupçon* of anchovy sauce.
O green and glorious! O herbaceous treat!
'T would tempt the dying anchorite to eat;
Back to the world he'd turn his fleeting soul,
And plunge his fingers in the salad-bowl;
Serenely full, the epicure would say,
"Fate cannot harm me,— I have dined to-day."
SYDNEY SMITH, *Recipe for Salad*

Salt.— I have eaten your bread and salt,
I have drunk your water and wine,
The deaths ye died I have watched beside,
And the lives that ye led were mine.
KIPLING, *Departmental Ditties*, Prelude, st. 1

Samaritan.— Yes! you find people ready enough to do the Samaritan without the oil and the twopence.
SYDNEY SMITH, *Wit and Wisdom: Table Talk*

Sands.— Come unto these yellow sands.
SHAKESPEARE, *The Tempest*, i, 2 (Ariel's Song)

Sandstone.— Then Abner Dean, of Angel's, rose to a point of order, when
A chunk of old red sandstone took him in the abdomen,
And he smiled a kind of sickly smile, and curled up on the floor
And the subsequent proceedings interested him no more.
BRET HARTE, *The Society upon the Stanislaus*, st. 7

Sandwich.— How Shem's proud children reared the Assyrian piles,
While Ham's were scattered through the Sandwich Isles.
HOLMES, *A Modest Request, The Speech*, lines 21, 22

Sarcastic.— He was a most sarcastic man, this quiet Mr. Brown,
And on several occasions he had cleaned out the town.
BRET HARTE, *The Society upon the Stanislaus*, st. 5

Satan. Satan trembles when he sees
The weakest saint upon his knees.
COWPER, *Exhortation to Prayer*, st. 3

Satire.— Fools are my theme, let satire be my song.
BYRON, *English Bards and Scotch Reviewers*, line 6

Satire should, like a polished razor keen,
Wound with a touch that's scarcely felt or seen.
LADY M. W. MONTAGU, *To the Imitator of the First Satire of Horace*, ii

Satire's my weapon, but I'm too discreet
To run amuck, and tilt at all I meet.
POPE, *Horace*, II, Satire i, line 69

Savage.— I am as free as nature first made man,
Ere the base laws of servitude began,
When wild in woods the noble savage ran.
DRYDEN, *The Conquest of Granada*, I, i, 1

I will take some savage woman, she shall rear my dusky race.

Iron-jointed, supple-sinewed, they shall dive, and they shall run,
Catch the wild goat by the hair, and hurl their lances in the sun;

Whistle back the parrot's call, and leap the rainbows of the brooks,
Not with blinded eyesight poring over miserable books.
TENNYSON, *Locksley Hall*, lines 168–172

Saviour.— Owning her weakness,
Her evil behaviour,
And leaving, with meekness,
Her sins to her Saviour!
HOOD, *The Bridge of Sighs*, st. 18

Say.— Though I say it that should not say it.
BEAUMONT AND FLETCHER, *Wit at Several Weapons*, ii, 2; FIELDING, *The Miser*, iii, 2; CIBBER, *Rival Fools*, ii; *Fall of British Tyranny*, iv, 2

Scaffold.— He is coming! he is coming!
Like a bridegroom from his room,
Came the hero from his prison
To the scaffold and the doom.
There was glory on his forehead,
There was lustre in his eye,
And he never walked to battle
More proudly than to die.
W. E. AYTOUN, *The Execution of Montrose*, st. 15

Scale.— A feather will turn the scale.[1]
SHAKESPEARE, *Measure for Measure*, iv, 2

Scandal.— No scandal about Queen Elizabeth, I hope.
R. B. SHERIDAN, *The Critic*, ii, 1

Scandals.— Dead scandals form good subjects for dissection.
BYRON, *Don Juan*, Canto i, st. 31

There's a lust in man no charm can tame
Of loudly publishing our neighbour's shame;
On eagles' wings immortal scandals fly,
While virtuous actions are but born and die.
STEPHEN HARVEY, *Juvenal's Satire, ix*

Scars.— He jests at scars that never felt a wound.
SHAKESPEARE, *Romeo and Juliet*, ii, 2

Scattered — All are scattered now and fled,
Some are married, some are dead.
LONGFELLOW, *The Old Clock on the Stairs*, st. 8

Schnapps.— Und he gife dem moral lessons,
How pefore de battle pops:
"Take a liddle brayer to Himmel,
Und a goot long trink of schnapps."
C. G. LELAND, *Breitmann in Bivouac*, st. 2

---

[1] The weight of a hair will turn the scales between their avoirdupois.
SHAKESPEARE, *King Henry IV, Part II*, ii, 4

Schoolboy.— A schoolboy's tale, the wonder of an hour.
BYRON, *Childe Harold's Pilgrimage*, Canto ii, st. 2

The whining schoolboy, with his satchel
And shining morning face, creeping like snail
Unwillingly to school.
SHAKESPEARE, *As You Like It*, ii, 7

Schoolmaster.— Let the soldier be abroad if he will, he can do nothing in this age. There is another personage, a personage less imposing in the eyes of some, perhaps insignificant. The schoolmaster is abroad, and I trust to him, armed with his primer, against the soldier in full military array.
LORD BROUGHAM, *Speech*, Jan. 29, 1828

Science.— Here about the beach I wandered, nourishing a youth sublime
With the fairy tales of science, and the long result of Time.
TENNYSON, *Locksley Hall*, lines 11, 12

Scoff.— Truth from his lips prevailed with double sway,
And fools, who came to scoff, remained to pray.
GOLDSMITH, *The Deserted Village*, st. 13

Scornful.— Never a scornful word should grieve ye,
I'd smile on ye sweet as the angels do;—
Sweet as your smile on me shone ever,
Douglas, Douglas, tender and true.
D. M. MULOCK CRAIK, *Too Late*, st. 2

Scotch.— Tell them . . . how well I speak of Scotch politeness, and Scotch hospitality, and Scotch beauty, and of everything Scotch, but Scotch oat-cakes, and Scotch prejudices.
SAMUEL JOHNSON, *Life*, by Boswell, May 27, 1775

Scotia.— From scenes like these old Scotia's grandeur springs,
That makes her loved at home, revered abroad.
BURNS, *The Cotter's Saturday Night*, st. 19

Scoundrels.— Some of the craftiest scoundrels that ever . . . crawled and crept through life by its dirtiest and narrowest ways will gravely jot down in diaries the events of every day, and keep a regular debtor and creditor account with Heaven, which shall always show a floating balance in their own favour.
DICKENS, *Nicholas Nickleby*, xliv

Screech-owls.— The time when screech-owls cry, and bandogs howl,
And spirits walk, and ghosts break up their graves.
SHAKESPEARE, *King Henry VI, Part II*, i, 4

Scribbler.— Who shames a scribbler? break one cobweb through,
He spins the slight, self-pleasing thread anew:
Destroy his fib or sophistry, in vain,
The creature's at his dirty work again,
Throned in the centre of his thin designs,
Proud of a vast extent of flimsy lines!
POPE, *Epistle to Dr. Arbuthnot*, lines 89–94

Scripture.— The devil can cite Scripture for his purpose.[1]
SHAKESPEARE, *Merchant of Venice*, i, 3

Scruple.— I will not bate thee a scruple.
SHAKESPEARE, *All's Well That Ends Well*, ii, 3

Scruples.—His scruples thus silenced, Tom felt more at ease,
And went with his comrades the apples to seize;
He blamed and protested, but joined in the plan:
He shared in the plunder, but pitied the man.
COWPER, *Pity for Poor Africans*, st. 11

Scylla.— When I shun Scylla . . . I fall into Charybdis.
SHAKESPEARE, *Merchant of Venice*, iii, 5

Sea.[2]— We were the first that ever burst
Into that silent sea.
COLERIDGE, *Ancient Mariner*, lines 105, 106

Safe in ourselves, while on ourselves we stand,
The sea is ours, and that defends the land.
Be, then, the naval stores the nation's care,
New ships to build, and battered to repair.
DRYDEN, *Epistle to John Dryden*, lines 146–149

In calm magnificence the sun declined,
And left a paradise of clouds behind:
Proud at his feet, with pomp of pearl and gold,
The billows in a sea of glory rolled.
JAMES MONTGOMERY, *The West Indies*, i, st. 5

When the loud trumpet of eternal doom
Shall break the mortal bondage of the tomb;
When with a mother's pangs the expiring earth
Shall bring her children forth to second birth;

---

[1] Satan uses Bible words.— WHITTIER, *The Witch of Wenham*, I, st. 14

[2] *Cf.* OCEAN.

Sea—*Continued*

Then shall the sea's mysterious caverns, spread
With human relics, render up their dead.[1]
JAMES MONTGOMERY, *The West Indies*, iii, st. 6

The sea! the sea! the open sea!
The blue, the fresh, the ever free!
B. W. PROCTER, *The Sea*, st. 1

A thousand miles from land are we,
Tossing about on the roaring [stormy] sea.
B. W. PROCTER, *The Stormy Petrel*, st. 1

Like the ocean-bird, our home
We'll find far out on the sea.
EPES SARGENT, *A Life on the Ocean Wave*, st. 2

The empire of the sea.
SHAKESPEARE, *Antony and Cleopatra*, i, 2

Now would I give a thousand furlongs of sea for an acre of barren ground, long heath, brown furze, any thing. SHAKESPEARE, *The Tempest*, i, 1

Rolled to starboard, rolled to larboard, when the surge was seething free,
Where the wallowing monster spouted his foam-fountains in the sea.
TENNYSON, *The Lotos-Eaters — Choric Song*, st. 8

And compassed by the inviolate sea.
TENNYSON, *To the Queen*

Of Christian souls more have been wrecked on shore
Than ever were lost at sea!
C. H. WEBB, *With a Nantucket Shell*, st. 4

---

[1] What hidest thou in thy treasure-caves and cells?
Thou hollow-sounding and mysterious main!
Pale glistening pearls and rainbow-coloured shells,
Bright things which gleam unrecked of and in vain! —
Keep, keep thy riches, melancholy sea!
We ask not such from thee.

. . . . .

Yet more! the billows and the depths have more!
High hearts and brave are gathered to thy breast!
They hear not now the booming waters roar,
The battle thunders will not break their rest.

. . . . .

To thee the love of woman hath gone down.
Dark flow thy tides o'er manhood's noble head,
O'er youth's bright locks, and beauty's flowery crown;
Yet must thou hear a voice — Restore the dead!
Earth shall reclaim her precious things from thee! —
Restore the dead, thou sea!
FELICIA HEMANS, *The Treasures of the Deep*, st. 1, 4, 6

Seamen. The church
And yard are full of seamen's graves, and few
Have any names.
JEAN INGELOW, *Brothers, and a Sermon*

Seas.— Ye gentlemen of England
That live at home at ease,
Ah! little do you think upon
The dangers of the seas.
MARTIN PARKER, *Ye Gentlemen of England*

See.— Oh, wad some power the giftie gie us
To see oursel's as others see us![1]
It wad frae monie a blunder free us
And foolish notion. BURNS, *To a Louse*, st. 8

To see and not be seen.— BEN JONSON, *Epithalamion*, st. 3; DRYDEN, *Ovid's Art of Love*, I, line 109; GOLDSMITH, *Citizen of the World*, Letter 71

Seed.— The seed ye sow, another reaps;
The wealth ye find, another keeps;
The robes ye weave, another wears;
The arms ye forge, another bears.

Sow seed,— but let no tyrant reap;[2]
Find wealth,— let no impostor heap;
Weave robes,— let not the idle wear;
Forge arms,— in your defence to bear.
SHELLEY, *Song to the Men of England*, st. 5, 6

Seeds.— We scatter seeds with careless hand,
And dream we ne'er shall see them more;
But for a thousand years
Their fruit appears,
In weeds that mar the land,
Or healthful store. KEBLE, *Example*, st. 1

Seek. 'T is in vain
To seek him here that means not to be found.
SHAKESPEARE, *Romeo and Juliet*, ii, 1

Seen. Oh, woe is me,
To have seen what I have seen, see what I see!
SHAKESPEARE, *Hamlet*, iii, 1

Self-approving.— One self-approving hour whole years outweighs
Of stupid starers, and of loud huzzas.
POPE, *Essay on Man*, Epistle iv, lines 255, 256

---

[1] Oh, that you could turn your eyes toward the napes of your necks, and make but an interior survey of your good selves.
SHAKESPEARE, *Coriolanus*, ii, 1

[2] *Cf.* WORKER.

Self-defence.— Self-defence is nature's eldest law.
DRYDEN, *Absalom and Achitophel*, I, line 458

Selfishness.— Selfishness, Love's cousin.
KEATS, *Isabella, or the Pot of Basil*, st. 31

Self-love.— Self-love, my liege, is not so vile a sin
As self-neglecting. SHAKESPEARE, *King Henry V*, ii, 4

Self-sacrifice.— The long self-sacrifice of life is o'er.
The great World-victor's victor will be seen no more.
TENNYSON, *Ode on the Death of the Duke of Wellington*, st. 4

Selleth.— When he that selleth house or land
Shows leak in roof or flaw in right.
HOLMES, *Latter-Day Warnings*, st. 2

Senator.— *Brabantio.* Thou art a villain.
Iago. You are — a senator.—SHAKESPEARE, *Othello*, i, 1

Sense.— Know, sense, like charity, begins at home.
POPE, *Umbra*, line 16

Sensible. A sensible man,
He stays to his home an' looks arter his folks;
He draws his furrer ez straight ez he can,
An' into nobody's tater-patch pokes.
LOWELL, *Biglow Papers*, I, iii, st. 1

Separation.— When, in the course of human events, it becomes necessary for one people to dissolve the political bonds which have connected them with another, and to assume among the powers of the earth the separate and equal station to which the laws of nature and of nature's God entitle them, a decent respect to the opinions of mankind requires that they should declare the causes which impel them to the separation.
THOMAS JEFFERSON, *Declaration of Independence*

Serpent.— The trail of the Serpent is over them all!
T. MOORE, *Lalla Rookh: Paradise and the Peri*

My serpent of old Nile.
SHAKESPEARE, *Antony and Cleopatra*, i, 5

The serpent that did sting thy father's life
Now wears his crown. SHAKESPEARE, *Hamlet*, i, 5

Wouldst thou have a serpent sting thee twice?
SHAKESPEARE, *Merchant of Venice*, iv, 1

Servant.— Servant of God, well done!
MILTON, *Paradise Lost*, VI, line 29

Let me be your servant:
Though I look old, yet I am strong and lusty;[1]
For in my youth I never did apply
Hot and rebellious liquors in my blood,
Nor did not with unbashful forehead woo
The means of weakness and debility;
Therefore my age is as a lusty winter,
Frosty, but kindly.—SHAKESPEARE, *As You Like It*, ii, 3

Served. O Cromwell, Cromwell!
Had I but served my God with half the zeal
I served my king, he would not in mine age
Have left me naked to mine enemies.
SHAKESPEARE, *King Henry VIII*, iii, 2

Serves.— Not thine, nor mine, to question or reply
When He commands us, asking "how?" or "why?"
He knows the cause; His ways are wise and just;
Who serves the King must serve with perfect trust.
HENRY VAN DYKE, *A Legend of Service*, st. 6

Service.— I'll do the service of a younger man.
SHAKESPEARE, *As You Like It*, ii, 3

Servitor.— Then rose the dumb old servitor, and the dead,
Steered [oared] by the dumb, went upward with the flood.
TENNYSON, *Launcelot and Elaine*, lines 1146, 1147

Sex. The masculine attire
In which they roughen to the sense, and all
The winning softness of their sex is lost.
THOMSON, *The Seasons*, Autumn, lines 576–578

Sexton.— Nigh to a grave that was newly made,
Leaned a sexton old on his earth-worn spade;

. . . . .

A relic of bygone days was he,
And his locks were white as the foamy sea;
And these words came from his lips so thin:
"I gather them in: I gather them in."
PARK BENJAMIN, *The Old Sexton*, st. 1

O sextant! there are one kermoddity
Wich's more than gold wich don't cost nothin',
Wuth more than anything except the sole of man!
I mean pewer are, sextant, I mean pewer are.
ARABELLA M. WILLSON, *To the Sextant*

[1] Old as I am, my lusty limbs appear
Like winter greens, that flourish all the year.
POPE, *January and May*, lines 135, 136

Shadow. Hence, horrible shadow!
Unreal mockery, hence! — SHAKESPEARE, *Macbeth*, iii, 4

Shadows.—'Tis the sunset of life gives me mystical lore,
And coming events cast their shadows before.[1]
THOMAS CAMPBELL, *Lochiel's Warning*, st. 5

Come like shadows, so depart.
SHAKESPEARE, *Macbeth*, iv, 1

Shaft.— Oh, many a shaft at random sent,
Finds mark the archer little meant!
And many a word, at random spoken,
May soothe or wound a heart that's broken.
SCOTT, *Lord of the Isles*, Canto v, st. 18

Shaken.— When taken
To be well shaken.
G. COLMAN, THE YOUNGER, *The Newcastle Apothecary*

Shakespeare.— *Kitty*. Shikspur? Shikspur? Who wrote it? No, I never read Shikspur.
Lady Bab. Then you have an immense pleasure to come. J. TOWNLEY, *High Life Below Stairs*, ii, 1

Shame.— As Mary rose at Jesus' word,
Redeemed and white before the Lord!
Reclaim thy lost soul! In His name,
Rise up, and break thy bonds of shame.
WHITTIER, *A Woman*

Shamed.— Whatever record leap to light
He never shall be shamed.—TENNYSON, *Ode on the Death of the Duke of Wellington*, st. 7

She.— Whoe'er she be,
That not impossible she,
That shall command my heart and me.
CRASHAW, *Wishes to His Supposed Mistress*, st. 1

The fair, the chaste, and unexpressive she.
SHAKESPEARE, *As You Like It*, iii, 2

Sheepfold.— De massa ob de sheepfol'
Dat guards de sheepfol' bin
Goes down in de gloomerin' meadows,
Wha'r de long night rain begin —
So he le' down de ba's ob de sheepfol',
Callin' sof', "Come in! Come in!"
Callin' sof', "Come in! Come in!"

---

[1] The spirits
Of great events stride on before the events.
S. T. COLERIDGE, *Death of Wallenstein*, v. 1, line 101

Den up t'ro' de gloomerin' meadows,
T'ro' de col' night rain and win',
And up t'ro' de gloomerin' rain-paf',
Wha'r de sleet fa' pie'cin' thin,
De po' los' sheep ob de sheepfol',
Dey all comes gadderin' in.
SARAH PRATT McLEAN GREEN, *De Sheepfol'*, st. 2, 3

Sheet.— A wet sheet and a flowing sea,
A wind that follows fast
And fills the white and rustling sail
And bends the gallant mast.
A. CUNNINGHAM, *A Wet Sheet and a Flowing Sea*, st. 1

Sheets.— After I saw him fumble with the sheets, and play with flowers, and smile upon his fingers' ends, I knew there was but one way; for his nose was as sharp as a pen, and a' babbled of green fields.
SHAKESPEARE, *King Henry V*, ii, 3

Sheridan.— Sighing that Nature formed but one such man,
And broke the die — in moulding Sheridan!
BYRON, *Monody on the Death of R. B. Sheridan*, st. 3

Shilling.— Happy the man who, void of cares and strife,
In silken or in leathern purse retains
A splendid shilling.
JOHN PHILIPS, *The Splendid Shilling*

Ship.— The ship was cheered, the harbour cleared.
COLERIDGE, *Ancient Mariner*, line 21

As idle as a painted ship
Upon a painted ocean. *Ibid.*, lines 117, 118

A ship is worse than a gaol. There is in a gaol, better air, better company, better conveniency of every kind; and a ship has the additional disadvantage of being in danger.[1] SAMUEL JOHNSON, *Life*, by Boswell, 1776

Don't give up the ship!— JAMES LAWRENCE, *Exclamation on being wounded on board the "Chesapeake"*

Thou, too, sail on, O Ship of State!
Sail on, O Union, strong and great!
LONGFELLOW, *Building of the Ship*, st. 25

---

[1] Ships are but boards, sailors but men: there be land-rats and water-rats, water-thieves and land-thieves, I mean pirates: and then there is the peril of waters, winds, and rocks. SHAKESPEARE, *Merchant of Venice*, i, 3

In case signals cannot be seen or clearly understood, no captain can do wrong if he places his ship alongside that of an enemy. — HORATIO, VISCOUNT NELSON,[1]
quoted by SOUTHEY, *Life of Nelson*, ix

Ships.— I have ships that went to sea
More than fifty years ago;
None have yet come home to me,
But are sailing to and fro.[2]
R. S. COFFIN, *Ships at Sea*, st. 1

Ships that pass in the night, and speak each other in passing,
Only a signal shown and a distant voice in the darkness;
So on the ocean of life we pass and speak one another,
Only a look and a voice, then darkness again and a silence.[3]
LONGFELLOW, *Elizabeth*, iv, lines 1–4

Spanish sailors with bearded lips,
And the beauty and mystery of the ships,
And the magic of the sea.
LONGFELLOW, *My Lost Youth*, st. 3

Shirt.— To treat a poor wretch with a bottle of Burgundy and fill his snuff-box is like giving a pair of laced ruffles to a man that has never a shirt on his back.[4]
TOM BROWN, *Laconics*

The loss of wealth is loss of dirt,
As sages in all times assert;
The happy man's without a shirt.
J. HEYWOOD, *Be Merry, Friends*

With fingers weary and worn,
With eyelids heavy and red,
A woman sat, in unwomanly rags,
Plying her needle and thread —
Stitch — stitch — stitch!

---

[1] Order issued by Nelson before the battle of Trafalgar. *Cf.* DUTY, quotation from NELSON; also FIRE, quotation from VILLENEUVE.

[2] To-day a song is on my lips:
Earth seems a paradise to me:
For God is good, and, lo, my ships
Are coming home from sea! G. ARNOLD, *Jubilate*, st. 3

[3] And soon, too soon, we part with pain,
To sail o'er silent seas again. T. MOORE, *Meeting of the Ships*, st. 3

[4] Such dainties to them, their health it might hurt;
It's like sending them ruffles when wanting a shirt.
GOLDSMITH, *The Haunch of Venison*, st. 2

In poverty, hunger, and dirt,
And still with a voice of dolorous pitch,—
Would that its tone could reach the rich!—
She sang this "Song of the Shirt!"[1]
HOOD, *The Song of the Shirt*

There's but a shirt and a half in all my company; and the half-shirt is two napkins tacked together and thrown over the shoulders like an herald's coat without sleeves.
SHAKESPEARE, *King Henry IV*, *Part I*, iv, 2

He always used to wear a shirt
For thirty days, all seasons, day and night:
Good man, he knew it was not right
For dust and ashes to fall out with dirt;
And then he only hung it out in the rain,
And put it on again. SOUTHEY, *Saint Romauld*, st. 2

Shoe.— No man knows so well where the shoe pinches as he who wears it.[2]—LINCOLN, *Letter to Secretary Chase*, June 28, 1864

Shoes.— Here's to the day when it is May,
And care as light as a feather,
When your little shoes and my big boots
Go tramping over the heather.

Here's to the night when our delight
Shall hold the stars in a tether,
And your little shoes and my big boots
Are under the bed together.— BLISS CARMAN, *A Toast*

Shop. Miss, the mercer's plague, from shop to shop
Wandering, and littering with unfolded silks
The polished counter, and approving none,
Or promising with smiles to call again.
COWPER, *The Task: Winter Walk at Noon*, lines 279–282

Shopkeepers.— To found a great empire for the sole purpose of raising up a people of customers, may at first sight appear a project fit only for a nation of shopkeepers.[3]
ADAM SMITH, *Wealth of Nations*, IV, vii, 3

Short.— This is the short and the long of it.
SHAKESPEARE, *Merry Wives of Windsor*, ii, 2

---

[1] "He sang The Song of the Shirt."
Inscription on Hood's monument in Kensal Green Cemetery

[2] This saying is, of course, proverbial.

[3] A nation of traders. NAPOLEON BONAPARTE, *Life*, by Sloane, II, 186

Shot.— By the rude bridge that arched the flood,
Their flag to April's breeze unfurled,
Here once the embattled farmers stood,
And fired the shot heard round the world.
EMERSON, *Concord Hymn*, st. 1

Shout. The inhuman shout which hailed the wretch who won.
BYRON, *Childe Harold's Pilgrimage*, Canto iv, st. 140

Showest.— Have more than thou showest,
Speak less than thou knowest,
Lend less than thou owest,
Ride more than thou goest,
Learn more than thou trowest,
Set less than thou throwest; . . .
And thou shalt have more
Than two tens to a score.
SHAKESPEARE, *King Lear*, i, 4

Shrew.— The veriest shrew of all.
SHAKESPEARE, *Taming of the Shrew*, v, 2

Shrieks.— Not louder shrieks to pitying heav'n are cast,
When husbands, or when lapdogs breathe their last;
Or when rich china vessels fall'n from high,
In glitt'ring dust and painted fragments lie![1]
POPE, *Rape of the Lock*, iii, lines 157–160

Shroud. When thoughts
Of the last bitter hour come like a blight
Over thy spirit, and sad images
Of the stern agony, and shroud, and pall,
And breathless darkness, and the narrow house,
Make thee to shudder, and grow sick at heart,—
Go forth, under the open sky, and list
To Nature's teachings.
BRYANT, *Thanatopsis*, lines 8–15

Sewing at once with a double thread
A shroud as well as a shirt.
HOOD, *The Song of the Shirt*

How swift the shuttle flies, that weaves thy shroud.
YOUNG, *Night Thoughts*, IV, line 810

Sick. You'll be sick to-morrow
For this night's watching.
SHAKESPEARE, *Romeo and Juliet*, iv, 4

---

[1] And mistress of herself, though china fall.
POPE, *Moral Essays*, Epistle ii, line 268

Sickness.— I'm sick of gruel, and the dietetics,
I'm sick of pills, and sicker of emetics,
I'm sick of pulses' tardiness or quickness,
I'm sick of blood, its thinness or its thickness,—
In short, within a word, I'm sick of sickness!
HOOD, *Fragment, Probably Written during Illness*

Side-curl.— When a young female wears a flat circular side-curl, gummed on each temple,— when she walks with a male, not arm in arm, but with his arm against the back of hers,— and when she says "Yes?" with the note of interrogation, you are generally safe in asking her what wages she gets, and who the "feller" was you saw her with. HOLMES, *Autocrat of the Breakfast-Table*, i

Sides.— Much may be said on both sides.
H. FIELDING, *The Covent Garden Tragedy*, i, 8

Sigh.— Here's a sigh to those who love me,
And a smile to those who hate;[1]
BYRON, *To Thomas Moore*, st. 2

What a sigh is there! The heart is sorely charged.[2]
SHAKESPEARE, *Macbeth*, v, 1

Sighed.— Had sighed to many, though he loved but one,[3]
And that loved one, alas! could ne'er be his.
BYRON, *Childe Harold's Pilgrimage*, Canto i, st. 5

Sighed and looked, and sighed again.
DRYDEN, *Alexander's Feast*, line 113

Sighs.—My story being done,
She gave me for my pains a world of sighs:
She swore, in faith, 't was strange, 't was passing strange,
'T was pitiful, 't was wondrous pitiful:
She wished she had not heard it, yet she wished
That heaven had made her such a man: she thanked me,
And bade me, if I had a friend that loved her,
I should but teach him how to tell my story,
And that would woo her. Upon this hint I spake:
She loved me for the dangers I had passed,
And I loved her that she did pity them.
SHAKESPEARE, *Othello*, i, 3

---

[1] With a pardon for the foes who hate,
And a prayer for those who love us.
ELIZA COOK, *Song for the New Year*, st. 3

[2] He raised a sigh so piteous and profound
That [as] it did seem to shatter all his bulk.— SHAKESPEARE, *Hamlet*, ii, 1

[3] He'd sparked it with full twenty gals,
He'd squired 'em, danced 'em, druv 'em,
Fust this one, an' then thet, by spells —
All is, he couldn't love 'em. LOWELL, *The Courtin'*, st. 9

Sight.— And out of mind, as soon as out of sight.[1]
LORD BROOKE, *Sonnet lvi*

Silence.— There was silence deep as death;
And the boldest held his breath
For a time. T. CAMPBELL, *Battle of the Baltic*, st. 2

Silence, like a poultice, comes
To heal the blows of sound.
HOLMES, *The Music-Grinders*, st. 10

Silence in love bewrays more woe
Than words, tho' ne'er so witty;
A beggar that is dumb you know,
May challenge double pity.
RALEIGH, *The Silent Lover*, st. 8

Silk.— And ye sall walk in silk attire,
And siller hae to spare,
Gin ye'll consent to be his bride,
Nor think o' Donald mair.
SUSANNA BLAMIRE, *The Siller Croun*, st. 1

Some marrowy crapes of China silk,
Like wrinkled skins on scalded milk.
HOLMES, *Contentment*, st. 6

Simile.— One simile, that solitary shines
In the dry desert of a thousand lines.
POPE, *Imitations of Horace*, II, Epistle i, lines 111, 112

Simon.— The real Simon Pure.
SUSANNA CENTLIVRE, *A Bold Stroke for a Wife*, v, 1

Simplicity.— Give me a look, give me a face,
That makes simplicity a grace:
Robes loosely flowing, hair as free:
Such sweet neglect more taketh me,
Than all the adulteries of art;
They strike mine eyes, but not my heart.[2]
BEN JONSON, *The Silent Woman*, i, 1

She 's modest as ony, and blithe as she 's bonnie,—
For guileless simplicity marks her its ain;
And far be the villain, divested of feeling,
Wha 'd blight in its bloom the sweet flower o' Dumblane.
R. TANNAHILL, *The Flower o' Dumblane*, st. 3

---

[1] To-day man is; to-morrow he is gone. And when he is out of sight, quickly also is he out of mind.
THOMAS À KEMPIS, *Imitation of Christ*, I, xxiii, 1

[2] A sweet disorder in the dress
Kindles in clothes a wantonness: . . .
A careless shoe-string, in whose tie
I see a wild civility:
Do more bewitch me, than when art
Is too precise in every part. HERRICK, *Delight in Disorder*

In the complicated agitation of modern existence, our wearied souls dream of simplicity.
CHARLES WAGNER, *The Simple Life*, Preface

Sin.— This uneradicable taint of sin.
BYRON, *Childe Harold's Pilgrimage*, Canto iv, st. 126

'Twas best, he said, mankind should cease to sin.
TIMOTHY DWIGHT, *The Smoothe Divine*, line 11

Said I not so, that I would sin no more?
Witness my God, I did;
Yet I am run again upon the score:
My faults cannot be hid.
GEORGE HERBERT, *Vows Broken and Renewed*, st. 1

The sin ye do by two and two ye must pay for one by one.
KIPLING, *Tomlinson*

Man-like is it to fall into sin,
Fiend-like is it to dwell therein,
Christ-like is it for sin to grieve,
God-like is it all sin to leave.
LONGFELLOW, *Sin*, from the German of F. von Logau

O Thou, who didst with pitfall and with gin
Beset the road I was to wander in,
Thou wilt not with predestined evil round
Enmesh, and then impute my fall to sin!
OMAR KHAYYÁM, *Rubáiyát* (trans. Fitzgerald), st. 80

For Charlie's sake I will arise;
I will anoint me where he lies,
And change my raiment, and go in
To the Lord's house, and leave my sin
Without, and seat me at his board,
Eat, and be glad, and praise the Lord.
For wherefore should I fast and weep,
And sullen moods of mourning keep?
I cannot bring him back, nor he,
For any calling, come to me.
The bond the angel Death did sign,
God sealed — for Charlie's sake, and mine.
J. W. PALMER, *For Charlie's Sake*, st. 4

Water cannot wash away your sin.
SHAKESPEARE, *King Richard II*, iv

Some rise by sin, and some by virtue fall.
SHAKESPEARE, *Measure for Measure*, ii, 1

God said of old to a woman like me,
"Go, sin no more," or your Bibles lie;
But you, you mangle his merciful words
To "Go, and sin till you die!"
R. H. STODDARD, *On the Town*, st. 15

No mercy now can clear her brow
  For this world's peace to pray;
For, as love's wild prayer dissolved in air,
  Her woman's heart gave way! —
But the sin forgiven by Christ in Heaven
  By man is cursed alway!

N. P. WILLIS, *Unseen Spirits*, st. 5

Sinful.— A sinful heart makes feeble hand.

SCOTT, *Marmion*, vi, 31

Sing.— Swans sing before they die,—'t were no bad thing
Did certain persons die before they sing.

S. T. COLERIDGE, *On a Bad Singer*

Single.— Nothing in the world is single,
All things by a law divine
In one another's being mingle—[1]
Why not I with thine?

SHELLEY, *Love's Philosophy*, st. 1

Oh, fie upon this single life! forego it.

J. WEBSTER, *Duchess of Malfi*, iii, 2

Sink.— Sink or swim, live or die, survive or perish, I give my hand and my heart to this vote.

DANIEL WEBSTER, *Eulogy on Adams and Jefferson*, delivered in Boston, Aug. 2, 1826

Sinned. Sinned I not
But in mistaking.

SHAKESPEARE, *Much Ado about Nothing*, v, 1

Sinning. I am a man
More sinned against than sinning.

SHAKESPEARE, *King Lear*, iii, 2

Sins.— Compound for sins they are inclined to,
By damning those they have no mind to.

BUTLER, *Hudibras*, I, i, lines 215, 216

When you break up housekeeping, you learn the extent
    of your treasures;
  Till he begins to reform, no one can number his sins.

JOHN HAY, *Distichs*, ix

Unto each man comes a day when his favourite sins all
    forsake him,
  And he complacently thinks he has forsaken his sins.

Ibid., xi

---

[1] Another reading is: In one spirit meet and mingle.

That frown upon Saint Giles's sins, but blink
The peccadilloes of all Piccadilly.[1]
HOOD, *Ode to Rae Wilson, Esquire*, st. 12

Commit
The oldest sins the newest kind of ways.
SHAKESPEARE, *King Henry IV, Part II*, iv, 5 [4]

Sires. Few sons attain the praise
Of their great sires, and most their sires disgrace.
POPE, *The Odyssey*, II, lines 315, 316

Sixpence.— I give thee sixpence! I will see thee damned first. CANNING, *The Friend of Humanity and the Knife-Grinder*, st. 9

Skies.— They change their skies above them,
But not their hearts that roam!
KIPLING, *The Native-Born*, st. 2

Skimble-skamble.— A deal of skimble-skamble stuff.
SHAKESPEARE, *King Henry IV, Part I*, iii, 1

Skin. That whiter skin of hers than snow,
And smooth as monumental alabaster.
SHAKESPEARE, *Othello*, v, 2

Skull.— Behold this ruin! 'Twas a skull[2]
Once of ethereal spirit full.
This narrow cell was Life's retreat;
This space was Thought's mysterious seat,
What beauteous visions filled this spot!
What dreams of pleasure long forgot!
Nor hope, nor joy, nor love, nor fear
Have left one trace of record here.
ANONYMOUS, *To a Skeleton*, st. 1

---

[1] Piccadilly,
A place where peccadilloes are unknown.
BYRON, *Don Juan*, Canto xiii, st. 27

[2] Remove yon skull from out the scattered heaps:
Is that a temple where a god may dwell?
Why even the worm at last disdains her shattered cell.

Look on its broken arch, its ruined wall,
Its chambers desolate, and portals foul:
Yes this was once ambition's airy hall,
The dome of thought, the palace of the soul:
Behold through each lack-lustre, eyeless hole,
The gay recess of wisdom and of wit,
And passion's host, that never brooked control:
Can all, saint, sage, or sophist ever writ,
People this lonely tower, this tenement refit?
BYRON, *Childe Harold's Pilgrimage*, Canto ii, st. 5, 6

The thoughts once chambered there,
Have gathered up their treasure and are gone.
FELICIA HEMANS, *Lines to a Butterfly Resting on a Skull*, st. 2

That skull had a tongue in it, and could sing once.
SHAKESPEARE, *Hamlet*, v, 1

Sky.— The sky, one blue, interminable arch,
Without a breeze, a wing, a cloud.—JAMES MONTGOMERY, *The Pelican Island*, Canto i, st. 2

That inverted bowl they call the sky.
OMAR KHAYYÁM, *Rubáiyát* (trans. Fitzgerald), st. 72

Slander.— Where it concerns himself,
Who's angry at a slander, makes it true.
BEN JONSON, *Catiline*, iii, 1

'Tis slander,
Whose edge is sharper than the sword; whose tongue
Outvenoms all the worms of Nile; whose breath
Rides on the posting winds and doth belie
All corners of the world: kings, queens, and states,
Maids, matrons, nay, the secrets of the grave
This viperous slander enters.
SHAKESPEARE, *Cymbeline*, iii, 4

Slander, meanest spawn of hell
(And women's slander is the worst).
TENNYSON, *The Letters*, st. 5

Slanderous.— Done to death by slanderous tongues.
SHAKESPEARE, *Much Ado about Nothing*, v, 3

Slaughter.— Forbade to wade through slaughter to a throne,
And shut the gates of mercy on mankind.
GRAY, *Elegy Written in a Country Churchyard*, st. 18

Slaves.— Slaves cannot breathe in England; if their lungs
Receive our air, that moment they are free;
They touch our country, and their shackles fall.
COWPER, *The Task: The Time-Piece*, lines 40–42

They are slaves who fear to speak
For the fallen and the weak;
They are slaves who will not choose
Hatred, scoffing, and abuse,
Rather than in silence shrink
From the truth they needs must think;
They are slaves who dare not be
In the right with two or three.
LOWELL, *Stanzas on Freedom*, st. 4

Mechanic slaves
With greasy aprons, rules, and hammers.
SHAKESPEARE, *Antony and Cleopatra*, v, 2

Slayer.— If the red slayer think he slays,
Or if the slain think he is slain,
They know not well the subtle ways
I keep, and pass, and turn again.
EMERSON, *Brahma*, st. 1

Sleep. Sleep hath its own world,
A boundary between the things misnamed
Death and existence. BYRON, *The Dream*, st. I

While I am sleeping, I neither fear nor hope, have neither pain nor pleasure: and well fare him that invented sleep, a cloak that covers all human thoughts; the food that slakes hunger; the water that quencheth thirst; and the fire that warmeth cold; the cold that tempers heat; and finally a current coin, with which all things are bought, a balance and weight that equals the king to the shepherd; the fool to the wiseman; only one thing (as I have heard) sleep hath ill, which is, that it is like death, in that between a man asleep, and a dead man, there is little difference.—CERVANTES, *Don Quixote* (Tudor Translation, ed Henley), II, lxviii

O sleep! it is a gentle thing,
Beloved from pole to pole!
To Mary Queen the praise be given!
She sent the gentle sleep from Heaven,
That slid into my soul.
COLERIDGE, *Ancient Mariner*, lines 292–296

Still let me sleep, embracing clouds in vain,
And never wake to feel the day's disdain.
SAMUEL DANIEL, *Sonnet liv*

We do not know what it is, dear, this sleep so deep and still;
The folded hands, the awful calm, the cheek so pale and chill;
The lids that will not lift again, though we may call and call;
The strange, white solitude of peace that settles over all.
MARY MAPES DODGE, *The Two Mysteries*, st. I

My fevered eyes I dared not close,
But stared aghast at sleep:
For sin had rendered unto her
The keys of hell to keep!
HOOD, *The Dream of Eugene Aram*

Be not afraid, ye doubting [waiting] hearts that weep,
For God still [still He] giveth his beloved sleep,
And if an endless sleep he wills, so best.
Epitaph of T. H. Huxley, from a poem by his wife, HENRIETTA A. HUXLEY

O, magic sleep! O comfortable bird,
That broodest o'er the troubled sea of the mind
Till it is hushed and smooth.
KEATS, *Endymion*, I, lines 453–455

How calm they sleep beneath the shade
  Who once were weary of the strife,
And bent, like us, beneath the load
    Of human life!
CRAMMOND KENNEDY, *Greenwood Cemetery*

Now I lay me down to take my sleep,
I pray the Lord my soul to keep:
If I should die before I wake,
I pray the Lord my soul to take.—*New England Primer*

No boy knows when he goes to sleep.[1]
J. W. RILEY, *No Boy Knows*

Give me to drink mandragora . . .
That I might sleep out this great gap of time.
SHAKESPEARE, *Antony and Cleopatra*, i, 5

    O sleep! O gentle sleep!
Nature's soft nurse, how have I frighted thee,
That thou no more wilt weigh my eyelids down[2]
And steep my senses in forgetfulness?
SHAKESPEARE, *King Henry IV, Part II*, iii, 1

Sleep that sometimes shuts up sorrow's eye.
SHAKESPEARE, *Midsummer-Night's Dream*, iii, 2

Tired nature's sweet restorer, balmy Sleep![3]
He, like the world, his ready visit pays
Where fortune smiles; the wretched he forsakes;
Swift on his downy pinions flies from woe,
And lights on lids unsullied with a tear.
YOUNG, *Night Thoughts*, I, lines 1–5

Sleeping.— Thus was I, sleeping, by a brother's hand
Of life, of crown, of queen, at once dispatched:
Cut off even in the blossoms of my sin,
Unhouseled, disappointed, unaneled,
No reckoning made, but sent to my account
With all my imperfections on my head.
SHAKESPEARE, *Hamlet*, i, 5

---

[1] If ignorance be indeed a bliss,
What blessed ignorance equals this,
  To sleep — and not to know it? — HOOD, *Miss Kilmansegg*, Her Dream

[2] The timely dew of sleep,
Now falling with soft slumbrous weight, inclines
Our eyelids. MILTON, *Paradise Lost*, IV, lines 614–616

Sleep shall neither night or day
Hang upon his pent-house lid. SHAKESPEARE, *Macbeth*, i, 3

[3] Innocent sleep,
Sleep that knits up the ravelled sleave of care,
The death of each day's life, sore labour's bath,
Balm of hurt minds, great nature's second course,
Chief nourisher in life's feast. SHAKESPEARE, *Macbeth*, ii, 2

Sleeps.— He that sleeps feels not the toothache.
SHAKESPEARE, *Cymbeline*, v, 4

There are a kind of men so loose of soul,
That in their sleeps will mutter their affairs.
SHAKESPEARE, *Othello*, iii, 3

Sleeve. I will wear my heart upon my sleeve
For daws to peck at. SHAKESPEARE, *Othello*, i, 1

Slept.— Then went to bed and slept as sound
As if I'd paid a note.—LANIER, *A Florida Ghost*, st. 15

God's finger touched him, and he slept.
TENNYSON, *In Memoriam*, lxxxv, st. 5

Slippery. So slippery that
The fear's as bad as falling.
SHAKESPEARE, *Cymbeline*, iii, 3

Sluggard.— 'Tis the voice of the sluggard, I heard him complain,
"You have waked me too soon, I must slumber again."
WATTS, *The Sluggard*

Slumbers.— To all, to each, a fair good night
And pleasing dreams and slumbers light.
SCOTT, *Marmion*, L'Envoy

Smart. *Leonato.* I will be heard.
Antonio. And shall, or some of us will smart for it.
SHAKESPEARE, *Much Ado about Nothing*, v, 1

Smell.— The smell of grain, or tedded grass, or kine.
MILTON, *Paradise Lost*, IX, line 450

A very ancient and fish-like smell.
SHAKESPEARE, *The Tempest*, ii, 2

Smile.— Too foolish for a tear, too wicked for a smile.
S. T. COLERIDGE, *Ode to Tranquillity*, st. 4

He smiled as he sat by the table,
With the smile that was childlike and bland.
BRET HARTE, *Plain Language from Truthful James*, st. 4

She looked down to blush, and she looked up to sigh,
With a smile on her lips and a tear in her eye.
SCOTT, *Marmion*, v, 12

Smitest.— Man of age, thou smitest sore.
SCOTT, *Lay of the Last Minstrel*, Canto iii, st. 10

Smoky.— Holding these smoky localities responsible for the conflagrations within them has a very salutary effect.
LINCOLN, *Letter to J. R. Underwood*, Oct. 26, 1864

Snake.— We have scotched the snake, not killed it.
SHAKESPEARE, *Macbeth*, iii, 2

Snakes.— There's not a mile in Ireland's isle
Where dirty varmin musters,
But there he put his dear fore-foot,
And murdered them in clusters.
The toads went pop, the frogs went hop,
Slap-dash into the water;
And the snakes committed suicide
To save themselves from slaughter.
HENRY BENNETT, *St. Patrick Was a Gentleman*

Snapper-up.— A snapper-up of unconsidered trifles.
SHAKESPEARE, *Winter's Tale*, iv, 3 [2]

Sneer.— There was a laughing devil in his sneer.
BYRON, *The Corsair*, Canto i, st. 9

Snow.— Now fades the last long streak of snow,
Now bourgeons every maze of quick.
TENNYSON, *In Memoriam*, cxv, st. 1

Snow-flakes.— Where the snow-flakes fall thickest there's nothing can freeze. HOLMES, *The Boys*, st. 2

Soap.— Seemed washing his hands with invisible soap,
In imperceptible water.
HOOD, *Miss Kilmansegg*, Her Christening

Sober.— And he that will to bed go sober,
Falls with the leaf still in October.
BEAUMONT AND FLETCHER, *The Bloody Brother*, ii, 2 (Song)

If I do not put on a sober habit,
Talk with respect, and swear but now and then,
Wear prayer-books in my pocket, look demurely,
Nay, more, while grace is saying, hood mine eyes
Thus with my hat, and sigh, and say "Amen,"
Use all the observance of civility,
Like one well studied in a sad ostent
To please his grandam, never trust me more.
SHAKESPEARE, *Merchant of Venice*, ii, 2

Soiling.— Soiling another, Annie, will never make one's self clean. TENNYSON, *The Grandmother*, st. 9

Soldier.— Providence and courage never abandon the good soldier.
COIGNY, cited by W. M. SLOANE, *Napoleon Bonaparte*, III, 248

When you 're wounded and left on Afghanistan's plains,
And the women come out to cut up what remains,
Jest roll to your rifle and blow out your brains
An' go to your Gawd like a soldier.
KIPLING, *The Young British Soldier*, st. 13

"A soldier of the Union mustered out"
Is the inscription on an unknown grave
At Newport News, beside the salt-sea wave,
Nameless and dateless.
LONGFELLOW, *A Nameless Grave*

Soldier, rest! thy warfare o'er,
Sleep the sleep that knows not breaking.
SCOTT, *Lady of the Lake*, Canto i, st. 31

A soldier,
Full of strange oaths and bearded like the pard,
Jealous in honour, sudden and quick in quarrel,
Seeking the bubble reputation
Even in the cannon's mouth.
SHAKESPEARE, *As You Like It*, ii, 7

Soldiers.— The worn white soldiers in khaki dress,

. . . . . .

Who gave up their lives at the Queen's command,
For the pride of their race, and the peace of the land.
KIPLING, *Ballad of Bon Da Thone*, st. 6, 8

Solitude.— He makes a solitude, and calls it — peace.
BYRON, *Bride of Abydos*, Canto ii, st. 20

O Solitude! where are the charms
That sages have seen in thy face?
COWPER, *Alexander Selkirk*, st. 1

Solitude sometimes is best society,
And short retirement urges sweet return.
MILTON, *Paradise Lost*, IX, lines 249, 250

Somebody.— Somebody 's courting somebody,
Somewhere or other to-night;
Somebody 's whispering to somebody,
Somebody 's listening to somebody,
Under this clear moonlight.—ANONYMOUS, *Somebody*

Son.— That unfeathered two-legged thing, a son.
DRYDEN, *Absalom and Achitophel*, I, line 170

Song.— Here lived the soul enchanted
By melody of song;
Here dwelt the spirit haunted
By a demoniac throng;
Here sang the lips elated;
Here grief and death were sated;
Here loved and here unmated
Was he, so frail, so strong.
J. H. BONER, *Poe's Cottage at Fordham*, st. 1

His song was only living aloud,
His work, a singing with his hand!
LANIER, *Life and Song*, st. 5

Be good, sweet maid, and let who will be clever;
Do noble things, not dream them, all day long:
And so make life, death, and that vast forever
One grand, sweet song.
KINGSLEY, *A Farewell*, st. 2

Songs.— Such songs have power to quiet
The restless pulse of care,
And come like the benediction
That follows after prayer.[1]
LONGFELLOW, *The Day Is Done*, st. 9

Sons.— Good wombs have borne bad sons.
SHAKESPEARE, *The Tempest*, i, 2

Sore. You rub the sore,
When you should bring the plaster.
SHAKESPEARE, *The Tempest*, ii, 1

Sorrow.— The path of sorrow, and that path alone,
Leads to the land where sorrow is unknown;
No traveller ever reached that blessed abode,
Who found not thorns and briers in his road.
COWPER, *Epistle to a Lady in France*, lines 9–12

They say 'tis a sin to sorrow,
That what God doth is best;
But 'tis only a month to-morrow
I buried it from my breast.
R. S. HAWKER, *Lament of a Cornish Mother*, st. 1

---

[1] It flooded the crimson twilight,
Like the close of an angel's psalm,
And it lay on my fevered spirit
With a touch of infinite calm.— A. A. PROCTER, *A Lost Chord*, st. 3

A feeling of sadness and longing,
  That is not akin to pain,
And resembles sorrow only
  As the mist resembles the rain.
LONGFELLOW, *The Day Is Done*, st. 3

Here bring your wounded hearts, here tell your anguish—
Earth has no sorrow that Heaven cannot heal.
T. MOORE, *Come, Ye Disconsolate*

A countenance more in sorrow than in anger.
SHAKESPEARE, *Hamlet*, i, 2

Gnarling sorrow hath less power to bite
The man that mocks at it and sets it light.
SHAKESPEARE, *King Richard II*, i, 3

If hearty sorrow
Be a sufficient ransom for offence,
I tender't here.
SHAKESPEARE, *Two Gentlemen of Verona*, v, 4

O Sorrow, wilt thou live with me,
  No casual mistress, but a wife.
TENNYSON, *In Memoriam*, lix, st. 1

Sorrow's crown of sorrow is remembering happier things.
TENNYSON, *Locksley Hall*, line 76

Sorrows.— Pity the sorrows of a poor old man!
  Whose trembling limbs have borne him to your door,
Whose days are dwindled to the shortest span,
  O, give relief, and Heaven will bless your store.
T. MOSS, *The Beggar*

When sorrows come, they come not single spies,
But in battalions. SHAKESPEARE, *Hamlet*, iv, 5

Soul.— Sweet friends! What the women lave
For its last bed of the grave
Is a tent which I am quitting,
Is a garment no more fitting,
Is a cage from which, at last,
Like a hawk my soul hath passed.

. . . . .

What ye lift upon the bier
Is not worth a wistful tear.
'Tis an empty sea-shell,— one
Out of which the pearl is gone;
The shell is broken, it lies there;
The pearl, the all, the soul, is here.
SIR EDWIN ARNOLD, *After Death in Arabia*, st. 3, 4

Soul—*Continued*

Part they must: body and soul must part;
Fond couple! linked more close than wedded pair.[1]

R. Blair, *The Grave*

O God! it is a fearful thing
To see the human soul take wing
In any shape, in any mood.

Byron, *Prisoner of Chillon*, st. 8

But whither went his soul, let such relate
Who search the secrets of the future state:
Divines can say but what themselves believe;
Strong proofs they have, but not demonstrative:
For, were all plain, then all sides must agree,
And faith itself be lost in certainty.
To live uprightly then is sure the best,
To save ourselves, and not to damn the rest.
The soul of Arcite went where heathens go,
Who better live than we, though less they know.

Dryden, *Palamon and Arcite*, lines 2120–2129

Out of the night that covers me,
  Black as the pit from pole to pole,
I thank whatever gods may be
  For my unconquerable soul.

W. E. Henley, *Out of the Night That Covers Me*, st. 1

Build thee more stately mansions, O my soul,
  As the swift seasons roll!
  Leave thy low-vaulted past!
Let each new temple, nobler than the last,
Shut thee from heaven with a dome more vast,
  Till thou at length art free,
Leaving thine outgrown shell by life's unresting sea!

Holmes, *The Chambered Nautilus*, st. 5

My soul is like the oar that momently
  Dies in a desperate stress beneath the wave,
Then glitters out again and sweeps the sea:
  Each second I'm new-born from some new grave.

Lanier, *Struggle*

The sun is but a spark of fire,
A transient meteor in the sky,
The soul, immortal as its sire,
  Shall never die.

James Montgomery, *The Grave*, st. 30

---

[1] Body and soul, like peevish man and wife,
United jar, and yet are loth to part.

Young, *Night Thoughts*, II, lines 175, 176

The look, the air, that frets thy sight,
May be a token, that below
The soul has closed in deadly fight
With some infernal fiery foe,
Whose glance would scorch thy smiling grace,
And cast thee shuddering on thy face.

A. A. Procter, *Judge Not*, st. 2

O limed soul, that, struggling to be free,
Art more engaged! Shakespeare, *Hamlet*, iii, 3

Now my soul hath elbow-room.

Shakespeare, *King John*, v, 7

Why should this worthless tegument endure
If its undying guest be lost forever?
Oh, let us keep the soul embalmed and pure
In living virtue; that when both must sever,
Although corruption may our frame consume,
The immortal spirit in the skies may bloom.

Horace Smith, *Address to a Mummy*, st. 13

For of the soule the bodie forme doth take;
For soule is forme, and doth the bodie make.

Spenser, *Hymne in Honour of Beautie*, lines 132, 133

So passed the strong heroic soul away.

Tennyson, *Enoch Arden*, line 909

Where wert thou, Soul, ere yet my body born
Became thy dwelling-place? Didst thou on earth,
Or in the clouds, await this body's birth?
Or by what chance upon that winter's morn
Didst thou this body find, a babe forlorn?
Didst thou in sorrow enter, or in mirth?
Or for a jest, perchance, to try its worth
Thou tookest flesh, ne'er from it to be torn?
Nay, Soul, I will not mock thee; well I know
Thou wert not on the earth, nor in the sky;
For with my body's growth thou too didst grow;
But with that body's death wilt thou too die?
I know not, and thou canst not tell me, so
In doubt we'll go together,— thou and I.

Samuel Waddington, *Soul and Body*

A soul immortal, spending all her fires,
Wasting her strength in strenuous idleness,
Thrown into tumult, raptured or alarmed
At aught this scene can threaten or indulge,
Resembles ocean into tempest wrought,
To waft a feather or to drown a fly.

Young, *Night Thoughts*, I, lines 149–154

Souls.— Of two souls — one must bend, one rule above.
R. Browning, *Beatrice Signorini*, line 86

'T is an awkward thing to play with souls,
And matter enough to save one's own:
Yet think of my friend, and the burning coals
He played with for bits of stone!
R. Browning, *A Light Woman*, st. 12

We are only we
While souls and bodies in one frame agree.
Dryden, *Translation of Lucretius*, III, lines 17, 18

These are the times that try men's souls.
T. Paine, *The Crisis*, No. 1

Thou almost mak'st me waver in my faith,
To hold opinion with Pythagoras,
That souls of animals infuse themselves
Into the trunks of men.
Shakespeare, *Merchant of Venice*, iv, 1

Sound.— A winged and wandering sound.
Maria Tesselschade Visscher, *The Nightingale* (trans. Sir John Bowring)

Sow.— He has the wrong sow by the ear.
Ben Jonson, *Every Man in His Humour*, ii, 1

The sow that was washed [is turned] to her wallowing in the mire. *2 Peter* ii, 22

Spaniel. You play the spaniel,
And think with wagging of your tongue to win me.
Shakespeare, *King Henry VIII*, v, 3 [2]

I am your spaniel; and, Demetrius,
The more you beat me, I will fawn on you:
Use me but as your spaniel, spurn me, strike me,
Neglect me, lose me; only give me leave,
Unworthy as I am, to follow you.
What worser place can I beg in your love
(And yet a place of high respect with me),
Than to be used as you use your dog?
Shakespeare, *Midsummer-Night's Dream*, ii, 1

Sparkled.— She sparkled, was exhaled, and went to heaven.[1]
Young, *Night Thoughts*, V, line 601

---

[1] That loving soul, which on the parent's breast
Had sparkled as a dew-drop, was exhaled,
To mingle mid the brightness of the skies.
L. H. Sigourney, *Dew-drops*

Speak. I trust I may have leave to speak;
And speak I will.
SHAKESPEARE, *Taming of the Shrew*, iv, 3

I speak as my understanding instructs me and as my honesty puts it to utterance.
SHAKESPEARE, *Winter's Tale*, i, 1

Spectres. They drink out of skulls newly torn from the grave,
Dancing 'round them the spectres are seen;
Their liquor is blood, and this horrible stave
They howl: "To the health of Alonzo the Brave,
And his consort, the Fair Imogene!"
M. G. LEWIS, *Alonzo the Brave and the Fair Imogene*

Speculation.— Speculation is a round game; the players see little or nothing of their cards at first starting; gains may be great — and so may losses. . . . A mania prevailed, a bubble burst, four stockbrokers took villa residences at Florence, four hundred nobodies were ruined, and among them Mr. Nickleby.
DICKENS, *Nicholas Nickleby*, i

Speech.— Men ever had, and ever will have, leave
To coin new words well suited to the age.
Words are like leaves, some wither every year,
And every year a younger race succeeds.
. . . . .
Use may revive the obsoletest words,
And banish those that now are most in vogue;
Use is the judge, the law, and rule of speech.
ROSCOMMON, *Art of Poetry*, lines 73–91

Speak the speech, I pray you, as I pronounced it to you, trippingly on the tongue: but if you mouth it, as many of your players do, I had as lief the town-crier spoke my lines. Nor do not saw the air too much with your hand, thus, but use all gently; for in the very torrent, tempest, and, as I may say, the whirlwind of passion,[1] you must acquire and beget a temperance that may give it smoothness. Oh, it offends me to the soul to hear a robustious periwig-pated fellow tear a passion to tatters, to very rags, to split the ears of the groundlings, who for the most part are capable of nothing but inexplicable dumb-shows and noise: I would have such a fellow whipped for o'erdoing Termagant.
SHAKESPEARE, *Hamlet*, iii, 2

---

[1] "As I may say, whirlwind of your passion" according to different versions.

Mend your speech a little,
Lest it [you] may mar your fortunes.
SHAKESPEARE, *King Lear*, i, 1

His speech was like a tangled chain; nothing impaired, but all disordered.
SHAKESPEARE, *Midsummer-Night's Dream*, v, 1

Rude am I in my speech,
And little blessed with the soft phrase of peace.
SHAKESPEARE, *Othello*, i, 3

Speech ventilates our intellectual fire;
Speech burnishes our mental magazine.
YOUNG, *Night Thoughts*, II, lines 478, 479

Spider.— The spider's touch, how exquisitely fine!
Feels at each thread, and lives along the line.[1]
POPE, *Essay on Man*, Epistle i, lines 217, 218

Spin.— Spin, spin, Clotho, spin!
Lachesis, twist! and, Atropos, sever!
Darkness is strong, and so is Sin,
But surely God endures for ever!
LOWELL, *Villa Franca*, st. 7

Spirit.— The letter kills, the spirit keeps alive[2]
In law and gospel.
R. BROWNING, *The Ring and the Book*, XI, lines 1531, 1532

O Lord! since we have feasted thus,
Which we so little merit,
Let Meg now take away the flesh,
And Jock bring in the spirit!
BURNS, *On a Sheep's Head*

I am thy father's spirit,
Doomed for a certain term to walk the night,
And for the day confined to fast in fires,
Till the foul crimes done in my days of nature
Are burnt and purged away. But that I am forbid
To tell the secrets of my prison-house,
I could a tale unfold whose lightest word
Would harrow up thy soul, freeze thy young blood,
Make thy two eyes, like stars, start from their spheres,
Thy knotted and combined locks to part,

---

[1] Much like a subtle spider which doth sit,
In middle of her web, which spreadeth wide;
If aught do touch the utmost thread of it,
She feels it instantly on every side.
SIR J. DAVIES, *The Immortality of the Soul*

[2] The letter killeth, but the spirit giveth life. 2 *Cor.* iii, 6

And each particular hair to stand on end,
Like quills upon the fretful porpentine [porcupine]:
But this eternal blazon must not be
To ears of flesh and blood.—SHAKESPEARE, *Hamlet*, i, 5

Rest, rest, perturbed spirit! *Ibid.*

When that this body did contain a spirit,
A kingdom for it was too small a bound;
But now two paces of the vilest earth
Is room enough: this earth that bears thee dead
Bears not alive so stout a gentleman.
SHAKESPEARE, *King Henry IV*, *Part I*, v, 4

These foolish drops do something [somewhat] drown my manly spirit.
SHAKESPEARE, *Merchant of Venice*, ii, 3

Our tastes, our needs, are never twice the same.
Nothing contents us long, however dear,
The spirit in us, like the grosser frame,
Outgrows the garments which it wore last year.
ELLA WHEELER WILCOX, *The Year Outgrows the Spring*, st. 4

Spirits. Spirits, when they please,
Can either sex assume, or both; so soft
And uncompounded is their essence pure,
Not tied or manacled with joint or limb,
Nor founded on the brittle strength of bones,
Like cumbrous flesh; but, in what shape they choose,
Dilated or condensed, bright or obscure,
Can execute their airy purposes,
And works of love or enmity fulfil.
MILTON, *Paradise Lost*, I, lines 423–431

Glendower. I can call spirits from the vasty deep.
Hotspur. Why, so can I, or so can any man;
But will they come when you do call for them?
SHAKESPEARE, *King Henry IV*, *Part I*, iii, 1

Spirits of peace, where are ye? are ye all gone,
And leave me here in wretchedness behind ye?
SHAKESPEARE, *King Henry VIII*, iv, 2

Take, O boatman, thrice thy fee,
Take, I give it willingly;
For, invisible to thee,
Spirits twain have crossed with me.
UHLAND, *The Passage* (trans. Sarah Austen), st. 6

Spiritual.— Millions of spiritual creatures walk the earth
Unseen, both when we wake and when we sleep.
MILTON, *Paradise Lost*, IV, lines 677, 678

Spleen.— You shall digest the venom of your spleen,
Though it do split you; for, from this day forth,
I 'll use you for my mirth, yea, for my laughter,
When you are waspish.
SHAKESPEARE, *Julius Cæsar*, iv, 3

Splendour.— The splendour falls on castle walls
And snowy summits old in story;
The long light shakes across the lakes,
And the wild cataract leaps in glory.
Blow, bugle, blow, set the wild echoes flying,
Blow, bugle; answer, echoes, dying, dying, dying.
TENNYSON, *The Princess*, iii

Spoke.— When I spoke that, I was ill-tempered too.
SHAKESPEARE, *Julius Cæsar*, iv, 3

Sport.— Sport that wrinkled Care derides,
And Laughter holding both his sides.
MILTON, *L'Allegro*, lines 31, 32

Spot.— My family . . . think it indispensable that [Mr. Micawber] should be upon the spot . . . in case of anything turning up.
DICKENS, *David Copperfield*, I, xii

Out, damned spot! out, I say.
SHAKESPEARE, *Macbeth*, v, 1

Spring.— The spring comes slowly up this way.
S. T. COLERIDGE, *Christabel*, I, line 22

Spring, the sweet spring, is the year's pleasant king.
T. NASH, *Spring, the Sweet Spring*

Come, gentle Spring, ethereal mildness, come.[1]
THOMSON, *The Seasons*, Spring, line 1

Spring-time.— Noiselessly as the spring-time
Her crown of verdure weaves,
And all the trees on all the hills
Open their thousand leaves.
C. F. ALEXANDER, *Burial of Moses*, st. 3

Squadron.— A fellow almost damned in a fair wife;
That never set a squadron in the field,
Nor the division of a battle knows
More than a spinster; . . .
Mere prattle, without practice,
Is all his soldiership. SHAKESPEARE, *Othello*, i, 1

---

[1] "Come, gentle spring! ethereal mildness! come."
O Thomson! void of rhyme as well as reason:
How couldst thou thus poor human nature hum?
There's no such season! HOOD, *Spring, A New Version*

Square.— Utopia is a pleasant place,
But how shall I get there?
"Straight down the crooked lane,
And all round the square."

HOOD, *A Plain Direction*, st. 2

Square Deal.— A man who is good enough to shed his blood for his country[1] is good enough to be given a square deal afterward. More than that no man is entitled to, and less than that no man shall have.

THEODORE ROOSEVELT, *Speech at Springfield, Ill.*, July 4, 1903

Squeezing.— What holds a pretty girl's
Hand without squeezing?

F. LOCKER-LAMPSON, *On an Old Muff*

Staff.— The boy was the very staff of my age.

SHAKESPEARE, *Merchant of Venice*, ii, 2

Stage. All the world 's a stage,
And all the men and women merely players:
They have their exits and their entrances;
And one man in his time plays many parts,
His acts being seven ages.[2]

SHAKESPEARE, *As You Like It*, ii, 7

A kingdom for a stage, princes to act
And monarchs to behold the swelling scene!

SHAKESPEARE, *King Henry V*, Prologue

Stammer.— I would thou couldst stammer, that thou mightst pour this concealed man out of thy mouth, as wine comes out of a narrow-mouthed bottle, either too much at once, or none at all. SHAKESPEARE, *As You Like It*, iii, 2

Stand.— Here I stand; I cannot do otherwise; God help me!

MARTIN LUTHER, *His Defence before the Diet of Worms*

Standard.— But still he waves the standard, and cries, amid the rout —
"For Church and King, fair gentlemen, spur on and fight it out!"
And now he wards a Roundhead's pike, and now he hums a stave,
And here he quotes a stage-play, and there he fells a knave. PRAED, *Sir Nicholas at Marston Moor*, st. 5

---

[1] Alluding to coloured troops.

[2] The world's a theatre, the earth a stage
Which God and nature do with actors fill.

T. HEYWOOD, *Apology for Actors*

Star.—"No sight? no sound?" "No; nothing save
The plover from the marshes calling,
And in yon western sky, about
An hour ago a star[1] was falling."

"A star? There's nothing strange in that."
"No, nothing; but, above the thicket,
Somehow it seemed to me that God
Somewhere has just relieved a picket."

BRET HARTE, *Relieving Guard*, st. 2, 3

Yet, if thou wilt remember one
Who never can forget,
Whose lonely life is not so lone
As if we had not met,
Believe that in the frosty sky
Whereon is writ his destiny,
Thy light is lingering yet,
A star before the darkened soul,
To guide, and gladden, and control.

PRAED, *A Farewell*, st. 7

It were all one
That I should love a bright particular star
And think to wed it, he is so above me:
In his bright radiance and collateral light
Must I be comforted, not in his sphere.
The ambition in my love thus plagues itself:
The hind that would be mated by the lion
Must die for love.

SHAKESPEARE, *All's Well That Ends Well*, i, 1

Stare. And then with a riding-whip
Leisurely tapping a glossy boot,
And curving a contumelious lip,
Gorgonized me from head to foot
With a stony British stare.—TENNYSON, *Maud*, xiii, st. 2

Stars. When the patient stars look down
On all their light discovers,
The traitor's smile, the murderer's frown,
The lips of lying lovers,

They try to shut their saddening eyes,
And in the vain endeavour
We see them twinkling in the skies,
And so they wink for ever.

HOLMES, *Album Verses*, st. 6, 7

Starve.— But still the great have kindness in reserve,
He helped to bury whom he helped to starve.

POPE, *Epistle to Dr. Arbuthnot*, lines 247, 248

---

[1] Thomas Starr King died in San Francisco, March 4, 1864.

State.— A thousand years scarce serve to form a state;
An hour may lay it in the dust.
BYRON, *Childe Harold's Pilgrimage*, Canto ii, st. 84

In friendship false, implacable in hate;
Resolved to ruin or to rule the state. DRYDEN,
Absalom and Achitophel, I, lines 173, 174

What constitutes a state?
Not high raised battlements or laboured mound,
Thick wall or moated gate;
Not cities proud with spires and turrets crowned;
Not bays and broad-armed ports,
Where, laughing at the storm, rich navies ride;
Not starred and spangled courts,
Where low-browed baseness wafts perfume to pride.
No: — men, high-minded men, . . .
Men, who their duties know,
But know their rights, and, knowing, dare maintain;
Prevent the long aimed blow
And crush the tyrant while they rend the chain:
These constitute a state,
And sovereign law, that state's collected will,
O'er thrones and globes elate
Sits empress, crowning good, repressing ill.
SIR WILLIAM JONES, *Ode in Imitation of Alcæus*

I have done the state some service, and they know 't.
SHAKESPEARE, *Othello*, v, 2

Statesman.— Statesman, yet friend to truth! of soul sincere,
In action faithful, and in honour clear;
Who broke no promise, served no private end,
Who gained no title, and who lost no friend;
Ennobled by himself, by all approved,
And praised, unenvied, by the Muse he loved.[1]
POPE, *Moral Essays*, Epistle v, lines 67–72

Statuary. She was one
Fit for the model of a statuary
(A race of mere impostors, when all's done —
I've seen much finer women, ripe and real,
Than all the nonsense of their stone ideal).
BYRON, *Don Juan*, Canto ii, st. 118

Statue.— The more the marble wastes
The more the statue grows.
MICHELANGELO BUONARROTI, *Sonnet*
(trans. Mrs. Henry Roscoe)

[1] This quotation was also used as an epitaph on the tomb of James Craggs in Westminster Abbey, with a change in the last line to
"Praised, wept, and honoured by the Muse he loved."

Stature.— *Jaques*. What stature is she of?
Orlando. Just as high as my heart.
SHAKESPEARE, *As You Like It*, iii, 2

Steal.— Thieves for their robbery have authority
When judges steal themselves.
SHAKESPEARE, *Measure for Measure*, ii, 2

"Convey," the wise it call. "Steal!" foh! a fico for the phrase! SHAKESPEARE, *Merry Wives of Windsor*, i, 3

We steal by line and level.
SHAKESPEARE, *The Tempest*, iv

Stealing.— In vain we call old notions fudge,
And bend our conscience to our dealing;
The Ten Commandments will not budge,
And stealing will continue stealing.
LOWELL, *Epigram: International Copyright*

B, taught by Pope to do his good by stealth,
'Twixt participle and noun no difference feeling,
In office placed to serve the Commonwealth,
Does himself all the good he can by stealing.
LOWELL, *Epigram: A Misconception*

When to bed the world are bobbing,
Then's the time for orchard-robbing;
Yet the fruit were scarce worth peeling
Were it not for stealing, stealing.
T. RANDOLPH, *Fairies' Song* (trans. from the Latin, by Leigh Hunt)

Steam.— Soon shall thy arm, unconquered steam! afar
Drag the slow barge, or drive the rapid car;
Or on wide waving wings expanded bear
The flying-chariot through the field of air.[1]
E. DARWIN, *A Botanic Garden*, I, i

Steed.— And there lay the steed with his nostril all wide,
And through it there rolled not the breath of his pride:
And the foam of his gasping lay white on the turf,
And cold as the spray of the rock-beating surf.
BYRON, *Destruction of Sennacherib*, st. 4

Like the impatient steed of war,
He snuffed the battle from afar.—SCOTT, *Marmion*, vi, 1

---

[1] I blow the bellows, I forge the steel,
In all the shops of trade;
I hammer the ore and turn the wheel
Where my arms of strength are made;
I manage the furnace, the mill, the mint,
I carry, I spin, I weave,
And all my doings I put into print
On every Saturday eve. G. W. CUTTER, *The Song of Steam*

Steeds.— The steeds are all bridled, and snort to the rein;
Curved is each neck, and flowing each mane;
White is the foam of their champ on the bit:
The spears are uplifted; the matches are lit;
The cannon are pointed and ready to roar,
And crush the wall they have crumbled before.
BYRON, *Siege of Corinth*, st. 22

Steer. I argue not
Against Heaven's hand or will, nor bate a jot
Of heart or hope; but still bear up, and steer
Right onward. MILTON, *Sonnet to Cyriac Skinner*

Stenches.— In Köhln, a town of monks and bones,
And pavements fanged with murderous stones,
And rags, and hags, and hideous wenches;
I counted two-and-seventy stenches,
All well defined, and several stinks!
S. T. COLERIDGE, *Cologne*, lines 1–5

Stephen.— King Stephen was a worthy peer,
His breeches cost him a crown;
He held them sixpence all too dear,
With that he called the tailor lown.
SHAKESPEARE, *Othello*, ii, 3

Steps.— He who, from zone to zone,
Guides through the boundless sky thy certain flight,
In the long way that I must tread alone,
Will lead my steps aright.
BRYANT, *To a Waterfowl*, st. 8

Stile.— I 'm sittin' on the stile, Mary,
Where we sat side by side.
. . . . .
And the red was on your lip, Mary,
And the love-light in your eye.
LADY DUFFERIN, *Lament of the Irish Immigrant*, st. 1

Stimulating.— There are companies of men of genius into which I sometimes go, where the atmosphere of intellect and sentiment is so much more stimulating than alcohol, that, if I thought fit to take wine, it would be to keep me sober.—HOLMES, *Autocrat of the Breakfast-Table*, viii

Stolen.— Stolen sweets are always sweeter;
Stolen kisses much completer.
T. RANDOLPH, *Fairies' Song* (trans. from the Latin, by Leigh Hunt)

Stolid.— A thing that grieves not and that never hopes,
Stolid and stunned, a brother to the ox.
EDWIN MARKHAM, *The Man With the Hoe*, st. 1

Stomach. He was a man
Of an unbounded stomach, ever ranking
Himself with princes.
SHAKESPEARE, *King Henry VIII*, iv, 2

Stomachs. Our stomachs
Will make what 's homely savoury.
SHAKESPEARE, *Cymbeline*, iii, 6

They have only stomachs to eat, and none to fight.
SHAKESPEARE, *King Henry V*, iii, 7

Stone.— As cold as any stone.
SHAKESPEARE, *King Henry V*, ii, 3

The earth upon her corpse was pressed,
This post was driven into her breast,
And a stone is on her face.
SOUTHEY, *The Cross-Roads*, st. 27

The stone that is rolling can gather no moss.
THOMAS TUSSER, *Five Hundred Points of Good Husbandry*, Good Husbandry Lessons, st. 46

Stonewall.— Appealing from his native sod,
In forma pauperis to God,
"Lay bare Thine arm! Stretch forth Thy rod:
Amen!"— That 's Stonewall's Way.
J. W. PALMER, *Stonewall Jackson's Way*, st. 3

Storm.— And, pleased the Almighty's orders to perform,
Rides in the whirlwind, and directs the storm.[1]
ADDISON, *The Campaign*, lines 291, 292

Poor creatures! how they envies us!
And wishes, I 've a notion,
For our good luck, in such a storm,
To be upon the ocean!
WILLIAM PITT (of Malta), *The Sailor's Consolation*, st. 2

So foul a sky clears not without a storm.
SHAKESPEARE, *King John*, iv, 2

Like a storm he came,
And shook the house, and like a storm he went.
TENNYSON, *Aylmer's Field*, lines 215, 216

---

[1] This line is frequently ascribed to Pope as it is found in the *Dunciad*, iii, line 264. *Cf.* GOD. Quotation from Cowper.

Stormy.— I 've seen your stormy seas and stormy women,[1]
And pity lovers rather more than seamen.
BYRON, *Don Juan*, Canto vi, st. 53

Story.— Story! God bless you! I have none to tell, sir.
CANNING, *The Friend of Humanity and the Knife-Grinder*, st. 6

A woman's story at a winter's fire,
Authorized by her grandam.
SHAKESPEARE, *Macbeth*, iii, 4

Straight.— There is no force however great
Can stretch a cord however fine
Into a horizontal line
That shall be accurately straight.
W. WHEWELL, *The Unconscious Poetizing of a Philosopher*

Strangers.— I do desire we may be better strangers.
SHAKESPEARE, *As You Like It*, iii, 2

Straw.— Take a straw and throw it up into the air, you may see by that which way the wind is.
JOHN SELDEN, *Table Talk: Libels*

Street.— A street there is in Paris famous,
For which no rhyme our language yields,
Rue Neuve des Petits Champs its name is —
The New Street of the Little Fields.
THACKERAY, *The Ballad of Bouillabaisse*, st. 1

Strength. If you had the strength
Of twenty men, it would dispatch you straight.
SHAKESPEARE, *Romeo and Juliet*, v, 1

Who trusts the strength will with the burden grow,
That God makes instruments to work his will,
If but that will we can arrive to know,
Nor tamper with the weights of good and ill.
TOM TAYLOR, *Abraham Lincoln*, st. 9

Strenuous.— I wish to preach, not the doctrine of ignoble ease, but the doctrine of the strenuous life, the life of toil and effort, of labour and strife; to preach that highest form of success which comes, not to the man who

---

[1] This only proved as a spark to the powder,
And the storm I had raised came faster and louder;
It blew and it rained, thundered, lightened, and hailed
Interjections, verbs, pronouns, till language quite failed
To express the abusive, and then its arrears
Were brought up all at once by a torrent of tears,
And my last faint, despairing attempt at an observation was lost in a tempest of sobs.
W. A. BUTLER, *Nothing to Wear*

desires mere easy peace, but to the man who does not shrink from danger, from hardship, or from bitter toil, and who out of these wins the splendid ultimate triumph.

THEODORE ROOSEVELT, *Speech before the Hamilton Club*, Chicago, April 10, 1899

Strife.— A man whose soul is pure and strong, whose sword is bright and keen,
Who knows the splendour of the fight and what its issues mean;
Who never takes one step aside, nor halts, though hope be dim,
But cleaves a pathway through the strife, and bids men follow him. —HENRY VAN DYKE, *Another Chance*, st. 7

Better a day of strife
Than a century of sleep.
A. J. RYAN, *The Rosary of My Tears*

Oh, hush thee, my baby, the time soon will come,
When thy sleep shall be broken by trumpet and drum;
Then hush thee, my darling, take rest while you may,
For strife comes with manhood, and waking with day.[1]
SCOTT, *Lullaby of an Infant Chief*, st. 3

Strike.— Strike when the iron is hot.
JOHN WEBSTER, *Westward Ho!* ii, 1;
G. FARQUHAR, *The Beaux Stratagem*, iv, 1

Strikes.— A mechanic his labour will often discard
If the rate of his pay he dislikes;
But a clock — and its case is uncommonly hard —
Will continue to work though it strikes.
HOOD, *Epigram on the Superiority of Machinery*

Strings.— 'Tis good in every case, you know,
To have two strings unto your bow.[2]
CHARLES CHURCHILL, *The Ghost*, IV

Stripes. Stripes, that Mercy, with a bleeding heart,
Weeps when she sees inflicted on a beast.
COWPER, *The Task: The Time-Piece*, lines 24, 25

Strokes. Hercules himself must yield to odds;
And many strokes, though with a little axe,
Hew down and fell the hardest-timbered oak.
SHAKESPEARE, *King Henry VI*, *Part III*, ii, 1

---

[1] Yet must they wake again,
Wake soon to all the bitterness of life,
The pang of sorrow, the temptation strife,
Aye to the conscience pain. G. W. BETHUNE, *Hymn to Night*

[2] He that has two strings to his bow. BUTLER, *Hudibras*, III, i, line 3
I had two strings to my bow. FIELDING, *Love in Several Masques*, v, 13

Strong.— Oh, East is East, and West is West, and never the twain shall meet,
Till Earth and Sky stand presently at God's great Judgment Seat;
But there is neither East nor West, Border, nor Breed, nor Birth,
When two strong men stand face to face, though they come from the ends of the earth.
KIPLING, *Ballad of East and West*

Know how sublime a thing it is
To suffer and be strong.
LONGFELLOW, *Light of the Stars*, st. 9

Struggle.— Hath hope been smitten in its early dawn?
Have clouds o'ercast thy purpose, trust, or plan?
Have faith, and struggle on!
R. S. S. ANDROS, *Perseverance*, st. 6

Say not the struggle nought availeth,
The labour and the wounds are vain.

. . . . .

If hopes were dupes, fears may be liars;
It may be, in yon smoke concealed
Your comrades chase e'en now the fliers,
And, but for you, possess the field.
A. H. CLOUGH, *Say not, the Struggle Nought Availeth*, st. 1, 2

Study.— No profit grows where is no pleasure ta 'en;
In brief, sir, study what you most affect.
SHAKESPEARE, *Taming of the Shrew*, i, 1

Style.— Style is the dress of thoughts.
CHESTERFIELD, *Letter to His Son*, Nov. 24, 1749

Sublime.— The sublime and the ridiculous are often so nearly related, that it is difficult to class them separately. One step above the sublime makes the ridiculous, and one step above the ridiculous makes the sublime.
THOMAS PAINE, *Age of Reason, II, ad finem*

Submission.— Yielded with coy submission, modest pride,
And sweet, reluctant, amorous delay.
MILTON, *Paradise Lost*, IV, lines 310, 311

Submission bondage, and resistance death.
JAMES MONTGOMERY, *The West Indies*, i, st. 16

Success.— 'Tis not in mortals to command success,
But we'll do more, Sempronius; we'll deserve it.[1]
ADDISON, *Cato*, i, 2

Such a nature,
Tickled with good success, disdains the shadow
Which he treads on at noon.
SHAKESPEARE, *Coriolanus*, i, 1

Sue.— Come not cringing to sue me!
Take me with triumph and power,
As a warrior storms a fortress!
I will not shrink or cower.
Come, as you came in the desert,
Ere we were women and men,
When the tiger passions were in us,
And love as you loved me then!
W. W. STORY, *Cleopatra*, st. 12

Suez.— Ship me somewhere east of Suez, where the best is like the worst,
Where there aren't no Ten Commandments an' a man can raise a thirst;
For the temple-bells are callin', and it's there that I would be —
By the old Moulmein Pagoda, looking lazy at the sea.
KIPLING, *Mandalay*

Sufferance.— Sufferance is the badge of all our tribe.
SHAKESPEARE, *Merchant of Venice*, i, 3

Sufferings.— To each his sufferings: all are men,
Condemned alike to groan;
The tender for another's pain,
Th' unfeeling for his own.
THOMAS GRAY, *Ode on a Distant Prospect of Eton College*, st. 10

Suggestion.— They'll take suggestion as a cat laps milk.
SHAKESPEARE, *The Tempest*, ii, 1

Sun.— Let others hail the rising sun:
I bow to that whose course is run.
DAVID GARRICK, *On the Death of Mr. Pelham*

Brushing with hasty steps the dews away,
To meet the sun upon the upland lawn.
GRAY, *Elegy Written in a Country Churchyard*, st. 26

---

[1] "'Tis not in mortals to command success;"
But do you more, Sempronius — *don't* deserve it.
And take my word, you won't have any less:
Be wary, watch the time, and always serve it.
BYRON, *Don Juan*, Canto xiii, st. 18

Taking the year together, my dear,
There is n't more cloud than sun.
R. Peale, *Faith and Hope*

The weary sun hath made a golden set,
And, by the bright track of his fiery car
Gives signal [token] of a goodly day to-morrow.
Shakespeare, *King Richard III*, v, 3

An hour before the worshipped sun
Peered forth the golden window of the east,
A troubled mind drave me to walk abroad.
Shakespeare, *Romeo and Juliet*, i, 1

Sunbeams.— He had been eight years upon a project for extracting sunbeams out of cucumbers, which were to be put in phials hermetically sealed, and let out to warm the air in raw, inclement summers.
Swift, *Gulliver's Travels: A Voyage to Laputa*, v

Sunday.— In spite of all hypocrisy can spin,
As surely as I am a Christian scion,
I cannot think it is a mortal sin —
(Unless he 's loose) to look upon a lion.
I really think that one may go, perchance,
To see a bear, as guiltless as on Monday —
(That is, provided that he did not dance)
Bruin 's no worse than bakin' on a Sunday —
But what is your opinion, Mrs. Grundy?
Hood, *An Open Question*, st. 11.

Sunflower.— The heart that has truly loved never forgets,
But as truly loves on to the close,
As the sunflower turns on her god, when he sets,
The same look which she turned when he rose.
Thomas Moore, *Believe Me, If All Those Endearing Young Charms*, st. 2

Superfluity.— Superfluity comes sooner by white hairs, but competency lives longer.
Shakespeare, *Merchant of Venice*, i, 2

Supper.— This night he makes a supper, and a great one.
Shakespeare, *King Henry VIII*, i, 3

About the sixth hour; when beasts most graze, birds best peck, and men sit down to that nourishment which is called supper.
Shakespeare, *Love's Labour's Lost*, i, 1

Being full of supper and distempering draughts.
Shakespeare, *Othello*, 1, i

Suspicion.— See what a ready tongue suspicion hath!
He that but fears the thing he would not know
Hath by instinct knowledge from others' eyes
That what he feared is chanced.
SHAKESPEARE, *King Henry IV, Part II*, i, 1

Suspicion always haunts the guilty mind;
The thief doth fear each bush an officer.
SHAKESPEARE, *King Henry VI, Part III*, v, 6

Swan.— Sweet swan of Avon! BEN JONSON,
To the Memory of Shakespeare, line 71

I will make thee think thy swan a crow.
SHAKESPEARE, *Romeo and Juliet*, i, 2

Swap.— It is not best to swap horses while crossing the river.
LINCOLN, *Reply to the National Union League*, June 9, 1864

Swashing.— We'll have a swashing and a martial outside,
As many other mannish cowards have
That do outface it with their semblances.
SHAKESPEARE, *As You Like It*, i, 3

Swear.— For though an oath obliges not,
Where any thing is to be got,
As thou hast proved, yet 'tis profane,
And sinful, when men swear in vain.
BUTLER, *Hudibras*, II, iii, lines 101–104

It's 'most enough to make a deacon swear.
LOWELL, *Biglow Papers*, II, ii, line 91

Do not swear at all;
Or, if thou wilt, swear by thy gracious self,
Which is the god of my idolatry,
And I'll believe thee.
SHAKESPEARE, *Romeo and Juliet*, ii, 2

Sweet.— How sad and bad and mad it was —
But then, how it was sweet!
R. BROWNING, *Confessions*, st. 9

Sweet are all things, when we learn to prize them,
Not for their sake, but His who grants them or denies
them! AUBREY DE VERE, *Sad Is Our Youth*

Sweetness.— And ever, against eating cares,
Lap me in soft Lydian airs,
Married to immortal verse,[1]
Such as the meeting soul may pierce,
In notes with many a winding bout
Of linkéd sweetness long drawn out.
MILTON, *L'Allegro*, lines 135–140

---

[1] Wisdom married to immortal verse.— WORDSWORTH, *The Excursion: Churchyard Among the Mountains* (Book VII), line 541

Sweets.— The fly that sips treacle is lost in the sweets.
GAY, *The Beggar's Opera*, ii, 2

Sweets to the sweet:[1] farewell!
SHAKESPEARE, *Hamlet*, v, 1

Swig. I 'll meet 'im later on
At the place where 'e is gone —
Where it 's always double drill and no canteen;
'E 'll be squattin' on the coals,
Givin' drink to poor damned souls,
An' I 'll get a swig in hell from Gunga Din.
KIPLING, *Gunga Din*, st. 5

Swimmer.— A solitary shriek — the bubbling cry
Of some strong swimmer in his agony.
BYRON, *Don Juan*, Canto ii, st. 53

Swine.— Or sheer swine, all cry and no wool.
BUTLER, *Hudibras*, I, i, line 852 [850]

Sword.— "I would," quoth grim old Oliver, "that Belial's trusty sword
This day were doing battle for the Saints and for the Lord!" PRAED, *Sir Nicholas at Marston Moor*, st. 6

Full bravely hast thou fleshed
Thy maiden sword.
SHAKESPEARE, *King Henry IV, Part I*, v, 4

Nay, never lay thy hand upon thy sword;[2]
I fear thee not.
SHAKESPEARE, *Much Ado about Nothing*, v, 1

Swords.— And sheathed their swords for lack of argument.
SHAKESPEARE, *King Henry V*, iii, 1

Swore.—"Our armies swore terribly in Flanders," cried my uncle Toby,—"but nothing to this. For my own part, I could not have a heart to curse my dog so."
STERNE, *Tristram Shandy*, III, xi

Syllables.— Syllables govern the world.
JOHN SELDEN, *Table Talk: Power*, 3

Table-talk. Let it serve for table-talk;
Then, howsoe'er thou speak'st, 'mong other things
I shall digest it.
SHAKESPEARE, *Merchant of Venice*, iii, 5

---

[1] The sweetest garland to the sweetest maid.
T. TICKELL, *To a Lady with a Present of Flowers*

[2] Nay, never look upon your lord
And lay your hands upon your sword. SCOTT, *Marmion*, vi, st. 14

Tailor.— Be sure your tailor is a man of sense;
But add a little care, a decent pride,
And always err upon the sober side.
HOLMES, *A Rhymed Lesson*, st. 47

Take. The good old rule
Sufficeth them, the simple plan,
That they should take, who have the power,
And they should keep who can.
WORDSWORTH, *Rob Roy's Gravc*, st. 10

Tale.— A tale should be judicious, clear, succinct;
The language plain, and incidents well linked.
COWPER, *Conversation*, lines 235, 236

I cannot tell how the truth may be;
I say the tale as 'twas said to me.
SCOTT, *Lay of the Last Minstrel*, Canto ii, st. 22

Mark now, how a plain tale [how plain a tale] shall put you down.
SHAKESPEARE, *King Henry IV, Part I*, ii, 4

Thereby hangs a tale.
SHAKESPEARE, *As You Like It*, ii, 7; *Merry Wives of Windsor*, i, 4; *Taming of the Shrew*, iv, 1

I will a round unvarnished tale deliver
Of my whole course of love.—SHAKESPEARE, *Othello*, i, 3

Talk. The herd of such,
Who think too little, and who talk too much.[1]
DRYDEN, *Absalom and Achitophel*, I, lines 533, 534

A gentleman, nurse, that loves to hear himself talk, and will speak more in a minute than he will stand to in a month. SHAKESPEARE, *Romeo and Juliet*, ii, 4

This gentleman will out-talk us all.
SHAKESPEARE, *Taming of the Shrew*, i, 2

In after-dinner talk
Across the walnuts and the wine.[2]
TENNYSON, *The Miller's Daughter*, lines 31, 32

Talked.— I be‥ve they talked of me, for they laughed consumedly.—G. FARQUHAR, *The Beaux Stratagem*, iii, 1

---

[1] E'en wit's a burthen, when it talks too long.
DRYDEN, *Juvenal*, Satire vi, line 573

[2] My lips let loose among the nuts and wine.
HOLMES, *A Rhymed Lesson*, st. 2

Talking.— Words learned by rote a parrot may rehearse,
But talking is not always to converse.
COWPER, *Conversation*, lines 7, 8

Talking is like playing on the harp; there is as much in laying the hand on the strings to stop their vibrations as in twanging them to bring out their music.
HOLMES, *Autocrat of the Breakfast-Table*, i

A good old man, sir; he will be talking.
SHAKESPEARE, *Much Ado about Nothing*, iii, 5

Tall.— I am more than common tall.
SHAKESPEARE, *As You Like It*, i, 3

Taste.—"I don't at all take it ill that you speak your sentiment; it is your sentiment only that I find bad. I have been most egregiously deceived in your narrow understanding. . . . Say no more, my child," said he; "you are yet too raw to make proper distinctions. Know that I never composed a better homily than that which you disapprove; for my genius (thank Heaven!) has as yet lost nothing of its vigour. Henceforth I will make a better choice of a confidant, and keep one of greater ability than you. . . . Adieu, Mr. Gil Blas; I wish you all manner of prosperity, with a little more taste!"[1]
LE SAGE, *Gil Blas*, lviii

Tastes.— Such and so various are the tastes of men.
MARK AKENSIDE, *Pleasures of the Imagination*, III, line 567

Tea.— Tea! thou soft, thou sober, sage, and venerable liquid; thou female-tongue-running, smile-smoothing, heart-opening, wink-tippling cordial, to whose glorious insipidity I owe the happiest moments of my life, let me fall prostrate. COLLEY CIBBER, *The Lady's Last Stake*, i, 1

Teach.— If I am right, thy grace impart,
Still in the right to stay;
If I am wrong, oh, teach my heart
To find that better way.
POPE, *The Universal Prayer*, st. 8

I can easier teach twenty what were good to be done, than to be one of the twenty to follow mine own teaching.
SHAKESPEARE, *Merchant of Venice*, i, 2

---

[1] Th' assuming Wit, who deems himself so wise,
As his mistaken patron to advise,
Let him not dare to vent his dang'rous thought,
A noble fool was never in a fault.
POPE, *January and May*, lines 162–165

Delightful task! to rear the tender thought,
To teach the young idea how to shoot.
THOMSON, *The Seasons*, Spring, lines 1152, 1153

Tear.— The lips may beguile,
With a dimple or smile,
But the test of affection 's a tear.
BYRON, *The Tear*, st. 1

Forgive this foolish tear,
But let the old oak stand.
G. P. MORRIS, *Woodman Spare That Tree*, st. 3

What a hell of witchcraft lies
In the small orb of one particular tear!
SHAKESPEARE, *A Lover's Complaint*, lines 288, 289

Tears.— More tears are shed in playhouses than in churches.
T. GUTHRIE, *The Gospel in Ezekiel*, XV

Tears, such as angels weep, burst forth.
MILTON, *Paradise Lost*, I, line 620

Some reckon their age by years,
Some measure their life by art;
But some tell their days by the flow of their tears,
And their lives by the moans of their heart.
A. J. RYAN, *The Rosary of My Tears*

The rose is sweetest washed with morning dew,
And love is loveliest when embalmed in tears.
SCOTT, *Lady of the Lake*, Canto iv, st. 1

A child will weep a bramble's smart,
A maid to see her sparrow part:
A stripling for a woman's heart:
But woe awaits a country when
She sees the tears of bearded men.[1]
Then, oh! what omen, dark and high,
When Douglas wets his manly eye!
SCOTT, *Marmion*, v, 16.

The tears live in an onion that should water this sorrow. SHAKESPEARE, *Antony and Cleopatra*, i, 2

The big round tears
Coursed one another down his innocent nose
In piteous chase. SHAKESPEARE, *As You Like It*, ii, 1

---

[1]A woman's tear-drop melts, a man's half sears,
Like molten lead, as if you thrust a pike in
His heart, to force it out, for (to be shorter)
To them [*women*] 'tis a relief, to us a torture.
BYRON, *Don Juan*, Canto v, st. 118

Ere yet the salt of most unrighteous tears
Had left the flushing in her galled eyes.
SHAKESPEARE, *Hamlet*, i, 2

If you have tears, prepare to shed them now.
SHAKESPEARE, *Julius Cæsar*, iii, 2

My tears,
The moist impediments unto my speech.[1]
SHAKESPEARE, *King Henry IV, Part II*, iv, 5 [4]

The pretty and sweet manner of it forced
Those waters from me which I would have stopped;
But I had not so much of man in me,
And all my mother came into mine eyes
And gave me up to tears.[2]
SHAKESPEARE, *King Henry V*, iv, 6

One whose subdued eyes,
Albeit unused to the melting mood,
Drop tears as fast as the Arabian trees,
Their medicinal gum. SHAKESPEARE, *Othello*, v, 2

She drinks no other drink but tears,
Brewed with her sorrows, mashed [sorrow, meshed] upon her cheeks. SHAKESPEARE, *Titus Andronicus*, iii, 2

A sea of melting pearl, which some call tears.
SHAKESPEARE, *Two Gentlemen of Verona*, iii, 1

Tears, idle tears, I know not what they mean.
TENNYSON, *The Princess*, iv, line 21

Tedious. He's as tedious
As is a tired horse, a railing wife;
Worse than a smoky house: I had rather live
With cheese and garlic in a windmill, far,
Than feed on cates and have him talk to me
In any summer house in Christendom.
SHAKESPEARE, *King Henry IV, Part I*, iii, 1

---

[1] He has strangled
His language in his tears. SHAKESPEARE, *King Henry VIII*, v, 1

[2] Too much of water hast thou, poor Ophelia,
And therefore I forbid my tears: but yet
It is our trick; nature her custom holds,
Let shame say what it will: when these are gone,
The woman will be out. SHAKESPEARE, *Hamlet*, iv, 7

Cromwell, I did not think to shed a tear
In all my miseries; but thou hast forced me,
Out of thy honest truth, to play the woman.
SHAKESPEARE, *King Henry VIII*, iii, 2

Oh! I could play the woman with mine eyes
And braggart with my tongue. SHAKESPEARE, *Macbeth*, iv, 3

Life is as tedious as a twice-told tale,[1]
Vexing the dull ear of a drowsy man.
SHAKESPEARE, *King John*, iii, 4

Tedious it were to tell, and harsh to hear.
SHAKESPEARE, *Taming of the Shrew*, iii, 2

Tediousness.— Our house is hell, and thou, a merry devil,
Didst rob it of some taste of tediousness.
SHAKESPEARE, *Merchant of Venice*, ii, 3

Tell.— All down the long and narrow street he went
Beating it in upon his weary brain
As though it were the burthen of a song,
Not to tell her, never to let her know.
TENNYSON, *Enoch Arden*, lines 791–794

Temper.— There was a stock of temper we both had for a start,
Although we never suspected 't would take us two apart.
W. CARLETON, *Betsey and I Are Out*, st. 4

Oh! blessed with temper, whose unclouded ray
Can make to-morrow cheerful as to-day;
She, who can love a sister's charms, or hear
Sighs for a daughter with unwounded ear;

. . . . .

Charms by accepting, by submitting sways,
Yet has her humour most, when she obeys.
POPE, *Moral Essays*, Epistle ii, lines 257–264

Tempest.— If after every tempest come such calms,
May the winds blow till they have wakened death!
And let the labouring bark climb hills of seas
Olympus-high, and duck again as low
As hell's from heaven. SHAKESPEARE, *Othello*, ii, 1

Temples.— The groves were God's first temples.
BRYANT, *A Forest Hymn*, line 1

Tempted.— 'Tis one thing to be tempted, Escalus,
Another thing to fall.
SHAKESPEARE, *Measure for Measure*, ii, 1

Tempter.— The tempter or the tempted, who sins most?
SHAKESPEARE, *Measure for Measure*, ii, 2

---

[1] What is so tedious as a twice-told tale? POPE, *Odyssey*, XII, *ad finem*

This act is as an ancient tale new told,
And in the last repeating troublesome.— SHAKESPEARE, *King John*, iv, 2

Tender.— More tender and more true.—SCOTT, *Marmion*, v, 16

Tennis. Renouncing clean
The faith they have in tennis, and tall stockings,
Short blistered breeches, and those types of travel.
SHAKESPEARE, *King Henry VIII*, i, 3

Tent.—'T is but a tent where takes his one day's rest
A Sultán to the realm of Death addressed;
The Sultán rises, and the dark Ferrash
Strikes, and prepares it for another guest.
OMAR KHAYYÁM, *Rubáiyát* (trans. Fitzgerald), st. 45

Terms.— Many holiday and lady terms.
SHAKESPEARE, *King Henry IV, Part I*, i, 3

Terrors.— The knell, the shroud, the mattock, and the grave;
The deep damp vault, the darkness, and the worm;
These are the bugbears of a winter's eve,
The terrors of the living, not the dead.
YOUNG, *Night Thoughts*, IV, lines 10–13

Text. Many a holy text around she strews,
That teach the rustic moralist to die.
GRAY, *Elegy Written in a Country Churchyard*, st. 22

Texts. Old Brown, . . .
Mad as he was, knew texts enough to wear a parson's gown. E. C. STEDMAN, *How Old Brown Took Harper's Ferry*, st. 7

Thankful.— I doubt whether that practice of piety, . . . to be thankful because we are better off than somebody else, be a very rational religious exercise.
THACKERAY, *Vanity Fair*, lxvi

Thanks.— Thanks, the exchequer of the poor.
SHAKESPEARE, *King Richard II*, ii, 3

Theoric.— The bookish theoric. SHAKESPEARE, *Othello*, i, 1

Thief.— *Dogberry*. If you meet a thief, you may suspect him, by virtue of your office, to be no true man; and, for such kind of men, the less you meddle or make with them, why, the more is for your honesty.

Second Watch. If we know him to be a thief, shall we not lay hands on him?

Dogberry. Truly, by your office, you may; but I think they that touch pitch will be defiled: the most peaceable way for you, if you do take a thief, is to let him show himself what he is and steal out of your company. SHAKESPEARE, *Much Ado about Nothing*, iii, 3

Thievery. I'll example you with thievery:
The sun's a thief, and with his great attraction
Robs the vast sea; the moon's an arrant thief,
And her pale fire she snatches from the sun:
The sea's a thief, whose liquid surge resolves
The moon into salt tears; the earth's a thief,
That feeds and breeds by a composture stolen
From general excrement: each thing's a thief.
SHAKESPEARE, *Timon of Athens*, iv, 3

Thieves.— A plague upon it when thieves cannot be true one to another.—SHAKESPEARE, *King Henry IV, Part I*, ii, 2

Thing.— Is this the Thing the Lord God made and gave
To have dominion over sea and land;
To trace the stars and search the heavens for power;
To feel the passion of Eternity?
EDWIN MARKHAM, *The Man With the Hoe*, st. 2

Think.— Could we but think with the intensity
We love with, we might do great things.
P. J. BAILEY, *Festus*, Scene — Home

What I think I utter, and spend my malice in my breath. SHAKESPEARE, *Coriolanus*, ii, 1

Thinking.— There is nothing either good or bad, but thinking makes it so. SHAKESPEARE, *Hamlet*, ii, 2

Thirsty.— When my thirsty soul I steep,
Every sorrow's lulled to sleep.
Talk of monarchs! I am then
Richest, happiest, first of men;
Careless o'er my cup I sing,
Fancy makes me more than king;
Gives me wealthy Crœsus' store,
Can I, can I wish for more?
T. MOORE, *Odes of Anacreon*, xlviii

Thorn.— If Heaven a draught of heavenly pleasure spare,
One cordial in this melancholy vale,
'T is when a youthful, loving, modest pair,
In other's arms breathe out the tender tale,
Beneath the milk-white thorn that scents the evening gale. BURNS, *The Cotter's Saturday Night*, st. 9

A weary lot is thine, fair maid,
A weary lot is thine!
To pull the thorn thy brow to braid,
And press the rue for wine!

A lightsome eye, a soldier's mien,
  A feather of the blue,
A doublet of the Lincoln green,—
  No more of me you knew,
      My love!
No more of me you knew.

SCOTT, *Rokeby*, Canto iii, st. 28

Thorns.— The rills of pleasure never run sincere,
  (Earth has no unpolluted spring);
From the cursed soil some dang'rous taint they bear,
  So roses grow on thorns, and honey wears a sting.

ISAAC WATTS, *Lyric Poems: Earth and Heaven*, lines 9–12

Thought.— Thought is deeper than all speech,
  Feeling deeper than all thought.

C. P. CRANCH, *Thought*, st. 1

Tic-tac! tic-tac! go the wheels of thought; our will cannot stop them; they cannot stop themselves; sleep cannot still them; madness only makes them go faster; death alone can break into the case, and, seizing the ever-swinging pendulum, which we call the heart, silence at last the clicking of the terrible escapement we have carried so long beneath our wrinkled foreheads. . . . Will nobody block those wheels, uncouple that pinion, cut the string that holds those weights, blow up the infernal machine with gunpowder? . . . If anybody would only contrive some kind of a lever that one could thrust in among the works of this horrid automaton and check them, or alter their rate of going, what would the world give for the discovery?

"From half a dime to a dime, according to the style of the place and the quality of the liquor,"— said the young fellow whom they call John.

HOLMES, *Autocrat of the Breakfast-Table*, viii

The weapons which your hands have found
  Are those which Heaven itself has wrought,
Light, Truth, and Love; your battle-ground
  The free, broad field of Thought.

WHITTIER, *To the Reformers of England*, st. 8

Thoughts.— And as I walk by the vast, calm river,
  The awful river so dread to see,
I say, "Thy breadth and thy depth for ever
  Are bridged by his thoughts that cross to me."

JEAN INGELOW, *Divided*, viii, st. 2

They are never alone that are accompanied with noble thoughts. SIR PHILIP SIDNEY, *Arcadia*, I

Thanks to the human heart by which we live,
Thanks to its tenderness, its joys, and fears,
To me the meanest flower that blows can give
Thoughts that do often lie too deep for tears.
WORDSWORTH, *Ode on Intimations of Immortality*, st. 11

Thoughts shut up want air,
And spoil, like bales unopened to the sun.
YOUNG, *Night Thoughts*, II, lines 467, 468

Threats.— There is no terror, Cassius, in your threats
For I am armed so strong in honesty
That they pass by me as the idle wind,
Which I respect not.
SHAKESPEARE, *Julius Cæsar*, iv, 3

Thrift.— Thrift is a blessing, if men steal it not.
SHAKESPEARE, *Merchant of Venice*, i, 3

Throats.— Men may sleep, and they may have their throats about them at that time; and some say knives have edges. SHAKESPEARE, *King Henry V*, ii, 1

Throne. A little shed
Where they shut up the lambs at night.
We looked in, and seen them huddled thar,
So warm and sleepy and white;
And thar sot Little Breeches, and chirped,
As peart as ever you see,
"I want a chaw of terbacker,
And that 's what 's the matter of me."

How did he git thar? Angels.
He could never have walked in that storm.
They just scooped down and toted him
To whar it was safe and warm.
And I think that saving a little child,
And bringing him to his own,
Is a derned sight better business
Than loafing around the Throne.
JOHN HAY, *Little Breeches*, st. 6, 7

In that fierce light which beats upon a throne.
TENNYSON, *Idylls of the King*, Dedication, line 26

Thumb.— Do you bite your thumb at us, sir?
SHAKESPEARE, *Romeo and Juliet*, i, 1

Thumbs.— By the pricking of my thumbs,
Something wicked this way comes.
SHAKESPEARE, *Macbeth*, iv, 1

Thumps.— The man that hails you Tom or Jack,
And proves by thumps upon your back
How he esteems your merit,[1]
Is such a friend that one had need
Be very much his friend indeed
To pardon or to bear it.
COWPER, *Friendship*, st. 29 [26]

Thunder.— From peak to peak, the rattling crags among
Leaps the live thunder!
BYRON, *Childe Harold's Pilgrimage*, Canto iii, st. 92

They will not let my play run; and yet they steal my thunder.
JOHN DENNIS, cited in *Biographia Britannica*, V

The thunder,
That deep and dreadful organ-pipe.
SHAKESPEARE, *The Tempest*, iii, 3

Thwack.— With many a stiff thwack, many a bang,
Hard crab-tree and old iron rang.
BUTLER, *Hudibras*, I, ii, lines 831, 832

Tickling.— Here comes the trout that must be caught with tickling. SHAKESPEARE, *Twelfth Night*, ii, 5

Tide.— There is a tide in the affairs of men,
Which, taken at the flood,[2] leads on to fortune.
SHAKESPEARE, *Julius Cæsar*, iv, 3

Even at the turning o' the tide.
SHAKESPEARE, *King Henry V*, ii, 3

Tiger.— Tiger! Tiger! burning bright,
In the forests of the night;
What immortal hand or eye
Could frame thy fearful symmetry?
WILLIAM BLAKE, *The Tiger*, st. 1

Timbrel.— Sound the loud timbrel o'er Egypt's dark sea!
Jehovah has triumphed — his people are free.
T. MOORE, *Sound the Loud Timbrel*

---

[1] Another reading is: "His sense of your great merit."

[2] "There is a tide in the affairs of men
Which, taken at the flood,"— you know the rest,
And most of us have found it, now and then;
At least we think so, though but few have guessed
The moment, till too late to come again.
BYRON, *Don Juan*, Canto vi, st. 1

Time.— Time writes no wrinkle on thine azure brow—
Such as creation's dawn beheld, thou rollest now.
BYRON, *Childe Harold's Pilgrimage*, Canto iv, st. 182

Rich with the spoils of time.
GRAY, *Elegy Written in a Country Churchyard*, st. 14

Time murders our youth with his sorrow and sin,
And pushes us on to the windowless inn.
EDWIN MARKHAM, *Youth and Time*, st. 4

Time was, Time is, but Time shall be no more.
W. MARSDEN, *What is Time?*

The Bird of Time has but a little way
To flutter.
OMAR KHAYYÁM, *Rubáiyát* (trans. Fitzgerald), st. 7

Who [*Time*], in the dark and silent grave,
When we have wandered all our ways,
Shuts up the story of our days:
But from this earth, this grave, this dust
My God shall raise me up, I trust![1]
SIR WALTER RALEIGH, *Even Such Is Time*[2]

Time is best measured by tears.
A. J. RYAN, *The Rosary of My Tears*

Time rolls his ceaseless course.[3]
SCOTT, *Lady of the Lake*, Canto iii, 1

The inaudible and noiseless foot of Time.[4]
SHAKESPEARE, *All's Well That Ends Well*, v, 3

Rosalind. Time travels in divers paces with divers persons. I'll tell you who Time ambles withal, who Time trots withal, who Time gallops withal, and who he stands still withal.

Orlando. I pr'ythee, who doth he trot withal?

---

[1] According to a London edition of 1751
And from which grave, and earth, and dust,
The Lord shall raise me up, I trust.

[2] Said by Oldys to have been written by Raleigh the night before his execution.

[3] Remorseless Time!
Fierce spirit of the glass and scythe! — what power
Can stay him in his silent course, or melt
His iron heart to pity? On, still on,
He presses, and forever. G. D. PRENTICE, *The Closing Year*, st. 5

[4] Too late I stayed,— forgive the crime!
Unheeded flew the hours:
How noiseless falls the foot of Time
That only treads on flowers.— W. R. SPENCER, *Too Late I Stayed*

Rosalind. Marry, he trots hard with a young maid between the contract of her marriage and the day it is solemnized: if the interim be but a se'nnight, Time's pace is so hard that it seems the length of seven year.

. . . . .

Orlando. Who doth he gallop withal?

Rosalind. With a thief to the gallows, for though he go as softly as foot can fall, he thinks himself too soon there. SHAKESPEARE, *As You Like It*, iii, 2

The time is out of joint. SHAKESPEARE, *Hamlet*, i, 5

We see which way the stream of time doth run.
SHAKESPEARE, *King Henry IV, Part II*, iv, 1

Old Time the clock-setter, that bald sexton Time.
SHAKESPEARE, *King John*, iii, 1

Time goes on crutches till Love have all his rites.
SHAKESPEARE, *Much Ado about Nothing*, ii, 1

What seest thou else
In the dark backward and abysm of time?
SHAKESPEARE, *The Tempest*, i, 2

Time hath, my lord, a wallet at his back,
Wherein he puts alms for oblivion,
A great-sized monster of ingratitudes:
Those scraps are good deeds past; which are devoured
As fast as they are made, forgot as soon
As done. SHAKESPEARE, *Troilus and Cressida*, iii, 3

Thus the whirligig of time brings in his revenges.
SHAKESPEARE, *Twelfth Night*, v

Time tries the troth in everything.
TUSSER, *Five Hundred Points of Good Husbandry*,
The Author's Epistle, i

We take no note of time
But from its loss.
YOUNG, *Night Thoughts*, I, lines 55, 56

Time wasted is existence; used, is life.[1]
Ibid., II, line 150

Times.— The times and titles now are altered strangely
With me since first you knew me.
SHAKESPEARE, *King Henry VIII*, iv, 2

---

[1] Dost thou love life, then do not squander time, for that is the stuff life is made of. FRANKLIN, *Poor Richard's Almanac*

Timid.— Then shrieked the timid, and stood still the brave.
BYRON, *Don Juan*, Canto ii, st. 52

Tintinnabulation. The tintinnabulation that so musically wells
From the bells, bells, bells, bells,
Bells, bells, bells —
From the jingling and the tinkling of the bells.
POE, *The Bells*, st. 1

Toad.— Squat like a toad, close at the ear of Eve.
MILTON, *Paradise Lost*, IV, line 800

Tobacco.— Sublime tobacco![1] which from east to west
Cheers the tar's labour or the Turkman's rest; . . .
Magnificent in Stamboul, but less grand,
Though not less loved, in Wapping or the Strand;
Divine in hookas, glorious in a pipe,[2]
When tipped with amber, yellow, rich, and ripe;
Like other charmers, wooing the caress
More dazzlingly when daring in full dress;
Yet thy true lovers more admire by far
Thy naked beauties — Give me a cigar!
BYRON, *The Island*, Canto ii, st. 19

What a glorious creature was he who first discovered the use of tobacco.
FIELDING, *The Grub Street Opera*, iii, 1

Peart and chipper and sassy,
Always ready to swear and fight,—
And I 'd larnt him ter chaw terbacker,
Jest to keep his milk-teeth white.
JOHN HAY, *Little Breeches*, st. 2

To-day. Happy the man, and happy he alone,
He, who can call to-day his own:
He who, secure within, can say,
To-morrow do thy worst, for I have lived to-day.[3]
DRYDEN, *Paraphrase of Horace*, III, Ode 29, lines 65–68

Never leave that till to-morrow which you can do to-day. FRANKLIN, *Poor Richard's Almanac*

---

[1] Divine tobacco! SPENSER, *Faerie Queene*, III, Canto v, 32

[2] A short frail pipe, which yet had blown
Its gentle odours over either zone,
And, puffed where'er winds rise or waters roll,
Had wafted smoke from Portsmouth to the Pole.
BYRON, *The Island*, Canto ii, st. 19

[3] Boldly say each night,
To-morrow let my sun his beams display,
Or in clouds hide them; I have lived to-day.
COWLEY, *Essay XI: Of Myself*

Cf. LIFE.

Rise from your dreams of the future,—
  Of gaining some hard-fought field;
Of storming some airy fortress,
  Or bidding some giant yield;
Your future has deeds of glory,
  Of honour (God grant it may!)
But your arm will never be stronger,
  Or the need so great as to-day.

A. A. PROCTER, *Now*, st. 2

Toe.— Come, and trip it as you go
On the light fantastic toe.[1]

MILTON, *L'Allegro*, lines 33, 34

Together.— I would change life's Spring for his roughest weather,
If we might bear the storm together;
And give my hopes for half thy fears,
And sell my smiles for half thy tears.

Give me one common bliss or woe,
One common friend, one common foe,
On the earth below, or the clouds above,
One thing we both may loathe, or love.

PRAED, *To* ——, st. 9, 10

They have seemed to be together, though absent; shook hands, as over a vast; and embraced, as it were, from the ends of opposed winds.

SHAKESPEARE, *Winter's Tale*, i. 1

Toil.— Heaven is blessed with perfect rest, but the blessing of Earth is toil.

HENRY VAN DYKE, *The Toiling of Felix*, Envoy, st. 5

He that will not live by toil
Has no right on English soil!
  God's word 's our warrant!

KINGSLEY, *Alton Locke's Song*, st. 2

Perchance, when long, long years are o'er —
  I care not how they flow —
Some note of me to that far shore
  Across the deep may go;
And thou wilt read, and turn to hide
The conscious blush of woman's pride;
  For thou alone wilt know
What spell inspired the silent toil
Of mid-day sun and midnight oil.

PRAED, *A Farewell*, st. 9

---

[1] Come, knit hands, and beat the ground
In a light fantastic round.

MILTON, *Comus*, lines 143, 144

Toiler.— Round swings the hammer of industry, quickly the sharp chisel rings,
And the heart of the toiler has throbbings that stir not the bosom of kings,—
He the true ruler and conqueror, he the true king of his race,
Who nerveth his arm for life's combat, and looks the strong world in the face.
D. F. MAC-CARTHY, *The Bell-Founder*

Toilet.— Rufa, whose eye quick-glancing o'er the Park,
Attracts each light gay meteor of a spark,
Agrees as ill with Rufa studying Locke,
As Sappho's di'monds with her dirty smock;
Or Sappho at her toilet's greasy task,
With Sappho fragrant at an ev'ning masque.
POPE, *Moral Essays*, Epistle ii, lines 21–26

Toiling.— Toiling, rejoicing, sorrowing,
Onward through life he goes;
Each morning sees some task begin,
Each evening sees it close;
Something attempted, something done,
Has earned a night's repose.
LONGFELLOW, *The Village Blacksmith*, st. 7

Toll.— Toll for the brave!
The brave that are no more!
COWPER, *On the Loss of the Royal George*, st. 1

Tolling.— Hear the tolling of the bells —
Iron bells!
What a world of solemn thought their monody compels.
POE, *The Bells*, st. 4

Tom.— Poor Tom's a-cold.—SHAKESPEARE, *King Lear*, iii, 4

Tomb.— When some proud son of man returns to earth,
Unknown to glory, but upheld by birth,
The sculptor's art exhausts the pomp of woe,
And storied urns record who rests below;
When all is done, upon the tomb is seen,
Not what he was, but what he should have been.
BYRON, *Inscription on the Monument of a Newfoundland Dog*, lines 1–6

Tombs.— Gilded tombs do worms enfold.
SHAKESPEARE, *Merchant of Venice*, ii, 7

Tommy. It's Tommy this, an' Tommy that, an' "Chuck him out, the brute!"
But it's "Saviour of 'is country," when the guns begin to shoot.
KIPLING, *Tommy*

To-morrow.— *To-morrow!*— Why, to-morrow I may be
Myself with Yesterday's seven thousand years.[1]
OMAR KHAYYÁM, *Rubáiyát* (trans. Fitzgerald), st. 21

And if the wine you drink, the lip you press,
End in what all begins and ends in — Yes;
Think then you are To-day what Yesterday
You were — To-morrow you shall not be less.
OMAR KHAYYÁM, *Rubáiyát* (trans. Fitzgerald), st. 42

To-morrow shall be like
To-day, but much more sweet.[2]
C. G. ROSSETTI, *The Unseen World*, st 2.

To-morrow, and to-morrow, and to-morrow,
Creeps in this petty pace from day to day
To the last syllable of recorded time,
And all our yesterdays have lighted fools
The way to dusty death. Out, out, brief candle!
Life 's but a walking shadow, a poor player
That struts and frets his hour upon the stage[3]
And then is heard no more: it is a tale
Told by an idiot, full of sound and fury,
Signifying nothing. SHAKESPEARE, *Macbeth*, v, 5

In human hearts what bolder thought can rise
Than man's presumption on to-morrow's dawn?
Where is to-morrow?
YOUNG, *Night Thoughts*, I, lines 373-375

Tongue.— Within this hollow cavern hung
The ready, swift, and tuneful tongue:
If Falsehood's honey it disdained,
And when it could not praise was chained;
If bold in Virtue's cause it spoke,
Yet gentle concord never broke,—
This silent tongue shall plead for thee
When Time unveils Eternity!
ANONYMOUS, *To a Skeleton*, st. 3

The firste vertue, sone, if thou wolt lere,
Is to restreyne, and kepe wel thy tonge.[4]
CHAUCER, *The Manciple's Tale*, lines 228, 229

---

[1] To-morrow, when You shall be You no more?
OMAR KHAYYÁM, *Rubáiyát* (trans. Fitzgerald), st. 53

[2] We were, fair queen,
Two lads that thought there was no more behind
But such a day to-morrow as to-day,
And to be boy eternal. SHAKESPEARE, *Winter's Tale*, i, 2

[3] Our little hour of strut and rave.— LOWELL, *Commemoration Ode*, st. 4

[4] Give thy thoughts no tongue,
Nor any unproportioned thought his act.— SHAKESPEARE, *Hamlet*, i, 3

When this poor lisping stammering tongue
  Lies silent in the grave.
COWPER, *Praise for the Fountain Opened*, st. 5

Let the candied tongue lick absurd pomp,
And crook the pregnant hinges of the knee,
Where thrift may follow fawning.
SHAKESPEARE, *Hamlet*, iii, 2

With doubler tongue
Than thine, thou serpent, never adder stung.
SHAKESPEARE, *Midsummer-Night's Dream*, iii, 2

Sir, would she give you so much of her lips
As of her tongue she oft bestows on me,
You'd have enough. SHAKESPEARE, *Othello*, ii, 1

My tongue will tell the anger of my heart,
Or else my heart, concealing it, will break;
And rather than it shall, I will be free
Even to the uttermost, as I please, in words.
SHAKESPEARE, *Taming of the Shrew*, iv, 3

What a spendthrift is he of his tongue!
SHAKESPEARE, *The Tempest*, ii, 1

The tongue is a fire,[1] as you know, my dear, the tongue is a fire. TENNYSON, *The Grandmother*, st. 7

We must be free or die, who speak the tongue
That Shakespeare spake, the faith and morals hold
Which Milton held.
WORDSWORTH, *It Is Not to Be Thought of*

Tongues.— Alas! they had been friends in youth;
But whispering tongues can poison truth;[2]
And constancy lives in realms above;
And life is thorny; and youth is vain;
And to be wroth with one we love
Doth work like madness in the brain.
S. T. COLERIDGE, *Christabel*, II, lines 408–413

How silver-sweet sound lovers' tongues by night,
Like softest music to attending ears!
SHAKESPEARE, *Romeo and Juliet*, ii, 2

Music of thousand tongues, formed by one tongue alone.
M. T. VISSCHER, *The Nightingale* (trans. Bowring)

---

[1] *James* iii, 6.

[2] A tonge cutteth frendship al a-two.
CHAUCER, *The Manciples Tale*, line 238

Toothache. There was never yet philosopher
That could endure the toothache patiently.
SHAKESPEARE, *Much Ado about Nothing*, v, 1

Tough.— He's hard-hearted, sir, is Joe — he's tough, sir, and de-vilish sly! DICKENS, *Dombey and Son*, vii

Tower. That tower of strength
Which stood four-square to all the winds that blew!
TENNYSON, *Ode on the Death of the Duke of Wellington*, st. 4

Tract.— I pray for grace — repent each sinful act —
Peruse, but underneath the rose, my Bible;
And love my neighbour, far too well, in fact,
To call and twit him with a godly tract
That's turned by application to a libel.
HOOD, *Ode to Rae Wilson, Esquire*, st. 4

Trade.— Hence merchants, unimpeachable of sin
Against the charities of domestic life,
Incorporated, seem at once to lose
Their nature; and, disclaiming all regard
For mercy and the common rights of man,
Build factories with blood, conducting trade
At the sword's point, and dyeing the white robe
Of innocent commercial justice red.[1]
COWPER, *The Task: The Winter Evening*, lines 676–683

Traders.— Within this hour it will be dinner-time:
Till that, I'll view the manners of the town,
Peruse the traders, gaze upon the buildings,
And then return and sleep within mine inn,
For with long travel I am stiff and weary.
SHAKESPEARE, *Comedy of Errors*, i, 2

Traveller.— A traveller between life and death.
WORDSWORTH, *She Was a Phantom of Delight*, st. 3

---

[1] How long, O cruel nation,
Will you stand, to move the world, on a child's heart,——
Stifle down with a mailed heel its palpitation,
And tread onward to your throne amid the mart?
Our blood splashes upward, O gold-heaper,
And your purple shows your path!
But the child's sob in the silence curses deeper
Than the strong man in his wrath.
E. B. BROWNING, *The Cry of the Children*, st. 13

The kilns and the curt-tongued mills say Go!
There's plenty that can, if you can't, we know.
Move out, if you think you're underpaid.
The poor are prolific; we're not afraid;
Trade is trade. LANIER, *The Symphony*, lines 46–50

Treason.— Treason doth never prosper: what's the reason?
Why, if it prosper, none dare call it treason.[1]
SIR JOHN HARRINGTON, *Epigrams*, iv, 3

Cæsar had his Brutus; Charles the First, his Cromwell; and George the Third —— (Treason! cried the Speaker . . . .) —— may profit by their example. If this be treason, make the most of it. PATRICK HENRY, *Speech on the Resolutions Concerning the Stamp Act, in the Virginia Assembly*, May, 1765

Tree.— And all amid them stood the Tree of Life,
High eminent, blooming ambrosial fruit
Of vegetable gold; and next to Life,
Our death, the Tree of Knowledge, grew fast by,
Knowledge of good, bought dear by knowing ill.
MILTON, *Paradise Lost*, IV, lines 218–222

Tremble.— I tremble for my country when I reflect that God is just. THOMAS JEFFERSON, *Notes on Virginia:* Query xviii

Trencher-man.— He is a very valiant trencher-man.
SHAKESPEARE, *Much Ado about Nothing*, i, 1

Trick.— I know a trick worth two of that.
SHAKESPEARE, *King Henry IV, Part I*, ii, 1

Trickled. His answer trickled through my head
Like water through a sieve.
C. L. DODGSON, *Through the Looking-Glass*, viii

Trifle.— Think naught a trifle, though it small appear;
Small sands the mountain, moments make the year,
And trifles life.
YOUNG, *Love of Fame*, Satire vi, lines 205–207 [208–211]

Triton.— This Triton of the minnows.
SHAKESPEARE, *Coriolanus*, iii, 1

Trivial.— What dire offence from am'rous causes springs,
What mighty contests rise from trivial things.
POPE, *Rape of the Lock*, Canto i, lines 1, 2

Troubadours.—Oh, the troubadours of old! with the gentle minstrelsie
Of hope and joy, or deep despair, whiche'er their lot might be;
For years they served their ladye-loves ere they their passions told,—
Oh, wondrous patience must have had those troubadours of old!
FRANCES BROWN, *Oh, the Pleasant Days of Old!*

---

[1] Let them call it mischief;
When it is past, and prospered, 't will be virtue.
BEN JONSON, *Catiline*, iii, 3

Trowel.— Well said: that was laid on with a trowel.
SHAKESPEARE, *As You Like It*, i, 2

True.— He serves all who dares be true.
EMERSON, *The Celestial Love*, st. 8

This above all: to thine own self be true,
And it must follow, as the night the day,
Thou canst not then be false to any man.
SHAKESPEARE, *Hamlet*, i, 3

'Tis true 'tis pity;
And pity 'tis 'tis true. *Ibid.*, ii, 2

My man's as true as steel.
SHAKESPEARE, *Romeo and Juliet*, ii, 4

Trumpet.— He has sounded forth the trumpet that shall never call retreat;
He is sifting out the hearts of men before his judgment-seat. JULIA WARD HOWE, *Battle-Hymn of the Republic*, st. 4

Trumps.— Like a man with eight trumps in his hand at a whist-table. LOWELL, *Fable for Critics*, line 40

Trust.— Put not your trust in money, but put your money in trust. HOLMES, *Autocrat of the Breakfast-Table*, ii

This be our motto, In God is our trust.
F. S. KEY, *The Star-Spangled Banner*, st. 4

What a fool Honesty is! and Trust, his sworn brother, a very simple gentleman! I have sold all my trumpery; . . . they throng who should buy first, as if my trinkets had been hallowed and brought a benediction to the buyer. SHAKESPEARE, *Winter's Tale*, iv, 4 [3]

Truth.— No pleasure is comparable to the standing upon the vantage ground of truth. BACON, *Essay I: Of Truth*

Truth is within ourselves; it takes no rise
From outward things. R. BROWNING, *Paracelsus*, i

Truth, crushed to earth, shall rise again;
Th' eternal years of God are hers;
But Error, wounded, writhes in pain,
And dies among his worshippers.[1]
BRYANT, *The Battle-Field*, st. 9

---

[1] Truth outlives pain, as the soul does life.
E. B. BROWNING, *Aurora Leigh*, VII, line 774

Does not Mr. Bryant say that Truth gets well if she is run over by a locomotive, while Error dies of lockjaw if she scratches her finger?
HOLMES, *Professor at the Breakfast-Table*, v

Whoever knew truth put to the worse in a free and open encounter?
MILTON, *Areopagitica*

Truth—*Continued*

'Tis strange,—but true; for truth is always strange;
Stranger than fiction.

BYRON, *Don Juan*, Canto xiv, st. 101

"Truth," I cried, "though the Heavens crush me for following her; no Falsehood! though a whole celestial Lubberland were the price of the apostasy."

CARLYLE, *Sartor Resartus*, II, vii

The good old bishops took a simpler way;
Each asked but what he heard his father say,
Or how he was instructed in his youth,
And by tradition's force upheld the truth.

DRYDEN, *The Hind and the Panther*, lines 736–739

I did n't know Truth was such an invalid. . . . How long is it since she could only take the air in a close carriage, with a gentleman in a black coat on the box?

HOLMES, *Professor at the Breakfast-Table*, v

Truth is invariable; but the Smithate of truth must always differ from the Brownate of truth. *Ibid.*, xii

The time is racked with birth-pangs; every hour
Brings forth some gasping truth, and truth new-born
Looks a misshapen and untimely growth,
The terror of the household and its shame,
A monster coiling in its nurse's lap
That some would strangle, some would only starve;
But still it breathes, and —

. . . . . .

— moves transfigured into angel guise,
Welcomed by all that cursed its hour of birth,
And folded in the same encircling arms
That cast it like a serpent from their hold.

HOLMES, *Truths*, lines 1–15

Many loved Truth, and lavished life's best oil
  Amid the dust of books to find her, . . .
    Many in sad faith sought for her,
    Many with crossed hands sighed for her;
    But these, our brothers, fought for her,
    At life's dear peril wrought for her,
    So loved her that they died for her.[1]

LOWELL, *Commemoration Ode*, st. 3

Men in earnest have no time to waste
In patching fig-leaves for the naked truth.

LOWELL, *A Glance Behind the Curtain*, lines 261, 262

---

[1] Immortal truth
That heroes fought for, martyrs died to save.

HOLMES, *Truths*, lines 31, 32

Truth for ever on the scaffold, Wrong for ever on the throne,—
Yet that scaffold sways the future, and, behind the dim unknown,
Standeth God within the shadow, keeping watch above his own.
LOWELL, *The Present Crisis*, st. 8

Were truth our uttered language, angels might talk with men,
And God-illumined earth should see the Golden Age again.—GERALD MASSEY, *This World is Full of Beauty*

Truth is as impossible to be soiled by any outward touch as the sunbeam. MILTON, *Doctrine and Discipline of Divorce*, Introduction

I do not know what I may appear to the world, but to myself I seem to have been only like a boy playing on the sea-shore, and diverting myself in now and then finding a smooth pebble, or a prettier shell than ordinary, whilst the great ocean of truth lay all undiscovered before me.
SIR ISAAC NEWTON, *Memoirs*, by Brewster, II, xxvii

'Tis not the many oaths that make the truth,
But the plain single vow that is vowed true.
SHAKESPEARE, *All's Well That Ends Well*, iv, 2

Power i' the truth o' the cause.
SHAKESPEARE, *Coriolanus*, iii, 3

If they speak more or less than truth, they are villains and the sons of darkness.
SHAKESPEARE, *King Henry IV, Part I*, ii, 4

Tell truth and shame the devil! *Ibid.*, iii, 1

The good I stand on is my truth and honesty.
SHAKESPEARE, *King Henry VIII*, v, 1

Truth hath a quiet breast.
SHAKESPEARE, *King Richard II*, i, 3

Truth is truth
To the end of reckoning.
SHAKESPEARE, *Measure for Measure*, v

Truth will come to light; . . . truth will out.
SHAKESPEARE, *Merchant of Venice*, ii, 2

---

[1] Showed worth on foot, and rascals in the coach.
DRYDEN, *Art of Poetry*, line 376

Wrong rules the land, and waiting justice sleeps.
J. G. HOLLAND, *Wanted*

Captive Good attending Captain Ill. SHAKESPEARE, *Sonnet lxvi*

Ring in the love of truth and right.
TENNYSON, *In Memoriam*, cvi, st. 6

Who never sold the truth to serve the hour,
Nor paltered with Eternal God for power.
TENNYSON, *Ode on the Death of the Duke of Wellington*, st. 7

The sages say, Dame Truth delights to dwell,
Strange mansion! in the bottom of a well.
JOHN WOLCOT, *Birthday Ode*

How happy is he born and taught
That serveth not another's will;
Whose armour is his honest thought
And simple truth his utmost skill!
SIR HENRY WOTTON, *Character of a Happy Life*, st. 1

Truths. Never earth's philosopher
Traced, with his golden pen,
On the deathless page, truths half so sage
As he wrote down for men.
C. F. ALEXANDER, *Burial of Moses*, st. 7

Truth-teller.— Truth-teller was our England's Alfred named.
TENNYSON, *Ode on the Death of the Duke of Wellington*, st. 7

Tub.— Every tub must stand upon its own bottom.
Bunyan's Pilgrim's Progress, I, Stage iii;
MACKLIN, *Man of the World*, i, 2

Turkey-cock.— Here he comes, swelling like a turkey-cock.
SHAKESPEARE, *King Henry V*, v, 1

Twain.— They two are twain.
SHAKESPEARE, *Troilus and Cressida*, iii, 1

Tweedle-dum— Strange! all this difference should be
'Twixt Tweedle-dum and Tweedle-dee![1]
JOHN BYROM, *Epigram on the Feuds about Handel and Bononcini*

Twin.— In form and feature, face and limb,
I grew so like my brother,
That folks got taking me for him,
And each for one another.
It puzzled all our kith and kin,
It reached an awful pitch;
For one of us was born a twin,
And not a soul knew which.
HENRY S. LEIGH, *The Twins*, st. 1

[1] These lines have also been attributed to Swift and Pope; they are assigned to Byrom in the Chalmers edition of *The English Poets* (1810).

Type.— So careful of the type she seems,
So carêless of the single life.
TENNYSON, *In Memoriam*, lv, st. 2

Tyranny. A name of fear
That tyranny shall quake to hear.[1]
BYRON, *The Giaour*, lines 119, 120

Where law ends, tyranny begins.
WILLIAM PITT, EARL OF CHATHAM, *Speech on Wilkes's Case*, Jan. 9, 1770

Tyrant. A tyrant throned in lonely pride,
Who loves himself, and cares for naught beside;
Who gave thee, summoned from primeval night,
A thousand laws, and not a single right,—
A heart to feel, and quivering nerves to thrill,
The sense of wrong, the death-defying will;
Who girt thy senses with this goodly frame,
Its earthly glories and its orbs of flame,
Not for thyself, unworthy of a thought,
Poor helpless victim of a life unsought,
But all for him, unchanging and supreme,
The heartless centre of thy frozen scheme!
HOLMES, *A Rhymed Lesson*, st. 10

Tyrants.—'Tis time to fear when tyrants seem to kiss.
SHAKESPEARE, *Pericles*, i, 2

Unborn.— The child may rue that is unborn
The hunting of that day.[2]
R. SHEALE, *Chevy-Chase*,[3] st. 2

Unction.— Lay not that flattering unction to your soul.
SHAKESPEARE, *Hamlet*, iii, 4

Undefiled.— Clear and cool, clear and cool,
By laughing shallow, and dreaming pool;
Cool and clear, cool and clear,
By shining shingle, and foaming weir;
Under the crag where the ouzel sings,
And the ivied wall where the church-bell rings,
Undefiled, for the undefiled;
Play by me, bathe in me, mother and child.
KINGSLEY, *Songs from the Water Babies*, I, st. 1

---

[1] [He] beckoned to the people, and in bold voice and clear
Poured thick and fast the burning words which tyrants quake to hear.
MACAULAY, *Virginia*, st. 5

[2] The woe's to come; the children yet unborn
Shall feel this day as sharp to them as thorn.
SHAKESPEARE, *King Richard II*, iv

[3] There are very many versions of this old ballad; the one here quoted belonging to the sixteenth or seventeenth century.

Undisputed.— Thou say 'st an undisputed thing
In such a solemn way. HOLMES, *To an Insect*, st. 1

Unfaltering.— And thus, with eyes that would not shrink,
With knee to man unbent,
Unfaltering on its dreadful brink,
To his red grave he went.
SIR F. H. DOYLE, *The Private of the Buffs*, st. 4

Unfortunate.— One more unfortunate,
Weary of breath,
Rashly importunate,
Gone to her death! HOOD, *The Bridge of Sighs*

Unhand. Unhand me, gentlemen!
By heaven I'll make a ghost of him that lets me!
SHAKESPEARE, *Hamlet*, i, 4

Uniform.— The uniform 'e wore
Was nothin' much before,
An' rather less than 'arf o' that be 'ind,
For a piece o' twisty rag
An' a goatskin water-bag
Was all the field-equipment 'e could find.
KIPLING, *Gunga Din*, st. 2

Union.— We join ourselves to no party that does not carry the flag and keep step to the music of the Union.
RUFUS CHOATE, *Letter to Massachusetts Whig Convention*, Oct. 1, 1855

The Federal Union — it must be preserved.
ANDREW JACKSON, *Toast on the Jefferson Birthday Celebration*, 1830

The flag of our Union for ever.
G. P. MORRIS, *The Flag of Our Union*

When my eyes shall be turned to behold for the last time the sun in heaven, may I not see him shining on the broken and dishonoured fragments of a once glorious Union, on States dissevered, discordant, belligerent; on a land rent with civil feuds, or drenched, it may be, in fraternal blood.—DANIEL WEBSTER, *Second Speech on Foote's Resolution* (*The Reply to Hayne*), Jan. 26, 1830

United.— United we stand — divided we fall![1] [2]
G. P. MORRIS, *The Flag of Our Union*

---

[1] The motto of the State of Missouri.

[2] By uniting we stand, by dividing we fall.
JOHN DICKINSON, *Liberty Song*

" We must indeed all hang together, or assuredly we shall all hang separately." BENJAMIN FRANKLIN,* cited in J. T. MORSE, *Benjamin Franklin*, viii

* Said at the time of the adoption of the Declaration of Independence.

Unkind.— Rich gifts wax poor when givers prove unkind.
SHAKESPEARE, *Hamlet*, iii, 1

Unkindliness.— Killed with inutterable unkindliness.
TENNYSON, *Merlin and Vivien*, line 884

Unkindness. Give me a bowl of wine.
In this I bury all unkindness.
SHAKESPEARE, *Julius Cæsar*, iv, 3

Unknown.— Not to know me argues yourselves unknown.
MILTON, *Paradise Lost*, IV, line 830

Unrewarded.— Nothing went unrewarded but desert.
DRYDEN, *Absalom and Achitophel*, I, line 560

Urn.— Can storied urn, or animated bust,
Back to its mansion call the fleeting breath?
Can honour's voice provoke the silent dust,
Or flattery soothe the dull, cold ear of death?
GRAY, *Elegy Written in a Country Churchyard*, st. 12

Usance.— I hate him for he is a Christian,
But more for that in low simplicity
He lends out money gratis and brings down
The rate of usance here with us in Venice.
SHAKESPEARE, *Merchant of Venice*, i, 3

Use.— Use almost can change the stamp of nature.
SHAKESPEARE, *Hamlet*, iii, 4

Use gave me fame at first, and fame again
Increasing gave me use. . . . .
I rather dread the loss of use than fame.
TENNYSON, *Merlin and Vivien*, lines 491, 492, 517

Uses.— To what base uses we may return, Horatio! Why may not imagination trace the noble dust of Alexander, till he find it stopping a bung-hole? . . . As thus: Alexander died, Alexander was buried, Alexander returneth into dust; the dust is earth; of earth we make loam; and why of that loam, whereto he was converted, might they not stop a beer-barrel?
Imperious [Imperial] Cæsar, dead and turned to clay,
Might stop a hole to keep the wind away:
Oh, that that [the] earth, which kept the world in awe,
Should patch a wall to expel the winter's flaw!
SHAKESPEARE, *Hamlet*, v, 1

Usurer.— The usurer is the greatest Sabbath-breaker, because his plough goeth every Sunday.
BACON, *Essay XLI: Of Usury*

Utopianism.— Utopianism: that is another of the devil's pet words. I believe the quiet admission which we are all of us so ready to make, that because things have long been wrong, it is impossible they should ever be right, is one of the most fatal sources of misery and crime.

RUSKIN, *Architecture and Painting*, iii

Vagrom.— *Dogberry.* You are thought here to be the most senseless and fit man for the constable of the watch; therefore bear you the lantern. This is your charge: you shall comprehend all vagrom men; you are to bid any man stand in the prince's name.

Second Watch. How if a' will not stand?

Dogberry. Why, then, take no note of him, but let him go; and presently call the rest of the watch together and thank God you are rid of a knave.

SHAKESPEARE, *Much Ado about Nothing*, iii, 3

Valentine.— To-morrow is Saint Valentine's Day,
All in the morning betime,
And I a maid at your window,
To be your Valentine. SHAKESPEARE, *Hamlet*, iv, 5

Valiant.— Thou may'st be valiant in a better cause;
But now thou seem'st a coward.

SHAKESPEARE, *Cymbeline*, iii, 4

I do not think a braver gentleman,
More active-valiant or more valiant-young,
More daring or more bold, is now alive
To grace this latter age with noble deeds.

SHAKESPEARE, *King Henry IV, Part I*, v, 1

As valiant as the wrathful dove or most magnanimous mouse. SHAKESPEARE, *King Henry IV, Part II*, iii, 2

Ring in the valiant man and free.

TENNYSON, *In Memoriam*, cvi, st. 8

Valley.— Love is of the valley.

TENNYSON, *The Princess*, line 183

Valour. He
That kills himself t' avoid misery, fears it,
And at the best shows but a bastard valour:
This life's a fort committed to my trust,
Which I must not yield up till it be forced;
Nor will I: he's not valiant that dares die,[1]
But he that nobly hears calamity.

P. MASSINGER, *The Maid of Honour*, iv. 3

---

[1] *Cf.* COWARD.

The better part of valour is discretion.
SHAKESPEARE, *King Henry IV, Part I*, v, 4

Ten to one is no impeach of valour.
SHAKESPEARE, *King Henry VI, Part III*, i, 4

You are the hare of whom the proverb goes,
Whose valour plucks dead lions by the beard.
SHAKESPEARE, *King John*, ii, 1

In a false quarrel there is no true valour.
SHAKESPEARE, *Much Ado about Nothing*, v, 1

My valour is certainly going! — it is sneaking off! I feel it oozing out, as it were, at the palms of my hands.
SHERIDAN, *The Rivals*, v, 3

Vampyrism.— Long illness is the real vampyrism; think of living a year or two after one is dead, by sucking the life-blood out of a frail young creature at one's bedside!
HOLMES, *Autocrat of the Breakfast-Table*, ix

Variety.— Variety 's the very spice of life,
That gives it all its flavour.[1]
COWPER, *The Task: The Time-Piece*, lines 606, 607

Vaux.— I wonder if Brougham thinks as much as he talks,
Said a punster, perusing a trial:
I vow, since his Lordship was made Baron Vaux,
He's been *Vaux et prœterea nihil!*
ANONYMOUS, *A Voice, and Nothing Else*

Veil.— There was the Door to which I found no Key;
There was the Veil through which I could not see;
Some little talk awhile of Me and Thee
There was — and then no more of Thee and Me.
OMAR KHAYYÁM, *Rubáiyát* (trans. Fitzgerald), st. 32

Veins.— But long o' her his veins 'ould run
All crinkly, like curled maple.
LOWELL, *The Courtin'*, st. 10

Vengeance.— Roused the vengeance blood alone could quell.
BYRON, *Childe Harold's Pilgrimage*, Canto iii, st. 23

Vengeance to God alone belongs;
But when I think on all my wrongs,
My blood is liquid flame! SCOTT, *Marmion*, vi, 7

---

[1] Variety alone gives joy;
The sweetest meats the soonest cloy.
PRIOR, *The Turtle and Sparrow*, lines 234, 235

Can vengeance be pursued further than death?
SHAKESPEARE, *Romeo and Juliet*, v, 3

Old Brown
Osawatomie Brown,
Raised his right hand up to heaven, calling Heaven's vengeance down.
E. C. STEDMAN, *How Old Brown Took Harper's Ferry*, st. 4

Venice.— I stood in Venice, on the Bridge of Sighs;
A palace and a prison on each hand.
BYRON, *Childe Harold's Pilgrimage*, Canto iv, st. 1

Venom.— We must supplant those rough rug-headed kerns,
Which live like venom where no venom else
But only they have privilege to live.
SHAKESPEARE, *King Richard II*, ii, 1

Venture.— Vessels large may venture more,
But little boats should keep near shore.
FRANKLIN, *Poor Richard's Almanac*

Ventures.— My ventures are not in one bottom trusted.
SHAKESPEARE, *Merchant of Venice*, i, 1

Venus.— Venus smiles not in a house of tears.
SHAKESPEARE, *Romeo and Juliet*, iv, 1

Verbosity.— He draweth out the thread of his verbosity finer than the staple of his argument.
SHAKESPEARE, *Love's Labour's Lost*, v, 1

Verse.— Who says in verse what others say in prose.[1]
POPE, *Imitations of Horace*, II, Epistle i, line 202

Verses.— Tear him for his bad verses.
SHAKESPEARE, *Julius Cæsar*, iii, 3

Veteran.— Superfluous lags the veteran on the stage.
SAMUEL JOHNSON, *Vanity of Human Wishes*, line 308

Vice.— When vice prevails, and impious men bear sway,
The post of honour is a private station.
ADDISON, *Cato*, iv, 4

Vice itself lost half its evil by losing all its grossness.
BURKE, *On the French Revolution*

---

[1] Prose poets like blank verse. BYRON, *Don Juan*, Canto i, st. 201

Prose is verse, and verse is merely prose.
BYRON, *English Bards and Scotch Reviewers*, line 236 [241]

Whose [*Emerson's*] prose is grand verse, while his verse, the Lord knows,
Is some of it pr—— no, 'tis not even prose.
LOWELL, *Fable for Critics*, lines 530, 531

Before any vice can fasten on a man, body, mind, or moral nature must be debilitated. The mosses and fungi gather on sickly trees, not thriving ones; and the odious parasites which fasten on the human frame choose that which is already enfeebled.

HOLMES, *Autocrat of the Breakfast-Table*, viii

If he does really think that there is no distinction between virtue and vice, why, sir, when he leaves our houses let us count our spoons.

SAMUEL JOHNSON, *Life*, by Boswell, 1763

Vice is a monster of so frightful mien,
As, to be hated, needs but to be seen;[1]
Yet seen too oft, familiar with her face,
We first endure, then pity, then embrace.

POPE, *Essay on Man*, Epistle ii, lines 217–220

There is no vice so simple but assumes
Some mark of virtue on his outward parts.

SHAKESPEARE, *Merchant of Venice*, iii, 2

Vices.— The gods are just, and of our pleasant vices
Make instruments to plague us.

SHAKESPEARE, *King Lear*, v, 3

Vicissitudes.— The sad vicissitudes of things.

R. GIFFORD, *Contemplation*

Victory.— A victory is twice itself when the achiever brings home full numbers.

SHAKESPEARE, *Much Ado about Nothing*, i, 1

"What they fought each other for,
I could not well make out;
But everybody said," quoth he,
"That 'twas a famous victory."

. . . . .

"With fire and sword the country round
Was wasted far and wide,
And many a childing mother then,
And new-born baby, died;
But things like that, you know, must be
At every famous victory."

. . . . .

"But what good came of it at last?"
Quoth little Peterkin.
"Why, that I cannot tell," said he;
"But 't was a famous victory."

SOUTHEY, *Battle of Blenheim*, st. 6, 8, 11

---

[1] Truth has such a face and such a mien
As to be loved needs only to be seen.

DRYDEN, *The Hind and the Panther*, lines 33, 34

Villain.— If God writes a legible hand, that fellow's a villain.
JAMES QUIN (speaking of Charles Macklin's features), cited in Watkins' Biographical Dictionary

O villain, villain, smiling damned villain!
My tables,— meet it is I set it down,
That one may smile, and smile, and be a villain.
SHAKESPEARE, *Hamlet*, i, 5

Hamlet. There's ne'er a villain dwelling in all Denmark
But he's an arrant knave.
Horatio. There needs no ghost, my lord, come from the grave
To tell us this. *Ibid.*

Villainy.— Trust not those cunning waters of his eyes,
For villainy is not without such rheum.
SHAKESPEARE, *King John*, iv, 3

Vine.— You know, my friends, with what a brave carouse
I made a second marriage in my house;
Divorced old barren Reason from my bed,
And took the Daughter of the Vine to spouse.
OMAR KHAYYÁM, *Rubáiyát* (trans. Fitzgerald), st. 55

Vintners. I wonder often what the vintners buy
One half so precious as the stuff they sell.
OMAR KHAYYÁM, *Rubáiyát* (trans. Fitzgerald), st. 95

Violet.— And from his ashes may be made
The violet of his native land.
TENNYSON, *In Memoriam*, xviii, st. 1

Violets.— Weep no more, lady, weep no more,
Thy sorrowe is in vaine;
For violets pluckt the sweetest showers
Will ne'er make grow againe.
THOMAS PERCY, *The Friars of Orders Gray*, st. 12

Lay her i' the earth:
And from her fair and unpolluted flesh
May violets spring! I tell thee, churlish priest,
A ministering angel shall my sister be,
When thou liest howling. SHAKESPEARE, *Hamlet*, v, 1

Virgins.— Where the virgins are soft as the roses they twine,
And all, save the spirit of man, is divine.
BYRON, *Bride of Abydos*, Canto i, st. 1

Virtue.— Virtue is like precious odours, most fragrant when they are incensed or crushed; for prosperity doth best discover vice, and adversity doth best discover virtue.
BACON, *Essay V: Of Adversity*

Virtue is its own reward![1] JOHN HOME, *Douglas*, iii, 1

Underneath this stone doth lie
As much beauty as could die:
Which in life did harbour give
To more virtue than doth live.
BEN JONSON, *Epitaph on Elizabeth L. H.*

Let this great maxim be my virtue's guide;
In part she is to blame that has been tried —
He comes too near that comes to be denied.
LADY MARY WORTLEY MONTAGU, *The Lady's Resolve*, lines 9–11

Know then this truth (enough for man to know)
"Virtue alone is happiness below."
POPE, *Essay on Man*, Epistle iv, lines 309, 310

Assume a virtue, if you have it not.
SHAKESPEARE, *Hamlet*, iii, 4

Virtuous.— For blessings ever wait on virtuous deeds;
And though a late a sure reward succeeds.
CONGREVE, *Mourning Bride*, v, 3

Sir Toby. Dost thou think, because thou art virtuous, there shall be no more cakes and ale?
Clown. Yes, by Saint Anne; and ginger shall be hot i' the mouth too. SHAKESPEARE, *Twelfth Night*, ii, 3

Visage. That large-moulded man,
His visage all agrin as at a wake,
Made at me through the press.
TENNYSON, *The Princess*, v, lines 509–511

Vision.— At the dead of the night a sweet vision I saw,
And thrice ere the morning I dreamt it again.
CAMPBELL, *The Soldier's Dream*, st. 2

---

[1] Why to true merit should they have regard?
They know that virtue is its own reward.
GAY, *Epistle to Paul Methuen*, lines 41, 42

Virtue is to herself the best reward. HENRY MORE, *Cupid's Conflict*

Our revels now are ended. These our actors,
As I foretold you, were all spirits, and
Are melted into air, into thin air:
And, like the baseless fabric of this vision,
The cloud-capped towers, the gorgeous palaces,
The solemn temples, the great globe itself,
Yea, all which it inherit, shall dissolve,
And, like this insubstantial pageant faded,
Leave not a rack behind. We are such stuff
As dreams are made on,[1] and our little life
Is rounded with a sleep.

SHAKESPEARE, *The Tempest*, iv, 1

Vital.— Vital spark of heavenly flame!
Quit, oh quit this mortal frame.[2]

POPE, *The Dying Christian to His Soul*, st. 1

Voice.— Give every man thy [thine] ear, but few thy voice.

SHAKESPEARE, *Hamlet*, i, 3

Her voice was ever soft,
Gentle, and low, an excellent thing in woman.

SHAKESPEARE, *King Lear*, v, 3

I hear a voice you cannot hear,
Which says I must not stay,
I see a hand you cannot see,
Which beckons me away.

TICKELL, *Colin and Lucy*

Vows.— Thy vows are all broken,
And light is thy fame;
I hear thy name spoken,
And share in its shame.

BYRON, *When We Two Parted*, st. 2

Yet now she says those words were air,
Those vows were written all in water,
And, by the lamp that saw her swear,
Has yielded to the first that sought her.

J. H. MERIVALE, *The Vow* (from the Greek of Meleager)

Those mouth-made vows,
Which break themselves in swearing!

SHAKESPEARE, *Antony and Cleopatra*, i, 3

---

[1] Wrought of such stuffs as dreams are; and as baseless
As the fantastic visions of the evening.

NATHANIEL COTTON, *To-Morrow*, lines 15, 16

[2] Soon may this fluttering spark of vital flame
Forsake its languid melancholy frame.

CAMPBELL, *Love and Madness*, st. 12

When the blood burns, how prodigal the soul
Lends the tongue vows.[1] SHAKESPEARE, *Hamlet*, i, 3

By all the vows that ever men have broke,
In number more than ever women spoke.
SHAKESPEARE, *Midsummer-Night's Dream*, i, 1

Vows are but breath, and breath a vapour is.
SHAKESPEARE, *Love's Labour's Lost*, iv, 3

Wager. Most men (till by losing rendered sager)
Will back their own opinions with a wager.
BYRON, *Beppo*, st. 27

Waist.— Her waist is ampler than her life,
For life is but a span. HOLMES, *My Aunt*, st. 1

Wait.— Those who wait the coming rider travel twice as far as he;
Tired wench and coming butter never did in time agree.
BRET HARTE, *Concepcion de Arguello*, iii, st. 13

They also serve who only stand and wait.
MILTON, *Sonnet on His Blindness*

Waiting.— Only waiting till the shadows
Are a little longer grown,
Only waiting till the glimmer
Of the day's last beam is flown;
Till the night of earth is faded
From the heart, once full of day;
Till the stars of heaven are breaking
Through the twilight soft and grey.
F. L. MACE, *"Only Waiting."*

---

[1] Fain would I say, "Forgive my foul offence!"
Fain promise never more to disobey;
But, should my Author health again dispense,
Again I might desert fair Virtue's way.
BURNS, *In the Prospect of Death*. st. 2

What shall I do? Make vows and break them still?
'Twill be but labor lost!
My good cannot prevail against mine ill:
The business will be crost.

O, say not so; thou canst not tell what strength
Thy God may give thee at the length:
Renew thy vows, and if thou keep the last,
Thy God will pardon all that 's past
Vow while thou canst; while thou canst vow, thou mayst
Perhaps perform it when thou thinkest least.

. . . . . .

Then once again
I vow to mend my ways;
Lord, say Amen,
And thine be all the praise.
GEORGE HERBERT, *Vows Broken and Renewed*, st. 2, 3

Walks.— She walks in beauty, like the night
Of cloudless climes and starry skies.
BYRON, *She Walks in Beauty*, st. 1

Wall.— The weakest goes to the wall.
SHAKESPEARE, *Romeo and Juliet*, i, 1

Walrus.— "The time has come," the Walrus said,
"To talk of many things:
Of shoes — and ships — and sealing-wax —
Of cabbages—and kings."
C. L. DODGSON ("LEWIS CARROLL"), *Through the Looking-Glass*, iv

Want.—For only one short hour
To feel as I used to feel,
Before I knew the woes of want
And the walk that costs a meal!
HOOD, *The Song of the Shirt*, st. 9

The more you have,
The more you want.
POPE, *Imitations of Horace*, II, Epistle ii, lines 213, 214

Ring out the want, the care, the sin.
TENNYSON, *In Memoriam*, cvi, st. 5

War. My voice is still for war.[1]
Gods! can a Roman senate long debate
Which of the two to choose, slavery or death!
ADDISON, *Cato*, ii, 1

Just fear of an imminent danger, though there be no blow given, is a lawful cause of a war.
BACON, *Essay XIX: Of Empire*

It hath been said that an unjust peace is to be preferred before a just war.[2]
S. BUTLER, *Speeches in the Rump Parliament*

War's a game, which, were their subjects wise,
Kings would not play at.
COWPER, *The Task: The Winter Morning Walk*, lines 187, 188

---

[1] War, war is still the cry, "war even to the knife!"*
BYRON, *Childe Harold's Pilgrimage*, Canto i, st. 86

My sentence is for open war. MILTON, *Paradise Lost*, II, line 51

[2] There never was a good war or a bad peace.
FRANKLIN, *Letter to Josiah Quincy*, Sept. 11, 1773

---

*This was the answer of General Palafox at Saragoza when summoned to surrender by the French besieging army.

War, he sung, is toil and trouble,
Honour but an empty bubble.
DRYDEN, *Alexander's Feast*, v, 5

Both parties deprecated war; but one of them would make war rather than let the nation survive; and the other would accept war rather than let it perish. And the war came.
LINCOLN, *Second Inaugural Address*, March 4, 1865

Ez fer war, I call it murder,—
There you hev it plain an' flat;
I don't want to go no furder
Than my testyment fer that:
. . . . .
An' you've gut to git up airly
Ef you want to take in God.
LOWELL, *Biglow Papers*, I, i, st. 5

With good old idees o' wut's right an' wut ain't,
We kind o' thought Christ went agin war an' pillage,
An' thet eppyletts worn't the best mark of a saint.
Ibid., iii, st. 5

Not but wut abstract war is horrid,
I sign to thet with all my heart,—
But civlyzation does git forrid
Sometimes upon a powder-cart. *Ibid.*, vii, st. 5

Long peace, I find,
But nurses dangerous humours up to strength,
License and wanton rage, which war alone
Can purge away. D. MALLET, *Mustapha*

War, then, war
Open or understood, must be resolved.
MILTON, *Paradise Lost*, I, lines 661, 662

In war the moral element and public opinion are half the battle.
NAPOLEON BONAPARTE, *Life*, by Sloane, IV, 28

War its thousands slays, Peace its ten thousands.
PORTEOUS, *Death*, line 178

I have seen war's lightning flashing,
Seen the claymore with bayonet clashing,
Seen through red blood the war-horse dashing,
And scorned, amid the reeling strife,
To yield a step for death or life.
SCOTT, *Lay of the Last Minstrel*, Canto v, st. 21

The harsh and boisterous tongue of war.
SHAKESPEARE, *King Henry IV, Part II*, iv, 1

The poor souls for whom this hungry war
Opens his vasty jaws.
SHAKESPEARE, *King Henry V*, ii, 4

In war was never lion raged more fierce,
In peace was never gentle lamb more mild.
SHAKESPEARE, *King Richard II*, ii, 1

The purple testament of bleeding war. *Ibid.*, iii, 3

Grim-visaged war hath smoothed his wrinkled front;
And now, instead of mounting barbed steeds
To fright the souls of fearful adversaries,
He capers nimbly in a lady's chamber
To the lascivious pleasing of a lute.
SHAKESPEARE, *King Richard III*, i, 1

War is a virtue,—weakness a sin.
C. D. SHANLY, *Civil War*

War is hell.[1] W. T. SHERMAN[2]

Satan gave thereat his tail
A twirl of admiration;
For he thought of his daughter War
And her suckling babe Taxation.
SOUTHEY, *The Devil's Walk*, st. 10

To be prepared for war is one of the most effectual means of preserving peace.
GEORGE WASHINGTON, *Speech to Both Houses of Congress*, Jan. 8, 1790

Warble. Sweetest Shakespeare, Fancy's child,
Warble his native wood-notes wild.
MILTON, *L'Allegro*, lines 133, 134

War-drum.— The war-drum of the white man 'round the world. KIPLING, *The Song of the Banjo*, st. 4

---

[1] This is the soldier brave enough to tell
The glory-dazzled world that "war is hell";
Lover of peace, he looks beyond the strife,
And rides through hell to save his country's life.
HENRY VAN DYKE, *On the St. Gaudens Statue of Sherman*

War is a terrible trade.
LONGFELLOW, *Courtship of Miles Standish*, iv, line 135

[2] This saying is commonly ascribed to Gen. Sherman, but has never been definitely located in any of his writings or speeches.

Till the war-drum throbbed no longer, and the battle-flags were furled
In the Parliament of Man, the Federation of the World.
TENNYSON, *Locksley Hall*, lines 127, 128

Warfare.— The world is full of warfare 'twixt the evil and the good;
I watched the battle from afar as one that understood
The shouting and confusion, the bloody, blundering fight —
How few they are that see it clear, how few that wage it right!
HENRY VAN DYKE, *Another Chancc*, st. 5

Warmth. What can match, to solve a learned doubt,
The warmth within that comes from "cold without"?
HOLMES, *A Modest Request: The Toast*, lines 49, 50

Warrant.— I hope your warrant will bear out the deed.
SHAKESPEARE, *King John*, iv, 1

Warrior.— But when the warrior dieth,
His comrades of the war,
With arms reversed and muffled drums,
Follow the funeral car.
They show the banners taken,
They tell his battles won,
And after him lead his masterless steed,
While peals the minute-gun.
C. F. ALEXANDER, *Burial of Moses*, st. 5

He lay like a warrior taking his rest
With his martial cloak around him.
CHARLES WOLFE, *Burial of Sir John Moore*, st. 3

Warriors.— The stern joy which warriors feel
In foemen worthy of their steel.
SCOTT, *Lady of the Lake*, Canto v, st. 10

Wars.— Why then are you not contented?
Why then will you hunt each other?
I am weary of your quarrels,
Weary of your wars and bloodshed,
Weary of your prayers for vengeance,
Of your wrangles and dissensions;
All your strength is in your union,
All your danger is in discord;
Therefore be at peace henceforward,
And as brothers live together.
LONGFELLOW, *Song of Hiawatha: The Peace-Pipe*, lines 106–115

What would you have me do? go to the wars, would you? where a man may serve seven years for the loss of a leg, and have not money enough in the end to buy him a wooden one? SHAKESPEARE, *Pericles*, iv, 6

Ring out the thousand wars of old.
TENNYSON, *In Memoriam*, cvi, st. 7

Washington.— Where may the wearied eye repose,
When gazing on the great;
Where neither guilty glory glows,
Nor despicable state?
Yes — one — the first — the last — the best —
The Cincinnatus of the West,
Whom envy dared not hate,
Bequeathed the name of Washington,
To make man blush there was but one!
BYRON, *Additional Stanzas to the Ode to Napoleon Bonaparte*, st. 19

Waspish.— If I be waspish, best beware my sting.
SHAKESPEARE, *Taming of the Shrew*, ii

Wasted.— Oh, the wasted hours of life
That have drifted by!
Oh, the good that might have been —
Lost, without a sigh!
Love that we might once have saved
By a single word,
Thoughts conceived, but never penned,
Perishing unheard;
Take the proverb to thine heart,
Take, and hold it fast —
"The mill cannot grind
With the water that is past."
SARAH DOUDNEY, *The Lesson of the Water Mill*, st. 5

Watch.—"Wal'r, . . . a parting gift, my lad. Put it back half an hour every morning, and about another quarter towards the arternoon, and it's a watch that'll do you credit." DICKENS, *Dombey and Son*, xix

For the watch to babble . . . is most tolerable and not to be endured.
SHAKESPEARE, *Much Ado about Nothing*, iii, 3

Watches.—'T is with our judgments as our watches, none
Go just alike, yet each believes his own.
POPE, *Essay on Criticism*, lines 9, 10

Watchman.—"What of the night, watchman?
What of the night?"
"Cloudy — all quiet;
No land yet — all's right."
Be wakeful, be vigilant;
Danger may be
At an hour when all seemeth
Securest to thee.
C. A. B. SOUTHEY, *Christian Mariner's Hymn*, st. 3

Water.— Water, water, every where,
And all the boards did shrink;
Water, water, every where
Nor any drop to drink.[1]
COLERIDGE, *Ancient Mariner*, lines 119-122

The conscious water saw its God and blushed.
R. CRASHAW, *Translation of Divine Epigram on John ii*

Oh, water for me! Bright water for me![2]
EDWARD JOHNSON, *The Water-Drinker*, st. 1

I came like water, and like wind I go.
OMAR KHAYYÁM, *Rubáiyát* (trans. Fitzgerald), st. 28

Smooth runs the water where the brook is deep.
SHAKESPEARE, *King Henry VI, Part II*, iii, 1

More water glideth by the mill
Than wots the miller of; and easy it is
Of a cut loaf to steal a shive.
SHAKESPEARE, *Titus Andronicus*, ii, 1

'T is a little thing
To give a cup of water; yet its draught
Of cool refreshment, drained by fevered lips,
May give a shock of pleasure to the frame
More exquisite than when nectarean juice
Renews the life of joy in happier hours.
SIR T. N. TALFOURD, *Ion*, i, 2

Waterloo.— The grave of France, the deadly Waterloo.
BYRON, *Childe Harold's Pilgrimage*, Canto iii, st. 18

---

[1] In midst of water I complain of thirst.
DRYDEN, *Iphis and Ianthe*, line 144

[2] Here's that which is too weak to be a sinner, honest water, which ne'er left man i' the mire. SHAKESPEARE, *Timon of Athens*, i, 2

Waters.— How gloriously her gallant course she goes!
Her white wings flying — never from her foes —
She walks the waters like a thing of life,[1]
And seems to dare the elements to strife.
BYRON, *The Corsair*, Canto i, st. 3

The hell of waters! where they howl and hiss,
And boil in endless torture.
BYRON, *Childe Harold's Pilgrimage*, Canto iv, st. 69

The world of waters is our home,
And merry men are we.
A. CUNNINGHAM, *A Wet Sheet and a Flowing Sea*

Unpathed waters, undreamed shores.
SHAKESPEARE, *Winter's Tale*, iv, 4 [3]

Waves.— Once more upon the waters! yet once more!
And the waves bound beneath me as a steed
That knows his rider.
BYRON, *Childe Harold's Pilgrimage*, Canto iii, st. 2

The waves with all their white crests dancing
Come, like thick-plumed squadrons, to the shore
Gallantly bounding.
AUBREY HUNT (Sir Aubrey de Vere), *Julian*.

Wax.— Since I nor wax nor honey can bring home,
I quickly were dissolved from my hive,
To give some labourers room.
SHAKESPEARE, *All's Well That Ends Well*, i, 2

Way. She hath a way,
Anne Hathaway;
To make grief bliss, Anne hath a way.
ANONYMOUS, *Anne Hathaway*

The way was long, the wind was cold,
The Minstrel was infirm and old.
SCOTT, *Lay of the Last Minstrel*, Introduction

Weak. To be weak is miserable,
Doing or suffering.
MILTON, *Paradise Lost*, I, lines 157, 158

And if my heart and flesh are weak
To bear an untried pain,
The bruised reed He will not break,
But strengthen and sustain.
WHITTIER, *The Eternal Goodness*, st. 17

---

[1] The master bold, . . .
Who ruled her like a thing of life
Amid the crested wave!— L. H. SIGOURNEY, *The Bell of the Wreck*, st. 2

Weakness.— Laments the weakness of these latter times.
THOMSON, *The Seasons: Autumn*, line 569

Weapons.— The race that shortens its weapons lengthens its boundaries. HOLMES, *Autocrat of the Breakfast-Table*, i

Wear. Really and truly — I've nothing to wear.
W. A. BUTLER, *Nothing to Wear*

Weariness. Weariness
Can snore upon the flint, when resty sloth
Finds the down pillow hard.
SHAKESPEARE, *Cymbeline*, iii, 6

Weary.— Well may the children weep before you!
They are weary ere they run;
They have never seen the sunshine, nor the glory
Which is brighter than the sun.
E. B. BROWNING, *The Cry of the Children*, st. 12

I will arise, O Christ, when thou callest me; but oh! let me rest awhile, for I am very weary.
Epitaph in a German churchyard, quoted by
W. E. H. LECKY, *Map of Life*, xvi

Web-feet.— Nor must Uncle Sam's web-feet be forgotten. . . . Not only on the deep sea, the broad bay, and the rapid river, but also up the narrow, muddy bayou, and wherever the ground was a little damp, they have been and made their tracks.
LINCOLN, *Letter to J. C. Conkling*, Aug. 26, 1863

Wed.— So these were wed, and merrily rang the bells.
TENNYSON, *Enoch Arden*, line 80

Wedded.— Hail, wedded love, mysterious law, true source
Of human offspring!
MILTON, *Paradise Lost*, IV, lines 750, 751

Wedding.— Wedding is great Juno's crown.
SHAKESPEARE, *As You Like It*, v, 4

Wedding-bells.— Hear the mellow wedding-bells,
Golden bells!
What a world of happiness their harmony foretells.
POE, *The Bells*, st. 2

Wedges.— Never an axe had seen their chips,
And the wedges flew from between their lips,
Their blunt ends frizzled like celery-tips.
HOLMES, *The Deacon's Masterpiece*, st. 5

Wedlock. Wedlock without love, some say,
Is but a lock without a key.
BUTLER, *Hudibras*, II, i, lines 321, 322

Lawful awful wedlock.
BYRON, *Don Juan*, Canto xi, st. 89

Weeds.— Great weeds do grow apace.
SHAKESPEARE, *King Richard III*, ii, 4

Idle weeds are fast in growth. *Ibid.*, iii, 1

Weep.— Mine eyes smell onions; I shall weep anon.
SHAKESPEARE, *All's Well That Ends Well*, v, 3

I cannot choose but weep, to think that they should lay him i' the cold ground.
SHAKESPEARE, *Hamlet*, iv, 5

Oh, I could weep
My spirit from mine eyes!
SHAKESPEARE, *Julius Cæsar*, iv, 3

Weeping.— A little weeping would ease my heart,
But in their briny bed
My tears must stop, for every drop
Hinders needle and thread!
HOOD, *The Song of the Shirt*

I am not prone to weeping, as our sex
Commonly are. SHAKESPEARE, *Winter's Tale*, ii, 1

Weeps. Look, the good man weeps!
He's honest, on mine honour. God's blest mother!
I swear he is true-hearted; and a soul
None better in my kingdom.
SHAKESPEARE, *King Henry VIII*, v, 1

Welcome.— 'T is sweet to hear the watch-dog's honest bark
Bay deep-mouthed welcome as we draw near home;
'T is sweet to know there is an eye will mark
Our coming, and look brighter when we come.
BYRON, *Don Juan*, Canto i, st. 123

To say you're [you are] welcome were superfluous.
SHAKESPEARE, *Pericles*, ii, 3

Welcome ever smiles,
And farewell goes out sighing.
SHAKESPEARE, *Troilus and Cressida*, iii, 3

Well.— Were 't the last drop in the well,
And I gasping on the brink,[1]
Ere my fainting spirit fell,
'T is to thee that I would drink.
BYRON, *Lines to Moore*, st. 4

Werther.— Werther had a love for Charlotte
Such as words could never utter;
Would you know how first he met her?
She was cutting bread and butter.
THACKERAY, *Sorrows of Werther*, st. 1

Westminster.— Westminster Abbey or victory!
HORATIO, VISCOUNT NELSON, Exclamation at the battle of Cape St. Vincent

Westward-Ho.— *Olivia.* There lies your way, due west.
Viola. Then westward-ho!
SHAKESPEARE, *Twelfth Night*, iii, 1

Wether.— I am a tainted wether of the flock,
Meetest for death.
SHAKESPEARE, *Merchant of Venice*, iv, 1

Wethers.— To return to our wethers.[2] RABELAIS, I, i

Whale.— His angle-rod made of a sturdy oak;
His line a cable which in storms ne'er broke;
His hook he baited with a dragon's tail,
And sat upon a rock, and bobbed for whale.
W. KING, *Upon a Giant's Angling*

Wheels.— All day the iron wheels go onward,
Grinding life down from its mark;
And the children's souls, which God is calling sunward,
Spin on blindly in the dark.
E. B. BROWNING, *The Cry of the Children*, st. 8

And wheels [*bicycles*] rush in where horses fear to tread.— HOLMES, *Autocrat of the Breakfast-Table*, vii, *Note*

Whip.— O heaven, that such companions thou'dst unfold,
And put in every honest hand a whip
To lash the rascals naked through the world.
SHAKESPEARE, *Othello*, iv, 2

Whipped.— Thou shalt be whipped with wire, and stewed in brine,
Smarting in lingering pickle.
SHAKESPEARE, *Antony and Cleopatra*, ii, 5

---

[1] Another reading is: As I gasped upon the brink.

[2] Usually quoted "muttons" from the French word *moutons*.

Whipping.— Use every man after his desert, and who should [shall] 'scape whipping? SHAKESPEARE, *Hamlet*, ii, 2

She shall have whipping—cheer enough.
SHAKESPEARE, *King Henry IV, Part II*, v, 4

Whiskey.— No wonder that those Irish lads
Should be so gay and frisky,
For sure St. Pat he taught them that,
As well as making whiskey;
No wonder that the saint himself
Should understand distilling,
Since his mother kept a shebeen shop
In the town of Enniskillen.
HENRY BENNETT, *St. Patrick Was a Gentleman*

Freedom and whiskey gang thegither!
BURNS, *Prayer to the Scotch Representatives, ad finem*

Peat whiskey hot,
Tempered with well-boiled water!
These make the long night shorter,—
Forgetting not
Good stout old English porter.
R. H. MESSINGER, *A Winter Wish*, st. 1

Whistle.— Oh, whistle, and I'll come to you, my lad;
Though father and mither and a' should gae mad.
BURNS, *Oh, Whistle, and I'll Come To You*, st. 1

As clear as a whistle.
JOHN BYROM, *Epistle to Lloyd*, st. 12

With mug in hand to wet his whistle.
COTTON, *Virgil Travestie*, line 6

He has paid dear, very dear, for his whistle.
FRANKLIN, *The Whistle*, November, 1719

The maiden laughed out in her innocent glee,—
"What a fool of yourself with your whistle you'd make!
For only consider, how silly 't would be
To sit there and whistle for — what you might take!"
ROBERT STORY, *The Whistle*

Whistled.— He trudged along, unknowing what he sought,
And whistled as he went, for want of thought.
DRYDEN, *Cymon and Iphigenia*, lines 84, 85

Whistling.— The school-boy, with his satchel in his hand,
Whistling aloud to bear his courage up.
R. BLAIR, *The Grave*

Whitewood.— The panels of whitewood, that cuts like cheese,
But lasts like iron for things like these.
HOLMES, *The Deacon's Masterpiece*, st. 5

Why.— Whatever skeptic could enquire for,
For ev'ry why he had a wherefore.[1]
BUTLER, *Hudibras*, I, i, lines 131, 132

The "why" is plain as way to parish church.
SHAKESPEARE, *As You Like It*, ii, 7

Wicked.— She never followed wicked ways —
Unless when she was sinning.
GOLDSMITH, *Elegy on Mrs. Mary Blaize*, st. 3

I's wicked — I is. I's mighty wicked, anyhow. I can't help it. H. B. STOWE, *Uncle Tom's Cabin*, xx

Wickliffe.— The Avon to the Severn runs,
The Severn to the sea;
And Wickliffe's dust shall spread abroad,
Wide as the waters be.[2]
DANIEL WEBSTER, *Address before the "Sons of New Hampshire"*

Widow.— He died of the slow fever called the tertian,
And left his widow to her own aversion.
BYRON, *Don Juan*, Canto i, st. 34

Widow Machree, and when winter comes in,
Och hone! Widow Machree,
To be poking the fire all alone is a sin,
Och hone! Widow Machree.
Sure the shovel and tongs
To each other belongs,
And the kettle sings songs
Full of family glee;
While alone with your cup,
Like a hermit, you sup,
Och hone! Widow Machree.
SAMUEL LOVER, *Widow Machree*, st. 3

---

[1] Every why hath a wherefore.

. . . . .

Was there ever any man thus beaten out of season,
When in the why and the wherefore is neither rhyme nor reason?
SHAKESPEARE, *Comedy of Errors*, ii, 2

[2] Flung to the heedless winds,
Or on the waters cast,
The martyrs' ashes, watched,
Shall gathered be at last;
And from that scattered dust,
Around us and abroad,
Shall spring a plenteous seed
Of witnesses for God.
MARTIN LUTHER, *The Martyrs' Hymn* (trans. W. J. Fox)

Is it for fear to wet a widow's eye
That thou consum'st thyself in single life?
SHAKESPEARE, *Sonnet ix*

I' faith, he'll have a lusty widow now,
That shall be wooed and wedded in a day.
SHAKESPEARE, *Taming of the Shrew*, iv, 2

Widower.— Tears of the widower, when he sees
A late-lost form that sleep reveals,
And moves his doubtful arms, and feels
Her place is empty.
TENNYSON, *In Memoriam*, xiii, st. 1

Widows.— If for widows you die,
Learn to kiss, not to sigh.
CHARLES LEVER, *Widow Malone*, st. 6

Widow-maker. It grieves my soul,
That I must draw this metal from my side
To be a widow-maker!— SHAKESPEARE, *King John*, v, 2

Wife.— He that hath wife and children hath given hostages to fortune; for they are impediments to great enterprises, either of virtue or mischief.
BACON, *Essay VIII: Of Marriage and Single Life*

What is it, then, to have or have no wife,
But single thraldom or a double strife?
BACON, *The World*, st. 3

What is there in the vale of life
Half so delightful as a wife,
When friendship, love, and peace combine
To stamp the marriage bond divine?
COWPER, *Love Abused*, lines 1–4

The faithful wife, without debate.
HENRY HOWARD, EARL OF SURREY, *The Means to Attain Happy Life*

The world goes up and the world goes down,
And the sunshine follows the rain;
And yesterday's sneer and yesterday's frown
Can never come over again,
Sweet wife;
No, never come over again.

For woman is warm though man be cold,
And the night will hallow the day;
Till the heart which at even was weary and old
Can rise in the morning gay,
Sweet wife;
To its work in the morning gay
KINGSLEY, *Dolcino to Margaret*

Sail forth into the sea of life,
O gentle, loving, trusting wife!
LONGFELLOW, *Building of the Ship*, st. 24

The wife, where danger or dishonour lurks,
Safest and seemliest by her husband stays,
Who guards her, or with her the worst endures.
MILTON, *Paradise Lost*, IX, lines 267–269

All these good parts a perfect woman make;
Add love to me, they make a perfect wife;[1]
Without her love, her beauty I should take,
As that of pictures, dead; *that* gives it life;
Till then her beauty, like the sun, doth shine
Alike to all; *that* only makes it mine.
SIR T. OVERBURY, *A Wife*

You are my true and honourable wife,
As dear to me as are the ruddy drops
That visit my sad heart.[2]
SHAKESPEARE, *Julius Cæsar*, ii, 1

Wilderness.— The wilderness shall blossom as the rose.[3]
TENNYSON, *Aylmer's Field*, line 649

Will.— Be there a will, and wisdom finds the way.
G. CRABBE, *The Birth of Flattery*, st. 18

At war 'twixt will and will not.[4]
SHAKESPEARE, *Measure for Measure*, ii, 2

Willie Winkie.— Wee Willie Winkie rins through the town,
Up stairs and doon stairs, in his nicht-gown,
Tirlin' at the window, cryin' at the lock,
"Are the weans in their bed? — for it's now ten o'clock."
W. MILLER, *Willie Winkie*, st. 1

Willing.— Barkis is willin'.— DICKENS, *David Copperfield*, I, v

---

[1] A guardian angel o'er his life presiding,
Doubling his pleasures and his cares dividing,
Winning him back when mingling in the throng,
Back from a world we love, alas! too long,
To fireside happiness, to hours of ease,
Blest with that charm, the certainty to please.
SAMUEL ROGERS, *Human Life*

[2] Dear as the light that visits these sad eyes,
Dear as the ruddy drops that warm my heart.— GRAY, *The Bard*, i, 3

Dear as the vital warmth that feeds my life;
Dear as these eyes, that weep in fondness o'er thee.
T. OTWAY, *Venice Preserved*, v, 1

[3] The desert shall rejoice, and blossom as the rose. *Isaiah* xxxv, 1

[4] What I will not, that I cannot do.
SHAKESPEARE, *Measure for Measure*, ii, 2

We would, and we would not. *Ibid.*, iv, 4

Willow.— There is a willow grows aslant a brook,
That shows his hoar leaves in the glassy stream.
SHAKESPEARE, *Hamlet*, iv, 7

Win.— Heads I win,— ditto tails.
LOWELL, *Biglow Papers*, II, ii, *Jonathan to John*, st. 4

Wind. 'T was but the wind
Or the car rattling o'er the stony street.
BYRON, *Childe Harold's Pilgrimage*, Canto iii, st. 22

Blow, blow, thou winter wind,
Thou art not so unkind
As man's ingratitude;
Thy tooth is not so keen,
Because thou art not seen,
Although thy breath be rude.
SHAKESPEARE, *As You Like It*, ii, 7

Ill blows the wind that profits nobody.[1]
SHAKESPEARE, *King Henry VI, Part III*, ii, 5

Plucking the grass, to know where sits the wind,
Peering in maps for ports and piers and roads.
SHAKESPEARE, *Merchant of Venice*, i, 1

More inconstant than the wind, who woos
Even now the frozen bosom of the north,
And, being angered, puffs away from thence,
Turning his face to the dew-dropping south.
SHAKESPEARE, *Romeo and Juliet*, i, 4

Windows.— Windows of her mind.
JOHN CHALKHILL, *The Dwelling of Orandra*

Wine.— Wine and Truth, is the saying.— BUCKLEY, *Theocritus*

Few things surpass old wine: and they may preach
Who please,— the more because they preach in vain,—
Let us have wine and women,[2] mirth and laughter,
Sermons and soda-water the day after.
BYRON, *Don Juan*, Canto ii, st. 178

---

[1] *Falstaff.* What wind blew you hither, Pistol?
Pistol. Not the ill wind which blows no man to good.
SHAKESPEARE, *King Henry IV, Part II*, v, 3

Except winde stands as never it stood,
It is an ill winde turnes none to good.— THOMAS TUSSER, *Five Hundred Points of Good Husbandry: The Properties of Winds*

[2] Then comes witching wine again,
With glorious woman in its train. T. MOORE, *Odes of Anacreon*

Who loves not wine, woman, and song,
He is a fool his whole life long! THACKERAY, *A Credo*

It [wine] helps the headache, cough, and phthisic,
And is for all diseases physic.
JOHN FLETCHER, *Drink To-Day*, st. 2

Fill every beaker up, my men,
Pour forth the cheering wine;
There's life and strength in every drop,—
Thanksgiving to the vine!
A. G. GREENE, *The Baron's Last Banquet*, st. 7

If with water you fill up your glasses,
You'll never write anything wise;
For wine's the true horse of Parnassus,
Which carries a bard to the skies!
T. MOORE, from the Anthologia, cited in note to *Odes of Anacreon*

A cup of hot wine with not a drop of allaying Tiber[1] in't.
SHAKESPEARE, *Coriolanus*, ii, 1

O thou invisible spirit of wine, if thou hast no name to be known by, let us call thee devil!
SHAKESPEARE, *Othello*, ii, 3

Jars were made to drain, I think,
Wine, I know, was made to drink.
R. H. STODDARD, *Persian Songs: The Jar*, st. 1

Wisdom.— The strongest plume in wisdom's pinion
Is the memory of past folly.
S. T. COLERIDGE, *To an Unfortunate Woman*, st. 6

As if wisdom's old potato could not flourish at its root?
HOLMES, *Nux Postcœnatica*, st. 7

To observations which ourselves we make,
We grow more partial for th' observer's sake;
To written wisdom, as another's, less.
POPE, *Moral Essays*, Epistle i, lines 11–13

Wisdom and goodness to the vile seem vile.
SHAKESPEARE, *King Lear*, iv, 2

With wisdom fraught,
Not such as books, but such as practice taught.
WALLER, *On the King's Return*

Wisdom is oft-times nearer when we stoop
Than when we soar.
WORDSWORTH, *The Excursion: Despondency*, lines 232, 233

The man of wisdom is the man of years.
YOUNG, *Night Thoughts*, V, line 775

---

[1] With no allaying Thames. LOVELACE, *To Althea from Prison*, st. 2

Wise. Much too wise to walk into a well.
POPE, *Imitations of Horace*, II, *Epistle* ii, line 191

Thou think'st it folly to be wise too soon.
YOUNG, *Night Thoughts*, II, line 47

Wiseacres.— Down deep in a hollow some wiseacres sit,
Like a toad in his cell in the stone;
Around them in daylight the blind owlets flit,
And their creeds are with ivy o'ergrown.
. . . . .
Contented to dwell deep down in the well
Or move like the snail in the crust of his shell,
Or live like the toad in his narrow abode,
With their souls closely wedged in a thick wall of stone,
By the grey weeds of prejudice rankly o'ergrown.
R. S. NICHOLS, *The Philosopher Toad*

Wisest. So well to know
Her own, that what she wills to do or say
Seems wisest, virtuousest, discreetest, best.
MILTON, *Paradise Lost*, VIII, lines 548-550

He is oft the wisest man,
Who is not wise at all.
WORDSWORTH, *The Oak and the Broom*, st. 7

Wish.— Thy wish was father, Harry, to that thought.
SHAKESPEARE, *King Henry IV*, *Part II*, iv, 5 [4]

A wish, that she hardly dared to own,
For something better than she had known.
WHITTIER, *Maud Muller*, st. 6

Wishes.— If wishes would prevail with me,
My purpose should not fail with me.
SHAKESPEARE, *King Henry V*, iii, 2

Wishing. Wishing, of all employments, is the worst.
YOUNG, *Night Thoughts*, IV, line 72

Wit. Although he had much wit,
He was very shy of using it;
As being loth to wear it out,
And therefore bore it not about,
Unless on holy-days, or so,
As men their best apparel do.
BUTLER, *Hudibras*, I, i, lines 45-50

Don't put too fine a point to your wit, for fear it should get blunted.
CERVANTES, *The Little Gipsy* (*La Gitanilla*)

His wit invites you by his looks to come,
But when you knock it never is at home.[1]

COWPER, *Conversation*, lines 303, 304

The greatest sharp some day will find another sharper wit;
It always makes the devil laugh to see a biter bit.

C. G. LELAND, *El Capitan-General*, st. 12

A wit with dunces, and a dunce with wits.[2]

POPE, *Dunciad*, iv, line 90

True wit is nature to advantage dressed,
What oft was thought, but ne'er so well expressed;
Something, whose truth convinced at sight we find,
That gives us back the image of our mind.
As shades more sweetly recommend the light,
So modest plainness sets off sprightly wit.
For works may have more wit than does 'em good,
As bodies perish through excess of blood.

POPE, *Essay on Criticism*, lines 297–304

You have a nimble wit.[3]

SHAKESPEARE, *As You Like It*, iii, 2

None are so surely caught, when they are catched,
As wit turned fool.

SHAKESPEARE, *Love's Labour's Lost*, v, 2

Wilt thou show the whole wealth of thy wit in an instant? SHAKESPEARE, *Merchant of Venice*, iii, 5

Look, he's winding up the watch of his wit; by and by it will strike. SHAKESPEARE, *The Tempest*, ii, 1

A sentence is but a cheveril glove to a good wit: how quickly the wrong side may be turned outward.

SHAKESPEARE, *Twelfth Night*, iii, 1

As full of wit as an egg is full of meat.

STERNE, *Tristram Shandy*, VII, xxxvii

---

[1] You beat you pate, and fancy wit will come:
Knock as you please, there's nobody at home. POPE, *Epigram*

[2] This man [*Lord Chesterfield*] I thought had been a lord among wits, but I find he is only a wit among lords.

SAMUEL JOHNSON, *Life*, by Boswell, 1754

[3] I have a pretty wit. SHAKESPEARE, *As You Like It*, v, 1

Your wit ambles well; it goes easily.

SHAKESPEARE, *Much Ado about Nothing*, v, 1

Witchcrafts.— And the Devil will fetch me now in fire,
My witchcrafts to atone;
And I, who have troubled [rifled] the dead man's grave,
Shall never have rest in my own.
SOUTHEY, *The Old Woman of Berkeley*, st. 9

Withered. What are these
So withered and so wild in their attire,
That look not like the inhabitants o' the earth,
And yet are on 't? SHAKESPEARE, *Macbeth*, i, 3

Wives.— Wives may be merry, and yet honest too.
SHAKESPEARE, *Merry Wives of Windsor*, iv, 2

Woe. He scorned his own, who felt another's woe.
CAMPBELL, *Gertrude of Wyoming*, I, st. 24

Alas! by some degree of woe
We every bliss must gain;
The heart can ne'er a transport know
That never feels a pain. LORD LYTTELTON,
Song: Say, Myra, Why is Gentle Love

What though no friends in sable weeds appear,
Grieve for an hour, perhaps, then mourn a year,
And bear about the mockery of woe[1]
To midnight dances and the public show?
POPE, *Elegy to an Unfortunate Lady*, lines 55-58

Woe worth the chase, woe worth the day,
That costs thy life, my gallant grey.
SCOTT, *Lady of the Lake*, Canto i, st. 9

One woe doth tread upon another's heel,
So fast they follow.[2] SHAKESPEARE, *Hamlet*, iv, 7

Woes.— The graceful tear that streams for other's woes.
AKENSIDE, *Pleasures of the Imagination*, I, line 6

---

[1] 'T is not alone my inky cloak, good mother,
Nor customary suits of solemn black,
Nor windy suspiration of forced breath,
No, nor the fruitful river in the eye,
Nor the dejected 'haviour of the visage,
Together with all forms, moods [modes], shapes [shows] of grief,
That can denote me truly: these indeed seem,
For they are actions that a man might play:
But I have that within which passeth show;
These but the trappings and the suits of woe.
SHAKESPEARE, *Hamlet*, i, 2

[2] Woes cluster: rare are solitary woes;
They love a train; they tread each other's heel.
YOUNG, *Night Thoughts*, III, lines 63, 64

Wolf.— The wolf's long howl from Oonalaska's shore.
THOMAS CAMPBELL, *Pleasures of Hope*, i, st. 7

You may as well use question with the wolf
Why he hath made the ewe bleat for the lamb.
SHAKESPEARE, *Merchant of Venice*, iv, 1

Woman.— When Eve brought woe to all mankind
Old Adam called her *wo-man;*
But when she wooed with love so kind,
He then pronounced her *woo-man.*
But now, with folly and with pride,
Their husbands' pockets trimming,
The women are so full of whims
That men pronounce them *wimmen!*
ANONYMOUS, *Woman*

Oh, woman! woman! thou should'st have few sins
Of thine own to answer for! Thou art the author
Of such a book of follies in a man,
That it would need the tears of all the angels
To blot the record out!
E. G. BULWER-LYTTON, *The Lady of Lyons*, v, 1

Say — the world is a nettle; disturb it, it stings:
Grasp it firmly, it stings not. On one of two things,
If you would not be stung, it behoves you to settle:
Avoid it or crush it. . . .
She tried
With the weak hand of woman to thrust it aside,
And it stung her. A woman is too slight a thing
To trample the world without feeling its sting.[1]
E. R. BULWER-LYTTON ("OWEN MEREDITH"),
Lucile, iii, 2

As father Adam first was fooled,
A case that's still too common,
Here lies a man a woman ruled —
The devil ruled the woman.
BURNS, *On a Hen-pecked Country Squire*

Extreme in love or hate, in good or ill,
The worst of crimes had left her woman still!
BYRON, *The Corsair*, Canto iii, st. 16

---

[1] Nor wife nor maiden, weak or brave,
Can stand and face the public stare,
And win the plaudits she may crave,
And stem the hisses she may dare,
And modest truth and beauty save.— J. G. HOLLAND, *The Mistress of the Manse: Love's Philosophies*, vii

Woman—*Continued*

Woman! thy vows are traced in sand.[1]
BYRON, *To Woman*

Till Hymen brought his love-delighted hour,
There dwelt no joy in Eden's rosy bower!
. . . . . .
The world was sad! — the garden was a wild!
And man, the hermit, sighed — till woman smiled!
CAMPBELL, *Pleasures of Hope*, ii, st. 4

But what is woman? Only one of
Nature's agreeable blunders.
HANNAH COWLEY, *Who's the Dupe?* ii, 2

She married,— well,— a woman needs
A mate, her life and love to share,—
And little cares sprang up like weeds
And played around her elbow-chair.
F. S. COZZENS, *An Experience and a Moral*

O woman, God beloved in old Jerusalem! The best among us need deal lightly with thy faults, if only for the punishment thy nature will endure, in bearing heavy evidence against us, on the Day of Judgment.
DICKENS, *Martin Chuzzlewit*, II, iii

First, then, a woman will, or won't, depend on 't;
If she will do 't, she will; and there's an end on 't.[2]
But if she won't, since safe and sound your trust is,
Fear is affront, and jealousy injustice.
AARON HILL, *Epilogue to Zara*

---

[1] Woman's faith, and woman's trust —
Write the characters in dust;
Stamp them on the running stream,
Print them on the moon's pale beam,
And each evanescent letter
Shall be clearer, firmer, better,
And more permanent, I ween,
Than the thing those letters mean. SCOTT, *The Truth of Woman*, st. 1

[2] Where is the man who has the power and skill
To stem the torrent of a woman's will?
For if she will, she will, you may depend on 't;
And if she won't, she won't; so there's an end on 't.
ANONYMOUS, Lines on a pillar in Dane John Field, Canterbury, quoted in *The Examiner* (London), May 31, 1829

Men, dying, make their wills, but wives
Escape a work so sad;
Why should they make what all their lives
The gentle dames have had? J. G. SAXE, *Woman's Will*

He is a fool who thinks by force or skill
To turn the current of a woman's will.
SIR S. TUKE, *Adventures of Five Hours*, v, 3

I would have a woman as true as Death. At the first real lie which works from the heart outward, she should be tenderly chloroformed into a better world.

HOLMES, *Autocrat of the Breakfast-Table*, xi

Hapless woman ne'er can say,
"My work is done," till judgment day.

ST. JOHN HONEYWOOD, *Darby and Joan*, i

It's oh! to be a slave
Along with the barbarous Turk,
Where woman has never a soul to save,
If this is Christian work!

HOOD, *The Song of the Shirt*, st. 2

Oh, the years we waste and the tears we waste
And the work of our head and hand
Belong to the woman who did not know . . .
And did not understand.

KIPLING, *The Vampire*, st. 2

Oh, the toil we lost and the spoil we lost
And the excellent things we planned
Belong to the woman who did n't know why
And did not understand. *Ibid.*, st. 4

It is the fate of woman
Long to be patient and silent, to wait like a ghost that is speechless,
Till some questioning voice dissolves the spell of its silence.
Hence is the inner life of so many suffering women
Sunless and silent and deep, like subterranean rivers
Running through caverns of darkness, unheard, unseen, and unfruitful,
Chafing their channels of stone, with endless and profitless murmurs.

LONGFELLOW, *Courtship of Miles Standish*, vi, lines 29–35

Praise of the virtuous woman, as she is described in the Proverbs,[1]—
How the heart of her husband doth safely trust in her always,
How all the days of her life she will do him good, and not evil,
How she seeketh the wool and the flax and worketh with gladness,
How she layeth her hand to the spindle and holdeth the distaff,
How she is not afraid of the snow for herself or her household,
Knowing her household are clothed with the scarlet cloth of her weaving! *Ibid.*, viii, lines 34–40

[1] *Proverbs* xxxi, 10–21.

Woman—*Continued*

A cunning woman is a knavish fool.
LORD LYTTELTON, *Advice to a Lady*

How sweetly sounds the voice of a good woman;
It is so seldom heard, that, when it speaks,
It ravishes all senses. MASSINGER, *The Old Law*, iv, 2

Thus it shall befall
Him who, to worth in woman overtrusting,
Lets her will rule; restraint she will not brook;
And, left to herself, if evil thence ensue,
She first his weak indulgence will accuse.
MILTON, *Paradise Lost*, IX, lines 1182–1186

Here woman reigns, the mother, daughter, wife,
Strews with fresh flowers the narrow way of life;
In the clear heaven of her delightful eye,
An angel-guard of loves and graces lie;
Around her knees domestic duties meet,
And fireside pleasures gambol at her feet.
JAMES MONTGOMERY, *The West Indies*, iii, 1

Who trusts himself to woman or to waves
Should never hazard what he fears to lose.
JOHN OLDMIXON, *The Governor of Cyprus*, iii

I'd leave the world for him that hates a woman.
Woman, the fountain of all human frailty!
What mighty ills have not been done by woman!
Who was 't betrayed the Capitol? A woman.
Who lost Mark Antony the world? A woman.
Who was the cause of a long ten years' war,
And laid at last old Troy in ashes? Woman,
Destructive, damnable, deceitful woman![1]
THOMAS OTWAY, *The Orphan*, iii, 1

O woman! lovely woman![2] Nature made thee
To temper man: we had been brutes without you;
Angels are painted fair, to look like you:
There's in you all that we believe of Heaven,
Amazing brightness, purity, and truth,
Eternal joy, and everlasting love.
THOMAS OTWAY, *Venice Preserved*, i, 1

Here rests a woman, good without pretence,
Blessed with plain reason and with sober sense:
No conquests she, but o'er herself, desired,
No arts essayed, but not to be admired.

---

[1] Oh, most pernicious woman! SHAKESPEARE, *Hamlet*, i, 5
[2] Woman, lovely woman! COWPER, *Progress of Error*, line 274

Passion and pride were to her soul unknown,
Convinced that virtue only is our own.
So unaffected, so composed a mind;
So firm, yet soft; so strong, yet so refined;
Heaven, as its purest gold, by tortures tried;[1]
The saint sustained it, but the woman died.

POPE, *Epitaph on Mrs. Corbet*

Woman, the last; the best reserved of God.[2]

POPE, *January and May*, line 64

O woman! in our hours of ease,
Uncertain, coy, and hard to please,
And variable as the shade
By the light quivering aspen made;
When pain and anguish wring the brow,
A ministering angel thou![3] SCOTT, *Marmion*, vi, 30

Do you know I am a woman? when I think, I must speak. SHAKESPEARE, *As You Like It*, iii, 2

A woman's thought runs before her actions.—*Ibid.*, iv, 1

'T is said a woman's fitness comes by fits.

SHAKESPEARE, *Cymbeline*, iv, 1

One that was a woman, sir; but, rest her soul! she's dead. SHAKESPEARE, *Hamlet*, v, 1

She's beautiful, and therefore to be wooed;
She is a woman, therefore to be won.[4]

SHAKESPEARE, *King Henry VI, Part I*, v, 3

Oh, tiger's heart wrapped in a woman's hide!

SHAKESPEARE, *King Henry VI, Part III*, i, 4

There was never yet fair woman but she made mouths in a glass.[5] SHAKESPEARE, *King Lear*, iii, 2

---

[1] Mrs. Corbet died of cancer.

[2] *Cf.* HEAVEN.

[3] Woman's at best a contradiction still.

POPE, *Moral Essays*, Epistle ii, line 270

Who is 't can read a woman? SHAKESPEARE, *Cymbeline*, v, 5

[4] She is a woman, therefore may be wooed;
She is a woman, therefore may be won;
She is Lavinia, therefore must be loved.

SHAKESPEARE, *Titus Andronicus*, ii, 1

[5] *Angelo.* Women are frail too.
Isabella. Ay; as the glasses where they view themselves.

. . . . . .

Nay, call us ten times frail,
For we are soft as our complexions are,
And credulous to false prints.— SHAKESPEARE, *Measure for Measure*, ii, 4

Was ever woman in this humour wooed?
Was ever woman in this humour won?
SHAKESPEARE, *King Richard III*, i, 2

She's a very tattling woman.
SHAKESPEARE, *Merry Wives of Windsor*, iii, 3

Such duty as the subject owes the prince
Even such a woman oweth to her husband;
And when she is froward, peevish, sullen, sour,
And not obedient to his honest will,
What is she but a foul contending rebel
And graceless traitor to her loving lord?
SHAKESPEARE, *Taming of the Shrew*, v, 2

Let still the woman take
An elder than herself: so wears she to him,
So sways she level in her husband's heart:
For, boy, however we do praise ourselves,
Our fancies are more giddy and unfirm,
More longing, wavering, sooner lost and worn [won],
Than women's are. SHAKESPEARE, *Twelfth Night*, ii, 4

That man that hath a tongue, I say, is no man,
If with his tongue he cannot win a woman.
SHAKESPEARE, *Two Gentlemen of Verona*, iii, 1

Nor ever yet was woman's life complete
Till at her breast the child of him she loved
Made life and love one name.
E. C. STEDMAN, *The Blameless Prince*, st. 134

Man for the field, and woman for the hearth;
Man for the sword, and for the needle she;
Man with the head, and woman with the heart;
Man to command, and woman to obey;
All else confusion.
TENNYSON, *The Princess*, v, lines 437-441

One half of woman's life is hope
And one half resignation.
M. A. TOWNSEND, *Her Horoscope*

A perfect woman, nobly planned,
To warn, to comfort, and command;
And yet a spirit still, and bright
With something of angelic light.
WORDSWORTH, *She Was a Phantom of Delight*, st. 3

Womanly.— Touch her not scornfully;
Think of her mournfully,
Gently and humanly;
Not of the stains of her;
All that remains of her
Now is pure womanly.—HOOD, *The Bridge of Sighs*, st. 4

Women.— Alas! the love of women! it is known
To be a lovely and a fearful thing;
For all of theirs upon that die is thrown,
And if 't is lost, life hath no more to bring
To them but mockeries of the past alone,
And their revenge is as the tiger's spring,
Deadly, and quick, and crushing; yet as real
Torture is theirs — what they inflict they feel.
BYRON, *Don Juan*, Canto ii, st. 199

Women are skeery, unless they have a home.
W. CARLETON, *Betsey and I Are Out*, st. 13

If women could be fair, and yet not fond,
Or that their love were firm, not fickle still,
I would not marvel that they make men bond
By service long to purchase their good will;
But when I see how frail those creatures are,
I muse that men forget themselves so far.
EDWARD DE VERE, EARL OF OXFORD,
A Renunciation, st. 1

No cause is tried at the litigious bar,
But women plaintiffs or defendants are,
They form the process, all the briefs they write;
The topics furnish, and the pleas indite.
DRYDEN, *Juvenal*, Satire vi, lines 341–344

O, weary fa' the women fo'k,
For they winna let a body be!
JAMES HOGG, *The Women Fo'k*

There are some very pretty . . . women who don't understand the law of the road with regard to handsome faces. Nature and custom . . . agree in conceding to all males the right of at least two distinct looks at every comely female countenance, without any infraction of the rules of courtesy or the sentiment of respect. HOLMES, *Autocrat of the Breakfast-Table*, viii

I sometimes think women have a sixth sense, which tells them that others, whom they cannot see or hear, are in suffering. . . . We . . . draw our first breath in their arms, as we sigh away our last upon their faithful breasts!
HOLMES, *Professor at the Breakfast-Table*, xi

Nothing so true as what you once let fall,
"Most women have no characters at all."
Matter too soft a lasting mark to bear,
And best distinguished by black, brown, or fair.
POPE, *Moral Essays*, Epistle ii, lines 1–4

If weak women went astray,
Their stars were more in fault than they.
MATTHEW PRIOR, *Hans Carvel*, lines 11, 12

Women are not
In their best fortunes strong.
SHAKESPEARE, *Antony and Cleopatra*, iii, 12[10]

The pleasing punishment that women bear.
SHAKESPEARE, *Comedy of Errors*, i, 1

Women are shrews, both short and tall.
SHAKESPEARE, *King Henry IV, Part II*, v, 3

Women's weapons, water-drops.
SHAKESPEARE, *King Lear*, ii, 4

I am ashamed that women are so simple
To offer war where they should kneel for peace,
Or seek for rule, supremacy, and sway,
When they are bound to serve, love, and obey.
Why are our bodies soft and weak and smooth,
Unapt to toil and trouble in the world,
But that our soft conditions and our hearts
Should well agree with our external parts?
SHAKESPEARE, *Taming of the Shrew*, v, 2

Women, not clothes, were loved
When this old flag was new. R. H. STODDARD,
When This Old Flag Was New, st. 9

Wonder.— And still they gazed, and still the wonder grew,
That one small head could carry all he knew.
GOLDSMITH, *The Deserted Village*, st. 14

Gloucester. Ten days' wonder at the least.
Clarence. That's a day longer than a wonder lasts.
SHAKESPEARE, *King Henry VI, Part III*, iii, 2

Woo.— Time to dance is not to woo;
Wooing light makes fickle troth.
E. B. BROWNING, *The Lady's Yes*, st. 4

If fond love thy heart can gain,
I never broke a vow;
Nae maiden lays her skaith to me,
I never loved but you.
For you alone I ride the ring,
For you I wear the blue;
For you alone I strive to sing,
Oh, tell me how to woo.
GRAHAM OF GARTMORE, *If Doughty Deeds My Lady Please*, st. 3

What is the greatest bliss
  That the tongue o' man can name?
'T is to woo a bonnie lassie
  When the kye comes hame!
JAMES HOGG, *When the Kye Comes Hame*, st. 1

Men are April when they woo, December when they wed: maids are May[1] when they are maids, but the sky changes when they are wives.
SHAKESPEARE, *As You Like It*, iv, 1

We cannot fight for love, as men may do;
We should be wooed, and were not made to woo.[2]
SHAKESPEARE, *Midsummer-Night's Dream*, ii, 1

Woodcock.— So strives the woodcock with the gin.[3]
SHAKESPEARE, *King Henry VI, Part III*, i, 4

Woodland.— Now rings the woodland loud and long,
  The distance takes a lovelier hue,
  And drowned in yonder living blue
The lark becomes a sightless song.
TENNYSON, *In Memoriam*, cxv, st. 2

Woodman.— Woodman, spare that tree![4]
  Touch not a single bough!
In youth it sheltered me,
  And I'll protect it now.
G. P. MORRIS, *Woodman Spare That Tree*, st. 1

Woodpecker.— The woodpecker tapping the hollow beech-tree. T. MOORE, *Ballad Stanzas*, st. 2

Woods.— There is a pleasure in the pathless woods,
There is a rapture on the lonely shore,
There is society, where none intrudes,
By the deep sea, and music in its roar.
BYRON, *Childe Harold's Pilgrimage*, Canto iv, st. 178

Into the woods my Master went,
Clean forespent, forespent.
Into the woods my Master came,
Forespent with love and shame.

---

[1] Women are angels, wooing. SHAKESPEARE, *Troilus and Cressida*, i, 2

[2] Her virtue, and the conscience of her worth,
That would be wooed, and not unsought be won.
MILTON, *Paradise Lost*, VIII, lines 502, 503

[3] Now is the woodcock near the gin. SHAKESPEARE, *Twelfth Night*, ii, 5

[4] Spare, woodman, spare the beechen tree.
CAMPBELL, *The Beech-Tree's Petition*, st. 1

But the olives they were not blind to Him,
The little grey leaves were kind to Him:
The thorn-tree had a mind to Him
When into the woods he came.

LANIER, *A Ballad of Trees and the Master*, st. 1

Fresh woods and pastures new.

MILTON, *Lycidas*, line 193

Wooer.— Last May a braw wooer cam' down the lang glen,
And sair wi' his love he did deave [*deafen*] me;
I said there was naething I hated like men,—
The deuce gae wi'm to believe me!

BURNS, *Last May a Braw Wooer*, st. 1

The wooer who can flatter most will bear away the belle.

G. W. THORNBURY, *The Jester's Sermon*

Wooing.— Never wedding, ever wooing,
Still a love-lorn heart pursuing,
Read you not the wrong you're doing
In my cheek's pale hue?
All my life with sorrow strewing,
Wed, or cease to woo.

CAMPBELL, *The Maid's Remonstrance*, st. 1

If I am not worth the wooing, I surely am not worth the winning.

LONGFELLOW, *Courtship of Miles Standish*, iii, line 111

Word.— A word and a blow.[1]

SHAKESPEARE, *Romeo and Juliet*, iii, 1

Word-catcher.— Each wight, who reads not, and but scans
and spells,
Each word-catcher, that lives on syllables,
Ev'n such small critics some regard may claim,
Preserved in Milton's or in Shakespeare's name.
Pretty! in amber to observe the forms
Of hairs, or straws, or dirt, or grubs, or worms!
The things, we know, are neither rich nor rare,
But wonder how the devil they got there.

POPE, *Epistle to Dr. Arbuthnot*, lines 165–172

Words. He could coin, or counterfeit
New words, with little or no wit;
Words so debased and hard, no stone
Was hard enough to touch them on;
And when with hasty noise he spoke 'em,
The ignorant for current took 'em.

BUTLER, *Hudibras*, I, i, lines 109–114

---

[1] All words came first, and after blows.

CHARLES LLOYD, *Speech of Courtney*

Words are women, deeds are men.[1]
GEORGE HERBERT, *Jacula Prudentum*

Words are wise men's counters, they do but reckon by them; but they are the money of fools.
HOBBES, *The Leviathan*, I, 4

Well-placed words of glozing courtesy,
Baited with reasons not unplausible.
MILTON, *Comus*, lines 161, 162

To those who know thee not no words can paint,
And those who know thee, know all words are faint.
HANNAH MORE, *Sensibility*

Words, words, words.[2] SHAKESPEARE, *Hamlet*, ii, 2

'T is a kind of good deed to say well:
And yet words are no deeds.
SHAKESPEARE, *King Henry VIII*, iii, 2

You have bereft me of all words.
SHAKESPEARE, *Merchant of Venice*, iii, 2

Words pay no debts.
SHAKESPEARE, *Troilus and Cressida*, iii, 2

Work.—Blessed is he who has found his work; let him ask no other blessedness.[3]
CARLYLE, *Past and Present: The Modern Worker*, xi

Now, by Saint Paul, the work goes bravely on!
COLLEY CIBBER, *Richard III*, iii, 1

Honest toil is holy service; faithful work is praise and prayer.
HENRY VAN DYKE, *Toiling of Felix*, Legend, st. 61

---

[1] I am not so lost in lexicography as to forget that words are the daughters of earth, and that things are the sons of heaven.
SAMUEL JOHNSON, *Preface to His Dictionary*

Words are men's daughters, but God's sons are things.
SAMUEL MADDEN, *Boulter's Monument* *

[2] Words, words, mere words. SHAKESPEARE, *Troilus and Cressida*, v, 3

[3] This is my work; my blessing, not my doom;
Of all who live, I am the one by whom
This work can best be done in the right way.
HENRY VAN DYKE, *Work*, st. 1

---

* These words have been supposed to be an interpolation by Dr. Johnson. See Boswell's *Life of Johnson*, 1756.

Work—work—work—
Till the brain begins to swim;
Work—work—work—
Till the eyes are heavy and dim!
Seam, and gusset, and band,—
Band, and gusset, and seam,
Till over the buttons I fall asleep,
And sew them on in a dream!

HOOD, *The Song of the Shirt*

Do the work that's nearest,
Though it's dull at whiles,
Helping, when we meet them,
Lame dogs over stiles;
See in every hedgerow
Marks of angels' feet,
Epics in each pebble
Underneath our feet.[1]

KINGSLEY, *The Invitation*, lines 97–104

The best way to live well is to work well. Good work is the daily test and safeguard of personal health.

JOSEPH MORTIMER-GRANVILLE, *How to Make the Best of Life*, i

To delight in doing one's work in life, that is what helps one on, though the road is sometimes very stiff and tiring — uphill rather, it would seem, than downhill, and yet downhill it is.

MAX MÜLLER, *Life*, by His Wife, II, xxv

No good work is ever lost; many labourers must be content to sow; others will come to reap the harvest.

MAX MÜLLER, *Letter to Mr. Nanjio*, Dec. 27, 1883, *Life*, by His Wife, II, xxvi

Work is life to me;[2] and when I am no longer able to work, life will be a heavy burden.

MAX MÜLLER, *Letter to Miss Byrd McCall*, Oct. 22, 1888, *Life*, by His Wife, II, xxix

I have never found the limit of my capacity for work.

NAPOLEON BONAPARTE, *Life*, by Sloane, III, 163

Worker. That which the worker winneth shall then be his indeed,
Nor shall half be reaped for nothing by him that sowed no seed.[3]—WILLIAM MORRIS, *The Day Is Coming*, st. 8

---

[1] *Cf.* ADVERSITY.

[2] Work done is the true happiness of life. MAX MÜLLER, *Letter to B. M. Malabari*, March 12, 1890, *Life*, by His Wife, II, xxx

[3] *Cf.* SEED.

Workers.— On we march then, we the workers, and the rumour that ye hear
Is the blended sound of battle and deliverance drawing near.
WILLIAM MORRIS, *The March of the Workers*, st. 4

Men, my brothers, men the workers, ever reaping something new;
That which they have done but earnest of the things that they shall do.
TENNYSON, *Locksley Hall*, lines 117, 118

Workman.— There the workman saw his labour taking form and bearing fruit,
Like a tree with splendid branches rising from a humble root.
HENRY VAN DYKE, *Toiling of Felix*, Legend, st. 57

Works.— Every one is the son of his own works.
CERVANTES, *Don Quixote*, I, iv

These are thy glorious works, Parent of good.
MILTON, *Paradise Lost*, V, line 153

World.— The world's a bubble, and the life of man
Less than a span.[1] BACON,[2] *The World*, st. 1

Let any man show the world that he feels
Afraid of its bark, and 't will fly at his heels:
Let him fearlessly face it, 't will leave him alone:
But 't will fawn at his feet if he flings 't a bone.
E. R. BULWER-LYTTON ("OWEN MEREDITH"),
Lucile, II, vii

Good-bye, proud world! I'm going home.
EMERSON, *Good-Bye*, st. 1

Into this world we come like ships,
Launched from the docks, and stocks, and slips,
For fortune fair or fatal.
HOOD, *Miss Kilmansegg*, Her Birth

There is another and a better world.
A. F. F. VON KOTZEBUE, *The Stranger*
(trans. R. Thompson), i, 1

Fer John P.
Robinson he
Sez the world'll go right, ef he hollers out Gee!
LOWELL, *The Biglow Papers*, I, iii, st. 9

---

[1] This life, which seems so fair,
Is like a bubble. W. DRUMMOND, *Madrigal: This Life*

[2] Ascribed also to Raleigh, Donne, and others.

World—*Continued*

This world is full of beauty, as other worlds above;
And, if we did our duty, it might be full of love.

GERALD MASSEY, *This World Is Full of Beauty*

The world was all before them, where to choose
Their place of rest, and Providence their guide.
They, hand in hand, with wandering steps and slow,
Through Eden took their solitary way.

MILTON, *Paradise Lost*, XII, lines 646–649

Chaos of thought and passion, all confused;
Still by himself abused, or disabused;
Created half to rise, and half to fall;
Great lord of all things, yet a prey to all;
Sole judge of truth, in endless error hurled:
The glory, jest, and riddle of the world!

POPE, *Essay on Man*, Epistle ii, lines 13–18

See how the world its veterans rewards!
A youth of frolics, an old age of cards;
Fair to no purpose, artful to no end,
Young without lovers, old without a friend;
A fop their passion, but their prize a sot;
Alive, ridiculous, and, dead forgot.

POPE, *Moral Essays*, Epistle ii, lines 243–248

I think, whatever mortals crave,
  With impotent endeavour,
A wreath—a rank—a throne—a grave—
  The world goes round for ever;
I think that life is not too long,
  And therefore I determine
That many people read a song,
  Who will not read a sermon.

. . . . .

I think the world, though dark it be
  Has aye one rapturous pleasure,
Concealed in life's monotony,
  For those who seek the treasure;
One planet in a starless night —
  One blossom on a brier —
One friend not quite a hypocrite —
  One woman not a liar!

PRAED, *Chant of the Brazen Head*, st. 1, 11

Hereafter, in a better world than this,
I shall desire more love and knowledge of you.

SHAKESPEARE, *As You Like It*, i, 2

How weary, stale, flat, and unprofitable,
Seem to me all the uses of this world!
SHAKESPEARE, *Hamlet*, i, 2

I hold the world but as the world, Gratiano;
A stage where every man must play a part.
And mine a sad one.
SHAKESPEARE, *Merchant of Venice*, i, 1

The world is not thy friend nor the world's law;
The world affords no law to make thee rich.
SHAKESPEARE, *Romeo and Juliet*, v, 1

Let the world slide.
SHAKESPEARE, *Taming of the Shrew*, Induction, 1

And o'er the hills, and far away
  Beyond their utmost purple rim,
Beyond the night, across the day,
  Through all the world she followed him.
TENNYSON, *The Day-Dream*, The Departure, st. 4

The world is too much with us; late and soon,
Getting and spending, we lay waste our powers.
WORDSWORTH, *The World Is Too Much With Us*, lines 1, 2

Worldly.— Be wisely worldly, be not worldly wise.
FRANCIS QUARLES, *Emblems*, II, 2

Worlds.— Yet not to earth's contracted span
  Thy goodness let me bound,
Or think Thee lord alone of man,
  When thousand worlds are round.
POPE, *The Universal Prayer*, st. 6

Worm.— I would not enter on my list of friends
(Though graced with polished manners and fine sense,
Yet wanting sensibility) the man
Who needlessly sets foot upon a worm.
COWPER, *The Task: Winter Walk at Noon*, lines 560–563

The smallest worm will turn, being trodden on,
And doves will peck in safeguard of their brood.
SHAKESPEARE, *King Henry VI, Part III*, ii, 2

Worms.— The worms they crept in, and the worms they crept out,
And sported his eyes and his temples about,
  While the spectre addressed Imogene.
M. G. LEWIS, *Alonzo the Brave and the Fair Imogene*, st. 12

Wormwood.— His [*cup*] had been quaffed too quickly, and
he found
The dregs were wormwood.
BYRON, *Childe Harold's Pilgrimage*, Canto iii, st. 9

Worship.— He wales [*chooses*] a portion with judicious care;
And "Let us worship God!" he says, with solemn air.
BURNS, *The Cotter's Saturday Night*, st. 12

What sought they thus afar?
Bright jewels of the mine?
The wealth of seas, the spoils of war?—
They sought a faith's pure shrine!

Ay, call it holy ground,
The soil where first they trod;
They have left unstained what there they found,—
Freedom to worship God.[1]
FELICIA HEMANS, *Landing of the Pilgrim Fathers*, st. 9, 10

One wishes worship freely given to God,
Another wants to make it statute-labour.
HOOD, *Ode to Rae Wilson, Esquire*, st. 11

Worst.— When things are at the worst, they sometimes
mend.[2] BYRON, *Don Juan*, Canto vi, st. 1

When the worst comes to the worst, no man is without a friend who is possessed of shaving-materials.
DICKENS, *David Copperfield*, I, xvii

In the worst inn's worst room.
POPE, *Moral Essays*, Epistle iii, line 299

We are not the first
Who, with best meaning, have incurred the worst.
SHAKESPEARE, *King Lear*, v, 3

When remedies are past, the griefs are ended
By seeing the worst, which late on hopes depended.
SHAKESPEARE, *Othello*, i, 3

---

[1] And now the aisles of the ancient church
By equal feet are trod,
And the bell that swings in its belfry rings
Freedom to worship God! WHITTIER, *In the Old South*, st. 9

[2] Would Heaven this mourning year were past!
She may have better luck at last;
Matters at worst are sure to mend,
The Devil's wife was but a fiend.
PRIOR, *Turtle and Sparrows*, lines 414-417

Things at the worst will cease, or else climb upward
To what they were before. SHAKESPEARE, *Macbeth*, iv, 2

Worth.— Worth makes the man, and want of it, the fellow;
The rest is all but leather or prunello.
POPE, *Essay on Man*, Epistle iv, lines 203, 204

Wrath. Our hame,
Whare sits our sulky, sullen dame,
Gathering her brows like gathering storm,
Nursing her wrath to keep it warm.
BURNS, *Tam O'Shanter*, st. 1

Come not within the measure of my wrath.
SHAKESPEARE, *Two Gentlemen of Verona*, v, 4

Wreck. All at once a sea broke over them,
And they that saw it from the shore have said
It struck the wreck and piecemeal scattered it,
Just as a woman might the lump of salt
That 'twixt her hands into the kneading-pan
She breaks and crumbles on her rising bread.
JEAN INGELOW, *Brothers and a Sermon*

Wrecked.— As men wrecked upon a sand, that look to be washed off the next tide.
SHAKESPEARE, *King Henry V*, iv, 1

Wrestled.— Sir, you have wrestled well and overthrown
More than your enemies.
SHAKESPEARE, *As You Like It*, i, 2

Wretched.— The wretched have no friends
DRYDEN, *All for Love*, iii, 1

Lest, when our latest hope is fled, ye taste of our despair,
And learn by proof, in some wild hour, how much the wretched dare.
MACAULAY, *Virginia*, st. 6

Wrinkles.— Wrinkles (the d—d democrats) won't flatter
BYRON, *Don Juan*, Canto x, st. 24

Writ.— The Moving Finger writes; and, having writ,
Moves on: nor all your piety nor wit
Shall lure it back to cancel half a line,
Nor all your tears wash out a word of it.[1]
OMAR KHAYYÁM, *Rubáiyát* (trans. Fitzgerald), st. 71

---

[1] What is writ, is writ,—
Would it were worthier!
BYRON, *Childe Harold's Pilgrimage*, Canto iv, st. 185

Whatever hath been written shall remain,
Nor be erased nor written o'er again;
The unwritten only still belongs to thee:
Take heed, and ponder well what that shall be.
LONGFELLOW, *Morituri Salutamus*, st. 18

Write.— He cannot write who knows not to give o'er.
DRYDEN, *Art of Poetry*, line 63

Learn to write well, or not to write at all.
DRYDEN, *Essay upon Satire*, line 281

It may be glorious to write
Thoughts that shall glad the two or three
High souls, like those far stars that come in sight
Once in a century;

But better far it is to speak
One simple word, which now and then
Shall waken their free nature in the weak
And friendless sons of men;

To write some earnest verse or line,
Which, seeking not the praise of art,
Shall make a clearer faith and manhood shine
In the untutored heart.
LOWELL, *Incident in a Railroad Car*, st. 19–21

Why did I write? what sin to me unknown
Dipped me in ink, my parents', or my own?
As yet a child, nor yet a fool to fame,
I lisped in numbers, for the numbers came.
I left no calling for this idle trade,
No duty broke, no father disobeyed.
POPE, *Epistle to Dr. Arbuthnot*, lines 125–130

But those who cannot write, and those who can,
All rhyme, and scrawl, and scribble, to a man
POPE, *Imitations of Horace*, II, Epistle i, lines 187, 188

Thither write, my queen,
And with mine eyes I'll drink the words you send,
Though ink be made of gall.
SHAKESPEARE, *Cymbeline*, i, 1 [2]

I once did hold it, as our statists do,
A baseness to write fair, and laboured much
How to forget that learning; but, sir, now
It did me yeoman's service.—SHAKESPEARE, *Hamlet*, v, 2

Devise, wit! write, pen! for I am for whole volumes in folio. SHAKESPEARE, *Love's Labour's Lost*, i, 2

To be a well-favoured man is the gift of fortune; but to write and read comes by nature.
SHAKESPEARE, *Much Ado about Nothing*, iii, 3

Writing.— This comes of drinking asses' milk and writing.
DRYDEN, *Absalom and Achitophel*, II, line 395

True ease in writing comes from art, not chance,
As those move easiest who have learned to dance.
POPE, *Essay on Criticism*, lines 362, 363;
Imitations of Horace, II, Epistle ii, lines 178, 179

Of all those arts in which the wise excel,
Nature's chief masterpiece is writing well.
SHEFFIELD, DUKE OF BUCKINGHAMSHIRE, *Essay on Poetry*, lines 1, 2

Wrong.— One wrong more to man, one more insult to God!
R. BROWNING, *The Lost Leader*, line 24

Time at last sets all things even —
And if we do but watch the hour,
There never yet was human power
Which could evade, if unforgiven,
The patient search and vigil long
Of him who treasures up a wrong.
BYRON, *Mazeppa*, st. 10

Wrongs.— On adamant our wrongs we all engrave,
But write our benefits upon the wave.
KING, *Art of Love*, lines 971, 972

How will you ever straighten up this shape;
Touch it again with immortality;
Give back the upward looking and the light;
Rebuild in it the music and the dream;
Make right the immemorial infamies,
Perfidious wrongs, immedicable woes?
EDWIN MARKHAM, *The Man With the Hoe*, st. 5

Xerxes.— Xerxes must die,
And so must I.
New England Primer

Yankee.— The Yankee boy, before he's sent to school,
Well knows the mysteries of that magic tool,
The pocket knife.

. . . . .

And in the education of the lad
No little part that implement hath had.
His pocket knife to the young whittler brings
A growing knowledge of material things.

. . . . .

Thus by his genius and his jack-knife driven,
Erelong he'll solve you any problem given;

. . . . .

Ay, when he undertakes it,
He'll make the thing and the machine that makes it.

. . . . .

For, there's go in it, you may know
That there's go in it, and he'll make it go
JOHN PIERPONT, *Whittling*

Yawp.— I sound my barbaric yawp over the roofs of the world. WALT WHITMAN, *Song of Myself*, 52

Year.— The old year lies a-dying.
TENNYSON, *Death of the Old Year*, st. 1

Yes.—"Yes," I answered you last night;
"No," this morning, sir, I say:[1]
Colours seen by candle-light
Will not look the same by day.

. . . . .

By your truth she shall be true,
Ever true, as wives of yore;
And her "yes," once said to you,
Shall be "yes" for evermore.
E. B. BROWNING, *The Lady's Yes*, st. 1, 7

Yesterday.— Oh, call back yesterday, bid time return!
SHAKESPEARE, *King Richard II*, iii, 2

Yesterdays.— Oh, for yesterdays to come!
YOUNG, *Night Thoughts*, II, line 312

Yester-year.— Where are the snows of yester-year?
DANTE GABRIEL ROSSETTI, *The Ballad of Dead Ladies*

Yew.— Old Yew, which graspest at the stones
That name the underlying dead,
Thy fibres net the dreamless head,[2]
Thy roots are wrapped about the bones.
TENNYSON, *In Memoriam*, ii, st. 1

Yorick.— Alas, poor Yorick! I knew him, Horatio: a fellow of infinite jest, of most excellent fancy: he hath borne me on his back a thousand times; and now, how abhorred in my imagination it is! my gorge rises at it. Here hung those lips that I have kissed I know not how oft. Where be your gibes now? your gambols? your songs? your flashes of merriment, that were wont to set the table on a roar? Not one now, to mock your grinning? quite chap-fallen? Now get you to my lady's chamber, and tell her, let her paint an inch thick, to this favour she must come.—SHAKESPEARE, *Hamlet*, v, 1

Young.— Young fellows will be young fellows.
ISAAC BICKERSTAFFE, *Love in a Village*, ii, 2

---

[1] Why, I pray,
Look "Yes" last night, and yet say "No" to-day?
BYRON, *Don Juan*, Canto xii, st. 34

[2] The dreamless sleep that lulls the dead. BYRON, *Euthanasia*, st. 1

The young lambs are bleating in the meadows,
  The young birds are chirping in the nest,
The young fawns are playing with the shadows,
  The young flowers are blowing toward the west —
But the young, young children, O my brothers,
  They are weeping bitterly!
They are weeping in the playtime of the others,
  In the country of the free.
E. B. BROWNING, *The Cry of the Children*, st. 1

And both were young, and one was beautiful.[1]
BYRON, *The Dream*, st. 2

Young men think old men fools, and old men know young men to be so.
Quoted by CAMDEN as a saying of one Dr. Metcalf

When all the world is young, lad,
  And all the trees are green;
And every goose a swan, lad,
  And every lass a queen;
Then hey for boot and horse, lad,
  And round the world away;
Young blood must have its course, lad,
  And every dog his day.
KINGSLEY, *Songs from the Water Babies*, II, st. 1

Young folks are smart, but all ain't good thet's new;
I guess the gran'thers they knowed sunthin' tu.
LOWELL, *Biglow Papers*, II, ii, lines 307, 308

The atrocious crime of being a young man.
WILLIAM PITT, EARL OF CHATHAM, *Speech*, March 6, 1741

  Young people now-a-days
Have fallen sadly off, I think, from all the good old ways.
BAYARD TAYLOR, *The Quaker Widow*, st. 15

Younger.— We shall ne'er be younger.
SHAKESPEARE, *Taming of the Shrew*, Induction, 2

Yourself.— Why don't you speak for yourself, John?
LONGFELLOW, *Courtship of Miles Standish*, iii, line 154

Youth.— A strappan youth; he taks the mother's eye.
BURNS, *The Cotter's Saturday Night*, st. 8

---

[1] Both young — and one how passing fair! BYRON, *Parisina*, st. 9

Fair laughs the morn, and soft the zephyr blows,
  While proudly riding o'er the azure realm
In gallant trim the gilded vessel goes;
  Youth on the prow, and Pleasure at the helm:
Regardless of the sweeping whirlwind's sway,
That hushed in grim repose expects his evening prey.

GRAY, *The Bard*, ii, 2

He doth not lack an almanac,
  Whose youth is in his soul.

HOLMES, *Remember—Forget*, st. 5

In youth the heart exults and sings,
The pulses leap, the feet have wings;
In age the cricket chirps, and brings
  The harvest home of day.

LONGFELLOW, *Kéramos*, st. 17

In the very May-morn of his youth,
Ripe for exploits and mighty enterprises.

SHAKESPEARE, *King Henry V*, i, 2

Cursed be the social wants that sin against the strength of youth![1]
Cursed be the social lies that warp us from the living truth!

TENNYSON, *Locksley Hall*, lines 59, 60

There are gains for all our losses,
  There are balms for all our pain,
But when youth, the dream departs,
It takes something from our hearts,
  And it never comes again.

R. H. STODDARD, *The Flight of Youth*, st. 1

God pity them both! and pity us all,
Who vainly the dreams of youth recall.

WHITTIER, *Maud Muller*, st. 52

Yule.— They bring me sorrow touched with joy,
The merry, merry bells of Yule.

TENNYSON, *In Memoriam*, xxviii, st. 5

Zaccheus.— Zaccheus he
Did climb the tree
Our Lord to see.

New England Primer

---

[1] This filthy marriage-hindering Mammon.

TENNYSON, *Aylmer's Field*, line 374

INDEX TO AUTHORS

Adams, John Quincy (1767–1848), 106, 172
Adams, Samuel (1722–1803), 8
Adams, Sarah Fuller Flower (1805–1848), 278
Addison, Joseph (1672–1719), 55, 85, 93, 132, 191, 216, 284, 303, 388, 392, 424, 430
Aïdé, Charles Hamilton (1830–1906), 72, 330
À Kempis, Thomas. See *Kempis, Thomas à,*
Akenside, Mark (1721–1770), 397, 448
Akerman, Lucy Evelina (–1874), 215
Aldrich, James (1810–1856), 105
Aldrich, Thomas Bailey (1836–1907), 12, 295
Alexander, Cecil Frances (1818–1895), 73, 154, 184, 264, 382, 418, 433
Allen, Elizabeth Akers (1832–), 340
Allison, Richard (18th Century), 343
Allston, Washington (1779–1843), 283
Anderson, Alexander (1845–), 16
Andros, R. S. S. (–1868), 391
Angelo, Michael. See *Buonarotti, Michael Angelo*
Anonymous, 14, 20, 23, 90, 106, 148, 149, 170, 183, 219, 231, 232, 246, 253, 261, 267, 283, 304, 320, 328, 361, 367, 373, 411, 423, 436, 437, 449, 450
Armstrong, John (1709–1779), 312
Arnold, Sir Edwin (1832–1904), 55, 74, 76, 231, 375
Arnold, George (1834–1865), 117, 172, 179, 313, 321, 360
Arnold, Matthew (1822–1888), 157
Askew, Anne (1521–1546), 140
Austin, Alfred (1835–), 103, 219, 220
Ayton, Sir Robert (1570–1638), 232
Aytoun, William Edmonstoune (1813-1865), 76, 351

Bacon, Francis, Lord Verulam (1561–1626), 8, 14, 30, 40, 50, 77, 88, 92, 153, 198, 206, 232, 248, 258, 266, 305, 310, 317, 318, 326, 334, 415, 421, 427, 430, 442, 461
Bailey, Philip James (1816–1902), 8, 157, 191, 198, 220, 227, 232, 248, 275, 309, 402
Ball, John (–1381), 149
Barbauld, Anna Letitia (1743–1825), 220
Barère de Vieuzac, Bertrand (1755–1841), 28
Barham, Richard Harris (1788–1845), 22
Barlow, George (1847–), 96, 112
Barnfield, Richard (1574–1627), 256
Baron, Robert (17th Century), 271
Barrett, Eaton Stannard (1785–1820), 67
Barrington, George (1755–*c.* 1840), 64
Barton, Bernard (1784–1849), 302
Baxter, Richard (1615–1691), 314
Bayly, Thomas Haynes (1797–1839), 1, 67, 265, 304, 319, 342, 343
Beattie, James (1735–1803), 172, 346
Beaumont, Francis (1584–1616) and Fletcher, John, 2, 41, 261, 270, 305, 309, 351, 372
Beddoes, Thomas Lovell (1803-1849), 232
Beecher, Henry Ward (1813–1887), 70, 135
Beers, Ethel Lynn (1827–1879), 311
Benjamin, Park (1809–1864), 357
Bennett, Henry (1785–18——), 348, 372, 440
Bennett, William Cox (1820–1895), 338
Berkeley, George (1685–1753), 109
Berners, Juliana (*c.* 1388–14——), 150
Bethune, George Washington (1805–1862), 390
Bickerstaffe, Isaac (1735–1812), 86, 185, 262, 468
Blacker, Colonel William (1777–1855), 311
Blair, Robert (1699–1746), 9, 162, 282, 376, 440
Blake, William (1757–1827), 405
Blamire, Susanna (1747–1794), 364
Bland, Robert (1779–1825), 182
Boker, George Henry (1823–1890), 190
Bonaparte, Napoleon. See *Napoleon Bonaparte*
Bonar, Horatius (1808–1889), 222

Boner, John Henry (1845–1903), 122, 244, 374
Booth, Barton (1681–1733), 88
Bourdillon, Francis William (1852–), 281
Bowles, Caroline Anne. See *Southey, Caroline Anne Bowles*
Brainard, John Gardiner Calkins (1796–1828), 56
Breton, Nicholas (1555–1624), 202
Bridges, Madeline. See *De Vere, Mary Ainge*
Brome, Alexander (1620–1666), 87
Brooke, Fulke Greville, Lord (1554–1628), 364
Brooks, Maria Gowen (1795–1845), 232
Brougham, Henry Peter, Lord (1778–1868), 33, 352
Brown, Frances (1818–1864), 414
Brown, Tom (1663–1704), 327, 360
Browne, Sir Thomas (1605–1682), 13
Browne, William (1591–1643), 180
Browning, Elizabeth Barrett (1806–1861), 120, 153, 154, 206, 220, 290, 413, 415, 437, 439, 456, 468, 469
Browning, Robert (1812–1889), 3, 24, 48, 71, 77, 78, 93, 130, 154, 155, 159, 206, 221, 222, 229, 230, 232, 233, 243, 256, 316, 318, 328, 336, 337, 378, 380, 394, 415, 467
Bryant, William Cullen (1794–1878), 74, 75, 86, 180, 227, 257, 268, 288, 322, 334, 362, 387, 400, 415
Buchanan, Robert William (1841–1901), 129, 176, 194, 284
Buckinghamshire, John Sheffield, Duke of (1648–1721), 467
Buckley, Theodore William Alois (1825–1856), 444
Bulwer-Lytton, Edward George Earle (1803–1873), 119, 301, 332, 449
Bulwer-Lytton, Edward Robert (1831–1891), 63, 140, 449, 461
Bunyan, John (1628–1688), 97, 159, 226, 317, 418
Buonarroti, Michelangelo (1475–1564), 247, 385
Burke, Edmund (1729–1797), 26, 50, 128, 138, 256, 265, 271, 280, 328, 424
Burleigh, George Shepard (1821–1903), 248
Burns, Robert (1759–1796), 14, 18, 19, 30, 37, 38, 44, 58, 77, 87, 103, 105, 119, 120, 130, 142, 145, 165, 172, 183, 184, 187, 188, 191, 192, 201, 203, 209, 211, 230, 244, 248, 249, 254, 257, 261, 263, 264, 270, 271, 294, 305, 307, 310, 311, 317, 324, 352, 355, 380, 402, 429, 440, 449, 458, 464, 465, 469
Burton, Robert (1577–1640), 232
Butler, —— (16th Century), 292
Butler, Samuel (1612–1680), 6, 20, 26, 36, 46, 47, 48, 54, 57, 62, 67, 86, 87, 88, 93, 95, 97, 130, 137, 151, 164, 165, 168, 184, 193, 216, 218, 230, 232, 241, 253, 261, 266, 269, 281, 287, 290, 302, 306, 310, 322, 325, 329, 335, 344, 345, 366, 390, 394, 395, 405, 430, 438, 441, 446, 458
Butler, William Allen (1825–1902), 389, 437
Byrd, William (*c.* 1538–1623), 262
Byrom, John (1692–1763), 183, 418, 440
Byron, George Gordon Noel, Lord (1788–1824), 2, 3, 4, 9, 12, 14, 15, 18, 19, 20, 24, 26, 28, 29, 30, 33, 34, 37, 40, 41, 51, 55, 57, 60, 62, 63, 64, 66, 67, 71, 72, 73, 76, 77, 79, 85, 92, 94, 95, 97, 98, 106, 107, 109, 110, 112, 117, 123, 124, 125, 129, 131, 135, 136, 142, 148, 150, 152, 154, 159, 160, 166, 168, 171, 172, 176, 177, 181, 189, 190, 192, 193, 203, 204, 206, 207, 210, 212, 216, 218, 219, 220, 223, 232, 233, 242, 245, 253, 256, 262, 264, 265, 269, 270, 271, 272, 274, 276, 277, 283, 285, 286, 288, 296, 304, 306, 309, 316, 323, 324, 328, 330, 333, 334, 344, 345, 350, 351, 352, 359, 362, 363, 365, 367, 369, 372, 373, 376, 385, 386, 387, 389, 392, 395, 398, 405, 406, 408, 410, 416, 419, 423, 424, 426, 428, 429, 430, 434, 435, 436, 438, 439, 441, 444, 449, 450, 455, 457, 464, 465, 467, 468, 469

Cable, George Washington (1844–), 73
Calidasa, 227
Calverley, Charles Stuart (1831–1884), 44, 139
Cambronne, Pierre Jacques Étienne (1770–1842), 166
Camden, William (1551–1623), 469
Camoens, Luis de (1524–1579), 233
Campbell, Thomas (1777–1844), 9, 13, 19, 31, 39, 60, 73, 93, 98, 110, 115, 142, 152, 203, 225, 233, 274, 287, 288, 300, 342, 358, 364, 427, 428, 448, 449, 450, 457, 458
Canning, George (1770–1827), 16, 145, 304, 310, 367, 389
Carew, Lady Elizabeth (*fl.* 1590), 234, 335
Carey, Henry (1692–1743), 6, 74, 201
Carleton, Will M. (1845–), 176, 286, 292, 310, 400, 455
Carlyle, Thomas (1795–1881), 416, 459
Carman, William Bliss (1861–), 361
Carpenter, Henry Bernard (1840–1890), 284
Carroll, Lewis. See *Dodgson, Charles Lutwidge*
Cary, Alice (1820–1871), 82, 145

Cary, Phœbe (1824–1871), 55, 58, 72, 220, 278
Centlivre, Susannah (*c.* 1667–1723), 364
Cervantes Saavedra, Miguel de (1547–1616), 249, 369, 446, 461
Chalkhill, John (17th Century), 444
Chapman, George (1557–1634), 28, 242
Chatham, Earl of. See *Pitt, William, Earl of Chatham*
Chaucer, Geoffrey (*c.* 1340–1400), 53, 150, 158, 271, 272, 279, 411, 412
Cherry, Andrew (1762–1812), 26
Chesterfield, Philip Dormer Stanhope, Earl of (1694–1773), 391
Choate, Rufus (1799–1859), 59, 149, 420
Chorley, Henry Fothergill (1808–1872), 286
Churchill, Charles (1731–1764), 6, 33, 123, 390
Cibber, Colley (1671–1757), 12, 110, 123, 171, 180, 351, 397, 459
Clare, John (1793–1864), 207
Clemens, Samuel Langhorne (1835–), 133
Cleveland, Mrs., 220
Cleveland, Stephen Grover (1837–), 289, 297
Clough, Arthur Hugh (1819–1861), 224, 391
Coffin, Robert Stevenson (1797–1827), 360
Coigny, Marie François (1737–1821), 373
Coke, Sir Edward (1552–1634), 44, 64, 327
Coleridge, Hartley (1796–1849), 117
Coleridge, Samuel Taylor (1772–1834), 5, 7, 27, 29, 36, 37, 58, 63, 77, 81, 84, 117, 128, 142, 154, 167, 172, 190, 200, 221, 234, 235, 253, 270, 288, 313, 314, 342, 346, 348, 353, 358, 359, 366, 369, 371, 382, 387, 412, 435, 445
Collins, Mortimer (1827–1876), 311
Collins, William (1721–1759), 34, 133, 272
Colman, George, the Younger (1762–1836), 150, 265, 358
Colton, Charles Caleb (*c.* 1780–1832), 41
Congreve, William (1670–1729), 84, 217, 272, 324, 427
Constable, Henry (1562–1613), 301
Conway, Katherine Eleanor (1853–), 67
Cook, Eliza (1818–1889), 1, 4, 12, 47, 110, 112, 113, 133, 143, 145, 173, 181, 226, 258, 317, 363
Coolidge, Susan. See *Woolsey, Sarah Chauncey*
Corinthians, Second Book of, 380
Corn-Law Rhymer, The. See *Elliott, Ebenezer*
Cornwall, Barry. See *Procter, Bryan Waller*
Cotton, Charles (1630–1687), 300
Cotton, Nathaniel (1705–1788), 182, 428, 440
Cowley, Abraham (1618–1667), 64, 101, 120, 408
Cowley, Hannah (1743–1809), 450
Cowper, William (1731–1800), 1, 3, 4, 12, 22, 29, 32, 36, 38, 39, 52, 54, 58, 62, 64, 66, 72, 86, 88, 92, 97, 102, 110, 116, 136, 138, 143, 144, 148, 154, 155, 171, 175, 183, 190, 201, 202, 217, 227, 229, 231, 254, 262, 266, 270, 274, 279, 281, 283, 284, 300, 319, 320, 333, 342, 345, 350, 353, 361, 368, 373, 374, 390, 396, 397, 405, 410, 412, 413, 423, 430, 442, 447, 452, 463
Cozzens, Frederick Swartwout (1818–1869), 450
Crabbe, George (1754–1832), 31, 295, 443
Craik, Dinah Maria Mulock (1826–1887), 35, 51, 80, 97, 108, 140, 184, 207, 208, 217, 221, 352
Cranch, Christopher Pearse (1813–1892), 403
Crashaw, Richard (*c.* 1613–1649), 221, 265, 312, 358, 435
Crawford, Julia, or Louisa Macartney (*c.* 1800–*c.* 1885), 116, 296
Cross, Marian Evans Lewes. See *Eliot, George*
Crowquill, Alfred. See *Forrester, Alfred Henry*
Cunningham, Allan (1784–1842), 286, 359, 436
Cutter, George Washington (1801–1865), 152, 386

Dana, Richard Henry (1787–1879), 88
Daniel, Samuel (1562–1619), 81, 369
Dante, Alighieri (1265–1321), 185
Darwin, Erasmus (1731–1802), 386
Davies, Sir John (1569–1626), 253, 380
Davis, Thomas Osborne (1814–1845), 59
Decatur, Stephen (1779–1820), 65
Defoe, Daniel (1661–1731), 87
Dekker, Thomas (*c.* 1570–*c.* 1641), 32, 61, 297
Democratic Party Slogan, 131
Denham, Sir John (1615–1669), 84
Dennis, John (1657–1734), 405
De Vere, Aubrey Thomas (1814–1902), 394
De Vere, Edward, Earl of Oxford (1550–1604), 455
De Vere, Mary Ainge (1840–), 242. See *Hunt, Aubrey*
Dibdin, Charles (1745–1814), 48
Dibdin, Thomas John (1771–1841), 194

Dickens, Charles (1812–1870), 28, 32, 42, 45, 48, 51, 54, 56, 62, 75, 85, 92, 122, 131, 166, 171, 187, 191, 192, 193, 195, 197, 198, 216, 225, 229, 230, 234, 257, 271, 273, 285, 287, 303, 309, 314, 315, 329, 352, 379, 382, 413, 434, 443, 450, 464
Dickinson, John (1732–1808), 420
Dobell, Sydney Thompson (1824–1874), 254, 277
Dobson, Henry Austin (1840–), 202
Doddridge, Philip (1702–1751), 227
Dodge, Mary Elizabeth Mapes (1831–1905), 77, 369
Dodgson, Charles Lutwidge (1832–1898), 198, 221, 414, 430
Dodsley, Robert (1703–1764), 203
Donne, John (1573–1631), 60
Doudney, Sarah (1843–), 88, 434
Dowling, Bartholomew (1823–1863), 91
Doyle, Sir Francis Hastings Charles (1810–1888), 39, 420
Drake, Joseph Rodman (1795–1820), 17, 147
Drayton, Michael (1563–1631), 203, 296
Drummond, William, of Hawthornden (1585–1649), 461
Dryden, John (1631–1700), 9, 13, 16, 19, 20, 30, 34, 39, 45, 51, 59, 71, 75, 77, 86, 89, 94, 98, 101, 102, 105, 114, 121, 132, 140, 148, 155, 158, 161, 162, 167, 168, 172, 177, 186, 192, 193, 202, 205, 221, 234, 245, 252, 256, 270, 272, 273, 277, 289, 294, 298, 302, 304, 305, 309, 311, 324, 330, 335, 345, 350, 353, 355, 356, 363, 374, 376, 378, 385, 396, 408, 416, 417, 421, 425, 431, 435, 440, 455, 465, 466
Dufferin, Lady Helen Selina (1807–1867), 387
Du Maurier, George Louis Palmella Busson (1834–1896), 237
Dunbar, Paul Laurence (1872–1906), 234
Dunlop, John (1755–1820), 234
Dwight, John Sullivan (1813–1893), 333
Dwight, Timothy (1752–1817), 58, 365
Dyer, Sir Edward (*c.* 1540–1607), 172, 262
Dyer, John (1700–1758), 257
Dyke, Henry van (1852–), 98, 155, 207, 221, 234, 324, 357, 390, 409, 432, 433, 459, 461

Eastman, Charles Gamage (1816–1861), 105
Ecclesiastes, Book of, 21, 136
Eliot, George (1819–1880), 50
Elizabeth, Queen of England (1533–1603), 55
Elliott, Ebenezer (1781–1849), 119, 173, 294, 301
Emerson, Ralph Waldo (1803–1882), 24, 39, 86, 104, 143, 159, 199, 234, 253, 362, 368, 415, 461
Emmet, Robert (1778–1803), 114
English, Thomas Dunn (1819–1902), 29
Erasmus, Desiderius (1467–1536), 130
Ettrick Shepherd, The. See *Hogg, James*
Everett, David (1769–1813), 2
Everett, Edward (1794–1865), 111

Faber, Frederick William (1814–1863), 337
Fanshawe, Catherine Maria (1765–1834), 167
Farquhar, George (1678–1707), 64, 279, 396
Ferguson, Sir Samuel (1810–1886), 8
Field, Eugene (1850–1895), 62, 280, 346
Fielding, Henry (1707–1754), 22, 102, 351, 363, 390, 408
Finch, Francis Miles (1827–), 28, 212
Finley, John (1797–1866), 16
Fitzgerald, Edward (1809–1883). See *Omar Khayyám*
Fletcher, Andrew, of Saltoun (1655–1716), 16
Fletcher, John (1579–1625), 101, 127, 257, 445. See also *Beaumont, Francis and Fletcher, John*
Ford, John (1586–1639), 88
Forrester, Alfred Henry (1804–1872), 285
Foster, Stephen Collins (1826–1864), 200
Fouché, Joseph, Duke of Otranto (1754–1820), 28
Francis I. of France (1494–1547), 231
Franklin, Benjamin (1706–1790), 117, 179, 183, 309, 332, 407, 408, 420, 424, 430, 440
Free Soil Party Slogan, 142
Freneau, Philip (1752–1832), 200
Fuller, Thomas (1608–1661), 31, 172, 254, 269

Garrick, David (1717–1779), 201, 286, 392
Garrison, William Lloyd (1805–1879), 262
Garth, Sir Samuel (1661–1719), 89
Gay, John (1685–1732), 47, 180, 185, 209, 215, 219, 270, 323, 347, 395, 427
Gibbon, Edward (1737–1794), 173, 180
Gibbons, Thomas (1720–1785), 26

Gifford, Richard (1725–1807), 425
Gilbert, William Schwenck (1836–), 189
Gilder, Richard Watson (1844–), 196
Gilmore, James Roberts (1822–1903), 94
Goldsmith, Oliver (1728–1774), 1, 12, 26, 68, 93, 95, 119, 130, 136, 141, 145, 159, 166, 168, 182, 185, 197, 202, 206, 211, 212, 214, 234, 249, 256, 261, 274, 282, 290, 294, 295, 300, 302, 303, 305, 316, 323, 332, 336, 349, 352, 355, 360, 441, 456
Graham, James, Marquis of Montrose (1612–1650), 124, 126, 234
Graham, Robert, of Gartmore (– c. 1797), 456
Gray, Barry. See *Coffin, Robert Stevenson*
Gray, David (1838–1861), 274
Gray, Thomas (1716–1771), 10, 11, 35, 44, 66, 68, 69, 108, 109, 122, 139, 141, 149, 158, 163, 168, 175, 190, 209, 257, 260, 269, 292, 293, 298, 301, 310, 368, 392, 401, 406 421, 443, 470
Green, Sarah Pratt McLean (1858–), 358, 359
Greene, Albert Gorton (1802–1868), 445
Greene, Robert (*c.* 1560–1592), 262
Guthrie, Thomas (1803–1873), 398

Habakkuk, Book of, 345
Hare, Julius Charles (1795–1855), 51
Harrington, Sir John (1561–1612), 141, 414
Harte, Francis Bret (1839–1902), 5, 31, 50, 141, 162, 171, 280, 304, 340, 346, 350, 371, 384, 429
Harvey, Stephen (17th Century), 351
Hawker, Robert Stephen (1803–1875), 63, 155, 374
Hay, John (1838–1905), 49, 77, 83, 104, 135, 186, 277, 301, 313, 319, 329, 330, 346, 366, 404, 408
Hayne, Paul Hamilton (1831–1886), 315
Heber, Reginald (1783–1826), 77, 163, 216
Hemans, Felicia Dorothea (1793–1835), 17, 113, 121, 149, 176, 209, 342, 354, 367, 464
Henley, William Ernest (1849–1903), 28, 126, 376
Henry, Patrick (1736–1799), 217, 414
Herbert, George (1593–1633), 3, 41, 73, 102, 140, 158, 193, 209, 218, 365, 429, 459
Herrick, Robert 1591–1674), 14, 100, 101, 129, 234, 254, 343, 364
Heywood, John (*c.* 1497–*c.* 1577), 360
Heywood, Thomas (*c.* 1597–*c.* 1650), 183, 383

H. H. See *Jackson, Helen Hunt Fiske*
Higginson, Francis (1588–1630), 281
Hill, Aaron (1685–1750), 280, 450
Hobart, Mrs. Charles, 56
Hobbes, Thomas (1588–1679), 459
Hogg, James (1770–1835), 455, 457
Holland, Josiah Gilbert (1819–1881), 15, 91, 175, 208, 259, 417, 449
Holmes, Oliver Wendell (1809–1894), 2, 5, 8, 10, 11, 13, 15, 21, 28, 31, 33, 40, 46, 55, 62, 64, 68, 74, 82, 85, 91, 94, 99, 102, 107, 114, 117, 124, 128, 129, 133, 153, 154, 155, 171, 175, 176, 181, 186, 187, 188, 194, 197, 198, 200, 201, 203, 208, 210, 212, 214, 216, 218, 230, 235, 237, 243, 249, 252, 254, 255, 264, 266, 269, 275, 279, 280, 294, 297, 298, 300, 303, 307, 309, 310, 312, 313, 315, 320, 321, 323, 325, 336, 342, 344, 345, 350, 356, 363, 364, 372, 376, 384, 387, 396, 397, 403, 415, 416, 419, 420, 423, 425, 429, 433, 437, 439, 441, 443, 445, 451, 455, 470
Home, John (1722–1808), 97, 427
Honeywood, St. John (1765–1798), 451
Hood, Thomas (1799–1845), 2, 4, 13, 15, 20, 21, 22, 25, 27, 28, 36, 38, 44, 45, 49, 52, 53, 61, 66, 67, 68, 69, 77, 78, 81, 86, 92, 96, 99, 103, 105, 106, 114, 115, 116, 120, 138, 151, 157, 165, 167, 169, 173, 176, 177, 182, 184, 188, 196, 200, 203, 204, 207, 210, 216, 226, 235, 244, 247, 252, 257, 260, 263, 265, 266, 270, 272, 276, 279, 282, 285, 290, 295, 308, 312, 316, 329, 330, 338, 339, 341, 343, 345, 347, 351, 360, 361, 362, 363, 367, 369, 370, 372, 382, 383, 390, 393, 413, 420, 430, 438, 451, 454, 460, 461, 464
Hooker, Richard (*c.* 1553–1600), 212
Hoole, John (1727–1803), 265
Hooper, Ellen Sturgis (1816–1841), 104
Hopkinson, Joseph (1770–1842), 58
Horatio, Viscount Nelson (1758–1805), 104, 360, 439
Houghton, Lord (1809–1885), 173
Hovell-Thurlow, Lord Edward. See *Thurlow*
Howard, Henry, Earl of Surrey, (*c.* 1517–1547), 442
Howarth, Ellen Clementine (1827–1899), 135
Howe, Julia Ward (1819–), 153, 225, 415
Hughes, Thomas (1823–1896), 131
Hunt, Aubrey (Sir Aubrey de Vere, 1788–1846), 436
Hunt, Helen Fiske. See *Jackson, Helen Hunt Fiske*
Hunt, James Henry Leigh (1784–1859), 204

Hurdis, James (1763–1801), 210
Huxley, Henrietta Anne, 369

Ingelow, Jean (1820–1897), 19, 35, 96, 97, 147, 166, 178, 244, 250, 355, 403, 465
Ingersoll, Robert Green (1833–1899), 222
Ingoldsby, Thomas. See *Barham, Richard Harris*
Irving, Washington (1783–1859), 96
Isaiah, Book of, 443

Jackson, Andrew (1767–1845), 420
Jackson, Helen Hunt Fiske (1831–1885), 78, 109
Jackson, Thomas Jonathan (Stonewall), (1824–1863), 333
James, Book of, 412
Jefferson, Thomas (1743–1826), 6, 161, 217, 289, 299, 307, 356, 414
Jenner, Edward (1749–1823), 324
Job, Book of, 334
Joel, Book of, 98
John, Gospel of, 154
Johnson, Edward, 435
Johnson, Samuel (1709–1784), 34, 126, 135, 171, 192, 193, 195, 206, 221, 266, 274, 298, 307, 312, 352, 359, 424, 425, 447, 459
Jones, Sir William (1746–1794), 227, 385
Jonson, Ben (1573–1637), 4, 99, 100, 211, 266, 355, 364, 368, 378, 394, 414, 427
Judson, Anne Hasseltine. See *Willson, Arabella M.*
Junius, 173

Kalidasa. See *Calidasa*
Keats, John (1795–1821), 20, 185, 191, 219, 235, 274, 356, 369
Keble, John (1792–1866), 355
Kemble, John Philip (1757–1823), 93
Kempis, Thomas à (*c.* 1380–1471), 116, 155, 287, 364
Kennedy, Crammond (1842–), 370
Kenyon, James Benjamin (1858–), 126
Keppel, Lady Caroline (*c.* 1735– ?), 340
Key, Francis Scott (1780–1843), 17, 276, 415
Khayyám, Omar. See *Omar Khayyám*
King, William (1663–1712), 279, 439, 467
Kingsley, Charles (1819–1875), 56, 96, 108, 113, 132, 136, 144, 148, 175, 203, 208, 221, 235, 247, 252, 254, 290, 323, 374, 409, 419, 442, 460
Kinney, Coates (1826–1904), 325
Kipling, Joseph Rudyard (1865–), 1, 13, 53, 54, 59, 60, 74, 75, 107, 111, 112, 113, 115, 136, 139, 147, 164, 169, 180, 187, 212, 215, 217, 242, 251, 252, 253, 259, 276, 280, 284, 287, 289, 301, 312, 339, 349, 365, 367, 373, 391, 392, 395, 410, 420, 432, 451, 469
Kirke, Edmund. See *Gilmore, James Roberts*
Knox, William (*c.* 1788–1825), 269
Körner, Karl Theodor (1791–1813), 151
Kotzebue, August Friedrich Ferdinand von (1761–1819), 461

Lamb, Charles (1775–1834), 158, 175, 210, 307
Lampman, Archibald (1861–1899), 344
Landor, Walter Savage (1775–1864), 78, 221
Lanier, Sidney (1842–1881), 18, 49, 78, 156, 194, 225, 273, 321, 371, 374, 376, 413, 457, 458
Lanigan, George Thomas (1845–1886), 261
Lawrence, James (1781–1813), 359
Lecky, William Edward Hartpole (1838–1903), 42
Lee, Henry (1756–1818), 132
Lee, Nathaniel (1653–1692), 165
Leigh, Henry Sambrooke (1837–1883), 68, 265, 320, 418
Leland, Charles Godfrey (1824–1903), 297, 351, 447
Le Sage, Alain-René (1668–1747), 397
L'Estrange, Sir Roger (1616–1704), 306, 318
Lincoln, Abraham (1809–1865), 6, 40, 58, 108, 109, 199, 276, 292, 302, 319, 332, 337, 361, 372, 394, 431, 437
Lindsay, Lady Anne (1750–1825), 68
Lloyd, Charles (1775–1839), 458
Locker-Lampson, Fredk. (1821–1895), 383
Lodge, Thomas (*c.* 1558–1625), 118
Longfellow, Henry Wadsworth (1807–1882), 1, 2, 3, 4, 10, 14, 24, 27, 28, 32, 33, 44, 48, 50, 55, 66, 69, 75, 76, 79, 84, 87, 94, 96, 108, 109, 130, 138, 139, 146, 147, 156, 157, 163, 170, 173, 177, 179, 191, 200, 201, 221, 222, 228, 235, 246, 255, 262, 276, 280, 282, 283, 292, 308, 313, 314, 331, 333, 334, 339, 351, 359, 360, 365, 373, 374, 375, 391, 410, 432, 433, 443, 451, 458, 465, 469, 470
Lord, William Wilberforce (1819–), 164
Lovelace, Richard (1618–1658), 133, 184, 318, 445
Lovell, Maria Anne (1803–1877), 224
Lover, Samuel (1797–1868), 9, 99, 286, 348, 441
Lowell, James Russell (1819–1891), 7, 8, 10, 19, 24, 27, 31, 34, 39, 40, 42, 46, 50, 60, 62, 67, 77, 83, 95, 102, 111, 114, 115, 131, 143, 146, 152,

156, 161, 171, 176, 177, 179, 181, 188, 191, 193, 199, 206, 208, 212, 213, 226, 245, 249, 250, 256, 259, 272, 277, 280, 281, 283, 288, 290, 299, 300, 306, 308, 314, 315, 319, 320, 323, 338, 344, 347, 356, 363, 368, 380, 386, 394, 411, 415, 416, 417, 423, 424, 431, 444, 461, 466, 469
Ludlow, Fitz Hugh (1836–1870), 211
Luke, Gospel of, 42, 140, 193, 320
Luther, Martin (1483–1546), 140, 383, 441
Lydgate, John (*c.* 1370–*c.* 1451), 158
Lyly, John (*c.* 1554–1606), 210
Lyttelton, George, Lord (1709–1773), 185, 235, 448, 452
Lytton, Earl of. See *Bulwer-Lytton, Edward George*; *Bulwer-Lytton, Edward Robert*

Macaulay, Thomas Babington (1800–1859), 17, 19, 37, 89, 111, 131, 179, 184, 308, 321, 341, 419, 465
MacCarthy, Denis Florence (1817–1882), 410
Macdonald, George (1824–1905), 16, 124, 203
Mace, Frances Parker Laughton (1836–1899), 429
Mackay, Charles (1814–1889), 48, 61, 109, 110, 143, 154, 159, 169, 175, 225, 235, 248, 249, 283
Macklin, Charles (1697–1797), 212, 418
Madden, Samuel (1686–1765), 459
Maginn, William (1793–1842), 194
Mallett, David (*c.* 1705–1765), 11, 431
Manners, Lord John (1818–1906), 284
Maria del Occidente. See *Brooks, Maria Gowen*
Mark, Gospel of, 42
Markham, Edwin (1852–), 38, 79, 147, 165, 180, 188, 195, 207, 388, 402, 406, 467
Mark Twain. See *Clemens, Samuel Langhorne*
Marlowe, Christopher (1564–1593), 205, 235, 242
Marsden, William (1754–1836), 406
Marvell, Andrew (1621–1678), 186, 286, 299
Mason, William (1724–1797), 181
Massey, Gerald (1828–), 38, 105, 186, 235, 255, 267, 417, 462
Massinger, Philip (1583–1640), 3, 79, 422, 452
Matthew, Gospel of, 42, 49, 184, 320
Meredith, Owen. See *Bulwer-Lytton, Edward Robert*
Merivale, John Herman (1779–1844), 428
Messinger, Robert Hinckley (1811–1874), 30, 440
Michael Angelo. See *Buonarotti, Michael Angelo*
Mickle, William Julius (1735–1788), 138, 244
Middleton, Thomas (*c.* 1570–1627), 158
Miller, William (1810–1872), 443
Milnes, Richard Monckton. See *Houghton, Lord*
Milton, John (1608–1674), 6, 7, 15, 18, 19, 29, 30, 40, 41, 46, 47, 49, 56, 63, 66, 70, 71, 72, 73, 84, 85, 90, 93, 94, 98, 106, 107, 108, 114, 116, 118, 121, 122, 123, 129, 134, 139, 147, 161, 165, 169, 170, 172, 177, 178, 186, 187, 188, 196, 199, 200, 213, 216, 217, 225, 228, 231, 256, 258, 263, 264, 268, 270, 277, 279, 281, 282, 291, 294, 295, 299, 303, 307, 312, 319, 329, 332, 335, 336, 343, 344, 357, 370, 371, 373, 381, 382, 387, 391, 394, 398, 408, 409, 414, 415, 417, 421, 429, 430, 431, 432, 436, 437, 446, 452, 457, 458, 459, 461, 462
Minor, Charles (1780–1865), 15
Mitchell, Silas Weir (1830–), 79
Montagu, Lady Mary Wortley (1689–1762), 350, 427
Montgomery, James (1771–1854), 61, 65, 123, 154, 157, 159, 182, 198, 217, 228, 236, 245, 249, 264, 267, 277, 278, 300, 313, 333, 341, 353, 354, 368, 376, 391, 452
Montgomery, Robert (1807–1855), 267
Montrose, Marquis of. See *Graham, James*
Moore, Clement Clarke (1779–1863), 24, 51
Moore, Thomas (1779–1852), 9, 17, 20, 23, 31, 47, 64, 74, 85, 100, 101, 106, 116, 118, 125, 143, 148, 149, 153, 158, 170, 173, 203, 204, 211, 222, 231, 236, 243, 257, 258, 274, 280, 286, 305, 327, 331, 339, 342, 344, 356, 360, 375, 393, 402, 405, 444, 445, 457
More, Hannah (1745–1833), 24, 28, 167, 285, 459
More, Henry (1614–1687), 427
Morris, Charles (1745–1838), 32
Morris, George Perkins (1802–1864), 398, 420, 457
Morris, William (1834–1896), 74, 207, 460, 461
Mortimer-Granville, Joseph, 460
Morton, Thomas (*c.* 1764–1838), 11, 166
Moss, Thomas (–1808), 375
Motherwell, William (1797–1835), 222
Muhlenberg, William Augustus (1796–1877), 228
Müller, Frederick Max (1823–1900), 79, 90, 96, 460
Mulock, Dinah Maria. See *Craik, Dinah Maria Mulock*

Nairne, Lady Carolina (1766–1845), 210, 215, 329
Napoleon Bonaparte (1769–1821), 34, 37, 171, 230, 247, 259, 322, 361, 431, 460
Nash, Thomas (1567–1601), 382
Nelson, Horatio. See *Horatio, Viscount Nelson*
New England Primer, 2, 305, 370, 467, 470
Newman, John Henry (1801–1890), 214
Newton, Isaac (1642–1727), 417
Nichols, Rebecca S. (1820–), 446
Noel, Thomas (1799–1861), 298
Norris, John (1657–1711), 9
Norton, Lady Caroline Elizabeth Sarah Sheridan (1808–1877), 146

O'Hara, Theodore (1820–1867), 26
Oldham, John (1653–1683), 195
Oldmixon, John (1673–1742), 452
Omar Khayyám (12th Century), 39, 44, 69, 72, 77, 82, 85, 100, 103, 107, 135, 152, 162, 178, 207, 311, 333, 334, 365, 368, 401, 406, 411, 423, 426, 435, 465
Orange, Prince of. See *William, Prince of Orange*
O'Reilly, John Boyle (1844–1890), 283
Osgood, Frances Sargent (1811–1850), 208
Osgood, Kate Putnam (1841–), 174
Otranto, Duke of. See *Fouché, Joseph*
Otway, Thomas (1652–1685), 83, 443, 452
Overbury, Sir Thomas (1581–1613), 443

Paine, Thomas (1737–1809), 340, 378, 391
Palmer, John Williamson (1825–1896), 365, 388
Parker, Martin (–*c.* 1656), 355
Parsons, Thomas William (1819–1892), 38
Paulding, James Kirke (1779–1860), 246
Payne, John Howard (1791–1852), 182
Peale, Rembrandt (1778–1860), 393
Percy, Florence. See *Allen, Elizabeth Akers*
Percy, Thomas (1729–1811), 145, 426
Perry, Nora (1841–1896), 30
Perry, Oliver Hazard (1785–1819), 110
Peter, Second Book of, 378
Pettee, G. W., 23
Philips, John (1676–1709), 359
Phillips, Wendell (1811–1884), 247
Philostratus (2nd Century), 100
Pierpont, John (1785–1866), 144, 407
Pike, Albert (1809–1891), 94
Pindar, Peter. See *Wolcot, John*
Pinkney, Edward Coate (1802–1828), 176
Piozzi, Hester Lynch Thrale. See *Thrale, Hester Lynch*
Pitt, William, Earl of Chatham (1708–1778), 8, 44, 60, 259, 279, 419, 469
Pitt, William, of Malta (–1840), 188, 285, 347, 388
Poe, Edgar Allan (1809–1849), 5, 17, 19, 23, 229, 236, 246, 261, 280, 325, 408, 410, 437
Pollok, Robert (1798–1827), 228, 288
Pomfret, John (1667–1702), 177
Pope, Alexander (1688–1744), 6, 14, 27, 30, 35, 36, 38, 41, 46, 49, 53, 57, 59, 61, 65, 66, 67, 68, 71, 75, 79, 84, 87, 91, 92, 94, 95, 100, 105, 107, 108, 113, 115, 117, 120, 123, 124, 126, 127, 128, 136, 137, 138, 139, 140, 141, 158, 161, 162, 163, 167, 168, 170, 174, 176, 178, 183, 184, 186, 189, 192, 195, 197, 200, 205, 206, 215, 216, 217, 218, 227, 228, 231, 233, 236, 237, 245, 248, 250, 252, 255, 259, 260, 265, 266, 269, 271, 278, 281, 282, 284, 289, 291, 292, 295, 297, 301, 306, 309, 316, 325, 327, 330, 332, 334, 336, 337, 338, 350, 353, 355, 356, 357, 362, 364, 367, 380, 384, 385, 397, 400, 410, 414, 424, 425, 427, 428, 430, 434, 445, 446, 447, 448, 452, 453, 455, 458, 462, 463, 464, 465, 466, 467
Porteous, Beilby (1731–1808), 272, 431
Powell, Sir John (1633–1696), 327
Praed, Winthrop Mackworth (1802–1839), 10, 63, 89, 104, 119, 125, 129, 146, 148, 174, 230, 237, 259, 269, 274, 293, 296, 308, 328, 331, 383, 384, 395, 409, 462
Prentice, George Denison (1802–1870), 406
Priest, Nancy Amelia Woodbury (1837–1870), 339
Prior, Sir James (*c.* 1790–1869), 298
Prior, Matthew (1664–1721), 1, 87, 109, 131, 190, 201, 317, 423, 450, 464
Procter, Adelaide Ann (1825–1864), 51, 127, 158, 198, 291, 293, 374, 377, 409
Procter, Bryan Waller (1787–1874), 219, 354
Proverbial Expressions, 87, 102, 120, 178
Proverbs, Book of, 199, 336, 451
Psalms, Book of, 35

Quarles, Francis (1592–1644), 403
Quin, James (1693–1766), 420

Rabelais, Francis (1483–1553), 11, 87, 100, 151, 270, 302, 439
Raleigh, Sir Walter (1552–1618), 55, 237, 364, 406

Ramsay, Allan (1686–1758), 229
Randall, James Ryder (1839–), 255
Randolph, Thomas (1605–1635), 386, 387
Ray, James (18th Century), 130
Republican Party Slogan, 142
Rice, Edward H., 340
Riley, James Whitcomb (1853–), 153, 309, 324, 370
Rochester, John Wilmot, Earl of (1647–1680), 202, 266
Rogers, Samuel (1763–1855), 158, 191, 443
Roland, Marie or Manon Jeanne Phlipon (1754–1793), 217
Roosevelt, Theodore (1858–), 54, 96, 117, 170, 222, 310, 338, 383, 389, 390
Roscommon, Wentworth Dillon, Earl of (c. 1633–1685), 83, 271, 379
Rossetti, Christina Georgina (1830–1894), 411
Rossetti, Dante Gabriel (1828–1882), 468
Rowe, Nicholas (1674–1718), 231, 265
Roydon, Matthew (1580–1622), 117
Ruskin, John (1819–1900), 302, 422
Russell, Lord John (1792–1878), 320
Russell, Irwin (1853–1879), 281
Ryan, Abram Joseph (1839–1886), 390, 398, 406

Sargent, Epes (1813–1880), 288, 354
Saxe, John Godfrey (1816–1887), 255, 316, 320, 450
Scott, Sir Walter (1771–1832), 3, 4, 6, 15, 16, 26, 39, 46, 47, 49, 58, 65, 79, 82, 83, 85, 97, 119, 129, 136, 138, 144, 214, 226, 229, 237, 267, 270, 272, 279, 299, 304, 306, 317, 326, 328, 342, 344, 358, 366, 371, 372, 373, 386, 390, 395, 396, 398, 401, 402, 403, 406, 423, 431, 433, 436, 448, 450, 453
Selden, John (1584–1654), 137, 146, 389, 395
Seward, William Henry (1801–1872), 60, 213
Sewell, George (–1726), 66
Shakespeare, William (1564–1616), 1, 2, 3, 4, 5, 6, 7, 8, 9, 10, 11, 12, 13, 14, 15, 16, 17, 18, 19, 20, 21, 22, 23, 24, 25, 27, 28, 29, 30, 31, 32, 33, 34, 35, 36, 37, 38, 39, 40, 41, 42, 43, 44, 45, 46, 47, 48, 49, 50, 51, 53, 54, 55, 56, 57, 58, 59, 60, 61, 62, 63, 64, 65, 66, 67, 68, 69, 70, 71, 72, 73, 74, 75, 79, 80, 82, 83, 84, 85, 86, 87, 88, 89, 90, 91, 93, 94, 95, 96, 97, 98, 99, 100, 101, 102, 103, 104, 105, 106, 107, 108, 109, 110, 111, 112, 113, 114, 116, 117, 118, 119, 120, 121, 122, 124, 125, 126, 127, 128, 129, 130, 131, 132, 133, 134, 135, 136, 137, 138, 139, 140, 141, 142, 144, 145, 146, 147, 148, 150, 151, 152, 153, 156, 157, 158, 159, 160, 161, 162, 163, 164, 165, 166, 167, 168, 169, 170, 171, 172, 174, 177, 178, 179, 180, 182, 183, 185, 186, 187, 188, 189, 190, 191, 192, 193, 194, 195, 196, 197, 198, 199, 201, 202, 204, 205, 206, 208, 209, 210, 211, 212, 213, 214, 215, 216, 217, 218, 219, 222, 223, 224, 225, 226, 227, 228, 229, 230, 231, 237, 238, 239, 240, 242, 243, 244, 245, 246, 247, 250, 251, 252, 253, 254, 255, 256, 257, 258, 259, 260, 261, 262, 263, 264, 266, 267, 268, 269, 270, 271, 272, 273, 275, 277, 278, 279, 280, 281, 282, 283, 285, 286, 287, 288, 289, 290, 291, 292, 293, 294, 295, 296, 297, 298, 299, 300, 301, 302, 303, 304, 305, 306, 307, 308, 309, 310, 311, 312, 313, 315, 316, 318, 319, 320, 321, 322, 323, 324, 325, 326, 327, 328, 330, 331, 332, 333, 334, 335, 336, 337, 338, 339, 340, 341, 342, 343, 344, 345, 346, 347, 349, 351, 352, 353, 354, 355, 356, 357, 358, 359, 361, 362, 363, 365, 366, 367, 368, 370, 371, 372, 373, 374, 375, 377, 378, 379, 380, 381, 382, 383, 384, 385, 386, 387, 388, 389, 390, 391, 392, 393, 394, 395, 396, 397, 398, 399, 400, 401, 402, 404, 405, 406, 407, 409, 410, 411, 412, 413, 414, 415, 417, 418, 419, 420, 421, 422, 423, 424, 425, 426, 427, 428, 429, 430, 432, 433, 434, 435, 436, 437, 438, 439, 440, 441, 442, 443, 444, 445, 446, 447, 448, 449, 452, 453, 454, 456, 457, 458, 459, 462, 463, 464, 465, 466, 468, 469, 470
Shanly, Charles Dawson (1811–1875), 432
Sheale, Richard (16th Century), 419
Shelley, Percy Bysshe (1792–1822), 27, 81, 175, 204, 205, 209, 219, 268, 279, 297, 355, 366
Shenstone, William (1714–1763), 192
Sheridan, Richard Brinsley (1751–1816), 6, 61, 114, 122, 191, 210, 246, 291, 293, 323, 351, 423
Sherman, William Tecumseh (1820–1891), 432
Shirley, James (1596–1666), 81, 103, 127, 199
Sidney, Sir Philip (1554–1586), 168, 235, 251, 403
Sigourney, Lydia Huntley (1791–1865), 34, 73, 151, 304, 332, 378, 436
Skipsey, Joseph (1832–1903), 342
Smith, Adam (1723–1790), 361
Smith, Horace (1779–1849), 10, 115, 174, 377
Smith, Samuel Francis (1808–1895), 65

Smith, Sydney (1771-1845), 296, 297, 347
Smith, Walter Chalmers (1824-), 305
Solomon, King of Israel (c. 1000 B.C.), 343
Southerne, Thomas (1660-1746), 305
Southey, Caroline Anne Bowles (1786-1854), 435
Southey, Robert (1774-1843), 11, 57, 63, 69, 87, 92, 130, 183, 268, 288, 304, 316, 326, 348, 361, 388, 425, 432, 448
Spencer, William Robert (1769-1834), 406
Spenser, Edmund (c. 1552-1599), 29, 47, 62, 119, 150, 158, 166, 206, 335, 377, 408
Sprague, Charles (1791-1875), 278
Stedman, Edmund Clarence (1833-), 22, 33, 38, 206, 211, 240, 253, 401, 424, 454
Steele, Sir Richard (1672-1729), 108
Sterne, Laurence (1713-1768), 62, 82, 142, 156, 180, 189, 209, 278, 287, 298, 315, 395
Stevens, George Alexander (1710-1784), 346
Stevenson, Robert Louis (1850-1894), 163, 175, 182, 221
Still, John (c. 1543-1608), 6
Stoddard, Richard Henry (1825-1903), 171, 229, 365, 445, 456, 470
Story, Robert (1795-1860), 440
Story, William Wetmore (1819-1895), 61, 120, 392
Stowe, Harriet Beecher (1811-1896), 166, 441
Stowell, William Scott, Lord (1745-1836), 92
Suckling, Sir John (1609-1642), 117, 129, 226, 240, 294
Surrey, Earl of. See *Howard, Henry*
Swift, Jonathan (1667-1745), 11, 35, 46, 134, 162, 252, 280, 281, 393
Sylvester, Joshua (1563-1618), 240

Tabley, John Byrne Leicester, Baron de (1835-1895), 57
Talfourd, Sir Thomas Noon (1795-1854), 435
Tannahill, Robert (1774-1810), 364
Tarlton, Richard (-1588), 202
Taylor, James Bayard (1825-1878), 34, 86, 223, 240, 241, 276, 312, 469
Taylor, Jefferys (1792-1853), 48
Taylor, Sir Henry (1800-1886), 259
Taylor, Tom (1817-1880), 118, 180, 198, 225, 287, 312, 324, 389
Tennyson, Alfred (1809-1892), 1, 7, 9, 12, 17, 18, 19, 20, 23, 25, 26, 32, 35, 37, 38, 40, 42, 43, 45, 46, 51, 52, 53, 54, 56, 59, 69, 72, 73, 76, 80, 81, 90, 93, 94, 97, 101, 104, 105, 106, 107, 108, 112, 113, 116, 119, 120, 122, 124, 128, 130, 132, 133, 135, 137, 140, 141, 144, 145, 146, 148, 150, 158, 160, 161, 162, 166, 167, 169, 170, 171, 174, 175, 181, 182, 185, 187, 189, 190, 192, 193, 200, 204, 205, 211, 214, 219, 224, 225, 226, 230, 231, 241, 242, 243, 244, 246, 252, 253, 256, 259, 267, 268, 271, 273, 275, 284, 287, 290, 291, 292, 297, 300, 301, 302, 310, 313, 316, 319, 322, 323, 328, 333, 334, 336, 337, 338, 339, 341, 343, 347, 350, 352, 354, 356, 357, 358, 368, 371, 372, 373, 375, 377, 382, 384, 388, 396, 399, 400, 404, 412, 413, 418, 419, 421, 422, 426, 427, 430, 433, 437, 442, 443, 454, 457, 461, 463, 468, 470
Terrett, William B., 241
Thackeray, William Makepeace (1811-1863), 32, 70, 82, 130, 150, 164, 255, 264, 292, 294, 318, 319, 343, 348, 389, 401, 439, 444
Thaxter, Celia (1836-1894), 155
Theobald, Lewis (1688-1744), 295
Thessalonians, First Book of, 320
Thomson, James (1700-1748), 3, 11, 18, 27, 37, 40, 43, 46, 53, 55, 102, 114, 127, 152, 160, 162, 230, 288, 289, 357, 382, 398, 437
Thornbury, George Walter (1828-1876), 1, 152, 219, 458
Thrale, Hester Lynch (1741-1821), 224
Thurlow, Lord (1781-1829), 277
Tickell, Thomas (1686-1740), 91, 395, 428
Timothy, First Book of, 267
Timothy, Second Book of, 131
Titcomb, Timothy. See *Holland, Josiah Gilbert*
Tobin, John (1770-1804), 66
Tourneur, Cyril (c. 1575-1626), 16, 93, 335
Townley, James (1714-1778), 358
Townsend, Mary Ashley (1836-1901), 454
Trumbull, John (1750-1831), 311
Tucker, St. George (1752-1828), 5
Tuke, Sir Samuel (-1674), 450
Tusser, Thomas (c. 1524-1580), 31, 52, 211, 230, 255, 261, 271, 388, 407, 444
Twain, Mark. See *Clemens, Samuel Langhorne*

Uhland, Johann Ludwig (1787-1862), 381

Van Dyke, Henry. See *Dyke, Henry van*
Verulam, Baron. See *Bacon, Francis, Lord Verulam*
Villeneuve, Pierre Charles (1763-1806), 132
Visscher, Maria Tesselschade (1597-1649), 378, 412

Waddington, Samuel (1844-), 377
Wagner, Charles (1852-), 190, 208, 229, 279, 365
Waller, Edmund (1606–1687), 106, 343, 445
Walsh, William (1663–1708), 339
Walton, Izaak (1593–1683), 7, 9, 10
Warburton, Thomas, 291
Washington, George (1732–1799), 432
Watts, Isaac (1674–1748), 95, 170, 190, 218, 263, 371, 403
Weatherly, Frederick Edward (1848-), 347
Webb, Charles Henry (1834-), 21, 354
Webster, Daniel (1782–1852), 112, 192, 218, 340, 366, 420, 441
Webster, John (*c.* 1580–*c.* 1640), 366 390
Welby, Amelia B. (1819–1852), 258
Wellesley, Arthur. See *Wellington, Duke of*
Wellington, Duke of (1769–1852), 166
Wesley, John (1703–1791), 55
Westcott, Edward Noyes (1847–1898), ?2, 133, 134, 187
Whewell, William (1794–1866), 389
Whitman, Walt (1819–1892), 43, 51, 178, 180, 229, 307, 468
Whittier, Elizabeth Hussey (1815–1864), 242
Whittier, John Greenleaf (1807–1892), 23, 32, 43, 90, 109, 120, 121, 134, 144, 147, 154, 160, 172, 185, 186, 214, 300, 314, 321, 346, 353, 358, 403, 436, 446, 464, 470
Wilcox, Ella Wheeler (1855-), 46, 129, 152, 175, 212, 242, 313, 329, 381
Willard, Emma Hart (1787–1870), 84
William, Prince of Orange (1533–1584), 93
Williams, Sir Charles Hanbury (1708–1759), 205
Willis, Nathaniel Parker (1806–1867), 47, 366
Willson, Arabella M. (1789–1826), 357
Wilson, John (1785–1854), 21
Wither, George (1588–1667), 120, 201, 260
Wolcot, John (1738–1819), 123, 326, 418
Wolfe, Charles (1791–1823), 102, 153, 313, 433
Woodworth, Samuel (1785–1842), 39, 49
Wordsworth, William (1770–1850), 25, 48, 49, 69, 73, 74, 91, 101, 121, 128, 164, 180, 182, 188, 201, 225, 229, 293, 301, 302, 316, 394, 396, 404, 412, 413, 445, 446, 454, 463
Wotton, Sir Henry (1568–1639), 7, 418
Wyatt, Sir Thomas (*c.* 1503–1542), 215, 256

Young, Edward (1683–1765), 12, 13, 14, 20, 24, 27, 28, 51, 59, 73, 76, 81, 82, 84, 92, 94, 98, 104, 124, 127, 137, 138, 146, 147, 157, 191, 198, 210, 224, 227, 249, 251, 265, 269, 272, 302, 305, 312, 316, 317, 318, 322, 327, 336, 346, 362, 370, 376, 377, 378, 380, 401, 404, 407, 411, 414, 445, 446, 448, 468

Zacharias, Pope (–752), 202

INDEX

A

Abandon, all hope, 185
  the good soldier, never, 373
Abashed for that, be not, 96
Abbey, 1
A B C, 1
  like a schoolboy that had lost his, 239
Abdallah's dead, ye say, 74
Abdomen, took him in the, 350
Abed, 1
  after midnight, not to be, 24
Abhor each other, 110
Abhorred, in my imagination it is, how, 468
  perish hopeless and, 342
Abhorrent of a calculation crossed, 161
Abide in my mother's house, I, 276
Abides no handling, 44
Ability, and keep one of greater, 397
Abject spirit, doubting in his, 34
Able and willing to pull his weight, 54
  to work, when I am no longer, 460
Abner Dean, of Angel's, 350
Abode, ever reached that blessed, 374
  like the toad in his narrow, 446
  the strong gods pine for my, 159
Abodes, aiming at the blessed, 316
Aboding luckless time, 25
About, about, in reel and rout, 81
Above, but 't is not so, 289
  me, he is so, 384
  you, below or else, 240
Abra, 1
Abreast of truth, who would keep, 281
Abridgment, 1
Abroad, no news so bad, 281
  our peace at home and safety, 299
  that I should be, 64
  the schoolmaster is, 352
Absalom, 1
Absence, 1, 2
  of occupation, 333
Absent child, of my, 165
  together though, 409
Absolute, that can with logic, 162
  the knave is, 43
Abstain, the colt who is wise will, 253
Abstemious, be more, 70
Abstract war is horrid, not but wut, 431
Abuse, he bore without, 150
  scoffing and, 368
Abused, still by himself, 462
Abusing of God's patience, 113
Abusive, to express the, 389
Abysm of time, the dark backward and, 407
Abyss may be, the depth of the, 293
Academes, the arts, the, 118
Accent, that not a single, 210
  with swaggering, 287
Accents, in still small, 298
  loved, are soon forgot, 209
Accept their part, 150
  war, the other would, 431
Acceptance, forge another to take up the, 82
Accepting, charms by, 400
Accompanied with noble thoughts, that are, 403
Accompt, 2
Account, but sent to my, 370
  keep a regular debtor and creditor, 352
  of empty boxes, a beggarly, 33
Accumulate, on horror's head horrors, 186
Accumulates, where wealth, 300
Accursed, prove, 159
  the traitor most, 188
Accuse, his weak indulgence will, 452
Accused, by fools, 320
Accusing spirit, the, which flew up to heaven's chancery, 287
Ace for me, he trumped death's, 77
Ache, charm, with air, 5
Acheron, on the shores of, 333
Aches, 2
Achieve and cherish, all which may, 337
  greatness, some, 164
Achiever brings home full numbers, when the, 425
Achieving, 2
Aching in the potter's hand, clay bleeding and, 107
  of heart, all the, 109
  void, they have left an, 300
Acknowledged, there can be no less, 212

Acorns, 2
Acquainted, when we were first, 311
Acquaintance be forgot, should auld, 14
decrease it upon better, 238
Acre of barren ground, for an, 354
Acres, over whose, 67
Act a lover's or a Roman's part, to, 236
for him, God bade me, 93
free to think and, 220
incurs no blame, a necessary, 279
is as an ancient tale new told, this, 400
pleasure in the, 103
nor any unproportioned thought his, 411
of God, think himself an, 248
princes to, 383
the kingliest, 144
thyself shall see the, 199
well your part, 184
Acting bravely, 61
Action, 2
and pious, 88
brave, asks word or, 144
faithful, in, 385
fine, makes that and the, 102
in the tented field, 130
lies, there the, 289
lose the name of, 61
men of, 225
of battery, tell him of his, 214
the fairest, 335
Actions, a woman's thought runs before her, 453
of the just, only the, 199
that a man might play, 448
Actor stops, a moment yet the, 70
Actors fill, God and nature do with, 383
these our, 428
Acts, 2
already past, the first four, 109
his, being seven ages, 383
little nameless unremembered, 201
so or so, why gals, 283
the best, 227
the man for a' that, 248
unknown facts of guilty, 99
Adage, poor cat i' the, 45
Adam, 2
and his wife, 148
and of Eve, the son of, 317
called her woman, 449
dolve, when, 149
first was fooled, as father, 449
sat under the tree, 13
Adamant, on, our wrongs we all engrave, 467
that Adam was not, 2
Adam's profession, they hold up, 15c
Add a little care, but, 396
another hue, or, 152
Adder stung, thou serpent never, 412
Adder's fork and blind-worm's sting, 179
Adding fuel to the flame, 147
Addle as an egg, beaten as, 322
Addressed, to the realm of death, 401
Adieu, 2, 3
Ad infinitum, so proceed, 134
Adjust it, we never can, 172
Administered, whate'er is best, 161
Admiralty, the price of, 113
Admiration, 3
gave his tail a twirl of, 432
Admire by far, more, 408
that riches grow in hell, none, 336
Admired, but not to be, 452
never more, 46
Admission to our hearts, pleads, 85
Admittance, no, at this wicket, 345
Admitted to that equal sky, 176
Ado, no more, 158
Adore, and infidels, 197
you, the more I'll, 59
Adored, in every clime, 127
Adores the Maker, who, 247
Adorn a tale, or, 274
Adorned, 3
thy humble grave, 139
Adorns and cheers the way, 185
with arts, and, 234
Adoption tried, and their, 146
Adulteries of art, than all the, 364
Advance the flag of Dixie, 94
Advanced so nobly, they thus far, 276
they have thus far so nobly, 276
Advantage dressed, nature to, 447
nailed for our, 67
Advantageous to life, everything, 223
Adventure of the diver, two points in the, 93
Adversaries do in law, do as, 214
the souls of fearful, 432
Adversary's heart, his, 335
Adversity, 3
doth best discover virtue, 427
Adversity's sweet milk, philosophy, 303
Advice, 3
has often stilled, 93
may take a knave's, 205
Advise, his mistaken patron to, 397
Æons, whirled for a million, 18
Ætna's breast of flame, in, 233
Afar, cometh from, 25
seeing each other, 339
Affairs, God prosper your, 319
in their sleeps will mutter their, 371
of men, a tide in the, 405
the privatest of men's, 120
Affect, study what you most, 391
Affection, 3, 4
limb, nor beauty, 336
preferment goes by letter and, 315
too much of amorous, 8
Affection's a tear, the test of, 398
Affections, and his, dark as Erebus, 273
mild, of, 252
passions, 197

Affects to nod, 155
Afflict me, how dost thou, 61
Affliction, 4
alters, 240
of all, 139
Afford to play cards for money, cannot, 234
Affords no law, the world, 463
such pity as my rapier's point, 305
Affright our souls, dreams, 99
Affrighted from his nest, 181
Affront, 4
fear is, 450
Afghanistan's plains, wounded and left on, 373
Afire with God, every common bush, 153
Afloat, 4
Afraid, and not a man, 181
be not, 369
not, even with the vineyard's best produce, 288
of, that I confess I'm, 283
show the world that he feels, 461
to strike, and yet, 71
we're not, 413
Afric maps, in, 252
African, to blanch an, 266
After-days, raise this soul to God in, 293
twine for me in, 104
After-dinner talk, in, 396
Afternoon, 4
another quarter toward the, 434
a wench married in an, 254
Afterthought, a mine of, 274
Again at Christmas did we weave, 52
that should applaud, 11
Age, 4, 5
be comfort to my, 326
before a sprightlier, 228
boy was the very staff of my, 383
by years, reckon their, 398
each, each kindred, 24
grow dim with, 191
has no honey, 4
he can do nothing in this, 352
he would not in mine, 357
in every, 127
in this iron, 194
lends the graces that are sure to please, 94
my, is as a lusty winter, 357
never an, 248
of chivalry is gone, the, 50
the cricket chirps, in, 470
the labour of an, 29
the toys of, 49
thou smitest sore, man of, 372
time-tutored, 65
to a gaping, 278
to grace this latter, 422
well suited to the, 379
Aged bosom, in an, 60
man, said the, 162
which means certainly, 4
Agencies vary, how widely its, 157
Agents of the people, servants and, 289
while night's black, 282
Ages, and to the next, 258
believe that in all, 156
his acts being seven, 383
in his face, the emptiness of, 180
in their hearts the feuds of, 130
in three distant, 309
look, the suffering, 188
one increasing purpose, through the, 322
past, hoary seers of, 334
past, once in the flight of, 228
rock of, cleft for me, 340
Agitation, in the complicated, 365
A-gley, gang aft, 261
Agog, and all, 72
Agonies, out of its, 210
we suffer, the, 172
Agony, 5
all night I lay in, 282
but conquers, 152
mirth cannot move a soul in, 264
of some strong swimmer in his, 395
of the stern, 362
of this life, the long, 222
Agree, never did in time, 429
oil, vinegar, sugar, and saltness, 349
then all sides must, 376
while souls and bodies in one frame, 378
with our external parts, should well, 456
with his peculiar whim, 171
Agrees as ill with Rufa studying Locke, 410
Agues, to find out, 306
Ahs, one stormy gust of long-suspended, 188
Aid, apt alliterations artful, 6
if men will call, saints will, 348
for some wretch's, 216
of my feller-critter's, 313
the freeman's laws, to, 144
the truth, cannon-balls may, 159
us, boys the Lord will, 38
we'll win our battle by its, 159
Aidenn, within the distant, 246
Aideth the poor, who, 181
Ails it now, something, 69
Aim, stick to your, 40
their horns, bulls, 14
Aiming at the blessed abodes, still is, 316
Aimless course, in wayward, 322
feet, nothing walks with, 160
Air, 5
all be lost in, 125
and fame, 123
and I found them, 302
a solemn stillness holds, all the, 209
a sup of New England's, 281
a vapour, 219
away! through the sightless, 152

Air
bombs bursting in, 17
charm ache with, 5
fills the silent, 268
he says with solemn, 464
if their lungs receive our, 368
I mean pewer, 357
into thin air, melted into, 428
let out to warm the, 393
lift their fronded palms in, 43
like the, 176
love can feed on the, 240
love free as, 233
mock our eyes with, 56
of night, in the icy, 23
on the desert, 149
only to kiss that, 100
out in the empty, 313
out in the midnight, 40
perfuming, the morning, 343
she could only take the, 416
she says those words were, 428
that do corrupt my, 69
the, the skies, 293
the look, the, 377
the sea and the, 196
there is in a gaol better, 359
thoughts shut up want, 404
through the field of, 386
throw it up into the, 389
trifles light as, 195
unwholesome, made the, 43
what is that honour, 185
when on the undulating, 52
with weary wing the, 340
Air-drawn dagger, the, 70
Airs of England, the martial, 112
Aisle, through the long-drawn, 10
Aisles of Christian Rome, and groined the, 39
of the ancient church, now the, 464
Ajax, this love is as mad as, 238
Alabaster, and smooth as monumental, 367
his grandsire cut in, 264
A-land, as men do, 133
Alarmed, raptured or, 377
Alarms, a blow which while it executes, 81
Alarum, 5
Albatross, 5
Alcalde, 5
Alchemist, the sovereign, 162
Alcohol, much more stimulating than, 387
Alcoholic, 5
Ale, 6
no more cakes and, 427
nor wanted they gude beef and, 267
take the size of pots of, 6
than a draught of Old England's, 281
the monks of St. Bothan's, 267
Alexander, the noble dust of, 421
Alexandrine, 6
Alfred named, Truth-teller was our England's, 418
Algebra, 6
Alice, don't you remember sweet, 29
Alike, come out, 220
Alive, bears not, 381
bricks are, 36
ridiculous, 462
the spirit keeps, 380
to grace this latter age, is now, 322
who think themselves, 75
All a dream, which was not, 98
a lie, a lie which is, 219
a muddle, 't is, 271
are but parts of one stupendous whole, 297
are made of clay, 55
be masters, we cannot, 255
hell broke loose, 178
her men, drawing force from, 277
I know is, 78
in all, and, 135
in all, take him for, 250
is not lost, 231
may do what has by man been done, 94
my pretty chickens, 49
night I lay in agony, 282
night, the sleeping woods, 37
sorts of people, golden opinions from, 290
that, a man's a man for, 248
that, and not a man for, 248
that, brothers be for, 38
that inhabit this great earth, 201
that in him lies, 54
that was, in, 18
the day, merry heart goes, 174
things, causes why and wherefore in, 288
things, free to prove, 320
things, great lord of, 462
things, prove, 320
things, see through, 57
things, there's music in, 212
things, sweet are, 394
things, though equal to, 141
things are bought, with which, 369
things both great and small, 314
things by a law divine, 366
things clad, 116
things in heaven and earth, 212
this, must I endure, 110
this is ours, 106
was ended now, 109
Alla Hu, 63
given by, 233
Illa Allah, la, 232
Allah's throne above, viewed from, 231
Allay the gust, to, 323
you would quench or but, 327
Alleged, when it is, 253
Allegiance swear, to these I do, 170
Allegory, 6
Alley, 6

Alley
and she lives in our, 74
Alliances, 6
Allied, are sure to madness near, 245
by birth, are kindred and, 201
Alliteration, 6
Allow, my good, 160
All-softening, o'erpowering knell, 92
Allured him, as the beacon-blaze allures, 25
Almanac, he doth not lack an, 470
Almighty, 6
dollar, the, 96
Master, do not tell me the, 155
Almighty's orders to perform, pleased the, 388
Alms, 7
for oblivion, wherein he puts, 407
should sue, for, 126
who gives himself with his, 181
Aloft, that sits up, 48
Alone, 7
and warming his five wits, 292
blind and wailing and, 15
heart is left, 172
I am, 146
in his glory, we left him, 153
in the cold I end, 57
they are never, 403
you must drink life's gall, 152
Alonzo the Brave, to the health of, 379
Alps, the soaring eagle of the, 332
though perched on, 322
Altar of Mammon, before the, 253
one nearer to God's, 312
Altar's God, the other to the, 312
Altars, a priest at her, 63
the hush of our dread high, 1
Altar-stairs, 7
Alter a decree established, can, 315
their rate of going, or, 403
Altered strangely, titles now are, 407
Alum and plaster, chalk and, 35
Alway, I would not live, 228
Amazement, what a strange delicious, 76
Amazon, a cruel, haughty, blood-stained, 143
Ambassador, 7
Amber, pretty in, 458
when tipped with, 408
Ambition, 7
death for his, 7
fame, love, wine, 274
in my love, the, 384
mock, let not, 310
to reign is worth, 329
virtue, that make, 125
Ambition's airy hall, was once, 367
ladder, lowliness is young, 7
Ambitious, 7, 8
Ambles well, your wit, 447
withal, who time, 406
Amen, 8
like the sound of a great, 51
Lord say, 429
Amen
sigh and say, 372
Amends, by way of, 318
America, 8
American, 8
Amiss, though there's nothing, 203
Amorous, 8
causes springs, dire offence from, 414
Amos Cottle, Phœbus! what a name, 274
Amount o' fleas, a reasonable, 134
Amuse themselves and other children, they, 321
Anarchy and wrath, tears and, 143
institute and digest of, 338
Ancestors no shame, done our, 89
Ancestral thirst, vengeance, the, 130
tree, on my, 342
Anchor, 8, 9
Anchoret, no prisoner but an, 318
Anchorite, could tempt the dying, 349
Anchors, great, 102
Anchovy sauce, a magic *soupçon* of, 349
Ancient as the sun, 180
days, deeds she wrought in, 111
form, keep an, 140
mariner, I fear thee, 253
people, they that marry, 254
tale new told, as an, 400
Andrew and his love of law, Sir, 235
Angel, 9
a guardian, o'er his life presiding, 443
a ministering, shall my sister be, 426
dropped down from the clouds, 187
guise, transfigured into, 416
it may be that Death's bright, 51
of death spread his wings, 77
of Life winds them up, the, 33
of the Resurrection, hand of the, 33
rolls the stone away, till the last, 13
the recording, as he wrote it down, 287
thou, a ministering, 453
till you find the deathless, 338
was a cruel, that the, 143
Angel-guard of loves and graces lie, 452
Angelic light, with something of, 454
Angel's, Abner Dean of, 350
finger rest, where shall the, 91
psalm, like the close of an, 374
touch remain, where, 91
wing, a quill from an, 301
wing, dropped from an, 301
wing, he asks no, 176
Angels, 9
are, our acts our, 2
are painted fair, 452
could no more, 24
do, sweet as the, 352
face, her, 119
fear to tread, where, 138

Angels
fell the, 7
guardian, sung this strain, 37
how did he git thar, 404
I b'lieve in God and the, 330
in heaven above, the, 236
lackey her, 47
may, and in the hereafter, 186
might talk with men, 417
name Lenore, whom the, 246
need the tears of all the, 449
of deliverance, knows not its, 255
sad as, 287
say, Sister Spirit, 170
shared, with, 233
those evil, 325
till our passion dies, ne'er like, 297
uncurtained that repose, 105
wait, while, 184
weep, as make the, 251
weep, tears such as, 398
within it, 292
wooing, women are, 457
would, be gods, 316
Angels' feet, marks of, 460
Anger, 9
at peace, 208
countenance more in sorrow than in, 375
in their, was a sin, 141
of my heart, will tell the, 412
of the wise, fear not the, 332
that carries, 209
they banish our, 212
Angered, puffs away from thence, and being, 444
Angle, 9
Angle-rod made of a sturdy oak, his, 439
Angling, 10
Angry at a slander, who's, 368
Anguish, 10
here tell your, 375
lessened by another's, 131
of patience, constant, 109
to discover, what, 242
when pain and, 453
Animal at best, is but an, 248
unfledged, man is an, 249
Animals, that souls of, 378
too, and rampant, 56
Animate the whole, 349
Annabel Lee, of the beautiful, 236
Annals of the human race, the, 228
of the poor, 310
Anne Hathaway, 436
Annie Laurie, but all sang, 241
Annual income, twenty pounds, 192
Anoint me, I will, 365
Anointed, 10
I am the Lord's, 108
Another blow, to strike, 130
Helen, like, 177
man's doxy, heterodoxy is, 291
man's eyes, through, 170
man's ground, built on, 187
Another morn than ours, 105
one, know from, 57
place there is, 114
sailing o'er life's solemn main, 138
star, emigrated to, 109
still, 53
then here goes, 286
though I called, 1
who'd give her booby for, 270
Another's gain, or but subserves, 160
Answer, 10
and cannot, 82
a letter, may, 216
be to them, what will thine, 151
each other in the mist, 52
for, few sins of thine own to, 449
for it, guv'ment ain't to, 156
him, ye owls, 282
his brute question, how, 147
in his own, finds a, 144
me, deep caverns of darkness, 163
no, dared not, 283
that, I'll not, 103
trickled through my head, his, 414
Answerable, how his spirit stands, 298
Answered so, will not be, 195
the wilt thou, 290
you last night, yes I, 468
Answers, 10
life's great end, which, 224
she who ne'er, 189
where, an echo, 107
Anthem, 10
swells the note of praise, 10
Anti, 10
Antic the law, old father, 213
Antidote, with some sweet oblivious, 263
Antidotes are poison, his, 303
Antiquity, 10
from all, 78
Any, enough to, 141
man, or so can, 381
thing is to be got, where, 394
Anywhere out of the world, 244
Apart, standing with mute lips, 115
Ape and tiger die, let the, 20
like an angry, 251
there was an, 311
Apes, 10
humility, is pride that, 316
Apollyon shoots darts, and, 226
Apology, 11
Apostasy, were the price of, 416
Apostles, 11
shrank, while, 67
would have done, all the, 51
Apostolic blows and knocks, by, 329
Apothecary, 11
Appal the devil, which might, 251
Apparatus of the system, all the, 33
Apparel, 11
do, as men their best, 446
wears out more, 126
Apparition, a lovely, 302
Appealing from his native sod, 388

Appear the better reason, 122
to the world, what I may, 417
Appeared, wheresoever he, 128
Appears, Roman honour more, 145
Appease thee, prayers cannot, 15
Appeased, the Eternal's wrath, 301
Appetite, 11
for emetics, contract so strong an, 109
for moral good, whets his, 312
may sicken, the, 273
the hungry edge of, 191
wait on, 91
you have, with what, 35
Appetites, other women cloy the, 5
Applaud, 11
Applause, 11
Apple, 11
had she, only one, 115
pressed with specious cant, 2
Apples, 11
hearts like, 175
on the Dead Sea's shore, 76
to seize, the, 353
Appliance, by desperate, 86
Application on it, lays in the, 287
that's turned by, 413
Appointed end, rolls to its, 322
Appreciate heaven well, to, 176
Apprehend more than cool reason comprehends, 243
Apprehension, is most in, 80
Apprentice hand, her, 211
Approach thou like the rugged, 72
thy grave, 227
Approbation, 11, 12
gives manhood more, 287
Approve it, will bless it and, 330
Approved, by all, 385
Approving none, and, 361
April day, of an, 240
when they woo, men are, 457
April's breeze unfurled, their flag to, 362
Aprons, mechanic slaves with greasy, 368
Apron-strings of an American mother, the, 8
Apt alliterations artful aid, 6
and punctual, are very, 122
Aptest, the harshest word comes, 114
Arab, 12
tents are rude for thee, 85
Arabia, all the perfumes of, 169
Arabian trees, drop tears as fast as the, 399
Arabs, like the, 44
Arbitrator, that old common, 109
Arcades ambo, 26
Arch Fear, the, where he stands, 78
look on its broken, 367
the sky one blue interminable, 368
Archangel call archangel, 275
the strong, 248
Arched the flood, by the rude bridge that, 362
Archer, 12
little meant, mark the, 358
Arcite, the soul of, 376
Are, 12
Argosies of magic sails, 59
Argue, 12
down or mask your passions, can, 298
not against heaven's hand, I, 387
plead, expound and, 283
Argues a monstrous life, 80
yourselves unknown, not to know me, 421
Arguing too, in, 12
Argument, finer than the staple of his, 424
for a week, 196
for lack of, 395
of tyrants, necessity is the, 279
stir without great, 164
Arguments, ear-kissing, 106
use wagers, fools for, 137
Arise, Columbia, to glory, 58
for Charlie's sake I will, 365
or be for ever fallen, 15
O Christ, I will, 437
O soul, 126
the happier to, 121
these stones, 145
ye Goths, 193
Arising, at break of day, 210
Arithmetic, reading, writing and, 187
Ark, 12
Arm, 12
alone, to thy, 156
because his strong right, 248
brought the freeman's, 144
for life's combat, nerveth his, 410
lay bare thine, 388
in arm, not, 363
my soul I, 311
or an, 184
should conquer twenty worlds, though mine, 61
slumbers in a peasant's, 300
soon shall thy, 386
was there, thy, 156
will never be stronger, your, 409
wi' the auld moon in her, 267
would wither, there is an, 10
Arm-chair, 12
saw her die in that old, 173
Armed, 12
camp, Christendom is an, 42
so strong in honesty, I am, 404
Armies swore terribly in Flanders, our, 395
Armour against fate, there is no, 127
is his honest thought, whose, 418
Arms, 12, 13
about my dearie, 44
and fleet in my, 47
and moves his doubtful, 442
corners of the world in, 112
first that ever bore, 150
fold thine, 35

Arms
forge, in your defence to bear, 355
gold provokes the world to, 158
hug it in mine, 90
in other's, 402
in the same encircling, 416
more strong than traitors', 192
never would lay down my, 8
of strength are made, where my, 386
or to take, 19
other, may press thee, 331
our first breath in their, 455
outstretched, with his, 167
reversed, with, 433
rolled in one another's, 108
strength in her, 142
take your last embrace, 118
to, in Dixie, 94
to front a lie in, 146
we start from the Mother's, 56
ye forge, the, 355
Army, an Austrian, 14
head of the, 171
of collectors, quite an, 92
Arose from out the azure main, 37
Around, the ice was all, 190
't was ice, 190
Array, battle's magnificently stern, 19
change his bed of fiery rich, 8
in grim, 282
Arrayed, awfully, 14
Arrears, pay glad life's, 78
were brought up, then its, 389
Arrest, strict in his, 80
Arrows, the slings and, 19
Art, 13
all nature is but, 337
but heart which wins, not, 175
can copy, cherub no, 96
can wash her guilt away, what, 136
is long, 163
is of ending, greater the, 109
is too precise, than when, 364
I want that glib and oily, 321
may err, 277
measure their life by, 398
no magical, 72
not chance, comes from, 467
not what thou wast, thou, 232
of beginning, great is the, 109
of hearts, love is the, 232
of perceiving, in the, 54
o' letter-writin', that's the great, 216
seeking not the praise of, 466
than all the adulteries of, 364
the only, 136
the sculptor's, 410
't is all thou, 334
war's glorious, 272
whatever thou, 236
with curious, 33
without poetry, music, and, 63
Artful aid, apt alliterations, 6
to no end, 462
Articles of ladies fair, 20
Artificer, 13
Artificial, all things are, 13
tears, with, 118
Artillery, 13
by infallible, 329
Artist wills, made to be fashioned as the, 107
Arts, 13
and adorns with, 234
and heart of, 232
essayed, no, 452
in which the wise excel, of all those, 467
of peace, the inglorious, 299
the books, the, 118
Ascend, a muse of fire that would, 272
by which he did, 7
Ascent to high office is steep, the, 305
Ascribe to heaven, which we, 330
we all, 156
Ashamed to confess it, nor am I, 283
Ashes, 13
and mingle with forgotten, 81
and of embers spent, 4
and praty-skins, 16
burn, in itself to, 48
e'en in our, 35
laid at last old Troy in, 452
lay, where Milton's, 29
may be made, and from his, 426
of his father, for the, 89
to the taste, 76
watched, the martyrs', 441
Ashore, till the last soul got, 329
Aside she threw, her old-world moulds, 179
Ask it o' yoursel', 234
me how many I'd have, 205
me no questions, 323
me to take none, don't, 32
nay do not, 328
not, I, 236
not if neighbour grind, 207
not such from thee, 354
vainly, you should not, 76
where's the North, 284
Asked but what he heard his father say, 416
enough, I'm sure he has been, 290
one another the reason, but they, 242
the Wilt thou, 290
you, sir, nobody, 246
Askew sets, somehow, 60
Asking, had for only the, 3
how or why, 357
may be had for the, 177
to be done agin it's ollers, 40
Asleep, between a man, 369
in the sun, that hath lain, 322
over the buttons I fall, 460
tide as moving seems, 18
Aspect, distraction in 's, 307
he rose, with grave, 85
nothing in nature's, 75

Aspen made, by the light quivering, 453
Aspire, but light and will, 240
Aspireth to it, honour, 77
Aspires, who, 7
Ass, 13
to say another is an, 340
whose back with ingots bows, 336
will not mend his pace, 33
Assent with civil leer, 71
Asses, 14
nations like o'erloaded, 55
Asses' milk and writing, this comes of drinking, 466
Assume among the powers of the earth, and to, 356
a virtue if you have it not, 427
Assumes some mark of virtue, 425
the god, 155
Assurance, 14
to give the world, 250
Assured alone that life and death, 147
of what he 's most, 251
Assyrian, 14
piles, Shem's proud children reared the, 350
Astray, if weak women went, 456
Astronomer, 14
Ate by his side, with, 335
Ate into itself, for lack, 26
Atheism, 14
and religion, and, 330
Atheist, 14
Athena 's wisest son, 206
A-tiptoe when this day is named, 66
Atlantic Ocean, the, beat Mrs. Partington, 297
Atlantis, 14
Atmosphere of intellect, where the, 387
Atoms or systems into ruin, 38
Atone, fully and well, 172
my witchcrafts to, 448
Atones, blood for blood, 15
Atropos, sever, 380
Attain, to something nobler we, 170
Attains the upmost round, 7
Attaint, since Lucifer 's, 316
Attempt, 14
by fearing to, 97
my last faint, despairing, 389
that dares love, 239
Attempted, something, 410
Attempting to do well, dissuading you from, 302
Attend all ye who list to hear, 111
Attendance on their lordships' pleasure, 71
Attending Captain Ill, Captive Good, 417
Attention, enforce, 105
Attire doth show her wit, 20
so wild in their, 448
walk in silk, 364
Attraction, with his great, 402
Attractive, 14
Attracts each light gay meteor, 410
Attribute to awe and majesty, 260
to God himself, an, 260
Audit here, whoso seeks an, 36
Augurs because they were bores, 31
Augustine, well hast thou said, 170
Auld Lang Syne, 14
Aunt, they braced my, 208
was an O'Shaughnessy, his, 348
Austrian, 14
Author health again dispense, should my, 429
in the world, any, 118
of such a book of follies, the, 449
Authority, a little brief, 251
and show by sanction of, 92
be a stubborn bear, 158
for their robbery have, 386
of the circumlocution office, 54
wrest once the law to your, 213
Authorized by her grandam, 389
Authors, 14
Automaton, the works of this horrid, 403
Autumn hath blown, when, 216
of adversity, in the, 3
't was, 32
Autumnal leaves that strow the brooks, 216
Avail the plough or sail, what, 143
Availed on high, 125
Availeth, say not the struggle nought, 391
Avails thee not, 334
Avalanche of men, 119
Avarice, 15
Avenge even a look, to, 50
Avenged, 15
Avenging, 15
Aversion, and left his widow to her own, 441
Avert, courage can, 189
Averted gaze, with, 121
Avoid, all these you may, 218
it, or crush it, 449
the man I should, 126
what is to come, 60
Avoided, trouble afterwards may be, 96
what can be, 157
what cannot be, 65
Avoirdupois, turn the scales between their, 351
Avon, sweet swan of, 394
to the Severn runs, the, 441
Avowed foe, give me the, 145
Await alike the inevitable hour, 163
Awake, 15
Awakens, when he, 91
Awakes, and the soul, 77
Awards it, the court, 134
Awe and majesty, the attribute to, 260
the lifted hand in, 272
to keep the strong in, 61
which kept the world in, 421

Aweary, 15
Awes if seen, and, 316
Awful cope, beneath that, 115
voice, the, 28
will, bow before the, 150
Awfully arrayed, an Austrian army, 14
Awkward hand in a row, and, 135
thing, 't is an, 378
Awoke one morning, I, 124
Awry, their currents turn, 61
Axe, 15
a butcher with an, 41
had seen their chips, never an, 437
many strokes though with a little, 390
the, the mill, 212
Axis, 15
Axle-tree, on the, 309
Azure main, arose from out the, 37

B

Baal, the golden calf of, 42
Babble, for the watch to, 434
Babbled of green fields, and a', 359
Babe again, awakens my, 91
forlorn, a, 377
like a testy, 341
taxation, and her suckling, 432
Babes, a blessing on his wife and, 313
Baboon and monkey, bred out into, 267
Baby, 15, 16
died, and new-born, 425
his, at her breast, 89
oh hush thee my, 390
some blamed the, 348
Baby's dimple be, where shall the, 91
nest, when he comes down to the, 91
Bacchus, 16
Back against a rock he bore, his, 136
and side go bare, 6
a wallet at his, 407
daily burden for the, 40
harness on our, 90
has never a shirt on his, 360
hath borne me on his, 468
one who never turned his, 337
on heaven, find me and turn thy, 159
the burden of the world, on his, 180
their own opinions with a wager, 429
thumps upon your, 405
to back in God's name, stand, 131
unto the ladder turns his, 7
yard, it's jest your own, 288
Backed like a weasel, 56
Background of God, there's a, 314
Backs his rigid Sabbath, who, 247
proudly on their, 141
Backward and abysm of time, the dark, 407
Backward, turn backward, 340
Back-wounding calumny strikes, 42
Bacon shined, think how, 123
Bachelor, 16
Bachelor's Hall, 16
Bad, 16
abroad, no news so, 281
a death, so, 80
and mad it was, how sad and, 394
angel fire my good one, 9
a thousandfold, good or, 157
man, a bold, 29
man, this bold, 29
news, to bring, 281
nothing either good or, 402
of every land, something good and, 8
one, never fails to see a, 70
peace, a good war or a, 430
so you o'ergreen my, 160
sons, good wombs have borne, 374
the poor in a loomp is, 310
things in this world, but two, 24
wiser being good than, 159
work follers ye ez long 's ye live, 40
workman, is a, 208
would make good of, 24
your sentiment only that I find, 397
Bade him go, and they, 183
it blossom there, and, 77
Badge of all our tribe, sufferance is the, 392
Baffle his design, may, 262
Baffled oft, though, 142
to fight better, are, 337
Bag and baggage, not with, 334
Baggage, not with bag and, 334
Bail, a good conscience is my, 318
Bairns, 16
Bait, 16
thy hook, with saints dost, 347
Baited, his hook he, 439
with reasons not unplausible, 459
Baits, while good news, 281
Bake, there's bread in the, 254
Baker, see you a-shaving of a, 225
Bakers, we can't go beyond, 225
Baking on the Sunday, no worse than, 393
Balance, 16
and weight, a, 369
then at the, 172
which shall show a floating, 352
Balcony, the rose upon my, 343
Bald, but now your brow is, 311
unjointed chat, 47
Bales, dropping down with costly, 59
unopened to the sun, like, 404
Ball, that melts the, 227
Ballad, with a woeful, 242
Ballad-makers, increase tailors, and breed, 299
Ballad-mongers, one of these same metre, 205
Ballads, 16
Ball-room's belle, she was not the, 296

Balm, 17
of hurt minds, 370
Balms for all our pain, there are, 470
Balsams, give it all sorts of, 64
Ban, heaven's benison or, 328
Band, find leash or, 344
heaven-born, 58
its children a happy, 209
seam and gusset and, 460
Ban-dogs howl, and, 352
Bane, that soil may best deserve the precious, 336
Baned, ten thousand ducats to have it, 325
Bang, many a stiff thwack, many a, 405
Banish our anger, they, 212
those, and, 379
you, I, 69
Banished who returned, the, 332
yet a trueborn Englishman, 113
Banishment, 17
Banjo an' de 'possum, dar's de, 281
Bank, 17
hold her nozzle agin the, 329
of violets, that breathes upon a, 273
Banker, beggar and, 21
Bankrupt quite the wits, but, 298
Banks dispense with bolts and locks, when, 216
of Seine, to the sunny, 332
of that lonely river, on the, 296
of the Nile, an allegory on the, 6
Banner, 17
freedom's, 17
in the sky, danced to see that, 114
of England blew, our, 112
that glances, the tree in his, 49
the royal, 125
Banner's massy fold, unfurled that, 111
Banners, 17
taken, they show the, 433
that host with their, 216
Banquet, the joys of his, 153
the mind shall, 263
there no forced, 333
Banquet-hall, 17
Baptist, a kind of maddened John the, 114
Bar, 17, 18
and the leaping, 247
between us, save for the, 243
'cross Bilbao, 115
good-bye to the, 132
it out, right to, 110
the harbour, be moaning, 132
tried at the litigious, 455
Barbarians, there were his young, 181
Barbarism, 18
Barbered, 18
Barbers shave, no, 345
Barcan wilderness, pierce the, 74
Bard, 18
to the skies, which carries a, 445
Bards are not chameleons, 123
Bards burn, and, 123
Bare, albeit the place be, 96
and shiny head, nothing like a, 94
him to the blast, may, 328
the gift without the giver is, 181
without it, meeting were, 129
Barefaced on the bier, 24
Barefoot on her wedding-day, 10
Bargain, 18
a dateless, 118
for the graves, we, 176
with a holy kiss, seal the, 204
Bargains, on me, my, 193
Barge, drag the slow, 386
Bark, 18
and bite, delight to, 95
and leaves, 308
at me, they, 95
feels afraid of its, 461
grows sharp and savage, 64
is my bride, my, 4
is on the sea, 28
let no dog, 291
let the labouring, 400
our poor devoted, 26
the watch-dog's honest, 438
Barkis is willin', 443
Barleycorn, 18, 19
Barnaby, yet whoop, 26
Baron's retainers, and the, 265
Barracks, but single men in, 349
Barred from real life, and, 76
my gates with iron, I, 284
Barrel, there's beer in the, 254
Barriers fall, the, 78
strong, parted by, 339
Bars, and solitude, locks, 318
forty flags with their crimson, 134
nor iron, a cage, 318
ob de sheepfol', he le' down de, 358
Barter away that precious jewel, 42
prey for prey, to, 10
Bartered, hoarded, 157
Base degrees, scorning the, 7
from its firm, 136
is he who 'neath the shade, most, 64
so, that would be a bondman, 29
uses, to what, 421
Baseless as the fantastic visions, as, 428
Baseness to write fair, a, 466
where low-browed, 385
Bastard Latin, that soft, 210
Bastion, 19
Bat night has flown, black, 148
wool of, 179
Bate a jot of heart or hope, nor, 387
his usual height, 135
me some, 318
thee a scruple, I will not, 353
Bated breath and whispering humbleness, 35
Bath, sore labour's, 370
Bathe in fiery floods, 90
in me, mother and child, 247, 419

Battalions, not single spies but in, 375
Batten on this moor, and, 269
Battered to repair, 353
Battery, boldly by, 14
tell him of his action of, 214
Battle, 19
and strife, hatred, 215
and the breeze, braved the, 110
are half the, 431
by its aid, we 'll win our, 159
driven, rushed the steed to, 13
for the saints and for the Lord, 395
from afar, he sniffed the, 386
from afar, I watched the, 433
he has fought may not be won, 62
he never walked to, 351
he that is in, 130
he who is in, 130
in the lost, 83
is the blended sound of, 461
knows, nor the division of a, 382
of life, who fell in the, 61
once begun, freedom 's, 142
pops, how pefore de, 351
strikes him dead, in fair, 12
thunders will not break their rest, 35
who shall have borne the, 337
Battle-flags were furled, and the, 433
Battle-ground the free broad field of thought, 403
Battlements, not high raised, 385
sheer o'er the crystal, 122
Battle 's lost and won, when the, 257
to fight, though a, 78
Battles, 19
on her side, and he who, 199
won, they tell his, 433
Battle-sword, swing the, 151
Battling Irishman, the rattling, 194
Bauble still, pleased with this, 49
Bay, decked his brows instead of, 282
deep-mouthed welcome, 438
in some near port or, 73
of Biscay, in the, 26
on the Bolivar south across the, 60
out across the, 215
outer China 'crost the, 252
the broad, and the rapid river, 437
the moon, 36
toward me o'er the, 315
threshed the Bolivar out across the, 54
Bayonet clashing, seen the claymore with, 431
Bayou, up the narrow, muddy, 437
Bays, deck thee with all, 124
and broad-armed ports, not, 385
Bay-tides rise and fall, and her, 32
Be, 19
not so to me, if she, 201
the best is yet to, 24
the Christ that is to, 51
to, contents his natural desire, 176
without body, 76
with us yet, 139
Be
wi' you, God, 156
Beach, go stand upon the, 135
I wandered, here about the, 352
night sank upon the dusky, 111
Beacon peerless, holdin' up a, 290
Beacon-blaze allures the bird of passage, 25
Beadroll, on Fame 's eternal, 47
Beads and prayer-books, 49
to tell his, 145
Beak, 19
with unbloodied, 41
Beaker, no playmate shares my, 146
up, fill every, 445
Beam, a light about to, 225
at the full midday, 277
from the solar, 101
of milder, calmer, 236
of the day 's last, 429
on the moon 's pale, 450
Beams, candle throws his, 42
display, let my sun his, 408
Bear, 19
another 's misfortunes, who could not, 265
an untried pain, to, 436
authority be a stubborn, 158
away the belle, will, 458
bush supposed a, 128
gave pain to the, 321
him best, which doth, 213
his comment, every nice offence should, 289
his courage up, whistling aloud to, 440
his friend 's infirmities, 145
how much the heart can, 173
it at first, one can, 31
it that the opposed may beware, 322
it, to pardon or to, 405
it with an honest heart, 150
melancholy as . . . a lugged, 258
or lion, a, 56
out the deed, hope your warrant will, 433
the brunt, 78
the flying-chariot, 386
the gree, 38
them, we get them, 311
the rugged Russian, 72
those ills we have, 79
to see a, 393
up and steer right onward, 387
Bear-baiting, the Puritans hated, 321
Beard, a hair more, or a hair less, in his, 322
and wiped his yellow, 181
neglected, a, 239
of formal cut, 199
plucks dead lions by the, 423
the lion in his den, 85
Bearded like the pard, 373
Beards unmown, and, 345
wag all, when, 261

Bearing heavy evidence against us, in, 450
the intent of, 13
Bearings of this observation, the, 287
Bears and lions, let, 95
another, 355
calamity, he that nobly, 422
down truth, appear that malice, 247
no fruit, the tree that, 147
not alive so stout a gentleman, 381
unfeeling, 259
us along, strongly it, 288
Beast, 20
are but beast, bird, man, 316
both man and bird and, 313
I cotched a vild, 200
inflicted on a, 390
lived, while the, 226
Beastly fury, in that, 101
Beasts by his body, of kin to the, 248
most graze, when, 393
the birds, the, 345
to know their friends, nature teaches, 278
Beat as one, two hearts that, 224
down the gate, as he would, 206
his music out, 97
his pate four days, I will, 216
me, the more you, 378
the ground, knit hands and, 409
your pate and fancy wit will come, 447
Beaten, 20
hymn of the, 61
may be said, he that is, 184
out of season, any man thus, 441
out of them, the dear breath, 35
Beatified, sings like a soul, 210
Beating funeral marches, are, 163
it in upon his weary brain, 400
mend his pace with, 33
of my own heart, the, 173
Beats and blows his numbing hands, 207
upon a throne, that fierce light which, 404
with weary wing, 340
Beau, every Miss but me has got a, 290
Beauteous eye, seek the, 152
looks, not their, 201
Beauties, more admire by far thy naked, 408
of the North, pale unripened, 284
Beautiful, 20
and both were young and one was, 469
and gallant craft, 66
and therefore to be wooed, she's, 453
my dreams were always, 98
the, the pure, the bright, 88
Beautifully less, fine by degrees and, 131
Beauty, 20, 21
a land of, 65
Beauty
and all that, 163
and mystery of the ships, 360
and rustic health, simple, 172
and Scotch, 352
as could die, as much, 427
bless, one brief gleam of, 230
bright, when, 236
could I come near your, 59
draws us with a single hair, 168
grew, the conscious stone to, 39
her, and her chivalry, 334
I should take her, 443
Isle of, 1
limb nor, 336
nor saw the, 145
nothing but bowls and, 308
of fresh, 233
of the lilies, in the, 225
of the sun, shows all the, 240
of youth and love and, 204
reigns, nature in all the pomp of, 217
save, modest truth and, 449
she walks in, 430
teaches such, 118
that life was, 104
this world is full of, 462
thy more than, 236
till then her, 443
was far beyond, her, 149
was my vision, whose, 274
what once had, 334
Beauty's chain, and, 233
flowery crown, and, 354
Became him like the leaving it, 223
Beckon to me, over the river they, 339
Beckoned him, hands that madly, 321
smiling sweet, 194
to the people, he, 419
Beckons me away, which, 428
Becks and wreathed smiles, 196
Become a fool and jester, 137
a man, all that may, 72
her, it doth so well, 20
of him, nor do I know what is, 310
that lion's robe, well did he, 226
them with one half so good a grace, 260
Becomes the throned monarch, it, 260
Becoming mirth, within the limit of, 196
Bed, 21
and sickened and went to her, 326
and went to, 123
and with the lark to, 210
are the weans in their, 443
but in their briny, 438
by night, a, 295
divorced old barren Reason from my, 426
go sober, he that will to, 372
lamp and gone to, 108
lies in his, 165
my grave is like to be my wedding, 254

Bed
now, or up in my, 68
of fiery rich array, change his, 8
of honour lain, be in the, 184
of pain, on the thorny, 293
of straw, a, 207
of the grave, for its last, 375
of time, becomes a, 151
one heart, one, 174
that lighted me to, 167
then went to, 371
the world, when to, 386
to call him from his warm, 210
together, are under the, 361
when by my, 283
who quitt'st thy narrow, 115
Bedclothes, 21
Bedfellows, 21
Beds, while folks are in their, 44
Bedside, a frail young creature at one's, 423
Bee, 21
had stung it newly, some, 226
in a hive, with one, 184
of her honey, rob the, 133
Beechen tree, spare the, 457
Beech-tree, the woodpecker tapping the hollow, 457
Beef, 22
and ale, nor wanted they gude, 267
and riot, very fond of, 249
Beefsteak, I like a, 110
Beelzebub lurks, says that, 226
Beelzebub's black rod, ushers of, 347
Been, my dear where have you, 68
thou art no more as thou hast, 342
Beer, 22
a cask of good old, 57
and chronicle small, 138
a parson much bemused in, 295
in a pot of, 310
in the barrel, there's, 254
no objection to a pot of, 110
to drink small, 130
undrawn, and, 345
Beer-barrel, might they not stop a, 421
Bees and such like hums, 151
no butterflies, no, 285
where wasps instead of, 330
Beetle, 22
that we tread upon, 80
Beeves, and driven the, 267
Befall, thus it shall, 452
Befell, at forty-odd, 22
Before, around, behind, 190
me, even as behind, 154
not dead but gone, 158
Beforehand, the circumlocution office was, 54
Beg a cheese, would, 92
when he might earn, or, 248
Began best, that what, 159
ere England's griefs, 166
where faith, law, morals, all, 269
Beggar, 22
and banker, 21
at Hallowmas, like a, 239
he prepares to plunge, 93
is taxed, 176
that is dumb, a, 364
thou, no, 126
you big black boundin', 147
Beggarly account of empty boxes, 33
Beggars, 22
worse in kings than, 122
Beggary, no vice but, 22
in the love, there's, 237
Begged his bread, the living Homer, 183
Begin it, I'll, 124
it with weak straws, 131
sees some task, 410
to think, at which he can, 210
Beginning, a kiss at love's, 203
as it was in the, 289
build sure in the, 39
great is the art of, 109
no great love in the, 238
of a higher life, 79
of the world, from the, 253
of our end, 109
Begins and ends in, what all, 411
at home, sense like charity, 356
man's general infancy, then . . . , 318
where law ends, tyranny, 419
within himself, when the fight, 130
Begot, by whom, 334
how, 124
in the ventricle of memory, 258
of nothing but, 99
upon itself, 195
Beguile, the lips may, 398
Beguiled, expectation every day, 92
Begun, antiquity appears to have, 10
freedom's battle once, 142
Behaviour, check on loose, 108
of the visage, dejected, 448
Behind, before, around, 190
even as, 154
one must ride, 337
Behold a cat, mad if they, 304
bright Phœbus in his strength, 316
her, to, 108
shall be turned to, 420
Being frantic and unquiet, a, 249
man is a moral accountable, 249
strongly framed, a, 189
this intellectual, 90
this pleasing, anxious, 139
Belfries rock and reel, how the, 23
Belfry, sits the white owl in the, 292
the bell that swings in its, 464
Belgium's capital, and, 334
Belgrade, boldly by battery besieged, 14
Belial's trusty sword, that, 395
Belie all corners of the world, and doth, 368
Belied him, malice that, 122
our fears, hopes, 105

Belief, as when 't is in a wrong, 287
in whom persuasion and, 121
trembling doubt and certain-sure, 234
Believe a woman or an epitaph, 67
but what themselves, 376
he did, 219
in princerple, I don't, 193
me, the deuce gae wi'm to, 459
not what the landsmen say, 347
of heaven, all that we, 452
promise, hope, 124
that in all ages, 156
thee, and I'll, 394
they talked of me, I, 396
Believed, I long, 92
these juggling fiends no more, 318
Believes a God, by night an atheist half, 14
his own, yet each, 434
Believing old signs, there is no, 239
Bell, 22, 23
ding, dong, 124
go fetch me a, 22
heart as sound as a, 174
in a cowslip's, 21
invites me, the, 205
mock the midnight, 33
slow falling to the prompter's, 70
struck in the night, I hear the, 200
that swings in its belfry, the, 464
they've hushed the minster, 264
tolls out, the minster, 264
twilight and evening, 18
Belle, she was not the ball-room's, 296
will bear away the, 458
Belles had faults to hide, if, 128
Bellows blows up sin, 134
I blow the, 386
'thout them to blow the, 156
Bells, 23
and all, 133
and merrily rang the, 437
brazen, 5
from hill to hill, 52
golden, 437
hear the loud alarum, 5
hear the tolling of the, 410
how sweet the sounds of village, 52
I hear, the, 43
iron, 410
jangled, like sweet, 327
jingling and the tinkling of the, 408
of these convent, 222
of Yule, the merry, 470
soft the music of those village, 52
that so musically wells from the, 408
the dead leaf trembles to the, 275
the sound of cheerful, 52
Belly, 24
God send thee good ale enough, 6
in fair round, 199
Bellyful of fighting, his, 131
Belongs, to each other, 441
to thee, the unwritten only still, 465
Beloved by heaven, 65
from pole to pole, 369
one, if anguish, 10
sleep, God still giveth his, 369
Below or else above you, 240
Bemused in beer, a parson much, 295
Ben Bolt, don't you remember, 29
Bench, great on the, 164
Bend a knotted oak, or, 272
of two souls, one must, 378
our conscience to our dealing, 386
Bending forward, and, 345
staff, I would not break a, 120
Bends over all, the blue sky, 348
the gallant mast, and, 359
Benedick, the married man, 254
Benediction, and brought a, 415
and come like the, 374
Benefit of the people, for the, 289
Benefits, 24
upon the wave, write our, 467
Benison, 24
and breathes a, 157
or ban, heaven's, 328
Bent in heaven, a silver bow new, 268
just as the twig is, 107
like us, beneath the load, 370
they fool me to the top of my, 137
Bequeathed by bleeding sire to son, 142
Bereft me of all words, you have, 459
Berkeley said there was no matter, 256
Berries, two lovely, 224
Berry, could have made a better, 10
that's as brown as a, 246
Berth, which happened in his, 22
Beseems, more fat than bard, 18
Beset the road, 365
Besieged Belgrade, 14
Best, 24
among us, the, 450
and hold fast the, 320
blood that hath most iron, 27
can bear reproof, those, 332
coat, a hole made in your, 57
contentment has, the noblest mind the, 62
friend, his own, 249
he prayeth, 314
if an endless sleep he wills, so, 369
is he, the, 248
is like the worst, where the, 392
king, fellow with the, 130
married that dies married young, 254
men, men of few words are the, 259
of all ways to lengthen our days, 74
of rest is sleep, 80
old friends are, 146
portion of a good man's life, 201
that what began, 159
that what God doth is, 374
the, the first, the last, 434
the greatest, worst and, 147
then is sure the, 376

Best
the worst turns the, 78
to die, 't is, 89
to weigh, 't is, 84
who loves another, 243
Bestial, and what remains is, 332
Best-laid schemes o' mice and men, the, 261
Bestow, the world has nothing to, 182
Bestowed, know'st if best, 35
Bestows on me, as of her tongue she oft, 412
Bestride the world like a colossus, 58
Bet, a saving, 247
Beteem the winds of heaven, he might not, 243
Betides, whate'er, 328
Betime, we rise, 40
Betimes, 24
Betoken love, 233
Betray, that men, 136
Betrayed for gold, 15
by nothing is so well, 150
humanity, 188
the Capitol, who was 't, 452
Betsey and I are out, 292
Better and grander, something, 190
a thousand times told, 203
but given unsought is, 240
by their presence, 50
cheer ere you depart, 48
days, looked on, 23
days, we have seen, 74
fifty years of Europe, 45
foot before, the, 171
for ane I'll get, 329
half, my, 168
how can man die, 89
is in some degree, 54
land, I hear thee speak of the, 209
made, the good are, 191
man, I could have better spared a, 250
no, and no worse, 80
off than somebody else, we are, 401
part of valour is discretion, 423
reason, appear the, 122
reckoned, 't is no, 158
some, and some worse, 316
spared a better man, I could have, 250
than he knew, builded, 39
than his dog, something, 297
than she had known, for something, 446
than well, all shall be, 74
the excess, 28
the instruction, but I will, 197
the more than less, 28
. . . the right way to go, 159
to have loved and lost, 242
to sink, 28
world, there is another and a, 461
world than this, hereafter in a, 462
Better-furnished gown, a, 161
Betters always have their will, 66
Betty, give this cheek, 75
Between the dragon and his wrath, 98
Beverage to the swelling deep, 101
Beware, 24
my fangs, 95
my lord, of jealousy, 195
my sting, if I be waspish, best, 434
of desperate steps, 86
of entrance to a quarrel, 322
of his echoing growl, 226
of that man, 302
of thee, that the opposed may, 322
the ides of March, 190
Bewared, once warned is well, 205
Bewitch me, do more, 364
Bewrays more woe, silence in love, 364
Bias, against his sinful, 247
its various, 172
Bible, 24
underneath the rose my, 413
with his ledger, binding up his, 247
words, Satan uses, 353
Bibles lie, or your, 365
Bid defiance to all the force of the crown, 44
the main flood, 135
time return, 468
you, if the devil, 156
Bidding some giant yield, 409
Bier, 24
on murdered Lincoln 's, 225
to wave, over his, 184
what ye lift upon the, 375
Bigger than the moon, no, 63
Bilbao bar, 'cross, 115
Bile, 24
Bilious, 25
Bill discounters, money-brokers and, 193
the weekly, 94
to you, God 'll send the, 156
when you were, 230
Billiards, 25
Billings of Louisville, Mr., 346
Billows and the depths have more, 354
and trusted to thy, 288
in a sea of glory, the, 353
in swelling and limitless, 288
never break, where, 89
on the shore, roar of the, 19
proud, rode in his shroud the, 332
roll, the, 245
Bills, virtue suffering from protested, 269
Bind, in body and in soul can, 237
it, no chains can, 262
fast find, 126
men down, which, 122
up my wounds, 187
up the nation's wounds, to, 337
Bird, 25
and beast, both man and, 313
as storm-tossed, 340
beast, are but beast, bird, man, 316
comes abroad, every foul, 332

Bird
curseth the warning, 319
in vain in the sight of the, 280
not reckoned a religious, 52
of time has but a little way to flutter, 406
O magic sleep, O comfortable, 369
on every tree, there sits a, 254
was dead, how the, 41
Birdie, 25
Birds begin to sing, and, 343
best peck, 393
betray, we the, 168
I love the song of, 235
in last year's nest, no, 280
no leaves, no, 285
the, the beasts, 345
the young, are chirping in the nest, 469
Birnam, 25
Birth, 25
and at my, 277
a pride of, 316
are kindred and allied by, 201
await this body's, 377
at his, 283
border nor breed nor, 391
bring her children to second, 353
but upheld by, 410
cursed its hour of, 416
excuses for his, 250
is nothing but our death begun, 81
not on his humble, 257
of Christ, near the, 52
of each new era, 115
of freedom, shall have a new, 276
of our new soil, new, 8
the nation's later, 276
Birthdays, 25
Birth-pangs, the time is racked with, 416
Birthplace of our fathers, the, 111
Birthright, 25
Birthrights proudly, bearing their, 141
Biscay, 26
Bishop, a church without a, 59
Bishops took a simpler way, the good old, 416
Bit me, though he had, 95
of their champ on the, 387
the man, went mad and, 95
Bite, 26
delight to bark and, 95
his nails, when you see Ned Cuttle, 273
I pray you, 216
'm, smaller still to, 134
so nigh, thou dost not, 24
sorrow hath less power to, 375
the man recovered of the, 95
the man that mocks at it, 375
this fish will, 16
your thumb at us, do you, 404
Biter bit, to see a, 447
Bits make rich the ribs, dainty, 298
of stone, he played with for, 378
Bitter a thing it is, 170
cold, 't is, 57
death must be, then, 241
experience is, 117
fancy, sweet and, 124
indeed, experience is, 117
love thou art, 241
make my own less, 1
sky, freeze thou, 24
sure the most, 195
Bitterer than a thousand years of fire, 83
Bitterest loss, ours is the, 1
Bitterness of life, to all the, 390
Bivouac, 26
Black as the pit, 376
dress, a, or a white dress, 295
dwells in white and, 3
eye, the bright, 117
eye, white wench's, 118
not, nor yet too light, 153
pinch him, 304
rod, ushers of Beelzebub's, 347
suits of solemn, 448
to red began to turn, from, 269
was white, affirmed that, 66
we call it, 48
Blackberries, reasons were as plentiful as, 327
Blackbird 't is to whistle, than to a, 165
Blackest of lies, is ever the, 219
Blackguards, 26
too, nor we aren't no, 349
Black-jack, 26
Black-leg saint, a, 247
Blackness of darkness, 313
of night, all is for these but the, 207
Bladders, boys that swim on, 153
Blade, 26
at that shade-made, 115
fragment of his, 47
Blades, between two, 213
of grass, two, 162
Blaize, 26
Blame, a necessary act incurs no, 279
as is the, 232
in part she is to, 427
dreading praise not, 8
on the 'other's, or a-passin', 314
that none might doubt or, 274
yet not afraid to, 46
Blamed and protested, he, 353
the babby, some, 348
Blameless, 26
for thy sake, 104
Blanch an African, to, 266
and Sweet-heart, Tray, 95
Bland, their juices rich and, 175
the smile that was childlike and, 371
Blandishments of life are gone, 66
Blank, 26
verse, prose poets like, 424
Blaspheme custard through the nose, 322

Blaspheme the twisted tendril, 69
Blasphemy, is flat, 43
shrink not from, 67
Blast, I cut them down with my, 284
like a rushing, 151
of a life, in the, 314
of that dread horn, 39
spread his wings on the, 77
threescore years and ten, keeps in, 28
upon his bugle-horn, one, 39
Blasts denote, and the, 78
Blaze, burst out into sudden, 123
can but, 123
of noon, not the, 4
Blazed the helmet of Navarre, 179
Blazon, but this eternal, 381
Blazoned on the panes, the prophets, 291
on the stately tomb, 264
Bleach, he helped to, 266
Bleat for the lamb, made the ewe, 448
Bleating in the meadows, the young lambs are, 469
Bleed, do we not, 197
Bleeding and aching in the potter's hand, clay, 107
fresh, dead and, 41
Blenches first, foul fall him that, 214
Blend, how sweetly those conditions, 242
shall, shall change, 78
Blent, in one red burial, 40
Bless heaven, see this and, 50
it and approve it, will, 330
one brief gleam of beauty, 230
the turf that wraps their clay, 34
to curse, to, 157
Blessed, 27
always to be, 186
be he who took and gave, 164
feet, walked those, 67
is he who has found his work, 459
once, what God, 159
part to heaven, his, 185
the memory of the just is, 199
with perfect rest, heaven is, 409
with temper, 400
with the soft phrase of peace, 380
yea thrice, 266
Blessedness, let him ask no other, 459
Blesseth him that gives, it, 260
Blessing, and with her, 283
dear, 't is expectation makes a, 117
her, praying for her, 243
my, not my doom, 459
of earth is toil, but the, 409
prayed for a, 313
thee, the power of, 27
thrift is a, 404
we should use it, a, 69
Blessings, 27
are a treasure, 16
ever wait on virtuous deeds, 427
on your frosty pow, 311
they say barnes are, 16
Blest be the man, 29
by all their country's wishes, 34
I have been, 233
in the mansions of the, 221
it is twice, 260
too, if it tells me, 116
too, is he who can divine, 337
Blew, four-square to all the winds that, 413
free ere the spirit passed, 284
it, and it rained, 389
our banner of England, 112
out the light within this brain, 195
the fire that burns ye, 131
you hither, what wind, 444
Blight, come like a, 362
ere sin could, 77
in its bloom, wha'd, 364
Blighted love shall never blow, 233
the root may not be, 149
Blighting was nearest, when, 326
Blind, 27
and wailing and alone, 15
be a little, nay intensely, 201
because love is, 240
be to her faults a little, 201
bow-boy's butt-shaft, 118
love is, 243
to him, the olives they were not, 458
to light, 70
winged Cupid painted, 69
Blindly, had we never loved sae, 37
Blind-worm's sting, 179
Blink the peccadilloes of all Piccadilly, 367
Bliss, 27
below, virtue only makes our, 250
called me thy angel in moments of, 9
exceeds all earthly, 262
has a price for its, 253
if ignorance be indeed a, 370
must gain, we every, 448
of dying, the, 105
or woe, mine never shall be parted, 139
or woe, one common, 409
that such a dream should be, 293
to make grief, 436
what is the greatest, 457
where ignorance is, 190
Blisses, her lip so rich in, 204
in the midst of my, 205
Blithe, and debonair, buxom, 41
and gay, were, 265
as she's bonnie, 364
Block those wheels, will nobody, 403
Blocked up the pass, 76
Blockhead, the bookful, 30
Blocks, 27
Blood, 27
alone could quell, the vengeance, 423
and drop my, 267
and the quick round of, 220

Blood
and virtue contend for empire, 25
are cold in, 233
a very river of sluggish, 133
be the price of admiralty, if, 113
build factories with, 413
burns, when the, 429
but taste his, 18
devise laws for the, 33
drenched . . . in fraternal, 420
drop of Christian, 134
enriched our, 22
every drop of, 199
false pride in place and, 54
fire i' the, 70
for blood atone, 15
for his country, to shed his, 383
for wine, who drinks hot, 301
freeze thy young, 380
from your veins, better to lose a pint of, 280
guiltless of his country's, 168
hot and rebelious liquors in my, 357
I'm sick of, 363
is cold, thy, 29
is liquid flame, my, 423
is warm within, whose, 264
must have its course, lad, young, 469
of all the Howards, 113
on the game, there's, 148
on your new foreign shrubs, there's, 148
perish through excess of, 447
rose in, 142
run chill, it makes my, 282
simple faith than Norman, 148
so cheap, flesh and, 78
splashes upward, our, 413
sucks and drains a people's, 64
taints of, 160
that she has spilt, in the, 342
the Douglas, 4
their liquor is, 379
thicker than itself with brother's, 169
through red, the war-horse dashing, 431
where civil, 54
Blood-avenging, 28
Bloodless lay the untrodden snow, all, 225
Blood's lava, and the, 204
Bloodshed, weary of your wars and, 433
Bloody Mary, now of a, 157
my head is, 28
sun at noon, 63
Bloom, in their, 252
in the skies may, 377
like a rose, till she, 226
new hope may, 236
on its fadeless, 209
wha'd blight in its, 364
with all the mimicry of, 64
Blooming alone, left, 342
old rag over'ead, to the, 112
Blooms a rose, 105
Blossom as the rose, the wilderness shall, 443
in their dust, smell sweet and, 199
one, on a brier, 462
that hangs on the bough, 21
there, and bade it, 77
Blossoms fall, the, 154
of my sin, even in the, 370
to-morrow, 164
Blot, creation's, 26
it, can burn or, 155
the record out, to, 449
Blotted it out forever, and, 287
Blow a bubble, propose to, 38
a flower about to, 225
and the stormy winds do, 19
and a word and a, 458
a signal, a shining mark, 81
blighted love shall never, 233
bugle, blow, 382
but give the cock a, 283
by th', 20
given, though there be no, 430
his wreathed horn, Triton, 293
let the pealing organ, 291
may the winds, 400
on whom I please, to, 217
out fire and all, 132
out your brains, and, 373
own genius gave the final, 106
perhaps may turn his, 145
prevent the long aimed, 385
strike another, 130
that made all England tremble, 87
the bellerses, 'thout them to, 156
the bellows, I, 386
them at the moon, 110
themselves must strike the, 29
thou winter wind, 444
't is Pallas gives this deadly, 294
up the infernal machine, 403
wind! come, wrack, 90
Blowing, a strong nor'wester's, 285
toward the west, the young flowers are, 469
Blown, flower that once has, 135
overboard, the mast be now, 231
was ever feather so lightly, 271
with restless violence, 90
Blows, and after, 458
and buffets of the world, vile, 328
and knocks, by apostolic, 329
his nail, 190
his numbing hands, 207
no man to good, not the ill wind which, 444
of a lumberer, like the, 314
of sound, comes to heal the, 364
soft the zephyr, 470
the wind that profits nobody, ill, 444
up sin, bellows, 134
Bludgeonings, 28

Blue, 28
  a feather of the, 403
  and drowned in yonder living, 457
  and his breeches were, 87
  darkly, deeply, beautifully, 288
  for you I wear the, 456
  pinch him, 304
  the, the fresh, the ever free, 354
  the melting, 117
Bluffed the eternal sea, 115
Blunder, 28
  free us, it wad frae monie a, 355
  guilt 's, 336
Blundered, some one had, 90
Blunders are all out, when I hope his, 284
  one of nature's agreeable, 450
Blunt, 28
Blunted, for fear it should get, 446
Blush of woman 's pride, the conscious, 409
  she looked down to, 371
  to find it fame, 123
  to give it in, and, 287
  to make man, 434
  unseen, born to, 149
Blushed and oft did say, laughed and, 306
  as he gave it in, 287
  saw its God and, 435
  with wine, 100
Blushes, 28
Blushing honours, bears his, 164
  to a brook, dogrose, 95
Board, against a, 208
  allots thee for thy, 182
  and seat me at his, 365
  he steps on, 102
  of grave responsible directors, 92
Boards did shrink, and all the, 435
  ships are but, 359
Boast of heraldry, 163
  all earthly pomp and, 228
  his wit, to, 304
  of this, 156
  of this I can, 113
  such is the patriot 's, 182
Boasted powers, tarnish all your, 58
Boasts two soul-sides, 243
Boat, 28
  embarked upon that little, 173
Boatman, take O, 381
Boats, fortune brings in some, 141
  little, should keep near shore, 424
  't is lucky for the, 244
Bobbed for whale, and, 439
Bobbing, to bed the world are, 386
Bode, what should that, 239
Bodies, 28
  forth, as imagination, 308
  in one frame agree, while souls and, 378
  perish through excess of blood, as, 447
  soft and weak and smooth, why are our, 456
Bodies
  with two seeming, 224
Bodkin, with a bare, 323
Body, 28
  and in soul can bind, in, 237
  and soul, like peevish man and wife, 376
  and soul must part, 376
  be, they winna let a, 455
  born, ere yet my, 377
  did contain the spirit, this, 38
  flexible and limber, his, 249
  follow, make the, 142
  forme doth take, the, 377
  his soul and, 273
  I 'll prove it on his, 320
  is wholesome for the, 209
  kiss a body, gin a, 203
  knew so young a, 171
  love is a, 232
  make, and doth the, 377
  may confine, the, 262
  meet a body, gin a, 203
  mind or moral nature, 425
  of kin to the beasts by his, 248
  pent, here in the, 278
  pine, though the, 263
  to be without, 76
Body 's death, with that, 377
  growth, for with my, 377
  work's expired, when, 21
Boil and bubble, hell-broth, 179
  . . . an egg, the vulgar, 108
  in endless torture, and, 436
Bold, 28, 29
  dare not be so, 120
  I can meet, 145
  one, aye and a, 251
  quick, ingenious, 33
  stern looks, with, 119
Bolder thought can rise, what, 411
Boldly by battery, 14
  let 's kill him, 201
Bolivar out across the Bay, threshed the, 54
  out we took the, 215
  south across the Bay, on the, 60
Bolt, 29
  a fool 's, 137
  till famine drew the, 110
Bolts and locks, when banks dispense with, 216
  and massive, 262
  of heaven, and louder than the, 13
  to throw, presume thy, 71
Bombs bursting in air, 17
Bond, 29
  at suspicion of a, 233
  forfeit of my, 83
  here appeareth due upon the, 213
  I 'll seal to such a, 197
  I would have my, 103
  marvel that they make men, 455
  merely justice and his, 199
  of brotherhood, natural, 38
  of fate, take a, 14

Bond
of love, the very, 240
take then thy, 134
the angel Death did sign, the, 356
Bondage and resistance death, submission, 391
of the tomb, the mortal, 353
Bondman, 29
checked like a, 15
Bonds, 29
cancels all, 82
of shame, and break thy, 358
Bondsman's two hundred and fifty years, 199
Bondsmen, 29
Bone and a hank of hair, a, 136
if he flings it a, 461
of my bone, 134
that phantom of grisly, 78
Bones, 29
a town of monks and, 387
are laid, the warrior's, 264
with aches, fill thy, 2
interred with their, 116
of the English, because on the, 113
on the brittle strength of, 381
rattle his, over the stones, 298
sharp misery had worn him to the, 264
thy roots are wrapped about the, 468
world shall see his, 15
Bonnet, 30
is trimming, while the, 211
unbanded, your, 239
Booby for another, who'd give her, 270
Book, 30
and volume of my brain, the, 331
been gilded, the world's, 207
and candle, bell, 22
go fetch me a, 22
he read aloud the, 280
of fate, hides the, 127
of fate, read the, 127
of follies, of such a, 449
of nature getteth short of leaves, 216
of time, in the, 142
of verses, a, 85
that fashioned others, 263
Bookful, 30
Bookish theoric, the, 401
Book-learned, 30
Books, 30, 31
all saws of, 331
amid the dust of, 416
and music, with, 101
as schoolboys from their, 239
dead he lay among his, 75
had they, or, 220
hath thy toil o'er, 215
in running brooks, 3
my only, 118
not such as, 445
old, old wine, 290
Books
our forefathers had no other, 317
poring over miserable, 350
their own faults', 119
they are the, 118
too much, read as well as, 259
we may live without, 63
Bookseller's hack, who once was a, 168
Boot and horse, lad, then hey for, 469
pitched into with a, 44
tapping a glossy, 384
Booth, can set up a small, 67
Boots are green, whiles your, 96
it at one gate, 84
like new, 161
your little shoes and my big, 361
Booty, the lust of, 171
Bo-peep, as if they started at, 129
Border, let that aye be your, 184
nor breed nor birth, 391
Bore, 31
arms, first that ever, 150
him off the field, 138
in vain, against her, 111
it not about, and therefore, 446
without abuse, he, 150
Boreas, cease, rude, 346
Bores, 31
Born and die, are but, 351
a twin, one of us, 418
every moment one is, 69
for liberty, proclaims that man was, 217
great, some are, 164
in Dublin, the editor was, 294
in the garret, 148
I've been, 21
natural to die as to be, 88
on Christmas Day, was, 51
on itself, 195
so, men are to be, 10
the house where I was, 330
though yourself had never been, 277
to be hanged, 169
to write, 107
't was the ninth he was, 348
under a rhyming planet, not, 336
with, that thou wast, 137
Borne down by the flying, 83
me on his back, he hath, 468
my breath away, had, 331
on thy breast to be, 288
so ill is, 195
Borrow its mirth, earth must, 212
Borrowed, squandered, doled, stolen, 157
Borrower, 31
Borrowing dulls the edge of husbandry, 31
who goeth a, 31
Bosom, 31
and one truth, one, 174
and wring his, 136
cannot char, my, 339

Bosom
carry it round in your, 64
cleanse the stuffed, 263
hidden in a mother's, 129
lifeless head to her, 109
in an aged, 60
of kings, that stir not the, 410
of the north, the frozen, 444
lodge, that in her, 270
of darkness, so from the, 138
of God, her seat is the, 212
of snow, and the, 246
of snow, the maid with a, 246
of the earth, 164
that slumber in its, 74
thought that perhaps in its, 163
was fretting, her stately, 316
with a glory in his, 225
Bosoms, home to men's business and, 40
two, and one troth, 174
Boston, 31, 32
man, pry that out of a, 188
State-House is the hub, 188
Both sides, dough on, 41
were young and one was beautiful, 469
young and one how passing fair, 469
Both-sides rogue, damnable, 341
Bottle, 32
comes out of a narrow-mouthed, 383
of Burgundy, with a, 360
to give him, nor a, 285
Bottom, must stand upon its own, 418
of a well, in the, 418
of the sea, in the, 102
stir, from the, 178
trusted, my ventures are not in one, 424
Bottomless pit, underneath the, 178
Bough, blossom that hangs on the, 21
there grows a flower on every, 203
touch not a single, 457
underneath the, 85
Boughs unite, where the fragrant limes their, 296
Bought, all things are, 369
and sold, hoarded, bartered, 157
and sold, is, 27
dear by knowing ill, 414
golden opinions, I have, 290
judges and senates have been, 158
nor sold, the manhood never, 185
Bouillabaisse, 32
Bound beneath me as a steed, and the waves, 436
by a solemn oath, but that he was, 287
fast in one, two lives, 224
heaven is not reached at a single, 208
I'll clear at a single, 152
in to saucy doubts, 41
of life, nearer the, 278
Bound so fairly, 30
thy goodness let me, 463
to do, a man is, 105
was too small a, 381
who can be, 287
Boundaries, lengthens its, 437
Boundary between the things misnamed, 369
Bounding, to the shore gallantly, 436
Boundless his wealth, 65
Bounds divide, thin partitions do their, 245
of modesty, not stepping o'er the, 266
Bounteous beauteous earth, enjoy this, 196
Bounty, 32
is as boundless as the sea, 239
judgment guide his, 84
those his former, 86
Bourbon or Nassau go higher, can, 317
Bourgeons every maze of quick, 372
Bourn, from whose, 79
Bout, with many a winding, 394
Bow before the awful will, 150
he that has two strings to his, 390
I had two strings to my, 390
new bent in heaven, a silver, 268
to have two strings unto your, 390
to that whose course is run, I, 392
Bow-boy's butt-shaft, 118
Bowed, 32
by the weight of centuries he leans, 180
her own, meekly she, 109
himself down, 313
Bowels of the deep, into the fatal, 346
Bower, dwelt no joy in Eden's rosy, 450
mirth in your, 125
wandering near her secret, 292
Bowl, 32
curse on the bonny brown, 26
fills with milk the, 182
fill up the, 101
full of jelly, like a, 24
has poured, Saki from that, 39
lurk within the, 349
mingles with my friendly, 327
of wine, give me a, 421
they call the sky, that inverted, 368
while we drain the, 55
would break the, 107
Bowls, 33
and beauty, nothing but, 308
Bows, for a hammock at the roaring, 8
Box, 33
a gentleman in a black coat on the, 416
Boxes, 33
Boy, 33
eternal, and to be, 411
from a, I wantoned with thy breakers, 288
her, belongs where he is wanted, 8

Boy
knows when he goes to sleep, no, 370
ne'er a peevish, 107
playing on the sea-shore, a, 417
than when I was a, 331
the Yankee, before he's sent to school, 467
thou comest, darling, 18
was the very staff of my age, 383
Boyhood, the blithe days of, 331
Boyhood's years, of, 258
Boyish love, perhaps 't was, 33
Boys, cheer, 48
get at one end, what the, 135
like little wanton, 153
liquor for, 34
or women tell their dreams, 99
people that make puns are like wanton, 321
the Lord will aid us, 38
Boys' copies, setting of, 63
Brace of game, for a few more, 208
Braced my aunt, they, 208
Brady, his mother was a, 348
Brag of, this vault to, 270
one went to, 312
Braggart with my tongue, and, 399
Bragh, Erin go, 115
Brain, 33
a fire in thy, 69
begins to swim, till the, 460
better store of love than, 232
children of an idle, 99
like madness in the, 412
memory the warder of the, 258
shallow draughts intoxicate the, 215
that hath a mint of phrases in his, 303
the book and volume of my, 331
the heat-oppressed, 70
the light within this, 195
the workings of his, 198
the written troubles of the, 263
upon his weary, 400
Brains, 33
and blow out your, 373
have such seething, 243
were out, when the, 90
Bramble's smart, will weep a, 398
Bran and water, fast a week with, 312
Branches, like a tree with splendid, 461
of an elm, the springy, 219
Brandy, 34
taste a little, 15
umbrellas, 44
Brandy-punchy feeling, old particular, 129
Brass, 34
and a' that, 249
and then his auld, 294
collar, braw, 58
resemble copper wire or, 276
Brave, 34
and stood still the, 408
but men less, 145
could danger, 67
hearts though stout and, 163
home of the, 17
live on, the, 66
man's moniment, a, 299
men, to all, 39
on ye, 152
our soldiers were, 22
over the unreturning, 166
that are no more, the, 410
the flag of the, 110
the palm of the, 133
the peace of dead men or of, 299
the worst turns the best to the, 78
toll for the, 410
where they, the, 276
Braved a thousand years, whose flag has, 110
by his brother, 15
Bravely, as for life and death, 120
Bravest, 34
of the brave, the, 34
Brazen bells, 5
mouth, with his, 22
Breach, more honoured in the, 70
set upon a little, 128
Bread, 34, 35
a loaf of, 85
and butter, she was cutting, 439
and liberty, a crust of, 217
and rags, a crust of, 207
and salt, I have eaten your, 349
and tastes his salt, who breaks his, 12
as the touch of holy, 205
but one halfpenny-worth of, 346
crumbles on her rising, 465
having looked to government for, 26
in the bake, there's, 254
like eating new, 31
no wife prepares the, 182
of banishment, the bitter, 17
or butter wanted weight, if, 6
should be so dear, that, 78
the living Homer begged his, 183
the same pleasure that he gives him, 12
unsavoury, 182
when he might earn his, 248
Breadth and thy depth, thy, 403
Break, 35
a bending staff, I would not, 120
a country heart, thought to, 174
and bids it, 165
break, break, 161
ere it rise and, 82
his heart in splinters, and, 317
into foam, chafe and, 138
into the case, death alone can, 403
it to our hope, and, 318
my heart concealing it will, 412

Break
nor would I, for your sweet sake, 246
of day, at, 210
of the wave, a, 269
the bowl, boy would, 107
the bruised reed he will not, 436
the heart will, 172
themselves in swearing, vows which, 428
them still, make vows and, 429
then the cords will, 173
thy bonds of shame, and, 358
up their graves, and ghosts, 352
up housekeeping, when you, 366
where billows never, 89
whose very strings would, 10
. . . the vase, you may, 258
Breakers, 35
I wantoned with thy, 288
roar, the, 2
Breakfast, 35
dare eat his, 134
Breaking, patch hearts that are, 175
the sleep that knows not, 373
till the stars of heaven are, 429
Breaks a butterfly, 41
away, lightly and brightly, 269
down but does n't wear out, a chaise, 46
forth, diseased nature oftentimes, 277
his bread and tastes his salt, 12
light through yonder window, 225
some heart indignant, 143
till your proud heart, 144
Breast, 35
a cheer then for the noble, 145
are gathered to thy, 354
as I lie upon your, 334
as in her, 36
comes upon the robin's, 241
eternal in the human, 186
filled her, 109
gnawing in the, 64
he rises in my, 333
hide thy grief within thy, 234
his baby at her, 89
his hands upon his, 62
I buried it from my, 374
in the green earth's, 108
murmur in the, 23
on her white, 197
over her, 169
that trembles in the, 313
that with dauntless, 168
the broad earth 's aching, 143
the child of him she loved, till at her, 454
throbbed beneath that leathern, 174
truth hath a quiet, 417
two hands upon the, 208
was driven into her, 388
was on thy, 288
win maiden's, 83
Breast
with a dream of her brooding, 97
within our, 182
Breast-milk, the Rhine's, 344
Breasts, can envy dwell in heavenly, 114
our last upon their faithful, 455
heads stood in their, 88
Breath, 35
a lightning-flash of, 123
and spend my malice in my, 402
and the boldest held his, 364
a vapour is, 429
away, had borne my, 331
beaten out of them, the dear, 35
be rude, although thy, 444
blew out the light within this brain, 195
breathe without, 76
by summer's ripening, 239
call the fleeting, 421
can float, a, 144
can make them, a, 300
death is that first, 76
in Italy, draws, 145
is sweet, you ask me why her, 343
life's more than, 220
love, wine, a little, 274
mouth-honour, 223
no means of stopping for, 229
of God, his life a, 248
of his pride, not the, 386
rides on the posting winds, 368
suspiration of forced, 448
the doors of, 118
the last, 91
vows are but, 429
weary of, 420
we draw our first, 455
what is death but parting, 77
when the good man yields his, 159
who draw living, 114
with his departing, 61
Breathe and walk again, 293
in England, slaves cannot, 368
not his name, oh, 274
on its fadeless bloom, 209
their last, or when lapdogs, 362
their words in pain, 105
thereon didst only, 99
will share thy destiny, all that, 86
without breath, 76
with syllables which, 210
Breathed, as it were, 160
her last, she has, 105
in the face of the foe, 77
of him, 100
the long, long night away, 105
Breathes a benison, and, 157
but still it, 416
labours, fights, lives, 176
no more, spirit, 140
there the man, 65
upon a bank of violets, that, 273
Breathing, 36
less of earth than heaven, 176

Breathing
of roses only, 100
these only words, 62
Breaths I hate, whose, 69
in thoughts not, 227
Bred in a book, dainties that are, 30
in the kitchen, 148
out, the strain of man's, 267
where is fancy, 124
Breech, 36
Breeches, and all that, the, 323
cost him but a crown, his, 387
short blistered, 401
were blue, and his, 87
Breed a habit, use doth, 167
and nurse, 311
ballad-makers, and, 299
nor birth, border nor, 391
of men, this happy, 112
Breeds hard English men, 113
like the old heroic, 250
that feeds and, 402
very valiant creatures, 111
Breeze, a wing a cloud, without a, 368
blow, we felt the same, 230
braved the battle and the, 110
death rides on every passing, 77
of eve unfurled, the freshening, 111
the joy to every wandering, 275
unfurled, their flag to April's, 362
without a, 200
Breezy dells, all about the, 52
Brevity, 36
Brew, soup or broth, or, 32
Brewed with her sorrows, 399
Brewer's horse, a, 53
Brewing toward my rest, 98
Bribe, 36
or prayer, no, 274
too poor for a, 141
Bribed their liberties away, that, 106
Bribery's golden sky, 64
Bribes, 36
Brick, deadlier than stone or, 114
Bricks, 36
Bridal of the earth and sky, 73
time of law and love, the, 300
Bride, 36
and my bark is my, 4
and sought me for his, 68
came forth on her wedding night, 55
consent to be his, 364
darkness as a, 90
or maid, mother or, 113
Bride-bed, 36
Bridegroom from his room, like a, 331
stood at the open door, the, 194
Bridge, 37
of Sighs, I stood in Venice on the, 424
that arched the flood, by the rude, 362
Bridged by his thoughts, are, 403
Bridled, the steeds are all, 387
Bridle-reins, a shake, 3
Brief, 37
. . . as woman's love, 't is, 238
in goodness, makes beauty, 21
Briefs they write, all the, 455
Brier, one blossom on a, 462
Briers, 37
who found not thorns, 374
Bright and yellow, 157
be it gloomy or, 116
beyond the gulf of death, 159
day so cool so calm so, 73
may our wine be as, 257
my Burgundy, made, 274
ones disappear, see my, 19
short and, 9
that outward sheweth, 158
the, the pure, the beautiful, 88
things which gleam, 354
to-morrow, shows the, 48
Brighten as they take their flight, 27
Brightens, how the wit, 231
Brighter, look, when we come, 438
ray, emits a, 185
suns dispense serener light, 65
Brightest thunderbolt from the darkest storm, 41
Brightness of the skies, mid the, 378
purity and truth, amazing, 452
Brim, a primrose by a river's, 316
but sparkles near the, 220
with the bubbles on its, 321
Brine, and stewed in, 439
Bring bad news, to, 281
but so much money as 't will, 266
forth, a gaoler to, 41
forth a mouse, the labouring mountain must, 270
him back, I cannot, 365
in great logs, 230
in the spirit, and Jock, 380
out their music, to, 397
such fishes back, to, 132
the plaster, when you should, 374
the treasure back, will, 149
with thee, and, 196
Bringer, the first, of unwelcome news, 281
Bringing him to his own, and, 404
Brings down the rate of usance, 421
in his revenge, whirligig of time, 407
in some boats, 141
the light, memory, 258
within him hell he, 178
Brink, and I gasping on the, 439
unfaltering on its dreadful, 420
Brinks, that hit at bothe, 53
Britain, 37
Britain's glory, forgot was, 241
British, 37
man, blood of a, 27
soldier, come you back you, 252
square, for you broke a, 147
stare, with a stony, 384
Briton may traverse the pole, 112
Britons, 37
have a tongue and free quill, 110

Britons
never will be slaves, 37
Brittle one, was at best a, 266
Broad face, he had a, 24
they lie so, 155
Broadcloth without, 183
Broadens slowly down, freedom, 144
Brogue, with his wonderful, 194
Broke a British square, for you, 147
all the vows that ever men have, 429
and robbed a house below, 306
a vow, I never, 456
his leg then, 216
loose, all hell, 178
moulded to be, 107
no promise, who, 385
over them, all at once a sea, 465
the die in moulding Sheridan, 359
the good meeting, 264
the Sabbath, never, 345
under me, at length, 153
vows for thee, 157
which in storms ne'er, 439
Broken in heart, the, 61
into shards if we offend, and, 107
me, grief and solitude have, 32
oh, pain, that it is, 293
than kept, bad promises are better, 319
the cheerful hearts now, 258
thy vows are all, 428
vow, renew the, 179
when the lute is, 209
when thy sleep shall be, 390
with storms of state, 29
Broken-hearted, 37
and languish, 295
half, 296
Brokenly live on, yet, 172
Brood, doves will peck in safeguard of their, 463
Broodest o'er the troubled sea of the mind, 369
Brooding on fancy's eggs, 124
over bein' a dog, 134
Brook, 37
and river meet, where the, 246
a willow grows aslant a, 444
dogrose blushin' to a, 95
drowned in the, 137
is deep, where the, 435
restraint she will not, 452
Brooks, books in running, 3
leap the rainbows of the, 350
in Vallombrosa, that strow the, 216
make rivers, as, 167
Broth, or brew, soup or, 32
Brother, 37
and trust his sworn, 415
braved by his, 15
forlorn and shipwrecked, 138
I grew so like my, 418
John, came and buried, 265
like a vera, 37
man, gently scan your, 188
Brother
shall be a friend and, 38
Sleep, death and his, 81
though the younger, 216
to Death, 81
to the ox, a, 388
Brotherhood, 38
Brother's blood, were thicker than itself with, 169
hand, by a, 370
murder, a, 272
Brothers, 38
his, and thy own, 314
live together, and as, 433
men the workers, men my, 461
Romans were like, 341
sisters, 129
the counterfeit presentment of two, 303
they our, 416
Broths, and sauced our, 62
Brougham thinks as much as he talks, if, 423
Brought to min', never, 14
Brow, 38
but some sober, 330
consents to death, 152
dat float on de mountains, 297
is beld, but now your, 311
grace was seated on his brow, 250
no mercy now can clear her, 366
of the foeman should scowl, if the, 226
shed upon my, 76
the hand that slanted back this, 195
there are no signs of care on my, 331
pain and anguish wring the, 453
to braid, thy, 402
was brent, your bonnie, 311
writes no wrinkles on thine azure, 406
Brown, 38
a little white amidst the, 68
all the trees are, 290
as a berry, that's as, 246
mad as he was, 401
raised his right hand up to heaven, 424
this quiet Mr., 350
Brownate of truth, the, 416
Brows, a nightcap decked his, 282
gathering her, 465
on either of our, 296
Browse on that, we'll, 257
Bruin's no worse thän bakin', 393
Bruised reed, he will not break, the, 436
Brunt, bear the, 78
Brush, needs no painter's, 152
suggestive of a wet, 171
Brushes his hat, a', 239
Brushing with hasty steps, 392
Brussels lace, chintz and, 75
Brute, 38
an' chuck him out, the, 410

Brute
man that blushes is not quite a, 28
question, how answer his, 147
Brutes no longer, deem our nation, 58
we quarrelled like, 323
without you, we had been, 452
Brutus, Cæsar had his, 414
is, no orator as, 291
makes mine greater, 145
Bryant say, does not Mr., 415
Bubble, 38
air, a vapour, 219
burst, a, 379
hell-broth boil and, 179
honour but an empty, 431
is like a, 461
reputation, seeking the, 373
the world's a, 461
Bubbles, 39
borne like thy, 288
do when they burst, just as, 303
on its brim, with the, 321
we buy, 177
Bubbling and loud-hissing urn, 116
Bucket, 39
Buckets, 39
Buckingham, so much for, 171
Bud, like a worm i' the, 298
of love, this, 239
to heaven conveyed, the opening, 77
Budge, 39
the Ten Commandments will not, 386
Buffets of the world, the vile blows and, 328
Buffoon, a hired, 245
statesman and, 114
Bugbears of a winter's eve, the, 401
Bugle, blow, 382
Bugle-horn, 39
Bugles, 39
Build, 39
factories with blood, 413
his monument, go, 267
me a nest, behold I will, 156
my faith on that, I, 155
new ships to, 353
thee more stately mansions, 376
the ladder by which we rise, 208
Builded, 39
Builders have builded, the, 207
Building, 40
man can raise, the stateliest, 195
Buildings, gaze upon the, 413
Builds a church to God, who, 53
among the stars, 316
himself, each man . . . , 322
on the earth, the earth, 106
on the watery sod, the marsh-hen, 156
stronger than . . . the mason, 164
Built, 40
a paper-mill, thou hast, 317
in your parlour or study, 212
Built
on another man's ground, 187
their temple walls, 155
Bulk, seem to shatter all his, 363
Bulldog, 40
Bullets, I'm not afraid of, 283
Bulls aim their horns, 14
dewlapped like, 88
Bully, like a tall, 59
Bumper I drain, a, 51
Bunch of radish, I am a, 324
Bung-hole, till he find it stopping a, 421
Bunker's Hill, 40
Burden, 40
grow, will with the, 389
life will be a heavy, 460
of the world, on his back, the, 180
Burdens down, where we lay our, 278
of the Bible, old, 24
Burgundy, 40
health made bright, my, 274
in all its sunset glow, 344
with a bottle of, 360
Burial, 40
sod, and fill the, 177
sod, beneath the, 114
Burial-ground God's-acre, 157
Buried, Alexander was, 421
because not, 75
Brother John, came and, 265
from human eyes, lies deeply, 186
in a cave, though he's, 15
in thy eyes, be, 174
it from my breast, I, 374
Burma girl a-settin', there's a, 251
Burn, but not enough to, 4
him, pinch him and, 304
in itself to ashes, 48
I smoke but do not, 339
or blot it, can, 155
the blazing hearth shall, 175
the embers that still, 108
the heart to cinders, doth, 298
to the socket, 91
when once their slumbering passions, 300
Burned each other, Christians have, 51
if with love thy heart has, 234
Burning and consuming element, 4
bright, tiger, 405
burns out another's, 131
core below, up from the, 24
for fear of, 131
Burnished sun, livery of the, 60
Burns most of all, 131
out another's burning, 131
when the blood, 429
ye, blew the fire that, 131
Burnt and purged away, 380
green and blue, 81
Burrs, when you stick on conversation's, 62
Burst all flowery chains, has, 321
and in they, 179

Burst his mighty heart, then, 192
into that silent sea, 353
just as bubbles do when they, 303
now a bubble, 38
of happy song, hear the, 23
out into sudden blaze, 123
till they, 248
Bursts full-blossomed, century, 143
Burthen, 40
e'en wit's a, 396
of a song, as though it were the, 400
our remembrance, 177
Burthens, kick off their, 55
Bury all unkindness, in this I, 421
Cæsar, I come to, 341
its dead, the dead Past, 147
the Great Duke, let us, 271
them, in expectation to, 254
whom he helped to starve, 384
Bush, 40
and every common, 153
an officer, thief doth fear each, 394
a shelter yields, no, 207
bird that hath been limed in a, 25
misdoubteth every, 25
supposed a bear, 128
Bushels of chaff, hid in two, 327
Bushes green, time shall make the, 233
Business, 40
be set apart for, 102
dinner lubricates, 92
feeling of his, 70
is a derned sight better, 404
no public, 54
of the day, the, 102
some to, 325
will be crost, the, 429
Bust, and worse, 123
can storied urn or animated, 421
of Pallas, perched upon a, 325
Busting out, with the meanness, 256
Busy in all, than to be, 92
But, 41
Butcher, 41
Butchered to make a Roman holiday, 181
Butchery, furious close of civil, 54
Butler, cook, pantler, 71
Butter, fat as, 126
smell of bread and, 34
tired wench and coming, 429
to plain bread and, 34
wanted weight, if bread or, 6
Butterflies, no, no bees, 285
Butterfly, 41
from flower to flower, the, 342
Buttock of the night, 282
Buttons I fall asleep, over the, 460
when we've matched our, 211
Butt-shaft, the blind bow-boy's, 118
Buxom, 41
Buy, 41
a knot that gold and silver can, 206
as thy purse can, 11
a world of happy days, 99
Buy
first, they throng who should, 415
gingerbread, thou should'st have it to, 301
him a wooden one to, 434
me a new pan, will, 294
the horse, to, 187
the spoils of office cannot, 259
Buyer, a benediction to the, 415
Buys, he sells, he steals for gold, 157
out the law, 289
who, who is the pot, 311
Buzz for a period, 64
Bygone days, a relic of, 357

C

C—— lies, here Francis, 87
Cabbages and kings, of, 430
Cabin-window bright, I see the, 200
Cabined, 41
Cable broke, the, 231
his line a, 439
Cad, here I come to be a farmer's, 200
Cadence sweet, in, 52
Cæsar, 41
coffin there with, 174
had his Brutus, 414
I come to bury, 341
imperious, 421
loved me, as, 7
Cæsar's hair, the exact shade of Julius, 58
spirit, 335
Cage from which, is a, 375
nor iron bars a, 318
Caged and captured, when, 233
Cages, 'tis wiser to make, 280
not in making, 280
Cain, and the first city, 64
Cake, 41
we'll eat our, 254
Cakes and ale, no more, 427
Calculation crossed, abhorrent of a 161
Calamity, 41
he that nobly bears, 422
Calculators, sophists, economists and, 50
Calf, 42
Calf's-skin on those recreant limbs, 226
Call a conscience, thing they, 61
again, promising with smiles to, 361
all things by their names, 275
and call, though we may, 369
at Number One, to, 290
back yesterday, bid time return, 468
for me, one clear, 17
for needful rest, each, 304
for them, come when you do, 381
him Peter, I'll, 275
me early, mother dear, 256
me fool, dost thou, 137
me not fool, 137

Call my own, all I dare now, 340
of incense-breathing morn, the breezy, 269
our own but death, 80
saints will aid if men will, 348
spirits from the vasty deep, 381
the devil over his own coals, 347
thee devil, let us, 445
the fleeting breath, 421
the Muezza's, 154
the rest, and presently, 422
thou wilt not slight my, 84
to-day his own, 408
unmoved can hear the, 227
you, hear your country, 94
Call'dst me dog before thou hadst a cause, 95
Called her his lady fair, 136
her woman, 449
that softly, sadly, 321
the tailor lown, he, 387
Callest me, I will arise . . . when thou, 437
Calling heaven's vengeance down, 424
if you've heard the East a-, 107
I left no, 466
nor he for any, 365
sof' come in, come in, 358
up and down, love goes, 290
Calls it peace, makes a solitude and, 373
Calm and peaceful shall I sleep, 84
and tempest, through, 245
for those who weep, a, 333
lying so straightly in an icy, 80
so bright, day so cool, so, 73
that breathes around, the holy, 298
the awful, 369
they sleep, how, 370
unfit, for a, 304
with a touch of infinite, 374
Calmed, soon, 84
Calmness about its nap, an unnatural, 171
to remember, for, 330
Calms, after every tempest come such, 400
so much the spirit, 344
Calumny, 42
Came, and the war, 431
down agen, and so, 202
down like a wolf, 14
down the lang glen, 458
faster and louder, 389
he mad, how, 245
into the woods my Master, 457
know not whence you, 100
like a storm he, 388
like water and like wind I go, 435
to scoff, fools who, 352
through, a hole where his tail, 87
Camel, 42
Death, though the black, 126
in shape of a, 56
Camp, 42
the grove, the court, the, 237
Camp-fires before us gleam, her, 281
Camping-ground, on fame's eternal, 26
Camps a leader sage, in, 46
Can, fill the cup, and fill the, 69
still be done, 96
such things be, 56
the youth replies I, 104
we'll drink our, 254
Cancel all our vows, 296
half a line, lure it back to, 465
Cancer, 42
Candid censor, a, 91
friend, save me from the, 145
Candidate, 42
Candied tongue lick absurd pomp, let the, 412
Candle, 42
as well, 22
bell, book and, 22
out, out, brief, 411
Candle-light, colours seen by, 468
Candles shine, and the many, 194
and starlight and moonshine, 304
Canker, the, and the grief, 223
Cankers wasting town and state, all the, 325
Cannikin clink, let me the, 100
Cannon, 42
are pointed, the, 387
not so loud as that of a, 203
shot from the mouth of a, 283
that speaks from the mouth of the, 314
Cannon-balls may aid the truth, 159
Cannon's mouth, even in the, 373
opening roar, the, 12
Cannon-shot, 42
Cannot be undone, what's done, 96
write and those who can, those who, 466
Canon 'gainst self-slaughter, 134
Canopy, 43
Canst, vow while thou, 429
Canstick turned, a brazen, 309
Cant of a Saviour's name, where they, 208
of not men, but measures, 256
pressed with specious, 2
Can't, plenty that can if you, 413
Can't-be gentlemen, would-be wits and, 150
Canteen, double drill and no, 395
Canticles of love and woe, the, 24
Cap and bells, for a, 177
by night, a, 282
Capacity for work, I have never found out the limit of my, 460
of loving, man who . . . has the largest, 243
Capable of nothing, for the most are, 379
ingenious, forward, 33
Capers nimbly, he, 432
Capital, and Belgium's, 334
Capitol, who was't betrayed the, 452

Capon lined, with good, 199
Caps, 43
Captain, 43
any, not under fire, 132
can do wrong, no, 360
Ill, Captive Good attending, 417
of my soul, I am the, 126
still, be the proud, 126
Captains and the kings depart, the, 139
the remark, should, 219
Captive Good attending Captain Ill, 417
Captured, when caged and, 233
Car, and the clattering, 271
by the bright track of his fiery, 393
of day, gilded, 73
or drive the rapid, 386
rattling o'er the stony street, 444
Caravan, join the innumerable, 227
Carcass fit for hounds, a, 201
is, wheresoever the, 184
Carcasses, prize as the dead, 69
Card, 43
insipid as the queen upon a, 193
Cardinal rose with a dignified look, the, 22
Cards, an old age of, 462
for money, cannot afford to play, 234
little or nothing of their, 379
two players playing at, 77
Care, 43
age is full of, 5
and melancholy, dull with, 196
and public, 85
and weep away the life of, 81
as feeling her, 212
as light as a feather, 361
but add a little, 396
by the chimney with, 51
crazed with, 66
death came with friendly, 77
derides, sport that wrinkled, 382
for him who shall have borne the battle, to, 337
housewife ply her evening, 175
how compounded, with what, 78
I, how kind she be, what, 201
I neither know nor, 295
mettle enough to kill, 45
killed a cat, 45
not for feeling, 67
not how they flow, I, 409
o' th' main chance, have a, 46
painter who made it his, 294
take, 24
the furrows of, 340
the ravelled sleave of, 370
there are no signs of, 331
there's neither cauld nor, 215
the restless pulse of, 374
the sin, ring out the want, 430
the woman who did not, 136
wales a portion with judicious, 464
without grief or, 219
Care-charmer Sleep, son of the sable night, 81
Career, curbed her high, 142
quitting the busy, 333
Careful of the type she seems, so, 419
Careless of censure, 46
of the single life, so, 419
word, drops some, 173
Cares, 44
against eating, 394
all the torments, all the, 339
and pleasures, what, 338
and strife, void of, 359
dividing, and his, 443
for naught beside, 419
for thee, one that, 189
little, sprang up like weeds, 450
of life, they increase the, 50
on God, cast all your, 9
Caress thee, dearer friends, 331
wooing the, 408
Caressed, hated yet, 67
Careworn brow, to smooth the, 297
Carnage, amid the thickest, 179
Carnal part, a very heathen in the, 330
Carnivorous production, man is a, 256
Carouse, with what a brave, 426
Carousing, there's no, 101
Carpenter, shipwright or the, 164
Carpet knight so trim, 46
Carriage, improving the manners and, 253
take the air in a close, 416
Carried so high, the head she, 316
on, which always must be, 329
Carries anger, that, 209
Carrion flesh, a weight of, 103
where'er ye fling the, 184
Carry all he knew, could, 456
gentle peace, in thy right hand, 299
I, I spin, 386
me to unknown lands, to, 186
the flag, party that does not, 420
where winds can, 161
Cart, I cannot draw a, 251
Carve him as a dish, let's, 201
Carved for many a year, have been, 252
it, twenty years later we have, 275
not a line, we, 153
Case, 44
can be no worse, for where your, 86
can break into the, 403
is uncommonly hard, its, 390
let us consider the reason of the, 327
o' gowd, I'd locked my heart in a, 231
that's still too common, a, 449
then closes the, 33
this appears the common, 345
when a lady's in the, 209
Cases, his, his tenures, 214
of defence, in, 84
suppose a change o', 142
Cash, 44

Cask of good old beer, 57
ran sour, my, 57
Cassius, as that spare, 126
is aweary of the world, 15
Cassock, unbidden from the, 312
Cast, 44
all your cares on God, 9
as rubbish to the void, 160
away, the other, 265
into my teeth, 15
it at his feet, and when he will to, 107
it like a serpent, that, 416
of thought, the pale, 61
off his friends, he, 145
or on the waters, 441
thee shuddering, and, 377
their shadows before, coming events 358
when once, 127
yet, your colt's tooth is not, 58
Castle, 44
hall, the mistletoe hung in the, 265
walls, the splendour falls on, 382
Castle's strength, our, 17
Castles and towers, the earth builds, 106
Castor, smoothing its dilapidated, 171
Casuists doubt, and soundest, 94
Cat, 44, 45
at play, like a, 60
if your mother's, 277
laps milk, take suggestion as a, 392
mad if they behold a, 304
melancholy as a gib, 258
Cataract, the wild, leaps in glory, 382
Catarrhs, to find out agues, coughs, 306
Catastrophe, 45
Catch a saint, to, 347
him once upon the hip, 166
that the one doth, 196
the conscience of the king, 306
the driving gale, and, 278
the wild goat, 350
Catched a vild beast, then I, 200
caught when they are, 447
with mouldy corn, that is, 206
Catechism, 45
so ends my, 185
Caters for the sparrow, providently, 326
Caterwauls, squalls, mauls, 44
Cates, than feed on, 399
Cathay, 45
Catherine Street, the paper is published in, 294
Cats, 45
Cattle, be not like dumb driven, 179
'tain't a knowing kind of, 206
Caty do, what did, 200
Caught it, when at last he, 342
when they are catched, 447
with glare, maidens, like moths, are ever, 270
Caught with tickling, trout that must be, 405
Cauldron, 45
Cause, 45
are not ever jealous for the, 195
a worthier, 144
before thou had'st a, 95
be valiant in a better, 422
bring fame and profit, ere her, 34
dared for a high, 120
for God, for the, 19
good or evil times, which, 317
he knows the, 357
if bold in virtue's, 411
increased devotion to that, 276
in freedom's, 58
magnificent and awful, 12
no, is tried, 455
o' 'er munny, 241
of a long ten years' war, the, 452
of my love and my hate, the, 327
of policy, to any, 161
of war, a lawful, 430
power i' the truth of the, 417
ring out a slowly dying, 339
undertake the noblest, 143
Caused printing to be used, thou hast, 317
Causes springs, dire offence from am'rous, 414
which impelled them, the, 356
why and wherefore in all things, 288
Cave, in yon, Honorius long did dwell, 177
there is cold meat i' the, 257
though he's buried in a, 15
Caved the head of Thompson in, 141
Cavern, within this hollow, 411
Caverns of darkness, running through, 451
the sea's mysterious, 354
voices from the deep, 163
Caves of ocean, the dark unfathomed, 149
of the north, from the, 284
Caviare, 45
Cavil, 45
Cawing from a steeple, keeps a-, 52
Cease, and all tears, 208
every fierce tumultuous passion, 298
rude Boreas, 346
things at the worst will, 464
thy counsel, 64
to follow him, lamb will never, 226
to sin, mankind should, 365
your tears, 74
Cecilia, 45
Celerity, 46
Celery tips, their blunt ends frizzled like, 437
Celestial fire, pregnant with, 109
stuff, the true, 5
Cell, disdains her shattered, 367
each in his narrow, 108
in my heart's most secret, 296
like a toad in his, 446

Cell, no, enclose, 262
this narrow, was life's retreat, 367
Cells, as in honeyed, 330
in thy treasure-caves and, 354
Celt said of purgatory, as the, 321
Cenotaphed his fame, have, 122
Censor, a candid, 91
Censors who sniff out our moral taints, 347
Censure, 46
more tongued with, 165
'scape, no might can, 42
Centre, life which is of all life, 76
moved, the, 53
the heartless, 419
throned in the, 353
Centuries, after the silence of the, 147
bowed by the weight of, 180
forty, look down upon you, 322
more gave a thumb, 311
Century, come in sight once in a, 466
energy sublime of a, 143
fruit, their, 31
of sleep, than a, 390
Ceremony, it useth an enforced, 238
sauce to meat is, 129
that to great ones 'longs, no, 260
Certain age, lady of a, 4
one thing is, 135
that the earth was square, 106
Certainly aged, which means, 4
Certainty, faith itself be lost in, 376
to please, the, 443
Chadbands, Mr., he wos a-prayin' wunst, 374
Chafe and break into foam, 138
as at a personal wrong, 161
Chaff behind, and leave the, 193
corn in, 67
for corn, receiving, 103
hid in two bushels of, 327
Chafing their channels of stone, 451
Chain, ere slumber's, 258
his speech was like a tangled, 380
while they rend the, 385
wove, my heart's, 236
Chained, the lions were, 226
when it could not praise was, 411
Chains and slavery, the price of, 217
but he saw not the, 226
has burst all flowery, 321
no, can bind it, 262
with leaden, 122
Chair, 46
fall back into my, 284
shall fa', last beside his, 201
she sat in, jumping from the, 204
Chaise, 46
Chalk and alum and plaster, 35
proud of knowing cheese from, 320
Challenge double pity, may, 364
each torn flag wavin', 299
so much I, 189
to his end, dares send a, 221
Chamber, capers nimbly in a lady's, 432
clothed in white, from that, 55
door, open thy, 240
door, perched above my, 325
door, rapping at my, 261
get you to my lady's, 468
made, thy nightly visits to my, 283
where each shall take his, 227
Chamberlain, guilt was my grim, 167
Chambers desolate, its, 367
opens at once into the secret, 129
Chameleon love can feed on the air, 240
Chameleons quite, bards are not, 123
Champ on the bit, of their, 387
Champagne, 46
soul of the foaming grape, 344
Champagny old-particular brandy-punchy feeling, 129
Champion, 46
Chance, 46
all, direction, 337
be right by, 136
comes from art not, 467
it be shaken, if by, 173
or by what, 377
under the bludgeonings of, 28
without a fair, 292
Chanced, what he feared is, 394
Chancery, which flew up to heaven's, 287
Chances, enhances life and all its, 284
Change, 46
and fate fulfill, 154
by to-morrow, were to, 47
came o'er the spirit, 98
life's spring, I would, 409
o' cases, suppose a, 142
of place, fly by, 178
shall, shall blend, 78
the stamp of nature, use almost can, 421
their skies above them, they, 367
to cheers, the hisses, 180
Changed, the law is also, 327
Changeful as the light, 73
Changeless law, changing world of, 224
Changes on the wind, four, 52
that monthly, 268
we have seen, what, 338
when they are wives, the sky, 457
well, rung her, 244
Changing the word, by, 85
world of changeless law, 224
Channels of stone, chafing their, 451
run thus far in separate, 339
Chant thy praise, hypocrisy, power to, 190
Chants a doleful hymn, 273
Chaos, 46
of thought and passion, 462
is come again, 239
of insane hurrahs, one whirlwind, 188
Chapel there, devil always builds a, 87

Chap-fallen, quite, 468
Chapped hands, clapped their, 43
Char, my bosom cannot, 339
Character be vindicated, than shall my, 114
 genius should marry a person of, 254
Characteristic, has nothing so, 171
Characters at all, most women have no, 455
 in dust, write the, 450
 our roots in, 62
Charge, 47
 for the golden lilies, 179
 this is your, 422
Charged, the heart is sorely, 363
Charger, he turned his, 3
Charging line, rises along the, 19
Chariot of fire, the God mount his, 255
Charities of domestic life, against the, 413
Charity remains, gracious, 219
 a little earth for, 29
 began, pity gave ere, 305
 begins at home, sense like, 356
 for all, with, 337
 for melting, 161
 rarity of Christian, 182
Charlatan, defamed by every, 150
Charles, King, that to, 39
 King of England, for, 19
 the First, his Cromwell, 414
 why should your mother, 164
Charlie's sake, for, 365
Charlotte, Werther had a love for, 439
Charm ache with air, 5
 blest with that, 443
 can soothe, what, 136
 can tame, no, 351
 from the sky, 182
 of powerful trouble, 179
Charmer, 47
Charmers, like other, 408
Charming, chaste, and twenty-three, 253
Charms, 47
 and spells around him flung, 283
 by accepting, 400
 remove the very, 342
 solitude, where are the, 373
 strike the sight, 260
 that dotes on truer, 246
 to soothe a savage breast, 272
 to show, a thousand, 143
 who can love a sister's, 400
Charter, 47
 as large a, 217
 of the land, 37
Chartered libertine, a, 5
Charybdis, I fall into, 353
Chase, gloom to, 219
 in piteous, 398
 its tail, the compass, 60
 the glowing hours, to, 71
 woe worth the, 448
Chased, the urchin, 342
Chaste, 47
 and twenty-three, married, charming, 253
 as ice, 42
Chasten and share, to, 153
Chastises those whom most he likes, 177
Chastity, 47
Chat, 47
Chattering pies in dismal discords sung, 25
Chaucer, 47
Chaw of terbacker, I want a, 404
 terbacker, I'd larnt him ter, 408
Cheap, 47
 flesh and blood so, 78
 in beauty, goodness that is, 21
Cheat, 47
 I, I lie, 247
 is plain, the, 249
 the thirsty moments, to, 288
Cheated as to cheat, of being, 47
Check, is an immediate, 108
 them, and, 403
Cheek, 47
 a lean, 239
 a little red, 75
 as it flits across thy, 293
 a something on her, 204
 a villain with a smiling, 11
 feed on her damask, 298
 have rolled, tears adown that dusky, 174
 if changing, 233
 is blooming, and why her, 343
 or chin, 91
 pale grew thy, 296
 something upon the soldier's, 312
 so pale and chill, the, 369
 the crimson streak on ocean's, 73
 the rose of her, 153
Cheek's pale hue, in my, 458
Cheeks, mashed upon her, 399
 than one, or kiss more, 200
 with artificial tears, 118
Cheer, 48
 at Christmas play and make good, 52
 but not inebriate, 116
 his soul, to, 182
 'mid the gay, 116
 then for the noble breast, a, 145
 up, my lads, 286
 with festal, 101
Cheered, the ship was, 359
Cheerful, 48
 as to-day, can make to-morrow, 400
 bells, the sound of, 52
Cheerfulness, no warmth, no, 285
Cheers for this Christmas old, give three, 51
 the hisses change to, 180
 the tar's labour, 408
 the way, adorns and, 185
Cheese, 48
 and garlic, live with, 399

Cheese
from chalk, proud of knowing, 320
mouldy like their, 94
to him who wants a, 265
whitewood that cuts like, 441
would beg a, 92
Chequered shade, dancing in the, 71
Cherish, 48
factions, and, 101
which may achieve, and, 337
Cherries, 48
those kissing, 226
Cherry and a fig, a, 162
like to a double, 224
Cherub, 48
no art can copy, 96
Cherubim, fluttered by the wings of, 52
Cherubs on its face, and may the, 68
Chess-board, 48
Chest contrived a double debt to pay, the, 295
Chester, charge, 47
Cheveril glove, a sentence is but a, 447
Chew and choke as much as possible, 40
Chewed and digested, some few to be, 30
Chickens, 48, 49
Chide me for loving, dare to, 12
Chides his infamous delay, 251
Chief, 49
a requiem for the, 332
in her halls, a, 63
o' Scotia's food, 310
Chiefest surprise, was the, 76
Chief's a rod, and a, 183
Chieftain treats a foe, an Arab, 12
Chiels, facts are, 119
Child, 49
again, make me a, 340
a naked new-born, 227
and never spares the, 341
and spoil the, 232
an old man is twice a, 250
as yet a, 466
bathe in me, mother and, 247, 419
could love it like a, 169
even from a, 92
he never spoils the, 341
I could lie down like a tired, 81
may rue that is unborn, the, 419
of doubt and death, poor, 330
of him she loved, till at her breast the, 454
of many prayers, thou, 313
of my absent, 165
of thee, I was as it were a, 288
of the skies, the, 58
out of the deep, 18
saving a little, 404
simplicity a, 252
sweetest Shakespeare, Fancy's, 432
that bids the world good-night, 96
that knows his own, 127
thou show'st thee in a, 192
Child
was too fast, if the, 348
where is my, 107
who enters life, 77
will weep a bramble's smart, 398
Childhood, 49
fleet, womanhood and childhood, 246
fleeted by, how my, 331
in my days of, 307
shows the man, 49
through, 58
Childhood's pleasures were, what, 331
Childish days, sweet, 74
weakness, 't were, 65
Childishness, 49
Childlike and bland, the smile that was, 371
Children, 50
at my heels, a troop of little, 167
but the young, young, 469
fear to go into the dark, 77
forth, shall bring her, 353
had the measles, if the, 198
he that hath wife and, 442
lodging, wife and, 187
must go as little, 77
nature fits all her, 67
not more the, 59
of an idle brain, 99
pride of a mother in her, 315
reared the Assyrian piles, Shem's proud, 350
run to lisp, no, 175
spare . . . my poor, 15
stood watching them, the, 132
they amuse themselves and other, 321
thou call'st its, 209
two, in two neighbour villages, 224
weep before you, well may the, 437
yet unborn, the, 419
Children's children, our, 50
children, they enslave their, 60
early words, and the, 235
souls which God is calling sunward, 439
Child's heart, on a, 413
Chill, dark the night, and, 211
it makes my blood run, 282
't would keep away the, 40
waxed deadly and, 77
with early showers, 105
Chills, the moral market had the usual, 269
Chimæras dire, hydras and, 161
Chime, all the way to guide their, 286
faintly as tolls the evening, 286
rang out Tintagel, 155
sounding from the, 115
to chime, from weary, 282
when last I heard their soothing, 23
Chimes at midnight, we have heard the, 262
Chimings, a few more, 222

Chimney, 50
by the, with care, 51
in my father's house, 36
Chimney-piece, leave the bottle on the, 32
Chimney's top, raven rooked her on the, 25
Chimney-sweepers, as, 103
Chin, cheek or, 91
close-buttoned to the, 183
compared to that was next her, 226
under her, 30
China 'crost the Bay, 252
fall, though, 362
silk, some marrowy crapes of, 364
vessels, or when rich, 362
Chinee, 50
Chinese, 50
Chiney's mended, the sooner the, 260
Chink, for he made the guineas, 183
to keep the, 92
Chintz, let a charming, 75
Chips, never an axe had seen their, 343
Chirped as peart as ever you see, 404
Chirping in the nest, the young birds are, 469
on my kitchen hearth, 175
Chirps, in age the cricket, 470
Chisel rings, quickly the sharp, 410
Chiselled, upon the tomb be, 329
Chivalry, 50
her beauty and her, 334
Chloroformed into a better world, 451
Choice, and in my, 329
in rotten apples, small, 11
love is not in our, 86
of a confidant, I will make a better, 3
what heart can doubt, 85
while he doth make his, 273
Choir, 50
led earth's most happy, 244
sings, and the sweet, 264
Choke as much as possible, chew and, 40
Choler, 50
Choleric word, but a, 43
Choose aright, and, 89
between the two, I cannot, 117
but hear, cannot, 172
but weep, I cannot, 438
debate which of the two to, 43[illegible]
executors, let's, 117
not half a kiss to, 243
'tain't for me to, 321
their place of rest, where to, 462
they are slaves who will not, 368
why I rather, 103
Choosing, two pleasures for your, 306
Chord, 51
in melancholy, but has its, 257
of self, smote the, 241
Chords, smote on all the, 241
Chortled in his joy, he, 118
Chorus, was ready, 209
Chose to Congriss, when one's, 60
Chosen, the less is always to be, 116
Chowder-kettle, 51
Christ, 51
above, faith in the, 242
ain't a-going to be too hard, 104
in Heaven, forgiven by, 366
in the name of, 242
is a God, if Jesus, 196
is a man, if Jesus, 196
draws near the birth of, 23
our Saviour was born, Jesus, 51
the Saviour died, who in, 220
was born, 225
went agin war an' pillage, thought, 431
Christ-Church bells, oh, the merry, 23
Christendom, any summer house in, 399
is an armed camp, 42
never a man in, 119
Christian, 51
blood, one drop of, 134
charity, rarity of, 182
England, a labourer in, 208
example, by, 197
faithful man, a, 77
if a Jew wrong a, 197
I hate him for he is a, 421
is, as a, 197
perfectly like a, 265
scion, as surely as I am a, 393
still a sad, good, 330
the true, is the true citizen, 54
work, if this, 451
wrong a Jew, if a, 197
Christians, 51
in converting Jews to, 310
want, so many, 188
Christ-like is it for sin to grieve, 365
Christmas, 51–52
at the season of, 48
holiday, keeping their, 265
Christmas-eve, strangely falls our, 181
Christ's righteousness, all had put on, 220
Chronicle, his own, 320
small beer, and, 138
Chuck him out, the brute, 410
Chunk of old red sandstone, a, 350
Church, 52–53
and King, for, 383
and mart, press too close in, 220
and state, than be true to, 213
and yard are full of seamen's graves, 355
below the hill, 23
for the cause, for the, 19
high on the roof of the, 314
in Dublin town, he built a, 348
is a little heaven below, 312
Militant, to be the true, 329
steeple, bells, and all, 133
the aisles of the ancient, 464
the holy, 342
where bells have knolled to, 23
with his presence glowed, 87
without a bishop, a, 59

Church-bell rings, where the, 419
Church-door, nor so wide as a, 189
Church-doors, because outside, 217
Churches, in playhouses than in, 398
Church-going bell, sound of the, 22
Church-tower, beside a grey, 224
Church-way paths to glide, in the, 282
Churchyard mould, verge of the, 157
  sod, beneath the, 108
  stone, some lie beneath the, 146
  to the, a pauper is going, 298
Churchyards yawn, when, 282
Chymist, fiddler, statesman, 114
Cider, 53
Cigar, 53
  give me a, 408
  so I have my, 339
Cigar-box, 53
Cimmerian desert, in dark, 85
Cincinnatus of the West, the, 434
Cinder wench and the white-handed lady, 21
Cinders, ashes, dust, is, 235
  doth burn the heart to, 298
Cipher too, he could write and, 206
Circle, 53
  close in firm, 102
  of the earth, perish from the, 276
  the world around, let it, 152
Circles the earth, 112
Circumstance allows, does the best his, 24
  in the fell clutch of, 28
  pride, pomp and, 125
  the lie with, the sixth, 218
Circular, no sign that it was, 106
Circulation, the stock of your lies in, 82
Circumlocution, 54
Cis, the downright loving of pretty, 203
Citadel, a towered, 56
Cite Scripture, the devil can, 353
Cities, far from gay, 68
  proud, not, 385
  seven, warred for Homer, 183
Citizen, 54
  before man made us, 259
City, and the first, 64
  as is usual in our, 92
  full, near a whole, 182
  of Cologne, doth wash your, 58
  of kites and crows, 43
  through the centre of every town or, 15
City's rout, tolls out above the, 264
Civet, 54
Civic, 54
Civil, 54
  be, 87
  discord flow, effects from, 93
  feuds, a land rent with, 420
  leer, assent with, 71
  or over, 324
  right, law an' order, honour, 212
  sort of lie, the most, 219
Civility, I see a wild, 364
  use all the observance of, 372
Civilization does git forrid, 431
  the fly-wheel in modern, 55
Civilized man cannot live without cooks, 63
Civilizes, 54
Clad, the naked every day he, 274
Claim his wage, yet, 248
Claims, a thousand, to reverence, 323
  himself a sole exclusive heaven, 176
  of long descent, 148
Clamours, immortal Jove's dread, 125
Clan, among such a, 247
  the last of its, 342
Clang, begins the clash and, 275
  of bell and roar of gun, 23
Clanging, 54
Clap hands and a bargain, 18
Clapped their chapped hands, 43
Clapper, tongue is the, 174
Clapper-clawing, 54
Claps her wings, she, 210
  the gate behind thee, 148
Claret, 55
  is the liquor for boys, 34
Clash and clang, begins the, 275
  and the shout, the, 136
Clashed and hammered from a hundred towers, 284
Clasp, and clasp it with a, 263
  a sainted maiden, it shall, 246
  something with passion, 48
  the hand of such as Marmion, 97
Clasped the phantoms, I, 302
Clasps the earth, the sunlight, 204
Class, in the same, 309
  them separately, that it is difficult to, 391
Classes, 55
  her noblest work she, 211
Classic, 55
Classical dish, an ancient, 96
Clause, a servant with this, 102
Claw, in a wile-cat's, 212
Clay, 55
  and made of the same, 201
  an oozy couch of, 8
  a pit of, for to be made, 303
  around, rank grass overhead and damp, 229
  bleeding and aching in the potter's hand, 107
  choosing sweet, 179
  dead and turned to, 421
  growing coarse to sympathize with, 56
  if we are only as the potter's, 107
  in, shovel the, 103
  to bless the turf that wraps their, 34
  touched the lifeless, 27
Clay-cold heads, ye whose, 298
Claymore with bayonet clashing, 431
Clean, 55
  and decent, . . . the politician who is, 310

Clean
from my hand, 169
hearth, a, a clear fire, 175
hearth and a clear fire, 175
the palm is hardly, 36
these hands ne'er be, 169
will never make one's self, 373
Cleaned out the town, he had, 350
Cleanliness, 55
Cleanse the stuffed bosom, 263
Cleansing my streams, 247
Clear, a conscience, 61
all doctrine plain and, 95
and cool, 419
as a whistle, as, 440
at a single bound, I'll, 152
fire, a, a clean hearth, 175
fire, a clean hearth and a, 175
the way, jingle, jingle, 23
the way, men of action, 225
though deep yet, 84
Cleared, all debts are, 82
some great truth, 91
the harbour, 359
Clearer one never was seen, a, 348
Clears not without a storm, so foul a sky, 388
Cleave alway, to him will I, 196
the wood, 207
Cleaves a pathway through the strife, 390
cleft for me, rock of ages, 340
with the blind bow-boy's butt-shaft, 118
Clergy, 55
Clever, let who will be, 374
Clicked behind the door, clock that, 295
Clicking, silence at last the, 403
Client still will be, such, 184
Climb, 55
feels the soul within him, 143
hills of seas, 400
his knees, or, 175
spurs them to, 46
the tree, Zaccheus he did, 470
to eminence, kings, 202
upward, will cease or else, 464
Climber-upward turns his face, 7
Clime adored, in every, 127
in some brighter, 220
the cold in, 233
through many a, 328
Climes and starry skies, cloudless, 430
Cling to thy home, 182
Clink, let me the cannikin, 100
Clip him, love will not, 4
Cloak around him, with his martial, 433
that covers all human thoughts, a, 369
'tis not alone my inky, 448
who 't was that nimmed a, 306
Clock, 55–56
and some blamed the, 348
back, put the, 111
but a, 390
Clock
does strike by algebra, 6
tells of a life to be, 280
the varnished, 295
was too slow, or the, 348
Clocks, our brains are seventy-year, 33
Clock-setter, old Time the, 407
Clod, become a kneaded, 90
Cloister, 56
Close against the sky, were, 331
and like a lily her life did, 105
as truly loves on to the, 393
behind him tread, 128
each evening sees it, 410
his eyes, to, 86
in firm circle, 102
intestine shock and furious, 54
lived she at its, 105
my mind, could I so, 263
of an angel's psalm, like the, 374
one stands up, 312
up his eyes, 80
the gates are mine to, 276
the shutters fast, 116
wish our happy life to, 89
Close-buttoned to the chin, 183
Closed her bright eye, 142
her quiet eyelids, 105
in deadly fight, the soul has, 377
in her, a thousand claims to reverence, 323
the door, and, 221
thy dying eyes were, 139
Closer walk with God, 155
Closest kept, burns most of all, 131
Closet, a private, is to me, 318
Closing eye requires, the, 35
Cloth, with the scarlet, of her weaving, 451
Clothed in white, from that chamber, 55
knowing her household are, 451
Clothes a wantonness, kindles in, 364
gars auld, 270
meat, fire and, 336
were loved, women not, 456
when he put on his, 274
Clotho, spin, 380
Cloud, 56
a fast-flying, 269
can o'ercast, the smile that no, 31
is scattered, when the, 209
nor speck, nor stain, 268
stooping through a fleecy, 268
sunshine, storm and, 141
takes all away, a, 240
than sun, there is n't more, 393
the thickest, earth ever stretched, 159
where ish de lofely golden, 297
without a breeze, a wing, a, 368
Cloudiness, of storm and, 119
Cloudless climes and starry skies, 430
Clouds, 56
above, or the, 409
are my minions, the, 284

Clouds
beyond the, 209
down from the, 187
hide them, or in, 408
in vain, embracing, 369
left a paradise of, 353
looks in the, 7
o'ercast thy purpose, have, 391
of glory, trailing, 25
on earth or in the, 377
sees God in, 176
to soar again, through rolling, 106
were rent asunder, 26
would break, never doubted, 337
Cloudy, all quiet, 435
Cloven in vain, not a worm is, 160
Clover, and kissing was, 240
Clown, master of lord and, 103
thou art mated with a, 189
Cloy the appetites they feed, 5
the hungry edge, 191
the sweetest meats the soonest, 423
Clubs typical of strife, 88.
Clung into a kiss, 204
Cluster, woes, 448
Clusters, murdered them in, 372
Clutch, denying to his frantic, 115
of circumstance, in the fell, 28
thee, let me, 70
Coach, rascals in the, 417
Coaches, 56
Coal that must be cooled, 4
Coals adrift a-deck, all the, 215
and rice, with handfuls of, 175
and the burning, 378
call the devil over his own, 347
'e'll be squattin' on the, 395
milk, 44
Coarse, 56
Coat, 57
for a riband to stick in his, 336
thet sets well here, a, 60
was red, his, 87
with a gentleman in a black, 416
Coats, rigged out in their swaller-tail, 11
Coats-of-arms, is worth a hundred, 246
Cobweb through, break one, 353
Cobwebs, 57
faster than gnats in, 168
Cock, 57
a blow, but give the, 283
crew, as the, 77
till the first, 135
to crow like a, 239
crows, the, 283
Cockle, 57
Code of marriage, in the modern, 253
Codeless myriad of precedent, the, 214
Coffee, 57
Coffin is shielded, the, 317
my heart is in the, 174
Cohorts were gleaming, his, 14
Coil, this mortal, 98
Coin, and finally a current, 369
my heart, I had rather, 267
Coin new words, to, 379
or counterfeit new words, he could, 458
Coinage of your brain, 33
Coins, authors like, 14
express, even its minted, 157
like these, for, 265
Coin-weights shut, two eyes with, 208
Cold, 57
again, and straight is, 209
as any stone, as, 388
as snow, 74
bitter, taunting truths, 122
decree, hot temper leaps o'er a, 33
find one out in the, 64
hard and, 157
in clime, the, 233
it is very, 5
nor care, there's neither, 215
of pain, darkness, and, 78
poor Tom's a-, 410
that tempers heat, the, 369
the day in, 189
the fire that warmeth, 369
the soup gets, 211
the weather being, 120
thy blood is, 29
till the sun grows, 240
when yule is, 132
without, that comes from, 433
Colder thy kiss 296
Coldly turns away, all, 125
would I shape reply, 274
Coliseum, 57
Collar, 58
grows right round his neck, a, 60
Collectors, quite an army of, 92
College fanes, heard once more in, 291
Collop of my flesh, 134
Coln there was never a knight, from Trier to, 221
Cologne, 58
Colonel, 58
Colossus, 58
Colour, 58
and form, let thy future give, 127
the wars for my, 301
to mark the changing, 293
Colours, 58
out, until water takes their, 5
seen by candle-light, 468
Colt, 58
who is wise, the, 253
Columbia, 58
she an', 111
Column, 59
throws up a steamy, 116
Comb, 59
have formed the, 330
Combat deepens, 152
nerveth his arm for life's, 410
Combination, a, and a form, 250
Combine, when friendship, love and peace, 442
Come, 59
again, chaos is, 239

Come
avoid what is to, 60
away, kiss her and leave her, 55
away, Sister Spirit, 170
back, could find out when to, 140
back from the echoless shore, 340
back, for those who will never, 132
back, he 'll ne'er, 168
back, wish to, 168
back to me, Douglas, 97
back to me, will never, 161
beat your pate and fancy wit will, 447
bravely onward, and, 232
from the ends of the earth, though they, 391
from the heart, all offences, 289
from, where did you, 16
gentle spring, ethereal mildness, 382
his wit invites you by his looks to, 447
hither, lads, and hearken, 74
home to men 's business and bosoms, 40
in, come in, callin' sof,' 358
it may, as come it will, 38
like shadows, so depart, 358
look brighter when we, 438
men may, 116
night, end, day, 282
no more, once departed, 334
of nothing, nothing will, 285
not when I am dead, 76
oh for yesterdays to, 468
one, come all, 136
out, 't will hardly, 214
out of the west, young Lochinvar is, 229
over again, can never, 442
the ides of March are, 190
the melancholy days are, 257
then let it, 46
they come, 136
to good, cannot, 159
to judgment, a Daniel, 72
to light, truth will, 417
to me, for any calling, 365
to my heart again, 340
to thee, from the desert I, 86
to their own, the people will, 301
to this favour she must, 468
to thy God in time, 155
to you, my lad, whistle and I 'll, 440
unto these yellow sands, 349
what's to, 239
when it will come, 80
when you do call for them, 381
with a ring, pray, 338
ye in peace here, or come ye in war, 299
you back, you British soldier, 252
Comer, by the poorest, 177
grasps in the, 167
Comers must go, when such, 338
Comes abroad, every foul bird, 332
again, and it never, 470
Comes at last, death that, 79
in the light, 224
something wicked this way, 404
slowly up this way, spring, 382
sooner by white hairs, superfluity, 393
to do and say, what he, 315
swelling like a turkey-cock, here he, 418
to the worst, when the worst, 464
with eating, appetite, 11
your book forth, when, 30
Comest, darling boy, thou, 18
Comfort, 59
and command, to warn, to, 454
and for happiness, for, 125
comes a man of, 93
flows, from ignorance our, 190
the weaker vessel, 68
to my age, be, 326
Comfortable man, a, 32
Comforted, must I be, 384
Comfortless for lack of plenishing, 96
Comic muse, the subject of the, 234
Coming, a good time, 159
an eye will mark our, 438
butter, tired wench and, 429
events cast their shadows before, 358
he is, 351
hither, even as their, 157
of the Lord, 153
rider, those who wait the, 429
she 's, 264
welcome the, speed the going guest, 167
the wonderful days a-, 74
through the rye, 203
yet, it 's, 38
Command, applause of listening senates to, 11
and some, 55
at Heaven 's, 37
gave up their lives at the Queen 's, 373
man to, 454
to obey, to endure, 113
more invitation than, 108
my heart and me, that shall, 358
success, not in mortals to, 392
to warn, to comfort and, 454
Commandment on the pulse of life, 86
thy, all alone shall live, 331
Commandments, 59
Commands all light, 127
us, when he, 357
Commas and points, 67
Commendable, nor more, 161
Comment, every nice offence should bear his, 289
one other, is necessary, 291
Commerce, 59
and honest friendships, 6
let wealth and, 284
Commit, pretty follies that themselves, 243

Commit the oldest kind of sins, 367
Commits his body, 189
Committee, sort of managing, 92
Commodities, an' such grasy, 16
Commodity, I will turn diseases to, 301
there are one, 357
Common, 59
a case that's still too, 449
because 't is so, 16
bliss or woe, give me one, 409
grief, that 't is a, 1
law, the . . . is nothing but reason, 327
make it too, 160
men, the roll of, 59
men, to the crowd of, 81
my lips are no, 227
natures, 't is the same with, 280
realm shall be in, 130
selfishness, too high for, 159
sense, rich in saving, 43
tall, I am more than, 397
that loss is, 1
Commonwealth, 59
set up an ordinary, 266
to serve the, 386
Compact of fire, love is a spirit all, 240
sweet, and the, 253
Companies of men of genius, there are, 387
Companions, all her lovely, 342
I have had, 307
slept, while their, 177
thou'dst unfold, that such, 439
Company, 60
and steal out of your, 401
better, better air, 359
but a shirt and a half in all my, 361
say to yourself in, 85
shall bear him, 176
than saved in vulgar, 149
Comparable to the standing upon the vantage-ground, 415
Comparisons, 60
Compared, is not to be, 112
to that was next her chin, 226
Compass, 60
fro roundel to, 53
though a wide, 159
Compassed by the inviolate sea, 354
Compassion in your hearts, heavenly, 75
Compassionate, Christ the, 242
Compelled, and we ourselves, 289
Compels, solemn thought their monody, 410
Competency lives longer, 393
Complain, does to the moon, 292
I heard him, 371
of thirst, in midst of water I, 435
writhe but not, 233
Complaining, work without, 207
Complete, is not, 253
Completeness, what she knew not, of, 204
Complexion, 60
whose fresh, 240
Complexions are, soft as our, 453
Complicate, how wonderful is man, how, 251
Complies against his will, he that, 290
Compose a tragedy, and some compose a rondo, 146
Composed, thy decent limbs, 139
Compost, do not spread the, 60
Composture stolen, by a, 402
Compound for sins they are inclined to, 366
o'er the flavoured, 349
of oddity rare, 197
of two cardinal virtues, 315
Compounded, look how, 78
Compounds, than these poor, 158
Comprehend all vagrom men, you shall, 422
not, the good they, 156
Comprehends, more than cool reason ever, 243
Compromise, 60
Compulsion, give no man a reason upon, 327
Compute, we partly may, 172
Comrade, new-hatched unfledged, 146
Comrades, and went with his, 353
chase e'en now the fliers, your, 391
of the war, his, 433
Concave and beyond, Hell's, 46
Conceal the mind, to, 210
Concealed, from man, 245
in yon smoke, 391
Concealment, but let, 298
Conceding, nature and custom agree in, 455
Conceit, profound, of wisdom, gravity, 291
sell us his petty, 67
so to his own, 307
Conceive, a heart to, 173
Concentrating, all, like rays, 204
Concentred all in self, 65
Concerns himself, where it, 368
Concert move, in, 204
Concludes her noblest song, 104
Conclusion, 60
Concord never broke, gentle, 411
of sweet sounds, with, 273
Concur to general use, 117
Condemn, both the golden mean alike, 237
it, is to, 191
to slaughter I, 305
Condemned himself, has, in a word, 321
Condiment that bites too soon, distrust the, 349
Condition, on any one, 274
rise, honour and shame from no, 184
Conditions blend, how sweetly those, 242
govern our, 127
our new, 8
our soft, and our hearts, 456

Conduct is n't all your fancy paints, if our, 349
they must stand or fall, 202
under them, but for his, 298
Conference a ready man, 326
Confess, 60
I'm afraid of, that I, 283
Confessed a flush, the east hath, 225
Confidant, a better choice of a, 397
Confidence, 60
Confident to-morrows, and, 48
they erred, nor am I, 139
Confined, cabined, cribbed, 41
from home, 186
their wishes all, 68
to fast in fires, 380
Confines shall in these, 335
Confirmation strong as proofs of holy writ, 195
Confiscate unto the state, 134
Conflagrations, responsible for the, 372
Conflict, 60
Confounded, confusion worse, 344
Confront the visage of offence, to, 260
Confusion, all else, 454
calamity and, 41
understood the shouting and, 433
worse confounded, 344
Confute, jarring sects, 162
Congenial, 60
Congregation, has the largest, 87
Congregations poor and small, 217
Congress, 60
Connected them with another, which have, 356
Conned by rote, 15
Conquer, 61
again and again, we'll, 286
America, you cannot, 8
go lose or, 150
like Douglas, 97
love who run away, only they, 234
we fight and we, 130
Conquered, 61
at last, the fever called living is, 229
he, and he fell, 130
man, and has died a, 321
Conqueror, he the true ruler and, 410
the proud foot of a, 112
Conquerors, a lean fellow beats all, 61
Conquers agony, but, 152
evermore, justice, 199
every wrong, peace unweaponed, 300
reason still, the ruling passion, 297
Conquest and subjugation, of foreign, 112
't is a firmer, 335
Conquests she but o'er herself, no, 452
Conscience, 61–62
a good, is my bail, 318
a still and quiet, 299
be honest and clean, 55
chills her, now, 330
corrupted with injustice, 12
of her worth, and the, 457
Conscience
of the king, catch the, 306
pain, aye to the, 390
slept, while, 215
to our dealing, bend our, 386
was strong, 183
we may live without, 63
Consecrates each grave, it, 157
Consent, 62
of the governed, from the, 161
to be his bride, gin ye'll, 364
Consented, whispering, "I will ne'er consent," 62
Consents, my poverty but not my will, 311
to death, brow, 152
Consideration, another half-hour's good, 210
Considering, 62
Consistency, 62
Consort, and his, 379
Constable, 62
of the watch, for the, 422
Constancy in wind, hope, 67
lives in realms above, 412
Constant, 62
never, to one thing, 83
then, if thou wilt be, 124
too, I will be, 340
Constitutes a state, what, 385
Constitution which they have established, 289
a higher law than the, 213
Constitutions, man is more than, 213
Constrained to love thee, 110
Construction, a Pickwickian, 303
Consume, corruption may our frame, 377
the thing that feeds, 132
Consumed the midnight oil, 215
Consuming element, burning and, 4
Consummation have, quiet, 163
Consumption, discontent, the nobleman's, 93
of the purse, 322
Consum'st thyself in single life, that thou, 442
Contagion to this world, 282
Contain, and nourish, 118
Contaminate our fingers, 36
Contempt, will grow more, 238
Contend for Homer dead, 183
to the uttermost, let a man, 318
Contending nations know, let fierce, 93
Content, 62
a mind, 262
farewell, 125
to sit by little fires, 132
with few will be ever, 205
with poverty, my soul I arm, 311
Contented, slaves howe'er, 143
well-breakfasted juryman, 92
why then are you not, 433
Contentment, 62
springs, from health, 172
Contents us long, nothing, 381

Contest, let fools, 161
was unequal, the, 297
Contests rise from trivial things, what mighty, 414
Contiguity of shame, some boundless, 229
Continuate goodness, untirable and, 160
Continue, if God wills that it, 199
Continuous unbroken strain, with one, 112
Contract, a debt he never did, 82
of her marriage, the, 407
Contracting parties meet, till the high, 253
Contradiction still, woman's at best a, 453
Contraries, dhrames always go by, 99
Contrary with me, ev'rythink goes, 230
Contrite heart, an humble and a, 139
Contrive, a head to, 173
nor let thy soul, 270
some kind of a lever, would only, 403
wicked custom so, 140
Contrived by man, nothing yet been, 192
Control, gladden and, 384
his, stops with the shore, 288
such base, 262
that never brooked, 367
Controversies, decide all, 329
Contumely, the proud man's, 323
Convenience next suggested, 279
snug, 142
Conveniency of every kind, better, 359
Convent bells, chiming of these, 222
Conversation, 62
may upset a freight-train of, 321
Conversations, 62
Converse and live with ease, 107
formed by thy, 162
talking is not always to, 397
Converses more with the buttock, 282
Converted, that loam whereto he was, 421
Converting Jews to Christians, in, 310
Convey, the wise it call, 386
Conveyed, the opening bud to heaven, 77
Conviction, flashing, 314
Convinced at sight, whose truth, 447
Coo, dove, to thy married mate, 97
Cook, 62
pantler, butler, 71
Cookery, 62
Cooks, 63
Cool, so calm, day so, 73
than my heart, 264
Cooled, coal that must be, 4
warmed and, by the same winter and summer, 197
Coolly, we talked of love as, 241
Cools, till a husband, 189
Cope, beneath that awful, 115
Copied there, youth and observation, 331
Copies, 63
Copper, 63
brass and a' that, on, 249
wire, others rather resemble, 276
Coppers on the railroad tracks, boys that put, 321
Copy and book, 263
leave the world no, 21
Coral, true, needs no painter's brush, 152
Cord however fine, can stretch a, 389
he knows each, 172
Cordial gives, the dewy, 101
old and rare, a, 78
one, in this melancholy vale, 402
that sparkled for Helen, the, 100
to the soul, 269
wink-tippling, 397
Cords will break, and then the, 173
Core below, up from the burning, 24
of heat, to make a solid, 230
Corinth, 63
Coriolanus' exile, hooting at, 43
Cork, the sub-editor at, 294
Cormorant, 63
Corn in chaff, 67
receiving chaff for, 103
Ruth among the fields of, 120
so take the, 193
that is ketched with mouldy, 206
two ears of, 162
Corner to die in, for a, 176
Corners of the world, doth belie all, 368
of the world in arms, 112
Cornish lads can do, shall understand what, 63
Cornishmen, 63
Corns out, new ones hunt folks's, 161
Coronets, kind hearts are more than, 148
Corporal sufferance, in, 80
Corporation, shocking, as for our, 256
Corporations, 64
Corpse, disthroned, 80
of public, the dead, 340
the earth upon her, 388
to the rampart we hurried, as his, 102
Corpses, three, lay out on the shining sands, 132
Corrupt a saint, able to, 347
my air, that do, 69
what plea so tainted and, 213
Corrupted currents, in the, 289
the youth, most traitorously, 317
with injustice, 12
Corrupteth and embaseth it, wanton love, 23
Corruption, 64
he has touched, 36
may our frame consume, 377
wealth, vice, 18
which rank, 106

Corsair 64.
Corse, thou, dead, 268
Cost, learned at a heavy, 117
nothin', wich do n't, 357
price, a little below, 175
too much, who, 202
Costly bales, dropping down with, 59
thy habit as thy purse can buy, 11
Costs a meal, and the walk that, 430
thy life, that, 448
Cottage porch, at my, 162
the poorest man may in his, 44
Cottle, O Amos! Phœbus! what a name, 274
Couch as thine, no such, 334
more magnificent, 334
of clay, or an oozy, 8
of ever-welcome rest, the, 333
the drapery of his, 227
Cough and phthisic, helps the headache, 445
Coughing in the street, for, 322
Coughs, 64
catarrhs, to find out agues, 306
Could not, dared not answer no, 283
not, would not, durst not play, 306
Council, great in, 43
the hidings of his, 154
Councils might not want vigour, that their, 82
Counsel, 64
in his face, 85
Count ever so much, 178
how many sands, 205
our spoons, let us, 425
their chickens ere th 're hatched, 48
time by heart-throbs, we should, 227
Counted two-and-seventy stenches, 387
Countenance and profit, to receive, 318
cannot lie, 117
more in sorrow than in anger, 375
Counter, the polished, 361
throwing . . . goods on the, 15
Countercheck quarrelsome, the, the fifth, 218
Counterfeit, dread clamours, 125
fair Portia 's, 303
new words, coin or, 458
presentment, the, 303
the deep tragedian, I can, 307
Counters, words are wise men 's, 459
Countless price, a gem of, 73
Country, 64–65
but it's saviour of 'is, 410
call you, hear your, 94
claims our fealty, our, 259
foreign troop was landed in my, 8
heart, thought to break a, 174
his first best, 182
I tremble for my, 414
lie abroad for the good of his, 7
loss, to do our, 185
messes, herbs and other, 303
Country
more essential service to his, 162
of the free, in the, 469
round was wasted, the, 425
that land thy, 182
the undiscovered, 79
they touch our, 368
to shed his blood for his, 383
woe awaits a, 398
Countrymen, fall was there, my, 121
first in the hearts of his, 132
friends, Romans, 341
Country 's blood, guiltless of his, 168
flag is at home, his, 133
glory fast, for his, 58
gut her soul, Earth 's biggest, 277
life, to save his, 432
pride, their, 300
thirst, to quench a, 248
wishes blest, by all their, 34
Couple, fond, 376
Coupled and inseparable, still we went, 224
Courage, 65
but screw your, 119
can avert, that strength and, 189
man! the hurt cannot be much, 189
never abandon the good soldier, 373
never to submit or yield, 231
party, is party expediency, 297
rise, make your, 18
to forget, or, 330
true hearts, 48
up, to bear his, 440
Courageous, to show itself, 68
Course, directing its, 102
great nature 's second, 370
how gloriously her gallant, 436
in his silent, 406
is run, to that whose, 392
it is the wisest, 3
lad, young blood must have its, 469
of empire, the, 109
of human events, when in the, 356
of love, of my whole, 396
of nature is the art of God, 13
of one revolving moon, 114
of true love never did run smooth, 238
others may take, what, 217
the desp'rat'st the wisest, 86
time rolls his, 406
to steer, the wise, 91
Coursed one another, the big round tears, 398
Courses, like ships they steer their, 335
Court, 65
awards it, the, 134
of heaven, the livery of the, 228
refused it in the open, 199
the camp, the grove, 237
was pure, her, 323
Courtesies, 65
in doing, 145
Courtesy, 65
the rules of, 455

Courtesy
use the devil himself with, 88
well-placed words of glozing, 459
Courtier, 66
Courtier 's, the, soldier 's, scholar 's, 263
Courtiers, our, were good, 22
Courting somebody, somebody 's, 373
Courtly sword, from a, 42
Courts his love, as I do thee, 254
not starred and spangled, 385
of heaven, before the, 313
Courtship, love and matrimony, of, 255
pleasant the snaffle of, 253
Cousin, and everybody 's, 319
selfishness, love 's, 356
Sleep, and not his, 81
Cousinship, will virtue, and all return, 319
Cover crimes, men can, 119
her guilt to, 136
my head now, to, 68
serves as paste and, 80
up the embers, stays to, 108
Covercle, broad as a, 53
Covers close, strained the dusky, 263
out of the night that, 376
Covet honour, a sin to, 185
Coward, 66
conscience, how dost thou, 61
shaked like a, 277
nor slave, find neither, 110
stands aside, while the, 34
the gift of a, 323
thou seem'st a, 422
Cowards, 66
crave, sech peace ez only, 299
have, as many other mannish, 394
of us all, 61
sots or slaves or, 113
thet tarries long in hands o', 143
use, word that, 61
Cower, I will not shrink or, 392
Cowslip 's bell, in a, 21
Cozened twice, idiots only may be, 205
Coxcomb, and your ploody, 216
Crab-tree and old iron rang, hard, 405
Crack of timbers, with a, 99
through every hole and, 132
Cracked and growled, it, 190
Cracking nuts, quarrel with a man for, 322
Crackling pile, nor, 155
Cradle, England is the, 111
if drink rock not his, 100
is the starting-place, our, 221
of the deep, in the, 84
where it lies, 124
Cradles rock us nearer to the tomb, 81
Craft, 66
on the line, the oldest, 346
the queerest little, 73
Crag, under the, 419
Crags among, the rattling, 405
at the foot of thy, 161
Crammed rosin and pine, furnace, 346
Crammed up, as would be, 336
with heaven, earth 's, 153
Cramps, rack thee with old, 2
Cranmer 's at the stake, like, 169
Cranks and wanton wiles, 196
Crannied wall, flower in the, 135
Crannies, pluck you out of the, 135
Cranny, in every, 231
Crapes of China silk, some marrowy, 364
Cravat, virtue may flourish in an old, 171
Crave the austere virtues, we, 185
the more you, 100
whatever mortals, 462
Craving for more, I still shall be, 205
in the souls of men, this restless, 46
Crawled and crept through life, 352
Crawling foam, the cruel, 136
Crazed, 66
Crazy as a loon, 286
Cream and mantle, do, 291
vigilant as a cat to steal, 45
Creation, a false, 70
called the lords of the, 259
moves, to which the whole, 322
the tire of all, 188
Creation 's blot, creation 's blank, 26
dawn beheld, such as, 406
Creature be repaid, from his helpless, 82
cringe to any mortal, 42
dead, poor, speechless, 38
drink, pretty, 101
feels, each, 14
he is a base and ignoble, 248
I am a lone lorn, 230
kills a reasonable, 30
life-blood out of a frail young, 423
no, owns it in the first degree, 284
of earth, the poor, 135
smarts so little, no, 137
thet slow, 212
was stirring, not a, 51
what a glorious, 408
why should every, 101
Creature 's at his dirty work again, the, 353
Creatures are, see how frail these, 455
breeds very valiant, 111
heaven from all, 127
he serveth, the, 319
how they envies us, poor, 388
kings, and meaner, 186
millions of spiritual, 381
such unromantic, 259
the meanest of his, 243
Credit go, let the, 44
his own lie, to, 219
in being jolly, some, 198
in that, there ain't much, 197
it 's a watch that 'll do you, 434
the dead corpse of public, 340
Creditor severe, misfortune like a, 265
Credulous to false prints, 453

Creed, 66
nor cursing, 155
of peace, profession of the, 42
of slaves, the, 279
outworn, suckled in a, 293
Creeds, and framed their iron, 155
are with ivy o'ergrown, their, 446
other, will rise, 330
than in half the, 97
Creep a little out, did, 129
home, and take your place, 290
past, and bade me, 78
Creepeth o'er ruins old, that, 195
Creeping like snail, 352
nigher, as a lion, 301
where no life is seen, 195
Creeps this petty pace, 411
Crept in, the worms they, 463
silently to rest, one by one, 333
Crescent moon, waning, not the, 4
Cressets, of burning, 277
Crest and crowning of all good, the, 38
behind the snow-white, 179
gets himself another, 241
Crests dancing, with all their white, 436
Crew, and as the cock, 77
he was of that stubborn, 329
the cock, 57
Crews, an' all their, 299
Cribbed, as if they'd, 347
confined, cabined, 41
Cricket, 66
chirps, in age the, 470
Crickets, 66
cry, the, 83
Cried aloud, I have not winced nor, 28
"Ha, Ha," he, 342
Cries amid the rout, 383
protest to the judges, 188
such hideous, 98
Crime, 66
fatal sources of misery and, 422
forgive the, 406
is it in heaven a, 236
numbers sanctified the, 272
the atrocious, of being a young man, 469
untold, price of many a, 157
without a, 142
worse than a, 28
Crimes, and a thousand, 64
are committed, how many, 217
had left her woman still, the worst of, 449
may reach the dignity of, 167
men can cover, 119
the register of the, 180
till the foul, 380
Crimson, a fuller, 241
bars, forty flags with their, 134
streak on ocean's cheek, 73
Cringe to any mortal creature, 42
Cringing to sue me, come not, 392
Crisis does divine, tell what, 306
the, the danger is past, 229
Crispian, 66
Critic, 67
Critical, 67
Critic-dame, the, 30
Critics and cold water, loathing, 308
ev'n such small, 458
make, or, 219
Croak is loud, the raven's, 184
Croaked as she sate at her meal, the raven, 326
Crœsus' store, gives me wealthy, 402
Cromwell, Charles the First his, 414
guiltless of his country's blood, 168
I charge thee, 7
see, 123
Crook the pregnant hinges of the knee, 412
Crooked lane, straight down the, 383
Cropped, in fight is, 216
Crops the flowery food, 27
Cross, 67
e'en though it be a, 278
her hands humbly, 169
him, I'll, 294
my prayer, lest the devil, 87
nearer leaving the, 278
of England, 'neath the Red, 110
ours is the heaviest, 1
over the river, let us, 333
she wore, a sparkling, 197
the threshold, his forces dare not, 44
the Unknown water, 73
to me, his thoughts that, 403
with thine, my path might, 230
Cross-bow, with my, 5
Crossed, abhorent of a calculation, 161
in hopeless love, 66
in love, an oyster may be, 293
in rest, two pale feet, 208
to the farther side, who've, 339
with me, spirits twain have, 381
Crosses, no forms or, 220
Crossing the river, swap horses while, 394
Cross-questions, till with all their, 348
Crossways, for things are running, 53
Crotch-deep in the snow, 313
Crow, 67
make thee think thy swan a, 394
the night-, 25
Crowbar, straightened out for a, 188
Crowbars loose the bulldog's grip, only, 40
Crowd, 67, 68
all, 123
of common men, calls ye to the, 81
Crowd-drawing preacher, makes him the, 314
Crowded, feast and your halls are, 129
Crowds, and oft in, 274
Crown, 68
a fairer name than French, 332
and a' that, not his, 248
and beauty's flowery, 354
and deck thee, I'll, 124
and kingdom is, both, 262

Crown
an emperor without his, 73
better than his, 260
his breeches cost him but a, 387
his misery, then to, 317
it, and, 108
must tumble down, sceptre and, 103
nearing gaining the, 278
no, no cross, 67
not the king's, 260
now wears his, 356
of, of queen, 370
of his head, from the, 196
of life, death is the, 81
of sorrow, sorrow's, 375
of verdure weaves, her, 382
ourselves with rosebuds, let us, 343
the frost is my, 284
to all the force of the, 44
wedding is great Juno's, 437
Crowner's quest law, 213
Crowning fact, the, 144
of all good, the crest and, 38
Crowns all, the end, 109
him victor glorified, 199
murders on their, 90
Crows, city of kites and, 43
the cock, 283
Crucified, till his Lord is, 34
Cruel, 68
and inconstant, 83
Cruellest she alive, 21
Cruelty to load a falling man, 121
Crumbled before, they have, 387
Crumbles on her rising bread, she breaks and, 465
Crumping snows, and upon the, 207
Cruse of oil, this, 12
Crush it, avoid it or, 449
of worlds, the, 191
the tyrant, and, 385
the wall, and, 387
Crushed a flower, 149
and some were, 35
as odours, 191
at Waterloo, the, 332
by pain's resistless power, 175
to earth, truth, 415
when they are incensed or, 427
Crust of bread and liberty, 217
of bread and rags, a, 207
when we share her wretched, 34
with water and a, 235
Crutch, 68
Crutches, Time goes on, 407
Cry, 68
and no wool, all, 395
Church, church, 52
east and west, 242
is still They come, 17
let the nations fear our, 143
liberty, when they, 217
mew, be a kitten and, 205
need a body, 203
of battle rises, the, 19
of curs, you common, 69
Cry
of defiance, a, 84
of some strong swimmer, the bubbling, 395
of startled sleepers, 99
of that spectral host, the, 151
out itself, Enough, 4
raise ye no, 17
she nor swooned nor uttered, 76
the crickets, 83
the spirit's yearning, 88
war is still the, 430
will be, for ever the, 1
with no language but a, 192
Crying at the lock, 443
for the light, an infant, 192
Crystalline delight, twinkle with a, 23
Cuba, light me another, 339
stout, get me a, 53
Cuckolds, what made them, 306
Cucumbers, extracting sunbeams out of, 393
Cuddle doon, bairnies, 16
Cudgel thy brains no more, 33
Cudgel's of, know what wood a, 20
Cultured and capable of sober thought, 262
Culverin's signal is fired, 63
Cunning hand laid on, 21
to thrive in, 88
woman is a knavish fool, a, 452
Cup, 68–69
alone with your, 441
each heart and each, 116
drink of this, 100
hand me the, 78
have drunk their, 333
I sing, careless o'er my, 402
leave a kiss but in the, 99
life's enchanted, 220
o'erflow the, 101
of hot wine, a, 445
o' kindness, we'll tak' a, 14
one, to the dead all ready, 91
was a fiction, her, 100
Cupboard's a storehouse, 16
Cupid, 69
might wander, wherever, 240
Cupid's name, to seal on, 336
Cups freshly remembered, in their flowing, 275
that cheer but not inebriate, 116
Cur can lend three thousand ducats, 95
would lick my hand, 169
Curb a runaway young star, 9
this cruel devil of his will, 213
Curbed her bright career, 142
Cure love with love, 88
of souls, in the, 347
the wise for, 172
thine heart, wilt thou, 232
Curfew, 69
he begins at, 135
Curious, it seemed so, 73
art, with, 33
Curled darlings of our nation, 72

Curled, the least ringlet that, 339
up on the floor, and, 350
Curlier, his hair grew, 311
Curls, Hyperion 's, 250
Current, 69
of a woman 's will, turn the, 450
of the soul, froze the genial, 301
took 'em, the ignorant for, 458
Currents turn awry, 61
Curs, 69
Curse, 69
an oath to vent or, 345
doing nothing was his, 285
it hath the primal eldest, 272
laid a swingeing long, 26
my dog so, a heart to, 395
of mankind, the common, 252
of service, 't is the, 315
on all laws but those, 233
to bless, to, 157
upon his tongue, laid a, 283
Cursed, 69
alway, by man is, 366
and tainted thing, was a, 143
be he, 29
be the social lies that warp us, 470
its hour of birth, all that, 416
with which our lives are, 339
Curses dark, rigged with, 18
deeper than the strong man, 413
not loud but deep, 223
on the spoiler 's head, 157
Curseth the warning bird, 319
Cursing creed, nor, 155
Curtain, 69–70
Curtains close, draw the, 80
let fall the, 116
round, drew my midnight, 167
Curuck-coo, you love me and I love you, 235
Curve at yonder pig, turned up in scornful, 304
Curves, last in kindly, 18
Cushion and soft dean invite, 178
Custard, and blaspheme, 322
Custom, 70
agree, nature and, 455
always of the afternoon, 4
holds, nature her, 399
so contrive, wicked, 140
stale her infinite variety, 5
the ancient Goths had a wise, 82
Customers, folks that want to be, 266
merchant over-polite to his, 15
raising up a people of, 361
Customs, 70
Cut, 70
a throat, ever scuttled ship or, 262
beard of formal, 199
diamonds, diamonds, 88
loaf to steal a shive, of a, 435
our names in big letters, to, 275
out the purity of his, I, 321
the halter, will come and, 254
them down with my blast, I, 284
Cut
up what remains, women come out to, 373
the string that holds those weights, 403
Cuts it quite, and, 96
like cheese, whitewood that, 441
Cutteth friendship al a'-two, a' tonge, 412
Cut-throat, dog, 147
Cutting bread and butter, she was, 439
of it, in the, 134
Cuttle bite his nails, when you see Ned, 273
Cuttle 's aground, you may know Ned, 273
Cycle of Cathay, than a, 45
Cygnet to this pale, faint swan, 273
Cynic, 70
Cynosure, 70
Cynthia howls, while Ralph to, 282
Czar, this emperor, this, 80

D

Dace, roach and, 32
Dacian mother, there was their, 181
Dagger, 70
at the drawn, 191
Daggers, 70
Daggers-drawing, have always been at, 54
Daguerreotype, the twenty-five-cent, 124
Daily burden for the back, 40
do, what men, 259
that we are dying, 79
Daintier sense, hath the, 70
Dainties that are bred in a book, 30
to them, such, 360
Dainty bits make rich the ribs, 298
Daisies pied, meadows trim with, 256
Daisy-blossom washed with still rains and, 224
Dale, under the hawthorn in the, 307
Dales and fields, 235
Dalliance, 70
silken, 111
Dam, chickens and their, 49
Dame, 71
that loves to rove, for, 344
whare sits our sulky, sullen, 465
Dames have had, the gentle, 450
ye high, exalted, virtuous, 142
Damn, 71
his treacherous flatteries, 259
itself, the world would, 198
the rest, not to, 376
Damnation, 71
to sip, calls it, 226
Damnations, 71
Damned be him that first cries, 214
beside a duke, genteelly, 149
better be, than mentioned not at all, 123

Damned first, I will see thee, 367
in a fair wife, almost, 382
to everlasting fame, 123
to fame, 123
many an old host that I know is, 290
minutes tells he o'er, what, 243
souls, givin' drink to poor, 395
villain, smiling, 426
Damning those they have no mind to, 366
Damp, wherever the ground was a little, 437
Damsel that 's merry, to the, 246
Dan Chaucer, well of English undefiled, 47
Dance, 71
and jollity, tipsy, 129
as those move easiest who have learned to, 467
barefoot on her wedding-day, 10
her turn, and, 71
is not to woo, time to, 456
provided that he did not, 393
Danced, and then she, 129
at night, death-fires, 81
'em, he 'd squired 'em, druv 'em, 363
to see that banner in the sky, 114
Dances and the public show, midnight, 448
such a way, she, 129
Dancing, 71
after, the New came, 119
oh heaven! her, 129
'round them the spectres are seen, 379
Dandled him to rest, who, 89
Dane slain, the Drury Lane, 115
Danger and reproof, the taste of, 332
brave, could, 67
breathe, does only death and, 300
in that hour of, 39
is in discord, all your, 433
is past, the, 229
just fear of an imminent, 430
may be at any hour, 435
of being in, 359
of detection increases every day, 82
or dishonour lurks, where, 443
on the deep, there 's, 304
out of this nettle, 280
pleased with the, 304
soft, making the nettle, 280
we are in great, 65
who does not shrink from, 390
Dangerous, 71
and his drink, 101
humours, nurses, 431
most, is that temptation, 347
such men are, 126
thing, a little learning is a, 215
to disturb a hornet 's nest, 186
Danger 's post, breast that fears not, 145
Dangers I had passed, for the; 363
of the sea, sing the, 346
of the seas, think upon the, 355
Dangers thou canst mak' us scorn, 19
Daniel, 72
Danny Deever in the mornin', they 're hanging, 169
Danube, 72
Dare, 72
a heart to feel and, 173
call it treason, none, 414
come to us, ere death, 79
do, what men, 259
eat his breakfast, 134
how much the wretched, 465
look on that, that, 251
maintain them, they have rights who, 338
more than the strongest, 133
never grudge the throe, 328
not be so bold, 120
not, fain deny, and, 223
not, letting I, 45
not be in the right, who, 368
not perch, where eagles, 106
not throne above, I, 160
not, with such a proposal I, 283
the elements to strife, seems to, 436
to do our duty, 337
to lay bare, none ever, 284
to vent his dang'rous thought, let him not, 397
Dared for a high cause, who have, 120
not answer no, 283
not close, my fevered eyes I, 369
not disobey, I, 93
Dares be true, he serves all who, 415
do more, who, 72
love attempt, that, 239
not lend his eye, th' other, 321
not put it to the touch, 126
rush on death, 191
send a challenge to his end, 221
to take the side, and, 337
Darest thou, then, 85
Daring, 72
last look of despairing, 86
more, or more bold, 422
the loving are the, 34
Dark, 72
and after that the, 18
and the daylight, between the, 50
as Erebus, his affections, 273
benighted way, upon the, 75
despite the, 145
fear to go into the, 77
for ways that are, 50
her silver mantle threw, o'er the, 268
no, still 'tis, 283
spin on blindly in the, 439
the night and chill, 211
the night both drear and, 26
though to-day be, 186
Dark-blue ocean, thou deep and, 288
Darker grows the night, as, 185
Darkest day, the, 86
storm, from the, 41

Darkness, 72
a distant voice in the, 360
again and a silence, then, 360
again, sink into, 138
and breathless, 362
and cold, of pain, 78
and to me, to, 69
as a bride, 90
a voice in the, 84
deep caverns of, 163
blackness of, 313
encompass, sorrows and, 163
falls from the wings of Night, the, 282
groping blindly in the, 156
in secret, 154
is strong, 380
of to-day, let us forget the, 48
right hand in that, 156
running through caverns of, 451
so from the bosom of, 138
swept across the sky, 76
the, and the worm, 401
the raven down of, 282
there's a midnight, 225
they who walk in, 324
up to God, slope through, 7
vigilant in, 70
villains and the sons of, 417
Darling, 72
of my heart, she is the, 6, 74
the Frenchman's, 144
Darling's grave, be weeping at her, 164
Darlings, 72
Darned long row to hoe, a, 344
sight better business, is a, 404
Dart, to wing the, 106
feather on the fatal, 106
too often Love's insidious, 236
Darts, and Apollyon shoots, 226
Dash, 72
Dashest 73
Dashing, through red blood the war-horse, 431
Dashings, save his own, 75
Dastard in war, and a, 237
Dateless bargain, a, 118
nameless and, 373
Dates are thine, these tamarinds and, 12
Daubed with red, nor need be, 152
Daughter, 73
am I in mother's house, 276
of Chaos and eternal Night, 46
of the gods, 94
of the Vine, and took the, 426
or hear sighs for a, 400
still harping on my, 171
War, he thought of his, 432
wife, the mother, 452
Daughters of earth, words are the, 459
words are men's, 459
Daunted, mystery the spirit, 69
Dauntless breast, that with, 168
spirit and a press, he had a, 315
David, Josias, young Obadias, 305
Daw, no wiser than a, 213
Dawn and dusk were mine, thy, 230
beheld, such as creation's, 406
comes up like thunder, the, 252
grows bright, the, 283
in the, 56
man's presumption on to-morrow's, 411
no, no dust, 285
on their rest, ere life shall, 97
smitten in its early, 391
the rift of, 207
through the vast waste, 18
Dawned in heaven, and the next waking, 105
Dawning of morn, with the, 98
Dawn's early light, 17
Daw's not reckoned a religious bird, 52
Daws to peck at, for, 371
Day, 73
a chest of drawers by, 295
after, sermons and soda-water the, 444
a hand open as, 161
a hundred years to a, 46
all the next, 169
and a new morning brings eternal, 13
and brings the harvest home of, 470
and every dog his, 469
and for the, confined to fast in fires, 380
and night, all seasons, 361
and night, stuck to me, 286
and waking with, 390
as it fell upon a, 256
as morning shows the, 49
a stocking all the, 282
a summer's, 122
as sharp to them as thorn, this, 419
at least one meal a, 256
be bread and peace, 35
been, I hae mony, 229
beguiled, expectation every, 92
beyond the night, across the, 463
bricks are alive at this, 36
brought back my night, 98
business of the, 102
but his eternal, 155
but one, the, 281
by day, lower to his level, 56
by day, that see we, 272
cares that infest the, 44
close the drama with the, 109
come night, end, 282
comes a frost, third, 164
dog will have his, 45
dozing all the, 101
end it, will one, 109
ended with the, 105
fight another, 130
follow as the night the, 415
for America, is a glorious, 8
for ever and a, 116
forget the luve o' life's young, 222
for killing folks, ninepence a, 272

Day
forth, from this, 382
good things of, 282
he first saw the, 348
here's to the, 361
he that outlives this, 66
in cold, the, 189
in June, rare as a, 199
in the light of fuller, 252
in the spring of, 161
into the light of, 15
is aye fair, the, 215
is called the feast of Crispian, 66
is done and the darkness, 282
is done, happy the man that when his, 62
is long, as merry as the, 261
is named, when this, 66
it is not yet near, 283
it is solemnized, the, 407
I dearly love but one, 74
knell of parting, 69
long, not dream them all, 374
longer than a wonder lasts, a, 456
men that in a narrower, 106
must win, right the, 337
nest at peep of, 25
next, the fatal precedent, 84
night is long that never finds the, 282
nor brought too long a, 331
of judgment, on the, 450
of strife, better a, 390
once full of, 429
precincts of the cheerful, 139
'round the chowder-kettle, that, 51
sleep shall neither night or, 370
tell what hour o' th', 6
that is dead, 161
the darkest, 86
the events of every, 352
the hunting of that, 419
the iron wheels go onward, all, 439
the maddest, merriest, 256
the meanest have their, 123
the night will hallow the, 442
the pleasures of the present, 227
this, she was both pantler, 71
to-morrow as to-day, such a, 411
to day, this petty pace from, 411
to shine by night and, 245
unto each man comes a, 366
we keep the, 101
we may not live to see the, 159
will look on a sultry, 269
will not look the same by, 468
woe worth the, 448
wooed and wedded in a, 442
Daylight, 73
around them in, 446
between the dark and the, 50
comes, when, 224
Daylight's past, and the, 344
Day's disasters in his morning face, 93
disdain, to feel the, 369
last beam is flown, the, 429
Day's life, the death of each, 370
march nearer home, a, 278
occupations, pause in the, 50
rest, where takes his one, 401
work, done thy long, 35
Days, 74
and live laborious, 123
are come, the melancholy, 257
are dwindled, whose, 375
are foul, his, 101
are gone when beauty bright, the, 236
are past, when these dark, 237
as belonged to early, 204
a world of happy, 99
come roaring and gleaming, 138
halcyon, 168
happy mixtures of more happy, 264
lived a courtier all my, 66
looked on better, 23
may come, and, 236
my salad, 349
of boyhood perished, the blithe, 331
of childhood, in my, 307
of her life, all the, 451
of long-ago, the lusty, 230
my, are in the yellow leaf, 223
of my life, kape me from such all the, 16
of nature, done in my, 380
of old, in the brave, 341
of yore, of the saintly, 325
past our dancing, 71
peat his pate for, 216
shuts up the story of our, 406
some tell their, 398
that length of, 223
that were earlier, in the, 311
the light of other, 258
then if ever come perfect, 199
Deacon, 74
swear, 'most enough to make a, 394
Deacons do, the Deacon swore, as, 74
Dead, 74–76
already, one cup to the, 91
and never dream we're, 235
and turned to clay, 421
but marks our English, 113
contend for Homer, 183
earth that bears thee, 381
fame, to his, 121
forgot, and, 462
for Homer being, 183
gazed on the face of the, 313
grace of a day that is, 161
how can he be, 191
how the bird was, 41
if I were, 76
if only the, 140
immortal of the, 115
in fair battle strikes him, 12
laurel the graves of our, 212
lay in his shroud of snow, 55
lions by the beard, plucks, 423
living a year or two after one is, 423

Dead
man, between a man asleep and a, 369
man 's face, sometimes in a, 225
man 's grave, I who have troubled the, 448
men, the peace of, 299
men, down among the, 172
not, but gone before, 158
now, oh would I were, 68
of the night a sweet vision I saw, 427
of those immortal, 50
once, you never shall return, 100
on the face of the, 311
poor, speechless creature, 38
render up their, 354
rest her soul, she 's, 453
restore the, thou sea, 354
say I 'm sick, I 'm, 206
scandals form good subjects, 351
selves, on stepping-stones of their, 170
shall not have died in vain, these, 276
so death is to the, 77
some are, 351
some flung up, 35
steered by the dumb, the, 357
take up thy, 28
that from these honoured, 276
that lull the, 468
that name the underlying, 468
the bivouac of the, 26
the devil to fetch the, 87
the heifer, 41
the light in the dust lies, 209
they said to him, she is, 55
till you 're, 112
unnoted, and for ever, 65
whose garlands, 17
when it goes out, we are, 28
where rest not England 's, 113
who rose again, the, 332
yea to the, 185
Deadlier than stone or brick, 114
Dead-low-tide, seen except at, 175
Deadly and chill, waxed, 77
Dead Sea, 76
Dead-sure thing, duty a, 104
Deaf as the sea, in rage, 324
Deal damnation round the land, 71
lightly with thy faults, need, 450
of sack, to this intolerable, 346
of skimble-skamble stuff, a, 367
Dealers in watered milk, 325
Dealing, bend our conscience to our, 386
out flannel and sheeting, 175
Dealings, whose sordid, 58
Dean invite, the cushion and soft, 178
Deans, dowagers for, 162
Dear and only love, my, 234
as remembered kisses after death, 205
as the light that visits, 443
as the ruddy drops, 443
Dear as the vital warmth, 443
as they grow old, 14
for earth too, 21
for my possessing too, 125
for what makes manhood, 27
he held them sixpence all too, 387
none so, 57
oh, how fondly, 135
ones wasted, an', 299
sea-coal fire when not too, 110
that bread should be so, 78
they will still be, 179
'tis expectation makes a blessing, 117
to heaven is saintly chastity, 47
to me as are the ruddy drops, 443
to me as life itself, 223
to the heart of our Lord, 160
Dearer than his horse, a little, 297
Dearest action in the tented field, 130
bliss, that, 27
foe in heaven, 73
friend to me, 145
truest the nearest and, 146
when joys are, 331
Dearie, my arms about my, 44
Dears, swears the lovely, 211
Death, 76–81
a glad relief, make our, 89
a Sultan to the realm of, 401
a woman as true as, 451
alone can break into the case, 403
and danger breathe, does only, 300
and existence, the things misnamed, 369
and pain, victor over, 199
and that vast forever, make life, 374
are all the same, life and, 155
assured alone that life and, 147
a thunder-clap, 123
a traveller between life and, 413
be sweeter, if, 241
befall you, lest worse than, 94
bravely as for life and, 120
bright beyond the gulf of, 159
by slanderous tongues, done to, 368
can vengeance be pursued further than, 424
come soon or late, 89
comes, so that when, 54
dares rush on, 191
dear as remembered kisses after, 205
did sign, the angel, 365
ere thou hast slain, 180
Falstaff sweats to, 210
for his ambition, 7
gone to her, 420
hail him at the gates of, 61
has left on her, 20
hymn to his own, 273
in battle, for the great prize o', 19
in that sleep of, 98
in the Revelation, 11
in the silent halls of, 227
into the world, brought, 93
into the valley of, 90

Death
is master of lord and clown, 103
is nigh, when, 273
lays his icy hand on kings, 127
leaves to its eternal rest, 221
life is perfected by, 206
made way for liberty, 217
mankind are equalized by, 114
manly brow consents to, 152
mature, for, 228
may not enter there, 209
meetest for, 439
mitigate the remembrance of, 50
must be, then bitter, 241
never taste of, 66
no certain life achieved by others, 27
no drinking after, 101
not guilty of his own, 213
of each day's life, 370
or give me, 217
or life, yield a step for, 431
our, the tree of knowledge, 414
poor child of doubt and, 330
proclaimed through our host, 156
run their horse to, 22
should sing, 't is strange that, 273
slavery or, 430
submission bondage and resistance, 391
succeeded life in her, 105
that it is light, 369
that none but, 206
the coward sneaks to, 66
the dull, cold ear of, 421
the old, old fashion, 191
the postman, or the bore, can keep out, 31
there was silence deep as, 364
the way to dusty, 411
those by, are few, 289
thou shalt seek, 69
though the black camel, 126
till they have wakened, 400
to engrossing, 118
to me, sweet is, 241
to us, 't is, 306
uncertain life and sure, 222
unloads thee, 336
was not the worst of all, 90
we owe God a, 89
were sated, here grief and, 374
what ugly sights of, 102
where is thy sting, 163
which happened in his berth, 22
with a rust, eaten to, 345
with that body's, 377
your ruling passion strong in, 297
Death-bed, 81
Death-fires, 81
Death-hymn, the wild swan's, 273
Death's bright angel, it may be that, 51
door, is brought to, 31
mystery, glad to, 244
Deaths, many times before their, 66
ye died I have watched beside, 349
Debased and hard, words so, 458
Debate, after much, 245
can a Roman senate long, 430
the faithful wife without, 442
Debating, 82
Debilitated, body, mind or moral nature must be, 425
Debility, the means of weakness and, 357
Debonair, buxom, blithe and, 41
Debt, 82
but Nature's, 89
but the debt of nature, I have no, 278
dread no foe but, 184
for so great a, 189
Debtor to his profession, every man a, 318
to you for courtesies, 65
Debtors do, and as most, 318
Debts, 82
are paid, my, 89
to pay, my, 232
with, to pay full-weight-dollar, 96
words pay no, 459
Decay, 82
and men, 300
and the dearest hopes, 125
are tainted to, 148
though the forms, 256
when love begins to sicken and, 238
Decayed fortune, the last effort of, 171
Deceit, 82
rumor of oppression and, 229
should dwell, 30
with a tear, and forgive her, 333
Deceits, 82
Deceive, 82
Deceived, 83
most egregiously, 397
was still, 92
Deceiver, 83
Deceivers, 83
Deceiving, what is hope but, 63
December, seek roses in, 67
the mirth of its, 331
when they wed, 457
Decency, 83
Decent, I hold it is not, 340
people, who came of, 348
priest, where monkeys were the gods, 316
Decide, 83
when doctors disagree, 94
Deck it was their field of fame, the, 288
my captain lies, where on the, 43
thee with all bays, 124
the lion-spirits that tread the, 133
Decked his brows, a nightcap, 282
thought thy bride-bed to have, 36
Decks, many a one on our, 133
Declaration, for the support of this, 307
(of Independence), what the, 8
of Independence, which make up the, 149

Declare, winds of the world, 111
Declared how much he knew, all, 206
Decline your nectared wine, none to, 152
Declined, end of language is, 210
Decrease it, yet heaven may, 238
 life is in, 81
 that now dilate and now, 52
Decree established, can alter a, 315
 hot temper leaps o'er a cold, 33
Decrees of Venice, no force in the, 213
Decried him, envy that, 122
Dedicate ourselves, rather, 276
Dedicated, rather to be, 276
Dee, lived on the river, 262
Deed, 83
 hope your warrant will bear out the, 433
 in fiery word or, 248
 is done for freedom, 143
 of shame, beneath our feet each, 170
 would he do, not a, 34
Deedless in his tongue, 84
Deeds, 83, 84
 are men, words are women, 459
 but pure in, 97
 by great thoughts and the good, 248
 displayed, his martial, 264
 I tell of the thrice-famous, 111
 not in words, but, 227
 not years, we live in, 227
 of men, through the, 126
 of mercy, to render the, 260
 ready for a hero's, 54
 that doth gentil, 150
 turnpikes leading to free, 31
 words are no, 459
Deemed of them, if we better, 191
Deep, 84
 across the, may go, 409
 a home on the rolling, 288
 and still, this sleep so, 369
 as a well, 't is not so, 189
 call spirits from the vasty, 381
 caverns, voices from the, 163
 drew from out the boundless, 18
 fishes that tipple in the, 133
 from the great, 18
 in ruin as in guilt, 342
 in the lowest, 178
 into the fatal bowels of the, 346
 my love as, 239
 out of the, 18
 there's danger on the, 304
 to that last, 18
 to the great, 18
 to the swelling, 101
 where the brook is, 435
Deeper than all speech, thought is, 403
Deep-tangled wildwood, the, 49
Deer, 84
 mice and rats and such small, 261
 my own stricken, 31
Defamed by every charlatan, 150
Defect, than the, 28
Defects, exact my own, 260
 of doubt, 160
Defence, 84
 immodest words admit of no, 83
 to bear, in your, 355
Defend, foremost to, 176
 the right, God, 338
 the wronged and the weak to, 173
 us, angels and ministers, 9
Defendant, plaintiff or, 92
Defendants, women plaintiffs or, 455
Defended, oft have heard, 260
Defends the land, that, 353
Defensive to a house, 112
Defer, 84
Defiance, 84
 bid, to all the force of the crown, 44
 in their eye, 316
 in their faces stern, 130
Defiant, mad, but not, 244
Defies its point, 191
Defiled, they that touch pitch will be, 401
Defined, all well, 387
Definition of a proverb is, my, 320
Defy, and I, 218
 they will, 322
Degenerate, 84
Degree better, is in some, 54
 of delight, we have a, 265
 of woe, by some, 448
Degrees, and in these, 242
 fine by, 131
 gather by unseen, 167
 it grows up by, 261
 of the lie, the, 218
Dejected 'haviour of the visage, 448
Delay, chides his infamous, 251
 in, there lies no plenty, 239
 rises in demand for her, 265
 sweet, reluctant, amorous, 391
 the law's, 323
Deliberates, 85
Deliberation, 85
Delicious bed, 21
Delight, gives his youth, 49
 go to 't with, 40
 he drank, 295
 in doing one's work in life, to, 460
 she was a phantom of, 302
 their tales of, 207
 to bark and bite, let dogs, 95
 to the night when our, 361
 twinkle with a crystalline, 23
 we have a degree of, 265
Delighted spirit, the, 90
Delightful as a wife, half so, 442
 task, to rear the tender thought, 398
Delights, all thoughts, all passions, all, 234
 to scorn, 123
Deliver, will a round unvarnished tale, 396

Deliverance, blended sound of battle, and, 461
its angels of, 255
Delivered, a nation saved, a race, 277
upon the mellowing of occasion, 258
Delivers in such apt, 196
Dells, all about the breezy, 52
Deluge showers, the rain a, 26
Delve one yard below their mines, 110
Demagogue, who can stand before a, 259
Demand for her delay, rises in, 265
new measures, new times, 281
Demands, a time like this, 259
Dem'd, damp, moist, unpleasant body, 28
Demeanour, 85
Demi-paradise, 112
Democrats, wrinkles the damned, 465
Demon of Drunkenness, the wandering, 102
that tempts us within, the, 120
Demoniac throng, by, 374
Demons down under the sea, the, 236
Demonstrative, but not, 376
Demurely, look, 372
Den, 85
Denied him, fate that then, 122
him, not she, 67
in heaven the soul, 176
that comes to be, 427
to friends and visitors, 345
was death, 81
Denies them, grants them, or, 394
Denmark, ne'er a villain dwelling in all, 426
rotten in the State of, 344
Denote me truly, that can, 448
Deny, he that will this health, 172
me, fie upon your law, if you, 213
nothing, I, 60
would fain, 223
Depart, and I am ready to, 221
better cheer, ere you, 48
come like shadows, so, 358
the captains and the king, 139
then quick, 283
to drink deep, ere you, 100
Departed, and all but he, 17
may return no more, once, 334
once, come no more, 334
Departing breath, with his, 61
leave behind us, 138
Department, the most important, 54
Departments, with all the public, 54
Departs, he ne'er, 305
when youth, the dream, 470
Departure, a fair, 1
and no friend take note of thy, 86
Depend, on exercise, 172
Depended, late on hopes, 464
Deplore thee, but we will not, 163
Depolarize, 85
Deprecated war, both parties, 431
Depth, far beyond my, 153
Depth in philosophy bringeth men's minds, 14
of the abyss may be, the, 293
thy breadth and thy, 403
Depths, 85
have more, the, 354
like a pebble, into its, 173
sounded all the, 140
through the dark blue, 268
Deputy of oak, had got a, 216
Derides, sport that wrinkled care, 382
Derive, this doctrine I, 118
Deriving their just powers, 161
Descend, into the dust, 103
to, ambition and revenge, 7
Descends in love, heaven itself, 233
Descent, 85
claims of long, 148
precipitous, the, 305
Desert, 85
air, on the, 149
as you came in the, 392
fair virtue's way, I might, 429
faring, o'er life's drear, 232
I come to thee, from the, 86
nothing went unrewarded but, 421
shall rejoice, the, 443
shines in the dry, 364
use every man after his, 440
Desert-circle spreads, the, 268
Deserted, 86
mansion, the door of the, 91
some banquet-hall, 17
Deserts are small, or his, 126
Deserve better of mankind, would, 162
it, don't, 392
it, we'll, 392
not punishment, 157
the precious bane, that soil may best, 336
Deserved, as he, 183
Deserves no name, 147
the fair, 34
Design, may baffle his, 262
unfinished lies, the great, 79
who knows the inscrutable, 164
Designs, in the centre of his thin, 353
Desire, 86
but its surcease, not, 4
contents his natural, 176
in your true heart's, 83
liveth not in fierce, 237
Lorde, I thee, 140
more love and knowledge of you, I shall, 462
not a moth with vain, 160
our low, 233
prayer is the soul's sincere, 313
the utmost share of, 100
thou nurse of young, 185
thrills the fond soul with wild, 236
to hear her speak again, 238
to rest, and I, 333
too much, can one, 159
we may be better strangers, 389

Desire
with dead, it doth not die, 237
will be the, 190
Desired, hurts and is, 79
Desires, 86
thee, no German maid, 151
Desirest, more than thou, 199
Desolation, demonstrating a careless, 239
sword and, 329
Despair, and infinite, 177
in the jolly black-jack, 26
or hope, texts of, 24
the hurried question of, 107
there breathes, 125
wasting in, 120
where reason would, 185
where seraphs might, 270
ye taste of our, 465
Despairing, 86
of what it would, 232
Desperate, 86
men, often the resort of, 298
part, a silent and, 61
Desperatest is the wisest course, 86
Despicable state, nor, 434
Despise me, ay, do, 86
Despised, 86
love, the pangs of, 323
Despot's heel is on thy shore, the, 255
Destinies, all men's, 306
Destiny, 86
grasp of vengeful, 127
obscure, and, 310
whereon is writ his, 384
Destroy his fib or sophistry, 353
not in after wrath, 107
one to, 272
Destroyed, by himself, 306
by thought, 33
not one life shall be, 160
when once, 300
Destroyer, 87
Destroying others, 306
Destructive, damnable, deceitful woman, 452
Detect, by his look, 306
Detection increases every day, danger of, 82
Detector of the heart, a, 81
Determine, doctors cannot quite, 89
Detest th' offence, yet, 289
Detested a quarrel, and, 308
Detraction will not suffer it, 185
Deuce gae wi'm to believe me, 458
Devil, 87, 88
and thou a merry, 400
bid you, if the, 156
can cite Scripture, the, 353
get thee gone, go, poor, 189
himself, sugar o'er the, 88
how the, they got there, 458
if the, to serve his turn, 218
in his sneer, a laughing, 372
in, to serve the, 228
laugh, it always makes the, 447
Devil
let us call thee, 445
of his will, curb this cruel, 213
over his own coals, call the, 347
represent the, 115
ruled the woman, the, 449
some play the, 285
take her, the, 240
tell truth and shame the, 417
they bade him go . . . to the, 183
thought of his old friend, 11
we'll face the, 19
which might appal the, 251
whispered behind the leaves, 13
will fetch me now in fire, and the, 448
with him was God or, 324
Devil's booth, at the, 177
cellar, the, 178
pet words, another of the, 422
wife was but a fiend, 464
Devils are here, all the, 178
Devise, I give and I, 91
laws for the blood, 33
wit! write, pen, 466
Devoid of sense and motion, 90
Devotion, 88
dust, perhaps a name, 274
wafts the mind above, 233
the last full measure of, 276
we take increased 276
Devour the way, seemed in running to, 345
Devoured as fast, which are, 407
Devours them all, 133
Devoutly, love prays, 235
Dew, are cooling, 160
as sunlight drinketh, 204
drop forgiveness from heaven like, 140
falling like, 192
fresh-blown roses washed in, 343
morning roses newly washed with, 343
of sleep, the timely, 370
of yon high eastward hill, 269
resolve itself into a, 134
soft falls the, 311
the ripe ruddy, 226
trembling as the, 245
washed with morning, 398
Dewdrop, had sparkled as a, 378
from its wing, shook the, 210
shall lingering lie, like a, 203
Dewlapped, 88
Dews away, brushing . . . the, 392
drawn up like morning, 19
Dewy grass among, haste the, 151
eve, from noon to, 122
Dial, 88
Diamond, 88
Diamonds, 88
as Sappho's, 410
three times eight large, 73
Diaries, will bravely jot down in, 352
Dicers' oaths, as false as, 287

Dick the shepherd, and, 190
Dictates to be done, 61
Did it, alone I, 7
it, thou canst not say I, 229
Diddled, taste for being, 103
Die, 88–91
a bachelor, 16
a dry death, 80
are but born and, 351
as much beauty as could, 427
because a woman's fair, 120
because he cannot, 191
before they sing, persons, 366
but fools they cannot, 138
but that which wished to, 76
but to obtain or, 233
by God, he shall not, 287
by which we live and, 30
cry out . . . enough! and, 4
dear, die, 232
do we not, 197
even fools would wish to, 81
for Dixie, live or, 94
for her, to fight and, 189
for love, must, 384
glad did I live and gladly, 163
go and sin till you, 365
hazard of the, 44
if for widows you, 442
if I should, 370
if need be to, 120
if we are marked to, 185
in, for a corner to, 176
in moulding Sheridan, broke the, 359
in music, and, 273
in that old arm-chair, saw her, 173
in the last ditch, I will, 93
in thy lap, 174
is thrown, all of theirs upon that, 455
is to, 136
it was sure to, 148
laws and learning, 284
lay their eggs and, 64
let me, 241
let the ape and tiger, 20
like Hector in the field to, 28
live or, 366
love like ours can never, 242
many times before their deaths, 66
may sicken and so, 273
more proudly than to, 351
no man can help you, 129
not valiant that dares, 422
or like Douglas, 97
shaft that made him, 106
she must weep or she will, 76
sinks downward here to, 270
swans sing before they, 366
teach the rustic moralist to, 401
the fading flower shall, 327
the soul . . . shall never, 376
the wounded to, 39
to make men free, let us, 225
unknown, or, 124
Die
upon the hand, to, 169
was not made to, 104
we must be free or, 412
with dead desire it doth not, 237
with love and never dream we're dead, 235
wilt thou too, 377
Xerxes must, 467
Died, 91
a conquered man, and has, 321
Alexander, 421
and new-born baby, 425
and they, 284
and when I, 265
an' when the vartoos, 111
blessing her, tell her that I, 243
but the woman, 453
for her, that they, 416
for men, on a man that, 104
for thee, would God I had, 1
from time to time, men have, 238
made way for liberty and, 217
in bitter pains, 109
in Christ the Saviour, 220
in harness, he, 90
in harness here, 90
in vain, resolve they have not, 276
in vain, shall not have, 276
of the slow fever called the tertian, 441
or perish as they, 128
o' Wednesday, he that, 185
sleeping when she, 105
the dog it was that, 95
to make men holy, as he, 225
to save, martyrs, 416
what else can be foretold, 228
young, well, he, 151
Dies, 91
a man, every moment, 69
among his worshippers, 415
and fancy, 124
as when a giant, 80
at every word a reputation, 332
but never surrenders, the Guard, 166
he that, 82
in a desperate stress, 376
in single blessedness, 342
love never, 235
married young, best married that, 254
ne'er like angels till our passion, 297
of lockjaw, error, 415
once has blown for ever, 135
so when a great man, 138
the good man never, 159
the same, then, 251
to-day who, 75
when love is done, 281
with the dying sun, 281
yet never, 28
Diet, like one that takes, 239
Dieter, and he her, 62
Dietetics, gruel and the, 363

Dieth, when the warrior, 433
Differ as heaven and earth, men at most, 259
Difference feeling, no, 386
should be, strange all this, 418
there is little, 369
Different dooms our birthdays bring, 25
Difficile, Latin was no more, 165
Difficult, better, though, 159
Diffused from pole to pole, 161
Dig the dust, to, 29
the grave and let me lie, 163
Digest of anarchy, institute and, 338
it, I shall, 395
Digested, some few to be chewed and, 30
Digestion, 91
Dighton Rock, like that on, 175
Dignities, a peace above all earthly, 299
Dignity and love, in every gesture, 161
into it, interest or, 208
of crimes, may reach the, 167
Dilate and now decrease, that now, 52
Dim and sad, morn came, 105
my sandals, I would not, 152
religious light, casting a, 225
the sun himself grow, 191
those perplexed and patient eyes were, 118
Dime, from half a dime to a, 403
Dimensions, senses, 197
Diminished, 91
heads, hide their, 172
Dimmed and gone, now, 258
Dimmed the light of heaven, 155
Dimple, 91
or smile, beguile with a, 398
Dine, 92
Dined or supped on fame, who ever, 123
to-day, I have, 349
Dining, where is the man that can live without, 63
Ding, chiels that winna, 119
dong, bell, 124
Dinner, 92
it was presently after, 239
Dinner-bell, 92
Dinner-time, if it's near, 92
it will be, 413
Dinners by the dozen, I'd, 319
Dipped me in ink, 466
Dire effects from civil discord flow, 93
Direct, 92
and honest, to be, 183
the lie, the seventh, 218
the understanding to, 173
Direction, all chance, 337
I cannot leave you my, 89
Directly to say I love you, 238
Directors, 92
Directs the storm, and, 388
Dirge, hark to the, 298
is sung, by forms unseen their, 34
Dirge, sing a, for St. Hugh's soul, 32
Dirt, 92
in poverty, hunger and, 361
is loss of, 360
or, or grubs or worms, 458
rather turn to, 158
to fall out with 361
Dirty, 92
gods, who worship, 158
politics, construed to mean, 310
Disabused, by himself abused or, 462
Disadvantage, a ship has the additional, 359
Disagree, when doctors, 94
Disappear, to see my bright ones, 19
Disappointed, 92
Disapprove, than that which you, 397
Disaster, yield the other up to, 155
Disasters, 93
Discard, his labour will often, 390
Discern, living sparks we still, 4
Disciples fight, differing doctors and, 162
Discontent, 93
Discontented or hungry jurymen, 92
Discord, 93
all, harmony not understood, 338
all your danger is in, 433
Discords, in dismal, 25
Discourse, 93
is his, 196
of reason, a beast that wants, 20
Discover virtue, adversity doth best, 427
what anguish to, 242
which to, 72
Discovered the use of tobacco, who first, 408
Discovers, on all their light, 384
Discovery, the world give for the, 403
Discredit more in hiding, 128
Discreet, I'm too, 350
Discretion, 93
that they might not want, 82
the better part of valour is, 423
Disdain, to feel the day's, 369
Disdained if falsehood's honey it, 411
Disdainful smile, with a, 310
Disdains her shattered cell, 367
the shadow which he treads on, 392
Disease, 93
the remedy is worse than the, 330
Diseases desperate grown, 86
physic, is for all, 445
subject to the same, 197
to commodity, I will turn, 301
Disfavour, bring religion's self into, 52
Disgrace, and most their sires 367
hidden from the heart's, 108
my man's apparel, 68
saintly mountebanks the porch, 52
what a burnin', 16
would be a, 132
Disguised by philosophic names, murders, 272

Disgust, that inward, 176
Dish, an ancient classical, 96
a noble, 32
fit for the gods, a, 201
for a king, 6
in that one, 32
that tempts an o'ergorged epicure, 92
Dishes, pans, pots, 16
Dishonour lurks, where danger or, 443
not your mothers, 270
party faithlessness is party, 297
past all, 20
Dishonourable graves, find ourselves, 58
Dishonoured, lost for evermore, shattered, 107
Disinherited, profaned and, 188
Dislike, and hesitate, 71
Dislikes, the rate of his pay, he, 390
Dislimns, the rock, 56
Disloyalty, to doubt would be, 337
Dismal discords sung, in, 25
Dismay, let nothing you, 51
Disobedience, 93
Disobey, 93
fain promise never more to, 429
Disorder, a sweet, in the dress, 364
with most admired, 264
Disordered, nothing impaired but all, 380
Disparage their best and dearest friend, 322
Dispatch you straight, it would, 389
Dispatched, at once, 370
Dispense with bolts and locks, when banks, 216
Disperse to nought, it, 53
Displaced the mirth, you have, 264
Displayed, his martial deeds, 264
is the net of the fowler, 280
Dispose, the stars, they say cannot, 306
Disposed when so, 32
Disposes, man proposes but God, 155
Disposition, horridly to shake our, 268
Dispraised, of whom to be, 312
Dispute, my right there is none to, 266
Disputed, downa be, 119
Disrobe the lion of that robe, 226
Dissection, form good subjects for, 351
Dissemble, 93
pause to parley or, 87
Dissemblers, that are the greatest, 310
Dissembling, subtle, 83
Dissensions, of your wrangles and, 433
Dissever my soul, can ever, 236
Dissevered, discordant, belligerent, 420
Dissimulation drops her mask, tired, 81
Dissolve, the great globe itself . . . shall, 428
the political bonds, to, 356
Dissolved from my hive, I quickly were, 436
Dissolved in air, love's wild prayer, 366
in his wine, was, 153
Distaff, and holdeth the, 451
Distance, 93
takes a lovelier hue, the, 457
their lies an outer, 178
Distant drum, rumble of a, 44
mien, the, the lofty port, 316
Distil it out, observingly, 160
Distilled, earthlier happy is the rose, 342
in which roses have once been, 258
Distilling, should understand, 440
Distinction between virtue and vice, no, 425
Distinctions, to make proper, 397
Distinguish, 93
Distinguished by black, brown or fair, best, 455
Distraction in 's aspect, 307
Distress, and double thy, 265
Distressed, is a mind, 333
that harass the, 195
District, wen he gits to the, 60
Disturb a hornet's nest, dangerous to, 186
Ditch, 93
Ditchers and grave-makers, 150
Dithering stands, needy labour, 207
Divan, the dry, 102
Dive, they shall, 350
Diver, 93
Divers tones, in, 170
Divide a hair, distinguish and, 93
for ever can, 206
thin partitions do their bounds, 245
Divided duty, a, 104
excellence, a fair, 168
we fall, 420
Dividends, with, 32
Dividing, and his cares, 443
by, we fall, 420
Divine, 94
all save the spirit of man is, 426
he who can, 337
human face, 118
in hookas, 408
the highest human nature is, 338
in rapture brief almost, 234
makes drudgery, 102
may kill a sound, 201
of kings, the right, 161
Providence, the protection of, 307
thou love, 232
tobacco, 408
to forgive, 140
what crisis does, 306
Divinely, 94
Diviner's theme, the glad, 98
Divines can say, 376
Divinity, 94
doth hedge a king, 202
in odd numbers, there is, 286
Division of a battle knows, nor the, 382

Divorced old barren Reason, 426
Dixie, 94
Do, 94
a hand to, 173
and die, theirs but to, 90
anything, though you, 239
earnest of the things that they shall, 461
it, how not to, 54
it, if it be man's work, 251
it yourself, you must, 96
more, Sempronius, we'll, 392
noble things, not dream them, 374
that I cannot, 443
that I shall be sorry for, 315
the Samaritan, ready enough to, 349
to-day, which you can, 408
to me, for that they, 140
unto the other feller, 82
vum, I, 74
we must what force, 139
what few or none would, 159
what men may, 259
which he can never, 130
you more, Sempronius, 392
Docks and stocks and slips, launched from the, 461
Doctor, 94
but himself, therein, 200
than fee the, 172
Doctors, 94
and disciples fight, 162
cannot quite determine, 89
give what they would take, and, 214
Doctrine, 95
for of such, 200
from women's eyes this, 118
of ignoble ease, not the, 389
orthodox, prove their, 329
Documents, the things named pants in certain, 294
Doe, some draw pleas for John, 146
Does a wise one, nor ever, 202
Doff it for shame, 226
Dog, 95
bark, let no, 291
because he hath wakened thy, 322
broodin' over bein' a, 134
but the poor, 176
cut-throat, 147
his day, and every, 469
his faithful, 176
is good fer a, 134
or horse, 38
rather be a, 36
so, a heart to curse my, 395
something better than his, 297
think of that, my, 45
to be used as you use your, 378
tongue of, 179
will have his day, 45
Doggies gang to heaven, do, 176
Dogmatist, thou testy little, 200
Dogrose, 95
Dog's obeyed in office, a, 289
Dogs, 95
between two, 213
howled, 25
liable to be torn by, 292
of war, let slip the, 335
orses and, 187
shall drink him, men and, 248
throw physic to the, 303
Doing, 96
and still be, 329
battle for the saints, 395
be up and, 2
joy's soul lies in the, 198
nothing was his curse, 285
or suffering, 436
Doings, all my, 386
Dole, with a temporal, 114
Doled, stolen, borrowed, squandered, 157
Doleful dumps the mind oppress, 166
Doll, 96
Dollar, 96
Dolve, when Adam, 149
Domain his own, such a vast, 112
or extension of, 110
Dome, beneath some ample hallowed, 264
more vast, with a, 376
of thought, the, 367
that fired the Ephesian, 123
the hand that rounded Peter's, 39
yet be the, 267
Domestic life, the charities of, 413
Dominies there, and, 176
Dominion over sea and land, to have, 402
Dominions, mid the night's, 284
Donald mair, nor think o', 364
Dove, 96
agin', it's ollers askin' to be, 40
and labour's, 35
as they did, 51
forgot as soon as, 407
for us, what has posterity, 311
in the right way, can best be, 459
nay I have, 296
ne'er can say my work is, 451
so little, 94
something attempted, something, 410
still be doing, never, 329
the deed, I have, 83
things won are, 198
thy long day's work, 35
what has by man been, 94
what's, 172
when love is, 281
what were good to be, 397
will all be, 257
Doom, by which he meets his, 106
can half-control his, 338
did receive, hard, 115
my blessing, not my, 459
the loud trumpet of eternal, 353
to the scaffold and the, 351
unriddled, our, 103

Doomed for a certain term, 380
to pay, hourly, 106
Dooms one to those dreadful words, 68
our birthdays bring, 25
Doomsday, houses . . . last till, 164
Door, 96
a knock at the, 84
and closed the, 221
another name was on the, 275
good John, shut the, 206
have borne him to your, 375
his fiddle hehind the, 261
is brought to death's, 31
new face at the, 119
no spiked and panelled, 31
of darkness through, passed the, 72
of her house, at the, 296
of thy heart, open the, 240
open then the, 77
slam the, 94
stand within that holy, 115
stood at the open, 194
take thy form from off my, 19
the locking of the, 91
the Pale Horse, stands, at my, 186
there was the, 423
were shut, as if a, 52
write on your, 28
Doors, goings in and out these, 222
of breath, the, 118
to let out life, 79
with flame, I shuttered my, 284
Dormouse, 96
Dote on his very absence, 1
nature, they say, doth, 179
upon a jest, 196
when wit doth, 136
Dotes on truer charms, that, 246
yet doubts, who, 243
Double debt to pay, a, 295
drill, and no canteen, it's, 395
quantity of salt, to add a, 349
sense, in a, 318
set, a, 100
thread, sewing at once with a, 362
thy distress, and, 265
wrong, he does me, 134
Doubler tongue than thine, with, 412
Doublet and hose, when he goes in his, 251
and hose ought, 68
for wearing his new, 322
of the Lincoln green, a, 403
Doubling his pleasures, 443
Doubly dying, and, 65
sure, I'll make assurance, 14
Doubt, 97
against the shafts of, 120
and certain-sure belief, trembling, 234
and death, poor child of, 330
and soundest casuists, 94
beyond, all, 155
defects of, 160
Doubt
dimmed the light of heaven with, 155
distract, horror and, 178
I'll see before I, 195
in, we'll go together, 377
never stand to, 14
no, to be sure, 284
not through the ages, yet I, 322
or blame, that none might, 274
spout out, jealous, 115
to, would be disloyalty, 337
to solve a learned, 433
Doubted, never, clouds would break, 337
Doubting in his abject spirit, 34
Doubtless God never did, 10
Doubts, 97
and fears, saucy, 41
are fear, the littlest, 238
who dotes yet, 243
who tempt with, 347
Dough, my cake is, 41
on both sides, 41
Douglas, 97
blood, ne'er cools the, 4
in his hall, 85
tender and true, 140, 352
wets his manly eye, when, 398
Dove, 97
as valiant as the wrathful, 422
changes on the burnished, 241
more of the serpent than the, 205
roar you as gently as any sucking, 339
the hawk shall nestle with the, 300
with a fondness of a, 173
Dovecote, like an eagle in a, 106
Doves say, what do the, 235
will peck in safeguard of their brood, 463
Dowagers for deans, 162
Down, 97
as low as high, 7
it merrily, and, 32
now, now up, 39
or pardoned being, 260
quite, quite, 263
smoothing the raven, 282
Downhill it is, yet, 460
Downright loving, the, 203
Downs, and o'er unhabitable, 252
Downstairs, why did you kick me, 93
Doxy, heterodoxy is another man's, 291
orthodoxy . . . is my, 291
Dozing all the day, 101
Drachmas, drop my blood for, 207
Drag thee down, weight to, 189
the slow barge, 386
Dragon, 98
Dragonish, cloud that's, 56
Dragon's tail, baited with a, 439
Drags its slow length along, 6
Drain, a bumper I, 51
jars were made to, 445

Drain the bowl, while we, 55
Drained by fevered lips, 435
Drains a people's blood, sucks and, 64
Drama with the day, 109
Drank as 't were their mother's milk, 181
  delight, he, 295
  in joy, from which he, 107
  of the water again, and, 348
  your fill, eat and, 228
Drapery of his couch, wraps the, 227
Drat that cat, 44
Draught of cool refreshment, yet its, 435
  for a nauseous, 172
  he took a long and solemn, 181
  of heavenly pleasure, 402
  of Old England's ale, than a, 281
  sips the nearest, 232
Draughts, full of supper and distempering, 393
  intoxicate the brain, shallow, 215
Draw a cart, I cannot, 251
  a furrer straighter, nor, 249
  from the earth, 188
  in again, did soon, 129
  it, take a sword an', 156
  men as they ought to be, to, 294
  new mischief on, next way to, 271
  pleas for John Doe, some, 146
  sword for liberty, some, 146
  the curtain and show, 69
  the curtains close, 80
  the line somewheres, necessary to, 225
  them, I would not, 103
  this curtain, 69
  this metal from my side, that I must, 442
  up the papers, lawyer, 292
  you to her with a single hair, 168
Drawers, a chest of by day, 295
Draweth out the thread of his verbosity, he, 424
Drawing nothing up, growing old in, 39
Drawn mature and perfect, 288
  out, linked sweetness long, 394
  the wine of life is, 270
  to him, our eyes were, 244
  up like morning dews, 19
  upon his memory, the gentleman has, 291
  with the lash, 199
  with the sword, 199
Draws his furrer ez straight ez he can, 356
  the sword reluctant, who, 317
  us with a single hair, 168
Dray, steering like a, 215
Dread and fear of kings, the, 260
  doth walk in fear and, 128
  no foe but debt, 184
  of something after death, 79
  shape, through this, 188
  that man should, 21
Dread the loss of use, I rather, 421
  thing, the grave, 162
  to see, river so, 403
Dreaded of man, 87
Dreadful note, a deed of, 83
Dream, 98
  a, a shadow, 219
  a hope beyond the shadow of a, 185
  as love's young, 236
  departs, when youth, the, 470
  if this be all an idle, 237
  I wrought a murder in a, 272
  liberty, the prisoner's pleasing, 217
  life is an empty, 221
  life is but an empty, 222
  life, what is it but a, 221
  like the hand which ends a, 77
  of her brooding breast, with a, 97
  of heaven, she did but, 105
  of life, when my, 236
  of passion, in a, 307
  or grave apart, to keep a, 220
  rebuild in it the music and the, 467
  sew them on in a, 460
  should be, bliss that such a, 293
  them all day long, not, 374
  the old men's, 98
  we're dead, and never, 235
Dreamed, never, . . . wrong would triumph, 337
  that life was beauty, 104
Dreaming, 98
Dreams, 98, 99
  and lies down to pleasant, 227
  and slumbers light, pleasing, 371
  are, of such stuffs as, 428
  are made on, such stuff as, 428
  cannot picture, 209
  have boded, my, 211
  infest the grave, if, 98
  may come, what, 98
  of love and truth, 88
  of pleasure, what, 367
  of the future, rise from your, 409
  of youth recall, who vainly the, 470
  your old men shall dream, 98
Dreamt it again, thrice ere the morning I, 427
  of in your philosophy, than are, 303
Drear and dark, the night both, 26
Dregs were wormwood, he found the, 464
Drenched . . . in fraternal blood, 420
  me in the sea, 131
Dress, a black, or a white, 295
  a sweet disorder in the, 364
  of thoughts, style is the, 391
Dressed, 99
  all in my best, I'm, 74
  how then was the devil, 87
  in a little brief authority, 251
  in an opinion, to be, 291
Dresses, neat-handed Phyllis, 303
Dressings fit, for every season she hath, 20

Drew from out the boundless deep, 18
my midnight curtains round, 167
near, their lips, 204
them as they are, who, 294
with one long kiss, once he, 204
Dries them with his hair, 194
Drift beyond his love and care, I cannot, 43
Drifted by, that have, 434
Drink, 99–101
again, gapes for, 101
a man may, 249
as friends, eat and, 214
before his wife, shall, 348
below, wants but little, 249
but I, every creature, 101
but tears, she drinks no other, 399
deep or taste not, 215
is another's meat or, 309
it down, I'll, 78
John, 't will do you good, 40
nor any drop to, 435
of it first, if the wife should, 348
of schnapps, a goot long, 351
on my score, all shall eat and, 267
out of skulls, they, 379
small beer, to, 130
the toddy, 321
the words you send, with mine eyes I'll, 466
't is to thee that I would, 439
to me, wittles and, 187
to my flame, summoned to, 274
to poor damned souls, givin', 395
to the general joy, 172
to the lass, 210
wine was made to, 445
with him that wears a hood, 6
with you, I will not, 41
your honour's health, glad to, 310
Drinketh dew, as sunlight, 204
Drinking, 101, 102
asses' milk and writing, this comes of, 466
can do for him, what, 34
deep, call, 102
fresh and fair, with constant, 101
largely sobers us again, 215
is the soldier's pleasure, 16
joys did first ordain, 16
very merry, dancing, 71
Drinks, and, 101
all night, he that, 169
hot blood for wine, who, 301
no other drink but tears, 399
Drip of the suspended oar, the light, 286
Drive, the horse I, 186
the rapid car, or, 386
Driven into her breast, this post was, 388
to church as to the parish pound, 52
Driver sings, which the mad, 298
Drives, that the devil, 87
Driving far off each thing, 47
the poor fry, 133
Drones, purge the land of these, 133
Droop and drowse, begin to, 282
with heaviness, when they, 293
Drop be spilt, let not a, 78
every, hinders needle and thread, 438
in the well, were't the last, 439
into thy mother's lap, thou, 228
my blood, and, 267
of allaying Tiber in 't, not a, 445
of blood, until every, 199
of Christian blood, 134
of ink, a small, 192
tears as fast as the Arabian trees, 399
there's a spell in its every, 100
to drink, nor any, 435
Dropped a tear upon the word, 287
from an angel's wing, 301
Droppeth as the gentle rain, it, 260
Dropping buckets into empty wells, 39
Droppings of the sky, the, 101
Drops, dear as the ruddy, 443
dear to me as are the ruddy, 443
do something drown, these foolish, 381
her mask, tired dissimulation, 81
in his vast and wandering grave, 347
like kindred, 110
of rain, stones with, 252
two, two mites, 265
of red, the bleeding, 43
that warm my heart, ruddy, 443
the closing eye requires, 35
Dross, 102
and stuff, 266
each ounce of, 177
Dross-allayed, for what he lent him, 82
Drove 'em, danced 'em, 363
from out the mother's nest, 106
Drown, 102
a fly, or to, 377
my manly spirit, 381
Providence wun't, 320
Drowned in the brook, 137
in yonder living blue, and, 457
where I am, 131
Drowns him, sin that often, 101
Drowse, begin to droop and, 282
Drowsy ear of night, 22
man, vexing the dull ear of a, 400
Drudge, condemned to, 245
disobedient, for a, 141
into a kitchen, 232
Drudgery, 102
Drum, 102
an' a fife, in front of a, 11
broken by trumpet and, 390
rumble of a distant, 44
the spirit-stirring, 125
Drum-beat, whose morning, 112
Drums, arms reversed and muffled, 433
begin to roll, when the, 180
like muffled, 163

Drunk, 102
and no be, 249
and once sober, once, 82
must get, 193
my share of wine, I have, 221
their cup, have, 333
the monks of St. Bothan's ale, I have, 267
with choler, 50
your water and wine, I have, 349
Drunkenness, 102
Drury Lane Dane slain, 115
Dry, and keep your powder, 311
as summer dust, 91
death, fain die a, 80
if perhaps you're, 321
streaming tear to, 219
when mother earth is, 101
Dublin town, he built a church in, 348
Ducat, and every part a, 103
dead, for a, 75
in six thousand ducats, every, 103
Ducats, 103
lend three thousand, 95
ten thousand, to have it baned, 325
Duck again as low, 400
trailing like a wounded, 54
Due, give the devil his, 87
to the devil, and so give his, 87
to the devil, give his, 87
to the Moor my lord, 189
upon the bond, here appeareth, 213
Dug his fingers into the wet earth, 313
Duke, genteelly damned beside a, 149
he was indeed the, 219
let us bury the Great, 271
or lord, as, 248
Dukedom large enough, my library was, 218
volumes that I prize above my, 31
Dull and dry, conversations, 62
as night, 273
ass will not mend his pace, 33
at whiles, though it's, 460
though gentle yet not, 84
thy palm, do not, 146
when I am, 196
Dulled their eyes with sin, 155
Dulls the edge of husbandry, 31
Dumb, and the dead, steered by the, 357
driven cattle, be not like, 179
modest men are, 265
terror, when this, 147
when the lips are, 174
Dumblane, the sweet flower o', 364
Dumb-shows and noise, inexplicable, 379
Dump, game was n't worth a, 77
Dumps the mind oppress, 166
Dumpy woman, I hate a, 94
Duncan, hear it not, 205
Dunce with wits, and a, 447
Dunces, a wit with, 447
Dune and headland, on, 139
Dungeon, scourged to his, 227
Dunsinane, till Birnam wood remove to, 25
Dupe of to-morrow, 92
Duped people, the, 106
Dupes, 103
if hopes were, 391
Duplicates of it, often . . . have, 129
Durance, 103
Durst not play, could not, would not, 306
poet touch a pen to write, never, 308
Dusk, like the, 246
of evening, 4
were mine, thy dawn and, 230
Dust, 103, 104
a heap of, 334
Alexander returneth into, 421
and ashes, for, 361
and from that scattered, 441
an hour may lay it in the, 385
away, steal his, 29
bends above his, 145
benison o'er the sleeping, 157
but earth and, 89
dry as summer, 91
enclosed here, 29
every pinch of human, 115
in glitt'ring, 362
lay the summer's, 27
lies dead, in the, 209
no dawn, no, 285
of Alexander, the noble, 421
of books, amid the, 416
our paper, make, 164
perhaps a name, 274
provoke the silent, 421
returnest, to, 222
Shovel, and we run to the, 56
smell sweet and blossom in their, 199
so nigh is grandeur to our, 104
the knight's bones are, 29
this grave, this, 406
thou art, 222
thou would'st not save, 76
to kindred dust, ashes to ashes, 13
to the vile, 65
tread is on an empire's, 109
when the original is, 123
Wickliffe's, shall spread abroad, 441
write the characters in, 450
ye tamely tread, 152
Dustman's, as big as a, 22
Dutch cheese, heel of a, 48
Duties know, who their, 385
meet, domestic, 452
new occasions teach new, 281
Duty, 104, 105
and if we did our, 462
and love a simple, 236
and so much, 189
as the subject, such, 454
broke, no, 466
dare to do our, 337
for ever, the picket's off, 311

Duty
gives from a sense of, 7
in unobtrusive ways of, 145
joy was, 214
party honesty is party, 297
seemed to call, 90
so ought they of, 318
who thought his, 308
Dwell a weeping hermit there, to, 34
contented to, 446
dame truth delights to, 418
nor be where thou dost, 125
therein, fiend-like is it to, 365
where peace and rest can never, 299
Dwellest thou, where, 43
Dwelling in all Denmark, ne'er a villain, 426
Dwelling-place, became thy, 377
that the desert were my, 85
what kind of, 176
Dwelt, bard here, 18
Dwindle, shall, shall blend, 78
Dyeing scarlet, 102
Dying, 105
after, all reprieve's too late, 59
all away, now, 52
answer echoes, 382
cause, ring out a slowly, 339
daily, that we are, 79
eyes were closed, thy, 139
fire, behind a slowly, 301
groans of the, 83
hand, with, 47
man to dying men, and as a, 314
only fault was, 90
rich, rage canine of, 336
sigh, a sick man's, 119
sun, dies with the, 281
the old year lies a-, 468
thus around us, 75
to-morrow will be, 343
tongueless, good deed, 83
Dyspepsy, of a mental, 31

E

Each age, each kindred, 24
at some well-remembered grave, 163
thing's a thief, 402
Eager air, a nipping and an, 5
for the fray, 12
Eagle, 106
fly away, as an, 336
in his flight, from an, 282
methinks I see her as an, 277
pride like any, 316
the screaming, flew, 181
the soaring, of the Alps, 332
Eagles, 106
be gathered together, 184
Eagles' wings, on, 351
Ear, 106
enchant thine, 93
falling at intervals upon the, 52
Ear
give every man thy, 428
hath not heard, 209
he has the wrong sow by the, 378
into my, 78
it came o'er my, 273
keep the word of promise to our, 318
no Christian, can endure to hear, 317
of a drowsy man, vexing the dull, 400
of death, the dull, cold, 421
of Eve, close at the, 408
of him that hears it, in the, 196
pierced the fearful hollow of thine, 283
plain as whisper in the, 69
shot through the, 118
the drowsy, of night, 22
undulates upon the listening, 52
voice in my dreaming, 98
with unwounded, 400
Ear-kissing, 106
Earlier, in the days that were, 311
Earliest at his grave, 67
hour, to be the very, 210
to the ground, 146
years, pedigree traced to earth's, 300
Early and provident fear, 128
nothing to him falls, 127
reason I was up so, 211
riser Mr. Gray has drawn, 151
that we may call it, 211
you've gut to git up, 431
Earn his bread, when he might, 248
there's little to, 132
Earned a night's repose, 410
him, than ever proof itself would have, 287
Earnest ef you fight, gut to be in, 131
have no time to waste, men in, 416
in downright, 96
life is, 222
of the things that they shall do, 461
the grateful, of eternal peace, 298
to do it in, 210
Ear-piercing fife, the, 125
Ears, 106
fall together by the, 111
falls into mine, 64
howled in mine, 98
if men had, 272
lend me your, 341
like softest music to attending, 412
longer than anything else than their, 300
more learned than the, 2
noise of waters in mine, 102
of corn, two, 162
of flesh and blood, to, 381
of the groundlings, to split the, 379
polite, never mentions hell to, 178
that aged, 196
that are hoary, takes the, 326

Ears
who shut your saintly, 217
with ravished, 155
Earth, 106, 107
a few feet of cold, 229
again, loves never on, 117
a hell, by making, 177
all that inhabit this great, 201
all things in heaven and, 212
and dashest him again to, 73
and dust, but, 89
and heaven, 'twixt, 255
and lards the lean, 210
and sky, bridal of the, 73
and sky stand presently, till, 391
(as far) as heaven from, 29
a stage, the, 383
a turf of fresh, 269
below, on the, 409
but from this, 406
can yield me but a common grave, 163
circles the, 112
crime deemed innocent on, 66
deny it who can, star of, 113
didst thou on, 377
draw from the, 188
dug his fingers into the wet, 313
enjoy this bounteous, beauteous, 196
ever stretched, the thickest cloud, 159
flop 'round the, 112
from sullen, 210
gets its price, 176
give him a little, 29
gives us, for what, 176
has no sorrow, 375
has no unpolluted spring, 403
hath bubbles, the, 39
his furrow stands, and to the last of, 79
huge foundation of the, 277
in them than heaven, with less of, 129
is but an echo of the spheres, 272
is dry, when mother, 101
is faded, till the night of, 429
is nor of heaven nor, 332
is toil, but the blessing of, 409
lay her i' the, 426
look not like the inhabitants o' the, 448
loved and lost on, 179
man marks the, 288
men are spread about this, 75
men at most differ as heaven and, 259
model of the barren, 80
more things in heaven and, 303
must borrow its mirth, 212
no life was ever lived on, 98
o'er a' the, 38
of majesty, this, 112
oh that that, 421
on manhood's solid, 250
on the bare, 86
Earth
perish from the circle of the, 276
returns to, 410
round about the, 152
seems a paradise to me, 360
shall glisten in the ray, 159
shall not perish from the, 276
shall reclaim her precious things, 354
should see, and God-illumined, 417
suck in the, 101
than heaven, breathing less of, 176
than heaven, 'tis less of, 176
that bears thee dead, 381
that heaven upon, 21
the, the sea, 196
the axis of the, 15
the bosom of the, 164
the dust is, 421
the expiring, 353
the gayest soul on, 148
the poor creature of, 135
there be on, 316
the soul he had on, 176
the sunlight clasps the, 204
the thirsty, soaks up the rain, 101
this, 112
though they come from the ends of the, 391
thou wert not on the, 377
to every man upon this, 89
to heaven, from, 308
to heaven it goes, from, 262
to lift from, 233
too dear, for, 21
treads not the, 150
truth crushed to, 415
two paces of the vilest, 381
words are the daughters of, 459
unseen, spiritual creatures walk the, 381
upon her corpse, the, 388
upon the lap of, 257
was gay, when all the, 148
we rise from the lowly, 208
which bind men down to, 122
who on, 247
with her thousand voices, 154
Earthly dignities, a peace above all, 299
longings, died to all, 91
my vow was, 157
Earthquake's spoil is sepulchred below, 109
Earth's aching breast, the broad, 143
a thief, the, 402
biggest country's gut her soul, 277
breast, in the green, 108
contracted span, yet not to, 463
crammed with heaven, 153
earliest years, whose pedigree traced to, 300
highest station ends in, 104
woe, to endure life's sorrow and, 242
most happy choir, led, 244
philosopher, and never, 418

Ease, 107
and sweetness, graceful, 128
gathered, or be with, 228
give one another, 345
in hours of, 453
in mine inn, take mine, 193
in writing comes from art not chance, true, 467
my heart, a little weeping would, 438
no healthful, 285
not the doctrine of ignoble, 389
that live at home at, 355
they whom youth and, 105
to hours of, 443
Tom felt more at, 353
weary and ill at, 291
with golden, 224
Easier, it's a good sight, 133
Easiest for his feet, they were, 146
Easily, and can more, 166
Easiness, a property of, 70
East, 107
is east and west is west, 391
is unveiled, the, 225
it is the, 225
I've wandered, 222
nor west, there is neither, 391
of Suez, ship me somewhere, 392
peered forth the golden windows of the, 393
the great wind overhead is blowing, 279
to west, tobacco which from, 408
to west, trembling on from, 143
wind, but a soul goes out on the, 113
Easter day, no sun upon an, 129
wearing his new doublet before, 322
Eastern skies, illumed the, 105
windows only, not by, 224
Eastward hill, the dew of yon high, 269
to the sea, lookin', 251
Easy as lying, 'tis as, 244
gait, and, 186
getting up seems not so, 151
is a bush, how, 128
it is of a cut loaf, 435
man, good, 164
than wrong, though, 159
trips, that the rich by, 176
Eat, and be glad, 365
and drank your fill, 228
and drink as friends, 214
and drink on my score, all shall, 267
and some wad, 257
an oyster, to, 292
a rich juicy meal for the worms to, 229
but little meat, I cannot, 6
chat as well as, 47
dried oats, nor, 251
ha'e meat and we can, 257
it, stay and, 48
soft water through hard marble, 252
some part of my leek, make him, 216
Eat, tempt the dying anchorite to, 349
they have only stomachs to, 388
thy cake, would'st thou both, 41
together, we still have . . . , 224
up the little ones, 133
with the devil, that must, 87
with you, I will not, 41
Eaten, 107
them, and worms have, 238
to death with a rust, 345
your bread and salt, I have, 349
Eating, appetite comes with, 11
Eats into itself, which, 26
up himself, he that is proud, 320
Eaves, 107
Ebrew Jew, an, 197
Echo, 107
applaud thee to the very, 11
came, the welcome, 274
for evermore, word that shall, 84
lasts a deal longer, its, 203
I asked of, 255
of the spheres, earth is but an, 272
Echoes flying, set the wild, 382
on Fontarabian, 39
that start, cruelly sweet are the, 258
Eclipse, built in the, 18
Economists and calculators, sophists, 50
Ecstasies, out of its agonies and, 210
Ecstasy of love, the very, 238
the living lyre, waked to, 109
tide is in his, 18
Eddies of the mighty stream, are, 322
Eden, this other, 112
took their solitary way, through, 462
Eden's green and gold, 13
rosy bower, dwelt no joy in, 450
Edge, doth lose his, 206
is sharper than the sword, whose, 368
of appetite, the hungry, 191
of battle, on the perilous, 19
of husbandry, dulls the, 31
set my teeth nothing on, 309
Edges, and some say knives have, 404
Editor was born in Dublin, the, 294
Education, 107, 108
of the lad, in the, 467
Educing good, still, 160
Eel of science by the tail, holds the, 192
Effects from civil discord flow, 93
Effort, the last, of decayed fortune, 171
the life of toil and, 389
Egg, 108
is full of meat, as full of quarrels as an, 322
is full of meat, full of wit as an, 447
Eggs, 108
and die, lay their, 64
as a weasel sucks, 257
brooding on fancy's, 124
in her nest, she has two warm, 97

Eggs
yellow of two hard-boiled, 349
Egotism wrong side out, apology is only, 11
Egotist, 108
Egypt, I am dying, 105
Egypt's dark sea, loud timbrel o'er, 405
fall, when, 322
Eight, may lie abed till, 1
times to-day, that's, 286
to-morrow morn, I'm off at, 132
trumps in his hand, a man with, 415
with three times, 73
years, he had been, 393
years together, I'll rhyme you so, 335
Eighteen pence, offered twelve for, 326
hundred pounds, or even, 42
hundred years' profession, after, 42
shillings a week, for, 42
those, upon whom the tower, 193
thousand pounds, 42
Eighth day of March, on the, 348
Either, how happy could I be with, 47
Elate with a dream, 97
Elbow chair, played around her, 450
Elbow chairs, convenience next suggested, 279
Elbow-room, now my soul hath, 377
Elder, 108
race, a type of the true, 308
than herself, the woman take an, 454
Electricity, love, heat, 237
Elegy, swan sings her own, 273
Element, burning and consuming, 4
in luck, one constant, 307
one law, one, 322
Elements so mixed in him, and the, 250
the wars of, 191
to strife, to dare the, 436
Elements' rage, and the, 78
Elephants, place, for want of towns, 252
Ell in height, was but an, 331
Elm, the springy branches of an, 219
Elms, 108
Elohim, the strong archangel of the, 248
Eloquence, action is, 2
has drawn upon his memory for his, 291
Eloquent, 108
Elysian, suburb of the life, 76
Embalmed and pure, keep the soul, 377
in tears, 398
Embark, when I, 18
Embarked upon that little boat, 173
Embase him, love did, 232
Embaseth it, corrupteth and, 232
Embellished with He said, and So said I, 62
Embers, 108
spent of ashes and of, 4
Emblem of untimely graves, 88
Embrace, 108
me, as to, 98
take your last, 118
thee, sour adversity, 3
then pity, then, 425
Embraced . . . from the ends of opposed winds, 409
Embraces met, that ever since in love's, 294
Embracing clouds in vain, 369
Emetics, 109
and sicker of, 363
Emigrated, 109
Eminence, kings climb to, 202
raised to that bad, 107
Eminent, for being, 46
Emperor, this Czar, this, 80
without his crown, an, 73
Empire, 109
in thee, contend for, 25
of the sea, the, 354
on, builds what empire far outweighs, 317
to found a great, 361
Emotion, when the heart is so full of, 173
Employ, how fit to, 229
Employed, on selfish thoughts alone, 223
Employment, hand of little, 70
Employments' wishing, of all, 446
Empress, sits, crowning good, 385
Emptiness of ages in his face, the, 180
Empty, and fells her place is, 442
boxes, a beggarly account of, 33
glass, turn down an, 152
hell is, 178
quite, but as, 49
wells, dropping buckets into, 39
Emulation, shouting their, 43
Enchant thine ear, 93
Enchantment, 't is no spell of, 72
to the view, distance lends, 93
Enclose, and no cell, 262
Encompass the tomb, 163
Encounter darkness as a bride, 90
in a free and open, 415
Encumbered, galled, but what, 76
End, 109
and sans, 103
and there an, 90
artful to no, 462
attempt the, 14
dares send a challenge to his, 221
day, come, night, 282
death, a necessary, 80
death the journey's, 77
have not money enough in the, 434
he makes a swan-like, 273
in love of God, all, 269
in lovers' meetings, 198
in what all begins and ends in, 411
is purposed, whose, 157

End
is woe, where the end is, 159
let us to the, 337
long agony of this life will, 222
of fame, what is the, 123
of honest Jack, an, 168
of language, nature's, 210
of life cancels all bonds, 82
of reckoning, truth to the, 417
old Time shall lead him to his, 267
on't, and there's an, 450
on't, so there's an, 450
o' the table, 71
rolls to its appointed, 322
the black minute 's at, 78
the boys get at one, 135
them, by opposing, 19
this strife and sorrow will, 94
through life to the, 58
to end, lies frae, 30
to stand on, 381
try the man, let the, 251
which answers life's great, 224
worst, can't, 159
Endearing young charms, if all those, 47
Endeavour, and in the vain, 384
resolute in, 54
themselves, ought they of duty to, 318
with impotent, 462
Ended, 109
his cares are now all, 44
our revels now are, 428
the griefs are, 464
Ending, 109
in the frost, the old year is, 290
Endless sleep he wills, if an, 369
Ends and uses, produces noble, 284
by their privit, 111
divinity that shapes our, 94
frizzled like celery tips, their blunt, 437
in, what all begins and, 411
in Here he lies, 104
in place and power all public spirit, 305
marked, more are men's, 105
of opposed winds, from the, 409
of the earth, though they come from the, 391
their races, 345
to gain some private, 95
Endure, 110
a stuff will not, 239
but still, 35
life's sorrow and earth's woe, 242
the toothache patiently, 413
their going hence, 157
to hear, no Christian ear can, 317
to obey, to, 113
we first, 425
Endured, most tolerable and not to be, 434
Endures forever, surely God, 380
Endures, guards her or with her the worst, 443
Enduring forces, opposing and, 60
Enemies, 110
have left me naked to mine, 357
overthrown more than your, 465
Enemy, 110
his own worst, 249
men should put an, 33
ship alongside that of an, 360
to weigh the, 84
Enemy's dog, mine, 95
Energy sublime, as the, 143
Enfeebled, which is already, 425
Enfold, gilded tombs do worms, 410
Enforced ceremony, it useth an, 238
who much, 209
Enforcement be, let gentleness my strong, 23
Engaged, art more 377
Engendered in the eyes, 124
Engine well, to treat his, 329
Engine-driver of broad-gauge mail train, 315
Engineer, 110
Engines, O you mortal, 125
England, 110–112
a labourer in Christian, 208
expects every man to do his duty, 104
Germany, or Spain, 135
Greece, Italy and, 309
mother England, 48
not three good men unhanged in, 259
shall be in, 130
slaves cannot breathe in, 368
the flag of, 284
the King of, cannot enter, 44
the roast beef of, 22
thy name shall yet warrant thy fame, 226
tremble, made all, 87
England's ale, than a draught of Old, 281
Alfred named, truth-teller was our, 418
dead, where rest not, 113
greatest son, this is, 167
griefs began, ere, 166
English, 113
air could make her, sweet as, 343
gentleman, a fine old, 149
nation, trick of our, 160
gun, nor ever lost an, 167
labourer's wife, as an, 208
minds and manners, 110
pluck, the surly, 307
roast beef, 22
soil, has no right on, 409
tongue, all who speak the, 111
undefiled, well of, 47
Englishman, 113
American as I am an, 8
dear, more than all to an, 286
is proud, 90

Englishman
words I'm an, 47
Englishman's food, roast beef was the, 22
Engrave it, had taken half a lifetime to, 264
on adamant our wrongs we all, 467
Engraven, deep on his front, 85
Engrossing death, to, 118
Enhances life and all its chances, noble thought, 284
Enjoy my Malthus, I never can, 247
this bounteous beauteous earth, 196
Enjoyed, peaceful hours I once, 300
Enlarge itself, never ceaseth to, 53
Enmesh, with predestined evil round, 365
Enmity, proof against their, 302
works of love or, 381
Enniskillen, in the town of, 440
Ennoble, 113
Ennobled by himself, 385
our hearts, it, 22
Enoch as a brave God-fearing man, 313
Enormous weight could raise, 84
Enough, cry out itself, 4
it was not, 183
she never gave, 141
we are, 185
Enquire for, whatever skeptic could, 441
Enriched our blood, 22
Enriches, that which not, 275
Ensign, 114
'neath the shade of Freedom's, 64
Enslave their children's children, 60
Ensnare, tresses man's imperial race, 168
Ensue, if evil thence, 452
Entails twenty-nine distinct damnations, 71
Entangling alliances with none, 6
Entendeth ay, and most, 150
Enter death, those who, 77
here, ye who, 185
life, souls draw when we, 76
now, ye cannot, 211
on my list of friends, I would not 463
still, but we can, 211
the King of England cannot, 44
there, I will not, 348
Entereth, knowledge by suffering, 206
Entering a room, on, 85
Enterprise, of noble, 18
Enterprises, impediments to great, 442
of great pith, 61
ripe for exploits and mighty, 470
Enters, this viperous slander, 368
Entertain, a wilful stillness, 291
Entertainment, with, 146
Enthralled, by which men aye have been, 321
Enthroned in the hearts of kings, it is, 260
Entitle them, the laws of nature and of nature's God, 356
Entitled to, more than that no man is, 383
Entrance to a quarrel, beware of, 322
Entrances, their exits and their, 383
Entrap the hearts of men, 168
Entwine, laurel wreaths, 304
Envies us, poor creatures how they, 388
Envious tongues, to silence, 299
Environ, what perils do, 302
Environed me about, 98
Envy, 114
dared not hate, who, 434
of less happier lands, 112
that decried him, 122
Epaulets worn't the best mark of a saint, 431
Ephesian dome, that fired the, 123
Epics in each pebble underneath our feet, 460
Epicure, dish that tempts an o'er-gorged, 92
would say Fate cannot harm me, 349
would say, live while you live, 227
Epicurus' sty, in, 181
Epitaph, 114
believe a woman or an, 67
none wrote his, 145
Epitaphs, of worms and, 164
Epithet, 114
suffer love, a good, 239
Epitome, 114
Equal eye, who sees with, 38
feet are trod, by, 464
good produce, 117
made, and in the dust be, 103
in full-blown powers, 318
powers, can ne'er be, 241
to all things, though, 141
where all are, 114
Equalized, 114, 115
Equals the king to the shepherd, 369
this, what blessed ignorance, 370
Equivocation will undo us, 43
Era, 115
Erased, nor be, 465
Erebus, his affections dark as, 273
Erect, who stands, 248
Erecting a grammar school, in, 317
Erin, 115
Err is human, to, 140
art may, 277
upon the sober side, always, 396
weep for the frail that, 312
Errand, and in your joyous, 152
speeds, and his, 36
Erred, nor am I confident they, 139
Erring souls, who looks on, 52
Error, and many an, 315
dies of lockjaw, 415
hurled, in endless, 462
in religion, what damned, 330
lies, in reas'ning pride, our, 316
which some truth, the, 120

Error, wounded, writhes in pain, 415
Errors fall, some female, 128
Eruptions, breaks forth in strange, 277
Escape a work so sad, 450
  calumny, thou shalt not, 42
  not the thunderbolt, innocents, 193
  whipping, and who should, 440
Escaped my recollection, almost, 89
Escapement, the clicking of the terrible, 403
Espied a feather of his own, 106
Essence, his glassy, 251
  pure, so soft and uncompounded is their, 381
Established law, thet slow critter, 212
Estate and sunneshine flies of, 3
  fallen from his high, 121
  of very small, 175
  who had an old, 149
Esteem and love were never, 158
  to love, to know, to, 221
Esteemed above thy life, are not with me, 223
Esteems your merit, how he, 405
Eternal beadroll, on Fame's, 47
  day, and a new morning brings, 13
  in the human breast, 186
  Night, Chaos and, 46
  peace, earnest of, 298
Eternal's wrath appeased, by penitence the, 301
Eternities, peaks of two, 222
  two, the past, the future, 222
Eternity, that wander through, 90
  the clock tells of, 280
  through nature to, 89
  to feel the passion of, 402
  when time unveils, 411
Ethereal sky, all the blue, 132
Euchred, 115
Euclio said and sighed, 91
Euphrosyne, in heaven ycleped, 264
Europe, better fifty years of, 45
Evade, human power which could, 467
Eve, 115
  brought woe to all mankind when, 449
  close at the ear of, 408
  from noon to dewy, 122
  span, and, 149
  the bugbears of a winter's, 401
  the first of dupes, 103
  the son of Adam and of, 317
  upon the first of men, 2
Even, 115
  measure of immortal hope, 115
  was weary and old, which at, 442
Evening, 116
  bell, twilight and, 18
  bells, those, 23
  by the waters, many an, 226
  care, housewife ply her, 175
  come in the, 59
  dusk of, 4
  each, sees it close, 410
  exhalation in the, 122
Evening
  fantastic visions of the, 428
  skies, the dusk in, 246
  star, sunset and, 17
Event, one far-off divine, 322
  to himself, the final, 340
Events, coming, cast their shadows before, 358
  in the course of human, 356
  of every day, the, 352
  stride on before the, 358
Ever, 116
  and a good jest for, 196
  and ever, the curse shall be on thee for, 69
  and for ever, 125
  be friends, we must, 146
  for, and for ever, 334
  for, float that standard sheet, 17
  for, never, 55, 280
  independence for, 192
  still for, 125
  we parted for, 296
Ever-heightening life, every phase of, 224
Everlasting farewell take, our, 125
  the, had not fixed, 134
Evermore, adieu for, 3
  and shall be for, 289
  from his grey hairs gone for, 121
  shall be Yes for, 468
Every bush, misdoubteth, 25
  day, dying thus around us, 75
  day, the rain it raineth, 325
  day they live, something, 138
  ducat in six thousand ducats, 103
  heart best knoweth, 163
  hour, groaning, 56
  inch a king, 202
  man after his desert, use, 440
  man thy ear, give, 428
  man to do his duty, expects, 104
  minute, sighing, 56
  moment dies a man, 69
  one I knew, to, 320
  tongue brings in a several tale, 61
  word a reputation dies, at, 332
  word, church, church at, 52
Everything by starts, 114
  else, in, 187
  good in, 3
  is for the best, 24
  we meet, there's fun in, 147
  which now thou art, being, 236
  who has not a conscience in, 62
Everywhere, Be bold, 28
  I am with thee, 207
  out of the, 16
Evidence against us, in bearing heavy, 450
  to give in, 289
Evil, 116
  all partial, 338
  and the good, warfare 'twixt the, 433
  behaviour, her, 351

Evil
be thou my good, 186
do him good and not, 451
from seeming, 160
goodness in things, 160
justified in doing, 117
lost half its, 424
love of money is the root of all, 267
manners live in brass, 34
money, the root of, 266
news rides post, 281
no man means, 88
obscures the show of, 213
or extremely, 251
round, thou wilt not with predestined, 365
side, for the good or, 83
sign, an, 25
soul producing holy witness, 11
spirit, an, at his birth, 283
thence ensue, if, 452
turn, wants but one more, 173
we fear nae', 19
Evils, 116
Ewe bleat for the lamb, made the, 448
Ewigkeit, afay in de, 297
Exact man, and writing an, 326
shade of Julius Cæsar's hair, 58
Exactness, with, grinds he all, 262
Exalted sat, Satan, 107
Examination, 't will be found upon, 87
Examine Venus and the moon, 306
well his milk-white hand, 36
Example, by Christian, 197
by the same, 315
may profit by their, 414
you with thievery, I'll, 402
Exceeds all earthly bliss, as far, 262
Excel, of all those arts in which the wise, 467
Excellence a fair divided, 168
it cannot reach, and hates that, 114
Excellent, oh, it is, 151
Excess, better the, 28
of blood, perish through, 447
of ill-got, ill-kept pelf, 300
of it, give me, 273
wasteful and ridiculous, 152
Exchange a peaceful word, nor to, 229
joy is an, 198
Exchequer of the poor, thanks, the, 401
Exclusive heaven, a sole, 176
Excommunicated, nor, 64
Excrement, stolen from general, 402
Excuse for the glass, she'll prove an, 210
the worse by the, 128
Excuses, not forced to frame, 250
Excusing of a fault, 128
Execute, a hand to, 173
I will, 197
laws which the people have made, 289
Executes a freeman's will, 144
blow which while it, 81
Execution in the morn, that wait for, 333
like a pardon after, 59
Executors, 117
Exercise depend, on, 172
Exercises, to such preposterous, 210
Exhalation in the evening, 122
Exhaled, had sparkled as a dewdrop, was, 378
she sparkled, was, 378
Exile, hooting at Coriolanus', 43
return with her from, 319
Exist and to be glad, I manage to, 61
Existence, called the New World into, 16
is a merry treat, 147
secured in her, 191
the things misnamed death and, 369
time wasted is, 407
't is woman's whole, 232
Exits, they have their, 383
Expatiates in a life to come, 186
Expectancy and rose, the, 263
Expectation, 117
every day beguiled, 92
rise, bids, 185
to bury them, in, 254
Expects his evening prey, 470
every man to do his duty, 104
Expediency, 117
party courage is party, 297
Expedient, to pursue the, 141
Expenditure, annual, nineteen nineteen six, 192
Experience, 117
my, tell ye wut it's ben, 40
old, but his, 198
to make me sad, than, 261
Expire, persons died before they, 91
Explain his explanation, 117
it, by trying to, 323
Explained, is easily, 329
Explanation, 117
Exploits and mighty enterprises, ripe for, 470
Exposed he lies, 86
Expound, and argue, he could plead, 283
Express, even its minted coins, 157
Expressed, but ne'er so well, 447
in fancy, but not, 11
Exquisite to last, joys too, 198
Extension of domain, 110
Extent of your treasures, you learn the, 366
proud of a vast, 353
to any great, 340
Extenuate, 117
External parts, agree with our, 456
Extracting sunbeams out of cucumbers, for, 393
Extreme gusts will blow out, 132
hate in the like, 237
in love or hate, in good or ill, 449
Extremes, 117
both . . . in, 324

Extremes
is such, the fate of all, 259
of passion, 'twixt two, 297
Extremity, a daring pilot in, 304
Exulting, the people all, 43
Exults and sings, in youth the heart, 470
Eye, 117, 118
a blue and sunken, 239
a lightsome, 403
all of fire, the, 246
and a tear in her, 371
and listless, 274
and pride in her, 316
and the love-light in your, 387
begets occasion, his, 196
closed her bright, 142
could never see, a friendly, 128
dares not lend his, 312
defiance in their, 316
fruitful river in the, 448
has danced to see, many an, 114
hath not seen it, 209
heaven in her, 161
heaven of her delightful, 452
her, lost its light, 153
he taks the mother's, 469
hide her shame from every, 136
is it for fear to wet a widow's, 442
like Mars, an, 250
looks yellow to the jaundiced, 195
more peril in thine, 302
of heaven, as the great, 119
of heaven, the beauteous, 152
of him who made us, if we offend the, 107
of newt and toe of frog, 179
quick-glancing, whose, 410
requires, the closing, 35
repose, where may the wearied, 434
seems wrong to man's blindfold, 337
shoots darts from her merry black, 226
shuts up sorrow's, 370
squints the, 135
the poet's, 308
the postern of a small needle's, 42
there was lustre in his, 351
to guide the seaman's, 245
tongue, sword, 263
what eye but such an, 322
what immortal hand or, 405
when Douglas wets his manly, 398
which hath the merriest, 213
which would forget to wake, 10
who sees with equal, 38
will mark our coming, there is an, 438
with its soft black, 148
Eyebrow, made to his mistress', 242
Eyelids closed, her quiet, 105
Eyelids down, weigh my, 370
heavy and red, with, 360
if ever from your, 23
inclines our, 370
to kiss thine, 293
Eyes, 118
all my mother came into mine, 399
and feast upon her, 238
and his temples about, sported his, 463
and with rainy, 164
are heavy and dim, till the, 460
a stain, what looks to thy dim, 198
because thou hast hazel, 322
buried in thy, 174
close up his, 80
dear as these, 443
drink to me only with thine, 99
engendered in the, 124
grow dim, that made your, 176
hath not a Jew, 197
have dulled their, 155
hooded, shafts from, 23
hood mine, 372
I could play the woman with mine, 399
I could weep my spirit from mine, 438
I dared not close, my fevered, 369
I'll drink the words you send, with mine, 466
I strain my, 313
kindling her undazzled, 277
knowledge from others', 394
left the flushing in her galled, 399
lies deeply buried from human, 186
light that visits these sad, 443
love looks not with the, 69
make thy two, 380
might sometimes see, our, 321
mine, have seen the glory, 153
no speculation in those, 29
not a friend to close his, 86
of flame, in he came with, 87
of the ignorant, 2
of the sleepers waxed deadly, 77
revengeful, fix, 28
sans, 49
saw with his own, 106
sees with larger, other, 261
severe, with, 199
shall be turned to behold, when my, 420
sights of death within mine, 102
smell onions, mine, 438
soft, looked love, 334
tears in his, 307
that death bandaged my, 78
that shone, the, 258
that would not shrink, with, 420
that you could turn your, 355
the cynosure of neighbouring, 70
the mind has a thousand, 281
the night has a thousand, 281
the steady keel, while follow, 43
thet tell o' triumph, 299
they strike mine, 364
those cunning waters of his, 426
through another man's, 170
try to shut their saddening, 384
were closed, thy dying, 139

Eyes
were drawn to him, our, 244
with air, mock our, 56
with coin-weights shut, two, 208
with his half-shut, 57
with streaming, 76
with the meek, brown, 246
yawns before our, 178
Eyesight, not with blinded, 350
Eye-witness, against thine own, 150

F

Fabric of this vision, the baseless, 428
Face, 118, 119
and limb, 418
and may the cherubs on its, 68
as a nose on a man's, 285
a stone is on her, 388
counsel in his, 85
day's disasters in his morning, 93
familiar with her, 425
full of woe, with a, 246
give me a, 364
grows old, the, 211
he had a broad, 24
his council and his, 154
his furrowed, 225
it, let him fearlessly, 461
look on her, 128
looks the whole world in the, 292
must hide, false, 122
my, is my fortune, 246
my ten commandments in your, 59
o' fire, her, 71
of the dead, gazed on the, 313
of the dead, on the, 311
of the foe, breathed in the, 77
looks the strong world in the, 410
shade my lifeless, 75
shuddering on thy, 377
sometimes in a dead man's, 225
spit in my, 218
that can be given to a man's, 219
that sages have seen in thy, 373
that smiles in yeer, 212
the climber-upward turns his, 7
the flash, and, 227
the mist in my, 78
the emptiness of ages in his, 180
the public stare, can stand and, 449
there is a garden in her, 343
there, you find one, 290
to face, talked with us, 308
to face, when two strong men stand, 391
too roughly, visit her, 243
truth has such a, 425
which all men knew, honest, 171
voice, or form, or, 274
Faces, 119
all are gone, the old familiar, 307
full of kindly, 182
one of those, children loathe, 176
stern defiance, in their, 130
Facing fearful odds, 89
Fact, the crowning, 144
to put a, 218
Factions, and cherish, 101
Factories with blood, build, 413
Facts, 119
of guilty acts, unknown, 99
upon his imagination for his, 291
Fade away, the stars shall, 191
may flourish or may, 399
no more, the love that shall, 240
or sorrow, 77
Faded and gone, are, 342
flower, but a little, 135
till the night of earth is, 429
Fades o'er the waters blue 2
the glimmering landscape, 209
the last long streak of snow, 372
youth, 221
Fading away, like fairy-gifts, 47
in music, 273
Fail, 119
but if you, 150
ef we do n't, 320
or land or life, if freedom, 143
rather than, 322
swell out and, 52
with me, my purpose should not, 446
Failed him, one word for ever, 283
till language quite, 389
who strove and who, 61
Failings, 119
Fails, one sure if another, 71
to see a bad one, never, 70
Fain die a dry death, 80
have all men true, 150
would I climb, 55
Faint, 120
and yield, where thou would'st only, 198
know all words are, 459
now, as farewells, 52
praise, damn with, 71
weary and, 182
Fainting spirit fell, ere my, 439
Fair, 120
all thet's honest, honnable and, 111
and free, come, thou goddess, 264
and young, ever, 16
and young, was she very, 200
are kind, still the, 141
arms are, 13
deserves the, 34
forms, and hoary seers, 334
hand that writ, 169
house built on another man's ground, 187
if women could be, 455
most divinely, 94
lady, ne'er won, 120
learned and, 180
looks, but love, 189
loved the brightest, 185
or foul, be, 221
the, the chaste, and unexpressive she, 358

Fair
this life which seems so, 461
thoughts be your fair pillow, 304
to no purpose, 462
to see, a maiden, 24
woman, never a, 119
Fairer, 120
Fairies, none but, here are seen, 304
Fairly bound, so, 30
Fairy gifts fading away, like, 47
hands their knell is rung, by, 34
ring, or to tread our, 304
tales of science, with the, 352
Faith, 120, 121
almost mak'st me waver in my, 378
and hope, two cardinal virtues, 315
and love, works of, 267
and morals hold, the, 412
and pride, glows with, 173
and unfaith can ne'er be equal powers, 241
an' truth, wut's words to them whose, 19
fought for queen and, 105
have, and struggle on, 391
have thine own, 312
I build my, 155
in all, is want of, 241
in God and nature, 156
in honest doubt, more, 97
in the Christ, thou who hast, 242
is but the flower, 327
itself be lost, 376
law, morals, all began, 269
many in sad, 416
perplexed in, 97
shall make a clearer, 466
so long as, 219
teaches us little, 179
than Norman blood, simple, 148
that right makes might, let us have, 337
they had denied, of the, 34
they have in tennis, 401
true, and ready hands, 259
upon, such as do build their, 329
woman's, 450
Faithful, 121
I would be so, 97
of thy word, 124
wife, without debate, the, 442
Faithless, among the, 121
Faithlessness is party dishonour, party, 297
Faith's pure shrine, they sought a, 464
Falcon, 121
in our glove, our, 344
soar her swing, let the wild, 344
Fall, 121
and her bay-tides rise and, 32
and some by virtue, 365
and their shackles, 368
another thing to, 400
back into my chair, 284
by dividing, we, 420
divided we, 420
Fall
dost mark the sparrow's, 84
ere we come to, 260
full well he may, as, 308
half to rise and half to, 462
he that is down need fear no, 97
I fear to, 55
if we must, 259
in Adam's, 2
into Charybdis, I, 353
into sin, man-like is it to, 365
it had a dying, 273
lest we, 313
like a bright, 122
like men, let us, 259
no lower, can, 97
no use buildin' wut's a-goin' to, 40
of a sparrow, providence in the, 320
one of them shall not, 320
or a sparrow, 38
out with a tailor, didst thou not, 322
out with dirt, to, 361
startles thousands with a single, 81
successive, they, 250
take them as they, 309
the blossoms, 154
the curtains, let, 116
the weak that, 312
they must stand or, 202
together by the ears, 111
to rise, held we, 337
to sin, impute my, 365
upon the sod, as snow-flakes, 144
with gentlest, 18
wha' last beside his chair shall, 201
when Egypt's, 322
when their leaders, 271
where fall it may, 10
Fallen, 121
and the weak, for the, 368
arise, or be for ever, 15
cold and dead, 43
from high, rich china vessels, 362
from his fellow's side, 90
head, to trample round my, 76
on evil days, though, 116
sadly off, have, 469
Falling, 121
a star was, 384
prone, so that, 313
star, like a, 122
the fear's as bad as, 371
to the prompter's bell, slow, 70
with soft slumbrous weight, 370
Falling-off, 121
Falls, 121, 122
as I do, 164
asunder at the touch of fire, 38
before us, 17
from a steady heart, 265
from the wings of night, 282
the Coliseum, when, 57
the great man never, 164
with the leaf, 372
False, 122
again, proved, 95

False
and friendly be, both, 24
and hollow, all was, 122
any other thing that 's, 67
as dicers' oaths, as, 287
creation, a, 70
in friendship, 385
Latin, I smell, 211
of heart, never say that I was, 2
pride in place and blood, 54
prints, credulous to, 453
to God, while we are doubly, 213
to any man, canst not then be, 415
we are by nature, 83
Falsehood, 122
no, 416
strife of Truth with, 83
Falsehood 's honey it disdained, 411
Falsehoods, 122
for a magazine, furnish, 245
Falstaff sweats to death, 210
Falter, to, would be sin, 337
Faltering feet, often, 324
Fame, 122–124
again increasing, and, 421
and gives immortal, 272
and light is thy, 428
and not to, 53
and profit, ere her cause bring, 34
be mine, could, 275
fresh and gory, from the field of his, 153
he sought be just as fleeting yet, 62
is shrewdly gored, my, 332
I would give all my, 6
love, wine, ambition, 274
name shall yet warrant thy, 226
nor too fond of, 46
nor yet a fool to, 466
out to wealth and, 214
sang of love and not of, 241
shall twine for me, 104
the deck it was their field of, 288
the speaking-trump of future, 274
to his dead, 121
unknown, and to, 257
use gave me, 421
wade in wealth or soar in, 104
wealth, and honour, what are you, 237
well secured our, 89
were thine, that, 275
what once had . . . wealth and, 334
Fame 's eternal beadroll, on, 47
eternal camping-ground, 26
Familiar, 124
as his garter, 161
in his mouth as household words, 275
with her face, 425
Familiarity, I hope upon, 238
Family, 124
glee, full of, 441
my, think it indispensable, 382
one of Eve 's, 115
Family
wants of a young, 48
Famine drew the bolt, till, 110
Famous, 124
victory, 't was a, 425
Fanatic, foul-tongued, 108
Fancies are more giddy and unfirm, our, 454
Fancy, 124
bids, if so your, 153
but not expressed in, 11
feigned, sweet as those by hopeless, 205
free, in maiden meditation, 257
her, is so flexible, 319
is some men 's, 187
makes me more than king, 402
now my sere, 223
of most excellent, 468
paints, if our conduck is n't all your, 349
still my sense in Lethe, 98
the lips we press in sparkling, 55
Fancy 's child, sweetest Shakespeare, 432
Fane of God, the, 114
Fanged with murderous stones, 387
Fangs, beware my, 95
Fantasies that apprehend, such shaping, 243
Fantastic if too new, alike, 126
round, in a light, 409
toe, on the light, 409
tricks, plays such, 251
Fantasy, nothing but vain, 99
Fantasy 's hot fire, it is not, 237
Far and near, from, 52
as springs will, as, 173
away, and o'er the hills and, 463
away, and was it, 176
away, over the hills and, 180
between, few and, 9
between, short and, 9
from gay cities, 68
from home was he, 182
from the madding crowd, 68
see ever so, 178
that little candle, 42
til that hit be so, 53
Far-blazing from the rear of Philip 's house, 25
Far-called our navies melt away, 139
Fardels bear, who would, 79
Fare like my peers, 78
thee well, and if for ever, 125
thee well, beloved, 125
thee well, Isle of Beauty, 1
worse, one might go farther and, 321
Farewell, 124, 125
a long farewell, 164
and looks around to say, 70
and mercy sighed, 142
goes out sighing, and, 438
hope, and with hope farewell fear, 186

Farewell
hope . . . bade the world, 142
I only feel, 242
no sadness of, 18
remorse, 186
sweets to the sweet, 395
to Lochaber, 229
Farewells, faint now as, 52
Farmer, my father's a, 246
Farmer's cad, here I come to be a, 200
Farmers stood, here once the embattled, 362
Far-off divine event, one, 322
Farther, gets the narrower by going, 276
Farthest from the fear, the, 127
Farthing, two sparrows sold for a, 320
Farthings, five sparrows sold for two, 320
Fashion, 126
our own hands, 67
planted, in all the world's new, 303
the glass of, 263
the high Roman, 341
the old, 191
Fashioned as the artist wills, made to be, 107
others, that, 263
Fashions, 126
Fast, 126
and furious, grew, 264
and the world goes by, 129
and weep, wherefore should I, 365
an Œdipus-people is coming, 301
a week with bran and water, 312
come he, 79
if the child was too, 348
more grievous torment than a hermit's, 235
the horse I drive so, 186
to, like one that takes diet, 239
Fasted, on Fridays when they, 267
when you, 239
Fasten, before any vice can, 425
Fastened, unless it is tightly, 206
Faster, madness only makes them go, 403
than gnats in cobwebs, 168
than his tongue, 118
Fasting, thank heaven, 238
Fasts I keep, because of the, 78
Fat, 126
and grows old, one of them is, 259
more, than bard beseems, 18
oyster, 't was a, 292
paunches have lean pates, 298
Fatal and perfidious bark, 18
shadows that walk by us still, 2
dart, feather on the, 106
vision, art thou not, 70
word, that, 124
Fate, 126, 127
a heart for any, 2
a heart for every, 2
and mine are one, eagle's, 106
and wish agree, 15
Fate
but in our, 86
cannot harm me, 349
changeless sentence of mortal, 211
entailed the mother's throes, 59
fear no sudden, 227
forced by, 13
found a rare soul, 244
fulfil, change and, 154
in spite of, 221
master of his, 141
of all extremes is such, 259
of a nation was riding that night, 276
of the peasant, when a prince to the, 317
of woman, it is the, 451
reserves, which, 119
take a bond of, 14
that then denied him, 122
Fates, 127
may be, though far our, 237
when once the, 75
Father, 127
Adam sat under the tree, 13
and mither, though, 440
antic the law, old, 213
disobeyed, no, 466
forgive them, 140
hear my prayer, 313
is alcalde, he whose, 5
I thank thee, 109
no more like my, 37
of spirits, to the, 298
of the man, 49
preferring you before her, 189
say, asked but what he heard his, 416
take them, 13
to that thought, thy wish was, 446
was a Gallagher, his, 348
what is your, 246
without your, 320
Father's brother, but no more like my father, 37
grave did utter, 37
house, chimney in my, 36
house, nearer my, 278
life, the serpent that did sting thy, 356
spirit, I am thy, 380
Fathers, 128
brothers, sisters, 129
deemed it two, our, 139
died, land where my, 65
fools, we think our, 111
the ashes of his, 89
the birthplace of our, 111
the spirits of your, 288
Fatter, would he were, 126
Fattest hog, the, 181
Fault, 128
a noble fool was never in a, 397
dear Brutus, the, 127
deem it not a, 349
flies every, 231

Fault
he that does one, 218
his only, 90
holds him as one without a, 12
I see, to hide the, 260
just hint a, 71
than they, their stars were more in, 456
which needs it most, a, 218
Faultily faultless, 128
Faultless, 128
Faults, 128
a little blind, be to her, 201
and folly, your neebours', 305
England, with all thy, 110
lie gently on him, his, 333
need deal lightly with thy, 450
not free from, 46
observed, all his, 15
than hairs, more, 168
to scan, their merits or their, 305
were his own, his, 261
will not be hid, my, 365
Faults' books, their own, 119
Favour, a floating balance in their own, 352
to this, she must come, 468
Favours, when Fortune, 141
Fawn at his feet, 't will, 461
on you, I will, 378
Fawning publican he looks, how like a, 320
where thrift may follow, 412
Fawns, the young, are playing with the shadows, 469
upon the lamb, when the lion, 226
Fealty, our country claims our, 259
Fear, 128
above, all, 155
a name of, 419
and hope and longing unexpressed, 234
and not of, 84
and the sorrow, the, 109
and with hope, farewell, 186
a shadow and a, 69
a stranger to, 197
death, to feel the fog, 78
death as children fear, 77
each bush an officer, thief doth, 394
him not, but I, 126
his terrible shape, I hardly, 78
if my name were liable to, 126
is affront, 450
no fall, he that is down need, 97
no more the frown, 146
no more the heat o' the sun, 103
nor hope, I neither, 369
nor love, nor, 367
not guilt, those who, 123
not the anger of the wise, 332
of an imminent danger, just, 430
of burning, for, 131
of his trial hath no, 5
of kings, the dread and, 260
o' hell's a hangman's whip, 184
Fear
our cry, let the nations, 143
peace wun't keep house with, 299
preoccupateth it, 77
that men should, 80
the Arch, 78
thee, ancient mariner, I, 253
thee not, I, 395
the farthest from the, 127
the littlest doubts are, 238
there is not a word of, 78
thy skinny hand, I, 253
't is time to, 419
to lament or, 65
to speak, they are slaves who, 368
to tread, where angels, 138
to tread, wheels rush in where horses, 439
to wet a widow's eye, is it for, 442
we'll come to harm, I, 267
Feared, 128
that what he, 394
Fearful night, 't is a, 304
summons, upon a, 57
thing, it is a, 376
trip is done, 43
Fearing to attempt, by, 97
Fear's as bad as falling, the, 371
Fears grow great, where little, 238
he that but, 394
his fate too much, he either, 126
it, t' avoid misery, 422
its joys and, 404
may be liars, 391
my hopes for half thy, 409
not danger's post, breast that, 145
our hopes belied, 105
saucy doubts and, 41
to plunge with all your, 79
with hope, twining subtle, 186
Fear'st thy death, grossly, 80
Feast, 129
as you were going to a, 99
at any good man's, 23
bare imagination of a, 191
chief nourisher in life's, 370
is set, the, 167
of Crispian, is called the, 66
of reason and the flow of soul, 327
one, one house, 170
upon her eyes, and, 238
Feasted thus, since we have, 380
Feasts, compared to public, 253
Feather, a wit's a, 183
care as light as a, 361
is wafted downward, as a, 282
of his own, espied a, 106
of the blue, a, 403
on the fatal dart, 106
so lightly blown, was ever, 271
the, whence the pen, 301
to waft a, 377
will turn the scale, a, 351
Feathers plucked, their own, 106
to thy heels, set, 171
when fowls have no, 142

Feature, in form and, 418
to each hard-working, 314
Features, ah, the coarsest, 259
February face, such a, 119
Fed from within, 250
his former bounty, 86
on, grown by what it, 11
our sea for a thousand years, we have, 113
with gazing, 124
with the same food, 197
worse, than your hogs and your sheep, 323
Federal Union, the, it must be preserved, 420
Federation of the world, the, 433
Fee, set my life at a pin's, 223
the doctor, than, 172
the priest hath his, 176
thrice thy, 381
Feeble, 129
faith, a, I would not shake, 120
hand, a sinful heart makes, 366
hands and helpless, 156
Feed fat the ancient grudge, 166
he that doth the ravens, 326
his sacred flame, 234
my revenge, it will, 335
on cates, than, 399
on her damask cheek, 298
on the air, Love can, 240
on this fair mountain, leave to, 269
upon nothing, to, 308
were best at home, to, 129
what would thousand others, 300
Feeding, starve with, 9
upon them, to persist in, 109
Feeds and breeds, that, 402
three, 181
Feel and dare, a heart to, 173
another's woe, teach me to, 260
as I used to feel, to, 430
farewell, I only, 242
for man, it does not, 38
have felt and, 233
in any member, no comfortable, 285
instinctively I, 163
I only, 125
it, doth he, 185
it too well, I can, 327
like a child, don't, 49
much more the heart may, 174
she seems to, 200
that I am happier than I know, 170
the friendly stroke, ere we, 89
the infinite in me, I, 230
thy very wishes, to, 293
what they inflict they, 455
whether a shoe be Spanish or neat's leather, 20
within me a peace, and I, 299
Feeling, 129
as to sight, 70
care not for, 67
deeper than all thought, 403
divested of, 364
Feeling
has this fellow no, 70
from the Godhead, a, 233
of sadness and longing, 375
Feelings, 129
I had immortal, 230
not in figures on a dial, 227
prove that you have human, 58
wither, when the warmest, 125
Feels at each thread, 380
her place is empty, and, 442
his way, the mannikin, 15
it instantly, she, 380
not the toothache, he that sleeps, 371
the noblest, 227
Feet, 129
and fell at his, 194
and head, weeping at the, 74
and when he will to cast it at his, 107
are weary and sore, thy, 162
a stone at the, 229
blood on your pointer's, 148
crossed in rest, two pale, 208
epics in each pebble underneath our, 460
fireside pleasures gambol at her, 452
freedom's soil beneath our, 17
have trod the ground, blessed, 328
have wings, the, 470
Iscariot washes the bridegroom's, 194
nothing walks with aimless, 160
marks of angels', 460
of cold earth, a few, 229
of peace, war-sick at the, 300
proud at his, 353
standing with reluctant, 246
stays our hurrying, 79
they pinched her, 208
they were easiest for his, 146
tread beneath our, 170
't will fawn at his, 461
walked those blessed, 67
where my, have trod, 207
with flying, 71
Feigned, sweet as those by hopeless fancy, 205
Feigning, the truest poetry is the most, 309
Feline foe, mauls some, 44
Fell, 130
down, all of us, 121
ere my fainting spirit, 439
foremost fighting, 131
I do not love thee, Doctor, 327
in the battle of life, 61
like the stick, he, 340
my lady, 57
swoop, at one, 49
the hardest-timbered oak, 390
till from itself it, 112
upon a day, as it, 256
"Feller" was you saw her with, who the, 363

Fellow almost damned in a fair wife, a, 382
and want of it the, 465
a robustious periwig-pated, 379
beats all conquerors, a lean, 61
do unto the other, 82
he's a good, 178
in a market-town, a, 326
in the firmament, no, 62
may be straighter 'n a string, 187
no feeling, has this, 70
should have fewer words than a parrot, 295
suppose some, 279
thru, stick a, 156
whom they call John, the young, 403
worm, to trample my, 177
Fellow-creature's aid, of my, 313
Fellow-feeling makes one wondrous kind, a, 201
Fellow-man, to whale his, 171
Fellow's a villain, that, 426
side, fallen from his, 90
Fellows, 130
no patience with sech swellin', 156
young, will be young fellows, 468
Fells a knave, there he, 383
Felony, 130
Felt, all that I have, 233
another's woe, who, 448
as a man, though he, 346
a wound, that never, 351
I have, 221
or seen, a touch that's scarcely, 350
the lesser is scarce, 247
when more is, 178
Female countenance, at every comely, 455
errors fall, some, 128
heart can gold despise, what, 44
when a young, 363
Female-tongue-running, thou, 397
Fence, ox jumped half over a, 272
Fens, reek o' the rotten, 69
Ferrash strikes, the dark, 401
Ferryman, 130
Festal cheer, with, 101
Festival, meeting at a, 224
Fetch me now in fire, and the devil will, 448
the dead, the devil to, 87
Fetched, 'round be, 159
Feud, 130
Feuds, 130
Fever, after life's fitful, 223
called living is conquered at last, 229
called the tertian, he died of the slow, 441
once when I had a, 286
Few and far between, 9
and short were the prayers we said, 313
or none would do beside, 159
for the gain of a, 297
Few, their wants but, 68
they are that see it clear, how, 433
those by death are, 289
through which a, 214
thy voice, but, 428
to be chewed and digested, 30
will be ever content, with, 205
words are the best men, men of, 259
Fewer men, the, 185
words than a parrot, 295
Fevered lips, drained by, 435
Fiat millions slew, whose, 332
Fib becomes due, when one, 82
or sophistry, destroy his, 353
Fibres net the dreamless head, thy, 468
Fibs, I'll tell you no, 323
Fickle still, were firm, not, 455
Fico for the phrase, a, 386
Fiction, but in a, 307
her cup was a, 100
stranger than, 416
Fiddle behind the door, hangs up his, 261
Fiddler, statesman, and buffoon, 114
Fiddler's wife, kissed the, 263
Fie, foh, and fum, 27
upon "But yet!", 41
upon your law, 213
Field, 130
and the street, smacks of the, 314
an' hill, snow on, 152
a scar brought from some well-fought, 198
be lost, what though the, 231
bore him off the, 138
but for you possess the, 391
equipment 'e could find, was all the, 420
gaining some hard-fought, 409
he rushed into the, 131
he that tossed you down into the, 207
I grew up in the, 259
is slain, if he that in the, 184
man for the, 454
of air, through the, 386
of fame, the deck it was their, 288
of his fame fresh and gory, from the, 153
of thought, the free, broad, 403
that never set a squadron in the, 382
there be six Richmonds in the, 337
to die, like Hector in the, 28
where they, upon this, 276
Fields, and a' babbled of green, 359
below him, the green, 235
better to hunt in, 172
by quiet, 18
dales and, 235
floods the calm, 268
holy, over whose acres, 67
of corn, Ruth among the, 120
the little tyrant of his, 168
the new street of the little, 389

Fields, toiling in the naked, 207
were won, showed how, 68
Fiend, a frightful, 128
Flibbertigibbet, the foul, 135
the devil's wife was but a, 464
thou marble-hearted, 192
Fiend-like is it to dwell therein, 365
Fiends, a legion of foul, 98
be these juggling, 318
they flew, the, 57
Fiend-voices that rave, the, 78
Fierce, safer being meek than, 159
thing, that, 61
zeal, showed their, 144
Fierceness of the dove, 97
Fiery floods, to bathe in, 90
shapes, was full of, 277
Fife, in front of a drum an' a, 11
the ear-piercing, 125
Fifteen minutes of hell, to have some, 176
Fifth, a, shall close the drama, 109
Fifty, at, chides his infamous delay, 251
miles, he had journeyed, 106
of them, fought not with, 324
years, all o', 111
years ago, more than, 360
years of Europe, better, 45
'Fifty-three, runs north of, 212
Fifty-four-forty or fight, 131
Fig, a cherry and a, 162
for the vicar, and a, 26, 226
Fig-leaves for the naked truth, patching, 416
Fight, 130, 131
a harder matter to, 219
always ready to swear and, 408
a man may, 249
and die for her, to, 189
and none to, 388
better, are baffled to, 337
differing doctors and disciples, 162
for freedom, they that, 143
for love as men do, we cannot, 457
growl and, 95
have fought the good, 120
I dare not, 48
I have fought my, 221
it out, spur on and, 383
let graceless zealots, 120
not to the strong, the, 324
on to the last, 58
or tyranny to, 219
the bloody, blundering, 433
the soul has closed in, 377
through it, and we'll, 171
through the perilous, 17
to suffer, resist, 120
we'll, and we'll conquer, 286
when a shin in, 216
when glory leads the, 143
who knows the splendour of the, 390
wut is wuth a, 212
Fighting, 131
devotion, dust, perhaps a name, 274
had grown rusty, for want of, 26
man, but a first-class, 147
to show you're up to, 299
Fights, lives, breathes, labours, 176
he that, and runs away, 130
he that gained a hundred, 167
he who, and runs away, 130
Fig-tree, 131
Figure moulded, and to this, 107
Figures on a dial, not in, 227
Filches from me my good name, he that, 275
Fill a fair and honest cup, then, 68
and drank your, 228
another room in hell, 178
a pit as well as better, 312
every beaker up, 445
it high, 101
our bowls once more, 33
the cup and fill the can, 69
the speaking-trump of future fame, to, 274
the world can never, 300
up one monument, goodness and he, 267
with commerce, saw the heavens, 59
Filled that they o'erflow, 101
with signs and portents, more, 165
with such memories, 258
Fillip me with a three-man beetle, 22
Fills the room up, grief, 165
the white and rustling sail, 359
Film, though light as, 245
Fin, fish have no, 142
Final blow, own genius gave the, 106
goal of ill, 160
trump, to wait for the, 77
Find, didst thou this body, 377
fast bind, fast, 126
flowers, will, 135
her, amid the dust of books to, 416
he that sweetest rose will, 343
linen enough, they'll, 226
me, and thou shalt, 207
me and turn thy back on heaven, 159
out the way, love will, 231
that better way, to, 397
the wealth ye, 355
weeds, may, 135
Finding a smooth pebble, now and then, 417
Finds the day, night is long that never, 282
Fine, 131
a point upon it, not to put too, 309
a sight, is half so, 129
how exquisitely, 380
makes that and the action, 102
within thee growing coarse, 56
Finely wrought, too, 33
Finer than the staple of his argument, 424

Finger, from his ambitious, 8
if she scratches her, 415
its, was in the largest public pie, 54
rest, the angel's, 91
to lay his, 108
touched him and he slept, 371
writes, the moving, 465
Fingers bloody red, with, 167
cannot lick his own, 62
contaminate our, 36
he dug his, into the wet earth, 313
in the salad-bowl, plunge his, 349
pricking her, 304
wan, with, 110
wandered idly, my, 291
weary and worn, with, 360
Fingers' ends, smile upon his, 359
Finish off my lunch, to, 321
Finished by such as she, 168
Finite grasp infinity, how can, 192
Finny prey, surprise the, 168
Fire, 131, 132
a clean heart and a clear, 175
a clear, a clean heart, 175
against my, 95
all alone, to be poking the, 441
and clothes, meat, 336
and her pale, 402
and sword and desolation, call, 329
and sword, with, 425
and the devil will fetch me now in, 448
are as bad as a, 332
a spirit all compact of, 240
as tapers waste that instant they take, 81
as the flint bears, 209
asunder at the touch of, 38
a woman's story at a winter's, 389
bastion fringed with, 19
behind a slowly dying, 301
bitterer than a thousand years of, 83
gold must be tried by, 158
hasty as, 324
her face o', 71
if ever the Prairie Belle took, 329
immortal spark of that, 233
in thy heart and a fire in thy brain, 69
I sit beside my lonely, 330
i' the blood, 70
i' the flint, 135
laden, orbed maiden with white, 268
love's a, 233
must be the tongue of, 314
no seraph's, 176
not fantasy's hot, 237
not the fierce heat of, 4
now stir the, 116
of life, before the, 221
of passion, allay the, 327
oh for a muse of, 272
O love, O, 204
on a stallion shod with, 86
pale his ineffectual, 153
pregnant with celestial, 109
Fire
sat by his, 68
set the heart on, 4
shrivelled in a fruitless, 160
sinks the, 139
slackens, life declines, when the, 28
speech ventilates our intellectual, 380
stars are, 97
stranded with strings of, 244
that warmeth cold, the, 369
the eye all of, 246
the motion of a hidden, 313
the right Promethean, 118
the sun is but a spark of, 376
the tongue is a, 412
to touch the, 120
who can hold a, 191
with wit, 283
Fired another Troy, 177
the Ephesian dome, that, 123
the shot heard round the world, 362
Firelight fell, as the, 280
Fires, 132
confined to fast in, 380
live their wonted, 35
spending all her, 377
thee, no German Rhine-wine, 151
Fireside happiness, to, 443
pleasures gambol, 452
the light of its own, 173
Firm a heart, too tender or too, 236
as the land, 267
at his dangerous post, 304
keep the soldiers, 104
nerves, my, 72
so, yet soft, 453
Firmament, 132
and the wide, 191
no fellow in the, 62
now glowed the, 268
Firmer, better, shall be clearer, 450
Firmest friend, in life the, 176
Firmness in the right, with, 337
shakes off her wonted, 162
First, 132
a little more trouble at, 96
all words came, 458
American, the, 8
an' do it, 82
breath, we draw our, 455
by whom the new are tried, 126
city Cain, and the, 64
cries, Hold, enough, 214
degree, no creature owns it in the, 284
disobedience, of man's, 93
Eve, but if the, 115
falls, the ripest fruit, 146
fierce impulse unto crime, 66
garden made, God the, 64
garments, came in with our, 191
green peas, the, 32
is hailed, when the, 178
let me be ever the, 146
magnitude, thou liar of the, 217

First
of men, Eve upon the, 2
of men, richest, happiest, 402
passion woman loves her lover, in her, 232
rank of these, in the, 114
requisite, the, of a good citizen, 54
returns the, 159
rude sketch, 13
salmon, and the, 32
sight, that loved not at, 242
sight they loved, but at, 242
that came away, I was the, 189
that ever burst, we were the, 353
the, in loftiness of thought, 309
the good die, 91
they are the, 328
to welcome, the, 176
when Britain, 37
which mates him, 82
who with best meaning have incurred the worst, 464
Fir-trees dark and high, the, 331
Fish, 132
as is the osprey to the, 278
hangs in the net, here 's a, 214
have no fin, 142
this, will bite, 16
what cat 's averse to, 44
wild-fowl, or venison, 36
Fishers, 132
Fishes, 132, 133
all sorts of, 32
gnawed upon, men that, 102
Fish-hook, 133
Fishified, how art thou, 134
Fish-like smell, ancient and, 371
Fit, 133
for treasons, stratagems, and spoils, 273
the reason to the rhyme, hard to, 335
to employ, how, 229
Fitful fever he sleeps well, 223
Fitness comes by fits, a woman 's, 453
Fits, 133
all her children, nature, 67
a woman 's fitness comes by, 453
them all, the handle which, 218
Fitter being sane, it 's, 159
Fitting of self to its sphere, rest is the, 333
Five, arts that thrive at Number, 13
have I slain to-day, 337
I dine at, 92
sparrows sold for two farthings, 320
wits, alone and warming his, 292
Fix this thing for good an' all, 40
Fixed like a plant, 306
on futurity, 86
the brazen hasp, and, 263
Flag, 133
has braved a thousand years, whose, 110
has flown, an English, 113
is stayed, the English, 113
Flag
of Dixie, advance the, 94
of England, the meteor, 110
of England, what is the, 111
of England blew free, the, 284
of our union for ever, the, 420
of the brave, the, 110
our, was still there, 17
party that does not carry the, 420
to April 's breeze unfurled, their, 362
was new, when this old, 456
wavin' chellenge, each torn, 299
Flagon of sack, seven deadly sins in a, 26
Flags, 134
my labour never, 207
Flame, adding fuel to the, 147
and feed his sacred, 234
and its orbs of, 419
in Ætna 's breast of, 233
in he came with eyes of, 87
I shuttered my doors with, 284
lacks oil, after my, 228
my blood is liquid, 423
of love, the ardent, 339
summoned to drink to my, 274
the volcano's tongue of, 24
this fluttering spark of vital, 428
to qualify, absence seemed my, 2
vital spark of heavenly, 428
Flames, but endless, 347
in the light refulgent, 288
yet from those, 72
Flanders, our armies swore terribly in, 395
Flannel and sheeting, dealing out, 175
Flash, and face the, 227
and in a, 262
of the lightning, a, 269
Flashed the red artillery, far, 13
with Israfel, or, 244
Flashing, seen war 's lightning, 431
Flashes of merriment, your, 468
Flat and unprofitable, how weary, stale, 463
with a spade, laid them, 77
Flatter, averse alike to, 46
most, the wooer who can, 458
wrinkles . . . won't, 465
Flatteries, 134
damn his treacherous, 259
Flattering unction, lay not that, 419
Flattery, 134
a stranger to, 197
soothe, or, 421
whom 't were gross, 66
Flavour of mild decay, a general, 82
that gives it all its, 423
Flaw in right, or, 356
to expel the winter 's, 421
Flaws congealed, sudden as, 161
Flax, is severed as the, 38
seeketh the wool and the, 451
to scorch them up like, 347
Flea, 134

Fleas, 134
a flea has smaller, 134
Fled, all are scattered now and, 351
as if that soul were, 170
hope withering, 142
I waked, she, 98
whose lights are, 17
Fledge the shaft, to, 106
Fleet in my arms, and, 47
invincible, when that great, 111
one, 133
our years are, 79
Fleeting yet, fame . . . be just as, 62
time is, 163
Fleets, ten thousand, 288
time, 221
Flesh, 134
and blood, to ears of, 381
and blood so cheap, 78
are weak, and if my heart and, 436
a weight of carrion, 103
from her fair and unpolluted, 426
in man's obdurate heart, no, 38
like cumbrous, 381
neither fish nor, 132
now take away the, 380
rotted off his, 15
sinks downward, whilst my gross, 270
statue of, 115
thou tookest, 377
touches the, 77
wallets of, 88
Fleshed thy maiden sword, 395
Flew a trope, but out there, 335
from between their lips, the wedges, 437
thence up he, 63
Flibbertigibbet, 135
Fliers, your comrades chase e'en now the, 391
Flies, and in a moment, 233
every fault, 231
from pole to pole, it, 262
from woe, 370
of estate and sunneshine, 3
shoot folly as it, 136
will crowd, the buzzing, 184
with swallow's wings, 186
Flieth to it, grief, 77
Flight, an eagle in his, 282
brighten as they take their, 27
not attained by sudden, 177
of ages past, once in the, 228
of years began, since first the, 75
O time, in your, 340
thy certain, 387
Fling away ambition, 7
her old shoe after, shall, 244
Flings it a bone, if he, 461
Flint, 135
bears fire, as the, 209
being incensed he's, 161
weariness can snore upon the, 437
Flirt and flutter, with many a, 325
Float, a breath can, 144
a ship, there is water to, 37
for ever, 17
over a slave, never, 133
Floated on, they, 56
Floating by, ice mast-high came, 190
Flock, I am a tainted wether of the, 439
Flocking ghosts, hast thou met the, 151
Flocks that range the valley free, 305
Flog, 135
Flogging, 135
Flood, 135
by the rude bridge that arched the, 362
gates are open, the, 247
swallowed in the, 231
the calm fields, 268
went upward with the, 357
which taken at the, 405
Flooded the crimson twilight, it, 374
Floods foamed forth in, 6
to bathe in fiery, 90
Floor, and curled up on the, 350
kiver the, 16
new foot on the, 119
the nicely sanded, 295
Flop 'round the earth, 112
Flopped down on my marrow-bones, I jest, 313
Flourish all the year, that, 357
at its root, could not, 445
but thou shalt, 191
he, and still, 286
in an old cravat, virtue may, 171
princes and lords may, 300
the shelter and grace of our line, 49
Flourished over us, 121
Flow, and dark as winter was the, 225
backward, one moment, 82
of soul, feast of reason and the, 327
of their tears, by the, 398
you might have let them, 148
Flowed around our incompleteness, 154
Flower, 135
about to blow, there's a, 225
and thorn, 224
a simple maiden in her, 246
faith is but the, 327
he lurks in every, 77
if thou hast crushed a, 149
is born to blush unseen, many a, 149
is just a flower, a, 316
may prove a beauteous, 239
O'Dumblane, the sweet, 364
of a blameless life, 26
on every bough, there grows a, 203
safety, we pluck this, 280
that smiles to-day, the same, 343
the meanest, that blows, 404
to flower, the butterfly from, 342
was in flushing, our, 326
Floweret of the vale, the meanest, 293

Flowers, 135
and fruits of love, the, 223
and play with, 359
no fruits, no, 285
strews with fresh, 452
that only treads on, 406
the young, are blowing toward the west, 469
was it full of, 176
Flowery food, crops the, 27
Flowing asunder, swerving and, 339
Flown, an English flag has, 113
black bat night has, 148
the day's last beam is, 429
Flung magic o'er my way, 148
to the heedless winds, 441
up dead, some, 35
Flush of a new-born sun, 13
the east hath confessed a, 225
Flushing in her galled eyes, left the, 399
Flutter, bird of time has but a little way to, 406
Fluttered by the wings of Cherubim, 52
Flunked, 135
Fly, 136
as high as metaphysic wit can, 261
at his heels, 't will, 461
away, as an eagle, 336
betimes, then, 234
by change of place, 178
I, I mount, 163
immortal scandals, 351
like thought, 171
nor hurt a, 271
or to drown a, 377
soon as granted, 237
that sips treacle, the, 395
those that, may fight again, 130
to others that we know not of, 79
to the desert, fly with me, 85
turn and, 28
up, my words, 313
which way shall I, 177
Flying, borne down by the, 83
fast, and we are, 344
feet, with, 71
fishes play, where the, 252
her white wings, 436
old time is still a-, 343
set the wild echoes, 382
while nights and larks are, 151
Flying-chariot, bear the, 386
Fly-wheel in our modern civilization, 55
Foam, 136
chafe and break into, 138
of his gasping, the, 386
too full for sound and, 18
wave may not, 113
white is the, 387
Foam-fountains in the sea, his, 354
Foamed forth in floods, 6
Foams high and brave, 265
Focus, into one, 204
Foe, 136
an Arab chieftain treats a, 12
a pitying, 142
as soon for a trampled, 173
breathed in the face of the, 77
but debt, dread no, 184
could quell thy soul, no foreign, 112
each I judge thy, 71
furnace for your, 136
in one red burial blent, 40
mauls some feline, 44
my dearest, 73
of peace and law, 143
one common, 409
overcome but half his, 139
the avowed, the erect, the manly, 145
to let in the, 84
where breathes the, 17
who never made a, 145
with some infernal, 377
Foeman should scowl, if the brow of the, 226
will find neither coward nor slave, 110
Foemen worthy of their steel, 433
Foes, if there were no, 101
make friends of, 24
never from her, 436
of all the, 21
routed all his, 19
who hate, with a pardon for the, 363
Fog in my throat, to feel the, 78
Fold, like a wolf on the, 14
their tents, shall, 44
Folded in the same encircling arms, 416
Folio, for I am for whole volumes in, 466
Folks, and looks arter his, 356
are in their beds, while, 44
never understand the folks they hate, 171
on shore now, them unhappy, 285
Folks's corns out, new ones hunt, 161
Follies and misfortunes of mankind, 180
of such a book of, 449
that themselves commit, 243
Follow, and then let virtue, 266
as the night the day, it must, 415
him, bids men, 390
him, I will, 196
make the body, 142
mine own teaching, twenty to, 397
out his plan, 321
so fast they, 448
some must, 55
thee and make a heaven, 169
thee to the last gasp, 243
the funeral car, 433
this and come to dust, 103
where my feet have trod, 207
you, unworthy as I am, to, 378
you the star, 338

Followed her, the king himself has, 202
him, through all the world she, 463
in her path, ever, 143
wicked ways, she never, 441
yet are, 70
Following her, crush me for, 416
Follows after prayer, that, 374
fast, and a wind that, 359
his own instructions, 94
ye ez long 's ye live, 40
Folly, 136
and ignorance, 252
and with pride, with, 449
confess thy, 341
deem it not all a too presumptuous, 304
the memory of past, 445
to be wise, 'tis, 190
to be wise too soon, 446
your neebours' faults and, 305
Folly 's all they 've taught me, 118
Fond, fair and yet not, 455
kiss, ae, 203
of fame, are, 123
of fame, nor too, 46
of grief, to be, 165
of him, aren't you, 237
of him, are you so, 237
Fonder, absence makes the heart grow, 1
Fondly to-day, which I gaze on so, 47
Fondness o'er thee, that weep in, 443
of a dove, with the, 173
Fontarabian echoes, on, 39
Food at last is the ivy 's, 195
chief o' Scotia 's, 310
crops the flowery, 27
fed with the same, 197
for fools, flattery 's the, 134
for powder, 312
for seven long year, have been Tom 's, 261
for vermin, like Priam, 89
heavenly, is very light, 123
it likes, and other, 64
not ever craving for their, 31
of love, if music be the, 273
of sweet and bitter fancy, 124
of us that trade in love, moody, 273
pined and wanted, 182
slakes hunger, the, 369
they picked the luscious, 300
was the Englishman 's, 22
Fool, 136, 137
a noble, was never in a fault, 397
as wit turned, 447
beside that he 's a, 323
but the heart of the, 200
his whole life long, he is a, 444
honesty 's a, 183
is knavish, 452
is love, so true a, 239
let me play the, 264
man suspects himself a, 251
marry a, 255
Fool
more knave than, 205
of yourself, what a, 440
their love away, while unthrifts, 232
the pious, that raised it, 123
the prize be sometimes with the, 318
to fame, nor yet a, 466
to make me merry, rather have, 261
to the wiseman, the, 369
who thinks by force or skill, a, 450
yon brawny, 248
you would think truth were a, 218
Fooled, as father Adam first was, 449
Foolery, 137
in the wise, 136
Fooling thee, she is, 24
Foolish for a tear, too, 371
tears upon my grave, drop thy, 76
thing, never says a, 202
wit, than a, 137
Fool 's paradise, a, 295
paradise, in his, 295
Fools, 137, 138
all our yesterdays have lighted, 411
are as like husbands, 190
are my theme, 350
contest, let, 161
folly in, 136
have, for so, 217
like you, we thrive at Westminster on, 292
in spite of all the, 111
insulted by, 320
of nature, we, 268
or knaves, what, 306
that marry, they are, 255
the food for, 134
the paradise of, 295
they are the money of, 459
who came to scoff, 352
who roam, they are, 182
will learn in no other, 117
would wish to die, even, 81
Foot, 138
and hand go cold, both, 6
before, and firmly placed his, 136
can fall, as softly as, 407
gorgonized me from head to, 384
in the grave, with one, 164
of a conqueror, proud, 112
of night, hushed as the, 282
of thy crags, O sea, 161
of time, noiseless falls the, 406
of time, the inaudible and noiseless, 406
of time, the lazy, 56
o' man, he was six, 249
one, in sea, 83
on the floor, a new, 119
showed worth on, 417
to the sole of his, 196
upon a worm, man who needlessly sets, 463
Football game, in life, as in a, 222
Footpath way, jog on, the, 174
Footprints, 138

Footsteps he hath turned, 65
in the sea, his, 154
roam, howe'er thy, 182
Fop their passion, a, 462
Forage for herself alone, to, 106
Forbade to wade through slaughter, 368
Forbear, 138
for Jesus sake, 29
Forbearance, 138
Forbid, but that I am, 380
it, almighty God, 217
my tears, therefore I, 399
why was Caty not, 200
Forbidden tree, fruit of that, 93
Forbore, and, 78
Force, 139
but this twofold, 260
from all her men, drawing, 277
however great, there is no, 389
in the decrees of Venice, no, 213
it out, to, 398
my ramparts, to, 284
of nature, the, 309
of temporal power, the, 260
of the crown, to all the, 44
or skill, who thinks by, 450
shall have spent its novel, 297
upheld the truth, by tradition's 416
Forced by Fate, 13
gait, 't is like the, 309
me out of thy honest truth, 399
those waters from me, 399
till it be, 422
Forces, all his, dare not cross the threshold, 44
opposing and enduring, 60
Fordoes me quite, makes me or, 247
Forefathers had no other books, our, 317
of the hamlet, 108
Fore-foot, there he put his dear, 372
Forego it, this single life, 366
Foregone conclusion, a, 60
Forehead, did not with unbashful, 356
is wrinkled, because his, 309
kiss from my, 340
of our faults, the teeth and, 289
of the morning, than with the, 282
there was glory on his, 351
Foreheads, carried so long beneath our wrinkled, 403
Foreign, 139
foe could quell thy soul, no, 112
land, to what it is in a, 133
levy, nothing, 223
nations, intercourse with, 65
rivals, through fear of, 110
strand, from wandering on a, 65
troops, in my country, 8
Foreman smiles, the, 92
Foremost captain of his time, 43
fighting, fell, 131
man of all this world, 36
to defend, 176
Foreseeing man, brave, 8
Forespent, clean, 457
Forest, 139
a fool i' the, 137
like the leaves of the, 216
no true lover in the, 56
their trysting-place in the, 339
the old tree is leafless in the, 290
there's no clock i' the, 56
Forestalled to be, 260
Forests of the night, in the, 405
Foretell, I can, 315
Foretells the nature of a tragic volume, 38
world of happiness their harmony, 437
Foretold, truly that hour, 296
what else can be, 228
Forever, 139
one grand sweet song, that vast, 374
Forfeit of my bond, 83
Forfeits his own blood, he, 27
Forgave the offence, 289
Forge another to take up the old acceptance, 82
the arms ye, 355
the steel, I, 386
think God can't, 156
Forget, 139
it soon, I won't, 286
men's names, new-made honour doth, 275
never can I, 72
not that I am an ass, 13
or courage to, 330
so lost in lexicography as to, 459
that learning, laboured much how to, 466
the human race, 85
the luve o' life's young day, never can, 222
them all, you'll, 128
the man wholly, you, 314
themselves so far, muse that men, 455
this lost Lenore, and, 280
who never can, 384
Forgetful we are of death, how, 79
Forgetfulness, 139
not in entire, 25
steep my senses in, 370
Forgets, the heart that has truly loved never, 393
Forget'st, what thou hast, 170
Forgetting, 140
a sleep and a, 25
that even the sparrow falls, 177
Forgive, 140
forget and, 139
her deceit with a tear, and, 333
him, cursed be my tribe, if I, 193
me for lying, the Lord, 244
my foul offence, 429
this foolish tear, 398
to love and to, 260
to pity and perhaps, 138

Forgiven, 140
by Christ in Heaven, the sin, 366
hopes to be, 176
little to be, 312
Forgiveness, 140
Forgives, for who, 335
Forgiving, 140
Forgot as soon as done, 407
by the world, 140
his own griefs, and, 125
loved accents are soon, 209
should auld acquaintance be, 14
was Britain's glory, 241
Forgotten, 140
nor must Uncle Sam's web-feet be, 437
not one of them is, 320
what the inside of a church, 53
Fork, adder's, 179
Forked mountain, a, 56
Forlorn, that would make me less, 293
Form, 140
a combination and a, 250
and bearing fruit, taking, 461
and feature, in, 418
a state, scarce serve to, 385
doth take, the bodie, 377
from off my door, take thy, 19
for soule is, 377
his vacant garments with his, 165
let thy future give colour and, 127
in a visible, 78
in perfect rest, a perfect, 302
of prayer can serve my turn, 313
of success, that highest, 389
or face, 274
shall hail him at the gates of death, 61
so fair, a, 176
that sleep reveals, a late-lost, 442
the mould of, 263
Forma pauperis to God, in, 388
to God, sue in, 312
Formation of a demeanour, in the, 85
Formed the whole, who, 233
Forming, and swiftly, 271
Forms, all, all pressures past, 331
decay, though the, 256
moods, shapes of grief, 448
no, or crosses, 220
of government, for, 161
of hairs, to observe the, 458
of party strife, ancient, 339
of things unknown, the, 308
the common mind, education, 107
to his conceit, with, 307
unseen their dirge is sung, by, 34
Forsake him, his favourite sins all, 366
its languid melancholy frame, 428
Forsaken his sins, thinks he has, 366
when he's, 4
Forsakes, the wretched he, 370
Forswore, a woman I, 157
Fortress, 140
as a warrior storms a, 392
built by Nature, 112
Fortress
I can march up to a, 283
of storming some airy, 409
Fortunate, as he was, 7
Fortune, 141
fair or fatal, for, 461
hath given hostages to, 442
joy for his, 7
leads on to, 405
led, by wit or, 214
of outrageous, 19
sent me, 137
smiles, where, 370
the last effort of decayed, 171
to, and to fame, 257
to be a well-favoured man is the gift of, 466
to dispose, for, 89
to prey at, 168
what is your, 246
while he whose, 266
Fortune's power, I am not now in, 97
Fortunes, 141
lest it may mar your, 380
our, and our sacred honour, 307
strong, women are not in their best, 456
Forty, a fool at, 137
centuries look down upon you, 322
flags with their silver stars, 134
knows it at, 251
minutes, in, 152
pounds a year, passing rich with, 336
thousand men, with, 202
Forty-odd befell, at, 22
Forty-parson power to chaunt thy praise, 190
Forty-second Foot, and the, 138
Fossils, 141
Fought all his battles, 19
and bled in freedom's cause, 58
and prayed, the men that, 181
each of us, 113
each other for, what they, 425
for queen and faith, 105
for, that heroes, 416
for her, 416
he, he conquered, and he fell, 130
not with fifty of them, if I, 324
so well, they that had, 80
throughout a weary life, has, 321
with outright, met and, 219
Foul, 141
and don't shirk, don't, 222
be fair or, 221
deeds will rise, 83
fall him that blenches first, 114
his days are, 101
murder most, 272
Foul-tongued fanatic, you, 108
Found his work, he who has, 459
it, most of us have, 405
myself famous, 124
out the limit of my capacity for work, never, 460

Found that life was duty, 104
that means not to be, 355
thee a way, 140
them air, and I, 302
'twill be, 87
when, make a note of, 285
you, when I, 137
Foundation, no sure, set on blood, 27
the frame and huge, 277
Foundations lie, the strong, 267
Founder, meant to, 115
Fount about to stream, there's a, 225
Fountain of all human frailty, the, 452
spouting through his heir, 248
Fountains, large streams from little, 2
Four acts already past, the first, 109
days, those, 37
summers after, we met again, 296
things greater than all things are, 164
times the spoon, 349
hundred nobodies were ruined, 379
Four-square to all the winds that blew, 413
Fourteen hundred years ago were nailed, 67
Fowl by hatching the egg, sooner have the, 108
Fowler, is the net of the, 280
Fowls, 142
Fox, 142
Fractious indeed, and was very, 198
Fragment of his blade, 47
Fragments lie, and painted, 362
on the broken and dishonoured, 420
Fragrant, with Sappho, 410
Frail, it may be, 44
so, so strong, 374
that err, weep for the, 312
too, women are, 453
Frailty, 142
from the organ-pipe of, 273
the fountain of all human, 452
Frame agree, while souls and bodies in one, 378
a ladder, we can, 170
a shock of pleasure to the, 435
and huge foundation, the, 277
a shining, 132
forsake its languid melancholy, 428
like the grosser, 381
my face to all occasions, 118
the law unto my will, 213
thy fearful symmetry, could, 405
unequal laws, 115
when my whole, 331
with rapture-smitten, 274
with this goodly, 419
Framed, equal laws which it had, 59
their iron creeds, and, 155
to make women false, 122
France, 142
England, Germany, 135
fair gentlemen of, 179
the deadly Waterloo, the grave of, 435
France
the foaming grape of Eastern, 344
the king of, 202
Francis C—— lies, here, 87
Frantic clutch, denying to his, 115
Fraud, his heart as far from, 29
Fraught with menace, more, 165
Fray, in arms and eager for the, 12
of such a bloody, 308
Free, 142
and open nature, 183
and strong, 247
as air, love, 233
as aught but the, 133
as nature, I am as, 350
both open and both, 84
deeds, turnpikes leading to, 31
even to the uttermost, 412
for who are so, 286
from faults, not, 46
himself from God he could not, 39
his people are, 405
in the country of the, 469
I shall be, 78
let us die to make men, 225
o'er the land of the, 17,
only, he soars, 233
principles, refuge of, 111
proud fathers slumber at thy side, thy, 128
quill, Britons have a tongue and, 110
ring in the valiant man and, 422
so cleanly I myself can, 290
souls, we that have, 195
speech, turnpikes leading to, 31
that moment they are, 368
the blue, the fresh, the ever, 354
thought, turnpikes leading to, 31
till thou at length art, 376
to make thy music, 10
to prove all things, 320
to think and act, men are, 220
we must be, or die, 412
whom the truth makes, 144
who would be, 29
Freed, Ned Purdon from misery, 168
Freedom, 142–144
and then glory, 18
and whiskey gang thegither, 440
deed is done for, 143
in all the pride of, 217
of the press and quill, 110
reigns, faith with, 219
ring, let, 65
shall awhile repair, and, 34
shall have a new birth of, 276
stand in the Old South Church, 32
the kingliest act of, 144
the nation's later birth of, 276
to worship God, 464
Freedom's banner streaming o'er us, 17
cause, in, 58
ensign, 'neath the shade of, 64
soil beneath our feet, 17

Freedom 's tomb, vampire which from, 64
Freeman, 144
Freemen, we call you as, 286
Free-will, and that sort of thing, 330
Freeze, there 's nothing can, 372
thou bitter sky, 24
thy young blood, 380
Freezing the marrow with too late, 211
Freight, built for, 66
Freight-train of conversation, upset a, 321
Frémont and victory, 142
French crown, a fairer name than, 332
Frenchman, 144
Frenzy rolling, in a fine, 308
Fresh and simple, hearts are, 156
wild thrill, 33
woods and pastures new, 458
Fresh-blown roses washed in dew, 343
Freshness, a dewy, 268
Fret, 144
me, though you can, 305
Frets his hour, that struts and, 411
thy sight, that, 377
Fretted vault, long-drawn aisle and, 10
Fretting, her stately bosom was, 316
Friar, 145
Fridays when they fasted, on, 267
Friend, 145
a brute, 38
and I 've a, 167
and who lost no, 385
becomes her lover, when Psyche 's, 242
both itself and, 31
both leal and tried, and a, 57
death, good friend, 78
foe, in one red burial blent, 40
for a soul-bound, 173
found not a generous, 142
her lover has become her, 242
his own best, 249
indeed, be very much his, 405
in life the firmest, 176
in need, may we never want a, 285
is such a, 405
i' the court, a, 65
I trusted, but when the, 125
my guide, philosopher and, 167
no man is without a, 464
old without a, 462
one, not quite a hypocrite, 462
one common, 409
plain blunt man that love my, 291
remembered not, 24
save honour, seek no, 184
say Welcome, 221
severe, a, 91
shall be a, 38
take note of thy departure, and no, 86
that loved her, if I had a, 363
the Devil thought of his old, 11
Friend
their best and dearest, 322
then think of the, 125
the world is not thy, 463
the wretched has no, 465
to close his eyes, 86
to truth, statesman yet, 385
with her took my, 57
yet think of my, 378
Friendly be, both false and, 24
eye could never see, 128
grasp, never shall in, 97
love perfecteth, 232
Friends, 145, 146
and visitors, denied to, 345
are dear, when, 220
are many, be glad and your, 152
are wanted most, when, 145
boun' to be good, 111
but served our, 89
dearer, caress thee, 331
eat and drink as, 214
gut to be fas', 111
in sable weeds appear, 448
in youth they had been, 412
I would not enter on my list of, 463
like summer, 3
nature teaches beasts to know their, 278
of foes, make, 24
Romans, countrymen, 341
sisters and, 129
still as kind and constant, 345
troops of, 223
we may live without, 63
were poor but honest, my, 310
Friendship, 146
all a-two, a tonge cutteth, 412
false, in, 385
love and peace combine, when, 442
of all who offer you, 146
O summer, 3
Friendship 's solid mason-work below, needs, 242
Friendships, 146
honest with all nations, 6
Fright the souls, to, 432
Frighted thee, how have I, 370
Frightened when a madman stares, 50
Frightful when one 's dead, 75
Fringed with fire, bastion, 19
Frisky, should be so gay and, 440
Frith, intersected by a narrow, 110
Frizzled like celery tips, their blunt ends, 437
Frog, and toe of, 179
Frogs went hop, the, 372
Frolic and fun, 197
Frolics, a youth of, 462
Fronded palms in air, lift their, 43
Front, 146
engraven, deep on his, 85
hath smoothed his wrinkled, 432
now his honest, 288
of heaven, the, 277
of Jove himself, the, 250

Front
of them, cannon in, 42
Front-door and a side-door, have a, 129
Frost, comes a, 164
is my crown, the, 284
so full of, 119
the old year is ending in the, 290
Frosty, but kindly, 357
Caucasus, thinking on the, 191
Froth, sea was all a boiling seething, 147
Froward, peevish, when she is, 454
Frown, 146
and we smile, 141
and yesterday's, 442
the murderer's, 384
upon Saint Giles's sins, 367
Frowned not, fair science, 257
Frowning sky, from forth the, 28
Froze the genial current of the soul, 301
Frozen home, milk comes, 190
F. R. S. and LL. D., 1
Fruit, 146, 147
appears, their, 355
blooming ambrosial, 414
in garnered, 337
of that forbidden tree, 93
taking form and bearing, 461
till like ripe, 228
their century, 31
were scarce worth peeling, the, 386
Fruitless fire, shrivelled in a, 160
Fruits, no, no flowers, 285
of love, the flowers and, 223
Fruit-tree tops, all the, 268
Fry, driving the poor, 133
Fudge, in vain we call old notions, 386
Fuel, 147
fresh beauty for its, 233
Full dress, when daring in, 408
for sound and foam, too, 18
for weeks thegither, 37
I was na, 307
man, reading maketh a, 326
of briers, 37
of deceits, are, 82
of emotion, when the heart is so, 173
of jealousy, love . . . is, 240
of joy, my songs were, 148
of mirth, little inmate, 175
of supper, being, 393
or no, the moon shine at, 193
the moon is, 57
the moon is at her, 268
without o'erflowing, 84
Full-blossomed on the thorny stem, 143
Full-hot horse, like a, 9
Fullness of perfection lies in him, 168
Full-weight-dollar debts with, to pay, 96
Fumble with the sheets, after I saw him, 359
Fun, 147
frolic and, 197
the mirth and, 264
Function suiting, and his whole, 307
Funeral, 147
car, follow the, 433
marches to the grave, 163
note, not a, 102
Fungi gather, the mosses and, 425
Funnel and a mast, just a, 54
Furious close, intestine shock and, 54
Furled, and the battle-flags were, 433
Furnace crammed rosin and pine, 346
from the hottest, 41
heat not a, 136
I manage the, 386
red, like a fiery, 87
sighing like a, 242
the human body is a, 28
unshrinking, through the, 9
Furnaced, has been fierily, 314
Furnish forth the marriage tables, 147
Furrow ez straight ez he can, he draws his, 356
stands, and to the last of earth his, 79
straighter, nor draw a, 249
Furrowed face, his, 225
Furrows of care, the, 340
Further gone than he, his neighbour, 284
go, could no, 309
I don't want to go no, 431
Fury, comes the blind, 123
full of sound and, 411
in that beastly, 101
like a woman scorned, nor hell a, 324
of a patient man, beware the, 298
oppose my patience to his, 298
thing that feeds their, 132
Furze, brown, long heath, 354
Future, 147
give colour and form, let thy, 127
has deeds of glory, your, 409
hope links her to the, 258
shame, relief from, 89
should woo the angel virtue in the, 332
state, the secrets of the, 376
the, the past, 222
yet that scaffold sways the, 417
your dreams of the, 409
Future's heart, leaps beneath the, 115
portal, nor attempt the, 281
Futurity, fixed on, 86
Fuzzy-Wuzzy, 147

G

G—— lies under ground, 168
Gaberdine, 147
Gain, and the people's, 276
but for, 345
it gets, know for the, 206
love were clear, 232
of a few, for the, 297

Gain or but subserves another's, 160
some private ends, to, 95
Gained a hundred fights, he that, 167
a point, feel I had, 197
most, learning hath, 31
no title, who, 385
Gaining some hard-fought field, of, 409
the crown, nearer, 278
Gains for all our losses, there are, 470
may be great, 379
or loses, what, 306
Gait, an easy, 186
like the forced, 309
Galatians, a great text in, 71
Gale, 147
and catch the driving, 278
comes on, sonorous as the, 52
it's a stiff, 320
note that swells the, 293
that scents the evening, 402
the lightning and the, 133
Gall, 148
alone you must drink life's, 152
in the slanderous tongue, 42
though ink be made of, 466
Gallagher, his father was a, 348
Gallant craft, a beautiful and, 66
is this that haughty, 231
Gallantly streaming, were so, 17
Gallantry, no more to do with, 61
Galled, but what encumbered, 76
Gallery of family portraits, man with the, 124
Gallop, that still eternal, 324
withal, who doth he, 407
Gallows, with a thief to the, 407
Gambols, your, your songs, 468
Game, 148
a few more brace of, 208
for love, a quiet, 234
in life as in a football, 222
never seeing noble, 70
or fish, wild-fowl or venison, 36
speculation is a round, 379
the rigour of the, 175
war's a, 430
wasn't worth a dump, 77
Gammon, texts with trading, 247
Gander, she finds some honest, 255
Gangrened, 148
Gaol a ship is worse than a, 359
Gaoler, is as a, 41
to his pity, his injury the, 192
Gap of time, this great, 370
Gapes for drink again, 101
Gaping age, to a, 278
who never leave, 133
wide, that the graves all, 282
Gaps, fill their, 252
Garbage floats, down Tiber, 184
Garden, 148
for parsley, as she went to the, 254
had been, to mark where a, 342
in her face, there is a, 343
made, God the first, 64
was a wild, the, 450
Gardener, 148
Adam was a, 2
Gardeners, no ancient gentlemen but, 150
our wills are, 28
Gardens, our bodies are [our], 28
shut the, 345
Garland, the remains of the, 100
the sweetest, 395
Garlands dead, whose, 17
Garlic, live with cheese and, 399
roach and dace, 32
Garment no more fitting, is a, 375
Garments, his vacant, 165
which it wore last year, 381
Garnish, eye of heaven to, 152
Garret, 148
Garrick's a salad, our, 349
Garrison hung but on him, 113
Garter, familiar as his, 161
for the sake of a ribbon, star, or, 42
Garters, gold, scarfs, 49
Gasp, follow thee to the last, 243
Gasping on the brink, and I, 439
the foam of his, 386
Gate, 148
alone, at the, 148
and see through heaven's, 292
as he would beat down the, 206
boots it at one, 84
lock the latticed, 345
matters not how strait the, 126
my dog howls at the, 95
no iron, 31
now at heaven's, 210
sings, at heaven's, 210
sings hymns at heaven's, 210
the house with the narrow, 187
the old poor at the, 149
thick wall or moated, 385
through glory's morning, 105
Gates are mine to close, the, 276
are mine to open, the, 276
iron, obstruct the prisoner's gaze, 262
kneel at thy, 126
of death, hail him at the, 61
of hell, as the, 218
of mercy on mankind, shut the, 368
of mercy shall be all shut up, 260
with iron, I barred my, 284
Gather by unseen degrees, 167
them in, I, 357
ye rosebuds while ye may, 343
Gathered be at last, shall, 441
together, can never be, 173
together, the eagles be, 184
up their treasure, have, 367
Gathering her brows, 465
in, dey all comes, 359
Gaudy, rich, not, 11
Gave, blessed be he who took and. 164
ere charity began, his pity, 305
me fame, use, 421
me up to tears, and, 399
she only, 265

Gave thee, who, 419
up their lives at the Queen's command, 373
Gay, 148
as soft, 20
can rise in the morning, 442
cities, far from, 68
from grave to, 162
Lothario, that haughty gallant, 231
Gayest soul on earth, was the, 148
Gaze, obstruct the prisoner's, 262
on thee, I, 285
with averted, 121
Gazed, and still they, 456
on the face of the dead, we steadfastly, 313
Gazelle, 148
Gazes on the ground, and, 130
Gazing fed with, 124
Gem, 149
of countless price, 73
Gems, 149
in sparkling showers, 107
General joy of the whole table, 172
so likes your music, the, 273
'twas caviare to the, 45
use, concur to, 117
Generalities, 149
Generation, that each, 54
the cold lair of my dark, 284
Generations dead, said of all the, 228
Generous glass, inspired to wake, 152
open, sincere, whose temper was, 197
Genius and his jack-knife driven, by his, 467
companies of men of, 387
gave the final blow, thine own, 106
my, . . . has as yet lost nothing, 397
should marry a person of character, 254
Gent, for any scientific, 171
Gentility, shabby, 171
Genteelly.
Gentle dedes, to do the, 150
dedis, that doth, 150
deeds is known, by, 150
he is, 150
minde, the, 150
of manners, 252
ones, one of those, 88
thing, sleep, it is a, 369
yet not dull, 84
Gentleman, 149, 150
a fine puss, 54
and scholar, the, 58
a very simple, 415
a worthy, 326
bears not alive so stout a, 381
I do not think a braver, 422
in a black coat, with a, 416
is God Almighty's, 51
porter and, 21
St. Patrick was a, 348
that loves to hear himself talk, 396
Gentleman
that makes the king a, 248
the honourable, has said much, 291
will out-talk us all, 396
Gentlemanly vice, a good old, 15
Gentleman's study, in an old, 279
Gentlemen, 150
but gardeners, no ancient, 150
but gents, a word not made for, 294
God Almighty's, 51
God rest ye, merry, 51
my Lords and, 75
of England, ye, 355
of France, fair, 179
other, come down Tom-all-Alone's, 314
Gentleness my strong enforcement be, 23
Gentler, still, sister woman, 188
Gentlest fall, with, 18
Gently and humanly, 454
but use all, 379
scan your brother man, 188
she is sleeping, 105
steer, who in his verse can, 162
to hear, 198
Gents, a word not made for gentlemen but, 294
Geographers in Afric maps, 252
Geometric scale, he by, 6
George, and if his name be, 275
the Fourth could reign, as long as, 3
the Third may profit by their example, 414
Georgius Primus' reign, in, 31
German, 151
Germany or Spain, 135
Gesture in every dignity and love, 161
Get a fish-hook in, 133
at one end, what the boys, 135
away, you won't, 112
before, to, 344
forrid, civlyzation doos, 431
heavy to, 157
in, wish to, 253
money, still get money, boy, 266
no more of me, you, 296
on, but really can't, 247
out of a room, hard for some people to, 212
out, wish to, 253
still thou striv'st to, 170
thar, how did he, 404
thee gone, go poor devil, 189
thee to a nunnery, 286
them, we, bear them, 311
there, but how shall I, 383
up, start again, 220
up airly, you've gut to, 431
you gone, old opinions . . . , 110, 143
Gets mad, the one thet fust, 245
the narrower by going farther, 276
well, say that truth, 415
Getting and spending we lay waste our powers, 463
Getting-up, 151

Ghastly dreams, of, 99
Ghost, ay, thou poor, 331
  of him that lets me, I 'll make a, 420
  that is speechless, like a, 451
  there needs no, 426
Ghosts, 151
  break up their graves, and, 352
Giant, 151
  dies, as when a, 80
  wake not thou the, 301
  yield, bidding some, 409
Gib cat, melancholy as a, 258
Gibbets keep the lifted hand in awe, 272
Gibes now, where be your, 468
Giddy, 151
Gift, freedom ain't a, 143
  last, best, 177
  of a coward, but that he hath the, 323
  of a grave, he would quickly have, 323
  of fortune, is the, 466
  till happier hours restore the, 203
  true love 's the, 237
  without the giver, the, 181
Gift-horse, 151
Giftie, gie us, wad some power the, 355
Gifts, if sorrow could be won by, 10
  pounds and possibilities is good, 311
  wax poor, rich, 421
Gild, 152
Gilded car of day, 73
  bath the world 's book been, 207
Gilead, is there balm in, 17
Gilt o'erdusted, more laud than, 103
Gin, he smells of Hollands, 181
  now is the woodcock near the, 457
  so strives the woodcock with the, 457
  with pitfall and with, 365
Ginger shall be hot i' the mouth, 427
Gingerbread, thou should'st have it to buy, 301
Gird thee up anew, 126
Girdle, 152
Girdled with the sky, 268
Girl a settin', there 's a Burma, 251
  gave, sweeter sure never, 205
  here's to the, 246
Girl-graduates, and sweet, 162
Girl 's door, to knock at a pretty, 338
  hand, holds a pretty, 383
Girls acts so or so, why, 283
  between two, 213
  golden lads and, 103
  sitting like shopkeepers, 266
  that are so smart, of all the, 6
Give a cup of water, to, 435
  and I devise, I, 91
  a thousand furlongs of sea, 354
  back the upward looking, 467
  enough, enabled them to, 266
  grandam kingdom, 162
  her booby for another, who 'd, 270
  his due to the devil, and so, 87
Give, I 'd, to feel once more, 33
  in, do n't, 131
  it, the law doth, 134
  it in, blush to, 287
  it willingly, I, 381
  me liberty, 217
  me sixpence, if you will, 310
  me sweet kisses, Chloe, 205
  my hopes, and, 409
  no man a reason upon compulsion, 327
  no reason, so can I, 327
  not what we, 181
  o'er, who knows not to, 466
  place, all other things, 209
  succeed and, 129
  the devil his due, 87
  thee, what strength that God may, 429
  thee sixpence, I, 367
  thoughts, the meanest flower that blows can, 404
  to God each moment, 227
  too much, fortune . . . doth, 141
  unless their subjects, 202
  up, do n't, afore the ship goes down. 320
  up the ship, do n't, 359
  up the ship, never, 58
  us, what riches, 336
  way and room, must I, 50
  what they would take, and doctors. 214
  when lawyers take what they would, 214
Given away, thou hast, 137
  away, 'tis heaven alone, 177
  o'er, 't is not amiss ere ye 're, 86
  to God, and so was, 56
  to God, worship freely, 464
  to lying, how this world is, 244
  with it, alas, if none is, 129
  with welcome, 't is, 129
  you one face, God has, 118
Giver, the gift without the, 181
Givers prove unkind, when, 421
Gives a kiss, and, 203
  but nothing, 26
  from a sense of duty, 7
  him that, 260
  himself, who, 181
  only the worthless gold, 7
  us back the image of our mind, that, 447
  what he has he, 84
Glad, 152
  did I live and gladly die, 163
  eat and be, 365
  I manage to exist and to be, 61
  I should be, 310
  I was up so late, 211
  me with its soft black eye, to, 148
  the two or three, thoughts that shall, 466
  to death 's mystery, 244
  to-morrow, in that great, 94

Glad
with all my heart, 296
Gladden and control, 384
Gladiator, 152
Gladness, and all the, 331
of the world's release, the, 300
the lark is so brimful of, 235
worketh with, 451
Glance from heaven to earth, doth, 308
would scorch, whose, 377
Glances bright, see the gleam of, 23
Glare, maidens, like moths, are ever caught with, 270
the rocket's red, 17
with, which thou dost, 29
Glares at one that nods and winks, 301
Glass, 152
and scythe, fierce spirit of the, 406
an excuse for the, 210
but she made mouths in a, 453
of fashion, the, 263
of time, love took up the, 241
pride is his own, 320
Glasses, stand to your, 91
there, fill all the, 101
where they view themselves, as the, 453
with water you fill up your, 445
Gleam, and one brief, 230
her camp-fires, before us, 281
in the morning, 132
of glances bright, 23
of sunshine, the parting, 111
of their snowy robes, the, 339
unrecked of, 354
Gleamed upon my sight, when first she, 302
Gleaming, at the twilight's last, 17
our days come roaring and, 138
Glee, laughed out in her innocent, 440
laughed with counterfeited, 93
puzzling with a deal of, 1
Glen, cam' down the lang, 458
Glib and oily art, I want that, 321
Glide, in the church-way paths to, 282
how mirth can into folly, 136
Glideth by the mill, more water, 435
Gliding free, rivers, 228
Glimmer, only waiting till the, 429
Glimpses of the moon, 268
so might I . . . have, 293
Glisten, 152
in the ray, earth shall, 159
Glisteneth, all is not gold that, 158
Glisters, all is not gold that, 158
gold, nor all that, 158
is not gold, all that, 158
Glittering and sounding generalities, the, 149
eye, with his, 117
in gold, 106
Glitters, all, as they say, that, 158
out again, then, 376
in the west, 109
Globe, all that tread the, 74
in this distracted, 331
itself, the great, 428
over the surface of the whole, 112
round, search the, 194
elate, o'er thrones and, 385
Gloom, amid the encircling, 214
long as there lingers, 219
shrieking through the, 61
Gloomy as usual, 124
or bright, be it, 116
Glories fall, where lights like, 264
its earthly, 419
of this world, some for the, 44
Glorified, till they stand, 255
Glorious charter, deny it who can, 47
day for America, a, 8
I'll make thee, 124
in a pipe, 408
Tam was, 191
to write, it may be, 466
works, Parent of Good, thy, 461
Glory, 152, 153
and shame, through, 236
an' one shame, hev, 208
circling round the soul, a, 233
ez to my princerples I, 42
forgot was Britain's, 241
freedom and then, 18
from his grey hairs, the, 121
full meridian of my, 122
glows, where neither guilty, 434
go to war for, 110
guards, and, 26
he had sought, the very, 342
in a sea of, 353
in full-orbed, 268
in his bosom, with a, 225
is like a circle, 53
jest and riddle of the world, the, 462
leads the fight, when, 143
like a sea of, 216
of his works, through all the, 154
of philosophy, the, 269
of the northern sky, the, 245
on his forehead, there was, 351
Rome in the height of her, 112
stood for his country's, 58
that may raise, love and, 293
the grape, 193
the paths of, 163
the rainbow's, 209
the uncertain, 240
the way to, 104
the wild cataract leaps in, 382
to, arise, 58
trailing clouds of, 25
trod the ways of, 140
unknown to, 410
vain pomp and, 310
wails manhood in, 326
we steer, 't is to, 286
which is brighter than the sun, 437
your future has deeds of, 409
Glory-dazzled world, to tell the, 432

Glory's morning gate, through, 105
Gloss, an unwholesome, 171
Gloucester fisherman, the wife of some, 99
Glove, a sentence is but a cheveril, 447
our falcon in our, 344
upon that hand, 47
Gloves, 153
Glow, Burgundy in all its sunset, 344
leaps with a burning, 173
a warmth about to, 225
breast ne'er learned to, 35
my heart has learned to, 174
with wisdom, 283
Glowed the firmament, now, 268
with his presence, 87
Glowing hours, to chase the, 71
Glows with faith and pride, 173
Glow-worm, 153
Gloze, have taught to, 105
Glut your ire, and, 193
Gnarling sorrow hath less power to bite, 375
Gnats in cobwebs, faster than, 168
Gnawing in the breast, 64
Go, and like wind I, 435
and men may, 116
as good to die and, 89
at once, but, 157
before, if money, 267
but let him, 422
forth under the open sky, 362
from your presence forth I, 328
grieve, and they turn and, 329
higher, can Bourbon or Nassau, 317
in it, there's, 467
in they, 21
in, would fain, 253
I have been there and still would, 312
know not why you, 100
must needs, 87
nor sit nor stand but, 328
on for ever, I, 116
onward, all day the iron wheels, 439
out, would fain, 253
right, ef he hollers out Gee, 461
see ere thou, 230
so much on religion, I don't, 330
the curt-tongued mills say, 413
't is mine to, 328
togither, maäkin' 'em, 241
to heaven, by easy trips may, 1
to the wars, would you, 434
to your Gawd like a soldier, an', 373
we know not where, 90
when such comers must, 338
where munny is, but, 267
with you, may I, 246
Goad us on to sin, that doth, 347
Goal of ill, the final, 160
comes surest to the, 324
the grave is not its, 222
we reach the, 221
Goat, catch the wild, 350
shave like the, 153
Goatskin water-bag, an' a, 420
Goblet, 153
hallows all it holds, the, 68
has scorned the flashing, 321
Goblins, 153
God, 153–157
a death, we owe, 89
a little, round, fat, oily man of, 289
all end in love of, 269
Almighty's gentleman, 51
Almighty's gentlemen, 51
Almighty's guns were going off, 147
Almighty's storm, we euchred, 115
alone belongs, vengeance to, 423
a mighty fortress is our, 140
and blushed, saw its, 435
and good books, I trust in, 31
and Mammon, yon servitor of, 247
and man is, know what, 135
and nature, faith in, 156
and nature hath assigned, that, 262
and nature, which, 383
and our right, 338
and the angels, I b'lieve in, 330
and the Prophet, 63
are hers, the eternal years of, 415
as lightning does the will of, 144
at home with, 108
bade me act for him, 93
beloved in old Jerusalem, O woman, 450
be thanked, the meanest, 243
be this juice the growth of, 69
be ye fixed on your, 5
blessed once, what, 159
by his spirit, of kin to, 248
by night an atheist half believes a, 14
calls virtue, when, 227
cast all your cares on, 9
could have, doubtless, 10
daughter of the voice of, 73
defend the right, 338
do the holy will of, 207
do we come from, 25
doth is best, that what, 374
each moment, give to, 227
ef you want to take in, 431
endures forever, surely, 380
erects a house of prayer, wherever, 87
for, for the cause, 19
for power, nor paltered with eternal, 418
for spite, as if they worshipped, 302
for use had given, powers which, 142
freedom to worship, 464
gave her peace, 323
given to, 56
gives us to see the right, as, 337
gives wind by measure, 209
give us men, 259
God, archangel call archangel, and, 275
had I but served my, 357

God
had sifted three kingdoms, 276
has bowed me down, 32
has given, the gift which, 237
has given you one face, 118
has need of him, when, 248
hath made him, every man is as, 249
hath made them so, 95
he could not free, himself from, 39
help me, I cannot do otherwise, 383
helps them that help themselves, 179
her seat is the bosom of, 212
he 's true to, 249
himself, an attribute to, 260
his life a breath of, 248
if Jesus Christ is a, 196
in after-days, raise this soul to, 293
in clouds, 176
in forma pauperis to, 388
is calling sunward, souls which, 439
is God, since, 337
is good, 360
is just, when I reflect that, 414
is marching on, while, 225
is not mocked for ever, 301
is obedience to, 328
is our trust, in, 415
is overhead, I believe that, 77
is seen God, 3
it is and it is not the voice of, 301
justify the ways of, 200
knows, the rest, 87
let us worship, he says, 464
like a soldier, an' go to your, 373
made, the thing the Lord, 402
made him, and therefore, 251
made sech nights, 152
made the country, 64
makes instruments, that, 389
may dwell, where a, 367
may give thee, what strength thy, 429
mount his chariot of fire, 255
nature is the art of, 13
nearer my, 278
never did, doubtless, 10
never made his work, 172
not one of them is forgotten before, 320
not unmarked of, 177
of all, as, 38
of my idolatry, the, 394
of storms, and give her to the, 133
one, one law, 322
one man with, 247
one more insult to, 467
or devil, with him was, 324
or man, never a law of, 212
pity is the touch of, 305
pity them both and pity us all, 470
poetry is itself a thing of, 309
prosper your affairs, 319
pseudo Privy Councillors of, 347
put your trust in, 311

God
rest ye, merry gentlemen, 51
said, let Newton be, 281
said of old to a woman, 365
save our king, 201
save our lord the king, 308
sealed for Charlie 's sake, 365
seed of witnesses for, 441
see the hand of, 341
seen in dreams from, 99
sendeth and giveth, 271
sends me love, 232
send us peace, 299
servant of, well done, 357
shall raise me up, my, 406
shall reply to, 147
somewhere has just relieved a picket, 384
spontaneously to, 279
steadfast in the strength of, 179
still giveth his beloved sleep, 369
stoops, who thinks, 108
sue *in forma pauperis* to, 312
tempers the wind to the shorn lamb, 209
thank, you are rid of a knave, 422
that this nation under, 276
that under, 276
the fane of, 114
the first garden made, 64
the laws of nature and of nature 's 356
the noblest work of, 183
the other to the altar 's, 312
the peace of, 75
the protector, you will find in your, 1
there 's a background of, 314
the sunflower turns on her, 393
think himself an act of, 248
'tis only, 177
though the mills of, 262
though he were ten times slain, 199
to man, so near is, 104
to scan, presume not, 250
through darkness up to, 7
up to nature 's, 278
vindicate the ways of, 200
where every, 250
while we are doubly false to, 213
who builds a church to, 53
who gave us life, the, 217
who loveth us, the dear, 314
will pardon all that 's past, 429
will save thy sailor, praying, 347
wills, yet if, 199
within the light of, 334
within the shadow, standeth, 417
woman, the last the best reserved of, 453
worship freely given to, 464
writes a legible hand, if, 426
wun't leave us yit, 320
Goddess, 157
fair and free, come thou, 264
God-fearing man, as a brave, 313

Godhead, a feeling from the, 233
God-illumined earth should see, and, 417
God-in-man is one, where, 313
Godlike, 157
  is it all sin to leave, 365
Godliness, next to, 55
God's altar, one nearer to, 312
  benison go with you, 24
  doth then show likest, 260
  finger touched him, 371
  first temples, the groves were, 400
  great judgment seat, stand presently at, 391
  image, a reasonable creature, 30
  name, stand back to back in, 131
  own hand, and, 184
  patience, abusing of, 113
  plan and measure, 250
  pure light, in, 198
  right hand, touch, 156
  sons are things, 459
  to thee, and what thy, 151
  word's our warrant, 409
Gods, 157
  angels would be, 316
  are just, the, 425
  as a dish fit for the, 201
  call dross, and the, 102
  daughter of the, 94
  howling to his, 73
  kings it makes, 186
  must yield, even, 330
  pine for my abode, the strong, 159
  the, on murderers, 28
  the temples of his, 89
  where monkeys were the, 316
  worship dirty, 158
God's-acre, 157
Goes all the day, merry heart, 174
  as useless if it, 190
  bravely on, the work, 459
  easily, your wit ambles well, it, 447
  on the earth, the earth, 106
  out, a soul, 113
  out sighing, and farewell, 438
  round forever, the world, 462
  to my heart, the way he says darling that, 72
  to the earth, the earth, 106
  to the wall, the weakest, 430
  toward love, love, 239
  up, the world, 442
Goest, ride more than thou, 362
Goeth every Sunday, his plough, 421
Going, 157
  back on him, and I'm not, 77
  ech aboute other, 53
  guest, speed the, 167
  my valour is certainly, 423
  off, God Almighty's guns were, 147
  where are you, 246
Goings in and out, a few more, 222
Gold, 157, 158
  and silver can buy, a knot that, 206
Gold
  and the rocks pure, 197
  as its purest, 453
  barbaric pearl and, 107
  beauty provoketh thieves sooner than, 21
  betrayed for, 15
  despise, what female heart can, 44
  Eden's green and, 13
  for a' that, the man's the, 249
  for what he lent him, 82
  fruit of vegetable, 414
  gives only the worthless, 7
  glittering in, 106
  gleaming in purple and, 14
  I'd locked my heart in a case o', 231
  its ounce of, 177
  kissed that haughty scroll of, 111
  love, in these are sunk, 193
  not the, 14
  scarfs, garters, 49
  sell and mart your offices for, 294
  spared neither land nor, 341
  the honour proof to place or, 185
  the love that's linked with, 203
  they refused the, 183
  to gild refined, 152
  transmute, leaden metal into, 162
  wedges of, 102
  where blood with, 27
  wich's more than, 357
  with pomp of pearl and, 353
Golden age again, see the, 417
  bells, 437
  calf of Baal, 42
  hair, in their, 162
  lads and girls, 103
  mean alike condemn, both the, 237
  opinions, I have bought, 290
  seeme, gold al is not that doth, 158
Gone, 158
  afay all, mit de lager beer, 297
  and are, 367
  and he is, 46
  and what's past help, 166
  are faded and, 342
  are ye all, 381
  ay, Cæsar, but not, 190
  from his grey hairs, 121
  he is dead and, 75
  now dimmed and, 258
  the flowers and fruits of love are, 22
  the old familiar faces, all are, 307
  to bed, lamp and, 108
  to her death, 420
  to-morrow he is, 364
  to the grave, thou art, 163
  when these are, 399
  wilt thou be, 283
  with a heaviness that's, 177
Good, 159, 160
  a holy place, 52
  all partial evil, universal, 338
  and all, till they do for, 202
  and bad of every land, with something, 8

Good
and did too little, 202
and ill, the weights of, 389
and ill together, 222
and just, study to be, 104
and much that is, 291
and out of, 116
an ill winde turnes none to, 444
are better made, the, 191
as she, and, 180
at pen and ink, 92
attending Captain Ill, Captive, 417
book, a, 30
books, God and, 31
but rarely came from good advice, 3
came of it at last, what, 425
cannot prevail, my, 429
cheer, at Christmas play and make, 52
citizen, first requisite of a, 54
crowning, repressing ill, 385
deceit, that is, 82
deed, kind of, 459
deed dying tongueless, 83
deed in a naughty world, 42
deeds past, those scraps are, 407
die first, the, 91
digestion wait on appetite, 91
divine that follows, 94
do, by stealth, 123
easy man, 164
either excellently, 251
enough for man, not, 56
enough to be given a square deal, is, 383
evil, be thou my, 186
fellow, he 's a, 178
fellows, king of, 130
fer a dog, is, 134
fight, I have fought a, 131
fight, who have fought the, 120
for our country 's, 64
friend thou art, 78
gifts, pounds and possibilities is, 311
glow for others', 35
grandam, there 's a, 162
hater, a, 171
he can, does himself all the, 386
hold fast that which is, 320
however, 31
how kind, how, 46
husband, get thee a, 189
in every case, 't is, 390
in everything, 3
inspirations, have, 80
is not original, the, 291
is oft interred with their bones, 116
I stand on, the, 417
it is never, 281
jest git all the, 49
knowledge of, 414
labours for his country 's, 64
length of days is not a, 223
love sought is, 240
luck shall fling her old shoe after, 244

Good
luck would have it, as, 244
make us lose the, 97
manners won't let me tell, 22
man to be sad, impious in a, 346
man weeps, look, the, 438
man 's feast, at any, 23
man 's life, best portion of a, 201
man 's love, for a, 238
man 's sin, for the, 287
men, that these are, 176
men, the lives of these, 301
morning, bid me, 220
more wit than does 'em, 447
morrow, fool, 137
name in man and woman, 275
name is mine, your, 275
news baits, while, 281
not the ill wind which blows no man to, 444
of bad, would make, 24
of just and, 91
of my country, for the, 64
one out, fire my, 9
only noble to be, 148
or bad, nothing either, 402
or bad a thousandfold, 157
or evil side, for the, 83
or ill, come, 150
or ill, extreme in love or hate, in, 449
or ill, our angels are, or, 2
or ill, the prophet of, 319
our courtiers were, 22
produce, equal, 117
quality, never sees a, 70
resign his own for others', 159
rest, and so, 333
she will do him, 451
some said it might do, 317
spirits may be in, 197
sweet maid, be, 374
temper, in good spirits and, 197
that might have been, the, 434
the crest and crowning of all, 38
thet 's new, all ain't, 469
the wise, the, 334
they comprehend not, 156
thy glorious works, parent of, 461
to be noble we 'll be, 148
to die and go, 89
to do his, 386
to glow for others', 174
to me is lost, all, 186
't will do you, 40
uncouth, makes ancient, 281
war, there never was a, 430
warfare 'twixt the evil and the, 433
was spontaneous, what was, 261
whets his appetite for moral, 312
will, by service long to purchase their, 455
will, peace and, 52
wine needs no bush, 40
wombs have borne bad sons, 374
word, who never wanted a, 26

Good
work is ever lost, no, 460
yoursel', ye wha are sae, 305
Good-bye, proud world, 461
Goodly apple rotton at the heart, 11
day to-morrow, gives signs of a, 393
outside falsehood hath, 122
Goodman's awa', when our, 244
Good-natured things alive, 140
Goodness, 160
and he fill up one monument, 267
beauty brief in, 21
let me bound, thy, 463
share with thy birthright, 25
that is cheap in beauty, 21
to the vile seem vile, wisdom and, 445
Good-night, 160
bids the world, 96
I shall say, 296
kiss was given, she thought our, 105
say not, 220
to each a fair, 371
your vow, 70
Goods a man has, the more, 279
men looking at, 266
on the counter, throwing . . . , 15
thy lands and, 134
Goose a swan, lad, and every, 469
fat pig and, 322
so grey, there swims no, 255
to hear thee slandered, 304
Goose-pen, write with a, 148
Goose-quill, ink and paper, pay for, 317
Gordian, 161
Gore one way or kick the other, 292
Gored, my fame is shrewdly, 332
Gorge rises at it, my, 468
Gorgonized me from head to foot, 384
Gorgons, 161
Gorilla, distinguishable from a, 255
Gory locks at me, never shake thy, 229
Gossamer links, who can follow the, 15
Gospel, 161
in law and, 380
texts, blends, 247
Gossips, 161
Got there, how the devil they, 458
where any thing is to be, 394
Goths, and glut your ire, 193
had a wise custom, the ancient, 82
Govern, 161
our conditions, 127
the world, syllables, 395
Governed, from the consent of the, 161
Government, 161
ain't to answer for it, 156
for bread, having looked to, 26
land of settled, 144
most important department under, 54
Government
of the people, by the people, for the people, 276
preservation of the general, 299
unless against the, 345
Governments, 161
Governs the world, a little foolery, 137
Gown, 161
texts enough to wear a parson's, 401
who preaches in her, 295
Gowns of silk, no, 220
Grace, 161
and remembrance be to you both, 343
his mysteries of, 154
if possible with, 266
impart, if I am right, thy, 397
I pray for, 413
is saying, while, 372
not to the righteous perfect, 324
of our line, the shelter and, 49
supreme in, 154
that makes simplicity a, 364
the herb of, 179
the power of, 274
this latter age, to, 422
thy, thy more than beauty, 236
was seated on his brow, but a, 250
with one half so good a, 260
would scorch thy smiling, 377
Graced with polished manners and fine sense, though, 463
Graceful ease and sweetness, 128
Graces, an angel-guard of loves and, 452
that are sure to please, age lends the, 94
to the grave, lead these, 21
Gracious, 161
Gradation, not by the old, 315
Gradual steps, but by, 31
Graduates, 162
Grain, the smell of, 371
to refuse the needful, 110
Grains of wheat, are as two, 327
Grammar school, in erecting a, 317
Granary, 162
Grand, but less, 408
sweet song, one, 374
Grandam, 162
authorized by her, 389
that had buried her, 239
to please his, 372
Grander, something better and, 190
Grandeur hear, nor, 310
rolls, the moon's unclouded, 268
to our dust, so nigh is, 104
springs, old Scotia's, 352
Grandsire, sit like his, 264
Grant, 162
it so, but then, we, 259
me to see the light, 313
Granted, soon as, 237
Gran'thers they knowed sunthin' tu, 469

Grants them, but his who, 394
Grape, 162
glory, the, 193
of Eastern France, the foaming, 344
Grapes of wrath are stored, the, 153
sours ripe, 118
Grapple them to thy soul, 146
Grasp, dropped from her nerveless, 142
from the strong iron, 127
it firmly, 449
it like a man of mettle, 280
never shall in friendly, 97
the bones, trembled not to, 29
the ocean, or, 263
with a fast and fervent, 263
Grasped thus, as may be, 36
Graspest at the stones, old yew which, 468
Grasps in the comer, 167
Grass, 162
among, haste the dewy, 151
overhead and damp clay around, rank, 229
plucking the, 444
star-scattered on the, 152
the smell of tedded, 371
Grass-green turf, a, 75
Grate, or a dry wheel, 309
Gratify thy lover, inclined to, 100
Gratitude and love, hymns of, 173
Grave, 162–164
adorned, thy humble, 139
and ocean was their, 288
and on that, 304
apart, to keep a dream or, 220
approach thy, 227
aspect he rose, with, 85
a throne, a, 462
away, roll the stone from its, 186
calls virtue to the, 227
drop thy foolish tears upon my, 76
earliest at his, 67
for its last bed of the, 375
for me, this be the verse you, 163
he went, to his red, 420
if dreams infest the, 98
in his vast and wandering, 347
in the dark and silent, 406
is like to be my wedding bed, my, 254
is not its goal, the, 222
it consecrates each, 157
I who have troubled the dead man 's, 448
lead these graces to the, 21
lies silent in the, 412
low in his, 267
my father 's, did utter, 37
new-born, from some new, 376
newly torn from the, 379
no ghost come from the, 426
not have strewed thy, 36
of France, the deadly Waterloo, the, 435
on an unknown, 373
Grave
quickly have the gift of a, 323
rot asleep to the, 144
sleep with thee in the, 114
that folds thy, 334
that reached into the, 145
that was newly made, nigh to a, 357
the mattock and the, 401
the secrets of the, 368
the silent, 228
the steps of glory to the, 152
this, this dust, 406
to a welcome, 9
to glory o'er the, 152
to his rest in the, 269
to lay him in his, 184
without a, 85
Graved in paradise, 73
Grave-maker, 164
Grave-makers, ditchers and, 150
Grave-making, sings at, 70
Graven, hammered and rolled, molten, 157
Graves, 164
all gaping wide, that the, 282
and ghosts break up their, 352
church and yard are full of seamen 's, 355
emblem of untimely, 88
find ourselves dishonourable, 58
of our dead, when they laurel, 212
over men 's, 202
two, grass-green, 224
we lie in, for the, 176
Gravity, profound conceit, 291
with a loyal, 120
Gray has drawn, Mr., 151
Graze, when beasts most, 393
Grease, 164
Greasy commodities, an' such, 16
Great, 164
and small, attends both, 123
a pang as, 80
but our hearts are, 175
danger, we are in, 65
deal worse, and sometimes a, 249
deep, from the, to the great deep, 18
God is, 154
have kindness in reserve, the, 384
if I do grow, 346
in council and great in war, 43
is the art of beginning, 109
little fire grows, 132
love grows there, 238
man dies, so when a, 138
man helped the poor, 341
man was dead, that a, 75
man 's memory may outlive his life, 258
man 's smile, 42
men, lives of, 138
men, the heights by, 177
men may jest with saints, 196
men should drink, 100
none could be unhappy but the, 265
ones eat up the little ones, 133

Great
ones 'longs, that to, 260
right, to do a, 213
that prince . . . is truly, 317
the frown o' the, 146
the rule of men entirely, 301
things we might do, 402
toe, a Hottentot 's, 266
what makes men, 306
when gazing on the, 434
where little fears grow, 238
where love is, 238
wits are sure to madness, 245
Greater, 164
malady is fixed, where the, 247
share of honour, the, 185
sin to keep a sinful oath, 287
than they are, 145
the art is of ending, 109
therefore should our courage be, 65
Greatest, and the, 212
can but blaze, the, 123
gentilman, take him for the, 150
is untold, the, 30
men, knows nothing of its, 259
minds, productive of the, 41
nation, an' risen up earth 's, 277
only are, as the, 43
sailor since our world began, 347
son, this is England 's, 167
worst and best, the, 147
Greatly to find quarrel, 164
Greatness, 164
no, can censure 'scape, 42
of God, build me a nest on the, 156
of God, lay me a-hold of the, 156
some achieve, 164
the highest point of all my, 122
thrust upon 'em, 164
to think God 's, 154
Gree, bear the, 38
Greece, Italy and England did adorn, 309
Greed, 165
Greek, 165
and Latin, in, 30
small Latin and less, 211
Greeks, 165
Green, 165
and all the trees are, 469
and gold, Eden 's, 13
bedclothes, under, 21
dare you haunt our hallowed, 304
in judgment, when I was, 349
in youth, now, 250
misbegotten knaves in Kendal, 205
one red, making the, 169
peas, the first, 32
sleeves, thunder to the tune of, 311
that folds thy grave, as the, 334
when summer is, 216
whiles your boots are, 96
Green-eyed jealousy, 195
Greenland, Zembla, there at, 284
Greenwich never could outdo, 32
Greenwood, 165
Grew, and still the wonder, 456
the more by reaping, 32
together, so we, 224
up in the field, I, 259
Grey, changing into, 225
friar of orders, 145
from her mantle of, 269
hairs gone, from his, 121
head which all men knew, 171
mare is ill to live with, 253
mare is the better horse, 253
mare 's the better horse, when the, 253
my gallant, 448
my hair is, 168
or suits of, 220
swims no goose so, 255
the, under the willow, 28
Greyhound in our hand, we hold our, 344
Grief, 165, 166
and death were sated, here, 374
and solitude have broken me, 32
bliss, to make, 436
flieth to it, 77
forms, moods, shapes of, 448
from sickness and from, 89
holding that, 308
is mute, two lips where, 208
love is joy and, 234
must then be mute, 38
of a wound, take away the, 184
or care, without, 219
smiling at, 298
that 't is a common, 1
the canker and the, 223
thine be the, 232
two extremes of passion, joy and, 297
within thy breast, hide thy, 234
Griefs, 166
are ended by seeing the worst, 464
began, ere England 's, 166
forgot his own, 125
of all the, 195
Grieve and they turn and go, 329
Christ-like is it for sin to, 365
for an hour, 448
make the judicious, 199
ye, a scornful word should, 352
Grieves my soul that I must draw, it, 442
not, a thing that, 388
the spirit, 215
Grieving, 166
what is knowledge but, 63
Grim, a champion, 46
and daring, the vessel, 43
Grimace, through life 's, 81
Grim-visaged war hath smoothed, 432
Grin, for me to sit and, 323
he owned with a, 316
horrible, 282
Grind, 166
an axe to, 15
slowly, the mills of God, 262

Grind
the mill cannot, 434
the poor, laws, 214
your wheat all, 207
Grinding life down from its mark, 439
must needs tarry the, 41
Grinds he all, with exactness, 262
Grinning, not one now to mock your, 468
scorn, to, 195
Grip, a middlin' tight, 330
hold on with a bulldog, 40
only crowbars loose the bulldog's, 40
where ye feel your honour, 184
with firm, 55
Gripe of noose, our necks to, 311
Griping grief the heart, 166
Grit an' human natur', clear, 249
Groan, a hush and then a, 76
from shore to shore, 87
men condemned alike to, 392
with bubbling, 85
Groaning and paraphrasin', 309
every hour, 56
Groans a slave, wherever, 144
cool with mortifying, 264
of the dying, 83
Grog, I 'll take the, 321
Groined the aisles of Christian Rome, 39
Groping blindly in the darkness, 156
Grossly fear'st thy death, 80
Grossness, by losing all its, 424
hiding the, 330
of his nature, the, 189
Ground, 166
and gazes on the, 180
brave lodgings for one in holy, 229
built on another man's, 187
drops earliest to the, 146
feet have trod the, 328
for an acre of barren, 354
knit hands and beat the, 409
like water, spilt on the, 173
now withering on the, 250
of expediency, on the, 117
on the, that perfection is Utopian, 302
pleasure lark-like nests upon the, 316
shall not fall on the, 320
sleep low in the, 333
think they should lay him i' the cold, 438
thousands had sunk on the, 39
to quit the, 224
tread on classic, 55
was a little damp, wherever, 437
whispering from the, 298
Groundlings, split the ears of the, 379
Grove, the court, the camp, the, 237
Groves were God's first temples, the, 400
Grow againe, will ne'er make, 426
apace, great weeds do, 438
Grow, make . . . two blades of grass to, 162
the rashes, green, 165
thou too didst, 377
will with the burden, 389
Growed, 166
Growing, while man is, 81
Growl and fight, let bears and lions, 95
beware of his echoing, 226
Growled, it cracked and, 190
Grows a flower on every bough, there, 203
an' proputty, proputty, 319
aslant a brook, a willow, 444
into the great sun, 73
lives and dies in single blessedness, 342
since when it, 100
the more the statue, 385
Growth, a misshapen and untimely, 416
a plant of slow, 60
idle weeds are fast in, 438
of God, be this juice the, 69
with my body's, 377
Grubs, or, or worms, 458
Grudge, 166
Gruel, I 'm sick of, 363
Grumble drat that cat, 44
Grundy, 166
what is your opinion, Mrs., 345, 393
Grunt and sweat under a weary life, 79
Guaranteed his liberty, must be, 338
Guard, 166
our native seas, that, 110
their noses, people ought to, 285
Guardian angels sung this strain, 37
Guards, 166
and glory, 26
de sheepfol' bin, dat, 358
her, who, 443
the right, heaven still, 338
Gudgeons ere they 're catched, to swallow, 48
Guerdon be gained, ere the, 78
but the fair, 123
Guessed, but few have, 405
Guest, 167
because thou com'st a weary, 12
claims the sated, 333
if its undying, 377
is meet, for such a, 303
prepares it for another, 401
Guests, 167
star-scattered on the grass, 152
Guide, 167
be my virtue's, 427
their chime, all the way, to, 286
to, and gladden, 384
with providence their, 462
Guides through the boundless sky, 387
Guiding star, like a, 179
Guilt, 167
away, can wash her, 136

Guilt
deep in ruin as in, 342
each thing of sin and, 47
those who fear not, 123
to cover, her, 136
Guiltless as on Monday, as, 393
of his country's blood, 168
wife, spare my, 15
Guilt's blunder, 336
in that heart, if, 236
Guilty acts, unknown facts of, 99
glory glows, where neither, 434
man, thou, 28
mind, suspicion always haunts the, 394
of his own death, not, 213
thing, like a, 57
Guinea, 167
but the jingling of the, 185
Guinea's stamp, but the, 249
Guineas chink, he made the, 183
Gulf, hell to its last, 165
of death, bright beyond the, 159
Gull, to the shark and the sheering, 113
Gum, Arabian trees their medicinal, 399
Gun, 167
an' each dumb, 299
clang of bell and roar of, 23
hot gun-lip kissin', 347
one, 115
the holy text of pike and, 329
Gunga Din, a swig in hell from, 395
Gun-lip kissin' gun, hot, 347
Gunpowder, blow up the infernal machine with, 403
Guns begin to shoot, when the, 410
peal on peal, how the great, 23
were going off, God Almighty's, 147
Gurgling of water, a, 99
Gushed forth, streams of revenue, 340
out amain, the blood, 27
Gushes cold and bright, Rhine's breast-milk, 344
Gushing of a rill, there's music in the, 272
Gusset and band, seam and, 460
Gust of long-suspended Ahs, one stormy, 188
to allay the, 323
with the least, 3
Gusts will blow out fire, 132
Gutter caterwauls, who in the, 44
Guttural, whistling, grunting, 210

H

H, 167
Habit, 167
costly thy, 11
if I do not put on a sober, 372
of drinking, the, 102
Habitation, a local, 308
Habits, 167
Hack, 168
for lack of somebody to hew and, 26
Hacks and your pointers, worse housed than your, 323
Haggard, 168
Hags and hideous wenches, rags and, 387
Hail, Columbia, 58
the rising sun, let others, 392
to the chief, 49
wedded love, 437
Hailed it in God's name, we, 154
the wretch, the inhuman shout which, 362
thundered, lightened and, 389
what so proudly we, 17
Hails you Tom or Jack, that, 405
Hair, 168
a bone and a hank of, 136
and each particular, 381
as free, 364
distinguish and divide a, 93
dries them with his, 194
grew curlier, his, 311
her lovely floating, 30
in their golden, 162
more, or a hair less, that hath a, 322
the few silver threads out of my, 340
the ninth part of a, 45
they singed her, 208
the weight of a, 351
with your 'ayrick 'ead of, 147
Hairs, from his grey, 121
more faults than, 168
to observe the forms of, 458
Hairy springes, with, 168
Halcyon, 168
Half, 168
Half a dime to a dime, from, 403
after ten, we take ten or, 210
a kiss, I think there is not, 243
an hour every morning, put it back, 434
a truth, a lie which is, 219
a year, memory may outlive his life, 258
be reaped for nothing, nor shall, 460
his foe, overcome but, 139
its evil, vice itself lost, 424
resignation, and one, 454
the creeds, than in, 97
there's but a shirt and a, 361
the zeal, but served my God with, 357
thy fears, my hopes for, 409
thy tears, my smiles for, 409
Half-brother of the world, America, 8
Half-control his doom, man can, 338
Half-hour's good consideration, another, 210
Half-penny, two pence for every, 193
loaves, seven, 130
Halfpenny-worth of bread, but one, 346

Half-shirt is two napkins, the, 361
Half-shut eyes, with his, 57
Half-way down the slope to hell, 316
Hall, ambition's airy, 367
from its station in the, 280
logs into the, 190
raced into the, 36
round the dim-lighted, 317
sorrow darkens hamlet and, 271
the Douglas in his, 85
when beards wag all, merry in, 261
Halloo, the soldier's wild, 181
with that wild, 63
Hallow the day, the night will, 442
us there, seems to, 182
Hallows all it holds, the goblet, 68
Halls, a chief in her, 63
are crowded, feast and your, 129
of death, in the silent, 227
the harp that once through Tara's, 170
Halt, 't is no matter if I do, 301
Halter, will come and cut the, 254
Halts, nor, though hope be dim, 390
Halyard, staff or the, 112
Hamlet and hall, sorrow darkens, 271
forefathers of the, 108
two children in one, 224
Hamlets round, four voices of, 52
Hammer of industry, swings the, 410
the ore, I, 386
Hammered and rolled, molten, graven, 157
from a hundred towers, 284
Hammers, with greasy aprons, rules and, 368
Hammock at the roaring bows, for a, 8
Hammock-shroud, his heavy-shotted, 347
Hampden, 168
Ham's were scattered through the Sandwich Isles, 350
Hand, 169
a good sword and a trusty, 63
all thy own to the last, a, 31
and God's own, 184
and heart, take, 78
and my heart, I give my, 366
and with as delicate a, 57
a palace and a prison on each, 424
a sinful heart makes feeble, 366
as much in laying the, 397
can hold, which the, 7
clay bleeding and aching in the potter's, 107
could'st not see thy, 72
East with richest, 107
examine well his milk-white, 36
finds ready to, 54
glove upon that, 47
go cold, both foot and, 6
handle toward my, 70
he leans upon his, 152
her 'prentice, 211
his heart and, 84
his parting guest by the, 167

Hand
his work a singing with his, 374
hold a fire in his, 191
I argue not against heaven's, 387
I fear thy skinny, 253
if God writes a legible, 426
in a row, an awkward, 135
in hand they passed, the loveliest pair, 294
in hand, . . . through Eden took their solitary way, 462
in thine, or place my, 127
leans her cheek upon her, 47
man with eight trumps in his, 415
me the cup, 78
Nature's own sweet and cunning, 21
of Douglas is his own, 97
offence's gilded, 289
of God, see the, 341
of little employment, 70
of such as Marmion, 97
of the Angel of the Resurrection, 33
of the reaper, the, 326
of war, the, 112
of woman, with the weak, 449
on kings, Death lays his icy, 127
open as day, 161
or eye, what immortal, 405
outside of his, 158
root and all, in my, 135
saw the air too much with your, 379
she layeth her, 451
sorrow's heavy, 175
that fed them, bite the, 26
that hovers o'er her mate, 97
that kings have lipped, 205
that rounded Peter's dome, 39
that slanted back this brow, 195
the, just raised to shed his blood, 27
the kindlier, 174
the lifted, in awe, 272
the ploughman near at, 307
the sound in his, 183
the vessel made, with his, 107
then of the potter, 178
this weak unknowing, 71
though trembling, 265
to do, a, 173
to execute, 173
to me, stretch out your, 140
to pour sad tears upon thy, 293
touch God's right, 156
trembles, when his, 309
up to heaven, raised his right, 424
upon the ark, lay their, 12
upon the ocean's mane, laid his, 288
upon thy mane, laid my, 288
upon thy sword, never lay thy, 395
we cannot hold mortality's strong, 270
we hold our greyhound in our, 344
we scatter seeds with careless, 355
which ends a dream, like the, 77
who will stand on either, 37
with dying, above his head, 47
with dying, the rudder held, 304

Hand
with his satchel in his, 440
with mug in, 440
without squeezing, a pretty girl's, 383
work of our head and, 451
you cannot see, I see a, 428
Handful, are but a, 74
of men as we were, 113
of silver he left us, just for a, 336
o' things I know, the, 330
Handfuls of coals and rice, with, 175
Handle toward my hand, 70
which fits them all, is the, 218
you, thus our nails shall, 304
Handling, abides no, 44
Hands, 169
and beat the ground, knit, 409
and helpless, the feeble, 156
and ready, 259
and your conscience be honest, 55
are, whatsome'er their, 119
are weeping and wringing their, 132
at the palms of my, 423
blows his numbing, 207
by foreign, 139
clap, and a bargain, 18
clapped their chapped, 43
fashion, our own, 67
folding at last his, 62
hath not a Jew, 197
have found, the weapons which our, 403
his owne two, 206
his wee white, 176
in his glowing, 241
I warmed both, 221
lords of our own, 141
many with crossed, 416
o' cowards, thet tarries long in, 143
of a little child, like the, 49
on him, shall we not lay, 401
out, I stretch my, 313
that heaved, ill fare the, 29
that the rod of empire, 109
that 'twixt her, 465
the folded, 369
then with praying, 255
to do, for idle, 190
turned his back on jewelled, 321
unclean, makes civil, 54
upon his breast, folding at last his, 62
upon the breast, two, 208
upon your sword, lay your, 395
wants both, 190
with invisible soap, washing his, 372
wring from the hard, 267
Handsaw, I know a hawk from a, 245
Handsome faces, with regard to, 455
in three hundred pounds, 128
Handy, anything that's, 44
Hang, and wretches, 92
on him, she would, 11
out our banners, 17
Hang round it still, will, 258
separately, or assuredly we shall all, 420
themselves, 254
the panel, more ready to, 199
together, we must indeed all, 420
upon thy tongue, while listening senates, 11
Hanged, 169
him, they would have, 95
Hanging, 169
and wiving goes by destiny, 86
Hangman's whip, a, 184
Hangs as mute on Tara's walls, 170
a tale, thereby, 396
or saves, 306
Hank of hair, a bone and a, 136
Hanover, 170
Hans Breitmann gife a barty, 297
Happened, 170
Happening, in the way of things, 170
Happier, 170
hours restore the gift, till, 203
hours, the life of joy in, 435
things, is remembering, 375
to arise, the, 121
Happiest moments, I owe the, 397
pair, kindest and the, 138
Happily to steer, 162
Happiness, 170
below, virtue alone is, 427
for comfort and for, 125
is produced, by which so much, 192
of life, work done is the true, 460
result, 192
their harmony foretells, world of, 437
we prize, if solid, 182
Happy, 170
as this little island, so, 194
breed of men, this, 112
could I be with either, 47
days, a world of, 99
days, happy mixtures of more, 264
is he born and taught, how, 418
is the blameless vestal's lot, 140
is the rose distilled, earthlier, 342
land, hail Columbia, 58
man henceforth is he, a, 348
man's without a shirt, the, 360
moment I have had, von only, 200
ought the rich to feel, how, 266
the man that when his day is done, 62
the man who, void of cares and strife, 359
they who wait no more, 98
thou art not, 170
who in his verse, 162
why so few marriages are, 280
with you, to be, 125
years, ah, 33
Harbour bar be moaning, though the, 132
cleared, the, 359
give, which in life did, 427

Hard and cold, 157
 and it shall go, 197
 and sour, are, 175
 dealings teaches them, 51
 doom did receive, 115
 grey weather, 't is the, 113
 hurls back an epithet as, 114
 it is to hide the sparks of nature, 278
 it's very, to live in such a row, 290
 nothing 's so, 14
 to come as for a camel, 42
 't shall go, 110
 water is soft, and marble, 252
Harder matter to fight, is a, 219
Hardest knife ill-used, 206
 science to forget, 139
Hard-hearted is Joe, 413
Hardship, from danger, from, 390
Hare of whom the proverb goes, 423
Hare-lip, makes the, 135
Hark, 170
 and from the dark park, 115
Harm for love, hate hath no, 300
 I fear we 'll come to, 267
Harmony, 170
 foretells, world of happiness their, 437
 like deep, 105
 not understood, all discord, 338
 of the world, her voice the, 212
Harms, how to redress their, 231
Harness, he died in, 90
 in, here he died, 90
 mailed, in sombre, 87
 on our back, 90
 on their throats, with, 100
Harp, 170
 talking is like playing on the, 397
 of life, love took up the, 241
Harping, 171
Harrow up thy soul, would, 380
Harsh, out of tune and, 327
 to hear, and, 400
Harshest word comes aptest, 114
Hart ungalled play, 84
Harvest, come to reap the, 460
 home of day, and brings the, 470
Has been, what has been, 221
Hasp, and fixed the brazen, 263
Hassock, passing by the customary, 312
Hast, forget'st, what thou, 170
 those friends thou, 146
Haste, 171
 might tell a hundred, with moderate, 188
 mounting in hot, 271
 the dewy grass among, 151
 thee, nymph, 196
 those that with, 131
Hasty as fire, 324
 spark, shows a, 209
Hat, 171
 a' brushes his, 239
 his cockle, 57
Hat
 lay my head to any good man 's, 214
 the old three-cornered, 323
 thus with my, 372
Hatch a lark, the raven doth not, 326
Hatched, before they are, 48
 count their chickens ere th 're, 48
Hatching the egg, sooner have the fowl by, 108
Hate, 171
 and a certain loathing, a lodged, 327
 another nation, right to, 110
 a smile to those who, 363
 extreme in love or, 449
 from the creatures, meet, 319
 hath no harm for love, 300
 hide his love or, 119
 him for he is a Christian, I, 421
 I know not of his, 160
 immortal, 231
 implacable in, 385
 in the like extreme, 237
 Juno 's unrelenting, 13
 thee, I love thee and, 327
 thee, those hearts that, 48
 with a pardon for the foes who, 363
 whom envy dared not, 434
 whose breaths I, 69
Hated, as to be, 425
 bear-baiting, the Puritans, 321
 be to be, 126
 by one he loves, 15
 like men, there was naething I, 458
 yet caressed, 67
Hater, 171
Hates a woman, for him that, 452
 our sacred nation, he, 193
 that excellence it cannot reach, and 114
 the smell of roses, she, 343
Hathaway, Anne, 436
Hating no one, and, 85
Hatred, battle, and strife, 215
 scoffing and abuse, 368
 the hereditary, 130
 turned, like love to, 324
Haunch and the hump is Obey, and the, 287
Haunt, life exempt from public, 3
 our hallowed green, dare you, 304
Haunted, holy ground, 't is, 181
 the place is, 69
Haunts the guilty mind, suspicion always, 394
Have his day, dog, 45
 it, both eat thy cake and, 41
 it, 't is mine and I will, 263
 justice, thou shalt, 199
 less than that no man shall, 383
 more than thou showest, 362
 or have no wife, to, 442
 thee not, and yet, 70
 the more you, the more you want, 430
 us do, what force will, 139
Haven under the hill, to their, 169

Havoc, cry, 335
Hawk from a handsaw, I know a, 245
  like a, my soul, 375
  shall nestle with the dove, 300
Hawked at and killed, 121
Hawks, between two, 213
  nosegays from street to street, 343
Hawthorn in the dale, under the, 307
Hay, went to pieces like a lock of, 166
Hayrick 'ead of 'air, with your, 147
Hazard of new fortunes, a, 141
  of the die, 44
  what he fears to lose, should never, 452
Hazel eyes, because thou hast, 322
He said, and So said I, 62
  to Hecuba, or, 307
Head, 171
  above his, 47
  above us all, half a, 250
  a grass-green turf at his, 75
  a journey in my, 21
  all my imperfections on my, 370
  and hand, work of our, 451
  and shelter for thy, 182
  and the hoof of the law, the, 287
  a stone at the, 229
  be flung, snows may o'er his, 173
  beside my own, laid her, 243
  could carry all he knew, 456
  from the crown of his, 196
  gave his able horse the, 345
  has been beaten, yet thy, 322
  his answer trickled through my, 414
  his madness was not of the, 245
  here rests his, 257
  is as full of quarrels, 322
  is bloody but unbowed, my, 28
  is bowed, while thy, 347
  lifts the, 59
  lumber in his, 30
  man with the, 454
  my deeds upon my, 83
  now, to cover my, 68
  o'er manhood 's noble, 354
  of 'air, with your 'ayrick, 147
  of the host, at the, 63
  of Thompson in, caved the, 141
  on horror 's, 186
  on your puny, 108
  or in the, 124
  pressed once more the lifeless, 109
  she bowed, as if her, 268
  than overthrow the, 335
  that 's to be let unfurnished, 57
  there 's nothing like a bare and shiny, 94
  there was pride in the, 316
  thy, thy sovereign, 189
  thy fibres net the dreamless, 468
  to any good man 's hat, lay my, 214
  to contrive, a, 173
  to foot, gorgonized me from, 384
  to heel, an African, 266
  to plan, a, 173
  to shrowd his, 183
Head
  to trample round my fallen, 76
  to the weary, 21
  turns no more his, 128
  uneasy lies the, 68
  unmellowed, his, 198
  wears a precious jewel in his, 3
  weeping at the feet and, 74
Headache, cough and phthisic, it helps the, 445
Headed with a knob of timber, 249
Headland, on dune and, 139
Heads, 172
  beast with many, 20
  do grow beneath their shoulders, 88
  I win, ditto tails, 444
  nodding their, 36
  stood in their breasts, 88
  whose clay-cold, 298
Headstrong as an allegory, 6
Heal and do well, would, 334
  it up, his eye did, 118
  that heaven cannot, 375
  the blows of sound, comes to, 364
Healed by the same means, 197
  wounds I might have, 116
Health, 172
  again dispense, should my Author, 429
  and wealth have missed me, 204
  glad to drink your honour 's, 310
  goes round, an eternal, 101
  have mind upon your, 139
  it might hurt, their, 360
  made bright my Burgundy, whose, 274
  of Alonzo the Brave, to the, 379
  on both, and, 91
  test and safeguard of personal, 460
Healthful life, remainder of his, 109
Heap, in many a mouldering, 108
  of dust, a, 334
Heaps, from out the scattered, 367
Heaps of pearl, 102
Hear, 172
  a brazen canstick, I had rather, 309
  and harsh to, 400
  didst thou not, 83
  gently to, 198
  her speak again, desire to, 238
  himself talk, loves to, 396
  I hear a voice you cannot, 428
  it, doth he, 185
  it not, Duncan, 205
  no more, I 'll, 282
  not now the booming waters, 354
  nothing, thou wilt, 115
  old Triton, 293
  the mellow wedding-bells, 437
  thy uttered name, 274
  't is sweet to, 438
  whom they cannot see or, 455
  us sing, when you come to, 304
Heard before, was never, 124
  ear hath not, 209

Heard his father say, asked but what he, 416
in his life, he never, 11
it, she wished she had not, 363
I will be, 371
no more, then is, 411
not a drum was, 102
of, more must be, 140
thee last, roughly since I, 227
Hearings, and younger, 196
Hearken, come hither lads and, 74
Hears him in the wind, 176
it, of him that, 196
the monarch, 155
Hearse, a grim one-horse, 298
Heart, 172–175
absence makes the, 1
a detector of the, 81
a face without a, 118
again, come to my, 340
again, shall take, 138
a great spirit and a busy, 220
a little weeping would ease my, 438
all offences come from the, 289
all the aching of, 109
and a hand all thy own to the last, 31
and a' that, soul and, 248
and door, open thy, 242
and flesh are weak, and if my, 436
and hand, his, 84
and in limb, English in, 113
and live without, 63
and me, that shall command my, 358
and soul, where, 204
and that your, 237
and the soul, employ all the, 229
and true, a merry, 63
a pike in his, 398
a rake, is at, 325
a sad, good Christian at her, 330
as far from fraud, 29
a stripling for a woman's, 398
as well as want of, 116
bear it with an honest, 150
best knoweth its own loss, 163
be ye stout of, 232
bread which strengtheneth man's, 35
break not, O woman's, 35
breaks, till your, 144
but kills the, 236
but not my, 364
but one, and the, 281
by the moans of their, 398
can doubt, the choice what, 85
can gain, if fond love thy, 456
can ne'er a transport know, the, 448
concealing it will break, my, 412
cool, than my, 264
destines for their, 106
detests him, my, 218
did know, every word, 340
doth wound, the, 166
each, and each cup, 116
exults and sings, in youth the, 470
Heart
faded from the, 429
faint, ne'er won fair lady, 120
falls from a steady, 265
for any fate, 2
for every fate, a, 2
for falsehood framed, a, 122
forgiving at their, 140
gave way, her woman's, 366
goodly apple rotton at the, 11
gushed from my, 27
has burned, if with love thy, 234
hath ne'er within him burned, 65
his adversary's, 335
how dear to this, 49
I am sick at, 57
I could find in my, 68
if bursting, 233
if guilt's in that, 236
I give my hand and my, 366
I had rather coin my, 267
I hold a mouses, 271
in a case o' gowd, I'd locked my, 231
indignant breaks, some, 143
in splinters, and break his, 317
in 't, mine with my, 169
in the human, 114
's audible, in which her, 203
is human, every human, 156
I sign to thet with all my, 431
is left alone, 172
. . . is not of ice, her, 328
is pure, because my, 12
is sorely charged, the, 363
is still his master's own, 176
joy to his mighty, 13
just as high as my, 386
leaps beneath the Future's, 115
level in her husband's, 454
life's tale to many a feeling, 221
long, long be my, 258
makes feeble hand, a sinful, 366
memory plays an old tune on the, 258
mercy with a bleeding, 390
must be tried by pain, as a, 158
must have to cherish, 48
my true-love hath my, 235
never say that I was false of, 2
no flesh in man's obdurate, 38
nor venture to unmask man's, 328
of a man, all the good from the, 49
of arts, and, 232
of freedom, the throbbing, 144
of her husband, the, 451
of man, in the lip than in the, 14
of nature, out from the, 24
of the fool, but the, 200
of our Lord, dear to the, 160
of the toiler, and the, 410
oh teach my, 397
once pregnant, some, 109
on fire, set the, 4
on heart, and, 220
on your dead heart, lay my, 140

Heart
open the door of thy, 240
or hope, nor bate a jot of, 387
or in the, 124
outward, lie which works from the, 451
preaching down a daughter's, 73
preferred in his, 339
pure messengers sent from his, 29
pursuing, a love-lorn, 458
rebel, shall my, 125
recalled a different name, each, 241
ruddy drops that warm my, 443
shall truly love you, my, 240
shall you know his, 119
she is the darling of my, 74
shine in the untutored, 466
so strong, is thy, 215
susceptible of pity, 262
take hand and, 78
take me again to your, 340
take the proverb to thine, 434
take thy beak from out my, 19
tell me my, 235
thanks to the human, 404
that dotes, a, 246
that has truly loved, the, 393
that quivered in his, 106
that rends the, 185
that's broken, wound a, 358
the broken in, 61
the darling of my, 6
then burst his mighty, 192
then let thy, 236
the ruddy drops that visit my sad, 443
the way he says darling that goes to my, 72
the workings of his, 198
tied a young man's, 30
to cinders, doth burn the, 298
to curse my dog so, not have a, 395
to feel, a, 419
together, and whose, 240
to heart, which, 237
tongue will tell the anger of my, 412
too tender or too firm a, 236
to pity, melt his iron, 406
to win the, 335
two seeming bodies, but one, 221
upon my sleeve, wear my, 371
very pin of his, 118
was every woman's toy, my, 148
was not of the head but, 245
was that young faithful, 121
what the false, 122
which at even, the, 442
which we call the, 403
which weighs upon the, 263
whispers the o'er-fraught, 165
whose very strings would break, 10
wilt thou cure thine, 232
with a fire in thy, 69
with all my, 156
within, and a warm, 183
woman with the, 454

Heart
would fain deny, the poor, 223
wrapped in a woman's hide, tiger's, 453
Heartbreak him, until I, 294
Heart-easing mirth, and by men, 264
Hearth, 175
in her mansions, 63
holly round the Christmas, 52
the cricket on the, 66
woman for the, 454
yield thee a, 182
Heart-opening, wink-tippling cordial, 397
Heart-quake, each kiss a, 204
Heart's blood of the brave, 34
chain wove, my, 236
desire, in your true, 83
desires be with you, 86
disgrace, hidden from the, 108
most precious rain, the, 293
most secret cell, in my, 296
repose, more, 182
Hearts, 175
and lukewarm, 298
are dry as summer dust, 91
are fresh and simple, 156
are more than coronets, kind, 148
are sighing, two mutual, 203
a thousand, beat happily, 334
but once heaved, their, 77
ensanguined, 88
great, true faith, 259
heavenly compassion in your, 75
here bring your wounded, 375
high, and brave, 354
it takes something from our, 470
love is the art of, 232
of his countrymen, first in the, 132
of kings, it is enthroned in the, 260
of men, entrap the, 168
of men, in the, 191
of men, sifting out the, 415
of oak are our men, 286
of Spain, the stoutest, 111
of the heathen, right into the, 314
our, it ennobled, 22
our soft conditions and our, 456
pleads admission to our, 85
press the life from out young, 296
that roam, but not their, 367
the cheerful, now broken, 258
the feuds of ages, in their, 130
the touch of God in human, 305
that hate thee, those, 48
that stirred our, 88
that weep, ye doubting, 369
though stout and brave, 163
two, that beat as one, 224
what bolder thought, in human, 411
Heart-sick jesters weep behind the mask, 165
Heartsome Ireland, 194
with thee, where, 229
Heart-strings, were my dear, 168
Heart-throbs, count time by, 227

Heat, electricity, love, 237
not a furnace, 136
of fire, not the fierce, 4
on fantastic summer's, 191
o' the sun, the, 103
rank corruption's, 64
the cold that tempers, 369
thou hast neither, 336
to make a solid core of, 230
with wine, rather, 264
Heated hot in a moment, 50
Heath, long, brown furze, 354
my foot is on my native, 138
Heathen, a very, in the carnal part, 330
Chinee is peculiar, 50
go, where, 376
right into the hearts of the, 314
you're a pore benighted, 147
Heather, go tramping over the, 361
Heat-oppressed brain, the, 70
Heaved the stones where Milton's, 29
those fossils, the way they, 141
Heaven, 176, 177
above, the angels in, 236
a crime, is it in, 236
a draught, if, 402
allots thee, all that, 182
all that we believe of, 452
a man that hopes for, 40
and earth, all things in, 212
and earth, men at most differ as, 259
and earth, more things in, 303
and hell he touched at, 244
and hell myself am, 178
and hell through, 196
and hell women worst and best, as, 259
and the next waking dawned in, 105
a regular debtor and creditor account with, 352
a rose in, 105
a silver bow new bent in, 268
as its purest gold, 453
as low as hell's from, 400
as the gentle rain from, 260
as the great eye of, 119
beauteous eye of, 152
before high, 251
before the courts of, 313
beloved by, 65
below, Church is a little, 312
breaks the serene of, 268
cannot heal, that, 375
confess yourself to, 60
conveyed, the opening bud to, 77
dearest foe in, 73
dimmed the light of, 155
doomed to shed, by righteous, 157
drop forgiveness from, 140
earth's crammed with, 153
far from earth, 29
fasting, thank, 238
find me and turn thy back on, 159
first taught, 216
Heaven
for love is, 237
for the last time the sun in, 420
from all creatures hides, 127
go, words without thoughts never to, 313
God's in his, 154
had made her such a man, that, 363
has past, she to, 105
has no rage like love to hatred turned, 324
hath sent me fortune, 137
help the husband, 348
his blessed part to, 185
in a lady's lap, 209
in her eye, 161
in hope to merit, 177
in their own way, praise, 217
is blessed with perfect rest, 409
is love, and, 237
is not reached at a single bound, 208
is registered in, 66
it goes, from earth to, 262
it may be that only in, 51
itself descends, but, 233
itself has wrought, are those which, 403
itself upon the past, not, 221
it smells to, 272
leave her to, 270
light came from, 245
louder than the bolts of, 13
love indeed is light from, 233
make a hell of, 263
marriages are made in, 253
may decrease it, yet, 238
mend us all, 80
nor earth, is not of, 332
not beteem the winds of, 243
number the stars in the, 205
of hell, make a, 169
of her delightful eye, the clear, 452
of invention, the brightest, 272
on bright wings towards, 122
or hell for a man, that makes, 242
or to hell, summons thee to, 205
pursue, more than, 61
rains down, the questions that, 8
raised his right hand up to, 424
robe and my integrity to, 340
see this and bless, 50
she did but dream of, 105
she sent the gentle sleep from, 369
shut thee from, 376
so dear to, 47
still guards the, 338
than serve in, 329
the front of, 277
the hell I suffer seems a, 178
the livery of the court of, 228
themselves, sure of, 347
things are the sons of, 459
till the stars of, 429
to earth, from, 308
to know I'm farther off from, 331
to pitying, are cast, 362

Heaven
to show the most of, 248
'twixt earth and, 255
upon earth, that, 21
was exhaled and went to, 378
was whispered in, 167
were not heaven, 117
which we ascribe to, 330
will bless your store, 375
with less of earth in them than, 129
ycleped Euphrosyne, in, 264
Heaven-born band, 58
Heaven-kissing hill, on a, 250
Heavenly bodies, princes are like to, 317
breasts, can envy dwell in, 114
food is very light, 123
love, thou a, 157
't was, 211
Heaven's benison or ban, 328
chancery, which flew up to, 287
command, at, 37
ebon vaults, 268
first law, order is, 291
gate, and see through, 292
gate, now at, 210
gate, sings hymns at, 210
gate sings, the lark at, 210
hand, I argue not against, 387
topmost height, from the, 28
vengeance down, calling, 424
wide pathless way, the, 268
Heavens, and spangled, 132
crush me, though the, 416
fill with commerce, saw the, 59
for power, and search the, 402
rain enough in the sweet, 169
see, never shalt thou the, 49
stars that oversprinkle all the, 23
yon blue, 148
Heaviest cross of all, 67
cross, ours is the, 1
Heaviness, 177
when they droop with, 293
Heaving rocks at him, reply by, 340
to and fro, kept, 36
Heavy cost, learned at a, 117
looks, toward school with, 239
too, for a man, 40
to get, 157
Hector in the field to die, better like, 28
Hecuba to him, what's, 307
Hedge a king, divinity doth, 202
linen enough on every, 226
Hedger, a spiritual, 247
Hedgerow marks of angels' feet, see in every, 460
Heed naught else, you won't never, 107
take, and ponder well, 465
Heedless, 177
Heel, an African from head to, 266
of a Dutch cheese, 48
stifle down with a mailed, 413
the despot's, is on thy shore, 255
Heel, they tread each other's, 448
Heels, asses lift their, 14
at his, 75
a troop of little children at my, 167
of my presentment, upon the, 30
one woe doth tread upon another's, 448
set feathers to thy, 171
struck his armed, 345
't will fly at his, 461
Heifer dead and bleeding fresh, 41
Height, bate his usual, 135
from the Heaven's topmost, 28
he rose, how to occasion's, 287
of pain, the measure of the, 293
our honour at the, 89
tide is at his highest, 18
Heights, 177
sat Freedom on the, 144
Heir, a fountain spouting through his, 248
they made her, 111
to the first, stood, 315
Heirs of pain, sure, 59
Held his breath, and the boldest, 364
it fast, and, 342
Helen, 177
the cordial that sparkled for, 100
Hell, 177, 178
a fury like a woman scorned, nor, 324
and heretics, prate of, 217
and rides through, 432
as the gates of, 218
better to reign in, 329
but that I was in, 98
call thou hell, 275
come hot from, 335
down all the stretch of, 165
false as, 122
fell to shame and, 57
flames, gold hath the hue of, 157
for a man, makes heaven or, 242
from the mouth of, 80
half-way down the slope to, 316
he touched at heaven and, 244
I'll get a swig in, 395
is full of good meanings, 193
is paved with, 193
is worth ambition though in, 329
itself breathes out, 282
itself can make a heaven of, 263
lead apes in, 10
lead his apes into, 10
make a heaven of, 169
might sit for, 115
of heaven, make . . . a, 263
of waters, the, 436
of witchcraft lies, what a, 398
our house is, 400
quiet to quick bosoms is a, 323
slander meanest spawn of, 368
summons thee to heaven or to, 205
that riches grow in, 336
that's there, and view the, 328
the fear o', 184

Hell
the snare and scourge of, 157
to have some fifteen minutes of, 176
to keep, the keys of, 369
to shun, more than, 61
through heaven and, 196
'twas muttered in, 167
war is, 432
women worst and best, as heaven and, 259
Hell-broth, 179
Hell's concave, tore, 46
from heaven, as low as, 400
Helm, nor yields to men the, 86
pleasure at the, 470
takes the, 102
Helmet, 179
of Navarre, the, 308
Help, 179
and ornament thereunto, to be a, 318
between a hindrance and a, 180
it, I can't, 441
since there's no, 203
the feeble, not enough to, 129
what need of, 315
what's past, 166
you die, no man can, 129
Helping when we meet them, 460
Helpless, the feeble hands and, 156
Helps one on, that is what, 460
the hurt that honour feels, 185
you live, and it, 129
Hent the stile-a, merrily, 174
Heraldry, the boast of, 163
Herald's coat without sleeves, like an, 361
Herb, 179
Herb-grace o' Sundays, may call it, 344
Herbs and other country messes, 303
at the morning prime, 151
green, 32
reaping thee sweet, 78
that scattered grow, 182
Hercules himself do what he may, 45
himself must yield to odds, 390
than I to, 37
Herd have fled from the, 31
of such, the, 396
winds slowly o'er the lea, 69
Here, into the, 16
Hereafter, 179
angels may, and in the, 186
what is love, 'tis not, 239
Hereditary hatred, the, 130
propensity, almost irresistible, 102
Heretics, prate of hell and, 217
Heritage the sea, our, 286
Hermit, like a, you sup, 441
sighed till woman smiled, man the, 450
there, to dwell a weeping, 34
Hermit's fast, more grievous torment than a, 235
Hero, 179, 180
bold, John Barleycorn was a, 18
fell, horse and, 80
from his prison, came the, 351
millions a, 272
must drink brandy, 34
perish, a, 38
Herod, 180
Heroes, 180
fought for, that, 416
hail ye, 58
kill, 123
lawyers, priests, 218
of old, the, 78
we are n't no thin red, 349
He-rogue, the great, 194
Heroic breeds, like the old, 250
built, 40
soul away, so passed the strong, 377
Hero's deeds, ready for a, 54
Herring, nor good red, 132
Herrings, as pilchards are to, 190
Herse, 180
Herself and the woman I love, 274
Hesitate dislike, and, 71
Hesperus, that led the starry host, 268
Heterodoxy is another man's doxy, 291
Hew and hack, for lack of somebody to, 26
down and fell the hardest-timbered oak, 390
him as a carcass, not, 201
Hiawatha, this song of, 156
Hid in night, nature's laws lay, 281
it from my sight, 28
long, murder cannot be, 272
my faults will not be, 365
the moon is, 23
Hidden brook, like of a, 37
from the heart's disgrace, 108
soul of harmony, 170
Hide, and turn to, 409
false face must, 122
her faults, might, 128
her shame, to, 136
his love, can less, 119
me, must for ever, 153
myself in thee, let me, 340
the fault, to, 260
the sparks of nature, hard . . . to, 278
their diminished heads, 172
them, or in clouds, 408
thou wear a lion's, 226
thy grief within thy breast, 234
tiger's heart wrapped in a woman's, 453
your diminished rays, 91
Hideous, and makes night, 282
cries, such, 98
more, when thou show'st, 192
Hides the book of fate, 127
them deep, he, 154
Hidest thou, what, 354
Hiding, discredit more in, 128

Hidings of his council, the, 154
High and fine, my thoughts were, 98
and treads on, 312
as my heart, just as, 386
availed on, 125
classes, meaning the, 55
descent, preachment of your, 85
estate, fallen from his, 121
for common selfishness, 159
he soared, low as, 7
in pride, up so, 316
on a throne of royal state, 107
the spacious firmament on, 132
though his titles, 65
thy seat is up on, 270
High-blown pride, my, 153
Higher law, there is a, 213
life, the beginning of a, 79
things, to, 170
Highest height, tide is at his, 18
point, touched the, 122
style of man, 51
the middle tree and, 63
Highness' dog at Kew, his, 95
High-proof melancholy, we are, 258
Hill, and the hunter home from the, 163
on a heaven-kissing, 250
single church below the, 23
snow on field an', 152
the dew of yon high eastward, 269
to their haven under the, 169
to climbing up a, 123
to hill, bells from, 52
to the poor-house, over the, 310
went up a, 202
Hills, 180
all the trees on all the, 382
and far away, and o'er the, 463
and valleys, that, 235
of seas, 400
of yore, on thy seven, 342
to climb steep, 55
with thunder riven, 13
Hillside for a pall, the, 184
Himmel, take a liddle prayer to, 351
Himself, 180
his hungering neighbour and me, 188
no more than from, 178
Hind of princes peer, make me own this, 324
that would be mated with the lion, the, 384
Hinders needle and thread, 438
Hindmost, the devil take the, 87
Hindrance, 180
Hinges of the knee, crook the pregnant, 412
Hint a fault, just, 71
upon this, I spake, 363
Hip, I have you on the, 72
once upon the, 166
Hire, taste the, 140
His indeed, shall then be, 460
could ne'er be, 363
His, 't is, 275
Hiss, we're obliged to, 210
where they howl and, 436
Hisses, 180
she may dare, stem the, 449
Historians, I defy, 218
History, 180
ever hear by tale or, 238
mad from life's, 244
of the human-kind, 103
Hit, 180
seem a lucky, 67
the line hard, 222
Hive, I quickly were dissolved from my, 436
with one bee in a, 184
Hoard is little, our, 175
of maxims, with a little, 73
Hoarded, bartered, 157
Hoarse with having little else to do, 9
Hobby-horse, 180
Hock, which . . . the poet speaks of, 344
Hocus-pocus science, a sort of, 212
Hodge-podge together, clapped, 308
Hoe, 180
a darned long row to, 344
Hog, 181
Hogs and your sheep, worse fed than your, 323
Hoist with his own petar, 110
Hold, as 't were, the mirror, 278
and light to, 157
both thee and me, wide enough to, 189
enough! that first cries, 214
fast that which is good, 320
fast the best, and, 320
it fast, take and, 434
like a serpent from their, 416
love out, stony limits cannot, 239
mortality's strong hand, we, 270
on with a bulldog grip, 40
out mine iron, 48
thee, he will, 297
the faith and morals, 412
the same rule will, 126
the world but as the world, I, 463
will slip, the mongrel's, 40
you here, I, 135
Holding both his sides, laughter, 382
up a beacon peerless, 290
Holding-anchor lost, the, 231
Holds a pretty girl's hand, what, 383
him with his glittering eye, 117
its warped mirror, 278
that anchor, 9
the eel of science by the tail, 192
Hole and crack, through every, 132
each lack-lustre, eyeless, 367
made in your best coat, 57
might stop a, 421
that hath but oon, 271
trusts to one poor, 271
where his tail came through, 87

Holiday, 181
and lady terms, many, 401
Holier laws, of . . . , 252
Holiest thing alive, the, 270
Holland, France, England, 135
Hollands, 181
Hollers out Gee, world 'll go right ef he, 461
Hollow, all was false and, 122
down deep in a, 446
of thine ear, pierced the fearful, 283
Holly, 181
branch shone, the, 265
round the Christmas hearth, 52
where English oak and, 304
Holy, 181
Book by which we live and die, 30
bread, as the touch of, 205
Church incorporate two in one, 53
door, stand within that, 115
fields over whose acres, 67
ground, ay, call it, 464
ground, brave lodgings for one in, 229
he died to make men, 225
men at their death, 80
place, is a good, a, 52
sae pious and sae, 304
witness, an evil soul producing, 11
writ, strong as proofs of, 195
Holy-day, on a sunshine, 71
Holy-days or so, unless on, 446
Holy Supper, 181
is spread within, the, 194
Homage, do her, 212
Home, 182
a day's march nearer, 278
again, princes are come, 112
all in a blessed, 334
and comes safe, 66
and feels herself at, 330
and that sweet time, youth and, 23
are crossways, things at, 292
art gone, 103
bravely onward to your, 232
confined from, 186
creep, and take your place, 290
for the Old Kentucky, 200
from sea, my ships are coming, 360
from the hill, and the hunter, 163
full numbers, brings, 425
God, who is our, 25
had he a, 182
he stays to his, 356
his country's flag is at, 133
his footsteps he hath turned, 65
I'm going, 461
in the Soudan, Fuzzy-Wuzzy at your, 147
is the sailor home from sea, 163
is still here, thy, 31
itself, a vision of, 133
makes her loved at, 352
merriest when they are from, 261
no news so bad abroad as this at, 281
Home
nor wax nor honey can bring, 436
of an Englishman, the island, 113
of the brave, 17
of the pilgrims, the, 111
on the rolling deep, a, 288
our, we'll find far out on the sea, 354
our, whare sits our sulky, sullen dame, 465
our peace at, and safety abroad, 299
our souls at, 108
out of house and, 107
sense like charity begins at, 356
that live at, 355
the ocean's my, 4
the world of waters is our, 436
there's nobody at, 447
they brought her warrior dead, 76
to feed were best at, 129
to me, none have yet come, 360
to me, that is, 8
to men's business and bosoms, 40
turns again, 18
warm at, 189
welcome as we draw near, 438
when cats run, 45
wherever the stars and stripes, 8
when the kye comes, 457
women are skeery unless they have a, 455
when you knock it never is at, 447
Home-keeping youth have ever, 182
Homeless, 182
Homely, 182
savoury, will make what's, 388
Homer, 183
and Virgil quotes, 30
Homes, at their native, 141
homeless near a thousand, 182
Homeward plods his weary way, 69
Homily, I never composed a better, 397
Honest, 183
and a perfect man, an, 127
dollar, short-weight dollar is not an, 96
doubt, more faith in, 97
fame, grant an, 124
hand a whip, and put in very, 439
happy and laudable, most, 203
heart, bear it with an, 150
honnable and fair, all thet's, 111
knaves, whip me such, 205
man may take a knave's advice, 205
man sent to lie abroad for his country, 7
man's revenge, patience is the, 335
on mine honour, he's, 438
poor but, 310
though he be merry, . . . he's, 261
though it be, 281
too, wives may be merry and yet, 448
Honester than I, no, 183
Honesty, 183
I am armed so strong in, 404

Honesty
is, what a fool, 415
is his, and, 128
my truth and, 417
party, is party duty, 297
puts it to utterance, 379
the more is for your, 401
wins not more than, 64
Honey, 184
age has no, 4
can bring home, nor wax nor, 436
it disdained, if falsehood's, 411
rob the bee of her, 133
the sweeter the, 240
wears a sting, 403
with trade wax, mingling poetic, 308
Honey-fee of parting, the, 296
Honorius long did dwell, in yon cave, 177
Honour, 184, 185
all is lost save, 231
aspireth to it, 77
at the height, our, 89
but an empty bubble, 431
civil right, law an' order, 212
clear, and in, 385
comes, a pilgrim grey, there, 34
deeds of glory, of, 409
depths and shoals of, 140
doth forget men's names, new-made, 275
doubt, more faith in, 97
for his valour, 7
he's honest on mine, 438
him, I, 7
is a private station, post of, 424
jealous in, 373
lost, for, 299
love, and obey, 45
love, obedience, troops of friends, 223
men who have, 259
our fortunes and our sacred, 307
than deep wounds before, hurts, 36
the ancient Roman, 145
thee, how I do, 72
those who have reflected, 111
to direct in chief, more, 92
what are you to love, 237
we call you, to, 286
wisdom and, 136
Honourable, esteemed more, 216
and fair, all thet's honest, 111
and his quarrel, 45
thing to thrive by dirty ways, 92
Honoured, by strangers, 139
in the breach, more, 70
once, how, 334
praised, wept and, 385
well are charms to sell, 47
Honouring thee, not so much, 99
Honour's at the stake, 164
in the right, your, 66
lodged, in the place where, 36
voice provoke, can, 421
Honours, 185
bears his blushing, 164
in more substantial, 148
space of our large, 36
Hood, drink with him that wears a, 6
mine eyes, 372
Hooded eyes, shafts from, 23
Hoof of the law, the head and the, 287
the iron on the, 187
Hook, bait the, 16
he baited, his, 439
with saints dost bait thy, 347
Hookas, divine in, 408
Hoops of steel, with, 146
shall have ten, 130
Hooted, the rabblement, 43
Hooting at Coriolanus' exile, 43
Hop, the frogs went, 372
Hope, 185, 186
again, never to, 122
a great man's memory may outlive, 258
and joy, of, 414
and longing unexpressed, fear and, 234
and loyal, 219
and pray for all, 312
and purpose high, with, 321
and the fear, the, 109
as giving it a, 99
. . . bade the world farewell, 142
be dim, though, 390
been smitten, hath, 391
believe, promise, 124
break it to our, 318
constancy in wind, 67
fondly do we, 199
for mercy, how shalt thou, 260
for the garrison hung, 113
hang themselves in, 254
haply lies his petty, 73
I neither fear nor, 369
is built on reeds, whose, 330
is fled, lest when our latest, 465
is, my own, 159
life is the rose's, 219
links her to the future, 258
may bloom, new, 236
may live without, 63
measure of immortal, 115
my hope, thy, 104
noble hopes are part of, 284
nor bate a jot of heart or, 387
nor, nor joy, 367
not that wind or wave, 149
on, hope ever, 38
one half of woman's life is, 454
points before, 48
soured on me, all, 313
tender leaves of, 164
texts of despair or, 24
the old, is hardest to be lost, 290
to find, perfection none must, 128
to merit heaven, 177
two cardinal virtues, faith and, 315
was rife, still the shadowy, 230

Hope
withering fled, 142
Hopeless love, crossed in, 66
Hopes are part of hope, noble, 284
belied, fears our, 105
decay, and the dearest, 125
depended, late on, 464
for half thy fears, my, 409
in, that Saint Nicholas, 51
of all men, the, 193
of my age, 5
that grieves not and that never, 388
the strivings after better, 88
were dupes, if, 391
Horizontal line, 389
Horn, a blast of that dread, 39
blest south wind that toots his, 132
ere thrice yon moon had filled her, 12
Triton blow his wreathed, 293
Hornet, 186
Horns, bulls aim their, 14
know him by his, 88
o' the moon, 43
Horologe, he 'll watch the, 100
Horrible shadow, hence, 358
Horror, 186
and doubt distract, 178
Horrors of this, 'mid, 9
Horse, 186, 187
a brewer 's, 53
a little dearer than his, 297
and hero fell, 80
an two men ride of a, 337
as tedious as is a tired, 399
call me, 218
dog or, 38
in the stable, a good, 303
kick that scarce would move a, 201
lad, than hey for boot and, 469
like a full-hot, 9
of Parnassus, wine 's the true, 445
rider and, 40
that which is now a, 56
the grey mare is the better, 253
the head, gave his able, 345
the ways of a man with a, 187
to death, run their, 22
to ride, a gallant, 57
when the grey mare 's the better, 253
went lame, my, 57
Horse - laugh through the pews, spread a, 212
Horsemanship, 187
Horses, 187
between two, 213
fear to tread, wheels rush in where, 439
not best to swap, 394
our passions are the, 56
women and, 164
Horse-sense, plain, in poetry-writin', 309
Hose, his youthful, 294
doublet and, 68
Hose, should be ungartered, your, 239
when he goes in his doublet and, 251
Hospitable, 187
Hospitality, and Scotch, 352
Host, at the head of the, 63
death proclaimed through our, 156
like a fashionable, 167
of prides, a, 316
on the morrow, that, 216
that I know, many an old, 290
that led the starry, 268
the cry of that spectral, 151
with their banners that, 216
Hostages to fortune, hath given, 442
Hosts, Lord God of, 139
Hot, 187
and copper sky, 63
and soon, 50
as a basted turkey, I was, 286
for your foe so, 136
right hand grows raging, 169
temper leaps o'er a cold decree, 33
when the iron is, 390
Hotchpotch of all sorts of fishes, 32
Hottentet's great toe, to bleach a, 266
Hottest furnace, from the, 41
Hound has part, love in which my, 187
Hounds, as a carcass fit for, 201
Hour, 187
a canny, at e'en, 44
ago, an, a star was falling, 384
await alike the inevitable, 163
before the worshipped sun, an, 393
every, brings forth some gasping truth, 416
foretold, truly that, 296
for only one short, 430
grieve for an, 448
groaning every, 56
his brute question in that, 147
if we do but watch the, 467
I have had my, 221
learn by proof in some wild, 465
mark him every, 154
may lay it in the dust, an, 385
never sold the truth to serve the, 418
of danger, 39
of rest, wakens at this, 23
of strut and rave, our little, 411
one self-approving, 355
or place, whatso'er the, 274
o' th' day, tell what, 6
ten, grief makes one, 165
that struts and frets his, 411
the wonder of an, 352
thoughts of the last bitter, 362
till Hymen brought his love-delighted, 450
to hour, from, 224
toil for triumphs of an, 104
went by me, never an, 286
when all seemeth securest, at an, 435
whenever you welcome the, 125
within this, 413

Humming, the city's rout and noise and, 264
Humour, lightens my, 196
most, yet has her, 400
say it is my, 103
wooed, was ever woman in this, 454
Humours, nurses dangerous, 431
of the land, 141
Humourous as winter, as, 161
Hump, and without an absolute, 255
is Obey, and the haunch and the, 287
Hums a stave, now he, 383
bees and such like, 151
Hundred, 188
coats-of-arms, is worth a, 246
fights, he that gained a, 167
pounds a year, I've a, 61
towers, clashed and hammered from a, 284
years are gone, when a, 286
years of life, worth a, 39
years to a day, 46
years, ye make in a, 152
will subscribe for soap, 38
Hundredth Psalm, the, 10
Hung a shadow and a fear, 69
it out in the rain, he only, 361
Hunger and dirt, in poverty, 361
in his heart, a lifelong, 174
the food that slakes, 369
Hungry judges soon the sentence sign, 92
jurymen, discontented or, 92
people, slowly comes a, 301
savage, anti-everythings, lean, 10
where most she satisfies, 5
Hunt each other, why then will you, 433
folks's corns out, new ones, 161
in fields, better to, 172
Hunter home from the hill, and the, 163
Hunting him, was killed with, 226
of that day, the, 419
Hunts for flowers, he who, 135
Huntsman his pack, as a, 145
Hurl their lances, 350
Hurled, swift to be, 244
Hurls back an epithet as hard, 114
Hurlyburly's done, when the, 257
Hurrah for the next that dies, 91
Hurrahs, 188
Hurricane, 188
Hurry along, as I, 247
and shock, will occur in a, 348
Hurrying feet, stays our, 79
Hurt, 189
a fly, nor, 271
if . . . you were, 40
that honour feels, helps the, 185
the proper power to, 14
with the same weapons, 197
would do no, 186
Hurts and is desired, 79
honour than deep wounds before, 36
Hurts the poor creature, 135
Husband, 189
a woman oweth to her, 454
calls the name of her, 99
of this gifted well, if the, 348
out of, shape a, 255
stays, safest and seemliest by her, 443
the heart of her, 451
then, heaven help the, 348
Husbandry, the edge of, 31
Husband's heart, level in her, 454
Husbands, 190
when, or when lapdogs, 362
Hush of our dread high-altars, 1
and then a groan, a, 76
that followed the prayer, 55
thee my baby, thy sire was a knight, 16
thee my baby, the time soon will come, 390
Hushed and smooth, till it is, 369
as the foot of night, 282
the minster bell, they've, 264
Hut, and that dear, 182
love in a, 235
Huzzas, of stupid starers and of loud, 355
Hydras, and chimæras dire, 161
Hymen brought his love-delighted hour, till, 450
Hymn, chants a doleful, 273
of the conquered, 61
Hymns, chanting faint, 56
of gratitude and love, 173
sings, at heaven's gate, 210
Hyperion's curls, 250
Hypocrisy, 190
can spin, in spite of all, 393
Hypocrite, one friend not quite an, 462
Hyrcan tiger, the, 72

I

I am there, and, 207
am, wheresoe'er, 240
and you wonder, 75
it is not, 74
to Hercules, than, 37
where you once utter the, 319
Xerxes must die and so must, 467
Iago, the pity of it, 305
Ice, 190
as chaste as, 42
her heart is . . . not of, 328
in June, 67
region of thick-ribbed, 90
thick-ribbed, not to, 347
to smooth the, 152
Ice-ribbed pinions, on mine, 284
Icicles, 190
Icily regular, 128
Icy air of night, how they tinkle in the, 23
hand on kings, death lays his, 127

Idea, depolarize every fixed religious, 85
how to shoot, to teach the young, 398
Ideal, 190
all the nonsense of their stone, 385
Ideality, 190
Ideas, a man of nasty, 281
o' wut 's right, good old, 431
Ides, 190
Idiot, a tale told by an, 411
Idiots only may be cozened twice, 205
Idle, 190
as a painted ship, as, 359
brain, children of an, 99
tears, I know not what they mean, 399
Idleness, in strenuous, 377
Idler, 90
Idolatry, the god of my 394
Idols, home itself and all its, 133
If, avoid that too with an, 218
much virtue in, 218
Ignoble strife, madding crowd 's, 68
use, soiled with all, 150
Ignominy sleep with thee, thy, 114
Ignorance, 190
be indeed a bliss, if, 370
equals this, what, 370
folly and, 252
it was a childish, 331
Ignorant, eyes of the, 2
for current, took 'em, 458
most, of what he 's most assured, 251
Ignorantly read, the bookful blockhead, 30
Ill, 191
a-brewing toward my rest, 98
a part, to play so, 116
blows the wind that profits nobody, 444
bought dear by knowing, 414
calls me well or, 160
cannot prevail against mine, 429
Captive Good attending Captain, 417
come good or, 150
cook that cannot lick, 62
crowning good repressing, 385
deeds, means to do, 83
done, makes deeds, 83
extreme in love or hate, in good or, 449
fare the hands that heaved, 29
fares the land, 300
habits gather, 167
he thinks no, 239
I don't at all take it, 397
luck stirring, no, 244
name of augurs, got the, 31
only one thing sleep . . . hath, 369
or good or, 2
savour, gives it an, 52
the final goal of, 160
the weights of good and, 389
together, good and, 222
Ill
to live with, the grey mare is, 253
will, in shrill, 44
winde turnes none to good, an, 444
wind which blows no man to good, not the, 444
Ill-favoured faults, vile, 128
thing, but mine own, 263
Illinois, I was with Grant in, 152
Illness, during temporary, 109
is over at last, the lingering, 229
is the real vampyrism, long, 423
Ills, 191
all, that strength and courage, 189
a prey, to hastening, 300
have not been done by a woman, what mighty, 452
of mortality, 'gainst the, 100
we have, those, 79
Ill-starred, stone or brick, 114
Ill-tempered, when I spoke that I was, 382
Illumed the eastern skies, 105
Ill-used, the hardest knife, 206
Image, a reasonable creature, God 's 30
of good Queen Bess, 157
of his Maker, 7
of our mind, the, 447
Images, and sad, 362
Imagination, 191
bodies forth, as, 308
fondly stoops, 295
for his facts, upon his, 291
how abhorred in my, 468
trace, why may not, 421
Imagine how the bird was dead, 41
Imagining some fear, 128
Immaculate, his thoughts, 29
Immeasurable reality, 190
Immodest words admit of no defence, 83
Immortal, 191
as itself, a thing, 223
as its sire, the soul, 376
a soul, 377
dead, of those, 50
feelings, I had, 230
hope, measure of, 115
longings in me, I have, 230
of the dead, 115
part of myself, lost the, 332
reign, scenes where love and bliss, 27
trust, take them O Father in, 13
Immortality, 191
the shade of, 124
touch it again with, 467
Imogene, his consort, the Fair, 379
while the spectre addressed, 463
Impaired, nothing, but all disordered, 380
Impeach of valour, ten to one is no, 423
Impeachment, 191
Impediments, for they are, 442
unto my speech, the moist, 399

Impelled them to the separation, the causes which, 356
Imperfections on my head, all my, 370
Impious in a good man to be sad, 346
men bear sway, and, 424
Implacable in hate, 385
Implement has had, no little part that, 467
Imponderables move the world, the, 237
Importance twice, debating everything of, 82
Important department, the most, 54
Importunate, rashly, 420
Importune, too proud to, 141
Imposing, less, in the eyes of some, 352
Impossible, it was equally, 54
she, that not, 358
that I should live, it is, 82
Impostor heap, let no, 355
Impostors, a race of mere, 385
Impotent and loud, 9
conclusion, most lame and, 60
Impression, as sharp an, 264
of St. Peter's keys in wax, the, 347
such terrible, 98
Imprisoned in the viewless winds, 90
Improve, 191
by travel, some minds, 276
Improves our parts, 234
Impulse, like the first fierce, 66
still with strong, 245
to a wordless prayer, 88
Impute my fall to sin, and then, 365
Inanimate e'er grieves, if aught, 166
Incarnadine, the multitudinous seas, 169
Incense soars, vainly his, 330
Incense-breathing morn, breezy call of, 269
Incensed, he's flint, 161
me, have so, 328
or crushed, most fragrant when they are, 427
Inch a king, aye, every, 202
of rigging, without an, 73
thick, let her paint, 468
Incidents well linked, and, 396
Inclination, a treacherous, 142
Inclined, the tree's, 107
to, compound for sins they are, 366
to embrace me she, 98
Inclines our eyelids, 370
us more to laugh than scold, 212
Income, 192
Incomparable man, a most, 160
Incomplete, our lives are, 79
Incompleteness, flowed around our, 154
Inconstant, cruel and, 83
than the wind, more, 444
Incorporate two in one, 53
Incorporated, seem at once to lose their nature, 413
Increase of appetite had grown, 11
tailors, and breed ballad-makers, 279
Increased with years, 224
Increases every day, danger of detection, 82
Incurred the worst, who with best meaning have, 464
Incurs no blame, a necessary act, 279
Ind, of Ormus and of, 107
Indebted, 192
Independence, 192
make up the Declaration of, 149
Index-learning, 192
Indian, lo, the poor, 176
Indians fell, for which unpitied, 157
India-rubber apron-strings, 8
India's morning-bugle, 112
Indifferent honest, myself, 183
Indirection, by any, 267
Indispensable, my family think it, 382
Indistinct, makes it, 56
Individual, nor should the, 340
Indulge, can threaten or, 377
Indulgence, she first his weak, 452
Indus to the pole, from, 216
Industry, the hammer of, 410
Inebriate, cheer but not, 116
Inestimable stones, 102
Inevitable hour, await alike the, 163
Infamies, make right the immemorial, 467
Infamous, men the most, 123
Infancy, begins man's general, 318
knew, which my, 49
Infant, 192
Infant's idle laughter, an, 119
Infected spy, seems infected that th', 195
Infection, against, 112
Inferred to us, 'tis, 101
Infest the day, cares that, 44
the grave, if dreams, 98
Infidels adore, and, 197
Infinite, for both are, 239
ideality, 190
in me, I feel the, 230
in power, 154
rate, purchased at an, 117
Infinitely, promise you, 318
Infinity, 192
Infirm of purpose, 70
Infirmities, should bear his friend's, 145
Infirmity, the last, of noble mind, 123
Inflamed my soul, once, 20
Inflammation of the lungs, with an, 198
Inflict they feel, what they, 455
Inflicted on a beast, 390
Influence, all, all fate, 127
Information, know where we can find, 206
Infraction of the rules of courtesy, without an, 455

Infringe the rights of others, so long as he does not, 338
Infuse themselves, that souls of animals, 378
Inglorious Milton, some mute, 168
Ingots bows, whose back with, 336
Ingratitude, 192
unkind as man 's, 444
Ingratitudes, a great-sized monster of, 407
Inhabit this great earth, all that, 201
Inhabitants o' the earth, look not like the, 448
Inherit, all which it, 428
Inhuman, ev'ythin' thet 's done, 208
Inhumanity, 192
Iniquity, the hire of their, 140
Injure you, I ne'er could, 122
Injured, forgiveness to the, 140
Injures all on 'em the same, 208
Injury, 192
to revenge an, 335
Injustice, and jealousy, 450
conscience corrupted with, 12
Ink, 192
and paper, pay for goose-quill, 317
be made of gall, though, 466
dipped me in, 466
gall enough in thy, 148
good at pen and, 92
he hath not drunk, 30
were tempered with love 's sighs, 308
Inky cloak, good mother, 448
Inmate, full of mirth, little, 175
Inn, 192, 193
pushes us on to the windowless, 406
return and sleep within mine, 413
the world 's an, 77
Innocence my liberty, and, 318
oh, mirth and, 264
Innocent as gay, 20
on earth, crime deemed, 66
Innocents, 193
good and easy, 103
Inn 's worst room, in the worst, 464
Insane, delight in prose, 309
Insatiate archer, could not one suffice, 12
Inscription, and from the, 163
is the, 373
let there be no, 114
Inscriptions on our hearts, 175
Insect, while man, vain, 176
Insensible, 'tis, 185
Inseparable, one and, 218
Inside of a church, 53
of your purse, show the, 158
Insignificant, perhaps, 352
Insipid, 193
things, 204
Insipidity, to whose glorious, 397
Insolence of office, the, 323
Inspection, on a very slight, 320
Inspirations, have good, 80
Inspires my wit, still, 20
Inspires thee, no German song, 151
Inspiring, bold John Barleycorn, 19
Instances, wise saws and modern, 199
the wilderness of single, 214
Instant, show the whole wealth of thy wit in an, 447
Instinct, hath by, 394
Instils the stirring memory, 72
Institute and digest of anarchy, a sort of, 338
Instituted among men, governments are, 161
Institution, such as are in the, 253
Instructed in his youth, how he was, 416
Instruction, 193
but I will better the, 197
Instructions, follows his own, 94
Instructs me, as my understanding, 379
Instrument, 193
you will, call me what, 305
Instruments, that God makes, 389
to plague us, make, 425
Insult, threatened her with, 50
to God, one more, 467
Insulted, by fools, 320
Integrity to heaven, my robe and my, 340
Intellect, is not replenished, 30
or will, for, 220
the atmosphere of, 387
Intellectual being, this, 90
Intended, as if religion were, 329
Intends deceit, that first, 82
Intensity we love with, think with the, 402
Intent and purpose of the law, 213
at least, to all, 340
of bearing, 13
on hospitable thoughts, 187
with knowledge or, 77
Intentions, 193
as much to all, 75
Intercourse with foreign nations, in her, 65
speed the soft, 216
Interest, 193
does not put, 208
Interested him no more, 350
Interim be but a se'nnight, the, 407
Interjections, verbs, pronouns, 389
Interpose, those who in quarrels, 323
Interpret law, office is to, 198
Interpreter, God is his own, 155
Interred with their bones, 116
Interrogation, with the note of, 363
Intersected by a narrow frith, 110
Intervals upon the ear, falling at, 52
Intestine shock and furious close, 54
Intoxicate the brain, shallow draughts, 215
Intoxication, 193
Intrudes, society where none, 457
Intuition, become a passionate, 121

Invalid, I didn't know truth was such an, 416
Invented for our sins, surely were, 304
sleep, him that, 369
Invention, if necessity be the mother of, 279
of the enemy, a weak, 110
surest prompter of, 279
the brightest heaven of, 272
Inventress of the vocal frame, 45
Inverted bowl they call the sky, that, 368
Invisible as a nose on a man's face, 285
perfume, a strange, 302
soap, washing his hands with, 372
the choir, 50
to thee, 381
Invitation, much more, 108
Invite my soul, I loafe and, 229
the cushion and soft dean, 178
Invites you by his looks to come, his wit, 447
Ire, 193
Ireland, 194
Ireland's isle, not a mile in, 372
Iris, a livelier, 241
Irish lads, no wonder that those, 440
Irishman, 194
Iron, 194
bells, 410
best blood that hath most, 27
creeds, and framed their, 155
for things like these, lasts like, 441
gate, no, 31
grasp, from the strong, 127
hold out mine, 48
is hot, strike when the, 390
I barred my gates with, 284
nothing but to rust, 299
on the hoof, that holds the, 187
rang hard crab-tree and old, 405
the man that meddles with cold, 302
thread, stretch forth your, 152
tongue, the midnight bell with his, 22
tongue of midnight, the, 262
Iron-bound bucket, 39
Iron-jointed, supple-sinewed, 350
Irrepressible conflict, an, 60
Iscariot, 194
Is, it, but hadn't ought to be, 346
time, 406
Iser rolling rapidly, the flow of, 225
Island, 194
home of an Englishman, 113
of England breeds, that, 111
Islands lift their fronded palms in air, 43
Isle, 194
of beauty, 1
this sceptred, 112
so little, never was, 113
Isles, the Niobe of, 283
Israfel, or flashed with, 244
Issue, I'll put it to the, 187
Issues mean, and what its, 390
Isthmus, this narrow, 222
Italy and England, Greece, 309
draws breath in, 145
Itch, what gives or cures the, 306
Itching palm, much condemned to have an, 294
Itself and friend, 31
not of, 100
Ivy, 195
o'ergrown, their creeds are with, 446
Ivy-mantled tower, from yonder, 292

J

Jack, an end of honest, 168
for the life of poor, 48
Jack-knife driven, by his genius and his, 467
Jack-knives, carved it or shut up our, 275
Jacob, I do not like to see thy nose, 304
what is dirt, 92
Jade, 195
on a journey, an arrant, 303
the panting sides of his poor, 345
Jail, the world miscalls a, 318
James, King, used to call for his old shoes, 146
James's, King, men shall understand, 63
Jamie lo'ed me weel, young, 68
January, snowhid in, 323
Jar, united, 376
Jarring sects unite, principles your, 162
Jars were made to drain, 445
Jaundice and creep into the, 264
Jaundiced, 195
Jaunt must be put off to-morrow, 324
Jaw, 195
Jaws of death, out of the, 80
of death, came through the, 80
this hungry war opens his vasty, 432
Jays, 195
Jealous confirmation strong, are to the, 195
doubt spout out, 115
for they are jealous, 195
Jealousies, and his pettier, 67
and pride, local, 110
Jealousy, 195
injustice, and, 450
love . . . is full of, 240
Jean, and farewell my, 229
Jehovah has triumphed, 405
Jove, or Lord, 127
Jelly, like a bowl full of, 24
Jenny kissed me, 204
Jerusalem, all men that dwelt in, 193
God beloved in old, 450
Jesses were my dear heart-strings, 168

Jest, 195, 196
a fellow of infinite, 468
and riddle of the world, the glory, 462
every speech a, 147
life is a, 219
man's life is but a, 219
or for a, 377
pass your proper, 67
unseen, inscrutable, invisible, 285
Jester, a fool and, 137
Jesters weep behind the mask, 165
Jests at scars that never felt a wound, he, 351
is indebted to his memory for his, 291
with his merry, 196
Jesus, 196
Christ our Saviour was born, 51
sake, for, 29
that gentilman, 150
Jesus' word, as Mary rose at, 358
Jew, 197
Jewel, 197
lies, this, 182
of their souls, is the immediate, 275
to barter away that precious, 42
unless experience be a, 117
wears a precious, 3
Jewels, 197
of the mine, bright, 464
unvalued, 102
Jewish gaberdine, my, 147
Jews, 197
to Christians, in converting, 310
Jilt, the, but I can live, 53
Jim, a keerless man in his talk was, 135
Jingle, clear the way, 23
Jingling and the tinkling of the bells, 408
of the guineas, helps the hurt, 185
Jo, John, John Anderson, my, 311
poor, he had no friends, 145
Job, as poor as, 310
Jocund one, were a, 269
Joe, hard-hearted is, 413
when you were Bill and I was, 230
Jog on, the footpath way, 174
Jogging whiles your boots, 96
John Anderson my jo, John, 311
Barleycorn, 18, 19
Doe, some draw pleas for, 146
the Baptist, a kind of maddened, 114
print it, some said, 317
P. Robinson he sez the world 'll go right, 461
P. Robinson he sez they did n't know everythin', 11
Johnny, 197
Join, thy summons comes to, 227
in your revels, 116
ourselves to no party, we, 420
Joined Greeks, when Greeks, 165
in the plan, 353
the other two, she, 309
Joint, the time is out of, 407
or limb, with, 381
Joints, his square-turned, 46
Joke, 197
had he, for many a, 93
Jokes, at all his, 93
Jollity, jest and youthful, 196
tipsy dance and, 129
Jolly, 197, 198
place, said he, 69
Josias, young Obadias, David, 305
Jot of former love, one, 296
of heart or hope, nor bate a, 387
Journey, an arrant jade on a, 303
in my head, 21
is done, the, 78
of life, the toilsome, 220
thy heavy riches but a, 336
ye make, the, 152
Journeyed fifty miles, he had, 106
Journey's end, death the, 77
Journeys, 198
Jove but laughs at lovers' perjury, 302
himself, the front of, 250
laughs, at lovers' perjuries, 302
or Lord, Jehovah, 127
thrown by angry, 122
Jove's dread clamours, 125
't was, 330
Joy, 198
and feast, welcome, 129
and grief, love is, 234
and grief, two extremes of passion, 297
and sorrow learn, love and, 48
and temperance and repose, 94
and the senses for ever in, 229
approbation strikes the string of, 12
base envy withers at another's, 114
be unconfined, let, 71
but now 't is little, 331
eternal, and everlasting love, 452
for ever, thing of beauty is a, 20
for his fortune, 7
from town to town, fling the, 23
from which he drank in, 107
in Eden's rosy bower, dwelt no, 450
its deep songs of, 209
my songs were full of, 148
nor hope nor, 367
of hope and, 414
of the whole table, 172
of youthful sports, my, 288
or moan, of, 24
prophetic, runs a thrill of, 143
renews the life of, 435
that tells the, 275
therein I find, such perfect, 262
they bring me sorrow touched with, 470
through, and through torment, 236
to his mighty heart, 13
was duty and love was law, 214
which warriors feel, the stern, 433
variety alone, 423
Joyful in my praise, 104

Joyous meeting, here's our next, 257
Joys, 198
drinking, 16
I have possessed, the, 221
its, and fears, 404
knows he the titillating, 285
of his banquet, the, 153
that bless thee, all the, 331
their homely, 310
three parts pain, be our, 328
must flow, 182
Judas, 198
Iscariot, the soul of, 194
with a temporal dole, 114
Judea, they did n't know everythin' down in, 11
Judge, 198
forbear to, 80
of the nations, 139
of truth, sole, 462
O wise young, 72
thy foe, each I, 71
use is the, 379
Judged, 198
Judge's robe, nor the, 260
Judges, 198
and senates have been bought, 158
of the world, the, 188
soon the sentence sign, 92
steal themselves, when, 386
Judging, 198
Judgment, 198,
a Daniel come to, 72
book, the leaves of the, 240
day, till, 451
guide his bounty, 84
I stand for, 213
morning, till the, 115
on the day of, 450
seat, before his, 415
seat, stand presently at God's great, 391
some shallow spirit of, 213
temper the imagination with, 191
when I was green in, 349
Judgments, 199
as our watches, 'tis with our, 434
mercies and, 154
who write down, 347
Judicious, 199
a tale should be, 396
Jug of wine, a, 85
Juggle, who will elsewhere, 114
Juice the growth of God, be this, 69
when nectarean, 435
Juices, the noblest, of the vineyard, 344
July, the warmth of its, 331
Jumping from the chair, 204
June, 199
forget that night in, 72
ice in, 67
may be had, 177
the leafy month of, 37
Jungle, these are the laws of the, 287
Juno had been sick, 62
Juno's crown, wedding is great, 437
swans, like, 224
unrelenting hate, 13
Jury, 199
has retired, when the, 92
Juryman, a good, contented, well-breakfasted, 92
Jurymen, discontented or hungry, 92
may dine, that, 92
Just, 199
and good, 'twas there of, 91
and 'tis prosperous to be, 34
are the ways of God, 200
hath his quarrel, 12
his cause being, 45
intent of bearing them is, 13
pretence, are their, 67
study to be good and, 104
thou art, 104
war, to be preferred before a, 430
Justice, 199
alike 'tis, 227
by merely human, 155
can do them, 114
in the course of, 260
may shove by, 289
of innocent commercial, 413
of it, than the, 212
sleeps, and waiting, 417
so little, here he found, 168
when mercy seasons, 260
Justifiable to men, and, 200
Justified, no man is, 117
Justify, 200
the means, the end must, 109

K

Kail, the monks of Melrose made gude, 267
Kangaroos, 200
Kate has done, many a, 200
Katy did no more, I warrant, 200
do, what did, 200
Katydid, 200
Keel, 200
while follow eyes the steady, 43
Keep a dream or grave apart, to, 220
and many to, 132
a stiff upper lip, 55, 220
him from broodin', 134
house with fear, peace wun't, 299
my soul to, 370
near shore, little boats should, 424
the day, we, 101
out death, the postman or the bore, can, 31
step to the music of the Union, 420
the bridge with me, 37
the last, if thou, 429
the law, when legislators, 216
the subtle ways I, 368
'the word of promise, that, 318
time, and our oars, 286
wel thy tonge, and, 411

Keep who can, they should, 396
your powder dry, 311
Keeper, thy, thy life, 189
Keepers, and vigilant, 262
Keeping their Christmas holiday, 265
Keeps, another, 355
in blast threescore years and ten, 28
Kehama shall reign, while, 69
Ken, for years beyond our, 138
Kendal green, misbegotten knaves in, 205
Kennin wrang, may gang a, 188
Kent, no man can gather cherries in, 48
Kentucky, 200
Kept, better broken than, 319
but never, 215
by great men reached and, 177
the Holy Supper is, 181
the law, most truly, 213
the time, with falling oars they, 286
Kerchief so sly, in her, 226
Kerns, these rough rug-headed, 424
Kettle sings songs, the, 441
Kew, his highness' dog at, 95
Key, almost always at least one, 129
into the hand, gives the, 33
is but a lock without a, 438
to which I found no, 423
with the past 's blood-rusted, 281
Keys of hell to keep, the, 369
over the noisy, 291
the impression of St. Peter 's, 347
Khaki dress, the worn white soldiers in, 373
Khan and the pachas, the, 63
Kick, 201
in that part more, a, 36
me downstairs, why did you, 93
off their burthens, 55
the other, gore one way or, 292
Kicked until they can feel whether, 20
Kickshaws, 201
Kidney, 201
Kids, do n't neglect your, 153
Kill, 201
a good book, as, 30
a man, thou shalt, 250
and heroes, 123
a sound divine, may, 201
a wife with kindness, 201
ere doctors learned to, 94
or save, alike to, 227
that murder could not, 252
the lust of office does not, 259
were privileged to, 272
Killed a mouse, I never, 271
it, scotched the snake, not, 372
with hunting him, was, 226
with unutterable unkindliness, 4:1
Killeth, the letter, 380
Killing ain't perlite, to think thet, 131
folks, ninepence a day for, 272
Kills for gold, he steals, he, 157
himself, he that, 422
Kills reason itself, 30
the heart, but, 236
the letter, 380
Kill'st me, boy, thou shalt kill a man, 250
Kilns and the curt-tongued mills, 413
Kin, makes the whole world, 278
to God by his spirit, 248
Kind, 201
hearts are more than coronets, 148
hearts, the true hearts, the, 175
how good, how, 46
of a little Johnny, a, 197
of good deed, 459
of men, for such, 401
of men so loose in soul, 371
only to be, 68
still the fair are, 141
than the colour of our, 58
to Him, the little grey leaves were, 458
were perfect in our, 304
Kinder gentleman treads not the earth, 150
Kindest and the happiest pair, 138
man, the, 145
Kindled from above, 204
Kindlier hand, larger heart, the, 174
Kindling her undazzled eyes, 277
Kindly faces, full of, 182
had we never loved sae, 37
to judge, 198
use 'em, 280
Kindly-earnest, brave, foreseeing man, 8
Kindness, 201
cup o', 14
in reserve, the great have, 384
in the Jew, say there is much, 197
save in the way of, 66
the milk of human, 262
to make to a woman, an offer of, 315
Kindred, 201
Kindred drops, like, 110
each, each age, 24
shall be joyful, 104
Kinds, knowledge is of two, 206
o' labour, all, 212
Kine are to be loved, 126
the smell of, 371
King, 201, 202
a gentleman, that makes the, 248
catch the conscience of the, 306
Charles, that to, 39
contrary to the, 317
dish for a, 6
fellow with the best, 130
foe of magistrate and, 143
for Church and, 383
God save our lord the, 308
grew vain, 19
half the zeal I served my, 357
James used to call for his old shoes, 146
James 's men shall understand, 63
makes me more than, 402

King
of England, for Charles, 19
of England cannot enter, 44
of good fellows, the best, 130
of his race, he the true, 410
of men, this rail-splitter a true-born, 324
or nobles, a state without, 59
Simonides, the good, 133
so strong, what, 42
Stephen was a worthy peer, 387
the year's pleasant, 382
to the shepherd, equals the, 369
who serves the, 357
Kingdom, a soul none better in my, 438
for a horse, my, 187
for a stage, a, 383
for it was too small, a, 381
give grandam, 162
is, both crown and, 262
is, my mind to me a, 262
Kingdoms and with kings, with, 147
Kingliest act, the, 144
King's crown, not the, 260
English, and the, 113
Kings, 202
and meaner creatures, 186
but the breath of, 183
Death lays his icy hand on, 127
depart, the, 139
enthroned in the hearts of, 260
have lipped, a hand that, 205
have no such couch as thine, 334
it makes gods, 186
may be blessed, 191
of cabbages and, 430
queens and states, 368
showers on her, 107
than beggars, worse in, 122
that stir not the bosom of, 410
the dread and fear of, 260
the right divine of, 161
this royal throne of, 112
thou shalt lie down with 334
will be tyrants from policy, 328
with kingdoms and with, 147
would not play at, 430
Kiss, 202–204
a bonny lass, 249
and part, come let us, 296
but in the cup, 99
colder thy, 296
every, has a price, 253
from my forehead, 340
Gillian the quicker, 226
her and leave her, 55
I think there is not half a, 243
me, then come, 239
me, though you make believe, 82
more cheeks than one, or, 200
not she with trait'rous, 67
not to sigh, learn to, 442
seal with a righteous, 118
that air, only to, 100
the rod, all humbled, 341
Kiss
the rod, confess thy folly, 341
the rod, wilt thou, 341
the thing you, 74
thine eyelids to, 293
took her nightly, 283
to share, the envied, 175
was given, our good-night, 105
when tyrants seem to, 419
which Jews might, 197
Kissed, 204
had I wist before I, 231
him, so she, 338
me, before you have, 286
that haughty scroll of gold, 111
thee, that lately, 100
the fiddler's wife, the minister, 263
the rod, if right, I, 67
those lips that I have, 468
Kisses, 204, 205
and welcome you'll find here, 59
as belonged to early days, such, 204
plucked up, 204
shall teach thy lips, my, 240
stolen, much completer, 387
which melts like, 210
Kissing, 205
cherries, those, 226
gun, hot gun-lip, 347
to deceive, you are, 82
was clover, and, 240
Kissings worth, what are all these, 204
Kitchen bred, in the, 148
hearth, chirping on my, 175
Kite soar with unbloodied beak, 41
Kites and crows, city of, 43
Kith and kin, he taught to, 181
and kin, it puzzled all our, 418
Kitten, 205
Kittened, your mother's cat had but, 277
Knave, 205
but he's an arrant, 426
I'm not a, 326
is, how absolute the, 43
there he fells a, 383
why does he suffer this rude, 214
you are rid of a, 422
Knaves, 205
what fools or, 306
Kneaded clod, become a, 90
Kneading-pan, 'twixt her hands into the, 465
Knee, crook the pregnant hinges of the, 412
knuckle or, 91
to man unbent, with, 420
with one of timber, the, 216
Kneel, at some well-remembered grave, will, 163
down remote, 312
I saw my mother, 283
undisturbed, fair saint, 348
Knees, around her, 452
down on your, 238
on parent, 227

Knees, or climb his, 175
the weakest saint upon his, 350
were feeble, but that his, 313
Knell, 205
all ring fancy's, 124
is rung, by fairy hands their, 34
like a rising, 334
of parting day, 69
that all-softening, o'erpowering, 92
the, the shroud, 401
Knelt in the pure shrine, 269
there he would have, 313
Knew, 206
could carry all he, 456
head which all men, 171
he builded better than he, 39
him, poor Yorick, I, 468
honest face which all men, 171
it could not last, 211
me, since first you, 407
no more of me you, 403
texts enough to wear a parson's gown, 401
the woes of want, before I, 430
they could but die, 90
what he said, and the old woman, 326
what it were, if we, 117
what's what, 261
which, not a soul, 418
Knife, 206
nothin' for a cancer but the, 42
war even to the, 430
Knight, from Trier to Coln there was never a, 221
no carpet, 46
thy sire was a, 16
Knight's bones are dust, the, 29
Knights are pressing close, a thousand, 179
Knit hands and beat the ground, 409
the holy knotts did, 206
Knits up the ravelled sleave of care, 370
Knives have edges, and some say, 404
Knob of timber, headed with a, 249
Knock as you please, there's nobody at home, 447
at the door, a, 84
him about the sconce, to, 214
his leek about his pate, 216
I stand at the door and, 96
it never is at home, when you, 447
sentiment a-kitin', would jes, 309
with a smart double, 338
Knocker, 206
Knocks, 206
by apostolic blows and, 329
Knot, 206
of it, the Gordian, 161
of mouth-friends, you, 146
there's no untying, the, 203
Knots, 206
Know, 206
all our knowledge is ourselves to, 250
Know
a man in love, how to, 239
a subject ourselves, we, 206
a trick worth two of that, 414
don't never prophesy onless ye, 319
everythin' down in Judee, they didn't, 11
from me, they shall never, 274
full well, this alone I, 327
he made an instrument to, 193
him by his horns, 88
his heart, shall you, 119
howe'er contented never, 143
how little while, you, 77
how sublime a thing it is, 391
I am happier than I, 170
it, and they, 385
it, I thought so once but now I, 219
it, to sleep and not to, 370
me all, but as you, 291
me argues yourselves unknown, not to, 421
me safe and warmly laid, 283
me well, when it came to, 148
my price, I, 315
myself now, I, 300
never to let her, 400
nor care, I neither, 295
not, I, I ask not, 236
not of, that we, 79
not the bells I, 23
not well the subtle ways, they, 368
not what, I, 78
not what they do, they, 140
not what they mean, I, 399
not what thou art, I, 220
not what we may be, 12
not whence you came, 100
not where, go we, 90
not why I am so sad, I, 346
not why you go, 100
of England, what should they, 111
one another, more occasion to, 238
reason but from what we, 327
sure no one could, 348
't, let him not, 340
thee not, to those who, 459
the false heart doth, 122
the hand, I, 169
their friends, nature teaches beasts to, 278
then this truth 427
then thyself, presume not, 250
the reason why, will, 63
the sweet Roman hand, 169
the thing he would not, 394
the woman who did not, 451
this truth enough for man to, 427
thou alone wilt, 409
though less they, 376
to esteem, to love, to, 221
turtles from jays, teach him to, 195
we can arrive to, 389
well enough, wise men, 255
what God and man is, 135
what is become of him, do I, 310

Know
what it is, we do not, 369
what we are, 12
what wood a cudgel 's of, 20
where we can find information, 206
who only England, 111
why, the woman who did n't, 451
young men to do so, old men, 469
Knowed a Quaäker fellow, I, 267
how, I reckon he never, 135
sunthin' tu, the gran'thers they, 469
Knowest, speak less than thou, 362
Knoweth its own loss, best, 163
Knowing, 206
cheese from chalk, proud of, 320
dare maintain, 385
what they do, not, 259
Knowing 's sake, know not for, 206
Knowledge, 206
all our, 250
but greiving, what is, 62
comes not with, 7
from others' eyes, 394
of good, 414
of material things, a growing, 467
of you, I shall desire more love and, 462
our death, the tree of, 414
too high the price for, 91
upon the tree of, 63
with more zeal than, 279
Known, nothing can be, 206
nothing is, 77
Knuckle or knee, 91
Köhln, a town of monks and bones, 387
Koran teach thee, shall the, 242
Kosciusko fell, as, 142
Knows, 207
each chord, he, 172
it at forty, 251
he that never took a pinch, 285
himself to be a fool, 137
his own child, 127
his rider, as a steed that, 436
not how to spend it, who, 319
not to give o'er, who, 466
not why, he, 104
the cause, he, 357
the inscrutable design, who, 164
to live, he, 228
what 's Swat, he, 261
when he goes to sleep, no boy, 370
where is he who, 18
which my nose, 285
Know'st if best bestowed, 35
Kye comes hame, when the, 457

L

Labour, 207, 208
all kin 's o', 212
and strife, of, 389
and the wounds are vain, 391
and to wait, 2

Labour
by stern and lonely, 321
cheers the tar 's, 409
free, 142
health, from, 172
lost, 't will be but, 420
of an age, 29
o' fire with, 71
ruined by Chinese cheap, 50
shall be my lot, 104
taking from and bearing fruit, 461
there 's work for honest, 48
to painful, 189
wherever struggles, 144
with his property or his, 338
will often discard, his, 390
Laboured much how to forget that learning, 466
Labourer, 208
Labourers, many, must be content to sow, 460
room, to give some, 436
Labouring, 208
mountain must bring forth a mouse, 270
Labourious days, and live, 123
Labour 's bath, sore, 372
done, and, 35
Labours, children sweeten, 50
fights, lives, breathes, 176
Lace, chintz and Brussels, 75
Laced, 208
Laces, tied up in godly, 142
Lachesis, twist, 380
Lack an almanac, he doth not, 470
of argument, for, 375
of somebody to hew and hack, 26
Lacked, think all other kisses, 204
Lackey her, liveried angels, 47
Lacks a note, it, 248
oil, after my flame, 228
Lad, a dear-loved, 142
in the education of the, 467
Ladder, 208
the Jacob 's, of the treasury stairs, 325
turns his back, 7
we can frame a, 170
young ambition 's, 7
Laden, orbed maiden with white fire, 268
Ladies fair, articles of, 20
young, spend their time in making nets, 280
Ladies' love unfit, for, 20
Lads and girls, golden, 103
that thought there was no more behind, 411
Lady, 209
ev'ry, would be queen for life, 325
fair, called her his, 136
fair, he met with a, 145
fair, ne'er wan a, 120
my, fell to shame and hell, 57
ne'er won fair, 120
of "a certain age," 4

Lady
of the snows, said our, 276
patch hearts that are breaking, your, 175
protests too much, the, 319
sad, to make a sweet, 346
terms, many holiday and, 401
the white-handed, the cinder wench and, 21
thy mother a, 16
with mien of lord or, 325
Lady-love, of, 233
Lady-loves, for years they served their, 414
Lady's bower, caught it in my, 342
chamber, get you to my, 468
chamber, he capers nimbly in a, 432
faith, learn to win a, 120
mind, hard to move the, 141
Lager beer, all goned afay mit de, 297
bier, have given place to, 22
Laggard in love and a dastard in war, 237
Laid her head beside my own, when she, 243
him down, slowly and sadly we, 153
him low, 277
me down with a will, and I, 163
on with a trowel, that was, 415
thee low, wound that, 106
them down, have, 75
them flat with a spade, 77
Lair, the cold, of my dark generation, 284
Laird o' Cockpen, I was daft to refuse the, 329
Lake, pebble stirs the peaceful, 53
Lakes, shakes across the, 382
Lamb, 209
made the ewe bleat for the, 448
more mild, in peace was never gentle, 432
the skin of an innocent, 295
when the lion fawns upon the, 226
Lambs, the young, are bleating in the meadows, 469
to pasture, who lead us, 325
where they shut up the, 404
Lame and impotent conclusion, 60
dogs over stiles, helping 460
my horse went, 57
Lament for Madam Blaize, 26
or fear, weakness to, 65
Lamentable thing, is not this a, 295
Laments the weakness of these latter times, 437
Lamp, 209
hast but taken thy, 108
if thou hast quenched a, 149
that saw her swear, by the, 428
Lampoon, scribbler of some low, 245
Lamps shone, bright the, 334
Lance, upon them with the, 179
Lances, hurl their, 350
Land, 209
and the peace of the, 373
Land
are we, a thousand miles from, 354
both by sea and, 189[2]
deal damnation round the, 71
dominion over sea and, 402
firm as the, 267
humours of the, 141
ill fares the, 300
in that lonely, 184
in the new and happy, 48
is bright, the, 224
leads to the, 374
light that never was on sea or, 225
o'er the furrowed, 307
of beauty, virtue, valour, truth, 65
of every land the pride, 65
of just and old renown, 144
of liberty, sweet, 65
of promise lies, the, 159
of settled government, 144
of the free, o'er the, 17
of the Pilgrims, Plymouth the, 308
of the Pilgrims' pride, 65
or gold, spared neither, 341
or life, if freedom fail, 143
o' the leal, the, 215
rent with civil feuds, a, 420
reposed, her, 323
ring out the darkness of the, 72
something good and bad of every, 8
that bears a well-known name, 113
that defends the, 353
the charter of the, 37
thy country, that, 182
to what it is in a foreign, 133
trembled, and the, 147
weeds that mar the, 355
we live within the stranger's, 181
we would purge the, 133
whales . . . o' the, 133
when he that selleth house or, 356
where my fathers died, 65
where shadows reign, in the, 151
where shall that, 182
wrong rules the, 417
yet all her house and, 265
yet, no, 435
Landing on some silent shore, 89
Landlord, 209
Land-rats and water-rats, there be, 359
Lands and goods, thy, 134
and tenements to Ned, 91
Death the Ploughman wanders in all, 79
envy of less happier, 112
intersected by a narrow frith, 110
lords and rulers in all, 147
lords of many, 141
till in all, 104
to carry me to unknown, 186
were fairly portioned, 341
Landscape, 209
Landsmen, list ye, 346
run, what risks all, 347

Landsmen say, believe not what the, 347
Land-thieves, water-thieves and, 359
Language, 210
but a cry, with no, 192
in his own, 100
in his tears, strangled his, 399
of his strange, 78
oh, that those lips had, 227
plain, the, 396
quite failed, till, 389
were truth our uttered, 417
yields, for which no rhyme our, 389
Languish broken-hearted, and, 295
Lantern, therefore bear you the, 422
Lap, coiling in its nurse's, 416
die in thy, 174
into thy mother's, 228
me in soft Lydian airs, 394
my heaven in a lady's, 209
of earth, upon the, 257
of Thetis, in the, 269
poured in her, 107
Lapdog, as if it were a miniature, 64
Lapdogs breathe their last, or when, 362
Laps milk, take suggestion as a cat, 392
Lapwing, the wanton, 241
Larboard, rolled to, 354
Larder, not a scrap of anything in the, 48
Lards, 210
Large enough, my library was dukedom, 218
of heart, 175
streams from little fountains flow, 2
Larger heart, the kindlier hand, 174
Largest congregation, the latter has the, 87
Lark, 210
becomes a sightless song, the, 457
is so brimful of gladness, 235
it was the nightingale and not the, 283
more blithe than he, no, 262
sing so like a, 326
the raven doth not hatch a, 326
Larks are flying, while nights and, 151
Lash, drawn with the, 199
the rascals naked through the world, 439
Lashed by law, that must be, 52
Lass, 210
a queen, and every, 469
may kiss a bonny, 249
thou can luvv thy, 241
Lasses, 211
were spent amang the, 165
Lassie, 211
to woo a bonnie, 457
Last, 211
and fight it to the, 131
angel rolls the stone away, 13
are they the, 328
as we sigh away our, 455
Last
at his cross, 67
best gift, 177
bitter hour, thoughts of the, 362
come to thy God at, 155
death that comes at, 79
deep, to that, 18
effort, the, of decayed fortune, 171
embrace, silent in a, 108
embrace, take your, 118
eyes, look your, 118
her monuments shall, 322
if thou keep the, 429
in both the, 309
it is my, 237
look of despairing, 86
love thyself, 48
man, to the, 141
night, look yes, 468
night I wrought a murder, 272
not least in love, though, 238
of earth, this is the, 106
she has breathed her, 105
sleep, in their, 75
that after, 159
that man may, 26
the best reserved of God, woman, the, 453
the people will come to their own at, 301
time, to behold for the, 420
time's noblest offspring is the, 109
to lay the old aside, 126
too exquisite to, 198
unchanged, and will, 191
words of Marmion, 47
words that poor Narcissa, 75
year's nest, no birds in, 280
Lasted, as long's their neighbours', 267
Lasts, a day longer than a wonder, 456
a deal longer, its echo, 203
like iron for things like these, 441
Late, 211
and finds too, 136
early or too, 127
I led, life that, 223
till too, to come again, 405
too, repentance comes, 127
Latin, 211
in Greek and, 30
that soft bastard, 210
was no more difficile, 165
word for three farthings, 332
Laud, more, than gilt o'erdusted, 103
Lauderdale, and driven the beeves of, 267
Laugh, 211, 212
always makes the devil, 447
a siege to scorn, 17
do we not, 197
of hell, the loudest, 336
than scold, inclines us more to, 212
that she may, 189
the landlord's, 209
when boys or women, 99

Laughed and blushed and oft did say, 300
awhile he, 342
consumedly, for they, 396
I looked and, 73
out, the maiden, 440
when you, 239
with counterfeited glee, 93
Laughing at the storm, 385
quaffing and unthinking, 71
Laughs, Jove, at lovers' perjuries, 302
Jove but, at lovers' perjury, 302
the morn, fair, 470
with you, laugh and the world, 212
Laughter, 212
an infant's idle, 119
for a month, 196
holding both his sides, 382
our meeting was all mirth and, 296
present mirth hath present, 239
wine and women, mirth and, 444
with mirth and, 264
yea, for my, 382
Launcelot and I are out, 292
Launch our Mayflower, 281
Launched, 212
from the docks and stocks, 461
Laurel, 212
not a single straw for a, 308
under the, 28
wreaths entwine, 304
Lava, and the blood's, 204
flood, mine was like the, 233
Lave, what the women, 375
Lavished life's best oil, 416
Lavinia, she is, 453
Law, 212–214
and gospel, in, 380
and love, the bridal time of, 300
and not to make, 198
and rich men rule the, 214
and sovereign, 385
and virtue, foe of, 143
buys out the, 289
by nature's kindly, 49
changing world of changeless, 224
divine, all things by a, 366
doth give it, the, 134
ends, where, 419
however stern, 37
I crave the, 83
is drinking, nature's holy, 101
is murder by the, 272
is that the, 199
morals, all began, where faith, 269
nor the world's, 463
nothing is, that is not reason, 327
office is to interpret, 198
of life, progress is the, 318
of love, the Koran teach thee the, 242
of love, the Saviour with his, 235
of the road, understand the, 455
one, one element, 322
order is heaven's first, 291
reason is the light of the, 327
Law
reason is the soul of the, 327
self-defence is nature's eldest, 356
Sir Andrew and his love of, 235
that must be lashed by, 52
the, and rule of speech, 379
the head and the hoof of the, 287
the lion's paw is all the, 226
the reason of the, being changed, 327
to make thee rich, the world affords no, 463
wedded love, mysterious, 437
when legislators keep the, 216
Lawful, awful wedlock, 438
Lawless science of our law, the, 214
through the void, flame, 306
Lawn, sleeves of, 42
the sun upon the upland, 151
to meet the sun upon the upland, 392
Law's delay, the, 323
Laws, 214
and learning die, 284
a thousand, 419
but those which love has made, all, 233
for rich and poor, unequal, 115
for the, 19
for the blood, devise, 33
of a nation, who should make, 16
of . . . holier, 252
of servitude, the base, 350
of the jungle, these are the, 287
of Venice, by the, 134
lay hid in night, nature's, 281
of nature mine, I'll make the, 101
of nature, to which the, 356
to aid the freeman's, 144
which it had framed, equal, 59
which the people have made, 289
who sweeps a room as for thy, 102
with purer, 252
Lawyer, 214
draw up the papers, 292
Lawyers, 214
priests, 218
Lay, 214
bare, none ever dare to, 284
bare thine arm, 388
down my arms, never, 8
for that same member, to, 171
her i' the earth, 426
him in his grave, to, 184
him i' the cold ground, 438
his weary bones, come to, 29
it in the dust, an hour may, 385
like a warrior taking his rest, 433
me down to take my sleep, now I, 370
me a-hold, I will heartily, 156
on my fevered spirit, and it, 374
the old aside, last to, 126
there let him, 73
there she, 26
the steed, and there, 386

Lay
waste our powers, we, 463
your head well to the wind, 171
Lays her skaith to me, nae maiden, 456
in the application on it, 287
Lazy foot of Time, 56
Lea, slowly o'er the, 69
standing on this pleasant, 293
Lead, 214
apes in hell, 10
but to the grave, 163
his apes into hell, 10
like molten, 398
my steps aright, will, 387
Leaden metal into gold, 162
Leader sage, a, 46
Leaders fall, mourning when their, 271
Leads on to fortune, 405
the fight, when glory, 143
treads, 44
Leaf down, turn the, 45
falls into the yellow, 223
falls with the, 372
my days are in the yellow, 223
the one red, 342
the sear, the yellow, 223
trembles, the dead, 275
Leafless all the winter time, was, 343
Leafy month of June, 37
League-long roller thundering on the reef, 341
Leak in roof, shows, 356
Leaking, 215
Leal, 215
all men true and, 150
and tried, both, 57
Lean and hungry look, 126
and slippered pantaloon, the, 294
fellow beats all conquerors, a, 61
hungry, savage, anti-everythings, 10
kine are to be loved, 126
pates, fat paunches have, 298
to virtue's side, 119
Leaned a sexton old, 357
Leans her cheek upon her hand, 47
on this side, and neither, 228
upon his hand, he, 152
upon his hoe, he, 180
Leap from the rocks, as they, 339
look before you ere you, 230
look ere thou, 230
the pulses, 470
the rainbows of the brooks, 350
Leaps, a heart that, 173
beneath the Future's heart, 115
the live thunder, 405
Learn, 215
in no other, 117
more than thou trowest, 362
nor account the pang, 328
of the little nautilus to sail, 278
to live well, 228
to pity them, I, 305
to write well or not to write at all, 466
Learned and all drunk, 102
and fair, 180
and conned by rote, 15
gladly to obey, he that hath, 287
lumber, loads of, 30
played, eat together, 224
roast an egg, the, 108
than the ears, more, 2
there, less is, 135
to dance, as those move easiest who have, 467
to glow, my heart has, 174
to trace, the boding tremblers, 93
Learning, 215
a pride of, 316
and his wit, to match his, 329
and laboured much how to forget that, 466
die, laws and, 284
hath gained most, 31
physic, must, 103
with just enough of, 265
Leas, along the healthy, 224
Leash or band, where shall we find, 344
Least, although the last, not, 211
in love, though last, not, 238
the very, as feeling her care, 212
Leather, a shoe be Spanish or neat's, 20
or prunello, the rest is all but, 465
Leave, 215
and ever will have, 379
behind us, departing, 138
God-like is it all sin to, 365
her, kiss her and, 55
her to heaven, 270
her, ruin and, 83
him alone, 't will, 461
it to men's charitable speeches, 25
it to others, must not, 96
me here in wretchedness, 381
my second leg, 138
my sin without, 365
no more for fortune, 89
not in Corinth, 63
off, now Rory, 286
only give me, 378
sack I'll purge and, 346
that till to-morrow never, 408
the bottle on the chimley-piece, 32
thee, must I, Paradise, 295
the world for him, I'd, 452
this laurel, let us, 181
to speak, I trust I may have, 379
us in the dust, 104
us still our old nobility, 284
us yit, God wun't, 320
you my direction, I cannot, 89
Leaven lowly lives, to, 219
of a lie, without some, 218
Leaves, 215, 216
and not on paper, 24
devil whispered behind the, 13
flattering, that shadowed us, 3

Leaves
in the glassy stream, shows his hoar, 444
no, no birds, 285
off his wit, and, 251
of hope, the tender, 164
of stone, 24
of the judgment book unfold, the, 240
on trees, like, 250
open their thousand, 382
roots, wood, bark and, 308
that are serest, waft the, 326
the little grey, were kind to Him, 458
the well-built nest, 175
us so doubly serious, laughter, 212
words are like, 379
Leaving it, became him like the, 223
the cross, nearer, 278
with meekness her sins, 351
Lectures in her night-dress, 295
Led astray, like one that has been, 268
by the nose with gold, 158
Ledger, his Bible with his, 247
Leek, 216
nat worth a, 271
Leer, assent with civil, 71
Lees, and the mere, 270
the wine of life is on the, 270
Left behind, and the winds are, 86
but by submission, none, 332
it so, you might have, 148
me naked to mine enemies, 357
of six hundred, 80
of them, cannon to, 42
her woman still, the worst of crimes had, 449
on my lip, the kiss that she, 203
our country, for our country's good, 64
the name, he, 274
the rose, I on its stalk had, 342
us, for a handful of silver he, 336
while yet a nook is, 110
all we have, 91
Leg, 216
and one the, 108
can honour set to a, 184
for the loss of a, 434
leave my second, 138
lizard's, 179
Legacy, no, is so rich as honesty, 183
Legible hand, if God writes a, 426
in the eie, 117
Legion of foul fiends, a, 98
Legislators, 216
Legs a race, between two, 344
under his huge, 58
Lend, lend your wings, 163
less than thou owest, 362
me your ears, 341
three thousand ducats, 95
Lender, neither a borrower nor a, 31
Lends enchantment to the view, 93
his eye, dares not, 312
Lends out money gratis he, 421
Length along, drags its slow, 6
be reckoned by its, 204
of days, that, 223
of seven year, it seems the, 407
of shambling limb, his, 225
thy God, may give thee at the, 429
Lengthen our days, ways to, 74
Lengthens its boundaries, 437
Lenore, and forget this lost, 280
whom the angels name, 246
Lent him dross-allayed, 82
Less as is said, the, 260
better the more than, 28
fine by degrees and beautifully, 131
flogging, there is now, 135
foul profanation, but in the, 196
Greek, small Latin and, 211
happier lands, envy of, 112
I'll grow, 346
in size, this world far, 331
love not man the, 277
of earth than heaven, 'tis, 176
than 'arf o' that be'ind, rather, 420
the, of two evils, 116
to-morrow you shall not be, 411
you won't have any, 392
Lessened, one pain is, 131
Lesser is scarce felt, the, 247
Lessons, gif dem moral, 351
Let a body be, they winna, 455
down this brutal jaw, 195
her down the wind, 168
in the foe, to, 84
loose among the nuts and wine, my lips, 396
Newton be, and all was light, 281
Lethe steep, my sense in, 98
Let's to billiards, 25
Lets me, I'll make a ghost of him that, 420
forth his sprite, every one, 282
Letter, 216
and affection, preferment goes by, 315
and each evanescent, 450
and runs with a, 301
give 'im a, 301
killeth, the, 380
kills, the, 380
Lettered, braw brass collar, 58
Letters, 216
mean, the thing those, 450
this prints my, 36
to cut our names in big, 275
Letter-writing, 216
Level, 217
day by day, lower to his, 56
we steal by line and, 386
Lever, contrive some kind of a, 403
Levite, 217
Levy, foreign, 223
Lexicography, I am not so lost in, 459
Lexicon of youth, in the, 119
Liable to fear, if my name were, 126

Liar, 217
one woman not a, 462
truth to be a, 97
Liars, fears may be, 391
Libel, by application to a, 413
Liberal education, was a, 108
Liberties away, that bribed their, 106
Libertine, a chartered, 5
Liberty, 217, 218
a man is master of his, 250
and innocence my, 318
must be guaranteed his, 338
plucks justice by the nose, 199
some draw sword for, 146
sweet land of, 65
the school of religious, 111
Library, 218
furnished me from mine own, 31
Lick absurd pomp, let the candied tongue, 412
his own fingers, cannot, 62
my hand, veriest cur would, 169
Licked them off, the breakers, 35
Licks the hand just raised, 27
Lid, hang upon his pent-house, 370
Lids that will not lift again, the, 369
unsullied, lights on, 370
License and wanton rage, 431
they mean, 217
Lie, 218, 219
abroad for the good of his country, 7
among the dead men let him, 172
and let it, 74
and let them, 230
and sweetly sleep, they softly, 333
a party, or a thriving, 42
at the proud foot, 112
beneath the churchyard stone, 146
dig the grave and let me, 163
down, thou shalt, 334
down like a tired child, I could, 81
fear not to, 67
for every nail, without a, 187
I, I cheat, 247
in a cowslip's bell I, 21
in arms, to front a, 146
in cold obstruction, to, 90
is gross, the, 249
long enough, only, 151
men who will not, 259
that countenance cannot, 117
too deep for tears, thoughts that do often, 404
to see him, 96
under dust to, 103
underneath this stone doth, 427
which works from the heart outward, first real, 451
within the light of God, to, 334
with me, loves to, 165
Lied, and he never, 135
Lies a-dying, the old year, 468
and here he, 145
down to pleasant dreams, and, 227
ends in Here he, 104
Lies frae end to end, 30
here Francis C———, 87
he there now, 335
in circulation, the stock of your, 82
in his bed, 165
it, I know, 74
lifts the head and, 59
one whose name was traced in sand, below, 274
one whose name was writ in water, here, 274
poor Ned Purdon, here, 168
that warp us from the living truth, 470
there, it, 375
the rest is, 135
to hide it, 218
under ground, poor G———, 168
what once was Matthew Prior, here, 317
where he longed to be, here he, 163
Life, 219–224
all the days of her, 451
all your, 56
and all its chances, enhances, 284
and barred from real, 76
and death are all the same, 155
and death, assured alone that, 147
and death, a traveller between, 413
and death, bravely as for, 120
and love one name, made, 454
and love to share, her, 450
and next to, 414
and on the tree of, 63
and our little, 428
and strength in every drop, there is, 445
and trifles, 414
an' love an' youth, who ventered, 19
argues a monstrous, 80
a thing apart, man's love is of man's, 232
beats out his weary, 25
beyond life, to a, 30
but as a part of, 232
but the spirit giveth, 380
by art, measure their, 398
child who enters, 77
complete, nor ever yet was woman's, 454
cool sequestered vale of, 68
crawled and crept through, 352
days of my, 16
death, and that vast forever, 374
death is the crown of, 81
declines, when the fire slackens, 28
did close, and like a lily her, 105
did harbour give, which in, 427
dost thou love, 407
down from its mark, grinding, 439
elysian, a suburb of the, 76
exempt from public haunt, 3
fie upon this single, 366
flower of a blameless, 26
friendship's the wine of, 146

Life
from out young hearts, press the, 296
gives me mystical lore, sunset of, 358
has passed with me but roughly, 227
hath no more to bring, 455
he never heerd in his, 11
he passeth from, 269
her waist is ampler than her, 429
his, a breath of God, 248
how good is man's, 229
if freedom fail, or land or, 143
I have walked through, 177
I'm sure, was in the right, his, 120
in doing one's work in, 460
in our course through, 257
in the blast of a, 314
in the very means of, 35
in this world, a damnable, 168
is a lightning-flash, 123
is as tedious as a twice-told tale, 400
is but a span, 429
is dirty, the public path of, 92
is done, when, 229
is hope, one half of woman's, 454
is in decrease, 81
is in the right, whose, 120
is made of, the stuff, 407
is never the same again, 203
is not too long, I think that, 462
is o'er, long self-sacrifice of, 356
is one dem'd horrid grind, my, 166
is perfected by death, 206
is seen, creeping where no, 195
is the staff of, 35
is thorny, 412
is to the living, as, 77
it never could save us a, 230
language grows out of, 210
long, a fool his whole, 444
nearer the bound of, 278
never knew any man in my, 265
no certain, achieved by others' death, 27
nor limb nor, 341
nothing half so sweet in, 236
o'er a' the ills o', 191
of, of crown, of queen, 370
of care, and weep away the, 81
of joy, renews the, 435
of man less than a span, 461
of mortal breath, this, 76
of poor Jack, watch for the, 48
of so many suffering women, the inner, 451
oh the wasted hours of, 434
once in this waste weary, 230
one, 133
on the ocean wave, a, 288
on the pulse of, 86
on the walls of this tenement of, 27
onward through, 410
outlived of yore, some, 315
over a wasted, 215
presiding, o'er his, 443

Life
progress is the law of, 318
remainder of his healthful, 109
ring in the nobler modes of, 252
ruled her like a thing of, 436
sail forth into the sea of, 443
seems to feel the thrill of, 200
serene, her, 323
set by't more than by your, 42
shall be destroyed, not one, 160
shall dawn on their rest, ere, 97
shortens not his own, 213
slits the thin-spun, 123
so careless of the single, 419
so dear, is, 217
so on the ocean of, 360
so softly death succeeded, 105
so sweet, think of that who find, 343
stood the tree of, 414
that costs thy, 448
that gives it, 443
the best of, 193
the blandishments of, 66
the death of each day's, 370
the desire to transform, 190
the end of, cancels, 82
the fairest action of our human, 335
the firmest friend, in, 176
the God who gave us, 217
the happiest moments of my, 397
the harp of, 241
the light of a whole, 281
the load of human, 370
the narrow way of, 452
the serpent that did sting thy father's, 356
these struggling tides of, 322
the wave of, 36
the wine of, is drawn, 270
the wine of, is on the lees, 270
they increase the cares of, 50
throughout a weary, 321
thy, thy keeper, 189
till wisdom is pushed out of, 84
time used is, 407
to all the bitterness of, 390
to be, the clock tells of a, 280
to close, wish our happy, 89
to come, expatiates in a, 186
to let out, 79
to live would not be, 81
to me, work is, 460
to part, with, 185
to pour his, 248
to save his country's, 432
to the end, through, 58
truth outlives pain as the soul does, 415
under a weary, 79
unsought, victim of a, 419
upon a cast, 44
variety's the very spice of, 423
walks the waters like a thing of, 436
warmth that feeds my, 443
was beauty, 104
was duty, that, 104

Life
was ever lived on earth, no, 98
was gentle, his, 250
wept too much in my, 208
what is there in the vale of, 442
what we call, 79
when my dream of, 236
when the heart, moments in, 173
which is of all life centre, 76
which seems so fair, this, 461
while there is, 185
who fell in the battle of, 61
whose lonely, 384
will be a heavy burden, 460
winds them up, the Angel of, 33
with sorrow strewing, all my, 458
work done is the true happiness of, 460
worth a hundred years of, 39
would be queen for, 325
yield a step for death or, 431
Life-blood of a master spirit, 30
out of a frail young creature, 423
Lifeboat, and like the, 145
Lifeless clay, touched the, 27
face, shade my, 75
head, pressed once more the, 109
Lifelong hunger in his heart, 174
Life 's a fort, this, 422
arrears, pay glad, 78
best oil, lavished, 416
but a span, a, 100
but a walking shadow, 411
combat, nerveth his arm for, 410
dear peril, at, 416
drear desert faring, o'er, 232
dull round, traveled, 192
feast, chief nourisher in, 370
final star, is brotherhood, 38
gall, alone you must drink, 152
grimace, through, 81
history, mad from, 244
leaden metal into gold, 162
monotony, concealed in, 462
poor play is o'er, 49
retreat, this narrow cell was, 367
set prize, for his, 318
spring, I would change, 409
star, our, 25
solemn main, sailing o'er, 138
sorrow and earth 's woe, to endure, 242
unresting sea, by, 376
Lifetime to engrave it, taken half a, 264
Lift their fronded palms in air, 43
their heels, asses, 14
Lifted up and strengthened, 156
Lifts the head and lies, 59
Light, 224, 225
all changeful as the, 73
and collateral, 384
and maddening as her, 344
an infant crying for the, 192
as air, trifles, 195
as film, though, 245

Light
as if they feared the, 129
blind to, 70
by the dawn 's early, 17
came from heaven, 245
commands all, 127
dawn of multitudinous-eddying, 18
de shtar of de sphirit's, 297
discovers, on all their, 384
dispense serener, 65
ere it comes to, 231
floods the calm fields with, 268
follow, and do the right, 338
from grave to, 162
from heaven, love indeed is, 233
from those flames no, 72
grant me to see the, 313
has come, the, 75
heavenly food is very, 123
he leaves behind him, 138
her eye lost its, 153
in God 's pure, 198
in the dust, the, 209
is come, and, 45
is lingering yet, thy, 384
lead kindly, 214
let Newton be, and all was, 281
light love, how the, 233
me another Cuba, 339
memory brings the, 258
more sweetly recommend the, 447
not to the wise the, 324
of a whole life, the, 281
of day, into the, 15
of eternal, 154
of fuller day, in the, 252
of God, within the, 334
of heaven, dimmed the, 155
of its own fireside, 173
of love shines over all, 235
of the bright world, the, 281
of the law, reason is the, 327
refulgent, flames in the, 288
shakes, the long, 382
square of comfortable, 25
swifter than, 262
than a, 78
that lies in woman 's eyes, 118
that visits these sad eyes, 443
the glimmering taper 's, 185
to hold, and, 157
the upward looking and the, 467
truth, and love, 403
truth will come to, 417
unveiled her peerless, 268
whatever record leap to, 358
which beats upon a throne, that fierce, 404
within this brain, the, 195
withdrawn, the, 121
with something of angelic, 454
word part us now, shall a, 146
Lighted me to bed, that, 167
once more it may be, 149
Lightened and hailed, thundered, 389
Lightens my humour, 196

Lightly fall, not, 144
Lightning, a flash of the, 269
and the gale, the, 133
does the will of God, as, 144
flashing, seen war's, 431
in the breech, as quick as, 36
loosed the fateful, 153
or in rain, in thunder, 257
Lightning-flash of breath, 123
Lightning's vivid powers, 26
Lights are fled, whose, 17
burn bright and fair, the, 194
like glories fall, where, 264
of mild philosophy, the calm, 303
on lids unsullied, and, 370
on my shoulders, but what, 244
Like again, I shall not look upon his, 250
as eggs, 108
husbands, fools are as, 190
my father, no more, 37
to be despised, I, 86
to do unto you, 82
you in the rest, if we are, 197
Likeness, 225
that I knew, in the old, 97
Likes, chastises those whom most he, 177
may marry whom she, 255
your music, the general so, 273
Lilies, 225
blow, where roses and white, 343
charge for the golden, 179
Lily, 225
her life did close, like a, 105
to paint the, 152
Limb, lopping away of the, 230
a chief, of the statue, 308
face and, 418
his length of shambling, 225
in heart and in, 113
nor beauty, 336
nor, nor life, 341
strength of, 46
with joint or, 381
Limbed like the old heroic breeds, 250
Limbs, a calf's-skin on those recreant, 226
appear, my lusty, 357
at rest, with our, 108
composed, thy decent, 139
whose trembling, 375
with travel tired, 21
wrap my cold, 75
Limed in a bush, 25
soul that struggling to be free, 377
Limes, where the fragrant, 296
Limit of becoming mirth, within the, 196
of my capacity for work, never found out the, 460
there is however a, 138
Limitless space, there is, 178
time, there is, 178
Limits cannot hold love out, stony, 239
Limits of a constitution, within the, 289
of becoming mirth, within the, 196
Limping on, with swelled feet, 301
Lincoln, 225
green, a doublet of the, 403
Linden, 225
Line, 225
a cable, his, 439
and level, we steal by, 386
and lives along the, 380
down all our, 308
hard, hit the, 222
into a horizontal, 389
of 'eroes, but it's thin red, 180
rises along the charging, 19
some earnest verse or, 466
the oldest craft on the, 346
the power-house of the, 312
the shelter and grace of our, 49
to cancel half a, 465
we carved not a, 153
Linen, 226
Lines, a vast extent of flimsy, 353
desert of a thousand, 364
of hair, slight, 168
own the happy, 231
the town-crier spoke my, 379
Lingering a minute, 292
lie, like a dewdrop shall, 203
Lining, turn forth her silver, 56
Link that binds her, but the, 258
the silver, 237
Linked more close, 376
and incidents well, 396
sweetness long drawn out, 394
with gold, the love that's, 203
with one virtue, 64
Links, who can follow the gossamer, 15
Linnets, 226
sing their wonted strain, 233
Lion, 226
a bear or, 56
be to speak, 14
creeping nigher, as a, 301
in his den, 85
may, when many asses do, 14
on the lip of a, 134
raged more fierce, in war was never, 432
that would be mated by the, 384
to look upon a, 393
Lions by the beard, plucks dead, 423
in the way, he espied two, 226
let bears and, 95
to walk like one of the, 239
Lion-spirits that tread the deck, the, 133
Lip, 226
atheism is rather in the, 14
can speak, ere the feverish, 293
can speak, not all the, 172
curving a contumelious, 384
has left, kiss thy, 203
him, maids will not, 4
keep a stiff upper, 55, 220

Lip
Mary, the red was on your, 387
of a lion, on the, 134
pride in her, 316
reveal, or the, 174
so rich in blisses, her, 204
the kiss that she left on my, 203
the marge, till it, 53
which would be still, 10
with a stiff upper, 58
with lingering, 274
you press, the, 411
Lips, 227
apart, standing with mute, 115
are dumb, when the, 174
at the touching of the, 226
drew near, their, 204
elated, here sang the, 374
have spoken, when the, 209
here hung those, 468
how ripe in show, 226
let loose among the nuts and wine, my, 396
may beguile, the, 398
my kisses shall teach thy, 240
my whole soul through my, 204
of lying lovers, the, 384
of those ye love, by the, 179
O you, the doors of breath, 118
prevailed, truth from his, 352
refused to send farewell, 124
rest on the, 252
she give you so much of her, 412
so thin, these words came from his, 357
Spanish sailors with bearded, 360
taught to writhe, 233
that are for others, on, 205
the wedges flew from between their, 437
to it, let me put my, 32
we press, red as the, 55
were red, her, 226
when I ope my, 291
where grief is mute, two, 208
whispering with white, 136
who wipes her, 203
with a smile on her, 371
you have witchcraft in your, 226
Liquid be, whate'er the, 68
sober, sage and venerable, 397
Liquids, and gentle, 210
Liquor, and the quality of the, 403
for boys, claret is, the, 34
is blood, their, 379
toss off thy, 26
Liquors, I never did apply hot and rebelious, 357
Lisp their sire's return, run to, 175
Lisped in numbers, I, 466
Lisping stammering tongue, when this poor, 412
List of friends, I would not enter on my, 463
sweets into your, 204
ye landsmen, 346
Listen for the weakest word, to, 293
you can look or, 152
Listened more, is, 105
Listens once will listen twice, who, 328
Listening ear, undulates upon the, 52
senates hang upon thy tongue, 11
senates to command, 11
to somebody, somebody's, 373
Listless woman, O, 33
Litanies of nations came, 24
Litany, sing the lovers', 242
Littering with unfolded silks, 361
Little as a fool, 137
Breeches, and thar sot, 404
chimney, he is a, 50
dogs and all, 95
done, so much to do, so, 94
earth, give him a, 29
else to do, hoarse with having, 9
employment, hand of, 70
fears grow great, where, 238
fire grows great, 132
fire is quickly trodden out, 131
fires, to sit by, 132
here, teaches us, 179
isle so, 113
is this too, 336
learning is a dangerous thing, 215
love me, 234
men, to live in narrow ways with, 276
one, a Hottentot's great toe or, 266
ones, eat up the, 133
our hoard is, 175
philosophy, a, 14
said is soonest mended, 260
some times so, 172
thing, 't is a, 435
to earn, there's, 132
while we have to stay, 77
who think too, 396
wind, grows great with, 132
wrong, do a, 213
Live, 227, 228
again, of those immortal dead who, 50
all alone shall, 331
and die, by which we, 30
and if to, 185
and it helps you, 129
as they lived, 128
but never, 26
but only they have privilege to, 424
by making tarts, cooks must, 63
by toil, he that will not, 409
cleanly as a nobleman should do, 346
fools, men may, 138
glad did I, 163
impossible I should, 82
in narrow ways with little men, to, 276
in peace, adieu, 292
in such a row, to, 290
in thy pain, thou shalt, 69
in thy heart, will, 174

Live
in vain, poor man would, 81
like venom, which, 424
marvel how the fishes, 133
must please to, 307
on, the brave, 66
on, yet brokenly, 172
or die, survive or perish, 366
or die for Dixie, 94
our noble king, long, 201
save means to, 223
so I have my cigar, 53
taught us how to, 91
that she may, 189
the means whereby I, 223
to fight another day, 130
to fight again, shall, 130
together, cannot, 5
to more virtue than doth, 427
to please, we that, 307
to see the day, we may not, 159
we how we can, 89
well is to work well, to, 460
while you, drink, 100
who better, than we, 376
with cheese and garlic, I had rather, 399
with ease, and, 107
with her, her mother came to, 270
with me, come, 235
with me, wilt thou, 375
without dining, the man that can, 63
with thee, to, 237
with the living, will it not, 185
Lived, 228
and loved, and I have, 221
and loved, I've, 221
and toiled with men, I have, 259
because he has, 54
I have, 221
live as they, 128
long enough, I have, 223
my life, I have, 221
on the river Dee, 262
she at its close, 105
the soul enchanted, 374
to-day, I have, 408
while the beast, 226
with no other thought, she, 246
Livelier plaything gives his youth, 49
Livelong day, the, 73
Lively to severe, from, 162
Liver, and let my, 264
Liveried angels lackey her, 47
Livery, 228
in her sober, 116
of hell, the cunning, 178
of the burnished sun, 60
Lives, 228
after them, 116
all that, 89
along the line, and, 380
and dies in single blessedness, 342
are cursed, with which our, 339
are incomplete, our, 79
Lives
at the Queen's command, gave up their, 373
before, than their, 105
breathes, labours, fights, 176
but human creatures', 226
but reason, 327
by the moans of their heart, 398
he most, 227
immortal, who, 191
immortal Lord, 235
in Paternoster Row, the proprietor, 296
longer, competency, 393
make what all their, 450
no more, to our purposes he, 278
of great men, 138
of most, in the, 140
of these good men, the, 301
our pilot still, yet, 231
pledge to each other our, 307
religion, and feels herself at home, 330
so these, 339
sublime, make our, 138
that ye led were mine, 349
to leaven lowly, 219
to show that still she, 143
two, bound fast in one, 224
we might have led, 179
we pay, our, 177
yet waste men's, 208
Liveth not in fierce desire, it, 237
Living, 229
aloud, his song was only, 374
as life is to the, 77
a year or two after one is dead, 423
breath, who draw, 114
foretold of all the, 228
had no roofe, who, 183
Homer, through which the, 183
honest as any man, 183
if thou withdraw in silence from the, 86
it is for us, the, 276
let us, the, 276
live with the, 185
one, not in Corinth a, 63
rock, cut from the, 73
Lizard's leg and owlet's wing, 179
Load a falling man, 121
bent like us, beneath the, 370
kings a useless heavy, 202
would sink a navy, a, 278
Loads of learned lumber, 30
Loaf of bread, a, 85
to steal a shive, of a cut, 435
Loafe, 229
Loafing around the throne, than, 404
Loam, of earth we make, 421
Loan oft loses, 31
Loathe all men, I, 259
we both may, 409
without knowing why, 176
Loathed melancholy, hence, 258
Loathing critics and cold water, 308

Loaves, seven halfpenny, 130
Lobster boiled, and like a, 269
Lobster-pot, leaking like a, 215
Local jealousies and pride, 110
Lochaber, 229
Lochinvar, 229
Lock, crying at the, 443
of hay, went to pieces like a, 166
the latticed gate, 345
without a key, is but a, 438
Locke, Rufa studying, 410
Locked in yard, yard, 347
my heart in a case o' gowd, I 'd, 231
up in steel, 12
Locking of the door, the, 91
Lockjaw, error dies of, 415
Locks, 229
are like the snow, your, 311
bars and solitude, 318
or youth 's bright, 354
played familiar with his hoary, 288
shaking her invincible, 277
thy knotted and combined, 380
were like the raven, your, 311
were white, his, 357
when banks dispense with bolts and, 216
Locomotive, if she is run over by a, 415
Lodge, 229
Lodgers, there had been many other, 296
Lodging, wife and children, 187
Lodgings, 229
for rain or shine, he took, 21
in a head, such as take, 57
Loftiness of thought, in, 309
Lofty of purpose, 54
port, his was the, 316
Logic, 230
absolute, that can with, 162
with irresistible, 314
vociferated, kills me quite, 284
Logical way, built in such a, 46
Logs, 230
into the hall, 190
London pride, a, 316
London's column pointing to the skies, 59
voice, Get money, money still, 266
Lone, 230
sea so, 113
whose lonely life is not so, 384
Loneliness, 230
Lonely land, in that, 184
'twas, so, 154
Lonesome road, one that on a, 128
Long and lank and brown, thou art, 253
and nothing, 114
and wish to be a subject, 202
art is, 163
as merry as the day is, 261
been dead, some have, 75
be so, as, 75
days that were as, 74
descent, claims of, 148
Long live our noble king, 201
long kiss, a, 204
long night away, 105
long thoughts, are, 33
nor that little, 249
nor wants that little, 249
not well married that lives married, 254
of it, the short and the, 361
or a kiss too, 203
orations, make no, 32
potations, banish, 32
sometimes so, 172
spoon, must have a, 87
so you love me, 234
that never finds the day, night is, 282
when it talks too, 396
Long-ago, 230
Long-drawn aisle, through the, 10
Longed to be, where he, 163
to be a king, never subject, 202
to slumber beside him, 163
Longer grown, are a little, 429
I stay a little, 108
than anything else than their ears, 300
wait a little, 159
would have mourned, 20
Longing, a feeling of sadness and, 375
and a nameless, 109
lingering look, one, 139
the restless unsatisfied, 109
unexpressed, fear and hope and, 234
Longings, 230
after something lost, 88
died to all earthly, 91
yearning, strivings, 156
Look, 230
a gift-horse in the mouth, 151
a lean and hungry, 126
and a voice, only a, 360
back, speak and, 307
but in, 137
by his, detect, 306
down, when the patient stars, 384
down upon you from the Pyramids, 322
give me a, 364
here, upon this picture, 303
into happiness, to, 170
like you, to, 452
not like the inhabitants o' the earth, 448
of despairing, the daring, 86
one longing lingering, 139
on her face, 128
or listen, you can, 152
rose with a dignified, 22
the, the air, 377
there was a manhood in his, 252
the same, which she turned, 393
to avenge even a, 50
to have, I must not, 223
to his bond, 29

Look
upon a lion, to, 393
upon your lord, never, 395
yes last night, why I pray, 468
Looked, 230
sighed and, 363
but they, 242
down to blush, she, 371
for, when you 're, 59
up to sigh, she, 371
Looking at goods, men lingering and, 266
at the prize, when, 342
lazy at the sea, 392
ill prevail, 294
Looks arter his folks, 356
at least two distinct, 455
at nation, nation wildly, 115
beyond the strife, he, 432
not their beauteous, 201
of love, virgin 's sidelong, 234
peace of God was in his, 75
puts on his pretty, 165
quite through the deeds of men, 126
than thy, 108
the whole world in the face, 292
through nature, but, 278
to come, his wit invites you by his, 447
to thy dim eyes a stain, 198
were women 's, 118
with bold, stern, 119
Look'st thou so, why, 5
Looming bastion fringed with fire, 19
Loon, crazy as a, 286
Loose behaviour, check on, 108
the bulldog 's grip, only crowbars, 40
unless he 's, 393
Loosed the fateful lightning, he hath, 153
Loosened and let down this brutal jaw, 195
Lopped away, must be, 148
Lopping, 230
Lord, 230, 231
affirmed that black was white, 66
alone of man, or think thee, 463
among wits, had been a, 447
and clown, master of, 103
and praise the, 365
as duke or, 248
be thankit, sae the, 257
but lives immortal, 235
dear to the heart of our, 160
due to the Moor my, 189
forgi'e me for lying, the, 244
for the saints and for the, 395
for thou, O, 84
God made, the thing the, 402
God of Hosts, 139
graceless traitor to her loving, 454
I pray the, my soul to keep, 370
is crucified, till his, 34
is found, wheresoe'er such, 184
Jehovah, Jove or, 127
Lord
knows, his verse the, 424
knows where, or the, 284
love us, 11
never look upon your, 395
of all, love will still be, 237
of all things, great, 462
or lady, with mien of, 325
our, to see, 470
redeemed and white before the, 358
say Amen, 429
shall raise me up, the, 406
the coming of the, 153
the judgments of the, 199
thy husband is thy, 189
was nigher, she knowed the, 50
will aid us, 38
Lord 's anointed, the, 10
anointed, I am the, 108
house, and go in to the, 365
Lords, 231
and gentlemen, dead, 75
and rulers, O masters, 147
of our own hands, 141
of the creation, called the, 259
only a wit among, 447
princes and, are but the breath of kings, 183
princes and, may flourish, 300
Lordship was made Baron Vaux, since his, 423
Lordships pleasure, on their, 71
Lore, a prescient, 315
sunset of life gives me mystical, 358
volume of forgotten, 261
Lorn creetur, I am a lone, 230
Lose, 231
a brute, 38
a pint of blood from your veins, better to, 280
at the other, they, 135
by overrunning, and, 292
his edge, doth, 206
it, it do n't take twice to, 46
it all, to win or, 126
lest they their rights should, 311
me, neglect me, 378
myself in the infinite main, I, 247
or conquer, go, 150
our ventures, 69
that too, may I never, 331
the good, make us, 97
their nature, seem at once to, 413
them all, sad and you, 152
then, if he, 273
to watch and then to, 19
what he fears to, 452
who would, 90
you, I would not, 238
Loses both itself and friend, 31
that it works for, 183
what gains or, 306
Losing all its grossness, by, 424
and the other, 306
his wits, e'en with, 245
office, hath but a, 281

Losing rendered sager, till by, 429
Loss, 231
best knoweth its own, 163
but for its, 407
is common, that, 1
must be the pain supreme, its, 234
of a leg, for the, 434
of use, I rather dread the, 421
of wealth is loss of dirt, the, 360
ours is the bitterest, 1
to do our country, 185
whose, might leave the soul, 120
Losses, and so may, 379
there are gains for all our, 470
Lost, 231
a day, I 've, 73
all good to me is, 186
an English gun, nor ever, 167
and if 't is, 455
and the spoil we, 451
and won, when the battle 's, 257
and worn, sooner, 454
at sea, than ever were, 354
battle, in the, 83
better to have loved and, 242
but once your prime, having, 254
by which the printers have, 31
chord divine, that one, 51
forever, if its undying guest be, 377
for evermore, shattered, dishonoured, 107
for honour, 299
in air, mine will not all be, 125
in the other, one was, 339
in the sweets, is, 395
I too have loved and, 117
longings after something, 88
my reputation, I have, 332
lost! lost, 73
Mark Antony the world, who, 452
no friend, and who, 385
no good work is ever, 460
so, so fallen, 121
swallowed and, 90
the immortal part of myself, 332
their voices are, 339
the toil we, 451
the winning softness of their sex is, 357
to be swallowed up and, 228
to sight, th' ecstatic lark above, 210
we have loved and, 179
who deliberates is, 85
without a sigh, 434
Lot, a weary, is thine, 402
be cast, mortal, howe'er thy, 228
labour shall be my, 104
may be, whate'er my, 125
might be, whiche'er their, 414
of all, have but the, 202
peace my, 35
the blameless vestal 's, 140
't is the common, 59
whate'er thy, 341
Loth to wear it out, as being, 446
Lothario, 231
Lotos closes, never the, 113
Loud again, now pealing, 52
alike, all, 102
as welcomes, now, 52
laugh, the, 211
roared the dreadful thunder, 26
Louder, a little, 49
shrieks, not, 362
still, clear and sonorous, 52
Loud-hissing, bubbling and, 116
Louisville, Mr. Billings of, 346
Lout who 'd shirk, the, 248
Love, 231–242
a bright particular star, should, 384
acts of kindness and of, 201
a kiss of youth and, 204
alas too long, a world we, 443
a naughty man, did Katy, 200
and bliss immortal reign, scenes where, 27
and care, I cannot drift beyond his, 43
and glory that may raise, 293
and health to all, 172
and joy and sorrow learn, 48
and knowledge of you, I shall desire more, 462
and matrimony, of courtship, 255
and not to, more painful still, 243
and obey, bound to serve, 456
and peace combine, when friendship, 442
and service to you evermore, in, 192
and shame, forespent with, 457
and truth, dreams of, 88
and woe, the canticles of, 24
an oyster may be crossed in, 293
an' youth, who ventered life an', 19
as I do thee, and courts his, 254
a spring of, 27
as you loved me then, 392
a train, they, 448
bewrays more woe, silence in, 364
but one day, I dearly, 74
but only her, 85
can hope, 185
can I beg in your, 378
can less hide his, 119
crossed in hopeless, 66
'em, he could n't, 363
endures no tie, 302
esteem and, 158
eternal joy and everlasting, 452
everything that 's old, I, 290
exalted youth, 65
fair looks, 189
first leaves, 175
for Charlotte, Werther had a, 439
God is, 155
God, thou art, 155
goes calling up and down, 290
gold, in these are sunk, 193
hail, wedded, 437
hate hath no harm for, 300
have all his rites, till, 407
herself and the woman I, 274

Love
his country, that will not, 65
his labour, who does not, 208
his work, needs must, 247
honour, and obey, 45
how wayward is this foolish, 341
hymns of gratitude and, 173
if music be the food of, 273
I know his goodness and his, 160
in every gesture dignity and, 161
in her attire doth show her wit, my, 20
in rhyme, as much, 336
in search of a word, music is, 273
in which my hound has part, 187
is clay, thy, 55
is done, when, 281
is loveliest, and, 398
is not in our choice, 86
is of the valley, 422
is worth a million, thy, 292
it, I love it, 12
it breeds, the, 206
it is a manacle of, 251
it like a child, 169
it might be full of, 462
it nurtures a deep and honest, 173
its whole wealth of, 173
lest that thy, 268
like ours can never die, 242
life, dost thou, 407
light, truth and, 403
looks not with the eyes, 69
looks with the mind, 69
made bold, by, 277
may live without, 63
me, a sigh to those who, 363
me, to know me well and, 148
moody food of us that trade in, 273
most tenderly, that which they, 322
must die for, 384
my, adieu for evermore, 3
my friend, plain, blunt man that, 291
my neighbour, and, 413
never doubt I, 97
nor, nor fear, 367
not a gaping pig, 304
not man the less, but nature more, 277
not smiles around, where universal, 43
obedience, 223
O fire, O, 204
of God, all end in, 269
of good, the common, 160
of life, that, 224
of life appears, the greatest, 224
of man, in love of God and, 269
of money, the, 267
of my whole course of, 396
of truth and right, ring in the, 418
of woman, to thee the, 354
of women, alas the, 455
o' life's young day, forget the, 222
once pleads, when, 85

Love
one jot of former, 296
one name, made life and, 454
or enmity, works of, 381
or hate, extreme in, 449
or hate, hide his, 119
or jealousy, away at once with, 195
or thrones without, tents with, 85
perhaps 't was boyish, 33
pity melts the mind to, 305
pity swells the tide of, 305
pity 's akin to, 305
prayers of, 160
presume too much upon my, 315
right to dissemble your, 93
shall win my, 201
she never told her, 298
sincere, his, 29
sings, like a soul beatified of, 210
slights it, 77
soft eyes looked, 334
so kind, she wooed with, 449
so well, hand I, 169
so 's my, 310
teach me to, 260
tears for his, 7
that 's linked with gold, the, 203
that we might once have saved, 434
the ambition in my, 384
the ardent flame of, 339
the beauty of the pure, 145
the bridal time of law and, 300
thee and hate thee, I, 327
thee, Cassio, I, 289
thee, constrained to, 110
thee, dear, so much, I could not, 18;
thee evermore, and, 124
thee, I do not, Doctor Fell, 327
thee still, I, 110
the flowers and fruits of, 223
the language, I, 210
the man who . . . has the largest capacity of loving, 243
the pangs of despised, 323
the paths lead to a woman 's, 305
the very charms that wake his, 342
the words of, 258
th' offender, yet detest th' offence, 289
thou a heavenly, 157
thou owest me thy, 292
thy heart can gain, if fond, 456
thyself last, 48
to, and not be loved again, 243
to be wroth with one we, 412
to business that we, 40
to hatred turned, no rage like, 324
to know, to esteem, to, 221
to me, add, 443
to share, her life and, 450
unfit, for ladies', 20
us, and a prayer for those who, 363
was law, and, 214
we both may loathe or, 409
we cannot fight for, 457
wedlock without, 438

Love
were firm, or that their, 455
when one is truly in, 3
whom none can, 26
wi' his, he did deave me, 458
will not clip him, 4
wine, a little breath, 274
with, think with the intensity we, 402
with love, must cure, 88
without her, 443
woman wakes to, 124
works of faith and, 267
you so well, sweetheart, I, 275
your true, 57
young, likes to knock, 338
Loved, 242
again, to love and not to be, 243
and eat, and, 228
and here unmated, here, 374
and I have lived and, 221
and lost, I too have, 117
and lost, we have, 179
as to be, 425
at home, that makes her, 352
but one, sighed to many though he, 363
but you, I never, 456
by me, than to love and be, 246
Cæsar less, not that I, 41
'er her, fur I, 241
her, and I, 363
her, if I had a friend that, 363
her that they died for her, so, 416
him the best, the woman who, 132
how, 334
I not honour more, 184
I have, 221
I 've lived and, 221
Lavinia therefore must be, 453
lean kine are to be, 126
me, as Cæsar, 7
me for the dangers, she, 363
me weel, young Jamie, 68
my books, I, 31
none without hope e'er, 185
one, alas for the, 153
one, and that, 363
one face there you, 290
ones who 've crossed, 339
only what were worth your love, 232
or was avenged like me, 15
Rome more, I, 41
sae kindly, 37
some we, 333
so well, of him he, 154
spot, and every, 49
thee, ocean, I have, 288
thee once, I, 232
thee so long, that hath, 215
the heart that has truly, 393
the place of old, hearts that, 175
thou would'st be, 236
though not less, 408
till at her breast the child of him she, 454
Loved
to hear, the names he, 252
truth, many, 416
who once has, 117
with a love that was more than love, 236
women not clothes were, 456
Loveliest and the best, the, 333
Love-light in her eye, the, 117
in your eye, 387
Loveliness needs not the foreign aid of ornament, 3
Lovely woman, woman, 452
Lover, 242
bears, of all the plagues a, 339
in her first passion woman loves her, 232
no true, 56
of peace, 432
of the good, but thou, meek, 159
repentance to her, 136
some banished, 216
to gratify thy, 100
true, seeks to steal a, 304
weary, 33
yet, affliction taught a, 139
Lover 's lute, the little rift within the, 337
or a Roman 's part, to act a, 236
pinch, as a, 79
staff, hope is a, 186
Lovers, 242, 243
of virtue, all that are, 10
rather more than seamen, pity, 389
the lips of lying, 384
two, whispering by an orchard wall, 22
yet thy true, 408
young without, 462
Lovers' meetings, journeys end in, 198
perjuries, at, 302
perjury, Jove but laughs at, 302
tongues by night, silver-sweet sound, 412
Love 's beginning, a kiss at, 203
cousin, selfishness, 356
embraces met, that ever since in, 294
first snowdrop, 203
persistency, secret of, 117
prick and Rosalind, must find, 343
sighs, tempered with, 308
wild prayer, as, 366
Loves, 243
and graces, an angel-guard of, 452
hated by one he, 15
himself, who, 419
I prize, whose, 69
is love, all she, 232
me, and my love, 235
me, because I know my love, 235
never on earth again, 117
not wine, woman and song, who, 444
on to the close, as truly, 393

Loves
the poor, he who ordained the Sabbath, 310
to lie with me, 165
weeds, he who, 135
Love-song, with a, 118
Lovest, 243
Loveth all, he made and, 314
best, he prayeth best, who, 314
most, he serves thee best, who, 314
well, he prayeth well, who, 313
Loving, 243
are the daring, the, 34
of pretty Cis, 203
so faithful, so, 97
that old arm-chair, 12
virtue, in, 347
Low as high he soared, 7
for murder, comes kind o', 272
has married Mr. R———, Nancy, 53
her breathing soft and, 36
hymn of the, 61
if you speak love, speak, 239
Lower, can fall no, 97
deep, in the lowest deep a, 178
night is beginning to, 50
sphere, pledge of a, 179
the proud, and, 141
to his level day by day, 56
Lowest deep, in the, 178
Lowing herd winds slowly, 69
Lowliness is young ambition 's ladder, 7
Lowly, must work their passage, poor and, 176
Lown, he called the tailor, 387
Loyalty, 243
Lubberland, though a whole celestial, 416
Lubricates business, dinner, 92
Lucca, with oil from, 349
Lucifer, he falls like, 122
Lucifer's attaint, since, 316
Luck, 244
at last, one may have better, 464
in odd numbers, there 's, 286
in such a storm, for our good, 388
one constant element in, 307
should turn, if, 319
Luckless millions do, what will those, 75
time, aboding, 25
Lucky, 244
hit, seem a, 67
Lucy, so he called upon, 338
Lugged bear, melancholy as a . . . , 258
Lukewarm hearts, clay-cold heads, 298
Lulls the dead, the dreamless sleep that, 468
Lumber, loads of learned, 30
Lumberer, like the blows of a, 314
Lump is bad, the poor in a, 310
of salt, might the, 465
Lunch, to finish off my, 321
Lungs receive our air, if their, 368
with an inflammation of the, 198
Lurching through the spray, 54
Lure it back, shall, 465
Lurks in every flower, 77
where danger or dishonour, 443
Lust and plunder, 143
in man, there 's a, 351
of booty, the, 171
of gold, narrowing, 158
of office, whom the, 259
Lustre in his eye, there was, 351
Lute is broken, when the, 209
the lascivious pleasing of a, 432
the little rift within the, 337
Luxury of doing good, learn the, 159
Lydian airs, lap me in soft, 394
Lying, 244
better thou and I were, 108
so easy by half as, 151
so straightly in an icy calm, 80
the steed beneath is, 90
would that we two were, 108
Lyre, 244
waked to ecstasy the living, 109

M

Macairs, real Turpins and, 325
Macbeth raving at that shade-made blade, 115
Macduff, lay on, 214
MacGregor, my name is, 138
Machiavel had ne'er a trick, Nick, 281
Machine, blow up the infernal, 403
that makes it, and the, 467
Machinery of the State, the whole, 33
Machree, widow, och hone, 441
Mackerel, cheap as stinking, 47
Mad, 244, 245
and a' should gae, 440
an undevout astronomer is, 14
as Ajax, this love is as, 238
as he was, Old Brown, 401
fitter being sane than, 159
if they behold a cat, 304
it was, how sad and bad and, 394
marriage never was before, such a, 253
not poetry but prose run, 309
or I am, 98
Maddened John the Baptist, a kind of, 114
Maddening as her light, and, 344
Madding crowd 's ignoble strife, 68
Made, and from his ashes may be, 426
and loveth all, he, 314
and preserved us a nation, 276
as fast as they are, 407
at me through the press, 427
Baron Vaux, his lordship was, 423
but those which love has, 233
for, what was love, 236
for, what were they, 326
him, every man is as God hath, 249
him, thou hast, 104

Made in heaven, marriages are, 253
me, nobody never, 166
merely for money-making, not, 267
of the same clay, 201
out of nothing, nothing can be, 285
the heart, who, 172
them so, God hath, 95
the thing the Lord God, 402
to die, was not, 104
to mourn, man was, 271
us, offend the eye of him who, 107
us men, great Nature, 259
way for liberty and died, 217
with his hand the vessel, 107
ye one, her sweet I will has, 290
Madest man, thou, 104
Madly strikes against it, 25
Madman stares, when a, 50
Madmen, 245
have such seething brains, lovers and, 243
Madness, 245
in the brain, doth work like, 412
of many, party is the, 297
only makes them go faster, 403
to defer, 'tis, 84
Mæander's banks when death is nigh, on, 273
Maelstrom, straight for the, 102
Magazine, 245
Maggie and I are out, 53
will have no rival, if, 339
Maggotship, may parade your, 108
Magic o'er my way, flung, 148
of a name, the, 274
of the sea, and the, 360
sails, argosies of, 59
Magical art, no, 72
Magistrate, 245
and king, 143
Magistrates, people governed by grave, 59
Magnanimity of thought, in all the, 251
Magnanimous mouse, or most, 422
Magnet, 245
Magnificence, in calm, 353
Magnificent and awful cause, 12
in Stamboul, 408
Magnitude, thou liar of the first, 217
Mahomet's, 'tis, 330
Maid, 246
and many a, 71
at your window, and I a, 422
a weary lot is thine, fair, 402
be good, sweet, 374
mother or bride or, 113
no German, 151
or some captive, 216
sweet, bride-bed to have decked, 36
the ways of a man with a, 187
to see her sparrow part, a, 398
to the sweetest, 395
trots hard with a young, 407
was young, when music, heavenly, 272
Maiden, 246
fair to see, 24
laughed out, the, 440
lays her skaith to me, nae, 456
meditation, fancy free, in, 257
nor wife nor, 449
sword, fleshed thy, 395
true betrayed for gold, 15
with white fire laden, that orbed, 268
Maiden's breast, who could win, 83
veil, of a, 219
Maidens, like moths, are ever caught by glare, 270
watching said, all her, 76
Maids, a malady most incident to, 316
are May when they are maids, 457
matrons, 368
must kiss no men, 202
must marry, young, 203, 254
will not lip him, 4
would far whiter be, 321
Mail train, engine-driver of broad-gauge, 315
Mailed, in sombre harness, 87
Maimed among, the spent and, 290
Main, 247
chance, care o' th', 46
flood, bid the, 135
from out the azure, 37
o'er life's solemn, 138
thou hollow-sounding and mysterious, 354
Maintain, and knowing dare, 385
them, they have rights who dare, 338
Maintained its man, every rood of ground, 166
Maintenance, and for thy, 189
Majestic though in ruin, 85
Majesty, dead, your, 75
in, the next, 309
in death, virtue alone has, 81
rising in cloudy, 268
stoops from his high, 108
the attribute to awe and, 260
this earth of, 112
Majority, 247
Make a man, and cannot, 179
and doth the bodie, 377
a note of, when found, 285
believe, though you, 82
'em good and stout, 292
everything of it, 64
her light and small, to, 208
her, nothing can, 240
her straight and tall, to, 208
it go, there's go in it and he'll, 467
law, and not to, 198
no more noise with it, 273
out nothink on it, I couldn't, 314
ready, up Guards, 166
sure, says he, to, 286
them, a breath can, 300
the meat it feeds on, 195
the most of it, if this be treason, 414

Make the most of what, 103
the one verse for the other's sake, 335
the thing, he'll, 467
. . . two blades of grass to grow, 162
vows and break them still, 429
war, one of them would, 431
way for liberty, 217
what a fool of yourself with your whistle you'd, 440
what all their lives, why should they, 450
with them, meddle or, 401
yourselves another, 118
Maker, 247
he serveth his, 181
just, presence of a, 115
the image of his, 7
Makes, 247
a solitude and calls it peace, he, 373
a supper, this night he, 393
it, of him that, 196
it so, but thinking, 402
night hideous, and, 282
no friend, he, 145
no sign, dies and, 91
the man, worth, 465
who, who sells, who buys, 311
Maketh mankind, nuptial love, 232
Making night hideous, 268
whiskey, as well as, 440
Malady, 247
most incident to maids, a, 316
Malcontent, like a, 239
Male tiger, than there is milk in a, 260
when she walks with a, 363
Malefactor, some monstrous, 41
Males, agree in conceding to all, 455
Malice, 247
and with well-concocted, 283
domestic, foreign levy, 223
in my breath, and spend my, 402
set down aught in, 117
that belied him, 122
toward none, with, 337
Malthus, 247
Mammon, 247, 248
before the altar of, 253
this filthy marriage-hindering, 470
wins his way, and, 270
Mammoth, till the skull of an old, 141
Mammy yet, to tak' me frae my, 254
Man, 248–251
a, pays to the public, 46
a bold, bad, 29
abridgment of all . . . pleasant in, 1
a debtor to his profession every, 318
a good quality in a, 70
a habit in a, 167
all promise is poor dilatory, 318
all save the spirit of, 426
all that may become a, 72
all the good from the heart of a, 49
alone, to, 237
Man
a lost and lonely, 328
a most incomparable, 160
and a positivist, then he was a, 311
and bird and beast, both, 313
and nation, once to every, 83
and nature scorn the shocking hat, 171
and wife, like peevish, 376
and woman, good name in, 275
arms and the, 13
art thou a, 182
as free as nature first made, 350
as much to all intents, 75
a soldier's a, 100
a woman ruled, a, 449
been done, what has by, 94
be cold, though, 442
before thy mother, scarce be a, 270
before your mother, strive still to be a, 270
being reasonable, 193
bird, beast are but beast, 316
blest be the, 29
blush, to make, 434
but pitied the, 353
by man, forth in the van, 151
by man the world would damn itself, 198
by nothing is so well betrayd, 150
called the rights of, 338
can die but once, 89
can fasten on a, 425
can half-control his doom, 338
can have at stake, 143
cannot be strict, a, 60
cannot make a, 179
can pray unbidden, a, 312
can raise, the stateliest building, 195
childhood shows the, 49
Christian is the highest style of, 51
civilized, cannot live without cooks, 63
contend to the uttermost, let a, 318
contract so strong appetite for emetics, 109
dare, I dare, what, 72
did Katy love a, 200
dissuading you, whenever you hear a, 302
doth safely rule, no, 287
father of the, 49
dreaded of, 87
dreams of fame, 124
eloquent, that old, 108
every, must be guaranteed his liberty, 338
every, with him, 324
except the soul of, 357
extremes in, 117
for the field, 454
for the sword, 454
gently scan your brother, 188
happy the, 408
has, the more goods a, 279

Man
has an axe to grind, 15
has his fault, every, 128
has seldom an offer of kindness, 315
heaven had made her such a, 363
he is oft the wisest, 446
he seems of cheerful yesterdays, 48
he was the mildest-mannered, 262
here lies the, 294
if Jesus Christ is a, 196
immortal, rationally brave, 191
in all the world's new fashion planted, 303
in Christendom, never a, 119
in debt, poor is the, 82
in his wrath, than the strong, 413
in love of God and love of, 269
in me, I had not so much of, 399
in nothing trust that, 62
in the lip than in the heart of, 14
in the parliament of, 433
in wit, a, 252
is, know what God and, 135
is a carnivorous production, 256
is bound to do, 105
is cursed alway, by, 366
is growing, while, 81
is his own star, 127
I should avoid, 126
I should like to see any kind of a, 255
is man and master, 141
is more than Constitutions, 213
is not alive, that, 332
is not man as yet, 318
is not to be judged by man, 198
it does not feel for, 38
i' the mire, which ne'er left, 435
I was not good enough for, 56
labourin', an' labourin' woman, 208
less than a span, the life of, 461
like me troubles himself little, a, 259
made thee to temper, 452
made the town, 64
made us citizens, before, 259
makes a death, 81
makes heaven or hell for a, 242
makes his own statue, each, 322
marks the earth with ruin, 288
may cry, church, church, 52
may serve seven years, where a, 434
may write the thing he will, 221
means evil, no, 87
misery acquaints a, 21
more sinned against than sinning, 366
must play a part, a stage where every, 463
nature formed but one such, 359
never a law of God or, 212
never is but always to be blessed, 186
nothing yet been contrived by, 192
of age, thou smitest sore, 372
of an unbounded stomach, a, 388
of comfort, a, 93

Man
of God, a little, round, fat, oily, 289
of mettle, grasp it like a, 280
of morals, tell me why, 101
of my kidney, a, 201
of nasty ideas, a nice man is a, 281
of sense, your tailor is a, 396
of such a book of follies in a, 449
of wisdom is the man of years, 445
one, in his time, 383
one wrong more to, 467
or think thee lord alone of, 463
or woman or suckling, 113
picked out of ten thousand, 183
posthumous, 115
pour this concealed, 383
prevailed above the magistrate, 245
proposes, but God disposes, 155
really loves a woman, if a, 243
reckon with this, 147
recovered of the bite, the, 95
resembled thee, that, 228
salt that seasons right to, 312
shall learn, till, 330
she set herself to, 273
she tried on, 211
should dread, of all the foes that, 21
should have them, that, 298
should know, more than mortal, 277
should undo a, 295
show the world, let any, 461
some proud son of, 410
so near is God to, 104
so various, a, 114
such master, such, 255
than the, 126
that, may last, 26
that blushes is not quite a brute, 28
that can write, any, 216
that died for men, on a, 104
that hails you, the, 405
that has never a shirt, a, 360
that has not tried, lives a, 136
that hath a tongue, that, 454
that hath no music, the, 273
that hopes for heaven, 40
that large-moulded, 427
that lays his hand upon a woman, 66
that meddles with cold iron, 302
that mocks at it, the, 375
that never feared, 181
that once did sell, 226
that same, that runnith awaie, 130
that's marred, is a, 254
that studieth revenge, a, 334
that when his day is done, happy the, 62
the apparel oft proclaims the, 11
the common rights of, 413
the half part of a blessed, 168
the hermit sighed till woman smiled, 450
the image of his Maker, 7
the less, but nature more, love not, 277

Man
the standard of the, 263
the state of, 164
there lived a, 228
the strong, must go, 78
the tongue o', can name, 457
the ways of a, 187
the wit of one, 320
this bold, bad, 29
though he felt as a, 346
thou madest, 104
thou shalt never die, 88
thou wilt quarrel with a, 322
to command, 454
to have some fifteen minutes of hell, 176
to know, this truth, enough for, 427
to make a, 191
to man, 38
to mend, for, 172
trust not a, 83
unto each, comes a day, 366
upon this earth, every, 89
vain insect, while, 176
vindicate the ways of God to, 200
was born for liberty, proclaims that, 217
was made to mourn, 271
went mad and bit the, 95
what is a, 189
who . . . has the largest capacity of loving, 243
who has the power and skill, the, 450
who is good enough, a, 383
who kills a, 30
who needlessly sets foot upon a worm, 463
whose soul is pure and strong, a, 390
who stole the livery, a, 228
will do soonest for a, 34
with eight trumps in his hand, 415
with soul so dead, 65
with the gallery of family portraits, 124
with the head, 454
worth makes the, 465
would die, the, 90
would live in vain, poor, 81
you are to bid any, 422
you forget the, 314
Manacle, 251
Manacled, not tied or, 381
Manage the furnace, I, 386
Managing committee, sort of, 92
Man-child, truth's yet mightier, 115
Mandalay, 251, 252
Mandragora, give me to drink, 370
Mane, and flowing each, 387
laid his hand upon the ocean's, 288
laid my hand upon thy, 288
Mange in swine, or, 306
Mangle his merciful words, you, 365
Manhood, 252
a clearer faith and, 466
dear, for what makes, 27
Manhood
for a bright, 119
has left him, or that his, 309
in glory, wails, 326
more approbation, gives, 287
never bought nor sold, the, 185
old age past, youth, 155
strife comes with, 390
through, 58
to the awful verge of, 143
Manhood's noble head, o'er, 354
solid earth, on, 250
Mania prevailed, a, 379
Man-in-God, is one with, 313
Mankind, 252
alike is perfected, when all, 318
all think their little set, 28
are equalized by death, 114
brought woe to all, 449
good will to all, 52
is in some degree better, 54
is man, the only science of, 250
is man, the proper study of, 250
misfortunes of, 180
nuptial love maketh, 232
respect to the opinions of, 356
ring in redress to all, 328
should cease to sin, 't was best . . . , 365
shut the gates of mercy on, 368
that of all, 196
the mere waste-paper of, 309
the prayer of all, 313
the wisest, brightest, meanest of, 123
would deserve better of, 162
Mankind's epitome, all, 114
Man-like is it to fall into sin, 365
Manly brow consents to death, 152
spirit, drown my, 381
Manna, though his tongue dropped, 122
Manner born, to the, 70
the pretty and sweet, 399
Manners, 252
and carriage, improving the, 253
and fine sense, graced with polished, 463
and their ways, their, 66
as by his, 150
English minds and, 110
improves our parts with polished, 234
of the town, I'll view the, 413
old, old books, 290
Mannikin feels his way, 15
Mannish cowards have, as many other, 394
Manor, sir, the, 91
Man's apparel, disgrace my, 68
as true as steel, my, 415
blindfold eye, seems wrong to, 337
bred out, the strain of, 267
brow, like to a title-leaf, 38
face, as a nose on a, 285
face, given to a, 219

Man's ingratitude, unkind as, 444
feast, at any good, 23
first disobedience, of, 93
general infancy, begins, 318
half sears, a, 398
hat, lay my head to any good, 214
heart, bread which strengtheneth, 35
heart, nor venture to unmask, 328
hobby-horse is as tender, a, 180
house, a, is his castle, 44
imperial race ensnare, tresses, 168
inhumanity to man, 192
life a thing apart, is of, 232
life, how good is, 229
life is but a jest, 219
love, for a good, 238
love is of man's life a thing apart, 232
mind to atheism, inclineth, 14
obdurate heart, no flesh in, 38
peril comes of bed, 21
pie is freed, no, 8
presumption on to-morrow's dawn, 411
true touchstone, 41
wickedness, a method in, 261
worth something, a, 130
Mansion call, back to its, 421
strange, 418
the door of the deserted, 91
this cheerless, 182
who kept up his old, 149
Mansions, a hearth in her, 63
be, where the many, 278
build thee more stately, 376
of the blest, in the, 221
Mantle clad, the morn in russet, 269
do cream and, 291
of grey, from her, 269
threw, her silver, 268
Many, 252
a crime deemed innocent on earth, 66
a Kate has done, than, 200
a man hath more hair, 168
a one has started forth, 321
be glad and your friends are, 152
doth give too much to, 141
heads, beast with, 20
people read a song, 462
still must labour for the one, 207
taxes when they're not too, 110
the madness of, 297
the wisdom of, 320
times before their deaths, 66
things, to talk of, 430
to keep, and, 132
Many-headed multitude, the, 271
Many-twinkling feet, muse of the, 129
Maple, all crinkly like curled, 423
Maps, 252
for ports and piers, peering in, 444
Mar the land, in weeds that, 355
your fortunes, lest it may, 380
Marble, 252
sleep in dull, cold, 140
wastes, the more the, 385
with his name, 53
Marbles, 252
March are come, the ides of, 190
beware the ides of, 190
in a fortnight he might, 287
nearer home, a day's, 278
on the eighth day of, 348
then, on we, 461
up to a fortress, I can, 283
Marched breast forward, 337
round in front of a drum, 11
Marching on, his truth is, 153
on, while God is, 225
Mare, 253
Marge, till it lip the, 53
Margin, through a meadow of, 293
Marian pass him by, 4
Mariner, 253
curseth the warning bird, 319
Mariners of England, ye, 110
Marjoram of the salad, the sweet, 179
Mark and glass, the, 263
and tell, nought to do but, 305
death loves a shining, 81
grinding life down from its, 439
him well, 65
measures . . . have always been my, 256
of a saint, eppylets worn't the best, 431
of virtue, assumes some, 425
our coming, an eye will, 438
put the self-same, 249
the archer little meant, finds, 358
the changing colour, to, 293
the sparrow's fall, 84
to bear, a lasting, 455
where a garden had been, to, 342
Mark Antony the world, who lost, 452
Marked him for her own, melancholy, 257
Market had the usual chills, the moral, 269
Market-town, a fellow in a, 326
Marks, by these special, 239
her its ain, simplicity, 364
of angels' feet, 460
our English dead, but, 113
upon you, none of my uncle's, 239
Marmion, last words of, 47
such as, 97
Marred in making, he, 178
is a man that's, 254
many a poem is, 109
Marriage, 253
a pair of stairs to, 242
bond divine, to stamp the, 442
comes by destiny, 86
I made a second, 426
tables, the, 147
the contract of her, 407
Marriage-bell, merry as a, 334

Marriage-hindering mammon, this filthy, 470
Marriages, 253
are happy, why so few, 280
Married, 253, 254
live till I were, 16
man, Benedick the, 254
Mr. R———, Nancy Low has, 53
she, 450
some are, 351
to immortal verse, 394
when we are, 238
Marrow of a nation, the pith and, 277
with too late, freezing the, 211
Marrow-bones, flopped down on my, 313
Marrowless, thy bones are, 29
Marry, 254, 255
for munny, don't thou, 267
the best person she could, 243
you, then I won't, 246
young maids must, 203
Mars, an eye like, 250
me, this movement makes or, 247
they'll question, 306
this seat of, 112
Marshal's truncheon, the, 260
Marshes calling, the plover from the, 384
Marsh-grass sends into the sod, the, 156
Marsh-hen secretly builds, as the, 156
Mart, press too close in church and, 220
to your throne amid the, 413
your offices for gold, sell and, 294
Martial airs of England, 112
outside, a swashing and a, 394
Martin-haunted eaves, the, 107
Martin's summer, Saint, 168
Martyr, 255
Martyrs died to save, 416
Martyrs' ashes watched, the, 441
Marvel and a mystery to the world, a, 255
how the fishes live, 133
or surprise, of, 147
Mary, I'm sitting on the stile, 387
now of a bloody, 157
Queen, to, the praise be given, 369
rose at Jesus' word, as, 358
Maryland, 255
Masculine attire in which they roughen to the sense, 357
Mashed upon her cheeks, 399
Mask, jesters weep behind the, 165
tired dissimulation drops her, 81
put on his ugliest, 80
your passions, can argue down or, 298
Mason, builds stronger than the, 164
Masque, fragrant at an ev'ning, 410
Masquerade, the truth in, 218
Mass, that party-coloured, 64
Massachusetts, a coat thet sets well in ole, 60
Mast, and bends the gallant, 359
just a funnel and a, 54
her holy flag, nail to the, 133
like a drunken sailor on a, 346
nailed her colours to the, 58
right up above the, 63
what though the, 231
Master, 255
a grief, can, 165
bold, the, 436
do not tell me the Almighty, 155
for life, he shall be, 348
I can hardly think you my, 239
missed it, though thy, 140
ob de sheepfol', 358
of his fate, 141
of his liberty, a man is, 250
of lord and clown, 103
of my fate, I am the, 126
of what is mine own, 263
Spirit, life-blood of a, 30
the book wherein the, 280
went, into the woods my, 457
Master-passion, since love is held the, 234
Masterpiece is writing well, nature's chief, 467
Master's own, heart is still his, 176
Masters, 255
lords and rulers, 147
of their fates, 127
Mast-high came floating by, ice, 190
Match, it was fit to, 329
those dreams of mine, to, 98
to solve a learned doubt, what can, 433
Matched our buttons, when we've, 211
Matches are lit, the, 387
Mate, a woman needs a, 450
choose not alone a proper, 254
coo dove to thy married, 97
hovers o'er her, 97
some honest gander for her, 255
to thee, and here, kind, 32
Mated by the lion, that would be, 384
with a clown, thou art, 189
Material things, a growing knowledge of, 467
Mates him first, 82
Matin to be near, 153
Matins, to tune up his unseasonable, 210
Matrimony, 255
Matrons, maids, 368
Matter, 256
better in France, they order this, 142
book containing such vile, 30
enough, and, 378
if, why the delicate dish, 92
of me, that's what's the, 404
of right, is a, 289
the wrecks of, 191
too soft, 455
what's the, 119

Matter-o'-money, quoth echo plainly, 255
Matters at worst are sure to mend, 464
  none of theirs, thrust them into, 285
Mattock, the, and the grave, 401
Maud and Marian pass him by, 4
  come into the garden, 148
Mauls some feline foe, 44
Mavournin, Erin, 115
Maxim, observed this useful, 66
  let this great, 427
Maxims, with a little hoard of, 73
May, 256
  be, what we, 12
  go marry, and while ye, 254
  last, a braw wooer, 458
  love whose month is ever, 238
  the day when it is, 361
  when they are maids, 457
Mayflower, launch our, 281
May-morn of his youth, in the very, 470
Mayor, 256
Maze of quick, now bourgeons every, 372
Me, himself, his hungering neighbour and, 181
  is not the rose for, 342
  then no more of thee and, 423
Mead and moor, from, 52
Meadow of margin, through a, 293
  the, the orchard, 49
Meadows, 256
  are bleating in the, 469
  brown and sere, and, 257
  goes down in de gloomerin', 358
  up t'ro' the gloomerin', 359
Meal a day, at least one, 256
  and the walk that costs a, 430
  for the worms to eat, a rich juicy, 229
  the raven croaked as she sate at her, 326
Meals, 256
Mean, and party leaders all they, 315
  alike condemn, both the golden, 237
  I know not what they, 399
  meaning, a very, 256
  the thing that is, 55
  the thing those letters, 450
  what may this, 268
  yes, mebby to, 283
Meander through a meadow of margin, shall, 293
Meaner creatures kings, and, 186
Meanest have their day, the, 123
  of mankind, 123
  of the mean, the, 245
Meaning, 256
  have incurred the worst, who with best, 464
Meanings and wishings, full of good, 193
Meanness, 256
Means enabled them, whose, 266
  get wealth and place, by any, 266
Means, healed by the same, 197
  he'll soon find, 142
  is one of the most effectual, 432
  no matter by what, 266
  not to be found, that, 355
  of evil, still to find, 116
  of life, in the very, 35
  the end must justify the, 109
  the happier to arise, 121
  to do ill deeds, 83
  to live, save, 223
  whereby I live, take the, 223
Meant, 256
  finds mark the archer little, 358
  who happens to be, 340
Measles and that, if the children had the, 19
Measure, God gives wind by, 209
  of all your pleasure, full, 329
  of an unmade grave, 163
  of a stalwart man, 250
  of devotion, the last full, 276
  of immortal hope, 115
  of my wrath, come not within the, 465
  of the height of pain, the, 293
  their life by art, some, 398
  twenty miles to-day, we must, 262
Measured by my soul, I must be, 263
  by tears, time is best, 406
Measures, 256
  new times demand new, 281
Meat, 257
  anger's my, 9
  and would fain have, 240
  as full of quarrels as an egg is full of, 322
  as full of wit as an egg is full of, 447
  both mouth and the, 271
  fire, and clothes, 336
  for your master, I am, 255
  I cannot eat but little, 6
  it feeds on, make the, 195
  or drink, is another's, 309
  sauce to, 129
Meats, the funeral baked, 147
  the sweetest, the soonest cloy, 423
Mechanic his labour will often discard, a, 390
  slaves with greasy aprons, 368
Med'cinable, some griefs are, 166
Meddle or make with them, the less you, 401
  with politics, I never love to, 310
Meddled with a tempest, should not have, 297
Meddles with cold iron, the man that, 302
Medicine more, to try one desperate, 86
Meditation, 257
  let us all to, 80
Meed, perseverance gains it, 302
Meek than fierce, it's safer being, 159
Meekly she bowed her own, 109
Meekness her sins, and leaving with, 351

Meet, 257
a body, gin a body, 203
again beyond the tomb, 61
again, congenial spirits part to, 60
again, Tom, we shall, 89
again, whether we shall, 125
and mingle, in one spirit, 366
and never the twain shall, 391
and oh, when we, 257
at any time again, when we, 296
for such a guest is, 303
'im later on, I'll, 395
it is I set it down, 426
that every nice offence, it is not, 289
them like necessities, let us, 279
the sun, to, 151
the sun upon the upland lawn, to, 392
when next we, 239
where two raging fires, 132
Meetest for death, 439
Meeting, 257
broke the good, 264
our, was all mirth and laughter, 296
was bliss, the, 338
were bare without it, 129
Meetings, journeys end in lovers', 198
Meets the ear, meant than, 106
Melancholy, 257, 258
a green and yellow, 298
and to be, 239
can soothe her, 136
slow, remote, unfriended, 332
with care and, 196
Mellowing of occasion, upon the, 258
Mellow-tasted Burgundy, the, 40
Melody foretells, world of merriment their, 23
of song, by, 374
Melrose made gude kail, the monks of. 267
Melt at others' woe, 174
away, our navies, 139
flesh would, 134
his iron heart to pity, or, 406
Melted away, voice in my dreaming ear, 98
him in his own grease, 164
into air, are, 428
Melting mood, unused to the, 399
Melts, a woman's tear-drop, 398
like kisses, which, 210
the ball, that, 227
the mind to love, pity, 305
Member do n't agree, if a, 171
no comfortable feel in any, 285
to lay for that same, 171
Members, gangrened, 148
Memories, 258
Memory, 258
a sinner of his, 219
for his jests, indebted to his, 291
from the table of my, 331
green in our souls, keep his, 274
has drawn upon his, 291
holds a seat, while, 331
Memory
now have I but their, 331
of a thousand years, 72
of past folly, the, 445
of the just, the, 199
of the man, to the, 132
pluck from the, 263
still, how sweet their, 300
Men, 259
about me that are fat, 126
about thee, thou hast, 317
an avalanche of, 119
and dogs shall drink him, 248
and justifiable to, 200
and studied, 66
and the ways of, 68
and women, all the, 383
and women, dead, 75
angels might talk with, 417
an' I 've seen things an', 40
an' warly, 44
are April when they woo, 457
are dangerous, such, 126
are free to think, and, 220
are merriest when they are from home, 261
are the tastes of, 397
are to be born so, 10
a sea of, 119
as he wrote down for, 418
as its exposing, 195
as live, such, 84
as they ought to be, to draw, 294
at some time, 127
below and saints above, and, 237
betray, that, 136
bond, marvel that they make, 455
breeds hard English, 113
call treasure, what, 102
can cover crimes, 119
car asses of unburied, 69
condemned alike to groan, 392
decay, and, 300
deeds are, 459
do, the evil that, 116
do a-land, as, 133
down, which bind, 122
drawing force from all her, 277
dying make their wills, 450
entirely great, the rule of, 301
entrap the hearts of, 168
ere we were women and, 392
ever had and ever will have leave, 379
Eve upon the first of, 2
fair women and brave, 334
fear death as children fear, 77
follow him, bids, 390
for ever, a star to, 206
forget themselves so far, muse that, 455
free, 142
governments are instituted among, 161
had ears, if, 272
handful of, 113

Men
have broke, all the vows that ever, 429
have died from time to time, 238
have done, what, 96
have dulled their eyes, 155
have their price, all those, 315
heart-easing Mirth, and by, 264
hearts of oak are our, 286
high-minded, 385
honest, that thinks, 183
in barricks do n't grow into plaster saints, 349
in earnest have no time to waste, 416
in the affairs of, 405
in the hearts of, 191
into the trunks of, 378
justify the ways of God to, 200
know love, most, 232
know well enough, wise, 255
less brave, but, 145
lies upon the paths of, 138
lingering and looking at goods, 266
maids in purity, see, 321
maids must kiss no, 202
may come, and men may go, 116
may do, fight for love as, 457
may live fools, 138
may rise on stepping-stones, 170
may sleep, 404
measures not, 256
might be better if we better deemed, 191
mortal but themselves, all, 269
mount, on which, 122
must endure their going hence, 157
must work, 132
my brothers, men the workers, 461
naething I hated like, 458
new measures and new, 281
not, but measures, 256
not two strong, 84
observingly distil it out, 160
of course do seek, 318
of death, work forth, 79
of genius, companies of, 387
of most renowned virtue, 213
of thought and men of action, 225
on a man that died for, 104
one of Plutarch 's, 308
other times and other, 114
port for, 34
prize the thing ungained, 318
pronounce them wimmen, 449
propose, why do n't the, 319
sailors but, 359
schemes o' mice and, 261
shall understand, King James 's, 63
shiver when thou'rt named, 162
should fear, that, 80
should put an enemy, 33
sifting out the hearts, 415
sit down to that nourishment, 393
so loose in soul, a kind of, 371
some to bus'ness, 325
talk only, and, 210

Men
that do the world 's rough work, 306
that dwelt in Jerusalem, above all, 193
that fishes gnawed upon, 102
that in a narrower day, 106
the busy hum of, 188
that women marry, the, 255
the helm, nor yields to, 86
the hopes of all, 193
their best apparel do, as, 446
the lives of most women and, 140
the most infamous, 123
there are a sort of, 291
there are love not a gaping pig, 304
the tears of bearded, 398
the thoughts of, are widened, 322
the tongues of, 82
this blunder still you find, in, 28
this happy breed of, 112
this rail-splitter a true-born king of, 324
this restless craving in the souls of, 46
through the deeds of, 126
to all brave, 39
true and leal, have all, 150
twelve good, into a box, 33
we petty, 58
were deceivers ever, 83
whose heads do grow, 88
whose heads stood, 88
. . . will back their own opinions with a wager, 429
will call, saints will aid if, 348
will seek you, rejoice and, 329
with forty thousand, 202
would be angels, 316
wrecked upon a sand, as, 465
write, for this, 123
Menace, more fraught with, 165
Mend, at the worst they sometimes, 464
for man to, 172
his pace, will not, 33
matters at worst are sure to, 464
my ways, I vow to, 429
too vain to, 46
your speech a little, 380
Mended, 260
for nothing else but to be, 329
Mends their morals, it, 135
Men 's affairs, the privatest of, 120
business and bosoms, home to, 40
charitable speeches, leave it to, 258
daughters, words are, 459
ends marked, more are, 105
evil manners live in brass, 34
faces are true, 119
graves, over, 202
lives, yet waste, 208
minds about to religion, 14
names, new-made honor doth forget, 275
souls, poison to, 158
souls, the times that try, 378

Mental dyspepsy, of a, 31
Mention her name, why I never once, 274
of me, where no, 140
Mentioned not at all, than, 123
Mentions hell to ears polite, never, 178
Mercer's plague, Miss, the, 361
Merchant over-polite to his customers, 15
Merchant's flesh, that same, 134
Merchants most do congregate, where, 193
unimpeachable of sin, 413
Mercies and judgments mark him, 154
Merciful one, the compassionate and, 242
Mercury, be, 171
like the herald, 250
Mercy, 260
alike to kill or save, 227
disclaiming all regard for, 413
in her woe, 142
is a God unjust, a God all, 157
no, now can clear her brow, 366
of a rude stream, 153
on mankind, shut the gates of, 368
sighed farewell, 142
temper, so justice with, 199
underlies, life and death his, 147
with a bleeding heart, stripes that, 390
Mere words, words, 459
Meridian of my glory, full, 122
Merit, 260
heaven by making earth a hell, 177
his sense of your great, 405
how he esteems your, 405
praise, who, 332
raised, by, 107
shall bring his, 187
should they have regard, to true, 427
spurns that patient, 323
which we so little, 380
Merits, 261
on their own, 265
or their faults to scan, 305
Merrier life than mine, led a, 221
man, a, 196
Merriest, 261
Merrily hent the stile-a, 174
shall I live now, 21
Merriment their melody foretells, what a world of, 23
your flashes of, 468
Merry, 261
dancing, drinking, 71
and yet honest too, wives may be, 448
as a marriage-bell, 334
heart goes all the day, 174
if to be old and, 290
men are we, and, 436
the damsel that's, 246
when I hear sweet music, never, 273
Mesh to entrap the hearts, 168
Messengers, his tears pure, 29
Messes, herbs and other country, 303
Messmates, hear a brother sailor, 346
Met again four summers after, 296
and fought with, may be, 219
and we parted for ever, 296
as it we had not, 384
her, would you know how first he, 439
never, 37
no sooner, 242
the enemy, we have, 110
the guests are, 167
the night that first we, 343
we, 't was in a crowd, 67
we, 't was in a mob, 67
when or how or where we, 220
when we, 204
with elsewhere, ne'er, 182
Metal from my side, that I must draw this, 442
more attractive, 14
into gold, life's leaden, 162
on war's red techstone rang true, 19
Metamorphosed with a mistress, now you are, 239
Metaphysic, 261
Meteor flag of England, the, 110
in the sky, a transient, 376
like a swift-fleeting, 269
of a spark, each light gay, 410
Meteor-like flame lawless through the void, 306
Metes to ev'ry pinch of human dust, 115
Method, 261
in 't, yet there's, 245
of making a fortune, the, 141
Metre ballad-mongers, one of these same, 205
Metropolis and see of Rome, the great, 342
Mettle enough to kill care, 45
grasp it like a man of, 280
Mew, be a kitten and cry, 205
the cat will, 45
Mewed, in shady cloister, 56
the brinded cat hath, 45
Mewing her mighty youth, an eagle, 277
Mexico, the richest spoils of, 111
Micawber, Mr., I never will desert, 85
Mice, 261
her feet fell patter, cheep, like little, 129
like little, stole in and out, 129
Mid-day beam, at the full, 277
Middle, now i' the, 71
of her web, in, 380
of the night, the dead vast and, 282
state, who keeps the, 228
tree and highest, the, 63
Midnight, 261, 262
abed after, 24
air, out in the, 40

Midnight
and morn, a mistake between, 348
bell, if the, 22
bell, mock the, 33
curtains round, drew my, 167
oil, consumed the, 215
oil, of mid-day sun and, 409
pillow, sighed upon a, 242
shout and revelry, 129
taper, beneath a, 317
taper, what they call their, 123
Midst of my blisses, in the, 205
of water I complain of thirst, in, 435
Mien, a monster of so frightful, 425
carries, though her, 108
such a face and such a, 425
the lofty port, the distant, 316
Might, faith that right makes, 337
have been, saddest are these, it, 346
no, can censure 'scape, 42
of his sunbeam, death with the, 77
on all the chords with, 241
that slumbers, the, 300
the sun never sets on his, 112
Mightier man-child, truth's yet, 115
than the sword, the pen is, 301
Mightiest in the mightiest, 'tis, 260
Mighty fire, will make a, 131
fortress is our God, a, 140
space of our large honours, 36
than he seems, more, 84
yearning, like the first, 66
Mild decay, a general flavour of, 82
not by nature, 341
of affections, 252
Milder moons emparadise the night, 65
Mildest, 262
Mildews the white wheat, 135
Mildness, come gentle spring, ethereal, 382
Mile in Ireland's isle, not a, 372
Mile-a, sad tires in a, 174
Miles, 262
he had journeyed fifty, 106
Military array, against the soldier in full, 352
posts, her possessions and, 112
Milk, 262
and marry, I shall, 254
and water, oh, 264
coals, 44
comes frozen home, 190
dealers in watered, 325
in a male tiger, than there is, 260
like wrinkled skins on scalded, 364
philosophy, adversity's sweet, 303
take suggestion as a cat laps, 392
the bowl, fills with, 182
Milking, I am going a-, 246
Milkmaid singeth blithe, the, 307
Milk-teeth white, to keep his, 408
Milk-white hand examine well his, 36
Mill cannot grind, the, 434
more water glideth by the, 435
the, the mint, 386
Mill, the, the plough, the axe, 212
Miller, 262
of, that wots the, 435
Millions æons, whirled for a, 18
men, troubles himself little about a, 259
piers, up on its, 152
pleased not the, 45
thy love is worth a, 292
Millions a hero, 272
do, what will those luckless, 75
in those solitudes, 75
of bubbles like us, 39
of spiritual creatures, 381
slew, whose fiat, 332
thousands, perhaps, 192
Mills, 262
the curt-tongued, 413
Milton held, which, 412
some mute inglorious, 168
Milton's ashes lay, where, 29
or in Shakespeare's name, in, 458
Mimicry of bloom, with all the, 64
Minaret, doth shake the, 154
Mince it in love, no ways to, 238
Minced-pies, quarrel with, 322
Mind, 262, 263
above, wafts the, 233
a dagger of the, 70
a thought, his, 248
education forms the common, 107
fail thee, if thy, 55
grief that saps the, 166
hard to move the lady's, 141
has a thousand eyes, the, 281
love looks with the, 69
methinks I see in my, 277
never brought to, 14
nobler in the, 19
so unaffected, so composed a, 453
stale in thrifty, 126
taint not thy, 270
tempt with doubts thy constant, 347
that never meant amiss, the, 256
that spoke the vacant, 211
the American, 8
the best contentment has, the noblest, 62
the gentle, 150
the image of our, 447
the last infirmity of noble, 123
the pain, never, 135
quite vacant, a, 333
the troubled sea of the, 369
to, by damning those they have no, 366
to atheism, inclineth man's, 14
to conceal the, 210
to him, the thorn-tree had a, 458
to love, pity melts the, 305
to mind, and, 237
to work my, 21
oppress, dumps the, 166
or moral nature, body, 425
out of, 364

Mind
quickly also is he out of, 364
upon your health, have, 139
were of my, 133
whose untutored, 176
windows of her, 444
Minds about to religion, 14
and manners, English, 110
are not ever craving, 31
balm of hurt, 370
improve by travel, some, 276
made better, in, 50
productive of the greatest, 41
strong, great hearts, 259
Mine, 263
and thine, love that says not, 235
bright jewels of the, 464
entered into, 51
in spite of fate are, 221
it was, it is not I, 74
now thine, is closelier, 275
of afterthought to me, 274
own, she is, 197
own, which is, 147
that only makes it, 443
't was, 't is his, 275
with my heart in 't, 169
Mines, one yard below their, 110
Mingle, in one another's being, 366
in one spirit meet and, 366
mid the brightness of the skies, 378
with forgotten ashes, and, 81
Mingled, hearts have once, 175
into one, 56
into one, been, 110
Mingles with my friendly bowl, 327
Mingling poetic honey with trade wax, 308
Minions, the clouds are my, 284
Minister, 263
one fair spirit for my, 85
to a mind diseased, 263
Ministers of grace, defend us, 9
of love, all are but, 234
Minnows, this Triton of the, 414
Minster, 264
Minstrel in, ring the fuller, 336
raptures swell, no, 65
was infirm and old, 436
Minstrelsy, the merry, 36
with the gentle, 414
Mint of phrases in his brain, that hath a, 303
the mill, the, 386
Minted coins express, even its, 157
Minute, at what precise, 210
in a, pay, 78
lingering a, 292
sighing every, 56
stopped, not a, 325
will speak more in a, 396
Minute-gun, while peals the, 433
Minute 's, the black, at end, 78
Minutes, in forty, 152
of hell, to have some fifteen, 176
tells he o'er, what damned, 243
Miracle, would work a, 155
Mire, to her wallowing in the, 378
which ne'er left man i' the, 435
Mirror, holds its warped, 278
up to nature, to hold . . . the, 278
Mirth, 264
and laughter, our meeting was all, 296
and laughter, wine and women, 444
can into folly glide, how, 136
earth must borrow its, 212
he is all, 196
I 'll use you for my, 382
in sorrow enter or in, 377
lady, when first your, 148
little inmate, full of, 175
not a string attuned to, 257
of its December, the, 331
present, hath present laughter, 239
the limits of becoming, 196
the night-song of, 125
within the limit of becoming, 196
Mirth-moving jest, turns to a, 196
Misapprehension of our new conditions, 8
Misbegotten knaves in Kendal green, 205
Misbeliever, call me, 147
Mischief, either of virtue or, 442
let them call it, 414
Satan finds some, 190
that is past and gone, mourn a, 271
Misdeeds, avenged on my, 15
Misdoubteth every bush, 25
Miser, rich honesty dwells like a, 183
Miserable, me, 177
night, passed a, 99
to be weak is, 436
Miseries, think to shed a tear in all my, 399
Misers, compare our rich, 133
Misery, 264
acquaints a man with strange bedfellows, 21
and crime, fatal sources of, 422
freed, Ned Purdon from, 168
must I lose that too, 231
result, 192
t' avoid, 422
to crown his, 317
Misfortune, 265
more bitter, they make, 50
sometimes a, 102
Misfortunes, 265
of mankind, follies and, 180
Mislike me not for my complexion, 60
Misquote, 265
Miss but me, that every, 290
but nature cannot, 277
him, till you, 49
no beauty she doth, 20
thou shalt not, 179
Missed it, though thy master, 140
should ever anything be, 44
Misses or who wins, who, 150

Mist and a weeping rain, there follows a, 203
answer each other in the, 52
folded in the, 23
in my face, 78
obscures, no, 268
resembles the rain, as the, 375
Mistake, they also lie too under a, 219
't was all a, 348
you lie under a, 219
Mistakes, 265
will occur, for, 348
Mistaking, sinned I not but in, 366
Mistletoe, 265
Mistress find, in every port a, 347
in my own, but, 276
Nature, a jealous, 277
no casual, 375
now you are metamorphosed with a, 239
of herself, and, 362
of the scene, that, 81
such Nan, such, 255
Mistress' eyebrow, made to his, 242
Mite, 265
by mite, who, 92
rob them of their, 67
Mite's, 265
Mix the punch, while you, 321
Mixtures of more happy days, happy, 264
Mizzled, and then he, 329
Moan be made, let no, 17
of joy or, 24
Moaning, and groanin' and paraphrasin', 309
of the bar, no, 17
to the bar and its, 132
Moans of their heart, by the, 398
Meat defensive to a house, 112
Mob of rascals, the, 325
we met, 't was in a, 67
Mock, let not ambition, 310
our eyes with air, 56
thee soul, I will not, 377
the meat it feeds on, 195
the midnight bell, 33
Mocked and scorned, by nature is, 277
for ever, God is not, 301
Mockeries of the past, but, 455
Mockery of woe, bear about the, 448
unreal, hence, 358
Mocking pencil, who with, 225
Mocks at it, bite the man that, 375
he who nature scorns and, 277
Model of a statuary, fit for the, 385
of the barren earth, 80
Moderate haste might tell a hundred, with, 188
Modern civilization, in our, 55
existence, agitation of, 365
nations vainly aim, at which all, 110
Modes of faith, for, 120
Modest, 265
as ony, she's, 364
Modester nor sweeter, ain't, 95
Modesty, 266
of nature, o'erstep not the, 278
Molasses, the product distilled from, 344
Molest her ancient, solitary reign, 292
Molten, graven, hammered and rolled, 157
Moment, every, dies a man, 69
every, lightly shaken, 241
every, one is born, 69
few have guessed the, 405
flies, and in a, 233
flow, the tide one, 82
give to God each, 227
heated hot in a, 50
I have had, von only happy, 200
of great pith and, 61
there's a, 140
to decide, comes the, 83
they are free, that, 368
will come, the, 338
yet the actor stops, a, 70
Momentary, the fit is, 133
Moment's ornament, to be a, 302
Moments before, a presentiment of it some, 315
in life when the heart, 173
make the year, 414
of bliss, called me thy angel in, 9
to cheat the thirsty, 288
Monarch, 266
hears, the, 155
it becomes the throned, 260
Monarch's voice, with a, 335
Monarchs die, how, 329
must obey, you proud, 81
talk of, 402
to behold the swelling scene, 383
Monarchy, 266
Monday, as guiltless as on, 393
comes betwixt the Saturday and, 74
denied to friends and visitors till, 345
Money, 266, 267
cannot afford to play cards for, 234
enough, and have not, 434
gratis, he lends out, 421
hath a dog, 95
in thy purse, put, 322
in trust, but put your, 415
it was for want of, 239
laaïd by, cause o' 'er, 241
love was love and better than, 240
of fools, they are the, 459
put not your trust in, 415
sir, your, 91
too, luvv thy lass an' 'er, 241
too, play for love and, 241
Money-bags, I did dream of, 98
Money-brokers and bill discounters, 193
Money-making, 267
Mongrel's hold will slip, the, 40
Monk, 267
would be, the devil a, 87

Monkey, 267
God help thee, poor, 127
with his tail abridged, a, 249
Monkeys were the gods, where, 316
Monks, 267
and bones, a town of, 387
Monody compels, solemn thought their, 410
Monopolists, joy flies, 198
Monotony, concealed in life 's, 462
Monster begot upon itself, a, 195
coiling in its nurse 's lap, a, 416
of ingratitudes, a great-sized, 407
of so frightful mien, vice is a, 425
spouted, where the wallowing, 354
which doth mock the meat, 195
Monsters you make of them, what, 255
Monstrous, is it not, 307
life, argues a, 80
Month, is ever May, love whose, 238
laughter for a, 196
of May, in the merry, 256
of June, in the leafy, 37
than he will stand to in a, 396
Months and years rolled by, 296
of every year, two, 110
to-morrow, but 't is only a, 374
that have not an R in their name, 292
Monument, 267
a brave man 's, 299
like patience on a, 298
Monuments, her, shall last, 322
Mood, in any shape, in any, 376
of melancholy, a kindly, 257
unused to the melting, 399
with Palinure 's unaltered, 304
Moods of mourning, sullen, 365
shapes of grief, 448
Moon, 267, 268
bay the, 36
blow them at the, 110
cold, fruitless, 56
complain, does to the, 292
course of one revolving, 114
examine Venus and the, 306
had filled her horn, ere thrice yon, 12
hang them on the horns o' the, 43
is full, when the, 57
into salt tears, 402
is hid, the, 23, 52
no bigger than the, 63
no sun, no, 285
pale as the, 344
shine at full or no, if the, 19
too quaffs the, 101
to wind up the sun and, 9
waning, not the crescent, 4
was round, the, 106
with this ninth, 18
Moonbeams kiss the sea, and the, 204
Moonlight, 268
under this clear, 373
Moon 's an arrant thief, the, 402
pale beam, print them on the, 450
Moons, milder, emparadise the night, 65
Moonshine an' snow on field an' hill, 152
be out, 304
Moor, 269
from mead and, 52
herself within my room, 73
my lord, due to the, 189
Mop and pattens with, 296
Moral, 269
accountable being, man is a, 249
element and public opinion, in war, the, 431
. . . may be safely attached, 48
nature, body, mind or, 425
of all human tales, 18
sensible, and well-bred man, 4
taints, sniff out our, 347
to point a, 274
Moralist to die, teach the rustic, 401
Moralists apply, unwashed, 344
Morals, 269
hold, the faith and, 412
it mends their, 135
More attractive, metal, 14
but nature, 277
faults than hairs, 168
goods a man has, the, 279
hair than wit, 168
I give to thee, the, 239
I have, the, 239
I 'll love no, 232
is felt, when, 178
is meant than meets the ear, 106
is no, 92
mighty than he seems, 84
much more, the heart may feel, 174
than less, better the, 28
of that, Hal, no, 243
of thee and me, then no, 423
than my brothers are to me, 38
time shall be no, 406
they thought they might get, 183
thou shalt have, 362
who dares do, 72
you drink, the, 100
you have the more you want, 430
Morn, 269
a mistake between midnight and, 348
as if that, 269
came dim and sad, 105
came peeping in at, 330
fair laughs the, 470
have a rouse before the, 69
I 'm off at eight to-morrow, 132
mute symbols of a joyful, 275
no, no noon, 285
no sleep till, 71
salutation to the, 57
than ours, another, 105
that wait for execution in the, 333
till night, my dream of life from, 262

Morn
till night, worked and sung from, 236
to noon he fell, from, 122
upon that winter's, 377
with the dawning of, 98
youth like summer, 5
Morning, 269
air, methinks I scent the, 269
almost at odds with, 282
away, from the voice of the, 57
betime, all in the, 422
breezy, preach upon a, 151
brings eternal day, and a new, 13
can rise in the, 442
come in the, 59
dews, drawn up like, 19
drum-beat, whose, 112
each, sees some task begin, 410
face, and shining, 352
face, day's disasters in his, 93
gate, through glory's, 105
gleam, in the, 132
half an hour every, 434
hanged betimes in the, 169
I awoke one, 124
prime, herbs at the, 151
roses newly washed with dew, 343
shine, to bid thy, 10
shows the day, as, 49
sir I say, No this, 468
than with the forehead of the, 282
the wings o' the, 112
they 're hanging Danny Deever in the, 169
thrice ere the, 427
true, the sun is to the, 245
two clouds at, 56
Morning-bugle, from India's, 112
Mornings, a' brushes his hat o', 239
Morrow morn, he rose the, 346
say good-night till it be, 296
that host on the, 216
we bitterly thought of the, 313
Morsel that stuffs him to the throat-gates, 92
Mortal, 269
breath, this life of, 76
coil, this, 98
creature, cringe to any, 42
engines, O you, 125
frame, quit this, 428
frame, whatever stirs this, 234
howe'er thy lot be cast, 228
suffered more, never, 208
taste, tree whose, 93
thread, cut the, 75
Mortality, 269, 270
'gainst the ills of, 100
no might nor greatness in, 42
Mortals be, what fools these, 138
call the moon, whom, 268
crave, whatever, 462
given, some feelings are to, 129
to command success, not in, 392
Moss, can gather no, 388
Moss, wipe the weeds and, 163
Moss-covered bucket, 39
Mosses and fungi gather, the, 425
Most strange, seems to me, 80
unkindest cut of all, 70
Moth with vain desire, not a, 160
Motes, 270
Mother, 270
a lady, thy, 16
and child, bathe in me, 247, 419
and for the tender, 89
and many a childing, 425
came into mine eyes, all my, 399
Charles, why should your, 164
could'n I luvv thy, 241
daughter, wife, the, 452
earth is dry, when, 101
England, for England, 48
for him no, 182
I'm his, 237
in her children, the pride of a, 315
isle, our little, 194
kept a shebeen shop, his, 440
kneel, I saw my, 283
of invention, necessity be the, 279
of safety, the, 128
of the world, necessity, thou, 279
or bride or maid, 113
Pembroke's, 180
praying God will save, 347
rock me to sleep, 340
sat there, a, 12
showed, as my, 189
so loving to my, 243
the apron-strings of an American, 8
there was their Dacian, 181
though father and, 440
was a Brady, his, 348
wife, and queen, in her as, 323
Mother (in law), 270
Mother's arms, we start from the, 56
bosom, hidden in a, 129
cat, if your, 277
eye, he taks the, 469
house, in my, 276
lap, into thy, 228
milk, as 't were their, 181
nest, drove from out the, 106
pangs, when with a, 353
throes, has Fate entailed the, 59
Mothers, 270
Moths, 270
Motio , devoid of sense and, 90
of a hidden fire, the, 313
scoured to death with perpetual, 345
this sensible warm, 90
Motions of his spirit, the, 273
Motives, let my character and my, 114
Motley's the only wear, 137
Motto, this be our, 415
Mould of form, the, 263
scratched with a stick in the, 13
though of terrestrial, 40
verge of the churchyard, 157
Moulded, and to this figure, 107
Moulder piecemeal on the rock, 28

Mouldering heap, in many a, 108
Moulders all, slowly, 337
Moulding Sheridan, broke the die in, 359
Moulds, her old-world, 179
Mouldy corn, that is ketched with, 206
want their doctors, 94
Mountain of its snows, as any, 285
Moulmein pagoda, by the old, 251, 392
Mound, or laboured, 385
Mount, 270
I, I fly, 163
to its summit, and we, 208
Mountain, 270
a forked, 56
brow, the river brink or, 182
leave to feed, on this fair, 269
small sands the, 414
view, climb and seek the, 46
yields, woods or steepy, 235
Mountaineers, believe that there were, 88
Mountain's prow, dat float on de, 297
Mountains and luxuriant plains, o'er the wild, 217
interposed make enemies, 110
rise, where'er the, 245
rolling, the sea was, 188
Mountain-side, from every, 65
Mountebanks the porch disgrace, 52
Mounted beggars, 22
Mounteth with occasion, courage, 65
Mounting, 271
barbed steeds, instead of, 432
Mourn, 271
a year, then, 448
for her, to weep and, 189
makes countless thousands, 192
where thou dost weep, 125
Mourned, and by strangers, 139
longer, would have, 20
Mourner bowed, not like a, 299
Mournful rhymes, ring out my, 336
Mournfully, think of her, 454
Mourning, 271
by, the Old Year went, 119
keep, sullen moods of, 365
year were past, would heaven this, 464
Mouse, 271
labouring mountain must bring forth a, 270
or most magnanimous, 422
not even a, 51
Mousing for vermin, 70
Mouth, 271
as household words, familiar in his, 275
even in the cannon's, 373
for rhetoric he could not ope his, 335
from a female, 210
ginger shall be hot i' the, 427
he always looked a gift-horse in the, 151
it, but if you, 379
look a gift-horse in the, 151
Mouth
of a woman, point-blank from the, 283
of hell, back from the, 80
of the cannon, that speaks from the, 314
this concealed man out of thy, 383
which hath the deeper, 213
with his brazen, 22
Mouth-filling oath, a good, 287
Mouth-friends, you knot of, 146
Mouthful, all at a, 133
Mouth-honour, breath, 223
Mouth-made vows, those, 428
Mouths in a glass, but she made, 453
into their, 33
Move a horse, kick that scarce would, 201
a soul in agony, mirth cannot, 264
easiest who have learned to dance, as those, 467
her, when looking well can't, 294
like the snail, or, 446
out if you think you're underpaid, 413
sun doth, 97
the world, the imponderables, 237
upward, working out the beast, 20
wheresoe'er thou, 244
Moved, nor is not, 273
Movement makes or mars me, this, 247
Moves his doubtful arms, and, 442
on, having writ, 465
she, 200
the whole creation, 322
Moving seems asleep, tide as, 18
Mower whets his scythe, the, 307
MSS., no creeds, . . . or, 220
Much at once, either to, 383
receives, who, 26
the hurt cannot be, 189
the lady protests too, 319
to do, so, 94
who love too, 237
who talk too, 396
Muck, money is like, 266
Muddle, 271
Muezza's call, the, 154
Muffled drums, like, 163
Mug in hand, with, 440
Multiplied with theirs the weekly bill, 94
Multiplies, stock of lies in circulation, 82
Multiplying ever-more, 53
Multitude, 271
make virtue of the faith, 34
Multitude's hum, and the, 136
Multitudinous seas incarnadine, 169
Multitudinous-eddying light, dawn of, 18
Murder, 272
could not kill, that, 252
ez fer war I call it, 431
works, the spirit of, 35
Murdered them in clusters, 372

Murderer's frown, the, 384
Murderers, gods on, 28
Murders, 272
doing more, 158
our youth with his sorrow and sin, 406
twenty mortal, 90
Murmur in the breast, in the, 23
Murmured, Father, I thank thee, 109
some kind voice had, 116
Murmurs, with endless and profitless, 451
Muse, 272
he loved, by the, 385
of the many-twinkling feet, 129
the poet's, 217
the subject of the comic, 234
Music, 272, 273
and art, without poetry, 63
and die in, 273
arose, and when, 334
and the dream, rebuild in it the, 567
free, to make thy, 10
in its roar, and, 457
in't, his very foot has, 138
I struck one chord of, 51
mute, will make the, 337
night shall be filled with, 44
of humanity, the still, sad, 188
of the union, step to the, 420
of those village bells, 52
of thousand tongues, 412
out, beat his, 97
passed in, 241
shed, the soul of, 170
tells, how many a tale their, 23
to attending ears, like softest, 412
to bring out their, 397
with books and, 101
Musician, that little airy, 210
Musketeers, one by one the, 181
Musket-shot, volley on volley, 42
Mussels, saffron, red peppers, 32
Must, 273
but what we, 229
not be, it, 315
when duty whispers low thou, 104
yet die we, 89
Mustard, piece of beef and, 22
of mordant, 349
Mustered out, a soldier of the Union, 373
Mute, and pages stand, 317
grief must then be, 38
inglorious Milton, some, 168
let's be, 172
lips apart, standing with, 115
on Tara's walls, hangs as, 170
will make the music, 337
would be still and, 10
Mutiny rash and undutiful, 20
Mutter their affairs, in their sleeps will, 371
Muttered in hell, 't was, 167
Mutton and porridge, pray a month with, 312
Muttons, to return to our, 439
Mutual admiration, a society of, 3
happiness, one, 170
Myriads who, that of the, 72
Myself am heaven and hell, 178
am hell, 178
I sup upon, 9
with yesterday's seven thousand years, 411
Mysteries, athwart all, 261
of grace, God hath his, 154
of that magic tool, knows the, 467
Mysterious one, and proud, 151
way, God moves in a, 154
Mystery, a sense of, 69
and in that, 313
of the ships, beauty and, 360
swift to be hurled, to death's, 244
to the world, marvel and a, 255

N

Nag, the forced gait of a shuffling, 309
Nail, a lie for every, 187
blows his, 190
the conscious needle, 279
to the mast her holy flag, 133
Nailed for our advantage, 67
her colours to the mast, 58
Nails, 273
come near your beauty with my, 59
shall handle you, thus our, 304
Naked, 274
in December snow, wallow, 191
though locked up in steel, 12
through the world, lash the rascals, 439
truth, patching fig-leaves for the, 416
Nakedness, not in utter, 25
Name, 274, 275
a deed without a, 83
a local habitation and a, 308
and memory, for my, 258
are committed in thy, 217
before his sacred, 231
beyond the sky, waft thy, 125
cant of a Saviour's, 208
cup of water in His, 69
deserves no, 147
each heart recalled a different, 241
have not an R in their, 292
he who once has won a, 1
in print, to see one's, 30
is a tower of strength, the king's, 202
is Death, a Reaper whose, 79
is MacGregor, and my, 138
is woman, thy, 142
land that bears a well-known, 113
left a corsair's, 64
made life and love one, 454
mark the marble with his, 53
of action, lose the, 61
of augurs, got the ill, 31

Name
of Christ, in the, 242
of Crispian, rouse him at the, 66
of fear, a, 419
of gentleman, grand old, 150
of her husband, calls the, 99
of Washington, bequeathed the, 434
proud his, 65
rise up, in his, 358
rum I take to be the, 344
shall yet warrant thy fame, 226
spoken, I hear thy, 428
stand back to back in God 's, 131
takes a specious, 272
than French crown, a fairer, 332
their love can scarce deserve the, 233
the tongue o' man can, 457
to be known by, if thou hast no, 445
to have . . . a, 123
to our Old Nick, gave 's, 281
the underlying dead, stones that, 468
upon a, 123
were liable to fear, 126
with the whistling of a, 123
we hailed it in God 's, 154
without a stone, a, 334
Named, when thou 'rt, 162
Names, 275
and calls sweet, 255
but few have any, 355
have left great, 145
he loved to hear, the, 252
I name no, 163
murders disguised by philosophic, 272
ye gi'e poor frailty, 142
Nameless and dateless, 373
grave, sat by some, 163
unremembered acts, little, 201
Nan, such mistress such, 255
Nancy Low has married Mr. R———, 53
Nap, calmness about its, 171
taken out his, 269
Napes of your necks, toward the, 355
Napkin, while we send for the, 211
Napkins tacked together, two, 361
Napping, while I nodded, nearly, 261
Narcissa spoke, that poor, 75
Narrow, 276
frith, intersected by a, 110
gate, the house with the, 187
house, and the, 362
Narrower, 276
day, men that in a, 106
Nassau, can Bourbon or, 317
Nasty ideas, a man of, 281
Nation, 276, 277
and of every, 193
brutes no longer, deem our, 58
darlings of our, 72
he hates our sacred, 193
how long, O cruel, 413
of shopkeepers, fit only for a, 361
Nation
of traders, a, 361
once to every man and, 83
survive, rather than let the, 431
the mourning of a mighty, 271
to hate another, 110
wildly looks at nation, 115
who should make the laws of a, 16
Nation 's care, the naval stores the, 353
prey, were every, 157
wounds, to bind up the, 337
Nations, and with all, 337
fear our cry, let the, 143
friendships with all, 6
intercourse with foreign, 65
judge of the, 139
know, let fierce contending, 93
like o'erloaded asses, 55
make enemies of, 110
the ingenious youth of, 135
the litanies of, 24
the Niobe of, 283
to foreign, 258
vainly aim, at which all modern, 110
Native daring which instils, 72
heath, my foot is on my, 138
here, though I am, 70
land, good-night, my, 160
land, my, my own, 65
land, the violet of his, 426
sod, appealing from his, 388
Nativity, 277
Natural to die as to be born, 88
right, generalities of, 149
to women, comes, 283
Naturalists enough, we are not, 210
observe, so, 134
Nature, 277, 278
all, is but art, 337
and custom agree, 455
and nature 's laws lay hid, 281
and time and change, 154
appalled, 162
but to write and read comes by, 466
change the stamp of, 421
cries, the voice of, 35
diseased, oftentimes breaks forth, 277
done in my days of, 380
extremes in, 117
faith in God and, 156
first made man, as free as, 350
fits all her children, 67
formed but one such man, 359
fortress built by, 112
free and open, 183
free proclaims that man, 217
getteth short of leaves, book of, 216
hath assigned, that God and, 263
her custom holds, 399
in all the pomp of beauty reigns, 217
is the art of God, 13
lies in his true, 289
made thee, to temper man, 452
made us men, great, 259
might stand up, that, 250

Nature
mild, not by, 341
never made, a death which, 81
of a tragic volume, 38
out from the heart of, 24
passing through, 89
scorn the shocking hat, man and, 171
seem at once to lose their, 413
shall waken their free, 466
sink in years, 191
swears, auld, 211
the force of, 309
the grossness of his, 189
the laws of, 101
they say, doth dote, 179
tickled with success, such a, 392
to pangs of, 160
to, 't is their, 95
to which the laws of, 356
true wit is, 447
we are by, 83
we fools of, 268
wherever outraged, 144
which God and, 383
will endure, the punishment thy, 450
Nature's agreeable blunders, one of, 450
aspect, nothing in, 75
chief masterpiece is writing well, 467
debt, but, 89
eldest law, self-defence is, 356
end of language, 210
holy law is drinking, 101
kindly law, by, 49
laws lay hid in night, 281
own sweet and cunning hand, 21
second course, great, 370
sober found, nothing in, 101
soft nurse, 370
teachings, list to, 362
Natures never vary, whose, 323
the same with common, 280
with sweet kind, 330
Naughty night to swim in, a, 282
world, good deed in a, 42
Nauseous draught, for a, 172
Nautilus, 278
Naval stores the nation's care, the, 353
Navarre, blazed the helmet of, 179
the helmet of, 308
Navies came, your nutshell, 284
our, melt away, 139
ride, rich, 385
Navigation's soul, 60
Navy, 278
Near bred, a neighbour and, 60
from far and, 52
he comes too, 427
is God to man, so, 104
port or bay, in some, 73
the matin to be, 153
the time of universal peace is, 299
your beauty with my nails, 59
Nearer, 278
and nearer, drawing, 339
Nearest and dearest, truest, the, 146
do the work that's, 460
to the stroke, 127
when friends are, 331
Nearing the place, I am, 78
Neat cookery, but his, 62
or leave them, 20
still to be, 99
Neat's leather, a shoe be Spanish or, 20
Nebulæ, as we talked of, 241
Necessary, 279
cat, harmless, 45
end, death a, 80
for one people, it becomes, 356
Necessities, 279
Necessity, 279
Neck, a collar grows right round his, 60
curved is each, 387
down her exquisite, 339
'round Donald's, 176
Necks, should trust our, 311
Nectar, the water, 197
Ned Cuttle bite his nail, when you see, 273
Cuttle's aground, you may know, 273
lands and tenements to, 91
Need a lie, nothing can, 218
deserted at his utmost, 86
for her time of, 277
is great, whoever thou art whose, 242
of drink, but little, 101
of help, what, 315
of property, he hath no, 319
predestined by that, 248
so great, or the, 409
with another's, 181
your woe, they do not, 329
Needed, the treasure back when, 149
Needle, 279
and thread, hinders, 438
and thread, plying her, 360
she, for the, 454
the mother wi' her, 270
to the pole, true as the, 88
Needle's eye, the postern of a, 42
Needless Alexandrine ends the song, 6
Needlessly sets foot upon a worm, man who, 463
Needs, 279
friendship's solid mason-work below, 242
it most, a fault which, 218
our tastes, our, 381
Neglect, 280
me, lose me, 378
such sweet, more taketh me, 364
Negligent, than by the, 46
Neigh of the steed, and the, 136
Neighbour, and love my, 413
further gone than he, thinks his, 284
grind great or small, if, 207

Neighbour, his hungering, 181
to whom I am a, 60
Neighbouring eyes, the cynosure of, 70
Neighbour's shame, publishing our, 351
Neighbours came and buried Brother John, 265
things that had niver been, 16
Neighbours' faults and folly, your, 305
lasted, as long 's their, 267
Nell, 280
Nepenthe, 280
Neptune's ocean, will all great, 169
Nerve, 280
tends their strength to, 37
Nerveless grasp, dropped from her, 142
Nerves, he shoots his thoughts by hidden, 86
my firm, 72
to thrill, quivering, 419
Nerveth his arm for life's combat, who, 410
Nest, 280
affrighted from his, 181
are chirping in the, 469
at peep of day, 25
behold I will build me a, 156
dangerous to disturb a hornet's, 186
down to the baby's, 91
drove from out the mother's, 106
in the puttock's, 41
leaves the well-built, 175
she has two warm eggs in her, 97
Nestle with the dove, the hawk shall, 300
Nestling so long, where he has been, 64
Nests upon the ground, pleasure lark-like, 316
Net, here's a fish hangs in the, 214
the dreamless head, thy fibres, 468
this, was twisted by the sisters three, 127
of the fowler, is the, 280
Nets, 280
Nettle, 280
the world is a, 449
Never, 280
at all to be getting a wife, 16
better late than, 211
better once than, 290
ceaseth to enlarge itself, 53
did this England, 112
for ever, 55
met, or never parted, 37
to have loved at all, 242
visit thee, 69
was on sea or land, 225
would lay down my arms, 8
Nevermore, quoth the raven, 17, 19, 246
New, 281
all ain't good thet's, 469
and happy land, in the, 48
are tried, by whom the, 126
birth of our new soil, 8
boots, like, 161
New
books, reading, 31
came dancing after, 119
customs, 70
era, birth of each, 115
face at the door, 119
friendship, is neither strong nor pure, 146
fortunes, a hazard of, 141
look amaist as weel 's the, 270
moon late yestreen, I saw the, 267
ones hunt folks 's corns out, 161
or old, if too, 126
ring in the, 339
shoes with old riband, tying his, 322
told, an ancient tale, 400
we seek for, 46
when this old ring was, 338
world into existence, 16
Year, of all the glad, 256
New-born and truth, 416
each second, I 'm, 376
sun, flush of a, 13
New England, 281
Newest kind of ways, the, 367
New-hatched unfledged comrade, 146
New-lighted, like the herald Mercury, 250
New-made honour doth forget men 's names, 275
Newport News, an unknown grave at, 373
News, 281
on the Rialto, what, 336
who bringeth him, 319
Newt, eye of, 179
Newton, 281
Next day, till, 26
the, in majesty, 309
time you come, the, 338
Ney, Marshal, 34
Nice, 281
too delicately, 345
Nicholas, Saint, soon would be there, 51
Nick, 281
Nickleby, and among them Mr., 379
Nigger, 281
squat on her safety-valve, 346
Nigh, thou dost not bite so, 24
Nigher, she knowed the Lord was, 50
Night, 281, 282
a bed by, 295
a cap by, 282
across the day, beyond the, 463
all seasons, day and, 361
an atheist half believes a God, by, 14
and day, to shine by, 245
another such a, 99
as darker grows the, 185
a sound of revelry by, 334
a sweet vision I saw, 427
and chill, dark the, 211
an infant crying in the, 192
and it is, 18

Night
are dull as, 273
away, talked the, 68
away, the long, long, 105
before Christmas, 't was the, 51
boldly say each, 408
both drear and dark, 26
breathing through the, 36
but the blackness of, 207
came forth on her wedding, 55
came on a hurricane, one, 188
Chaos and eternal, 46
day brought back my, 98
death-fires danced at, 81
drinking all, 101
emparadise the, 65
ever sence one, 330
fate of a nation was riding that, 276
from primeval, 419
gear, doffs his, 210
has flown, black bat, 148
he makes a supper, this, 393
he that drinks all, 169
here's to the, 361
hideous, making, 268
how beautiful is, 268
in England ne'er had been, such, 111
in storms, to watch the, 189
in June, forget that, 72
in the icy air of, 23
in the forests of the, 405
in the, imagining, 128
into the heavy, 313
is beginning to lower, 50
is done, comes when the, 73
is still, the, 23, 52
is past, the, 269
like the quarry-slave, at, 227
my dream of life from morn till, 236
nature's laws lay hid in, 281
now I often wish the, 331
of cloudless climes and starry skies, 430
of earth is faded, till the, 429
oft in the stilly, 258
of uncreated, 90
one planet in a starless, 462
or day, sleep shall neither, 370
passed a miserable, 99
sank upon the dusky beach, 111
shall be filled with music, 44
shall be with you that, 116
she came tearin' along that, 346
ships that pass in the, 360
shorter, these make the long, 440
should have stood that, 95
shut up the lambs at, 404
silver lining on the, 56
silver-sweet sound lovers' tongues by, 412
sleeping woods all, 37
son of the sable, 81
steal a few hours from the, 74
stuck to me day and, 286
that, affrighted from his nest, 181
that, at Bunker's Hill, 40

Night
that covers me, out of the, 376
that first we met, the, 343
that makes me, this is the, 247
the bell struck in the, 200
the day, follow as the, 415
the drowsy ear of, 22
through the, 17
toiling upward in the, 177
to walk the, 380
unseen, in the, 87
we parted by, 296
what of the, watchman, 435
will hallow the day, the, 442
worked and sung from morn till, 262
Nightcap, 282
Nightcaps, threw up their sweaty, 43
Night-cloud had lowered, for the, 39
Night-crow cried, the, 25
Night-dress, lectures in her, 295
Night-gown, in his, 443
Nightingale, 283
roar you an 't were any, 339
Nightly, 283
Night's dominions, mid the, 284
repose, has earned a, 410
watching, for this, 362
Nights and larks are flying, 151
God made sech, 152
such as sleep o', 126
Night-song of mirth, the, 125
Night-winds sigh, the, 2
Nihil, has been Vaux et præterea, 423
Nile, an allegory on the banks of the, 6
my serpent of old, 356
Nimble wit, you have a, 447
Nimmed a cloak, who 't was, that, 306
Ninepence a day for killing folks, 272
Nineteen nineteen six, annual expenditure, 192
Nineveh and Tyre, is one with, 139
Ninth he was born, 't was the, 348
moon, with this, 18
part of a hair, 45
Niobe, 283
Nipping and an eager air, 5
Nips his root, 164
No, 283
birds in last year's nest, 280
creeds to guide them, 220
man can gather cherries in Kent, 48
man can help you die, 129
man relies on, whose word, 202
man see me more, 122
man's pie is freed, 8
man's pleasure, for, 39
man therein doctor, and, 200
more, may return, 77
sun, no moon, 285
to-day, and yet say, 468
Nobility, 284
Noble, 284
and to be, 148
deeds, this latter age with, 422
dish, a, 32

Noble
fool, a, was never in a fault, 397
game, never seeing, 70
he's as, 248
horsemanship, the world with, 187
nook, grant him now some, 149
savage ran, the, 350
things, not dream them, do, 374
thoughts, accompanied with, 403
to be good, only, 148
words, like perfect music unto, 273
Nobleman should do, live cleanly as a, 346
Nobleman's consumption, discontent the, 93
Noblemen to tailors, from, 347
Nobler modes of life, ring in the, 252
parts, before the, 148
than the last, 376
we attain, to something, 170
whether 't is, 19
Nobles, a state without king or, 59
Noblest cause, undertake the, 143
mind the best contentment has, 62
offspring, time's, 109
Roman of them all, 341
thing which perished there, the, 121
work, her, 211
work of God, 183
Nobly, acts, 24
as the thing is high, 120
Nobodies, four hundred, were ruined, 379
Nobody never made me, do n't think, 166
Nobody's tater-patch pokes, an' into, 356
Nod, affects to, 155
to tumble down, with every, 346
who at thy, 151
Nodding their heads, 36
Noddle, comb your, 59
Noddy, our mayor's a, 256
Nods and becks, 196
and winks, one that, 301
Noise about thy keel, I hear the, 200
and humming, the city's rout and, 264
hear a, 83
he spoke 'em, when with hasty, 458
inexplicable dumb-shows and, 379
like of a hidden brook, 37
of the mourning, to the, 271
of waters, what dreadful, 102
that with the very, 98
with it, make no more, 273
Noiseless falls the foot of time, 406
tenor of their way, 68
Noiselessly as the daylight, 73
as the spring-time, 382
Noises in a swound, like, 190
Noisy, 284
Nominated in the bond, 29
"Non nobis," let there be sung, 156
None at all, or, 383
are so surely caught, 447
None but himself can be his parallel, 295
but the brave, 34
by resignation, 289
can love, whom, 26
dares do more is, 72
go just alike, 434
or grant me, 124
would do beside, few or, 159
Nonsense of their stone ideal, 385
Nook, grant him now some noble, 149
is left, while yet a, 110
Noon, 284
he fell, from morn to, 122
no morn, no, 285
not the blaze of, 4
riding near her highest, 268
the bloody sun at, 63
shadow, which he treads on at, 392
will look, the, 269
Noose, to gripe of, 311
Norman blood, simple faith than, 148
North, 284
nail the conscious needle to the, 279
of 'Fifty-three, runs, 212
the frozen bosom of the, 444
Northern sky, the pale glory of the, 245
star, constant as the, 62
whistling, like our harsh, 210
North-northwest, I am but mad, 245
Nor'wester, 285
Nose, 285
blaspheme custard through the, 322
down his innocent, 398
got in his, 142
led by the, 158
liberty plucks justice by the, 199
must often wipe a bloody, 323
on the doctor's, 94
turned up in scornful curve, 304
was as sharp as a pen, his, 359
with spectacle on, 294
Nosegays from street to street, hawks, 343
Noses, 285
Nostril all wide, with his, 386
Not enough to help the feeble, 129
to be, to be or, 19
one to throw at a dog, 95
Note, 285
deed of dreadful, 83
every, with sorrow stirred, 340
for a' that, it lacks a, 248
not a funeral, 102
not so strong a, 136
of him, why then take no, 422
of me, some, 409
of praise, swells the, 10
of thy departure, and no friend take, 86
of time, we take no, 407
slept as sound as if I'd paid a, 371
the simplest, 293
Note-book, set in a 15
Notes a chiel's amang you, taking, 317
with many a winding bout, in, 394

Nothing, 285
and gives to airy, 308
before and nothing behind, 288
but leaves, 215
but talk of his horse, 187
can be known, 206
can we call our own, 80
first, all at once and, 303
gives, but, 26
I confess, 60
in 't, although there 's, 30
in the world is single, 366
in this age, he can do, 352
is dead, 76
is known, 77
long, and, 114
more, and it was, 316
more, only this and, 261
much before, was, 420
o' the sort, 42
speaks an infinite deal of, 327
'tis something, 275
to wear, really and truly I 've, 437
trust that man in, 62
up, in drawing, 39
went unrewarded but desert, 421
which thou art not, be, 236
Nothing 's so hard, 14
Notice, and hang a wooden, 345
Notion, and foolish, 355
and wishes, I 've a, 388
so unholy, will not own a, 176
Notions fudge, in vain we call old, 386
Nought, it disperse to, 53
shall make us rue, 112
to do, ye 've, 305
Noun, 'twixt participle and, 386
Nourish all the world, 118
Nourished by my victuals, one that am, 240
how, 124
in the womb of pia mater, 258
Nourisher in life 's feast, chief, 370
Nourishing a youth sublime, 352
Nourishment which is called supper, 393
Novel, 285
November, 285
Novice she could say, what to a, 255
Now and forever, 218
Nozzle agin the bank, he 'd hold her, 329
Null, splendidly, 128
Number his kisses, who can, 205
his sins, no one can, 366
more than ever women spoke, in, 429
One, to call at, 290
the stars in the heaven, 205
Numbers, 286
brings home full, 425
I lisped in, 466
in mournful, 222
sanctified the crime, 272
Numbing hands, beats and blows his, 207
Nunnery, 286
Nuptial love maketh mankind, 232
Nurse it, take it up and, 64
breed and, 311
nature 's soft, 370
of young desire, hope thou, 185
to rear, to bear, to, 19
will scratch the, 341
Nursed, 286
a dear gazelle, I never, 148
Nursery, go to their, 247
Nurse 's lap, a monster coiling in its, 416
Nurses dangerous humours, 431
the wife who, 89
Nursing her wrath, 465
Nurtures a deep and honest love, 173
Nut, 286
Nut-brown ale, the, 6
ale, the spicy, 6
bowl, the jolly, 32
Nutmeg-graters, be rough as, 280
Nuts and wine, among the, 396
quarrel with a man for cracking, 322
Nutrition, to draw, 306
Nymph, haste thee, 196
Nymphs, tell me, what power divine, 58

O

Oak, 286
a lumberer felling an, 314
and holly, where English, 304
fell the hardest-timbered, 390
had got a deputy of, 216
his angle-rod made of a sturdy, 439
or bend a knotted, 272
stand, let the old, 398
Oaken bucket, the old, 39
Oaks, tall, from little acorns grow, 2
Oar, 286
my soul is like the, 376
spread the thin, 278
Oars, 286, 287
Oat-cakes, but Scotch, 352
Oath, 287
by yea and nay, her pretty, 306
obliges not, though an, 394
that I will have my bond, 29
to vent, nor was he ever known an, 345
Oaths, 287
are oracles, 29
are straw, the strongest, 70
full of strange, 373
that make the truth, not the many, 417
they swear fierce, 259
Oats, nor eat dried, 251
Obadias, young, David, Josias, 305
Obdurate heart, no flesh in man 's, 38
Obedience, and true, 189
to God, is, 328
troops of friends, 223
Obedient to his honest will, not, 454
Obeisance made he, not the least, 325

Obey, 287
bound to serve, love and, 456
love, honour and, 45
to endure, command, to, 113
woman to, 454
you proud monarchs must, 81
you well, the rogues, 280
Obeyed in office, a dog 's, 289
Obeys, when she, 400
Object, for every, 196
Objection to a pot of beer, have no, 110
Obligation to posterity, 311
Obliges not, though an oath, 394
Oblivion, alms for, 407
and mere, 49
Obscure, they walk, 200
Obscures, no mist, 268
the show of evil, 213
Obscurity, repose in, 114
Observance of civility, use all the, 372
than in the, 70
Observation, 287
attempt at an, 389
that youth and, 331
Observations which ourselves we make, to, 445
Observed, if he be, 161
of all observers, the, 263
he is a great, 126
Observer 's sake, we grow more partial for th', 445
Observers, the observed of all, 263
Obsoletest words, revive the, 379
Obstinacy, 287
Obstruction, to lie in cold, 90
Obtain or die, I knew but to, 233
Occasion, 287
and have more, 238
courage mounteth with, 65
for his wit, 196
to forbear, 138
upon the mellowing of, 258
Occasions, 288
flog them upon all, 135
frame my face to all, 118
he had cleaned out the town, on several, 350
new, teach new duties, 281
Occupation, absence of, 333
Occupation 's gone, Othello 's, 125
Occupations, pause in the day 's, 50
Ocean, 288
like the round, 268
naked breadth of the, 99
of life, so on the, 360
of truth, the great, 417
or grasp the, 263
paths, long lay the, 245
resembles, 377
ship upon a painted, 359
the dark unfathomed caves of, 149
to be upon the, 388
will all great Neptune 's, 169
Ocean-bird, like the, 354
Ocean 's cheek, the crimson streak on, 73
dreamless ooze, in, 299
misty tears, 101
my home, the, 4
October, 288
falls with the leaf . . . in, 372
Odd numbers, divinity in, 286
numbers, there 's luck in, 286
the people 's voice is, 301
Oddities, storehouse of comical, 16
Oddity, frolic and fun, 197
Odds, facing fearful, 89
with morning, almost at, 282
Odious, in woollen, 75
she and comparisons are, 60
Odour, stealing and giving, 273
Odourous, comparisons are, 60
Odours crushed, as, 191
had blown its gentle, 408
virtue is like precious, 427
Œdipus-people is coming fast, 301
O'er again, all his battles, 19
when it 's, 94
O'ercast, the smile that no cloud can, 31
O'erdoing Termagant, for, 379
O'erdriven, pity for a horse, 187
O'erdusted, gilt, 103
O'erflowing, without, full, 84
O'ergreen my bad, so you, 160
O'erleaps itself, vaulting ambition which, 7
O'erloaded asses, nations like, 55
O'er-perch these walls, did I, 239
O'erstep not the modesty of nature, 278
O'erthrown, what a noble mind is here, 263
Off with his head, 171
Offence, 289
and forgave the, 289
be pardoned and retain the, 295
forgive my foul, 429
from amorous causes springs, dire, 414
is a sour, 346
is rank, my, 272
sufficient ransom for, 375
the visage of, 260
tongue did make, 118
yet detest th', 289
Offences, 289
Offend, broken into shards if we, 107
to flatter or, 46
Offender, 289
the, never pardons, 140
Offending soul alive, the most, 185
Offends me to the soul, it, 379
Offer of kindness to make to a woman, 315
you friendship, of all who, 146
Office, 289
by virtue of your, 401
hath but a losing, 281
is to interpret law, 198

Office
of a wall, 112
placed, in, 386
the ascent to high, 305
the insolence of, 323
the lust of, 259
the spoils of, 259
to git some on 'em, 11
truly by your, 401
Officer, 289
thief doth fear each bush an, 394
Offices for gold, sell and mart your, 294
Official, 289
Officials, 289
Offspring, time's noblest, 109
true source of human, 437
Oft, yet seen too, 425
Often told, and, 15
Oftener you come here, 59
O'Grady, his uncle an, 348
Oil, after my flame lacks, 228
and the twopence, without the, 349
consumed the midnight, 215
from Lucca crown, the spoon with, 349
lavished life's best, 416
of mid-day sun and midnight, 409
this cruse of, 12
vinegar, sugar and saltness agree, 349
Oils, like a witch's, 81
Oily, 289
Old, 290
age, accompany, 223
age is still old age, 4
age ne'er cools, 4
age of cards, and, 462
age past, 155
age, that which should accompany, 223
a head, body with so, 171
and rich, when thou art, 336
and the stars are, 240
as I am, for ladies' love unfit, 20
as I am, my lusty limbs appear, 357
aside, last to lay the, 126
as the ten commandments, 59
but his experience, 198
but she may learn, not yet so, 215
clock on the stair, 55
come forth to play, 71
days, the reverence of, 121
fashions please me best, 126
friends are best, 146
grow, along with me, 24
grow dear as they grow, 14
growing in drawing nothing up, 39
hugged by the, 157
Hundred ring, when he made, 50
if too new or, 126
in the brave days of, 341
in times of, 69
let young and, 150
loved the place of, 175
man, a good, 397
Old
man, a poor, infirm, weak and despised, 310
man, a very foolish fond, 251
man, broken with storms, 29
man do but die, 4
man, do n't think the poetry is dead in an, 309
man, do wi' an, 211
man eloquent, that, 108
man is twice a child, an, 250
man, that is an, 183
man, the sorrows of a poor, 375
men, wale of, 130
men are to this vice of lying, 244
men fools, young men think, 469
men's dream, the, 98
men shall dream dreams, 98
oaken bucket, the, 39
of all the living, young or, 228
old fashion, the, 191
one, no fool like the, 137
one of them is fat and grows, 259
opinions, rags and tatters, 110, 143
read in story, 15
riband, tying his new shoes with, 322
ring out the, 339
sakes' sake, for, 96
sat Freedom, of, 144
say I'm growing, 204
shoes, used to call for his, 146
South Church, shall freedom stand in the, 32
tale and often told, 15
the face grows, 211
the saying wise and, 28
the troubadours of, 414
though I look, 357
when you are, 131
without a friend, 462
with service, weary and, 153
woman knew what he said, the, 326
world, redress the balance of the, 16
Year went mourning by, 119
Olden time, all of the, 149
Older a guv'ment is, th', 161
fashion yet, for that, 191
than we, of those who were, 236
that one grows, the, 212
Oldest kind of sins, commit the, 367
Old-particular brandy-punchy feeling, 129
Old-world moulds aside she threw, 179
Olives they were not blind to Him, the, 458
Olympus-high, hills of seas, 400
Omen, dark and high, what, 398
Once, 290
a year, for Christmas comes but, 52
departed, and, 77
has loved, who, 117
heaved, hearts but, 77
I'll play the housewife for this, 188
in doubt, to be, 97

Once
man can die but, 89
that Peter was respected, 128
to every man and nation, 83
utter the I, where you, 319
One, 290
and inseparable, 218
and the heart but, 281
another, and each for, 418
apple had she, only, 115
bee in a hive, with, 184
blush there was but, 434
bottom trusted, not in, 424
by one, ye must pay for, 365
day end it, will, 109
don't take at Number, 13
eagle's fate and mine are, 106
feast, one house, 170
fell swoop, 49
foot in the grave, 164
for sense and one for rhyme, 335
God, one law, one element, 322
grew before, where only, 162
heart, I have, 174
heart, one bed, 174
he seemed to be not, 114
hour ten, grief makes, 165
I'll get better, for, 329
incorporate two in, 53
I never knew but, 145
I shall find, 79
life shall be destroyed, not, 160
life, one flag, one fleet, one throne, 133
man, the wit of, 320
man picked out of, 183
man's poison, what's, 309
man with God is a majority, 247
many still must labour for the, 207
more evil turn, wants but, 173
of the twenty, than to be, 397
of two things, on, 449
of us, shall, 36
party, he's been true to, 62
place there is, 114
planet in a starless night, 462
poor hole, trusts to, 271
returns to tell us, not, 72
small head could carry, 456
spot where I made, 152
step, nor from hell, 178
the day but, 281
thing, now it is not, 308
thing to be tempted, 't is, 400
thing we both may loathe, 409
thought no more of being, 241
touch of nature, 278
virtue, linked with, 64
with Nineveh and Tyre, 139
yard below their mines, 110
One-horse shay, the wonderful, 46
Onion atoms lurk, let, 349
the tears live in an, 398
Onions, garlic, roach and dace, 32
mine eyes smell, 438
Onward, they must upward still and, 281
Oonalaska's shore, wolf's long howl from, 449
Ooze, in ocean's dreamless, 299
Oozing out, I feel it, 423
Ope his mouth, he could not, 335
my lips, when I, 291
Open air, God of the, 155
all ways do lie, 267
and both free, 84
as day, a hand, 161
as the sea, 267
or understood, war, 431
question, is not marriage an, 253
the door is, 96
the door of thy heart, 240
the door with shame, 96
the gates are mine to, 276
their thousand leaves, 382
then the door, 77
the old cigar-box, 53
thy heart and door, 242
war, my sentence is for, 430
which I with sword will, 293
Opened, and kept open, 31
Opening in the thatch, an, 68
paradise, to him are, 293
roar, the cannon's, 12
Opens his vasty jaws, this hungry war, 432
wide, threatening to devour me, 178
Opinion, 290
he gave it for his, 162
of God, better to have no, 153
to be dressed in an, 291
what is your, Mrs. Grundy, 345, 393
with Pythagoras to hold, 378
Opinions, 290
and a will, who possess, 259
of mankind, respect to the, 356
old, 110, 143
stiff in, 114
with a wager, back their own, 429
Opportunities, a woman with fair, 255
Oppose, fat pig and goose itself, 322
my patience to his fury, 298
Opposed may beware of thee, that the, 322
Opposing, and by, 19
and enduring forces, 60
Opposite, still so perverse and, 302
Oppress, dumps the mind, 166
Oppressed, 290
Oppression and deceit, rumor of, 229
Oppressor's wrong, the, 323
Oracle, 291
Oracles, his oaths are, 29
Orations, make no long, 32
Orator, 291
Orb, in her circled, 268
of one particular tear, in the small, 398
Orbed maiden with white fire laden, that, 268

Orbs of flame, and its, 419
a shadow lies, in whose, 246
Orcades, in Scotland, at the, 284
Orchard, sleeping within my, 4
the meadow, the, 49
Orchard-robbing, then 's the time for, 386
Orchestra business, that has no, 210
Ordain, drinking joys did first, 16
Ordained the Sabbath, he who, 310
Order, 291
honour, civil right, law an', 212
nominate in, 218
of your going, stand not upon the, 157
Reverends of every, 75
this matter better in France, they, 142
to haud the wretch in, 184
Orders grey, friar of, 145
to perform, the Almighty 's, 388
Ore, I hammer the, 386
the purest, 41
Oregon, where rolls the, 74
Organ, 291
came from the soul of the, 51
'gins to swell, the, 264
rings, and the, 264
will speak with most miraculous, 272
Organ-pipe of frailty, from the, 273
thunder that deep and dreadful, 405
Organs, 291
dimensions, 197
Oriflamme to-day, be your, 308
Original, 291
is dust, when the, 123
proclaim, their great, 132
Orion, 291
Ormus and of Ind, wealth of, 107
Ornament, needs not the foreign aid of, 3
thereunto, a help and a, 318
to be a moment 's, 302
with fair, 330
Orphan, for his widow and his, 337
Orpheus, who found no remedy, 279
Orthodox, flashing conviction, 314
prove their doctrine, 329
Orthodoxy, 291
Osawatomie Brown raised his right hand, 424
Brown said, Boys, the Lord will aid us, 38
O'Shaughnessy, his aunt was an, 348
Osprey to the fish, as is the, 278
Ostent, well studied in a sad, 372
Othello 's jealous doubt spout out, 115
occupation 's gone, 125
Other dear charmer away, 47
people, no more piety than, 52
things give place, all, 209
Others . . . because they never parted, 295
declare, while, 348
does not infringe the rights of, 338
Others misfortunes and pains of, 265
must not leave it to, 96
on lips that are for, 205
roar aloud, 36
said No, 317
see us, as, 355
show, that mercy I to, 260
suspect the thoughts of, 51
that we know not of, 79
where are the, 163
Others' good, glow for, 174
Otherwise, I cannot do, 383
Ought, not because he, 159
to, an' so we 'd, 111
to be, it is but had n't, 346
Ounce of dross costs its ounce of gold, each, 177
Our country, right or wrong, 65
Ours, and they are, 110
for ours is thine and mine, 235
the sea is, 353
Ourselves, but in, 127
do lie, our remedies oft, 330
to see, 355
't is in, 127
Out, 292
and Maggie and I are, 53
and such as are, 253
damned spot, out I say, 382
mordre wol, 272
of the jaws of death, 80
truth will, 417
Outbuilds the pyramids, virtue alone, 322
Outcast, 292
Outdone, human justice thus, 155
Outer distance, there lies an, 178
Outface it with their semblances, 394
them and outswear them too, 292
Outgrows the garments which it wore, 381
Out-herods Herod, it, 180
Outlawed, nor be, 64
Outlive his life half a year, 258
Outlived in fame, 123
Outlives pain, truth, 415
this day, he that, 66
Outrages, known to commit, 101
Outrun by violent swiftness, we may, 292
the constable at last, thou hast, 62
Outshone the wealth of Ormus, 107
Outside, a swashing and a martial, 394
of that, limitless space, 178
of his hand, 158
what a goodly, 122
Outstretched, with his arms, 167
Outswear, 292
Out-talk us all, this gentleman will, 396
Outvenoms all the worms of Nile, 368
Outward walls, banners on the, 17
Outweighs, what empire far, 317
Ouzel sings, where the, 419
Oven stopped, like an, 298
Oven 's mouth, sing at the, 66

Overcome him, enough to, 101
us like a summer's cloud, 56
Overcomes by force, who, 139
Overflows, and its secret, 173
Overhaul your catechism, 45
Overhead, that God is, 77
Overloaded, undermanned, meant to founder, 115
Over-polite to his customers, 15
Overpowered, thousands had sunk on the ground, 39
Overrunning, 292
Overthrow the head, than, 335
Overthrowing me, by, you threw me higher, 316
Overthrown more than your enemies, 465
Overtrusting, to worth in woman, 452
Overwhelmed in the strife, 61
Owe, 292
God a death, we, 89
Owes, 292
that dear perfection which he, 275
Owest, lend less than thou, 362
me thy love, thou, 292
Oweth to her husband, such a woman, 454
Owl, 292
he is the human, 70
scream, heard the, 83
shrieked at thy birth, 25
was by a mousing, 121
Owlet's wing, 179
Owlets flit, the blind, 446
Owls, answer him, ye, 282
Own, 292
a wish that she had hardly dared to, 446
blood, he forfeits his, 27
feather on the fatal dart, 106
hand of Douglas is his, 97
it seems so like my, 78
the happy lines, let a lord once, 231
the ocean, tu, we, 288
the soft impeachment, 191
this hind of princes peer, make me, 324
Owning her weakness, 351
Owns, he's only a pauper whom nobody, 298
it in the first degree, no creature, 284
Ox, 292
a brother to the, 388
might fell an, 248
Oxen, who drives fat, 126
Oxlips, and the nodding violet, 17
Oyster, 292, 293
as your pearl in your foul, 183

P

Pace at first, requires slow, 55
creeps in this petty, 411
in running, every, 344
'round the forbidden place, 292
Pace, time's, is so hard, 407
will not mend his, 33
Paced into the hall, 36
Paces, travels in divers, 406
two, of the vilest earth, 381
Pachas, the khan and the, 63
Pack, as a huntsman his, 145
o' rotten plates, 115
Pagan, 293
Page, 293
on the deathless, 418
prescribed, all but the, 127
Pageant, like this insubstantial, 428
Pages stand mute, and, 317
vacant, every life has, 221
Pagoda, by the old Moulmein, 251
Paid, 293
by another, shall be, 199
dear, very dear for his whistle, 440
in full, Lord God, we ha', 113
pleasure will be, 307
Paul, by robbing Peter he, 302
Pail, frozen home in, 190
Pain, 293
all the dull deep, 109
and anguish wring the brow, when, 453
a peace out of, 78
and woe, source of all his, 283
as a heart must be tried by, 158
aye, to the conscience, 390
balms for all our, 470
breathe their words in, 105
but wretchedness and, 76
darkness and cold, 78
error wounded writhes in, 415
is lessened, one, 131
it is the worst of, 243
it was to drown, 102
most human, in, 234
never mind the, 135
nor pleasure, have neither, 369
sure heirs of, 59
supreme, its loss must be the, 234
sweet is pleasure after, 16
that is not akin to, 375
that never feels a, 448
the bliss of dying, the, 105
the tender for another's, 392
thou shalt live in thy, 69
though full of, 90
to bear an untried, 436
to the bear, not because it gave, 321
too soon we part with, 360
truth outlives, 415
victor over death and, 199
Painful still, not to love nor, 243
Pain's resistless power, 175
Pains, died in bitter, 109
grow sharp, when, 224
it stings you for your, 280
my soul below, the wrong that, 160
of others, misfortunes and, 265
pay me for my, 104
reading, study, 67
she gave me for my, 363

Paint an inch thick, let her, 468
  no words can, 459
  the lily, to, 152
  the town red, 102
Painted blind, winged Cupid, 69
  fair, angels are, 452
  ship, as idle as a, 359
Painter, 294
  plays the spider, 168
Painter's brush, needs no, 152
Painters have fashioned, the, 207
Painting of a sorrow, 118
Paintings too, heard of your, 118
Pair, 294
  a youthful, loving, modest, 402
  kindest and the happiest, 138
  more close than wedded, 376
  of stairs, have they made a, 242
  that once was white, the, 153
Palace and a prison on each hand, a, 424
  in such a gorgeous, 30
  is, the hollow oak our, 286
  love in a, 235
  of the soul, the, 367
Palaces, the gorgeous, 428
Pale, 294
  and white and cold, 74
  at the raven's tale, and she grew, 326
  at which the world grew, 274
  cast of thought, 61
  grew thy cheek and cold, 296
  his ineffectual fire, 153
  index-learning turns no student, 192
  unripened beauties of the North, 284
Palinure's unaltered mood, with, 304
Pall, and shroud and, 362
  carry the warrior's, 271
  mute by the canopied, 317
  the hillside for a, 184
Pallas, 294
  perched upon a bust of, 325
Pall Mall, 294
Palm, 294
  bear the, 38
  do not dull thy, 146
  is hardly clean, 36
  of the brave, have carried the, 133
Palms across thy breast, 35
  in air, lift their fronded, 43
  of my hands, at the, 423
Palm-trees, but over the scud and the, 113
  the wind is in the, 252
Palmy well, Rachel by the, 120
Palpable hit, a very, 180
Palpitation, with a mailed heel its, 413
Palter with us, that, 318
Paltered with eternal God for power, nor, 418
Pan, 294
  out on the prophets, I don't, 330
Panel, more ready to hang the, 199
Panes, blazoned on the, 291
Pang, and every, 185
  as great, a, 80
  from thine, to steal one, 10
  nor account the, 328
  of sorrow, the, 390
Pangs of despised love, 323
  of nature, to, 160
Pannelled door, no spiked and, 31
Pans, pots, dishes, 16
Pansies, 294
Pantaloon, 294
Pantler, she was both, 71
Pants, 294
Papa, potatoes, poultry, prunes and prism, 85
Paper, goose-quill, ink and, 317
  he hath not eat, 30
  in a sheet of, 336
  is published in Catherine Street, the, 294
  leaves, and not on, 24
  make dust our, 164
  of uncertain, 123
  whiter than the, 169
Paper-mill, thou hast built a, 317
Papers, lawyer, draw up the, 292
Parade, you henceforth may, 108
Paradise, 295
  and walked in, 105
  enow, wilderness were, 85
  graved in, 73
  of clouds, and left a, 353
  sigh for the Prophet's, 44
  to him are opening, 293
  to me, earth seems a, 360
Parallel, 295
Paraphrasing, moanin' and groanin' and, 309
Parasites, the odious, 425
Parchment, 295
Pard, bearded like the, 373
Pardon after execution, like a, 59
  all that's past, thy God will, 429
  but they ne'er, 140
  for the foes who hate, with a, 363
  left, none for, 332
  or to bear it, to, 405
Pardoned, 295
  again, has sinned and is, 247
  being down, or, 260
Pardons, the offender never, 140
Parent, but be a, 153
  knees, on, 227
  of good, thy glorious works, 461
Parent's breast, which on the, 378
Parents', my, or my own, 466
Paris famous, a street there is in, 389
  like a perfumed, 28
Parish church, plain as way to, 441
  pound, driven to church as to the, 52
  swallowed the whole, 133
Park, and from the dark, 115
  quick-glancing o'er the, 410
Parley or dissemble, pause to, 87

Parliament, a seat in, 42
of man, in the, 433
Parlour, 295
or study, built in your, 212
Parlous boy, 33
Parnassus, the true horse of, 445
Parrot, 295
may rehearse, a, 397
Parrot's call, whistle back the, 350
Parsley to stuff a rabbit, 254
Parson, 295
he's a rare man, our, 250
made it his text, the, 219
owned his skill, the, 12
Wilbur sez he never heerd, 11
Parson's gown, texts enough to wear a, 401
Part, 295, 296
accept their, 150
act well your, 184
again, never to, 340
always wise in every, 277
and then to, 221
and yet are loth to, 376
a silent and desperate, 61
a stage where every man must play a, 463
as he has about him, as tender a, 180
a truth, a lie which is, 219
before we, 203
come let us kisse and, 203
for ever, to-night, 211
from mine, shall never, 203
is too precise in every, 364
know that thou and I must, 220
love in which my hound has, 187
no little, that implement hath had, 467
not, from its present pathway, 236
of his plan, consistency still was a, 62
of life, but as a, 232
they must, 376
thy knotted and combined locks to, 380
't is hard to, 220
to act a lover's or a Roman's, 236
to play so ill a, 116
us now, shall a light word, 146
to see her sparrow, 398
with life to, 185
with that, I cannot, 91
with pain, too soon we, 360
Parted, 296
by barriers strong, 339
from us, 110
mine never shall be, 134
or never, 37
others . . . because they never, 295
seeming, 224
Partial for the observer's sake, we grow, 445
Participation of office, if a due, 289
Participle and noun, 'twixt, 386
Parties, both, deprecated war, 431
meet, the high contracting, 253
Parting, 296
breath, what is death but, 77
day, knell of, 69
gleam of sunshine, the, 111
guest by the hand, shakes his, 167
guest, speed the, 167
our, was all sob and sigh, 296
soul relies, the, 35
was well made, 125
was woe, the, 338
Partings, 296
Partington, 296, 297
Partitions do their bounds divide, thin, 245
thin, sense from thought divide, 245
Partridge in the puttock's nest, 41
Partridge-breeders of a thousand years, 231
Parts, 297
all his gracious, 165
all these good, 443
allure thee, if, 123
before the nobler, 148
plays many, 383
some mark of virtue on his outward, 425
were in six, 103
with polished manners, improves our, 234
Party, 297
a, or a thriving lie, 42
he's been true to one, 62
leaders all they mean, and, 315
none was for a, 341
strife, ancient forms of, 339
we join ourselves to no, 420
Pass among the guests, 152
and repass, obstinately sullen, 282
and speak one another, we, 360
and turn again, and, 368
away, blaze and, 123
away, war may speedily, 199
blocked up the, 76
by me as the idle wind, they, 404
for a man, let him, 251
for a' that, will not, 249
in the night, ships that, 360
to bring such visionary scenes to, 266
your proper jest, 67
Passage, allures the bird of, 25
a quiet, 9
leaves some trace of its, 138
must work their, 176
until you find that, 45
Passed all pleasure by, 321
away, will have, 86
beside the reverend walls, 161
in music, 241
my soul hath, 375
o'er me and you, have, 338
on the river, never be, 329
the loveliest pair, 294
the strong heroic soul away, so, 377
Passenger, he shall not be a mere, 54
Passeth show, that within that, 448

Passing by the customary hassock, 312
fair, is she not, 120
through nature to eternity, 89
wise, I know him, 28
Passion, 297
a fop their, 462
allay the fire of, 327
all vile degraded, 143
and pride were to her soul unknown, 453
burns, and now, 330
but pining, 63
chaos of thought and, 462
clasp, something with, 48
every fierce tumultuous, 298
his, and his theme, 217
in a dream of, 307
move, might my, 237
of eternity, to feel the, 402
there is not a, 114
the whirlwind of, 379
the wine of, 324
to tatters, tear a, 379
woman loves her lover, in her first, 232
Passionate intuition, become a, 121
Passion's host, and, 367
Passions, 297, 298
all, all thoughts, 234
are the horses, our, 56
burn, when once their slumbering, 300
senses, affections, 197
told, ere they their, 414
were in us, when the tiger, 392
Past all dishonour, 20
and gone, mourn a mischief that is, 271
as wholly wasted, 170
bury its dead, 147
but mockeries of the, 455
but 'tis, 211
grief, should be, 166
has power, upon the, 221
leave thy low-vaulted, 376
our dancing days, 71
rehearsal of the, 18
repent what's, 60
she to heaven has, 105
the, the future, 222
the link that binds her to the, 258
the tyrant's stroke, 146
these dark days are, 237
who seeks repentence for the, 332
with the water that is, 434
Paste and cover, 80
Pastime, break a country heart for, 174
Past's blood-rusted key, with the, 281
Pasture now, they sell the, 187
on the rocks, to, 325
Pastures new, fresh woods and, 458
Pat in, gliding all so, 210
Patch a wall, should, 421
grief with proverbs, 165
Patch hearts that are breaking, 175
I have a trifling, 68
Patched, before it was so, 128
Patches, a king of shreds and, 202
set upon a little breach, 128
Patching fig-leaves for the naked truth, 416
Pate and fancy wit will come, beat your, 447
knock his leek about his, 216
made by a good old, 149
or I will peat his, 216
Paternoster Row, the proprietor lives in, 294
Pates, fat paunches have lean, 298
Path, 298
each one its devious, 339
ever followed in her, 143
in yon straight, 37
lies, where'er my, 116
my, might cross with thine, 230
of duty be the way to glory, 104
of duty, to the straight, 104
of labour, they who tread the, 207
of life is dirty, the public, 92
of sorrow, the, 374
your purple shows your, 413
Paths, of all the, 305
of glory lead, 163
of men, lies upon the, 138
to glide, in the church-way, 282
Pathway, from its present, 236
may beat a, 214
the star that lights a desert, 338
through the strife, cleaves a, 390
white, flashing o'er the, 23
with those dreadful *urs*, do n't strew your, 62
Patience, 298
abusing of God's, 113
constant anguish of, 109
he stands waiting, with, 262
is the honest man's revenge, 335
must have had, wondrous, 414
of her, and I want but, 278
wins the race, 302
with sech swellin' fellers, no, 156
Patient, 298
dreading praise, 8
eyes, perplexed and, 118
showed us, there, 91
Patriarchs of the infant world, with, 334
Patriot, art thou a man, a, 182
the profession of a, 298
too cool, for a, 141
Patriotism, 298
Patriot's boast, such is the, 182
Patriots all, true, 64
Patron to advise, his mistaken, 397
Pattens, with mop and, 296
Patter, cheep, like little mice, her feet fell, 129
of the rain, by the, 325
Pattern is sold, the, 211
of mine own thoughts, by the, 321

Paul. by robbing Peter he paid, 302
I give it, 91
preaches that Peter and, 26
Paunches, 298
Pauper, 298
Pause, must give us, 98
in the day's occupations, 50
to parley or dissemble, 87
Paved with good intentions, 193
Pavements fanged with murderous stones, 387
Paw is all the law, the lion's, 226
Pay for one by one, ye must, 365
for what they stole before, and, 320
full-weight-dollar debts with, 96
her every farthing I owe her, I will, 278
I will be ever to, 65
me for my pains, 104
my debts to, 232
no debts, words, 459
the rate of his, 390
our lives we, 177
still, and yet, 65
thy poverty, I, 311
you some, and I will, 318
Payment, too little, 189
Pays all debts, 82
Peace, 298–300
adieu, live in, 292
a good war or a bad, 430
among ourselves, a just and lasting, 337
and good will, 52
and slept in, 185
anger at, 208
bread and, 35
combine, when friendship, love and, 442
commerce and honest friendships, 6
desires mere easy, 390
first in, 132
foe of, 143
God gave her, 323
henceforward, therefore be at, 433
I knew, all the, 331
in obscurity, in, 114
its ten thousands, 431
little blessed with the soft phrase of, 380
long, I find, 431
lover of, 432
makes a solitude and calls it, 373
means of preserving, 432
of God was in his looks, 75
of the land, and the, 373
out of pain, shall become, 78
profession of the creed of, 42
said that an unjust, 430
so sweet, or, 217
spirits of, where are, 381
the strange, white solitude of, 369
to pray, for this world's, 366
to sleep, in, 84
waits us, 333
Peace
was never gentle lamb more mild, in, 432
was slain, thrice my, 12
went with them, 167
where they should kneel for, 456
Peaceable way for you, the most, 401
Peaceful, 300
evening in, welcome, 116
lake, pebble stirs the, 53
shall I sleep, 84
Peace-maker, your if is the only, 218
Peacemakers, necessity, thou best of, 279
Peach that's got the yellers, like a, 256
Peak to peak, from, 405
Peaks, between the cold and barren, 222
of song, the long reaches of the, 207
Peal of bells below, a single, 23
on peal, how the great guns, 23
Pealing anthem swells the note of praise, 10
folded in the mist, 23
loud again, now, 52
Pearl, 300
and gold, barbaric, 107
and gold, with pomp of, 353
a sea of melting, 399
heaps of, 102
if all their sand were, 197
in your foul oyster, as your, 183
is gone, out of which the, 375
prince he rises with his, 93
the all, the, 375
Pearls, pale glistening, 354
Peasant, 300
has yielded, to the fate of the, 317
Peasantry, 300
Peasants, from the hard hands of, 267
Peat whiskey hot, 440
Pebble, finding a smooth, 417
into its depths like a, 173
stirs the peaceful lake, 53
underneath our feet, epics in each, 460
Peccadilloes are unknown, where, 367
of all Piccadilly, 367
Peck at the shells, the young shall, 97
at, for daws to, 371
birds best, 393
in safeguard of their brood, doves will, 463
Pecking the hand that hovers, 97
Pedigree, 300
wi' a lang, 210
Peeling, the fruit were scarce worth, 386
Peep about, and, 58
of day, nest at, 25
to what it would, can but, 202
Peeping in at morn, the sun came, 330
Peer, King Stephen was a worthy, 387
make me own this hind of princes, 324

Peered forth the golden windows of the east, 393
Peering in maps for ports and piers, 444
Peers, fare like my, 78
Peevish boy, ne'er a, 107
by being, 264
Pegasus, a fiery, 187
Peggie hawks nosegays from street to street, 343
Pelf, 300
despite those titles, power and, 65
do anything for, 247
on all sides that give places or, 62
Pembroke 's mother, 180
Pen, 301
and ink, good at, 92
devise, wit, write, 466
glorious by my, 124
hard-nibbed, with a, 347
his nose was as sharp as a, 359
if of all words of tongue and, 346
may write, than the, 174
of all sad words of tongue or, 346
the poet 's, 308
saddest of tongue or, 346
traced with his golden, 418
Tre, Pol and, 63
Penalty and forfeit of my bond, 83
hath full relation to the, 213
Penance for her sins, in, 208
Pence, although he gave but, 266
Pendent rock, a, 56
world, the, 90
Pendulum, seizing the ever-swinging, 403
Penitence, 301
Penned, conceived but never, 434
Penniless lass, a, 210
Penny, 301
in purse, a, 65
sold for a, 130
Pension, 301
Pent-house lid, hang upon his, 370
Penury, 301
People, 301
all exulting, the, 43
are free, his, 405
for the benefit of the, 289
golden opinions from all sorts of, 290
governed by grave magistrates, 59
government of the, 276
have made, laws which the, 289
he beckoned to the, 419
I am not of this, 4
necessary for one, 356
now-a-days, young, 469
of customers, raising up a, 361
officials are the trustees of the, 289
ought to guard their noses, 285
proud, to meet a, 299
ready enough, you find, 349
that make puns are like wanton boys, 321
the duped, 106
People
the servants and agents of the, 289
the sunbeams, the gay motes that, 270
they that marry ancient, 254
who cannot afford to play cards for money, 234
we shall meet the, 257
People 's blood, sucks and drains a, 64
gain, and the, 276
prayer, the, 98
Peoples, wherever rise the, 144
Peppercorn, I am a, 53
Peppers, red, 32
Pequot 's ringing whoop, the, 181
Perceive here a divided duty, 104
Perceiving, in the art of, 54
Perch, where eagles dare not, 106
Perched and sat and nothing more, 325
Perdition catch my soul, 239
Perfect, 302
days, then if ever come, 199
in our kind, were, 304
man, an honest and a, 127
may be, singly, 308
music unto noble words, like, 273
picture to see him lie, 96
wife, they make a, 443
woman nobly planned, a, 454
Perfected, all mankind alike is, 318
by death, life is, 206
Perfecteth it, friendly love, 232
Perfection, 302
dead, 128
lies in him, fullness of, 168
none must hope to find, 128
of reason, the law which is the, 327
retain that dear, 275
Perfidious bark, fatal and, 18
Perform, his wonders to, 154
it, thou mayst perhaps, 429
the Almighty 's orders to, 388
Perfume, 302
on the violet, 152
that 's all, 54
to pride, wafts, 385
Perfumed Paris, than like a, 28
Perfumes of Arabia, all the, 169
Peril, 302
all for thee, before I, 127
all of man 's, 21
at life 's dear, 416
of water, wind and rocks, there is the, 359
Perilous edge of battle, 19
Perils, 302
Periods fall on you, his, 314
Perish, a hero, 38
all, whose breast, 35
as they died, or, 128
clasp or, 48
from the earth, shall not, 276
rather than let it, 431
rather, to, 90
Rome shall, 342

Perish, shall never wane and, 276
survive or, 366
there too, or, 9
Perished, the blithe days of boyhood, 331
there, the noblest thing which, 121
Perishing unheard, 434
Perjuries, 302
Perjury, 302
Jove, but laughs at lovers', 302
Permanent, better and more, 450
Pernicious woman, O most, 452
Perplexed and patient, 118
in faith, but pure in deeds, 97
Perseverance, 302
Persevering ones, many of those, 92
Persistency, secret of love's, 117
Person of genius should marry a person of character, 254
she could . . . marry, the best, 243
Personage, there is another, 352
Personal wrong, chafe as at a, 161
Personality, infinite, 190
Person's feelings, every, 129
Persons die before they sing, 366
divers paces with divers, 406
Persuaded, quite, 51
Persuasion and belief, in whom, 121
Pert and chipper and sassy, 408
Perturbed spirit, rest, 381
Peruse, but underneath the rose, 413
the traders, 413
Pervading, the something, 308
Perverse, 302
Perversity of thought, strange, 159
Pestilence on him for a mad rogue, 341
like one that has the, 239
Petals kiss, I'll show you how, 203
Petar, hoist with his own, 110
Peter, 302
and Poule, preaches that, 26
feared, twenty times was, 128
I'll call him, 275
Peterkin, quoth little, 425
Peter's dome, the hand that rounded, 39
keys in wax, Saint, 347
Petitioner for kisses, sweet, 204
Petticoat, beneath her, 129
courageous to, 68
Petty conceit, sell us his, 67
hope, haply lies, 73
men, we, 58
Pews of a tabernacle, through the, 212
Phantom, 302
of grisly bone, that, 78
Phantoms, 302
Pharaoh's lean kine, 126
Phase of ever-heightening life, every, 224
Pheasant-lords, these old, 231
Pheasant's wing, one likes the, 108
Phials, which were to be put in, 393
Philip's house, from the rear of, 25
Philosopher and friend, my guide, 167
Philosopher that could endure the toothache, 413
traced with his golden pen, 418
Philosophy, 303
a little, inclineth man's mind to atheism, 14
the glory of, 269
Phœbus in his strength, bright, 316
Phrase, a fico for the, 386
of peace, little blessed with the soft, 380
that ancient Saxon, 157
Phrases, 303
Phyllis, 303
Physic, 303
is for all diseases, 445
must all follow this, 103
Physician, 303
Physicians, quacks not, 347
Physiognomies o' th' planets, i' th', 306
Pia mater, the womb of, 258
Piccadilly, a place where, 367
the peccadilloes of all, 367
Pickaxe, 303
Picked her pouch, and, 200
out of ten thousand, 183
shall have my pocket, 193
the luscious food, they, 300
Pickers, 303
Picket, has just relieved a, 384
Picket's off duty, the, 311
Pickle, smarting in lingering, 439
Picks your pocket, while it, 212
Pickwickian, 303
Picture, 303
a wretched, 123
dreams cannot, 209
grows, thought he, as the, 342
he is a proper man's, 250
in the book of time, bloodiest, 142
let's see your, 69
show you the, 69
to see him lie, 96
Pictures, as that of, 443
with savage, 252
Pie is freed, no man's, 8
supped on dormouse, 96
was in the largest public, 54
Piece of beef and mustard, 22
of twisty rag, for a, 420
to see, thinks a faultless, 128
Piecemeal on the rock, 28
Pieces, 303
like a lock of hay, went to, 166
Pierce, a sun will, 159
Pierced the fearful hollow of thine ear, 283
Piercing cider, the, 53
Piers and roads, for ports and, 444
on its million, 152
Pies, chattering, 25
Piety nor wit, nor all your, 465
than other people, no more, 52
that practice of, 400
Pig, 304
fat, and goose itself oppose, 322

Pigeon tumbling, a, 219
Pigs, erring souls as straying, 52
  squeak, as naturally as, 165
Pike and gun, the holy text on, 329
  in, as if you thrust a, 398
  ye see, the speedy, 184
Pilchards are to herrings, as, 190
Pile, nor crackling, 155
Piled stones, in, 29
  until all the wealth, 199
Pilgrim grey, there Honour comes a, 34
Pilgrim's weeds, clad in a, 145
Pilgrims be, we ourselves must, 281
  found, a rest for weary, 333
  in Plymouth the land of the, 308
  the home of the, 111
Pilgrims' pride, land of the, 65
Pillage, thought Christ went agin war an', 431
Pillar of State, a, 85
Pillars, on crystal, 267
Pillow, 304
  hard, when resty sloth finds the down, 437
  sighed upon a midnight, 242
  spread, and each calm, 167
  think of abandoning his, 210
  upon her lonely, 99
Pills, I 'm sick of, 363
Pilot, 304
  no thoughtful, 102
  still, yet lives our, 231
Pilot 's bell, to mind the, 329
Pilots of the purple twilight, 59
Pin, and pinned it wi' a siller, 231
  of his heart cleft, 118
  the web and the, 135
Pinch, 304
  as a lover 's, 79
  he that never took a, 285
  of human dust, every, 115
Pinched her feet, they, 208
Pinches, knows so well where the shoe, 361
Pinder, that spiritual, 52
Pine, 304
  blessed be the evergreen, 49
  for my abode, the strong gods, 159
  her furnace crammed rosin and, 346
  though the body, 263
  who see pale mammon, 248
Pined and wanted food, 182
  in thought, she, 298
Pining for the spring, 343
  twenty years of, 208
  what is passion but, 63
Pinion, the strongest plume in wisdom 's, 445
  uncouple that, 403
Pinions, on mine ice-ribbed, 284
  swift on his downy, 370
Pink of courtesy, the very, 65
  of perfection, the very, 302
Pinned it wi' a siller pin, and, 231
Pin 's fee, set my life at a, 223
Pins, 304
  they screwed it up with, 208
Pint of blood from your veins, better to lose a, 280
Pious, 305
  action, and, 88
  drops the closing eye requires, 35
  can say I am not, 247
  nor think I 'm, 25
Pipchin, Mrs., always used that form, 62
Pipe, 305
  a short frail, 408
  but as the linnets sing, 226
  glorious in a, 408
Pipes and whistles in his sound, 294
Piping time of peace, in this weak, 300
Pirates, I mean, 359
Pit as well as better, they 'll fill a, 312
  black as the, 376
  into one, 21
  of clay for to be made, a, 303
  underneath the bottomless, 178
Pitch a ton, none could n't quicker, 249
  it reached an awful, 418
  my moving tent, yet nightly, 278
  they that touch, 401
  which flies the higher, 213
  with a voice of dolorous, 361
Pitched into, the cat 's, 44
Pitchers have ears, 106
Pitchfork, hay tossed from a, 166
Piteous and profound, a sigh so, 363
Pitfall, with, and with gin, 365
Pith and marrow of a nation, the, 277
  and moment, of great, 61
Pitied the man, but, 353
  to pity and be, 23
Pities them, how I, 285
  then, what a thousand, 2
Pitiful, it was, 182
  oh, pitiful, 42
  't was wondrous, 363
Pitiful-pitiless knife, by the, 230
Pittance that would scarcely pay, 317
Pity, 305
  a heart susceptible of, 262
  and be pitied, 23
  and perhaps forgive, 138
  but not in, 159
  for a horse o'er-driven, 187
  hath a tear for, 161
  his iron heart to, 406
  injury the gaoler to his, 192
  lovers rather more than seamen, 389
  may challenge double, 364
  tears of, 160
  them, that she did, 363
  them both and pity us all, God, 470
  then embrace, 425
  the sorrows of a poor old man, 375
  't is, 't is true, 415
Pitying foe, a, 142
Pity 's sake, for poor, 82
Place, 305
  a, a party, or a thriving lie, 42

Place
according to the style of the, 403
and blood, false pride in, 54
and wealth, get, 266
and takes, 216
be bare for poverty, albeit the, 96
beneath, upon the, 260
by any means get wealth and, 266
do not all go to one, 21
fly by change of, 178
I am nearing the, 78
in her pride of, 121
is empty, and feels her, 442
is haunted, the, 69
left for repentance, no, 332
like home, no, 182
my hand in thine, or, 127
of high respect, yet a, 378
of old, hearts that loved the, 175
of rest, where to choose their, 462
of that festive, 295
or gold, the honour proof to, 185
pace 'round the forbidden, 292
shall serve, when time and, 13
the mind is its own, 263
there, and take your, 290
there is, one, 114
to lager bier, have given, 22
what a quare-lookin', 16
whatsoe'er the hour or, 274
where 'e is gone, at the, 395
where honour's lodged, in the, 36
worth no worse a, 315
Placed his foot before, and firmly, 136
Places, and hold their, 289
from many strange, 257
his ship alongside, if he, 360
or pelf, on all sides that give, 62
Plague, 306
Miss, the mercer's, 361
of all cowards, 66
us, make instruments to, 425
us worse, is there a vice can, 285
Plagues a lover bears, of all the, 339
but of all, good Heaven, 145
itself, thus, 384
of all, the greatest is untold, 30
Plain, 306
and clear, what makes all doctrine, 95
and He will make it, 155
an' flat, there you hev it, 431
as way to parish church, 441
as whisper, said as, 69
blunt man, a, 291
eagle stretched upon the, 106
for were all, 376
living and high thinking, 229
tale shall put you down, how a, 396
upon tables, make it, 345
Plainest right, to do the, 54
wrong, to undo the, 54
Plainness, so modest, 447
Plains of the water, 18
the wild mountains and luxuriant, 217
Plains, wounded and left on Afghanistan's, 373
Plain-song, 306
Plaint, pour out your praise or, 348
Plaintiff, always find for the, 92
Plaintiff's the man, I rather think, 92
Plaintiffs or defendants, women, 455
Plan, a head to, 173
and measure, God's, 250
and reforms his, 251
but joined in the, 353
condemned himself to follow out his, 321
it is not a proper, 171
obedient to some, 31
save on some worn-out, 179
the simple, 396
the surest, 191
thy purpose, trust or, 391
was a part of his, 62
Planet, 306
not born under a rhyming, 336
one, in a starless night, 462
Planets, and all the, 216
Planned, a perfect woman nobly, 454
the excellent things we, 451
Plant, 306
is the ivy green, a dainty, 195
of slow growth, a, 60
the wound, helped to, 106
to every thirsty, 101
Planting, the wheat for this, 276
Plants his footsteps in the sea, 154
suck in the earth, 101
Plaster, chalk and alum and, 35
saints, men in barricks don't grow into, 349
when you should bring the, 374
Plates, pack o' rotten, 115
Plato and the swing of Pleiades, 207
Plaudits she may crave, win the, 449
Play, 306
Play, actions that a man might, 448
and make good cheer, at Christmas, 52
a part, a stage where every man must, 463
at, kings would not, 430
by me, bathe in me, 247, 419
cards for money, cannot afford to, 234
come forth to, 71
for love and money too, 241
is done, the, 70
is o'er, life's poor, 49
like a cat at, 60
on, if music be the food of love, 273
run, they will not let my, 405
so ill a part, to, 116
the, I remember, pleased not, 45
the devil, some, 285
the hart ungalled, 84
the housewife for this once, 188
the spaniel, you, 378
the swan, I will, 273
the woman, to, 399

Play, the woman with mine eyes, I could, 399
upon me, you cannot, 305
with souls, to, 378
young barbarians all at, 181
Played and loved, you 've, 228
around her elbow-chair, 450
eat together, 224
familiar, and, 288
on, easier to be, 305
with for bits of stone, he, 378
Player, 307
a poor, 411
Players, all the men and women merely, 383
do, as many of your, 379
playing at cards, two, 77
see little or nothing, 379
Playful spray, in thy, 73
Playhouses, more tears are shed in, 398
Playing mad pranks, 224
on the harp, talking is like, 397
on the sea-shore, a boy, 417
the Judas, 114
with the shadows, the young fawns are, 469
Playmate shares my beaker, no, 146
Playmates, 307
Plays and tumbles, a', 133
an old tune on the heart, memory, 258
many parts, in his time, 383
Plaything gives his youth delight, 49
Playtime of the others, are weeping in the, 469
Plea, necessity the tyrant 's, 279
so tainted and corrupt, what, 213
the mightiest, for erring souls, 313
Plead, expound and argue, he could, 283
for thee, this silent tongue shall, 411
precedent will, 84
Pleadingly and prayerfully, 340
Pleads admission to our hearts, 85
Pleas for John Doe, some draw, 146
indite, and the, 455
Pleasance, youth is full of, 5
Pleasant in man, 1
future howe'er, 147
place, Utopia is a, 383
sure, to see one 's name, 30
the snaffle of courtship, 253
to make thy riches, 336
to severe, from, 162
vices, and of our, 425
weaving nets, 't is, 280
Please, 307
age lends the graces that are sure to, 94
books cannot always, 31
coy and hard to, 453
his grandam, to, 372
love, studious how to, 234
me best, old fashions, 126
the certainty to, 443
Please
thee with my answers, 10
Pleased, he knew when he, 145
not the million, 45
to give ten thousand ducats, 325
to the last, 27
with a rattle, 49
with the danger, 304
Pleasing, anxious being, this, 139
more, more quaint, 161
of a lute, the lascivious, 432
punishment that women bear, the, 456
Pleasure, 307
a draught of heavenly, 402
after pain, 16
at the helm, 470
by, passed all, 321
drinking is the soldier 's, 16
fills up, when, 116
for no man 's, 39
full measure of all your, 329
has aye one rapturous, 462
have neither pain nor, 369
I live in, 227
in the act, 103
in the house, there 's little, 244
in the pathless woods, there is a, 457
is as great, doubtless the, 47
is comparable, no, 415
lark-like nests upon the ground, 316
may give a shock of, 435
meet, youth and, 71
on their lordships', 71
some to, 325
sweet the, 16
ta'en, where is no, 391
that he gives him bread, the same, 12
thence which flows, the, 285
the rills of, 403
to be drunk, 102
to come, you have an immense, 358
to the spectators, because it gave, 321
what dreams of, 367
with instruction, 193
Pleasures and palaces, 182
and seize the, 227
doubling his, 443
for your choosing, two, 306
might, these, 237
my, are not now, 331
prove, we will all the, 235
what cares and, 338
Pledge, 307
of a lower sphere, 179
the universe in wine, 101
with mine, I will, 99
Pleiades, Plato and the swing of, 207
Plenishing, comfortless for lack of, 96
Plentiful as blackberries, if reasons were as, 327
Plenty, 307
in delay there lies no, 239
that can, there 's, 413

Plies corruption's trade, 64
Plods his weary way, 69
Plot, and some poor, 182
this blessed, 112
Plough goeth every Sunday, his, 421
or sail, what avail the, 143
the, the axe, the mill, 212
Ploughman, 307
homeward plods, 69
wanders in all lands, Death the, 79
Plover from the marshes calling, the, 384
Pluck, 307
a crow together, 67
away, nor even rashly, 120
this flower safety, we, 280
you out of the crannies, 135
Plucked and shorn, being, 103
for violets, 426
not harshly, 228
their own feathers, 106
up kisses by the roots, 204
Plucking the grass, 444
Plucks dead lions by the beard, 423
justice by the nose, liberty, 199
Plum, a cherry and a fig, 162
give it a, 162
Plume, 308
in wisdom's pinion, the strongest, 445
who have lent his, 106
Plumes, like tossing, 184
Plum-porridge, their best and dearest friend, 322
Plunder, he shared in the, 353
lust and, 143
Plundered, profaned, 188
Plunge, a beggar he prepares to, 93
with all your fears, 79
Plutarch, 308
Plying her needle and thread, 360
Plymouth, 308
Pocket knife, that magic tool, the, 467
picked, shall have my, 193
wear prayer-books in my, 372
while it picks your, 212
Pockets trimming, their husband's, 449
Poem, 308
is marred, many a, 109
Poet, 308
begs, your, 349
Poetic, 308
souls, delight in prose insane, 309
Poetry, 309
angling is somewhat like, 10
music and art, without, 63
Poetry-writing, plain hoss-sense in, 309
Poet's muse, the, 217
Poets, 309
prose, like blank verse, 424
sing, 123
styled, by, 232
write of, which, 130
Point, 309
Point
affords, such pity as my rapier's, 305
a moral, to, 274
and defies its, 191
don't put too fine a, 446
feel I had gained a, 197
of order, rose to a, 350
touched the highest, 122
Point-blank from the mouth of a woman, 283
Pointer's feet, blood on your, 148
Pointers, worse housed than your hacks and your, 323
Points, commas and, 67
in the adventure of the diver, 93
Poison, 309
his antidotes are, 303
nor steel nor, 223
to men's souls, 158
truth, can, 412
us, if you, 197
Pokes, an' into nobody's tater-patch, 356
Poking the fire all alone, to be, 441
Pol and Pen, by Tre, 63
Pole, from Portsmouth to the, 408
Indus to the, 216
so tall to reach the, 263
the magnetic needle to the, 279
to pole, beloved from, 369
to pole, diffused from, 161
to pole, it flies from, 262
to pole, it spreads from, 216
to pole, spread the truth from, 216
traverse the, 112
trembling vassal of the, 60
true as the needle to the, 88
turning to the, 245
Policy, any cause of, 161
honesty is the best, 183
tyrants from, 328
Polished manners, improves our parts with, 234
Polite, never mentions hell to ears, 178
to think thet killin' ain't, 131
Politeness, how well I speak of Scotch, 352
Political bonds, to dissolve the, 356
Politician who is clean, the, 310
wise, makes the, 57
Politicians, 310
the most practical of all, 310
the whole race of, 162
Politics, 310
than it has with, 61
Pomp, 310
and boast, all earthly, 228
and circumstance, 125
let the candied tongue lick absurd, 412
of beauty reigns, nature in all the, 217
of pearl and gold, with, 353
of power, 163
of woe, exhausts the, 410
of yesterday, all our, 139

Pomp
what is, 89
Pond, like a standing, 291
Ponder well what that shall be, 465
Pondered, while I, 261
Pool, and dreaming, 419
Poor, 310
a backward steward, for the, 248
and lowly must work their passage, 176
are prolific, the, 413
feud of rich and, 130
for a bribe, too, 141
for bread, sold to the, 35
house, dwells like a miser in a, 183
if thou art rich, thou'rt, 336
indeed, and makes me, 275
is the man in debt, 82
laws grind the, 214
lone woman, 230
man, a blind man is a, 27
man loved the great, 341
man's right in the law, like a, 214
men, when yule is cold, 132
rich gifts wax, 421
the exchequer of the, 401
to do him reverence, none so, 335
to relieve the old, 149
to the wandering, 242
unequal laws for rich and, 115
whether he be rich or, 248
who aideth the, 181
Poorest comer, by the, 177
man may in his cottage, 44
Poor-house, 310
Pop, the toads went, 372
Pope, 310
Poppy, sauce cf syrup of, 96
Porch, at my cottage, 162
disgrace, the, 52
Porcupine, making a woman like a, 304
upon the fretful, 381
Pork, 310
Porridge, 310
pray a month with mutton and, 312
Port, his was the lofty, 316
in every, a mistress find, 347
is near, the, 43
for men, 34
or bay, in some near, 73
pride in their, 316
the lazy gossips of the, 161
Portal, nor attempt the future's, 281
we call death, whose, 76
Portals foul, and, 367
Portents, more filled with signs and, 165
Porter and gentleman, 21
good stout old English, 440
with a good old, 149
Portia's counterfeit, fair, 303
Portion, he wales a, 464
of a good man's life, best, 201
of the human race, 103
to fill a certain, 123
Portioned, lands were fairly, 341
Portraits, man with the gallery of family, 124
Ports and piers and roads, for, 444
not bays and broad-armed, 385
Portsmouth to the pole, from, 408
Positivist, 311
Possess the field, but for you, 391
Possessed, but first I have, 233
joys I have, 221
of shaving-materials, who is, 464
Possessing, too dear for my, 125
Possession, while they can keep, 170
Possessions and military posts, 112
Possibilities, 311
'Possum, dar's de banjo an' de, 281
Post, and win the, 344
breast that fears not danger's, 145
evil news rides, 281
firm at his dangerous, 304
is not at his, 132
of honour is a private station, 424
pachas are all at their, 63
was driven into her breast, this, 388
Posterity, 311
Postern of a small needle's eye, 42
Posthumous man, 115
Postman or the bore, can keep out death, the, 31
Pot of ale and safety, 6
of beer, in a, 310
of beer, no objection to a, 110
the three-hooped, 130
were not I a little, 50
who is the potter . . . and who the, 311
Potations, banish long, 32
banish, strong, 32
Potato could not flourish at its root, wisdom's old, 445
Potatoes, 311
two boiled, 349
Potato-patch pokes, an' into nobody's, 356
Potent in potting, most, 112
Potomac, 311
Pots, dishes, pans, 16
of ale, take the size of, 6
the luckless, 178
Potter, 311
the hand then of the, 178
Potter's clay, if we are only as the, 107
hand, clay bleeding and aching in the, 107
Potting, most potent in, 112
Pouch, and picked her, 200
on side, and, 294
Poultice comes, silence like a, 364
Pound, driven to church as to the parish, 52
of flesh, thy, 134
of that same merchant's, 134
Pound were baith for me, the croun and the, 68
Pounds a year, in three hundred, 128
a year, I've a hundred, 61

Pounds a year, two hundred, 95
eighteen thousand, 42
seven hundred, and possibilities, 311
Pour, and will, 39
forth the cheering wine, 445
this concealed man, thou mightst, 383
Poured in her lap all gems, 107
the fiery Hollands in, 181
the wine, before I, 194
thick and fast the burning words, 419
Pouring forward, went, 271
without stint, 27
Poverty, 311
albeit the place be bare for, 96
hunger and dirt, in, 361
nothing in, 195
Pow, 311
Powder, 311, 312
as a spark to the, 389
Powder-cart, git forrid sometimes upon a, 431
Power, a, to which, 112
and earthly, 260
and pelf, despite those titles, 65
and search the heavens for, 402
and skill, who has the, 450
and war, 164
a slowly-dying, 18
can stay him, what, 406
divine, what, 58
he is king who has the, 202
infinite in, 154
in place and, 305
in Venice, there is no, 315
i' the truth of the cause, 417
knowledge itself is a, 206
not exempted from her, 212
not now in fortune's, 97
of beauty, the, 20
of blessing thee, the, 27
of grace, the, 274
oh, for a forty-parson, 190
oh wad some, 355
pain's resistless, 175
that has made and preserved us, 276
that pities me, that, 305
the force of temporal, 260
the pomp of, 163
there never yet was human, 467
the seeds of godlike, 157
they should take who have the, 396
to bite, sorrow hath less, 375
to hurt, the proper, 14
to place and, 305
to quiet, such songs have, 374
to save, hast, 84
to tell, one hath, 178
upon the past has, 221
with triumph and, 392
Powerful of the earth, the, 334
Power-house, 312
Powers, and exercise their, 289
by lightning's vivid, 26
can ne'er be equal, 241
Powers, deriving their just, 161
equal in full-blown, 318
of the earth, among the, 356
tarnish all your boasted, 58
we lay waste our, 463
which God for use had given, 142
Practical politics must not be construed, 310
Practice, mere prattle without, 382
of piety, that, 401
taught as, but such as, 445
Practise to deceive, first we, 82
to deceive, I will not, 82
Practised, 312
Prairie Belle took fire, if ever the, 329
Praise, 312
and endless theme of, 236
and prayer, faithful work is, 459
and thine be all the, 429
and when it could not, 411
be given, to Mary Queen the, 369
damn with faint, 71
few sons attain the, 367
from God, take that, 156
from those who spoke her, 26
heaven in their own way, 217
him, not to, 341
hypocrisy, power to chant thy, 190
indeed, is, 11
it brings, the, 206
joyful in my, 104
my, will be your proudest theme, 237
not blame, dreading, 8
of art, seeking not the, 466
of the virtuous woman, 451
or plaint, pour out your, 348
ourselves, however we do, 454
still pleased to, 46
swells the note of, 10
the Lord, and, 365
to hear our noble England's, 111
who merit, 332
Praised me at a time, he, 312
unenvied, and, 385
Praises God, earth, 154
Praising, railing and, 324
the rose that all are, 342
Pranks, playing mad, 224
Prate in puling strain, I cannot, 233
of hell and heretics, 217
Prattle, mere, without practice, 382
Praty-skins, ashes and, 16
Pray, 312
because 't is lucky for the boats, 244
fervently do we, 199
for grace, I, 413
for mercy, we do, 260
for this world's peace to, 366
for wisdom yet, 330
the Lord my soul to keep, 370
remained to, 352
then let us, 38
with you, I will not, 41
Prayed, 313
a lot, he, 314

Prayed
the men that fought and, 181
the prayer of all mankind, he who, 313
Prayer, 313
and he made his, 136
as love's wild, 366
doth teach, that same, 260
erects a house of, 87
every syllable a, 340
faithful work is praise and, 459
for those who love us, and a, 363
hush that followed the, 55
if ever fondest, 125
lest the devil cross my, 87
no bribe or, 274
that follows after, 374
the people's, 98
to, 154
to a wordless, 88
to Himmel, take a liddle, 351
to sully your pure, 348
to thee I make my, 155
what's in, 260
Prayer-books, beads and, 49
in my pocket, wear, 372
Prayers, 313, 314
cannot appease thee, 15
a few more, 222
for vengeance, weary of your, 433
I consider faith and, 120
of love, 160
they seldom say their, 259
your sighs and, 74
Prayeth, 313, 314
Praying, 314
dumbly, as if, 169
for her, loving her, 243
God will save thy sailor, 347
hands, then with, 255
the yearning back of the, 313
Prays for love, when it, 235
Preach again, as never sure to, 314
an' could na, 263
I wish to, 389
for this men write, speak, 123
upon a morning breezy, 151
who please, they may, 444
Preached, 314
he practised what he, 312
Preacher, 314
cries, the sacred, 227
Preachers, 315
Preaches in her gown, a wife who, 295
that Peter and Poule, 26
Preaching down a daughter's heart, 73
Preachment, made a, 85
Precedence, allay the good, 41
Precedent, 315
the codeless myriad of, 214
to precedent, from, 144
will plead, 84
Precedents, shelter him with noble and right-reverend, 92
Precept, a familiar, 193
Precincts of the cheerful day, 139
Precious as the stuff they sell, half so, 426
jewel, to barter away that, 42
souls, six, 72
stone, this, 112
the more, for the struggles, 111
Precise, than when art is too, 364
Preferment, 315
Preferred before a just war, is to be, 430
in his heart, the least ringlet, 339
Preferring you before her father, 189
Pregnant with celestial fire, 109
Prejudice, by the grey weeds of, 446
Prejudices, and Scotch, 352
Preoccupateth it, fear, 77
Prepare to shed them now, 399
Prepared for war, to be, 432
Prepares it for another guest, 401
Presbyterian, true blue, 't was, 329
Prescient, 315
Prescribed, all but the page, 127
Presence, made better by their, 50
civilizes ours, sex whose, 54
glowed, with his, 87
of a Maker, in the dread, 115
the sun from their, 284
within our, 115
Present state, their, 127
Presentiment, 315
Presentment, the counterfeit, 303
upon the heels of my, 30
Preservation of the general government, the, 299
Preserved in Milton's or in Shakespeare's name, 458
the Federal Union, it must be, 420
us a nation, made and, 276
Preserving peace, means of, 432
President, 315
Presiding, o'er his life, 443
Press, 315
and quill, freedom of the, 110
free, 142
made at me through the, 427
not a falling man, 121
thee, other arms may, 331
the life from out young hearts, 296
the rue for wine, 402
too close in church and mart, 220
where ye see my white plume, 308
Pressed once more the lifeless head, 109
the earth upon her corpse was, 388
the lips that he has, 252
Presses, on, still on he, 406
Pressing close, a thousand knights are, 179
Pressures past, all forms, all, 331
Presume, 315
not God to scan, 250
thy bolts to throw, 71
to lay their hand, 12
Presuming, 'ould be, 283
Presumption on to-morrow's dawn, man's, 411

Pretence, are their just, 67
good without, 452
Prettiest doll in the world, the, 96
Pretty, but is it art, 13
creature, drink, 101
looks, puts on his, 165
maid, my, 246
quarrel, the quarrel is a very, 323
thing man is, what a, 251
well, considering, I 'm, 62
wit, I have a, 447
Prevail, looking ill, 294
with me, if wishes would, 446
Prevailed above the magistrate, the man, 245
with double sway, 352
Prevails, when vice, 424
Prevaricate, Ralpho, thou dost, 325
Prevent the long aimed blow, 385
Prey at fortune, to, 168
expects his evening, 470
for prey, to barter, 10
must have, 256
surprise the finny, 168
that on him, 134
to all, yet a, 462
to dumb forgetfulness a, 139
to hastening ills a, 300
were every nation 's, 157
where eagles, wrens make, 106
Preys do rouse, to their, 282
on herself, 33
Priam, food for vermin, like, 89
Price, 315
a gem of countless, 73
a little below cost, 175
earth gets its, 176
every kiss has a, 253
no, is set on the lavish summer, 177
of admiralty, if blood be the, 113
of apostasy, were the, 416
of chains and slavery, at the, 217
of many a crime untold, 157
of pork, you raise the, 310
the, too high, 91
Prick and Rosalind, must find love 's, 343
and sting her, to, 270
me off, how if honour, 184
us, if you, 197
Pricking her fingers, 304
of my thumbs, by the, 404
Pricks me on, honour, 184
Pride, 315, 316
a decent, 396
alone, who stands in his, 286
and worse ambition, till, 7
and spite of, 338
a Roman knows, that, 285
a tyrant throned in lonely, 419
blush of woman 's, 409
glows with faith and, 173
he that is low no, 97
in place and blood, false, 54
is his own glass, 320
land of the Pilgrims', 65
Pride
local jealousies and, 110
most provoked by, 319
my high-blown, 153
not the breath of his, 386
of freedom, in all the, 217
of place, in her, 121
of their race, for the, 373
onward with a secret, 159
passion and, were to her soul unknown, 453
pomp and circumstance, 125
sweetness void of, 128
the banner of our, 17
their country 's, 300
wafts perfume to, 385
with coy submission, modest, 391
with folly and with, 449
Prides, a host of, 316
Priest, 316
at her altars, a, 63
hath his fee, the, 176
I tell thee, churlish, 426
Priests, lawyers, 218
the selling do, 47
Prime, having lost but once your, 254
time, 115
Primer, armed with his, 352
Primeval race was run, long after thy, 10
this is the forest, 139
Primrose, 316
Primroses, 316
Prince, 317
as the subject owes the, 454
he rises with his pearl, 93
who nobly cried, the, 73
Princely counsel in his face, 85
Prince 's name, stand in the, 422
ransom in the pearl, left a, 300
Princes, 317
and lords are but the breath of kings, 183
and lords may flourish, 300
are come home again, 112
ever ranking himself with, 388
peer, this hind of, 324
to act, 383
were privileged to kill, 272
Principle, are rebels from, 328
I do n't believe in, 193
Principles I glory, ez to my, 42
the refuge of free, 111
your jarring sects unite, 162
Print, 317
I put into, 386
them on the moon 's pale beam, 450
to see one 's name in 30
Printers, 317
have last, 31
Printing, 317
Prints my letters, this, 36
Prior, 317
Prison, 318
came the hero from his, 351
on each hand, a palace and a, 424

Prison
so I were out of, 261
Prisoner, make me no, 318
takes his valour, 101
Prisoner's gaze, obstruct the, 262
pleasing dream, liberty, the, 217
Prison-house, the secrets of my, 380
Private end, served no, 385
ends, by their, 111
station, post of honour is a, 424
Privatest of men's affairs, 120
Privilege, anger hath a, 9
to live, but only they have, 424
Privileged, Princes were, 272
Privy Councillors of God, pseudo, 347
Prize, 318
a sot, but their, 462
he'd caught, the, 342
if solid happiness we, 182
itself, the wicked, 289
left to, 91
more than all to an Englishman, dear, 286
o' death in battle, for the great, 19
them, when we learn to, 394
unseduced by the, 120
we sought is won, the, 43
whose loves I, 69
who misses or who wins the, 150
Prizes you're running, if when for life's, 220
Problem given, he'll solve you any, 467
Proceed ad infinitum, 134
Proceedings, and the subsequent, 350
Process, they form the, 455
of the suns, widened with the, 322
Proclaim, their great Original, 132
Proclaimed through our host, 156
Proclaims the man, the apparel oft, 11
Procrastination, 318
Proctors, with prudes for, 162
Produce, the vineyard's best, 288
Produces noble ends and uses, noble thought, 284
Product distilled from molasses, the, 344
Production, man is a carnivorous, 256
Productive of the greatest minds, 41
Profanation, but in the less foul, 196
Profane, yet 't is, 394
Profaned and disinherited, 188
Profess, that I may, 189
Profession, 318
of a patriot, the, 298
of the creed of peace, 42
they hold up Adam's, 150
Professors, of mair use to the, 212
Profit by their example, may, 414
ere her cause bring fame and, 34
grows, no, 391
to receive countenance and, 318
Profitless, falls into mine ears as, 64
Profits nobody, ill blows the wind that, 444
Progeny of learning, a, 215
Progress, 318
Progression, change is the watchword of, 46
Project, eight years upon a, 393
may at first sight appear a, 361
Prologue to his sleep, the, 100
Promethean fire, the right, 118
Promise, 318
howe'er we, 124
lies, the land of, 159
never more to disobey, fain, 429
who broke no, 385
yet, never saw I, 308
Promised on a time, I was, 335
Promises, 319
made, 215
Promising with smiles, or, 361
Promontory, or blue, 56
Prompter of invention, surest, 279
Prompter's bell, slow falling to the, 70
Prone to weeping, I am not, 438
Pronounced her wooman, he then, 449
Pronouns, 319
interjections, verbs, 389
Proof against their enmity, I am, 302
and on the, 195
bring his merit to the, 187
in some wild hour, and learn by, 465
itself would have earned him, than ever, 287
through the night, gave, 17
Proofs, his, his publishers and printers, 317
of holy writ, strong as, 195
strong, they have, 376
Prop, when you do take the, 223
Propagate and rot, 306
Propensity, almost irresistible hereditary, 102
to stick, has a, 114
Proper jest, pass your, 67
man's picture, he is a, 250
mate, choose not alone a, 254
plan, it is not a, 171
power to hurt, 14
time to marry, but, 254
Property, 319
of easiness, a, 70
or his labour, with his, 338
Prophecy, protest that is also, 188
Prophesy, 319
Prophet, 319
God and the, 63
Prophetic, runs a thrill of joy, 143
Prophet's paradise, sigh for the, 44
Prophets, I don't pan out on the, 330
blazoned on the panes, the, 291
Proposal, to a woman with such a, 283
Propose, 319
Proposes, but God disposes, man, 155
Proposition, the truth of its own fundamental, 8
Propped, with one of timber's, 216
Proprietor lives in Paternoster Row, the, 294

Prose, 319
and verse is merely, 424
insane, delight in, 309
is verse, 424
poets like blank verse, 424
run mad, not poetry but, 309
't is not even, 424
what others say in, 424
whose, is grand verse, 424
Prosper, 319
treason doth never, 414
Prospered, when it is past and, 414
Prosperity, a jest's, 196
doth best discover vice, 427
I wish you all manner of, 397
she makes a scourge of past, 265
that shadowed us in our, 3
Prosperity's the very bond of love, 240
Prosperous, 319
to be just, 't is, 34
Prospers, for the world, 111
Prostrate, let me fall, 397
Protect her from all ills, 189
it now, and I'll, 457
Protection of Divine Providence, the, 307
Protector, in your God the, 144
Protest, a, that is also prophecy, 188
Protestant succession, and, 170
Protested, he blamed and, 353
Protests, 319
Proteus, have sight of, 293
Protracted life, 221
Proud, 319, 320
and lower the, 141
heart breaks, fret till your, 144
his name, 65
mad, but not defiant, 244
man's contumely, 323
of a vast extent of flimsy lines, 353
of thee. O nose, I am as, 285
shall be, all the, 334
the Englishman is, 90
the spirit of mortal be, 269
to importune, too, 141
to meet a people proud, 299
Prouder for it, ay I'm the, 86
Proudly, more, than to die, 351
question ours, ere you, 58
we hailed, 17
Prove, 320
when I doubt, 195
Proved false again, 95
it, said there was no matter and, 256
to thy face, it will be, 317
Proverb, 320
goes, the hare of whom the, 423
never stale, 126
to thine heart, take the, 434
you know the, 260
Proverbs, as she is described in the, 451
of Solomon, in the, 285
patch grief with, 165
Proves by thumps upon your back, 405
Providence, 320
and courage never abandon, 373
their guide, and, 462
then Bill let us thank, 347
Provoke the silent dust, 421
Provoked by pride, the proud are always most, 319
not soon, 84
Provokes the world to arms, gold, 158
Provoketh thieves, beauty, 21
Provok'st, that thou oft, 80
Prow, youth on the, 470
Prudent, 't is thought among the, 323
Prudes, 320
for proctors, with, 162
Prunello, the rest is all but leather or, 465
Pry on every side, and, 307
that out of a Boston man, you could n't, 188
Psalm, like the close of an angel's 374
the hundredth, 10
up in the spire, send the, 244
Psalter, the full heart's a, 173
Psyche's friend becomes her lover, when, 242
Phthisic, helps the headache, cough and, 445
Public, a man pays to the, 46
business, no, 54
care, and, 85
departments, with all the, 54
haunt, life exempt from, 3
officers are the servants, 289
officials trustees of the people, 289
opinion, in war the moral element and, 431
path of life is dirty, 92
pie, was in the largest, 54
rout, where meet a, 253
spirit ends, all, 305
tart, in the smallest, 54
Publican, 320
Published in Catherine Street, the paper is, 294
Publishers, 320
his, and printers, his proofs, 317
Publishing, of loudly, 351
Puddle, at a slop or a, 297
Puffed where'er winds rise, 408
Puffs away from thence, being angered, 444
Puissant nation, a noble and, 277
Puling, to speak, 239
Pull a crow, you and I must, 67
his weight, to, 54
the thorn, to, 402
Pulled out, with a single hair, 168
Pulse ablaze, and the, 204
of care, the restless, 374
of life, on the, 86
of racing oars, the measured, 287
Pulses leap, the, 470
of the stars, they'll feel the, 306
when your castigated, 324

Pulses' tardiness or quickness, 363
Pulsing it again through them, 277
Pun, rejoiced in a, 197
Punch, 321
Punctual, are very apt and, 122
Punishment, deserve not, 157
new, what a, 115
oftenest of all a, 102
that women bear, the pleasing, 456
thy nature will endure, the, 450
Punishments the scroll, how charged with, 126
Puns, 321
Punster, said a, 423
Puny head, on your, 108
Purchase their good will, by service long to, 455
Purchased, as to be, 217
at an infinite rate, 117
Purdon, here lies poor Ned, 168
Pure, all women, 150
as snow, as, 42
because my heart is, 12
gold for what he lent him, 82
hold on to the, 55
in deeds, but, 97
neither strong nor, 146
the, the bright, the beautiful, 88
the real Simon, 364
the statesman, 104
Purer laws, with . . . , 252
science, of, 252
Purest oar, the . . . from the hottest furnace, 41
Purest ray, many a gem of, 149
Purgatory, 321
Purge and leave sack, I 'll, 346
away, which war alone can, 431
the land, we would, 133
Purged away, are burnt and, 380
Puritan anthem, the grand old, 10
Puritans, 321
stern-eyed, 31
Purity, 321
and truth, brightness, 452
Purple and gold, gleaming in, 14
shows your path, 413
twilight, pilots of the, 59
Purpose, 321, 322
a preacher who speaks to the, 314
can cite Scripture for his, 353
can there be, what, 265
fair to no, 462
for the sole, 361
have clouds o'ercast thy, 391
infirm of, 70
lofty of, 54
of the law, the intent and, 213
pushes his prudent, 251
should not fail with me, my, 446
was strong in moral, 269
to be dressed in an opinion, 291
Purposed, whose end is, 157
Purposes, can execute their airy, 381
he lives no more, to our, 278
the Almighty has his own, 6
Purse, 322
a penny in, 65
a pride of, 316
can buy, as thy, 11
in silken or in leather, 359
the inside of your, 158
who steals my, 275
Pursue, more than heaven, 61
Pursued betimes, small habits well, 167
further than death, can vengeance be, 424
Pursuing, a love-lorn heart, 458
still achieving, still, 2
Push us from our stools, 90
Pushes his prudent purpose, 251
us on to the windowless inn, 406
Pushing away the Atlantic Ocean, 296
Puss gentleman, a fine, 54
while folks are in their beds, 44
Put a girdle round about, 152
a head on him, for to, 171
it back half an hour, 434
it on again, 361
it on your finger first, since I, 338
it to the issue, I 'll, 187
it to the touch, dares not, 126
on his clothes, when he, 274
out to sea, when I, 17
that in, 204
to the worse, knew truth, 415
too fine a point to your wit, don't, 446
too fine point upon it, not to, 309
you down, how a plain tale shall, 396
Puts forth the tender leaves, 164
Puttied up with tar, pack o' rotten plates, 115
Puttock 's nest, the partridge, 41
Puzzled all our kith and kin, it, 418
Puzzles the will, 79
Pygmies, 322
Pyramid, under a star -ypointing, 29
Pyramids, 322
are pryamids in vales, 322
virtue alone outbuilds the, 322
Pythagoras, to hold opinion with, 378

Q

Quacking only gives it an ill savour, 52
Quacks, not physicians, 347
Quadrangular of diamond form, spots, 88
Quaff this kind nepenthe, 280
Quaffed too quickly, his (cup) had been, 464
Quaffs her paly stream, 101
Quaint, more, more pleasing, 161
Quake to hear, that tyranny shall, 419
to hear, words that tyrants, 419
Quaker fellow as often 'as towd ma this, 267
Qualify, absence seemed my flame to, 2

Quality, 322
and all, 125
never sees a good, 70
of mercy, the, 260
of the liquor, and the, 403
true-fixed and resting, 62
Quarrel, 322, 323
and detested a, 308
greatly to find, 164
honourable, and his, 45
just, hath his, 12
sudden and quick in, 373
there is no true valour, in a false, 423
Quarrelled, 323
with a man, thou hast, 322
Quarreller, he 's a great, 323
Quarrelling, 323
as addle as an egg for, 322
wilt tutor me from, 322
Quarrels, 323
Romans in Rome 's, 341
thy head is as full of, 322
Quarry-slave, go not like the, 227
Quart of ale, 6
Quarter toward the arternoon, another, 434
Quarto page, a beautiful, 293
Queen, 323
and every lass a, 469
and faith, fought for, 105
an' Gawd save the, 301
at length apparent, 268
Bess, image of good, 157
Elizabeth, no scandal about, 351
for life, ev'ry lady would be, 325
of crown, of, 370
of the world, the, 58
o' the May, I 'm to be, 256
sent word, a, 276
thou sat'st a, 342
upon a card, insipid as the, 193
Queen 's command, gave up their lives at the, 373
Queens and states, kings, 368
Queer, 323
Queerest little craft, 73
Queer-looking place, what a, 16
Quell, the vengeance blood alone could, 423
thy soul, no foreign foe could, 112
Quench it, she took to, 71
rivers cannot, 131
or but allay, you would, 327
Quenched a lamp, if thou hast, 149
Question everything, the right to, 8
his brute, 147
hopelessly, I put this, 320
is not marriage an open, 253
Mars, they 'll, 306
of despair, the hurried, 107
or reply, not thine nor mine to, 357
ours, ere you proudly, 58
staying no longer, 345
that is the, 19
thy soul to-night for me, 127
Question with the wolf, may as well use, 448
Questions, 323
that Heaven rains down, 8
Quick as is the wit it gives, 46
as lightning in the breech, 36
bosoms is a hell, quiet to, 323
now bourgeons every maze of, 372
Quickly, well it were done, 96
Quickness, pulses' tardiness or, 363
Quiddities, thy quips and thy, 324
where be his, 214
Quiet, 323
along the Potomac, all, 311
be, and go a-angling, 10
breast, truth hath a, 417
cloudy, all, 435
consummation have, 163
eyelids closed, her, 105
fields, by, 18
have power to, 274
passage, a, 9
some to, 325
to have an hour 's, 229
tune, singeth a, 37
Quietus, 323
Quill, Britons have a tongue and free, 110
freedom of the press and, 110
from an angel 's wing, made of a, 301
Quillets, his, his cases, 214
of the law, these nice sharp, 213
Quills upon the fretful porcupine, 381
Quip modest, the, the second, 218
Quips, 324
and cranks, 196
Quire below, to the full-voiced, 291
Quit for the next, 91
it, the very rats instinctively had, 325
the ground, least willing still to, 224
their sphere, all, 316
this mortal frame, 428
Quitteth both riches and wisdom, 8
Quitting the busy career, rest is not, 333
Quitt 'st thy narrow bed, 115
Quotes a stage-play, here he, 383
Homer and Virgil, 30
Quoth echo, plainly, 255

R

R in their name, have not an, 292
Rabbit, for parsley to stuff a, 254
would be a, 212
Rabblement hooted, 43
Race, 324
another, the following spring supplies, 250
a type of the true elder, 308
a younger, succeeds, 379
between two legs a, 344
delivered, a nation saved, a, 277
ensnare, tresses man 's imperial, 168

Race
forget the human, 85
for the pride of their, 373
has run its course, our, 191
is won, the, 208
life is the running of the, 221
not always to the swift, 318
of man is found, the, 250
of mere impostors, a, 385
of politicians, the whole, 162
patience wins the, 302
portion of the human, 103
she shall rear my dusky, 350
that shortens its weapons, the, 437
the annals of the human, 228
the Bible of the, 24
the true king of his, 410
to command, to obey, the, 113
was run, long after thy primeval, 10
Races' ends, when they 're at their, 345
Rachel by the palmy well, 120
Racing oars, the measured pulse of, 287
the same, selling or, 187
Rack behind, leave not a, 428
the ship has weathered every, 43
Racketing her rivets loose, 215
Radiance in his bright, 384
Radish, 324
Rag and a bone and a hank of hair, 136
for a piece of twisty, 420
over'ead, the bloomin' old, 112
Rage, 324
and the elements', 78
canine of dying rich, 336
for fame, what, 123
license and wanton, 431
penury repressed their noble, 301
strong without, 84
Raged more fierce, in war was never lion, 432
Rages loud and long, while the battle, 19
the furious winter's, 103
Ragged, if I was very, 197
Raggedy-man, 324
Raging hot, hand grows, 169
Ragings, 324
Rags, a crust of bread and, 207
and hags and hideous wenches, 387
and tatters, old opinions, 110, 143 143
in unwomanly, 360
to very, 379
virtue though in, 311
Rail, whiles I am a beggar, I will, 22
Railer, rude Boreas, blustering, 346
Railing, 324
Railroad tracks, boys that put coppers on the, 321
Rails, and he, 193
below, half the, 215
Rail-splitter, 324
Raiment, and change my, 365
Rain, 324, 325
a deluge showers, 26
Rain
a mist and a weeping, 203
and win', t'ro' de col' night, 359
as the mist resembles the, 375
begin, wha'r de long night, 358
droppeth as the gentle, 260
enough, is there not, 169
he only hung it out in the, 361
in thunder, lightning, or in, 257
may enter, 44
or shine, or, 221
or shine, took lodgings for, 21
potatoes, let the sky, 311
soaks up the, 101
stones with drops of, 252
sunshine still must follow, 76
the heart's most precious, 293
the sunshine follows the, 442
wears the marble, much, 252
Rainbow, hue unto the, 152
Rainbow's glory is shed, the, 209
Rainbows of the brooks, leap the, 350
Rain-drops fall, like, 160
Rained, it blew and it, 389
Raineth every day, the rain it, 325
Rain-paf', up t'ro' de gloomerin'. 359
Rains, washed with still, 224
Rainy eyes, and with, 164
when it is not, 110
Raise a thirst, an' a man can, 392
me up, my God shall, 406
no money by vile means, I can, 267
th' enormous weight, could, 84
the price of pork, you, 310
the stateliest building man can, 195
the stone, 207
this soul to God in after-days, 293
Raised a sigh so piteous, he, 363
his right hand up to heaven, 424
it, the pious fool that, 123
not a stone, and we, 153
some serious song, 91
thee anew, ever we, 112
to shed his blood, the hand just, 27
to that bad eminence, 107
Raiseth me, a cross that, 278
Raising up a people of customers, 361
Rake, 325
Ralph to Cynthia howls, while, 282
Rampant animals, too, 56
Rampart wall had scaled, 87
we hurried, as his corpse to the, 102
Ramparts, because to force my, 284
o'er the, 17
Ramrod down, and he shoved his, 38
Random sent, many a shaft at, 358
spoken, many a word at, 358
Rang, hard crab-tree and old iron, 405
the bells, and merrily, 437
Range the valley free, flocks that, 305
Ranging for revenge, 335
Rank, a pride there is of, 316
a wreath, a, 462
of these, in the first, 114
is but the guinea's stamp, 249
or worth, whatever be their, 201

Ranker, to make them, 60
Ranking himself with princes, ever, 388
Ranks of war, amidst the, 308
of war, in the, 271
Rank-scented many, the mutable, 252
Ransom for offence, be a sufficient, 375
in the pearl, left a prince's, 300
Rapids are near, the, 344
Rapier's point affords, such pity as my, 305
Rapine, war and, 143
Rapping, as of some one gently, 261
Rapture brief, almost divine, 234
on the lonely shore, there is a, 457
Raptured or alarmed, 377
Raptures swell, no minstrel, 65
Rapture-smitten frame, with, 274
Rare and radiant maiden, clasp a, 246
as a day in June, 199
bedfellows, 21
man, he's a, 250
Rarity of Christian charity, 182
Rascals, 325
in the coach, 417
naked through the world, to lash the, 439
Rash and undutiful, 20
choler, way and room to your, 50
splenitive and, 71
Rashes, green grow the, 165
Rat, 325
Rate, at a bountiful old, 149
of going, alter their, 403
of his pay he dislikes, if the, 390
of usance, brings down the, 421
purchased at an infinite, 117
Rats, 325
and such small deer, mice and, 261
Rattle his bones over the stones, 298
pleased with a, 49
where mingles war's, 83
Rattling o'er the stony street, the car, 444
Rave, our little hour of strut and, 411
where the scattered waters, 288
Raven, 325, 326
down, smoothing the, 282
nevermore, quoth the, 17, 19, 246
ringlets, her, 30
rooked her on the chimney's top, 25
your locks were like the, 311
Raven's croak is loud, the, 184
Ravens, 326
on high, storms rock the, 297
Raving at that shade-made blade, 115
Ravished, are quite, 196
ears, with, 155
with the whistling of a name, 123
Ravishes all senses, it, 452
Raw, inclement summers, in, 393
you are yet too, 397
Ray, beneath her steady, 268
earth shall glisten in the, 159
emits a brighter, 185
many a gem of purest, 149
Ray of him, a, 233
whose unclouded, 400
with unsetting, 245
Rays, hide your diminished, 91
like, into one focus, 204
Raze out the written troubles, 263
Razor keen, like a polished, 350
Razors, 326
Reach me more, might never, 229
that excellence it cannot, 114
the longest, is past, 344
the pole, to, 263
the spot, 152
Reached and kept, by great men, 177
that blessed abode, ever, 374
Reaches of our souls, beyond the, 268
of the peaks of song, the long, 207
Read, 326
aloud the book, he, 280
and thou wilt, 409
a sermon, who will not, 462
as well as books, men may be, 259
a woman, who is 't can, 453
comes by nature, but to write and, 466
he that runs may, 345
I want to, 247
much, not read at all, 309
Shikspur, no, I never, 358
the book of fate, 127
which shall be, 275
write and, 2
Readeth it, he may run that, 345
Reading, 326
of an ever changing tale, the, 219
study, pains, 67
writing and 'rithmetic, 187
Reads much, he, 126
Ready ere I called her name, Abra was, 1
for a hero's deeds, 54
man, conference a, 326
to hand, finds, 54
to try our fortunes, 141
we always are, 286
Real, life is, 222
much finer women, ripe and, 385
Reality, but this is, 100
immeasurable, 190
Realm, riding o'er the azure, 470
shall be in common, 130
that moves to that mysterious, 227
this, 112
throughout the solid, 86
Realms above, constancy lives in, 412
Reap, as you sow, y're like to, 230
the harvest, others will come to, 460
Reaped for nothing, nor shall half be, 460
Reaper, 326
whose name is Death, 79
Reaping, grew the more by, 32
something new, ever, 461
thee sweet herbs, 78
Reaps, another, 355
Rear of Philip's house, 25

Rear the tender thought, to, 398
to bear, to nurse, to, 19
Reason, 327
and have no other, 287
appear the better, 122
blessed with plain, 452
divorced old barren, 426
ever comprehends, more than cool, 243
for my rhyme, to have, 335
having no other, 322
I received nor rhyme nor, 335
itself, kills, 30
I was up so early, 211
neither rhyme nor, 335
no sooner knew the, 242
still, the ruling passion conquers, 297
that wants discourse of, 20
the wherefore is neither rhyme nor, 441
't is you that have the, 335
to be fond of grief, 165
to the rhyme, hard to fit the, 335
upon compulsion, give no man a, 327
void of rhyme as well as, 382
what, I should be the same, 232
what 's the, 414
why, Cornishmen will know the, 63
why, theirs not to, 90
why, there 's little, 218
why, they scarcely asked, 90
would despair, where, 185
ye shall find, till some, 58
Reasonable amount o' fleas, a, 134
creature, kills a, 30
my pension shall seem the more, 301
Reasoned strong, he, 91
Reasoning with yourself, what are you, 335
Reason 's spite, in erring, 338
Reasons, 327
not unplausible, baited with, 459
Rebel, a foul contending, 454
shall my heart, 125
use 'em kindly, they, 280
Rebellion, 328
whirlwinds of, 147
Rebels, 328
Rebuff, 328
and one refusal no, 328
Rebuild in it the music and the dream, 467
Recall, beyond, 144
him, a signal to, 132
who vainly the dreams of youth, 470
Recalled a different name, each heart, 241
Received nor rhyme nor reason, 335
Receives, who much, 26
Recess, the gay, of wisdom and of wit, 367
Reckless, 328
Reckon by them, they do but, 459
not on your chickens, 48
Reckon their age by years, some, 398
with this man, the future, 147
Reckoned by its length, it must be, 204
the love that can be, 237
Reckoning, a trim, 185
made, no, 370
truth to the end of, 417
Reclaim her precious things, earth shall, 354
thy lost soul, 358
Recognizing start, with a, 115
Recoils, back on itself, 335
suffers, 232
Recollection, almost escaped my, 89
presents them to view, 49
Recommend the light, more sweetly, 447
Recommended to the notice of, 193
Reconciled, deems he is, 341
Record here, have left one trace of, 367
leap to light, whatever, 358
of reply, lives no, 37
out, to blot the, 449
weep to, 287
who rest below, storied urns, 410
Recorded for a precedent, 't will be, 315
they made and, 338
Recording angel, the, as he wrote it down, 287
Records, all trivial fond, 331
Recovered of the bite, the man, 95
Recreant limbs, calf 's-skin on those, 226
Recreation, more calm, quiet, innocent, 10
Rector, the mealy-mouthed, 144
Red and white, whose, 21
artillery, far flashed the, 13
as a rose is she, 36
as the lips we press, 55
began to turn, from black to, 269
burial blent, in one, 40
cheek a little, 75
Cross of England, 'neath the, 110
her lips were, 226
herring, nor good, 132
his coat was, 87
making the green one, 169
nor need be daubed with, 152
of innocent commercial justice, 413
paint the town, 102
right hand, his, 169
right hand grows raging hot, 169
the bleeding drops of, 43
the winding rivers be, 212
was on your lip Mary, the, 387
Reddening of the rose, the, 200
Redeemed and white before the Lord, 358
Redeemer, 328
Redress, 328
the balance of the old, 16
their harms, how to, 231

Reed he will not break, the bruised, 436
there's music in the sighing of a, 272
Reeds, whose hope is built on, 330
Reef, roller thundering on the, 341
Reek o' the rotten fens, 69
Reel and rout, in, 81
how the belfries rock and, 23
Refines, how the style, 231
Refit, this tenement, 367
Reflect that God is just, 414
Reform, till he begins to, 366
Reformation, a godly, thorough, 329
Reforms his plan, 251
Refrain, from expensive sins, 345
I list to this, 325
Refreshment, its draught of cool, 435
Refuge of a scoundrel, the last, 298
of free principles, 111
Refusal, 328
Refuse, 329
the shilling, 345
though I can't, 321
Refused it, he hath, 199
the gold, they, 183
to send farewell, 124
Regard, and stronger, worthier of, 58
for mercy, disclaiming all, 413
may claim, some, 458
to true merit should they have, 427
with this, 61
Region of thick-ribbed ice, 90
Register of the crimes, little more than the, 180
Registered in heaven, is, 66
Regret, sleep with nothing of, 62
Regular, icily, 128
Rehearsal of the past, 18
Rehearse, a parrot may, 397
Reign, 329
in Georgius Primus', 31
molest her ancient, solitary, 292
of Chaos and old Night, 46
pomp, rule, 89
there alone, the dead, 75
unless their subjects give, 202
while Kehama shall, 69
Reigned, could reign he, 329
Reigneth, God, 154
Reigns, here woman, 452
nature in all the pomp of beauty, 217
over all, a good God, 154
Rein, and snort to the, 387
too much the, 70
Rejoice 329
at it, I, 7
oft in crowds I might, 274
the desert shall, 443
Rejoiced in a pun, 197
Rejoicing, sorrowing, toiling, 410
Related, are often so nearly, 391
to whom, 334
Relation to plain bread and butter, 34
Relation to the penalty, hath full, 213
Release, the gladness of the world's, 300
Reliance, with a firm, 307
Relic of bygone days was he, a, 357
Relics are laid, cold and unhonoured his, 274
spread with human, 354
Relief, bringeth but slight, 1
make our death a glad, 89
much thanks, for this, 57
O give, 375
to them 'tis a, 398
Relies on, no man, 202
still on hope, 185
Relieved a picket, has just, 384
by desperate appliance are, 86
from a world of woe, 105
Religion, 329, 330
as rum and true, 344
men's minds about to 14
Religion's self into disfavour, 52
Religions, 330
Religious bird, not reckoned a, 52
exercise, be a very rational, 401
idea, depolarize every fixed, 85
liberty, the school of, 111
light, casting a dim, 225
Reliques, his hallowed, 29
Relish a love-song, to, 239
of the saltness of time, 5
Relished a joke, who, 197
Remain below, my thoughts, 313
whatever hath been written shall, 465
Remained to pray, 352
Remains is bestial, and what, 332
of her, all that, 454
of thee, alone, 334
to mark a friend's, 145
women come out to cut up what, 373
Remark, first I would, 171
should captains the, 219
Remarked before, I should have, 162
Remedies, 330
are past, when, 464
Remedy, 330
but they sought the, 242
Orpheus who found no, 279
Remember, 330, 331
March, the ides of March, 190
one, if thou wilt, 384
that I am an ass, 13
the pledge, 179
yet, the power of beauty, I, 20
Remembered, in their flowing cups freshly, 275
in thy epitaph, not, 114
kisses after death, dear as, 205
not, sweet tones are, 209
Remembering happier things, in, 375
Remembers me of all, 165
Remembrance, grace and, be to you both, 343
not burthen our, 177
of death, mitigate the, 50

Remembrance, rosemary, that's for, 343
Remind us, all, 138
Remnant of the week, the wicked, 247
Remorse, farewell, 186
Remote, 332
Remove to Dunsinane, till Birnam wood, 25
why should man's success, 342
Removes, 332
Removing this trifle, just in, 308
Remuneration, 332
Rend the chain, while they, 385
Render, teach us all to, 260
up their dead, 354
Rendered unto her, for sin had, 369
Rendering none, hope for mercy, 260
Renew the broken vow, 179
thy vows, 429
Renewal, a fire that needs, 233
Renews the life of joy, 435
Renouncing clean the faith they have in tennis, 401
Renown, of just and old, 144
shall forfeit fair, 65
Renowned be thy grave, 163
than war, no less, 299
Rent asunder, the clouds were, 26
with civil feuds, 420
Repaid, from his helpless creature be, 82
Repair, and battered to, 353
his vigour lost, 293
Repeating troublesome, and in the last, 400
us by rote, 179
Repeats his words, 165
Repelled, each call for needful rest, 304
Repent each sinful act, 413
what's past, 60
Repentance, 332
comes, too late, 127
to her lover, to give, 136
Replevy cannot be, 127
Reply churlish, the, the third, 218
coldly would I shape, 274
discreetly, 284
lives no record of, 37
not thine nor mine to question or, 357
theirs not to make, 90
to God, shall, 147
Repose, angels uncurtained that, 105
has earned a night's, 410
hushed in grim, 470
for limbs with travel tired, 21
may the wearied eye, 434
in statue-like, 105
joy and temperance and, 94
more heart's, 182
Reposed, her land, 323
Represent the Devil, 115
Repressed their noble rage, penury, 301
Reprieve's too late, all, 59
Reproof, 332
valiant, the, the fourth, 218
Reptile, 332
race, and all the, 345
Republic of ours, in this, 54
Reputation, 332
for wisdom, 136
seeking the bubble, 373
Requiem, 332
Requires that they should declare, 356
Requisite, the first, of a good citizen, 54
Resemble copper wire, others rather, 276
her to thee, when I, 343
you in that, we will, 197
Resembled thee, that man, 228
Resembles sorrow only, and, 375
Reserve, the great have kindness in, 384
Reserved of God, woman the last, the best, 453
Reservoir, this year, a, 248
Reside in thrilling region, 90
Resign, 333
his own for others' good, 159
Resignation, and one half, 454
none, by, 289
Resigned, being e'er, 139
Resist, fight, to suffer, 120
Resistance death, submission bondage and, 391
Resisted, know not what's, 172
Resolute, 333
in endeavour, 54
Resolution, the native hue of, 61
Resolve, a heart to, 173
by sines and tangents straight, 6
itself, thaw and, 134
purpose to, 251
that we here highly, 276
with, to edge, 27
Resolved, once to be, 97
war open or understood must be, 431
Resolves and re-resolves, 251
the moon into salt tears, 402
Resort of desperate men, often the, 298
Resources, the rock of the national, 340
Respect, a decent, to the opinions of mankind, 356
or the sentiment of, 455
talk with, 372
yet a place of high, 378
Respectability, the *ultimum moriens* of, 171
Respected, once that Peter was, 128
Responsible for the conflagrations, 372
Rest, 333, 334
a perfect form in perfect, 302
a thousand spears in, 179
awhile, but oh, let me, 437
can never dwell, where peace and, 299

Rest
dandled him to, 89
each call for needful, 304
ere life shall dawn on their, 97
God knows, the, 87
heaven is blessed with perfect, 409
her soul she's dead, but, 453
he sinks into the last eternal, 62
he was already at, 163
His, 'round our restlessness, 154
how sleep the brave who sink to, 34
I bid thee, 12
ill a-brewing toward my, 98
in my own, shall never have, 448
in the grave to his, 269
in this bosom, 31
is lies, the, 135
leaves to its eternal, 221
like a warrior taking his, 433
much veneration, but no, 317
or the Turkman's, 408
our limbs at, 108
you know the, 405
perturbed spirit, 381
shall the traitor, 83
sweet clay from the, 179
takes his one day's, 401
that she may, 189
the cushion and soft dean invite to, 178
thee here, but, 162
thy best of, 80
thy warfare o'er, 373
to sneer, teach the, 71
will not break their, 354
to their lasting, 273
turn to thy, 35
two pale feet crossed in, 208
wakens at this hour of, 23
we shall be with those that, 222
where to choose their place of, 462
while you may, take, 390
Resting from above, 267
quality, true-fixed and, 62
Resting-place, 334
Restless, unsatisfied longing, the, 109
violence, blown with, 90
Restlessness, round our, 154
Restore the dead, thou sea, 354
the gift, till happier hours, 203
Restorer, tired nature's sweet, 370
Restrain and kepe wel thy tonge, is to, 411
Restraint she will not brook, 452
Rests, 334
and expatiates in a life to come, 186
a woman, here, 452
Result happiness, 192
of Time, and the long, 352
Resurrection, hand of the Angel of the, 33
Retain, but its teachings we, 117
one jot of former love, 296
that dear perfection, 275
the offence, be pardoned and, 295
Retire alone, shalt thou, 334
Retirement, short, urges sweet return, 373
Retort courteous, the, the first, 218
Retreat, 334
from his dark, 288
that shall never call, 415
was life's, 367
Retrieved, is ne'er, 122
Retrospection cursed, with many a, 328
Return, 334
bid time, 468
once dead, you never shall, 100
no more, may, 77
run to lisp their sire's, 175
short retirement urges sweet, 373
to Lochaber no more, we'll maybe, 229
to me, and, 116
to our muttons, to, 439
to our wethers, to, 439
to what base uses we may, 421
truant husband should, 189
with her from exile, 319
Returns, no traveller, 79
to tell us of the road, 72
Reveal, or the lip, 174
Revealed, the magnet was, 245
Reveals, a late-lost form that sleep, 442
Revelation, friend Death in the, 11
Revelry, 334
midnight shout and, 129
Revels keep, the winds their, 288
now are ended, our, 428
shall join in your, 116
Revenge, 334, 335
and study of, 231
descend to, 7
is as the tiger's spring, their, 455
shall we not, 197
triumphs over death, 77
whirligig of time brings in his, 407
will not ambition and, 7
Revengeful eyes, fix, 28
Revenue, abundant streams of, 340
Reverence, 335
a thousand claims to, 323
for the Sabbath day, your holy, 345
pay the, 121
Revered abroad, loved at home, 352
Reverend walls, I passed beside the, 161
Reverends, Right and Wrong, 75
Review, can surely, 67
Revisit'st thus the glimpses, 268
Revive, use may, 379
Revived might be, so thine, 10
Reward of it all, the, 78
succeeds, a sure, 427
virtue is its own, 427
virtue is to herself the best, 427
Rewards, how the world its veterans, 462
Rhetoric, 335

Rheum, villainy is not without such, 426
Rhine, and Rupert of the, 19
it is well known, river, 58
shall henceforth wash the river, 58
Rhine's breast-milk, the, 344
Rhine-wine, no German, 151
Rhinoceros, the armed, 72
Rhyme, 335, 336
and scrawl and scribble, all, 466
it hath taught me to, 239
nor reason, the wherefore is neither, 441
our language yields, for which no, 389
things unattempted yet in prose or, 319
void of, as well as reason, 382
who worshipped a, 308
Rhymes, 336
Rhyming, 336
nay, I was, 335
Rialto, 336
Riband, 336
Ribbed sea-sand, as is the, 253
Ribbon, for the sake of a, 42
Ribs, dainty bits make rich the, 298
Rice, with handfuls of coals and, 175
Rich, 336
affords no law to make thee, 463
and poor, feud of, 130
and poor, unequal laws for, 115
and rare were the gems she wore, 149
being, 22
by easy trips, that the, 176
for use, too, 21
honesty dwells like a miser, 183
how happy ought the, 266
in blisses, her lip so, 204
in deep hymns, 173
in having such a jewel, as, 197
in saving common sense, 43
men rule the law, and, 214
misers, compare our, 133
no sin but to be, 22
not gaudy, 11
or poor, whether he be, 248
that its tone could reach the, 361
the ribs, dainty bits make, 298
the treasure, 16
with the spoils of time, 406
Richard's himself again, 180
Richer than my tongue, more, 238
Riches, 336
and wisdom, quitteth both, 8
keep thy, 354
pleasant, to make thy, 336
thou bar'st thy heavy, 336
Richest hand, East with, 107
Richly dight, storied windows, 225
Richmonds, 337
Rid of a knave, you are, 422
Riddle of the world, the glory, jest and, 462
Ride, 337
more than thou goest, 362
the ring, for you alone I, 456
Rider and horse, 40
as a steed that knows his, 436
those who wait the coming, 429
Rides in the whirlwind, 388
on every passing breeze, death, 77
post, evil news, 281
through hell, and, 432
upon the storm, 154
Ridiculous excess, wasteful and, 152
never so, 70
one step above the, 391
Riding high, at her full and, 268
near her highest noon, 268
o'er the azure realm, proudly, 470
that night, fate of a nation was, 276
the springy branches, 219
Riding-whip, then with a, 384
Rifle, just roll to your, 373
Rift, 337
of dawn, the, 207
Rigged out in their swaller-tail coats, 11
Rigging, without an inch of, 73
Right, 337, 338
and not a single, 419
a noisy man is always in the, 284
an' wut ain't, idees o' wut 's, 431
boldly claim his, 112
by chance, be, 136
every cranny but the, 231
by him, to du wut 's, 320
divine of kings to govern wrong, 161
freedom and the, 143
hand carry gentle peace, in thy, 299
hand grows raging hot, 169
hand, his red, 169
hand, the willing strong, 48
have boded all too, 211
he knew it was not, 361
his life, I'm sure was in the, 120
hold on to the, 55
I kissed the rod, if, 67
impossible that they should ever be, 422
in the law, like a poor man's, 214
is a matter of, 289
law an' order, honour, civil, 212
little, tight little island, a, 194
make, the immemorial infamies, 467
may she always be, 65
no land yet, all 's, 435
of at least two distinct looks, the, 455
of them, cannon to, 42
once we thought it, 110
on English soil, has no, 409
or flaw in, 356
or wrong, our country, 65
Reverends and Wrong Reverends, 75
ring in the love of truth and, 418
so long as there is wrong to, 219
sounding generalities of natural, 149
there is none to dispute, my, 266

Right
they set exactly, 67
to dissemble your love, 93
to do, as they 've good, 241
to do a great, 213
to do as he likes, his, 338
to do the plainest, 54
to man, salt that seasons, 312
too fond of the, 141
to one, conveys a, 129
to question everything, the, 8
to stay, still in the, 397
way, be done in the, 459
way to go, better . . . the, 159
whose life is in the, 120
with the world, all 's, 154
with two or three, in the, 368
your honour 's in the, 66
Righteous altogether, are true and, 199
kiss, seal with a, 118
not to the, 324
Righteousness, put on Christ 's, 220
Rightly to be great, 164
Rights, 338
but know their, 385
of all, and plead for the, 32
of man, and the common, 413
should lose, lest they their, 311
to secure these, 161
was won, I recollect how sailors', 347
Rigour of the game, the, 175
Rill, there 's music in the gushing of a, 272
Rills of pleasure, the, 403
Rim, beyond their utmost purple, 463
Rind, sweetest nut hath sourest, 286
Ring, 338, 339
and a bright gold, 149
for you alone I ride the, 456
he made Ole Hundred, 50
in redress to all mankind, 328
in the common love of good, 160
in the Christ that is to be, 51
in the love of truth and right, 418
in the nobler modes of life, 252
in the thousand years of peace, 300
in the true, 122
in the valiant man and free, 422
is on, the, 290
out false pride in place and blood, 54
out my mournful rhymes, 336
out old shapes, 93
out the darkness of the land, 72
out the false, 122
out the feud of rich and poor, 130
out the grief, 166
out the narrowing lust, 158
out the thousand wars of old, 434
out the want, the care, the sin, 430
out, wild bells, 23
the fuller minstrel in, 336
Ringlet, 339
Ringlets, her raven, 30
Rings of rogues, the, 325
Rings, quickly the sharp chisel, 410
the bell that swings in its belfry, 464
the woodland loud and long, now, 457
Riot, very fond of beef and, 249
Ripe and rotten-ripe, time is, 46
but his judgment, 198
for exploits and mighty enterprises, 470
grapes, sours, 118
in show thy lips, how, 226
Ripened into faith, had, 121
Ripeness is all, 157
Ripening, greatness is a-, 164
Riper stage, amuse his, 49
Ripest fruit first falls, 146
Rise again, but now they, 90
again, truth crushed to earth shall, 415
and break, ere it, 82
and fall, and her bay-tides, 32
and successive, 250
betime, we, 40
by sin, some, 365
can never, and fight again, 130
created half to, 462
foul deeds will, 83
from outward things, takes no, 415
from your dreams of the future, 409
held we fall to, 337
in, a way . . . to, 140
make your courage, 18
on stepping-stones, 170
or if you, 150
the peoples, wherever, 144
to-morrow 's sun to thee may never, 84
up, in his name, 358
we build the ladder by which we, 208
while nights and larks are flying, 151
will never, to fight again, 130
with the lark, 210
Risen up earth 's greatest nation, an', 277
Riser, an early, 151
Rises dark o'er the way, 228
in my breast, he, 333
the Sultan, 401
up, and every dirty reptile, 332
with his pearl, a prince he, 93
Rising from a humble root, 461
from the sea, Proteus, 293
in cloudy majesty, 268
in his, 85
on its wrecks, if, 170
sun, let others hail the, 392
sun, tinged with the, 56
to great place is by a winding stair, 305
Risks all landsmen run, know what, 347
Rites, till love have all his, 407
Rival, 339
Rivals, 339
through fear of foreign, 110

Riven, then shook the hills with thunder, 13
River, 339
adown the Danube, 72
brink, wild on the, 182
in the eye, fruitful, 448
let us cross over the, 333
meet, the brook and, 246
never be passed on the, 329
of sluggish blood, a very, 133
on the banks of that lonely, 296
Rhine, shall henceforth wash the, 58
save the rush of the, 311
shore, upon the, 3
swap horses while crossing the, 394
the broad bay and the rapid, 437
the vast, calm, 403
River 's brim, a primrose by a, 316
Rivers be red, or the winding, 212
cannot quench, 131
like subterranean, 451
our lives are, 228
shed of tears, 38
run to seas, 167
up, drinks twice, 101
Rivets loose, racketing her, 215
Rivulet of text, a neat, 293
Rivulets, 339
Roach and dace, 32
Road is sometimes very stiff and tiring, 460
it is rough, the, 298
I was to wander in, the, 365
one that on a lonesome, 128
returns to tell us of the, 72
thorns and briars in his, 374
to Mandalay, on the, 252
understand the law of the, 455
who takes no private, 278
Roads, by many strange, 257
for ports and piers and, 444
we cannot see his, 155
Roam, absent from Him I, 278
but not their hearts, that, 367
where'er we, 182
fools who, 182
howe'er thy footsteps, 182
though we may, 182
Roar, 339
aloud, others, 36
and music in its, 457
and ready to, 387
nor tempests, 89
now, hark do n't ye hear it, 285
of gun, clang of bell and, 23
the breakers, 2
the cannon 's opening, 12
wont to set the table on a, 468
of the billows on the shore, 19
Roared and howled, and, 190
Roaring and gleaming, our days come, 138
bows, for a hammock at the, 8
Roast an egg, the learned, 108
beef of old England, 22
Rob it of some taste of tediousness, 400
the bee of her honey, 133
the luckless town, that, 325
Robbed, 340
the whole tree, have, 115
who broke and, a house below, 306
Robbers, but for supporting, 36
Robbery have authority, for their, 386
Robbing, like one that fears, 239
Peter he paid Paul, by, 302
Robe, 340
disrobe the lion of that, 226
dyeing the white, 413
nor the judge 's, 260
the snows are my, 284
well did he become that lion 's, 226
Robes are on, when all her, 20
loosely flowing, 364
the gleam of their snowy, 339
weave, let not the idle wear, 355
Robin Adair, 340
Robin-redbreast, like a, 239
Robin 's breast, comes upon the, 241
Robinson he, but John P., 11, 461
Robs me of that which not enriches him, 275
the vast sea, 402
Rock, 340
and reel, how the belfries, 23
and sat upon a, 439
a pendent, 56
cut from the living, 73
dislimns, the, 56
he bore, his back against a, 136
moulder piecemeal on the, 28
not his cradle, if drink, 100
shall fly, this, 136
thee, its passions will, 297
Rocked in the cradle of the deep, 84
Rocket, 340
Rocket 's red glare, 17
Rock-pines, and the dark, 184
Rock-ribbed and ancient as the sun, 180
Rocks, 340
pure gold, and the, 197
the peril of water, winds and, 359
to pasture on the, 325
to soften, 272
Rod, 341
and a chief 's a, 183
if right I kissed the, 67
of empire might have swayed, 109
stretch forth thy, 388
then spare the, 232
Rode brightest, till the moon, 268
by on his vocation, 11
in his shroud, and, 332
the six hundred, 90
Roderick then, where was, 39
Rogers, only Mrs. Something, 296
Rogue, 341
that I am, 247
Rogues obey you well, the, 280
Roll, a few more years shall, 222

Roll all earthly pomp and boast, 228
like a smithy-shop after every, 54
of common men, 59
on, thou deep and dark-blue ocean, 288
the stone from its grave away, 186
to your rifle, just, 373
when the drums begin to, 180
where waves can, 161
Rolled from wing to wing, 308
in one another's arms, 108
into one, 150
molten, graven, hammered and, 157
not, through it there, 386
tears adown that dusky cheek have, 174
to starboard, rolled to larboard, 354
up like a scroll, is, 191
Roller, 341
Rollest now, thou, 406
Rolling rapidly, the flow of Iser, 225
the sea was mountains, 188
the stone that is, 388
Rolls his ceaseless course, time, 406
the moon's unclouded grandeur, 268
through the dark blue depths, 268
to its appointed end, that, 322
Roman, 341
hand, the sweet, 169
holiday, to make a, 181
honour, the ancient, 145
knows, that pride a, 285
senate long debate, can a, 430
such a, 36
Roman's part, to act a lover's or a, 236
Romans, 341
were like brothers, 341
Rome, 342
and groined the aisles of Christian, 39
falls, and when, 57
in the height of her glory, 112
more than the Pope of, 310
more, that I loved, 41
Romeo, 342
called, were he not, 275
Rome's quarrels, Romans in, 341
Rondo, and some compose a, 146
Rood of ground, when every, 166
Roof, ever upon the topmost, 112
may shake, 44
of the church, high on the, 314
shows leak in, 356
who living had no, 183
Roofs of the world, over the, 468
Rooked her on the chimney's top, 25
Room as for thy laws, who sweeps a, 102
below, in that silent, 55
enough, is, 381
for wit, no, 172
hard for some people to get out of a, 212
in hell, another, 178
in the worst inn's worst, 464
like a bridegroom from his, 351
Room, moor herself within my, 73
must I give way and, 50
no wit for so much, 172
on entering a, 85
to give some labourers, 436
up, grief fills the, 165
with civet in the, 54
Root and all, in my hand, 135
could not flourish at its, 445
nips his, 164
of all evil, love of money is the, 267
of evil, money, the, 266
reason the, 327
rising from a humble, 461
the, may not be blighted, 149
the tree of deepest, 224
Rooted, so strongly, 114
Roots are wrapped about the bones, thy, 468
began to spread their, 31
by so many, 156
he cut our, 62
plucked up kisses by the, 204
wood, bark and leaves, 308
Rope of sand, as tough a, 57
Rory O'More, said, 286
Rosalind, such a nut is, 286
Rose, 342, 343
and blooms a, 105
and blossoms as the, 443
at an instant, 224
at Jesus' word, as Mary, 358
but underneath the, 413
how to occasion's height he, 287
in blood, 142
is she, red as a, 36
is sweetest, the, 398
like a rocket, as he, 340
of her cheek, the, 153
that which we call a, 275
the dumb old servitor, then, 357
the expectancy and, 263
the lark, merrily, 210
the morrow morn, he, 346
the reddening of the, 207
the wilderness shall blossom as the, 443
till she bloom like a, 226
when he, 393
with grave aspect he, 85
Rosebud, 343
Rosebuds, 343
Rosemary, 343
Rose's hope, life is the, 219
Roses, 343
grow on thorns, so, 403
in December, seek, 67
like the vase in which, 258
only, breathing of, 100
the scent of the, 258
they twine, soft as the, 426
Rosin and pine, and her furnace crammed, 346
Rot, and to, 90
asleep to the grave, 144
beneath the sod, better, 213

Rot, clear that I shall, 89
in sheep, the, 306
propagate and, 306
the very deep did, 84
Rote, learned and conned by, 15
repeating us by, 179
words learned by, 397
Rotted off his flesh, 15
Rotten, 344
apples, small choice in, 11
at the heart, 11
case abides no handling, 44
fens, reek o' the, 69
Rotten-ripe, time is ripe and, 46
Rotting inward, that, 337
Rough as nutmeg-graters, be, 280
turns earth's smoothness, 328
work, men that do the world's, 306
Roughen to the sense, in which they, 357
Roughest weather, life's spring for his, 409
Rough-hew them how we will, 94
Roughly since I heard thee last, 227
Round about the cauldron go, 45
attains the upmost, 7
belly, a little, 24
by round, we mount . . . , 208
in a light fantastic, 409
of blood, and the quick, 220
of life, so runs the, 224
or two before, a, 333
the moon was, 106
the square, and all, 383
the world away, and, 469
thinks the world turns, 151
travelled life's dull, 192
with solemn, 26
Rounded with a sleep, is, 428
Roundel, a little, 53
Roundhead's pike, now he wards a, 383
Rouse before the morn, have a, 69
him at the name of Crispian, 66
to their preys do, 282
Roused from their slumbers, 282
the Atlantic was, 296
Rousing herself like a strong man, 277
Rout, cries amid the, 383
in reel and, 81
on rout, ruin upon ruin, 344
tolls out above the city's, 264
where meet a public, 253
Routed all his foes, 19
Rove, 344
Row, 344
an awkward hand in a, 135
to live in such a, 290
Rowel-head, up to the, 345
Royal banner, the, 125
state, throne of, 107
throne of kings, this, 112
Rub, there's the, 98
the sore, you, 374
Rubbish to the void, or cast as, 160
Rudder held, with dying hand the, 304
Rudder is of verses, rhyme the, 335
Rude am I in my speech, 380
forefathers of the hamlet, 108
that would not be a Roman, so, 341
Rudely as before, not so, 183
Rue, 344
for wine, press the, 402
nought shall make us, 112
the child may, 419
there's rosemary and, 343
Rufa, whose eye quick-glancing, 410
Ruffles, is like giving a pair of laced, 360
it's like sending them, 360
Rugged elms, beneath those, 108
Ruin, 344
Ruin and leave her, 83
behold this, 367
deep in, 342
hurled, systems into, 38
majestic though in, 85
marks the earth with, 288
or to rule the state, 385
swept, found he had to, 342
to save, to, 157
Ruined by Chinese cheap labour, 50
Ruins of the noblest man, the, 250
old, that creepeth o'er, 195
since the world began, their, 228
Rule above, one, 378
and so with holy, 341
no man doth safely, 287
of interest, his simple, 193
of men, beneath the, 301
of speech, the law and, 379
severe by, 341
sufficeth them, the good old, 396
supremacy and sway, seek for, 456
the law, and rich men, 214
the Sachem learned the, 181
the state, ruin or to, 385
the waves, Britannia, 37
what is pomp, 89
will hold, the same, 126
Ruled, a man a woman, 449
her like a thing of life who, 436
Ruler and conqueror, he the true, 410
Rulers in all lands, 147
they, unprophetic, 106
Rules and hammers, with greasy aprons, 368
him, if she, 189
of courtesy, the, 455
the court, the camp, the grove, 237
the land, wrong, 417
Ruling passion, be it what it will, 297
passion strong in death, your, 297
Rum, 344
Rumble of a distant drum, 44
Rumour of oppression and deceit, where, 229
that ye hear, the, 461
Run again upon the score, yet I am, 365
all crinkly like curled maple, 423
amuck, too discreet to, 350

Run, and they shall, 350
at, that which we, 292
away, only they conquer love who, 234
down, and all the wheels, 290
from the white man, 181
its course, until our race has, 191
over by a locomotive, if she is, 415
they are weary ere they, 437
smooth, course of true love never did, 238
that readeth it, he may, 345
we fight and we, 130
Runaway young star, curb a, 9
Rung her changes well, 244
Runneth awaie, man that, 130
Running, 344, 345
crossways, for things are, 53
if when for life's prizes you're, 220
of the race, life is the, 221
through caverns of darkness, 451
Runs, 345
a thrill of joy prophetic, 143
away, fights and, 130
before her actions, a woman's thought, 453
fast, the stream, 344
one increasing purpose, 322
the world away, 84
through the town, wee Willie Winkie, 443
with a letter, and, 301
Rupert of the Rhine, and, 19
where was, 39
Rush in, fools, 138
into the secret house, 79
into the skies, and, 316
into the state, will, 315
in where horses fear to tread, wheels, 439
of the river, save the, 311
together at last, 339
Rushed, and on they, 179
into the field, he, 131
the steed to battle driven, then, 13
together, and our spirits, 226
together at last, 339
Russet mantle clad, the morn in, 269
Russian bear, the rugged, 72
Rust, 345
and his good sword, 29
iron, this peace is nothing but to, 299
we value, it is the, 14
Rustic health, simple beauty and, 172
Rusts ingloriously, 26
Rusty, 345
for want of fighting had grown, 26
Ruth among the fields of corn, 120
Rye, coming through the, 203

S

Sabbath, 345
he who ordained the, 310
who backs his rigid, 247
Sabbath-breaker, the greatest, 421
Sable cloud, there does a, 56
Sable-coloured melancholy, 258
Sachem learned the rule, the, 181
Sack, 346
seven deadly sins in a flagon of, 26
Sacred thing is that old arm-chair, 12
Sacrifice, thine ancient, 139
Sacrifices, considering her, 62
Sad, 346
and bad and mad it was, how, 394
and you lose them all, 152
are these we daily see, more, 346
by fits, 't was, 133
morn came dim and, 105
music of humanity, the still, 188
one, and mine a, 463
say I'm, 204
than experience to make me, 261
sincerity, wrought in a, 39
tires in a mile-a, 174
vicissitudes of things, the, 425
words of tongue or pen, of all, 346
Sadder, 346
Saddest, 346
of the year, the, 257
Saddle, great in the, 164
Sadly, when you looked, 239
Sadness and longing, feeling of, 375
of farewell, no, 18
Safe and warm, to whar it was, 404
and warmly laid, know me, 283
home, and comes, 66
in ourselves, 353
to be direct and honest is not, 183
Safeguard of personal health, test and, 460
of their brood, doves will peck in, 463
Safer being meek, it's, 159
Safest and seemliest by her husband stays, 443
Safety abroad, our peace at home and, 299
the mother of, 128
pot of ale and, 6
we pluck this flower, 280
Safety-valve, 346
Saffron, red peppers, mussels, 32
Sagacious, patient, dreading praise, 8
Sage, 346
and by, 127
a leader, 46
or sophist, saint, 367
truths half so, 418
Sager, till by losing, rendered, 429
Sages have seen in thy face, 373
in all time assert, as, 360
said by ancient, 224
Said, after all is, 94
but they all mostly, 314
little, is soonest mended, 260
more easily be thought than, 166
much that is original, has, 291
on both sides, much may be, 363
to me, say the tale as 't was, 396
't was no matter what he, 256

Said, what further can be, 228
who never to himself hath, 65
Sail, and fills the white and rustling, 359
learn of the little nautilus to, 278
o'er silent seas again, to, 360
forth into the sea of life, 443
on, O ship of state, 359
set every threadbare, 133
what avail the plough or, 143
Sailing away to the west, 132
o'er life's solemn main, 138
to and fro, but are, 360
Sailor, 346
at the wheel, I see the, 200
home from sea, home is the, 163
said the, though I can't refuse, 321
Sailors, 347
and half our, 231
but men, 359
with bearded lips, Spanish, 360
Sails, argosies of magic, 59
no steady wind in its, 102
toward me, one, 315
Saint, 347, 348
a blackleg, 247
a self-elected, 316
by, by savage, 127
eppylets worn't the best mark of a, 431
himself, no wonder that the, 440
provoke, 't would a, 75
run mad, is a, 245
sage, or sophist, can all, 367
Saint Andrew's College, fresh from, 279
Saint Augustine, well hast thou said, 170
Saint Bothan's ale, the monks of, 267
Saint Davy's day, upon, 216
Saint Giles's sins, frown upon, 367
Saint John mingles with my friendly bowl, 327
Saint Keyne, 348
Saint Martin's summer, 168
Saint Nicholas, soon would be there, 51
Saint Pat, he taught them that, 440
Saint Patrick, 348
Sainted man, sure he must be, 328
Saintly mountebanks the porch disgrace, 52
Saints, 348, 349
above, and men below and, 237
and for the Lord, for the, 395
great men may jest with, 196
one of those self-constituted, 347
reforming, 345
should scorn, why the, 218
soul is with the, 29
that stubborn crew of errant, 329
with, dost bait thy hook, 347
Saint-seducing gold, 158
Sake, blameless for thy, 104
break for your sweet, 246
Sake, make the one verse for the other's, 335
not for their, 394
that died for England's, 113
wear this, for my, 251
we grow more partial for th' observer's, 445
Sake's sake, yet for old, 96
Sáki from that bowl has poured, 39
you shall pass, 152
Salad, 349
marjoram of the, 179
Salad-bowl, plunge his fingers in the, 349
Sale, one that hath a horse on, 187
Sally, there's none like pretty, 6
to walk abroad with, 74
Salmon, and the first, 32
Salt, 349
breaks his bread and tastes his, 12
might the lump of, 465
of most unrighteous tears, the, 399
that seasons right to man, 312
to add a double quantity of, 349
Saltness agree, oil, vinegar, sugar and, 349
of time, 5
Salutary effect, has a very, 372
neglect, a wise and, 280
Salutation to the morn, 57
Salutes, but sisterly, 204
Salvation, none of us should see, 260
Samaritan, 349
Same again, life is never the, 203
are never twice the, 381
by day, will not look the, 468
if 't is not the, 236
what reason I should be the, 232
with God, are all the, 155
woman I love are the, 274
Sanctified the crime, 272
Sanctimonious face, no solemn, 25
Sanction of authority, and show by, 92
Sanctity, his kissing is as full of, 205
Sand, as men wrecked upon a, 465
as tough a rope of, 57
if all their, 197
thy vows are traced in, 450
washes it out from the, 138
whose name was traced in, 274
Sandal shoon, and his, 57
Sandals fair, I would not dim my, 152
Sands, 349
betwixt two tides, these, 222
of time, on the, 138
on the shore, count how many, 205
out on the shining, 132
ran itself in golden, 241
small, the mountain, 414
to the golden, 247
would steer too nigh the, 304
Sandstone, 350
Sandwich, 350
Sandwiches of veal, like, 204
Sane than mad, it 's fitter being, 159

Sang of love and not of fame, 241
the lips elated, here, 374
the song of the shirt, he, 361
this song of the shirt, she, 361
Sans end, 103
everything, 49
Sap of reason, if with the, 327
Sapphires set in snow, her eyes are, 118
with living, 268
Sappho at her toilet's greasy task, 410
Sapping a solemn creed, 66
Saps the mind, grief that, 166
Sarcastic, 350
Sarmatia fell, 142
Sat down beneath our tree, 182
like a cormorant, 63
perched and, and nothing more, 325
side by side, where we, 387
there, a mother, 12
Satan, 350
exalted sat, 107
finds some mischief, 190
gave thereat his tail, 432
uses Bible words, 353
Satchel in his hand, with his, 440
the whining schoolboy with his, 352
Sate like a cormorant once, 63
Sated guest, claims the, 333
here grief and death were, 374
Satin, should be writ on, 210
Satire, 350
Satirist, a would-be, 245
Satisfied, well paid that is well, 293
who by repentance is not, 332
Satisfies, where most she, 5
Saturday and Monday, comes betwixt the, 74
eve, on every, 386
Sauce of syrup of poppy, 96
to meat is ceremony, 129
Sauced our broths, and, 62
Savage, 350
anti-everythings, lean, hungry, 10
bark grows sharp and, 64
bosoms, that in even, 156
breast, charms to soothe a, 272
by, by saint, 127
that is understood by the, 314
Savageness out of a bear, she will sing the, 19
Save, alike to kill or, 227
has never a soul to, 451
hast power to, 84
his country's life to, 432
me from the candid friend, 145
modest truth and beauty, 449
one's own, to, 378
our gracious king, God, 201
ourselves, to, 376
our sinful souls to, 345
the austere virtues strong to, 185
thee, and shield thee and, 9
the imperilled state, and, 276
themselves from slaughter, to, 372
the one, to, 155
Save thy sailor, praying God will, 347
to ruin, to, 157
unhappy dust thou would'st not, 76
us a life, it never could, 230
us from being tempted, 313
Saved, a race delivered, a nation, 277
in vulgar company, than, 149
without it, states can be, 301
Saves, hangs or, 306
Saving a little child, I think that, 404
common sense, rich in, 43
Saviour, 351
of 'is country, but it's, 410
stung her, 67
was born on Christmas Day, 51
who in Christ the, 220
with his law of love, the, 235
Saviour's name, where they cant of a, 208
Savour, gives it an ill, 52
these keep seeming and, 343
Savoury, will make what's homely, 388
Saw its God and blushed, 435
the air, nor do not, 379
the day, he first, 348
with his own eyes, 106
Saws, full of wise, 199
of books, all, 331
Saxon phrase, that ancient, 157
Say, 351
each night, boldly, 408
fain would I, 429
farewell, and looks around to, 70
hapless woman ne'er can, 451
he that no more must, 105
logic is logic, that's all I, 230
nay, 215
no, to mean yes an', 283
no more, 162
secure within, can, 408
that's what I always, 96
the tale as 't was said to me, 396
they are fools that marry, 255
to all the world, and, 250
to yourself, if you sometimes, 85
well, to, 459
what will Mrs. Grundy, 166
you 're welcome, to, 438
Saying, wine and truth is the, 444
wise and old, 28
Says a foolish thing, he never, 202
in verse what others say in prose, 424
to all, an ancient timepiece, 280
to the earth, the earth, 106
Scabbards, would have leaped from their, 50
Scaffold, 351
sways the future, yet that, 417
to the skies, his throne a, 317
truth for ever on the, 417
Scale, 351
he by geometric, 6
if that ain't Judas on the largest, 198

Scaled, the rampart wall had, 87
Scales, will turn the, 351
Scan, exact my own defects to, 260
presume not God to, 250
their merits or their faults to, 305
Scandal, 351
Scandalous and poor, a merry monarch, 266
Scandals, 351
Scans and spells, but, 458
Scar brought from some well-fought field, 198
Scarce, where words are, 105
Scarcity, in the very first, 26
Scarfs, garters, gold, 49
Scarlet, dyeing, 102
Scars, 351
Scarse in that, 117
Scatter seeds, we, with careless hand, 355
Scattered, 351
it, and piecemeal, 465
through the Sandwich Isles, Ham's were, 350
when the cloud is, 209
Scene, at aught this, 377
monarchs to behold the swelling, 383
that mistress of the, 81
Scenes like these, from, 352
of my childhood, 49
where love and bliss immortal reign, 27
to bring such visionary, 266
Scent of the roses, the, 258
the morning air, methinks I, 269
Scents the evening gale, that, 402
Sceptre and crown must tumble down, 103
learning, physic must, 103
shows the force, his, 260
Sceptred isle, this, 112
Scheme, centre of thy frozen, 419
Schemes o' mice and men, 261
Schnapps, 351
Scholar, the gentleman and, 58
Scholar's, the courtier's, soldier's, 263
Scholars, wherein your worldly, 122
School, before he's sent to, 467
experience keeps a dear, 117
never was there, 200
of religious liberty, 111
unwillingly to, 352
with heavy looks, toward, 239
Schoolboy, 352
a laughing, 219
to sigh like a, 239
with his satchel in his hand, 440
Schoolboys from their books, as, 239
Schooldays, in my joyful, 307
Schoolmaster, 352
Schools, less flogging in our great, 135
and were there, 176
Science, 352
a sort of hocus-pocus, 212
frowned not, fair, 257
Science
of mankind is man, the only, 250
of our law, the lawless, 214
of purer, 252
seeds of, 1
talk of your, 94
the eel of, 192
to forget, hardest, 139
Scientific gent, for any, 171
gent, not decent for a, 340
Scoff, 352
Scoffing and abuse, 368
Scold, inclines us more to laugh than, 212
Sconce, to knock him about the, 214
Scooped down, they just, 404
Scorch them up like flax, to, 347
thy smiling grace, whose glance would, 377
Score and the tally, the, 317
all shall eat and drink on my, 267
more than two tens to a, 362
yet I am run again upon the, 365
Scorn, dangers thou canst mak' us, 19
delights, to, 123
the shocking hat, man and nature, 171
to grinning, 195
to touch . . . the thing that is mean, 55
Tre, Pol and Pen, will they, 63
why the saints should, 218
will laugh a siege to, 17
Scorned amid the reeling strife, 431
his own, he, 448
by nature is mocked and, 277
the flashing goblet, has, 321
Scornful, 352
curve, thy nose turned up in, 304
jest, is a, 195
Scornfully, touch her not, 454
Scorning the base degrees, 7
to revenge, is, 335
Scorns and mocks, he who nature, 277
of time, the whips and, 323
the immortal mind, but, 262
Scotch, 352
Scotched the snake, not killed it, 372
Scotia, 352
Scotia's food, chief of, 310
Scotland, in, at the Orcades, 284
Scoundrel the refuge of a, 298
Scoundrels, 352
Scour a tribe, enough to, 266
Scoured to nothing with perpetual motion, 345
Scourge of hell, the snare and, 157
of past prosperity, she makes a, 265
of war, this mighty, 199
Scourged to his dungeon, 227
Scowl, if the brow of the foeman should, 226
Scrap of anything, really not a, 48
Scraps are good deeds past, those, 407
Scratch the nurse, will, 341
Scratched with a stick, 13

Scratches her finger, if she, 415
Scrawl and scribble, all rhyme and, 466
Scream, heard the owl, 83
Screech-owl shrieks, again the, 282
Screech-owls, 352
Screw your courage, but, 119
Screwed it up with pins, they, 208
Scribble, all rhyme and scrawl and, 466
Scribbled o'er, parchment being, 295
Scribbler, 353
a monthly, 245
Scripture, 353
Scroll, how charged with punishments the, 126
is rolled up like a, 191
of gold, kissed that haughty, 111
Scrolls a breath can float the, 144
Scruple, 353
Scruples, 353
Scrutiny, make no deep, 20
Scud and the palm-trees, but over the, 113
Scuds along, as it swiftly, 23
Scullery, shrills from tile to, 253
Sculptor's art, the, 410
Scutcheon, honour is a mere, 185
Scutcheons of silver, with, 317
Scuttled ship or cut a throat, ever, 262
Scylla, 353
Scythe and spade, with the poor crooked 103
raise not your, 345
spirit of the glass and, 406
the mower whets his, 307
Sea, 353, 354
across the, 225
and if we gang to, 267
and land, both by, 189
and land, dominion over, 402
and on the purple, 111
and sweeps the, 376
and the magic of the, 360
and the moonbeams kiss the, 204
away to the, 247
a wet sheet and a flowing, 359
bluffed the eternal, 115
bounty is as boundless as the, 239
broke over them, all at once a, 465
but if upon the troubled, 149
by life's unresting, 376
by the deep, 457
down yon dark, 18
drenched me in the, 131
foot of thy crags, O, 161
for a thousand years, we have fed our, 113
his footsteps in the, 154
home is the sailor home from, 163
I have ships that went to, 360
in rage deaf as the, 324
in the bottom of the, 102
itself, the, 101
lookin' eastward to the, 251
looking lazy at the, 392
Sea
loud timbrel o'er Egypt's dark, 405
my bark is on the, 28
my fortunes are at, 141
my God! there is no, 190
nearer the crystal, 278
not only on the deep, 437
of glory, in a, 153
of glory, like a, 216
of life, sail forth into the, 443
of melting pearl, a, 399
of men, a, 119
of the mind, the troubled, 369
of troubles, 19
of upturned faces, 119
on a wide, wide, 7
one foot in, 83
or land, light that never was on, 225
open as the, 267
our heritage the, 286
Proteus rising from the, 293
robs the vast, 402
set in the silver, 112
sing the dangers of the, 346
so lone, never was, 113
the, and the air, 196
the demons down under the, 236
the Severn to the, 441
through the desperate winter, 281
thy cold grey stones, O, 35
to that unfathomed, boundless, 228
was all a boiling seething froth, 147
was mountains rolling, the, 188
waves o'er every, 133
when I put out to, 17
white as the foamy, 357
young Jamie ga'ed to, 68
Sea-coal fire when not too dear, 110
Seal, did seem to set his, 250
that he was fain to, 336
the bargain with a holy kiss, 204
to such a bond, I'll, 197
Sealed, in phials hermetically, 393
Sealing-wax, of shoes and ships and, 430
Seam and gusset and band, 460
Seaman's eye, to guide the, 245
knell, ring the dead, 205
Seamen, 355
pity lovers rather more than, 389
Sea-mew, and shrieks the wild, 2
Sea-monster, than the, 192
Sea-water, squeezing out the, 296
Sear, the yellow leaf, is fallen into the, 223
Search a planet's house, they'll, 306
forbear, in pity from the, 328
of a word, love in, 273
the globe round, 194
the heavens for power, and, 402
the patient, and vigil long, 467
will find it out, 14
Sears, a man's half, 398
Sea's a thief, the, 402
Seas, 355
again, to sail o'er silent, 360

Seas
as twenty, 197
climb hills of, 400
incarnadine, the multitudinous, 169
I've seen your stormy, 389
rivers run to, 167
that guard our native, 110
the wealth of, 464
'twixt two boundless, 222
Sea-sand, as is the ribbed, 253
Sea-shell, 't is an empty, 375
Sea-shore, like a boy playing on the, 417
Season after, and for a, 98
from that time unto this, 335
of Christmas, at the, 48
she hath dressings fit, for every, 20
so it would have done at the same, 277
there's no such, 382
thus beaten out of, 441
Seasoned with a gracious voice, 213
Seasons, all, day and night, 361
come, a few more, 222
justice, when mercy, 260
right to man, salt that, 312
roll, as the swift, 376
Seat in parliament, a, 42
is the bosom of God, her, 212
is up on high, thy, 270
made the throne her, 265
me at his board, and, 365
of Mars, this, 112
was thought's mysterious, 367
while memory holds a, 331
Seated one day at the organ, 291
Sea-water, squeezing out the, 296
Second birth, bring her children forth to, 353
childishness and mere oblivion, 49
Daniel, a, 72
each, I'm new-born, 376
each, stood heir to the first, 315
leg, leave my, 138
marriage, I made a, 426
Seconds less, some, 186
Secret darkness, in, 154
house of death, 79
it rolls, though in, 274
of love's persistency, 117
Secret prepossession, a, 79
should be told, lest her, 277
sleep, like the, 154
spilt on the ground like water, 173
yet, to me's a, 220
Secretary, good at pen and ink, 92
Secrets of the grave, the, 368
to tell the, 380
who search the, 376
Sect, slave to no, 278
Sects, the two-and-seventy jarring, 162
unite, principles your jarring, 162
Secure and safe, 189
here we may reign, 329
I rest, 84
Secure these rights, to, 161
within, can say, 408
Secured our fame, well, 89
Securest to thee, when all seemeth, 435
See, 355
a bear, may go . . . to, 393
a friendly eye could never, 128
and lovers cannot, 243
before I doubt, I'll, 195
ere thou go, 230
her, when you shall, 243
her, you cannot, 240
him, and you shall, 137
his roads, we cannot, 155
in every hedgerow marks of angels' feet, 460
in my mind, methinks I, 277
I see a hand you cannot, 428
it clear, how few they are, 433
it is to have a vision of home, to, 133
me more, no man, 122
more sad are these we daily, 346
of Rome, the great metropolis and, 342
oh say can you, 17
or hear, whom they cannot, 455
our eyes might sometimes, 321
our Lord to, 470
the human soul take wing, to, 376
the right, as God gives us to, 337
thee still, I, 70
the veil through which I could not, 423
them more, dream we ne'er shall, 355
this and bless heaven, 50
through all things, 57
through heaven's gate, 292
thy hand, could'st not, 72
what I see, 355
which thou canst not, 337
while you can stand and, 131
Seed, 355
by him that sowed no, 460
of a nation, as the living, 276
shall spring a plenteous, 441
Seeing, shall take heart again, 138
the worst, by, 464
Seeds, 355
of godlike power, 157
of science called his A B C, 1
Seek, 355
all day, you shall, 327
but cheerly, 231
death, thou shalt, 69
it, shall we not, 209
it, we, 231
it vainly, I have sought but I, 51
me, never more thou neede st, 207
no friend save honour, 184
roses in December, 67
sech peace, than, 299
the treasure, for those who, 462
to receive countenance and profit, 318

Seek
through the world, 182
you, rejoice and men will, 329
Seeking for a fool, 137
Seeks repentance, he who, 332
Seem, are not what they, 222
to be so, that but, 183
to myself I, 417
Seemed, death it, 81
there to be, scarce, 154
to be together, they have, 409
Seeming and savour, these keep, 343
Seemly gloves, wear, 153
Seems infected that th' infected spy, 195
love, all, 231
so careful of the type she, 419
Seem'st a coward, now thou, 422
Seen, 355
as to be loved needs only to be, 425
because thou art not, 444
before, likeness hardly, 225
be it not, 296
his duty, he, 104
in dreams from God, 99
it, eye hath not, 209
no more, World-victor's victor will be, 356
scarcely felt or, 350
that day, or ever I had, 73
the days that we have, 74
the sunshine, they have never, 437
their chips, never an axe had, 437
things an' men, an' I've, 40
think what 'e's, 301
to be hated needs but to be, 425
to see and not be, 355
war's lightning flashing, I have, 431
Seers, hoary, of ages past, 334
Sees God in clouds, 176
with larger, other eyes, he, 261
Seest thou else, what, 407
Seething brains, have such, 243
free, when the surge was, 354
Seine, to the sunny banks of, 332
Seldom heard, it is so, 452
Selected, magistrates which it had, 59
Self be true, to thine own, 415
is noble song, and noble, 284
smote the chord of, 241
swear by thy gracious, 394
to wean from, 233
Self-approving, 355
Self-defence, 356
Self-elected saint, a, 316
Self-esteem, that precious jewel, 42
Selfish thoughts, on, 223
Selfishness, 356
too high for common, 159
Selfless man, O, 150
Self-love, 356
Self-mettle tires him, 9
Self-neglecting, not so vile a sin as, 356
Self-poised, who stands, 250
Self-possessed, and calm and, 333
Self-respect could we keep, what, 323
erect in, 248
Self-sacrifice, 356
Self-same mark, put the, 249
thing, the, 123
Self-slaughter, canon 'gainst, 134
Sell and mart your offices for gold, 294
blood on the game you, 148
half so precious as the stuff they, 426
made . . . to, 326
my smiles, and, 409
that thou may'st not, 158
the mighty space, 36
the lion's skin, once did, 226
the pasture now to buy the horse, 187
us his petty conceit, 67
with you, I will, 41
Selleth, 356
Selling do, if priests the, 47
or racing the same, 187
Sells, who, who buys, who makes, 311
he steals, he kills for gold, 157
Selves, an interior survey of your good, 355
from our own, 182
stepping-stones of their dead, 170
Semblances, outface it with their, 394
Semper eadem, our glorious, 17
Senates hang upon thy tongue, while listening, 11
have been bought, judges and, 158
the applause of listening, 11
Senator, 356
Send him back the . . . garland, 100
him, I'll, 22
Sendeth and giveth, God, 271
Sending them ruffles, it's like, 360
Sense, 356
and motion, devoid of, 90
and one for rhyme, one for, 335
and worth, 38
from thought divide, 245
hath the daintier, 70
in a double, 318
in Lethe steep, 98
in which they roughen to the, 357
of death is most in apprehension, 80
of duty, gives from a, 7
of mystery, a, 69
of something lost, the quiet, 231
of wrong, the, 419
of your great merit, his, 405
plain reason and with sober, 452
spirit, taste and, 67
think women have a sixth, 455
though graced with polished manners and fine, 463
want of decency is want of, 83
where heart and soul and, 204
your tailor is a man of, 396
Senseless and fit man, the most, 422
things, you worse than, 27
Senses, affections, passions, 197
for ever in joy, and the, 229
in forgetfulness, steep my, 370
it ravishes all, 452

Senses, who girt thy, 419
Sensible, 356
and well-bred man, 4
to feeling as to sight, 70
warm motion, this, 90
Sensibility, yet wanting, 463
Sent the gentle sleep from heaven, she, 369
Sentence, comprised in the one golden, 193
is but a cheveril glove, a, 447
is for open war, my, 430
of mortal fate, changeless, 211
sign, judges soon the, 92
Sentiment a-kitin', knock, 309
of respect, or the, 455
only that I find bad, your, 397
the atmosphere of intellect and, 387
Sentinel stars set their watch in the sky, 39
Sent'st it back to me, 99
Separation, 356
Sepulchre, all in one mighty, 334
Sepulchred below, earthquake's spoil is, 109
Sequestered vale of life, 68
Seraph's fire, no, 176
Seraphs might despair, where, 270
Serene and resolute and still, 333
of heaven, breaks the, 268
Serener light, dispense, 65
Sergeant death, this fell, 80
Series of trifles, life's but a, 219
Serious drinking, set ardent in for, 102
in mortality, there's nothing, 270
laughter leaves us doubly, 212
Sermon, who will not read a, 462
Sermons and soda-water the day after, 444
in stones, 3
Serpent, 356
cast it like a, 416
thou, never adder stung, 412
to have more of the, 205
Serpent's tooth, sharper than a, 49
Servant, 357
both dame and, 71
with this clause, a, 102
Servants of the people, 289
Serve God, that will not, 156
his turn, to, 218
in heaven, than, 329
it, and always, 392
love and obey, bound to, 456
my turn, what form of prayer can, 313
seven years, may, 434
the Commonwealth, to, 386
the devil in, to, 228
thee, I'll, 124
the hour, never sold the truth to, 418
't will, 189
who only stand and wait, they also, 429
Served, 357
all, 71
no private end, 385
our friends, but, 89
Serves, 357
all who dares be true, he, 415
mercy, whereto, 260
take the current when it, 69
thee best, he, 314
theirs, when it, 218
Serveth his maker, he, 181
not another's will, that, 418
still, the creatures he, 319
Service, 357
do more essential, 162
done the state some, 385
honest toil is holy, 459
long to purchase their good will, by, 455
now it did me yeoman's, 466
't is the curse of, 315
to you evermore, in love and, 192
weary and old with, 153
Serviceable, you will find it, 85
Servitor, 357
of God and Mammon, yon, 247
Servitude, the base laws of, 350
Set, a double, 100
apart for business, 102
by't more than by your life, 42
down aught in malice, nor, 117
every threadbare sail, 133
he knew how types were, 315
herself to man, she, 273
it down, meet it is I, 426
it there, who, 69
less than thou trowest, 362
mankind, all think their little, 28
my life, I have, 44
my teeth nothing on edge, that would, 309
round with three times eight, 73
the feast is, 167
the weary sun hath made a golden, 393
to a leg, can honour, 184
to them, what it is, 257
up an ordinary commonwealth, would, 266
with little wilful thorns, a rosebud, 343
Sets all things even, time at last, 467
it light, and, 375
off sprightly wit, 447
when he, 393
Setting, hath had elsewhere its, 25
haste now to my, 122
of boys' copies, 63
sun, and with the, 122
sun, signal of the, 115
Settle, it behoves you to, 449
Settled government, land of, 144
Settles over all, that, 369
Seven ages, his acts being, 383
and pine in vain the sacred, 159
cities warred for Homer, 183

Seven deadly sins in a flagon, 26
halfpenny loaves sold, 130
hills of yore, on thy, 342
hundred pounds and possibilities, 311
long year, have been Tom's food for, 261
thousand years, with yesterday's, 411
wealthy towns contend, 183
year, it seems the length of, 407
years, may serve, 434
Seventy-year clocks, our brains are, 33
Sever, and then we, 203
Atropos, 380
for years, to, 296
no more shall the war-cry, 212
that when both must, 377
Several tale, brings in a, 61
they be, though, 227
Severe, a friend, 91
by rule, 341
from lively to, 162
from pleasant to, 162
Severed as the flax, is, 38
now, those who are, 179
Severn runs, the Avon to the, 441
to the sea, the, 441
Sew them on in a dream, 460
Sewing at once with a double thread, 362
Sex, 357
are still forgiving, 140
assume, can either, 381
commonly are, weeping as our, 438
to the last, 289
whose presence civilizes ours, 54
Sexton, 357
Time, that bald, 407
went and told the, 22
Shabby gentility, 171
Shackles fall, and their, 368
Shade, dancing in the chequered, 71
let it sleep in the, 274
no, no shine, 285
of Freedom's ensign, 'neath the, 64
of immortality, fame is the, 124
of Julius Cæsar's hair, the exact, 58
of the trees, and rest under the, 333
on it, sit under the, 131
sleep beneath the, 370
some boundless contiguity of, 229
that yew-tree's, 108
variable as the, 453
Shade-made blade, at that, 115
Shades more sweetly recommend, as, 447
Shadow, 358
a, bubble, air, 219
and a fear, hung a, 69
and in itself a, 124
and shine is life, 224
lies, in whose orbs a, 246
life's but a walking, 411
of a dream, a hope beyond the, 185
standeth God within the, 417
Shadow
which he treads on at noon, 392
Shadows, 358
are playing with the, 469
gathered faster, while round them, 280
only waiting till the, 429
reign, in the land where, 151
that walk by us still, 2
Shady cloister mewed, in, 56
place, made a sunshine in the, 119
Shaft, 358
flew thrice, thy, 12
that quivered in his heart, 106
that made him die, 106
to fledge the, 106
Shafts from hooded eyes, 23
of doubt, a shield against the, 120
Shake, did the hand then of the potter, 178
hands and part, fit that we, 296
hands for ever, 296
he gave his bridle-reins a, 3
I would not, 120
our disposition, horridly to, 268
the roof may, 44
the spheres, seems to, 155
the world, 147
thunder-music, rolling, 291
thy gory locks at me, never, 229
Shaked like a coward, 277
Shaken, 358
withered and, 4
if by chance it be, 173
Shakes off her wonted firmness, 162
that slightly, 167
Shakespeare, 358
Fancy's child, sweetest, 432
spake, that, 412
what needs my, 29
Shakespeare's name, in Milton's or in, 458
Shaking her invincible locks, 277
Shall be, what must be, 273
Shallow, by, 419
draughts intoxicate the brain, 215
Shame, 358
and hell, fell to, 57
and hide the, 121
and its, 416
and share in its, 428
beneath our feet each deed of, 170
be thine, could, 275
doff it for, 226
done our ancestors no, 89
forespent with love and, 457
from no condition rise, honour and, 184
hev one glory an' one, 208
open the door with, 96
publishing our neighbour's, 351
relief from future, 89
say what it will, let, 399
the devil, tell truth and, 417
through glory and, 236
to be bad, 'tis no, 16

Shame
to hide her, 136
were mine, that, 275
yet start at, 123
Shamed, 358
Shames a scribbler, who, 353
Shank, for shrunk, 294
Shape, I hardly fear his terrible, 78
a husband out of, woman could not, 255
but that, take any, 72
ever straighten up this, 467
in any mood, in any, 376
more terrible than this, there is no, 165
of a camel, 56
or in that, in this, 59
they choose, in what, 381
through this dread, 188
Shaped a hero new, 179
him, those who, 147
whence the pen was, 301
Shapeless earth, trampled back to, 107
Shapes of foul disease, old, 93
of grief, 448
our ends, divinity that, 94
turns them to, 308
was full of fiery, 277
Shards if we offend, and broken into, 107
Share, if to her, 128
in its shame, and, 428
in the work, shall do his, 54
in whatso we, 181
of honour, the greater, 185
of wine, I have drunk my, 221
the envied kiss to, 175
the utmost, of my desire, 100
thy destiny, all that breathe will, 86
to chasten and, 153
Shared in the plunder, he, 353
Shares my beaker, no playmate, 146
Shark and the sheering gull, to the, 113
and tiger, like the, 256
Sharp, likes to have her religion rather, 329
the greatest, 447
thy sting is not so, 24
to them as thorn, as, 419
Sharper than a serpent's tooth, 49
wit, will find another, 447
Shatter all his bulk, seem to, 363
the vase, you may 258
Shattered, dishonoured, lost for evermore, 107
when the lamp is, 209
Shave, I never thought that they would, 326
like the goat, 153
Shaving of a baker, I see you a, 225
Shaving-materials, who is possessed of, 464
Shay, the wonderful one-hoss, 46
She, 358
Shear swine, all cry and no wool, 395
Shearing, welcome to our, 343
Shears of destiny, bear the, 86
wi' her needle an' her, 270
with the abhorred, 123
Sheathed their swords for lack of argument, 395
Sheaths, gladly, 317
Shebeen shop, his mother kept a, 440
Shed, a little, 404
a tear in all my miseries, think to, 399
his blood for his country, to, 383
if there the meanest, 182
one drop, dost, 134
the honey, where'er ye, 184
them now, prepare to, 399
the rainbow's glory is, 209
Sheep, and kept, 261
de po' los', ob de sheepfol', 359
the rot in, 306
to a close-shorn, 209
worse fed than your hogs and your, 323
Sheepfold, 358, 359
Sheer o'er the crystal battlements, 122
Sheet, 359
anchor of our peace at home, 299
for and a shrouding, 303
of paper, crammed up in a, 336
that standard, 17
Sheeting, by dealing out flannel and, 175
Sheets, 359
Shelf, on every, 297
Shell, a prettier, than ordinary, 417
in the crust of his, 446
is broken, the, 375
leaving thine outgrown, 376
shot and, 80
take ye each a, 292
they picked the luscious food, from the rough, 300
Shell-like ear, her small and, 106
Shells, and rainbow-coloured, 354
the young shall peck at the, 97
Shelter and grace of our line, 49
for thy head, and, 182
him with noble and right-reverend precedents, 92
yields, where no bush a, 207
Sheltered me, in youth it, 457
Shem's proud children reared the Assyrian piles, 350
Shepherd, and Dick the, 190
equals the king to the, 369
tells his tale, every, 307
Shepherd's tongue, truth on every, 237
Sheppards, Jack, of their city flocks, 325
Sheridan, 359
Shield thee and save thee, 9
the soul without a, 120
Shift, for any marketable, 265
Shilling, 359
refuse the, 345

Shillings, for eighteen a week, 42
Shin in fight, when a, 216
Shine alike to all, doth, 443
at full or no, if the moon, 193
by night and day, to, 245
in more substantial honours, we 'll, 148
is life, shadow and, 224
my white plume, 308
no shade, no, 285
or rain or, 221
that his goblet might, 153
took lodgings for rain or, 21
to bid thy morning, 10
Shined bright and made a sunshine, 119
think how Bacon, 123
upon, although it is not, 88
Shines a good deed, 42
one simile that solitary, 364
over all, light of love, 235
Shineth as the gold, al thing which that, 158
Shingle, by shining, 419
Shingles, which is played upon the, 325
Shining frame, a, 132
mark, death loves a, 81
may I not see him, 420
Ship, 359, 360
adrift, finds a, 102
goes down, afore the, 320
has weathered every rack, 43
me somewhere east of Suez, 392
never give up the, 58
or cut a throat, ever scuttled, 262
there is water to float a, 37
Ships, 360
and sealing-wax, of shoes and, 430
are but boards, 359
better thet all our, 299
did we watch the stately, 226
go on, the stately, 169
hearts of oak are our, 286
into this world we come like, 461
new, to build, 353
they steer their courses, like, 335
work their passage as they do in, 176
Shipwrecked brother, forlorn and, 138
Shipwright or the carpenter, 164
Shirk, do n't foul and do n't, 222
his daily work, who 'd, 248
Shirt, 360, 361
a shroud as well as a, 362
Shirt-sleeves, human nature in its, 188
Shive, of a cut loaf to steal a, 435
Shiver when thou 'rt named, 162
Shivering, sends him, 73
Shoals of honour, 140
Shock, intestine and furious close, 54
of pleasure, may give a, 435
sink beneath the, 28
them, and we shall, 112
will occur in a hurry and, 348
Shocking hat, man and nature scorn the, 171
Shocks of sound, with twelve great 284
Shoe, 361
after, luck shall fling her old, 244
be Spanish or neat 's leather, 20
untied, your, 239
Shoes, 361
and ships and sealing-wax, of, 430
used to call for his old, 146
Shoe-string a careless, 364
Shone ever, as your smile on me, 352
Shook hands as over a vast, 409
the hills with thunder riven, then, 13
the house, and, 388
the world, monk who, 267
when he laughed, 24
Shoon, and his sandal, 57
Shoot folly as it flies, 136
let others, 138
to teach the young idea how to, 398
when the guns begin to, 410
Shoots his thought by hidden nerves, he, 86
Shop, 361
Shopkeepers, 361
girls sitting like, 266
Shops of trade, in all the, 386
Shore, and one on, 83
apples on the Dead Sea 's, 76
a rapture on the lonely, 457
come back from the echoless, 340
fades, my native, 2
his control stops with the, 288
how many sands on the, 205
landing on some silent, 89
little boats should keep near, 424
more have been wrecked on, 354
my boat is on the, 28
now, them unhappy folks on, 285
of the great unknown, from the, 15
roar of the billows on the, 19
the despot 's heel is on thy, 255
they that saw it from the, 465
to shore, groan from, 87
to that far, 409
to that unknown and silent, 158
to the, gallantly bounding, 436
upon the river, 3
where is that radiant, 209
wolf 's long howl from Oonalaska 's, 449
Shores of Acheron, on the, 333
of time, but on the, 138
unpathed waters, undreamed, 436
Shorn lamb, tempers the wind to the, 209
of being plucked and, 103
Short, 361
and bright, 9
and far between, 9
of leaves, getteth, 216
Shortens its weapons, the race that, 437
not his own life, 213
Shorter, these make the long night, 440

Short-weight dollar is not an honest dollar, 96
Shot, 362
and shell, stormed at with, 80
fool's bolt is soon, 137
from the mouth of a cannon, 283
the albatross, I, 5
through the ear, 118
through the staff, 112
Shot-torn wreck, may sink with a, 133
Should have been, but what he, 410
not say it, that, 351
Shoulder, a tap upon the, 42
on his, and his, 71
Shouldered his crutch and showed, 68
Shoulders, and thrown over the, 361
but what lights on my, 244
do grow beneath their, 88
Shout, 362
Shout and revelry, midnight, 129
and the clash and the, 136
down all our line a deafening, 308
that tore Hell's concave, 46
Shouting and confusion, understood the, 433
dies, the, 139
their emulation, 43
Shove by justice, may, 289
Shoved his ramrod down, and he, 38
Shovel and tongs, sure the, 441
and we run to the Dust, 56
the clay in, 103
with a dirty, 214
Shoves you from the stage, and, 228
Show a woman when he loves her, one to, 243
contains and nourish, 118
dances and the public, 448
himself what he is, to let him, 401
I never ain't had no, 330
it, and all things, 219
itself courageous, 68
myself, now will I, 205
of evil, obscures the, 213
the most of heaven, to, 248
the whole wealth of thy wit in an instant, 447
thy lips, how ripe in, 226
to me, that mercy, 260
you how, its petals kiss, I'll, 203
you're up to fightin' tu, 299
Showed him more, she, 277
us the wise course to steer, 91
Showers, chill with early, 105
gems in sparkling, 107
of blood, lay the summer's dust with, 27
on her kings, 107
violets pluckt the sweetest, 426
Showest, 362
Showeth bright, that outward, 158
Shows but a bastard valour, 422
his hoar leaves in the glassy stream, 444
leak in roof or flaw in right, 356
not till it be struck, 135
Shows she rules, never, 189
what thinks, he, 84
Shrank, while apostles, 67
Shreds and patches, a king of, 202
Shrew, 362
Shrewdly, the air bites, 5
Shrews both short and tall, women are, 456
Shriek, a solitary, 395
wakes with a, 99
Shrieked, and freedom, 142
the timid, then, 408
Shrieks, 362
the wild sea-mew, 2
Shrine of truth, in the pure, 269
sought a faith's pure, 464
Shrink, and all the boards did, 435
from danger, the man who does not, 390
from what we cannot shun, 206
not from blasphemy, 67
or cower, I will not, 392
rather than in silence, 368
with eyes that would not, 420
Shrill and clear, the lark so, 210
Shrills, when her whinny, 253
Shrivelled in a fruitless fire, 160
Shrives us, who comes and, 176
Shroud, 362
and rode in his, 332
the knell, the, 401
of snow, lay in his, 55
Shrouding sheet, a, 303
Shrubs, blood on your new foreign, 148
Shudder, make thee to, 362
Shuffled off this mortal coil, 98
Shuffling, there is no, 289
Shun, here he seems to, 290
more than hell to, 61
Scylla, when I, 353
shrink from what we cannot, 206
the sight, that seems to, 316
Shunned the fire, thus have I, 131
Shut the door, good John, 206
thee from heaven, 376
the Gardens, 345
thee in, their temple walls to, 155
thee out, their iron creeds to, 155
the gates of mercy on mankind, 368
the ponderous tome, he, 263
their saddening eyes, try to, 384
two eyes with coin-weights, 208
up, the gates of mercy shall be all, 260
up our jack-knives, carved it or, 275
your saintly ears, who, 217
Shuts up sorrow's eye, sleep that sometimes, 370
up the story of our days, 406
Shutter, open here I flung the, 325
Shuttered my doors with flame, I, 284
Shutters fast, close the, 116
Shuttle flies, how swift the, 362
Shy of using it, he was very, 446
Sick, 362
at heart, and grow, 362

Sick
at heart, I am, 57
I'm dead, say I'm, 206
man's dying sigh, a, 119
of sickness, I'm, 363
of time, I am, 333
the devil was, 87
Sicken and decay, when love begins to, the appetite may, 273
Sickened and went to her bed, 326 326
Sicklied o'er with the pale cast, 61
Sickly trees, gather on, 425
Sickness, 363
rages, and, 224
from, and from grief, 89
Side, a hair 'twixt south and southwest, 93
and neither leans on this, 228
and pouch on, 294
by side, for the way was one, 220
dares to take the, 337
fallen from his fellow's, 90
feels it instantly on every, 380
go bare, back and, 6
of the law, keep o' the windy, 214
on the other, 220
that I must draw this metal from my, 442
who've crossed to the farther, 339
with Truth is noble, 34
Side-curl, 363
Side-door, have a front-door and a, 129
Sides, 363
against the panting, 345
dough on both, 41
laughter holding both his, 382
that give places or pelf, on all, 62
the leaf, writ o' both, 336
Sidney's sister, 180
Siege to scorn, will laugh a, 17
Sieve, like water through a, 414
passed through kitchen, 349
water in a, 64
Sifted the wheat, then had, 276
three kingdoms, God hath, 276
Sifting out the hearts of men, he is, 415
Sigh, 363
and say Amen, 372
and waft a, 216
a sick man's dying, 119
a world of pride in the very, 316
I resign, with a, 333
learn to kiss not to, 442
lost without a, 434
no more, ladies, 83
not whine nor, 233
she looked up to, 371
the night-winds, 2
to, like a schoolboy, 239
too much, a, 203
to think, may, 192
was all sob and, 296
Sighed, 363
and looked unutterable things, 230
but they, 242
Sighed
or her, 416
old Euclio said and, 91
till woman smiled, man the hermit, 450
upon a midnight pillow, as ever, 242
Sighing, and farewell goes out, 438
every minute, 56
like a furnace, 242
of a reed, there's music in the, 272
that nature formed but one such man, 359
Sighs, 363
and prayers, I can hear your, 74
and tears, a few more, 222
for a daughter, or hear, 400
if ye be sorry open it with, 96
tempered with love's, 308
Sight, 364
at whose, 172
charms strike the, 260
glimmering landscape on the, 209
half so fine a, 129
hide it from my, 28
how tame a, 133
lost to, th' ecstatic lark, 210
may at first, 361
more, luvved 'er a vast, 241
no, no sound, 384
of each other, coming in, 339
of human ties, at, 233
of means to do ill deeds, 83
of Proteus, have, 293
of the bird, in vain in the, 280
passed in music out of, 241
that loved not at first, 242
that seems to shun the, 316
they loved, but at first, 242
those far stars that come in, 466
to feeling as to, 70
veiled from human, 154
when first she gleamed upon my, 302
when she was out of, 286
Sightless song, the lark becomes a, 457
Sights of death, ugly, 102
so full of ugly, 99
Sign, an evil, 25
dies and makes no, 91
no, that it was circular, 106
shown by many a bitter, 233
to thet with all my heart, 431
your names, 275
Signal blow, a, a shining mark, 81
is fired, the culverin's, 63
of a goodly day to-morrow, 393
of the setting sun, 115
shown, only a, 360
to recall him, a, 132
Signals cannot be seen, in case, 360
Signed, the names are, 275
Signifying nothing, 411
Signs and portents, more filled with, 165
of care, there are no, 331
there is no believing, 239

Silence, 364
all, slowly, 337
an' all glisten, 152
and tears, parted in, 296
at last the clicking, 403
darkness again and a, 360
dissolves the spell of it, 451
envious tongues, to, 299
from the living, if thou withdraw in, 86
in the, 413
of the centuries, after the, 147
of the heart, the, 172
shrink, rather than in, 368
spreads the couch, 333
though quite in, 204
we parted in, 296
ye wolves, while Ralph to Cynthia howls, 282
Silenced, his scruples thus, 353
Silent and desperate part, 61
in a last embrace, 108
in the grave, lies, 412
long to be patient and, 451
room below, in that, 55
sea, ever burst into that, 353
shore, to that unknown and, 158
tents are spread, 26
Silently steal away, 44
Silk, 364
no gowns of, 220
remains, it soft as, 280
soft for us as, 280
Silken dalliance in the wardrobe lies, 111
snare, in the, 30
Silks, littering with unfolded, 361
Silly 't would be, consider how, 440
Siloam fell, the tower in, 193
Silver, all gold and, 158
bells, 23
can buy, a knot that gold and, 206
hae to spare, 364
he left us, for a handful of, 336
lining, turn forth her, 56
mantle threw, her, 268
pin, and pinned it wi' a, 231
stars, forty flags with their, 134
that tips with, 268
with scutcheons of, 317
Simile, 364
Simon, 364
Simonides, the good king, 133
Simple and tame, yet, 187
ashamed that women are so, 456
faith than Norman blood, 148
hearts are fresh and, 156
one, it is a, 48
Simplicity, 364, 365
a child, 252
more for that in low, 421
sublime, in his, 43
our weary souls dream of, 365
Sin, 365, 366
against the strength of youth, wants that, 470
Sin
and bile, 24
and folly into, 136
and guilt, each thing of, 47
and so is, 380
bellows blows up, 134
by that, 7
cherubs on its face protect me from the, 68
committed while conscience slept, 215
could blight or sorrow fade, ere, 77
even in the blossoms of my, 370
for the good man's, 287
had rendered unto her, for, 369
has many tools, 218
have dulled their eyes with, 155
I cannot think it is a mortal, 393
if to be old and merry be a, 290
I know it is a, 323
in their anger was a, 141
is it, 79
it is great, 287
murders our youth with his sorrow and, 406
no, but to be rich, 22
of humanity, every, 172
poking the fire all alone is a, 441
ring out the want, the care, the, 430
self-love . . . is not so vile a, 356
that doth goad us on to, 347
that his favourite, 316
that often drowns him, 101
to covet honour, if it be a, 185
to falter would be, 337
to me unknown, what, 466
to rob them of their mite, 67
to sorrow, they say 'tis a, 374
to swear unto a, 287
'twad be a, 254
unimpeachable of, 413
weakness a, 432
who make compromise with, 60
Sincere, his love, 29
never run, 403
Sincerely so, a soul is found, 47
Sincerity, wrought in a sad, 39
Sines and tangents straight, resolve by, 6
Sinful, 366
act, repent each, 413
oath, to keep a, 287
Sing, 366
arms and the man I, 13
at the oven's mouth, 66
because I must, I do but, 226
careless o'er my cup I, 402
for you alone I strive to, 456
heigh-ho and heigh-ho, 203, 254
her song, 71
once, and could, 367
so like a lark, 326
strange that death should, 273
the dangers of the sea, 346
the savageness, 19
the songs he loved to hear, 101

Sing
when you come to hear us, 304
wherewith thou dost so heavenly, 301
Singe yourself, that it do, 136
Singed her hair, they, 208
Singer, sans, 103
Singers have sung, the, 207
Singeth a quiet tune, 37
blithe, the milkmaid, 307
Singing in the wilderness, 85
out of tune, all were, 9
with his hand, his work a, 374
Single, 366
blessedness, lives and dies in, 342
bound, I'll clear at a, 152
church below the hill, 23
gentlemen, like two, 150
hair, beauty draws us with a, 168
hair, draw you to her with a, 168
hair pulled out, with a, 168
instances, the wilderness of, 214
life, that thou consum'st thyself in, 442
man, like a spruce, 338
word, 'tis a, 139
Sings at grave-making, 70
and he sings, that he, 235
from the organ-pipe of frailty, 273
her own elegy, swan, 273
in youth the heart exults and, 470
like a soul beatified, of love, 210
the lark at heaven's gate, 210
to one clear harp, 170
Sink, 366
a navy, a load would, 278
beneath the shock, 28
into darkness again, 138
not gross to, 240
or swim, leave us yit to, 320
to rot, should, 299
with a shot-torn wreck, that flag may, 13
Sinking in thy last long sleep, 227
Sinks a throne, wherever, 144
downward, whilst my gross flesh, 270
into the last eternal rest, he, 62
it, and I am ready to depart, 221
Sinned, 366
against than sinning, more, 366
all, 2
a soul that has, 247
if ye have, 96
Sinner, made such a, 219
too weak to be a, 435
Sinners above all men, 193
all, we are, 80
commending, 347
Sinning, 366
is to-day official, 289
unless when she was, 441
Sins, 366, 367
against this life, he, 224
in a flagon of sack, seven deadly, 26
in penance for her, 208
Sins
most, who, 400
of thine own, should'st have few, 449
of will, 160
pride is one of the seven deadly, 315
to her Saviour, her, 351
were invented for our, 304
wisely from expensive, 345
Sip the ripe ruddy dew, 226
would to each one, 71
Sips the nearest draught, 232
Sire, he, their, 181
to son, by bleeding, 142
the soul immortal as its, 376
was a knight, thy, 16
Sire's return, run to lisp their, 175
Sires, 367
so lived our, 94
Sister be, a ministering angel shall my, 426
live a barren, 56
Sidney's, 180
Spirit, come away, 170
Sisterly salutes to feel, but, 204
Sister's charms, who can love a, 400
Sisters and friends, 129
three, twisted by the, 127
Sit and grin, for me to, 323
beside my lonely fire, I, 330
down to a quiet game for love, 234
for Hell, might, 115
nor, nor stand, 328
Sits the wind, to know where, 444
Sitting on the stile, I'm, 387
Six foot o' man, A1, 249
hundred, left of, 80
hundred, rode the, 90
is sounding from the chime, 115
parts, were in, 103
precious souls, and all agog, 72
Richmonds in the field, there be, 337
thousand ducats, every ducat in, 103
Sixpence, 367
all too dear, he held them, 387
if you will give me, 310
Sixth hour, about the, 393
sense, think women have a, 455
Sixty smaller ones, each with, 73
Size of pots of ale, take the, 6
Skaith to me, nae maiden lays her, 456
Skeptic could enquire for, whatever, 441
Sketch, the first rude, 13
Skies, 367
and points her to the, 257
and rush into the, 316
a scaffold to the, 317
cloudless climes and starry, 430
earth to the vaulted, 208
illumed the eastern, 105
mid the brightness of the, 378
pointing to the, 59
serene, and, 233
the air, the, 293

Skies
the child of the, 58
twinkling in the, 384
up to the, 63
which carries a bard to the, 445
Skill, and simple truth his utmost, 418
an' kin 's o', 212
in surgery, honour hath no, 184
the parson owned his, 12
who has the power and, 450
who thinks by force or, 450
Skimble-skamble, 367
Skin, 367
of an innocent lamb, 295
of wine, this, 12
once did sell the lion 's, 226
Skins may differ, but affection, 3
on scalded milk, like wrinkled, 364
Skipper, some coasting, 99
Skull, 367
of a lawyer, may not that be the, 214
of an old mammoth, till the, 141
weave fine cobwebs fit for, 57
Skulls, they drink out of, 379
Sky, 368
above, the blue, 235
a hot and copper, 63
and in yon western, 384
and the ocean but the, 288
a transient meteor in the, 376
believe that in the, 384
bends over all, the blue, 348
bribery 's golden, 64
bridal of the earth and, 73
changes when they are wives, the, 457
charm from the, 182
clears not without a storm, so foul a, 388
danced to see that banner in the, 114
darkness swept across the, 70
expansive as the, 267
freeze, thou bitter, 24
from forth the frowning, 28
girdled with the, 268
guides through the boundless, 387
nor in the, 377
rain potatoes, let the, 311
stand presently, till earth and, 391
stars set their watch in the, 39
that equal, 176
the droppings of the, 101
to the wild, 23
under the open, 362
under the wide and starry, 163
waft thy name beyond the, 125
were close against the, 331
with all the blue ethereal, 132
Slain, and no be, 249
another, ere thou hast, 180
at thy nod were, 151
he can never do that 's, 130
he slew the, 19
he that is in battle, 130
Slain, he who is in battle, 130
if he that in the field is, 184
the Drury Lane Dane, 115
thinks he is slain, or if the, 368
though he were ten times, 199
to-day, five have I, 337
Slam the door, 94
Slander, 368
and the spite, the civic, 54
Slandered, goose, to hear thee, 304
Slanderous, 368
tongue, gall in the, 42
Slanted back this brow, the hand that, 195
Slap-dash into the water, 372
Slaughter, 368
he that made the, 41
I condemn, to, 305
to save themselves from, 372
Slaughters a thousand, 83
Slave, find neither coward nor, 110
I have set my life, 44
never float over a, 133
of the wheel of labour, 207
oh to be a, 451
to no sect, 278
to thousands, has been, 275
where'er he cowers, the, 143
wherever groans, a, 144
you fancied your, 144
Slavery or death, 430
the price of chains and, 217
Slaves, 368
as freemen, not, 286
beside, all are, 144
Britons never will be, 37
howe'er contented, 143
kings must have, 202
of gold, whose sordid dealings, 58
or cowards, sots or, 113
the creed of, 279
Slayer, 368
Slays, if the red slayer thinks he, 368
war its thousands, 431
Sleave of care, the ravelled, 370
Sledges with the bells, hear the, 23
Sleek-headed men, 126
Sleep, 369, 370
and a forgetting, 25
and his brother, 81
and not his cousin, 81
a time, though it, 28
best of rest, 80
calm and peaceful shall I, 84
cannot still them, 403
care-charmer, 81
Death 's twin-brother, 81
down and, 304
every sorrow 's lulled to, 402
forefathers of the hamlet, 108
in dull cold marble, 140
in peace to, 84
in their last, 75
in the shade, let it, 274
is rounded with a, 428
like a strong man after, 277

Sleep
like the secret, 154
men may, 404
might steal on me, like, 81
of death, in that, 98
o' nights, such as, 126
reveals, a late-lost form that, 442
rock me to, 340
shall be broken, thy, 390
shall obey me, 69
sinking in thy last long, 227
snuff, tobacker and, 187
some must, 84
still let me, 98
than a century of, 390
that knows not breaking, 373
the brave who sink to rest, how, 34
the dreamless, that lulls the dead, 468
the prologue to his, 100
the sooner to, 132
the sounder, may, 169
the weary to, 39
the world may, 254
they, 163
they all lie in uncomplaining, 21
they softly lie and sweetly, 333
till morn, no, 71
to, perchance to dream, 98
to wake, 337
when he wakes, 264
when we wake and when we, 381
within mine inn, 413
with nothing of regret, 62
with thee, thy ignominy, 114
Sleepers, and the eyes of the, 77
waking, grumble, 44
Sleeping, 370
dust, benison o'er the, 157
she is, 105
tarn, into some, 53
when she died, 105
while I am, 369
within my orchard, 4
woods all night, 37
Sleeps, 371
and waiting justice, 417
till tired he, 49
well, he, 223
Sleet fa' pie'cin' thin, wha'r de, 359
Sleeve, 371
unbuttoned, your, 239
Sleeves, like an herald's coat without, 361
of lawn, 42
Sleigh, 't is the merry, 23
Slept, 371
and dreamed, 104
dying when she, 105
in peace, and, 185
together, we still have, 224
while conscience, 215
while their companions, 177
Slew him, I, 7
him, then, 277
them, and, 193
Slew the slain, he, 19
whose fiat millions, 332
Slide, let the world, 463
Slight a thing, a woman is too, 449
my call, thou wilt not, 84
Slights it, love, 77
the next, who, 224
Slings and arrows, 19
Slip the dogs of war, let, 335
the mongrel's hold will, 40
Slippery, 371
Slits the thin-spun life, 123
Slop, she was excellent at a, 297
Slope to hell, half-way down the, 316
Sloping slowly to the west, great Orion, 291
Sloth finds the down pillow hard, 437
Slow, come he, 79
critter, thet, 212
growth, a plant of, 60
length along, drags its, 6
or the clock was too, 348
pace at first, requires, 55
the sun climbs, 224
Slowly, comes a hungry people, 301
the Bible of the race is writ, 24
the mills of God grind, 262
Slowly-dying power, a, 18
Sluggard, 371
Sluggish blood, a very river of, 133
Slumber again, I must, 371
at thy side, thy free proud fathers, 128
beside him, longed to, 163
in its bosom, 74
Slumbering passions burn, when once their, 300
Slumber's chain, ere, 258
Slumbers, 371
dead that, 222
in a peasant's arm, 300
over my, 340
roused from their, 282
sinks back to uneasy, 99
Sly, tough and devilish, 413
Smack of age, some, 5
Smacked on her cheek, that, 204
Smacks of the field and the street, a preacher who, 314
Small appear, though it, 414
attends both great and, 123
beer, and chronicle, 138
beer, to desire, 22
beer, to drink, 130
booth, can set up a, 67
choice in rotten apples, 11
estate, of very, 175
habits, well pursued betimes, 167
Latin and less Greek, 211
or his deserts are, 126
praise, were no, 312
too, for any marketable shift, 265
when I was very, 331
yet they grind exceeding, 262
Smaller still, and these have, 134

Smart, 371
human sorrow and, 116
love and all its, 232
of all the girls that are so, 6
will weep a bramble's, 398
young folks are, 469
Smarting in lingering pickle, 439
Smarts so little, no creature, 137
Smashing it, hatching the egg than by, 108
Smell, 371
a rat, I, 325
as sweet, would, 275
false Latin, I, 211
of bread and butter, 34
of roses, she hates the, 343
of sweet herbs, the, 151
onions, mine eyes, 438
sweet and blossom in their dust, 199
the blood of a British man, 27
to turf, to, 269
Smells, grows and, 100
of Hollands gin, when you find he, 181
to heaven, it, 272
Smile, 371
a great man's, 42
and be a villain, one may, 426
and we smile, 141
at the claims, 148
beguile with a dimple or, 398
calm thou mayst, 227
frown and we, 141
he smiled a kind of sickly, 350
on thee to-morrow, sunburst may, 186
on ye sweet, I'd, 352
so many, 38
sweet as your, 352
that no cloud can o'ercast, 31
the traitor's, 384
to those who hate, a, 363
we shall, 125
upon his finger's ends, 359
yet I, 74
Smiled as he sat by the table, 371
if wrong, I, 67
on us, right graciously he, 308
sighed till woman, 450
while all around thee, 227
Smiles around, cannot go where universal love not, 43
as we draw nigh, that, 219
at the drawn dagger, 191
beaming all o'er with your, 116
becks and wreathed, 196
in yeer face, that, 212
not in a house of tears, Venus, 424
the, the tears, 258
welcome ever, 438
Smile-smoothing, heart-opening, 397
Smiling cheek, a villain with a, 11
Smilingly, drink it down right, 78
Smitest, 372
Smithate of truth, the, 416
Smithy-shop after every roll, 54
Smitten, hath hope been, 391
Smock, with her dirty, 410
Smoke and stir, above the, 107
but a good cigar's a, 53
cannot, but the, 302
concealed, in yon, 391
had wafted, 408
I, but do not burn, 339
Smoke-stack white as snow, 215
Smoky, 372
Smooth and even, all would go, 140
runs the water, 435
the careworn brow, to, 297
the few silver threads, 340
the ice, to, 152
Smoothed his wrinkled front, 432
Smoothing its dilapidated castor, 171
Smoothness and softness, 349
rough, that turns earth's, 328
that may give it, 379
Smooth-shaven green, on the dry, 165
Smote on all the chords with might, 241
the rock of the national resources, 340
the warden hoar, 87
Smutch appears, an ugly, 36
Snaffle of courtship, pleasant the, 253
Snagsby's, wos a-prayin' wunst at Mr., 314
Snail, creeping like, 352
or move like the, 446
Snails, like, 129
Snake, 372
like a wounded, 6
Snakes, 372
Snapper-up, 372
Snare and scourge of hell, the, 157
in the silken, 30
the twisted tendril as a, 69
Snatches from the sun, she, 402
Sneaking off, it is, 423
Sneaks to death, the coward, 66
Sneer, 372
teach the rest to, 71
the self-complacent British, 225
with solemn, 66
yesterday's, 442
Sneering and without, 71
Sniffed the battle from afar, he, 386
Snooze, cotched a vild beast in a, 200
Snore upon the flint, weariness can, 437
Snort to the rein, 387
Snow, 372
all bloodless lay the untrodden, 225
and the bosom of, 246
as pure as, 42
chaste as unsunned, 47
crotch-deep in the, 313
her eyes are sapphires set in, 118
lay in his shroud of, 55
naked in December, 191
on field an' hill, 152
pale and white and cold as, 74
she is not afraid of the, 451

Snow
smoke-stack white as, 215
that whiter skin of hers than, 367
the maid with a bosom of, 246
time dissolve the winter, 233
wash it white as, 169
when it's thaw, like, 215
your locks are like the, 311
Snowdrop, love's first, 203
Snow-flakes, 372
fall, as, 144
Snowhid in Jenooary, 323
Snows, and upon the crumping, 207
as any mountain of its, 285
are my robe, the, 284
begin, when the, 78
may o'er his head be flung, 123
of yester-year, where are the, 468
said our Lady of the, 276
Snow-white crest, behind the, 179
wand, or, 149
Snuff of younger spirits, 228
tobacker and sleep, 187
Snuff-box, and fill his, 360
Snug little island, it's a, 194
So said I, He said and, 62
Soap, 372
hundreds will subscribe for, 38
Soar again, through rolling clouds to, 106
in fame, wade in wealth or, 104
so high, wherewith he wont to, 106
when we stoop than when we, 445
Soars enraptured, he, 233
Sob and sigh, our parting was all, 296
Sober, 372
critic come abroad, some more, 67
found, nothing in nature's, 101
it would be to keep me, 387
livery, in her, 116
once drunk and once, 82
side, always err upon the, 396
thinking, hence with all your, 101
wishes never learned to stray, 68
Sobers us again, drinking largely, 215
Sobriety's daughter, that grief was, 308
sobs, was lost in a tempest of, 389
Society of mutual admiration, a, 3
where none intrudes, there is, 457
solitude sometimes is best, 373
Socket, burn to the, 91
Sod, and fill the burial, 177
beneath the burial, 114
beneath the churchyard, 108
better rot beneath the, 213
builds on the watery, 156
dread ye not the cold, 5
fall upon the, 144
remote upon the simple, 312
the marsh-grass sends into the, 156
Soda-water, sermons and, the day after, 444
Sofa round, wheel the, 116
Soft and low, her breathing, 36
making the nettle danger, 280
Soft the music of those village bells, 52
as silk remains, it, 280
as the roses they twine, virgins are, 426
as young, 20
gentle and low, ever, 428
Soften rocks or bend a knotted oak, to, 272
Softly as foot can fall, go as, 407
death succeeded life, so, 105
Softness of their sex is lost, the winning, 357
smoothness and, 349
Soil, free, 142
from the cursed, 403
has no right on English, 409
may best deserve the precious bane, that, 336
new birth of our new, 8
where first they trod, the, 464
with Freedom's, 17
Soiled with all ignoble use, 150
truth is as impossible to be, 417
Soiling, 373
Solace is to know, all my, 328
Solar beam, from the, 101
system, the hub of the, 188
Sold, are all things, 177
bought and, 157
is bought and, 27
spoils were fairly, 341
the feast is, 129
their fortunes, have, 141
the manhood never bought nor, 185
the pattern is, 211
the truth to serve the hour, never, 418
were never to be, 158
Soldier, 373
be abroad, let the, 352
brave enough, this is the, 432
come you back, you British, 252
drink, let a, 100
knew, not though the, 90
the broken, 68
which in the, 43
Soldier's a man, a, 100
cheek, something upon the, 312
mien, a, 403
our, were brave, 22
pleasure, drinking is the, 16
the courtier's, scholar's, 263
wild halloo, the, 181
Soldiers, 373
firm, keep the, 104
Soldiership, is all his, 382
Sole of his foot, to the, 196
Solemn creed, sapping a, 66
round, with, 26
thing, language is a, 210
thought, what a world of, 410
way, in such a, 420
Solemnized, the day it is, 407
Soles, onions, garlic, 32
Solid core of heat, to make a, 230
flesh, this too too, 134

Solid man of Boston, 32
men of Boston, 32
Solitary shines, one simile that, 364
woes, rare are, 448
Solitude, 373
have broken me, grief and, 32
locks, bars and, 318
of peace, the strange, white, 369
Solitudes, millions in those, 75
Solve a learned doubt, to, 433
you any problem given, he 'll, 467
Sombre harness mailed, in, 87
Some must follow, and some command, 55
must watch, while some must sleep, 84
of us will smart for it, 371
people are more nice than wise, 281
people to get out of a room, hard for, 212
said It might do good, 317
weep because they part, 295
Somebody, 373
else, better off than, 401
Something in me dangerous, 71
lost, the quiet sense of, 231
tells me, there 's, 238
'tis, 275
to do, children with, 67
upon the soldier 's cheek, 312
Somewhere or other, 373
Son, 374
Athena 's wisest, 206
by bleeding sire to, 142
love you my, 237
nor, nor wife, 341
O Absalom, my, 1
of Adam and of Eve, the, 317
of a woman, and yet the, 295
of his own works, the, 461
of man, some proud, 410
of the sable Night, Sleep, 81
this is England 's greatest, 167
Song, 374
Alexandrine ends the, 6
and noble self is noble, 284
as though it were the burthen of a, 400
be clear and strong, though the, 248
concludes her noblest, 104
he had to write his, 317
I can suck melancholy out of a, 257
is on my lips, to-day a, 360
I troll out for Christmas stout, 51
let satire be my, 350
many people read a, 462
no German, 151
of birds, I love the, 235
of Hiawatha, this, 156
of the shirt, he sang the, 361
of the shirt, she sang this, 361
raised some serious, 91
rose the, 340
sans, 103
shall be, still all my, 278
sunshine and of, 74
Song
the burst of happy, 23
the lark becomes a sightless, 457
the long reaches of the peaks of, 207
we 'll sing one, 200
who loves not wine, woman and, 444
would sing her, 71
Songful, soulful, sorrowful Ireland, 194
Songs, 374
he loved to hear, 101
of joy, its deep, 209
were full of joy, my, 148
your gambols, your, 468
Sonorous, clear and, 52
Sons, 374
are things, God 's, 459
attain the praise, few, 367
no doubt, our wiser, 137
of darkness, villains and the, 417
of heaven, things are the, 459
of men, in the weak and friendless, 466
of the waves, so free as the, 286
Soon shall be, not mad but, 244
or late, death cometh, 89
Sooner it 's over, the, 132
the chiney 's mended, the, 260
Soonest mended, little said is, 260
Soothe a savage breast, music hath charms to, 272
her melancholy, 136
or flattery, 421
or wound a heart that 's broken, 358
Soothed with the sound, 19
Soothing chime, when last I heard their, 23
Sophist ever writ, or, 367
Sophisters, economists and calculators, 50
Sophistry, destroy his fib or, 353
Sordid dealings, whose, 58
Sore, 374
critics who themselves are, 67
thy feet are weary and, 162
Sorely charged, the heart is, 363
Sorest, the old wound if stricken is the, 290
Sorrow, 374, 375
a bitter, 38
and death may not enter, 209
and earth 's woe, to endure life's, 242
and sin, murders our youth with his, 406
and smart, human, 116
a rooted, 263
concealed, like an oven stopped, 298
could be won by gifts, 10
darkens hamlet and hall, 271
done, tales of, 68
enter, didst thou in, 377
fade, ere sin could blight or, 77
I see with, 324
is in vaine, thy, 426
laden, this soul with, 246
learn, love and joy and, 48

Sorrow
no more of idle, 48
on the bosom, 164
parting is such sweet, 296
returned with the dawning, 98
stirred, every note with, 340
strewing, all my life with, 458
that should water this, 398
the fear and the, 109
the painting of a, 118
the pang of, 390
there, there's nae, 215
this strife and, 94
to this, 296
touched with joy, they bring me, 470
weep and wrestle with our, 155
we spoke not a word of, 312
words, give, 165
Sorrowing face, one, 219
goeth a, 31
toiling, rejoicing, 410
Sorrow's eye, shuts up, 370
heavy hand, 175
lulled to sleep, every, 402
Sorrows, 375
and darkness, 163
brewed with her, 399
see in thy chastening, 341
Sorry for, that I shall be, 315
if ye be, 96
trade, oh, the, 82
Sort of men, there are a, 291
of thing, free-will and that, 330
Sorting and puzzling with a deal of glee, 1
Sot, but their prize a, 462
Sots, what can ennoble, 113
Soudan, Fuzzy-Wuzzy at your 'ome in the, 147
Sought for her, 416
her, has yielded to the first that, 428
in vain, they never, 230
is good, love, 240
the Lord aright, that, 230
the storms, he, 304
the remedy, but they, 242
they thus afar, what, 464
unknowing what he, 440
Soul, 375-377
a glory circling round the, 233
a kind of men so loose in, 371
alive, the most offending, 185
a mouse of any, 271
and body, his, 273
and for my, 223
and heart, 'tis, 248
and sense, where heart and, 204
an evil, producing holy witness, 11
arise O, 126
a star before the darkened, 384
awakes, and the, 77
away, the Spaniard cast his, 157
beatified, sings like a, 210
below, the wrong that pains my, 160
but merit wins the, 260
Soul
contrive, nor let thy, 270
cordial to the, 269
could force his, 307
does life, as the, 415
Earth's biggest country's gut her, 277
employ all the heart and the, 229
enchanted, lived the, 374
feast of reason and the flow of, 327
from the soul, dissever my, 236
froze the genial current of the, 301
goes out on the east wind, but a, 113
got ashore, till the last, 329
grapple them to thy, 146
he'd turned his fleeting, 349
he had on earth, 176
I am the captain of my, 126
I arm, my, 311
I loafe and invite my, 229
I must be measured by my, 263
in agony, mirth cannot move a, 264
in body and in, 237
is dead, for the, 222
is found sincerely so, 47
is pure and strong, whose, 390
I steep, when my thirsty, 402
is with the saints I trust, 29
knew which, not a, 418
lends, how prodigal, 429
lies in the doing, joy's, 198
many a, 232
may pierce, such as the meeting, 394
meet the sunrise of the, 324
mount, mount, my, 270
my, happy friends, 116
navigation's, 60
never was in my, 116
no foreign foe could quell thy, 112
none better in my kingdom, 438
of decent wit, 152
of goodness, some, 160
of harmony, hidden, 170
of Judas Iscariot, 'twas the, 194
of man, except the, 357
of music shed, the, 170
of the foaming grape, 344
of the law, reason is the, 327
of the organ, which came from the, 51
of wit, the, 36
oh! then, my, 94
once inflamed my, 20
perdition catch my, 239
pliant, found a rare, 244
reclaim thy lost, 358
relies, the parting, 35
rot asleep, lets your, 144
secured in her existence, 191
should tend the, 279
signs and portents for the, 165
sincere, of, 385
sing a dirge for St. Hugh's, 32
so dead, 65
tell me, my, 79
that can render, the, 127

Soul
that flattering unction to your, 419
that has sinned, like a, 247
that I must draw, it grieves my, 442
that loving, 378
that rises with us, 25
that slid into my, 369
that wings the, 257
the, uneasy and confined from home, 186
the before unconceived, unconceivable, 308
the palace of the, 367
the poor, will die, 287
the tocsin of the, 92
the weary, 221
thrills the fond, 236
through my lips, my whole, 204
to cheer his, 182
to God in after-days, raise this, 293
to keep, pray the Lord my, 370
Tommy, 'ow's yer, 180
to-night for me, question thy, 127
to save, where woman has never a, 451
to soul, from, 216
to take, I pray the Lord my, 370
unbowed, with, 115
was not spoken of the, 222
were fled, as if that, 170
whose youth is in his, 470
with his own, 114
within him climb, feels the, 143
without a shield, the, 120
with sorrow laden, tell this, 246
working out her, 54
would harrow up thy, 380
Soul-bound friend, as it does for a, 173
Soul's in arms, my, 12
sincere desire, prayer is the, 313
tasking, with a whole, 177
Souls, 378
at home, and our, 108
beyond the reaches of our, 268
closely wedged, with their, 446
draw, breath which our, 76
dreams affright our, 99
for whom this hungry war, the poor, 432
from getting rusty, to keep our, 345
in the cure of, 347
jealous, will not be answered so, 195
keep his memory green in our, 274
of Christian, 354
of men, this restless craving in the, 46
our weary, dream of simplicity, 365
poison to men's, 158
six precious, 72
the immediate jewel of their, 275
the mightiest plea for erring, 313
the two or three high, 466
they have no, 64
to fright the, 432
to save, our sinful, 345
two, with but a single thought, 224
Souls
we that have free, 195
which God is calling sunward, 439
who looks on erring, 52
Soul-sides, boasts two, 243
Sound, 378
and foam, too full for, 18
and fury, full of, 411
and hears no, 74
as a bell, heart as, 174
as if I'd paid a note, 371
I heard, all the, 173
in his hand, the, 183
like the sweet, 273
my barbaric yawp, I, 468
no sight, no, 384
of a great Amen, like the, 51
of a kiss, the, 203
of a voice that is still, 169
of battle, is the blended, 461
of cheerful bells just undulates, 52
of revelry, there was a, 334
of the church-going bell, 22
save the rush of the river, no, 311
shut between me and the, 52
soothed with the, 19
strikes, a deep, 334
the gospel's, 161
the loud timbrel o'er Egypt's dark sea, 405
there was another heavy, 76
to heal the blows of, 364
with twelve great shocks of, 284
Sounded all the depths, 140
forth the trumpet, he has, 415
Sounder, may sleep the, 169
Sounds as if it should be writ, 210
of village bells, 52
the voice of a good woman, sweetly, 452
Soup gets cold, 211
or broth, or brew, 32
Soupçon, a magic, 349
Sour, are hard and, 175
my cask ran, 57
offence, is a, 346
Source of all his pain and woe, 283
of human offspring, true, 437
Sources, from distant and separate, 339
one of the most fatal, 422
Soured on me, all hope, 313
Sourest rind, sweetest nut hath, 286
Sours ripe grapes, 118
South and southwest side, 'twixt, 93
breathe of the sweet, 210
like the sweet, 273
turning his face to the dew-dropping, 444
wind that toots his horn, O blest, 132
Southerly, when the wind is, 245
Southrons, hear your country, 94
Southwest side, 'twixt south and, 93
Sovereign alchemist, the, 162
lord the king, our, 202

Sovereign reason, that noble and most, 327
thy, thy head, 189
Sovereignty, grander than, 80
of nature, takes it by, 278
of their own, 276
Sow, 378
as you, y're like to reap, 230
many labourers must be content to, 460
seed, but let no tyrant reap, 355
the seed ye, 355
Sowed no seed, by him that, 460
Space of our large honours, 36
there is limitless, 178
this, was thought's mysterious seat, 367
Spacious firmament on high, 132
Spade, a pickaxe and a, 303
laid them flat with a, 77
on his earth-worn, 357
with the poor crooked scythe and, 103
Spades, the emblem of untimely graves, 88
Spake again, to eyes that, 334
methinks an angel, 9
my brother, there, 37
Spain, England, Germany or, 135
the stoutest hearts of, 111
Span, a life's but a, 100
and Eve, 149
dwindled to the shortest, 375
grasp the ocean with my, 263
life is but a, 429
the life of man less than a, 461
yet not to earth's contracted, 463
Spaniard cast his soul away, the, 157
Spanish or neat's leather, a shoe be, 20
Spanish sailors with bearded lips, 360
Spaniel, 378
Spare my guiltless wife, 15
not your labour, 207
siller hae to, 364
that tree, woodman, 457
the beechen tree, 457
the rod, then, 232
us yet, 139
Spared neither land nor gold, 341
a better man, I could have better, 250
Spares the child, and never, 341
the rod, and, 341
Spark, each light gay meteor of a, 410
of fire, the sun is but a, 376
of heavenly flame, vital, 428
of that immortal fire, a, 233
of vital flame, this fluttering, 428
shows a hasty, 209
to the powder, proved as a, 389
Sparked it with full twenty gals, he'd, 363
Sparkle still the right Promethean fire, 118
to the highest top, 116
Sparkled, 378
for Helen, the cordial that, 100
Sparkles near the brim, but, 220
Sparkling showers, gems in, 107
Sparks, living, we still discern, 4
of nature, hard . . . to hide the, 278
Sparrow fall, or a, 38
falls, forgetting that even, 177
part, to see her, 398
providence in the fall of a, 320
providently caters for the, 326
Sparrow's fall, dost mark the, 84
Sparrows, five, sold for two farthings, 320
two, sold for a farthing, 320
Spawn of hell, slander meanest, 368
Speak, 379
all the lip can, 172
and look back, 307
and purpose not, art to, 321
by the card, 43
each other in passing, and, 360
ere the feverish lip can, 293
for yourself, why don't you, 469
Greek, 'tis known he could, 165
if the lion be to, 14
less than thou knowest, 362
love, speak low if you, 239
more in a minute, will, 396
more or less than truth, 417
one simple word, better far it is to, 466
preach, for this men write, 123
the grief that does not, 165
the heart must, 174
the speech, I pray you, 379
the tongue, 412
well did'st thou, 206
when I think, I must, 453
who fear to, 368
with most miraculous organ, will, 272
your sentiment, that you, 397
Speaker, and some before the, 146
Speakest, than howsoe'er thou, 395
Speaking in deeds, 84
to hisself, sounded as if he wos a-, 314
Speaking-trump of future fame, the, 274
Speaks, his tongue, 174
Spear, the shattered, 142
Spears are uplifted, the, 387
in rest, a thousand, 179
Special wonder, without our, 56
Specify, do not forget to, 13
Speck of life, this, 222
or little pitted, 337
nor stain, 268
Spectacle on nose, with, 294
Spectator, the tame, 265
Spectators, gave pleasure to the, 321
Spectral host, the cry of that, 151
Spectre addressed Imogene, while the, 403

Spectre Conscience, shrieking through the gloom, 61
Spectres, 379
rise, the grisly, 282
Speculation, 379
thou hast no, 29
Speech, 379, 380
every, a jest, 147
free, 142
the moist impediments unto my, 399
thought is deeper than all, 403
Speeches, leave it to men's charitable, 258
Speechless creature dead, 38
Speed, and yet for, 66
be wise with, 137
of my desire, in the, 86
the going guest, 167
the parting guest, 167
the soft intercourse, 216
with impetuous, 271
Spell awoke within me, that, 274
in its every drop, there's a, 100
inspired the silent toil, what, 409
of enchantment, 'tis no, 72
of its silence, dissolves the, 451
would ye learn the, 12
Spells around him flung, 283
by, this one, an' then thet, 363
but scans and, 458
Spend another such a night, 99
it, who knows not how to, 319
I've a guinea I can, 167
my malice in my breath, 402
what we yet may, 103
Spending all her fires, 377
we lay waste our powers, getting and, 463
Spendthrift is he of his tongue, what a, 412
Spent amang the lasses, 165
and maimed among, the, 290
in vain, seldom, 105
its novel force, his passion shall have, 297
Sphere, all quit their, 316
not in his, 384
pledge of a lower, 179
the fitting of self to its, 333
Spheres, earth is but an echo of the, 272
music of the, 272
seems to shake the, 155
start from their, 380
Spice of life, variety's the very, 423
Spicy nut-brown ale, 6
Spider, 380
painter plays the, 168
Spies, they come not single, 375
Spiked and panelled door, no, 31
Spills another, that, 27
Spilt on the ground like water, 173
Spin, 380
all hypocrisy, 393
I, I weave, 386
on blindly in the dark, 439
Spindle, layeth her hand to the, 451
Spins the slight, self-pleasing thread, he, 353
Spinster, more than a, 382
Spire, from which the sound, 52
send the psalm up in the, 244
Spires and turrets crowned, with, 385
Spirit, 380, 381
all compact of fire, love is a, 240
and a busy heart, a great, 220
and it lay on my fevered, 374
and unwearied, 145
an unquestionable, 239
calms, so much the, 344
come away, 170
daunted, mystery the, 69
doth raise, the clear, 123
doubting in his abject, 34
fell, ere my fainting, 439
for my minister, one fair, 85
from mine eyes, I could weep my, 438
full, once of ethereal, 367
God is a, 154
grieves, the, 215
haunted, here dwelt the, 374
life-blood of a master, 30
like a blight over thy, 362
meet and mingle, in one, 366
Mrs. Partington's, was up, 297
of judgment, some shallow, 213
of kin to God by his, 248
of man is divine, all save the, 426
of mortal, the, 269
of murder works, the, 35
of my dream, o'er the, 98
of the glass and scythe, fierce, 405
of wine, O thou invisible, 445
out of the deep, 18
passed, ere the, 284
stands answerable, how his, 298
still and bright, and yet a, 454
taste, and sense, 67
the accusing, which flew up to heaven's chancery, 287
the delighted, 90
the immortal, in the skies may bloom, 377
the motions of the, 273
through which the, 140
turns to thee, 125
Spirit-level, that pure, 115
Spirit's utter loneliness, my, 230
yearning cry, 88
Spirits, 381
congenial, part to meet again, 60
may be in good, 197
of great events stride on, 358
of your fathers, the, 288
rushed together, and our, 226
the snuff of younger, 228
to the father of, 298
walk, and, 352
were all, 428
who wait, like outcast, 292
Spirit-stirring drum, the, 125

Spiritual, 381
pinder, that, 52
Spit and sputter all, and, 210
in my face, 218
upon my Jewish gaberdine, 147
Spite, as if they worshipped God for, 302
of all the virtue, in, 85
the civic slander and the, 54
the world, reckless what I do to, 328
Spleen, 382
Splendid shilling, retains a, 359
Splendidly null, 128
Splendour, 382
of God, by the, 156
of the fight, who knows the, 390
Splendours, the parlour, 295
Splenitive and rash, 71
Splinters, and break his heart in, 317
Split the ears of the groundlings, to, 379
you, though it do, 382
Spoil, an earthquake's, 109
it, we should only, 323
like bales unopened, 404
of me, hath been the, 60
the child, and, 232
we lost, and the, 451
Spoiler's head, curses on the, 157
Spoils of Mexico, the richest, 111
of office, whom the, 259
of time, rich with the, 406
of war, the, 464
the child, he never, 341
the pleasure of the time, it, 307
the rod, but, 341
treasons, stratagems, and, 273
were fairly sold, 341
Spoke, 382
'em, when with hasty noise he, 458
in number more than ever women, 429
in virtue's cause it, 411
to a nation, a nation, 276
Spoken, I hear thy name, 428
of the soul, was not, 222
when the lips have, 209
Spontaneous, what was good was, 261
Spontaneously to God, 279
Spoon, add a single, 349
must have a long, 87
who stole a thimble or a, 306
with oil, four times the, 349
Spoons, let us count our, 425
Sport, 382
is stale, all the, 290
to have the enginer, 110
Sported his eyes and his temple about, 463
Sports, my joy of youthful, 288
your, and your wiles, 116
Spot, 382
and every loved, 49
beauteous visions filled this, 367
is cursed the 69
of earth be found, that, 182
Spot
on his peculiar, 306
stir of this dim, 107
of ground, to grow upon a, 162
though 'tis but a little, 113
thy home, and that, 182
where I made one, 152
Spotless and fair, too, 153
Spots quadrangular of diamond form, 88
Spouse, I will have no Maggie for, 339
took the Daughter of the Vine to, 426
Spout out, jealous doubt, 115
Spouted, where the wallowing monster, 354
Sprang up like weeds, little cares, 450
Spray, and cold as the, 386
in thy playful, 73
lurching through the, 54
of Western pine, this, 304
Spread abroad, Wickliffe's dust shall, 441
a horse-laugh through the pews, 212
not good except it be, 266
the thin oar, 278
twelve hundred million men are, 75
Spreadeth wide, which, 380
Spreading, till by broad, 53
Spreads, and still another, 53
his light wings, 233
Sprightlier age, before a, 228
Spring, 382
and summer, for winter, 20
a plenteous seed, shall, 44
as the tiger's, 455
each, 172
earth has no unpolluted, 403
ever sence one night last, 330
from A B C, can only, 1
in the, 241
I would change life's, 409
love's pure congenial, 232
of day, in the, 161
of love gushed, 27
of love, how this, 240
pining for the, 343
supplies, the following, 250
Springes, with hairy, 168
Springs eternal, hope, 186
the hearse has no, 298
will take, as far as, 173
Spring-time, 382
Sprite, every one lets forth his, 282
of the blood-avenging, 28
the fierce avenging, 15
Sprung upon its feet, and it, 340
Spur, fame is the, 123
on and fight it out, 383
Spurn me, strike me, 378
Spurned, and worships what it, 255
by the young, 157
Spurns that patient merit, 323
Spurs are striking deep, a thousand, 179
Spurt, for just a single, 186

Sputter all, spit and, 210
Spy out such a quarrel, would, 322
seems infected that th' infected, 195
Squadron, 382
the mustering, 271
Squadrons, come like thick-plumed, 436
Squalls, caterwauls, 44
Squander time, then do not, 407
Squandered, doled, stolen, borrowed, 157
Square, 383
and we parted on the, 217
certain that the earth was, 106
for you broke a British, 147
of comfortable light, 25
Square Deal, 383
Square-turned joints, his, 46
Squat like a toad, 408
on her safety-valve, a nigger, 346
Squatting on the coals, 'e'll be, 395
Squeak, as naturally as pigs, 165
Squeezing, 383
out the sea-water, 296
Squints the eye, 135
Squired 'em, he'd, 363
Stabbed with a white wench's, 118
Stable, a good horse in the, 303
Staff, 383
a bending, I would not break, 120
his cockle hat and, 57
hope is a lover's, 186
of life, bread is the, 35
or the halyard, 112
Stage, 383
amuse his riper, 49
and shoves you from the, 228
his hour upon the, 411
not, but real, 325
the poor, degraded, 278
the veteran on the, 424
where every man must play a part, a, 463
Stage-play, here he quotes a, 383
Stages, in our later, 224
where'er his, 192
Stain, nor cloud, nor speck, 268
what looks to thy dim eyes a, 198
Stainless gentleman, and, 150
Stains of her, not of the, 454
of powder, washed off the, 312
Stair, as he comes up the, 138
rising to great place is by a winding, 305
the old clock on the, 55
Stairs, have they made a pair of, 242
up, and doon stairs, 443
Stake, honour's at the, 164
like Cranmer's at the, 169
my reputation is at, 332
that man can have at, 143
Stale, all the sport is, 290
flat and unprofitable, how weary, 463
proverb never, 126
Stalk had left the rose, I on its, 342
Stalk, left on its, 342
Stallion shod with fire, on a, 86
Stamboul, magnificent in, 408
Stammer, 383
Stamp, but the guinea's, 249
of nature, change the, 421
on us in an hour, misery puts a new, 264
the marriage bond divine, to, 442
them on the running stream, 450
Stamped with the image, now, 157
Stamps in vain, 207
Stand, 383
and see, while you can, 131
and wait, who only, 429
a-tiptoe when this day is named, 66
at the door and knock, I, 96
back to back in God's name, 131
by uniting we, 420
by your colours, my friend, 58
for judgment, I, 213
for your own, 292
in the prince's name, 422
let this holly, 181
nor sit nor, 328
on either hand, who will, 37
or fall, they must, 202
let the old oak, 398
presently at God's great judgment seat, 391
they could not, 183
to in a month, than he will, 396
to doubt, never, 14
to your glasses, 91
united we, 420
upon its own bottom, must, 418
up, that Nature might, 250
we take our, 94
while on ourselves we, 353
Standard, 383
of the man, the mind's the, 263
sheet, 17
to be found a British, 37
up with our, 143
Standard-bearer fall, if my, 308
Standeth God within the shadow, 417
Standing upon the vantage-ground of truth, 415
with reluctant feet, 246
Stands above me, Death, 78
and to the last of earth his furrow 79
as if it, 190
as never it stood, except winde, 444
a very pretty quarrel as it, 323
in his pride alone, who, 286
still withal, who he, 406
the Coliseum, while, 57
with you, the bottle, 32
Stanley, approbation from Sir Hubert, 11
on, 47
Stanza, and each exalted, 231
Staple of his argument, finer than the, 424

Star, 384
constant as the northern, 62
curb a runaway young, 9
emigrated to another, 109
is brotherhood, life's final, 38
like a falling, 122
like a guiding, 179
man is his own, 127
of de sphirit's light, 297
of earth, deny it who can, 113
of empire, the, 109
of the unconquered will, 333
or garter, for the sake of a ribbon, 42
our life's, 25
shall be, the sailor's, 347
shine, and saw the same, 230
sunset and evening, 17
that lights a desert pathway, the, 338
to guide, a surer, 245
to men for ever, to become a, 206
Starboard, rolled to, 354
Stare, 384
a distressful, 284
face the public, 449
folks must stop and, 186
Stared aghast at sleep, 369
Starers and of loud huzzas, of stupid, 355
Star-gazing, mostly poets is all, 309
Starlight and moonshine, candles and, 304
Starry skies, cloudless climes and, 186
Stars, 384
above us, the, 127
and stripes, home wherever the, 8
and stripes overhead, 8
are fire, 97
are old, and the, 240
broad stripes and bright, 17
builds among the, 316
for tapers tall, 184
forty flags with their silver, 134
hide their diminished heads, 172
in a tether, shall hold the, 361
in the heaven, number the, 205
like those far, 466
make thy two eyes, like, 380
not in our, 127
of heaven are breaking, till the, 429
set their watch in the sky, the sentinel, 39
shall fade away, the, 191
studded with, 268
that oversprinkle all the heavens, 23
they say, cannot dispose, 306
to trace the, 402
were more in fault than they, their, 456
whilst all the, 216
ye little, 91
Star-scattered on the grass, 152
Star-spangled banner, that, 17
Star-ypointing pyramid, under a, 29
Start again, get up, 220
alas, you now must, 283
Start, a stock of temper we both had for a, 400
at shame, 123
from every wave, shall, 288
from their spheres, 380
tremble and, 307
with a recognizing, 115
Started forth, many a one has, 321
like a guilty thing, 57
Starting, at first, 379
Starting-place, our cradle is the, 221
Startles thousands with a single fall, 81
Startling word, speaks the, 88
Starts, by, 't was wild, 133
everything by, 114
she, 200
Starve, 384
some would only, 416
with feeding, 9
Starves himself, one rich worldling, 300
State, 385
a knave to me in every, 205
all were for the, 341
and from thy, 134
and save the imperilled, 276
a pillar of, 85
broken with storms of, 29
nor despicable, 434
of Denmark, rotten in the, 344
of man, the, 164
of Venice, unto the, 134
rose of the fair, 263
sail on, O ship of, 359
than be true to church and, 213
the sun in all his, 105
throne of royal, 107
to lie in, 184
wasting town and, 325
whole machinery of the, 33
will rush into the, 315
without king or nobles, a, 59
State-House is the hub of the solar system, 188
State's collected will, that, 385
States can be saved without it, 301
dissevered, discordant, belligerent, on, 420
kings, queens and, 368
Statesman, 385
and buffoon, 114
pure, the, 104
too nice for a, 141
Station ends in, earth's highest, 104
in the hall, from its, 280
like the herald Mercury, a, 250
the separate and equal, 356
Statists do, I once did hold it as our 466
Statuary, 385
Statue, 385
a chief limb of the, 308
makes his own, 322
of flesh, 115
Statue-like repose, in, 105

Stature, 386
tall, her, 94
Statute labour, another wants to make it, 464
Stave, now he hums a, 383
this horrible, 379
Stay a little longer, I, 108
and eat it, 48
as die and, 89
him, what power can, 406
how little while we have to, 77
I ask not to, 228
know how little while we have to, 334
some truth may, 120
still in the right to, 397
which says I must not, 428
Stayed he, stopped or, 325
the English flag is, 113
too late I, 406
Staying no longer a question, 345
Stays our hurrying feet, 79
safest and seemliest by her husband, 443
to his home, he, 356
Steadfast in the strength of God, 179
Steadies with upright keel, 200
Steal, 386
a few hours from the night, 74
a lover true, seeks to, 304
a shive, of a cut loaf to, 435
away, silently, 44
away their brains, 33
away, then, 220
cream, vigilant as a cat to, 45
his dust away, 29
it not, if men, 404
my thunder, yet, 405
one pang from thine, 10
on me, till death like sleep might, 81
out of your company, and, 401
when publishers no longer, 320
Stealers, these pickers and, 303
Stealing, 386
Steals, he kills for gold, he, 157
my purse, who, 275
Stealth, do good by, 123
to do his good by, 386
Steam, 386
Steamy column, throws up a, 116
Steed, 386
after him lead his masterless, 433
and the neigh of the, 136
beneath is lying, 90
farewell the neighing, 125
that knows his rider, as a, 436
the, the mustering squadron, 271
the waves bound beneath me as a, 436
to battle driven, rushed the, 13
Steeds, 387
instead of mounting barbed, 432
Steel, again in complete, 268
and vengeful, 233
foemen worthy of their, 433
heart is true as, 174
Steel, I forged the, 386
locked up in, 12
my man's as true as, 415
nor poison, nor, 223
with hoops of, 146
Steep hills, to climb, 55
my senses in forgetfulness, and, 370
my thirsty soul I, 402
Steeple, and on it put a, 348
bells, and all, 133
keeps a-cawing from a, 52
or a weathercock on a, 285
Steer, 387
boldly through the desperate winter sea, 281
can gently, 162
happily to, 162
their courses, like ships they, 335
'tis to glory we, 286
too nigh the sands, would, 304
Steered, boats that are not, 141
by the dumb, and the dead, 357
Steering, caused of otheres, 53
like a dray, 215
Steers straight for the maelstrom, 102
Stem, moulded on one, 224
the hisses, and, 449
the torrent of a woman's will, to, 450
of time, on the thorny, 143
Stenches, 387
Step aside, to, is human, 188
aside, who never takes one, 390
for death or life, yield a, 431
judging each, 198
nor from hell one, 178
one, above the ridiculous, 391
one, above the sublime, 391
one false, 122
Stephen, 387
Stepped a stately raven, in there, 325
Stepping o'er the bounds of modesty, not, 266
Stepping-stones, men may rise on, 170
Steps, 387
beware of desperate, 86
brushing with hasty, 392
but by gradual, 31
grace was in all her, 161
of glory, who track the, 152
to pursue, thy, 9
wandering, and slow, 462
Stern array, battle's magnificently, 19
daughter of the voice of God, 73
de himmelstrahlende, 297
Sterner stuff, ambition should be made of, 7
Stern-eyed Puritans, 31
Steward, sees but a backward, 248
Stewed in brine, and, 439
Stick a feller thru, an' go, 156
has a propensity to, 114
he fell like the, 340
on conversation's burrs, when you, 62
scratched with a, 13

Stick to your aim, 40
Sticking-place, courage to the, 119
Sticks out visibly, the axis of the earth, 15
proputty, proputty, 319
Stiff in opinions, 114
obstinacy's ne'er so, 287
upper lip, keep a, 220
Stifle down with a mailed heel, 413
Stile, 387
Stiles, helping . . . lame dogs over, 460
Still, all white and, 152
and for ever grew, 77
and mute, would be, 10
sad music of humanity, 188
sound of a voice that is, 169
suffer and be, 79
that comes down as, 144
the night is, 23, 52
the plains of the water be, 18
them, sleep cannot, 403
Stilled, advice has often, 93
Stillness entertain, a wilful, 291
holds, a solemn, 209
Stimulating, 387
Sting, blind-worm's, 179
each, that bids, 328
her, to prick and, 270
honey wears a, 403
if I be waspish, best beware my, 434
is not so sharp, 24
thee more, to, 265
thee twice, would'st thou have a serpent, 356
thy father's life, the serpent that did, 356
where is thy, 163
without feeling its, 449
Stings not, grasp it firmly, it, 449
you for your pains, it, 280
Stinking, greasy caps, 43
mackerel, cheap as, 47
Stinks, and several, 387
Stint, pouring without, 27
Stir, above the smoke and, 107
a very river, that would, 133
for this, all hell shall, 178
the fire, now, 116
the hell within him, 178
without great argument, not to, 164
Stirred by too daring a word, lion be, 226
Stirring memory of a thousand years, 72
not a creature was, 51
Stirrup-cup to me, thy rich, 78
Stirs, see, she, 200
this mortal frame, whatever, 234
Stitch, stitch, stitch, 360
Stithy, foul as Vulcan's, 141
Stock of temper we both had for a start, 400
of your lies in circulation, the, 82
Stockbrokers, four, took villa residences, 379
Stocking all the day, a, 282
Stockings, and tall, 401
were hung, 51
Stocks and slips, from the docks and, 461
watered milk and watered, 325
Stole a thimble or a spoon, who, 306
before, pay for what they, 320
in, the soul of Judas Iscariot, 194
in and out, 129
the livery of the court of heaven, 228
Stolen, 387
borrowed, squandered, doled, 157
not wanting what is, 340
Stolid, 388
Stomach, 388
is not good, my, 6
Stomachs, 388
Stone, 388
and we raised not a, 153
at his heels a, 75
at the head, and a stone at the feet, 229
away, till the last angel rolls the, 13
chafing their channels of, 451
doth lie, underneath this, 427
for bits of, 378
from its grave away, roll the, 186
ideal, all the nonsense of their, 385
in a thick wall of, 446
in his cell in the, 446
is flung, as when a, 53
no, was hard enough, 458
on her walls, a, 63
or brick, deadlier than, 114
or leaves of, 24
raise the, 207
some lie beneath the churchyard, 146
this precious, 112
throw on water now a, 53
to beauty grew, the conscious, 39
without a, 334
Stone-deaf has been, 321
Stones, arise, these, 145
inestimable, 102
in piled, 29
old yew which graspest at the, 468
pavements fanged with murderous, 387
rattle his bones over the, 298
sermons in, 3
that spares these, 29
the martyr, it, 255
thy cold grey, 35
trodden down with, 15
where Milton's ashes lay, 29
with drops of rain, 252
you blocks, you, 27
Stonewall, 388
Stony limits cannot hold love out, 239
Stood against the world, might have, 335
before the Tavern, 77
here once the embattled farmers, 362

Stood in Venice on the Bridge of Sighs, 424
still the brave, and, 408
that night, should have, 95
Stool, with a three-legged, 59
Stools, necessity invented, 279
push us from our, 90
Stoop, is in that aching, 188
she'll, when she has tired her wing, 344
wisdom is oft-times nearer when we, 445
Stooping through a fleecy cloud, 268
Stoops from His high majesty, 108
to folly, woman, 136
Stop a beer-barrel, might they not, 421
a hole, might, 421
for thy tread, 109
my tears must, 438
their vibrations, to, 397
themselves, they cannot, 403
your mouth, I will, 271
Stopped by three, a thousand may well be, 37
or stayed he, not a minute, 325
which I would have, 399
Stopping a bung-hole, till he find it, 421
for breath, no means of, 229
Stops with the shore, his control, 288
Store, gives me wealthy Crœsus', 402
heaven will bless your, 375
of love, hath better, 232
or healthful, 355
pine amidst his, 248
Storehouse, his cupboard's a, 16
Storied urn or animated bust, can, 421
Storm, 388
after storm, where, 228
and cloud, sunshine, 141
and cloudiness, of, 119
could never have walked in that, 404
from the darkest, 41
her brows like gathering, 465
I had raised, the, 389
rides upon the, 154
their high-built organs make, the, 291
the pilot that weathered the, 304
this sublime and terrible, 296
together, if we might bear the, 409
unheard, news of the, 319
we euchred God Almighty's, 115
Stormed at with shot and shell, 80
Storming some airy fortress, of, 409
Storms, and give her to the god of, 133
he sought the, 304
may enter, 44
ne'er broke, which in, 439
of state, broken with, 29
rock the ravens on high, as the, 297
the night in, 189
Stormy, 389
gust of long suspended Ahs, one, 188
Story, 389
being done, my, 363
Story
how to tell my, 363
in all human, 104
listen to this simple, 156
of our days, shuts up the, 406
old, read in, 15
snow summits old in, 382
that's not in Tom Moore, 338
Stout and brave, hearts though, 163
of heart, be ye, 232
Straight, 389
down the crooked lane, 383
ez he can, he draws his furrer ez, 356
path of duty, to the, 104
to me, bear it, 68
Straighten up this shape, how will you ever, 467
Straightened out for a crowbar, 188
Straighter 'n a string, may be, 187
Straightest, pity's the, 305
Strain again, that, 273
angels sung this, 37
hold cheap the, 328
I cannot prate in puling, 233
linnets sing their wonted, 233
my eyes, I, 313
of man's bred out, the, 267
one continuous and unbroken, 112
Strained the dusky covered close, he, 263
the quality of mercy is not, 260
Strait the gate, how, 126
path, in yon, 37
Strand, in Wapping or the, 408
Stranded with strings of fire, his lyre, 244
Strange all this difference should be, 418
and unnatural, most foul, 272
bed-fellows, 21
delicious amazement, what a, 76
in that, there's nothing, 384
is it not, 72
seems to me most, 80
't is, but true, 416
't was passing, 363
with a maid be, 187
Strangely falls our Christmas-eve, 181
Stranger said, the, 162
stooped to the well, the, 348
than fiction, 416
to fear, a, 197
to flattery, a, 197
Stranger's land, we live within the, 181
Strangers, 389
ask of me, when, 237
honoured, by, 139
two, meeting at a festival, 224
Strangle, some would, 416
Strangled his language in his tears, 399
Stratagems and spoils, 273
Straw, 389
a bed of, 207
at wagging of a, 307
cared not a single, 308
find quarrel in a, 164

Straw
strongest oaths are, 70
tickled with a, 49
Strawberries, as Dr. Boteler said of, 10
Strawed our best to the weed 's unrest, 113
Straws, begin it with, 131
the forms of hairs or, 458
Stray, wishes never learned to, 68
Straying pigs, erring souls as, 52
Streak of snow, fades the last long, 372
on ocean 's cheek, the crimson, 73
Stream, a fount about to, 225
are eddies of the mighty, 322
her paly, 101
mercy of a rude, 153
of time doth run, which way the, 407
runs fast, the, 344
runs swift, the, 344
shows his hoar leaves in the glassy, 444
stamp them on the running, 450
Streaming eyes, with, 76
o'er us, 17
were so gallantly, 17
Streams, cleansing my, 247
for other 's woes, that, 448
in lavish, 248
large, from little fountains flow, 2
of revenue, abundant, 340
that keep a summer mind, 323
Street, 389
all down the long and narrow, 400
smacks of the field and the, 314
the car rattling o'er the stony, 444
the front-door is on the, 129
to street, hawks nosegays from, 343
Strength, 389
and courage can avert, 189
but weakness, not, 4
dangerous humours up to, 431
for a kiss 's, 204
he needs, with all the, 250
in every drop, there 's life and, 445
in her arms, 142
is in your union, all your, 433
king 's name is a tower of, 202
my arms of, 386
of bones, nor founded on the brittle, 381
of God, steadfast in the, 179
of limb, 46
of ten, as the, 12
of the race, 113
of youth, wants that sin against the, 470
that tower of, 413
thou canst not tell what, 429
to have a giant 's, 151
to nerve, tends their, 37
wasting her, 377
Strengthen and sustain, but, 436
Strengthened, are lifted up and, 156
Strengtheneth man 's heart, 35
Strenuous, 389, 390
Stress, dies in a desperate, 376
Stretch a cord, can, 389
forth thy rod, 388
my hands out, I, 313
of hell, down all the, 165
forth your iron thread, 152
out your hand to me, 140
Stretched upon the plain, eagle, 106
Strewed thy grave, not have, 36
Strews, many a holy text around she 401
with fresh flowers, 452
Stricken deer, my own, 31
deer go weep, 84
Strict in his arrest, 80
Stride on before the events, 358
Strife, 390
ancient forms of party, 339
and sorrow, this, 94
be a hero in the, 179
clubs typical of, 88
hatred, battle and, 215
he looks beyond the, 432
hour of danger, toil and, 39
madding crowd 's ignoble, 68
of labour and, 389
of Truth with Falsehood, 83
once were weary of the, 370
overwhelmed in the, 61
scorned amid the reeling, 431
some to public, 325
the single thraldom or a double, 442
to dare the elements to, 436
void of cares and, 359
without a further, 335
Strike, 390
and yet afraid to, 71
another blow, to, 130
by and by it will, 447
me, spurn me, 378
mine eyes, they, 364
the blow, themselves must, 29
Strikes, 390
as soon, and, 173
heaven is not always angry when he, 177
him dead, in fair battle, 12
the dark Ferrash, 401
Striking deep, a thousand spurs are, 179
String attuned to mirth, there 's not a, 257
of joy, approbation strikes the, 12
straighter 'n a, 187
that holds those weights, the, 403
Strings, 390
a harp of thousand, 170
laying the hand on the, 397
of fire, stranded with, 244
would break, whose very, 10
Stripes, 390
broad, and bright stars, 17
Stripling for woman 's heart, a, 398
Strive, and hold cheap the strain, 328
mightily, but eat and drink as friends, 214

Strive on to finish the work, let us, 337
Strives the woodcock with the gin, so, 457
Strivings after better hopes, 88
longings, yearnings, 156
Striv'st to get, still thou, 170
Stroke after stroke, 314
a nettle, 280
ere we feel the friendly, 89
of death is as a lover's pinch, 79
of fate, nearest to the, 127
the tyrant's, 146
Strokes, 390
Strong, 391
and free, 247
and lusty, yet I am, 357
a note, not so, 136
but wants that little, 249
enforcement be, gentleness my, 23
in awe, keep the, 61
is thy heart so, 215
man, rousing herself like a, 277
man must go, 78
men, not two, 84
nor pure, neither, 146
not to the, 324
potations, banish, 32
so, yet so refined, 453
the peaceful are the, 300
wail of the weak against the, 219
what king so, 42
without rage, 84
with the strength, 113
women are not in their best fortunes, 456
Stronger, our love it was, 236
than . . . the mason, 164
thought's a weapon, 159
worthier of regard and, 58
Strongest dare, is more than the, 133
oaths are straw, 70
Strongly framed, a being, 189
Strow the brooks in Vallombrosa, 216
Strown, lay withered and, 216
Struck by stone or brick, 114
eagle, so the, 106
one chord of music, 51
the foremost man, 36
the wreck, have said it, 465
till it be, 135
Struggle, 391
bravely, 58
Struggled in earnest, that has, 314
Struggles labour, wherever, 144
through which it has passed, 111
Struggling to be free, limed soul that, 377
Strut and rave, our little hour of, 411
Struts and frets his hour, that, 411
Stubborn bear, authority be a, 158
Stuck in my throat, 8
to me day and night, 286
Studded with stars, 268
Student pale, index-learning turns no, 192
Studied in a sad ostent, well, 372
Studieth revenge, a man that, 334
Studious how to please, love, 234
Study, 391
built in your parlour or, 212
in an old gentleman's, 279
of mankind is man, the proper, 250
of revenge, and, 231
pains, reading, 67
to be good and just, 104
Stuff, a deal of skimble-skamble, 367
ambition should be made of sterner, 7
as dreams are made, we are, 428
dross and, 266
for that is the, 407
of that perilous, 263
the true celestial, 5
they sell, half so precious as the, 426
untainted, with, 179
Stuffs as dreams are, of such, 428
him to the throat-gates, morsel that, 92
out his vacant garments, 165
Stung her, and it, 449
if you would not be, 449
it newly, some bee had, 226
thou serpent, never adder, 412
Sty, the fattest in Epicurus', 181
Style, 391
of man, Christian is the highest, 51
of the place, according to the, 403
refines, how the, 231
Sub-editor at Cork, 294
Subject, long and wish to be a, 202
of all verse, lies the, 180
of the comic muse, love's the, 234
ourselves, we know a, 206
owes the prince, as the, 454
to the same diseases, 197
we old men are to this vice, 244
Subjects are rebels from principle, when, 328
for dissection, form good, 351
give, unless their, 202
wise, which were their, 430
Subjugation, foreign conquest and, 112
Sublime, 391
as the energy, 143
a thing it is to suffer, 391
in his simplicity, 43
make our lives, 138
Submission, 391
none left but by, 332
Submit or yield, never to, 231
Submitting sways, by, 400
Subscribe enough, to, 266
for soap, hundreds will, 38
subscribe, 36
Subserves another's gain, 160
Substance of the common earth, my, 107
Subtle, cruel and inconstant, 83
Suburb of the life elysian, 76
Succeed and give, 129
in the world, who would, 319

Succeeding wave washes, though the, 138
Succeeds, a sure reward, 427
Success, 392
remove, why should man's, 342
which comes, that form of, 389
Succession, and Protestant, 170
Successive, they fall, 250
Such, heaven is full of, 176
things be, can, 56
Suck in the earth, 101
melancholy out of a song, I can, 257
Sucking the life-blood, by, 423
Suckle fools and chronicle, 138
Suckled in a creed outworn, 293
Suckling, man or woman or, 113
Sucks and drains a people's blood, 64
where the bee, 21
Suction, like woodcocks upon, 256
Sudden as flaws congealed, 161
flight, not attained by, 177
Suddenly, there is no man, 251
Sue, 392
for a debt he never, 82
in forma pauperis to God, 312
Suez, 392
Suicide, the snakes committed, 372
Suffer and be still, 79
and be strong, to, 391
for a high cause to, 120
in the mind to, 19
it, detraction will not, 185
like him, all who, 160
love, a good epithet, 239
the agonies we, 172
Sufferance, 392
be, what should his, 197
in corporal, 80
Suffered more, never mortal, 208
which, being, 131
Suffering ages look, the, 188
are in, 455
doing or, 436
ended with the day, 105
entereth, knowledge by, 206
from protested bills, virtue, 269
Sufferings, 392
Suffers, recoils, 232
Suffice, could not one, 12
Sufficeth them, the good old rule, 396
Sufficient at one time, I think's, 335
Sugar and saltness agree, oil, vinegar, 349
o'er the devil, 88
Suggestion, 392
Suited to the age, well, 379
Suits of grey, or, 220
of solemn black, customary, 448
of woe, the, 448
the better't, 161
Sully your pure prayer, to, 348
Sultan rises, the, 401
to the realm of death, a, 401
Sultry day, will look on a, 269
Sum of living, makes up the, 229
Summed in those few brief words, 313
Summer air, in clear, 219
brave, youth like, 5
by the same winter and, 197
days, and, 74
dust, dry as, 91
for winter, spring and, 20
friends, like, 3
friendship, 3
house, in any, 399
is green, when, 216
mind, streams that keep a, 323
morn, youth like, 5
no price is set on the lavish, 177
Saint Martin's, 168
the last rose of, 342
Summer's cloud, like a, 56
day, a, 122
dust, lay the, 27
heat, on fantastic, 191
ripening breath, by, 239
Summers in a sea of glory, 153
in raw, inclement, 393
not a few, 338
Summit, and we mount to its, 208
attained, the, 78
of my crown, upon the, 68
slippery, the, 305
whose, like all hills, 123
Summits, snowy, old in story, 382
Summon the place to surrender, 283
Summoned from some primeval night, 419
to drink to my flame, 274
Summons comes to join, when thy, 227
thee to heaven or to hell, 205
upon a fearful, 57
Sums, doomed to pay the, 106
Sun, 392, 393
all else beneath the, 35
ancient as the, 180
and moon, to wind up the, 9
and shines the, 269
and with the setting, 122
appears, when the rosy, 101
at noon, the bloody, 63
bales unopened to the, 404
came peeping in at morn, 330
climbs slow, in front the, 224
declines, the, 353
dies with the dying, 281
doth move, 97
flush of a new-born, 13
following the, 112
from their presence, I took the, 284
glory which is brighter than the, 437
grows cold, till the, 240
grows into the great, 73
had long since, the, 269
himself grow dim, the, 191
his beams display, let my, 408
hurl their lances in the, 350
in all his state, 105
in heaven, for the last time the, 420
is but a spark of fire, the, 376
is out, it is because the, 343
Juliet is the, 225

Sun
like the, doth shine, 443
livery of the burnished, 60
never sets on his might, the, 112
no, no moon, 285
no, upon an Easter day, 129
O blessed breathing, 188
of mid-day, 409
she snatches from the, 402
shows all the beauty of the, 240
signal of the setting, 115
that rose on freedom, 142
that sends the hidden, 18
the common, 293
the heat o' the, 103
tinged with the rising, 56
to thee may never rise, to-morrow's, 84
true as the, 245
true as the dial to the, 88
under the, 182
was low, on Linden when the, 225
upon the upland lawn, 151
went down, as the, 132
will pierce, a, 159
Sunbeam, death with the might of his, 77
soiled by outward touch as the, 417
Sunbeams, 393
the gay motes that people the, 270
Sunburst may smile on thee to-morrow, 186
Sunday, 393
his plough goeth every, 421
night, last, 73
putting too much Sabbath into, 345
tankards foam, no, 345
Sunday's best, he was in his, 87
Sundays, may call it herb-grace o', 344
on, no admittance at this wicket, 345
Sunflower, 393
Sung, he worked and, 262
let there be, 156
of Chaos, I, 46
Sunk the hopes of all men, in these are, 193
unrequited toil shall be, 199
Sunless and silent and deep, 451
Sunlight, as moonlight unto, 268
clasps the earth, the, 204
drinketh dew, as, 204
Sunny, youth it is, 4
Sunrise of the soul, meet the, 324
Sun's a thief, the, 402
Suns, brighter, dispense serener light, 65
widened with the process of the, 322
Sunset and evening star, 17
glow, Burgundy in all its, 344
of life gives me mystical lore, 358
were seen, at, 216
Sunset-gun, to the last, 112
Sunshine, flies of estate and, 3
follows the rain, 442
holy-day, on a, 71
Sunshine in the shady place, 119
still must follow rain, 76
storm and cloud, 141
the parting gleam of, 111
they have never seen the, 437
we'll talk of, 74
Sunward, souls which God is calling, 439
Sup, like a hermit you, 441
of New England's air, a, 281
upon myself, 9
with thee, take Him in that comes to, 96
Superfluity, 393
Superfluous lags the veteran, 424
to say you're welcome were, 438
verse, marred by a, 109
Supped on dormouse pie, 96
on fame, dined or, 123
Supper, 393
wine is poured at last, the, 194
Supplant those rough rug-headed kerns, 424
Supplied, can never be, 300
Support him after, but to, 129
of this declaration, for the, 307
Supporters, its sole, 267
Supposed a bear, a bush, 128
Suppressors of our vice, 345
Supremacy and sway, seek for rule, 456
Supreme, all for him, unchanging and, 419
in grace, 154
Surcease, not desire, but its, 4
Sure and safe one, a, 140
death, uncertain life and, 222
foundation, no, set on blood, 27
I'll make assurance doubly, 14
one, if another fails, 71
Surf, of the rock-beating, 386
Surface of the whole globe, 112
Surfeiting, the appetite may sicken, 273
Surge resolves, whose liquid, 402
was seething free, when the, 354
Surgery, hath no skill in, 184
Surges, the mournful, 205
Surnamed the Destroyer, 87
Surpass old wine, few things, 444
Surpassed, in loftiness of thought, 309
Surprise, death takes us by, 79
of marvel or, 147
was the chiefest, 76
Surrender, summon the place to, 283
Surrenders, the Guard dies but never, 166
Survey, I am monarch of all I, 266
make but an interior, 355
Survive or perish, 366
rather than let the nation, 431
Survives, loyal hope, 219
Susan came to live with me, when, 270
Suspect him, you may, 401
the thoughts of others, 51
't was he that made the slaughter, 41

Suspected, to be, 64
't would take us two apart, never, 400
Suspects himself a fool, 251
yet strongly loves, 243
Suspended oar, the light drip of the, 286
Suspicion, 394
intending deep, 307
of a bond, at, 233
Suspiration of forced breath, windy, 448
Sustain, but strengthen and, 436
my house, the prop that doth, 223
Sustained and soothed, but, 227
it, the saint, 453
Swaggers, swears, who, 248
Swaller-tail coats, rigged out in their, 11
Swallow gudgeons ere th're catched, 48
Swallowed in the flood, half our sailors, 231
in the yeast, some, 35
others to be, 30
the whole parish, 133
up and lost in the wide womb, 90
up and lost, to be, 228
Swallow's wings, and flies with, 186
Swan, 394
I'll play the, 273
lad, and every goose a, 469
sings her own elegy, the mournful, 273
this pale, faint, 273
Swan-like end, he makes a, 273
Swan's death-hymn, the wild, 273
Swans sing before they die, 366
Swap, 394
Swash of an Irishman, leathering, 194
Swashing, 394
Swat, he knows what's, 261
Sway, and impious men bear, 424
mercy is above this sceptred, 260
prevailed with double, 352
rule, supremacy and, 456
the sweeping whirlwind's, 470
Swayed him onward, that, 159
rod of empire might have, 109
Sways, by submitting, 400
she level, so, 454
the future, yet that scaffold, 417
Swear, 394
and fight, always ready to, 408
and lie to, 218
but now and then, 372
by the lamp that saw her, 428
not by the moon, 268
unto a sin, to, 287
Swearing, vows which break themselves in, 428
Swears, and a' that, 248
Sweat under a weary life, 79
Sweats to death, Falstaff, 210
Sweaty night-caps, threw up their, 43
Sweep, nor wild wind, 113
over thee in vain, 288
Sweeps a room as for thy laws, who, 102
the sea, 376
Sweet, 394
Alice, don't you remember, 29
and bitter fancy, 124
and fair she seems to be, 343
and our union as, 257
are the uses of adversity, 3
as English air could make her, 343
as lovely melancholy, nothing's so dainty, 257
as those by hopeless fancy feigned, 205
beautiful as, 20
but much more, 411
day, so cool, so calm, 73
girl-graduates, 162
is death to me, 241
is pleasure after pain, 16
is revenge, especially to women, 334
look thou but, 302
love art thou, 241
maid, bride-bed to have decked, 36
revenge, at first though, 335
sorrow, parting is such, 296
sweet home, 182
sweets to the, 395
the pleasure, 16
there's nothing half so, 236
the sounds of village bells, 52
time, youth and home and that, 23
to know, how, 266
to the weary death is, 79
would smell as, 275
Sweet-and-twenty, then come kiss me, 239
Sweeten this little hand, will not, 169
Sweeter, ain't modester nor, 95
far may be, 331
manners, with, 252
still, odours crushed are, 191
sure never girl gave, 205
Sweetest garland to the sweetest maid, the, 395
hours, the, 165
nut hath sourest rind, 286
Sweetheart, I were unmannerly, 204
Tray, Blanch and, 95
Sweet-marjoram of the salad, 179
Sweetness, 394
and waste its, 149
graceful ease and, 128
of ambrosial, 204
Sweets, 395
into your list, love to get, 204
stolen, are always sweeter, 387
Swell out and fail, 52
the organ 'gins to, 264
with its voluptuous, 334
Swelling like a turkey-cock, 418
Swells a self-elected saint, the proudest, 316
the gale, note that, 293
the tide of love, pity, 305
Swerve from law, Britons rarely, 37

Swerved, their honesty never, 183
Swerves, destiny never, 86
Swerving and flowing asunder, 339
Swift, not to the, 324
the race not always to the, 318
true hope is, 186
Swiftness, we may outrun by violent, 292
Swig, 395
Swim, how we apples, 11
in, a naughty night to, 282
leave us yit to sink or, 320
on bladders, boys that, 153
sink or, 366
till the brain begins to, 460
Swimmer, 395
Swine, 395
or mange in, 306
Swing, no v'ice hed sech a, 50
of Pleiades, Plato and the, 207
the battle-sword, 151
the wild falcon soar her, 344
Swingeing long curse, laid a, 26
Swings the hammer of industry, round, 410
Swinish multitude, a, 271
Switzerland again was free, 217
Swooned nor uttered cry, she nor, 76
Swoop, at one fell, 49
Sword, 395
and a trusty hand, a good, 63
and desolation, 329
drawn with the, 199
ef you take a, 156
eye, tongue, 263
for liberty, some draw, 146
from a courtly, 42
his terrible swift, 153
is bright and keen, whose, 390
laid by, 26
man for the, 454
nor the deputed, 260
reluctant, who draws the, 317
rust, and his good, 29
sharper than the, 368
the pen is mightier than the, 301
will open, which I with, 293
with fire and, 425
Sword 's point, conducting trade at the, 413
Swords, 395
than twenty of their, 302
would have leaped, ten thousand, 50
Swore, 395
as deacons do, the Deacon, 74
a thousand times he, 329
she, in faith, 363
Sworn an oath, I have, 29
Swound, like noises in a, 190
Syllable, every, a prayer, 340
of recorded time, the last, 411
Syllables, 395
that lives on, 458
which breathe, with, 210
Symbols, mute, of a joyful morn, 275
Symmetry, could frame thy fearful, 405
Sympathize with clay, 56
Sympathy, it is the secret, 237
Syrup of poppy, sauce of, 96
System, all the apparatus of the, 33
the hub of the solar, 188
Systems into ruin, atoms or, 38

T

Tabernacle, through the pews of a, 212
Table, joy of the whole, 172
of my memory, from the, 331
on a roar, that were wont to set the, 468
smiled as he sat by the, 371
upper end o' the, 71
who at her, 30
Tables, and near a thousand, 182
make it plain upon, 345
my, 426
the marriage, 147
Table-talk, 395
Tail abridged, with his, 249
came through, a hole where his, 87
holds the eel of science by the, 192
Satan gave thereat his, 432
watched the compass chase its, 60
Tailor, 396
lown, he called the, 387
Tailors, from noblemen to, 347
increase, and breed ballad-makers, 299
Tails, heads I win, ditto, 444
Taint of sin, this uneradicable, 365
not thy mind, 270
they bare, some dang'rous, 403
Tainted and corrupt, what plea so, 213
to decay, 148
wether of the flock, I am a, 439
Taints of blood, 160
Take, 396
and doctors give what they would, 214
all there is, 78
arms against a sea, 19
at Number One, do n't, 13
away . . . a chief limb of the statue, 308
away the flesh, let Meg now, 380
away the grief of a wound, 184
away the sword, 301
her, the Devil, 240
her without her answer, 10
Him in that comes to sup, 96
in God, ef you want to, 431
it hard, you mus 'n', 288
me again to your heart, 340
my house, you, 223
my life, you, 223
my soul to, 370
'old o' the wings o' the mornin', 112
the cash, ah, 44
the grog, I 'll, 321

Take
the hindmost, the devil, 87
the wings of morning, 74
their flight, 27
what they would give, when lawyers, 214
whistle for what you might, 440
ye each a shell, 292
you out, unmannerly to, 204
Taken thy lamp, hast but, 108
when, to be well shaken, 358
Takes all away, a cloud, 240
and him that, 260
it by sovereignty of nature, 278
no rise from outward things, 415
something from our hearts, it, 470
the kiss, and, 203
us by surprise, death, 79
Taking me for him, folks got, 418
notes, a chiel 's amang you, 317
off, damnation of his, 71
Tale, 396
an ancient, new told, 400
an ever changing, 219
and she grew pale at the raven 's, 326
an old, 15
a schoolboy 's, 352
as tedious as a twice-told, 400
breathe out the tender, 402
every, condemns me, 61
every shepherd tells his, 307
makes up life 's, 221
of terror now, what a, 5
or adorn a, 274
or history, ever hear by, 238
so tedious as a twice-told, 400
their music tells, how many a, 23
there is to tell, for a, 74
told by an idiot, a, 411
unfold, I could a, 389
Tales, moral of all human, 18
of delight, have fashioned their, 207
of sorrow done, 68
truant at his, 196
Talk, 396
a keerless man in his, 135
awhile of me and thee, some little, 423
I cannot, with civet in the room, 54
of a noun and a verb, that usually, 317
of death, why do I, 78
of his horse, nothing but, 187
of many things, to, 430
of wills, and, 117
proud of her, 320
to me, and have him, 399
with men, angels might, 417
with you, I will, 41
Talked, 396
of love as coolly, we, 241
the night away, 68
with us, one of Plutarch 's men, 308
Talking, 397
to theirselves, mostly sounded to be a-, 314
Talks, thinks as much as he, 423
too long, when it, 396
Tall, 397
divinely, 94
her stature, 94
oaks from little acorns grow, 2
were I so, 263
Tally, the score and the, 317
Tam lo'ed him, 37
was glorious, 191
Tamarinds and dates are thine, 12
Tame a sight, how, 133
spectator, the, 265
yet simple and, 187
Tamper with the weights, nor, 389
Tangents straight, resolve by sines and, 6
Tangled chain, speech was like a, 380
web, what a, 82
Tankards foam, no Sunday, 345
Tap upon the shoulder, a, 42
Taper, beneath a midnight, 317
what they call their midnight, 123
Taper-light, or with, 152
Taper 's light, like the glimmering, 185
Tapers tall, stars for, 184
waste that instant they take fire, 81
Tapestry waves dark, the, 317
Tapped, than to have a nerve, 280
Tapping a glossy boot, leisurely, 384
at my chamber door, 261
the hollow beech-tree, the woodpecker, 457
Taps that in our day were famous, 22
Tapsalteerie, may a' gae, 44
Tar, puttied up with, 115
Tara 's halls, the harp that once through, 170
Tardiness or quickness, pulses', 363
Tarn, into some sleeping, 53
Tarries long in hands o' cowards, thet, 143
Tarry the grinding, must needs, 41
you may for ever, 254
Tar 's labour, cheers the, 408
Tart, in the smallest public, 54
Tartness of his face, 118
Tarts, cooks must live by making, 63
Task, and though hard be the, 55
begin, sees some, 410
dedicated to the great, 276
grief was writhing o'er its, 165
hast done, thy worldly, 103
her toilet 's greasy, 410
Tasking, with a whole soul's, 177
Taste, 397
and sense, spirit, 67
ashes to the, 76
for being diddled, 103
his blood, but, 18
not the Pierian spring, 215
of danger and reproof, without the, 332
of death, never, 66
of our despair, ye, 465
of tediousness, rob it of some, 400

Taste
of your quality, give us a, 322
sans, 49
the hire, let them not, 140
the whole of it, let me, 78
tree whose mortal, 93
Tasted, some books are to be, 30
Tastes, 397
his salt, who breaks his bread and, 12
our needs, our, 381
the coarsest, 259
Tasting, have robbed the whole tree, 115
Tattered ensign down, tear her, 114
Tatters, old opinions, rags and, 110, 143
tear a passion to, 379
Tattling woman, she's a very, 454
Taught, but such as practice, 445
by Pope, 386
by that power that pities me, 305
by time, my heart, 174
how happy is he born and, 418
letters, heaven first, 216
me, folly's all they've, 118
me this, it has, 117
me to rhyme, it hath, 239
thee, say I, 140
them that, St. Pat, 440
us how to die, 91
Taunting truths, cold, bitter, 122
Tavern or inn, as a good, 192
you eat at Terré's, 32
Tax, censure is the, 46
Taxation, and her suckling babe, 432
Taxed, the beggar is, 176
Taxes, I like the, 110
Taylor preach upon a morning, 151
"Te Deum," "Non nobis" and, 156
Tea, 397
Teach, 397, 398
him, I should but, 363
O ye who, 135
thee, shall the Koran, 242
the rustic moralist to die, 401
you to drink, deep, 100
Teaches beasts to know their friends, nature, 278
us little here, 179
Teaching me that word, 72
twenty to follow mine own, 397
Teachings, and list to nature's, 362
we retain, its, 117
Tear, 398
and forgive her deceit with a, 333
a passion to tatters, 379
for pity, hath a, 161
from your eyelids wiped a, 23
her tattered ensign down, 114
him for his bad verses, 424
in all my miseries, think to shed a, 399
in her eye, and a, 371
is not worth a wistful, 375
or streaming, 219
that we shed, and the, 274
Tear
thee unexpressed, though it, 234
the graceful, 448
too foolish for a, 371
unsullied with a, 370
upon the word, dropped a, 287
Tear-drop melts, a woman's, 398
Tearing along that night, she came, 346
Tears, 398, 399
adown that dusky cheek have rolled, 174
and anarchy and wrath, 143
and 't were your hot, 76
blame not these, 328
by a torrent of, 389
cease, and all, 208
cease your, 74
for his love, 7
I can see your falling, 74
in his eyes, 307
lie too deep for, 404
must stop, my, 438
my smiles for half thy, 409
nor all your, 465
of all the angels, it would need the, 449
of pity, 160
of the widower when he sees, 442
parted in silence, and, 296
pure messengers, 29
rivers shed of, 38
the, the smiles, 258
the moon into salt, 402
the ocean's misty, 101
they shed no, 259
time is best measured by, 406
to pour sad, 293
upon my grave, drop thy foolish, 76
Venus smiles not in a house of, 424
we waste, and the, 451
with artificial, 118
Tedded grass, the smell of, 371
Tedious, 399, 400
as a twice-told tale, life is as, 400
Tediousness, 400
Teeth and forehead of our faults, the, 289
nothing on edge, set my, 309
proud of her, 320
sans, 49
to cast into my, 15
Tegument endure, this worthless, 377
Tell, 400
a hundred, might, 188
and another, 218
her that I died, 243
her that wastes her time and me, 343
I daurna, 234
if I can, 327
I want it to, 279
me, and thou canst not, 377
me, I implore, 17
me how to woo, oh, 456
me, my heart, if this be love, 235

Tell
me, my soul, 79
me not in mournful numbers, 222
nought to do but mark and, 305
one hath power to, 178
sir, I have none to, 389
tedious it were to, 400
that I cannot, 425
the anger of my heart, my tongue will, 412
thee a lie, if I, 218
their days, some, 398
the reason why I cannot, 327
the soldier brave enough to, 432
truth and shame the devil, 417
us all they think, when preachers, 315
us of the road, returns to, 72
us this, to, 426
ways we cannot, 154
why, but cannot, 327
yeou, with an I dew vum or an I, 74
you, I would, 76
you no fibs, I 'll, 323
Telling of it, by, 219
Tells he o'er, what damned minutes, 243
his tale, every shepherd, 307
me, there 's something, 238
them that others, which, 455
Temper, 400
a hot, leaps o'er a cold decree, 33
in good spirits and good, 197
man, made thee to, 452
oft has vent, in bad, 235
so justice with mercy, 199
the imagination with judgment, 191
was generous, whose, 197
which bears the better, 213
Temperance and repose, joy and, 94
you must acquire and beget a, 379
Tempered with love 's sighs, ink were, 308
with well-boiled water, 440
Tempers the wind to the shorn lamb, 209
Tempest, 400
for in the very torrent, 379
of sobs, was lost in a, 389
should not have meddled with a, 297
through calm and, 245
wrought, ocean into, 377
Tempesting forth, I come, 284
Tempest 's worst, who has known the, 328
Tempests roar, nor, 89
shook down trees, 25
Temple door, his torch is at thy, 255
gummed on each, 363
is a good, a holy place, 52
is that a, 367
let each new, 376
of my youth, 269
walls, built their, 155
Temple-bells are callin', for the, 392
they say, the, 252
Temples, 400
about, sported his eyes and his, 463
of his god, 89
the solemn, 428
Temporal dole, with a, 114
Tempt me no further, 139
the dying anchorite, 't would, 349
with doubts, who, 347
Temptation, most dangerous is that, 347
strife, the, 390
ye 're aiblins nae, 142
Tempted, 400
him as you have done, 332
save us from being, 313
the tempter or the, 400
Tempter, 400
Tempting grow, 226
Ten, as the strength of, 12
Commandments in your face, I'd set my, 59
Commandments, old as the, 59
Commandments, where there are n't no, 392
Commandments will not budge, the, 386
days' wonder at the least, 456
grief makes one hour, 165
hoops, shall have, 130
it 's waur I 'll get, 329
minutes to five, I declare, 92
o'clock, for it 's now, 443
or half after ten, we take, 210
thousand ducats to have it baned, 325
thousand fleets sweep over thee, 288
thousand men that fishes, 102
thousand, picked out of, 183
thousand swords would have leaped, 50
thousands, peace its, 431
times frail, call us, 453
times o'er, barbered, 18
times slain, though he were, 199
to one is no impeach of valour, 423
to one, 't is, 168
touched me for, 346
Tender, 401
and true, Douglas, 97
a part as he has about him, as, 180
comely, valiant Ireland, 194
fierceness of the dove, 97
for another 's pain, the, 392
or too firm a heart, too, 236
Tenderest, the bravest are the, 34
Tender-handed stroke a nettle, 280
Tenderness, thanks to its, 404
Tendril, who dare blaspheme the twisted, 69
Tends, to place and power all public spirit, 305
Tenement of life, on the walls of this, 275
refit, this, 367
the threshold of the ruined, 44
Tenements to Ned, lands and, 91

Tenets might be wrong, in some nice, 120
Tennis, 401
Tenor of their way, 68
Tens, two, to a score, 362
Tent, 401
nightly pitch my moving, 278
unto my, 12
which I am quitting, is a, 375
Tented field, action in the, 130
Tents are rude for thee, our Arab, 85
are spread, their silent, 26
shall fold their, 44
with love or thrones without, 85
Tenures, his, and his tricks, 214
Term, doomed for a certain, 380
Termagant, for o'erdoing, 379
Terms, 401
Terrestrial mould, though of, 40
Terrible impression, such, 98
oath, a, 287
shape, I hardly fear his, 78
swift sword, 153
than this, no shape more, 165
trade, war is a, 432
Terror, Cassius in your threats, no, 404
now, what a tale of, 5
of the household, the, 416
so full of dismal, 99
when this dumb, 147
Terrors, 401
Tertian, the slow fever called the, 441
Test, good work is the daily, 460
of affection's a tear, the, 398
Testament, go no furder than my, 431
of bleeding war, the purple, 432
Testify, alive at this day to, 36
Tether, shall hold the stars in a, 361
Teutonic pluck, is genuine, solid, old, 307
Text, 401
a neat rivulet of, 293
approve it with a, 330
in Galatians, a great, 71
of pike and gun, the holy, 329
one unquestioned, 155
that week, made it his, 219
Texts, 401
blends gospel, 247
of despair or hope, 24
Thames, with no allaying, 445
Thank God you are rid of a knave, 422
heaven, fasting, 238
heaven the crisis, 229
Providence, then Bill let us, 347
thee, Father, I, 109
thee, Jew, I, 72
whatever gods may be, I, 376
whom none can, 26
Thanked me, she, 363
Thankful, 401
to meet, you 're, 314
Thankless child, to have a, 49
Thanks, 401
for this relief much, 57
to stay and eat it, 48
Thanks
to the human heart, 404
Thanksgiving to the vine, 445
Thatch, an opening in the, 68
Thaw and resolve itself, 134
like snaw when it 's, 215
Theatre, the world 's a, 383
Thee and me, then no more of, 423
not of itself but, 100
when I live to, 227
Theft, the slyer the, 240
Theme, fools are my, 350
his passion and his, 217
of praise, an endless, 236
or guess that idle, 274
the glad diviner 's, 98
Themes, were his usual, 324
Theoric, 401
There, and she was, 105
it is, my child, 209
Thessalian bulls, dewlapped like, 88
Thetis, in the lap of, 269
Thick and thin, to dash through, 72
as autumnal leaves, 216
upon him, honours, 164
Thicker than itself, were, 169
Thickest, where the snow-flakes fall, 372
Thicket, above the, 384
Thickness, its thinness or its, 363
Thick-ribbed ice, region of, 90
Thief, 401
doth fear each bush an officer, the, 394
each thing's a, 402
of time, procrastination is the, 318
time you, 204
to the gallows, with a, 407
Thievery, 402
Thieves, 402
beauty provoketh, 21
for their robbery have authority, 386
little and great, 325
Thimble or a spoon, who stole a, 306
Thin, and one was, 226
partitions do their bounds divide, 245
partitions, sense from thought divide, 245
red line of 'eroes, but it's, 180
to dash through thick and, 72
Thine, love that says not mine and, 235
my name once mine, now, 275
why not I with, 366
Thing, 402
a cursed and tainted, 143
a lovely and a fearful, 455
an ill-favoured, 263
apart, of man's life a, 232
he is, to the, 147
he 'll make the, 467
he would not know, the, 394
I am not the, 74
immortal as itself, being a, 223
is certain, one, 135

Thing
is high, nobly as the, 120
is lost, whatsoever, 231
like a guilty, 57
man is, what a pretty, 251
of beauty is a joy, 20
of custom, a, 70
of God, poetry is itself a, 309
of life, ruled her like a, 436
of life, walks the waters like a, 436
one, was requisite, 266
she took to quench, 71
that feeds their fury, 132
that grieves not, a, 388
that very, 188
the play's the, 306
the self-same, 123
those letters mean, the, 450
to be asked for, not a, 3
to be well done, wish a, 96
ungained, men prize the, 318
Things alive, best good-natured, 140
an' men, an' I've seen, 40
are artificial, all, 13
are at the worst, when, 464
. . . are neither rich nor rare, the, 458
are not what they seem, 222
are running crossways, for, 53
are the sons of heaven, 459
at home are crossways, 292
at the worst will cease, 464
be, can such, 56
but words are, 192
by their names, call all, 275
can never die, these, 88
give place, all other, 209
God's sons are, 459
go wrong, how easily, 203
happening, in the way of, 170
have long been wrong, because, 422
I know, the handful o', 330
in heaven and earth, more, 303
like that, you know, must be, 425
like these, lasts like iron for, 441
misnamed death and existence, 369
named pants in certain documents, 294
of day, good, 282
that had neuer been neighbours before, 16
that they shall do, earnest of the, 461
then necessities, are these, 279
the sad vicissitudes of, 425
unattempted yet in prose or rhyme, 319
we planned, and the excellent, 451
won are done, 198
you worse than senseless, 27
Think, 402
all men mortal but themselves, 269
and act, free to, 220
him so, because I think him so 327
him so, is, 191
how little we, 79
Think
if he does really, 425
I must speak, when I, 453
it odd, none of those who, 312
naught a trifle, 414
not God at all, 200
o' Donald mair, nor, 364
of her mournfully, 454
of his pension, 301
of that, my cat, 45
old men fools, young men, 469
on all my wrongs, but when I, 423
one thing, who dares, 218
our fathers fools, we, 137
so, at least, we, 405
that they should lay him, to, 438
that you will love me still, I, 237
themselves alive, who, 75
then you are to-day what yesterday, 411
the poetry is dead in an old man, do n't, 309
thet killin' ain't perlite, 131
the truth they needs must, 368
that one may go, I really, 393
thousands, perhaps millions, 192
thy swan a crow, make thee, 394
too little, who, 396
upon, little do you, 355
when preachers tell us all they, 315
with you, ef we can't, 288
Thinker has a seat in the first-class cars, 315
Thinkest least, perform it when thou, 429
thou little, 137
Thinking, 402
on fantastic summer's heat, 191
on the frosty Caucasus, 191
o't, for, 263
plain living and high, 229
Thinks, and he complacently, 366
as much as he talks, if Brougham, 423
he needs, the more he, 279
he slays, if the red slayer, 368
himself too soon there, he, 407
men honest, that, 183
most, he most lives who, 227
o' me, and I know she, 251
the world turns round, 151
too much, he, 126
what his heart, 174
what ne'er was, 128
who can tell what a baby, 15
Thinness or its thickness, its, 363
Thin-spun life, slits the, 123
Third, and that the, 53
day comes a frost, 164
to make a, 309
Thirst, a man can raise a, 392
in midst of water I complain of, 435
of hate, 171
of vengeance, the ancestral, 130
the water that quencheth, 369
to quench a country's, 248

Thirsty, 402
moments, to cheat the, 288
plant, to every, 101
tongue, the piercing cider for the, 53
Thirty, at, man suspects himself a fool, 251
at, we are trying to cut our names, 275
days, to wear a shirt for, 361
years, his dark retreat of, 288
Thompson in, caved the head of, 141
Thomson, O, void of rhyme as well as reason, 382
Thorn, 402, 403
as sharp to them as, 419
flower and, 224
withering on the virgin, 342
Thorn-bit of marriage, the terrible, 253
Thorns, 403
and briers, who found not, 374
and to those, 270
a rosebud set with little wilful, 343
so roses grow on, 403
Thorn-tree had a mind to Him, the, 458
Thorny stem of time, on the, 143
Those days, those days, 74
Thou beside me, 85
Thought, 403
and passion, chaos of, 462
as a sage, he, 346
by hidden nerves, he shoots his, 86
can rise, what bolder, 411
capable of sober, 262
Christ went agin war an' pillage, 431
dare to vent his dang'rous, 397
divide, sense from, 245
even with a, 56
fly like, 171
for reposeful, 229
for want of, 440
from self each, 233
his act, nor any unproportioned, 411
his mind a, 248
in all the magnanimity of, 251
I never, that they would shave, 326
in loftiness of, 309
is destroyed by, 33
like dew upon a, 192
men of, 225
more easily be, 166
noble, enhances life and all its chances, 284
of his daughter War, he, 432
of love, lightly turns to, 241
of the morrow, we bitterly, 313
runs before her actions, a woman's, 453
she lived with no other, 246
strange perversity of, 159
teems with, 231
the dome of, 367
their monody compels, solemn, 410
the pale cast of, 61
there was no more behind, 411
Thought
thy wish was father to that, 446
to rear the tender, 398
unworthy of a, 419
upon a, 133
was mine, what I once, 333
what oft was, 447
whose armour is his honest, 418
with but a single, 224
wrought by want of, 116
Thought's a weapon stronger, 159
mysterious seat, was, 367
Thoughts, 403, 404
all passions, all, 234
are legible, whose, 117
beyond the reaches of our souls, 268
be your fair pillow, fair, 304
by great, and good deeds, 248
by the pattern of mine own, 321
conceived, but never penned, 434
distract his troubled, 178
immaculate, 29
intent, on hospitable, 187
not breaths, in, 227
no tongue, give thy, 411
of men are widened, 322
of mortality, no less are, 269
of my age, 5
of others, 51
of the last bitter hour, when, 362
of youth are long, 33
once chambered here, the, 367
pansies, that's for, 294
remain below, my, 313
style is the dress of, 391
that arise in me, 35
that shall glad the two or three, 466
that wander through eternity, 90
unruly, with, 348
were high and fine, my, 98
words without, 313
Thousand charms to show, 143
claims to reverence, 323
crimes, and a, 64
doors, death hath a, 79
eyes, the mind has a, 281
eyes, the night has a, 281
fearful wrecks, a, 102
furlongs of sea, give a, 354
homes, homeless near a, 182
knights, a, 179
leaves, open their, 382
lines, dry desert of a, 364
liveried angels lackey her, 47
may well be stopped by three, 37
men, were worth a, 39
miles from land are we, a, 354
others feed, what would, 300
pities then, what a, 2
pound, do I owe you a, 292
several tongues, hath a, 61
strings, a harp of, 170
tables, and near a, 182
times, borne me on his back a, 468
times he swore, a, 329
times told, better a, 203

Thousand tongues, music of, 412
voices, earth with her, 154
waiting upon that, 83
wars of old, ring out the, 434
worlds are round, when, 463
years, but for a, 355
years, memory of a, 72
years ago, died a, 75
years of fire, bitterer than a, 83
years of peace, ring in the, 300
years, partridge-breeders of a, 231
years scarce serve to form a state, 385
years, we have fed our sea for a, 113
years, whose flag has braved a, 110
Thousandfold, good or bad, a, 157
Thousands had sunk on the ground overpowered, 39
has been slave to, 275
mourn, makes countless, 192
slays, war its, 431
that which makes, 192
to murder, 272
with a single fall, startles, 81
Thraldom or a double strife, the single, 442
Thread, cut the mortal, 75
feels at each, 380
hinders needle and, 438
of his verbosity, the, 424
of it, the utmost, 380
plying her needle and, 360
sewing at once with a double, 362
the postern of a small needle's eye, 42
the slight, self-pleasing, 353
your iron, 152
Threads, smooth the few silver, 340
Threaten or indulge, can, 377
Threatening to devour me, 178
Threatens, of one who, 178
Threats, 404
Three, a thousand may well be stopped by, 37
cheers for this Christmas old, give, 51
corners of the world, 112
corpses lay out on the shining sands, 132
farthings, the Latin word for, 332
feeds, 181
fishers went sailing, 132
good men unhanged in England, not, 259
hundred pounds a year, 128
kingdoms, God had sifted, 276
meet again, when shall we, 257
misbegotten knaves in Kendal green, 205
ought to have dined at, 92
poets in three distant ages, 309
removes are as bad as a fire, 332
than we did of being, 241
the king amang us, 201
thousand ducats, lend, 95
thousand ducats, to receive, 103
Three thousand years ago, as was said, 199
times eight large diamonds, 73
years before the war, 162
Three-hooped pot, the, 130
Three-legged stool, with a, 59
Three-man beetle, with a, 22
Threescore years and ten, keeps in blast, 28
Threshed the Bolivar out across the Bay, 54
Threshold of the ruined tenement, 44
Threw me down, ambition, 7
me higher, by overthrowing me, you, 316
their caps, they, 43
Thrice ere the morning I dreamt it again, 427
he routed all his foes, 19
is he armed, 12
the brinded cat hath mewed, 45
thy fee, 381
thy shaft flew, 12
yon moon had filled her horn, ere, 12
Thrift, 404
may follow fawning, where, 412
my well-won, 193
thus charitable, 265
Thrifty mind, stale in, 126
Thrill, and feel a, 133
fresh wild, 33
loving is a painful, 243
of joy prophetic, runs a, 143
of life, seems to feel the, 200
thee with its warning, 115
will fondly, 237
Thrills the fond soul, 236
Thrive by dirty ways, 92
at Number Five, arts that, 13
at Westminster, we, 292
in cunning, to, 88
Thrived, was the ones thet, 40
Thriving lie, a party, or a, 42
ones, sickly trees not, 425
Throat, Amen stuck in my, 8
ever scuttled ship or cut a, 262
the fog in my, 78
you lie in your, 219
Throat-gates, morsel that stuffs him to the, 92
Throats, 404
had hanging at them, whose, 88
whose rude, 125
with harness on their, 100
Throb she gives, the only, 143
Throbbed beneath that leathern breast, 174
no longer, till the war-drum, 433
Throbbings, the heart of the toiler has, 410
Throe, never grudge the, 328
Throes, has Fate entailed the mother's, 59
Throne, 404
above, from Allah's, 231
above, I dare not, 160

Throne
amid the mart, to your, 413
and makes his, 317
a rank, a, 462
her seat, made the, 265
nearer the great white, 278
of kings, this royal, 112
of royal state, 107
of the world, to the, 339
one, 133
sent word to a, 276
wade through slaughter to a, 368
wherever sinks a, 144
wrong for ever on the, 417
Thrones and globes elate, o'er, 385
without, tents with love or, 85
Throng, when mingling in the, 443
Through, when thou art, 78
Throw at a dog, not one to, 95
it up into the air, 389
physic to the dogs, 303
Throwest, set less than thou, 362
Thrown a gem unheeded, thou hast, 149
by angry Jove, 122
upon that die is, 455
Thrust in among the works, that one could, 403
it aside, she tried . . . to, 449
them into matters none of theirs, who, 285
upon 'em, greatness, 164
Thumb, 404
to his wrist, gave a, 311
Thumbs, 404
I twirl my, 284
Thumps, 405
Thunder, 405
lightning, or in rain, in, 257
loud roared the dreadful, 26
riven, then shook the hills with, 13
the dawn comes up like, 252
to the tune of Green Sleeves, 311
Thunderbolt, innocents 'scape not the, 193
the brightest, 41
Thunder-clap at death, a, 123
Thundered, lightened and hailed, 389
volleyed and, 42
Thundering on the reef, roller, 341
Thunder-music, rolling, 291
Thus or thus, that we are, 127
Thwack, 405
Thwarted and withstood, 64
love, in bad temper oft has vent, 235
Thyme blows, where the wild, 17
Tiber in't, not a drop of allaying, 445
where'er down, 184
Ticket, and the Fellow's, 345
Tickle us, if you, 197
your catastrophe, I'll, 45
Tickled with a straw, 49
with good success, 392
Tickling, 405
Tick-tock, tick-tock, 280
Tide, 405
and the taintless, 247
but such a, 18
I'm afloat on the fierce rolling, 4
in the affairs of men, 405
is at his highest height, 18
is in his ecstasy, 18
look to be washed off the next, 465
lost in the dashing, 339
of love, pity swells the, 305
of times, in the, 250
one moment flow, let the, 82
parted from us by a, 110
without a, 200
Tides, and her bay-, 32
betwixt two, 222
dark flow thy, 354
of life, these struggling, 322
Tidings, confirm the, 216
up and down, send the, 23
Tie, a careless shoe-string in whose, 364
as though there were a, 311
love endures no, 302
the silken, 237
to him doth, 335
up the knocker, 206
Tied or manacled, not, 381
Ties, at sight of human, 233
Tiger, 405
die, let the ape and, 20
like the shark and, 256
passions were in us, when the, 392
than there is milk in a male, 260
the Hyrcan, 72
Tiger's heart wrapped in a woman's hide, 453
spring, their revenge is as the, 455
Tight little island, a, 194
Tile to scullery, shrills from, 253
Tilt at all I meet, and, 350
Timber, headed with a knob of, 249
Timber's propped, with one of, 216
Timbrel, 405
Time, 406, 407
aboding luckless, 25
agree, never did in, 429
all of the olden, 149
and change, 154
and me, tell her that wastes her, 343
and our oars keep, 286
and place shall serve, 13
and the long result of, 352
as this, in such a, 289
at last sets all things even, 467
bed becomes a bed of, 151
be not coy but use your, 254
but on the shores of, 138
by heart-throbs, count, 227
choose thine own, 220
come to thy God in, 155
could we choose the, 89
dissolve the winter snow, 233
doth not breathe, 209
draws near the birth of Christ, 23, 52
enough, in we came an', 115

Time
fleets, youth fades, 220
for all, 4
foremost captain of his, 43
for orchard-robbing, then 's the, 386
gave us liberty at the same, 217
has come, the walrus said, 430
has pressed, rolling, 333
held his breath for a, 364
I am sick of, 333
'ill be the happiest, 256
in the book of, 142
is fleeting, 163
is like a fashionable host, 167
is racked with birth-pangs, the, 416
is ripe and rotten-ripe, 46
I think 's sufficient at one, 335
it spoils the pleasure of the, 307
let not a drop be spilt, 78
like this, a, 259
makes ancient good uncouth, 281
may have their throats about them at that, 464
men at some, 127
of day, no proper, 285
of need, for her, 277
of night, now it is the, 282
of night, the very witching, 282
of peace, in this weak piping, 300
of universal peace is near, the, 299
old, is still a-flying, 343
old common arbitrator, 109
on the sands of, 138
on the thorny stem of, 143
prime, 115
quaffing and unthinking, 71
return, bid, 468
saltness of, 5
shall come, yet the, 38
shall lead him to his end, 267
shall make the bushes green, 233
soon will come, the, 390
spend their, in making nets, 280
taught by, 174
terror was the, 99
that, 74
the glass of, 241
the last syllable of recorded, 411
the lazy foot of, 56
there is limitless, 178
there was a, 331
there was ere England's griefs began, 166
the thief of, 318
the whips and scorns of, 323
this great gap of, 370
though it sleep a, 28
to dance is not to woo, 456
to fear when tyrants seem to kiss, 419
to marry, but proper, 254
to time, men have died from, 238
to waste, men in earnest have no, 416
turn backward, O, 340
unto this season, from that, 335

Time
unveils eternity, when, 411
watch the, and always serve it, 392
were twins, nature and, 277
when screech-owls cry, the, 352
with falling oars they kept the, 286
youth and home and that sweet, 23
you thief, 204
Timepiece says to all, an ancient, 280
Time 's great wilderness, in, 222
noblest offspring, 109
tragedy is in that aching stoop, 188
Times, 407
corsair 's name to other, 64
have been, the, 90
in the tide of, 250
new, demand new measures and new men, 281
O, 74
of general calamity, 41
of old, in, 69
old, old manners, 290
resign his own at, 159
that try men 's souls, the, 378
the weakness of these latter, 437
till other, 114
which cause good or evil, 317
Time-tutored age, 65
Timid, 408
Tinker, I can drink with any, 100
Tinkle in the icy air of night, how they, 23
Tinkling of the bells, the jingling and the, 408
Tintagel chime, rang out, 155
Tintinnabulation, 408
Tints are very much like, 5
Tiny kickshaws, any pretty little, 201
Tipped with amber, when, 408
Tippeny, wi', we fear nae evil, 19
Tipple in the deep, fishes that, 133
Tips with silver, that, 268
Tire of all creation, the, 188
Tired he sleeps, till, 49
her wing, when she has, 344
limbs with travel, 21
wench and coming butter, 429
Tires him, self-mettle, 9
in a mile-a, 174
Tirling at the window, 443
Titillating joys, knows he the, 285
Tittering on, comes, 228
Title, who gained no, 385
without that, 275
Title-leaf, like to a, 38
Titles, all thy other, 137
high though his, 65
now are altered strangely, 407
power and pelf, despite those, 65
wealth and fame, 334
To and fro, kept heaving, 36
be, or not to be, 19
Toad, 408
in his cell, like a, 446
or live like the, 446
ugly and venomous, 3

Toads went pop, the, 372
Toast cheese, it will, 48
pass, let the, 210
Tobacco, 408
and sleep, snuff, 187
I want a chaw of, 404
Tocsin of the soul, the, 92
To-day, 408, 409
and shall be done, 96
be dark, though, 186
be wise, 84
can make to-morrow cheerful as, 400
he puts forth, 164
it is our pleasure, 102
man is, 364
official sinning, is, 289
such a day to-morrow as, 411
the darkness of, 48
to-morrow shall be like, 411
we must measure twenty miles, 262
what yesterday you were, 411
who dies, 75
yet say No, 468
Toddy, and drink the, 321
Toe, 409
a Hottentot's great, 266
of frog, and, 179
Toes, to warm his, 207
Together, 409
cannot live, 5
in doubt we'll go, 377
we've been long, 220
Toil, 409
and effort, the life of, 389
and strife, hour of danger, 39
and trouble, unapt to, 456
and trouble, war . . . is, 431
for her, to work and, 189
for triumphs of an hour, 104
is holy service, honest, 459
mock their useful, 310
o'er books, hath thy, 215
of dropping buckets, 39
of unrequited, 199
or from bitter, 390
weary with, 21
we lost, the, 451
Toiled with men, I have lived and, 259
Toiler, 410
Toilet, 410
Toiling, 410
upward in the night, 177
Token, may be a, 377
watch for the lightest, 293
Told, great griefe will not be, 166
her love, she never, 298
lest her secret should be, 277
the sexton, they went and, 22
Toledo trusty, the trenchant blade, 26
Tolerable and not to be endured, most, 434
Toll, 410
Tolled the bell, the sexton, 22
Tolling, 410
Tolls out, the minster bell, 264
Tolls the knell, the curfew, 69
the evening chime, faintly as, 286
Tom, 410
bears logs, and, 190
Tom - all - Alone's, other gentlemen come down, 314
Tomb, 410
asleep within the, 222
beyond the, 209
blazoned on the stately, 264
cradles rock us nearer to the, 81
e'en from the, 35
encompass the, 163
is found, where the Redeemer's, 328
meet again beyond the, 61
on the, 252
seated in the vacant, 338
shall break the mortal bondage of the, 353
thus it might upon the, 329
upon my, 114
vampire which from Freedom's, 64
Tombs, 410
in the, 101
of those who have reflected honour, 111
Tome, he shut the ponderous, 263
Tommy, 410
'ow's yer soul, 180
Tom's food for seven long year, have been, 261
To-morrow, 411
blossoms, 164
but one more, 79
cheerful as to-day, make, 400
defer not till, 84
do thy worst, 408
dupe of, 92
he is gone, 364
in that great, glad, 94
is Saint Valentine's Day, 422
knows no, 155
let my sun his beams display, 408
live till, 86
'll be the happiest time, 256
morn, I'm off at eight, 132
never leave that till, 408
our jaunt must be put off, 324
shows the bright, 48
sunburst may smile on thee, 186
you'll be sick, 362
To-morrows, and confident, 48
Ton, none couldn't quicker pitch a, 249
Tone, but rather the general, 308
could reach the rich, would that its, 361
its various, 172
Tones, in divers, 170
sweet, are remembered not, 209
Tongs, sure the shovel and, 441
Tongue, 411, 412
all who speak the English, 111
alone, formed by one, 412
and braggart with my, 399
and free quill, Britons have a, 110

Tongue
and pen, if of all words of, 346
could utter, that my, 35
cutteth friendship al a-two, a, 412
deedless in his, 84
dropped manna, though his, 122
every, brings in, 61
faster than his, 118
flatteries of his, 134
gall in the slanderous, 42
if with his, 454
in it, that skull had a, 367
is the clapper, 174
laid a curse upon his, 283
midnight bell with his iron, 22
more richer than my, 238
murder, though it have no, 272
never in the, 196
of dog, 179
of fire, must be the, 314
of flame, like the volcano 's, 24
of midnight, the iron, 262
of war, the harsh and boisterous, 432
o' man can name, the, 457
or pen, of all sad words of, 346
or pen, saddest of, 346
outvenoms, whose, 368
see what a ready, 394
speaks, his, 174
sword, eye, 263
take her without her, 10
that man that hath a, 454
the piercing cider for the thirsty, 53
think with wagging of your, 378
trippingly on the, 379
truly the only, 314
truth on every shepherd 's, 237
vows, lends the, 429
which his fair, 196
while listening senates hang upon thy, 11
with unholy, 67
Tongued with censure, more, 165
Tongueless, one good deed dying, 83
Tongues, 412
a thousand several, 61
and evil, 116
done to death by slanderous, 368
in trees, 3
of dying men, 105
of men are full, 82
to silence envious, 299
To-night, a child again just for, 340
dream of money-bags, 98
Too heavy for a man, 40
late, after dying all reprieve's, 59
late, that comfort comes, 59
much of a good thing, 159
Took and gave, blessed be he who, 164
my friend, with her, 57
the ground, when she, 166
Tool, the mysteries of that magic, 467
Tools, sin has many, 218
Tooth is not so keen, thy, 444
sharper than a serpent 's, 49
Toothache, 413
he that sleeps feels not the, 371
Toots his horn, south wind that, 132
Top of my bent, they fool me to the, 137
Topics furnish, the, 455
Topmost height, from the Heaven 's, 28
roof, ever upon the, 112
Tops, all the fruit-tree, 268
I used to think their slender, 331
Torch is at thy temple door, his, 255
Torment, no, is so bad as love, 232
than a hermit 's fast, more grievous, 235
through joy and through, 236
Torments, of all the, 339
Torn by dogs, liable to be, 292
ne'er from it to be, 377
Torrent of a woman 's will, to stem the, 450
of tears, by a, 389
tempest, for in the very, 379
Torture, and boil in endless, 436
and trouble in vain, 230
as real, is theirs, 455
may be called a hell, 178
to us a, 398
Tory, I ain't a, 42
Toss to hell, he will, 178
Tossed from a pitchfork, hay, 166
on the thorny bed of pain, 293
you down into the field, 207
Tossing about on the roaring sea, 354
Toted him, scooped down and, 404
Touch, dares not put it to the, 126
God 's right hand, 156
her not scornfully, 454
him further, nothing can, 223
if aught do, 380
it again with immortality, 467
much, 115
not a single bough, 457
of a vanished hand, for the, 169
of fire, asunder at the, 38
of God, pity is the, 305
of holy bread, as the, 205
of infinite calm, with a, 374
of nature, one, 278
our country, they, 368
pitch, they that, 401
remain, where shall the angel 's, 91
soiled by any outward, 417
that cheek, might, 47
the fire, to, 120
them on, hard enough to, 458
the spider 's, 380
the underpinnin', do n't never, 39
which in Death 's, 76
wound with a, 350
Touched corruption, he has, 36
him, God 's finger, 371
me for ten, 346
not rashly to be, 304
the dead corpse, he, 340
with joy, they bring me sorrow, 470

Touches the flesh, 77
us not, it, 195
Touching of the lips, at the, 226
Touchstone, man's true, 41
on war's red, 19
Tough, 413
conscience was, 183
Tougher or truer, there is no, 307
Tower, 413
from yonder ivy-mantled, 292
in Siloam fell, the, 193
of strength, king's name is a, 202
people this lonely, 367
Towered citadel, a, 56
Towering in her pride of place, 121
Towers, clashed and hammered from a hundred, 284
the cloud-capped, 428
the earth builds . . . castles and, 106
Town and state, wasting, 325
ere you went to, 174
he had cleaned out the, 350
man made the, 64
of monks and bones, a, 387
or city, through the centre of every, 15
procured from, 349
red, paint the, 102
to town, fling the joy from, 23
view the manners of the, 413
watching them out of the, 132
wee Willie Winkie rins through the, 443
who will never come back to the, 132
Town-crier, as lief the, 379
Towns, for want of, 252
seven wealthy, contend, 183
Toy, my heart was every woman's, 148
Toys of age, 49
Trace, fondly stoops to, 295
his works we, 154
of him afford no other, 228
of its passage, leaves some, 138
of record here, have left one, 367
the boding tremblers learned to, 93
the stars, to, 402
with mocking pencil wont to, 225
Traced in sand, thy vows are, 450
in sand, whose name was, 274
the lives of the good men, that, 301
to earth's earliest years, whose pedigree, 300
with his golden pen, 418
Track of his fiery car, by the bright, 393
the steps of glory to the grave, 152
Tracks, they have been and made their, 437
Tract, 413
while there is one untrodden, 220
Trade, 413
in all the shops of, 386
left no calling for this idle, 466
oh, the sorry, 82
Trade
or employment, no, 180
plies corruption's, 64
war is a terrible, 432
wax, mingling poetic honey with, 308
Traders, 413
a nation of, 361
Tradition's force upheld the truth, by, 416
Tragedian, counterfeit the deep, 307
Tragedy, and some compose a, 146
time's, 188
Tragic volume, nature of a, 38
Trail of the serpent is over them all, 356
Trailing clouds of glory, 25
like a wounded duck, 54
Train, glorious woman in its, 444
they love a, 448
up a fig-tree, 131
Traitor, and graceless, 454
most accursed, is the, 188
rest, shall the, 83
to humanity, the, 188
Traitorous kiss, not she with, 67
Traitor's smile, the, 384
Traitors, our doubts are, 97
Traitors' arms, more strong than, 192
Tramping over the heather, go, 361
Trample my fellow worm, helping to, 177
round my fallen head, to, 76
the world, to, 449
Trampled back to shapeless earth, 107
foe, as soon for a, 173
Trampling out the vintage, he is, 153
Tranquil mind, farewell the, 125
Transept, in the great minster, 264
Transfigured into angel guise, 416
Transfigures you and me, 225
Transform life, the desire to, 190
Transgressing, have some times by, 213
Transition, what seems so is, 76
Transmute, leaden metal into gold, 162
Transport know, can ne'er a, 448
Trappings and the suits of woe, 448
of a monarchy, the, 266
Trash, so much, 36
their vile, 267
who steals my purse steals, 275
Travail, had my labour for my, 208
Travel, some minds improve by, 276
those types of, 401
tired, limbs with, 21
too, we must, 72
twice as far as he, 429
with long, 413
Travels in divers paces, time, 406
Traveller, 413
no, ever reached that blessed abode, 374
returns, no, 79
Traverse the pole or the zone, 112
Tray, Branch and Sweetheart, 95

Tre, Pol and Pen, by, 63
Treacle, the fly that sips, 395
Tread alone, that I must, 387
doth close behind him, 128
each other's heel, they, 448
if we will but, 170
is on an empire's dust, 109
it down, 103
on classic ground, 55
onward to your throne, and, 413
our fairy ring, to, 304
the globe, all that, 74
upon another's heels, one woe doth, 448
upon, beetle that we, 80
wheels rush in where horses fear to, 439
where angels fear to, 138
where'er we, 181
Treads alone some banquet-hall deserted, 17
leads, 44
not the earth, 150
on flowers, that only, 406
on high, and, 312
on life, life, 220
Treason, 414
can but peep to what it would, 202
cannot commit, 64
has done his worst, 223
while bloody, 121
Treasons, stratagems and spoils, 273
Treasure, Bacchus' blessings are a, 16
back, will bring the, 149
for those who seek the, 462
have gathered their, 367
rich the, 16
what men call, 102
Treasure-caves and cells, in thy, 354
Treasured up, to a life beyond life, 30
Treasurer, of course, 92
Treasures up a wrong, of him who, 467
you learn the extent of your, 366
Treasury stairs, the Jacob's ladder of the, 325
Treat a poor wretch, to, 360
existence is a merry, 147
it as he will, yet all his own to, 107
O herbaceous, 349
Treble, turning again toward childish, 294
Tree, 414
Adam sat under the, 13
a hale green, 286
and highest, the middle, 63
fruit of that forbidden, 93
give me again my hollow, 217
have robbed the whole, 115
in his banner that glances, 49
of deepest root, the, 224
of Knowledge, fast by the, 63
of Life, and on the, 63
on my ancestral, 342
sat down beneath our, 182
that bears no fruit, the, 147
the old, is leafless in the forest, 290
Tree
there sits a bird on every, 254
they don't make a, 308
under the greenwood, 165
with splendid branches, like a, 461
woodman, spare that, 457
Zaccheus he did climb the, 470
Tree's inclined, the, 107
Trees, and on the, 275
are brown, and all the, 290
are green, and all the, 469
gather on sickly, 425
like leaves on, 250
on all the hills, all the, 382
tempests shook down, 25
their medicinal gum, Arabian, 399
tongues in, 3
under the shade of the, 333
upon 't, with, 56
Trelawney die, and shall, 63
Tremble, 414
and start, 307
made all England, 87
shall never, 72
Trembled, and the land, 147
kissing, and, 205
Tremblers learned to trace, the boding, 93
Trembles when he sees, Satan, 350
in the breast, that, 313
when his hand, 309
Trembling all about the breezy dells, 52
as the dew, 245
on from east to west, 143
the chord of self, 241
vassal of the Pole, 60
waked, I, 98
wings misdoubteth every bush, 25
Trench, this working in the dismal, 40
Trenchant blade, Toledo trusty, the, 26
Trencher-man, 414
Tresses man's imperial race ensnare, 168
Tresspass is it, tell me what, 298
Trial hath no fear, of his, 5
perusing a, 423
Tribe, enough to scour a, 266
his, were God Almighty's gentlemen, 51
sufferance is the badge of all our, 392
Tribes, a handful to the, 74
Tribute, craves no other, 189
pays his, 36
Trice, alchemist that in a, 162
Trick, 414
Nick Machiavel had ne'er a, 281
of our English nation, 160
may upset a freight-train of conversation, 321
yet it is our, 399
Trickled, 414
Tricks, his tenures and his, 214
plays such fantastic, 251

Tricks that are vain, 50
Tried, both leal and, 57
by fire, gold must be, 158
by whom the new are, 126
that has been, 427
Trier to Coln there was never a knight, from, 221
Tries the troth in everything, time, 407
Trifle, 414
in removing this, 308
Trifles, a series of, 219
a snapper-up of unconsidered, 372
life, and, 414
light as air, 195
Trim, in gallant, 470
no carpet knight so, 46
Trimming, while the bonnet is, 211
Trinkets had been hallowed, as if my, 415
Trip is done, our fearful, 43
it as you go, come and, 409
on it, once you, 71
you're running, you, 220
Trippingly on the tongue, 379
Trips, that the rich by easy, 176
Triton, 414
or hear old, 293
Triumph advances, the chief who in, 49
and power, take me with, 392
tasted, thet tell o', 299
wins the splendid ultimate, 390
wrong would, 337
Triumphed, Jehovah has, 405
Triumphs of an hour, toil for, 104
over death, revenge, 77
Trivial, 414
Trod, by equal feet are, 464
one nearer to God's altar, 312
the ground, blessed feet have, 328
the soil where first they, 464
the ways of glory, 140
too heedless where I, 177
upon a worm, I, 271
Trodden down with stones, 15
on, will turn being, 463
out, little fire is quickly, 131
Troll out for Christmas stout, song I, 51
the bowl, 32
Troop, farewell the plumed, 125
of little children at my heels, 167
was landed in my country, foreign, 8
Troop-sergeant-major, late, 301
Trope, but out there flew a, 335
Trot, in a jolly round, 298
withal, who doth he, 406
Troth in everything, time tries the, 407
two bosoms and one, 174
wooing light makes fickle, 456
Trots hard with a young maid, he, 407
withal, who time, 406
Troubadours, 414
Trouble afterwards, may be avoided, 96
Trouble, charm of powerful, 179
in vain, torture and, 230
little Caty-did, 200
of my own, filled with a, 295
unapt to toil and, 456
war . . . is toil and, 431
you, did she mean to, 200
Troubled mind drave me to walk abroad, 393
the dead man's grave, I who have, 448
with a rat, if my house be, 325
Troubles, a sea of, 19
enough of its own, but has, 212
himself little about a million men, 259
of the brain, the written, 263
Troublesome, and in the last repeating, 400
Troubling, the wicked cease from, 334
Trout, and though it be a two-foot, 168
that must be caught with tickling, 405
Trowel, 415
Trowest, learn more than thou, 362
Troy, fired another, 177
in ashes, laid at last old, 452
Truant at his tale, play, 196
husband should return, and, 189
in the law, a, 213
Truce, our bugles sang, 39
Truckle-bed, to lie in honour's, 184
Trudged along, unknowing what he sought, 440
Trudging my weary way, I'm, 310
True, 415
all men's faces are, 119
alms which the hand can hold, no, 7
a lover as ever sighed, 242
and if thou still art, 340
and leal, all men, 150
and righteous altogether, are, 199
and tender, she nursed me, 286
as death, a woman as, 451
as steel, heart is, 174
as the dial to the sun, 88
as the needle to the pole, 88
as the sun, 245
as what you once let fall, nothing so, 455
a valiant man and, 105
before, that which was proved, 95
by your truth she shall be, 468
citizen, true Christian is the, 54
dare to be, 218
do rest but, 112
face, has a, 119
hearts, the, 175
he serves all who dares be, 415
look thou be, 70
love, the course of, 238
lover in the forest, no, 56
love's the gift, 237
makes it, 368
man, to be no, 401

True
more tender and more, 401
one to another, when thieves cannot be, 402
patriots all, 64
plain single vow that is vowed, 417
ring in the, 122
steadfast in the strength of God and, 179
to church and state, than be, 213
to man, he 's true to God who 's, 249
to one party, he 's been, 62
valour, in a false quarrel there is no, 423
Trueborn Englishman, yet a, 113
True-fixed and resting quality, 62
True-hearted, I swear he is, 438
True-love hath my heart, my, 235
I had a, 57
Truer, there is no tougher or, 307
Truest poetry is the most feigning, 309
the nearest, and dearest, 146
Truly blent, beauty, 21
mourn, they, 271
Trump, the shrill, 125
to wait for the final, 77
when the great, 115
Trumped death 's ace for me, he, 77
Trumpet, 415
and drum, broken by, 390
his own, 320
when the loud, 353
Trumps, 415
Truncheon, the marshal 's, 260
Trundling her mop, 296
Trunks of men, into the, 378
Trust, 415
and woman 's, 450
by an unfaltering, 227
committed to my, 422
her not, 24
in critics, before you, 67
in God, put your, 311
in God and good books, I, 31
in her always, doth safely, 451
is, safe and sound your, 450
me more, never, 372
me not at all or all in all, 275
must serve with perfect, 357
my fate to thee, before I, 127
my trust, thy, 104
no future howe'er pleasant, 147
not a man, 83
not the physician, 303
not those cunning waters of his eyes, 426
or plan, thy purpose, 391
our necks, should, 311
take them O Father in immortal, 13
that man in nothing, 62
to him, and I, 352
Trusted, let no such man be 273
not in one bottom, 424
to thy billows, 288
Trustees of the people, officials, 289
Trusting wife, gentle loving, 443
Trusts himself to woman or to waves, who, 452
the strength, who, 389
to one poor hole, 271
Trusty, Toledo, the trenchant blade, 26
Truth, 415–418
a land of . . . , 65
a lie which is half a, 219
and love, light, 403
and loyalty, with, 243
and never tell the, 187
and spread the, 216
brightness, purity and, 452
by your, she shall be true, 468
cannon-balls may aid the, 159
can poison, 412
can tell, 218
cleared some great, 91
convinced at sight, whose, 447
dreams of love and, 88
enough for man to know, 427
for they breathe, 105
forced me out of thy honest, 399
from his lips prevailed, 352
has such a face, 425
I hold it, 170
in masquerade, but the, 218
in the pure shrine of, 269
is marching on, his, 153
is noble, to side with, 34
is old, the, 249
makes free, whom the, 144
malice bears down, 247
may be, tell how the, 396
may stay, which some, 120
modest, and beauty save, 449
of its own fundamental proposition, 8
one, is clear, 338
one bosom and one, 174
on every shepherd 's tongue, 237
one who having into, 219
sole judge of, 462
that warp us from the living, 470
they needs must think, the, 368
this I set down as a positive, 255
to be a liar, 97
well known to most, 231
were a fool, you would think, 218
who would keep abreast of, 281
wine and, is the saying, 444
with Falsehood, strife of, 83
wut 's words to them whose faith an', 19
yet friend to, 385
Truth 's yet mightier man-child, 115
Truths, 418
there are some, 122
Truth-teller, 418
Try men 's souls, that, 378
one desperate medicine more, to, 86
our fortunes, 141
the man, let the end, 251
us, decidedly can, 172
Trying to cut our names, at thirty we are, 275

Trysting-place in the forest, at their, 339
Tub, 418
Tug of war, then was the, 165
Tumble down, ready with every nod to, 346
down, sceptre and crown must, 103
Tumbles, a' plays and, 133
Tumbling, a pigeon, 219
Tumult and the shouting dies, 139
thrown into, 377
Tune, all were singing out of, 9
and harsh, out of, 327
of Green Sleeves, thunder to the, 311
on the heart, memory plays an old, 258
our voices keep, 286
singeth a quiet, 37
that they play, from the, 112
up, and prepares to, 210
Turbulency tells, their, 5
Turf, a grass-green, 75
lay white on the, 386
that wraps their clay, to bless the, 34
to smell to a, 269
where heaves the, 108
Turk, along with the barbarous, 451
Turkey, hot as a basted, 286
Turkey-cock, 418
Turkman's rest, or the, 408
Turn again, and pass and, 368
and dance her, 71
and fly, 28
and go, grieve and they, 329
down an empty glass, 152
Fortune, turn thy wheel, 141
him about, and, 304
his blow, perhaps may, 145
in their, 216
may, and fight another day, 130
religions take their, 330
that he can take hold of and, 279
the current of a woman's will, to, 450
the leaf down, 45
the scale, a feather will, 351
the scales, a hair will, 351
the smallest worm will, 463
the wheel, and, 386
thy back on heaven, 159
to serve his, 218
to thee, I, 155
to the straight path, 104
wants but one more evil, 173
what form of prayer can serve my, 313
your eyes, that you could, 355
Turned fool, as wit, 447
his back on jewelled hands, has, 321
it in his glowing hands, 241
outward, the wrong side may be, 447
round, having once, 128
up in scornful curve, thy nose, 304
Turning his face to the dew-dropping south, 444
o' the tide, even at the, 405
up, in case of anything, 382
Turnpikes leading to free thought, 31
Turns, atheism and religion take their, 330
again home, 18
away, all coldly, 125
by, give one another ease, 345
no more his head, 128
on her god, the sunflower, 393
none to good, an ill winde, 444
to a mirth-moving jest, the other, 196
to thee, my spirit, 125
to thought of love, 241
Turpins and Macaires, real, 325
Turrets crowned, with spires and, 385
Turtles from jays, teach him to know, 195
Tutor, own discretion be your, 93
me from quarrelling, yet thou wilt, 32
Twain, 418
till out of, 290
Twal, ayont the, 187
Twanged off, sharply, 287
Twanging them, as in, 397
Tweed, at York, 'tis on the, 284
Tweedle-dee, 'twixt Tweedle-dum and, 418
Tweedle-dum, 418
Twelve for eighteen pence, offered, 326
great shocks of sound, with, 284
good men into a box, 33
hundred million men are spread, 75
tongue of midnight hath told, 262
Twenty days are now, 74
gals, with full, 363
men, if you had the strength of, 389
miles to-day, we must measure, 262
mortal murders, 90
of their swords, than, 302
pounds, annual income, 192
pounds ought and six, annual expenditure, 192
thousand Cornishmen will know the reason why, 63
times, utter the You, 319
times was Peter feared, 128
what were good to be done, teach, 307
worlds, though mine arm should conquer, 61
years later we have carved it, 275
years of pining, I've had, 208
Twenty-five-cent daguerreotype, the, 124
Twenty-nine distinct damnations, 71
Twenty-three, married, charming, chaste and, 253
Twice done salutation to the morn, 57
ten thousand rivers up, drinks, 101
to lose it, it don't take, 46
would'st thou have a serpent sting thee, 356

Twice-told tale, as tedious as a, 400
tale, what is so tedious as a, 400
Twig is bent, just as the, 107
Twilight and evening bell, 18
grey, and, 116
it flooded the crimson, 374
pilots of the purple, 59
soft and grey, through the, 429
Twilight's last gleaming, 17
Twin, 418
Twin-brother, Sleep, Death's, 81
Twine, whose inmost, 100
Twining subtle fears with hope, 186
Twinkle with a crystalline delight, 23
Twinkling in the skies, we see them, 384
Twins, let the four, 247
nature and time were, 277
Twirl my thumbs, I, 284
of admiration, gave his tail a, 432
Twist, Lachesis, 380
Twisted by the sisters three, 127
Twit him, to call and, 413
Twitch, Hudibras gave him a, 36
Two and two, the sin ye do by, 365
are twain, they, 418
blades of grass, 162
boundless seas, 'twixt, 222
cardinal virtues, compound of, 315
bad things in this world, 24
bosoms, and one troth, 174
clouds at morning, 56
distinct looks, at least, 455
ears of corn, 162
eternities, peaks of, 222
eternities, the past, the future, 222
evils the less, of, 116
extremes of passion, joy and grief, 297
farthings, five sparrows sold for, 320
forty-five, an easy gait, 186
hands upon the breast, 35
hundred and fifty years of unrequited toil, 199
hundred more, 95
hundred pounds a year, 95
I cannot choose between the, 117
in one, incorporate, 53
it calls for, 198
kinds, knowledge is of, 206
lads that thought, 411
makes it, 218
men ride of a horse, an, 337
months of every year, 110
mutual hearts, when, 203
of that, a trick worth, 414
or three, in the right with, 368
our fathers deemed it, 139
paces of the vilest earth, now, 381
pence for every half-penny, 193
pleasures for your choosing, 306
points in the adventure of the diver, 93
raging fires meet, 132
she joined the other, 309
single gentlemen, like, 150
Two souls one must bend, of, 378
souls with but a single thought, 224
sparrows sold for a farthing, 320
strings to his bow, he that has, 390
strings to my bow, I had, 390
strings unto your bow, to have, 390
strong men stand face to face, when, 391
tens to a score, more than, 362
thereby, grows, 218
tides, betwixt, 222
to choose, debate which of the, 430
warm eggs in her nest, she has, 97
went to pray, 312
Two-and-seventy jarring sects, 162
stenches, I counted, 387
Two-foot trout, and though it be a, 168
Two-legged thing, unfeathered, 374
Twopence, without the oil and the, 349
Tying her bonnet, 30
his new shoes, for, 322
Type, 419
of evanescence, 115
of the true elder race, a, 308
Types of travel, those, 401
were set, he knew how, 315
Tyrannous to use it, 151
Tyranny, 419
to fight, or, 219
Tyrant, 419
and crush the, 385
of his fields, the little, 168
reap, let no, 355
Tyrant's plea, necessity the, 279
stroke, past the, 146
Tyrants, 419
from policy, 328
quake to hear, which, 419
rebellion to, 328
the argument of, 279
Tyre, is one with Nineveh and, 139

U

Ugliest mask, put on his, 80
Ugly sights of death, 102
smutch appears, an, 36
Ultimum moriens of respectability, 171
Umbrella, chance is like an, 46
Umbrellas, brandy, 44
Unadorned, adorned the most, but is when, 3
Unattempted yet in prose or rhyme, 319
Unaware, I blessed them, 27
Unbent, with knee to man, 420
Unbidden, a man can pray, 312
Unblemished let me live, 124
Unbloodied beak, the kite soar with, 41
Unblown, while yet, 219
Unborn, 419
by a village eyes as yet, 275

Unbought, for health, 172
Unbowed, bloody but, 28
by that pure spirit-level, 115
Unburied men, carcasses of, 69
Uncertain, coy and hard to please, 453
life and sure death, 222
Uncertainty of it, the glorious, 212
Uncle an O'Grady, his, 348
Sam's web-feet be forgotten, nor must, 43
Toby, cried my, 287
Unclean, makes civil hands, 54
Uncoffined and unknown, unknelled, 85
Uncomplaining sleep, they all lie in, 21
Unconfined, let joy be, 71
Unconquerable soul, for my, 376
Uncouple that pinion, 403
Uncouth, makes ancient good, 281
not a single accent seems, 210
Unction, 419
Uncurtained that repose, angels, 105
Undecayed, and standest, 115
Undefiled, 419
for the undefiled, 247
well of English, 47
Underlies, life and death his mercy, 147
Underlings, that we are, 127
Undermanned, meant to founder, we, 115
Underpaid, if you think you're, 413
Underpinning, do n't never tech the, 39
Understand, and did not, 451
it, our duty as we, 337
I cannot, I love, 241
if I could, 135
the folks they hate, 171
Understanding instructs me, as my, 379
deceived in your narrow, 397
to direct, the, 173
Understood, as one that, 433
be it, 64
by the savage, that is, 314
unless their use be, 223
Undeservers, mart your offices for gold to, 294
Undevout astronomer is mad, an, 14
Undiscovered before me, lay all, 417
country, the, 79
Undisputed, 420
Undo a man, should, 295
us, equivocation will, 43
Undone, cannot be, 96
Undreamed shores, unpathed waters, 436
Undulates upon the listening ear, 52
Undulating air, when on the, 52
Undutiful, rash and, 20
Uneasy lies the head, 68
the soul, 186
Unenvied, and praised, 385
Unequal laws for rich and pure, 115
the contest was, 297
Unexhausted west, the, 179
Unexpressed, though it tear thee, 234
Unexpressive she, the chaste and, 358
Unfaith can ne'er be equal powers, faith and, 241
Unfaltering, 420
Unfathomed caves of ocean, the dark, 149
Unfeathered two-legged thing a son, 374
Unfed, calls us still, 113
Unfeeling for his own, th', 392
Unfinished lies, the great design, 79
Unfit, for a calm, 304
for all things, 141
for ladies' love, 20
Unfledged comrade, new-hatched, 146
Unfold, the leaves of the judgment book, 240
Unforgiven, could evade if, 467
Unforgiving, even though, 125
Unfortunate, 420
Unfound, unquaffed, 232
Unfriended, melancholy, slow, remote, 332
Unfurled that banner's massy fold, 111
their flag to April's breeze, 362
Unfurnished, a head that's to be let, 57
Ungained, men prize the thing, 318
Ungalled, the hart, 84
Ungathered let us leave, to-night, 181
rose, one sad, 342
Ungrateful things, coughs are, 64
Unhand, 420
Unhanged in England, not three good men, 259
Unhappy, and none could be, 265
dust thou would'st not save, 76
Unheeded flew the hours, 406
thrown a gem, 149
Unholy tongue, with, 67
will not own a notion so, 176
Unhonoured and unsung, 65
falls, 176
his relics are laid, cold and, 274
Unhurt amidst the wars of elements, 191
Uniform, 420
Union, 420
all your strength is in your, 433
a soldier of the, 373
as sweet, and our, 257
in partition, an, 224
liberty and, 218
strong and great, O, 359
Unite, principles your jarring sects, 162
United, 420
be, let both, 227
United States, the President of the, 315
Uniting, by, we stand, 420
the whole, 308
Universal love not smiles around, 43
peace is near, the time of, 299
Universe in wine, pledge the, 101

Universe, menace to the, 165
Unjointed chat, bald, 47
Unjust, is a God, 157
peace, said that an, 430
Unkind, 421
thou art not so, 444
Unkindest cut of all, 70
Unkindliness, 421
Unkindness, 421
Unknelled, uncoffined and unknown, 85
Unknowing hand, this weak, 71
what he sought, 440
Unknown, 421
and behind the dim, 417
and silent shore, to that, 158
facts of guilty acts, 99
from the shore of the great, 15
lands, to carry me to, 186
or die, 124
the forms of things, 308
the land where sorrow is, 374
unknelled, uncoffined and, 85
unknowing, 154
voice, haply from an, 274
water, should cross the, 73
were to her soul, 453
Unloose, familiar as his garter, 161
Unloved again, he that can love, 232
Unmade grave, measure of an, 163
Unmanly, let them be, 70
Unmannerly to take you out, 204
Unmarked of God, not, 177
Unmarried, pale primroses that die, 316
Unmask, nor venture to, 328
Unmated, here loved and here, 374
Unmellowed, his head, 198
Unmixed with baser matter, 331
Unnatural, most foul, strange, and, 272
Unnoted, and for ever dead, 65
Unnoticed all his worth, 176
Unpathed waters, undreamed shores, 436
Unpleasant body, a dem'd, damp, moist, 28
Unprofitable, how weary, stale, flat and, 463
Unprophetic rulers they, 106
Unquestioned text, one, 155
Unrelenting hate, Juno's, 13
Unremembered acts, little nameless, 201
Unrest, a vague, 109
we have strawed our best to the weed's, 113
Unreturned, if thy love is, 234
Unreturning brave, over the, 166
Unrewarded, 421
Unriddled, our doom, 103
Unsatisfied longing, the restless, 109
Unseasonable, it is, 292
Unseduced by the prize, 120
Unseen, born to blush, 149
in the night, 87
Unsettled humours of the land, 141
Unshrinking, through the furnace, 9
Unsought be won, wooed and not, 457
is better, but given, 240
Unspotted lily, a most, 225
Unstained what there they found, they have left, 464
Unsung, unwept, unhonoured, and, 65
Unsunned snow, as chaste as, 47
Unsure, what's to come is still, 239
Untainted back to thine, 203
Unthrifts fool their love away, 232
Untie, gold and silver can yet, 206
Untimely graves, emblem of, 88
Untirable and continuate goodness, 160
Untold, the greatest is, 30
Untying, the knot there's no, 203
Unutterable things, looked, 230
Unveiled her peerless light, 268
Unwashed artificer, another lean, 13
Unwearied spirit, and, 145
Unwelcome news, the first bringer of, 281
Unwept, unhonoured and unsung, 65
unnoted and for ever dead, 65
Unwholesome, it is unseasonable and, 292
made the air, 43
Unworthy of Him, as is, 153
takes, patient merit of the, 323
Unwounded ear, with, 400
Unwritten only still belongs to thee, the, 465
Up betimes, is to be, 24
now, now down, 39
the game is, 148
Upheld the truth, by tradition's force, 416
Uphill rather, it would seem, 460
Upland lawn, the sun upon the, 151
Uplifting, the light, 219
Upmost round, attains the, 7
Upper end o' the table, 71
Upright keel, steadies with, 200
the politician who is . . . , 310
Uprightly, live, 376
Upsees out, drink, 26
Upset a freight-train of conversation, may, 321
Upward looking, give back the, 461
still, they must, 281
Urchin chased, the, 342
Urge me no more, 139
Urgest justice, as thou, 199
Urn, 421
bubbling and loud-hissing, 116
Urns, storied, record who rests below, 410
Urs, don't strew your pathway with those dreadful, 62
Usance, 421
Use, 421
beauty too rich for, 21
be understood, unless their, 223
concur to general, 117

Use
doth breed a habit, 167
had given, powers which God for, 142
him as he uses thee, 189
is of mair, 212
is the judge, 379
it, a blessing we should, 69
it like a giant, to, 151
me but as your spaniel, 378
of all the powers, the unfettered, 142
of anything, a good wit will make, 301
of his pronouns, wise in the, 319
of that which is, 147
of tobacco, first discovered the, 408
soiled with all ignoble, 150
the devil himself with courtesy, 88
Used is life, time, 407
Useless, as, if it goes, 190
heavy load, kings a, 202
Uses, 421
of adversity, 3
of this world, seem to me all the, 463
produces noble ends and, 284
Ushers of Beelzebub's Black Rod, 347
Using it, he was very shy of, 446
Usquebae, wi', we 'll face the devil, 19
Usurer, 421
Utmost, an, that is veiled, 178
Utopia is a pleasant place, 383
Utopian, on the ground that perfection is, 302
Utopianism, 422
Utter nakedness, not in, 25
such as words could never, 439
the thoughts that arise, 35
the You twenty times, 319
what I think, I, 402
Utterance, honesty puts it to, 379
Uttered cry, she nor swooned nor, 76
Uttermost, free even to the, 412
in which both do their, 344

V

Vacancies to be obtained, how are, 289
Vacant chair, to see the, 46
garments, stuffs out his, 165
mind, that spoke the, 211
Vagrom, 422
Vague unrest, a, 109
Vain, as wholly wasted, wholly, 170
because they preach in, 444
desire, not a moth with, 160
in, in the sight of the bird, 280
I only know we loved in, 242
not a worm is cloven in, 160
seldom spent in, 105
shall not have died in, 276
surely not in, 107
sweep over thee in, 288
the king grew, 19
the labour and the wounds are, 391
they never sought in, 230
Vain, thou shalt seek death in, 69
thy sorrowe is in, 426
to mend, too, 46
torture and trouble in, 230
to seek him here, 't is in, 355
tricks that are, 50
we loved in, 125
when men swear in, 394
yet that were, 98
Vainly aim, all modern nations, 110
his incense soars, 330
I seek it, 51
Vale, in this melancholy, 402
life is a narrow, 222
of life, sequestered, 68
of life, what is there in the, 442
the meanest floweret of the, 293
Valentine, 422
Vales, pyramids are pyramids in, 322
Valiant, 422
as he was, 7
creatures, breeds very, 111
flea, that 's a, 134
man and true, 105
never taste of death but once, 66
that dares die, he 's not, 422
trencher-man, a very, 414
Valley, 422
free, flocks that range the, 305
of Death, into the, 90
Valleys, that hills and, 235
Vallombrosa, that strow the brooks in, 216
Valour, 422, 423
a land of . . . , 65
honour for his, 7
prisoner, takes his, 101
Value, the rust we, 14
to me, when praise was of, 312
Vampire, that greedy, 64
Vampyrism, 423
Van, forth in the, 151
Vane shall point west, the, 279
Vanish friendships only made in wine, 146
Vanished hand, touch of a, 169
Vanquished, for e'en though, 12
him, quite, 192
the demon, and have, 120
Vantage-ground of truth, standing upon the, 415
Vapour, a, at the best, 219
is, breath a, 429
is lost in, 123
sometime like a, 56
Vapours, which at evening weep, 101
Variable as the shade, 453
thy love prove likewise, 268
Varied workings, its, 33
Variety, 423
her infinite, 5
Various, a man so, 114
such and so, 397
Vary, how widely its agencies, 157
whose naturs never, 323
Vase, like the, 258

Vase, you may shatter the, 258
Vassal of the Pole, 60
Vast and middle of the night, the dead, 282
domain his own, such a, 112
shook hands as over a, 409
Vault, is left this, 270
long-drawn aisle and fretted, 10
the deep damp, 401
Vaulting ambition, which o'erleaps itself, 7
Vaults, heaven's ebon, 268
Vaux, 423
Veal, like sandwiches of, 204
Vegetables stored, with, 182
Veil, 423
uplifting of a maiden's, 219
Veiled, an utmost that is, 178
from human sight, 154
Vein, and scorching, 233
Veins, 423
better to lose a pint of blood from your, 280
convulse, what ragings must his, 324
to feed its putrid, 64
Veneration, which have much, 317
Vengeance, 423, 424
the ancestral thirst of, 130
weary of your prayers for, 433
Venice, 424
by the laws of, 134
no force in the decrees of, 213
the rate of usance here with us in, 421
there is no power in, 315
unto the State of, 134
Venison, fish, wild-fowl, or, 36
Venom, 424
of your spleen, you shall digest the, 382
Vent, in bad temper oft has, 235
Ventilates our intellectual fire, speech, 380
Venture, 424
Ventured life an' love an' youth, who 19
like little wanton boys, 153
Ventures, 424
lose our, 69
Venus, 424
and the moon, examine, 306
Verb, talk of a noun and a, 317
Verbosity, 424
Verbs, pronouns, interjections, 389
Verdure weaves, her crown of, 382
Vere de Vere, Clara, 148
Verge of manhood, to the awful, 143
of the churchyard mould, 157
Veriest shrew of all, the, 362
Vermin, like Priam, food for, 89
mousing for, 70
musters, where dirty, 372
Vermin's, like the, 208
Verse, 424
for the other's sake, make the one, 335
Verse
happy who in his, 162
Lydian airs married to immortal, 394
marred by a superfluous, 109
or line, to write some earnest, 466
the subject of all, 180
to it, adds a, 24
wisdom married to immortal, 394
you grave for me, this be the, 163
Verses, 424
a book of, 85
rhyme the rudder is of, 335
wits by making, 63
Very late, that we may call it early, 211
Vessel, a large may venture more, 424
comfort the weaker, 68
goes, the gilded, 470
grim and daring, the, 43
made, that with his hand the, 107
Vessels passing close to each other, 99
Vestal's lot, the blameless, 140
Veteran, 424
Veterans reward, how the world its, 462
Vex the unhappy dust thou would'st not save, 76
Vexation, I'm sick with mere, 259
Vibrations, to stop their, 397
Vicar, a fig for the, 26, 226
he calls it damnation, our, 226
still preaches, our, 26
Vice, 424, 425
a good old gentlemanly, 15
but beggary, no, 22
can plague us worse, is there a, 285
corruption, wealth, 18
is often a, 102
of lying, to this, 244
prosperity doth best discover, 427
suppressors of our, 345
Vices, 425
we can frame, of our, 170
Vicissitudes, 425
Victim bleeds, his, 330
poor helpless, 419
Victor glorified, crowns him, 199
over death and pain, 199
will be seen no more, world-victor's, 356
Victories, peace hath her, 299
Victorious, o'er a' the ills o' life, 191
Victory, 425
and shouted, 47
Frémont and, 142
Westminster Abbey or, 439
where is thy, 163
win, they only the, 120
won, the, 94
Victuals and drink to me, 187
one that am nourished by my, 240
Vie, with the vineyards best produce to, 288
View, climb and seek the mountain, 46

View, distance lends enchantment to the, 93
presents them to, 49
Viewless winds, imprisoned in the, 90
Views, lord in my, 227
Vigil long, the patient search and, 467
Vigilant as a cat to steal cream, 45
be, 435
in darkness, 70
Vigour, in its whole constitutional, 299
lost, repair his, 293
lost nothing of its, 397
that their councils might not want, 82
Vile a sin, self-love . . . is not so, 356
ill-favoured faults, 128
in durance, 103
matter, book containing such, 30
means, raise no money by, 267
seem vile, wisdom and goodness to the, 445
who is here so, 65
Vilely, doth it not show, 22
Villa residences at Florence, took, 379
Village all declared how much he knew, 206
bells, how sweet the sounds of, 52
bells, soft the music of those, 52
cock, the early, 57
eyes, by, 275
Hampden, some, 168
Villages, in two neighbour, 224
Villain, 426
a trusty, 196
condemns me for a, 61
far be the, 364
one murder made a, 272
thou art a, 356
with a smiling cheek, 11
Villainous company hath been the spoil, 60
Villains and the sons of darkness, 417
Villainy, 426
you teach me, 197
Vindicate the ways of God to man, 200
Vindicated, shall my character be, 114
Vine, 426
thanksgiving to the, 445
Vinegar, and twice with, 349
sugar and saltness agree, oil, 349
Vineyard, the noblest juices of the, 344
Vineyard's best produce, even with the, 288
Vintage, he is trampling out the, 153
that from his, 333
Vintners, 426
Violence, blown with restless, 90
Violent, so over, 324
Violet, 426
perfume on the, 152
grows, the nodding, 17
Violets, 426
that breathes upon a bank of, 273
Virgil quotes, Homer and, 30
Virgin kiss, 203
Virgin's sidelong looks of love, 234
Virgins, 426
Virtue, 427
a land of . . . , 65
all that are lovers of, 10
alone outbuilds the pyramids, 322
alone has majesty in death, 81
and the conscience of her worth, her, 457
and vice, no distinction between, 425
but assumes some mark of, 425
calumny strikes the whitest, 42
contend, thy blood and, 25
cousinship and all return, will, 319
fall, and some by, 365
foe of peace and law and, 143
follow, then let, 266
forbearance ceases to be a, 138
he did make of necessity, 279
in living, 377
in loving, 347
like necessity, there is no, 279
linked with one, 64
may flourish in an old cravat, 171
men of most renowned, 213
much, in if, 218
of necessitee, maken, 279
of necessity, made, 279
of necessity, to make a, 279
of the faith, make, 34
only is our own, convinced that, 453
only makes our bliss below, 250
or mischief, either of, 442
of your office, by, 401
should woo the angel, 332
that make ambition, 125
suffering from protested bills, 269
the firste, sone, 411
then, being rich, 22
though in rags, 311
't will be, 414
unmoved can hear the call, 227
war is a, 432
we can boast, all the, 85
when God calls, 227
worth, what were that intrinsic, 279
Virtue's cause it spoke, if bold in, 411
self, for, 245
side, lean to, 119
way, I might desert fair, 429
Virtues, compound of two cardinal, 315
considering her, 62
died, and when the, 111
don't wash, the alcoholic, 5
very kind, be to her, 201
we crave the austere, 185
we write in water, 34
Virtuous, 427
actions are but born and die, 351
alway, loke who that is most, 150
dames, ye high, exalted, 142
Visage, 427
dejected 'haviour of the, 448
of offence, the, 260
wanned, all his, 307
with devotion's, 88

Visages do cream and mantle, whose, 291
Visible, rather darkness, 72
Vision, 427, 428
art thou not, fatal, 70
of home itself, a, 133
the young men's, 98
whose beauty was my, 274
Visions of the evening, the fantastic, 428
what beauteous, filled this spot, 367
your young men shall see, 98
Visit her face too roughly, 243
is really over, after their, 212
my sad heart, the ruddy drops that, 443
only on a formal, 330
pays, his ready, 370
thee never, 69
Visitor, 't is some, 261
Visits, few and far between, like angel, 9
short and bright, like angels, 9
these sad eyes, light that, 443
to my chamber made, thy nightly, 283
Vital, 428
Vizier himself at the head, 63
Vocal frame, inventress of the, 45
Vocation, rode by on his, 11
Vociferated logic kills me quite, 284
Vogue, that now are most in, 379
Voice, 428
a broken, 307
a distant, in the darkness, 360
and clear, and in bold, 419
and his big manly, 294
grave did utter forth a, 37
had murmured, some kind, 116
haply from an unknown, 274
hed sech a swing, no, 50
I heard a, 28
in my dreaming ear melted away, 98
in the darkness, 84
is odd, the people's, 301
is still for war, my, 430
London's, 266
low and sweet, and a loving woman s, 235
of a good woman, the, 452
of dolorous pitch, with a, 361
of God, daughter of the, 73
of God, it is and it is not the, 301
of Nature cries, 35
of the morning away, from the, 57
of the sluggard, 't is the, 371
of the weeper, the, 326
only a look and a, 360
provoke, can honour's, 421
seasoned with a gracious, 213
sweet and low, with a, 246
that is still, sound of a, 169
the harmony of the world, 212
till some questioning, 451
to say whose, 274
with a monarch's, 335
Voice
within us, a, 88
yet must thou hear a, 354
Voices are lost, their, 339
from the deep caverns, 163
keep tune, our, 286
of four hamlets, 52
sweet, stone-deaf to, 321
with her thousand, 154
Void, cast as rubbish to the, 160
flame lawless through the, 306
life is all a, 223
of pride, sweetness, 128
they have left an aching, 300
Volcano's tongue of flame, 24
Volley on volley, 42
Volleyed and thundered, 42
Volubility, lie with such, 218
Voluble, so sweet and, 196
Volume, many a quaint and curious, 261
nature of a tragic, 38
of my brain, the book and, 331
Volumes in folio, for I am for whole, 466
that I prize, 31
Vote, is the freeman's, 144
my hand and my heart to this, 366
Votes, an' some on 'em, 11
Vow, bound by any solemn, 287
but the plain single, 417
good-night your, 70
I never broke a, 456
renew the broken, 179
to mend my ways, once again I, 429
was earthly, my, 157
Vows, 428, 429
are traced in sand, thy, 450
cancel all our, 296
for thee broke, 157
I hold to my first-sworn, 339
Vulcan's stithy, foul as, 141
Vulgar, by no means, 124
boil, the, 108
company, than saved in, 149

W

Wade in wealth, what though we, 104
through slaughter to a throne, 368
Waft a feather, to, 377
thy name beyond the sky, 125
Wafted downward, as a feather is, 282
smoke, had, 408
Wafts the mind above, 233
Wag all, when beards, 261
Wage it right, how few that, 433
yet claim his, 248
Wager, 429
Wagers, fools for arguments use, 137
Wages, and what are its, 207
she gets, in asking her what, 363
ta'en thy, 103
Wagging of your tongue, with, 378
Wail of the weak, 219
their loss, sit and, 231

Wailing and alone, blind and, 15
and whining, long past, 208
Wainscot, fix on the, 284
Waist, 429
Wait, 429
a little longer, 159
and there to, 334
for execution in the morn, that, 333
for thee I, 242
like a ghost, to, 451
like outcast spirits who, 292
on each, 116
on virtuous deeds, blessings ever, 427
on woman, to, 189
to labour and to, 2
the hours are few to, 97
Waited long for thee, I have, 194
Waiting, 429
with patience he stands, 262
Waits thee, go where glory, 153
Wake again, yet must they, 390
and call me early, you must, 256
and never, 369
and weep, 103
and when we sleep, when we, 381
eye which would forget to, 10
his visage all agrin as at a, 427
if I should die before I, 370
not thou the giant, 301
sleep to, 337
the life-refining soul of decent wit, 152
the world may, 254
Waked, I, she fled, 98
I trembling, 98
to ecstasy the living lyre, 109
me too soon, you have, 371
Wakeful, be, 435
Waken their free nature, shall, 466
Wakened death, till they have, 400
thy dog, because he hath, 322
Wakens at this hour of rest, 23
Wakes, freedom now so seldom, 143
with a shriek, 99
Waking dawned in heaven, and the next, 105
grumble drat that cat, 44
with day, and, 390
Wale of auld men, 130
Walk abroad, a troubled mind drave me to, 393
abroad with Sally, to, 74
again, breathe and, 293
alone, to, 239
and proud of her, 320
backward, 121
by the vast calm river, 403
in fear and dread, 128
into a well, much too wise to, 446
sober off, 228
that costs a meal, and the, 430
the earth unseen, spiritual creatures, 381
the long path with you, I will, 298
the night, to, 380
Walk with God, closer, 155
with you, I will, 41
Walked before, when she has, 202
forth to tell his beads, 145
in paradise, 105
in that storm, could never have, 404
on his way, 145
the way of nature, he 's, 278
through life, I have, 177
when you, 239
Walks, 430
along, as he, 210
o'er the dew of yon high eastward hill, 269
on and turns no more, 128
the waters, she, 436
till the first cock, 135
up and down with me, 165
with aimless feet, nothing, 160
Wall, 430
along the emblazoned, 264
and crush the, 387
and the ivied, 419
flower in the crannied, 135
had scaled, the rampart, 87
in the office of a, 112
its ruined, 367
of stone, wedged in a thick, 446
rocks, the blind, 275
shone on the old oak, 265
should patch a, 421
the whitewashed, 295
thick, or moated gate, 385
when icicles hang by the, 190
whispering by an orchard, 224
Wallet at his back, a, 407
Wallets of flesh, 88
Wallop, gi'es now and then a, 324
Wallowing in the mire, to her, 378
Walls, a stone on her, 63
did I o'er-perch these, 239
each grave within its, 157
hangs as mute on Tara 's, 170
high and huge, 262
I passed beside the reverend, 161
of this tenement of life, on the, 273
on the outward, 17
stone, do not a prison make, 318
Walnuts and the wine, across the, 396
Walrus, 430
Wan, why so pale and, 294
Wane and perish, shall never, 276
Wand, or snow-white, 149
Wander, wherever Cupid might, 240
where'er I, 113
Wandered all our ways, when we have, 406
east, I 've wandered west, I've, 222
here about the beach I, 352
idly, my fingers, 291
Wandering from shop to shop, 361
moon, the, 268
near her secret bower, such as, 292
on a foreign strand, 65
poet, a, 308

Wanders in all lands, Death the Ploughman, 79
Waning, not the crescent moon, 4
Wanned, all his visage, 307
Want, 430
a friend in need, may we never, 285
but patience of her, and I, 278
full measure of all your pleasure, they, 329
it, wad eat that, 257
its man, shall, 248
of decency is want of sense, 83
of faith in all, is, 241
of fighting had grown rusty, for, 26
of thought, for, 440
of thought, wrought by, 116
of it the fellow, and, 465
of money, it was for, 239
of towns, for, 252
that glib and oily art, I, 321
so many Christians, 188
wealth or, 150
Wanted food, pined and, 182
they gude beef and ale, nor, 267
Wanting a shirt, ruffles when, 360
is the brown October, nor, 288
sensibility, yet, 463
what is stolen, not, 340
Wanton boys, like little, 153
love corrupteth and embaseth it, 232
Wantoned with thy breakers, I, 288
Wantonness, kindles in clothes a, 364
Wants and its weariness, its, 210
both hands, that, 190
but few, their, 68
but little drink below, man, 249
but little, man, 249
but little here below, man, 249
of a young family, 48
that sin against the strength of youth, 470
Wapping or the Strand, in, 408
War, 430–432
amidst the ranks of, 308
and a dastard in, 237
and great in, 43
and rapine, 143
circumstance of glorious, 125
first in, 132
his comrades of the, 433
in the ranks of, 271
let slip the dogs of, 335
like the impatient steed of, 386
of unsuccessful or successful, 229
or come ye in, 299
power and, 164
right to go to, 110
the cause of a long ten years', 452
the hand of, 112
then was the tug of, 164
the spoils of, 464
'twixt will and will not, at, 443
this mighty scourge of, 199
three years before the, 162
to offer, 456
War
victories no less renowned than, 299
Warble, 432
War-cry sever, no more shall the, 212
Warden hoar, smote the, 87
Warder of the brain, memory the, 258
Wardrobe lies, in the, 111
War-drum, 432, 433
Wards a Roundhead's pike, now he, 383
Warfare, 433
o'er, soldier rest thy, 373
Warm at home, thou liest, 189
champagny old-particular brandy-punchy feeling, 129
dress it up, 64
enough to, 4
heart within, and a, 183
his toes, 207
my heart, ruddy drops that, 443
nursing her wrath to keep it, 465
the air, let out, 393
virtue . . . will keep me, 311
Warmed and cooled by the same winter and summer, 197
both hands, I, 221
Warmest feelings wither, when the, 125
Warming his five wits, alone and, 292
Warmly laid, know me safe and, 283
Warmth, 433
about to glow, there's a, 225
no, no cheerfulness, 285
of its July, the, 331
that feeds my life, the vital, 443
Warn, to, to comfort and command, 454
Warned is well bewared, once, 205
Warning, come without, 59
dreams, echoed in, 99
give little, 220
shall thrill thee with its, 115
Warns me not to do, 61
Warp, though thou the waters, 24
us from the living truth, 470
Warrant, 433
God's word's our, 409
Warred for Homer, seven cities, 183
Warrior, 433
a single, 87
dead, home they brought her, 76
storms the fortress, as a, 392
Warrior's bones are laid, the, 264
Warriors, 433
carry the warrior's pall, 271
War's glorious art, 272
rattle, where mingles, 83
red techstone rang true metal, on, 19
Wars, 433, 434
and the big, 125
for my colour, I have the, 301
of elements, the, 191
of old, the thousand, 434
War-sick, at the feet of peace, 300
Wary, be, watch the time, 392
Was, not what he, 410

Was time, 406
Wash away your sin, water cannot, 365
her guilt away, 136
it white, to, 169
out a word of it, nor all your tears, 465
the alcoholic virtues don't, 5
the river Rhine, shall henceforth, 58
Washed away, with drops of rain are, 252
in dew, fresh-blown roses, 343
off the next tide, look to be, 465
off the stains of powder, 312
the sow that was, 378
with dew, morning roses newly, 343
with morning dew, 398
Washes it out from the sand, 138
the bridegroom's feet, Iscariot, 194
Washing his hands with invisible soap, 372
Washington, 434
when it gits on to, 60
Waspish, 434
when you are, 382
Wasps instead of bees, where, 330
Waste, and the tears we, 451
dawn, through the vast, 18
its sweetness, and, 149
men in earnest have no time to, 416
men's lives, yet, 208
old ocean's grey and melancholy, 288
that instant they take fire, tapers, 81
the years we, 451
Wasted, 434
an' dear ones, 299
far and wide, was, 425
irrevocable past as wholly, 170
is existence, time, 407
Wasteful and ridiculous excess, 152
Waste-paper, they are the mere, 309
Wastes her time and me, tell her that, 343
the more the marble, 385
Wasting in despair, 120
Watch, 434
above his own, keeping, 417
an idler is a, 190
for the constable of the, 422
for the lightest token, 293
in the sky, the sentinel stars set their, 39
it more and more, those that, 225
keep, your loving, 340
of his wit, winding up the, 447
out, gobble'uns 'll get you ef you don't, 153
some must, 84
the foreman takes out his, 92
the horologe a double set, 100
the hour, if we do but, 467
the night in storms, 189
the stately ships, did we, 226
the time, be wary, 392
Watch
to, and then to lose, 19
to, like one that fears robbing, 239
to keep, 48
wound up just like a, 173
Watch-dog's honest bark, to hear the, 438
Watched beside, deaths ye died I have, 349
her breathing, we, 36
o'er the ramparts we, 17
the battle from afar, I, 433
Watches, 434
Watching, for this night's, 362
them out of the town, 132
Watchman, 435
Watchword of progression, change is the, 46
Water, 435
and a crust, with, 235
and wine, I have drunk your, 349
both sides the, 111
cannot wash away your sin, 365
critics and cold, 308
fast a week with bran and, 312
hast thou, too much of, 399
hath, as the, 39
if that thou throw on, 53
in a sieve, 64
in His name, 69
is in water, as, 56
like a circle in the, 53
like a witch's oils, 81
nectar, the, 197
oh milk and, 264
should cross the unknown, 73
slap-dash into the, 372
spilt on the ground like, 173
takes their colours out, until, 5
tempered with well-boiled, 440
that is past, with the, 434
that quencheth thirst, the, 369
their virtues we write in, 34
this sorrow, that should, 398
through a sieve, like, 414
through hard marble eat, 252
to float a ship, wherever there is, 37
unto wine, and as, 268
were written all in, 428
whose name was writ in, 274
with invisible soap in imperceptible, 372
you fill up your glasses, if with, 445
Water-bag, an' a goatskin, 420
Water-drops, women's weapons, 456
Waterloo, 435
the crushed at, 332
Waterproof the American mind, trying to, 8
Water-rats, there be land-rats and, 359
Waters, 436
be, wide as the, 441
blue, fades o'er the, 2
cast, or on the, 441
forced those, 399

Waters
in mine ears, noise of, 102
many an evening by the, 226
of his eyes, those cunning, 426
once more upon the, 436
rave, where the scattered, 288
roar, the booming, 354
roll, winds rise or, 408
warp, though thou the, 24
wind and rocks, the peril of, 359
Water-thieves and land-thieves, 359
Wave, a break of the, 269
a life on the ocean, 288
amid the crested, 436
beneath the, 376
beside the salt-sea, 373
lost in one dark, 228
may not foam, 113
of life, the, 36
of all her waves, there's never a, 113
over his bier to, 184
shall start from every, 288
that star-spangled banner yet, 17
upon the, 84
washes, though the succeeding, 138
will bring, wind or, 149
write our benefits upon the, 467
Waved on high, long has it, 114
Waver in my faith, almost mak'st me, 378
Wavered not long, they, 183
Waves, 436
Britannia, rule the, 37
can roll, where, 161
dark, the tapestry, 317
o'er every sea, a flag that, 133
so free as the sons of the, 286
there 's never a wave of all her, 113
the standard, but still he, 383
trusts himself to woman or to, 452
went high, when the, 304
Wax, 436
mingling poetic honey with trade, 308
St. Peter's keys in, 347
Way, 436
adorns and cheers the, 185
and Mammon wins his, 270
and room, must I give, 50
and wisdom finds the, 443
being allowed his, 9
built in such a logical, 46
comes, something wicked this, 404
due west, there lies your, 439
flung magic o'er my, 148
found thee, a, 140
good old bishops took a simpler, 416
he ever trod, from that, 305
he says darling that goes to my heart, 72
I fly is hell, which, 178
I knew there was but one, 359
I 'm trudging my weary, 310
in a mysterious, 154
in the long, 387
it should go, in the, 131
Way
jingle, jingle, clear the, 23
jog on, the footpath, 174
love will find out the, 231
men of action clear the, 225
of kindness, save in the, 66
of life, my, 223
of life, the narrow, 452
of nature, he 's walked the, 278
of things happening, in the, 170
plods his weary, 69
rises dark o'er the, 228
shall bear us on our, 48
takes its, 109
tenor of their, 68
that 's Stonewall 's, 388
the heaven 's wide pathless, 268
the, he 'd like to do unto you, 82
the mannikin feels his, 15
there is a lion in the, 226
there lies your, 96
the stream of time doth run, which, 407
the wind is, you may see by that which, 389
they heaved those fossils, 141
through Eden took their solitary, 462
through many a weary, 222
to draw new mischief on, the next, 271
to devour the, 345
to dusty death, 411
to find that better, 397
to flutter, bird of time has but a little, 406
to glory, 104
to go, the right, 159
to improve the world, the worst, 191
to kill a wife with kindness, 201
to parish church, plain as, 441
two lions in the way, 226
upon the dark benighted, 75
walked on his, 145
was one, for the, 220
were plain, as though the, 198
Ways are wise and just, his, 357
by its dirtiest and narrowest, 352
do lie open, all, 267
from all the good old, 469
I keep, the subtle, 368
in such noble, 124
I vow to mend my, 429
of duty he kept, 145
of glory, trod the, 140
of a man, the, 187
of God, just are the, 200
of God, justify the, 200
of God, vindicate the, 200
of men, and the, 68
she never followed wicked, 441
that are dark, for, 50
their manners and their, 66
the newest kind of, 367
thy gentle, 236
to lengthen our days, 74

Ways to mince it in love, no, 238
to thrive by dirty, 92
wandered all our, 406
watch his devious, 262
we cannot tell, 154
when we tire of well-worn, 46
with little men, to live in narrow, 276
Wayward is this foolish love, how, 341
We, where the Abbey makes us, 1
Weak, 436
and weary, while I pondered, 261
for the fallen and the, 368
straws, begin it with, 131
that fall, the, 312
to be a sinner, too, 435
to defend, the, 173
wail of the, 219
Weaker sort of politicians, the, 310
vessel, comfort the, 68
Weakest goes to the wall, the, 430
kind of fruit, 146
saint upon his knees, 350
Weakness, 437
and debility, means of, 357
a sin, 432
not strength but, 4
owning her, 351
to lament or fear, 65
Weal or woe, reckless alike of, 328
prayer for other's, 125
Wealth accumulates, where, 300
and commerce, let, 284
and fame, beauty, titles, 334
and fame, out to, 214
and honour, what are you to love, 237
and place, by any means get, 266
and woe among, in, 215
boundless his, 65
find, let no impostor heap, 355
get place and, 266
have missed me, health and, 204
of love, its whole, 173
of Ormus and of Ind, 107
of seas, the, 464
of simple beauty and rustic health, 172
of thy wit in an instant, show the whole, 447
or want, come, 150
the loss of, 360
the other's wanton, 265
until all the, 199
vice, corruption, 18
what though we wade in, 104
ye find, the, 355
Wealthy curled darlings of our nation, 72
Weans in their bed, are the, 443
Weapon, a, that comes down as still, 144
satire's my, 350
stronger, thought's a, 159
Weapons, 437
hurt with the same, 197
Weapons
water-drops, women's, 456
which your hands have found, the, 403
Wear, 437
a lion's hide, thou, 226
a shirt, he always used to, 361
it out, as being loth to, 446
let not the idle, 355
motley's the only, 137
my heart upon my sleeve, 371
not much the worse for, 171
out, a chaise breaks down but does n't, 46
the blue, for you I, 456
this, for my sake, 251
whether a parson ought to, 295
Weariness, 437
its wants and its, 210
to relieve their, 345
Wearing his new doublet, for, 322
awa', I'm, 215
out, not linen you're, 226
Wears a crown, that, 68
another, 355
away, eternal matter never, 256
his crown, now, 356
it, as he who, 361
out more apparel, 126
she to him, so, 454
the marble, much rain, 252
Weary, 437
and faint, 182
and ill at ease, I was, 291
and old, which at even was, 442
and old with service, 153
and sore, thy feet are, 162
are at rest, the, 334
bones, come to lay his, 29
fa' the women fo'k, 455
guest, because thou com'st, 12
head, to the, 21
I am stiff and, 413
lover, 33
of breath, 420
of the strife, who once were, 370
of your quarrels, I am, 433
say I'm, 204
the, the broken in heart, 61
to sleep, 39
to the, death is sweet, 79
way, plods his, 69
with toil, 21
Weasel, like a, 56
sucks eggs, as a, 257
Weather being cold, the, 120
I like the, 110
through pleasant and through cloudy, 220
't is the hard grey, 113
Weathercock on a steeple, or a, 285
if I put a, 279
Weathered every rack, the ship has, 43
the storm, the pilot that, 304
Weave, again at Christmas did we, 52
I spin, I, 386

Weave, the robes ye, 355
Weaves, her crown of verdure, 382
thy shroud, shuttle flies that, 362
Weaving, the scarlet cloth of her, 451
Web and the pin, the, 135
in middle of her, 380
of our life is of a mingled yarn, 222
what a tangled, 82
Web-feet, 437
Wed, 437
December when they, 457
it, and think to, 384
I 've been, 21
none but you, and will, 340
or cease to woo, 458
Wedded, 437
in a day, wooed and, 442
Wedding, 437
bed, my grave is like to be my, 254
never, ever wooing, 458
night, came forth on her, 55
Wedding-bells, 437
Wedding-day, dance barefoot on her, 10
Wedding-ring, the, conveys a right to one, 129
your, wears thin, 338
Wedged, with their souls closely, 446
Wedges, 437
of gold, 102
Wedlock, 438
. . . hath oft been compared, 253
Wednesday, he that died o', 185
Wee short hour, some, 187
Weed's unrest, we have strawed our best to the, 113
Weeds, 438
appear, friends in sable, 448
clad in a pilgrim's, 145
he who loves, 135
of prejudice, by the grey, 446
sprang up like, 450
spread the compost on the, 60
that marred the land, in, 355
Week, argument for a, 196
of all the days that's in the, 74
for eighteen shillings, a, 42
his text that, 219
the wicked remnant of the, 247
Weekly bill, the, 94
Weeks thegither, fou for, 37
Weep, 438
a bramble's smart, will, 398
a calm for those who, 333
and mourn for her, to, 189
and women must, 132
and wrestle, vainly we, 155
and you weep alone, 212
as make the angels, 251
away the life of care, and, 81
awhile if ye are fain, 76
because they part, 295
before you, well may the children, 437
behind the mask, jesters, 165
for her, that he should, 307
Weep
for him, I, 7
for the frail that err, 312
here must I wake and, 103
in fondness, that, 443
mourn where thou dost, 125
no more, lady, 426
no more, seek it and, 209
she must, 76
stricken deer go, 84
to, like a young wench, 239
to record, 287
wherefore should I fast and, 365
while all around thee, 227
ye doubting hearts that, 369
Weeper, the voice of the, 326
Weeping, 438
and wringing their hands, 132
at her darling's grave, be, 164
at the feet and head, 74
bitterly, they are, 469
hermit there, to dwell a, 34
thou sat'st, 227
while you 're, 105
Weeps, 438
when she sees inflicted on a beast, 390
Weigh my eyelids down, thou no more wilt, 37
the enemy, to, 84
Weighed its relation, till he, 34
Weighs their wits, and, 30
upon the heart, which, 263
Weight, a balance and, 369
could raise, th' enormous, 84
falling with soft slumbrous, 370
if bread or butter wanted, 6
of a hair will turn the scales, 351
of carrion flesh, a, 103
of centuries he leans, bowed by the, 180
to drag thee down, 189
to pull his, 54
Weights of good and ill, the, 389
the string that holds those, 403
Weir, and foaming, 419
Welcome, 438
back again, aye be, 249
each rebuff, 328
found the warmest, 192
friend, 221
grave, to a, 9
joy and feast, 129
kisses and, you 'll find here, 59
peaceful evening in, 116
sir, you 're kindly, 246
the coming, speed the going, 167
the coming, speed the parting, 167
the first to, 176
the hour, whenever you, 125
't is given with, 129
to our shearing, 343
Welcomed all, served all, 71
by all that cursed, 416
it too, who once, 125
Welcomes, now loud as, 52

Well, 439
all is, 154
and 't will all be, 178
as buckets in a, 39
attempting to do, 302
bucket which hung in the, 39
deep down in the, 446
does, 24
done, servant of God, 357
done, wish a thing to be, 96
dressed, when he's, 197
fare him that invented sleep, 369
he prayeth, 313
ill will never said, 191
in the bottom of a, 418
is worth doing, 96
it were done quickly, 96
loved not wisely but too, 242
made, this parting was, 125
much too wise to walk into a, 446
of English undefiled, 47
of Saint Keyne, has heard of the, 348
or ill, calls me, 160
paid that is well satisfied, 293
Rachel by the palmy, 120
read, exceedingly, 326
the devil was, 87
'tis not so deep as a, 189
will again be, 133
would heal and do, 334
Well-breakfasted juryman, a good, contented, 92
Well-bred man, sensible and, 4
witty, virtuous, was, 319
Well-built nest, leaves the, 175
Well-favoured man is the gift of fortune, to be a, 466
Well-placed words of glozing courtesy, 459
Well-remembered grave, at some, 163
Wells, dropping buckets into empty, 39
the tintinnabulation that so musically, 408
Well-worn ways, we tire of, 46
Wench and coming butter, tired, 429
married in an afternoon, 254
the cinder, and the white-handed lady, 21
to weep like a young, 239
Wench's black eye, white, 118
Wenches, rags and hags and hideous, 387
Went agin war an' pillage, thought Christ, 431
and like a storm he, 388
astray, if weak women, 456
for it thar and then, and, 104
into the woods my Master, 457
to heaven, was exhaled and, 378
to pieces all at once, it, 303
to pieces like a lock of hay, 166
to the garden for parsley, as she, 254
up a hill, 202
upward with the flood, 357
Went where duty seemed to call, they, 90
Wept and honoured, praised, 385
but soon he, 342
for it, but I, 271
o'er his wounds, 68
too much, I have, 208
Werther, 439
West, are blowing toward the, 469
away to the, 132
country, a well there is in the, 348
glitters in the, 109
great Orion sloping slowly to the, 291
is west, east is east and, 391
I've wandered east, 222
that young eagle of the, 106
the Cincinnatus of the, 434
there is neither east nor, 391
there lies your way due, 439
the unexhausted, 179
the vane shall point, 279
trembling on from east to, 143
which from east to, 408
young Lochinvar is come out of the, 229
Western pine, this spray of, 304
Westminster, 439
we thrive at, 292
Westward look, but, 224
the course of empire, 109
Westward-Ho! 439
Wet his whistle, to, 440
Wether, 439
Wethers, 439
Wets his manly eye, when Douglas 398
Whale, 439
his fellow-man, to, 171
like a, 56
so fitly as to a, 133
Whales . . . o' the land, 133
Whatever is, is right, 338
What's Swat, he knows, 261
what, he knew, 261
Wheat, a cake out of the, 41
all, grind your, 207
as two grains of, 327
for this planting, to find the, 276
mildews the white, 135
then had sifted the, 276
Wheel, and turn the, 386
butterfly upon a, 41
grate, or a dry, 309
of labour, slave of the, 207
the sailor at the, 200
the sofa round, 116
turn thy, 141
wol cause another wheel, 53
Wheels, 439
of thought, go the, 403
run down, and all the, 290
will nobody block those, 403
Whelp, a wolf's, 64
When or where, no matter, 133

Where and when, the, have they fixed, 63
an echo answers, 107
but, 79
Wherefore, every why hath a, 441
for every why he had a, 441
in the why and the, 441
Whets his appetite for moral good, 312
Which is which, at odds with morning, 282
Whig, I ain't a, 42
Whim, agree with his peculiar, 171
Whims, the women are so full of, 449
Whine nor sigh, I could not, 233
Whining, long past wailing and, 208
Whinny shrills, when her, 253
Whip, 439
and put in every honest hand a, 439
a hangman's, 184
me such honest knaves, 205
Whipped, 439
I would have such a fellow, 379
Whipping, 440
Whips and scorns of time, 323
Whirled for a million æons, 18
Whirligig of time brings in his revenge, 407
Whirlwind chaos of insane hurrahs, one, 188
of passion, 379
rides in the, 388
Whirlwind's sway, regardless of the sweeping, 470
Whirlwinds of rebellion, 147
Whiskey, 440
Whiskey-devouring Irishman, the, 194
Whisper, hark, they, 170
I' your lug, let me, 142
said as plain as, 69
this, smile and, 74
Whispered in heaven, 't was, 167
Whispering from the ground, 298
humbleness, 35
low, 78
tongues, but, 412
to somebody, somebody's, 373
with thee, the angels are, 9
with white lips, 136
Whispers breathing less of earth than heaven, 176
low thou must, when duty, 104
the o'er-fraught heart, 165
Whist table, at a, 415
Whistle, 440
back the parrot's call, 350
her off, I'd, 168
let the law go, 214
than to a blackbird 't is to, 165
them back, he could, 145
Whistled, 440
Whistles in his sound, pipes and, 294
o'er the furrowed land, 307
Whistling, 440
of a name, with the, 123
White, affirmed that black was, 66
amidst the brown, a little, 68
White and black, dwells in, 3
and still, all, 152
as snow, wash it, 169
as the foamy sea, his locks were, 357
dress, a black dress or a, 295
flower of a blameless life, 26
from that chamber clothed in, 55
hairs, how ill, 137
hairs, superfluity comes sooner by, 393
horse, an apothecary on a, 11
lips, whispering with, 136
man, run from the, 181
man round the world, the war-drum of the, 432
man, the poor, 182
soldiers in khaki dress, the worn, 373
the pair that once was, 153
to keep his milk-teeth, 408
we called the chess-board, 48
wench's black eye, 118
wheat, mildews the, 135
whose red and, 21
White-handed lady, the cinder wench and the, 21
Whiter skin of hers than snow, that, 367
than the paper, 169
Whitest virtue, calumny strikes, 42
Whitewood, 441
Whittler, his pocket knife to the young, 467
Whole of it, let me taste, 78
parts of one stupendous, 297
table, joy of the, 172
tree, have robbed the, 115
uniting the, 308
Wholesome for the body, is, 269
Whoop, the Pequot's ringing, 181
Why, 441
man of morals, tell me, 101
Wicked, 441
cease from troubling, the, 334
custom, did not, 140
far, seemed to me less, 331
for a smile, too, 371
this way comes, something, 404
too, and yet so, 200
Wickedness, a method in man's, 201
Wicket, no admittance at this, 345
Wickliffe, 441
Wide as a church door, nor so, 189
as the waters be, 441
enough to hold both thee and me, 189
wide sea, on a, 7
Widened with the process of the suns, 322
Widening, and ever, 337
Widens, the circle, 53
Wider than himselve was, 53
Widow, 441, 442
and for his, 337
nor wife, neither maid, 246
upon her lonely pillow, a, 99

Widower, 442
Widow-maker, 442
Widows, 442
Wife, 442, 443
Adam and his, 148
almost damned in a fair, 382
and babes, a blessing on his, 313
and children, lodging, 187
and for the, 89
and queen, in her as mother, 323
as an English labourer's, 208
a tired horse, a railing, 399
but life itself, my, 223
credit in being jolly with a, 198
here's to the, 246
I am married to a, 223
is, as the husband is, 189
I've a, 167
kissed the fiddler's, 263
like peevish man and, 376
neither maid, widow, nor, 246
niver at all to be gettin' a, 16
no, prepares the bread, 182
no casual mistress, but a, 375
nor maiden, nor, 449
nor son nor, 341
should drink of it first, if the, 348
since you became my own dear, 338
spare my guiltless, 15
the book-learned, 30
the devil's, was but a fiend, 464
the mother, daughter, 452
there is not a, 348
the sailor's, the sailor's star, 347
when my old, 71
with kindness, kill a, 201
who preaches in her gown, a, 295
Wight, a graceless, worthless, 151
each, who reads not, 458
she was a, 138
Wilbur sez he never heerd, Parson, 11
Wild bells, ring out, 23
by starts 't was, 133
in their attire, so withered and so, 448
the garden was a, 450
thrill, fresh, 33
thyme blows, 17
tremendous Irishman, a, 194
Wild-cat's claw, in a, 212
Wilderness, 443
a lodge in some vast, 229
in time's great, 222
of single instances, the, 214
one rose of the, 342
pierce the Barcan, 74
were paradise enow, 85
Wild-fowl or venison, 36
wake, never the, 113
Wildwood, the deep-tangled, 49
Wiles, cranks and wanton, 196
your sports and your, 116
Will, 443
a boy's, is the wind's will, 33
against heaven's hand or, 387
against my, 271
Will
and I laid me down with a, 163
be done, let thy, 35
betters always have their, 66
bow before the awful, 150
cannot stop them, our, 403
consents, my poverty but not my 311
curb this cruel devil of his, 213
do 't, if she, 450
executes a freeman's, 144
fairly make your, 228
for if she, 450
for intellect or, 220
he that complies against his, 290
his mysterious, 154
in shrill ill, 44
instruments to work his, 389
I pay thy poverty and not thy, 311
not obedient to his honest, 454
of God, as lightning does the, 144
of God, do the, 207
or won't, a woman, 450
puzzles the, 79
rule, lets her, 452
sins of, 160
star of the unconquered, 333
that in your, 239
that serveth not another's, 418
that state's collected, 385
the current of a woman's, 450
the death defying, 419
therefore frame the law unto my, 213
the torrent of a woman's, 450
the unconquerable, 231
to it, could frame my, 213
we can arrive to know, if but that, 389
who possess opinions and a, 259
work forth your, 79
Willie Winkie, 443
Willing, 443
able and, to pull his weight, 54
strong right hand, 48
to wound, and yet, 71
Willingly receiving chaff for corn, 103
Willow, 444
bends, not a, 145
under the, 28
Wills, and talk of, 117
are gardeners, our, 28
made to be fashioned as the artist, 107
men dying make their, 450
Wilt thou answered, the, 290
Wimmen, men pronounce them, 449
Win, 444
a lady's faith, learn to, 120
a woman, if with his tongue he cannot, 454
by it, hope to, 7
good we oft might, 97
maiden's breast, 83
me, with wagging of your tongue to, 378

Win
my love, shall, 201
or lose it all, to, 126
our battle by its aid, we'll, 159
right the day must, 337
that love had been sae ill to, 231
the heart, to, 335
the plaudits, and, 449
the post, and, 344
they laugh that, 212
Wince, let the galled jade, 195
Winced nor cried aloud, I have not, 28
Winch, a weathercock with a, 279
Wind, 444
a fiery Pegasus, 187
as large a charter as a, 217
away, to keep the, 421
blow, come, wrack, 90
blows, when the, 154
blows, which way the, 279
but a soul goes out on the east, 113
by measure, God gives, 209
de col' night rain and, 359
four changes on the, 52
grows great with little, 132
hears him in the, 176
I go, and like, 435
in its sails, no steady, 102
is, which way the, 389
is in the palm-trees, the, 252
is southerly, when the, 245
lay your head well to the, 171
let her down the, 168
or wave will bring, 149
may blow through it, 44
overhead, when the great, 279
pass by me as the idle, 404
sweep, nor wild, 113
that follows fast, and a, 359
to the shorn lamb, 209
up the sun and moon, 9
was cold, the, 436
Winding up the watch of his wit, 447
Windmill, with cheese and garlic in a, 399
Window, and I a maid at your, 422
breaks, light through yonder, 225
the little, where the sun, 330
tirlin' at the, 443
you can see from this, 314
Windows, 444
of the east, peered forth the golden, 393
richly dight, storied, 225
Wind's will, is the, 33
Winds and naked woods, of wailing, 257
and rocks, the peril of water, 359
are left behind, and the, 86
be soft, 233
blow, may the, 400
flung to the heedless, 441
from the ends of opposed, 409
in the viewless, 90
of heaven, beteem the, 243
of the world, declare, 111
Wind, rides on the posting, 368
rise, or waters roll, where'er, 408
sigh, the night, 2
slowly o'er the lea, 69
that blew, four-square to all the, 413
the autumn, rushing, 326
their revels keep, the, 288
them up, the Angel of Life, 33
do blow, and the stormy, 19
Windy side of the law, keep o' the, 214
Wine, 444, 445
across the walnuts and the, 396
a jug of, 85
ambition, fame, 274
among the nuts and, 396
and as water unto, 268
and blushed with, 100
be as bright, may our, 257
before I poured the, 194
comes out of a narrow-mouthed bottle as, 383
give me a bowl of, 421
good, needs no bush, 40
if I thought it fit to take, 387
I'll not look for, 99
I have drunk my share of, 221
I have drunk your water and, 349
none to decline your nectared, 152
of life, friendship's the, 146
of life is drawn, 270
of life is on the lees, 270
of passion, rage, 324
old books, old, 290
only made in, 146
press the rue for, 402
rather heat with, 264
sans, 103
the universe in, 101
this skin of, 12
was dissolved in his, 153
who drinks hot blood for, 301
you drink, and if the, 411
Wing, a cloud, without a breeze, a, 368
a quill from an angel's, 301
and owlet's, 179
beats with weary, 340
dropped from an angel's, 301
he asks no angel's, 176
moults, love's, 233
one likes the pheasant's, 108
shook the dewdrop from its, 210
the dart, to, 106
to see the human soul take, 376
to wing, as rolled from, 308
when she has tired her, 344
Winged and wandering sound, a, 378
Cupid painted blind, 69
the shaft, and, 106
Wings, and flies with swallow's, 186
as on bright, 122
flying, her white, 436
of a dove, had I, 97
of Cherubim, fluttered by the, 52
of morning, take the, 74
of night, falls from the, 282
on eagles', 351

Wings on the blast spread his, 77
or on wide waving, 386
o' the mornin', take 'old o' the, 112
riches make them, 336
she claps her, 210
spreads his light, 233
the feet have, 470
the soul, that, 257
to fly, he has, 233
with love's light, 239
with trembling, 25
Wink for ever, so they, 384
I will, 48
too soon, he never came a, 331
Winking, damn his treacherous flatteries without, 259
Winks, one that nods and, 301
Wink-tippling cordial, 397
Winneth, that which the worker, 460
Winning him back, 443
how delicious is the, 203
I surely am not worth the, 458
one is, 306
Wins, not art but heart which, 175
not more than honesty, 64
the prize, or who, 150
the race, patience, 302
the soul, but merit, 260
the splendid ultimate triumph, 390
Winsome Ireland, 194
Winter and summer, by the same, 197
as humourous as, 161
bare, age like, 5
comes in, when, 441
greens, like, 357
in 't, no, 32
long, all the, 343
my age is as a lusty, 357
snow, time dissolve the, 233
spring and summer, for, 20
time, was leafless all the, 343
was the flow, and dark as, 225
weather, age like, 5
wind, blow thou, 444
Winter's eve, the bugbears of a, 401
fire, a woman's story at a, 389
flaw, to expel the, 421
rages, the furious, 103
Wipe a bloody nose, must often, 323
away all trivial fond records, I'll, 31
the weeds and moss, 163
Wiped his yellow beard, and, 181
Wire, others rather resemble copper, 276
thou shalt be whipped with, 439
Wisdom, 445
and of wit, recess of, 367
finds the way, and, 443
glow with, 283
gravity, profound conceit, of, 291
married to immortal verse, 394
is pushed out of life, 84
of many, the, 320
quitteth both riches and, 8
reputation for, 136
Wise, 446
and old, the saying, 28
and salutary neglect, a, 280
at all, the wisest man who is not, 446
be not worldly, 463
but not what, 306
course to steer, 91
defer not till to-morrow to be, 84
excel, of all those arts in which the, 467
father that knows, 127
foolery in the, 136
for cure, the, 172
I know him passing, 28
it call, the, 386
makes the politician, 57
one, nor ever does a, 202
only wretched are the, 190
man, I knew a very, 16
man knows himself, 137
men know well enough what monsters, 255
men ne'er sit, 231
men say it is the wisest course, 3
men's counters, words are, 459
nature is always, 277
not to the, 324
some people are more nice than, 281
steadfast in the strength of God, 179
the, the good, 334
the anger of the, 332
think he is, 137
'tis folly to be, 190
to-day, be, 84
too soon, folly to be, 446
we grow, so, 137
who deems himself so, 397
with speed, be, 137
young judge, O, 72
Wiseacres, 446
Wisely, one that loved not, 242
worldly, be, 463
Wise man, the fool to the, 369
Wiseness fear, let thy, 71
Wiser being good, it's, 159
man, a sadder and a, 346
sons, no doubt, our, 137
than a daw, no, 213
than we, of many far, 236
to make cages, 't is, 280
Wisest, 446
brightest, meanest of mankind, 123
course, it is the, 3
course, the desp'rat'st is the, 86
Wish, 446
agree, fate and, 15
for more, can I, 402
he were here, I, 116
to come back, think he'll, 168
the night, now I often, 331
there was more, she'll, 216
Wished, what ardently I, 92
Wishes, 446
all confined, 68
blest, by all their country's, 34
I've a notion, and, 388

Wishes
never learned to stray, 68
to feel thy very, 293
whose, soon as granted, 237
Wishing, 446
Wishings, full of good meanings and, 193
Wist before I kissed, had I, 231
Wit, 446, 447
a good, will make use of anything, 301
a man, in, 252
and leaves off his, 251
brightens, how the, 231
can fly, as high as metaphysic, 261
devise, write pen, 466
doth dote, when, 136
for so much room, no, 172
fire with, 283
in her attire doth show her, 20
in them, 'tis, 196
is out, 5
is stored, where, 297
it gives, quick as is the, 46
more hair than, 168
nor all your piety nor, 465
no room for, 172
occasion for his, 196
of one man, the, 320
or fortune led, by, 214
proud of her, 320
recess of wisdom and of, 367
still inspires my, 20
than a foolish, 137
th' assuming, 397
the life-refining soul of decent, 152
the soul of, 36
to boast his, 304
to match his learning and his, 329
too proud for a, 141
't will pass for, 67
with little or no, 458
Witch the world with noble horsemanship, 187
Witchcraft in your lips, 226
lies, what a hell of, 398
Witchcrafts, 448
Witching wine again, then comes, 444
time of night, the very, 282
Witch's oils, water like a, 81
Withdrawn, the light, 121
Wither, an arm would, 10
every year, some, 179
her, age cannot, 5
when the warmest feelings, 125
Withered, 448
and shaken, 4
and strown, lay, 216
be, it could not, 99
before they be, 343
Withering on the ground, now, 250
on the virgin thorn, 342
Withers are unwrung, our, 195
at another's joy, base envy, 114
Within that passeth show, that, 448
they that are, 253
Without, they that are, 253
Withstood, e'en when he labours, 64
tyrant of his fields, 168
Witness my God, I did, 365
that mourn without a, 271
Witnesses for God, seed of, 441
may commit perjury, the, 302
Wit's a burthen when it talks too long, 396
a feather, 183
Wits, alone and warming his five, 292
and a dunce with, 447
and weighs their, 30
are sure to madness, great, 245
but bankrupt quite the, 298
by making verses, 63
e'en with losing his, 245
had been a lord among, 447
have ever homely, 182
Witticism, for the sake of a battered, 321
Witty fool, better a, 137
though ne'er so, 364
Wives, 448
escape a work so sad, 450
of yore, ever true as, 468
the sky changes when they are, 457
Wiving goes by destiny, 86
Woe, 448
among, in wealth and, 215
and all our, 93
and melt at others', 174
awaits the country, 398
bear about the mockery of, 448
bliss or, 134
exhausts the pomp of, 410
flies from, 370
is protracted, 221
nor mercy in her, 142
of another's, 265
one common bliss or, 409
one kindred, 219
reckless alike of weal or, 328
silence in love bewrays more, 364
source of all his pain and, 283
the canticles of love and, 24
they do not need your, 329
to endure life's sorrow and earth's, 242
to feel another's, 260
when Eve brought, 449
where the end is, 159
with a face full of, 246
who did begin our, 283
world of, 105
Woe's to come, the, 419
Woes, 448
cluster, 448
of want, before I knew the, 430
perfidious wrongs, immedicable, 467
Woke and found, I, 104
Wolf, 449
on the fold, like a, 14
Wolf's whelp, you find it is a, 64
Wolsey, that once trod, 140
Wolves, silence, ye, 282

Woman, 449–454
a poor lone, 230
an excellent thing in, 428
an offer of kindness to make to a, 315
and song, who loves not wine, 444
and yet the son of a, 295
born, on all of, 59
but march up to a, 283
could not shape a husband out of, 255
every, is at heart a rake, 325
from the mouth of a, 283
good name in man and, 275
if a man really loves a, 243
I forswore, a, 157
I hate a dumpy, 94
I love, herself and the, 274
I'm glad I am a, 189
in its train, glorious, 444
in love with some, 239
is only a woman, a, 53
is warm, for, 442
I will take some savage, 350
knew what he said, and the old, 326
labourin', labourin' man an', 208
lays his hand upon a, 66
like a porcupine, making a, 304
like me, to a, 365
loves her lover, in her first passion, 232
make, a perfect, 443
marry, the men that, 255
might the lump of salt, as a, 465
my little, said Mr. Snagsby, 329
never a fair, 119
O listless, 33
one, not a liar, 462
or an epitaph, believe a, 67
or suckling, man or, 113
sat in unwomanly rags, 360
scorned, nor hell a fury like a, 324
still gentler sister, 188
stoops to folly, when lovely, 136
sung them now, 't was a, 340
thy name is, 142
to cry like a, 68
to play the, 399
to thee the love of, 354
to wait on, 189
wakes to love, 124
when he loves her, one to show a, 243
who deliberates, the, 85
who did not care, the, 136
who loved him the best, 132
will be out, the, 399
with fair opportunities, a, 255
with mine eyes, I could play the, 399
Womanhood and childhood fleet, 246
Womankind, much less in, 128
Womanly, 454
Woman's affection, surely a, 3
anger, like, 9
dear lip, dew of a, 226
eye, as a, 118
Woman's eyes, lies in, 118
faith, and woman's trust, 450
fair, because a, 120
heart, a, and its whole wealth, 173
heart, a stripling for a, 398
heart, break not, O, 35
heart gave way, her, 366
life, one half of, 454
love, the paths lead to a, 305
love, 't is brief as, 238
pride, blush of, 409
reason, no other but a, 327
slander is the worst, 368
story at a winter's fire, 389
tear-drop melts, a, 398
toy, my heart was every, 148
voice, and a loving, 235
whole existence, 't is, 232
will, the current of a, 450
will, to stem the torrent of a, 450
Womb, in the wide, 90
of pia mater, 258
Wombs have borne bad sons, good, 374
Women, 455, 456
all the men and, 383
and horses and power and war, 164
and men, ere we were, 392
and men, the lives of most, 140
are angels, wooing, 457
are apt to love the men, 243
are so full of whims, the, 449
are weeping, and they, 132
comes nateral to, 283
come out to cut up what remains, 373
deeds are men, words are, 459
false, to make, 122
I've seen much finer, 385
kindness in, 201
lave what the, 375
let us have wine and, 444
life of so many suffering, 451
men and, 75
must weep, 132
o'er fair, 334
other, cloy the appetites, 5
pure, all, 150
spoke, in number more than ever, 429
stormy seas and stormy, 389
sweet is revenge, especially to, 334
tell their dreams, 99
worst and best, 259
Women's are, sooner lost and worn than, 454
eyes this doctrine, 118
faces, poor, 119
looks, were, 118
Won are done, things, 198
hailed the wretch who, 362
her, he wooed and, 277
I recollect how sailors' rights was, 347
is ever, 142
she is a woman, therefore to be, 453

Won, showed how fields were, 68
the battle he has fought may not be, 62
the prize we sought is, 43
the race is, 208
was ever woman in this humour, 454
when the battle 's lost and, 257
wooed and not unsought be, 457
Wonder, 456
it inspires, the, 206
of an hour, the, 352
often what the vintners buy, I, 426
when you and I are dead, 75
without our special, 56
Wonderful is Death, how, 81
is man, how complicate, how, 251
Wondering eyes, quoth Hodge with, 326
Wonders, his, to perform, 154
Won't, and if she, 450
a woman will or, 450
Wont, you were, 239
Wonted fires, live their, 35
Woo, 456, 457
and were not made to, 457
her, and that would, 363
the angel virtue, should, 332
wed or cease to, 458
Wood a cudgel 's of, know what, 20
bark, and leaves, 308
cleave the, 207
till Birnam, 25
Woodcock, 457
Woodcocks, he cannot live like, 256
Wooden one, to buy him a, 434
Woodland, 457
Woodman, 457
Wood-notes wild, warble his native, 432
Woodpecker, 457
Woods, 457, 458
all night, sleeping, 37
lose thyself in the continuous, 74
of wailing winds and naked, 257
or steepy mountain yields, 235
when wild in, 350
Wooed and won her, he, 277
and wedded in a day, 442
a woman therefore may be, 453
but when she, 449
she 's beautiful and therefore to be, 453
that would be, 457
was ever woman in this humour, 454
we should be, 457
Wooer, 458
Wooing, 458
light makes fickle troth, 456
the caress more dazzlingly, 408
women are angels, 457
Wool, all cry and no, 395
and the flax, she seeketh the, 451
of bat, 179
Woollen, odious, in, 75
Wooman, he then pronounced her, 449
Woos even now the frozen bosom of the north, 444
Word, 458
action to the, 2
a, that cowards use, 61
and every jest but a, 196
as Mary rose at Jesus', 358
at every, 52
at random spoken, many a, 358
but a choleric, 43
comes aptest, the harshest, 114
dropped a tear upon the, 287
drops some careless, 173
every, her heart did know, 340
every, that he speaks, 314
faithful of thy, 124
for in that, 124
for it Sammy, take my, 310
for three farthings, the Latin, 332
honour, what is in that, 185
in short, within a, 363
lion be stirred by too daring a, 226
love in search of a, 273
no man relies on, whose, 202
nor to exchange a peaceful, 229
not a, 95
not made for gentlemen, but gents, 294
of Cæsar might have stood against the world, 335
of fear, there is not a, 78
of it, wash out a, 465
of promise, that keep the, 318
of sorrow, we spoke not a, 313
one, for ever failed him, 283
or action brave, asks, 144
or deed, in fiery, 248
saved by a single, 434
shall a light, 146
should grieve ye, a scornful, 352
speaks the startling, 88
take my, 392
teaching me that, 72
that shall echo for evermore, 84
'tis a single, 139
there is no such, 119
to a throne, a queen sent, 276
to listen for the weakest, 293
to speak one simple, 466
to the action, 2
was this, my, 66
what is honour? — a, 184
which stands for it, 85
who never wanted a good, 26
whose lightest, 380
with him but a jest, not, 196
would he utter, not a, 34
write that, 342
Word-catcher, 458
Wordless prayer, to a, 88
Word 's our warrant, God 's, 409
Words, 458, 459
admit of no defence, immodest, 83
and such abominable, 317
and the children 's early, 235
another of the devil 's pet, 422

Words
are bonds, 29
are few, whose, 255
are like leaves, 379
are scarce, where, 105
are the best men, men of few, 259
are the saddest of tongue or pen, 346
are things, but, 192
bewrays more woe than, 364
breathing these only, 62
came first, all, 458
came from his lips, these, 357
charm agony with, 5
could never utter, such as, 439
dooms one to those dreadful, 68
free . . . as I please in, 412
give sorrow, 165
I'm an Englishman, is breathed in, 47
in, as fashions, 126
in pain, breathe their, 105
in such apt and gracious, 196
learned by rote, 397
like perfect music unto noble, 273
of love then spoken, the, 258
of Marmion, the last, 47
of the prayer, it is not the, 313
of tongue and pen, if of all, 346
of tongue or pen, of all sad, 346
poured thick and fast the burning, 419
repeats his, 165
summed in those few brief, 313
than a parrot, should have fewer, 295
that form of, 62
that poor Narcissa spoke, 75
to coin new, 379
to them whose faith an' truth, wut's, 19
trust not in, 227
were air, she says those, 428
without thoughts never to heaven go, 313
you mangle his merciful, 365
you send, I'll drink the, 466
you will find the following, 285
Wore last year, garments which it, 381
the gown, of old I, 161
the uniform 'e, 420
were the gems she, 149
Work, 459, 460
again, at his dirty, 353
and toil for her, to, 189
a singing with his hand, his, 374
bad, follers ye ez long 's ye live, 40
dedicate ourselves to the unfinished, 27
do his share in the, 54
done thy long, 35
here to the unfinished, 276
if it be man's, 251
if this is Christian, 451
for honest labour, 48
for man to mend, 172
her noblest, 211
Work
his will, instruments to, 389
is done, ne'er can say my, 451
men must, 132
men that do the world's rough, 306
my mind when body's work's expired, 21
needs must love his, 247
of death was done, the, 76
of God, the noblest, 183
of our head and hand, the, 451
so sad, wives escape, 450
their passage, as they do in ships, 176
to do, there must be somewhere, 78
to its, in the morning gay, 442
we are in, to finish the, 331
who 'd shirk his daily, 248
will continue to, 390
without complaining, they who, 207
work, work, 207
worth, what is all this sweet, 204
Worked and sung, he, 262
I have, 221
thorough, folks thet, 40
Worker, 460
Workers, 461
Worketh with gladness, 451
Working for, is worth, 222
in the dismal trench, 40
out her soul, 54
out the beast, 20
that from her, 307
Working-day world, this, 37
Workings, its varied, 33
Workman, 461
Work's expired, when body's, 21
Works, 461
all the glory of his, 154
could thrust in among the, 403
for, loses that it, 183
from the heart outward, lie which, 451
may have more wit, for, 447
of love or enmity fulfill, 381
World, 461–463
again, gave his honours to the, 185
a little foolery governs the, 137
a marvel and a mystery to the, 255
and in this, 54
and nourish all the, 118
and now a, 38
and say to all the, 250
an I had but one penny in the, 301
any author in the, 118
anywhere out of the, 244
are bobbing, to bed the, 386
around, let it circle the, 152
assurance, to give the, 250
away, runs the, 84
back from a, 443
back to the, 349
began, the greatest sailor since our, 347
began, their ruins since the, 228
beside, o'er all the, 65

World
beside, than all the, 182
bestride the, 58
brought death into the, 93
can never fill, the, 300
Cassius is aweary of the, 15
chloroformed into a better, 451
contagion to this, 282
damnable life in this, 168
declare, winds of the, 111
ever the blind, 255
far less in size, seemed to me this, 331
fired the shot heard round the, 362
foremost man of all this, 36
forgetting, the, 140
from the beginning of the, 253
give for the discovery, what would the, 403
glory of this, 310
goes, as this, 183
goes by, fast and the, 129
goes up, and the world goes down, the, 442
good deed in a naughty, 42
good-night, bids the, 96
grew pale, at which the, 274
half-brother of the, 8
has nothing to bestow, 182
he like the, 370
he will never march in this, 287
holds on high, that the, 120
I'd leave the, 452
if all the, 237
in all this, 128
in awe, which kept the, 421
in the face, looks the strong, 410
in the face, looks the whole, 292
is a nettle, the, 449
is full of warfare, the, 433
is given to lying, how this, 244
is old, when all the, 290
is single, nothing in the, 366
is young, lad, when all the, 469
kin, makes the whole, 278
knows nothing of its greatest men, 259
lash the rascals naked through the, 439
laughs with you, laugh and the, 212
may sleep, the, 254
might have stood against the, 335
miscalls a jail, that which the, 318
monk who shook the, 267
murders in this loathsome, 158
my wife and all the, 223
necessity, thou mother of the, 279
no copy, leave the, 21
o'er, the, 38
of changeless law, changing, 224
of happiness their harmony foretells, 437
of happy days, a, 99
of merriment their melody foretells, 23
of pride, a, 316

World
of sighs, a, 363
of solemn thought, what a, 410
of vile ill-favoured faults, 128
of waters is our home, the, 436
of woe, from a, 105
on his back the burden of the, 180
over, kissing was clover all the, 240
over, which wins the wide, 175
over the roofs of the, 468
patriarchs of the infant, 334
prospers, the, 111
reckless what I do to spite the, 328
seek through the, 182
shake the, 147
shall see his bones, 15
sleep hath its own, 369
so fair, picture a, 209
some for the glories of this, 44
so with the, 236
succeed in the, 319
surely is wide enough, this, 189
syllables govern the, 395
that nod unto the, 56
the corrupted current of this, 289
the exhaustless granary of a, 162
the federation of the, 433
the harmony of the, 212
the imponderables move the, 237
the judges of the, 188
the light of the bright, 281
the pendent, 90
the prettiest doll in the, 96
the queen of the, 58
the vile blows and buffets of the, 328
the war-drum of the white man round the, 432
this little, 112
this working-day, 37
three corners of the, 112
throughout the wondering, 108
to arms, gold provokes the, 158
to darkness, leaves the, 69
toil and trouble in the, 456
to move the, 413
too wide, a, 294
to tell the glory-dazzled, 432
to the oppressed of all the, 290
to the throne of the, 339
to trample the, 449
turns round, thinks the, 151
was sad, the, 450
what I may appear to the, 417
when Rome falls, the, 57
who lost Mark Anthony the, 452
with, one to face the, 243
with noble horsemanship, 187
worst way to improve the, 191
would damn itself, the, 198
Worldling, one rich, 300
Worldly, 463
cares, an' warly men, 44
task hast done, 103
World's altar-stairs, the great, 7
an inn, the, 77
a stage, all the, 383

World's a theatre, the, 383
blind greed, censure of the, 165
book been gilded, for what and for whom, 207
mine oyster, the, 293
new fashion planted, man in all the, 303
peace to pray, for this, 366
release, the gladness of the, 300
rough work, men that do the, 306
Worlds, 463
should conquer twenty, 61
the crush of, 191
World-victor's victor will be seen no more, 356
Worm, 463
even the, 367
is cloven in vain, not a, 160
i' the bud, 298
I trod upon a, 271
the, the canker, 223
the darkness and the, 401
Worms, 463
and epitaphs, of, 164
enfold, gilded tombs do, 410
of Nile, outvenoms all the, 368
or grubs, or, 458
Wormwood, 464
Worn him to the bones, sharp misery had, 264
sooner lost and, 454
Worn-out plan, save on some, 179
Worse, and sometimes a great deal, 249
appear the better reason, 122
for wear, not much the, 171
I'll get ten, it's, 329
in kings than beggars, 122
make the fault the, 128
no better and no, 80
poison to men's souls, 158
some better and some, 316
than a crime, 28
than death, lest, 94
than senseless things, you, 27
Worser place, what, 378
Worship, 464
dirty gods, who, 158
labour is, 208
the golden calf, 42
Worshipped a rhyme, who, 308
God for spite, as if they, 302
Worshippers, dies among his, 415
Worships what it spurned, and, 255
Worst, 464
and best, the greatest, 147
can't end, 159
enemy, his own, 249
for sudden the, 78
I've known the, 328
of all, death was not the, 90
of madmen is a saint, 245
one, the first and, 21
sure rivals are the, 339
to-morrow do thy, 408
treason has done his, 223
Worst
where the best is like the, 392
who has known the tempest's, 328
Worsted, though right were, 337
Worth, 465
a dump, game was n't, 77
a fight, wut is, 212
a hundred years of life, 39
and the conscience of her, 457
a thousand men, 39
doing, what is, 96
in anything, what is, 266
in woman overtrusting, to, 452
living, is life, 219
living, the life that is, 222
more than anything, 357
no worse a place, 315
on foot, showed, 417
something, a man's, 130
that sense and, 38
the search, they are not, 327
the silence of the heart, 172
the wooing, if I am not, 458
to try its, 377
unnoticed all his, 176
whatever be their rank or, 201
working for, is, 222
Worthier cause, a, 144
of regard and stronger, 58
would it were, 465
Worthless gold, gives only the, 7
wight, a graceless, 151
Worthy to be filed, on Fame's eternal beadroll, 47
Would and we would not, we, 443
be, it's there that I, 392
not, durst not play, 306
not what we, 229
wait upon I, 45
Would-be wits and can't-be gentlemen, 150
Wound a heart that's broken, 358
goot for your green, 216
helped to plant the, 106
itself, help to, 112
that never felt a, 351
the grief of a, 184
the heart doth, 166
the old, if stricken is the sorest, 290
up just like a watch, 173
willing to, 71
with a touch, 350
Wounded and left on Afghanistan's plains, 373
hymn of the, 61
snake, like a, 6
to die, 39
Wounds before, hurts honour than deep, 36
bind up my, 187
green, keeps his own, 334
I might have healed, 116
me with the flatteries, 134
the labour and the, 391
to bind up the nation's, 337
wept o'er his, 68

Woven a golden mesh, 168
Wrack, blow, wind! come, 90
him, cross him and, 294
Wrangles and dissensions, of your, 433
Wrapped about the bones, thy roots are, 468
Wraps the drapery of his couch, one who, 227
Wrath, 465
and despair in the jolly black-jack, 26
appeased, the Eternal 's, 301
can send, thy, 145
destroy, not in after, 107
execute thy, 15
infinite, 177
tears and anarchy, 143
than the strong man in his, 413
the dragon and his, 98
the grapes of, 153
Wrathfully, but not, 201
Wreath, a, a rank, 462
I covet not, a, 104
I sent thee late a rosie, 99
I took the, 100
of roses, she wore a, 343
you lay a, 225
Wreathe your arms, to, 239
Wreaths entwine, and laurel, 304
Wreck, 465
may sink with a shot-torn, 133
out of his, 140
Wrecked, 465
on shore, more have been, 354
Wrecks, a thousand fearful, 102
if rising on its, 170
of matter, the, 191
Wrens make prey where eagles, 106
Wrest once the law to your authority, 213
Wrestle, vainly we weep and, 155
Wrestled, 465
Wretch, cast o'er hardened, 127
concentred all in self, 65
condemned with life to part, 185
excellent, 239
is a, 66
to haud the, 184
to treat a poor, 360
who can number his kisses, 205
who long has tossed, 293
who won, hailed the, 362
Wretched, 465
he forsakes, the, 370
the only, 190
Wretchedness, and leave me here in, 381
and pain, but, 76
Wretch 's aid, for some, 216
Wretches betray, so many of the little, 176
hang, and, 92
have o'ernight, as, 333
Wring from the hard hands, than to, 267
his bosom, and, 136
Wring the brow, pain and anguish, 453
Wringing their hands, are weeping and, 132
Wrinkled, because his forehead is, 309
Wrinkles, 465
come, let old, 264
on thine azure brow, writes no, 406
time got his, 78
Wrist, gave a thumb to his, 311
Writ, 465
in water, whose name was, 274
o' both sides the leaf, 336
of little Nell, had, 280
the fair hand that, 169
Write, 466
and cipher too, he could, 206
and read, 2
a novel, some play the devil and then, 285
any man that can, 216
anything wise, you 'll never, 445
converse, and live with ease, 107
he who would, 67
in rhyme, those that, 335
me down an ass, 13
of me, not, 109
on your door, 28
our benefits upon the wave, 467
sorrow on the bosom, 164
speak, preach, for this, 123
than the pen may, 174
that word, 342
the characters in dust, 450
the thing he will, 221
touch a pen to, 308
Writes no wrinkles on thine azure brow, 406
the moving finger, 465
Writhe, lips taught to, 233
Writhes in pain, error wounded, 415
Writhing o'er its task, Grief was, 165
Writing, 466, 467
and 'rithmetic, reading, 187
an exact man, and, 326
Written all in water, those vows were, 428
down, though it be not, 13
o'er again, erased nor, 465
then may my epitaph be, 114
whatever hath been, 465
Wrong, 467
a Christian, if a Jew, 197
always in the, 114
chafe as at a personal, 161
do a little, 213
for ever on the throne, 417
his can't be, 120
how easily things go, 203
in some nice tenets might be, 120
I smiled, if, 67
may gang a kennin, 188
no captain can do, 360
no other reason for this, 287
our country, right or, 65

Wrong
peace unweaponed conquers every, 300
rules the land, 417
side may be turned outward, 447
side out, egotism, 11
's most ollers, 245
sow by the ear, he has the, 378
that pains my soul below, 160
the multitude is always in the, 271
the oppressor's, 323
the sense of, 419
the side that seems, 337
the t'other wuns prayed, 314
things have long been, 422
though easy, 159
to right, so long as there is, 219
to undo the plainest, 54
us, if you, 197
who had done the, 140
would triumph, 337
you're doing, read you not the, 458
Wronged and the weak to defend, 173
Wrongs, 467
but when I think on all my, 423
Wrote down for men, as he, 418
it, who, 358
Wroth with one we love, to be, 412
Wrought a murder in a dream, I, 272
are those which heaven itself has, 403
for her, 416
of such stuffs as dreams are, 428
that night at Bunker's Hill well he, 40

X

Xerxes, 467

Y

Yankee, 467
Yard are full of seamen's graves, the church and, 355
below their mines, one, 110
locked in yard, 347
Yarn, web of our life is of a mingled, 222
Yawn, when churchyards, 282
Yawns before our eyes, 178
Yawp, 468
Yea and nay, her pretty oath by, 306
Year 468
after year the same absurd mistakes, 265
carved for many a, 252
for Christmas comes but once a, 52
he that dies this, 91
I've a hundred pounds a, 61
like two months of every, 110
memory may outlive his life half a, 258
moments make the, 414
passing rich with forty pounds a, 336
some wither every, 379
that flourish all the, 357
Year
then mourn a, 448
the saddest of the, 257
this, a reservoir, 248
three hundred pounds a, 128
together, taking the, 393
two hundred pounds a, 95
were past, would heaven this mourning, 464
Yearning back of the praying, the, 313
like the first fierce impulse, 66
Yearnings, strivings, longings, 156
Yearns with the fondness of a dove, 173
Year's pleasant king, spring is the, 382
Years, a few more, 222
and nature sink in, 191
are fleet, our, 79
are o'er when long, long, 409
beyond our ken, for, 138
but not with, 168
but young, his, 198
increased with, 224
it may be for, 116
man of wisdom is the man of, 445
of God are hers, the eternal, 415
outweighs of stupid starers, whole, 355
pedigree traced to earth's earliest, 300
reckon their age by, 398
rise with other, 330
the flight of, 75
they served, for, 414
to sever for, 296
we live in deeds not, 227
we waste, the, 451
Yeast, some swallowed in the, 35
Yell upon yell, 42
Yellow, bright and, 157
leaf, falls into the, 223
leaf, my days are in the, 223
leaf, the sear, the, 223
of two hard-boiled eggs, the, 349
primrose was to him, 316
sands, come unto these, 349
to the jaundiced eye, 195
Yellows, like a peach that's got the, 256
Yeoman's service, now it did me, 466
Yes, 468
mebby to mean, 283
when she says, 363
Yesterday, 468
all our pomp of, 139
the word of Cæsar might, 335
you were, to-day what, 411
Yesterday's have lighted fools, all our, 411
seven thousand years, with, 411
sneer and yesterday's frown, 442
Yesterdays, 468
seems of cheerful, 48
Yester-year, 468
Yestreen, I saw the new moon late, 267

Yew, 468
Yew-tree's shade, that, 108
Yield, and not to, 146
a step for death or life, 431
even gods must, 330
me but a common grave, 163
never to submit or, 231
their juices, 175
up, which I must not, 422
when you must, only, 58
where thou would'st only faint and, 198
Yielded to the first that sought her, has, 428
with coy submission, 391
Yields, for which no rhyme our language, 389
his breath, when the good man, 159
to men the helm, nor, 86
Yoked with a lamb, you are, 209
Yonder cloud, do you see, 56
Yore, of the saintly days of, 325
some life outlived of, 315
Yorick, 468
York, at, 't is on the Tweed, 284
You and I are dead, when, 75
shall be you no more, when, 411
twenty times, utter the, 319
were you, to prove that, 320
Young, 468, 469
a body, knew so, 171
all the world and love were, 237
and old come forth to play, 71
and old, let, 150
as beautiful, 20
best married that dies married, 254
but his heart is, 173
eagle of the West, 106
ever fair and, 16
family, the wants of a, 48
his years but, 198
idea how to shoot, to teach the, 398
lassie, what can a, 211
man following it, 180
man married is a man that's marred, 254
man's fancy, a, 241
man's heart, tied a, 30
men shall see visions, your, 98
men's vision, the, 98
or old, of all the living, 228
shall peck at the shells elate, 97
spurned by the, 157
to marry yet, I 'm o 'er, 254
well, he died, 151
when music, heavenly maid, was, 272
when we were, 74
without lovers, 462
you loved when all was, 290
Younger, 469
brother, though the, 216
man, I'll do the service of a, 357
spirits, the snuff of, 228
Youngest, when your, 144
Yours is mine, and what is, 263
Yourself, 469
Youth, 469, 470
a, to fortune and to fame unknown, 257
and ease, they whom, 105
and home and that sweet time, 23
and love, a kiss of, 204
and observation copied there, 331
and pleasure meet, 71
an eagle mewing her mighty, 277
crabbed age and, 5
delight, gives his, 49
fades, time fleets, 221
for in my, 357
home-keeping, 182
how he was instructed in his, 416
in, it sheltered me, 457
in immortal, 191
in the lexicon of, 119
is full of pleasance, 5
is vain, 412
it is sunny, 4
like summer brave, 5
lost Atlantis of our, 14
love-exalted, 65
manhood, old age past, 155
many a, 71
not clean past your, 5
now green in, 250
of England are on fire, 111
of frolics, a, 462
of nations, the ingenious, 135
of the realm, corrupted the, 317
over, who can live, 33
replies I can, the, 104
stirred our hearts in, 88
sublime, nourishing a, 352
the aspiring, 123
the temple of my, 269
the thoughts of, 33
they had been friends in, 412
ventered life an' love an', 19
with his sorrow and sin, murders our, 406
Youth's a stuff will not endure, 239
bright locks, o'er, 354
Yule, 470
is cold, when, 132

Z

Zaccheus, 470
Zeal be had, may too much, 245
but served my God with half the, 357
showed their fierce, 144
than knowledge, with more, 279
Zealots fight, let graceless, 120
Zembla, there at Greenland, 284
Zenith, dropped from the, 122
Zephyr blows soft the, 470
Zimri stand, did, 114
Zone, its gentle odours over either, 408
the pole or the, 112
to zone, he who from, 387